TABLE OF CONTENTS

The Burning Legion Returns

We who fought in the Third War never deceived ourselves that the war had put an end to the Burning Legion. Kil'jaeden and his vast army were cut off from Azeroth, but not indefinitely. Yet with the threat of all-out war between Horde and Alliance, and the continuing danger of the Scourge, what could we do about the Legion? How could we prepare for a war that might be millennia in the future when so much conflict was already at our doorstep?

Now that the Dark Portal has been reactivated, we must reevaluate our priorities. The world of Draenor did not, after all, perish under the strain of the magical portals Ner'zhul created eighteen years ago. Rather, Draenor has been reduced to the shattered territories of Outland, where, just as rumor had it, the demon Illidan Stormrage is fighting to solidify his power base.

Many of the loved ones we thought had perished with Draenor may in fact have survived the hardships of life on Outland. Sizable tracts of land have been largely untouched by either fel magic or Ner'zhul's reckless sorcery. Better still, the Alliance and Horde have recently gained new allies in the draenei and blood elves, respectively.

Nonetheless, the reactivation of the Dark Portal is a two-edged sword. Illidan and his allies are fighting to keep all the other portals of Outland closed, but his loyalties and capabilities remain an open question. Should even one portal be reopened, the forces of the Legion would pour into Outland. Their almost inevitable triumph over Illidan would set off a chain reaction—countless worlds falling to the Legion—that Azeroth has little hope of withstanding.

In the interests of preventing such a scenario, we have dispatched a number of scouts to bring back information from Outland. Today we understand the current layout and disposition of the enemies waiting beyond the Dark Portal. We have compiled maps, bestiaries, and strategies, all of which are provided herein. Knowledge will be the key to our conquest of Outland.

Make no mistake: the tensions between Horde and Alliance did not arise overnight. They were not the work of a whim, and they cannot be lightly set aside. I think of the lives lost, and I grieve bitterly; I, too, wish to kill. But we cannot afford to be blinded by bloodlust. Remember who first set our people at one another's throats. We cannot permit the Burning Crusade to engulf other worlds.

We must bring it to an end. We must find a way.

Within These Pages

- A Breakdown of Gameplay Changes Integrated Into Burning Crusade
- Strategies and Information About New Abilities and Talents (Expanded Talent Trees With Two New Tiers)
- Updated Crafting Tables With Jewelcrafting, New Recipes, and a New Tier of Mastery
- Full Explanations of the New Races (Blood Elves and Draenei)
- Leveling Guides for Twenty Levels of Unique New Content (Start New Characters and Savor the Blood Elf and Draenei Territory)
- Developed Maps for New Zones in Azeroth and Outland (NPC Locations, Trainers, Crafters, Vendors, Monsters, and Points of Interest)
- Tables, Monster Information, and Anything Else That We Could Fit Between the Covers

Burning Crusade brings with it a number of major and minor gameplay changes. Not only is there new content to discover and conquer, but higher character levels, flying mounts, interface improvements, and many other more subtle changes.

This chapter's goal is to help everyone understand all of the differences. It makes it easier to refine your characters and get the most out of the new system without taking too much time away from your exploration! After explaining the new terminology and general changes, we'll move into class additions, player versus player combat in Outland, and a zone-by-zone introduction of the newest territory.

Gameplay Changes

No matter what your interests, be they PvP combat, dungeon delving, roleplaying, and so forth, the first thing that you might notice is that the game feels different. There are new options, areas, levels, abilities, Talents, creatures, and more. Read this section to learn about all of this fresh material.

INTERFACE AND STATISTIC CHANGES

Many of the new options and terms nestled in the various menus can be easy to miss. Though less trumpeted than graphical improvements, raid zones, and fresh items, these things make a big impact on how people relate to the game.

New Terminology and Statistics

Before you spend too much time in the new game, it is likely that you will come across some new or updated terms. Critical Rating? Dodge Rating? Haste?

Don't worry; though these terms are new, it won't take you long to figure them out. After you have learned what everything affects, we'll explain how the numbers add up!

New Terminology

Term	Improves These Stat(s)
Bonus Damage	Bonus Damage to Spell Effects
Bonus Healing	Bonus Healing to Healing Effects
Critical Rating	Melee and Ranged Critical Chance
Defense Rating	Block Percentage, Dodge Percentage, Parry Percentage
Dodge Rating	Dodge Percentage
Haste	Attack Speed
Hit Rating	Hit Percentage
Parry Rating	Parry Percentage
Resilience	Decreased Chance of Receiving Critical Hits, Decreased Damage from Critical Hits

With the Burning Crusade's increased level cap, players will finally be able to earn *experience* again.

THE NEW CHARACTER SCREEN

The Character Screen in World of Warcraft has been upgraded, and it is now amazing. Stats that were previously more troublesome for new players to find (e.g. Dodge, Parry, Critical Rate) are shown without any difficulty. Even better, stats that needed to be tested and calculated (e.g. Spell Critical Rates) are shown too!!!

By selecting the information displayed in your Character Screen, via the drop-down menu that is in place, you have the power to learn everything about your new and old stats. Highlighting each attribute of your character reveals even more. As before, this information is updated in real-time, so it is very simple to judge the value of various equipment changes. Even the new point system for Criticals, Spell Damage, and other statistics is easy to understand if you use the Character Screen heavily and watch for the appropriate value changes.

GRADED ON A CURVE NOW

As a World of Warcraft player, you've already dealt with the idea of having a growth curve, whether you've known it or not. For instance, you might have gained a level and had your Critical Chance go down. This might have confused you at first, but in time it becomes clear that you need to keep your Agility up to a certain value to maintain a given Critical Chance. If you just rely on gear that is 30 levels out of date, your values fall as your character is falling farther under the par value for Agility.

The new system adds par values for many other types of statistics. Instead of having equipment that adds +1% to Dodge, you get a Dodge Rating from your equipment. Four points of Dodge Rating at level 20 can be pretty darn nice, giving you a very noticeable chance in your Dodge Chance. At level 60, however, it will add far less. This is true for items that raise your Defense, Dodge, Parry, Hit Rate, Critical Rates, Attack Speed, or Resilience.

This may seem like a nerf, but you won't log in to find your characters in worse shape than they were before. The system has been well balanced to provide more flexibility in most equipment, and your characters are going to be just fine. In fact, the system allows for lower-level items to get these effects, and that is an awesome improvement for the early stages of the game.

In the older days of WoW, you wouldn't see many +Hit, +Crit, or other such items until well into the second half of your leveling. Even then, cheesy greens wouldn't be able to give you anything to raise such stats; you needed to wait for the right items of Superior quality. That limited the customization of some characters in the early game.

Because the system scales on a much finer basis now, items are being added that give characters more options. One has only to play around in the new Blood Elf or Draenei lands to see this. This brings the option for far more customization into the hands of casual players, who aren't always decked out in Superior or Epic gear. Very nice indeed.

The Percents Are Still There

Not only does the new character screen still let you see the final percentages for your Block, Parry, Dodge, Criticals, Spell Criticals, and so forth, but these percentages are still altered by Talents in the same way they were before. So, the changes are not affecting everything about your character; they just alter the way items affect your final percentages.

OFFENSIVE RATINGS

Most of the Ratings control statistics are already very familiar to most players. Weapon Skill, Criticals, Dodge, Parry, and other such statistics have been in use for a very long time.

To help give players an idea of what to expect at level 60, Blizzard provided a number of conversions. These figures provide a baseline (so that you don't go into the field without a general idea of what these points are "worth").

Specifically, Weapon Skill has been dramatically changed in how it functions (not just how it is gained). Weapon Skill Rating adds to Weapon Skill; Weapon Skill itself no longer determines whether a melee character gets Glancing Blows and other forms of damage mitigation against a higher-level opponent. This is a very major change for Warriors and Rogues, and is somewhat significant to any melee user. With regard to creatures above the player's level, Weapon Skill Rating is far less important in the expansion than it was in the old system. Against creatures at the same level or lower than the player, Weapon Skill Rating is just as useful as before because Glancing Blows are not an issue. You now receive Crit Rating bonuses from having a high Weapon Skill, but this is a minor increase rather than something major to rely on. You can get more bang for your buck with Crit Rating improvements than by upping your Weapon Skill Rating.

Sample Rating Points at Level 60

Rating Type	Value in Traditional Statistics
Weapon Skill Rating	2.5 Rating grants 1 Weapon Skill
Hit Rating	10 Rating grants 1% Hit Chance
Spell Hit Rating	8 Rating grants 1% Spell Hit Chance
Critical Strike Rating	14 Rating grants 1% Critical Chance
Spell Critical Strike Rating	14 Rating grants 1% Spell Critical Strike Chance
Haste	10 Rating for 1% Haste (1% Improvement to Physical Attack Speed)
Spell Haste	10 Rating grants 1% Spell Haste (1% Improvement to Spell Casting Speed)

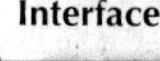

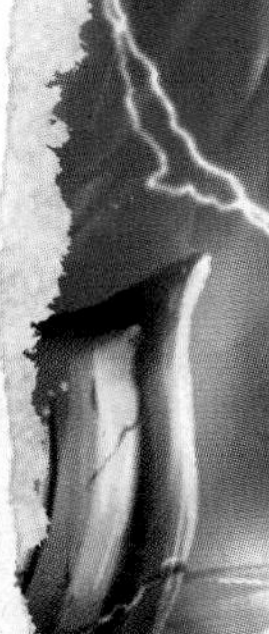

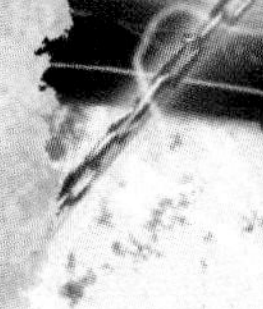
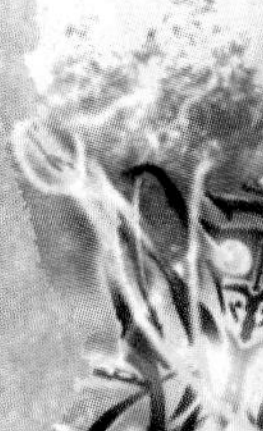

DEFENSE RATING

Defense has changed too, such that items that add bonuses to Defense are on a Rating that is converted into actual Defense Skill bonuses. As before, Defense Skill controls the percentage chances for a character to Dodge, Parry, Block, be missed, or be Critically Struck.

Weapon Skills follow suit, with their Ratings being converted into actual Weapon Skill improvements. These alter the chance for a character to successfully strike their targets.

Sample Defense Values at 60

Rating Type	Value in Traditional Statistics
Defense Skill Rating	1.5 Rating grants 1 Defense Skill
Dodge Rating	12 Rating grants 1% Dodge
Parry Rating	20 Rating grants 1% Parry
Block Rating	5 Rating grants 1% Block chance

RESILIENCE

Resilience is a new stat that is being added to help mitigate burst damage against characters. While Defense works to reduce general damage (by avoiding attacks more often), it is a stat that does nothing to stop damage that gets through. That is where Resilience comes in.

Not only does Resilience reduce the chance that your character will be hit critically but it also reduces the damage done to your character by a Critical Hit. Note that the damage reduction of Resilience is a percentage that is twice as high as the reduction in chance for an enemy Critical Hit (thus, enough Resilience to lower an enemy's Critical Hit value by 10% would also reduce Critical damage to your character by 20%).

Sample Resilience Values at 60

Rating Type	Value in Traditional Statistics
Resilience	25 Rating grants 1% Reduction to Critical Hit Damage Received

BONUS DAMAGE AND BONUS HEALING

Casters of all classes have seen bonuses to various damage types before. A few items have always given a boost to spell damage and/or healing, so these aren't new concepts at all (or even new terms). What has changed is that these bonuses are found on a wealth of high-level items, to the point where it is now easy to start accumulating a substantial pool of bonuses.

One reflection of this change is the inclusion of new Talents that give characters improvements to their Bonus Damage values. The difference this makes is quite noticeable for casters. It is much easier to seek items that raise casting DPS or healing capabilities without making gigantic sacrifices in survivability. Weapons and armor alike have high numbers to add into Bonus Healing or Damage.

It is also far less common that you will find items with only one type of Bonus Damage. Instead of something adding +Fire Damage, it is likely that you will find items with just a generic Bonus Damage value. For quite some time casters have had to live with itemization that was not entirely ideal, and this change makes up for it. Caster gear now *feels* far more important toward specialization and effectiveness, rather than being kind of a blunt improvement.

Instant Looting

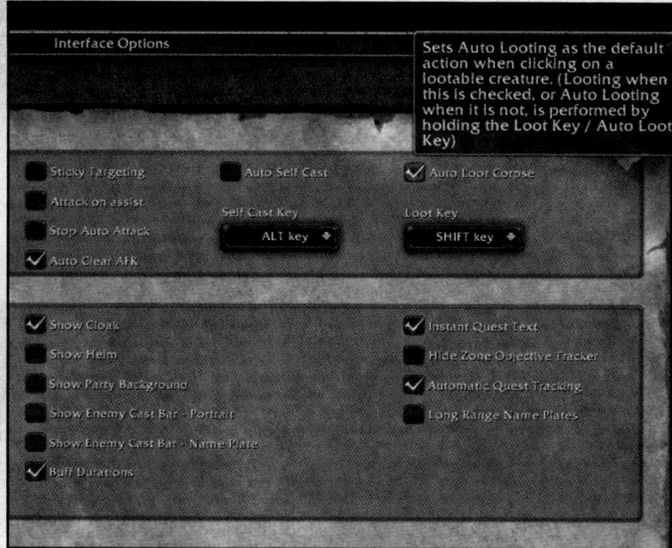

This new Interface Option is wonderful. People who are shift-click addicts no longer have to worry about their looting problem any longer. You can now set a default Instant Loot for your character. This saves a bit of time as you plow through waves of creatures while soloing. And, this doesn't force you to grab everything in sight either (for example, if you enter a group with Free-For-All looting in place). This is because you can use Shift+Click to loot the old piece-by-piece way. Put simply, this option is wonderful and effective.

Spell Updates After Training

Unlike the earlier days of WoW, your spells now automatically update after gaining a new rank. Though you can always access you lower-rank spells (via your spellbook), any of the spells that are already on your quickbar update to the highest rank when a new rank is purchased.

Improved Looking For Group Options

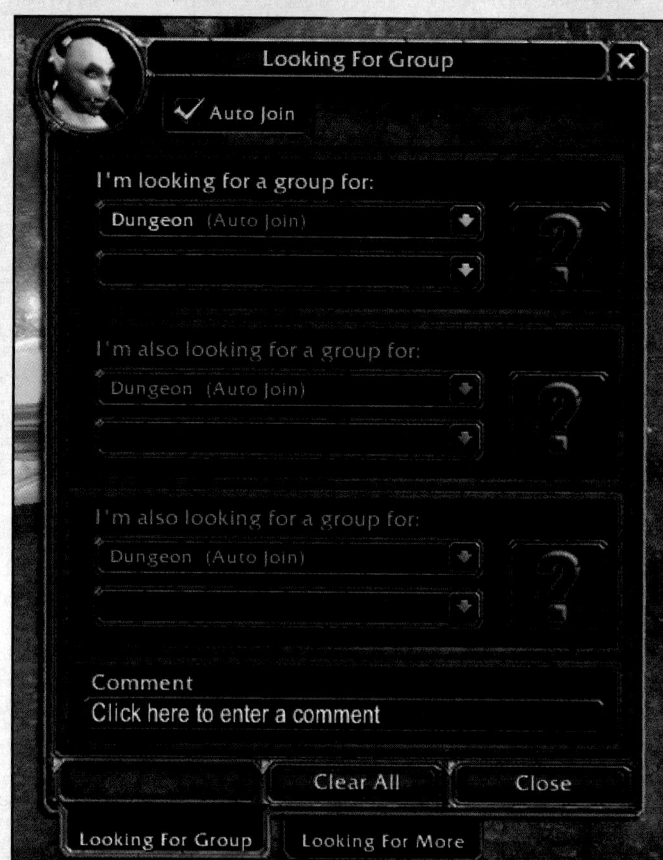

The new Looking For Group functionality is a sweeping change, allowing players to look for specific dungeon, quest, or fighting groups with only a few moments of selecting options. Using the /lfg option brings up the page, and from there you can start searching. You can also use the new icon on the bottom of the screen to access this (Click on Looking For Group/Looking For More). This system is even refined enough to allow searches for Heroic Dungeon runs, specific Elite Quests, and so forth.

FINDING A GROUP

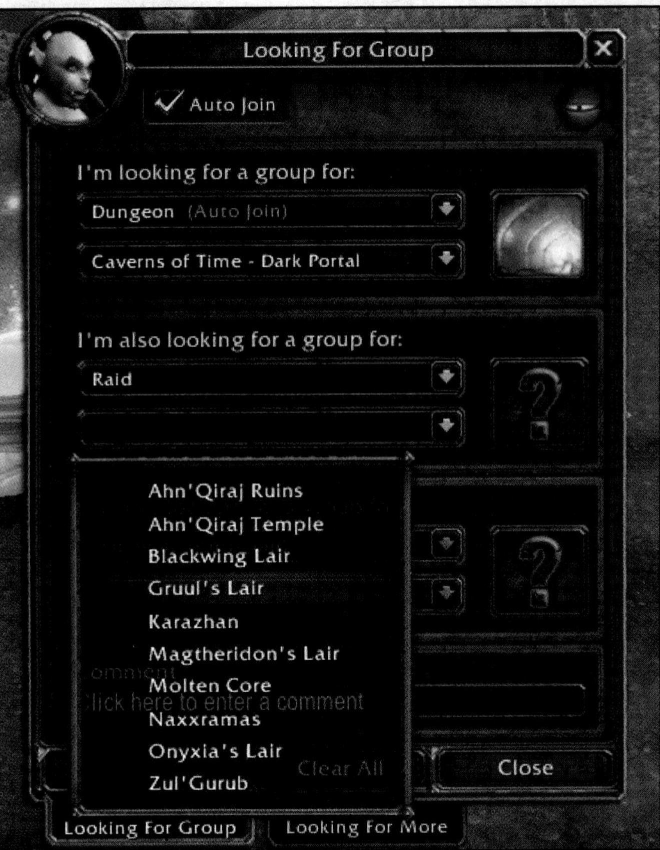

The Looking for Group interface now has primary and secondary drop-down menus that allow players to refine their searches for comrades. This search can be made on the basis of a given dungeon, raid, battleground, or zone. Or, you can search for buddies even for a given quest.

All of these choices, only selected in the primary field, provide a level-appropriate group of options in the second field. In the case of quests, the system even provides a list from your current quest log.

Use the bottom of the screen to enter any comments that would help people to figure out what you are looking for.

At the top of the screen is the Auto Join toggle. This determines whether you are interested in being thrown automatically into groups that are interested in the same goals. If you want to screen for the better pick-up-groups, leave this option off. If you just want a group of any sort to get your quest/dungeon run started, leave it on for convenience.

Once you have entered the information for your first goal, the second set of menus lights up. This allows you to look for multiple groups simultaneously; up to three search flags can be up as you travel around!

LOOKING FOR MORE

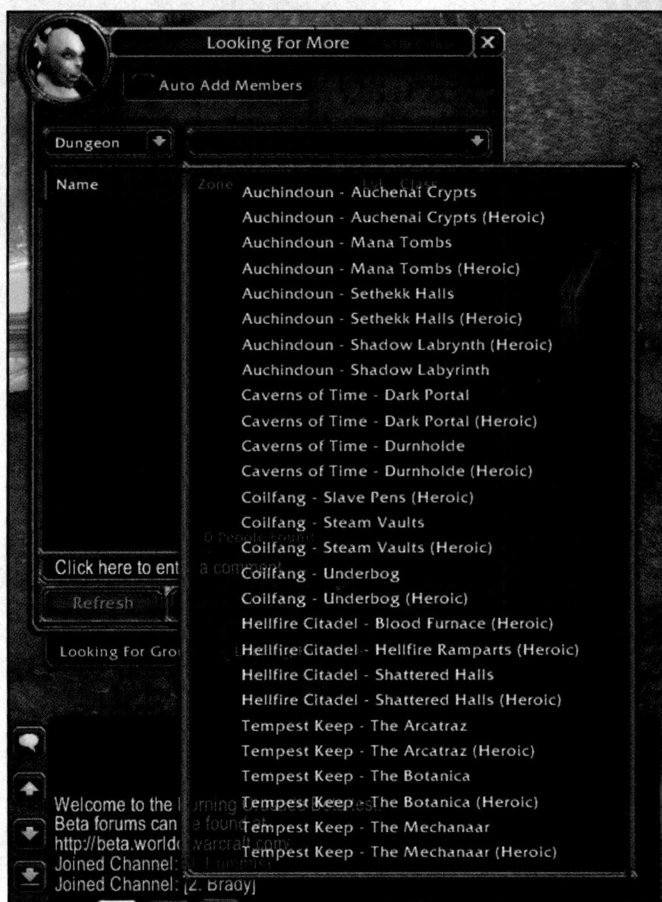

The Looking For More tab is at the bottom of the /lfg page. This tool lets you search the active list of interested characters and invite them directly into your group if they meet your qualifications.

If you choose to toggle Automatically Add Members at the top of the page, your group can be filled quickly with any of the available people in the list. With that off, it's much easier to search and find people that you might already know or even have grouped with previously.

Without even leaving the screen to type, you can click on the available buttons to invite characters individually or send the players messages.

Want a Challenge? Try Heroic Mode!

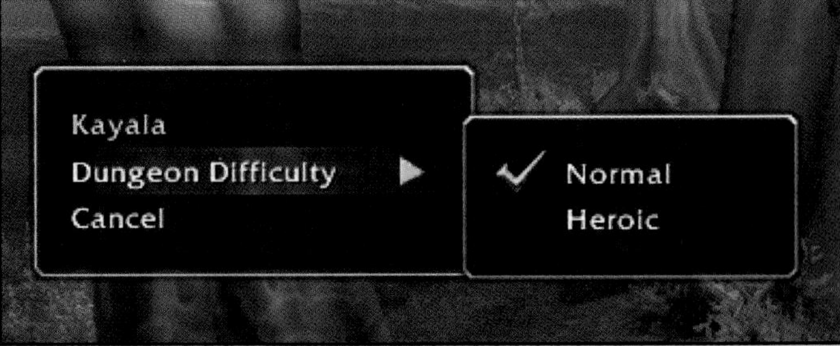

Dungeons are now going to have a mode for capped players. Heroic Mode allows for new rewards, adds a ton of difficulty, and lets you build up toward purchasing epic armor for 5-man groups. This is an awesome change, and it really helps to give non-raiders even more content and challenges to look forward to. This won't be free epic time, but your work will get you the goodies you want in the end. Finally, a fair system for all players concerned.

The idea is that your group leader can use the normal group interface to select Heroic Mode. This means that any Instance Dungeon you enter will be set for a level 70 group. Expect the monsters to be a couple levels above you, and their bosses might even have new tricks up their sleeves.

Be aware that you need to unlock Heroic Dungeons. The keys for each are going to be unique, such that you may need higher Reputation to be able to use them. Being Revered in Honor Hold/Thrallmar might be required for your Heroic Hellfire Citadel runs, just as Revered Reputation with Sha'tar may be required for Tempest Keep Instances.

When you defeat a boss, they drop epic gear for the level 70s, and they also drop a token for each person in the group. These tokens are used to purchase Tier 4 Epic armor for level 70s.

Heroic Mode instances have a raid timer similar to normal raid instances; you can run any Heroic Mode instance only once per day.

Resetting Instances

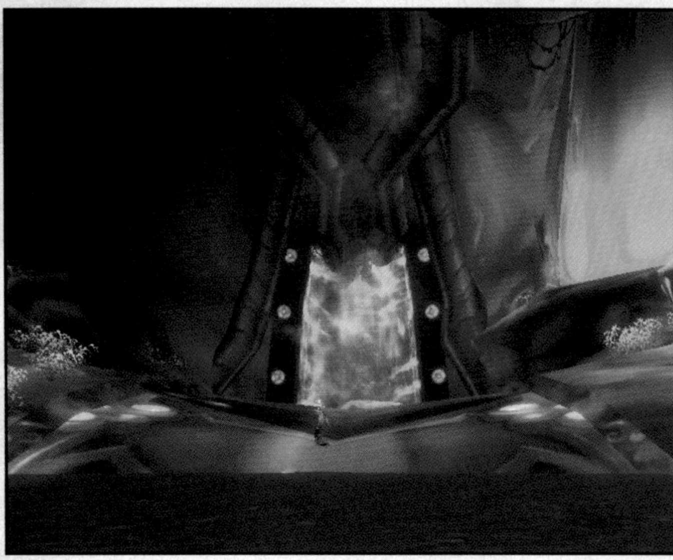

There have always been odd ways to change Instances so that players can rerun them without waiting for a full respawn of enemies and bosses. Now, things are much more convenient than they used to be, as Blizzard has added the Reset Instance feature.

To access this feature the leader clicks on their own portrait, and then they select the option to Reset Instance. From there, they will get a query for whether to reset all Instances. Once they select "Yes," the chat box will list all of the Instances that have been reset. After that point, the group can return to any Instance and start from the beginning.

So, when your group finishes an Instance and wants to run it again, all you have to do is head out and use this option before returning. However, note that there is a maximum number of times you can reset an instance per hour.

CRAFTING AND FINDING NEW GEAR

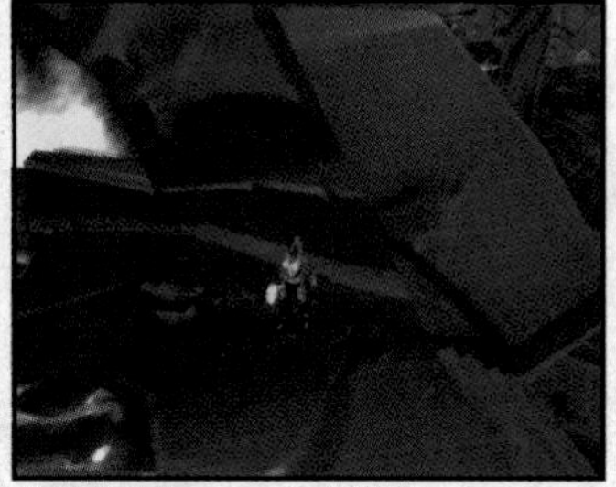

Equipment statistics have changed, and their creation and effects have as well. Master-tier crafting has been added to the game, opening an entirely new set of pieces for the dedicated crafters of WoW. There are more Superior and Epic pieces than before that can be learned, and just a glance at your trainer's recipes lets you know that these are serious pieces.

Beyond the new recipes for various professions, there is also an entirely new profession to master: Jewelcrafting.

And if that isn't enough, non-crafters can join in the fun with Socketed Items. These are found in Outland, and they are pieces that can be improved by adding various gems to the item.

Another perk for non-crafters is the change in gear quality during the post-60 levels. Even a number of simple green drop items start to look good as you travel through Outland. The equipment curve rises substantially, to help a number of more casual players partially compete with the raiders who have their second- or third-tier sets completed. This won't overcome the equipment gap in a level or two, but it helps to soften the difference.

Master Tier Crafting

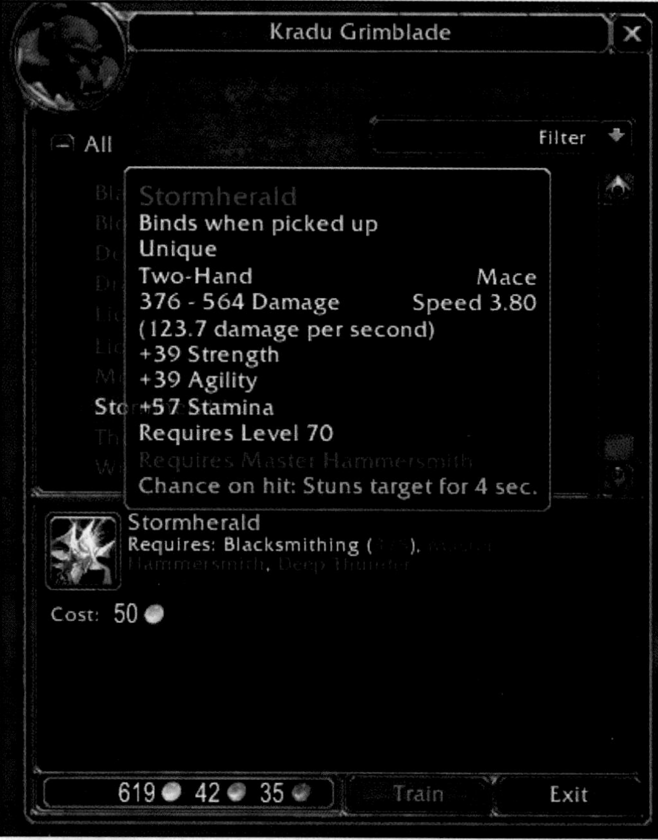

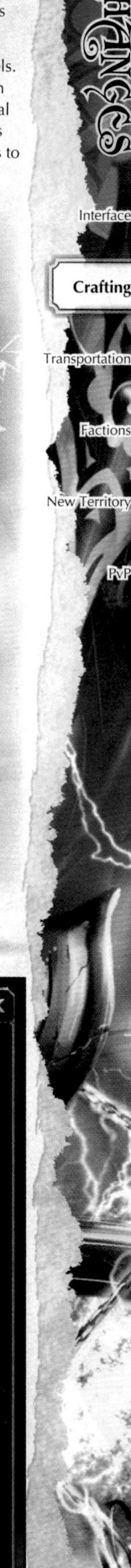

For those who have been waiting at 300 in their chosen Professions, it is time to move on. Seek the new Grand Master Trainers, and have them teach you the secrets of Master Crafting.

After purchasing this new rank, your crafter will be able to start gaining points again. This new tier, like all of the ones that came before it, stretches for 75 points (capping at 375). In many of the Professions, there are some incredible new options for what you can harvest or create.

Beyond doing more of the same, the Burning Crusade additions attempt to relieve some of the burden on Professions that had a hard time previously. For example, Blacksmiths suffered from having only a few pieces that many players were interested in purchasing.

Now, there are not only good pieces of weapons and armor to sell (even for high-end players) but there are also bind-on-pickup recipes that allow Blacksmiths of the highest skill to create upgradeable equipment for themselves. Epic-quality gear is just on the horizon for dedicated crafters, and these pieces are pretty impressive.

There is also a far better distribution of stats for the items that some Professions make. You used to see some recipes that added +Agility/Spirit and other such odd combinations. Things like this are rarely see anymore (if at all).

Alliance Grand Masters

Trade	Location
Alchemy	Honor Hold Tower, Hellfire Peninsula
Blacksmithing	Honor Hold Blacksmith, Hellfire Peninsula
Cooking	Honor Hold Inn, Hellfire Peninsula (Purchase Book)
Enchanting	Honor Hold Tower, Hellfire Peninsula
Engineering	Telredor, Zangarmarsh
First Aid	Temple of Telhamut, Hellfire Peninsula
Fishing	Cenarion Post, Zangarmarsh
Herbalism	Honor Hold Tower, Hellfire Peninsula
Jewelcrafting	Honor Hold Inn, Hellfire Peninsula
Leatherworking	Outside Honor Hold Inn, Hellfire Peninsula
Mining	Honor Hold Blacksmith, Hellfire Peninsula
Skinning	Honor Hold Inn, Hellfire Peninsula
Tailoring	Honor Hold Inn, Hellfire Peninsula

Horde Grand Masters

Trade	Location
Alchemy	Bat Tower of Thrallmar, Hellfire Peninsula
Blacksmithing	Thrallmar Smith, Hellfire Peninsula
Cooking	Thrallmar Inn, Hellfire Peninsula (Purchase Book)
Enchanting	Bat Tower of Thrallmar, Hellfire Peninsula
Engineering	Thrallmar, Hellfire Peninsula
First Aid	Falcon Watch, Hellfire Peninsula
Fishing	Cenarion Post, Zangarmarsh
Herbalism	Bat Tower of Thrallmar, Hellfire Peninsula
Jewelcrafting	Inside Inn of Thrallmar, Hellfire Peninsula
Leatherworking	Near Inn in Thrallmar, Hellfire Peninsula
Mining	Outside Barracks of Thrallmar, Hellfire Peninsula
Skinning	Thrallmar
Tailoring	Thrallmar, Hellfire Peninsula

Jewelcrafting

Jewelcrafting is an entirely new Profession that has recipes for Rings, Necklaces, some Trinkets, and gems for Socketed Items. Because some of the rare equipment with Sockets can be upgraded to have very high stats and a wonderful degree of customization, Jewelcrafting is going to be in fairly high demand.

For those who desire this new trade, consider raising Mining along with it. Having a Miner to get easy metal and gemstones is going to decrease the expense of leveling Jewelcrafting by an immense margin. A huge number of Jewelcrafting recipes have a need for both metal and stones, so the Auction House is going to be a familiar place to you if you don't have Mining or a supportive guild behind you.

One very interesting thing about the products from this Profession is that some of them are quite group friendly. Some items have on-use effects that buff your character and any party members within range. Consider the Thick Felsteel Necklace: beyond its +36 Stamina, this necklace has a use that buff party members for +20 Stamina for 30 minutes. That buff may not be huge, but a couple hundred Health can make the difference in those close matches.

Socketed Items

Socketed Items are found in Outland, and they offer unprecedented item customization. When highlighting and item that has Sockets, you will quickly notice that those open slots are listed in grey and state what form of gems they take.

From there, you can research the gems available for those slots. Use the tables in this guide to get an idea of what you can have. Once you know which gems sound exciting, look up the materials required for Jewelcrafters to do their work and gather/buy these. It's always nice to be able to give crafters what they need (it saves money in the long run). This way, you escape with only a tip most of the time, rather than paying for the time, hassle, and profit of the crafter.

There are several major types of Socketed Gems. Most of these count as having one or two colors, and there are also Meta Gems that can only be used when your items have a certain level of several colors. This is complex enough that it requires some explanation for those who aren't yet familiar with the system.

The four types of Sockets are as follows: Blue, Red, Yellow, and Meta. The first three are the most common types, and they appear as Sockets in a fair number of Outland rewards. You character can use any gems of a corresponding color in those slots. Or, they can use any gem that has a mixed color where one of the two colors matches that slot. The table below expands on this.

Socketed Gem Types

Gem Type	Where Used	Requirements
Blue	Any Blue Sockets	N/A
Red	Any Red Sockets	N/A
Yellow	Any Yellow Sockets	N/A
Green	Any Blue or Yellow Sockets	N/A
Orange	Any Red or Yellow Sockets	N/A
Purple	Any Blue or Red Sockets	N/A
Meta	Head Pieces w/ Meta Slots	Various Points in Multiple Primary Colors (* Explained Below)

Meta Gems and their Sockets are the most complex of these new bonuses. Head pieces are the primary equipment that have Meta Sockets; you won't see chest pieces, legs, and so forth with these. In addition, you won't be able to use these slots even if you do have a Meta Gem unless you meet certain requirements.

The key to having an active Meta Bonus is in having multiple pieces of Socketed gear. The Meta Gem itself determines how many of other colored gems you need. For instance, a Meta Gem might say (2 Red, 1 Yellow). This would mean that the Meta Gem would only function as long as your character has equipment with 2 or more Red Gems and 1 or more Yellow Gems.

One piece of good news is that Green, Orange, and Purple stones count twice! Thus, your character would need 15 Sockets to activate a 5/5/5 Meta Slot if you only used primary colors (5 Blues, 5 Reds, and 5 Yellows). But with Green, Orange, and Purple stones you could get away with fewer.

Example: (3 Greens, 3 Oranges, and 2 Purples would give you enough points in all colors to activate a 5/5/5 Meta Slot). Any 3-3-2 combination of multi-colored gems should succeed in this example.

Samples of Common Gems

Gem Name	Gem Type	Bonuses Conveyed
Bold Blood Garnet	Red	+6 Strength
Luminous Flame Spessarite	Yellow	+7 Healing Bonus, +3 Intellect
Sparkling Azure Moonstone	Blue	+6 Spirit
Mystical Skyfire Diamond	Meta	2% Chance on Spellcast to make next spell Instant

Enchanting Change: Disenchant Has Skill Requirements

It won't be as easy for players to create casual Enchanters for the purpose of disenchanting items without bothering to skill up actual item enchanting. Now, items have certain skill requirements for an Enchanter to be able to break them into their component parts.

To find out what skill is required for breaking a given item, click on Disenchant and bring the mouse to hover over the item that you are considering. This brings up a listing for the required skill.

A New Grade of Equipment: Items Post 60

Boulderfist Gloves of the Beast
Soulbound
Hands Plate
606 Armor
+15 Strength
+18 Strength
+18 Agility
+28 Stamina
Durability 12 / 40
Requires Level 65

When Will My Old Gear Be Obsolete?

Quality of Equipment	When You Might Find Better Gear	Where to Go for a Challenge/Some Loot
Tier .5/Level 60 Rares	60+	Hellfire Peninsula/Hellfire Citadel: Ramparts
Tier 1 Epics	62+	Zangarmarsh/Coilfang
Tier 2 Epics	65+	Nagrand Outdoor Quests
Tier 3 Epics	Late 60s	Karazhan, Netherstorm Instances

Equipment in the post 60 environment is incredible; the scale is entirely different, and it doesn't take long before even casual players are able to find gear that rivals tier 1/tier 2 equipment from before the expansion. Only those who are equipped in the absolute best gear pre-expansion are going to be overly picky about some of the quest items that are found in Outland.

After several days of play, people will be seeing green items that rival things that were epic before. This is the way of things, and it should be understood that what was once the cap has no real meaning now. 90 DPS weaponry is not end-game now. 10,000 Health is not crazy wonderful. You get the idea.

There are so many quests with multiple item choices that it is very easy to gear up for the Outland content just by going through even the safer outdoor quests that you find all over the place. Take a buddy or two with you into Outland and it gets even easier.

So, be careful of letting colors decide whether you are interested in gear. Even if you have blue or purple piece of equipment for a given slot, start training yourself not to immediately pass or Disenchant the greens that you find. When your tank finds a 3000 Armor green shield with tons of Stamina and Block, it should become clear that things are changing quickly.

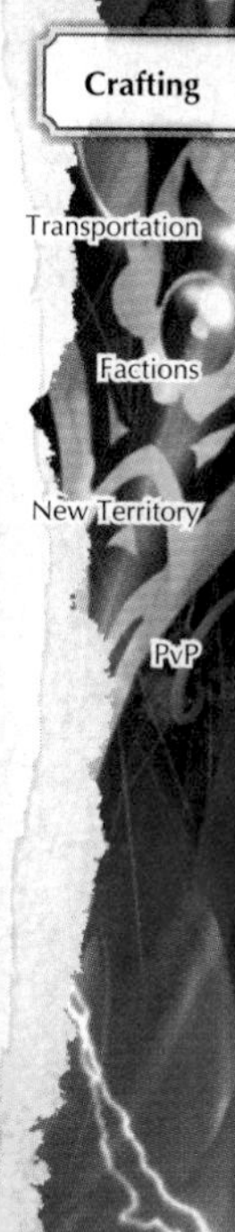

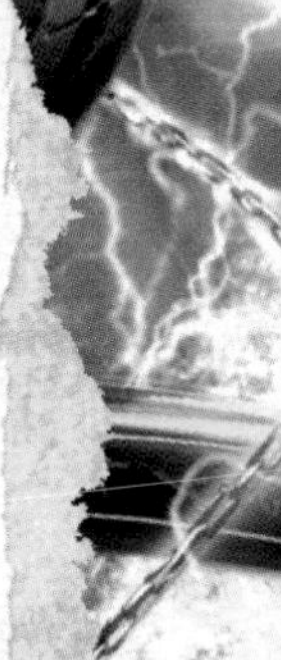

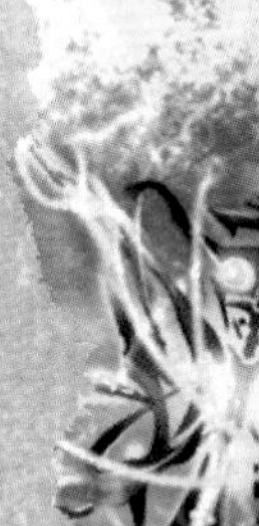

TRANSPORTATION CHANGES

With so much new territory added to the game, it's important to understand how to get around! Most of the new content has been added as Outland, as a section of 7 outdoor zones, 1 major city (with plenty of smaller towns), and more World Dungeons than you can shake a stick at.

The Dark Portal and Travel in Outland

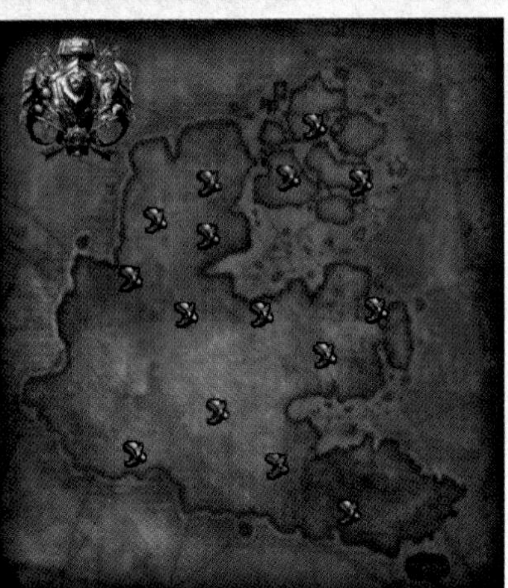

The Dark Portal, located in the southern part of the Blasted Lands, is your key to Outland. This massive gate will be seized by both Alliance and Horde troops, who hold the line against the darkness so that champions from both factions can freely come back and forth between the worlds.

To reach the Dark Portal, keep heading south from Stonard if you are a Horde player and keep going until you pass into Blasted Lands and eventually on to Outland. For Alliance, you can fly from Stormwind directly down to Blasted Lands and make a short run to the Portal.

Some important things to know about Outland: you can get back through the Dark Portal at any time by walking in the opposite direction, there are gateways to all of the major cities (for both factions) in the center of Shattrath City, and there are plenty of Flight Points.

Even in the first zone of Outland, there are multiple Flight Points! Make sure to grab the first one just outside of the Dark Portal. There are separate Flight Points for the Horde and Alliance here, so be sure you are getting the correct flight point.

Meeting Stones

Meeting Stones these days are so much better than they were in the old days. You can use them to teleport grouped members to the Stone's location, and you only need the help of one other group member! This means that Warlocks no longer are forced to rush to sites ahead of time just to wait for two more people to help summon any stragglers. Now, anybody can arrive near the dungeon and summon everyone else as soon as a second member arrives. No wasted time, no wasted effort, and no massive delays if you don't have a Warlock. It doesn't get much easier than this!

Flying Mounts

At level 70, players get the ability to learn how to ride Flying Mounts. These are only usable and available in Outland, and they are the key to safe and fast exploration of any and all outdoor areas. This includes several parcels of land that are entirely unreachable without Flying Mounts! Thus, you can return to Hellfire Peninsula, Terokkar Forest, and all of the other Outland zones and re-explore to see what you missed the first time around. Hard-to-find Herbs, interesting locales, and other surprises wait for those who are able to pay the hefty price for learning this new skill.

Flying Mounts are purchased in Shadowmoon Valley, the final zone that many players seek in Outland. Though the mounts themselves aren't terribly pricey (100 gold for normal Flying Mounts and 200 gold for Swift ones, before discounts), it is quite expensive to master the art of riding them. For training your character to 225 Riding, it costs 800 gold; this allows you to use the standard Flying Mounts. Then, as a necessary progression, you need 5000 gold more to get to 300 Riding. Though money comes in quite easily in Outland, you are still likely to be saving money for a short while at level 70 before you can afford everything.

On PvP servers, Flying Mounts make it much easier to get around regions without being hassled. It is very hard for anyone to get you off of your Mount, as these creatures make your character Immune to a number of crowd control effects. Beyond that, you can avoid damage by flying high enough that grounded characters don't have the range to do anything to you. And, other flying characters can't attack you because those actions aren't allowed while you are mounted.

Druid Flying Form

At level 68, Druids can learn how to shift into a Flying Form! This is a wonderful gift for the class; even though many characters are going to be able to fly a few levels after, it is still wonderful to be able to take to the skies early on and explore the content that is reserved for those who can fly out to seek it. This is also a very inexpensive method of gaining flight!

As with normal flight, this mode is restricted to Outland; you won't be able to dominate Warsong Gulch, fly over Orgrimmar, or otherwise use this new ability to alter the way that earlier content was dealt with.

The Undercity/Silvermoon City Teleporter

For fast transport between the Blood Elven lands and the other sections of Horde territory, use the Teleporter in Undercity and the northern throne room of Silvermoon City. This two-way Teleporter prevents young players from needing to corpse drag themselves all the way across the Plaguelands to reach the comfort of Tirisfal.

Mage Portal Training

There are four new transportation spells added to the Mage repertoire: two teleports and two portals. Horde Mages can use the Undercity/Silvermoon City teleporter to find the Blood Elven Portal trainer nearby and learn how to magic yourself and others to Silvermoon City. The Shattrath City portal trainer, found near the portals to the major cities in the central area (The Terrace of Light), teaches the Shattrath City spells, as do the Portal Trainers in the Aldor/Scryer terraces. Alliance Mages gain the equivalent spells for the Exodar.

More Factions Than Ever

There are many new factions in Outland. Gaining Reputation with these groups is something that crafters and normal players alike are going to enjoy, at least to a fair extend. Many of the Rep systems in Outland are much easier than some of the immensely time-consuming factions that were seen in the earlier game. Read through here to find out what rewards are available and to get a start on what your characters need to achieve their various goals.

Honor Hold (Alliance Only)

Honor Hold is the first major bastion of Alliance might in Outland. It should be the first stop for any Alliance characters who come through the portal and wish to look for adventure. There are many quests there (ideal for level 60+ characters), and there are two types of rewards for people to consider.

Warrant Officer Tracy Proudwell is a PvP reward NPC; she lets you turn in Marks of Honor Hold for Socketed Gems or one of a few other items. The Honor Hold Favor is wonderful for Reputation grinding, and its boost to experience gained is truly a nifty perk. She is found along the road near the northeast side of Honor Hold.

Only a short distance away, Logistics Officer Ulrike is the Faction NPC for Honor Hold rewards. There are more items there, and you purchase them normally, with gold. Early rewards cover some interesting crafting pieces, including the Elixir of Major Agility and some sweet Enchantments. By the time you reach Exalted there are a few epics items to consider.

Warrant Officer Tracy Proudwell Rewards

Name	Cost	Requirements	Stats
Mighty Blood Garnet	10 Marks of Honor Hold	None	Red Socket Gem (+14 Attack Power)
Stark Blood Garnet	10 Marks of Honor Hold	None	Red Socket Gem (+8 Spell Damage)
Barbed Deep Peridot	10 Marks of Honor Hold	None	Yellow or Blue Socket Gem (+3 STAM, +4 Crit Rating)
Notched Deep Peridot	10 Marks of Honor Hold	None	Yellow or Blue Socket Gem (+3 STAM, +4 Spell Crit Rating)
Band of the Victor	15 Marks of Honor Hold	None	Finger (+25 STAM, Equip for +13 Crit Rating) +1 Red Socket, Unique
Circlet of the Victory	15 Marks of Honor Hold	None	Finger (+25 STAM, Equip for +13 Spell Crit Rating) +1 Red Socket, Unique
Honor Hold Favor	5 Marks of Honor Hold	None	Use in Hellfire Peninsula and Hellfire Citadel to increase Honor Hold Reputation gained from killing monsters by 25% and experience by 5% (lasts 30 Minutes)

Honor Hold Reputation Rewards

Name	Cost	Requirements	Stats
Pattern: Felstalker Belt	10 Gold 80 Silver	Friendly, Leatherworking (350)	Mail Waist (357 Armor +18 AGI, Equip for +50 Attack Power, 7 Mana/5 Seconds) +1 Blue Socket, +1 Red Socket, Felstalker Set
Footman's Waterskin	18 Silver/5	Friendly	Restores 4200 Mana over 30 Seconds
Formula: Enchant Bracer Superior Healing	5 Gold 40 Silver	Friendly, Enchanting (325)	Adds +30 to Healing Bonus Enchantment for Bracers
Dried Mushroom Rations	54 Silver/5	Honored	Restores 3888 Health over 27 Seconds, +10 Stamina for 10 Minutes
Recipe: Elixir of Major Agility	4 Gold 50 Silver	Honored, Alchemy (330)	Use to Add 35 Agility for 1 Hour
Pattern: Felstalker Bracers	14 Gold 40 Silver	Honored, Leatherworking (360)	Mail Wrist (283 Armor +18 AGI, Equip for +38 Attack Power, +4 Mana/5 Seconds) +1 Blue Socket, Felstalker Set
Footman's Longsword	26 Gold 73 Silver	Honored	1h Sword (47.1 DPS +12 STAM, Equip for +9 Hit Rating, +18 Attack Power)
Glyph of Fire Warding	90 Gold	Honored	Permanently Adds +20 Fire Resistance to a Head Item
Sage's Band	10 Gold 33 Silver	Honored	Finger (+12 INT, Equip for +12 Spell Crit Rating, +14 to Damage and Healing Bonus), Unique
Recipe: Transmute Skyfire Diamond	7 Gold 20 Silver	Honored, Alchemy (350)	Teaches your Alchemist how to Transmute a Skyfire Diamond
Pattern: Felstalker Breastplate	14 Gold 40 Silver	Honored, Leatherworking (360)	Mail Chest (646 Armor +26 AGI, Equip for +52 Attack Power, 10 Mana/5 Seconds) +1 Blue Socket, +2 Red Sockets, Felstalker Set
Formula: Enchant Chest Exceptional Stats	5 Gold 40 Silver	Revered, Enchanting (345)	Adds +6 to All Stats Enchantment for Chest
Glyph of Renewal	90 Gold	Revered	Permanently Adds +35 to Healing Bonus and 7 Mana/5 Seconds to a Head Item

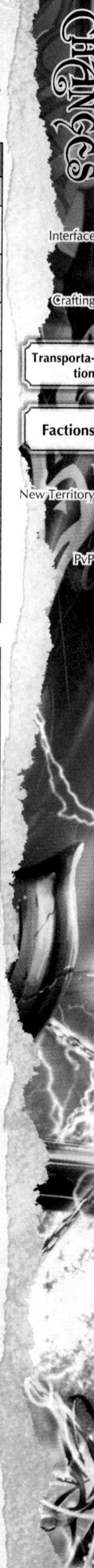

Honor Hold Reputation Rewards

Name	Cost	Requirements	Stats
Ring of Convalescence	15 Gold 84 Silver	Revered	Finger (+15 INT, Equip for +57 to Healing Bonus, 4 Mana/5 Seconds), Unique
Hellforged Halberd	50 Gold 13 Silver	Revered	Polearm (93.3 DPS +26 AGI, Equip for +19 Hit Rating, +92 Attack Power)
Plans: Felsteel Shield Spike	5 Gold 40 Silver	Exalted, Blacksmithing (360)	Use to attach this crafted Shield Spike (deals 26-38 Damage)
Veteran's Musket	144 Gold	Exalted	Gun (72.0 DPS +11 AGI, Equip for +11 Hit Rating, +22 Attack Power)
Blade of the Archmage	185 Gold 35 Silver	Exalted	Mh Dagger (41.4 DPS +12 STAM, +11 INT, Equip for +21 Spell Crit Rating, +150 to Damage and Healing Bonus), Unique
Honor's Call	178 Gold 81 Silver	Exalted	1h Sword (78.9 DPS +12 STAM, Equip for +16 Defense Rating, +6 Hit Rating), Unique
Honor Hold Tabard	90 Silver	Exalted	A Unique Honor Hold Tabard

Thrallmar (Horde Only)

The forward base of the Horde in Outland is at Thrallmar. These Orcs are extremely loyal to Thrall and to the cause of retaking Outland, so they won't be impressed just because you are a hero back in Orgrimmar. They want fresh blood, eager songs of victory, and a push against the Burning Legion such as rarely been seen before. Triumph against the Hellfire Orcs and the Demons of the area, and perhaps, they will sing of you.

To improve your Reputation with the Orcs of Thrallmar, get to work killing the Hellfire Orcs. Early on, the non-elite Orcs of the area provide more than enough Reputation gain to keep things going quickly. Once these enemies stop giving Reputation gain, move into the early Hellfire Instances and fight those Elites. For the highest advancement of Reputation, you must then shift to the Shattered Halls.

Not far from the Inn of Thrallmar is Battlecryer Blackeye. Speak to this NPC once you have accumulated a modest number of Marks of Thrallmar; these are them used for getting useful Socket Gems or one of a couple rings. For those who wish to grind Thrallmar Reputation more effectively, the Thrallmar Favor is absolutely wonderful. Use this when going into Hellfire Instances for a major boost to your Reputation.

For the actual rewards gained by improving Thrallmar Reputation, speak to Quartermaster Urgronn; this NPC stands just outside of the main barracks in Thrallmar.

Battlecryer Blackeye's Rewards

Name	Cost	Requirements	Stats
Mighty Blood Garnet	10 Marks of Thrallmar	None	Red Socket Gem (+14 Attack Power)
Stark Blood Garnet	10 Marks of Thrallmar	None	Red Socket Gem (+8 Spell Damage)
Barbed Deep Peridot	10 Marks of Thrallmar	None	Yellow or Blue Socket Gem (+3 STAM, +4 Crit Rating)
Notched Deep Peridot	10 Marks of Thrallmar	None	Yellow or Blue Socket Gem (+3 STAM, +4 Spell Crit Rating)
Band of the Victor	15 Marks of Thrallmar	None	Finger (+25 STAM, Equip for +13 Crit Rating) +1 Red Socket, Unique
Circlet of the Victory	15 Marks of Thrallmar	None	Finger (+25 STAM, Equip for +13 Spell Crit Rating) +1 Red Socket, Unique
Thrallmar Favor	5 Marks of Thrallmar	None	Use in Hellfire Peninsula and Hellfire Citadel to increase Thrallmar Reputation gained from killing monsters by 25% and experience by 5% (lasts 30 Minutes)

Thrallmar Reputation Rewards

Name	Cost	Requirements	Stats
Pattern: Felstalker Belt	10 Gold 80 Silver	Friendly, Leatherworking (350)	Mail Waist (357 Armor +18 AGI, Equip for +50 Attack Power, 7 Mana/5 Seconds) +1 Blue Socket, +1 Red Socket, Felstalker Set
Grunt's Waterskin	18 Silver/5	Friendly	Restores 2934 Mana over 30 Seconds
Dried Fruit Rations	54 Silver/5	Honored	Restores 3888 Health over 27 Seconds, +10 Stamina for 10 Minutes
Formula: Enchant Bracer Superior Healing	5 Gold 40 Silver	Friendly, Enchanting (325)	Adds +30 to Healing Bonus Enchantment for Bracers
Recipe: Elixir of Major Agility	4 Gold 50 Silver	Honored, Alchemy (330)	Use to Add 35 Agility for 1 Hour
Formula: Enchant Chest Exceptional Stats	5 Gold 40 Silver	Revered, Enchanting (345)	Adds +6 to All Stats Enchantment for Chest
Pattern: Felstalker Bracers	14 Gold 40 Silver	Honored, Leatherworking (360)	Mail Wrist (283 Armor +18 AGI, Equip for +38 Attack Power, +4 Mana/5 Seconds) +1 Blue Socket, Felstalker Set
Grunt's Waraxe	26 Gold 73 Silver	Honored	1h Axe (47.1 DPS +12 STAM, Equip for +9 Hit Rating, +18 Attack Power)
Glyph of Fire Warding	90 Gold	Honored	Permanently Adds +20 Fire Resistance to a Head Item
Farseer's Band	10 Gold 33 Silver	Honored	Finger (+12 INT, Equip for +12 Spell Crit Rating, +14 to Damage and Healing Bonus), Unique
Recipe: Transmute Skyfire Diamond	7 Gold 20 Silver	Honored, Alchemy (350)	Teaches your Alchemist how to Transmute a Skyfire Diamond
Pattern: Felstalker Breastplate	14 Gold 40 Silver	Honored, Leatherworking (360)	Mail Chest (646 Armor +26 AGI, Equip for +52 Attack Power, 10 Mana/5 Seconds) +1 Blue Socket, +2 Red Sockets, Felstalker Set
Glyph of Renewal	90 Gold	Revered	Permanently Adds +35 to Healing Bonus and 7 Mana/5 Seconds to a Head Item
Ancestral Band	15 Gold 84 Silver	Revered	Finger (+15 INT, Equip for +57 to Healing Bonus, 4 Mana/5 Seconds), Unique
Blackened Spear	50 Gold 13 Silver	Revered	Polearm (93.3 DPS +26 AGI, Equip for +19 Hit Rating, +92 Attack Power)

Thrallmar Reputation Rewards			
Name	**Cost**	**Requirements**	**Stats**
Plans: Felsteel Shield Spike	5 Gold 40 Silver	Exalted, Blacksmithing (360)	Use to attach this crafted Shield Spike (deals 26-38 Damage)
Marksman's Bow	144 Gold	Exalted	Bow (73.7 DPS +11 AGI, Equip for +11 Hit Rating, +22 Attack Power)
Stormcaller	185 Gold 35 Silver	Exalted	Mh Dagger (41.4 DPS +12 STAM, +11 INT, Equip for +21 Spell Crit Rating, +150 to Damage and Healing Bonus), Unique
Warbringer	178 Gold 81 Silver	Exalted	1h Axe (78.9 DPS +12 STAM, Equip for +16 Defense Rating, +6 Hit Rating), Unique
Thrallmar Tabard	90 Silver	Exalted	A Unique Thrallmar Tabard

Kurenai (Alliance Only)

The Kurenai are a group of the Broken that have clawed their way back from the brink of slavery. Exerting themselves now, they are helping the Alliance to push back the various nasty forces that cover Outland.

You can find the Kurenai in Zangarmarsh and in Nagrand, but their heaviest concentration of quests and their reward NPC are all found in Telaar, in southern Nagrand. Trade Narasu, west of the inn, has the various goodies that you earn by fighting for the Kurenai. Slaying the foul Ogres and Kilsorrow Orcs of Nagrand is a very fast way to earn a fine Reputation. Then, once the Kurenai are Friendly, turn in the Obsidean Warbeads that you collect from the Ogres for even more Reputation gain.

Kurenai Reputation Rewards			
Name	**Cost**	**Requirements**	**Stats**
Pattern: Netherfury Belt	10 Gold 80 Silver	Friendly, Leatherworking (340)	Mail Waist (339 Armor +27 STAM, Equip for +21 to Damage and Healing Bonus, 9 Mana/5 Seconds) +1 Blue Socket, +1 Red Socket, Netherfury Set
Pattern: Reinforced Mining Bag	4 Gold 50 Silver	Honored, Leatherworking (325)	28 Slot Mining Bag
Pattern: Netherfury Leggings	10 Gold 80 Silver	Honored, Leatherworking (340)	Mail Legs (527 Armor +37 STAM, Equip for +29 to Damage and Healing Bonus, 10 Mana/5 Seconds) +2 Blue Sockets, +1 Red Socket, Netherfury Set
Band of Elemental Spirits	15 Gold 84 Silver	Revered	Finger (+15 STAM, +26 INT, +15 SPI), Unique
Kurenai Kilt	19 Gold 62 Silver	Revered	Leather Legs (256 Armor +11 INT, Equip for +18 Spell Crit Rating, +44 to Damage and Healing Bonus), +1 Red Socket, +2 Yellow Sockets
Recipe: Transmute Primal Fire to Earth	7 Gold 20 Silver	Revered	It does exactly what you would expect
Pattern Netherfury Boots	10 Gold 80 Silver	Revered, Leatherworking (350)	Mail Feet (392 Armor +36 STAM, Equip for +21 to Damage and Healing Bonus, 7 Mana/5 Seconds) +1 Blue Socket, +1 Red Socket, Netherfury Set
Cloak of the Ancient Spirits	45 Gold 48 Silver	Exalted	Back (78 Armor +15 STAM, +26 INT, Equip for 6 Mana/5 Seconds)
Arechron's Gift	188 Gold 5 Silver	Exalted	2h Mace (93.3 DPS Equip for +42 Hit Rating, +84 Attack Power)
Far Seer's Helm	74 Gold 30 Silver	Exalted	Mail Head (530 Armor +37 STAM, +25 INT, Equip for +50 Attack Power) +1 Blue Socket, +1 Red Socket, +1 Yellow Socket
Epic Talbuks	90 Gold	Exalted	There are 5 colors of Epic Talbuk Mounts Here

Mag'har (Horde Only)

The Mag'har Orcs are a tough breed; they have lived and fought in Outland, and done all that they can to resist the lure of the demonic taint. They aren't overly found of the Alliance (and vice versa), but they'll be glad to make friends with any of the Horde troops that come through the portal.

There are a few initial quests to ingratiate yourself with the Mag'har in Hellfire Peninsula, if you are a Horde character. Their rewards, more quests, and the monsters that raise Mag'har Reputation are primarily in Nagrand. Clear Sunspring Post of its enemies or fight against the Ogres of Nagrand to raise Reputation. Save the Obsidian Warbeads that you fight from the Ogres, as these too can be used for Mag'har Rep (or Consortium Rep once you reach Friendly with that group).

On the western side of Garadar is Provisioner Nasela; seek her for any of the Reputation rewards that interest you. The equipment is primarily leather or mail, and Warrriors/Paladins have the least to gain there. What might interest anyone, however, is that Epic Talbuks are sold there. The grind to Exalted isn't too bad with these guys, and having a special mount at low cost is certainly interesting to some players!

Mag'har Reputation Rewards

Name	Cost	Requirements	Stats
Pattern: Netherfury Belt	10 Gold 80 Silver	Friendly, Leatherworking (340)	Mail Waist (339 Armor +27 STAM, Equip for +21 to Damage and Healing Bonus, 9 Mana/5 Seconds) +1 Blue Socket, +1 Red Socket, Netherfury Set
Pattern: Reinforced Mining Bag	4 Gold 50 Silver	Honored, Leatherworking (325)	28 Slot Mining Bag
Pattern: Netherfury Leggings	10 Gold 80 Silver	Honored, Leatherworking (340)	Mail Legs (527 Armor +37 STAM, Equip for +29 to Damage and Healing Bonus, 10 Mana/5 Seconds) +2 Blue Sockets, +1 Red Socket, Netherfury Set
Band of Ancestral Spirits	15 Gold 84 Silver	Revered	Finger (+15 STAM, +26 INT, +15 SPI), Unique
Tempest Leggings	19 Gold 62 Silver	Revered	Leather Legs (256 Armor +11 INT, Equip for +18 Spell Crit Rating, +44 to Damage and Healing Bonus), +1 Red Socket, +2 Yellow Sockets
Talbuk Hide Spaulders	15 Gold 4 Silver	Revered	Leather Shoulder (219 Armor +20 AGI, Equip for +15 Hit Rating, +70 Attack Power)
Pattern Netherfury Boots	10 Gold 80 Silver	Revered, Leatherworking (350)	Mail Feet (392 Armor +36 STAM, Equip for +21 to Damage and Healing Bonus, 7 Mana/5 Seconds) +1 Blue Socket, +1 Red Socket, Netherfury Set
Ceremonial Cover	45 Gold 48 Silver	Exalted	Back (78 Armor +15 STAM, +26 INT, Equip for 6 Mana/5 Seconds)
Hellscream's Will	188 Gold 5 Silver	Exalted	2h Axe (93.3 DPS Equip for +42 Hit Rating, +84 Attack Power)
Earthcaller's Headdress	74 Gold 30 Silver	Exalted	Mail Head (530 Armor +37 STAM, +25 INT, Equip for +50 Attack Power) +1 Blue Socket, +1 Red Socket, +1 Yellow Socket
Epic Talbuks	90 Gold	Exalted	There are 5 colors of Epic Talbuk Mounts Here

Cenarion Expedition (Both Factions)

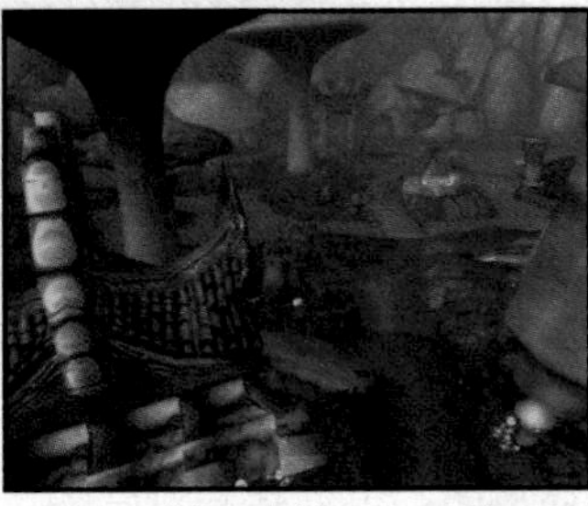

The Cenarion Expedition in Outland has an entirely different Reputation than that of the Cenarion Circle members back in Azeroth. So, you need to start from scratch. Luckily, there are a ton of quests to do for these characters in Zangarmarsh (with a bit in western Hellfire Peninsula as well).

As with all members of the Cenarion Circle, these people are friendly to both the Horde and the Alliance. Dark lines on a map of the world mean nothing to those who care for nature and beauty. Come one and come all, for the greater good of Outland.

If you really want to raise faction with the Expedition, run through the Coilfang Instances consistently. Collecting Unidentified Plant Parts while fighting the native creatures of the area will help too, as those can be turned in to Lauranna Thar'well (at the southern side of the Cenarion Refuge).

Fedryen Swiftspear is the Quartermaster for the Cenarion Expedition. Look for him outside the Inn at the Cenarion Refuge in Zangarmarsh.

Cenarion Expedition Reputation Rewards

Name	Cost	Requirements	Stats
Pattern: Heavy Netherweave Net	2 Gold 70 Silver	Friendly., Tailoring (325)	Use to capture a target up to 35 Yards away for 3 Seconds.
Pattern: Heavy Clefthoof Boots	12 Gold 60 Silver	Friendly, Leatherworking (355)	Leather Feet (198 Armor +37 STAM, Equip for +24 Defense) +1 Blue Socket, +1 Yellow Socket, Clefthoof Set
Schematic: Green Smoke Flare	5 Gold 40 Silver	Friendly, Engineering (335)	Use to throw a Green Smoke Flare at a location for 5 Minutes
Expedition Flare	72 Silver	Friendly	Use to call a Cenarion Expedition unit to your aid (works only in Zangarmarsh)
Pattern: Heavy Clefthoof Leggings	12 Gold 60 Silver	Honored, Leatherworking (355)	Leather Legs (251 Armor +42 STAM, Equip for +34 Defense) +2 Blue Sockets, +1 Yellow Socket, Clefthoof Set
Plans: Adamantite Sharpening Stone	5 Gold 40 Silver	Honored, Blacksmithing (350)	Use to add +12 Damage and +14 Crit Rating to a weapon for 30 Minutes (Edged Weapons)
Plans: Adamantite Weightstone	5 Gold 40 Silver	Honored, Blacksmithing (350)	Use to add +12 Damage and +14 Crit Rating to a weapon for 30 Minutes (Blunt Weapons)
Scout's Arrows	18 Silver	Honored	26 DPS Arrows
Preserver's Cudgel	27 Gold 32 Silver	Honored	Mh Mace (41.3 DPS +15 STAM, +9 INT, Equip for +57 to Healing Bonus, 4 Mana/5 Seconds)
Warden's Hauberk	13 Gold 76 Silver	Honored	Leather Chest (204 Armor +17 AGI, +25 STAM) +2 Red Sockets, +1 Yellow Socket
Explorer's Walking Stick	34 Gold 3 Silver	Honored	Staff (63.7 DPS +42 STAM, Equip for +54 Attack Power, Slight Run Speed Increase)
Glyph of Nature Warding	90 Gold	Honored	Adds +20 Nature Resistance to a Head Slot Item
Design: Nightseye Panther	10 Gold 80 Silver	Revered, Jewelcrafting (370)	Trinket (Equip for +1 Stealth Level, +54 Attack Power, Use: +320 Attack Power for 12 Seconds)
Pattern: Heavy Clefthoof Vest	14 Gold 40 Silver	Honored, Leatherworking (360)	Leather Chest (290 Armor +52 STAM, Equip for +28 Defense) +1 Blue Socket, +2 Yellow Sockets, Clefthoof Set
Warden's Arrow	45 Silver	Revered	37 DPS Arrows
Recipe: Major Nature Protection Potion	9 Gold	Exalted, Alchemy (360)	Use to Absorb 2800 to 4000 Nature Damage over 1 Hour
Glyph of Ferocity	90 Gold	Revered	Adds +34 Attack Power and +16 Hit Rating for a Head Slot Item
Watcher's Cowl	11 Gold 46 Silver	Revered	Cloth Head (127 Armor +21 STAM, +36 INT, +14 SPI, Equip for +79 Healing Bonus)
Strength of the Untamed	15 Gold 84 Silver	Revered	Neck (+27 STAM, Equip for +19 Defense Rating, +18 Dodge Rating)
Recipe: Transmute Primal Water to Air	7 Gold 20 Silver	Revered	It does exactly what you would expect
Windcaller's Orb	71 Gold 11 Silver	Exalted	Off-Hand Item (+15 INT, +11 SPI, Equip for +62 Healing Bonus)
Earthwarden	228 Gold 40 Silver	Exalted	2h Mace (102.5 DPS +500 Armor, Equip for +24 Defense Rating, +24 Feral Combat, +525 Attack Power in Cat, Bear, Dire Bear, and Moonkin Forms); Clearly a Paladin Mace

Sporeggar (Both Factions)

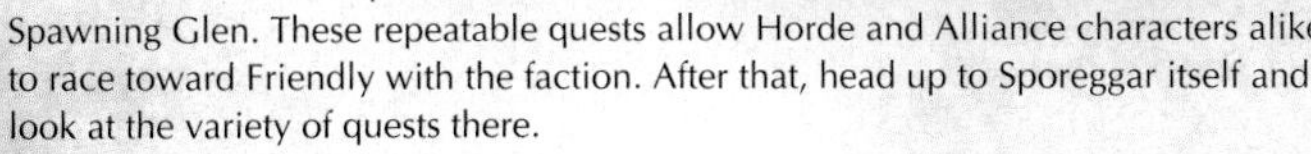

The cute little fungus-people of Sporeggar are always in need of help. These friendly creatures live in several areas of Zangarmarsh, and they are hunted by many of the Giants that also share that zone. Neither Horde grunts nor Alliance soldiers should be able to resist the lure of helping these cute humanoids.

To ingratiate yourself with Sporeggar, travel to the southwestern part of the zone and look for the quests beside The Spawning Glen. These repeatable quests allow Horde and Alliance characters alike to race toward Friendly with the faction. After that, head up to Sporeggar itself and look at the variety of quests there.

For continued Reputation gain, run the kill quest against the Naga at least once (Now That We're Friends). Then, form large groups to chain-kill Giants in the south for rapid advancement.

As far as rewards go, your characters should collect the bright Glowcap Mushrooms that are found throughout the area, as ground spawns. It does not require Herbalism to pick these! The mushrooms act as currency with the Sporeggar. Alchemists and Cooks are going to be most interested in some of the rewards. To purchase reward items, look in a small building on the western side of Sporeggar.

Sporeggar Reputation Rewards

Name	Cost	Requirements	Stats
Recipe: Sporeling Snack	2 Gold	Cooking (310)	Turns Strange Spores into Sporeling Snacks (+20 STAM/SPI for pets), Lasts 30 Minutes
Recipe: Clam Bar	1 Glowcap Mushroom	Cooking (300)	Food that restores 4320 Health/30 Seconds, After 10 Seconds it adds +20 STAM/SPI for 30 Minutes
Marsh Lichen	2 Glowcap Mushrooms	None	Use to restore 4320 Health/30 Seconds, After 10 Seconds it adds +10 Spirit for 10 Minutes
Tallstalk Mushroom	1 Glowcap Mushroom	Friendly	Use to show the location of Giants on the Minimap, Lasts for 1 Hour
Redcap Toadstool	1 Glowcap Mushroom	Honored	Use to remove 1 Poison Effect, Lowers Nature Resistance by 50 for 1 Minute
Petrified Lichen Guard	15 Glowcap Mushrooms	Honored	Shield (2534 Armor 48 Block +24 STAM, Equip Effect: Afflicts attacker with Deadly Poison when you are struck)
Sporeling's Firestick	20 Glowcap Mushrooms	Revered	Wand (96.9 DPS +12 STAM, +9 INT, Equip for +11 to Damage and Healing Bonus)
Hardened Stone Shard	45 Glowcap Mushrooms	Revered	1h Dagger (55.3 DPS +16 STAM, Equip for +12 Hit Rating, +22 Attack Power), Unique
Recipe: Transmute Primal Earth to Water	25 Glowcap Mushrooms	Revered, Alchemy (350)	It does exactly what you would expect
Muck-Covered Drape	25 Glowcap Mushrooms	Honored	Back (66 Armor +30 STAM, Use to reduce Threat with nearby enemies)
Recipe: Shrouding Potion	30 Glowcap Mushrooms	Exalted, Alchemy (335)	Use to reduce Threat with nearby enemies

The Aldor (Either Faction)

The Aldor are Draenei who are fully loyal to the Naaru of Shattrath City (the Sha'tar). This loyalty does not extend to the Scryers, who also dwell in Shattrath City; these two factions work toward some common goals, but they do not get along! Peace is kept within the city, but neither side is going to be happy if someone aids the other. Thus, even though Horde or Alliance members can aid the Aldor, it comes at the price of alienating the Scryers.

Seek the upper tier of the Aldor on the western side of Shattrath. There, you can find NPCs who provide various repeatable quests to earn favor with this group. Slaying Demons of the Burning Legion is the most stable way to do this, as there are Insignias and Artifacts to be found and turned in by doing so. Good areas for finding the Burning Legion include western Nagrand and several spots of Netherstorm.

For Aldor Enchantments, turn in the Artifacts in exchange for Reputation and Holy Dust. This Holy Dust is taken to Inscriber Saalyn (at the Aldor bank, on the northern side of the city). This NPC places Enchantments on Shoulder pieces. Nearby is Quartermaster Endarin, who controls the purchasable rewards from the faction.

Aldor Enchantment Rewards

Name	Cost	Requirements	Stats
Inscription of Discipline	1 Holy Dust	Honored	Adds +15 to Damage and Healing Bonus to a Shoulder Item
Inscription of Faith	1 Holy Dust	Honored	Adds +29 Healing Bonus to a Shoulder Item
Inscription of Vengeance	1 Holy Dust	Honored	Adds +26 Attack Power to a Shoulder Item
Inscription of Warding	1 Holy Dust	Honored	Adds +13 Dodge Rating to a Shoulder Item
Greater Inscription of Discipline	5 Holy Dust	Exalted	Adds +18 to Damage and Healing Bonus to a Shoulder Item
Greater Inscription of Faith	5 Holy Dust	Exalted	Adds +33 Healing Bonus and 4 Mana/5 Seconds to a Shoulder Item
Greater Inscription of Vengeance	5 Holy Dust	Exalted	Adds +30 Attack Power and +10 Crit Rating to a Shoulder Item
Greater Inscription of Warding	5 Holy Dust	Exalted	Adds +15 Dodge Rating and +10 Defense Rating to a Shoulder Item

Aldor Faction Rewards

Name	Cost	Requirements	Stats
Design: Gleaming Golden Draenite	4 Gold 50 Silver	Friendly, Jewelcrafting (305)	Yellow Socket Gem, +6 Spell Crit Rating
Pattern: Shadowguard Belt	7 Gold 20 Silver	Honored, Leatherworking (350)	Leather Waist (146 Armor +27 STAM, +30 Shadow Resistance) +2 Blue Sockets
Pattern: Shadowscale Belt	7 Gold 20 Silver	Honored, Leatherworking (350)	Mail Waist (325 Armor +27 STAM, +30 Shadow Resistance) +2 Blue Sockets
Plans: Shadowbane Bracers	5 Gold 40 Silver	Friendly, Blacksmithing (350)	Plate Wrist (497 Armor +15 STAM, +28 Shadow Resistance) +1 Blue Socket, Shadow Guard Set
Design: Royal Shadow Draenite	4 Gold 50 Silver	Honored, Jewelcrafting (305)	Red or Blue Gem, +7 to Healing Bonus, 1 Mana/5 Seconds
Plans: Shadowbane Gloves	5 Gold 40 Silver	Honored, Blacksmithing (360)	Plate Hands (722 Armor +21 STAM, +30 Shadow Resistance) +1 Blue Socket, +1 Yellow Socket, Shadow Guard Set
Pattern: Mystic Spellthread	5 Gold 40 Silver	Honored, Tailoring (335)	Use to add +25 to Spell Bonus and +15 STAM to a Leg Item

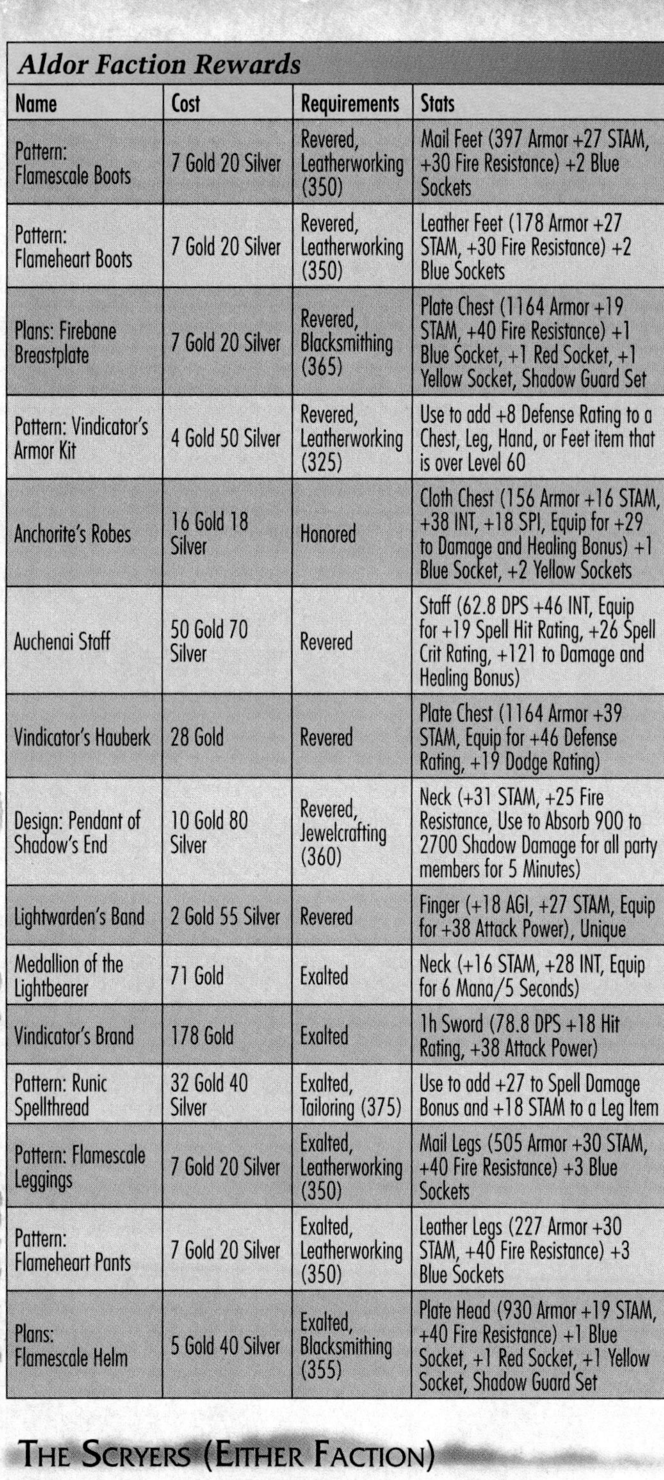

Aldor Faction Rewards			
Name	**Cost**	**Requirements**	**Stats**
Pattern: Flamescale Boots	7 Gold 20 Silver	Revered, Leatherworking (350)	Mail Feet (397 Armor +27 STAM, +30 Fire Resistance) +2 Blue Sockets
Pattern: Flameheart Boots	7 Gold 20 Silver	Revered, Leatherworking (350)	Leather Feet (178 Armor +27 STAM, +30 Fire Resistance) +2 Blue Sockets
Plans: Firebane Breastplate	7 Gold 20 Silver	Revered, Blacksmithing (365)	Plate Chest (1164 Armor +19 STAM, +40 Fire Resistance) +1 Blue Socket, +1 Red Socket, +1 Yellow Socket, Shadow Guard Set
Pattern: Vindicator's Armor Kit	4 Gold 50 Silver	Revered, Leatherworking (325)	Use to add +8 Defense Rating to a Chest, Leg, Hand, or Feet item that is over Level 60
Anchorite's Robes	16 Gold 18 Silver	Honored	Cloth Chest (156 Armor +16 STAM, +38 INT, +18 SPI, Equip for +29 to Damage and Healing Bonus) +1 Blue Socket, +2 Yellow Sockets
Auchenai Staff	50 Gold 70 Silver	Revered	Staff (62.8 DPS +46 INT, Equip for +19 Spell Hit Rating, +26 Spell Crit Rating, +121 to Damage and Healing Bonus)
Vindicator's Hauberk	28 Gold	Revered	Plate Chest (1164 Armor +39 STAM, Equip for +46 Defense Rating, +19 Dodge Rating)
Design: Pendant of Shadow's End	10 Gold 80 Silver	Revered, Jewelcrafting (360)	Neck (+31 STAM, +25 Fire Resistance, Use to Absorb 900 to 2700 Shadow Damage for all party members for 5 Minutes)
Lightwarden's Band	2 Gold 55 Silver	Revered	Finger (+18 AGI, +27 STAM, Equip for +38 Attack Power), Unique
Medallion of the Lightbearer	71 Gold	Exalted	Neck (+16 STAM, +28 INT, Equip for 6 Mana/5 Seconds)
Vindicator's Brand	178 Gold	Exalted	1h Sword (78.8 DPS +18 Hit Rating, +38 Attack Power)
Pattern: Runic Spellthread	32 Gold 40 Silver	Exalted, Tailoring (375)	Use to add +27 to Spell Damage Bonus and +18 STAM to a Leg Item
Pattern: Flamescale Leggings	7 Gold 20 Silver	Exalted, Leatherworking (350)	Mail Legs (505 Armor +30 STAM, +40 Fire Resistance) +3 Blue Sockets
Pattern: Flameheart Pants	7 Gold 20 Silver	Exalted, Leatherworking (350)	Leather Legs (227 Armor +30 STAM, +40 Fire Resistance) +3 Blue Sockets
Plans: Flamescale Helm	5 Gold 40 Silver	Exalted, Blacksmithing (355)	Plate Head (930 Armor +19 STAM, +40 Fire Resistance) +1 Blue Socket, +1 Red Socket, +1 Yellow Socket, Shadow Guard Set

The Scryers (Either Faction)

This Blood Elven faction is open to members of the Alliance or the Horde, though it's most likely to be chosen by Horde players. As with the Aldor, you must dedicate to one side or the other here. Everything that pushes Scryer Reputation forward will push Aldor Reputation back considerably.

Look in the Scryer's area of Shattrath for small quests and repeatable quests for Reputation. The biggest bread-winners come from hunting Blood Elves in eastern Terrokar or in Netherstorm. The Marks of Kael'thas that drop from these foes are turned in for considerable Rep. In addition, the same targets drop Arcane Tomes; those are turned in for even more Reputation. You also receive Arcane Runes for these turn ins.

Arcane Runes are taken to the Scryers Bank in the city. Look at the back of that building for Inscriber Veredis. This NPC takes Arcane Runes and enchants Shoulder items in return. At Honored, he'll turn a single Arcane Rune into a moderate bonus. At Exalted with Scryers, he'll accept 5 Arcane Runes in exchange for a major enchantment. The table below lists these effects.

Also in the Scryer's Bank is Quartermaster Enuril, the NPC who sells items for those who have proven themselves with the faction. The next table shows what is available from him.

Scryer Enchantment Rewards			
Name	**Cost**	**Requirements**	**Stats**
Inscription of the Blade	1 Arcane Rune	Honored Reputation	Adds +13 Crit Rating to a Shoulder Item
Inscription of the Knight	1 Arcane Rune	Honored Reputation	Adds +13 Defense Rating to a Shoulder Item
Inscription of the Oracle	1 Arcane Rune	Honored Reputation	Adds +5 Mana per 5 Seconds to a Shoulder Item
Inscription of the Orb	1 Arcane Rune	Honored Reputation	Adds +13 Spell Crit Rating to a Shoulder Item
Greater Inscription of the Blade	5 Arcane Runes	Exalted Reputation	Adds +15 Crit Rating and +20 Attack Power to a Shoulder Item
Greater Inscription of the Knight	5 Arcane Runes	Exalted Reputation	Adds +15 Defense Rating and +10 Dodge Rating to a Shoulder Item
Greater Inscription of the Oracle	5 Arcane Runes	Exalted Reputation	Adds +6 Mana per 5 Seconds and up to 22 Healing to a Shoulder Item
Greater Inscription of the Orb	5 Arcane Runes	Exalted Reputation	Adds +15 Spell Crit Rating and up to 12 Spell Damage Bonus to a Shoulder Item

Scryer Faction Rewards			
Name	**Cost**	**Requirements**	**Stats**
Design: Runed Blood Garnet	6 Gold	Friendly, Jewelcrafting 315	Red Socket Gem, +7 Spell Damage
Design: Dazzling Deep Peridot	6 Gold	Honored, Jewelcrafting 325	Yellow or Red Socket Gem, +1 Mana/5 Seconds, +3 Int
Plans: Enchanted Adamantite Belt	6 Gold	Friendly, Blacksmithing (355)	Plate Waist (644 Armor +21 STAM, +30 Arcane Resistance) +1 Blue Socket, +1 Yellow Socket, Enchanted Adamantite Armor Set
Pattern: Enchanted Felscale Gloves	8 Gold	Honored, Leatherworking (350)	Mail Hands (361 Armor +27 STAM, +30 Arcane Resistance) +2 Blue Sockets
Pattern: Enchanted Clefthoof Boots	8 Gold	Honored, Leatherworking (350)	Leather Feet (178 Armor +27 STAM, +30 Arcane Resistance) +2 Blue Sockets
Pattern: Silver Spellthread	6 Gold	Honored, Tailoring (335)	Use to Enchant Leggings with +46 Healing Bonus and +15 STAM
Design: Pendant of Withering	12 Gold	Revered, Jewelcrafting (360)	Necklace (+31 STAM, +25 Nature Resistance, Use to Absorb 900 to 2700 Nature Damage for all Nearby Party Members/10 Charges)
Recipe: Elixir of Major Firepower	6 Gold	Revered, Alchemy (345)	Use to Increase Fire Spell Damage by up to 65 for 1 Hour
Plans: Enchanted Adamantite Boots	6 Gold	Honored, Blacksmithing (355)	Plate Feet (787 Armor +21 STAM, +30 Arcane Resistance) +1 Red Socket, +1 Blue Socket, Enchanted Adamantite Armor Set
Pattern: Enchanted Felscale Boots	8 Gold	Revered, Leatherworking (350)	Mail Feet (397 Armor +27 STAM, +30 Arcane Resistance) +2 Blue Sockets
Pattern: Enchanted Clefthoof Gloves	8 Gold	Revered, Leatherworking (350)	Leather Hands (162 Armor +27 STAM, +30 Arcane Resistance) +2 Blue Sockets

Scryer Faction Rewards

Name	Cost	Requirements	Stats
Plans: Enchanted Adamantite Breastplate	6 Gold	Revered, Blacksmithing (360)	Plate Chest (1154 Armor +27 STAM, +40 Arcane Resistance) +2 Blue Sockets, +1 Yellow Socket, Enchanted Adamantite Armor Set
Gauntlets of the Chosen	16 Gold 9 Silver	Revered	Plate Hands (728 Armor +15 AGI, +30 STAM, Equip for +35 Defense Rating)
Retainer's Leggings	22 Gold 61 Silver	Revered	Leather Legs (256 Armor +28 STAM, Equip for +26 Hit Rating, +92 Attack Power)
Seer's Cane	56 Gold 93 Silver	Revered	Staff (62.8 DPS +28 STAM, +46 INT, Equip for +228 Healing Bonus, +10 Mana/5 Seconds)
Scryer's Bloodgem	17 Gold 60 Silver	Revered	Trinket (Equip for +32 Spell Hit Rating, Use for +150 Spell Damage Bonus and +280 Healing Bonus for 15 Seconds)
Pattern: Magister's Armor Kit	5 Gold	Revered, Leatherworking (325)	Patch to Add +3 Mana/5 Seconds to a Chest, Leg, Hand, or Feet Item Over Level 60
Pattern: Golden Spellthread	36 Gold	Exalted, Tailoring (375)	Teaches You to Create Golden Spellthread
Pattern: Enchanted Felscale Leggings	8 Gold	Exalted, Leatherworking (350)	Mail Legs (505 Armor +30 STAM, +40 Arcane Resistance) +3 Blue Sockets
Plans: Enchanted Adamantite Leggings	8 Gold	Exalted, Blacksmithing (365)	Plate Legs (1019 Armor +27 STAM, +40 Arcane Resistance) +2 Blue Sockets, +1 Red Socket, Adamantite Armor Set
Pattern: Enchanted Clefthoof Leggings	8 Gold	Exalted, Leatherworking (350)	Leather Legs (227 Armor +30 STAM, +40 Arcane Resistance) +3 Blue Sockets
Retainer's Blade	198 Gold 71 Silver	Exalted	1h Dagger (78.7 DPS +21 AGI, +21 STAM)
Seer's Signet	79 Gold 1 Silver	Exalted	Finger (+22 STAM, Equip for +11 Spell Crit Rating, +33 to Damage and Healing Bonus), Unique

The Sha'tar (Both Factions)

Shattrath City is the only place in Outland that has survived war against Illidan and the Burning Legion. The Naaru that peacefully rule this city are known as the Sha'tar. More than willing to befriend Horde or Alliance, Aldor or Scryer, these powerful beings are pivotal in the struggle to save Outland from the forces of evil.

When you reach level 70, look for G'eras in the Terrace of Light (on the western side of the main room). This Naaru sells the rewards for turning in Badges of Justice.

Sha'tar Rewards for Badges of Justice

Name	Cost	Requirements	Stats
Khadgar's Backpack	30 Badges of Justice	None	Off-Hand (Adds +43 to Damage and Healing Bonus)
Talisman of Kalecgos	30 Badges of Justice	None	Off-Hand (Adds +12 INT, +46 to Damage by Arcane Spells/Effects)
Mazthoril Honor Shield	40 Badges of Justice	None	Shield (4058 Armor 94 Block +15 STAM, +15 INT, Equip for +19 Spell Crit Rating, +22 to Damage and Healing Bonus)
Searing Sunblade	60 Badges of Justice	None	Off-Hand Dagger (78.5 DPS +21 AGI, +21 STAM)
Flametongue Seal	30 Badges of Justice	None	Off-Hand (Equip for +13 Spell Crit Rating, +44 Damage to Fire Spells/Effects)
Sapphiron's Wing Bone	30 Badges of Justice	None	Off-Hand (Equip for +10 to Spell Hit Rating, +47 Damage to Frost Spells/Effects)
Tears of Heaven	30 Badges of Justice	None	Off-Hand (Equip for +68 to Healing Bonus, 5 Mana/5 Seconds)
Light-Bearer's Faith Shield	40 Badges of Justice	None	Shield (4058 Armor 94 Block +18 STAM, +20 INT, Equip for +53 to Healing Bonus)
Orb of the Soul Eater	30 Badges of Justice	None	Off-Hand (+15 STAM, Equip for +47 Shadow Damage for Spells/Effects)
Azure-Shield of Coldarra	40 Badges of Justice	None	Shield (4058 Armor +28 STAM, Equip for +19 Defense Rating, +30 Block)
Ring of Cryptic Dreams	30 Badges of Justice	None	Finger (+15 STAM, +16 INT, Equip for +18 Crit Rating, +21 to Damage and Healing Bonus), Unique
Band of Halos	30 Badges of Justice	None	Finger (+19 STAM, +19 INT, Equip for +42 to Healing Bonus, 6 Mana/5 Seconds), Unique
Ring of Arathi Warlords	30 Badges of Justice	None	Finger (+21 STAM, Equip for +21 Crit Rating, +44 Attack Power), Unique
Ring of Unyielding Force	30 Badges of Justice	None	Finger (200 Armor, +25 STAM, Equip for +21 Defense Rating), Unique
Manasurge Pendant	30 Badges of Justice	None	Neck (+21 STAM, +20 INT, Equip for +27 to Damage and Healing Bonus)
Necklace of Eternal Hope	30 Badges of Justice	None	Neck (+21 STAM, +21 INT, Equip for +44 to Healing Bonus, 3 Mana/5 Seconds)
Choker of Vile Intent	30 Badges of Justice	None	Neck (+19 AGI, +16 STAM, Equip for +16 Hit Rating, +38 Attack Power)
Necklace of the Juggernaut	30 Badges of Justice	None	Neck (+18 AGI, +30 STAM, Equip for +20 Defense)
Shawl of Shifting Probabilities	30 Badges of Justice	None	Back (81 Armor +16 STAM, +15 INT, Equip for +21 Spell Crit Rating, +18 to Damage and Healing Bonus)
Bishop's Cloak	30 Badges of Justice	None	Back (81 Armor +15 STAM, +16 INT, Equip for +40 to Healing Bonus, 8 Mana/5 Seconds)
Blood Knight War Cloak	30 Badges of Justice	None	Back (81 Armor +20 AGI, +21 STAM, +46 Attack Power)
Farstrider Defender's Cloak	30 Badges of Justice	None	Back (231 Armor +28 STAM, Equip for +35 Block)
Icon of the Silver Crescent	50 Badges of Justice	None	Trinket (Equip for +40 to Damage and Healing Bonus, Use for +153 to Damage and Healing Bonus for 20 Seconds)
Essence of the Martyr	50 Badges of Justice	None	Trinket (Equip for +75 to Healing Bonus, Use for +288 to Healing Bonus for 20 Seconds)
Bloodlust Brooch	50 Badges of Justice	None	Trinket (Equip for +66 Attack Power, Use for +270 Attack Power for 20 Seconds)
Gnomeregan Auto-Blocker 600	50 Badges of Justice	None	Trinket (Equip for +51 Block, Use for +200 Block for 20 Seconds)

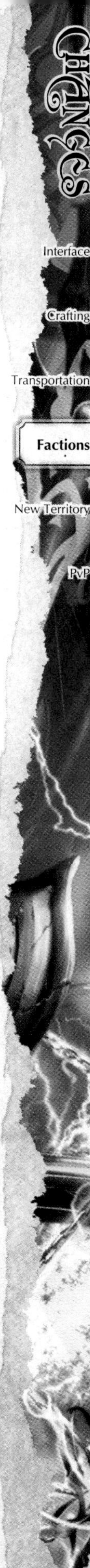

Sha'tar Lower City (Both Factions)

The refugees of Outland gather in Sha'tar, and they too have their own Reputation. These people won't care a bit whether you are loyal to the Aldor or Scryers; they are quite ready to take help wherever it can be found.

Allerian Stronghold (Alliance Only)

Just on the eastern side of Terokkar is the Allerian Stronghold, an Alliance fortress in southern Outland. This area has no faction of its own, as it is linked with the major Alliance push based out of Honor Hold, but there are still some independent rewards here. When the Alliance is in control of the PvP goals in Terokkar Forest, characters from that faction are able to gain Spirit Shards when they kill bosses inside of the area's Instance Dungeons. These Spirit Shards are turned in to Spirit Sage Zran, in the northwestern part of town.

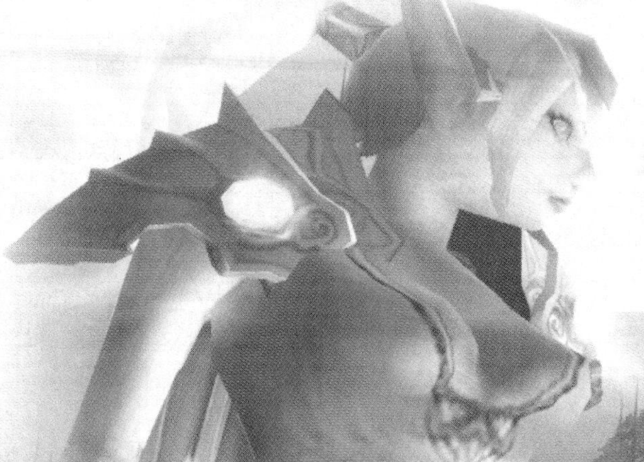

Spirit Sage Zran Rewards

Name	Cost	Requirements	Stats
Band of the Exorcist	100 Spirit Shards	None	Ring (+24 STAM, Equip for +10 Hit Rating, +16 Crit Rating, +11 Resilience Rating, +34 Attack Power), Unique
Seal of the Exorcist	100 Spirit Shards	None	Ring (+24 STAM, Equip for +12 Spell Hit Rating, +11 Resilience Rating, +28 to Bonus Damage and Healing), Unique
Exorcist's Plate Helm	30 Spirit Shards	None	Plate Head (827 Armor +25 STR, +30 STAM, Equip for +25 Crit Rating, +11 Resilience Rating) +1 Meta Socket
Exorcist's Lamellar Helm	30 Spirit Shards	None	Plate Head (827 Armor +30 STAM, +16 INT, Equip for +16 Spell Crit Rating, +11 Resilience Rating, +29 to Damage and Healing Bonus) +1 Meta Socket
Exorcist's Scaled Helm	30 Spirit Shards	None	Plate Head (827 Armor +20 STR, +30 STAM, +15 INT, Equip for +18 Crit Rating, +22 to Damage and Healing Bonus) +1 Meta Socket
Exorcist's Chain Helm	30 Spirit Shards	None	Mail Head (463 Armor +20 AGI, +35 STAM, +15 INT, Equip for +10 Crit Rating, +12 Resilience Rating, +20 Attack Power) +1 Meta Socket
Exorcist's Linked Helm	30 Spirit Shards	None	Mail Head (463 Armor +24 STR, +30 STAM, +13 INT, Equip for +22 Crit Rating, +13 Resilience Rating) +1 Meta Socket
Exorcist's Mail Helm	30 Spirit Shards	None	Mail Head (463 Armor +30 STAM, +16 INT, Equip for +24 Spell Crit Rating, +17 Resilience Rating, +29 Damage and Healing Bonus) +1 Meta Socket
Exorcist's Leather Helm	30 Spirit Shards	None	Leather Head (208 Armor +27 AGI, +33 STAM, Equip for +10 Crit Rating, +14 Resilience Rating, +20 Attack Power) +1 Meta Socket
Exorcist's Dragonhide Helm	30 Spirit Shards	None	Leather Head (248 Armor +23 STR, +17 AGI, +30 STAM, Equip for +11 Resilience Rating, +37 to Healing Bonus) +1 Meta Socket
Exorcist's Wyrmhide Helm	30 Spirit Shards	None	Leather Head (248 Armor +35 STAM, +16 INT, Equip for +10 Resilience Rating, +34 to Damage and Healing Bonus) +1 Meta Socket
Exorcist's Silk Hood	30 Spirit Shards	None	Cloth Head (111 Armor +34 STAM, +14 INT, Equip for +25 Spell Crit Rating, +14 Resilience Rating, +29 to Damage and Healing Bonus) +1 Meta Socket
Exorcist's Dreadweave Hood	30 Spirit Shards	None	Cloth Head (111 Armor +34 STAM, +25 INT, Equip for +20 Resilience Rating, +29 to Damage and Healing Bonus) +1 Meta Socket
Swift Wind Diamond	20 Spirit Shards	None	Meta Gem (+20 Attack Power and Minor Run Speed Increase), Requires 2 Yellow/1 Red
Swift Starfire Diamond	20 Spirit Shards	None	Meta Gem (+12 Spell Damage and Minor Run Speed Increase), Requires 2 Yellow/1 Red

Stonebreaker Hold (Horde Only)

Stonebreaker Hold is an Orcish camp in Terokkar Forest. This is not a faction unto itself, but there are several things that you can do with the people there. For one, you can turn in groups of 30 Arakkoa Feathers to Malukaz in the southern part of the camp. This nets you some free magical items with each turn in (and Rare items are possible). These Feather are farmed by killing many of the birdlike humanoids in Terokkar at their camps.

Speak to Spirit Sage Gartok, also in the southern part of the camp, to see what other items are available at Stonebreaker. To pay for the Sage's items, you must go into the Instance dungeons of the area while your faction has control of the PvP areas around the Bone Wastes. Killing each boss inside a Terokkar Instance nets each party member a Spirit Shard. Gartok accepts these are payment for his items.

Spirit Sage Gartok Rewards

Name	Cost	Requirements	Stats
Band of the Exorcist	100 Spirit Shards	None	Ring (+24 STAM, Equip for +10 Hit Rating, +16 Crit Rating, +11 Resilience Rating, +34 Attack Power), Unique
Seal of the Exorcist	100 Spirit Shards	None	Ring (+24 STAM, Equip for +12 Spell Hit Rating, +11 Resilience Rating, +28 to Bonus Damage and Healing), Unique
Exorcist's Plate Helm	30 Spirit Shards	None	Plate Head (827 Armor +25 STR, +30 STAM, Equip for +25 Crit Rating, +11 Resilience Rating) +1 Meta Socket
Exorcist's Lamellar Helm	30 Spirit Shards	None	Plate Head (827 Armor +30 STAM, +16 INT, Equip for +16 Spell Crit Rating, +11 Resilience Rating, +29 to Damage and Healing Bonus) +1 Meta Socket
Exorcist's Scaled Helm	30 Spirit Shards	None	Plate Head (827 Armor +20 STR, +30 STAM, +15 INT, Equip for +18 Crit Rating, +22 to Damage and Healing Bonus) +1 Meta Socket
Exorcist's Chain Helm	30 Spirit Shards	None	Mail Head (463 Armor +20 AGI, +35 STAM, +15 INT, Equip for +10 Crit Rating, +12 Resilience Rating, +20 Attack Power) +1 Meta Socket
Exorcist's Linked Helm	30 Spirit Shards	None	Mail Head (463 Armor +24 STR, +30 STAM, +13 INT, Equip for +22 Crit Rating, +13 Resilience Rating) +1 Meta Socket
Exorcist's Mail Helm	30 Spirit Shards	None	Mail Head (463 Armor +30 STAM, +16 INT, Equip for +24 Spell Crit Rating, +17 Resilience Rating, +29 Damage and Healing Bonus) +1 Meta Socket
Exorcist's Leather Helm	30 Spirit Shards	None	Leather Head (208 Armor +27 AGI, +33 STAM, Equip for +10 Crit Rating, +14 Resilience Rating, +20 Attack Power) +1 Meta Socket
Exorcist's Dragonhide Helm	30 Spirit Shards	None	Leather Head (248 Armor +23 STR, +17 AGI, +30 STAM, Equip for +11 Resilience Rating, +37 to Healing Bonus) +1 Meta Socket
Exorcist's Wyrmhide Helm	30 Spirit Shards	None	Leather Head (248 Armor +35 STAM, +16 INT, Equip for +10 Resilience Rating, +34 to Damage and Healing Bonus) +1 Meta Socket
Exorcist's Silk Hood	30 Spirit Shards	None	Cloth Head (111 Armor +34 STAM, +14 INT, Equip for +25 Spell Crit Rating, +14 Resilience Rating, +29 to Damage and Healing Bonus) +1 Meta Socket
Exorcist's Dreadweave Hood	30 Spirit Shards	None	Cloth Head (111 Armor +34 STAM, +25 INT, Equip for +20 Resilience Rating, +29 to Damage and Healing Bonus) +1 Meta Socket
Swift Wind Diamond	20 Spirit Shards	None	Meta Gem (+20 Attack Power and Minor Run Speed Increase), Requires 2 Yellow/1 Red
Swift Starfire Diamond	20 Spirit Shards	None	Meta Gem (+12 Spell Damage and Minor Run Speed Increase), Requires 2 Yellow/1 Red

Halaa (Dominant PvP Faction)

Though not a proper faction, there are rewards for the fighting that is done in and around the city of Halaa, in Nagrand. Whether soloing, grouped, or in a raid, you receive a Battle Token for each killing blow made by you or your team. When Halaa itself is under your faction's control, travel to the larger building on the western side of town and look for Chief Researcher Amereldine (Alliance: Chief Researcher Kartos). She accepts Oshu'gun Crystal Powder Samples; these are gained from standard monster fighting throughout the entire region, from just about every creature you might fight.

With a mixture of Battle Tokens and Research Tokens (that she gives you for every 20 Samples you turn in), your character can purchase Halaa rewards. These are grabbed from Quartermaster Jaffrey Noreliqe (Alliance: Quartermaster Davian Vaclav), who is standing just beside the Chief Researcher. The following table lists the rewards for these turn ins.

Halaa Rewards

Name	Cost	Requirements	Stats
Avenger's Waistguard	20 Battle Tokens, 1 Research Token	None	Plate Waist (573 Armor +16 STR, +24 STAM, +11 INT, Equip for +12 Crit Rating, +17 Resilience Rating, and +20 to Damage and Healing Bonus)
Avenger's Legguards	40 Battle Tokens, 2 Research Tokens	None	Plate Legs (891 Armor +22 STR, +33 STAM, Equip for +14 Crit Rating, +22 Resilience Rating, +27 to Damage and Healing Bonus) +1 Yellow Socket

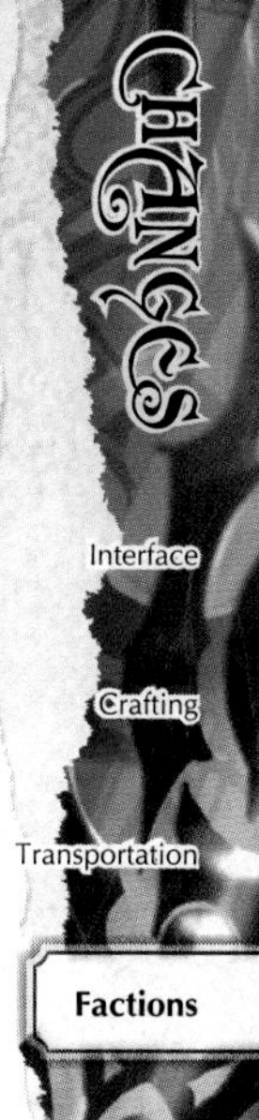

Halaa Rewards

Name	Cost	Requirements	Stats
Marksman's Belt	20 Battle Tokens, 1 Research Token	None	Mail Waist (321 Armor +19 AGI, +28 STAM, +12 INT, Equip for +9 Crit Rating, +13 Resilience Rating, +20 Attack Power)
Marksman's Leggaurds	40 Battle Tokens, 2 Research Tokens	None	Mail Legs (499 Armor +25 AGI, +39 STAM, +13 INT, Equip for +11 Crit Rating, +13 Resilience Rating, +22 Attack Power) +1 Yellow Socket
Hierophant's Sash	20 Battle Tokens, 1 Research Token	None	Cloth Waist (77 Armor +28 STAM, +19 INT, Equip for +19 Resilience Rating, +22 to Damage and Healing Bonus)
Hierophant's Leggings	40 Battle Tokens, 2 Research Tokens	None	Cloth Legs (119 Armor +39 STAM, +17 INT, Equip for +25 Resilience Rating, +29 to Damage and Healing Bonus) +1 Yellow Socket
Shadowstalker's Sash	20 Battle Tokens, 1 Research Token	None	Leather Waist (144 Armor +17 AGI, +24 STAM, Equip for +13 Crit Rating, +16 Resilience Rating, +26 Attack Power)
Shadowstalker's Leggings	40 Battle Tokens, 2 Research Tokens	None	Leather Legs (224 Armor +23 AGI, +33 STAM, Equip for +15 Crit Rating, +17 Resilience Rating, +30 Attack Power) +1 Yellow Socket
Slayer's Waistguard	20 Battle Tokens, 1 Research Token	None	Plate Waist (573 Armor +22 STR, +24 STAM, Equip for +19 Melee Crit Rating, +19 Resilience Rating)
Slayer's Legguards	40 Battle Tokens, 2 Research Tokens	None	Plate Legs (891 Armor +25 STR, +39 STAM, Equip for +17 Crit Rating, +25 Resilience Rating) +1 Yellow Socket
Stormbreaker's Girdle	20 Battle Tokens, 1 Research Token	None	Mail Waist (321 Armor +28 STAM, +19 INT, Equip for +19 Spell Crit Rating, +19 Resilience Rating)
Stormbreaker's Leggings	40 Battle Tokens, 2 Research Tokens	None	Mail Legs (499 Armor +39 STAM, +16 INT, Equip for +14 Spell Crit Rating, +22 Resilience Rating, +27 to Damage and Healing Bonus) +1 Yellow Socket
Dreamstalker Sash	20 Battle Tokens, 1 Research Token	None	Leather Waist (184 Armor +15 STR, +13 AGI, +24 STAM, +15 INT, Equip for +15 Resilience Rating, +31 to Healing Bonus)
Dreamstalker Leggings	40 Battle Tokens, 2 Research Tokens	None	Leather Legs (284 Armor +20 STR, +6 AGI, +30 STAM, +10 INT, Equip for +20 Resilience Rating, +44 to Healing Bonus) +1 Yellow Socket, +1 Red Socket
Halaani Bag	8 Research Tokens	None	An 18 Slot Bag! (It Binds on Pickup)
Sublime Mystic Dawnstone	500 Battle Tokens	None	Yellow Socket Gem, +10 Resilience

The Consortium (Both Factions)

The Consortium is a band of dimensional travelers with a colored reputation. These merchants are neutral to just about anyone who comes along, and they can certainly be swayed to your side through various profitable deeds. Early quests in Nagrand make it easy to reach Friendly with the Constortium; with very little time, you can hunt crystals near the Aeris Landing camp and grab tusks from the wandering Elekks as well. Once that is done, the only options are to turn in the Obsidian Warbeads that drop from the Ogres of Nagrand or to return to Terokkar Forest and hit the Mana Tombs (where the monsters provide Consortium Reputation when they die).

Later, however, you reach Netherstorm, where there are many more Consortium quests. Save these for the later end of your Consortium work to get an easy boost. That is also the area where you can purchase Reputation rewards from this group. Seek the Stormspire for these (it is in one of the strange domes on the northern side of the zone), especially if you are a Rogue.

Consortium Faction Rewards

Name	Cost	Requirements	Stats
Pattern: Fel Leather Gloves	12 Gold	Friendly, Leatherworking (340)	Leather Hands (169 Armor, Equip for +17 Hit Rating, +24 Crit Rating, +36 Attack Power) +1 Red Socket, +1 Yellow Socket, Fel Skin Set
Pattern: Bag of Jewels	4 Gold	Honored, Tailoring (340)	24 Slot Gem Bag
Pattern: Fel Leather Boots	14 Gold	Honored, Leatherworking (350)	Leather Feet (196 Armor, Equip for +25 Hit Rating, +17 Crit Rating, +36 Attack Power) +1 Red Socket, +1 Yellow Socket, Fel Skin Set
Pattern: Fel Leather Leggings	14 Gold	Revered, Leatherworking (350)	Leather Legs (249 Armor Equip for +25 Hit Rating, +25 Crit Rating, +52 Attack Power) +1 Red Socket, +2 Yellow Sockets, Fel Skin Set
Consortium Blaster	34 Gold 41 Silver	Revered	Gun (66.2 DPS +15 STAM, Equip for +7 Crit Rating, +36 Attack Power)
Nomad's Leggings	23 Gold 2 Silver	Honored	Leather Legs (256 Armor +33 AGI, +49 STAM, Equip for +66 Attack Power)
Haramad's Bargain	79 Gold 1 Silver	Exalted	Neck (+25 STR, +24 AGI)
Guile of Khoraazi	190 Gold 57 Silver	Exalted	1h Dagger (79.1 DPS +24 AGI, Equip for +50 Attack Power)

A Quick List of New Zones, Dungeons, and Raids

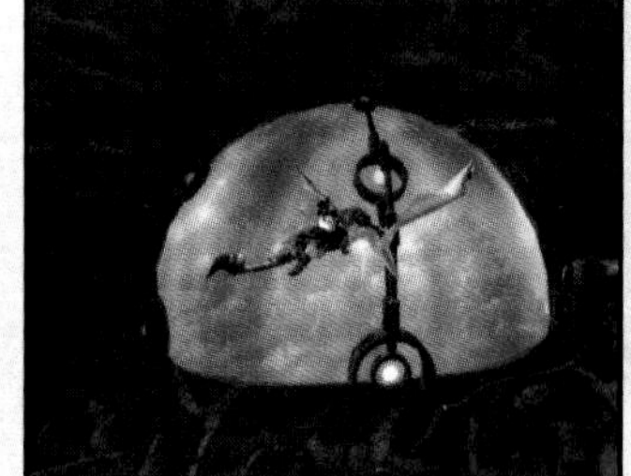

New Zones

Azeroth

Zone Name	Level Range	Location	Notes
Eversong Woods	1-13	Top of Eastern Kingdoms (Above the Plaguelands and Ghostlands)	
Ghostlands	10-21	Top of Eastern Kingdoms (Above Eastern Plaguelands)	
Silvermoon City	Any	Center of Eversong Woods	Capital City of Blood Elves
Azuremyst Isle	1-13	Island Off of Kalimdor	
Bloodmyst Isle	10-21	Island Off of Kalimdor	
The Exodar	Any	Western Side of Azuremyst Isle	Capital City of Draenei

Outland			
Zone Name	**Level Range**	**Location**	**Notes**
Hellfire Peninsula	58-63	First Zone of Outland, Outside the Dark Portal	Reputation With Thrallmar and Mag'Har for Horde/ Honor Hold for Alliance
Zangarmarsh	60-64	West of Hellfire Peninsula	Reputation for Both Factions with Sporeggar and the Cenarion Refuge
Terokkar Forest	62-65	South of Hellfire Peninsula	Location of Shattrath City
Shattrath City	58+	Western Side of Terokkar Forest	Ruled by the Sha'tar
Nagrand	64-67	Southwestern Part of Outland	Telaar Faction for Alliance/ Garadar for Horde; Halaa is a PvP Location for Both Factions; Aeris is a Consortium Location
Blade's Edge Mountains	65-68	North of Zangarmarsh	Home of Sylvanaar (Alliance), Thunderlord Stronghold (Horde), and the Gronn'bor Shrine (Both Factions)
Shadowmoon Valley	67-70	Southeastern Side of Outland	Home of Wildhammer Stronghold (Alliance), Shadowmoon Village (Horde), and Altar of Sha'tar (Both Factions)
Netherstorm	67-70	Northern End of Outland	Home of the Neutral Cities: Area 52 and The Stormspire

New Dungeons (5 Man Content)		
Dungeon Name	**Level Range**	**Location**
Hellfire Ramparts	60-62	Hellfire Peninsula
The Blood Furnace	61-63	Hellfire Peninsula
The Shattered Halls	70+	Hellfire Peninsula
The Slave Pens	62-64	Zangarmarsh
The Underbog	63-65	Zangarmarsh
The Steamvault	70+	Zangarmarsh
Auchenai Crypts	64-66	Terokkar Forest
Shadow Labyrinth	65-67	Terokkar Forest
Sethekk Halls	67-69	Terokkar Forest
Mana-Tombs	70+	Terokkar Forest
The Mechanar	69-72	Netherstorm
The Botanica	70+	Netherstorm
The Arcatraz	70+	Netherstorm
Durnholde Keep	66-70	Caverns of Time (Tanaris)
Black Morass	68-70	Caverns of Time (Tanaris)

New Raids (25 Man Dungeons, 10 Man for Karazhan)		
Raid Name	**Level Range**	**Location**
Magtheridon's Lair	70+	Hellfire Peninsula
Serpentshrine Cavern	70+	Zangarmarsh
Gruul's Lair	70+	Blade's Edge Mountains
Tempest Keep	70+	Netherstorm
Black Temple	70+	Shadowmoon Valley
Battle of Mount Hyjal	70+	Caverns of Time (Tanaris)
Karazhan	70+	Deadwind Pass (Between Duskwood and Swamp of Sorrows)
Zul'Aman	70+	Karazhan

New Battlegrounds/PvP Areas		
Name	**Location**	**Rewards**
Arena	Multiple/Battleground NPCs	Full Reward System
Eye of the Storm	Netherstorm/Battleground NPCs	Marks/Full Reward System
Hellfire Peninsula PvP	Central Hellfire Peninsula	Marks/5% Damage Bonus to Leading Faction
Zangarmarsh PvP	South-Central Zangarmarsh	5% Damage Bonus to Leading Faction
Terokkar Forest PvP	The Bone Wastes	5% Damage/XP Bonus, Ability to Gather Spirit Shards for Leading Faction
Nagrand PvP	Halaa	5% Damage Bonus/Ability to Turn in PvP and PvE Items for Halaa Rewards for Leading Faction

PvP in Outland

World PvP is a much greater focus in the expansion. Though there is new Battleground content (Eye of the Storm and the new Arena System), there is even more to find with the PvP for several of the outdoor areas. Hellfire Peninsula, Zangarmarsh, Terokkar Forest, and Nagrand each have prominent outdoor PvP features, including a number of rewards that are in place for those who participate.

This section explains what PvP is found in Outland (and the expansion in general); it also explains some of the new combat dynamics that are involved in PvP during the post 60 levels.

SEIZING TERRITORY

Seizing territory is done in a very different way in the new content that Blizzard is introducing. Primarily gone are the days of finding flags and clicking on them to take something (with the vulnerability that one shot against your character can spoil the whole affair).

Instead, Blizzard's more recent PvP additions are based on controlling an area through force of numbers. The more PvP-flagged characters that are up on one side, the stronger their control of the area. Whichever side is stronger in this way will be able to take the land after a certain amount of time.

A progress bar appears for this, with the Alliance having control if the bar moves to the left side, and the Horde gaining control if it moves to the right. By killing off any of the enemies who arrive while you are trying to seize an area, you ensure that the bar goes where you want.

Some of the tricks that you might think of to control areas have already been defeated by Blizzard, to keep the fight fair for both sides. For instance, a Rogue or Druid cannot stay in Stealth to help in seizing an area. Nor can a Night Elf with Shadow Meld accomplish this. These characters do not count toward PvP control.

FLIGHT CHANGES THINGS

During outdoor PvP, the addition of Flying Mounts makes for some new tactics. Characters are able to stay out of fights as they wish, or enter battle late without the risk of having someone jump on their backs at any moment. This allows the DPS classes and healers to pick their best moments and enter existing skirmishes near their desired targets.

Ganking gets taken to an all new level as well. The bad news is that someone can safely observe your character from a high altitude, then wait for you to try to quest or grind a few monsters before they come to attack. That is a major pain when you are just interested in relaxing and having a good time (luckily, it's not an issue for PvE servers, and if you like sudden PvP it isn't an issue anyway, right?).

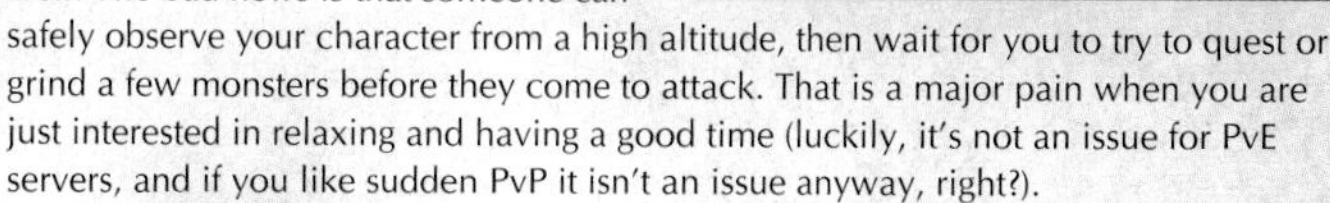

The good news is that no low-level characters are going to come to Outland for very long, so that person flapping above you isn't that many levels out of your league, at worst. Grab a partner as soon as possible if a level 70 person has singled you out, and together the two of you might be able to avoid too much harassment.

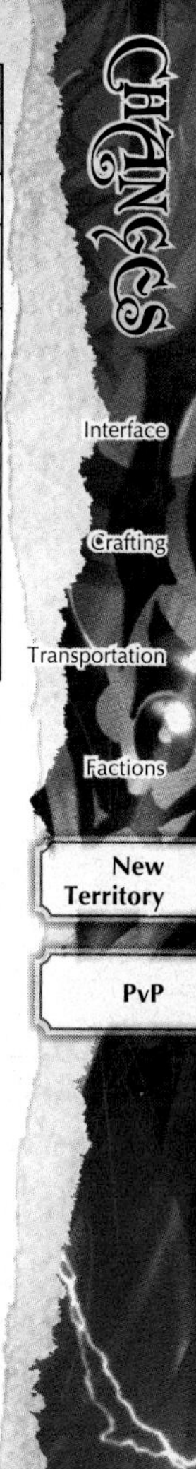

THE OLD HONOR SYSTEM IS DEAD; LONG LIVE THE NEW HONOR SYSTEM

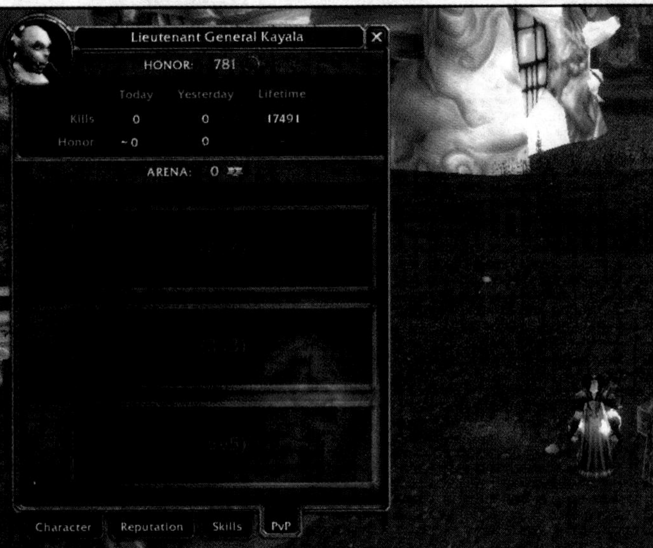

There are now Arena rewards, Eye of the Storm rewards, and new items for higher-level characters throughout the world. In addition to this, players are going to be purchasing these through the new Honor system. Because this system is already incorporated into the live servers before The Burning Crusade, it is likely that you are already familiar with the changes it makes to PvP.

The old Honor system was based on reaching certain ranks by playing consistently (and heavily) over a consecutive number of weeks. It was exciting, but also sometimes tedious or outright tiring if you wanted to achieve the highest ranks and their powerful epic gear.

Now, your characters do not need to play heavily during a given week to accumulate what is needed. Instead, combinations of Marks from the various Battlegrounds are used with Honor to purchase items. This means that is takes a fair bit of time to build up to major purchases, but that it can be done over any period that you like, without fear of Honor Decay! Thank the beautiful fates; it's a much healthier system for all of us who love going after PvP rewards.

Some rewards, such as PvP mounts, require that you collect Marks from multiple Battlegrounds. To make things easier, Blizzard changed the stacking values for all of the Battleground Marks; gone are the stacks of 20! You can now hold huge stacks of Marks without even taking a second slot in your inventory.

HELLFIRE PENINSULA

In the first zone of Outland, fighting takes place in a relatively tight area. Because there are modest faction rewards just for PvPing here, the action is often volatile in Hellfire. The Horde and Alliance have special NPCs in Thrallmar and Honor Hold (respectively) that give items to characters in exchange for turning in their PvP Marks. Because one such reward offers a temporary buff to Experience and Reputation gained, people are quite happy to rush out and join the PvP groups for a time, even if they aren't heavily into PvP in general.

Hellfire Superiority is a buff that adds 5% more damage from all attacks that characters in the leading faction make. You maintain this buff by controlling all three of the towers in the region of Hellfire Peninsula. These towers are named (The Stadium, Broken Hill, and The Overlook). Though it is quite hard to maintain such control, your allies in the region are quite happy when it happens; not only is this buff valid for everyone in the region but it also applies to characters in Hellfire Peninsula Instances.

ZANGARMARSH

Zangarmarsh has a fairly complex system of combat. The Twinspire Graveyard at the center is what controls the buff for the area. Twinspire Blessing conveys a 5% damage bonus to the side that controls the zone, and grants faster corpse runs while doing Coil Fang Reservoir. The way it works is that each side vies for the two Beacons in the region. When one side controls both of them, the Field Scout for that faction starts to hand out Battle Standards. By looking on the zone map, you can clearly see where your Field Scout is standing. The Horde Scout is to the west, and the Alliance Scout is to the east. Both Field Scouts are Elite, so it is not entirely easy to make a direct run against your enemy's Scout without a substantial party.

When someone takes a Battle Standard from the Field Scout and moves it to the Twinspire Graveyard, they can seize the Graveyard, turning control of it over to their faction. The buff is granted to the side at that time, and it lasts until the other faction wrests control from them.

Battle Standards function in much the same way as carrying a Flag in Warsong Gulch; you cannot Mount or use abilities that make you immune to damage while carrying them. You won't have to maintain control of both Beacons for the buff to stay on your team; it's all about the Graveyard.

Zangarmarsh doesn't have quite as much PvP. This is due to the temporary aspect of the rewards. While Hellfire and Nagrand offer extra benefits for activity in PvP, Zangarmarsh does not. Maintaining the buff and having a good time are the only major perks to participation in this area.

TEROKKAR FOREST

Terokkar Forest has a very interesting system of PvP; the 5 PvP goals of the area are on a single timer, and normally these goals aren't available. When the timer runs out, whichever side was in control loses their buff and all of the sites turn grey. It is then a free-for-all to see which faction can first grab all of the goals (through the standard capturing process). Once this happens, the buff goes up for those on the winning side, and this lasts until the timer again expires.

The faction that is currently in charge of the area gains the Blessing of Auchindoun. This conveys a buff with +5% to Experience Gain and Damage Dealt. It also allows the capture of Spirit Shards.

Not only is the buff here better than in the other open PvP areas, but the ability to capture Spirit Shards is very nice for getting some interesting rewards. The Alliance and Horde each have an NPC in their Terokkar bases that accept Spirit Shards. The rewards focus heavily on several cool Socketed items.

To get Spirit Shards, wait until your faction has Blessing of Auchidoun and head into the Terokkar Instances. All of them are affected by the buff and cause defeated bosses in the various dungeons to drop Spirit Shards when they die. Each member of the victorious party gets a Spirit Shard!

NAGRAND

Nagrand has one of the coolest world PvP systems to date. There is a central camp, called Halaa; this town is captured by either faction in the same way as all of the other world PvP goals in Outland. Thus, only those who come across the bridges while PvP flagged will count toward ownership of the town.

Halaa is protected by up to 15 guards. These are loyal to the current team in control, and all of them have very high Health. You won't be able to quickly rush the town and trash them with a small group. Instead, it is easier (and far more fun) to use the four Wyvern Camps that surround the cliffs beyond Halaa. These allow attackers to launch bombing runs on Halaa, taking out both its NPC defenders and any characters that get in the way! Note that starting such a run flags your character for PvP whether you like it or not, so there aren't any blue wall options here.

Halaa guards are on a very long timer, taking about an hour to respawn. This prevents the sieges from being an especially frustrating affair (and frankly, it's quite a blast to have the town turn back and forth heavily throughout the day).

The bombs that are dropped from the Wyverns have an initial blast and then deal damage-over-time as a percentage of the target's Health. The DOT ticks are the most important part of taking out the guards, because each tick knocks off thousands of Health. One technique is to have a single character collect a few of the guards and bring them out onto a bridge. Once the guards are close together, those making bombing runs can deliver even more punishment. And, if any of the enemies inside town come out to help, your forces can ambush them on the bridge.

The buff provided by control of Halaa is Strength of the Halaani (+5% Damage Dealt). Beyond that buff, the controlling side can safely move through Halaa, which reduces the travel time in the area considerably.

If you have a considerable amount of Oshu'gun Crystal Powder Samples from PvE fighting in the area, talk to the NPCs in Halaa while it is under your team's control. These can be turned in for experience. They are also an essential part of the reward system for Halaa; turn in the Samples and PvP Marks from the fighting here for a couple of good armor pieces and the potential for some 18-slot bags.

THE ARENA SYSTEM

Arena fighting is almost the opposite of the old way that Battlegrounds were used. Instead of trying to run as many fights as possible, this system dramatically encourages that you sign up for only a few matches and do everything in your power to excel at them. Forming small groups (2v2, 3v3, 5v5); you take your character into a situation where the fighting will be at its most challenging.

Expect people to break out their timers quite heavily (though long-term abilities, such as Warrior's Retaliation or a Paladin's Lay on Hands are greyed out). Short-term abilities are used all the time, and anything that gives you an edge in the fight is worth using. Arena matches are rated, and your win-loss ratio is quite important.

To play Rated Matches in the Arena, you form teams and create your own tabard. Characters under level 70 can practice in the Arena, but rated matches are available only after reaching cap at level 70. If you plan on working toward Arena rewards, it is very wise to practice with your friends. Arena fighting feels fairly different from outdoor PvP and the other Battleground environments, so it takes some getting used to.

EYE OF THE STORM

- Once the game begins, don't jump straight down from the starting location; it is a long way down. Use the floating rocks to make your way safely to the ground
- As long as your team has more people at a tower than your opponents, your team will begin to capture or keep that tower
- The amount of Victory Points you receive goes up drastically with the number of towers you control (Thus, having 4 Towers is well over twice as useful as having 2 Towers)
- The area of influence around a Tower is big enough that a group could gain control of the tower without ever being seen; defenders should patrol or use Hunters to find enemies who may be doing this
- The Human tower is the easiest to defend because there is only one path leading up to it
- Flying Mounts are not allowed in Eye of the Storm

Eye of the Storm is a more traditional Battleground, and it has opened in Netherstorm. This BG is a combination of Warsong Gulch and Arathi Basin. Each team is trying to reach a point goal, but they do it through both a Capture the Flag effort and through controlling terrain. You can reach this Battleground quickly by looking for a new Battlemasters for it; they appear in the same areas as the other Battlemasters throughout the world, and queuing functions just as it normally does.

There are four areas to be seized on the map, and this is done by having a consistent number of characters near the desired sites. These provide points over time, and the heaviest focus is on holding three of the sites. A team that can hold three points for the match will win consistently, even if their efforts for the flag are a near or full failure.

As with Arathi Basin, your team needs to be able to flow and stay dynamic throughout each engagement. A predictable team will lose sites to sudden hits with greater numbers, then find little resistance when they go to take it back (discovering instead that a different point is falling even before they fully take back the site they are zerging). Keep a consistent flow of information running; this allows attack forces on your team to know the best places and times to strike.

Even if your team is going to almost ignore the flag in its win strategy, take at least some effort to stymie the enemy's pursuit of it. If you don't have anyone working on the flag, the enemy team can toss a single person out to just rake in the points. Leaving a single person on flag capturing is enough to ensure that the enemy needs to pull two or three members from capturing territory just to have a similar rate of point income. This leaves enough of an opening that your main force should be able to capitalize on it and keep that third point under control.

TEN MORE LEVELS TO GAIN

Because the level cap is changing from 60 to 70, players are going to have 10 more Talent points to work with. Also, the class trainers are certainly ready to teach your advancing champions more about both their old abilities and about a few new ones as well.

NEW CLASS ABILITIES

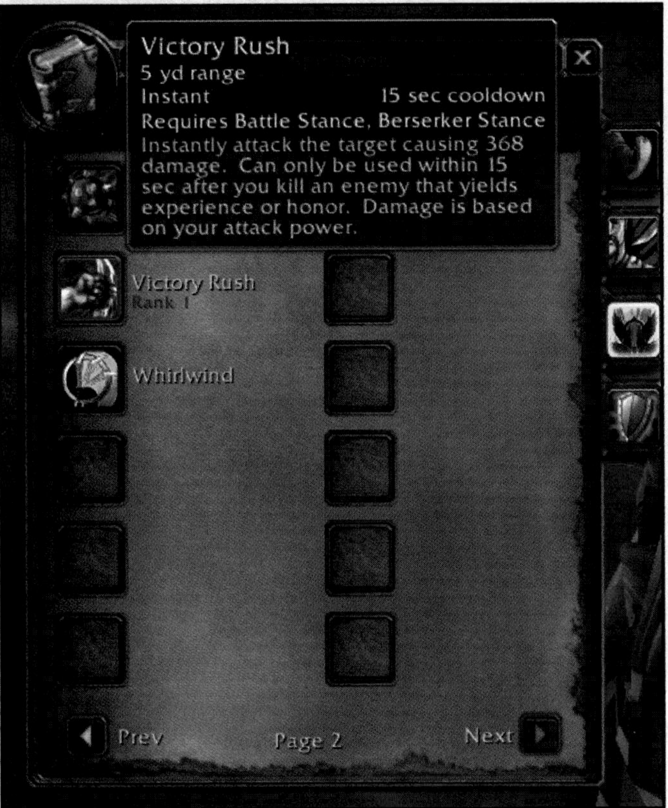

There are new class abilities being added to the game. Most of these are not available until your character passes beyond the old 60 level cap and into the highest tier of advancement. Yet, there are a few new abilities in the earlier levels as well. For example, Warriors are getting a couple points worth of Tactical Mastery free of charge now, as a trainable ability at level 20!

A number of classes have additional spells to learn at level 60 (that weren't there before). Consider stopping by your trainer before heading to Outland as there are no trainers in that besieged world.

No Outland Class Trainers?!

Those who have passed into Outland have far more critical activities and time-consuming arts to practice without spending their moments with Class training. Therefore, you must return to the older realms to train. Shattrath City has portals to the major cities of both the Horde and Alliance, or you can return through the Dark Portal. You might also be able to convince a friendly Mage to portal you. Because you will need to transport yourself, keep your Hearthstone linked to a sensible place (Shattrath City or one of your faction's central towns) to cut back on your travel time.

NEW AND REVISED TALENTS

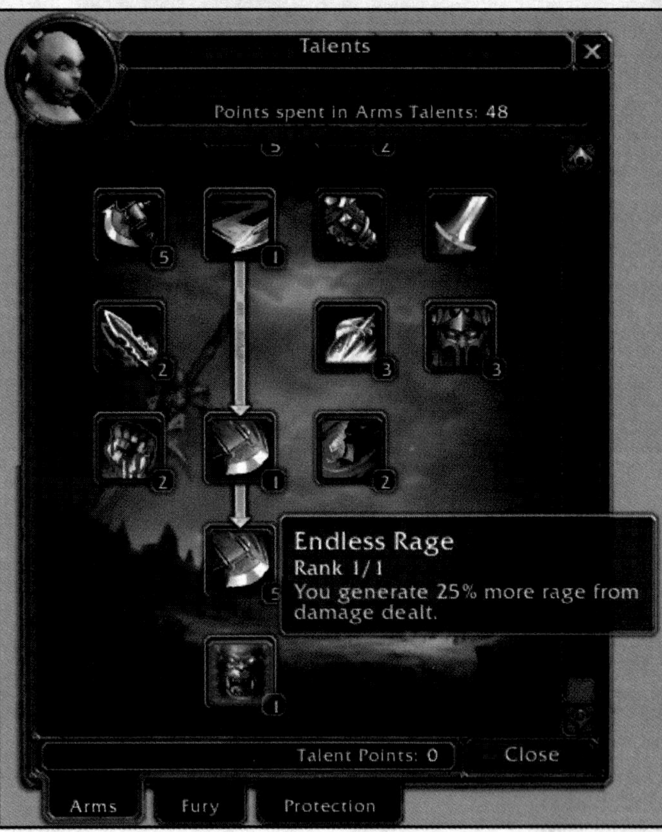

Though your characters are going to grab 10 more Talent points, it won't be easy to decide where to spend them. Two new tiers of Talents are being added to every single Talent line in the game, and with so many powerful choices it is quite hard to come up with a single "perfect spec" no matter how hard you try.

These new Talents are often immensely powerful. It now takes at least 41 Talent points to be able to get to the end of a single Talent line, and the material at the end of the chain is so tempting that single Talent-line specializations are somewhat alluring now, depending on what you are looking for.

Beyond that, cross-Talent builds can do things that would have been impossible before. Do you want to grab Mortal Strike and Flurry? Go ahead! But can you resist the lure of Rampage or Endless Rage? If you find yourself staring at Talent lines for 30 minutes while drooling a little, don't be embarrassed. It happens.

While considering things, be certain to check all of your old Talents to see which ones have changed. There are a lot of buffs in there, and the nerf bat was applied so sparingly that you can honestly say that Blizzardclaus came early. Don't worry about things getting too easy; Outland is a harsh place, and you'll need the love.

New Class Abilities and Talents

With the increase in level cap to 70, all of the classes in World of Warcraft have been given both new abilities to train and many new Talents as many. This changes the entire dynamic of the Talent trees, and introduces a massive shift in how some of the classes can be played.

This section explains these new selections in a class-by-class style, giving as much detail as possible to help players plan out their incredible push from 60 onward.

DRUID ABILITIES

Cyclone

Ability Line	Balance
Requirements	Level 70
Cost	249 Mana
Casting Time/Cooldown	1.5 Seconds/Global Cooldown
Range	30 Yards

Tosses the enemy target into the air, preventing all action but making them invulnerable for up to 6 sec. Only one target can be affected by your Cyclone at a time.

Cyclone opens the door for wider crowd control (something that Druids have rarely had in such a universal or direct fashion). Instead of hindering movement or stopping specific foes, Druids now can take single targets out of a fight during a much wider variety of encounters!

Though quite brief in duration, Cyclone is relatively inexpensive. For such a modest price, your character now has the potential to put the second target for a group out of commission until the first foe is down. Longer crowd control is still going to be used on major adds, but the healing and added order that Cyclone brings to a fight is noticeable.

This is also a strong spell for player versus player combat. Six seconds can be quite an eternity for another player. Killing a foe in PvP is something far less effective than slowing them down. Use Cyclone to protect an ally from an enemy that might disrupt their flag capture or catch up during an important escape. This is very nice against targets with strong ranged potential (where Entangling Roots was always only half a crowd control spell).

Maim

Ability Line	Feral Combat
Requirements	Level 62, Cat Form
Cost	35 Energy
Casting Time/Cooldown	Instant/10 Second Cooldown
Range	9 Yards

Finishing move that causes damage plus an additional amount and Incapacitates the opponent. Any damage caused will revive the target. Causes more damage and lasts longer per combo point:

1 point	129 damage and 2 seconds
2 points	213 damage and 3 seconds
3 points	297 damage and 4 seconds
4 points	381 damage and 5 seconds
5 points	465 damage and 6 seconds

Maim gives your Cat Form greater potential to stop an enemy cold for a fair period; use this Incapacitation period to get some Caster Form work done or to prepare a different stage of your assault against a target. For example, your Druid could lay on a four-point Maim, switch to Caster Form, snag Regrowth and Rejuventation, then be back to Cat Form just as your opponent is getting back into the action.

Cat Form has always been a good way for Druids to mimic the Rogue style of DPS melee combat, but the diminished ability for Stun or Incapacitation effects was sorely felt. This helps considerably. You still won't be able to stunlock in the way that a Rogue can, but with greater options for healing and ranged assault, your character should be more than able to compensate.

Lacerate

Ability Line	Feral Combat
Requirements	Level 66, Bear Form or Dire Bear Form
Cost	15 Rage
Casting Time/Cooldown	Instant Cast/Global Cooldown
Range	Melee

Lacerates the enemy target, making them bleed for 155 damage over 15 sec and causing a high amount of Threat. This effect stacks up to five times on the same target.

Lacerate won't win the fight on damage alone, as Warrior-style DOTs just aren't intended to bring enemies down directly. Instead, Lacerate offers a relatively inexpensive way to keep a DOT on your foe (a great perk when fighting against Rogues).

In addition, the added Threat from Lacerate is quite important when you are offtanking for a group. If aggro control has been somewhat disrupted, and an enemy is starting to ping-pong out toward your healers, Lacerate gives your Bear a chance to grab aggro in a much faster way than Maul. Beyond that, you can stack these by selecting Maul and using additional Rage to slap on Lacerate in the meanwhile. This gives your tank much more time and comfort in regaining aggro, and leaves your Druid with mana in the event that healing *is* needed later in the fight.

Flight Form (Shapeshift)

Ability Line	Feral Combat
Requirements	Level 68
Cost	498 Mana
Casting Time/Cooldown	Instant/Global Cooldown
Range	Self

Transforms your Druid into a Flight Form, increasing movement speed by 60% and allowing you to fly. Can only use this form in Outland. The act of shapeshifting frees the caster of Polymorph and Movement Impairing effects.

Having a Flight Form is another boon that is just amazing. Beyond the usefulness of this, few can discount the coolness factor involved with getting the potential for flight so easily (in a relative sense).

Lifebloom

Ability Line	Restoration
Requirements	Level 64
Cost	220 Mana
Casting Time/Cooldown	Instant/Global Cooldown
Range	40 Yards

Heals the target for 273 over 7 sec. When Lifebloom completes its duration or is dispelled, the target is instantly healed for 600. This effect can stack up to 3 times on the same target.

Lifebloom offers more survival over time to Druids. This was already a field that they excelled in, being able to tackle enemies while soloing that few other classes could hope to beat.

When used to heal others, Lifebloom adds to the aspect of supplementary health restoration that is also a strong element of the Druid class. While Priests can lay on health in massive doses, the use of Druid heal-over-time powers tends to smooth out the incoming damage. This makes it easier for all types of healers to react to sudden criticals and other problems that cannot be stopped with burst healing.

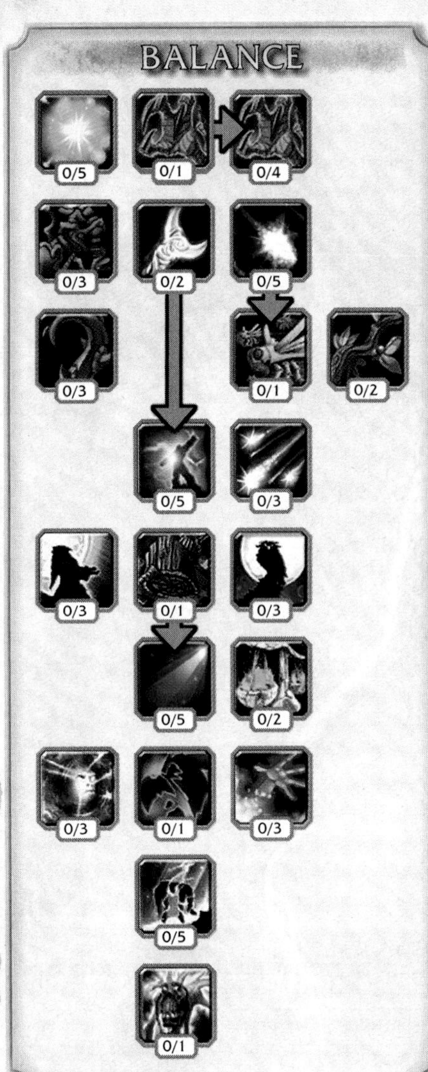

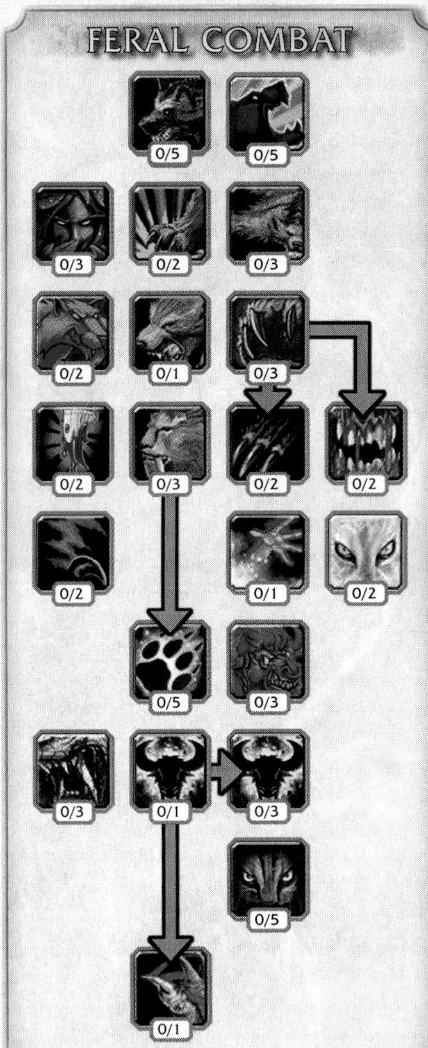

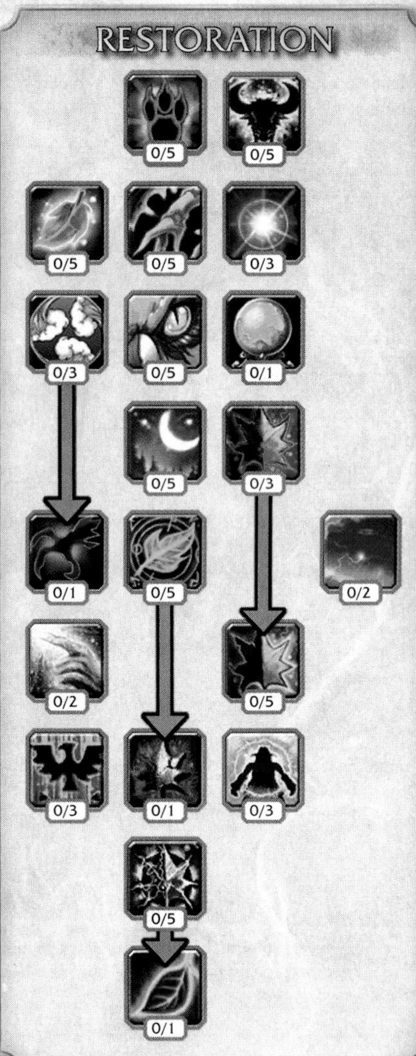

DRUID TALENTS

BALANCE

Starlight Wrath (Revised Talent)

Ranks	5
Requires	Nothing

Reduces the casting time of Wrath and Starfire spells by .1 seconds (per rank). This takes the place of Improved Wrath, which only changed the casting time of Wrath.

Control of Nature (Revised Talent)

Ranks	3
Requires	5 Points in Balance

Improved Entangling Roots has been replaced with this Talent. Though keeping the 40%/70%/100% progression of avoiding Interruption caused by damage while casting Entangling Roots, this Talent now affects Cyclone as well.

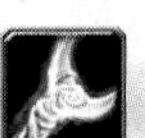

Focused Starlight (New Talent)

Ranks	2
Requires	5 Points in Balance

This Talent increases the Critical Chance of Wrath and Starfire by 2% (per rank). It also acts as the prerequisite Talent for Vengeance.

Brambles (Revised Talent)

Ranks	3
Requires	10 Points in Balance

This changes Improved Thorns so that it adds the 25% damage bonus (per rank) to both Thorns and Entangling Roots.

Insect Swarm (Revised Talent)

Ranks	1
Requires	10 Points in Balance

This was a Restoration Talent in the past, but it has moved to this tree. The function of the spell, to lower the Hit Chance of your target and deal Nature damage, is unchanged.

Nature's Reach (Revised Talent)

Ranks	2
Requires	10 Points in Balance

As a slight change, this Talent provides its 10% range bonus to all Balance spells and additionally to Faerie Fire (Feral) as well.

Celestial Focus (Revised Talent)

Ranks	3
Requires	15 Points in Balance

Improved Starfire has been removed and changed into this Talent. It still has a 5% chance (per rank) to grant a 3 Second Stun on a target that is hit with Starfire. In addition, this talent also grants a chance to resist being interrupted while casting Wrath (25%/50%/75%).

Lunar Guidance (New Talent)

Ranks	3
Requires	20 Points in Balance

This Talent increases spell damage and healing by 8% of your character's total Intellect (per rank).

Balance of Power (New Talent)

Ranks	2
Requires	25 Points in Balance

This increases your Druid's chance to Hit with all spells while reducing the chance that your character is Hit by spells. This effect improves both stats by 2% (per rank).

Dreamstate (New Talent)

Ranks	3
Requires	30 Points in Balance

Every 5 seconds, even while casting, your Druid will now regenerate 4% of their Intellect in Mana. The progression for this Talent is 4%/7%/10%.

Moonkin Form (Revised Talent)

Ranks	1
Requires	30 Points in Balance

The buff to group member Spell Critical Rates has been increased from 3% to 5% for Druids in Moonkin Form. Also, Attack Power for the Druid is increased to 150% of your character's level. Melee attacks made by a Moonkin Druid have a chance on Hit to regenerate Mana based on Attack Power.

Improved Faerie Fire (New Talent)

Ranks	3
Requires	30 Points in Balance

Faerie Fire, when used with this Talent, increases the chance for the target to be Hit by melee and ranged attacks by 1% (per rank).

Wrath of Cenarius (New Talent)

Ranks	5
Requires	35 Points in Balance

Starfire spells gain an additional 4% improvement (per rank) from Bonus Damage Effects and your Druid's Wrath spells gain an additional 2% (per rank).

Force of Nature (New Talent)

Ranks	1
Requires	40 Points in Balance

This Talent teaches your Druid a spell that summons 3 Treants to attack the enemy target for 30 seconds. This summoning spell is an Instant ability, but it rests on a 3-minute Cooldown.

FERAL COMBAT

Feral Instinct (Revised Talent)

Ranks	3
Requires	5 Points in Feral Combat

Mastering this Talent now costs 3 Talent points instead of 5. The total effect of Feral Instinct remains the same.

Thick Hide (Revised Talent)

Ranks	3
Requires	5 Points in Feral Combat

Increases your Armor contribution from items by a progression of 4%/7%/10% (rather than the old 2% per rank for 5 ranks).

Shredding Attacks (Revised Talent)

Ranks	2
Requires	15 Points in Feral Combat

This Talent now improves Shred and Lacerate. Shred is reduced by 6 Energy (per rank), and Lacerate is reduced by 1 Rage (per rank).

Nurturing Instinct (New Talent)

Ranks	2
Requires	20 Points in Feral Combat

When coming out of Feral Form, your Druid adds 25% of their Strength (per rank) as a bonus to any Healing spells that are cast. This effect lasts for 6 seconds.

Survival of the Fittest (New Talent)

Ranks	3
Requires	25 Points in Feral Combat

Increases all attributes of your Druid by 1% (per rank) and reduces the chance that they will be Critically Hit by melee attacks by 1% (per rank).

Primal Tenacity (New Talent)

Ranks	3
Requires	30 Points in Feral Combat

Increases your Druid's chance to Resist Stun and Fear effects by 5% (per rank).

Leader of the Pack (Revised Talent)

Ranks	1
Requires	30 Points in Feral Combat

The buff to party members' ranged and melee Critical Chance has changed from 3% to 5%!

Improved Leader of the Pack (New Talent)

Ranks	2
Requires	1 Point in Leader of the Pack, 30 Points in Feral Combat

Your Druid's Leader of the Pack aura also causes affected characters to heal themselves for 2% of their total Health (per rank) when they are Critically Hit with a melee or ranged attack. This can only occur as much as once every 6 seconds.

Predatory Instincts (New Talent)

Ranks	5
Requires	35 Points in Feral Combat

This improves your Druid's Critical Strike damage in melee by 3% (per rank); it also conveys a 3% chance (per rank) to avoid area-of-effect attacks.

Mangle (New Talent)

Ranks	1
Requires	1 Point in Leader of the Pack, 40 Points in Feral Combat

Mangle adds a new ability for your Druid to use in both Dire Bear and Cat Forms. The Dire Bear form of Mangle generates a significant amount of threat. This ability deals Instant damage; it has a 6-second Cooldown in Dire Bear Form, and no Cooldown at all for Cat Form.

Dire Bear Mangle	
Cost	20 Rage
Casting Time	Instant/6 Second Cooldown
Range	5 Yards
Effect	130% Damage + Bonus + 25% Bleed Damage Over Time
Rank One	+98 Damage
Rank Two	+137 Damage
Rank Three	+176 Damage

Cat Mangle	
Cost	45 Energy
Casting Time	Instant/Global Cooldown
Range	5 Yards
Effect	150% Damage + Bonus + 25% Bleed Damage Over Time
Rank One	+140 Damage
Rank Two	+180 Damage
Rank Three	+233 Damage

RESTORATION

Naturalist (Revised Talent)

Ranks	5
Requires	5 Points in Restoration

Improved Healing Touch has evolved. While retaining the .1 second reduction in the casting time of Healing Touch, your Druid also gets to put some mean hits on enemies, doing 2% more damage (per rank) with physical attacks.

Natural Shapeshifter (Revised Talent)

Ranks	3
Requires	5 Points in Restoration

Now a Restoration Talent, this still reduces the Mana cost of Shapeshifting by 10% (per rank).

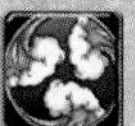

Intensity (Revised Talent)

Ranks	3
Requires	10 Points in Restoration

Improved Enrage and Reflection have been combined into this Talent. Your Druid still gets a 5% Mana regeneration (per rank), even while casting spells. When using Enrage, your character generates Instant Rage, in a progression of 4/7/10.

Subtlety (Revised Talent)

Ranks	5
Requires	10 Points in Restoration

Beyond its original 4% reduction in Threat (per rank) from Druid Healing, this Talent now adds a 6% chance (per rank) for your Healing effect to avoid being Dispelled.

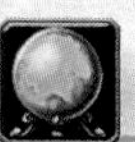

Omen of Clarity (Revised Talent)

Ranks	1
Requires	10 Points in Restoration

Though unchanged in effect, Omen of Clarity has been moved from Balance to Restoration.

Improved Tranquility (Revised Talent)

Ranks	2
Requires	20 Points in Restoration

The reduction in Threat caused by Tranquility spells has changed from 40% (per rank) to 50% (per rank), effectively eliminating all Threat generated by this spell.

Empowered Touch (New Talent)

Ranks	2
Requires	25 Points in Restoration

This gives your Druid's Healing Touch spells an additional 10% boost from your Bonus Healing Effects.

Living Spirit (New Talent)

Ranks	3
Requires	30 Points in Restoration

Increases your Druid's total Spirit by 5% (per rank).

Swiftmend (Revised Talent)

Ranks	1
Requires	5 Points in Gift of Nature, 30 Points in Restoration

The amount of Instant healing done by Swiftmend is currently equal to 18 seconds of Regrowth, not the 15 seconds that was listed in the second Master Guide.

Natural Perfection (New Talent)

Ranks	3
Requires	30 Points in Restoration

Your Druid's Critical Chance with all spells is increased by 1% (per rank); melee and ranged Critical Hits that land on your character are reduced in damage by a progression of 4%/7%/10%.

Empowered Rejuvenation (New Talent)

Ranks	5
Requires	35 Points in Restoration

Bonus Healing Effects are increased by 4% (per rank) for all of your Druid's Heal-over-time spells.

Tree of Life (New Talent)

Ranks	1
Requires	5 Points in Empowered Rejuvenation, 40 Points in Restoration

This Talent teaches your Druid how to Shapeshift into the Tree of Life Form. In this state, all Healing done by the Druid's group is improved by 25% of their total Spirit. Only Swiftmend and Heal-over-time spells can be cast, and your character's movement rate is reduced by 20%. The good news is that your spells cost 20% less Mana.

HUNTER PET ABILITIES

New Tamable Beasts

Before long, eager Hunters are going to charge into Outland, looking for anything that they can Tame. Even in Azeroth, there are changes, so take a look at the table below.

New Tamable Pets		
Race	**Diet**	**What They Can Learn**
Dragonhawk	Meat, Fish, Fruit, Raw Meat, Raw Fish	Bite, Cover, Dive, Fire Breath, Growl
Nether Ray	Meat, Raw Meat	Bite, Cower, Dive, Growl
Ravager	Meat, Raw Meat	Bite, Cower, Dash, Gore, Growl
Serpent	Meat, Fish	Bite, Cower, Growl, Poison Spit
Sporebat	Cheese, Bread, Fungus, Fruit	Cower, Growl
Warp Stalker	Fish, Fruit, Raw Fish	Warp

Great Stamina (Rank 11)

Requires	Level 70, Great Stamina (Rank 10)
Cost	90 Silver, 220 Training Points

Increases Stamina by 64

Natural Armor (Rank 11)

Requires	Level 70, Natural Armor (Rank 10)
Cost	90 Silver, 220 Training Points

Armor Increased by 1600

Growl (Rank 8)

Requires	Level 70, Growl (Rank 7)
Cost	90 Silver

Taunt the target, increasing the likelihood the creature will focus attacks on you.

Arcane Resistance (Rank 5)

Requires	Level 60, Arcane Resistance (Rank 4)
Cost	90 Silver, 105 Training Points

Increases Arcane Resistance by 140

Fire Resistance (Rank 5)

Requires	Level 60, Fire Resistance (Rank 4)
Cost	90 Silver, 105 Training Points

Increases Fire Resistance by 140

Frost Resistance (Rank 5)

Requires	Level 60, Frost Resistance (Rank 4)
Cost	90 Silver, 105 Training Points

Increases Frost Resistance by 140

Nature Resistance (Rank 5)

Requires	Level 60, Nature Resistance (Rank 4)
Cost	90 Silver, 105 Training Points

Increases Nature Resistance by 140

Shadow Resistance (Rank 5)

Requires	Level 60, Shadow Resistance (Rank 4)
Cost	90 Silver, 105 Training Points

Increases Shadow Resistance by 140

HUNTER ABILITIES

Aspect of the Viper

Ability Line	Beast Mastery
Requirements	Level 64
Cost	40 Mana
Casting Time/Cooldown	Instant/Global Cooldown
Range	Self

The Hunter takes on the aspects of a viper, regenerating Mana equal to 25% of her Intellect every five seconds. Only one Aspect can be active at a time.

For short fights, Aspect of the Viper isn't going to make a huge difference. You can get far more burst survival by increasing your character's Dodge rate, realize even more ranged damage with extra Attack Power from Aspect of the Hawk, and so forth. Indeed, Aspect of the Viper is clearly made for extremely long fights *or* for chain fights where your character is not interested in resting or does not have the luxury of downtime.

Because Aspect of the Viper is directly linked to your character's Intellect value, a specific configuration of gear makes this Aspect even more powerful than it would otherwise be. With a higher percentage of epic gear, this Aspect takes on more and more value.

Kill Command (Rank 1)

Ability Line	Beast Mastery
Requirements	Level 66
Cost	75 Mana
Casting Time/Cooldown	Instant/5 Second Cooldown
Range	40 Yards

Give the command to kill, causing your pet to instantly attack for an additional 127 damage. Can only be used after the Hunter lands a critical strike on the target. Being able to keep more aggro on your pet and do extra damage with almost no cost is almost too good to be true. Keep Kill Command at a convenient place on your quickbar, so that it can be tapped easily any time it lights up.

Though the damage done may not seem dramatic by itself, this ability adds to the "death of one-thousand cuts" aspect of Hunter play. As if the DOT, autoshot, ranged abilities, and pet weren't enough.

Steady Shot

Ability Line	Marksmanship
Requirements	Level 62, Ranged Weapon
Cost	110 Mana
Casting Time/Cooldown	1.5 Seconds/Global Cooldown
Range	8-35 Yards

A steady shot that causes 100 damage. Causes an additional 175 damage against Dazed targets. 30% of your Ranged Attack Power is added to Steady Shot's damage.

Steady Shot is a very mean ability to slip in-between your existing routine of attacks. Though possessing a casting time, this is short enough that you can use it just after an existing autofire attack and avoid losing any damage whatsoever (because your casting time falls in-between the natural cooldown of the autoshots, and the timer is *not* disrupted by the Steady Shot).

Concussive Shot was already an ability of immense use in PvE and PvP. Once you get Steady Shot there is yet another reason to use Concussive Shot early in the fight. Daze your target with the Concuss, then enjoy free bonus damage when the Steady Shot lands.

All Hunters stand to gain from this attack; once its timing is mastered, there are very few downsides.

Misdirection

Ability Line	Survival
Requirements	Level 70
Cost	326 Mana
Casting Time/Cooldown	Instant/2 Minute Cooldown
Range	100 Yards

Threat caused by your Hunter's next three attacks is redirected to a target raid member. Only one caster and target can be paired in this way at the same time, meaning that no person can have two Misdirections affecting them simultaneously. The effect itself lasts for 30 seconds.

In larger groups and raids, this is going to become a tool of immense importance. Being able to direct aggro onto a main tank, especially early in an encounter, is very powerful. This isn't simply a way to avoid getting aggro with an Aimed Shot or burst of damage. This is a way to have your main tank's Threat soar while they are still building Rage and settling into the encounter. Very nice indeed!

Snake Trap

Ability Line	Survival
Requirements	Level 68
Cost	305 Mana
Casting Time/Cooldown	Instant/30 Second Cooldown
Range	N/A

Place a trap that will release several venomous snakes to attack the first enemy to approach. The snakes will die after 15 sec. Trap will exist for 1 min. Only one trap can be active at a time.

HUNTER TALENTS

BEAST MASTERY

Improved Aspect of the Hawk (Revised Talent)

Ranks	5
Requires	Nothing

This Talent now gives you a 10% chance for all Ranged Attacks to increase Ranged Attack Speed by 3% (per rank). The effect lasts for 12 seconds now, rather than 8 seconds.

Endurance Training (Revised Talent)

Ranks	5
Requires	Nothing

Increases the Health of your pet by 2% (per rank) and of your Hunter by 1% (per rank). This Talent used to add 3% Health to your pet but did nothing for your Hunter.

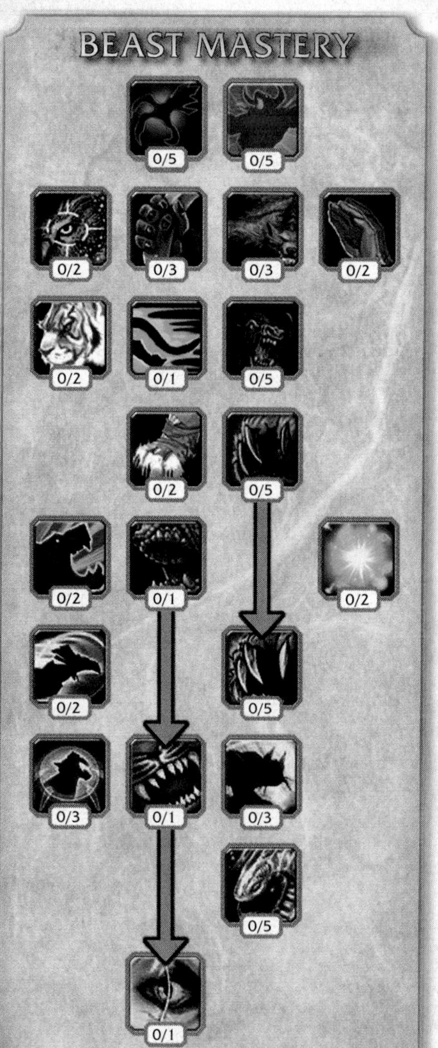

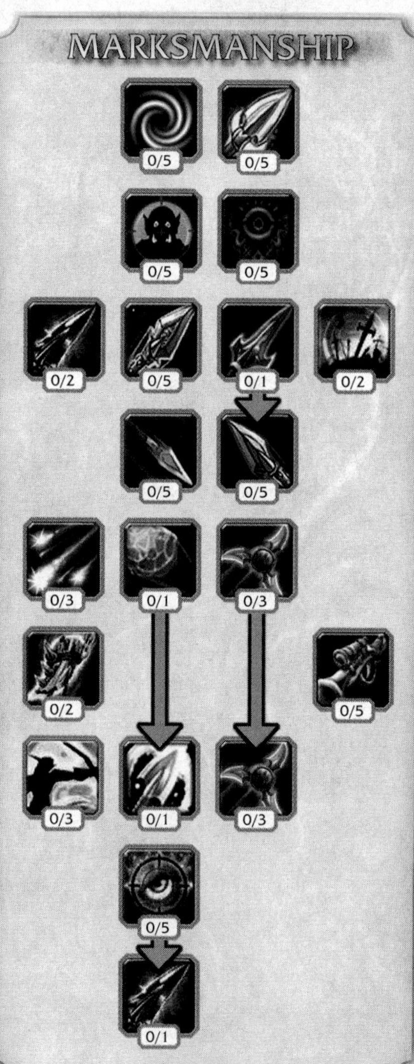

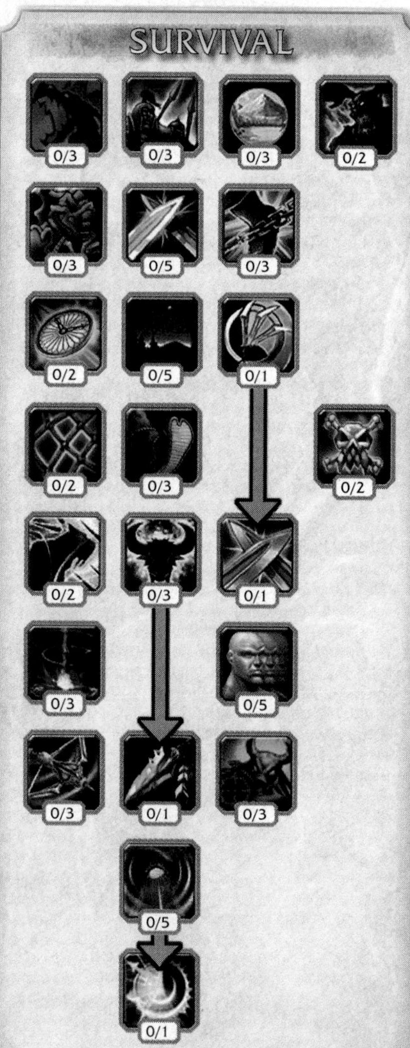

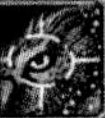

Focused Fire (New Talent)

Ranks	2
Requires	5 Points in Beast Mastery

All damage caused by your Hunter is increased by 1% (per rank) while your pet is active. Also, the Critical Strike chance of your Kill Commands is increased by 10% (per rank).

Improved Aspect of the Monkey (Revised Talent)

Ranks	3
Requires	5 Points in Beast Mastery

Increases the Dodge bonus of your Aspect of the Monkey by 2% (per rank).

Thick Hide (Revised Talent)

Ranks	3
Requires	5 Points in Beast Mastery

Thick Hide, much like Endurance Training, has been split so that one-third of its bonuses go directly to the Hunter. Currently, each rank gives your pet roughly a 6.7% gain in its Armor Rating while your Hunter gains about 3.3%. With three points invested, this gives +20% to your pet and +10% to your Hunter.

Rapid Killing (New Talent)

Ranks	2
Requires	10 Points in Marksmanship

After killing an opponent that yields experience or honor, your next Aimed Shot, Arcane Shot, or Auto Shot causes 10% additional damage (per rank). This effect lasts for 20 seconds. Also, the cooldown of your Rapid Fire ability is reduced by 1 minute.

Pathfinding (Revised Talent)

Ranks	2
Requires	10 Points in Beast Mastery

Now increases the speed bonus from Aspect of the Cheetah and Aspect of the Pack by 4% (per rank) instead of 3%.

Ferocity (Revised Talent)

Ranks	5
Requires	15 Points in Beast Mastery

Ferocity adds less of a critical strike chance bonus for your pet than it did in the listed in Master Guide II. It current adds 2% (per rank) to your pet's chance instead of 3%.

Bestial Discipline (Revised Talent)

Ranks	2
Requires	20 Points in Beast Mastery

Currently this Talent adds 50% (per rank) to your pet's Focus Regeneration. In Master Guide II, this was listed as adding 10% (per rank).

Animal Handler (New Talent)

Ranks	2
Requires	25 Points in Beast Mastery

Increases your speed while mounted by 4% (per rank), and adds 2% (per rank) to your pet's chance to hit. The mounted movement speed increase does not stack with other effects.

Ferocious Inspiration (New Talent)

Ranks	3
Requires	30 Points in Beast Mastery

When your pet scores a Critical Hit, all group members gain +1% (per rank) to all of their damage for 10 seconds.

Bestial Wrath (Revised Talent)

Ranks	1
Requires	30 Points in Beast Mastery

This ability adds 50% additional damage to your pet's attacks for 18 seconds, not for 15.

Catlike Reflexes (New Talent)

Ranks	3
Requires	30 Points in Beast Mastery

This powerful defensive Talent adds 3% to your pet's chance to Dodge (per rank) and additionally increases your Hunter's chance to Dodge by 1% (per rank).

Serpent's Swiftness (New Talent)

Ranks	5
Requires	35 Points in Beast Mastery

Increases your pet's Melee Attack Speed by 4% (per rank) and your Hunter's Ranged Attack Speed by the same amount.

The Beast Within (New Talent)

Ranks	1
Requires	40 Points in Beast Mastery

As long as your pet is under the effect of Bestial Wrath, your Hunter gains 10% additional damage. During this period, your Hunter cannot be affected by Fear and other forms of crowd control.

MARKSMANSHIP

Lethal Shots (Revised Talent)

Ranks	5
Requires	Nothing

Though unchanged in power, Lethal Shots is now a first-tier Talent.

Improved Hunter's Mark (Revised Talent)

Ranks	5
Requires	5 Points in Marksmanship

Now a tier-two Talent, Improved Hunter's Mark does not improve Ranged Attack Power any longer. Instead, it has a 20% chance to allow Hunter's Mark to affect Melee Attack Power as well as Ranged Attack Power. This aids in your pet's damage as well as that of any melee members who are aiding you in a fight.

Go for the Throat (New Talent)

Ranks	2
Requires	10 Points in Marksmanship

Critical hits at range give your pet a free and instant 25 Focus.

Improved Stings (New Talent)

Ranks	5
Requires	15 Points in Marksmanship

Increases the damage done by Serpent Sting and Wyvern Sting by 6% (per rank), and it raises the Mana drained by Viper Sting by 6% (per rank) as well.

Concussive Barrage (New Talent)

Ranks	3
Requires	20 Points in Marksmanship

Successful Auto Shot attacks by your Hunter gain a 2% chance (per rank) to Daze the target for 4 seconds.

Combat Experience (New Talent)

Ranks	2
Requires	25 Points in Marksmanship

Increases your total Agility, Stamina, and Intellect by 3% (per rank).

Careful Aim (New Talent)

Ranks	3
Requires	30 Points in Marksmanship

Increases your Ranged Attack Power by 15% of your total Intellect value (per rank).

Improved Barrage (New Talent)

Ranks	3
Requires	3 Points in Barrage, 30 Points in Marksmanship

Increases the chance to score a Critical Hit with Multi-Shot by 5% (per rank). This Talent also gives your Hunter a 33% chance (per rank) to avoid interruption caused by damage while Channeling Volley.

Master Marksman (New Talent)

Ranks	5
Requires	35 Points in Marksmanship

Increases your Ranged Attack Power by 2% (per rank).

Silencing Shot (New Talent)

Ranks	1
Requires	5 Points in Master Marksman, 40 Points in Marksmanship

This adds a new ability for your Hunter to use in combat. Silencing Shot has a low cost, attacks instantly (at an 8-35 yard range), and deals 75% weapon damage. An enemy hit with this attack is then Silenced for 3 seconds.

SURVIVAL

Hawk Eye (Revised Talent)

Ranks	3
Requires	Nothing

Though Hawk Eye still improved the range for your Hunter's missile weapons, it is now a first-tier Survival Talent.

Entrapment (Revised Talent)

Ranks	3
Requires	5 Points in Survival

The percentage chance for your Hunter's Immolation, Frost, and Explosive Traps to Immobilize targets has gone up from 5% (per rank) to 8% (per rank).

Improved Wing Clip (Revised Talent)

Ranks	3
Requires	5 Points in Survival

The cost to reach a 20% Immobilization chance when using Wing Clip is only 3 Talent points not 5, like it used to be.

Survival Instincts (New Talent)

Ranks	2
Requires	20 Points in Survival

Reduces all damage taken by 2% (per rank).

Resourcefulness (New Talent)

Ranks	3
Requires	25 Points in Survival

Reduces the Mana cost of all traps and melee abilities by 20% (per rank) and reduces the Cooldown of all traps by 2 seconds (per rank).

Thrill of the Hunt (New Talent)

Ranks	3
Requires	30 Points in Survival

Gives you a 33% chance (per rank) to regain 40% of the Mana cost of any shot when it Critically Hits its target.

Expose Weakness (New Talent)

Ranks	3
Requires	5 Points in Lightning Reflexes, 30 Points in Survival

Your Hunter's ranged Critical Hits have a 10% chance (per rank) to apply an Expose Weakness effect on the target. This increases the Attack Power of all attackers against the target by 25% of your Agility; this lasts for 7 seconds.

Master Tactician (New Talent)

Ranks	5
Requires	35 Points in Survival

Successful ranged attacks gain a 6% chance to increase your Hunter's Critical rate with all attacks by 2% (per rank); this lasts for 8 seconds.

Readiness (New Talent)

Ranks	1
Requires	5 Points in Master Tactician, 40 Points in Survival

This Talent gives your Hunter an Instant ability that immediately finishes the Cooldowns on all of your Hunter abilities. Readiness itself has a 5-minute Cooldown.

MAGE ABILITIES

Arcane Blast

Ability Line	Arcane
Requirements	Level 64
Cost	190 Mana
Casting Time/Cooldown	2.5 Seconds (Variable)/Global Cooldown
Range	30 Yards

Blasts the target with energy, dealing 575 to 665 Arcane damage. Each time you cast Arcane Blast, the casting time is reduced while mana cost is increased. Effect stacks up to 5 times and lasts 8 sec.

Invisibility

Ability Line	Arcane
Requirements	Level 68
Cost	263 Mana
Casting Time/Cooldown	Instant/5 Minute Cooldown
Range	Self

Fades the caster to invisibility over 8 sec. The effect is cancelled if you perform or receive any hostile actions. While invisible, you can only see other invisible targets and those who can see invisible. Lasts 20 sec.

Spellsteal

Ability Line	Arcane
Requirements	Level 70
Cost	474 Mana
Casting Time/Cooldown	Instant/Global Cooldown
Range	30 Yards

Steals a beneficial magic effect from the target. This effect lasts a maximum of 2 min.

Molten Armor

Ability Line	Fire
Requirements	Level 62
Cost	630 Mana
Casting Time/Cooldown	Instant/Global Cooldown
Range	Self

Causes 75 Fire damage when hit and reduces the chance you are critically hit by melee attacks and spells by 5%. However, it also increases the Mage's spell critical effect chance by 3%. Only one type of Armor spell can be active on the Mage at any time. Lasts 30 min.

Ice Lance

Ability Line	Ice
Requirements	Level 66
Cost	150 Mana
Casting Time/Cooldown	1.5 Seconds/Global Cooldown
Range	30 Yards

Deals 173 to 200 Frost damage to an enemy target. Causes triple damage against Frozen targets.

MAGE TALENTS

ARCANE

Improved Blink (New Talent)

Ranks	2
Requires	20 Points in Arcane

Reduces the Mana cost of Blink by 25% (per rank).

Arcane Mind (Revised Talent)

Ranks	5
Requires	20 Points in Arcane

The efficiency of this Talent has been raised. Instead of providing an Intellect boost of 2% (per rank), the value of this Talent is now a 3% boost (per rank).

Prismatic Cloak (Revised Talent)

Ranks	2
Requires	25 Points in Arcane

Reduces all damage taken by your Mage by 2% (per rank).

Arcane Potency (New Talent)

Ranks	3
Requires	5 Points in Arcane Concentration, 25 Points in Arcane

Increases your Mage's Critical Spell Chance while Clearcasting by 10% (per rank).

Empowered Arcane Missiles (New Talent)

Ranks	3
Requires	30 Points in Arcane

Though this Talent increases the Mana cost of your Mage's Arcane Missiles by 2% (per rank), it provides a 15% boost to Bonus Spell Damage (per rank) for that spell.

Arcane Power (Revised Talent)

Ranks	1
Requires	3 Pointsin Arcane Instability, 30 Points in Arcane

In a slight adjustment, this Talent now causes spells to deal 30% more damage and cost 30% more Mana.

Spell Power (New Talent)

Ranks	2
Requires	30 Points in Arcane

This increases the Critical damage bonus of all spells by 25% (per rank).

Mind Mastery (New Talent)

Ranks	5
Requires	35 Points in Arcane

Mind Mastery increases spell damage by up to 25% of your Mage's total Intellect.

Slow (New Talent)

Ranks	1
Requires	40 Points in Arcane

This Talent adds another spell to your Mage's arsenal. As an Instant spell without a Cooldown, Slow has desirable potential in crowd control. The target's movement speed is reduced by 50% and their time for ranged attacks and spells is increased by 50%. Slow lasts for 15 seconds and can only affect one target at a time.

Fire

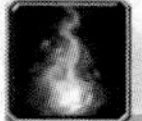

Burning Soul (Revised Talent)

Ranks	2
Requires	10 Points in Fire

Instead of reducing the Threat caused by your Fire spells by 15% (per rank), Burning Soul reduces this statistic by 5% (per rank).

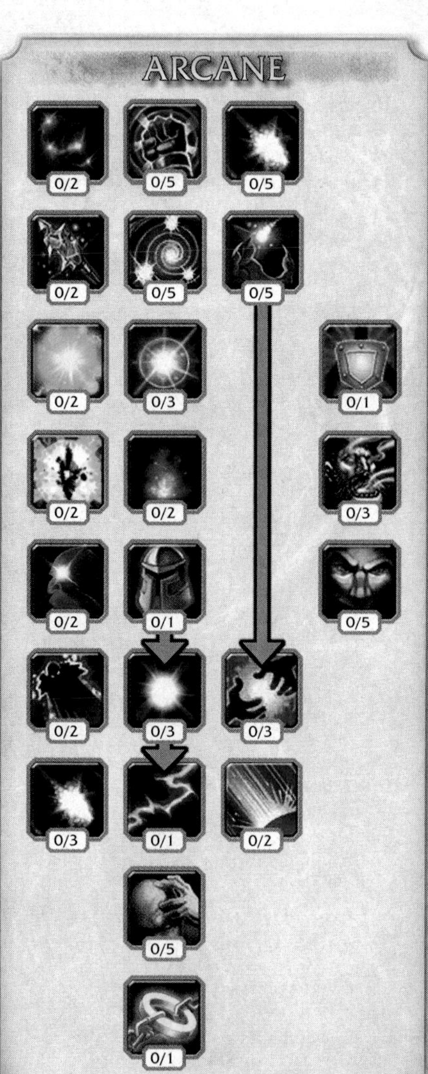

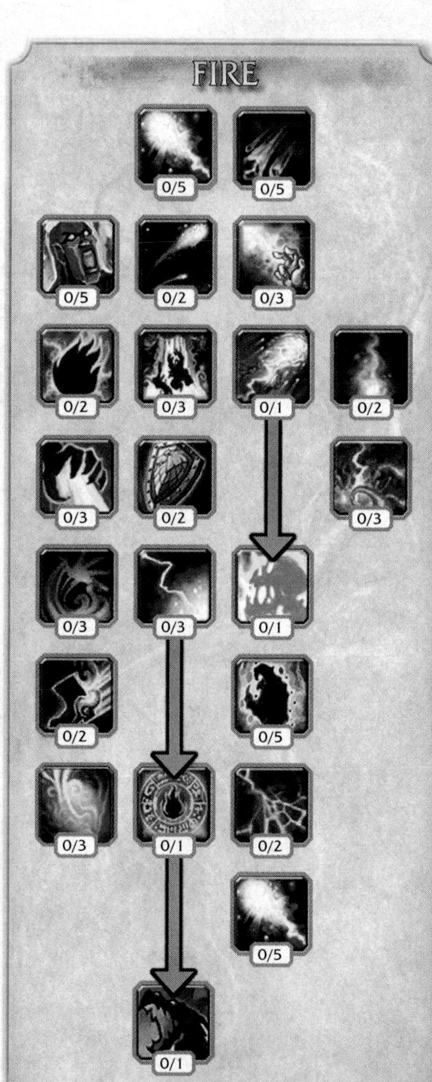

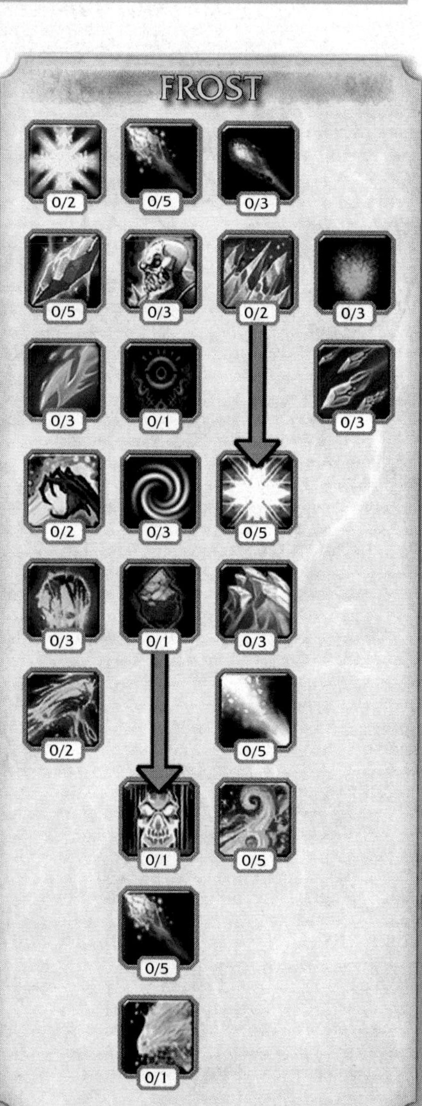

Improved Scorch (Revised Talent)

Ranks	3
Requires	15 Points in Fire

The duration for this Talent has doubled since the second Master Guide was published. The vulnerability to Fire damage lasts for 30 seconds, not 15.

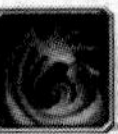

Playing With Fire (New Talent)

Ranks	3
Requires	20 Points in Fire

Increases all spell damage caused by your Mage by 1% (per rank), but also increases all spell damage taken by the same quantity.

Blazing Speed (New Talent)

Ranks	2
Requires	25 Points in Fire

Blazing Speed gives your Mage a 5% chance (per rank) to receive a buff when hit by a melee or ranged attack. This buff lasts for 8 seconds and increases movement speed by 50%; it also removes any movement-impairing effects.

Pyromaniac (New Talent)

Ranks	3
Requires	30 Points in Fire

This Talent improves all of your Mage's Fire spells by increasing their chance for a Critical Hit and reducing their Mana cost. Both of these stats chance by 1% (per rank).

Molten Fury (New Talent)

Ranks	3
Requires	30 Points in Fire

Molten Fury is like a passive Execute for Mages! When targets are below 20% Health, all of your character's spells deal 10% more damage (per rank).

Empowered Fireball (New Talent)

Ranks	5
Requires	35 Points in Fire

Your Mage's Fireballs gain an additional 4% from your Bonus Spell Damage (per rank).

Dragon's Breath (New Talent)

Ranks	1
Requires	1 Point in Combustion, 40 Points in Fire

This new spell is an Instant Fire spell with a 20-second Cooldown. Used at fairly close range, Mages are able to deliver moderate damage to a cone in front of themselves while Disorienting all affected targets for 3 seconds.

Rank One	370-430 Fire Damage/475 Mana
Rank Two	454-526 Fire Damage/575 Mana
Rank Three	574-666 Fire Damage/660 Mana
Rank Four	680-790 Fire Damage/700 Mana

Frost

Frost Channeling (Revised Talent)

Ranks	3
Requires	15 Points in Frost

The Threat Reduction of this Talent has changed since the printing of the second Master Guide. Instead of lowering Threat from Frost spells by 10% (per rank), this Talent follows a progression of 4%/7%/10%.

Frozen Core (New Talent)

Ranks	3
Requires	20 Points in Frost

Reduces the damage your Mage takes from Frost and Fire effects by 2% (per rank).

Ice Floes (New Talent)

Ranks	2
Requires	25 Points in Frost

Reduces the Cooldown for Cone of Cold, Cold Snap, Ice Barrier, and Ice Block by 10% (per rank).

Winter's Chill (Revised Talent)

Ranks	5
Requires	25 Points in Frost

With two more Ranks, Winter's Chill can be raised all the way to a 100% chance of adding its Frost vulnerability.

Arctic Winds (New Talent)

Ranks	5
Requires	30 Points in Frost

This new Talent reduces the chance that melee and ranged attacks will Hit your Mage by 1% (per rank).

Empowered Frostbolt (New Talent)

Ranks	5
Requires	35 Points in Frost

Your character's Frostbolts gain an additional 2% of your Bonus Spell Damage (per rank) and a 1% chance (per rank) to Critically Hit.

Summon Water Elemental (New Talent)

Ranks	1
Requires	40 Points in Frost

Your Mage can use this Talent to Instantly summon a Water Elemental, up to every 3 minutes. This ally fights by your character's side for 45 seconds.

PALADIN ABILITIES

Consecration (Rank 6)

Ability Line	Holy
Requirements	Level 70
Cost	670 Mana
Casting Time/Cooldown	Instant/8 Second Cooldown
Range	Point Blank Area-of-Effect

Consecrates the land beneath Paladin, doing 592 Holy damage over 8 sec to enemies who enter the area.

Spiritual Attunement (Rank 2)

Ability Line	Holy
Requirements	Level 66
Cost	None (Passive)
Casting Time/Cooldown	N/A
Range	N/A

Gives the Paladin mana when healed by other friendly targets. The amount of mana gained is equal to 10% of the amount healed.

Righteous Defense

Ability Line	Protection
Requirements	Level 20
Cost	86 Mana
Casting Time/Cooldown	Instant/15 Second Cooldown
Range	40 Yards

Come to the defense of a friendly target, commanding up to 3 enemies attacking the target to attack the Paladin instead.

Seal of Justice (Rank 2)

Ability Line	Protection
Requirements	Level 48
Cost	225 Mana
Casting Time/Cooldown	Instant/Global Cooldown
Range	Self

Fills the Paladin with the spirit of justice for 30 sec, giving each melee attack a chance to stun for 2 sec. Only one Seal can be active on the Paladin at any one time.

Unleashing this Seal's energy will judge an enemy for 10 sec, preventing them from fleeing and limiting their movement speed. Your melee strikes will refresh the spell's duration. Only one Judgement per Paladin can be active at any one time.

Crusader Aura

Ability Line	Retribution
Requirements	Level 64
Cost	None
Casting Time/Cooldown	Instant/Global Cooldown
Range	30 Yards

Increases the mounted speed by 20% for all party members within 30 yards. Players may only have one Aura on them per Paladin at any one time.

Seal of Blood

Ability Line	Retribution
Requirements	Level 64, Horde Paladin
Cost	210 Mana
Casting Time/Cooldown	Instant/Global Cooldown
Range	Self

All melee attacks deal additional Holy damage equal to 30% normal weapon damage, but the Paladin loses health equal to 10% of the total damage inflicted.

Unleashing this Seal's energy will judge an enemy, instantly causing 445 to 488 Holy damage at the cost of 148 to 163 health.

Seal of Vengeance

Ability Line	Retribution
Requirements	Level 64
Cost	250 Mana
Casting Time/Cooldown	Instant/Global Cooldown
Range	Self

Fills the Paladin with holy power, granting each melee attack a chance to cause 80 Holy damage over 12 sec. This effect can stack up to 5 times. Only one Seal can be active on the Paladin at any one time. Lasts 30 sec.

Unleashing this Seal's energy will judge an enemy, instantly causing 86 Holy damage per application of Holy Vengeance.

PALADIN TALENTS

HOLY

Aura Mastery (New Talent)

Ranks	1
Requires	10 Points in Holy

Increases the radius of your Paladin's Auras to 40 yards.

Pure of Heart (New Talent)

Ranks	3
Requires	20 Points in Holy

Increases your Paladin's Resistance to Curse and Disease effects by 5% (per rank).

Sanctified Light (New Talent)

Ranks	3
Requires	20 Points in Holy

Increases the Critical Chance of your Paladin's Holy Light spell by 2% (per rank).

Purifying Power (New Talent)

Ranks	2
Requires	25 Points in Holy

This Talent reduces the Mana cost of Cleanse and Consecration by 5% (per rank) and increases the Critical Chance of Exorcism and Holy Wraith by 10% (per rank).

Light's Grace (New Talent)

Ranks	3
Requires	30 Points in Holy

Holy Light spells gain a 33% chance (per rank) to reduce the casting time of your Paladin's next Holy Light by .5 seconds. This effect lasts for 15 seconds.

Blessed Life (New Talent)

Ranks	3
Requires	30 Points in Holy

All attacks against your Paladin have a 4% chance (with a 4%/7%/10% progression) of doing half damage.

Holy Guidance (New Talent)

Ranks	5
Requires	35 Points in Holy

This Talent increases Spell Damage and Healing by 7% (per rank) of your Paladin's total Intellect.

Divine Illumination (New Talent)

Ranks	1
Requires	40 Points in Holy

Divine Illumination is on a 3-minute Cooldown; when used, this Talent instantly reduces the Mana cost of all spells by 50% for 10 seconds.

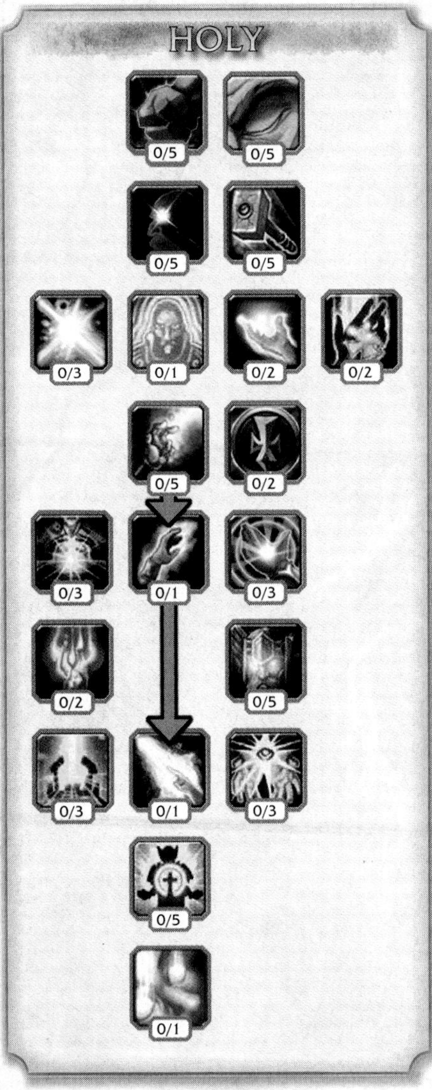

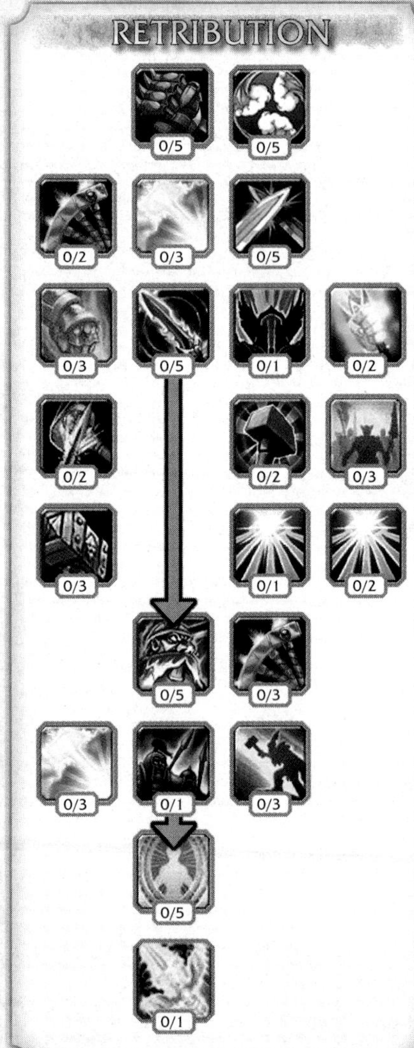

PROTECTION

Redoubt (Revised Talent)

Ranks	5
Requires	Nothing

When it procs, Redoubt still gives your Paladin a 6% increase to their Block Chance for either 10 seconds or 5 Blocks. Instead of proccing after a Critical Hit against your character, Redoubt now has a 10% chance to proc after any melee or ranged attack strikes your character.

Anticipation (Revised Talent)

Ranks	5
Requires	10 Points in Protection

This Talent adds 4 Defense (per rank) to your character. This is twice what it added during the time when the second Master Guide was printed.

Stoicism (New Talent)

Ranks	2
Requires	15 Points in Protection

Stoicism adds 5% (per rank) to your Paladin's chance to Resist Stun effects. It also gives your character's spells a 15% chance (per rank) to avoid being Dispelled.

Spell Warding (New Talent)

Ranks	2
Requires	20 Points in Protection

This Talent mitigates all spell damage taken by your Paladin by 2% (per rank).

Blessing of Sanctuary (Revised Talent)

Ranks	1
Requires	20 Points in Protection

The values for Blessing of Sanctuary have been improved since the second Master Guide. This Talent's effect deals about the same damage that is used to, but it reduces mores damage for the protected target.

Reckoning (Revised Talent)

Ranks	5
Requires	20 Points in Protection

The old Reckoning effect was to grant a free attack after being the victim of a Critical Hit. If you master this version of Reckoning, your Paladin gets a 10% chance after being hit by *any* damaging attack for a buff. This effect allows up to 4 free weapon swings over the next 8 seconds.

Except when fighting enemies with an very high Critical Chance, this is a buff to the Talent. Not only does Reckoning proc more often during fights against weaker enemies; it also maintains its rate even if you invest a great deal in equipment with high Resilience. The old version would have been punished by that because the enemies Critical Chance would have fallen in the process.

Improved Divine Shield (New Talent)

Ranks	2
Requires	25 Points in Protection

This reduces the Cooldown of Divine Shield by 30 seconds (per rank) and reduces the penalty to your Paladin's attack speed by 50% (per rank).

Ardent Defender (New Talent)

Ranks	5
Requires	30 Points in Protection

When your Paladins drops below 20% Health, this Talent kicks in to reduce all damage taken by 10% (per rank).

Weapon Expertise (New Talent)

Ranks	5
Requires	35 Points in Protection

This Talent increases your Paladin's Weapon Skill with all weapons by 2 points (per rank).

Avenger's Shield (New Talent)

Ranks	1
Requires	1 Point in Holy Shield, 40 Points in Protection

Avenger's Shield is an attack spell with only a 1-second casting time; it has a 30-second Cooldown and a moderately-heavy Mana cost. In return, this spell hits one enemy with Holy damage, then the effect tries to find another target to jump to. Avenger's Shield can strike up to 3 total targets over 3 seconds.

Rank One	270-330 Holy Damage/500 Mana
Rank Two	370-452 Holy Damage/615 Mana
Rank Three	581-709 Holy Damage/825 Mana

RETRIBUTION

Crusade (New Talent)

Ranks	3
Requires	15 Points in Retribution

Damage that your Paladin causes to Humanoids, Demons, Undead, and Elementals is increased by 1% (per rank).

Improved Sanctity Aura (New Talent)

Ranks	2
Requires	1 Point in Sanctity Aura, 20 Points in Retribution

Healing done to party members under the effect of your Paladin's Sanctity Aura is increased by 3% (per rank).

Sanctified Judgement (New Talent)

Ranks	3
Requires	25 Points in Retribution

This gives your Paladin's Judgement a 33% chance (per rank) to return 50% of the Mana cost from the Judged Seal.

Sanctified Crusader (New Talent)

Ranks	3
Requires	30 Points in Retribution

Judgement of the Crusader gains the additional benefit of raising the Critical Chance of all attacks made against the target by 1% (per rank).

Divine Purpose (New Talent)

Ranks	3
Requires	30 Points in Retribution

Melee and ranged Critical Hits against your Paladin cause less damage (in a progression of 4%/7%/10%).

Fanaticism (New Talent)

Ranks	5
Requires	1 Point in Repentance, 35 Points in Retribution

Fanaticism increases the chance for a Judgement to Critically Hit by 3% (per rank). This Talent has no effect in cases where a Judgement does not have a chance to Critically Hit.

Crusader Strike (New Talent)

Ranks	1
Requires	40 Points in Retribution

This melee ability is used Instantly to deal full weapon damage plus 40% of your Paladin's Holy Spell Damage; it also has the benefit of refreshing all Judgements on the target! Being Crusader Strike only has a 10-second Cooldown, there is quite the potential for maintaining a very aggressive series of attacks against a single foe, so long as your character can keep up the Mana cost.

PRIEST ABILITIES

Mass Dispel

Ability Line	Discipline
Requirements	Level 70
Cost	1181 Mana
Casting Time/Cooldown	1.5 Seconds/Global Cooldown
Range	30 Yards

Dispels magic in a 15 yard radius, removing 1 harmful spell from each friendly target and 1 beneficial spell from each enemy target. Affects a maximum of 5 friendly targets and 5 enemy targets. This dispel is potent enough to remove Magic effects that are normally undispellable.

Binding Heal

Ability Line	Holy
Requirements	Level 64
Cost	1034 Mana
Casting Time/Cooldown	1.5 Seconds/Global Cooldown
Range	40 Yards

Heals a friendly target and the caster for 1053 to 1350.

Prayer of Mending

Ability Line	Holy
Requirements	Level 68
Cost	976 Mana
Casting Time/Cooldown	Instant/Global Cooldown
Range	30 Yards

Places a spell on the target that heals them for 702 to 858 the next time they take damage. When the heal occurs, Prayer of Mending jumps to a nearby raid target. Jumps up to 5 times and lasts 1 min after each jump. This spell can only be placed on one target at a time.

Shadow Word: Death (Rank 1)

Ability Line	Shadow
Requirements	Level 62
Cost	243 Mana
Casting Time/Cooldown	Instant/6 Second Cooldown
Range	30 Yards

A word of dark binding that inflicts 450 to 522 Shadow damage to the target. If the target is not killed by Shadow Word: Death, the caster takes damage equal to the damage inflicted upon the target.

Shadow Word: Death (Rank 2)

Ability Line	Shadow
Requirements	Level 70
Cost	309 Mana
Casting Time/Cooldown	Instant/6 Second Cooldown
Range	30 Yards

A word of dark binding that inflicts 572 to 664 Shadow damage to the target. If the target is not killed by Shadow Word: Death, the caster takes damage equal to the damage inflicted upon the target.

Shadowfiend

Ability Line	Shadow
Requirements	Level 66
Cost	210 Mana
Casting Time/Cooldown	Instant/5 Minute Cooldown
Range	30 Yards

Creates a shadowy fiend to attack the target. Caster receives mana when the Shadowfiend deals damage. Lasts 15 sec.

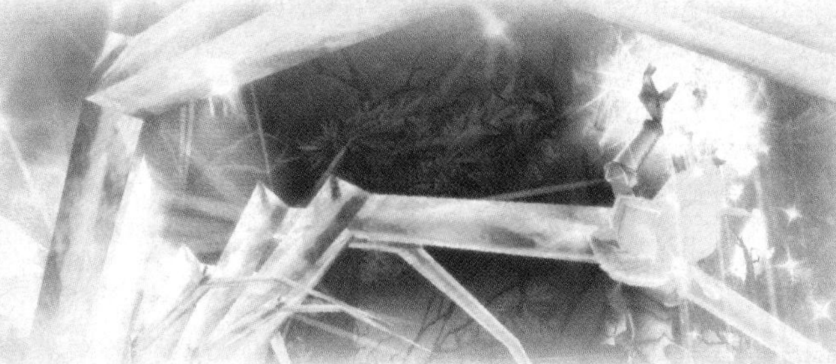

PRIEST TALENTS

Discipline

Silent Resolve (Revised Talent)

Ranks	5
Requires	5 Points in Discipline

In addition to reducing the Threat generated by your Priest's spells, this Talent now reduces the chance that your spells will be Dispelled by 4% (per rank).

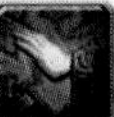

Absolution (New Talent)

Ranks	3
Requires	10 Points in Discipline

Absolution reduces the Mana cost of Dispel Magic, Cure Disease, Abolish Disease, and Mass Dispel by 5% (per rank).

Improved Mana Burn (Revised Talent)

Ranks	2
Requires	15 Points in Discipline

The effect of this Talent has doubled since the printing of the second Master Guide; it now reduces the casting time of Mana Burn by .5 seconds (per rank).

Improved Divine Spirit (New Talent)

Ranks	2
Requires	1 Point in Divine Spirit, 20 Points in Discipline

Your Priest's Divine Spirit/Prayer of Spirit not only improve the targets' Spirit, but also raise their Spell Damage and Healing by 5% of their total Spirit (per rank).

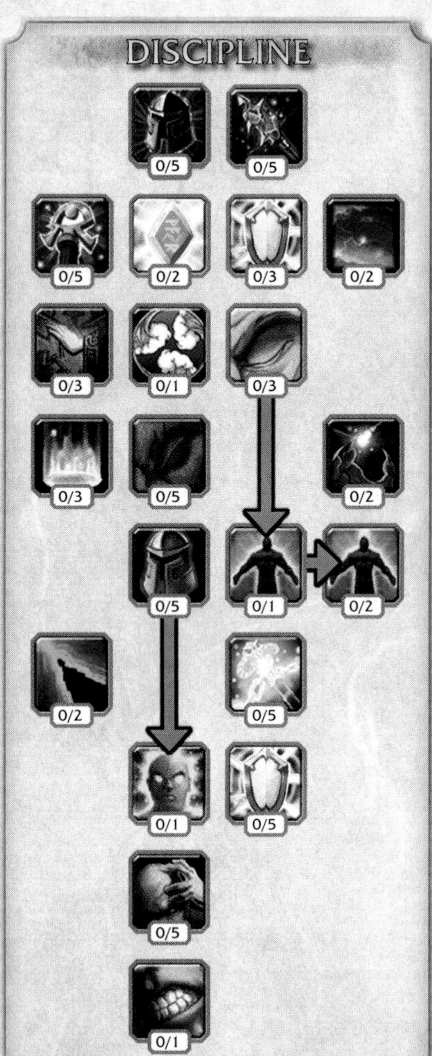

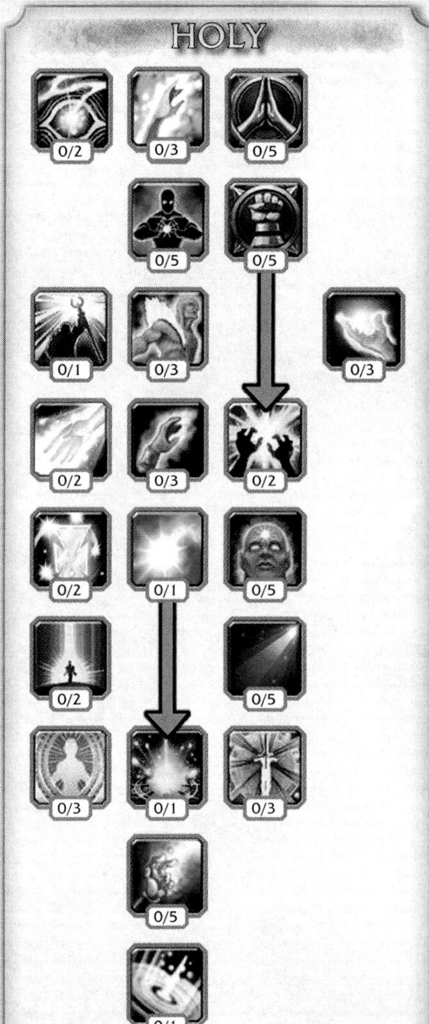

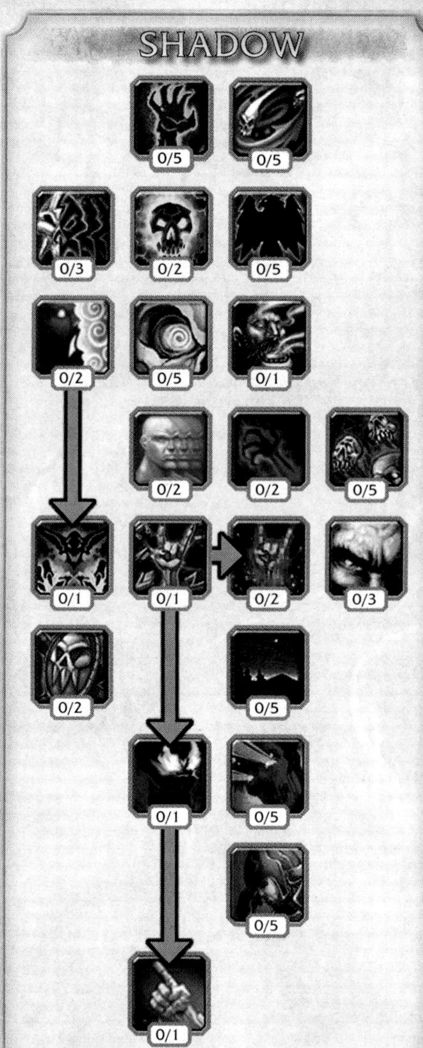

Focused Power (New Talent)

Ranks	2
Requires	25 Points in Discipline

Smite and Mind Blast both receive a 2% boost to Hit (per rank). These spells also cause 5% more damage (per rank) against Feared targets. Scream away.

Reflective Shield (New Talent)

Ranks	5
Requires	30 Points in Discipline

10% (per rank) of the damage absorbed by your Priest's Power Word Shield is reflected back at the attacker. This damage causes no Threat, which is very good when the spell is used on soft allies.

Enlightenment (New Talent)

Ranks	5
Requires	35 Points in Discipline

Increases your Priest's total Stamina, Intellect, and Spirit by 1% (per rank).

Pain Suppression (New Talent)

Ranks	1
Requires	40 Points in Discipline

Pain Suppression is an Instant ability that is used to give your Priest 8 seconds of reduced damage; it knocks off 60% of all damage dealt to your character, and the spell is on a 3-minute Cooldown.

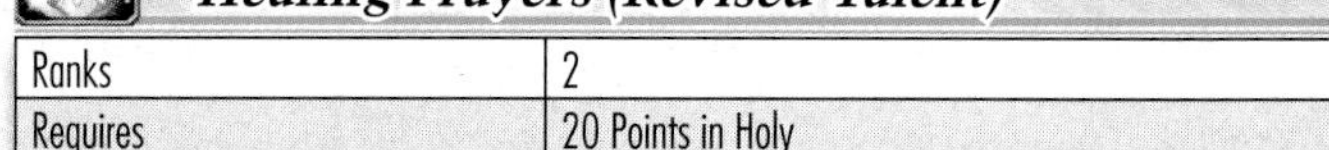

HOLY

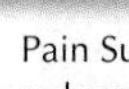

Healing Prayers (Revised Talent)

Ranks	2
Requires	20 Points in Holy

The older Talent, Improved Prayer of Healing has been renamed as Healing Prayers. It now reduces the Mana cost of both Prayer of Healing and Prayer of Mending by 10% (per rank).

Spirit of Redemption (Revised Talent)

Ranks	1
Requires	20 Points in Holy

The effect from this Talent currently lasts for 15 seconds. For the second Master Guide, this was listed at 10 seconds. All the more time to keep the team alive.

Surge of Light (New Talent)

Ranks	2
Requires	25 Points in Holy

Spell Criticals gain a 25% chance (per rank) to cause your Priest's next Smite to be both Instant and free of Mana cost. The effect lasts for up to 10 seconds, and the only penalty is that your Smite will never be a Critical.

Holy Concentration (New Talent)

Ranks	3
Requires	30 Points in Holy

Casting Flash Heal and Greater Healing gives your Priest a 2% chance (per rank) to enter a Clearcasting state. This reduces the Mana cost of the next Flash Heal or Greater Heal by 100%.

Blessed Resilience (New Talent)

Ranks	3
Requires	30 Points in Holy

Critical Hits against your Priest now have a 20% chance (per rank) of making your character immune to further Critical Hits for 6 seconds.

Empowered Healing (New Talent)

Ranks	5
Requires	35 Points in Holy

Greater Heal gains an additional 4% effectiveness (per rank) from your Priest's Bonus Healing effects. Flash Heal gets 2% of this (per rank).

Circle of Healing (New Talent)

Ranks	1
Requires	40 Points in Holy

This Talent teaches an Instant, ranged, area-of-effect Healing spell. The target and any allies within 15 yards are healed for a moderate sum of Health.

Rank One:	289-319 Healed/400 Mana
Rank Two	337-372 Healed/450 Mana
Rank Three	385-426 Healed/500 Mana
Rank Four	434-479 Healed/550 Mana
Rank Five	475-525 Healed/600 Mana

Shadow

Shadow Reach (Revised Talent)

Ranks	2
Requires	15 Points in Shadow

It only takes 2 Talent points to master this Talent, rather than the 3 points that it previously took.

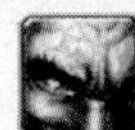

Focused Mind (New Talent)

Ranks	3
Requires	20 Points in Shadow

Focused Mind reduces the Mana cost of Mind Blast, Mind Control, and Mind Flay by 5% (per rank).

Shadow Resilience (New Talent)

Ranks	2
Requires	25 Points in Shadow

This Talent reduces the chance that your Priest will be Critically Hit with spells by 2% (per rank).

Shadow Power (New Talent)

Ranks	5
Requires	30 Points in Shadow

Shadow Power increases the Critical Chance of Mind Blast and Shadow Word Death by 3% (per rank).

Misery (New Talent)

Ranks	5
Requires	35 Points in Shadow

Shadow Word Pain, Mind Flay, and Vampiric Touch cause the target to additionally take 1% Spell Damage (per rank).

Vampiric Touch (New Talent)

Ranks	1
Requires	1 Point in Shadowform, 40 Points in Shadow

This new spell has a 1.5-second casting time but no Cooldown. Vampiric Touch causes respectable Shadow damage to a single target; it takes 15 seconds for the full sum to tick away, and all damage done by this attack causes all party members to gain an equal amount of Mana. Vampiric Embrace and Vampiric Touch are two great effects that work well together.

ROGUE ABILITIES

Deadly Throw

Ability Line	Assassination
Requirements	Level 64, Thrown Weapon
Cost	35 Energy
Casting Time/Cooldown	Instant/Global Cooldown
Range	8-30 Yards

Finishing move that reduces the movement of the target by 50% for 5 sec and causes thrown weapon damage plus additional damage per level per combo point:

1 point	215-232 damage
2 points	320-337 damage
3 points	425-442 damage
4 points	530-547 damage
5 points	635-652 damage

Envenom (Rank 1)

Ability Line	Assassination
Requirements	Level 62, Melee Weapon
Cost	25 Energy
Casting Time/Cooldown	Instant/Global Cooldown
Range	5 Yards

Consumes all Deadly Poison doses on the target, dealing Instant Poison damage for each dose consumed. Up to one dose is consumed for each combo point spent.

1 Dose	155 Damage
2 Doses	311 Damage
3 Doses	466 Damage
4 Doses	622 Damage
5 Doses	777 Damage

Envenom (Rank 2)

Ability Line	Assassination
Requirements	Level 69, Melee Weapon
Cost	25 Energy
Casting Time/Cooldown	Instant/Global Cooldown
Range	5 Yards

Consumes all Deadly Poison doses on the target, dealing Instant Poison damage for each dose consumed. Up to one dose is consumed for each combo point spent.

1 Dose	191 Damage
2 Doses	383 Damage
3 Doses	574 Damage
4 Doses	766 Damage
5 Doses	957 Damage

Cloak of Shadows

Ability Line	N/A
Requirements	Level 66
Cost	None
Casting Time/Cooldown	Instant/1 Minute Cooldown
Range	Self

Garrote (Rank 7)

Ability Line	Assassination
Requirements	Level 61, Stealth
Cost	50 Energy
Casting Time/Cooldown	Instant/Global Cooldown
Range	5 Yards

Garrote the enemy, Silencing them for 3 seconds and causing 666 damage over 18 sec, increased by Attack Power. Must be stealthed and behind the target. Awards 1 combo point.

Garrote (Rank 8)

Ability Line	Assassination
Requirements	Level 70, Stealth
Cost	50 Energy
Casting Time/Cooldown	Instant/Global Cooldown
Range	5 Yards

Garrote the enemy, Silencing them for 3 seconds and causing 810 damage over 18 sec, increased by Attack Power. Must be stealthed and behind the target. Awards 1 combo point.

Shiv

Ability Line	Combat
Requirements	Level 70, Melee Weapon
Cost	33-49 Energy (Varies By Weapon Type)
Casting Time/Cooldown	Instant/Global Cooldown
Range	5 Yards

Performs an instant off-hand weapon attack that automatically applies the poison from your off-hand weapon to the target. Slower weapons require more Energy. Awards 1 combo point.

Evasion (Rank 2)

Ability Line	Combat
Requirements	Level 66
Cost	None
Casting Time/Cooldown	Instant/5 Minute Cooldown
Range	Self

Increases the rogue's dodge chance by 50% and reduces the chance ranged attacks hit the rogue by 50%. Lasts 15 sec.

Anesthetic Poison

Ability Line	Poisons
Requirements	Level 68
Cost	None
Casting Time/Cooldown	None
Range	Melee

Coats a weapon with poison that lasts for 30 minutes. Each strike has a 20% chance of reducing Threat by a moderate amount. 120 charges.

ROGUE TALENTS

Assassination

Murder (Revised Talent)

Ranks	2
Requires	5 Points in Assassination

Increases all damage caused against Humanoid, Giant, Beast, and Dragonkin targets by 1% per rank (at the time of Master Guide II, this was listed as 2% per rank).

Improved Expose Armor (Revised Talent)

Ranks	2
Requires	10 Points in Assassination

Increases the armor reduced by your Expose Armor ability by 25% per rank (at the time of Master Guide II, this was listed at 15% per rank).

Fleet Footed (New Talent)

Ranks	2
Requires	20 Points in Assassination

Increases your chance to resist movement-impairing effects bt 5% and increases your movement speed by 4%. This does not stack with out movement speed increasing effects.

Quick Recovery (New Talent)

Ranks	2
Requires	20 Points in Assassination

All healing effects on you are increased by 10%. In addition, your finishing moves cost 40% less Energy when they fail to hit.

Master Poisoner (New Talent)

Ranks	2
Requires	25 Points in Assassination

Reduces the chance your Poisons will be resisted by 2% and increases your chance to resist Poison effects by an additional 15%.

Deadened Nerves (New Talent)

Ranks	5
Requires	30 Points in Assassination

Decreases all physical damage taken by 1%.

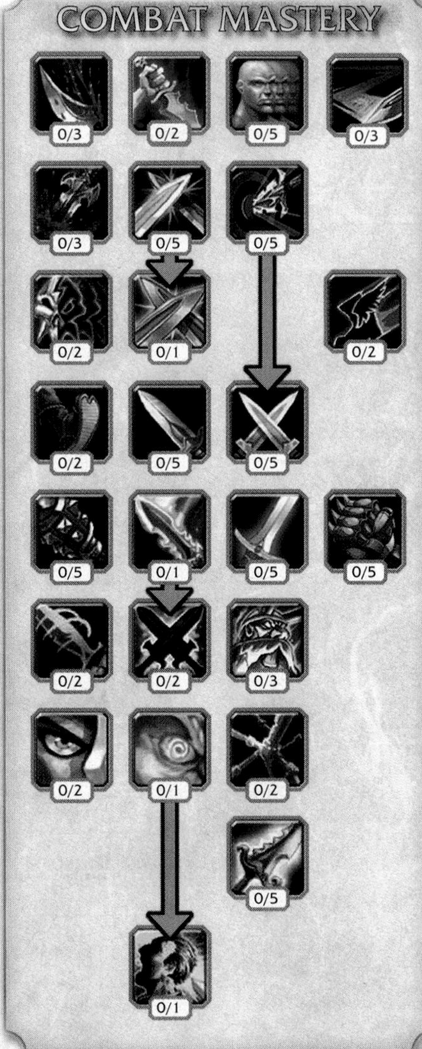

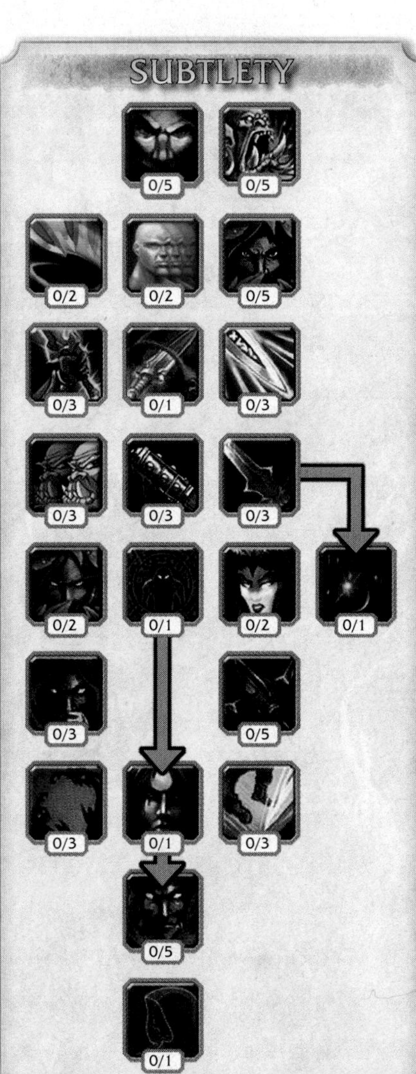

Find Weakness (New Talent)

Ranks	5
Requires	35 Points in Assassination

Your finishing moves increase the damage of all your offensive abilities by 2% for 10 seconds.

Mutilate (New Talent)

Ranks	1
Requires	1 Point in Vigor, 40 Points in Assassination

Adds an instant attack with daggers which costs 60 Energy and has a 5 yard range.

Instantly attacks with both weapons for an additional 44 with each weapon. Damage is increased by 50% against Poisoned targets. Must be behind the target for this attack to be possible. Awards two Combo Points when successful.

COMBAT MASTERY

Blade Flurry (Revised Talent)

Ranks	1
Requires	20 Points in Combat

Blade Flurry was listed as having a 5-minute cooldown in the second Master Guide. This Talent now has a 2-minute cooldown.

Vitality (New Talent)

Ranks	2
Requires	30 Points in Combat

Increases your total Stamina by 2% (per rank).

Adrenaline Rush (Revised Talent)

Ranks	1
Requires	30 Points in Combat

Adrenaline Rush was listed as having a 6-minute cooldown in the second Master Guide. This Talent now has a 5-minute cooldown.

Nerves of Steel (New Talent)

Ranks	2
Requires	30 Points in Combat

Increases your chance to resist Stun and Fear effects by an additional 5% (per rank).

Blade Twisting (New Talent)

Ranks	5
Requires	35 Points in Combat

Gives your Sinister Strike, Backstab, Gouge, and Shiv a 5% chance to Daze the target for 8 seconds.

Surprise Attacks (New Talent)

Ranks	1
Requires	1 Point in Adrenaline Rush, 40 Points in Combat

Your Sinister Strike, Backstab, Shiv, and Gouge can no longer be dodged, and damage caused by those abilities is increased by 10%.

SUBTLETY

Ghostly Strike (Revised Talent)

Ranks	1
Requires	10 Points in Subtlety

Ghostly Strike increases your chance to Dodge for 7 seconds and has a 5-yard range.

Heightened Senses (Revised Talent)

Ranks	2
Requires	20 Points in Subtlety

At the time of the second Master Guide, this Talent affected your chance to be hit by spells and ranged attack by 1% (per rank). That effect is now 2% (per rank).

Master of Subtlety (New Talent)

Ranks	3
Requires	25 Points in Subtlety

Attacks made while Stealthed and for 6 seconds after breaking Stealth cause an additional 4% damage (per rank).

Enveloping Shadows (New Talent)

Ranks	3
Requires	30 Points in Subtlety

Increases your chance to avoid area-of-effect attacks by an additional 5% (per rank).

Premeditation (Revised Talent)

Ranks	1
Requires	1 Point in Preparation, 30 Points in Subtlety

Premeditation currently has a 20-yard range and a 2-minute cooldown; it does not cost Energy to use. This instant ability, used from Stealth, still functions in a similar manner.

Cheat Death (New Talent)

Ranks	5
Requires	30 Points in Subtlety

You gain a 4% chance to completely avoid any damaging attack that would otherwise kill you.

Sinister Calling (New Talent)

Ranks	5
Requires	1 Point in Premeditation, 35 Points in Subtlety

Increases your Agility by 2% (per rank).

Shadowstep (New Talent)

Ranks	1
Requires	40 Points in Subtlety

Attempts to step through the shadows and appear behind the enemy. The damage of your next Ambush, Backstab, or Garrote ability is increased 20 %. Lasts 10 seconds, costs 10 Energy, and has a 20 second cooldown.

SHAMAN ABILITIES

Fire Elemental Totem

Ability Line	Elemental
Requirements	Level 70, Fire Totem
Cost	680 Mana
Casting Time/Cooldown	Instant/20 Minute Cooldown
Range	Point Blank

Summons an elemental totem that calls forth a greater fire elemental to rain destruction on the caster's enemies. Lasts 2 min.

Wrath of Air Totem

Ability Line	Enhancement
Requirements	Level 64, Air Totem
Cost	320 Mana
Casting Time/Cooldown	Instant/Global Cooldown
Range	Point Blank

Summons a Wrath of Air Totem with 5 health at the feet of the caster. Party members within 20 yards of the totem have their magical damage from spells and effects increased by up to 101. Lasts 2 min.

Bloodlust

Ability Line	Enhancement
Requirements	Level 70, Horde Shaman
Cost	750 Mana
Casting Time/Cooldown	Instant/10 Minute Cooldown
Range	Group

Increases melee, ranged, and spell casting speed by 30% for all party members. Lasts for 40 Seconds.

SHAMAN TALENTS

ELEMENTAL COMBAT

Unrelenting Storm (New Talent)

Ranks	5
Requires	20 Points in Elemental Combat

Your Shaman will regenerate 2% of their total Intellect in Mana (per Rank) every 5 seconds. This occurs even during casting.

Elemental Precision (New Talent)

Ranks	3
Requires	25 Points in Elemental Combat

This Talent increases the chance to Hit with Fire, Frost, and Nature spells by 2% (per rank).

Heroism

Ability Line	Enhancement
Requirements	Level 70, Alliance Shaman
Cost	750 Mana
Casting Time/Cooldown	Instant/10 Minute Cooldown
Range	Group

Increases melee, ranged, and spell casting speed by 30% for all party members. Lasts for 40 Seconds.

Water Shield (Rank 1)

Ability Line	Restoration
Requirements	Level 62
Cost	50 Mana
Casting Time/Cooldown	Instant/Global Cooldown
Range	Self

The caster is surrounded by 3 globes of water. When a spell, melee or ranged attack hits the caster, 95 mana is restored to the caster. This expends one water globe. Only one globe will activate every few seconds. Lasts 10 min.

Water Shield (Rank 2)

Ability Line	Restoration
Requirements	Level 62
Cost	50 Mana
Casting Time/Cooldown	Instant/Global Cooldown
Range	Self

The caster is surrounded by 3 globes of water. When a spell, melee or ranged attack hits the caster, 123-124 mana is restored to the caster. This expends one water globe. Only one globe will activate every few seconds. Lasts 10 min.

Earth Elemental Totem

Ability Line	Restoration
Requirements	Level 70, Earth Totem
Cost	705 Mana
Casting Time/Cooldown	Instant/20 Minute Cooldown
Range	Point Blank

Summons an elemental totem that calls forth a greater earth elemental to protect the caster and his allies. This lasts for 2 minutes.

Elemental Shields (New Talent)

Ranks	3
Requires	30 Points in Elemental Combat

Reduces the chance that your Shaman will be Critically Hit by melee and ranged attacks by 2% (per rank).

Lightning Overload (New Talent)

Ranks	5
Requires	35 Points in Elemental Combat

Your Shaman's Lightning Bolt and Chain Lightning gain a 1% chance (per rank) to cast a second, identical spell on the same target. This occur with no additional Mana cost.

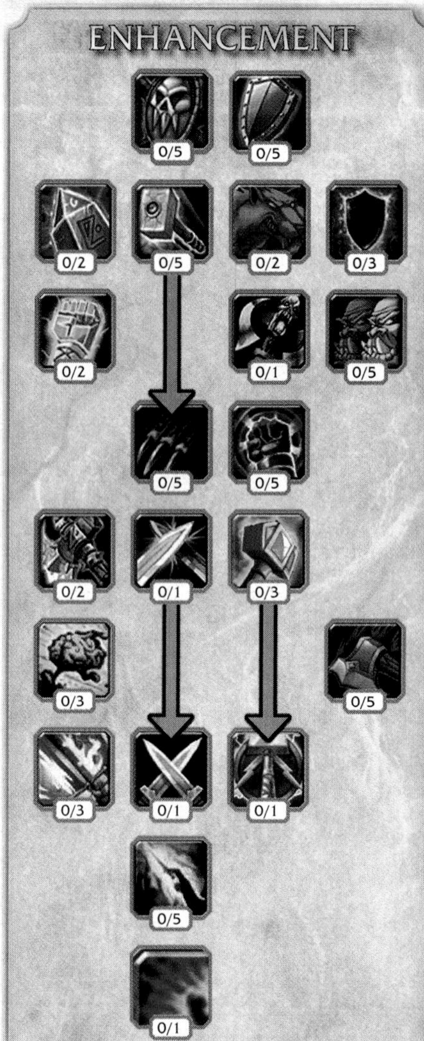

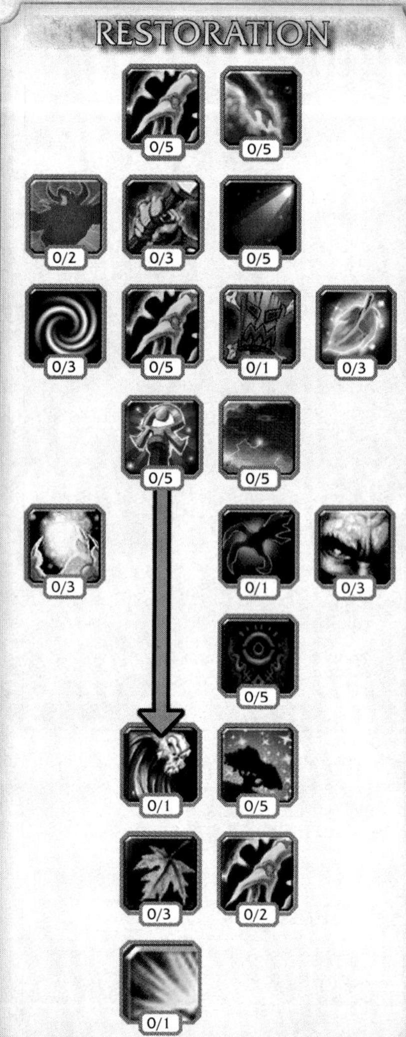

Totem of Wrath (New Talent)

Ranks	1
Requires	5 Points in Lightning Overload, 40 Points in Elemental Combat

This Talent adds a new form of Fire Totem ability. Totems of Wrath are summoned with 5 Health and last for 2 minutes. These Totems raise the chance to Critically Hit with spells by 3% for all party members within 20 yards.

ENHANCEMENT

Unleashed Rage (New Talent)

Ranks	5
Requires	25 Points in Enhancement

Unleashed Rage causes your Shaman's Critical Hits in melee to buff allies within 20 yards. This buff raises Attack Power by 2% (per rank) and lasts for 10 seconds.

Dual Wield (New Talent)

Ranks	1
Requires	1 Point in Parry, 30 Points in Enhancement

Allows Shamans to wield one-hand or off-hand weapons in their off-hand. Slashy slashy.

Mental Quickness (New Talent)

Ranks	3
Requires	30 Points in Enhancement

This Talent reduces the Mana cost of Instant spells by 2% (per rank).

Dual Wield Specialization (New Talent)

Ranks	5
Requires	1 Point in Dual Wield, 35 Points in Enhancement

This Talent adds a 2% chance to Hit (per rank) while dual wielding.

Shamanistic Rage (New Talent)

Ranks	1
Requires	40 Points in Enhancement

Shamanistic Rage gives your character a self-buff that they can cast on a 2-minute Cooldown. This buff, which lasts for 30 seconds, gives your melee attacks a chance to regenerate Mana equal to 15% of your Shaman's Attack Power.

RESTORATION

Focused Mind (New Talent)

Ranks	3
Requires	20 Points in Restoration

Learning this Talent increases your Shaman's Resistance to Silence and Interruption mechanics by an additional 5% (per rank).

Mana Tide Totem (Revised Talent)

Ranks	1
Requires	5 Points in Restorative Totems, 30 Points in Restoration

Mana Tide Totem no longer adds a set quantity of Mana to nearby party members. Instead, it adds 6% of their total Mana every 3 seconds, for a 12-second duration.

Nature's Guardian (New Talent)

Ranks	5
Requires	30 Points in Restoration

Any time that your Shaman receives a damaging attack that reduces their Health below 30%, there is a 10% chance (per rank) to Heal 10% of your character's total Health; this also reduces your Threat level with that target (if applicable). Nature's Guardian can only be triggered up to every 5 seconds.

Nature's Blessing (New Talent)

Ranks	3
Requires	35 Points in Restoration

This Talent increases your Shaman's Spell Damage and Healing by 10% of their Intellect (per rank).

Improved Chain Heal (New Talent)

Ranks	2
Requires	35 Points in Restoration

Chain Heal gains a 10% bonus (per rank) to its total amount Healed.

Earth Shield (New Talent)

Ranks	1
Requires	40 Points in Restoration

This Talent teaches your Shaman a special type of shield spell. As before, only one type of shield is effective for a given character, and a Shaman can only cast Earth Shield on one person at a time.

Earth Shield gives the target a 30% chance of ignoring Interruption while casting; it also causes melee attacks against the target to Heal the person for a given amount. This effect can only occur every few seconds, and after either 10 charges or 10 minutes, the effect will dissipate.

Though costly, Earth Shield lasts for such a long time that it has wonderful opportunities to be used with almost no downside. For example, a Shaman who knows that a boss is coming up in the next encounter casts Earth Shield on the main tank before the group rests to top off their Health/Mana. Thus, the fight starts with the Earth Shield at full power, but the Shaman has all of her Mana anyway!

Rank One	150 Health Per Tick/600 Mana
Rank Two	205 Health Per Tick/745 Mana
Rank Three	270 Health Per Tick/900 Mana

WARLOCK ABILITIES

Seed of Corruption

Ability Line	Affliction
Requirements	Level 70
Cost	882 Mana
Casting Time/Cooldown	2 Seconds/Global Cooldown
Range	30 Yards

Imbeds a demon seed in the enemy target, causing 1044 Shadow damage over 18 sec. When the target takes 1044 total damage, the seed will inflict 1110 to 1290 Shadow damage to all enemies within 15 yards of the target. Only one Corruption spell per Warlock can be active on any one target.

Fel Armor (Rank 1)

Ability Line	Demonology
Requirements	Level 62
Cost	637 Mana
Casting Time/Cooldown	Instant/Global Cooldown
Range	Self

Surrounds the caster with fel energy, increasing the amount of health generated through spells and effects by 20% and increasing spell damage by up to 50. Only one type of Armor spell can be active on the Warlock at any time. Lasts 30 min.

Fel Armor (Rank 2)

Ability Line	Demonology
Requirements	Level 69
Cost	637 Mana
Casting Time/Cooldown	Instant/Global Cooldown
Range	Self

Surrounds the caster with fel energy, increasing the amount of health generated through spells and effects by 20% and increasing spell damage by up to 100. Only one type of Armor spell can be active on the Warlock at any time. Lasts 30 min.

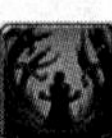

Ritual of Souls

Ability Line	Demonology
Requirements	Level 70, Soul Shard
Cost	1532 Mana
Casting Time/Cooldown	3 Seconds/5 Minute Cooldown
Range	30 Yards

Begins a ritual that creates a Soulwell. Raid members can click the Soulwell to acquire a Master Healthstone. The Soulwell lasts for 5 min or 10 charges. Requires the caster and 2 additional party members to complete the ritual. In order to participate, all players must be out of combat and right-click the soul portal and not move until the ritual is complete.

Soulshatter

Ability Line	Demonology
Requirements	Level 66, Soul Shard
Cost	193 Health
Casting Time/Cooldown	Instant/5 Minute Cooldown
Range	N/A

Reduces Threat by 50% for all enemies.

Incinerate (Rank 1)

Ability Line	Destruction
Requirements	Level 64
Cost	256 Mana
Casting Time/Cooldown	2.5 Seconds/Global Cooldown
Range	30 Yards

Deals 357 to 413 Fire damage to your target and an additional 89 to 104 Fire damage if the target is affected by an Immolate spell.

Incinerate (Rank 2)

Ability Line	Destruction
Requirements	Level 70
Cost	300 Mana
Casting Time/Cooldown	2.5 Seconds/Global Cooldown
Range	30 Yards

Deals 429 to 497 Fire damage to your target and an additional 107 to 125 Fire damage if the target is affected by an Immolate spell.

WARLOCK TALENTS

AFFLICTION

Improved Curse of Weakness (Revised Talent)

Ranks	2
Requires	5 Points in Affliction

It only takes 2 Talent points to get a 20% increase in Curse of Weakness' effect. Formerly, it took 3 Talent points to achieve this.

Improved Drain Soul (Revised Talent)

Ranks	2
Requires	5 Points in Affliction

If a target dies while you are using Drain Soul, 7% of your Warlock's maximum Mana is restored (the progression is 7%/15%). Also, your character's Affliction spells generate 5% less Threat (per rank).

Soul Siphon (New Talent)

Ranks	2
Requires	5 Points in Affliction

The amount that is taken by Drain Life and Drain Mana is increased for each Affliction effect on the target, up to a maximum value. The progression for this Talent is 2%/5% for the increased value, and 24%/60% for the improvement cap.

Improved Curse of Agony (Revised Talent)

Ranks	2
Requires	10 Points in Affliction

The efficiency of this Talent has been increased by a fair margin. The old Talent raised the damage from Curse of Agony by 2% (per rank). This version adds 5% (per rank) instead.

Nightfall (Revised Talent)

Ranks	2
Requires	15 Points in Affliction

The progression for your Warlock's chance to enter a Clearcasting state has changed from 2%/3% to 2%/4%, making this a slight buff to the Talent.

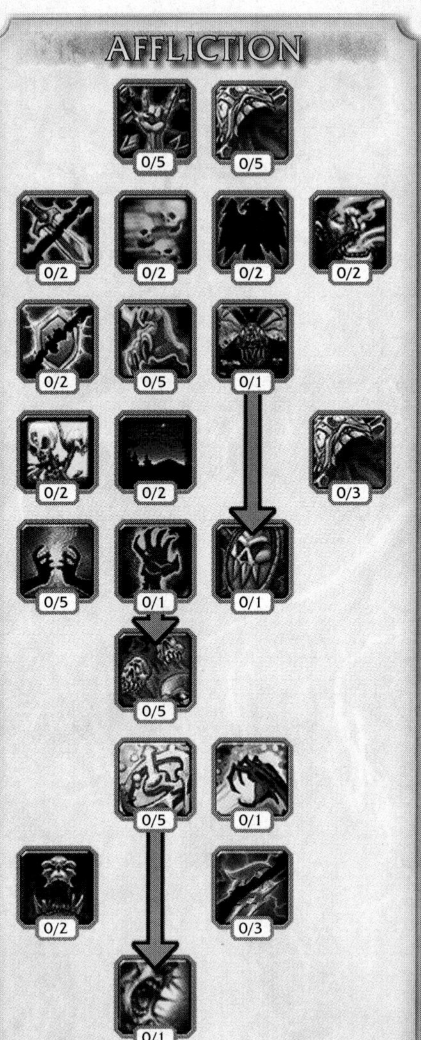

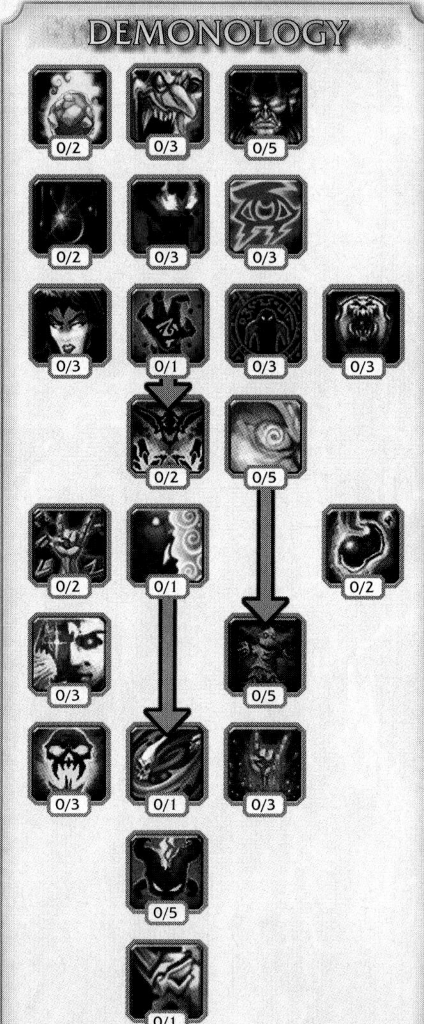

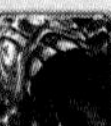

Empowered Corruption (New Talent)

Ranks	3
Requires	15 Points in Affliction

Corruption gains an additional 12% of your Warlock's Bonus Spell Damage effects (per rank).

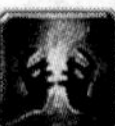

Shadow Embrace (New Talent)

Ranks	5
Requires	20 Points in Affliction

Corruption, Curse of Agony, Siphon Life, and Seed of Corruption cause the Shadow Embrace effect; this reduces the physical damage caused by the target by 1% (per rank).

Siphon Life (Revised Talent)

Ranks	1
Requires	20 Points in Affliction

Siphon Life was listed with a 1.5-second casting time in the second Master Guide. Currently, this Talent's ability has an Instant casting time.

Curse of Exhaustion (Revised Talent)

Ranks	1
Requires	1 Point in Amplify Curse, 20 Points in Affliction

Curse of Exhaustion used to require that you purchase 5 Talent points to reach a 30% reduction in target movement speed. This is all given to a Warlock in a single Talent point now, making the purchase far less painful for those who need to be able to Snare targets without allies around to help.

Contagion (New Talent)

Ranks	5
Requires	30 Points in Affliction

Contagion improves the damage from Curse of Agony, Corruption, and Speed of Corruption by 1% (per rank). This Talent also gives your Warlock's Affliction spells a 6% chance (per rank) to avoid being dispelled.

Dark Pact (Revised Talent)

Ranks	1
Requires	30 Points in Affliction

The range of this ability has been buffed to 30 yards, and the amount of Mana exchanged has also increased since the publishing of the second Master Guide.

Improved Howl of Terror (New Talent)

Ranks	2
Requires	35 Points in Affliction

This Talent reduces the casting time of Howl of Terror by a progression of .8 seconds/1.5 seconds.

Malediction (New Talent)

Ranks	3
Requires	35 Points in Affliction

Malediction increase the Damage Bonus effects for Curse of Shadows and Curse of the Elements by 1% (per rank).

Unstable Affliction (New Talent)

Ranks	1
Requires	5 Points in Contagion, 40 Points in Affliction

Could it be another DOT? It is!!! Unstable Affliction adds another damage-over-time ability to the already frightening lineup of an Affliction Warlock. This new spell has a 1.5-second casting time, but it has no Cooldown and is Mana efficient.

The target is nailed with a fairly mean Shadow DOT that takes 18 seconds to tick down. The most amusing and enjoyable part of all is that nobody can safely Dispel Unstable Affliction; if they dare, the Dispeller takes *even* more damage than the DOT would have done to the victim in the first place. Beyond that, the Dispelled is affected by Silence for 5 seconds.

Rank One	660 Shadow Damage/270 Mana (990 Damage if Dispelled)
Rank Two	930 Shadow Damage/315 Mana (1395 Damage if Dispelled)
Rank Three	1050 Shadow Damage/400 Mana (1575 Damage if Dispelled)

DEMONOLOGY

Improved Health Funnel (Revised Talent)

Ranks	2
Requires	5 Points in Demonology

This Talent continues to add 10% (per rank) to the amount of Health transferred by Health Funnel; it now also reduces the Health Cost of the ability by 10% (per rank).

Improved Voidwalker (Revised Talent)

Ranks	3
Requires	5 Points in Demonology

This Talent has received a slight buff, having a new progression of 10% (per rank), rather than the old 8%/16%/25%.

Improved Succubus (Revised Talent)

Ranks	3
Requires	10 Points in Demonology

Much like Improved Voidwalker, this Talent now advances with a 10% (per rank) progression.

Fel Stamina (Revised Talent)

Ranks	3
Requires	10 Points in Demonology

Fel Stamina is better than ever. With only 3 ranks instead of 5, this Talent now accomplishes a great deal more. The Stamina improvement for your pets is 5% (per rank), and your Warlock gets +1% Health (per rank). It's a very nice buff all around.

Demonic Aegis (New Talent)

Ranks	3
Requires	10 Points in Demonology

Your Warlock's Demon Armor and Fel Armor spells get a 10% (per rank) increase in their effectiveness.

Master Summoner (Revised Talent)

Ranks	2
Requires	1 Point in Fel Domination, 15 Points in Demonology

The reduction in casting time for your Warlock's pets is still 2 seconds (per rank). The new addition is that there is also a Mana reduction of 20% (per rank) as a Master Summoner.

Unholy Power (Revised Talent)

Ranks	5
Requires	15 Points in Demonology

Melee attack damage for your Warlock's Voidwalker, Succubus, Felhunter, and Felguard is improved by 4% now (per rank) instead of 3%. Another buff that has been added is that your Warlock also gets a boost, with +1% to Shadow and Fire damage (per rank).

Improved Enslave Demon (Revised Talent)

Ranks	2
Requires	20 Points in Demonology

It only takes 2 Talent points currently to get the same effect that 5 Talent points got your previously. Because there are a number of potent Demons to Enslave in Outland, this Talent is looking very tempting.

Maser Conjuror (Revised Talent)

Ranks	2
Requires	20 Points in Demonology

This Talent replaces the older Improved Firestone. It adds the existing 15% to Bonus Fire Damage (per rank) to a 15% Spell Critical Rating (per rank) for Spellstones.

Mana Feed (New Talent)

Ranks	3
Requires	25 Points in Demonology

When your Warlock gains Mana from Drain Mana or Life Tap spells, your pet gains 33% of that value (per rank). Who could say no to something that wonderful?

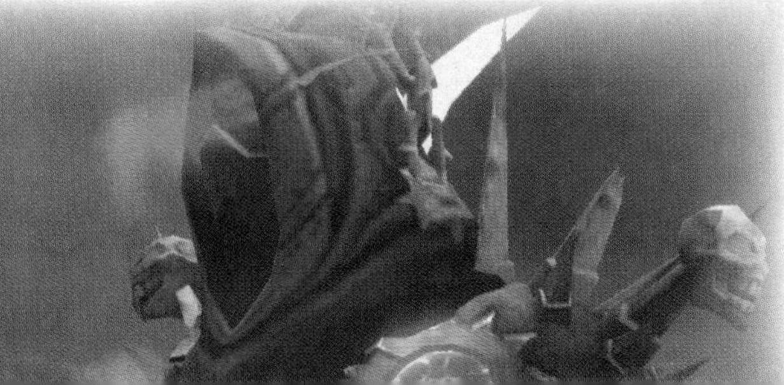

Master Demonologist (Revised Talent)

Ranks	5
Requires	5 Points in Unholy Power, 25 Points in Demonology

This Talent gives both your Warlock and the currently-summoned pet a slight buff.

Demonologist Buffs

Pet	Effect on Warlock and Pet
Imp	Reduces Threat Caused by 4% (per rank)
Voidwalker	Reduces Physical Damage Taken by 2% (per rank)
Succubus	Increases All Damage Caused by 2% (per rank)
Felhunter	Increases All Resistances by .2/Level (per rank)
Felguard	Increases All Damage Caused by 1% (per rank) and Raises All Resistances by .1/Level (per rank)

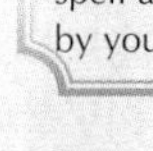

Demonic Resilience (Revised Talent)

Ranks	3
Requires	30 Points in Demonology

This reduces the chance that your Warlock will be Critically Hit by melee or spell attacks by 1% (per rank); Demonic Resilience also reduces damage taken by your pets by 5% (per rank).

Soul Link (Revised Talent)

Ranks	1
Requires	1 Point in Demonic Sacrifice, 30 Points in Demonology

This Talent no longer splits the damage evenly between your Warlock and their pet. Instead, 30% of the damage taken by your Warlock is transferred to your pet. Another change is that the active pet and your Warlock deal 3% more damage as long as the Demon is active.

Demonic Knowledge (New Talent)

Ranks	3
Requires	30 Points in Demonology

Demonic Knowledge adds to your Warlock's spell damage by 5% (per rank) of your current pet's Stamina plus Intellect.

Demonic Tactics (New Talent)

Ranks	5
Requires	35 Points in Demonology

Damage caused by your Warlock and their pet is increased by 1% (per rank).

Summon Felguard (New Talent)

Ranks	1
Requires	40 Points in Demonology

Without waste, muss, or fuss, your Demonology Warlock can call a Felguard. This takes 10 seconds and a Soul Shard (well, and a fair bit of Mana), but otherwise lacks the drawbacks of other summonings for this type of Demon.

Bane (Revised Talent)

Ranks	5
Requires	5 Points in Destruction

This Talent also effects Soul Fire now, with a .4-second reduction in casting time (per rank).

Shadowburn (Revised Talent)

Ranks	1
Requires	10 Points in Destruction

Shadowburn's damage has been slightly toned down in the earlier ranks. Instead of requiring that the target die directly to Shadowburn, your Warlock now gets the invested Soul Shard back if the target dies within 5 seconds (a very useful improvement).

Intensity (Revised Talent)

Ranks	2
Requires	15 Points in Destruction

The Resistance to Interruption given by this Talent now expands to cover any Destruction spell.

Destructive Reach (Revised Talent)

Ranks	2
Requires	15 Points in Destruction

This Talent still covers the increased range for Destruction spells, and it now adds a 5% reduction in accrued Threat (per rank) for these spells as well.

Improved Searing Pain (Revised Talent)

Ranks	3
Requires	15 Points in Destruction

It now only takes 3 Talent points to master Improved Searing Pain. The final bonus is still a 10% improvement to the Critical Chance of Searing Pain.

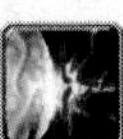

Nether Protection (New Talent)

Ranks	3
Requires	25 Points in Destruction

After being affected by a Fire or Shadow spell, your Warlock has a 10% chance (per rank) to become Immune to Shadow and Fire spells for 4 seconds.

Backlash (New Talent)

Ranks	3
Requires	30 Points in Destruction

Backlash increases your Warlock's Critical Spell Chance by 1% (per rank); it also provides an 8% chance (per rank) to grant a buff when your character is hit with a physical attack. This buff allows your next Shadow Bolt or Incinerate to be cast instantly. The buff only lasts for 8 seconds, and it can only occur up to once every 8 seconds.

Conflagrate (Revised Talent)

Ranks	1
Requires	5 Points in Improved Immolate, 30 Points in Destruction

Conflagrate has moved from a 1.5-second casting time into being an Instant spell; it also does more damage than it used to and has a lower cost as well.

Soul Leech (New Talent)

Ranks	3
Requires	30 Points in Destruction

Your Warlock's Shadow Bolt, Shadowburn, Soul Fire, Incinerate, Searing Pain, and Conflagrate gain a 10% chance (per rank) to return Health equal to 20% of the damage caused.

Shadow and Flame (New Talent)

Ranks	5
Requires	35 Points in Destruction

Shadow Bolt and Incinerate spells cast by your Warlock gain an additional 4% of your Bonus Spell Damage effects (per rank).

Shadowfury (New Talent)

Ranks	1
Requires	5 Points in Shadow and Flame, 40 Points in Destruction

This Talent teaches your Warlock a new spell; Shadowfury is an area-of-effect Shadow attack that has a .5-second casting time. Though on a 20 second Cooldown, Shadowfury is a great spell for delivering close-range damage while Stunning its victims for 2 seconds.

Though Shadowfury gets your Warlock a great deal of Threat, it is meant to be used during phases where that is a moot point anyway. Often, Warlocks are going to use this as a prelude to area-of-effect assaults anyway, giving themselves a faint moment of free time before the rush of attackers close in.

Rank One	343-407 Shadow Damage/440 Mana
Rank Two	459-547 Shadow Damage/545 Mana
Rank Three	612-728 Shadow Damage/710 Mana

WARRIOR ABILITIES

Heroic Strike (Rank 10)

Ability Line	Arms
Requirements	Level 66, Melee Weapon
Cost	15 Rage
Casting Time/Cooldown	Next Swing/Global Cooldown
Range	Melee

A strong attack that increases melee damage by 182 and causes a high amount of Threat. Causes additional damage against dazed targets.

Heroic Strike (Rank 11)

Ability Line	Arms
Requirements	Level 70, Melee Weapon
Cost	15 Rage
Casting Time/Cooldown	Next Swing/Global Cooldown
Range	Melee

A strong attack that increases melee damage by 247 and causes a high amount of Threat. Causes additional damage against dazed targets.

Victory Rush

Ability Line	Fury
Requirements	Level 62, Battle or Berserk Stance
Cost	10 Rage
Casting Time/Cooldown	Instant/5 Second Cooldown
Range	Self

Relish your victory after killing an enemy that yields experience or honor, increasing your chance to critically strike by 5% for 30 sec.

Commanding Shout

Ability Line	Fury
Requirements	Level 68
Cost	10 Rage
Casting Time/Cooldown	Instant/Global Cooldown
Range	20 Yards

Increases total health of all party members within 20 yards by 730. Lasts 2 min.

Stance Mastery

Ability Line	Protection
Requirements	Level 20
Cost	Passive
Casting Time/Cooldown	N/A
Range	Self

Stance Mastery allows your Warrior to retain up to 10 points of Rage while switching Stances. In conjunction with Tactical Mastery (now a Protection Talent), this enables Warriors to retain the full 25 Rage that they have become accustomed to. In essence, this is a compromise the frees two Talent points for Warriors who still have to have their full flexibility when switching Stances, and allows other Warriors to entirely spec their characters without taking Tactical Mastery.

Spell Reflection

Ability Line	Protection
Requirements	Level 64, Battle or Defensive Stance, Shield
Cost	25 Rage
Casting Time/Cooldown	Instant/10 Second Cooldown
Range	Self

Raises your shield, reflecting the next spell cast on you. Lasts 5 sec.

Intervene

Ability Line	Protection
Requirements	Level 70
Cost	10 Rage
Casting Time/Cooldown	Instant/30 Second Cooldown
Range	8-25 Yards

Run at high speed towards a party member, intercepting the next melee or ranged attack made against them.

Shield Bash (Rank 4)

Ability Line	Protection
Requirements	Level 64, Battle or Defensive Stance, Shield
Cost	10 Rage
Casting Time/Cooldown	Instant/12 Second Cooldown
Range	5 Yards

Bashes the target with your shield for 67 damage. It also dazes the target and interrupts spellcasting, preventing any spell in that school from being cast for 6 sec.

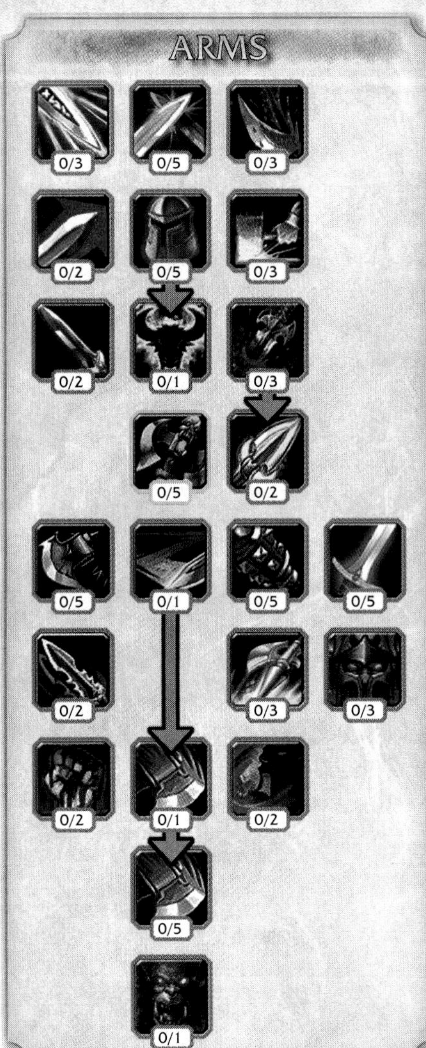

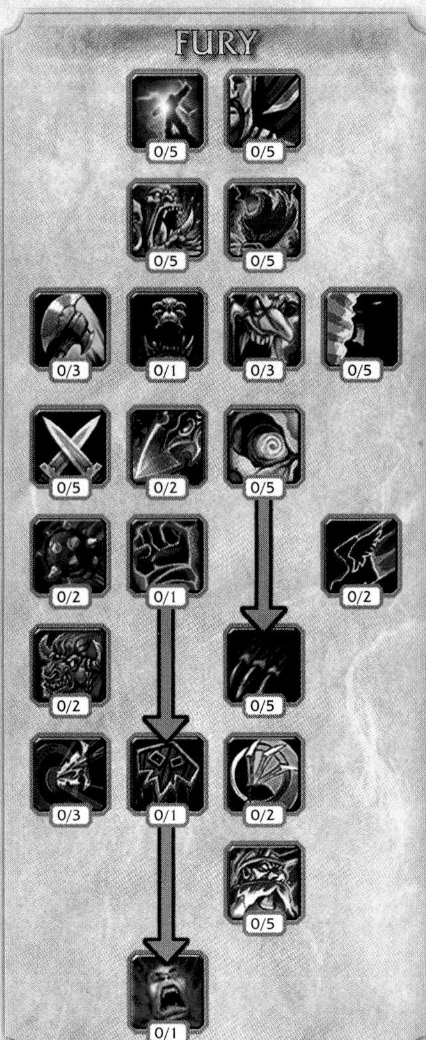

WARRIOR TALENTS

ARMS

Improved Rend (Revised Talent)

Ranks	3
Requires	Nothing

Has improved from a 15% bonus to Rend damage to a 25% improvement (per rank).

Iron Will (Revised Talent)

Ranks	5
Requires	5 Points in Arms

Iron Will has been moved from the Protection line into the Arms line of Talents. This was a trade for Tactical Mastery. The effect of Iron Will is still the same (increasing your chance to Resist Stun and Charm effects by 3% per rank).

Anger Management (Revised Talent)

Ranks	1
Requires	10 Points in Arms

Instead of reducing Rage decay, this Talent now functions in a better way by adding 1 point of Rage every three seconds. Outside of battle, this still works to mitigate the loss of Rage. Inside battle, this now helps to improve on Rage accrual.

Mace Specialization (Revised Talent)

Ranks	5
Requires	20 Points in Arms

This Talent now adds 6 points of Rage when its 3-second Stun procs. As before, additional ranks add to the chance that this proc will trigger.

Poleaxe Specialization (Revised Talent)

Ranks	5
Requires	20 Points in Arms

Axe and Polearm Specialization have now been combined into a single Talent. The effect of this is still a 1% increase in your Warrior's chance to score a Critical Hit while wielding one of these weapon types.

Improved Thunder Clap (Revised Talent)

Ranks	3
Requires	5 Points in Arms

This Talent has been greatly improved. The old version lowered the Rage cost of Thunder Clap by a 1/2/4 progression. While that is still true, this Talent also adds to Thunder Clap's damage in a 40%/70%/100% progression, and improves the Slowing effect of the ability by 4%/7%/10%. Suddenly, this Talent is almost up to the must-have level of quality for anyone interested in mitigating damage, whether in PvP or PvE.

Weapon Mastery (New Talent)

Ranks	2
Requires	25 Points in Arms

Increases skill with all weapons by 2 (per rank) and increases your chance to Resist Disarm effects by an additional 50% (per rank).

Improved Disciplines (New Talent)

Ranks	3
Requires	25 Points in Arms

Reduces the cooldown of your Warrior's Retaliation, Recklessness, and Shield Wall abilities by a progression of 4/7/10 minutes, and increases their duration by 2 seconds (per rank).

Blood Frenzy (New Talent)

Ranks	2
Requires	30 Points in Arms

Rend and Deep Wounds now increase all melee damage caused to the target by 2% (per rank). The larger the group of characters with your Warrior, the more effective this becomes.

Second Wind (New Talent)

Ranks	2
Requires	30 Points in Arms

Whenever your Warrior is struck by a Stun or Immobilize effect, 10 Rage and 5% of the character's total Health (per rank on both accounts) are gained over the next 10 seconds.

Improved Mortal Strike (New Talent)

Ranks	5
Requires	1 Point in Mortal Strike, 35 Points in Arms

Reduces the cooldown of Mortal Strike by .2 seconds (per rank) and increases the damage it causes by 1% (per rank).

Endless Rage (New Talent)

Ranks	1
Requires	40 Points in Arms

Adds 25% to the Rage your Warrior generates from damage dealt to enemies.

FURY

Improved Slam (Revised Talent)

Ranks	2
Requires	20 Points in Fury

Compared with the listing in the second Master Guide, this Talent now has two ranks, instead of five, and decreases the casting time of Slam by .5 seconds (per rank).

Death Wish (Revised Talent)

Ranks	1
Requires	20 Points in Fury

The negative aspect of Death Wish has changed a great deal. Currently, this ability increases all damage taken by your Warrior by 5%; this is greatly improved from the 20% decrease to Armor Rating and Resistances that was caused by the old version. The positive effects of the ability remain unchanged.

Precision (New Talent)

Ranks	3
Requires	30 Points in Fury

Warriors now get this Talent! Precision adds 1% to your base chance to Hit with melee weapons. This is a very valuable Talent for evening your Rage accrual and general effectiveness.

Bloodthirst (Revised Talent)

Ranks	1
Requires	1 Point in Death Wish, 30 Points in Fury

Bloodthirst has received a small buff since the printing of the second Master Guide. It now delivers a blow at 45% of your Warrior's Attack Power (rather than a 40% value).

Improved Whirlwind (New Talent)

Ranks	2
Requires	30 Points in Fury

Reduces the cooldown of Whirlwind by 1 second (per rank).

Improved Berserk Stance (New Talent)

Ranks	5
Requires	35 Points in Fury

Increases your Warrior's Attack Power while in Berserk Stance by 2% (per rank).

Rampage (New Talent)

Ranks	1
Requires	1 Point in Bloodthirst, 40 Points in Fury

For 30 Rage, this Instant ability adds an effect to your Warrior that increases Attack Power by 30. With each successful melee attack, this Attack Power increase improves, until the effect has stacked 5 times (for a 150 Attack Power increase). Rampage can only be triggered after delivering a Critical Hit.

Rank One	+30 Attack Power (+150 AP Total)
Rank Two	+40 Attack Power (+200 AP Total)
Rank Three	+50 Attack Power (+250 AP Total)

PROTECTION

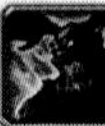

Improved Bloodrage (Revised Talent)

Ranks	2
Requires	Nothing

Instead of reducing the Health cost of Bloodrage, this Talent now increases the Rage generated by this ability by 3 (per rank).

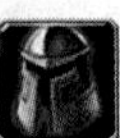

Tactical Mastery (Revised Talent)

Ranks	3
Requires	Nothing

Tactical Mastery has been moved into the Protection tree. In addition, 10 points of Rage can be kept when switching Stances by simply training your Warrior's abilities. Only 15 points are now dependant on this Talent. This frees Warriors to pursue builds without the ubiquitous Tactical Mastery investment for instant Intercepts and so forth. /cheer

Anticipation (Revised Talent)

Ranks	5
Requires	Nothing

Currently, Anticipation adds 4 Defense (per rank).

Improved Shield Block (Revised Talent)

Ranks	1
Requires	5 Points in Shield Specialization, 10 Points in Protection

Allows Shield Block to Block one additional attack and improves the duration of this ability by 1 second.

Improved Revenge (Revised Talent)

Ranks	3
Requires	10 Points in Protection

The Stun caused by this Talent used to have a progression of 20%/30%/40% for its chance to succeed. This new progression for Improved Revenge is 15%/30%/45%.

Defiance (Revised Talent)

Ranks	3
Requires	10 Points in Protection

Increases the Threat generated by your Warrior's attacks while in Defensive Stance by 5% (per rank) instead of the old 3%!

Shield Mastery (New Talent)

Ranks	3
Requires	25 Points in Protection

Increases the amount of damage absorbed by your Warrior's shields by 10% (per rank).

Improved Defensive Stance (New Talent)

Ranks	3
Requires	30 Points in Protection

Reduces all spell damage taken while in Defensive Stance by 2% (per rank).

Focused Rage (New Talent)

Ranks	3
Requires	30 Points in Protection

Reduces the Rage cost of all offensive abilities by 1 point (per rank).

Devastate (New Talent)

Ranks	1
Requires	40 Points in Protection

This Instant ability costs 15 Rage and can only be used with a One-Handed Melee Weapon. It causes an attack that deals 50% of your weapon damage, plus 15 damage, and adds additional Threat for each application of Sunder Armor that is on the target. Also, this attack renews the duration of Sunder Armor.

This effectively replaces Sunder Armor after the initial five applications! Certainly, this is worthwhile in longer fights to keep some extra damage moving on the target when you would normally be restoring Sunders periodically anwway.

Rank One	+15 Damage
Rank Two	+25 Damage
Rank Three	+35 Damage

Vitality (New Talent)

Ranks	5
Requires	35 Points in Protection

Increases your Warrior's total Stamina by 1% (per rank) and Strength by 2% (per rank).

TWO SURPRISING ALLIES

As the ceasefire between the Horde and Alliance continues to erode, both sides have begun enlisting aid for the coming war. Though goals may differ, no one wants to be the single empire against a united front. The Horde and Alliance alike are eager to find new forces that will grant them an edge they need to be victorious.

Blood Elves

A TALE TARNISHED WITH BLOOD

Countless centuries ago, ships landed on the shores of Lordaeron. The exiled High Elves, led by Dath'Remar Sunstrider tried to make a new home for themselves. Made mortal by the loss of contact with the Well of Eternity, many of the High Elves fell to starvation or illness in their trek across Tirisfal Glades. Insanity claimed many more before the cause was found. An evil influence within Tirisfal Glades itself was eroding what little was left of the High Elves.

Leaving Tirisfal Glades, the High Elves met the Trolls of Zul'Aman. The meeting went poorly and the Trolls vowed to exterminate the High Elves from lands the Trolls saw as theirs. The war continued while the refugee Elves looked for a land to call home. They came to forests so similar to their lost home in Kalimdor that there was no question where they would settle.

The kingdom of Quel'Thalas was founded when the last of the Amani Trolls were pushed out of the region. Using their greatest arcane arts and a vial of water stolen from the Well of Eternity, the High Elves crafted the Sunwell. This bastion of magic energy infused all High Elves with strength and vigor. So powerful was the Sunwell that spring would forever reign in Eversong Forest. The defenses would bring the High Elves four thousand years of peace.

It was during a terrible war with the Amani Trolls that the forces of Quel'Thalas sought aid from the human nation of Arathor. Though the Trolls vastly outnumbered the Elves, the combined forces of Quel'Thalas and Arathor, whom the Elves taught magic, ground the Amani empire into dust. In the wake of this wonderful victory, the alliance between Quel'Thalas and Arathor was celebrated by the founding of Dalaran. This nation of wizards would be home to both Elves and Humans looking to learn the arcane ways.

The Second War brought strife to Quel'Thalas once again. With the help of the Horde, the Amani Trolls torched the borderlands of the Elven nation and slaughtered any and all High Elves they could find. In response to this absurd destruction of life, the Elves committed their entire nation to the war effort.

The Horde was defeated by the combined forces of the Alliance. With the threat over and the Human nations bickering amongst themselves, the Elves withdrew from the Alliance to continue their isolationistic existence. The years drew on and the once warm friendships grew cold.

Perhaps it was the cooling of alliances that brought the downfall of Quel'Thalas. During the Third War, the undead armies overran the Elven nation and closed on the precious Sunwell. Betrayal created the opening and the Sunwell was shattered. The royal family was killed save for Prince Kael'thas Sunstrider, who was studying in Dalaran at the time.

The Elves survived the nightmarish attack of the Scourge, but the survivors found that life wasn't any easier than death. The High Elves quickly grew ill and lethargic. The power of the Sunwell had suffused their race for so long, that living without it brought symptoms of withdrawal.

The Prince was filled with a thirst for vengeance upon his return. Quel'Thalas was almost entirely obliterated and those of his people who weren't dead soon would be if an answer to the addiction wasn't found. To honor those who died to the Scourge, Kael'thas named his people the "Blood Elves." Taking his strongest warriors, he joined the campaign against the Scourge while Halduron Brightwing was left to defend the homeland.

Prejudice and suspicion led to the Blood Elves being given the most difficult missions possible. Though powerful and angry, the Blood Elves eventually accepted the assistance of the Naga, under Lady Vashj. Grand Marshal Garithos, who had been watching Kael'thas closely for some time, considered the alliance with the Naga high treason. His army descended on the smaller force of Blood Elves and imprisoned them in Dalaran.

The timing of Lady Vashj and her Naga were all that kept the Prince and his elves from execution. The freed Blood Elves fled with the Naga through the portal to Outland.

Kael'thas found the one thing that had eluded him in Azeroth. The hunger of the Elves could be brought to an end by a powerful demon named Illidan Stormrage. Most of the Elves stayed in Outland, but Rommath was sent back with a message of hope.

Since that time, the Blood Elves have worked to live with their addiction through strict mental discipline. They have begun rebuilding Silvermoon for the day when Kael'thas will return.

LIVING A NEW LIFE

Though their power diminished by the absence of the Sunwell, the Blood Elves have found ways to continue living. The constant hunger for magic has become a way to weed out the ranks of the Elves. The weak become the "Wretched" while the strongest work to rebuild that nation. Meeting a Blood Elf on the field of battle is to meet one of the most disciplined of an entire race.

Rogue

The Blood Elves have learned the art and power of subtlety and shadows. Though the only class of Blood Elves that doesn't use magic actively, they are not to be underestimated. The dedication and discipline of a Blood Elven rogue is nearly mystical in itself.

Mage, Warlock, Hunter

The Elves have used magic for longer than some races have used fire. It isn't a wonder that they excel in the arcane arts. Their contact with the Burning Legion has shown them the power of demons and their inherent love of nature has given the magically inclined more avenues of learning than the traditional wizard.

Paladin, Priest

Through trickery and magical enslavement, the Blood Elves have harnessed the power of the Light. Even the most holy magics of the Naaru are wielded by Elves determined to bring the resurrection of their kingdom. While taken unwillingly, the powers wielded by these Elves is no less potent than the most devout follower of the Light.

THE LEGACY OF THE SUNWELL

The destruction of the Sunwell changed the Blood Elves in as strong a way as the creation of the Sunwell changed the High Elves. Through generations of living with magic flowing in and about them, the Elves have become quite adept at its use. The lack of the Sunwell's energies has only driven them to become stronger.

Mana Tap

Classes	All
Target	Enemies with mana
Range	30 yards
Casting Time	Instant
Cooldown	30 seconds
Effect	Drains 50 mana+(1 per level) from your target and charges you with Arcane energy for 10 minutes. This effect stacks up to 3 times.

Through their mastery of magic energies, Blood Elves can pull mana from any opponent possessing it. This can be quite useful when facing powerful casting enemies. While the cooldown keeps a single Blood Elf from being able to completely drain a target, nothing stops that same Blood Elf from bringing friends.

As your Arcane Torrent's power is based on the number of Mana Tap charges you have accumulated, use Mana Tap at every opportunity. Once you have stacked all three Mana Tap charges, use it occasionally to renew the duration on the stack. This makes sure you have the most potent Arcane Torrent when you need it.

Arcane Torrent

A Blood Elf with mana coursing around him or her is quite dangerous. They have not only mastered pulling it from targets, they can also release it in quite a devastating way.

Classes	Rogue
Target	None
Range	Self
Casting Time	Instant
Cooldown	2 minutes
Effect	Silences all enemies within 8 yards for 2 seconds. In addition, you gain 10 energy for each Mana Tap currently affecting you.

Blood Elf Rogues can release an Arcane Torrent that silences all enemies within 8 yards and restores energy. This ability is best used after an enemy has started casting, but before they finish. That way they have wasted all the time they spent casting their spell, and now they are silenced for two seconds. Another excellent time to use it is right after a finishing move as it restores your energy and allows you to start the next combo set a few seconds earlier.

Classes	Mage, Paladin, Hunter, Priest, Warlock
Target	None
Range	Self
Casting Time	Instant
Cooldown	2 minutes
Effect	Silences all enemies within 8 yards for 2 seconds. In addition, you gain 10+(2 per level)+(2 per 10 levels) mana for each Mana Tap currently affecting you.

Mana-using Blood Elves use Arcane Torrent to silence enemies and restore their own mana. Use Arcane Torrent when an enemy is attempting to cast a spell near you. This interrupts their spell as well as silencing them for two seconds. If you aren't near enemies, release your Arcane Torrent to restore your mana should it ever drop to low levels while you are still in danger.

Arcane Affinity

Classes	All
Target	None
Range	None
Casting Time	Passive
Cooldown	None
Effect	Enchanting skill increased by 10.

Being enchanted by the Sunwell themselves, the Blood Elves have a unique affinity for Enchanting. They can intuitively sense the magical ties within an item and manipulate them.

The greatest power of this ability is allowing Blood Elves to learn recipes at a lower level than their counterparts. While your skill can only progress as quickly as you can collect the materials for it, the auction house can make this limitation moot.

Magic Resistance

Classes	All
Target	None
Range	None
Casting Time	Passive
Cooldown	None
Effect	All magical resists increased by 5.

Being infused with magic every minute of every day for years has given the Blood Elves a resistance to magic. While it isn't as strong as some of the other races resistances, Blood Elves are slightly resistant to *every* type of magic.

The benefit of increased magic resistance is the lower damage from magic-based attacks. Magic resistance increases your chance to resist partial damage from magical attacks as well as your chance to fully resist the effects. Being resistant to all schools of magic, these effects include both damage and crowd control abilities.

Draenei

THE CHASE

Thousands of years ago, on a world called Argus, the Eredar lived. Masters of their world, they used intelligence and magical affinity to craft a society brighter than the stars themselves. Very little seemed beyond the reach of these people and Argus shone like a beacon across the cosmos.

No beacon goes unseen. Sargeras, the Destroyer of Worlds, saw the accomplishments of the Eredar. They would fit nicely into his plans. Bent on destroying all life, Sargeras saw in the Eredar the power to lead his army of demons.

Contact was made between Sargeras and three of the Eredar's leaders. He offered what all demons offer: power and knowledge in exchange for loyalty. Sargeras didn't want just their loyalty though. He wanted the entire Eredar race. Kil'Jaeden and Archimonde were tempted by the offer while Velen was hesitant. They were given time to think it over.

Velen had cultivated the gift of foresight. He called upon the gift and was bestowed with a vision of the future. He saw the truth of Sargeras' words. The Eredar who accepted his offer would gain almost limitless power and knowledge. The price, Velen saw, would be terrible. The Eredar would be transformed into creatures of evil.

The vision continued and Velen saw the Burning Legion and the purpose for which it was created. He watched as the Legion destroyed civilization after civilization. He awoke from the vision terribly disturbed. Though he warned the others of his vision, Kil'Jaeden and Archimonde ignored Velen. The power that Sargeras offered was too great a temptation.

When next Sargeras contacted the three, Kil'Jaedan and Archimonde swore their allegiance. Velen fled as the others were transformed into creatures of unspeakable evil. To stand against such power would have been suicide.

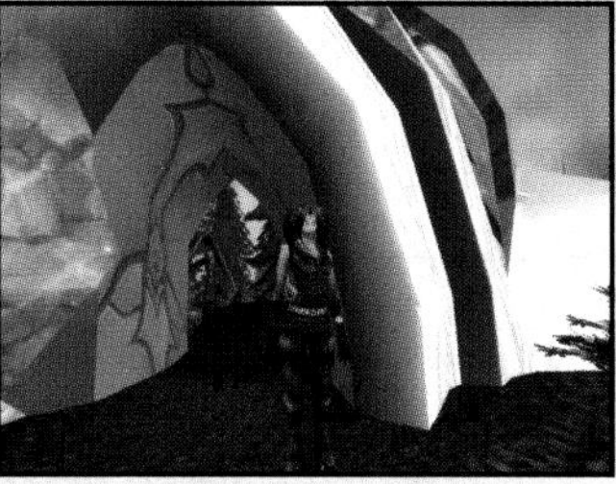

Once again, Velen attempted to call upon his foresight. His despair disturbed his concentration, but it was enough to call a strange creature before him. It explained that his prayer had been heard. Velen listened closely as the creature called itself a Naaru. The Naaru were a race of energy beings that had pledged themselves to stopping the Burning Crusade.

In time, the Naaru explained, Velen and others like him could become a force of great good. For now, they must flee. The Naaru offered to help Velen, and any Eredar who thought as him, flee Argus.

Velen made haste to gather the Eredar who had refused to join Sargeras. With the help of the Naaru, the refugees narrowly escaped the Burning Legion. Velen and the others chose to call them selves the Draenei; meaning "exiled ones."

Kil'jaeden's forces were minutes from the launch pads when the Draenei lifted off. Velen's betrayal would not go unpunished, he vowed. Kil'jaeden gathered his forces and promised to chase Velen until the latter paid for his treachery.

Thousands of years and dozens of worlds would pass as Kil'jaeden hunted the Draenei. Each time the Draenei found a new home, the Burning Legion would be upon them. The Draenei mapped much of the cosmos in the flight, but the hatred of Kil'jaeden knew no bounds.

The Naaru began to teach the Draenei, blessing them with powers and knowledge of the Light. The Naaru spoke of others in the universe that would stand against the Burning Legion. One day, the Naaru would join the forces together and create an army capable of stopping the Legion forever. This hope became a central tenant of life for the Draenei and they vowed to train for the day when they would help vanquish the great evil.

The Draenei landed on the world of Draenor. Over the many attempts at rebuilding, they had become quite good at hiding themselves from Kil'jaeden's forces mystically. They weren't alone on this world. The Orcs of the southern grasslands were peaceful enough and preferred to keep to themselves.

The good neighbors engaged in limited trade, but the peace didn't last long. Kil'jaeden had found the Draenei once again. Rather than rushing in, he took his time and observed first. In the Orcs he saw the instrument of his vengeance.

Through Ner'zhul and Gul'dan, Kil'jaeden corrupted the Orcs into bloodthirsty killers armed with terrible magics that would do more than kill the Draenei; they would warp them into lesser forms of themselves. Almost annihilated by the Orcs or by the magics they wielded, the Draenei were sent fleeing once again.

The battle was so close that the enemy was able to board the Draenei ship, the Exodar, before it could lift off. The fight continued onboard while the ship fled Draenor. The battle took its toll and the Draenei were forced to make an emergency landing on the closest habitable world. Sabotaged systems failed and the Exodar plummeted to the surface of Azeroth, killing even more of the surviving Draenei.

KNOWING YOURSELF

The Draenei have spent many lifetimes perfecting themselves. Their once brilliant civilization was a place of learning and what the Draenei didn't discover themselves, they learned from others. Perhaps it was this ability to absorb knowledge that Sargeras saw in them.

Warrior, Mage

Whether devoted to war or magic, the keen focus of the Draenei makes them quite adept. The endless days aboard the Exodar and the battles on Draenor have only served to hone these arts that have existed since Argus.

Shaman, Hunter

Though their time on Draenor wasn't long, the Draenei learned much from the Orcs. Their beliefs in the elements and nature, at first, seemed rather barbaric to the Draenei. Slowly, some of the Draenei accepted the beliefs and learned to wield the same powers as the Orcs.

Paladin, Priest

The Naaru may have saved the Draenei, but there was a price. The Draenei chose to become warriors of the Light and promised to fight against the Burning Legion. Their strength wasn't enough. That had been seen. The Naaru taught them to call upon the powers of the Light.

THE POWER OF THE NAARU

The Draenei have learned a great deal from the Naaru, but the changes don't start there. Being in the presence of sentient beings of pure energy and intentions, coupled with the constant fight to survive against the Burning Legion, has put a great deal of stress on the Draenei. Through conviction and a power deep inside the people, the Draenei have changed to meet these challenges.

Gift of the Naaru

Classes	All
Target	Self or friendly
Range	40 yards
Casting Time	1.5 seconds
Cooldown	3 minutes
Effect	Heals 35+(15 per level) health over 15 seconds.

The Naaru have taught the Draenei a great deal. With the blessing and tutelage of these great allies, every Draenei has learned rudimentary healing magic.

This ability is quite powerful for every character in every situation. Melee classes (tanks in particular) should use this ability before entering combat against a tough opponent. The healing provided isn't enough to make a healer unneeded in more difficult fights, but it allows you to build some aggro or deal some damage before your healer needs to worry.

Casters can use the ability on themselves (when soloing generally) in similar situations to melee classes, but its power is truly realized in group settings. At the cost of *zero* mana and very little time, you can throw a heal over time on the group tank or another party member in trouble. This keeps the healer from being over-taxed.

As Gift of the Naaru can stack with itself, you need not worry about 'wasting' it by casting it on a target that is already under the effects of another gift.

Inspiring Presence

Classes	Shaman, Priest, Mage
Target	Party Members
Range	30 yards
Casting Time	Passive
Cooldown	None
Effect	Increases chance to hit with spells by 1% for you and all party members within 30 yards.

Standing beside a Draenei in combat is quite motivating. These people have not only survived against the Burning Legion for hundreds of years, but they have explored much of the cosmos and still chosen to continue the fight against this menace.

All party members in range get the increase in hit chance for spells. While only one Inspiring Presence can be active at once (multiple Draenei cannot stack the same presence), both Heroic Presence and Inspiring Presence can be active at the same time.

While the ability is passive and affects the entire group, little strategy is involved in smaller group configurations. In raid situations, consider placing Draenei Shaman, Mages, or Priests in groups with your attacking casters to gain the most benefit from this ability.

Heroic Presence

Classes	Warrior, Paladin, Hunter
Target	Party Members
Range	30 yards
Casting Time	Passive
Cooldown	None
Effect	Increases chance to hit by 1% for you and all party members within 30 yards.

The noble Draenei neither back down nor run away from a fight. The driving courage of these people makes fighting with them an almost spiritual experience. Having explored much of the cosmos and still considering other races equals says a great deal of their character.

All party members in range get the increase in hit chance. While only one Heroic Presence can be active at once (multiple Draenei cannot stack the same presence), both Heroic Presence and Inspiring Presence can be active at the same time.

The only strategy in smaller groups involves Hunters or healing Paladins. These Draenei should make sure that the melee group members at the front lines are within range to receive the bonus. Raid groups should have a Draenei Warrior, Paladin, or Hunter in every group that will be dealing physical damage to make full use of the amazing ability.

Gemcutting

Classes	All
Target	None
Range	None
Casting Time	Passive
Cooldown	None
Effect	Jewelcrafting skill increased by 5.

The Draenei have used crystals and gems as power sources, jewelry, information storage, and healing for centuries. Every Draenei has a Jewelcrafter in their family and as such have picked up an affinity for working with pretty rocks.

The greatest power of this ability is allowing Draenei to learn recipes at a lower level than their counterparts. While your skill can only progress as quickly as you can collect the materials for it, the auction house can make this limitation moot.

Shadow Resistance

Classes	All
Target	None
Range	None
Casting Time	Passive
Cooldown	None
Effect	Shadow Resistance increased by 10.

The Draenei have so dedicated themselves to the Light and the teachings of the Naaru that every member of their civilization has become a beacon of hope that dispels darkness from around them. This infusing of the Light grants them a slight resistance to Shadow magic.

The benefit of increased Shadow Resistance is the lower damage from Shadow-based attacks. Shadow Resistance increases your chance to resist partial damage from Shadow attacks as well as your chance to fully resist the effects. Being resistant to Shadow magic is quite useful as damage and fear effects are often Shadow-based.

TRAINING THE NEWCOMERS

This chapter takes players, both new and old, through the creation of advancement of the new races. Rather than doing what we did with the master guides, and give you a modest walkthrough of the starting zones, we've gone much farther. This time, the walkthroughs cover the full path from creation to around level 20. Quel'Thalas and Ghostlands are covered first, then we'll start over and give you a tour of Azuremyst and Bloodmyst Isles with the Draenei.

Before starting, take a look at some of the methods used to call out information in this chapter. Throughout the writeups, **bold** text will signal the name of a quest. *Italic* text lets you know that something is used by a quest.

Then, the map legend divides each zone into larger areas (denoted by capital letters) and specific points of interest (shown with numbers). Read the map legends to find out where various monsters and NPCs are located. For fast perusal, notice that a • indicates a hostile creature. A • identifies a neutral creature that won't attack you automatically.

Blood Elves

The two new zones added for the starting Blood Elves are Eversong Woods and Ghostlands. Inside Eversong Woods is the partially razed capital city of the Blood Elves, known as Silvermoon City. These lands are stuffed with quests and content, far more than the starting areas we've already covered in earlier guides. It is very comfortable to level from 1 to 20 on quests alone, without needing to stop for grinding or to use quests from other zones.

EVERSONG WOODS MAP LEGEND

Eversong Woods Legend

	Location / Name	Info
A	**Sunstrider Isle**	
•	Feral Tender	3
	Mana Wyrm	1
	Springpaw Cub	1
	Springpaw Lynx	2-3
	Tender	2-3
B	**The Sunspire**	
	Jesthenis Sunstriker	Paladin Trainer
	Julia Sunstriker	Mage Trainer
	Matron Arena	Priest Trainer
	Pathstalker Kariel	Rogue Trainer
	Ranger Sallina	Hunter Trainer
	Shara Sunwing	General Supplies
	Summoner Teli'Larien	Warlock Trainer
	Sunstriker Guardian	65
	Well Watcher Solanian	Quest Giver
	Yasmine Teli'Larien	Demon Trainer
C	**Armory**	
	Arcanist Ithanas	Quest Giver
	Faraden Thelryn	Armorsmith
	Raelis Dawnstar	Weaponsmith
D	**The Pond**	
•	Feral Tender	3
	Solanian's Scrying Orb	Quest Item
	Tender	2-3
E	**The Fountain**	
•	Feral Tender	3
	Scroll of Scourge Magic	Quest Item
	Tender	2-3
F	**Burning Crystal**	
	Mana Wyrm	1
	Solanian's Journal	Quest Item
G	**Shrine of Dath'Remar**	
	Plaque	Quest Item
H	**Falthrien Academy**	
•	Arcane Wraith	3-4
•	Felendren the Banished	5 Quest Target
•	Tainted Arcane Wraith	4
I	**Ruins of Silvermoon**	
•	Arcane Patroller	5-6
	Unstable Mana Crystals (In Crates)	Quest Target
•	Wretched Urchin	4-5
J	**Falconwing Square**	
	Aeldon Sunbrand	Quest Giver
	Aleinia	Jewelcrafter
	Anathos	Stable Master
	Celoenus	Warlock Trainer
	Daestra	Demon Trainer
	Duelist Larenis	Weapon Master
	Farsil	Armor and Shield Merchant
	Garridel	Mage Trainer
	Geron	Weapon Merchant
	Hannovia	Hunter Trainer
	Innkeeper Delaniel	Innkeeper/Quest Target
	Kanaria	First Aid Trainer
	Kyrenna	Cheese Vendor
	Landraelanis	Tradesman
	Magister Jaronis	Quest Giver
	Mailbox	
	Noellene	Paladin Trainer
	Novice Ranger	
	Ponaris	Priest Trainer
	Quarelestra	Cooking Trainer
	Sergeant Kan'ren	
	Sheri	General Goods Vendor
	Silvermoon Guardian	24
	Sleyin	Weapon Vendor
	Tannaria	Rogue Trainer
	Telenus	Pet Trainer
	Vara	Cloth and Leather Merchant
	Wanted Poster	Quest Giver
K	**North Sanctum**	
	Apprentice Veya	
	Ley-Keeper Caidanis	Quest Giver
	Prospector Anvilward	Quest Target
L	**West Sanctum**	
	Crazed Dragonhawk	7-8
•	Darnassian Intruder	7 Drops Quest Item
•	Darnassian Scout	7
	Ley-Keeper Velania	Quest Giver
•	Mana Stalker	5
•	Mana Wraith	6-7
•	Springpaw Stalker	5-6
M	**The Dead Scar**	
•	Angershade	7-8
•	Darkwraith	9-10
•	Plagueborn Pillager	5-6
•	Rotlimb Cannibal	6-7
•	Rotlimb Marauder	8-9
N	**Stillwhisper Pond**	
	Instructor Antheol	Quest Giver
	Silvermoon Apprentice	8
O	**Skinner's Camp**	
	Kinamisa	Leatherworking Supplies
	Mathreyn	Skinning Trainer
	Sathein	Leatherworking Trainer
P	**Fairbreeze Village**	
	Anvil	
	Ardeyn Riverwind	Quest Giver
	Cooking Fires	
	Dragonhawk Hatchlings	2
	Eversong Ranger	12
	Forge	
	Halis Dawnstrider	General Goods
	Magistrix Landra Dawnstrider	Quest Giver
	Mailbox	
	Marniel Amberlight	Innkeeper, Quest Giver
	Ranger Degolien	Quest Giver
	Ranger Sareyn	Quest Giver
	Sathiel	Trade Goods Vendor
	Silvermoon Guardian	24-25
	Velan Brightoak	Quest Giver
Q	**Sunsail Anchorage**	
•	Aldaron the Reckless	8 Quest Target
	Captain Kelisendra	Quest Giver
	Eversong Ranger	12
	Sailor Melinan	Drink Vendor
	Sin'dorei Armament Boxes	Quest Target
	Velendris Whitemorn	Quest Giver
•	Wretched Hooligan	6-7
•	Wretched Thug	7-8
R	**Golden Strand**	
	Barrels of Captain Kelisendra's Cargo	Quest Target
•	Grimscale Murloc	7-8
•	Grimscale Oracle	7-8
•	Mmmmrrrggglll	9
S	**East Sanctum**	
•	Angershade	7-8
	Apprentice Mirveda	Quest Giver
•	Rotlimb Marauder	8-9
	Tainted Soil	Quest Target
T	**The Scorched Grove**	
	Crazed Dragonhawk	7-8
•	Old Whitebark	10 Quest Target
	Runestone	Quest Target
•	Withered Green Keeper	9-10
U	**Farstrider Retreat**	
	Arathel Sunforge	Journeyman Blacksmith, Quest Giver
	Areyn	General Goods Vendor
	Lieutenant Dawnrunner	Quest Giver
	Magister Duskwither	Quest Target
	Paelarin	Bowyer
	Silvermoon Guardian	25
	Zalene Firstlight	Food and Drink Vendor
V	**Tor'Watha**	
•	Amani Axethrower	9-10
•	Amani Berserker	10
•	Amani Shadowpriest	8-10
•	Spearcrafter Otembe	10 Quest Target
	Ven'jashi	Quest Giver
W	**Zeb'Watha**	
•	Amani Axethrower	9-10
•	Amani Berserker	10
•	Amani Shadowpriest	8-10
•	Chieftain Zul'Marosh	11 Quest Target
X	**Duskwither Grounds And Spire**	
	Apprentice Loralthalis	Quest Giver
•	Ether Fiend	9-10
•	Mana Serpent	9-10
	Power Sources	Quest Target
Y	**The Fallen Courier**	
	Apothecary Thedra	Quest Giver
	Courier Dawnstrider	Quest Giver
1	**Outrunner Alarion**	**Quest Giver**
2	**Master Kelerun Bloodmourn**	**Blood Knight**
3	**Slain Outrunner**	**Quest Target**
4	**Thaelis the Hungerer**	**6 Quest Target**
5	**Silanna**	
6	**Apprentice Meledor**	**Quest Giver**
7	**Apprentice Ralen**	**Quest Target**
8	**Ranger Jaela**	**Quest Giver**
9	**Skymistress Gloaming**	**Flight Merchant**
10	**Entrance to Silver Moon City**	
11	**Perascamin**	**Mount Trainer**
12	**Winaestra**	**Mount Merchant**
13	**Saltheril's Haven**	
14	**Larianna Riverwind**	**Quest Giver**
15	**Runewarden Deryan**	**Quest Giver**
16	**Eastern Runestone**	**Quest Target**
17	**Groundskeeper Wyllithen**	**Quest Giver**

EVERSONG WOODS

Eversong Woods is the home of the Blood Elven capital, Silvermoon City. Though still in the process of reclaiming this land, the Blood Elves possess relative safety here due to their recent efforts. Flights from Silvermoon have resumed, and the new union with the Horde makes it possible for the Blood Elves to spread out across Azeroth without the odds being stacked as heavily against them. That said, the Dead Scar is one of the greatest reminders that the doom and peril of the Scourge stands ready to push into Quel'Thalas during even the faintest moment of weakness.

SUNSTRIDER ISLE

Sunstrider Isle is a quiet place on the northwestern end of Eversong Woods. Characters begin here, with a series of quests that help to clear the isle of a few problems. As you first start to get your bearings, look for Magistrix Erona, who should be standing somewhat nearby. Erona has a golden exclamation point, meaning that the Magistrix has a quest for you! Speak to Erona and accept the quest, **Reclaiming Sunstrider Isle**.

Reclaiming Sunstrider Isle	
Faction	Horde
Location	Sunstrider Isle
Quest Giver	Magistrix Erona
Quest Completion	Magistrix Erona
Reward	Green Chain Boots (Mail Feet, 46 Armor), Wyrm Sash (Cloth Waist 6 Armor), Chain to Unfortunate Measures

Erona wants you to kill eight of the *Mana Wyrms* near the Burning Crystals of the area. These enemies practically infest the place, so finding them is a trifle. Luckily, these enemies are quite weak and won't last for more than a minute or two. Even without many abilities, your character should have a very easy time fighting through the Wyrms. Return to Erona when you are finished.

With the first quest done, Erona asks you to begin a new task, **Unfortunate Measures.**

Unfortunate Measures	
Faction	Horde
Location	Sunstrider Isle
Quest Giver	Magistrix Erona
Quest Completion	Magistrix Erona
Reward	Green Chain Vest (Mail Chest 67 Armor), Lynxskin Gloves (Leather Hands, 21 Armor), or Sunrise Bracers (Cloth Wrist, 4 Armor), Chain to Report to Lanthan Perilon

Look for the Springpaw Lynxes and Cubs in the area. These enemies are spread out, but they are also very common. Attack them and collect the *Lynx Collars* that drop with high frequency. When you have eight of the Collars, return to Erona and complete the quest.

No matter which your class, has chosen, there is a small quest to seek your trainer in the nearby building. This is a good time to do that because you are able to train for new abilities upon reaching level two. Read the text of the quest to find out where your trainer is located.

Instead of this tiny quest ending blandly with your trainers, it actually chains into a real quest, with more interesting consequences. Regardless of the trainer you use, the person will give you **Well Watcher Solanian** to accept. Go to the top of Sunspire, the central building, and look for Solanian out on the ledge above the main area. Solanian gives you the task of finding **Solanian's Belongings**. You are also asked to check on **The Shrine of Dath'Remar.** Also, talk to Erona again for the next step in that chain, **Report to Lanthan Perilon**.

Find Lanthan by following the road roughly southwest. Look for Lanthan by a large tree, and talk to him to get the quest, **Aggression**.

With these quests ready to go, you might notice that there are two other Blood Elves in the area who have taken interest in your activities. There are more golden exclamation points out there, and this is as good a time as any to collect them all. Search the areas nearby for Arcanist Helion and Arcanist Ithanas. The two of them have the quests, **Thirst Unending** and **A Fistful of Slivers**.

You should now have a group of five quests that can be done in a single run: **Solanian's Belongings, The Shrine of Dath'Remar, Aggression, Thirst Unending,** and **A Fistful of Slivers.** Set out and get some leveling done!

Solanian's Belongings	
Faction	Horde
Location	Sunstrider Isle
Quest Giver	Well Watcher Solanian
Quest Completion	Well Watcher Solanian
Reward	Sunspire Cord (Leather Waist, 19 Armor), Well Watcher Gloves (Cloth Hands, 6 Armor)

The Shrine of Dath'Remar	
Faction	Horde
Location	Sunstrider Isle
Quest Giver	Well Watcher Solanian
Quest Completion	Well Watcher Solanian
Reward	Experience

Aggression	
Faction	Horde
Location	Sunstrider Isle
Quest Giver	Lanthan Perilon
Quest Completion	Lanthan Perilon
Reward	Sunstrider Axe (MH Axe, 2.0 DPS), Sunstrider Dagger (1h Dagger, 2.1 DPS), Sunstrider Mace (MH Mace, 2.0 DPS), Sunstrider Staff (Staff, 2.6 DPS), Sunstrider Sword (MH Sword, 2.0 DPS)

Thirst Unending	
Faction	Horde
Location	Sunstrider Isle
Quest Giver	Arcanist Helion
Quest Completion	Arcanist Helion
Reward	Green Chain Gauntlets (Mail Hands, 42 Armor), Vigorous Bracers (Leather Wrists, 15 Armor), and Striding Pants (Cloth Legs, 9 Armor)

A Fistful of Slivers	
Faction	Horde
Location	Sunstrider Isle
Quest Giver	Arcanist Ithanas
Quest Completion	Arcanist Ithanas
Reward	Daylight Cloak (Back, 5 Armor)

There are three items that Well Watcher Solanian wants you to retrieve: *Solanian's Scrying Orb, Scroll of Scourge Magic,* and *Solanian's Journal.* These are found at three separate sites in the isle, so there isn't a good reason to race to retrieve all of them at once. Instead, you want to pick these up while getting some of the other quests in your log finished.

The *Orb* is at the pond (southwest from Sunspire). Kill the Tenders while you are there to satisfy the requirements for **Aggression.** After finishing your work at the pond, walk north toward the fountain. You will find the *Scroll* there. Then, get the *Journal* by one of the Burning Crystals in the area. When you see creatures with mana while doing your fighting, be certain to Mana Tap them!

For **Aggression**, kill 7 *Tenders* and 7 *Feral Tenders.* This is a weapon quest for young characters, so that you won't have to wield the starting equipment for very long. Tarry by the pond to finish off enough of these enemies.

Mana Tap six creatures to satisfy the goal of **Thirst Unending**. Because there is a 30-second cooldown on Mana Tap, you would have to spend a few minutes doing this if you tried to do it by itself. Instead, Mana Tap enemies as you go through the area.

Learning About Mana Tap and Arcane Torrent

Notice how your character can build up to three charges of Mana Tap in preparation for a stronger Arcane Torrent. Being able to give yourself a boost of Mana or Energy is a big deal for any fight that might go the wrong way. In addition, Arcane Torrent gives Blood Elves the ability to Silence nearby enemies. Because there is a two-minute cooldown on Arcane Torrent, you might as well build up a few charges for each use and get the most out of it! Besides, Mana Tap is free, so you don't have to invest Energy or Mana to steal from enemies in the first place.

Speaking of good targets to Mana Tap, there are Mana Wyrms at many of the sites you are passing. These drop the *Arcane Slivers* that you need for **A Fistful of Slivers**. Kill the Mana Wyrms after Mana Tapping them, and use the creatures as targets of opportunity while exploring.

One point of interest is that you get a +5 Stamina/Spirit buff when you complete this quest for Arcanist Ithanas. That will be useful during the final push against the denizens of the Academy (not far in your future).

When all of the other quests are completed, walk to the northwestern part of the isle and look for the Shrine of Dath'Remar. Read the *Plaque* there to complete your quest.

Go back to Sunspire and hand in all five of your completed quests. This gets you a burst of experience, and takes you up to the point where you can train for your level 4 class abilities. Sell any unneeded items that were picked up along the way and collect the last quest from Lanthan Perilon. He wishes you to eliminate **Felendren the Banished**, at the Falthrien Academy.

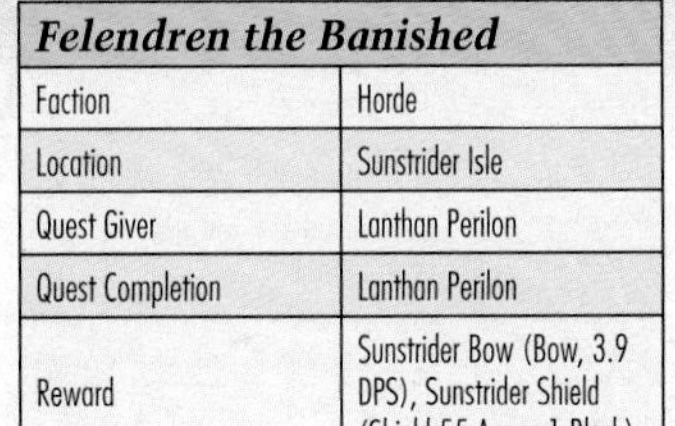

Felendren the Banished	
Faction	Horde
Location	Sunstrider Isle
Quest Giver	Lanthan Perilon
Quest Completion	Lanthan Perilon
Reward	Sunstrider Bow (Bow, 3.9 DPS), Sunstrider Shield (Shield 55 Armor 1 Block)

Walk to the southwest, the direct route to the Falthrien Academy. Do this while you still have the buffs from turning in A Fistful of Slivers. Your mission is to kill 8 *Arcane Wraiths* and 2 *Tainted Arcane Wraiths* and take *Felendren's Head* before returning.

Like a number of the places in the Blood Elven lands, this Academy is bursting with magic. Held aloft by the forces of the ether, the building is a beautiful sight. Climb carefully up the walkways and into the higher tiers, dealing with the various Wraiths that guard the way. Not many of them come at the same time, so long as you pull them back and away from the open areas.

Loot the corpses for a group drop in this area, the Tainted Arcane Sliver. Use this item to start the quest, **Tainted Arcane Sliver**. This item drops from the Tainted Arcane Wraiths, unsurprisingly.

Tainted Arcane Sliver	
Faction	Horde
Location	Sunstrider Isle
Quest Giver	Group Drop Item
Quest Completion	Arcanist Helion
Reward	Experience and Modest Money

It's a Great View, But Mind the Edge

Don't jump off of the higher tiers at the Falthrien Academy. Though there is water below, some of it is quite shallow; if you land in the wrong spot, your character is going to take full damage. And from that height, full damage is not going to make you look any prettier.

To be careful, hop down in stages when you are done with the quest.

Felendren is at the top of the Academy. Destroy this fool for his mockery of what the Academy should stand for. Go back to the Sunspire once you have his head. If you still need to kill a few of the Wraiths, stay for that, but enough of them are found on the way up that this is usually moot.

The Journey South

Aiding the Outrunners	
Faction	Horde
Location	Sunstrider Isle
Quest Giver	Lanthan Perilon
Quest Completion	Outrunner Alarion
Reward	Chain to Slain by the Wretched

This quest leads you away from your humble beginnings. Get it and take care of any parting business at the Sunspire before leaving. Talk to Outrunner Alarion on the road leaving south and away from Sunstrider Isle (toward the Ruins of Silvermoon). She offers you **Slain by the Wretched** in return.

Slain by the Wretched

Faction	Horde
Location	Dawning Lane
Quest Giver	Outrunner Alarion
Quest Completion	Slain Outrunner
Reward	Chain to Package Recovery

Look for the Slain Outrunner in Dawning Lane. Take the main route through the street into the city, and you will find the Slain Outrunner lying right there, not far in. After completing the quest, you start **Package Recovery**.

Package Recovery

Faction	Horde
Location	Dawning Lane
Quest Giver	Slain Outrunner
Quest Completion	Outrunner Alarion
Reward	Chain to Completing the Delivery

Take the package back to Outrunner Alarion. She'll give you a new quest, **Completing the Delivery**.

Completing the Delivery

Faction	Horde
Location	Dawning Lane
Quest Giver	Outrunner Alarion
Quest Completion	Innkeeper Delaniel
Reward	Refreshing Spring Water (5) or Shiny Red Apples (5)

The Inn is on the SE side of the ruins, in a section called Falconwing Square. Complete this quest by going over to Innkeeper Delaniel, bind there so that you can Hearthstone back to it in the future, and look around for the various trainers and vendors in the area. You can learn First Aid and Cooking, sell, repair your equipment, and so forth. There is a recipe for Lynx Steak at the Inn, for those aspiring toward culinary greatness.

Talk to Magister Jaronis to get the **Major Malfunction** quest after you are finished with any immediate errands. Look for Aeldon Sunbrand as well, who has the collection quest **Unstable Mana Crystals**. Finally, look near the eastern side of Falconwing Square for a Wanted Poster. This starts **Wanted: Thaelis the Hungerer**.

With this group of quests initiated, it's time to search through the ruins.

Major Malfunction

Faction	Horde
Location	Falconwing Square
Quest Giver	Magister Jaronis
Quest Completion	Magister Jaronis
Reward	Green Chain Belt (Mail Waist 38 Armor), Light Silk Robe (Cloth Chest 10 Armor), or Soft Leather Vest (Leather Chest 33 Armor), Chain to Delivery to the North Sanctum

Unstable Mana Crystals

Faction	Horde
Location	Falconwing Square
Quest Giver	Aeldon Sunbrand
Quest Completion	Aeldon Sunbrand
Reward	Experience

Wanted: Thaelis the Hungerer

Faction	Horde
Location	Falconwing Square
Quest Giver	Wanted Poster (East Side of Falconwing Square)
Quest Completion	Sergeant Kan'ren
Reward	Experience

Collect 6 *Arcane Cores* from the Arcane Patrollers that roam the city. These enemies are all over the city, but the best concentration of them is by the roads. You find them frequently there, sometimes with a couple close to each other. They have a very high drop rate, so it only takes six to get what you need.

While going after the Arcane Patrollers, collect six *Unstable Mana Crystals*. Look for crates that contain these. They are all over the place too, but the best area is near Thaelis' building, on the eastern side of the ruins. These crates have a faint glow to them, and that helps you to spot them even at range.

There is a large building that is still intact, and a number of monsters guard the place. Clear a spot for some safe fighting and get your health back to full before pulling Thaelis. He comes with one or two people, so pull carefully if you are nervous. Once you have his head, return to Falconwing Square and turn everything in.

Talk to Jaronis again. With his previous deed finished, he'll ask you to leave the ruins and check on the areas outside the walls. His **Delivery to the North Sanctum** sends you to a small area that is relatively quiet and close by. Also, grab **Darnassian Intrusions** from Aeldon Sunbrand. These are the only quests for the moment.

Spreading Out and Exploring the Wilderness

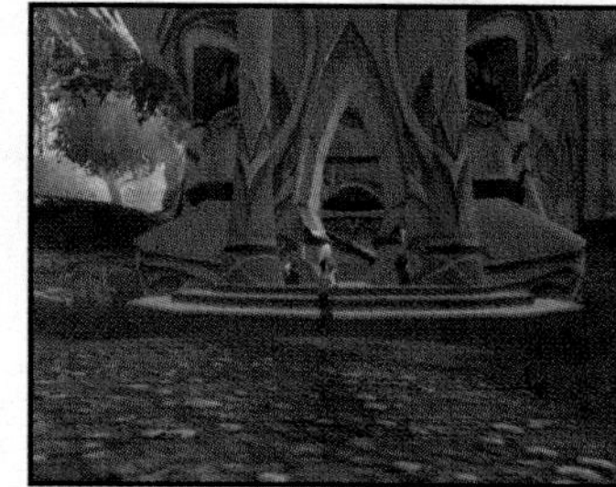

Delivery to the North Sanctum

Faction	Horde
Location	Falconwing Square
Quest Giver	Magister Jaronis
Quest Completion	Ley-Keeper Caidanis
Reward	Chain to Malfunction at the West Sanctum

Darnassian Intrusions

Faction	Horde
Location	Falconwing Square
Quest Giver	Aeldon Sunbrand
Quest Completion	Ley-Keeper Velania
Reward	Chain to Arcane Instability

Leave via the southern gate and head to the North Sanctum. All that you need to do there is switch **Delivery to the North Sanctum** over to **Malfunction at the West Sanctum** by talking to Ley-Keeper Caidanis. From there, continue on to the West Sanctum, off on its own island one a short distance away.

Malfunction at the West Sanctum

Faction	Horde
Location	North Sanctum
Quest Giver	Ley-Keeper Caidanis
Quest Completion	Ley-Keeper Velania
Reward	Experience

Now that you have two targets at the West Sanctum, look for Ley-Keeper Velania. She stands to the east of the Sanctum, run out of her area by the Mana Wraiths and Mana Stalkers that now infest the valley. Agree to help her out by killing 5 of each. As an added bonus the void creatures give power-boffs for magic users when they die

Arcane Instability	
Faction	Horde
Location	West Sanctum
Quest Giver	Ley-Keeper Velania
Quest Completion	Ley-Keeper Velania
Reward	Ley-Keeper's Blade (1H Sword, 2.4 DPS) or Velania's Walking Stick (Staff 3.2 DPS)

While doing this, keep an eye out for the Darnassians that are prowling around. The Darnassian Scouts should be dispatched whenever you see them; go after them as aggressively as possible. If you are lucky, the Darnassians will drop **Incriminating Documents** to begin a quest of the same name.

Mostly, the Darnassians stay up on the hills to avoid the Mana Wraiths. If you can't find the Incriminating Documents at first, search along the ridgeline that surrounds the West Sanctum until you find the right target.

Incriminating Documents	
Faction	Horde
Location	West Sanctum
Quest Giver	Incriminating Documents
Quest Completion	Aeldon Sunbrand
Reward	Chain to The Dwarven Spy

The Dwarven Spy	
Faction	Horde
Location	Falconwing Square
Quest Giver	Aeldon Sunbrand
Quest Completion	Aeldon Sunbrand
Reward	Bloodhawk Claymore (2H Sword, 3.6 DPS) or Long Knife (1H Sword, 2.9 DPS)

After activating these by right-clicking on them, you can take the papers back to Aeldon, at Falconwing Square. Wait until you have finished with your business at the West Sanctum though, since there won't be any need to come back this far for any return trips.

When you turn in the Incriminating Documents, Aeldon realizes their significance. To stop the flowing of dangerous information, he charges you with eliminating the insidious source, **The Dwarven Spy**.

Go back to the North Sanctum and talk to Prospector Anvilward. Convince him (using the text option that appears) to come inside and have a private chat with you. Far too late to save himself, the Dwarf recognizes that he is in grave danger. Lay into him with your best attacks, and watch this threat to Eversong go up in smoke (or fall to steel; your preference really). Return to Aeldon and tell him that the problem has been eliminated.

The Dead Scar and Some Naughty Apprentices

There are now a few assorted quests to gather, as your character moves down toward Fairbreeze Village. On the way are a few off-the-beaten-path chores that are pretty fun. Get **Fairbreeze Village** from Aeldon, at Falconwing Square. That is an introduction quest that is meant to get you where you are supposed to be.

Training From Time to Time

Players that have leveled characters before will be familiar with training. Even if you aren't as seasoned you should remember the class trainers are located in Falconwing Square and in the eastern part of Silvermoon City.

Looking on the map, Fairbreeze Village is not too long a trip to the south. Start walking down the road out of Silvermoon City but stop at the main bridge. Apprentice Meledor starts a chain there that should not be missed (the payoff at the end is wonderful, not in gold or experience, but in sheer amusement).

Fairbreeze Village	
Faction	Horde
Location	Falconwing Square
Quest Giver	Aeldon Sunbrand
Quest Completion	Ranger Degolien
Reward	More Quests

Soaked Pages	
Faction	Horde
Location	Eversong Woods
Quest Giver	Apprentice Meledor
Quest Completion	Apprentice Meledor
Reward	Chains to Taking the Fall

To retrieve *Antheol's Elemental Grimoire,* dive into the cool water behind the Apprentice and swim underneath the bridge. Still visible in the dirt at the bottom is the journal you are looking for. Right-click on it and swim back to the top. Talk to Meledor again, and he'll give you **Taking the Fall** this time.

Taking the Fall	
Faction	Horde
Location	Eversong Woods
Quest Giver	Apprentice Meledor
Quest Completion	Instructor Antheol
Reward	Chain to Swift Discipline

Take Antheol's Elemental Grimoire to Instructor Antheol at Stillwhisper Pond. This is to the southeast of Silvermoon. Getting there means you have to cross the Dead Scar, a place where you will soon return to fight. Once you reach Stillwhisper Pond, talk to Instructor Antheol and give him his Grimoire back. Nonplussed over the role his Apprentices played in the affair, Antheol hands you the role of **Swift Discipline**. This is where it all gets good!

Swift Discipline	
Faction	Horde
Location	Stillwhisper Pond
Quest Giver	Instructor Antheol
Quest Completion	Instructor Antheol
Reward	Magister's Pouch (4 Slot Bag)

Use *Antheol's Disciplinary Rod* on his two students. One of them you've already met, back at the bridge (Apprentice Meledor). The other is northeast up the road from Meledor (Apprentice Ralen). Using the Rod on the two of them causes an interesting effect to occur, as Ralen sadly laments.

When you return to Instructor Antheol, he'll reward you with a four-slot bag, called the Magister's Pouch. It's not much of a bag, but it might do if you don't have a few spare silver to fill out your allotment of six-slot bags.

Return to the Dead Scar and walk to the north, where the Dead Scar passes right through the center of Silvermoon City. The cursed event looks like it ripped right through everything, stopping for neither person nor building. It's no wonder that the Scourge litter the place now. By the city walls is a group of Rangers, led by Ranger Jaela (Jaela and her band are also needed for the priest-specific quest). Offer to help her clear **The Dead Scar**.

The Dead Scar	
Faction	Horde
Location	The Dead Scar
Quest Giver	Ranger Jaela
Quest Completion	Ranger Jaela
Reward	Black Leather Vest (Leather Chest 37), Gatewatcher's Chain Gloves (Mail Hands 46 Armor), or Guard's Leggings (Cloth Legs 10 Armor)

Kill 8 Plagueborn Pillagers in the areas either north or south of the Ranger. Plagueborn Pillagers are the Skeletons of this part of the Dead Scar, and most are close by. If you stray too far to the south along the Scar, you will soon find tougher Undead that are not needed for the quest.

On to Fairbreeze Village

Now it's perfectly fine to move southwest and enter Fairbreeze Village. It's just past another fork in the road and is only somewhat west of the Dead Scar. Within are a full range of quests to start.

Don't forget to repair, restock any supplies that are lagging, and rebind at the Inn here.

Complete Aeldon's quest to contact **Fairbreeze Village** by talking to Ranger Degolien. Degolien, who is on the second floor of the Fairbreeze Inn, tells you about the **Situation at Sunsail Anchorage**, which is an area to the west, where Wretched Thugs and Hooligans are taking over. Before hurrying out to do that, talk to Velan Brightoak as well. Velan needs some **Pelt Collection** done, and asks for you to find six *Springpaw Pelts* from the local Lynxes (Springpaw Stalkers). Because these creatures are only seen here or there, it's wise to get this quest right up front and get it done as a matter of opportunity (instead of hunting the creatures on their own). Just attack the Springpaws as you see them, and the quest will pretty much finish itself.

Questing for Lord Saltheril

There is a somewhat involved chain that has you go to several places on the map and pick up a few items in the chain. If you are interested in this, talk to Magistrix Landra Dawnstrider while you are still in town. You learn that there is a place called **Saltheril's Haven**, just to the west of town. There, Lord Saltheril is busy partying away while the other Blood Elves fight the good fight.

Go there and talk to Lord Saltheril next. **The Party Never Ends** is the Lord's claim, but for that to stay true a few items are needed. You must collect Suntouched Special Reserve, Springpaw Appetizers, and a Bundle of Fireworks. Doing all of this will get you an award of experience and the ability to talk to the party goers (some of them are trainers). You can also loot and interact with some of the very items that you brought to the party.

Saltheril's Haven	
Faction	Horde
Location	Fairbreeze Village
Quest Giver	Magistrix Landra Dawnstrider
Quest Completion	Lord Saltheril
Reward	Access to Party Items/ Interaction With Party Goers

The Party Never Ends	
Faction	Horde
Location	Saltheril's Haven
Quest Giver	Lord Saltheril
Quest Completion	Lord Saltheril
Reward	Saltheril's Haven Party Invitation

This quest should be done while adventuring. So, while doing other quests throughout Eversong Woods, keep an eye out for the following vendors.

For the *Suntouched Special Reserve*, trade with Vinemaster Suntouched in the Silvermoon City Inn, near the Royal Exchange. This is inside the actual capital of Silvermoon City, so look on that map instead of the Eversong Woods one. This item costs 3 silver, without any discounts for reputation.

Springpaw Appetizers only cost 1 silver and are purchased from Zalene Firstlight at the Farstrider Retreat. This is on the eastern side of the map and is the location for some of the anti-Troll questing later in the region.

A *Bundle of Fireworks* can be had for 1 silver and 50 copper. These are found directly at Fairbreeze Village, so you can pick them up at any time. Buy them from Halis Dawnstrider.

When you bring these back, you get a profit of a few silver, so don't worry about the out-of-pocket expenses. You can also use the Invitation that is given to you to pick up goodies from the tables; there are multiple spawns of these.

Situation at Sunsail Anchorage	
Faction	Horde
Location	Fairbreeze Village
Quest Giver	Ranger Degolien
Quest Completion	Ranger Degolien
Reward	Experience

Pelt Collection	
Faction	Horde
Location	Fairbreeze Village
Quest Giver	Velan Brightoak
Quest Completion	Velan Brightoak
Reward	Sprinpaw Hide Leggings (Leather Legs 36 Armor), Fur Lined Chain Shirt (Mail Chest 81 Armor), or Sprinpaw Hide Cloak (Back 7 Armor)

Now that you are on the lookout for easy *Pelts*, head west until you approach Sunsail Anchorage. Just before you reach the main area, where the Wretched Thugs and Hooligans patrol, you should spot Captain Kelisendra. The Captain's group has a few extra quests for you, while you are in the area. Start these now, in addition to fighting the *5 Wretched Thugs* and *5 Wretched Hooligans* for Ranger Degolien.

Lost Armaments	
Faction	Horde
Location	Sunsail Anchorage
Quest Giver	Velendris Whitemorn
Quest Completion	Velendris Whitemorn
Reward	Rusty Sin'dorei Sword (MH Sword 3.0 DPS), or Rusty Mace (1H Mace 2.6 DPS)

Captain Kelisendra gives you **Grimscale Pirates!** Velendris Whitemorn starts **Lost Armaments**. The Captain's quest takes you up north along the coast, to hit the Murloc camps. Velendris' quest chain has you attacking the Anchorage directly. For a few reasons, start with the Anchorage quests.

Move into the lower area of the Anchorage and fight against the Thugs and Hooligans. These foes are low level and spread out when you fight down on the docks. As you head up toward the building above the docks, their numbers begin to increase slightly, so more care is needed if you are alone or are poorly equipped.

While fighting against the enemies there, look for the boxes that are spread over the Anchorage. The highest concentration of them is in and around the main building, but the boxes stretch along the entire length of the docks. These contain the *Sin'dorei Armaments* that Velendris desires. Once you have killed the enemies you need and collected 8 Sin'dorei Armaments, return to Velendris to get the next step, **Wretched Ringleader**.

Dealing With Competition

It's wise to start with the Lost Armaments quest because there may not be enough of the boxes in the area to collect 8 Sin'dorei Armaments in a single run. When other people are in the area, you might need to wait a few minutes for a respawn of these boxes.

So, make your run, then divert farther west if competition causes you to cool your heels a little. Run the **Grimscale Pirates!** quest in the meanwhile, and there should be plenty of new boxes by the time you get back.

Wretched Ringleader	
Faction	Horde
Location	Sunsail Anchorage
Quest Giver	Velendris Whitemorn
Quest Completion	Velendris Whitemorn
Reward	Sunsail Bracers (Mail Wrist 39 Armor), Longshoreman's Bindings (Leather Wrist 20 Armor), or Silk Wristbands (Cloth Wrist 7 Armor)

Once you have this quest, walk in the main entrance of the building above the Anchorage and start to fight your way to the top. Avoid walking through the center of the rooms unless you want extra aggro from all of the enemies at once; though these are soft targets, the adds might not be healthy for you.

Aldaron is at the top of the tower, and it is possible to pull him by himself if you are careful. The leader has a two-handed sword for some decent DPS, and he casts fire spells on top of that not a lot of subtlety here to this guy. Mana Tap Aldaron early on, and Silence him with Arcane Torrent once he tries to use fire on you. In doing so, the fight should be a piece of cake. Snag *Aldaron's Head* and give it to Velendris at your convenience.

With the Anchorage in good shape, move north to fight the Murlocs (if you haven't done so already).

Grimscale Pirates!	
Faction	Horde
Location	Sunsail Anchorage
Quest Giver	Captain Kelisendra
Quest Completion	Captain Kelisendra
Reward	Experience

Look for six sets of *Captain Kelisendra's Cargo* by fighting the Murlocs in the Golden Strand, along the western coast. Not only do the little guys hold the *Cargo* directly, but there are barrels that have additional sets as well. This won't take terribly long, but be certain to fight enough that you get the Drop Quest Item, *Captain Kelisendra's Lost Rudders*. Also, look for the larger Murloc, Mmmmrrrggglll, as he is fun to fight.

Captain Kelisendra's Lost Rudders	
Faction	Horde
Location	Golden Strand
Quest Giver	Captain Kelisendra's Lost Rudders
Quest Completion	Captain Kelisendra
Reward	Experience

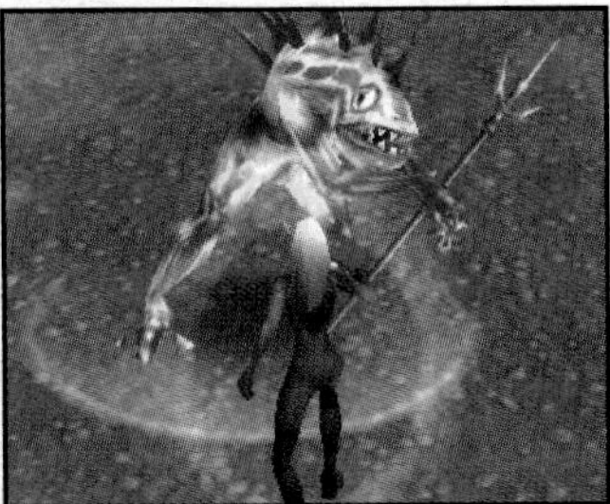

You get these as a random group drop off of the Murlocs. It usually doesn't take too many kills to discover, and it's easy experience when you return to item to Captain Kelisendra.

This completes the quests in and around the Anchorage. After turning in both quests to Kelisendra and finishing with Velendris, you should return to Fairbreeze Village and talk to Degolien again for your reward. If you've found all six *Sprinpaw Pelts* already, turn those in as well (though you'd have to be fairly lucky to have that done so soon).

Marniel Amberlight, the Innkeeper, sends you out to meet **Ranger Sareyn**. After greeting the Ranger, who is on the eastern road out of Fairbreeze, you receive **Defending Fairbreeze Village**. Also, ask Magistrix Landra Dawnstrider about **The Wayward Apprentice** before leaving town.

Ranger Sareyn	
Faction	Horde
Location	Fairbreeze Village
Quest Giver	Marniel Amberlight
Quest Completion	Ranger Sareyn
Reward	Chain to Defending Fairbreeze Village

Defending Fairbreeze Village	
Faction	Horde
Location	Fairbreeze Village
Quest Giver	Ranger Sareyn
Quest Completion	Ranger Sareyn
Reward	Experience

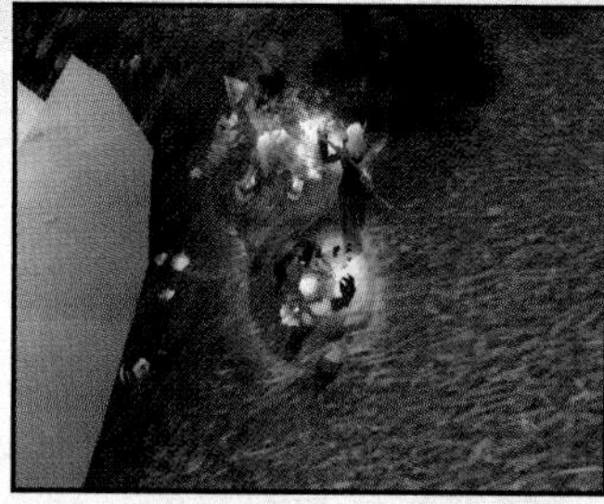

The Wayward Apprentice	
Faction	Horde
Location	Fairbreeze Village
Quest Giver	Magistrix Landra Dawnstrider
Quest Completion	Apprentice Mirveda
Reward	Chain to Corrupted Soil

The East Sanctum has the targets that you need for **Defending Fairbreeze Village**. So, follow your map and run over to East Sanctum. When you get there, look on the eastern side of the Dead Scar; behind the Sanctum itself is Apprentice Mirveda, who asks you to help her research the **Corrupted Soil**.

Corrupted Soil	
Faction	Horde
Location	East Sanctum
Quest Giver	Apprentice Mirveda
Quest Completion	Apprentice Mirveda
Reward	Chain to Unexpected Results

While grabbing the glowing green *Tainted Soil Samples* for Mirveda, you end up killing the *4 Rotlimb Marauders* and *4 Darkwraiths* that you wanted to fight anyway. If you end up short on *Darkwraiths*, the harder ones to find, then travel south later to pick up any stragglers.

Unexpected Results	
Faction	Horde
Location	East Sanctum
Quest Giver	Apprentice Mirveda
Quest Completion	Apprentice Mirveda
Reward	Chain to Research Notes

After turning in **Corrupted Soil**, wait for Mirveda to finish testing what you brought. Be certain to have full health when you talk to her again and receive **Unexpected Results**.

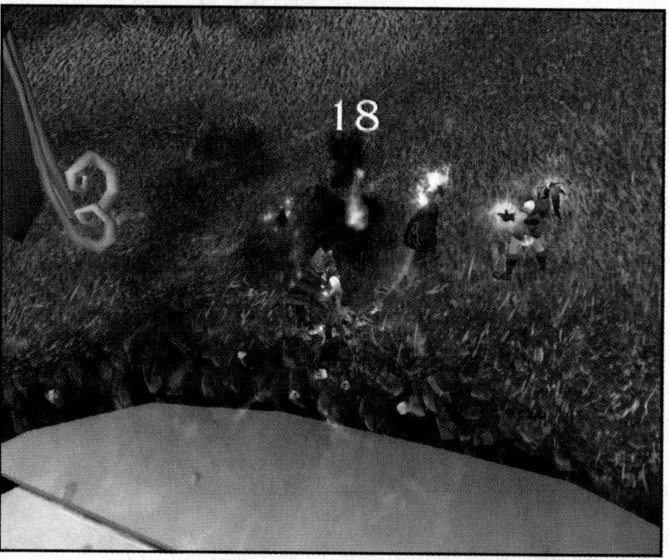

As soon as you start the quest, three enemies attack Apprentice Mirveda. Two of the enemies are Angerwraiths, and the third is Gharsul the Remorseless. If you didn't have Mirveda's help in the fight, things might be pretty dangerous indeed. Let her hold aggro for at least one of the enemies, as she is up to the challenge. Blast through the Angerwraiths, as they are very fast to drop. Then, focus on Gharsul, who is named but not Elite.

When the fight ends, Mirveda asks you to take her **Research Notes** back to Magistrix Landra Dawnstrider.

Research Notes	
Faction	Horde
Location	East Sanctum
Quest Giver	Apprentice Mirveda
Quest Completion	Magistrix Landra Dawnstrider
Reward	Experience

Take Mirveda's *Research Notes* back to Fairbreeze village and hand them over to Landra. This is already on your way, because there are some tasks at Fairbreeze that lead you to the southwest anyway, and those are perfectly fitting at this stage.

Once you are in Fairbreeze again, ask Ardeyn Riverwind about **The Scorched Grave**. You learn that Larianna Riverwind is near that area, at the bottom of Eversong Woods. With the problems there, it is likely that your assistance is needed as soon as possible.

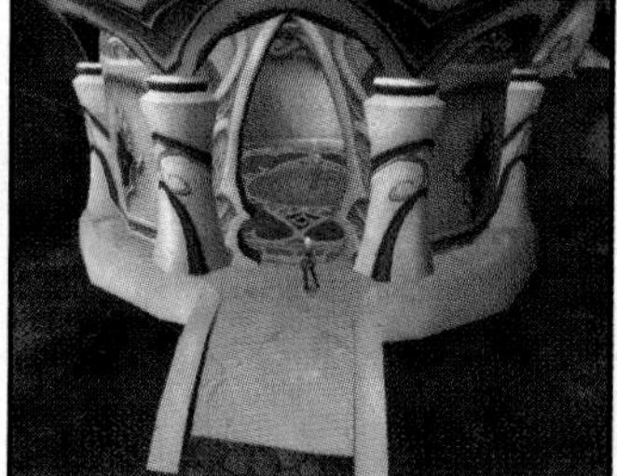

The Scorched Grave	
Faction	Horde
Location	Fairbreeze Village
Quest Giver	Ardeyn Riverwind
Quest Completion	Larianna Riverwind
Reward	Chain to A Somber Task

Travel to the south, to the map location marked with Larianna Riverwind. Talk with her and receive **A Somber Task**.

A Somber Task	
Faction	Horde
Location	The Scorched Grove
Quest Giver	Larianna Riverwind
Quest Completion	Larianna Riverwind
Reward	Experience

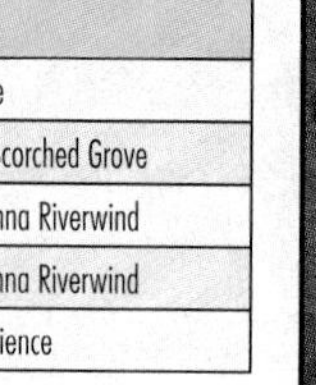

Kill 10 of the *Withered Green Keepers* that control The Scorched Grave. You can't swing a stick without hitting one; of course, that stick is probably one of their discarded limbs, so they might take it quite personally. Either way, look for a larger tree while doing this, a tougher elemental by the name of Old Whitebark. This one drops a quest item (*Old Whitebark's Pendant*). Right click on that to start a quest of the same name.

Old Whitebark's Pendant	
Faction	Horde
Location	The Scorched Grove
Quest Giver	Old Whitebark's Pendant
Quest Completion	Larianna Riverwind
Reward	Chain to Whitebark's Memory.

Return the item to Larianna Riverwind once you have destroyed all 10 of the required *Withered Green Keepers*. Hand in both quests, and receive **Whitebark's Memory**.

Whitebark's Memory	
Faction	Horde
Location	The Scorched Grove
Quest Giver	Larianna Riverwind
Quest Completion	Whitebark's Spirit
Reward	Experience

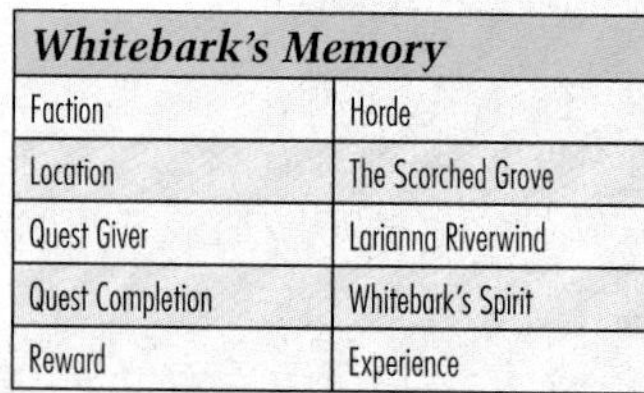

Bury Old Whitebark's Pendant at the blue Runestone that dominates the eastern part of the Scorched Grove. This summons Whitebark's Spirit, which will be aggressive at first. Start the fight at range to capitalize on the slow advancement that the Spirit makes. Not that you probably need to run and keep hitting it at range, but it is an option if you want to have fun. When the Spirit is almost defeated, it will turn Friendly and talk to you, completing the quest.

Instead of heading back, move farther to the east and look for the next Runestone on your map. This is the location of Runewarden Deryan, who is involved in **Powering Our Defenses**. He notes that two of the three Runestones in the area have been trashed by the recent wars. However, one of the Runestones might be activated again, he hopes. This final Runestone is to the east, and it won't take you long to reach it.

Powering Our Defenses	
Faction	Horde
Location	Eversong Woods
Quest Giver	Runewarden Deryan
Quest Completion	Runewarden Deryan
Reward	Experience

Attempt to *Energize the Runestone*, but keep your wits about you; Energized Wraiths attack in two waves. Though they have low health, you must face three of them at a time. After the first three drop, use any food or water that you have to restore yourself; otherwise, the next wave will hit before you are ready to deal with them. Once the task is complete, return to Runewarden Deryan.

Rolling Over to East Side

Stop back at Fairbreeze Village for any chores that need doing, and start Ranger Degolien's next quest, **Farstrider Retreat**. You are now high enough in level and equipment to be able to handle the monsters on the eastern side of the map. Travel northeast, across the river that feeds Stillwhisper Pond, and look for the large Farstrider building.

Farstrider Retreat	
Faction	Horde
Location	Fairbreeze Village
Quest Giver	Ranger Degolien
Quest Completion	Lieutenant Dawnrunner
Reward	Experience

Go inside the enclave and meet its residents. Lieutenant Dawnrunner is combatting the **Amani Encroachment**. Arathel Sunforge, the blacksmith of the Retreat, also wants you to combat the Trolls. We wants you to find and return **The Spearcrafter's Hammer**, which is in the hands of Spearcrafter Otembe.

Amani Encroachment	
Faction	Horde
Location	Farstrider Retreat
Quest Giver	Lieutenant Dawnrunner
Quest Completion	Lieutenant Dawnrunner
Reward	Experience

The Spearcrafter's Hammer	
Faction	Horde
Location	Farstrider Retreat
Quest Giver	Arathel Sunforge
Quest Completion	Arathel Sunforge
Reward	Farstrider Sword (2H Sword 5.8 DPS), Smooth Metal Staff (Staff 5.7 DPS), or Ranger's Pocketknife (1H Dagger 4.3 DPS)

Take the path up into the hills, to the region northwest of Tor'Watha on your map. These outlying areas are where you can find the *Amani Berserkers* and *Axe Throwers* that are needed for your quest. At the center of the first camp with actual buildings is *Spearcrafter Otembe*, another important target for you. Knock down all of these foes and speak with Ven'jashi, who is trapped in a cage not far from where Otembe lives. This conversation sparks the quest, **Zul'Marosh**.

Though Tor'Watha extends south for a great distance, you won't find any quest targets in the lower areas. All of the foes you need are up in the hills at the very beginning of the Tor'Watha area, as shown on the map.

Zul'Marosh	
Faction	Horde
Location	Tor'Watha
Quest Giver	Ven'jashi
Quest Completion	Ven'jashi
Reward	Ven'jashi's Bow (Bow 6.7 DPS), Hoodoo Wand (Wand 8.1 DPS)

Before returning to the Farstrider Retreat, come down from the hills and cross the Lake Elrendar. Zeb'Watha is on the other side, and that is where Chieftain Zul'Marosh lives. The largest building of the area is his hut, and you should see the big guy on the second floor of it even while standing outside the hut.

Fight your way in, clearing the lower floor. On top is a platform with three guards and the Chieftain. Keep an eye out for the patrolling guard who comes all the way up to the top. If you see that guy, nail him sooner rather than later.

Pull both of the peripheral guards ahead of time, to avoid complications. Then, attack the final guard and the Chieftain simultaneously. Go after the guard first, for the fast victory, then turn on Zul'Marosh. Mana Tap him and use Arcane Torrent for a boost.

Once he dies, you can return *Zul'Marosh's Head* to Ven'jashi, and take the *Amani Invasion Plans* that drop to Lieutenant Dawnrunner, back at the Farstrider Retreat. You have two other quests to turn in there anyway!

Amani Invasion	
Faction	Horde
Location	Zeb'Watha
Quest Giver	Amani Invasion Plans
Quest Completion	Lieutenant Dawnrunner
Reward	Chain to Warning Fairbreeze Village

Lieutenant Dawnrunner is concerned enough about the Amani's plans that it seems sensible to tell the good folks in Fairbreeze Village. The good news is that this can wait until you are down in that neck of the woods for other things. Instead, your next target is the Duskwither Spire. Purchase the *Springpaw Appetizers* from Zalene Firstlight if you are doing **The Party Never Ends**. After that, travel north and take the path out to the Duskwither Spire.

Warning Fairbreeze Village	
Faction	Horde
Location	Farstrider Retreat
Quest Giver	Lieutenant Dawnrunner
Quest Completion	Ranger Degolien
Reward	Blackened Chain Girdle (Mail Waist 61 Armor), Ranger's Vest (Leather Chest 55 Armor), or Satin Lined Boots (Cloth Feet 14 Armor)

The north road from Farstrider Retreat has an eastern branch. Take that and look for Apprentice Loralthalis, a sad student of the arcane who regrets the current state of the Spire. To cheer her up, you can take on the job of **Deactivating the Spire** and find out **Where's Wyllithen?**

Deactivating the Spire	
Faction	Horde
Location	Duskwither Spire
Quest Giver	Apprentice Loralthalis
Quest Completion	Apprentice Loralthalis
Reward	Chain To Word From The Spire

Where's Wyllithen	
Faction	Horde
Location	Duskwither Spire
Quest Giver	Apprentice Loralthalis
Quest Completion	Groundskeeper Wyllithen
Reward	Chain to Cleaning Up The Grounds

Stay on the northern path and follow it down in the gardens of the Spire. Ignore the Translocation Orb you pass on the way (for now), and look to see if you can spot old Willie. Surrounded by enemies, Groundskeeper Wyllithen is spitting mad with the chaos these things are causing. He wants 6 *Mana Serpents* and just as many *Ether Fiends* put down immediately. That is his way of **Cleaning the Grounds**.

Cleaning Up The Grounds	
Faction	Horde
Location	Duskwither Grounds
Quest Giver	Groundskeeper Wyllithen
Quest Completion	Groundskeeper Wyllithen
Reward	Experience

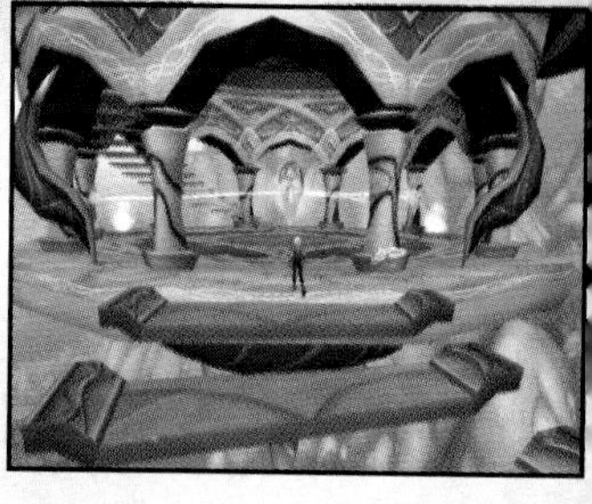

Fighting those targets as you go, return to the Translocation Orb and use it to enter the Spire. Take down all three power sources using the Jewel that Loralthalis gave you.

The inside of Duskwither Spire has modest fighting against the mystic creatures of the area, but they never come in too large a group. Thus, it is very safe to solo here. There are three floors to clear, and each has one of the *Power Sources* that you are trying to disable. On top, with the last *Power Source*, is another Translocation Orb that will spit you back outside.

Let Loralthalis know that all is well, and he'll have you send **Word From The Spire** to Magister Duskwither, back at the Farstrider Retreat. Hit that on the way for your just reward, and consider a stop at the capital as well. If you haven't already gotten the Flight Point from Skymistress Gloaming, do so now. Then head inside for class training, learning new weapon skills from the Weapon Master, and other such tasks. If you want to keep up with **The Party Never Ends**, look for the *Suntouched Special Reserve* at the Silvermoon City Inn.

Word From The Spire	
Faction	Horde
Location	Duskwither Grounds
Quest Giver	Apprentice Loralthalis
Quest Completion	Magister Duskwither
Reward	Fallen Apprentice's Robe (Cloth Chest 19 Armor, +1 Stam, +1 Int)

SILVERMOON CITY MAP LEGEND

Silvermoon City Legend

Location	Name	Role
A	**Front Gate**	
	Arcane Guardian	65
	Gatewatcher Aendor	
	Harassed Citizen	
	Silvermoon City Guardian	65
	Silvermoon Guardian	22
B	**Wayfarer's Rest**	**Shortcut Between Bazaar/Walk of Elders**
	Cooking Stove	
	Innkeeper Jovia	Innkeeper
	Mailbox	
	Quelis	Cooking Supplier
	Rarthein	
	Sylann	Cook
C	**Registrar of Guilds**	
	Kredis	Tabard Vendor
	Tandrine	Guild Master
D	**Skinner's Corner**	
	Lynalis	Expert Leatherworker
	Talmar	Journeyman Leatherworker
	Tyn	Skinner
	Zaralda	Leatherworking Supplier
E	**Jewelers**	
	Amin	Journeyman Jewelcrafter
	Blood Elf Magister	
	Gelanthis	Jewelcrafting Supplier
	Kalinda	Master Jewelcrafter
	Telia	Expert Jewelcrafter
	Toban	Artisan Jewelcrafter
	Worker Mo'rrisroe	Silvermoon Builder's Association
F	**Velanni's Arcane Goods**	
	Velanni	Arcane Goods Vendor
	Zathanna	Wand Vendor
G	**Elder's Park**	
	Conjurer Tyren	
	Harene Plainwalker	**Druid Trainer**
	Silvermoon City Guardian	65
H	**Silvermoon Finery**	
	Andra	Clothier
	Rathin	Bag Vendor
	Zyandrel	Cloth Armor Merchant
I	**Keelen's Trustworthy Tailoring**	
	Deynna	Tailoring Supplier
	Galana	Journeyman Tailor
	Leper Gnome Laborer	
	Sheets	Expert Tailor
	Sirigna'no	Sheets' Minion
J	**Blades by Rehein/Feledis' Axes**	
	Rahein	Blade Vendor
	Reledis	Axe Vendor
K	**The Auctionhouse**	
	Darise	Auctioneer
	Feynna	Auctioneer
	Jenath	Auctioneer
	Vynna	Auctioneer
L	**The Bank of Silvermoon**	
	Ceera	Banker
	Elana	Banker
	Hatheon	Banker
	Silvermoon City Guardian	65
M	**Shields of Silver/Plate and Mail Protection**	
	Keeli	Mail Armor Merchant
	Tynna	Plate Armor Merchant
	Winthren	Shield Merchant
N	**The Rabble**	
	Lyria Skystrider	
	Melaya Tassler	
	Priest Ennas	
	Silvermoon Citizen	
	Silvermoon Magister	
	Terric Brightwind	
	Vaeron Kormar	
O	**General Goods**	
	Rarthein	
	Sathren Azuredawn	General Goods
	Zalle	Reagent Vendor
P	**Tradesmen on the Corner**	
	Alestus	First Aid Trainer
	Drathen	Fishing Trainer
	Olirea	Fishing Supplier
Q	**Silvermoon City Inn**	**Shortcut Between Murder Row/Royal Exchange**
	Blood Knight Adept	
	Blood Knight Stillblade	
	Innkeeper Velandra	Innkeeper
	Vinemaster Suntouched	Wine and Spirits Merchant
R	**The Royal Exchange**	
	Caidori	Auctioneer
	Ithillan	Auctioneer
	Silvermoon City Guardian	65
	Tandron	Auctioneer
S	**Royal Exchange Bank**	
	Daenice	Banker
	Mailbox	
	Novia	Banker
	Periel	Banker
	Silvermoon City Guardian	65
T	**Farstrider Square**	
	Bipp Glizzitor	Arena Master
	Champion Vranesh	
	Duyash the Cruel	Eye of the Storm Battlemaster
	Gurak	Alterac Valley Battlemaster
	Ileda	Weapon Master (Bow/Dagger/Polearm/1H Sword/2H Sword/Thrown)
	Initiate Colin	
	Initiate Emeline	
	Ithelis	**Paladin Trainer**
	Karen Wentworth	Arathi Basin Battlemaster
	Knight-Lord Bloodvalor	
	Krukk	Warsong Gulch Battlemaster
	Osselan	**Paladin Trainer**
	Silvermoon City Guardian	65
	Wylaris	**Paladin Trainer**
U	**Entrance to Lady Liadrin's Area**	
	Blood Elf Magister	
	Blood Knight Adept	
	Lady Liadrin	Blood Knight Matriarch (Boss)
	Magister Astalor Bloodsworn	
V	**Hunter's Guild**	
	Halthenis	Pet Trainer
	Oninarth	**Hunter Trainer**
	Shalenn	Stable Master
	Silvermoon Ranger	
	Tana	**Hunter Trainer**
	Zandine	**Hunter Trainer**
W	**The Forge**	
	Anvil	
	Belil	**Mining Trainer**
	Bemarrin	Expert Blacksmith
	Eriden	Blacksmithing Supplier
	Forge	
	Mirvedon	Journeyman Blacksmith
	Zelan	Mining Supplies
X	**Engineer's Corner**	
	Anvil	
	Danwe	Expert Engineer
	Gloresse	Journeyman Engineer
	Yatheon	Engineering Supplier
Y	**Murderer's Row**	
	Alamma	**Warlock Trainer**
	Blood Elf Warlock	
	Darlia	Poison Supplier
	Elara	**Rogue Trainer**
	Instructor Cel	
	Keyanomir	
	Mailbox	
	Nerisen	**Rogue Trainer**
	Nimrida	Keyanomir's Minion
	Talionia	**Warlock Trainer**
	Torian	Demon Trainer
	Trainee Alcor	
	Trainee Firea	
	Zanien	**Warlock Trainer**
	Zelanis	**Rogue Trainer**
Z	**Sunfury Spire**	
	Aldrae	**Priest Trainer**
	Aurosalia	
	Belestra	**Priest Trainer**
	Elrodan	
	Inethven	**Mage Trainer**
	Lor'Themar Theron	Regent Lord of Quel'Thalas (Boss)
	Lotheolan	**Priest Trainer**
	Narinth	Portal Trainer
	Quithas	**Mage Trainer**
	Silvermoon City Guardian	65
	Teleporter to Undercity	
	Zaedana	**Mage Trainer**
1	**Bithrus**	**Fireworks Vendor**
2	**West Gate**	
3	**Welethelon**	**Blunt Weapon Merchant**
4	**Noraelath**	**Leather Armor Merchant**
5	**Parnis**	**Tradesman**
6	**Mathaleron**	**Gunsmith**
7	**Celana**	**Bowyer**
8	**Enchants Enhanced**	**Enchanting Training and Supplies**
9	**Silvermoon Alchemy**	**Herbalism and Alchemy Training and Supplies**

Return to Fairbreeze, turn in **Word From The Spire** and **Warning Fairbreeze Village**, and pick up the final ingredient for **The Party Never Ends**, if you like. This is the *Bundle of Fireworks*, from Halis Dawnstrider. Take those items over to Saltheril's Haven and turn in that considerable quest to keep the party going.

Very little is left to accomplish in Eversong Woods. You can fought long and hard, and now it's time to move on. Magistrix Landra Dawnstrider, in Fairbreeze, lets you know that a courier has been lost on the way to the Ghostlands. Accept the quest **Missing in the Ghostlands**, then leave the village.

The Ghostlands Call

Missing in the Ghostlands	
Faction	Horde
Location	Fairbreeze Village
Quest Giver	Magistrix Landra Dawnstrider
Quest Completion	Courier Dawnstrider
Reward	Chain to The Fallen Courier

Look on the eastern side of the Dead Scar, just on the border between the two zones. Courier Dawnstrider has been ambushed by the Scourge, and he now clings barely to life. With some luck, a Forsaken by the name of Apothecary Thedra is there to tend the Courier. Talk with both of these people, in turn, to get **The Fallen Courier** quest.

The Fallen Courier	
Faction	Horde
Location	Southern Tip of Eversong Woods
Quest Giver	Apothecary Thedra
Quest Completion	Apothecary Thedra
Reward	Chain to Delivery to Tranquillien

Keep going south, into Ghostlands. To "save" the Courier from his fate, kill the beasts of the area until you can collect *4 Plagued Blood Samples*. Any of the beasts from that area can drop the Blood you need, and their levels are comparable to what you've already been fighting and defeating.

Hasten back to the Apothecary when you are done. Hand her the Blood and talk to Courier Dawnstrider after his partial recovery. He'll transfer his duties over to you. Thus, you now have a **Delivery to Tranquillien** to take care of.

Delivery to Tranquillien	
Faction	Horde
Location	Southern Tip of Eversong Woods
Quest Giver	Courier Dawnstrider
Quest Completion	Arcanist Vandril
Reward	Courier's Wraps (Cloth Wrist 8 Armor, +1 Int), Tranquillien Scout's Bracers (Leather Wrist 24 Armor, +1 AGI), or Bronze Mail Bracers (Mail Wrist 47 Armor, +1 STR) AND Courier's Bag (6 Slot Bag)

GHOSTLANDS MAP LEGEND

Ghostlands Legend

	Name	Notes
A	**Tranquillien (East Side)**	
	Anvil	
	Apothecary Renzithen	Quest Giver
	Arcanist Vandril	Quest Giver
	Blacksmith Frances	Blacksmithing Supplies (Repairer)
	Eralan	Poison Vendor, Rogue Quest Giver
	Forge	
	Ghostlands Guardian	26-30
	Innkeeper Kalarin	Innkeeper
	Magistrix Aminel	Repeatable Quest Giver
	Mailbox	
	Master Chef Mouldier	Cooking Trainer and Supplier, Quest Giver
	Paniar	Stable Master
	Provisioner Vredigar	Factional Goods Vendor
	Quartermaster Lymel	General Goods
	Rathis Tomber	Quest Giver
	Terellia	Trade Goods Vendor
	Wanted Poster	Quest Giver
B	**Tranquillien (West Side)**	
	Advisor Valwyn	Quest Giver
	Dame Auriferous	Quest Giver
	Deathstalker Maltendis	Quest Giver
	Deathstalker Rathiel	Quest Giver
	Ghostlands Guardian	26-30
	High Executor Mavren	Quest Giver
	Magister Darenis	Quest Giver
	Ranger Lethvalin	Quest Giver
	Skymaster Sunwing	Flight Merchant, Quest Target
C	**Suncrown Village**	
•	Anok'suten	11 Elite Quest Target
	Dying Blood Elf	Quest Giver
•	Nerubis Guard	9-10 Quest Target
D	**An'daroth**	
•	Sentinel Leader	11 Quest Target
•	Sentinel Spy	10-11 Quest Target
E	**Goldenmist Village**	
•	Quel'dorei Ghost	10-11 Quest Target
•	Quel'dorei Wraith	11 Quest Target
	Rune of Summoning	
F	**The Plagued Coast**	
•	Withered Grimscale	12-13
•	Zombified Grimscale	12-13
G	**Shalandis Isle**	
•	Darnassian Druid	13-14
•	Darnassian Huntress	14-15
	Night Elf Plans	An'daroth Quest Target
	Night Elf Plans	An'owyn Quest Target
	Scrying on the Sin'dorei	Quest Target
H	**Sanctum of the Moon**	
•	Arcane Devourer	11-12
•	Mana Shifter	12
I	**The Dead Scar**	
•	Dreadbone Sentinel	17-18
•	Dreadbone Skeleton	10
•	Gangled Cannibal	12-13 Quest Target
•	Luzran	21 Elite
•	Phantasmal Watcher	12
•	Risen Creeper	9-10
•	Risen Hungerer	13-14 Quest Target
•	Risen Stalker	16-17
J	**Windrunner Village**	
•	Knucklerot	21 Elite (Patrols to the East)
•	Phantasmal Seeker	12-13
•	Stonewing Slayer	13-14
K	**Underlight Mines**	
	Apprentice Shatharia	Quest Giver
•	Blackpaw Gnoll	14 Quest Target
•	Blackpaw Scavenger	12-13 Quest Target
•	Blackpaw Shaman	12-14 Quest Target
L	**Amani Catacombs**	
	Mummified Remains	Quest Target
•	Mummified Headhunter	16-17
	Ranger Lilatha	Quest Giver
•	Shadowpine Oracle	15-16
M	**Valanna's Camp**	
	Lieutenant Tomathren	
	Ranger Valanna	Quest Giver
N	**Isle of Tribulations**	
	Brazier	
•	Nerubis Guard	9-10 Quest Target
O	**Lake Elrendar**	
•	Aquantion	13 Quest Target
	Glistening Mud	Quest Target
•	Ravening Apparition	11-12 Quest Target
•	Vengeful Apparition	12 Quest Target
P	**Zeb'Sora**	
•	Shadowpine Ripper	10-11
•	Shadowpine Witch	11-12
Q	**Dawnstar Spire**	
•	Arcane Reaver	15-16
	Dusty Journal	Quest Target
R	**Farstrider Enclave**	
	Apothecary Venustus	Quest Giver
	Captain Helios	Quest Giver
	Farstrider Dusking	
	Farstrider Sedina	Quest Giver
	Farstrider Solanna	Quest Giver
	Heron Skygaze	Food and Drink Vendor
	Narina	Bowyer
	Ranger Krenn'an	Quest Giver
	Ranger Vynna	Quest Giver
	Wanted Poster	Quest Giver
S	**Zeb'Tela**	
•	Shadowpine Headhunter	17-18
•	Shadowpine Shadowcaster	17-18
T	**An'telas**	
	Magister Sylastor	Quest Giver
	Night Elf Moon Crystal	
	Tranquillien Scout	16
U	**Sanctum of the Sun**	
	Arcanist Janeda	Quest Giver
	Ghostlands Guardian	30
	Magister Idonis	Quest Giver
	Magister Kaendris	Quest Giver
	Magister Quallestis	
V	**Zeb'Nowa**	
	Fresh Fish Rack	Quest Target
•	Ghostclaw Lynx	15-16
•	Kel'gash the Wicked	20 Elite Quest Target
	Raw Meat Rack	Quest Target
•	Shadowpine Catlord	18-19
•	Shadowpine Hexxer	17-19
	Smoked Meat Rack	Quest Target
W	**Windrunner Spire**	
•	Deatholme Acolyte	14-15 Quest Target
•	Fallen Ranger	15 Quest Target
X	**An'owyn**	
	Scrying Crystal	Quest Target
•	Sentinel Infiltrator	15-16
Y	**Deatholme**	
•	Deatholme Necromancer	18-19
•	Dreadbone Skeleton	18-19
•	Eye of Dar'Khan	19-20 Quest Target
•	Nerubis Centurion	18-19 Quest Target
•	Wailer	18-19 Quest Target
Z	**Dark Temples**	
	Apprentice Varnis	Quest Target (At Eastern Temple)
•	Borgoth the Bloodletter	Quest Target (spawn at either Temple)
•	Deatholme Necromancer	18-19
•	Dreadbone Skeleton	18-19
•	Eye of Dar'Khan	19-20 Quest Target
	Ranger Vedoran	Quest Target (At Southern Temple)
1	**Keltus Darkleaf**	**Rogue Quest Giver**
2	**Tomber's Cart**	
3	**Geranis Whitemorn**	**Quest Giver**
4	**Apprentice Vor'el**	**Quest Giver**
5	**Howling Ziggurat**	
6	**Bleeding Ziggurat**	
7	**Mirdoran the Fallen**	**20 Quest Target**
8	**Jurion the Deceiver and 20 Quest Target**	**Apothecary Enith**
9	**Masophet the Black**	**20 Quest Target (Can Spawn in 2 Places)**
10	**Dar'Khan Drathir**	**21 Elite Quest Target**

WALKTHROUGH FOR GHOSTLANDS

Greatly affected by the ravages of the plague, Ghostlands are currently dark and dangerous. Lurking within the shadows of the mist and trees are many animals that have been changed by the influence of the Scourge. Here too the Dead Scar runs horribly through the wilderness, a highway for the legions of unthinking monsters that serve The Lich King's will.

Attacking the Darkness

Despite these perils, it's time to advance. You have a job to do, and Tranquillien isn't that far away. Look on the provided map until you see the area of Tranquillien. This isn't more than a minute or so to the south from where you enter the region, and the hills surrounding it protect from attack on most sides. Use the road that leads in from the north and examine the town.

Split in the center by the road, the town is naturally divided into two halves. On the west side is the Flight Merchant, Skymaster Sunwing. Get the Flight Point from this person immediately, then look on the eastern side of town for the Inn. That is the only building there, as everything else is merely a glorified stand. Rebind at the Inn, then get down to business. Talk to Arcanist Vandril to learn more about the town and turn in **Delivery to Tranquillien**.

Tranquillien Reputation

The people who have chosen to make a stand here are quite independent, and as such will view your character on his or her own merits. If you do enough of the quests in the region, people here will not only offer you discounts, they will sell you special merchandise!

In return for helping the town, Arcanist Vandril recommends you to High Executor Mavren so that you can see more of the town's workings. Because **The Forsaken** are partially in charge here, it's best to get in good with them. High Executor Mavren is the guy to talk to for this.

The Forsaken	
Faction	Horde
Location	Tranquillien
Quest Giver	Arcanist Vandril
Quest Completion	High Executor Mavren
Reward	Chain to Return to Arcanist Vandril

Mavren is inside the building on the west side of town, and the group in there is always arguing over one thing or another. Mavren has you **Return to Arcanist Vandril** to begin your exciting quests for Tranquillien.

Return to Arcanist Vandril	
Faction	Horde
Location	Tranquillien
Quest Giver	High Executor Mavren
Quest Completion	Arcanist Vandril
Reward	Chain to Suncrown Village

Vandril does indeed have fun tasks for you. The first of these is to seek **Suncrown Village** and hunt ten of the *Nerubis Guards* that patrol the region. These Undead are quite foul to look upon, but they and their leader must be destroyed.

Learning to Fly

As with all areas adjacent to starting zones, there is a chain to learn about the Flight Merchants. This starts in Tranquillien, when you talk with Quartermaster Lymel. Don't rush off to do this until you have other chores in Silvermoon City; this lets you kill two birds with one Hearthstone. Wait until your character needs to train again, perhaps at level 14.

Goods From Silvermoon City	
Faction	Horde
Location	Tranquillien
Quest Giver	Quartermaster Lymel
Quest Completion	Skymaster Sunwing
Reward	Chain to Fly to Silvermoon City

Talk to the Skymaster and get the flight route for this area. Then, complete the quest by speaking to Skymaster Sunwing about the Quartermaster's Goods. This opens the quest to **Fly to Silvermoon City**.

Fly to Silvermoon City	
Faction	Horde
Location	Tranquillien
Quest Giver	Skymaster Sunwing
Quest Completion	Sathren Azuredawn
Reward	Chain to Skymistress Gloaming

Bind at the Inn in Tranquillien first. Then, take the flight that has just opened and go to Silvermoon City. Talk to Sathren Azuredawn there. On our map, Sathren is found by the "O" callout and is a General Goods Vendor. This step chains into **Skymistress Gloaming**.

Skymistress Gloaming	
Faction	Horde
Location	Silvermoon City
Quest Giver	Sathren Azuredawn
Quest Completion	Skymistress Gloaming
Reward	Chain to Return to Quartermaster Lymel

Move to speak with **Skymistress Gloaming**, just outside the gates of Silvermoon City. Talk to her to complete the quest and start the next step, but do not take her flight. Instead, use your Hearthstone to skip straight back to town.

Return to Quartermaster Lymel	
Faction	Horde
Location	Silvermoon City
Quest Giver	Skymistress Gloaming
Quest Completion	Quartermaster Lymel
Reward	Experience

Port back to Tranquillien and turn in the quest for a good experience boost. This is the end of the chain.

Suncrown Village	
Faction	Horde
Location	Tranquillien
Quest Giver	Arcanist Vandril
Quest Completion	Arcanist Vandril
Reward	Chain to Goldenmist Village

While approaching Suncrown Village, keep an eye out for the Dying Blood Elf. This NPC is lying on the road just west of the village. The Blood Elf gives you a charge of slaying **Anok'suten**, the Nerubis leader. Look on top of the southern building in the town to find *Anok'suten*. If he isn't there, be cautious, as he'll be patrolling the streets. Pull as many of the nearby Nerubis as possible ahead of time, to keep the area clear, then attack *Anok'Suten* directly. It might even be worthwhile to grab a friend for assisstance. Put all damage on any Nerubis that add to the fight, then slap as many DOTs, Sunder Armors, and other such effects onto *Anok'suten*. Though Elite, this leader is low in level, so it's likely that you can solo the fight even without a great deal of practice.

Anok'suten	
Faction	Horde
Location	Suncrown Village
Quest Giver	Dying Blood Elf
Quest Completion	Arcanist Vandril
Reward	Fortified Oven Mitts (Mail Hands 72 Armor, +1 STR), Stung (1H Sword 6.0 DPS, +1 STR), Vandril's Hand Me Down Pants (Cloth Legs 18 Armor, +1 SPI), or Tranquillien Breeches (Leather Legs, +1 AGI, +1 STAM)

When this is done, rest and polish off any remaining Nerubis guards to complete your primary quest here. Run back to town and turn in **Anok'suten** and **Suncrown Village**.

Arcanist Vandril receives both sets of good news and sends you right back out, this time to **Goldenmist Village**. Spirits of the fallen remain there, and many of them must be destroyed before the place can hope to be reclaimed. In addition, look into the western building and talk to Dame Auriferous. She wants you to **Investigate An'daroth**, which is close to Goldenmist Village.

Goldenmist Village	
Faction	Horde
Location	Tranquillien
Quest Giver	Arcanist Vandril
Quest Completion	Arcanist Vandril
Reward	Goldenmist Special Brew (Adds 70 Maximum Health for 1 Hour), Quel'Thalas (Bow 7.0 DPS, +1 AGI), Chain to Windrunner Village

Investigate An'daroth	
Faction	Horde
Location	Tranquillien
Quest Giver	Dame Auriferous
Quest Completion	Dame Auriferous
Reward	Lesser Healing Potions (2), Chain to Into Occupied Territory

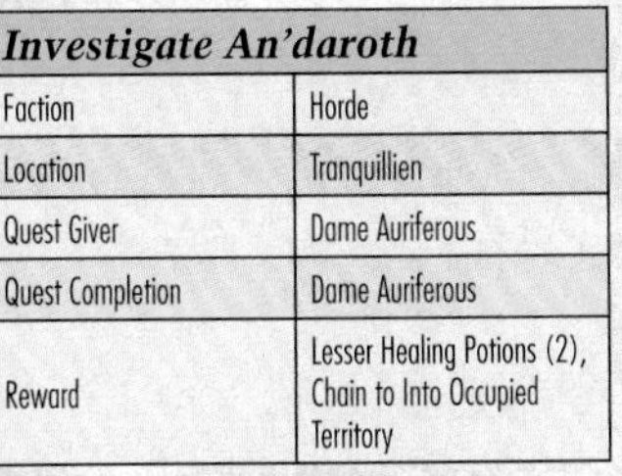

You have to cross the Dead Scar to reach the northwest, but you don't have to stay in it for very long, nor do you have to walk through the lower sections of that awful place. With each step to the south, the Dead Scar becomes stronger, carrying a greater influence on Ghostlands. For now, you can just run happily across it. This is good, because the Scourge in the lower section of the Dead Scar are much higher in level and can be quite aggressive. There is also an Elite Abomination that patrols up and down a fair length of the Dead Scar, and you won't want to run into him yet.

Investigate An'daroth is the first quest on your route. Use our map instead of the in-game one to find the area, as An'daroth is not that easy to see. The place is only a collection of stones normally. At the moment, however, it also has a wide range of *Sentinel Spies* and their Sentinel Leader! Go about the task of informing these arrogant Night Elves that their hopes of completing their mission, and indeed their lives, are over. Slay *12 Sentinel Spies* to get the idea across.

Because the Sentinel Spies and their Leader move around somewhat, pull at range if you are having any trouble with them. None of the enemies stealth, fortunately, so you are free to back away while fighting if anything unwanted draws near.

With that done, move to the west. Climb over the hills there and down into the valley beyond. When you arrive in **Goldenmist Village**, kill eight *Quel'dorei Ghosts* and just as many *Quel'dorei Wraiths*. The Wraiths are easier to get because they come out from the buildings of the village and patrol. There are many of them, and they like to aggro on people's backs when you aren't careful. Finding enough Ghosts is the real trick; look inside the buildings and on the upper levels to collect more of them.

Tricksy Spirits

The Quel'dorei spirits are tough to hit in the second half of their health bar. If you are a class with physical damage, especially if you are a Warrior, save some strength for the later part of the encounter. Put any DOTs on the Quel'dorei enemies early on, and get them debuffed before they fade into their evasive state.

Also, be ready to have them debuff you as well. The Ghostly Touch these guys lay on characters causes a -5 debuff to Stamina and Spirit.

Return to town and collect several quests this time. You have advanced enough in strength and reputation in town that there should be more that people are willing to trust you.

A Clean Sweep of the West

Talk to Arcanist Vandril and Dame Auriferous again, then seek Tomber, Apothecary Renzithen, Master Chef Mouldier (ick), and Deathstalker Rathiel. This accumulates a nice spread of quests, all within a moderate range of each other. When you are done in town, you should have **Windrunner Village**, **Tomber's Supplies**, **The Plagued Coast**, **Culinary Crunch**, and **Down the Dead Scar**.

Tomber's Supplies	
Faction	Horde
Location	Tranquillien
Quest Giver	Rathis Tomber
Quest Completion	Rathis Tomber
Reward	Tomber Becomes a Merchant

The Plagued Coast	
Faction	Horde
Location	Tranquillien
Quest Giver	Apothecary Renzithen
Quest Completion	Apothecary Renzithen
Reward	Swim Speed Potions (2) and Renzithen's Dusty Cloak (Back 12 Armor, +1 STAM)

Rogues and casters have to grit their teeth through this. The Murlocs have a 5-minute debuff called Decayed Agility. They can also slap people with Fevered Fatigue, which hits Intellect and Spirit.

Into Occupied Territory	
Faction	Horde
Location	Tranquillien
Quest Giver	Dame Auriferous
Quest Completion	Dame Auriferous
Reward	Experience

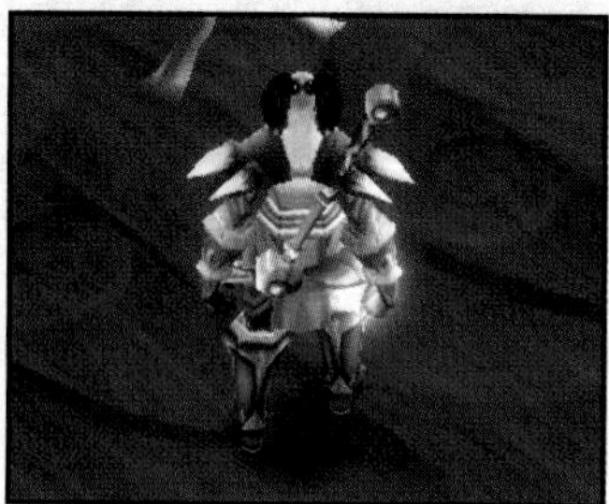

After getting enough of the *Plagued Murloc Spines*, swim to the nearby island; it should be within your immediate sight. This place is known as Shalandis Isle, and a ship of Night Elves has anchored near there. Even more audacious, the Darnassians have set up a camp. Clearly they are planning on staying for some time, so you should discover what they are doing coming **Into Occupied Territory**.

Because both the Darnassian Huntresses and Druids have ranged attacks, you won't want to be coy with them. Instead, hit them directly and use burst damage. This is especially important against the Druids, who would love to engage you in a long, drawn-out fight where their healing can make a big difference. Save your attacks that Stun or otherwise interrupt casting (Blood Elves can Silence on cue) and use those to prevent successful heals.

Culinary Crunch	
Faction	Horde
Location	Tranquillien
Quest Giver	Master Chef Mouldier
Quest Completion	Master Chef Mouldier
Reward	Crunchy Spider Surprise (5), Recipe Crunchy Spider Surprise

Two sets of the plans that you need are here on the island. Search inside the tents for the *Night Elf Plans for An'daroth* and *An'owyn*. Next, climb up the gangway onto the pretty ship by the western edge of Shalandis Isle. Clear your way to the top of the deck and steal the document *Scrying on the Sin'dorei*.

With that much intelligence gathered, you've done your part. Hop down off the ship, and turn to the south. Not only are there Spindleweb Lurkers to collect down there, for **Culinary Crunch**, but **Windrunner Village** is also in that neck of the woods. After a short swim, you can work on both.

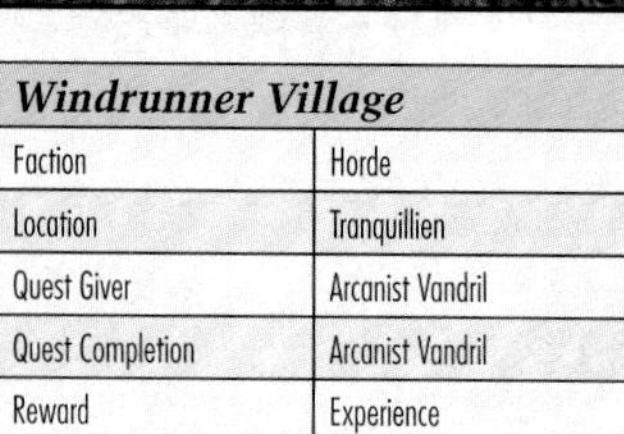

Windrunner Village	
Faction	Horde
Location	Tranquillien
Quest Giver	Arcanist Vandril
Quest Completion	Arcanist Vandril
Reward	Experience

Clear the area near Windrunner Village of as many Spindleweb Lurkers as possible. They are targets of opportunity, and you don't need to get all of their nice *Crunchy Spiders Legs* at once. When their numbers are diminished, walk into town and fight the Stonewing Slayers and Phantasmal Seekers.

Down the Dead Scar	
Faction	Horde
Location	Tranquillien
Quest Giver	Deathstalker Rathiel
Quest Completion	Deathstalker Rathiel
Reward	Experience

Next, look at our map again to find **Tomber's Supplies**. His cart is located just bit south from An'daroth. You'll know when you are getting close because of the Ghouls that are kicking back in the surrounding area. Kill one of those Undead to make room for your approach, then collect what you need from the cart. Simple!

Back in Business

Once you complete his quest, Tomber becomes a full merchant for you. Not only does he sell a variety of Trade Supplies, but he has a few rare goods as well. Sometimes you will see limited rare items such as Scrolls for various attributes, Copper Ore, and other useful goodies.

The Plagued Coast is off to the west. Keep going until you see the cute Murlocs playing on the happy beaches of Ghostlands. It looks just like it did in the travel brochures. Collect *6 Plagued Murloc Spines* from the Murlocs there. Many of them have ranged weapons, but you are lucky in that the Murlocs are fairly spread out. Avoid the huts to save yourself from fighting a few Murlocs at a time, and instead fight the loners on the beach and in the water.

Gather *6 Phantasmal Substances* and *4 Gargoyle Fragments*. The *Gargoyle Fragments* don't drop off of every Stonewing Slayer, but you have to cut through a lot of those Gargoyles to get deeper into the town anyway. The *Phantasmal Substances* fall at a one-per-kill drop rate, so you only need six of those Seekers to get everything you want. For a great cluster of the Phantasmal Seekers, climb up to the second floor of the southeast building.

Stay Paranoid

While fighting on the eastern side of Windrunner Village, or when you are out hunting the Spindleweb Lurkers, be alert. Knucklerot, another Elite patroller, comes to the outskirts of Windrunner Village. If he aggros on your back, it's probably going to end poorly. Run and pray if that happens, or perhaps elbow any buddies you have in the stomach and hope it winds them!

With backpack bursting, you have just finished two more quests. Stop at the Dead Scar on your way back to town. Most of the northern Scar is filled with Risen Hungerers and Gangled Cannibals. If the enemies are too tough, you've gone too far south. And only at the VERY top of the Scar is there anything weaker to fight. Kill *10 Risen Hungerers* and *10 Gangled Cannibals*.

Go into Tranquillien and turn in all of the quests that you've completed.

Repairing in Tranquillien

You might notice that there are not many people who can repair equipment in Tranquillien. On the eastern side of the town, nestled behind most of the vendors and such, is Blacksmith Frances. Ask the Blacksmith to repair anything that has been damaged during your recent fighting.

Accept **Salvaging The Past** from Magister Darenis and **Trouble at the Underlight Mines** from Deathstalker Maltendis. Take **Deliver the Plans to An'telas** as well, from Dame Auriferous, though you won't get around to this step in the chain for some time. These are saved for the last quests on this part of the western side because they are close together and because one of them is somewhat challenging. **Trouble at the Underlight Mines** requires you to go into a valley where aggro can be fierce. With the extra experience you've gained, it's probably doable. If not, this is a good time to pick up a companion to assist in the fighting.

Salvaging The Past	
Faction	Horde
Location	Tranquillien
Quest Giver	Magister Darenis
Quest Completion	Magister Darenis
Reward	Experience

Trouble at the Underlight Mines	
Faction	Horde
Location	Tranquillien
Quest Giver	Deathstalker Maltendis
Quest Completion	Deathstalker Maltendis
Reward	Experience

Travel west from town and seek the Sanctum of the Moon. **Salvaging the Past** requires you to collect *8 Crystalized Mana Essences* from Arcane Devourers and Mana Shifters. These are the only two types of enemies around the Sanctum of the Moon. Both of them are fun targets for Blood Elves, and you can Mana Tap to your heart's content. After **Salvaging the Past** is completed, move south and stay above the Underlight Mines until you see Apprentice Shatharia, who stands on the eastern side of the hill. Shatharia cannot stand a chance against the horde of Gnolls that have taken over the valley, and will beg for you to collect the **Underlight Ore Samples** in her stead. This can be done while slaying the Blackpaw Gnolls, Scavengers, and Shamans for **Trouble at the Underlight Mines**.

Underlight Ore Samples	
Faction	Horde
Location	Underlight Mines
Quest Giver	Apprentice Shatharia
Quest Completion	Magister Quallestis
Reward	Experience

Because the Gnolls wander, have a wide aggro radius, and like to bring friends, you could choose to be quite cautious in pulling them. Use Snares to keep runners from getting into other groups of Gnolls (e.g., Ice Bolt is your friend).

When fighting a pack, drop the Shamans first. Their high DPS and ranged capabilities make them the hardest to move around and control. They also have low health and won't survive for long. Use Arcane Torrent to Silence the Shamans if they become troublesome or petulant.

Collect *6 Underlight Ore* samples from the Gnolls. These samples must eventually go to Magister Quallestis, at the Sanctum of the Sun. If you want to get there quickly, take the back route from Tranquillien next time you are in town. A path through the hills, between Tranquillien and the Sanctum, can be seen by the faint torchlight that lines the path.

The Sanctum of the Sun	
Faction	Horde
Location	Tranquillien
Quest Giver	Magister Darenis
Quest Completion	Magister Idonis
Reward	Experience

When you do go, pick up **The Sanctum of the Sun** from Magister Darenis of Tranquillien. This is an introduction quest, so it doesn't have to do done, but there is no reason to skip it since you pass through Tranquillien anyway.

Time to Explore the East

You have cleared a huge amount of content in the west, and done it quite quickly at that! Now, it is time to push eastward and see more of what that region has to offer. Make one more trip to Tranquillien and stock up on supplies. You might be some time in the bush, so a training run to the capital could be in order as well. Either way, ask Ranger Lethvalin what is going on. The response: **Help Ranger Valanna**! It sounds like two of the Rangers have gone a bit missing, and you must find them to see if they are in trouble. Advisor Valwyn also has a quest for that region. **Investigate the Amani Catacombs** passes close to the Rangers' previous position. While there, you'll be able to collect **Troll Juju** for Deathstalker Maltendis as well.

Help Ranger Valanna	
Faction	Horde
Location	Tranquillien
Quest Giver	Ranger Lethvalin
Quest Completion	Ranger Valanna
Reward	Chain to Dealing With Zeb'Sora

Investigate the Amani Catacombs	
Faction	Horde
Location	Tranquillien
Quest Giver	Advisor Valwyn
Quest Completion	Advisor Valwyn
Reward	Experience

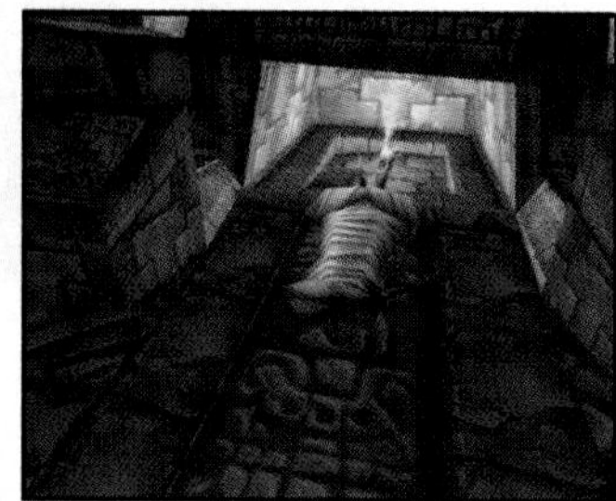

Troll Juju	
Faction	Horde
Location	Tranquillien
Quest Giver	Deathstalker Maltendis
Quest Completion	Deathstalker Maltendis
Reward	Rotting Handwraps (Cloth Hand 19 Armor, +2 STAM, +2 INT), Undertaker's Gloves (Leather Hands 45 Armor, +2 AGI, +2 STAM), Maltendis' Handguards (Mail Hands 99 Armor, +2 STAM, +2 INT)

Hit the Amani Catacombs first, as they are on the way. Stay on the northern side of the mountains, while leaving Tranquillien, and slip into the pass through the hills once you see the Trolls wandering about. There are two entrances to the Catacombs, and it doesn't matter which you take.

Inside, there are Mummified Headhunters and Shadowpine Oracles. The Oracles are very easy to dispatch, despite their casting abilities. Instead, it is the Undead that cause you the most problems. Mummified Headhunters deal plenty of damage on their own, plus they burst into a toxic gas when they die. Either loot immediately or come back and loot groups of them later, once the gas has dispersed. When fighting a few enemies at a time, retreat once the first Headhunter dies. This keeps you from standing around in the goo!

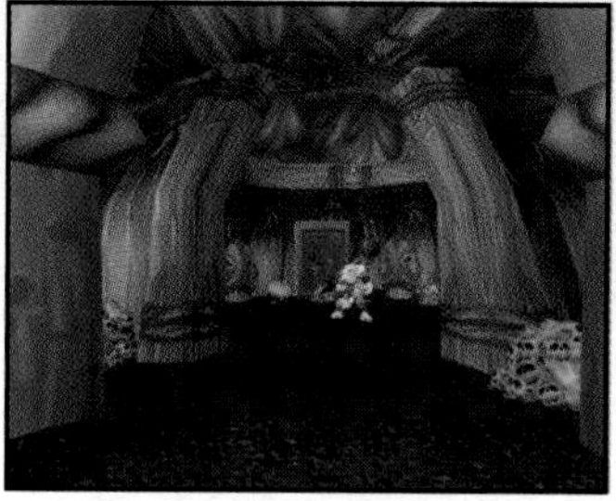

Collect the *8 Troll Juju* that you need during the fighting (Oracles and Headhunters alike drop the *Juju*), and right-click on the bodies that line the walls. Torching these will show that you are investigating in style. However, **Investigate the Amani Catacombs** won't be complete until you search the room at the far end of the upper corridor. This room has several enemies, but it also has a prisoner. When you have checked to ensure that **Troll Juju** is also completed, free Ranger Lilatha and receive the quest to help her to safety.

Corpse Bonfire

Everyone in a group receives credit when one member torches some remains in the Amani Catacombs. Because of this and the fact that the Torch has a cooldown, **Investigate the Amani Catacombs** is extremely group friendly. If you see other characters in the area, and they are competing with you for bodies, just ask them to join you. Everyone gets the quest done faster, and you won't have to wait for bodies to respawn.

Escape From The Catacombs	
Faction	Horde
Location	Amani Catacombs
Quest Giver	Ranger Lilatha
Quest Completion	Captain Helios
Reward	Troll Kickers (Mail Feet 109 Armor, +3 STR), Troll Kickers (Cloth Feet 21 Armor, +1 STAM, +1 INT, Increases damage and healing by 2), Troll Kickers (Leather Feet 50 Armor, +3 AGI)

This is an escort quest. Take Ranger Lilatha out of the Catacombs and get her over to the Farstrider Enclave. Captain Helios is there, and he'll reward you for your success. In addition, there are many quests based out of the Farstrider Enclave!

For now, accept **Spirits of the Drowned** from Ranger Krenn'an and **Bearers of the Plague** from Farstrider Sedina. The *Ghostclaw Lynxes* are your targets of opportunity now. You only need to kill 10 of them, and that can be done as you go about other tasks. Keep your best eye out for them while passing by the Farstrider Enclave or along the eastern side of the map, near the various Troll areas.

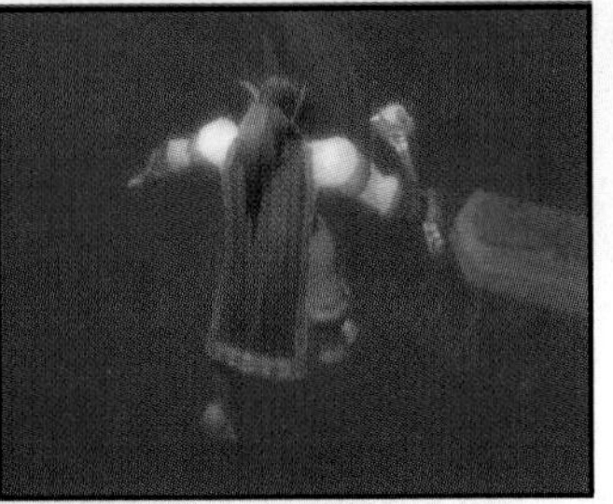

Spirits of the Drowned	
Faction	Horde
Location	Farstrider Enclave
Quest Giver	Ranger Krenn'an
Quest Completion	Ranger Krenn'an
Reward	Experience

Bearers of the Plague	
Faction	Horde
Location	Farstrider
Quest Giver	Farstrider Sedina
Quest Completion	Farstrider Sedina
Reward	Chains to Curbing the Plague

Travel north, along the western side of Lake Elrendar. Meet Ranger Valanna. This completes the quest, **Help Ranger Valanna**, and gets you the quest **Dealing With Zeb'Sora**.

Dealing With Zeb'Sora	
Faction	Horde
Location	Lake Elrendar
Quest Giver	Ranger Valanna
Quest Completion	Ranger Valanna
Reward	Chain to Report to Captain Helios

Because Zeb'Sora is just across the lake, swim there now and start slashing, blasting, and mashing the Trolls. The Witches and Rippers there drop *Troll Ears* for Ranger Valanna, but their drop rate is not terribly high. It'll take a number of kills to finish this group off, but the Trolls are so soft that it's rather relaxing.

Swim back when you are done, and fight any stray *Ravening Apparitions* or *Vengeful Apparitions* that you see; they will be your primary targets in such a moment. Talk to Ranger Valanna again, and she'll order you to **Report to Captain Helios**. You certainly know where he is, and on your next trip there that will be a free turn-in.

Report to Captain Helios	
Faction	Horde
Location	Lake Elrendar
Quest Giver	Ranger Valanna
Quest Completion	Captain Helios
Reward	Farstrider's Tunic (Leather Chest 62 Armor, +1 AGI, +1 STAM), Troll Handler Gloves (Cloth Hands 14 Armor, +1 INT, +1 SPI), or Farstrider's Shield (Shield 239 Armor 4 Block, +1 STAM)

Before reporting back to the Farstrider Enclave, swim to the tiny island southeast of Valanna's position; it's marked with a "3" on our map. Stand fast when you see the spirit of Geranis Whitemorn, and trust that he means you no harm. Talk to him and accept the quest **Forgotten Rituals**.

Forgotten Rituals	
Faction	Horde
Location	Lake Elrendar
Quest Giver	Geranis Whitemorn
Quest Completion	Geranis Whitemorn
Reward	Vanquishing Aquantion

Now you get to finish killing the various *Apparitions* of the lake while searching for *8 Wavefront Medallions.* Dig into the Glistening Mud at the bottom of the Lake while fighting. Remember to come up for air after every *Medallion* or two, and pull Apparitions to the top with ranged weapons if it makes you nervous to fight underwater.

When you are finished collecting these items for Geranis, return to him and hand them in. He'll teach you how to summon the elemental named *Aquantion.* Swim north, just a short distance, and look for the altar at the bottom of the Lake. Clear any Apparitions that are close by, then use the altar for your ritual. Attack the Water Elemental as soon as it appears, and swim to the top while engaging *Aquantion.* This prevents you from drowning if you take too long during the battle.

Vanquishing Aquantion	
Faction	Horde
Location	Lake Elrendar
Quest Giver	Geranis Whitemorn
Quest Completion	Geranis Whitemorn
Reward	Experience

When Aquantion collapses lifeless into the deep, swim again to Geranis and turn in his quest. Continue from there out to the Farstrider Enclave again.

Report to Captain Helios for a reward and see if you can finish **Bearers of the Plague** now. Having taken out a number of the Lynxes as targets of opportunity, there shouldn't be too many left to grab. Look south of the Enclave to find any that you need, then switch that quest into its next step, **Curbing the Plague**. That portion of the chain has you kill *8 Spindleweb Lurkers* and *10 Vampiric Mistbats.* Because the Lurkers are on the other side of the map, you won't complete this quest until later, when you have a few more reasons to head in that direction. The Mistbats, however, are close to the Enclave and can be fought now, while you are passing through the area constantly.

Talk to Captain Helios again to start **Shadowpine Weaponry**, and listen to Farstrider Solanna's suggestion to start the **Attack on Zeb'Tela**. Both of these quests should be within your grasp, though the chains lead into some difficult fighting. This should be clear when you use the Wanted Poster at the southern entrance to the Farstrider Enclave. That Poster starts the quest, **Bring Me Kel'Gash's Head!** You won't have to fight Kel'Gash quite yet, but that Elite Troll is coming up. This might be a good time to find a partner or two, unless you are happy to do most of these quests now and return later to finish the last bits off.

Curbing the Plague	
Faction	Horde
Location	Farstrider Enclave
Quest Giver	Farstrider Sedina
Quest Completion	Farstrider Sedina
Reward	Ranger's Sash (Cloth Waist 16 Armor, +2 STAM, +2 INT), Farstrider's Belt (Leather Waist 39 Armor, +2 AGI, +2 STAM), or Rusted Chain Girdle (Mail Belt 81 Armor, +2 STR, +2 STAM) AND Survival Knife (1H Dagger 7.7 DPS +1 AGI)

Shadowpine Weaponry

Shadowpine Weaponry	
Faction	Horde
Location	Farstrider Enclave
Quest Giver	Captain Helios
Quest Completion	Captain Helios
Reward	Experience

Attack on Zeb'Tela

Attack on Zeb'Tela	
Faction	Horde
Location	Farstrider Enclave
Quest Giver	Farstrider Solanna
Quest Completion	Farstrider Solanna
Reward	Chains to Assault on Zeb'Nowa

Bring Me Kel'Gash's Head!

Bring Me Kel'Gash's Head!	
Faction	Horde
Location	Farstrider Enclave
Quest Giver	Wanted Poster
Quest Completion	Captain Helios
Reward	Well Crafted Long Bow (Bow 10.9 DPS), Well Crafted Sword (MH Sword 10.2 DPS, +3 STR), or Well Crafted Staff (Staff 13.0 DPS, Increases Damage and Healing by up to 4)

Shadowpine Weaponry requires you to collect 3 weapons from each of the four Troll types found in the next two villages. Zeb'Tela has *Shadowpine Shadowcasters* and *Headhunters*; these drop *Shadowcaster Maces* and *Headhunter Axes*. You need to kill the Trolls there for **Attack on Zeb'Tela** anyway and can collect the weapons while you finish that quest.

While visiting this eastern Troll camp, keep your interrupt abilities at their best. The *Shadowcasters* use Mark of Shadow to increase the amount of damage taken from Shadow by a fair margin (20 points). Because of this, it's very useful to Silence casters with Arcane Torrent or to use abilities like Kick, Gouge, Hammer of Justice, and such to disable the casters before they finish their spells.

It's likely that you will finish the kill quest before you have the two sets of weapons needed from Zeb'Tela. Stay until both aspects are completed, then return to the Farstrider Enclave. Zeb'Nowa has the other weapons that you need, but there are two additional quests that you can get for that area. Turn in Attack on Zeb'Tela; this chains into the **Assault on Zeb'Nowa**. Also, talk to Apothecary Venustus, on the second floor of the Enclave. Chillingly, the Apothecary has some great ideas about how to deal with the Trolls. Accept **A Little Dash of Seasoning** before moving to the southeast.

Assault on Zeb'Nowa

Assault on Zeb'Nowa	
Faction	Horde
Location	Farstrider Enclave
Quest Giver	Farstrider Solanna
Quest Completion	Farstrider Solanna
Reward	Sentry Bracers (Mail Wrist 72 Armor, +2 STR, +2 STAM), Supple Cotton Bracers (Cloth Wrist 14 Armor, +1 STAM, +1 INT, Increases Damage and Healing by up to 2), and Farstrider's Bracers (Leather Wrist 33 Armor, +2 AGI, +2 STAM)

A Little Dash of Seasoning

A Little Dash of Seasoning	
Faction	Horde
Location	Farstrider Enclave
Quest Giver	Apothecary Venustus
Quest Completion	Apothecary Venustus
Reward	Experience

Fighting the *Hexxers* and *Catlords* is once again useful for two quests, as you work on the kill quest and the collection of weapons. From these two drop *Hexxer Staves* and *Catlord Claws*. Because the enemies in Zeb'Nowa are higher in level, you can expect the aggro to be somewhat fierce in this village. Draw enemies out from longer range, and fight where you know the area is clear. Don't approach the huts of Zeb'Nowa from the sides either, as the enemies aggro once they see you passing either their doors or windows.

While the numbers are stacking up for your first two quests, search for the three meat sources that need to be poisoned for **A Little Dash of Seasoning**. Zeb'Nowa is a big place, so it takes some work to find everything.

Tainting the Meat in Zeb'Nowa

Goal	Location
Raw Meat Rack	Outside Between Two Huts, South Side; Near the Road
Smoked Meat Rack	Almost at the Bottom of Zeb'Nowa; Also Outside Between Two Huts
Fresh Fish Rack	Inside Large Building, North Side (First Floor)

The *Hexxers* aren't skilled casters at range; they prefer to run up and smack you. What makes them troublesome is that they have mastered the art of Polymorph to Chicken. It is extremely likely that they will turn you into a chicken. This only lasts for a few moments, but it makes running away from *Hexxers* a bit edgy.

As for the *Catlords*, they are more a challenge of combined resources. Acting like Survival Hunters, they like to close as well, bringing their pet Lynxes with them. Attack the *Catlords* first, then switch to their kitties. This gets the combined damage of the pair down quickly enough that they shouldn't be too nasty.

Faster Recovery

Zeb'Nowa is the type of place where casual resting is a bit risky. Wandering Catlords have the potential to bump into you at almost any time, and that sure can spoil your day if you are at one-third Health.

Remember to practice First Aid; get into the better tiers of bandages as soon as possible. This makes it much easier to maintain a higher degree of Health.

For casters, drink that water whenever you can. If you are a Mage or bump into them often enough, get a few big stacks and use them like you mean it. Tip and thank Mages that are nice enough to help you out like this, because it makes a huge difference in leveling speed and general survivability of all casters.

Once you have killed enough of the Trolls to complete your assault and get your weapons, it's time for extra credit. Three quests here should be completed, but Kel'Gash still has his head. If you have a partner or two, or if you have done some extra leveling and think that you can take a level 20 Elite by yourself, look on the southern end of Zeb'Nowa. There is a small path, still guarded by Trolls, that leads into a narrow valley. A single building back there has two floors, and the balcony above is where you see Kel'Gash hanging about.

Clear all of the wandering Trolls from the area near the building, and kill everything on the lower floor and balcony. You can't afford to have an add during this fight, unless you are so powerful that the entire strategy is moot. While clearing, build up three charges with your Mana Tap.

Next, after healing and regaining mana, attack Kel'Gash with your best opener. Ambush him as a Rogue, hit him with your best Fireball, etc. From there, it's a rush to stay ahead of Kel'Gash's damage curve.

This Elite Troll is a caster, so your Arcane Torrent is best used late in one of the big guy's casting phases. Be sure to hold on just long enough that you receive the full use of the free Mana/Energy from hitting Arcane Torrent. As always with casters, other interrupts are essential to survival. Stun this creep as often as possible before his lightning completes.

At some point in the encounter, you are probably going to get Cursed with a Shrink ability. This takes 6 points off of your Strength and Stamina; it's bad for everyone, but especially cruel to Paladins and Rogues who are soloing the encounter. There isn't much that you can do to avoid this, so anticipate it and be ready to use a Healing Potion to keep your Health at a safe range in the later stage of the fight.

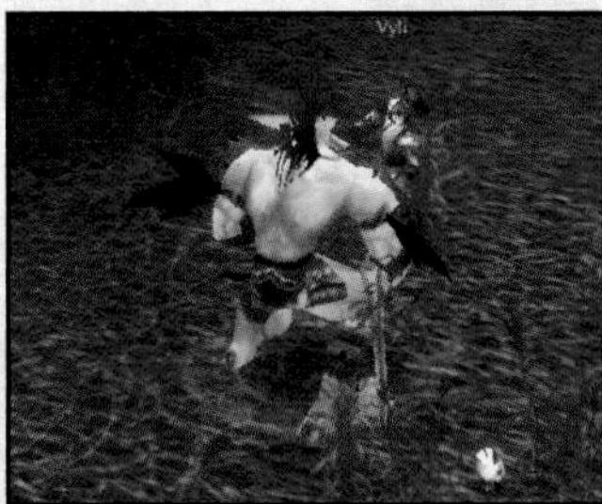

Once you happily collect *Kel'Gash's Head*, return to the Farstrider Enclave and turn in all four of your quests. This gets you a few nice items and quite a dose of experience as well!

Getting Close to the End

Start wrapping up the other loose ends and side quests of the Ghostlands. Dame Auriferous still has her chain for dealing with the Night Elves of Darnassus. Though you discovered the plans some time ago, you weren't in the right neighborhood to follow up on the issue. The next step, **Deliver The Plans to An'telas**, is now a good choice for your hero. Pick this up from Auriferous, in Tranquillien (if you don't have it already).

Deliver The Plans to An'telas	
Faction	Horde
Location	Tranquillien
Quest Giver	Dame Auriferous
Quest Completion	Magister Sylastor
Reward	Chain to Deactivate An'owyn

Look at the mountains northeast from the Sanctum of the Sun. In a tiny cubby of the land, there is a Night Elf site that has been taken over by Magister Sylastor and his companions. Give him the plans and hear what he has to say.

Even as you talk, two more of the Darnassian riders approach. Stay near the Magister's guards, to keep yourself safe while fighting these enemies. Focus on a single target with burst damage to ensure that you get experience credit when the foe goes down, then assist with the other.

With NPC allies there to help, there is no substantial danger, so you can afford to put all Energy/Mana into damage rather than crowd control or improved survival.

As soon as the Night Elves are down, talk to Magister Sylastor again and promise to **Deactivate An'owyn**. Your trip will be a short one, but the rewards are quite fair.

Deactivate An'owyn	
Faction	Horde
Location	An'telas
Quest Giver	Magister Sylastor
Quest Completion	Magister Sylastor
Reward	Sylastor's Cloak (Back 15 Armor, +2 STAM), Divining Crystal (Off-Hand +1 INT, Improves Spell Hit Rating by 1), or An'telas Scale Shirt (Mail Chest 151 Armor, +3 STR, +2 INT)

Travel south toward An'owyn. Walk past the road and over to the mountains at the base of the map. Slay a few of the Sentinels there, and you should find the *Crystal Controlling Orb* on one of their bodies. This is a random drop, but it is often fairly quick to achieve.

With that, you can *Deactivate the Scrying Crystal* at the center of the camp! That done, you should return to the Magister and let him know of your success.

Pick up another burst of quests from Tranquillien when this is done: **Retaking Windrunner Spire** from High Executor Mavren and both **Rotting Hearts** and **Spinal Dust** from Magistrix Aminel. If you don't already know where Magistrix Aminel is, climb to the second floor of the Tranquillien Inn and look for her on the left side. These should all be available now, and each takes you to the west, so it's a good loop to get done in a single sweep.

Retaking Windrunner Spire	
Faction	Horde
Location	Tranquillien
Quest Giver	High Executor Mavren
Quest Completion	High Executor Mavren
Reward	Experience

Rotting Hearts	
Faction	Horde
Location	Tranquillien
Quest Giver	Magistrix Aminel
Quest Completion	Magistrix Aminel
Reward	Scourgebane Draught (+30 Attack Power Vs. Undead for 30 Minutes)

Spinal Dust	
Faction	Horde
Location	Tranquillien
Quest Giver	Magistrix Aminel
Quest Completion	Magistrix Aminel
Reward	Scourgebane Infusion (Increases Spell Damage Vs. Undead by up to 15 for 30 Minutes)

You pass through the Dead Scar first, so collecting the *Rotting Hearts* and *Spinal Dust* might be better to get first, though it's purely a matter of interest. You need 10 of each item, so it's going to take a while to get everything.

Endlessly Roaming

Luzran is still happily running about the Dead Scar in his unending patrol. While fighting the Risen Stalkers, Dreadbone Sentinels, and Deathcage Sorcerers, stay by the eastern edge of the Dead Scar to give yourself a better sight of Luzran's route. Once you spot him, follow his trail visually and keep your character's orientation in that general direction so that he won't surprise you on the way back.

Of the three Scourge targets that you are hunting here, the Deathcage Sorcerers are the worst; they are able to aggro from long range, and their attacks are ice based. For Rogues, this can be troublesome if you don't see them until after they aggro. It is wise to scan the field ahead of time, pick out the Sorcerers, then use Stealth to get the drop on them.

The Fun Never Stops

Rotting Hearts and Spinal Dust can be collected before you get the quests for these items; they can also be found after you complete the quests for Magistrix Aminel. Turning these in to the Magistrix continues to get you Scourgebane Draughts and Infusions. Create a stockpile of these items if you plan on doing a lot of soloing against the Undead during your later fighting in Ghostlands.

Once you finish the quests, or if you tire of the Scourge momentarily and want a break and resume your westward journey. Windrunner Spire is by the coast, and it is a beautiful structure, despite the vermin that call it home currently. Your task is to cleanse the place, eradicating *8 Deatholme Acolytes* and *10 Fallen Rangers*.

If you have trouble fighting casters, be especially wary of this quest. Both the Acolytes and the Rangers are casters, and a few of them patrol. Don't engage in any fights before looking past your foe to see what might wander over in the near future. Mana Tap and Arcane Torrent are very useful here; save your Torrent for any fights where you suddenly find yourself in a pinch.

During the looting, it is likely that you will find **The Lady's Necklace**. This useful item is used to start a quest of the same name.

The Lady's Necklace	
Faction	Horde
Location	Windrunner Spire
Quest Giver	The Lady's Necklace
Quest Completion	High Executor Mavren
Reward	Chain to Journey to Undercity

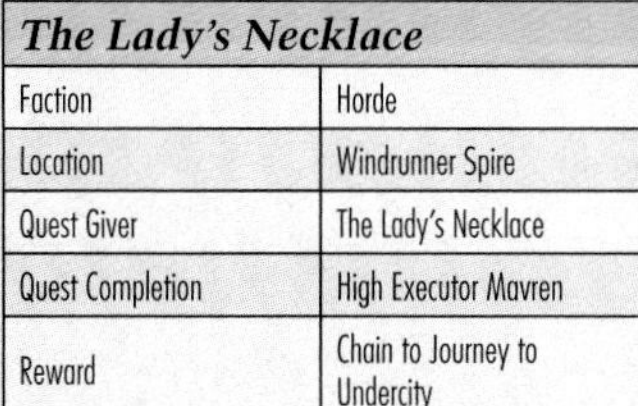

When you turn in Retaking Windrunner Spire, give Mavren this item as well. The immediate experience reward is a friendly boost, and he'll also ask that you **Journey to Undercity** and give the Necklace to Lady Sylvanas. You can do this now, if you want. However, there is going to be another quest that takes you to Lady Sylvanas before much time has passed. For efficiency, wait until you are done with the Ghostlands. Otherwise, go now and have fun! Either way, use the Teleporter to Undercity at the back of the Sunfury Spire to get you where you need to go.

Journey to Undercity	
Faction	Horde
Location	Tranquillien
Quest Giver	High Executor Mavren
Quest Completion	Lady Sylvanas
Reward	Experience

A small kill quest that you should pick up during your growing expeditions through the southern parts of the map is **Clearing the Way**. Apprentice Vor'el provides this, and he is found at the Andilien Estate. Look at our map, in the area south of Tranquillien to find this.

Clearing the Way	
Faction	Horde
Location	Andilien Estate
Quest Giver	Apprentice Vor'el
Quest Completion	Apprentice Vor'el
Reward	Experience

While running about, kill *10 Greater Spindlewebs and 10 Ghostclaw Ravagers*. As for primary quest chains, you are also ready to go into the coolest one of the Ghostlands. Begin **The Traitor's Shadow**, over at the Farstrider Enclave.

The Traitor's Shadow	
Faction	Horde
Location	Farstrider Enclave
Quest Giver	Ranger Vynna
Quest Completion	Dar'Khan
Reward	Chain to Hints of the Pest

Travel to Dawnstar Spire and look for the *Dusty Journal* on the second floor of the building there. You must fight through a number of Arcane Reavers; some of them are patrolling, so it's best to advance slowly, especially if you are alone.

Use bandages or food to keep Health as high as possible, and stick to the walls of the buildings so that you aren't in danger of having proximity aggro from multiple directions. Having a single Arcane Reaver attack isn't too bad, despite their high damage, but being Stunned (via knockdown) by two creatures is quite brutal.

Climb to the second story of the spire and out onto the ledge beyond. The *Dusty Journal* is there! Read it and accept the next step in the chain: **Hints of the Past**.

Hints of the Past	
Faction	Horde
Location	Dawnstar Spire
Quest Giver	Dusty Journal
Quest Completion	Ranger Vynna
Reward	Chain to Report to Magister Kaendris

Return to the Farstrider Enclave and talk to Ranger Vynna. You are quickly sent on from there to **Report to Magister Kaendris** at the Sanctum of the Sun.

Report to Magister Kaendris	
Faction	Horde
Location	Farstrider Enclave
Quest Giver	Ranger Vynna
Quest Completion	Magister Kaendris
Reward	Red Silk Trousers (Cloth Legs 25 Armor, +2 STAM, +3 INT), Black Leather Jerkin (Leather Chest 71 Armor, +3 AGI, +2 STAM), or Tranquillien Scale Leggings (Mail Legs 132 Armor, +3 STAM, +2 INT), and Chain to The Twin Ziggurats

This might seem like the end of the chain, considering that you get a nice choice of armor rewards here. That is far from the reality of things, however, as Magister Kaendris is only getting warmed up. This step chains into **The Twin Ziggurats**, which is a very fun quest.

The Twin Ziggurats	
Faction	Horde
Location	Sanctum of the Sun
Quest Giver	Magister Kaendris
Quest Completion	Magister Kaendris
Reward	Sunwell Blade (1H Sword 10.0 DPS, +3 STAM, Use on Dar'Khan Drathir to Deal 500 Damage + Silence), or Sunwell Orb (Off-Hand +3 INT, Use on Dar'Khan Drathir to Deal 500 Damage + Silence)

Both of the Ziggurats are marked clearly on the map, so finding them is a piece of cake. Stonewing Trackers guard the exterior of the buildings, and they can hit fairly hard. If you pull at range there won't be any chance for multiple Trackers to come at the same time, and that should be safe enough for easy entrance.

Inside, there are several Deatholme Darkmages. Fighting even a single Darkmage while standing out in the open is just foolish; they deal damage in heavy doses. Rather than risk a ranged duel or a charge that might aggro the rest of the Ziggurat, creep into the room from either side until one of the Darkmages proximity aggros. In response, slip back around the corner. This breaks line of sight and forces the Darkmage to run all the way to you. You thus avoid the dangers of multiple casters attacking you, and the issue of ranged damage is negated as well!

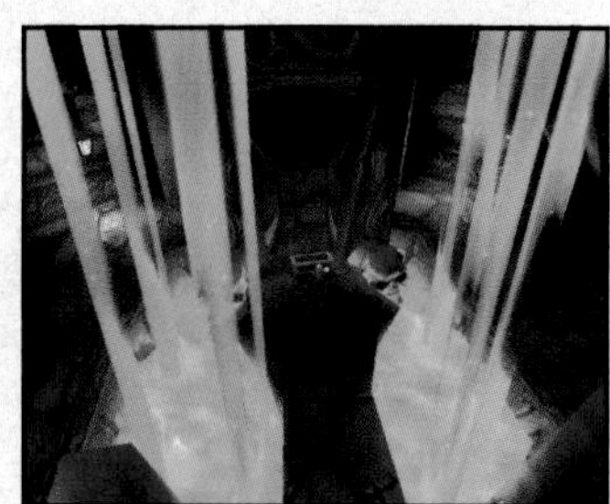

The *Stone of Flame* and the *Stone of Light* are placed in the same spots within the Ziggurats, so your strategy will be identical for each. Collect both items before heading back to the Sanctum of the Sun.

Bringing Destruction to the Scourge

With all in place, those at the Sanctum of the Sun are ready to make **War on Deatholme**. You too should gather your forces while accepting this quest. These final actions against the creatures of Deatholme and the surrounding area can be quite challenging. Though soloable for players with the right patience, equipment, and skill, it is far easier and just as rewarding to get a group of three or so characters and roll through the rest of the Ghostlands. Stop at Tranquillien as well, and receive the Wanted Poster quest for **Knucklerot and Luzran**. The Wanted Poster is just outside the Tranquillien Inn.

War on Deatholme	
Faction	Horde
Location	Sanctum of the Sun
Quest Giver	Magister Idonis
Quest Completion	Magister Idonis
Reward	Chain to Dar'Khan's Lieutenants and A Restorative Draught

Wanted: Knucklerot and Luzran	
Faction	Horde
Location	Tranquillien
Quest Giver	Wanted Poster
Quest Completion	Deathstalker Rathiel
Reward	Invoker's Signet (Ring +3 Int, +2 Spell Critical Rating), Slayer's Band (Ring +3 STAM, +2 Critical Rating)

For those forming a group, it's good to start getting everyone together during **War on Deatholme**. This is a quest that can be finished very quickly in a group. Beyond that, this is the easiest Deatholme quest to solo; you don't have to go inside or near any of the buildings, and that minimizes the risks to your soloist. While the group is forming, you can start on the quest and get extra experience without having to sit on your hindquarters.

There are three types of enemies needed for the quest (out of the five enemy types found in the open area of Deatholme). Search for *Eyes of Dar'Khan, Nerubis Centurions,* and *Wailers.* Stay away from Deatholme Necromancers and their Dreadbone Skeleton pets, as these are not needed.

When You Have Enough Levels or People

You can silence Luzran and Knucklerot at any time; they aren't part of the chain, and the reward for bringing justice to them is quite impressive! Having a solid ring at this stage of your character's development is sweet.

So, when you have gotten enough people to join your quest or when you have gotten up to level 20 or so, look for these foes. Luzran, as said, patrols the western part of the Dead Scar. He walks up and down relentlessly.

Knucklerot is much trickier to find, as his route between Windrunner Village and the Dead Scar goes over more uneven terrain. If you have buddies, get people to spread out and scout for the bad guy. Turn on Undead Tracking, if anyone has the ability at their disposal.

Once you spot an Abomination, estimate the path that it is taking. Because these fiends walk slowly, you have the time to run ahead of them and clear all of the possible adds out of the way. Finish that, rest, and organize people to get as many ranged attacks as possible. Have your most solid character stay in a defensive style of play throughout the fight, and try to keep aggro on them. Paladins are quite dependable for these fights.

Because Abominations are often slow kills, invest in anything that lessens armor, lands high-efficiency DOTs, or keeps character Health higher.

Once you finish, it's time for rings!

Eyes of Dar'Khan are the dark, Wraith-type enemies that you see quite commonly wandering about. They are one used as both patrollers in Deatholme and as static guards for buildings. Their meanest aspect is that they love to use an instant Curse of Agony. Because it's hard to avoid this Curse, you might as well take out the Eyes last when there is a group of mixed enemies.

Nerubis Centurions are the most melee capable of the enemies outside of the ziggurats and towers of Deatholme. These enemies are seen by the edges of the area, along the inner walls. Though they have a Deadly Poison DOT that they enjoy applying to their victims, it doesn't land as commonly as the Curse of Agony from the *Eyes of Dar'Khan.* For this reason, it's good to hit Centurions first in the hope that they won't get to use their DOT in time.

Wailers are Banshee-type creatures. Instead of using DOTs like many of their allies, they try to debuff targets with Wailing Dead, a general attribute-lowering attack. This has a short duration, and at least it's better than having them constantly Silence you (as many of their higher-level relatives would try). Still, this lowers all attributes by 9%.

Of all the generic enemies in Deatholme, it is the Necromancers and their Skeleton pets that do the most damage to a solo character. The Skeletons hit hard enough on their own, and the Necromancers are no slouches on Shadow attacks themselves. Always use corners and cover to force the Necromancers out of casting range, and take them out before worrying about their pets. Though these targets are avoidable in the outdoor areas, you are going to fight several of them when going after the Lieutenants and leader of the area.

With all right in the world, back up to the Sanctum of the Sun and turn in your quests. Accept **Dar'Khan's Lieutenants, The Traitor's Destruction,** and **A Restorative Draught** at this time. Make a short run to Tranquillien to advance **A Restorative Draught** into **Captives of Deatholme** and to turn in the Wanted Poster quest if you were able to take down both *Luzran* and *Knucklerot* already.

Dar'Khan's Lieutenants	
Faction	Horde
Location	Sanctum of the Sun
Quest Giver	Magister Idonis
Quest Completion	Magister Idonis
Reward	Reforged Quel'dorei Crest (Shield 411 Armor 7 Block, +2 STR, +2 STAM), Ley-Keeper's Wand (Wand 15.0 DPS), Ghostclaw Leggings (Leather Legs 68 Armor, +4 AGI, +4 STAM)

The Traitor's Destruction	
Faction	Horde
Location	Sanctum of the Sun
Quest Giver	Magister Kaendris
Quest Completion	Magister Kaendris
Reward	Staff of the Sun (Staff 18.3 DPS, +10 INT, +4 SPI), Farstrider's Longbow (Bow 14.4 DPS), Dawnblade (1H Dagger 13.7 DPS, +5 STAM), or Sin'dorei Warblade (2H Sword 18.2 DPS, +10 STR, +4 STAM)

A Restorative Draught	
Faction	Horde
Location	Sanctum of the Sun
Quest Giver	Arcanist Janeda
Quest Completion	Apothecary Renzithen
Reward	Chain to Captives at Deatholme

Captives of Deatholme	
Faction	Horde
Location	Tranquillien
Quest Giver	Apothecary Renzithen
Quest Completion	
Reward	Experience

Be certain that everyone keeps their quest reward from **The Twin Ziggurats** at the ready. You will soon be going after the leader of Deatholme, and both items from the earlier quest have a special ability that nails Dar'Khan for impressive damage. Even a soloer has a considerable chance of stopping this Elite caster if they use the class wisely in conjunction with the reward items.

Return to Deatholme and use to map to locate the Captives and the Lieutenants that you need. In the north, always in the same crypt, are *Jurion the Deceiver* and the innocent *Apothecary Enith*. Slay Jurion after clearing the way into the building, then rescue the Apothecary. Jurion is a named Wraith, but he doesn't have much more potential for carnage than one of the Eyes.

Next, walk along the road to the open-air structure in the northeastern part of the area. Wailers are frequent in that section, and at the center of the building is *Mirdoran the Fallen*. Ambush him, and notice that you are getting a faint amount of Argent Dawn Reputation from this work. That is kind of a nice perk! Fight Mirdoran inside the building, by over at a wall. This limits the number of wandering things that could trouble you.

The next two Lieutenants can be in a couple of spots. *Borgoth the Bloodletter* is always in one of the temples. There is one temple on the eastern side of Deatholme, up on a hill; the other temple is directly by the south wall of Deatholme. You need to get inside both of these anyway, because the other two Captives are inside those buildings. Search for *Apprentice Varnis* and *Ranger Vedoran*, and save them both.

When you do find *Borgoth the Bloodletter*, he'll always be standing behind the two altars in the lower level of each temple. Monsters love to patrol into these buildings from the outside, so wait for a moment at the top of the building and look to see if anyone is coming. If they are, wait for them and attack the patrollers before going downstairs.

Eyes are in the cubbies within the lower floor, so you won't want to take up a lot of space down there either. Pull Borgoth back to you, and destroy this non-Elite Abomination. His damage is impressive for a non-Elite, so you want a fast fight if there are no healers. Use damaging attacks and keep the action rapid rather than efficient. You can always rest afterward, since you avoided the patroller issue.

With **Captives of Deatholme** completed, you now want to finish off the last Lieutenant. *Masophet the Black* is inside one of the ziggurats on the south side of Deatholme. Look inside either of them. If you have a Rogue present, let them stealth behind the two Eye guards outside the building, then poke their head around the corner to see if Masophet is there. Done carefully, you don't need to fight at all to check while in Stealth.

When you do find this target, clear the fight against both Eyes at the entrance while standing around the side of the building (to save yourself from road wanderers). Then, have one person look inside and proximity aggro one of the casters. Slip back around the wall and fight the Necromancer and his pet. Repeat this on the other side. Carefully do this a third time to get the last Necromancer out of the way, then take on Masophet directly.

If any of the pulled Necromancers gets too close to him on the way out, he'll come earlier. If that happens, you'll get a fairly big fight, with two of the casters, their pets, and Masophet. Use crowd control on Masophet, eliminate the casters, then do the same on the Skeletons until Masophet breaks out of Poly (or whatever you are using). Turn the damage on him then, and clear the encounter.

There is only one quest left to worry about. To ensure **The Traitor's Destruction**, carefully approach the Tower of the Damned in the center of Deatholme. Eyes and Wailers patrol outside and inside the building. If you are soloing, hug the walls to avoid aggroing a wanderer and one of the Necromancers in the lower levels. This would bring three things at once, and you might be hard pressed to win such a fight without using potions or timed abilities.

The final room at the bottom has two more Necromancers and Dar'Khan himself. Pulling Dar'Khan directly does not cause the Necromancers to add, so you can ignore them entirely. That said, you can also pull the Necromancers one by one and clear the room beforehand (if it would make you more comfortable). As usual, the key is not to screw up and get too close to your targets until the pulls are done.

Whatever you are pulling, use the walls for cover to force the targets up the stairs and into your ambush. Once Dar'Khan enters the fray, use the weapons that you received from The Twin Ziggurats. Dar'Khan won't lost as long with that free damage hitting him in the face!

Use Arcane Torrent to Silence Dar'Khan as well, promising at least a couple of easy seconds and one spell interrupted in the process. Rely also on any Stuns or interrupts that your group can provide; these do a great deal to mitigate Dar'Khan's best actions.

Extract yourself from the Tower of the Damned, or even Hearth back to Tranquillien if you like. Turn in the quests there and at the Sanctum of the Sun. Fine work!

Seeing the World

Your actions have helped to save the Ghostlands, at least for now. However, with the Plaguelands so close, it would be near insanity to leave it at that. Listen to Magister Kaendris and take a flight to the capital so that you can meet Lor'Themar Theron, the leader of Quel'Thalas. This time, you arrive at in Silvermoon City as a **Hero of the Sin'dorei**.

Hero of the Sin'dorei	
Faction	Horde
Location	Sanctum of the Sun
Quest Giver	Magister Kaendris
Quest Completion	Lor'Themar Theron
Reward	Chain to Envoy of the Horde

Once you arrive in Silvermoon City, walk to the back of the Sunfury Spire. There, Lor'Themar Theron will give you a most honorable distinction. As an **Envoy to the Horde**, you will be able to travel to Undercity and see the sights in style. Use the teleporter on the right side of the Spire for a much faster (and safer) trip.

Envoy to the Horde	
Faction	Horde
Location	Silvermoon City
Quest Giver	Lor'Themar Theron
Quest Completion	Lady Sylvanas Windrunner
Reward	Chain to Meeting the Warchief

Lady Sylvanas is in the lower chambers of Undercity, just as she was before if you delivered **The Lady's Necklace** to her. Look for her in the Royal Quarter and greet her as an emissary of your people. Stick around as Sylvanas doesn't grant completion immediately. Returning the good will of the Blood Elves, she suggests that you also travel to Orgrimmar, to **Meet the Warchief**.

Meeting the Warchief	
Faction	Horde
Location	Royal Quarter, Undercity
Quest Giver	Lady Sylvanas Windrunner
Quest Completion	Thrall
Reward	Chain to Allegiance to the Horde

Exit Undercity and climb the hill toward the flight tower across from the city's entrance. Check to make sure you are taking the correct flight (the lower dock is the one you want for Orgrimmar, but it's always good to double check). Then, enter Orgrimmar after your flight arrives. Head to the back of the city and have an audience with Thrall, then return home to share the offer of **Allegiance to the Horde**.

Allegiance to the Horde	
Faction	Horde
Location	Orgrimmar
Quest Giver	Thrall
Quest Completion	Lor'Themar Theron
Reward	Experience

The chain ends with Lor'Themar, when you bring him up to speed about the current status of Horde relations. You receive a nice boost to your Silvermoon City Reputation, and the experience award is quite fair.

This ends you passage through the Blood Elven lands. It is now your character's duty to enter the other besieged regions of Kalimdor and Azeroth. If you continue to show the tenacity and devotion that you have here, it won't be long at all before you too pass through the Dark Portal, to aid your people in their fight for Outland.

In the meanwhile, try some of the questing in southern Barrens or Hillsbrad. Branch out, and start to work with the other Horde races. They may not look as pretty as your kin, but do not doubt their honor, strength, or courage. They won't let you down!

Draenei

The Exodar crashed on a small cluster of islands. The primary two are Azuremyst Isle and Bloodmyst Isle. While parts of the Exodar were scattered across the islands, the largest portion has become the hub of the Draenei civilization on Azuremyst Isle. The quests throughout these two zones teach you quite a bit about the Draenei and yourself. Be prepared to adventure in these islands until level 20 if you want to use them to their fullest.

AZUREMYST ISLE MAP LEGEND

Azuremyst Isle Legend

Map	Name	Info
A	**Ammen Vale**	
	Draenei Survivor	Quest Target
	Vale Moth	1
	Volatile Mutation	1-2
	Root Lasher	
B	**Crash Site**	
	Proenitus	Quest Giver
	Botanist Taerix	Quest Giver
	Apprentice Vishael	
	Apprentice Tedon	
	Aurok	Armorsmith Quest Giver
	Jaeleil	Quest Giver
	Jel	Cloth & Leather Merchant
	Aurelon	Paladin Trainer
	Zalduun	Priest Trainer
	Valaatu	Mage Trainer
	Firmanvaar	Shaman Trainer
	Kore	Warrior Trainer
	Keilnei	Hunter Trainer
	Ryosh	General Supplies
	Mura	Weaponsmith
	Vindicator Aldar	Quest Giver
	Technician Zhanaa	Quest Giver
C	**Nestlewood Thicket**	
	Nestlewood Owlkin	3-4
•	Mutated Owlkin	3-4
	Emitter Spare Part	Quest Target
D	**Shadow Ridge**	
•	Blood Elf Scout	4-5
•	Surveyor Candress	5 Quest Target
E	**Ammen Fields**	
	Volatile Mutation	1-2
•	Mutated Root Lasher	3
	Corrupted Flower	Quest Target
F	**The Sacred Grove**	
	Spirit of the Vale	70
	Spirit of Water	3
	Spirit of Fire	3
	Spirit of Air	3
•	Restless Spirit of Earth	4
G	**Azuremyst Isle East**	
	Skittering Crawler	7-8
	Moongraze Stag	6-7
•	Timberstrider Fledgling	6-7
•	Timberstrider	7-8
•	Root Trapper	5-6
	Azure Snapdragon Bulb	Quest Target
H	**Azure Watch**	
	Tullas	Paladin Trainer
	Caregiver Chellan	Innkeeper
	Guvan	Priest Trainer
	Esbina	Stable Master
	Semid	Mage Trainer
	Ruada	Warrior Trainer
	Cryptographer Aurren	Quest Giver
	Arugoo of the Stillpine	Quest Giver
	Totem of Akida	Quest Giver
	Buruk	Pet Trainer
	Acteon	Hunter Trainer
	Kioni	Cloth & Leather Merchant
	Nabek	Weapons & Armor Merchant
	Ziz	Tradesman
	Otonambusi	General Goods Vendor
	Anchorite Fateema	First Aid Trainer
	Daedal	Journeyman Alchemist
	Artificer Daelo	Journey Engineer
	Heur	Herbalist
	Exarch Menelaous	Quest Giver
	Tuluun	Shaman Trainer
	Technician Dyvuun	Quest Target
	Dulvi	Mining Trainer
	Azuremyst Peacekeeper	23
	Mailbox	
	Forge	
	Anvil	
I	**Odesyus' Landing**	
	Logan Daniel	General Goods Vendor
	Blacksmith Calypso	Blacksmithing Trainer & Supplies
	Erin Kelly	Journeyman Tailor
	"Cookie" McWeaksauce	Cooking Trainer & Supplies
	Admiral Odesyus	Quest Giver
	Priestess Kyleen Il'dinare	Quest Giver
	Archaeologist Adamant Ironheart	Quest Giver
	Engineer "Spark" Overgrind	Quest Target
	Alliance Axeman	10
	Skittering Crawler	5-7
J	**Geezle's Camp**	
•	Venture Co. Gemologist	6-7
•	Venture Co. Saboteur	7
	Nautical Compass	Quest Target
	Nautical Maps	Quest Target
K	**Wrathscale Point**	
	Skittering Crawler	5-7
•	Wrathscale Myrmidon	7-8
•	Wrathscale Naga	7-8
•	Wrathscale Siren	7-8
	Ancient Relic	Quest Target
L	**Tide's Hollow**	
•	Wrathscale Myrmidon	7-8
•	Wrathscale Naga	7-8
•	Wrathscale Siren	7-8
•	Warlord Sriss'tiz	10 Quest Target
M	**Moonwing Den**	
•	Aberrant Owlbeast	9-10
•	Deranged Owlbeast	8-9
•	Raving Owlbeast	9-10
N	**Silvermyst Isle**	
	Barbed Crawler	8-9
•	Siltfin Murloc	9-10
•	Siltfin Oracle	9-10
•	Siltfin Hunter	9-10
O	**Bristlelimb Village**	
	Totem of Vark	Quest Giver
	Stillpine Captive	6-9
•	Bristlelimb Ursa	7-8
•	Bristlelimb Windcaller	6-7
•	Bristlelimb Furbolg	6-7
P	**Azuremyst Isle Central**	
	Moongraze Buck	7-8
•	Infected Nightsaber Runt	7-8
•	Timberstrider	6-8
Q	**Azuremyst Isle West**	
	Moongraze Buck	7-8
•	Nightstalker	8-9
•	Root Thresher	7-8
•	Greater Timberstrider	7-9
R	**Silting Shore**	
•	Blood Elf Bandit	7 Drops Quest Item
•	Siltfin Murloc	9-10
•	Siltfin Oracle	9-10
•	Siltfin Hunter	9-10
•	Murgurgula	13 Drops Quest Item
S	**Menagerie Wreckage**	
•	Ravager Specimen	9-10
•	Death Ravager	11 Quest Target
T	**Stillpine Hold**	
	Parkat Steelfur	General Goods
	Moordo	Journeyman Leatherworker
	Gurf	Skinner
	Kurz the Revelator	
	Stillpine the Younger	
	High Chief Stillpine	
	Stillpine Hunter	10
	Stillpine Defender	9-10
	Crazed Wildkin	9-10
	Chieftain Oomooroo	11
	The Kurken	12
	The Blood Crystal	Quest Target
U	**Docks**	
	Huntress Kella Nightbow	
	Shalannius	Druid Trainer
	Boat to Auberdine	
1	**Megelon**	**Quest Giver**
2	**Tolaan**	**Quest Giver**
3	**Aeun**	**Quest Giver**
4	**Dyktynna**	**Fishing Trainer & Supplies**
5	**Totem of Tikti**	**Quest Giver**
6	**Cowlen**	**Quest Giver**
7	**Magwin**	**Quest Giver**
8	**Totem of Coo**	**Quest Giver**
9	**Totem of Yor**	**Quest Giver**
10	**Temper**	**Quest Giver**
11	**Ammen Vale Guard**	**65**

WALKTHROUGH FOR AZUREMYST ISLE

The quiet tranquility of Azuremyst Isle was shattered when the burning and fragmenting hulk of the Exodar plummeted to Azeroth. Much of the wildlife was killed when the flaming pieces of metal and crystal hit the ground. Even more were mutated and corrupted when the systems that were vital to the Exodar's functions proved toxic to the plants and wildlife of Azeroth.

Ammen Vale

Your pod crashed in the small valley of Ammen Vale. While you are not alone, there are only a few other Draenei who have landed here. With much of the technology from the Exodar in ruins, you'll have to rely on your own abilities to survive and help others.

Megelon is standing just down the path from your pod. Above him floats a yellow "!" NPCs with quests you can obtain have these. If the "!" is grey, you are not yet high enough level for the quest. Speak with Megelon by right-clicking on him. He's not in the greatest shape, but he directs you to follow the path to a larger spot of wreckage called the Crash Site and speak with Proenitus (**You Survived!**). Follow his instructions and head southwest to find other survivors.

You Survived!	
Faction	Alliance
Location	Ammen Vale
Quest Giver	Megelon
Quest Completion	Proenitus
Reward	Chains to Replenish the Healing Crystals

Proenitus has a yellow "?" floating above him. This shows that you have a completed quest that Proenitus will reward you for. NPCs with grey "?" above them are waiting for you to complete a quest before they can reward you. Proenitus also shows on your mini-map as a yellow dot. This makes it very easy to obtain rewards for work done.

Proenitus needs your help **Replenishing the Healing Crystals**. He's found the blood of some of the local wildlife to be a suitable replacement, but needs you to hunt them. Head north and hunt the *Vale Moths* to collect the blood. Once an enemy is dead, its body will have gold sparkles rising off it to show that there is loot to be collected. Right-click on the body to open the loot window and then left-click on each item to put it in your inventory. To speed your looting, hold shift when you right-click the corpse to automatically put all the loot in your backpack or initiate the auto-loot function from the interface menu as a shortcut. The *Vials of Moth Blood* (like many quest items) are items that drop from the Vale Moths and must be looted to be collected.

Replenish the Healing Crystals	
Faction	Alliance
Location	Crash Site
Quest Giver	Proenitus
Quest Completion	Proenitus
Reward	Choice of Salvaged Leather Belt (Leather Waist, 19 Armor), Slightly Rusted Bracers (Mail Wrist, 29 Armor), or Worn Slippers (Cloth Feet, 7 Armor).

Return to Proenitus for your reward. With the blood gathered, he asks you to bring it to Zalduun (**Urgent Delivery**). Zalduun is in the largest part of the Crash Site tending the wounded. He's so grateful to you that he wants you to help him **Rescue the Survivors!** He gives you a *Healing Crystal* and sends you to find the scattered wounded, while he tends to the ones here. Speak with your trainer before using the southwest exit. Mura is there and will buy any excess items you've accumulated. Proenitus (back outside) also asks you to speak with **Botanist Taerix** on the west side of the crash site.

Urgent Delivery	
Faction	Alliance
Location	Crash Site
Quest Giver	Proenitus
Quest Completion	Zalduun
Reward	Chains to Rescue the Survivors

Rescue the Survivors!	
Faction	Alliance
Location	Crash Site
Quest Giver	Zalduun
Quest Completion	Zalduun
Reward	Empty Draenei Supply Pouch (4 Slot Bag).

Botanist Taerix	
Faction	Alliance
Location	Crash Site
Quest Giver	Proenitus
Quest Completion	Botanist Taerix
Reward	Chains to Volatile Mutations

The Spoils of War

Your backpack is nearly full. First, take the time to look through it and see if there is any usable equipment for you. Second, become familiar with any recover items (potions, food, drink, etc.) you've accumulated. Everything else that can be sold to vendors should be.

With new abilities learned and your inventory cleared, head out and around to the west side of the Crash Site. Botanist Taerix also needs help. Before she starts to cure the wildlife, you need to prune back the **Volatile Mutations**. Head west and kill eight of the mutations before returning to Taerix.

Volatile Mutations	
Faction	Alliance
Location	Crash Site
Quest Giver	Botanist Taerix
Quest Completion	Botanist Taerix
Reward	Chains to What Must Be Done...

Taerix's team needs samples of the plants and wildlife to help find a way to cure the contamination. Apprentice Vishael asks you to do some **Botanical Legwork** while Taerix tells you **What Must Be Done...** You can hunt the *Mutated Root Lashers* while looking for survivors and *Corrupted Flowers*, so accept the quests.

What Must Be Done...	
Faction	Alliance
Location	Crash Site
Quest Giver	Botanist Taerix
Quest Completion	Botanist Taerix
Reward	Chains to Healing the Lake

Botanical Legwork	
Faction	Alliance
Location	Crash Site
Quest Giver	Apprentice Vishael
Quest Completion	Apprentice Vishael
Reward	Chains to Experience

The Draenei that need your assistance are the ones that can't make it to the Crash Site. Look around the wreckage of pods for the *Draenei Survivors*. To heal the survivors, select them by left-clicking on the body and then open your inventory. Right-click on the *Healing Crystal* to activate it. An alternate way to use items in your inventory is to drag them onto one of your quickbars and push the appropriate hotkey. Once the survivors can move on their own, they'll go to the Crash Site for better care.

The *Corrupted Flowers* are in the Ammen Fields to the west, but they don't drop from enemies. They are a ground spawn and you need to right-click on them when the cursor turns into a gold gear to collect them (a grey gear means you are not close enough). Wait for a loot window to open and left-click on the flower to put it in your inventory. With *Mutated Root Lashers* and survivors here also, you can accomplish all three quests at once!

Traveling the Bloody Way

As you are traveling from point A to point B, kill everything your level or lower that gets near you. The enemies in Ammen Vale are fairly weak and the additional experience and usable equipment make it worth your time. Don't deviate too much from your path (unless you really enjoy the slaughter), but the extra kills give practice and loot.

With some good work done, return to the Crash Site. Botanist Taerix has more work for you now that the samples have been collected (**Healing the Lake**). Inside, Zalduun gives you a small bag as a reward. As your backpack fills up quite quickly, even a bag this small is very useful. To equip it, open your inventory and drag the bag onto one of the slots to the left of your backpack. The bag locks into place and items can now be store inside it. Zalduun is finished with you for now, but there are others who need help outside the southern exit.

Technician Zhanaa is working to restore a communications device, but needs you to collect some **Spare Parts** while Vindicator Aldar asks you to do some **Inoculation**. Sell any excess items before moving south to Silverline Lake.

Healing the Lake	
Faction	Alliance
Location	Crash Site
Quest Giver	Botanist Taerix
Quest Completion	Botanist Taerix
Reward	Experience

Inoculation	
Faction	Alliance
Location	Crash Site
Quest Giver	Vindicator Aldar
Quest Completion	Vindicator Aldar
Reward	3 Minor Healing Potions (Use Restores 70 to 90 health) and the choice of 3 Elixir of Minor Defense (Use Increases armor by 50 for 1 hour) or 3 Elixir of Lion's Strength (Use Increases Strength by 4 for 1 hour).

Spare Parts	
Faction	Alliance
Location	Crash Site
Quest Giver	Technician Zhanaa
Quest Completion	Technician Zhanaa
Reward	Choice of Beaten Chain Leggings (Mail Legs, 58 Armor), Rough Leather Leggings (Leather Legs, 29 Armor), or Hand Sewn Pants (Cloth Legs, 9 Armor)

The *Irradiated Power Crystal* polluting the lake is quite large. Dive into the water and disperse the *Neutralizing Agent* on it. With the source dealt with, you need to deal with the affected. Northeast of the lake is Nestlewood Thicket. You have much to do. Use the *Inoculating Crystal* on the *Nestlewood Owlkin*. The Mutated Owlkin have become aggressive and will attack you on sight. Be prepared to defend yourself. Follow the winding path through the hills and look for the *Emitter Spare Parts*. Finish the remainder of your quests before heading back to the Crash Site for your well-deserved rewards. That was a lot!

Taerix thanks you for your work and asks you to speak with **Vindicator Aldar**. Head to the south edge of the Crash Site and speak with Aldar about a couple things. Aldar asks you to find **The Missing Scout** near Shadow Ridge.

Vindicator Aldar	
Faction	Alliance
Location	Crash Site
Quest Giver	Botanist Taerix
Quest Completion	Vindicator Aldar
Reward	Experience

The Missing Scout

Faction	Alliance
Location	Crash Site
Quest Giver	Vindicator Aldar
Quest Completion	Tolaan
Reward	Chains to The Blood Elves

Tolaan is near the entrance to Shadow Ridge and in dire need of medical attention. He waves you off and insists that you instead deal with **The Blood Elves**. Travel up the paths slaying the *Blood Elf Scouts*.

The Blood Elves

Faction	Alliance
Location	Shadow Ridge
Quest Giver	Tolaan
Quest Completion	Tolaan
Reward	Choice of Weathered Cloth Armor (Cloth Chest, 9 Armor), Weathered Leather Vest (Leather Chest, 31 Armor), or Weathered Mail Tunic (Mail Chest, 63 Armor)

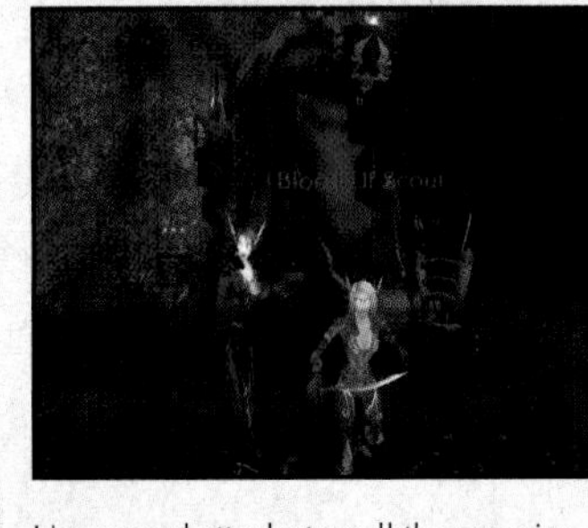

Use ranged attacks to pull the enemies away from each other to avoid larger fights. When you've slain all 10 of the scouts, return to Tolaan. With the scouts dead, Tolaan asks you to deal with the **Blood Elf Spy**.

Blood Elf Spy

Faction	Alliance
Location	Shadow Ridge
Quest Giver	Tolaan
Quest Completion	Vindicator Aldar
Reward	Choice of Exodar Bastard Sword (Two-hand Sword, 2.7 DPS), or Exodar Dagger (One-hand Dagger, 1.9 DPS), Exodar Maul (Main-hand Mace, 2.1 DPS), Exodar Shortsword (Main-hand Sword, 2.1 DPS), Exodar Crossbow (Crossbow, 4.0 DPS), or Exodar Staff (Two-hand Staff, 2.7 DPS)

Make your way back up the paths to the very top of the camp. *Candress* stands with a body guard, so it is impossible to fight only her. When you start the fight, kill *Candress* first. She does more damage then her partner and is weaker. With Candress dead, loot the **Blood Elf Plans** from her body and return to Vindicator Aldar.

The *Blood Elf Plans* are a quest-starting item. With it in your inventory, right-click on it to bring up the quest. Click "Accept" to add the quest to your log.

Blood Elf Plans

Faction	Alliance
Location	Shadow Ridge
Quest Giver	Blood Elf Plans
Quest Completion	Vindicator Aldar
Reward	Experience

While you were gone, Zhanaa has been working on **The Emitter**. Other Draenei have survived the crash! With tentative contact made with others, it's time to **Travel to Azure Watch** to establish more formal communications. Take care of any last errands you have at the Crash Site and take the pass to the southwest.

The Emitter

Faction	Alliance
Location	Crash Site
Quest Giver	Vindicator Aldar
Quest Completion	Technician Zhanaa
Reward	Chains to Travel to Azure Watch

Travel to Azure Watch

Faction	Alliance
Location	Crash Site
Quest Giver	Technician Zhanaa
Quest Completion	Technician Dyvuun
Reward	Experience

The Path to Azure Watch

On the road to Azure Watch is Aeun. He was attacked by some of the mutated creatures in the area and can't take the **Request for Emergency Supplies** to Azure Watch in his condition. Accept the quest and continue west across the river.

Request for Emergency Supplies

Faction	Alliance
Location	Azuremyst Isle
Quest Giver	Aeun
Quest Completion	Caregiver Chellan
Reward	Choice of 5 Brilliant Smallfish (Use Restores 61 health over 18 sec. Must remain seated while eating) or 5 Refreshing Spring Water (Use Restores 151 mana over 18 sec. Must remain seated while drinking)

Take a short break from your journey and speak to Diktynna. She can teach you to fish and has work for you. Help her catch some **Red Snapper – Very Tasty!** and she'll give you a fishing pole. Use her fishing net on the nearby schools of red snapper and be ready for a fight as Angry Murlocs are after the same fish you are. Angry Murlocs also have a decent chance to drop a 6 slot bag. Return to her and Diktynna asks you to **Find Acteon!** As Acteon is at Azure Watch, you're in luck! Follow the road west.

Red Snapper – Very Tasty!	
Faction	Alliance
Location	Azuremyst Isle
Quest Giver	Diktynna
Quest Completion	Diktynna
Reward	Fishing Pole and Shiny Bauble (Use When applied to your fishing pole, increases Fishing by 25 for 10 min.)

Find Acteon!	
Faction	Alliance
Location	Azuremyst Isle
Quest Giver	Diktynna
Quest Completion	Acteon
Reward	Chains to The Great Moongraze Hunt

Azure Watch

Without missing a beat, Acteon gives you more work to do. He asks you to join **The Great Moongraze Hunt**, but speak with everyone in town before you head out. Anchorite Fateema speaks about the **Medicinal Purpose** of hunting lashers, while a number of Draenei here can teach you various professions or class abilities.

The Great Moongraze Hunt	
Faction	Alliance
Location	Azure Watch
Quest Giver	Acteon
Quest Completion	Acteon
Reward	5 Roasted Moongraze Tenderloin (Use Restores 61 health over 18 sec. Must remain seated while eating. If you spend at least 10 seconds eating you will become well fed and gain 2 Stamina and Spirit for 15 min.), Recipe Roasted Moongraze Tenderloin, and choice of Moongraze Fur Cloak (Back, 8 Armor) or Moongraze Hide Boots (Leather Feet, 31 Armor)

Medicinal Purpose	
Faction	Alliance
Location	Azure Watch
Quest Giver	Anchorite Fateema
Quest Completion	Anchorite Fateema
Reward	Chains to An Alternative Alternative

Speak with Caregiver Chellan and "Make this inn your home." This will allow you to use your Hearthstone to return here from across great distances. With errands done, head west to hunt the *Moongraze Stags* and *Root Trappers*. Both sides of the road hold your targets. The enemies here are tougher than in Ammen Vale. The timber striders and root trappers are aggressive and will attack you on sight. Keep your health and mana above half by resting, eating, or drinking between fights. This gives you the staying power to pull through a difficult encounter if things go poorly.

Return to Azure Watch once you have collected the lasher roots. You'll be going back out shortly, so don't worry about collecting all the meat. Fateema's ointment is ineffective, but Daedal has **An Alternative Alternative.** He needs 5 *Azure Snapdragon Bulbs* for his concoction. They grow near the trees north of the road to Ammen Vale.

An Alternative Alternative	
Faction	Alliance
Location	Azure Watch
Quest Giver	Daedal
Quest Completion	Daedal
Reward	Chains to The Prophecy of Velen

Bring the bulbs back to Daedal and he will tell you of **The Prophecy of Velen**. He charges you with traveling south to find the kin of the wounded creature, but first you need to finish **The Great Moongraze Hunt**. Exit to the northwest of Azure Watch and climb the hill to look for the *Moongraze Bucks*. Return when you have the hides you need.

The Prophecy of Velen	
Faction	Alliance
Location	Azure Watch
Quest Giver	Daedal
Quest Completion	Admiral Odesyus
Reward	Experience

Odesyus' Landing

Follow the south road until you find a hastily constructed fort bearing odd blue banners. Though the people are strange, they will not attack you. Introduce yourself to their commander Admiral Odesyus. He is very appreciative of your efforts to help his crewmember. Most of the camp doesn't trust you yet, but Admiral Odesyus tells you how to make **A Small Start** toward earning that trust.

A Small Start	
Faction	Alliance
Location	Odesyus' Landing
Quest Giver	Admiral Odesyus
Quest Completion	Admiral Odesyus
Reward	Opens a number of quests

Follow the shoreline east in search of the goblins and their allies. Search the camp near the ruins first. The *Nautical Compass* is sitting on one of the crates. The *Nautical Map*, however, is in the primary camp is more difficult to obtain.

The Venture Company Saboteurs and Gemologists stick together like Draenei and, unless you are careful, will overwhelm you when one of them is in trouble. Use ranged attacks to pull the enemies away from the camp one at a time and make your way slowly to the center of the camp. With both pieces in hand, return to Odesyus.

With Admiral Odesyus' trust on your side, the rest of his crew is willing to speak with you about their difficulties. Look around and grab **Cookie's Jumbo Gumbo**, **Precious and Fragile Things Need Special Handling**, and **Reclaiming the Ruins**. Follow the shoreline west toward Wrathscale Point and hunt the *Skittering Crawlers* for **Cookie's Jumbo Gumbo** on the way.

Cookie's Jumbo Gumbo	
Faction	Alliance
Location	Odesyus' Landing
Quest Giver	"Cookie" McWeaksauce
Quest Completion	"Cookie" McWeaksauce
Reward	10 Cookie's Jumbo Gumbo (Use Restores 61 health over 18 sec. Must remain seated while eating. If you spend at least 10 seconds eating you will become well fed and gain 2 Stamina and Spirit for 15 min.)

Precious and Fragile Things Need Special Handling	
Faction	Alliance
Location	Odesyus' Landing
Quest Giver	Archaeologist Adamant Ironheart
Quest Completion	Archaeologist Adamant Ironheart
Reward	Experience

Reclaiming the Ruins	
Faction	Alliance
Location	Odesyus' Landing
Quest Giver	Priestess Kyleen Il'dinare
Quest Completion	Priestess Kyleen Il'dinare
Reward	Experience

While **Reclaiming the Ruins**, by killing the Wrathscale, keep your eyes out for the *Ancient Relics*. These **Precious and Fragile Things Need Special Handling**. The Wrathscale are very aggressive and fairly dangerous. Pull each one away from any others as a fight against two will be your doom. Some of the Naga and relics are found underwater. When you dive below the surface, a breath meter will show in the center of the screen. Do not let this run out as you take damage very quickly when it does. The Naga also carry a **Rune Covered Tablet**. Priestess Kyleen Il'dinare will want to see this when you return to the landing.

Rune Covered Tablet	
Faction	Alliance
Location	Wrathscale Point
Quest Giver	Rune Covered Tablet
Quest Completion	Priestess Kyleen Il'dinare
Reward	Chains to Warlord Sriss'tiz

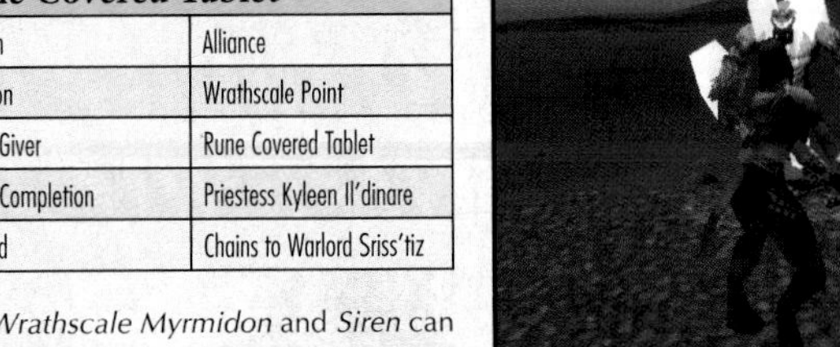

The *Wrathscale Myrmidon* and *Siren* can be found on the beach, but the *Naga* are found in the ruins. As the Ancient Relics are found all over, it's a win-win situation. Continue killing and collecting until your quests are completed before traveling back to the landing. You probably haven't collected all the *Skittering Crawler Meat* you need, so do a bit of hunting before you enter Odesyus' Landing.

The people of the landing are warming up to you, but there is still a long way to go before they can call you friend. Priestess Kyleen Il'dinare asks you to kill **Warlord Sriss'tiz**. Return to Wrathscale point and continue east until you find Tides' Hollow.

Warlord Sriss'tiz	
Faction	Alliance
Location	Odesyus' Landing
Quest Giver	Priestess Kyleen Il'dinare
Quest Completion	Priestess Kyleen Il'dinare
Reward	Choice of Battle Tested Blade (Main-hand Sword, 4.3 DPS) or Naga Scale Boots (Mail Feet, 70 Armor)

With nowhere to run, the cave can be very dangerous. If there are other Draenei close by, ask to join them, but don't fret if no help is found. The cave can be taken alone. Follow the downward slope to the left. Be ready to call upon the Gift of the Naaru if more than one enemy attacks you. The Naga are quite strong and can fell even the proudest of warriors.

At the bottom of the down slope, head west into some ruins. **Warlord Sriss'tiz** is in sight, but do not engage him yet. Clear the guards from around him to ensure that you only fight him when the time comes. Without an army of Naga behind him, *Sriss'tiz* is just a bully. The Gift of the Naaru should be more than enough to tip the balance in your favor and make the fight as difficult as any other. Slay him and bring word of the deed back to Odesyus' Landing.

The relationship between your people and the strangers has been aided greatly by your actions. Now it is time to return to your people. Travel north to Azure Watch with the news of new friends.

The Path to Stillpine Hold

Aurren is **Learning the Language** of the Furbolg and wants you to as well. Use the *Stillpine Furbolg Language Primer* he gives you and speak with the Totem of Akida. The Stillpine Ancestor Akida will appear before you and show you the way to the **Totem of Coo**. Follow him up the hill and speak with the totem. Skirt the north edge of the hill and kill a couple Infected Nightsaber Runts until you find the *Faintly Glowing Crystal*. Open you inventory and use the item to start the quest **Strange Findings**. You don't need to follow the spirit if you know where you're going.

Learning the Language	
Faction	Alliance
Location	Azure Watch
Quest Giver	Cryptographer Aurren
Quest Completion	Totem of Akida
Reward	Chains to Totem of Coo

Totem of Coo	
Faction	Alliance
Location	Azure Watch
Quest Giver	Totem of Akida
Quest Completion	Totem of Coo
Reward	Chains to Totem of Tikti

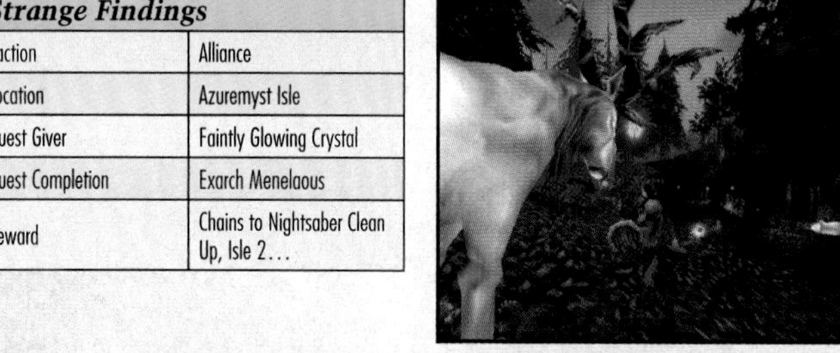

Strange Findings	
Faction	Alliance
Location	Azuremyst Isle
Quest Giver	Faintly Glowing Crystal
Quest Completion	Exarch Menelaous
Reward	Chains to Nightsaber Clean Up, Isle 2...

Totem of Tikti	
Faction	Alliance
Location	Azuremyst Isle
Quest Giver	Totem of Coo
Quest Completion	Totem of Tikit
Reward	Chains to Totem of Yor

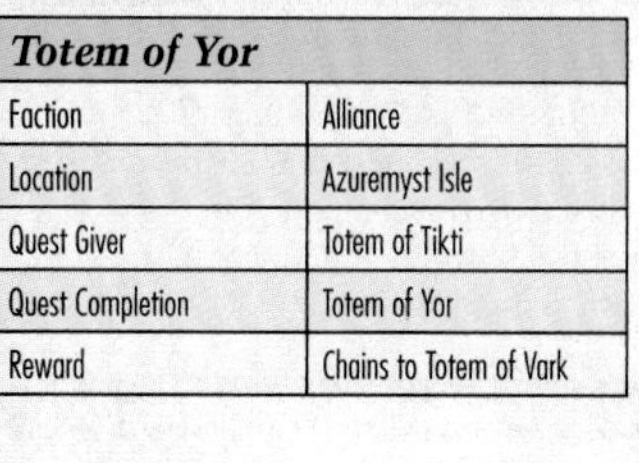

Totem of Yor	
Faction	Alliance
Location	Azuremyst Isle
Quest Giver	Totem of Tikti
Quest Completion	Totem of Yor
Reward	Chains to Totem of Vark

Totem of Vark	
Faction	Alliance
Location	Azuremyst Isle
Quest Giver	Totem of Yor
Quest Completion	Totem of Vark
Reward	Chains to The Prophecy of Akida

The totem of Coo stands on the top of the hill amongst the ruins. Speak with it to receive aid getting to the **Totem of Tikti**. The Stillpine Ancestor Coo gives you the ability to survive falls and walk on water. Jump off the cliff to the east and make your way across the river to the Totem of Tikti.

As you speak with each totem, the symbols of the Stillpine language make more sense to you. The Totem of Tikti is far from your final destination and sends you down the river to look along the bottom for the **Totem of Yor**. The Stillpine Ancestor Tikti allows you to swim at great speeds and breathe underwater.

Understanding Stillpine Ancestor Yor is much easier than the others so far. He grants you an amazing power and leads you to the final totem. He gives you the form of a cat, invisibility, and increased speed. He becomes difficult to see once you are transformed, so select him before hand and follow his name through the world of shadows to the **Totem of Vark** that shows you **The Prophecy of Akida.**

The Prophecy of Akida	
Faction	Alliance
Location	Azuremyst Isle
Quest Giver	Totem of Vark
Quest Completion	Arugoo of the Stillpine
Reward	Choice of Stillpine Defender (Shield, 239 Armor, 4 Block, +1 STA), Stillpine Shocker (Wand, 8.6 DPS, +1 INT), or Arugoo's Crossbow of Destruction (Crossbow, 7.3 DPS, +1 AGI)

The Totem of Vark has much to say now that you fully grasp the language of the Stillpine. It shows you a war between the Stillpine and the Bristlelimb and charges you with freeing the captive Stillpine Furbolg. They are in cages throughout the camp and the keys are kept by the Bristlelimb Furbolg. Kill them one at a time and set a captive free as soon as you have a key and an opening. Using the cage with a *Bristlelimb Key* in your inventory will open the cage. The keys are automatically put into your key ring, so don't panic if they don't show up in your bag. When all captives are freed, use your Hearthstone for a quick return to Azure Watch. Arugoo is very happy to see you and hear of your deeds. He asks you to visit **Stillpine Hold** to the north.

Before you head out, speak with Exarch Menelaous and give him the *Faintly Glowing Shard.* While he believes he knows what caused the problem, the damage is done and the tainted must be killed before they can spread. He asks for a **Nightsaber Clean Up, Isle 2...**

Stillpine Hold	
Faction	Alliance
Location	Azure Watch
Quest Giver	Arugoo of the Stillpine
Quest Completion	Speak with High Chief Stillpine at Stillpine Hold
Reward	Chains to Searching Stillpine Hold

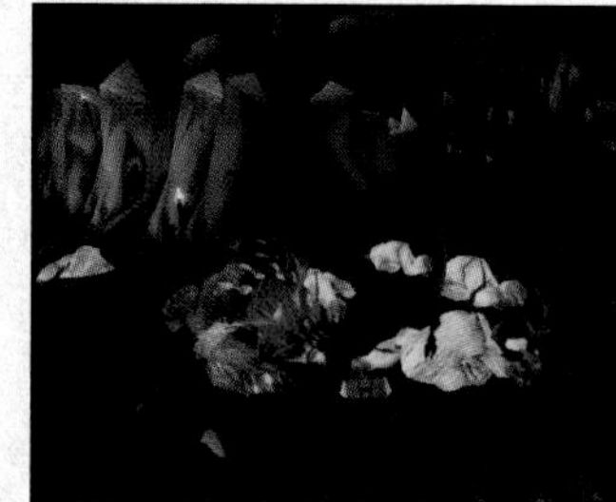

Nightsaber Clean Up, Isle 2...	
Faction	Alliance
Location	Azure Watch
Quest Giver	Exarch Menelaous
Quest Completion	Exarch Menelaous
Reward	Choice of Huntsman's Bracers (Leather Wrist, 18 Armor), Reinforced Mail Boots (Mail Feet, 56 Armor), or Slightly Worn Bracer (Cloth Wrist, 6 Armor)

While Stillpine Hold is your ultimate goal, there are many *Infected Nightsaber Runts* in the woods on the way. Avoid the road and kill the runts (and anything else that looks tasty) to complete your quest. It will be a while before you turn it in, but killing the targets while you travel makes it much faster.

Stillpine Hold

The Stillpine Furbolg have been forced out of their home by aggressive Owlkin. Warriors stand behind fortifications and corpses litter the entrance to the hold. Speak with High Chief Stillpine about **Searching Stillpine Hold**. He knows something's wrong, but none of his warriors are strong enough to get inside the hold.

Nearby, Stillpine the Younger and Kurz the Revelator also have work for you. **Chieftain Oomooroo** has taken command of the Wildkin and appears to be the mastermind behind the attacks. Kill him and the rest of the infected Owlkin would be easy prey. Kurz has had a disturbing vision of a monster deep within Stillpine Hold. No Furbolg is safe as long as **The Kurken is Lurkin'**. Fortify yourself and sell excess loot before descending into the darkness.

Searching Stillpine Hold	
Faction	Alliance
Location	Stillpine Hold
Quest Giver	High Chief Stillpine
Quest Completion	Blood Crystal
Reward	Chains to Blood Crystals

Chieftain Oomooroo	
Faction	Alliance
Location	Stillpine Hold
Quest Giver	Stillpine the Younger
Quest Completion	Stillpine the Younger
Reward	Sturdy Belt (Leather Waist, 29 Armor) or Fortified Wristguards (Mail Wrist, 45 Armor)

The Kurken is Lurkin'	
Faction	Alliance
Location	Stillpine Hold
Quest Giver	Kurz the Revelator
Quest Completion	Kurz the Revelator
Reward	Chains to The Kurken's Hide

The Owlkin move slowly and are vulnerable to long-ange attacks. If you have these, use them as the Owlkin have high health and do a good bit of damage. Avoid fighting more than one at a time and joining with others makes this area much easier. Take the right path up to the second level.

Fight your way along the left side of this level until you find the bridge going northwest. *Oomooroo* is just across the bridge and to the left. Pull him to the bridge to avoid getting more monsters than you can handle. At low health, Oomooroo enrages and inflicts even more damage. Use potions if you need to keep your health high and finish your opponent.

Continue killing the *Crazed Wildkin* along the path to the northeast until the path ends. Down a short cliff is a pool of water and the *Kurken*. Drop down away from the Kurken and prepare yourself. Like Oomooroo, the Kurken has high health and deals a good bit of damage. Pull and kill the two wandering Owlkin before you engage the Kurken. Having either of them attack your back during the fight with the *Kurken* is death.

With the area clear, rest to full health and mana. If you're alone, be ready to use Gift of the Naaru when your health falls to half. Pound away at the Kurken and be ready to use more potions. Even the Kurken will eventually fall and victory is yours.

Rest to full again before wading into the water and examining the *Blood Crystal*. It looks like a piece of the Exodar, but it's dissolving into the water supply. Two enemies attack when you get too close to the crystal. Kill them one at a time to minimize the damage you take. With an understanding about the **Blood Crystals**, take the only path up and out of the cave.

Blood Crystals	
Faction	Alliance
Location	Stillpine Hold
Quest Giver	Blood Crystal
Quest Completion	High Chief Stillpine
Reward	Experience

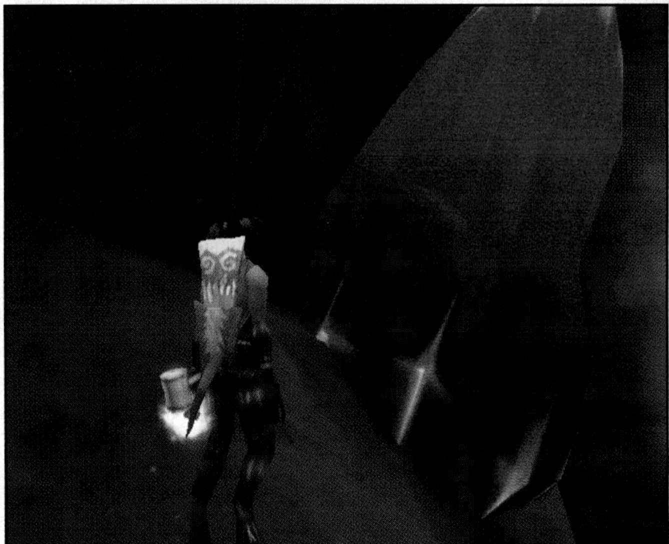

Don't waste time exiting the cave as several Owlkin will likely be right on your heels. A fight of five to one isn't in your favor, but the Stillpine are very close. Keep running and let the Furbolg stop the Owlkin. Turn in all your quests. Kurz gives you **The Kurken's Hide** as a reward for your valiant efforts. Take it to the west side of the camp and have a piece of armor made for you. High Chief Stillpine tells you to **Warn Your People**, but there is still much to do up here.

Collect **Beasts of the Apocalypse** and **Murlocs...Why Here? Why Now?** These quests involve hunting in the northern part of Azuremyst Isle and should be done before you head south again.

The Kurken's Hide	
Faction	Alliance
Location	Stillpine Hold
Quest Giver	Kurz the Revelator
Quest Completion	Moordo
Reward	Kurkenstoks (Cloth Feet, 13 Armor, +1 STA) or Kurken Hide Jerkin (Leather Chest, 55 Armor, +1 AGI)

Warn Your People	
Faction	Alliance
Location	Stillpine Hold
Quest Giver	High Chief Stillpine
Quest Completion	Exarch Menelaous
Reward	Experience

Beasts of the Apocalypse	
Faction	Alliance
Location	Stillpine Hold
Quest Giver	Moordo
Quest Completion	Moordo
Reward	Ravager Hide Leggings (Leather Legs, 48 Armor, +1 AGI) or Ravager Chitin Tunic (Mail Chest, 108 Armor, +1 STR) or Thick Ravager Belt (Cloth Waist, 11 Armor, +1 INT)

Murlocs...Why Here? Why Now?	
Faction	Alliance
Location	Stillpine Hold
Quest Giver	Gurf
Quest Completion	Gurf
Reward	Experience

When you've sold your loot and are ready to leave, head east toward the Menagerie Wreckage. The Ravagers in the area do a good bit of damage and will sense you from a good range. They also use a Rend ability that causes damage over time. Don't try to bandage while you are taking damage as the next tick will interrupt your bandaging and leave you with the recently bandaged debuff. Kill them one at a time and collect the *Ravager Hides*. Move north through the wreckage as you kill them.

When you've acquired enough hides, take the road north and west toward the Silting Shore. Skinners, Miners, and Herbalists should avoid walking on the road as resources in this area are plentiful.

The Silting Shore has several dangers for you. Murloc guard the *Sacks of Stillpine Grain*. Several of the Murloc used ranged attacks or spells. This makes them very difficult to pull away from others and battles with two or more are likely unless you're very careful. Use your longest range attack and then back up. As long as you stay out of their range, they will try to get closer. When they stray away from their friends run toward them and finish the job. You'll take damage before the fight even begins, but it's better than fighting an entire camp.

If these were the only dangers, the Silting Shore wouldn't be the place of woe that it is. Murgurgula is a large and particularly fierce Murloc. He wanders along the shore so keep an eye out for him. The other danger can't be seen until it's very close. Blood Elf Bandits sneak around the area ready to attack when you least expect it.

When you see either a bandit or Murgurgula, take the time to clear them out of the way before continuing your hunt of the Murloc. Murgurgula carries **Gurf's Dignity** while the bandit carries a **Blood Elf Communication**. Both of these items begin quests. The *Sacks of Stillpine Grain* can be found against the buildings in the Murloc camps or on the Murlocs themselves.

Gurf's Dignity	
Faction	Alliance
Location	Silting Shore
Quest Giver	Gurf's Dignity
Quest Completion	Gurf
Reward	Choice of Heavy Chain Leggings (Mail Legs, 101 Armor, +1 STR, +1 STA) or Savage Leggings (Leather Legs, 51 Armor, +1 AGI, +1 STA) or Fur Covered Robe (Cloth Chest, 21 Armor, +1 STA, +1 SPI)

Blood Elf Communication	
Faction	Alliance
Location	Silting Shore
Quest Giver	Blood Elf Communication
Quest Completion	Exarch Menelaous
Reward	Choice of Battle Worn Gauntlets (Mail Hands, 55 Armor), Battle Worn Gloves (Leather Hands, 28 Armor), or Battle Worn Handguards (Cloth Hands, 9 Armor).

Kill your way south along the Silting Shore until you have everything you need. Cut east through the woods to arrive at Stillpine Hold. Speak with everyone you need and sell any excess loot you have accumulated before following the road south to Azure Watch.

At first glance, there is only one person to speak with in Azure Watch: Exarch Menelaous. You have several quests to speak with him. Also, seek out your trainer; you've gained enough levels that you should be ready to train, and many classes gain a class-specific quest at level 10.

Becoming More Talented

Every level (starting at level 10), you gain a Talent Point. These can be used to increase your abilities or learn new ones. Open your talent window (defaulted to 'n'). There are three panels in the window. Look at each talent carefully before choosing as once you spend your points, it takes gold to relearn them. There is more about the benefits of each talent in the Class section.

Menelaous believes you are **Coming of Age**. He asks you to travel to the Exodar and speak with the pack handler. If your inventory has been filling up recently, take the time to buy a bag or two from the General Goods merchant. While the cost seems substantial at first, it will be made up quickly by selling the extra loot you bring back each time.

Coming of Age	
Faction	Alliance
Location	Azure Watch
Quest Giver	Exarch Menelaous
Quest Completion	Torallius the Pack Handler
Reward	Experience

THE EXODAR MAP LEGEND

The Exodar Legend

	Location / NPC	Role / Level
A	**Flightpoint**	
	Stephanos	Hippogryph Master
	Exodar Peacekeeper	65
	Miglik Blotstrom	Arena Master
B	**Mailbox**	
	Exodar Peacekeeper	65
	Exodar Proselyte	30
	Mailbox	
C	**Elekk Herd**	
	Torallius the Pack Handler	Quest Giver
	Exodar Peacekeeper	65
	Elekk	10
D	**Inn**	
	Caregiver Breel	Innkeeper
	Arthaid	Stable Master
	Mailbox	
E	**Cooking**	
	Mumman	Cook
	Phea	Cooking Supplier
F	**Jewelcrafting**	
	Farii	Master Jewelcrafter
	Arred	Jewelcrafting Supplier
	Padaar	Expert Jewelcrafter
	ElaandoArtisan Jewelcrafter	
	Driaan	Journeyman Jewelcrafter
G	**First Aid**	
	Nus	First Aid Trainer
	Duumehi	
	Ereuso	
H	**Fishing**	
	Erett	Fishing Trainer
	Dekin	Fishing Supplier
I	**Enchanting**	
	Kudrii	Journeyman Enchanter
	Egomis	Enchanting Supplier
	NahoggExpert Enchanter	
J	**General Goods**	
	Onnis	General Goods Vendor
	Cuzi	Bag Vendor
K	**Auction House**	
	Eoch	Auctioneer
	Iressa	Auctioneer
	Fanin	Auctioneer
	Mailbox	
L	**Anchorites Sanctum**	
	Fallat	Priest Trainer
	Izmir	Priest Trainer
	Caedmos	Priest Trainer
M	**Alchemy & Herbalism**	
	Cemmorhan	Herbalist
	Deriz	Journeyman Alchemist
	Lucc	Expert Alchemist
	Altaa	Alchemy Supplier
N	**Vindicator's Sanctum**	
	Jol	Paladin Trainer
	Baatun	Paladin Trainer
	Kavaan	Paladin Trainer
O	**Hall of Mystics**	
	Oss	Wand Vendor
	Lunaraa	Portal Trainer
	Bati	Mage Trainer
	Harnan	Mage Trainer
	Edirah	Mage Trainer
	Musal	Arcane Goods Vendor
P	**Guild Master & Tabards**	
	Issca	Tabard Vendor
	Funaam	Guild Master
Q	**Hunters' Sanctum**	
	Vord	Hunter Trainer
	Deremiis	Hunter Trainer
	Killac	Hunter Trainer
	Muhaa	Gunsmith
	Ganaar	Pet Trainer
	Avelii	Bowyer
R	**Ring of Arms**	
	Kazi	Warrior Trainer
	Behomat	Warrior Trainer
	Ahonan	Warrior Trainer
	Handiir	Weapon Master (Dagger)
	Fingin	Poison Supplier
S	**Engineering**	
	Ghermas	Journeyman Engineer
	Feera	Engineering Supplier
	Ockil	Expert Engineer
T	**Mining & Smithing**	
	Muaat	Mining Trainer
	Merran	Mining Supplies
	Arras	Blacksmithing Supplier
	Miall	Expert Blacksmith
	Edrem	Journeyman Blacksmith
	Forge	
	Anvil	
U	**Plate Armor & Shields**	
	Yil	Mail Armor Merchant (Top Floor)
	Gotaan	Plate Armor Merchant
	Treall	Shield Merchant
V	**Bladed Weapons**	
	Mahri	Leather Armor Merchant (Top Floor)
	Gornii	Cloth Armor Merchant (Top Floor)
	Ven	Blade Vendor
W	**Leatherworking & Skinning**	
	Remere	Skinner
	Haferet	Leatherworking Supplier
	Akham	Expert Leatherworker
	Feruul	Journeyman Leatherworker
X	**Tailoring**	
	Kayaart	Journeyman Tailor
	Neii	Tailoring Supplier
	Refik	Expert Tailor
1	**Primary Entrance**	
2	**Sulaa**	**Shaman Trainer**
3	**Bildine**	**Reagent Vendor**
4	**Hobahken**	**Shaman Trainer**
5	**Foreman Dunaer**	
6	**Farseer Nobundo**	**Shaman Trainer**
7	**Gurrag**	**Shaman Trainer**
8	**Nurguni**	**Tradesman**
9	**Jihi**	**Warsong Gulch Battlemaster**
10	**Mahul**	**Alterac Valley Battlemaster**
11	**Tolo**	**Arathi Basin Battlemaster**
12	**Prophet Velen**	**Quest Giver**
13	**Back Exit**	
14	**Ellomin**	**Blunt Weapon Merchant**
15	**O'ros**	

What's left of the Exodar stands as testament to the strength of the Draenei. Not even crashing into a planet can stop them!

It's *So* Big!

Ironforge is a rather impressive town, but its dwarfed compared with the Exodar. Exploring all of it would take quite a bit of effort, but you're not the first to get lost in this city. The guards are accustomed to newcomers needing directions and they give them freely. To find things in a hurry, ask a guard and they will plot it on your minimap.

There are a great many people you may want to talk with in the Exodar. Every craft and professions is represented as is every class. Take the time to choose your professions (if you haven't already) and set your Hearthstone to the inn here.

Speak with Torallius the Pack Handler outside, but don't get **Elekks are Serious Business** just yet. You have other business to attend to. Speak with Hippogryph Master Stephanos on your way out to collect the flight point (this will be important later). Take the road south and west from the Exodar to the docks. To the south is Silvermyst Isle and your destination. Follow the coastline and swim to the island.

Hiding near a log is Magwin. She's a younger elf and fairly frightened. Speak with her. Her story is **A Cry for Help** that can't be ignored.

A Cry For Help	
Faction	Alliance
Location	Silvermyst Isle
Quest Giver	Magwin
Quest Completion	Cowlen
Reward	Cowlen's Bracer's of Kinship (Cloth Wrist, 8 Armor, + 1 STA)

As soon as you accept the quest, Magwin will start walking south. This is an escort quest. You have to follow Magwin and keep her safe from harm until she reaches her destination. Don't stray too far from her and don't worry about being attacked. She'll stop to help you fight but continue on her journey as soon as the immediate threat is gone.

Cowlen is her final goal and he is very relieved to see his daughter. Get your reward from him and listen to his story. **All that Remains** now is to avenge the death of his wife and bring her remains back to him.

All That Remains	
Faction	Alliance
Location	Silvermyst Isle
Quest Giver	Cowlen
Quest Completion	Cowlen
Reward	Experience

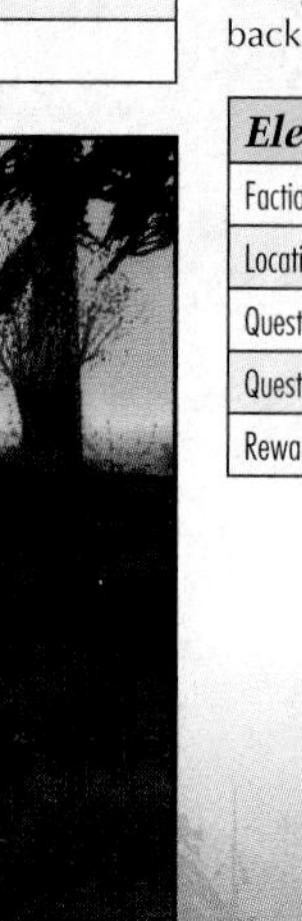

Head back into the Moonwing Den and begin slaying the Owlkin. The *Remains of Cowlen's Family* can be dropped by any of the beasts, so keep killing until you have them. With the deed done, return to Cowlen for your reward before using your Hearthstone to return to the Exodar.

Now it's time to take the Elekk ride to Kessel's Crossing. Speak with Torallius and accept **Elekks are Serious Business**. You can't control the Elekk in the least, so just sit back and enjoy the ride.

Elekks are Serious Business	
Faction	Alliance
Location	The Exodar
Quest Giver	Torallius the Pack Handler
Quest Completion	Vorkhan the Elekk Herder
Reward	Experience

BLOODMYST ISLE MAP LEGEND

Bloodmyst Isle Legend

A Kessel's Landing

	Name	Info
	Aonar	Quest Giver
	Vorkhan the Elekk Herder	Quest Giver
	Kessel Elekk Lord	Quest Giver

B Bloodmyst Isle South

	Name	Info
	Brown Bear	9
	Bloodmyst Hatchling	10-11
	Blue Flutterer	9-10
	Sand Pear	Quest Item

C Bristlelimb Enclave

	Name	Info
	Princess Stillpine	Quest Giver
•	Bristlelimb Warrior	10-11
•	Bristlelimb Shaman	10-11
•	High Chief Bristlelimb	13 Drops Quest Item

D Wrathscale Lair

	Name	Info
•	Wrathscale Shorestalker	12-13
•	Wrathscale Screamer	12-13
•	Lord Xiz	13 Quest Target

E Bloodcurse Isle

	Name	Info
•	Bloodcursed Naga	15-16

F Wyrmscar Island

	Name	Info
	Prince Toreth	Quest Giver
•	Veridian Broodling	17-18
•	Veridian Whelp	16-17

G Talon Stand

	Name	Info
•	Veridian Broodling	17-18
•	Veridian Whelp	16-17
•	Razormaw	20 Elite Quest Target

H Bloodcursed Reef

	Name	Info
	Captain Edward Hanes	Quest Giver
•	Bloodcursed Naga	15-16
•	Bloodcursed Voyager	16-17

I Ragefeather Ridge

	Name	Info
•	Irradiated Wildkin	13-15
•	Infected Wildkin	13-14
•	Contaminated Wildkin	14-15

J Bloodmyst Isle Central

	Name	Info
•	Mutated Lasher	11-12
•	Corrupted Treant	11-13
•	Grizzled Brown Bear	12-13
	Blood Mushroom	Quest Item
	Aquatic Stinkhorn	Quest Item

K Ruins of Loreth'Aran

	Name	Info
•	Wrathscale Sorceress	13-14
•	Wrathscale Marauder	13-14
	Draenei Cartographer	Quest Giver
	Ruinous Polyspore	Quest Item

L Nazzivian

	Name	Info
•	Nazzivus Felsworn	14
•	Nazzivus Satyr	12
•	Nazzivus Rogue	13-14
•	Tzerak	14
	Fel Cone Fungus	Quest Item
	Nazzivus Monument Glyph	Quest Item

M Blacksilt Shore

	Name	Info
•	Blacksilt Forager	11-12
•	Blacksilt Tidecaller	11-12
•	Blacksilt Scout	12-13

N Bloodmyst Isle West

	Name	Info
•	Enraged Ravager	17
•	Corrupted Stomper	16-17
•	Mutated Tangler	17-18

O The Cryo-Core

	Name	Info
	Galaen's Corpse	Quest Giver
	Galaen's Journal	Quest Giver
•	Sunhawk Reclaimer	16-17

P Bloodmyst Isle North

	Name	Info
•	Mutated Constrictor	14-15
•	Elder Brown Bear	15-16
•	Royal Blue Flutterer	16

Q Bladewood

	Name	Info
•	Sunhawk Spy	13-14

R The Warp Piston

	Name	Info
•	Void Anomaly	15-16

S Coastline

	Name	Info
•	Blacksilt Shorestriker	15-16
•	Blacksilt Warrior	16-17
•	Blacksilt Seer	16-17
	Clopper Wizbang	Quest Giver
	Clopper's Equipment	Quest Item

T Bloodmyst Isle Waterfall

	Name	Info
•	Mutated Constrictor	14-15
•	Elder Brown Bear	15-16
•	Royal Blue Flutterer	16
•	Deathclaw Quest Target	17

U Axxarien

	Name	Info
•	Axxarien Shadowstalker	15-16
•	Axxarien Hellcaller	15-17
•	Axxarien Trickster	16
	Zevrax	18 Quest Target
	Corrupted Crystal	Quest Item

V Vindicator's Rest

	Name	Info
	Scout Loryi	Quest Giver
	Scout Jorli	Quest Giver
	Demolitionist Legoso	Quest Giver
	Vindicator Corin	Quest Giver

W Amberweb Pass

	Name	Info
•	Myst Spinner	16-17
•	Myst Leecher	17-18
•	Webbed Creature	15
•	Zarakh	19 Quest Target

X Sunhawk Camps

	Name	Info
•	Sunhawk Pyromancer	17-18
•	Sunhawk Defender	16-17
•	Matis the Cruel	18 Elite Quest Target

Y The Portal

	Name	Info
•	Sunhawk Pyromancer	17-18
•	Sunhawk Defender	16-17
•	Void Critter	4
•	Void Anomaly	3
•	Sunhawk Portal Controller	17-18 Elite

Z The Vector Coil

	Name	Info
•	Sunhawk Agent	18-19 Elite
•	Sunhawk Saboteur	17-18 Elite
•	Sironas	20 Elite Quest Target

AA Blood Watch

	Name	Info
	Morae	Herbalism Trainer
	Achelus	Quest Giver
	Beega	Bowyer
	Fazu	Tradesman
	Harbinger Mikolaas	Quest Giver
	Exarch Admetius	Quest Giver
	Interrogator Elysia	Quest Giver
	Anchorite Paetheus	Quest Giver
	Messenger Hermesius	Quest Giver
	Prospector Nachlan	Quest Giver
	Vindicator Boros	Quest Giver
	Vindicator Aesom	Quest Giver
	Vindicator Kuros	Quest Giver
	Stillpine Ambassador Frasaboo	Quest Target
	Loando	Hippogryph Master
	Jessera of Mac'Aree	Quest Giver
	Tracker Lyceon	Quest Giver
	Vindicator Aalesia	Quest Giver
	Meriaad	General Goods
	Astur	Stable Master
	Caregiver Topher Loaal	Innkeeper
	Wanted Poster	Quest Giver
	Mailbox	
	Forge	
	Anvil	
	Blade of Argus	14
	Blood Watch Peacekeeper	31

1 Tel'athion's Camp

WALKTHROUGH FOR BLOODMYST ISLE

While the bulk of the Exodar landed on Azuremyst Isle, many of the more toxic systems landed on what is now Bloodmyst Isle. The Draenei have had the unfortunate experience of watching the land become corrupted before their very eyes.

Kessel's Crossing

There isn't much to Kessel's Crossing. It's just a few Draenei, some Elekk, and a lot of work to do. Speak with Kessel first and grab **The Kessel Run**. This is a timed quest, so don't delay. Begin heading south back into Azuremyst Isle as soon as you mount the Elekk.

The Kessel Run	
Faction	Alliance
Location	Kessel's Crossing
Quest Giver	Kessel
Quest Completion	Kessel
Reward	Chains to Declaration of Power

Take the west (right) fork in the road and swing around the mountains to Stillpine Hold. The Elekk allows you to move at incredible speeds. Avoid running right through enemies and they'll never be able to catch you. Warn High Chief Stillpine of the coming invasion and take the road south.

Quick stops at Azure Watch and Odesyus' Landing complete the quest, but you're on the wrong side of the island now! You have plenty of time before you lose the help of the Elekk, so cruise back to Kessel in style.

Kessel is pleased with your performance and gives you a more challenging task. The Naga have been getting uppity and Kessel wants you to make a **Declaration of Power** to show them who's the boss. Grab **Alien Predators** and **A Favorite Treat** before you head out.

Declaration of Power	
Faction	Alliance
Location	Kessel's Crossing
Quest Giver	Kessel
Quest Completion	Kessel
Reward	Choice of Kessel's Cinch Wrap (Cloth Waist, 16 Armor, +2 STA, +2 INT), Kessel's Sweat Stained Elekk Leash (Leather Waist, 39 Armor, +3 STA), and Kessel's Sturdy Riding Handle (Mail Waist, 81 Armor, +3 STA)

A Favorite Treat	
Faction	Alliance
Location	Kessel's Crossing
Quest Giver	Aonar
Quest Completion	Aonar
Reward	Choice of Elekk Handler's Leathers (Leather Chest, 58 Armor, +1 AGI, +1 STA), Farmhand's Vest (Cloth Chest, 21 Armor, +1 STA, +1 INT), or Elekk Rider's Mail (Mail Chest, 115 Armor, +1 STR, +1 STA) and 20 Sand Pear Pie (Use Restores 243 health over 21 sec. Must remain seated while eating.)

Alien Predators	
Faction	Alliance
Location	Kessel's Crossing
Quest Giver	Aonar
Quest Completion	Aonar
Reward	Choice of 2 Stone Sledgehammer (Two-hand Mace, 7.7 DPS, +1 STR, +1 STA) or Elekk Handler's Blade (Main-hand Sword, 6.0 DPS, +1 STR) or Old Elekk Prod (One-hand Mace, 5.8 DPS, +1 STA) or Surplus Bastard Sword (Two-hand Sword, 7.8 DPS, +1 STR, +1 AGI)

Head into the woods to the east. The *Sand Pears* can be found on the ground near the trees, while the *Bloodmyst Hatchlings* can be found trying to kill you. All the enemies in this area are aggressive. This isn't new, but there is one difference from previous areas: the Bloodmyst Hatchlings will run away in fear when they get low in health. They need to be killed before they find help, so keep a damaging attack held in reserve to finish them off.

An alternative is using movement-impairing abilities such as Hamstring or Frost Bolt. These keep the enemy from running very far before you finish the job.

The appearance of Furbolg between the trees heralds a change in plans. You aren't done with any of your quests and don't have one for the Furbolg. In the center of the easternmost camp stands a large cage with Princess Stillpine in it. She has a quest mark above her head, so kill your way to her.

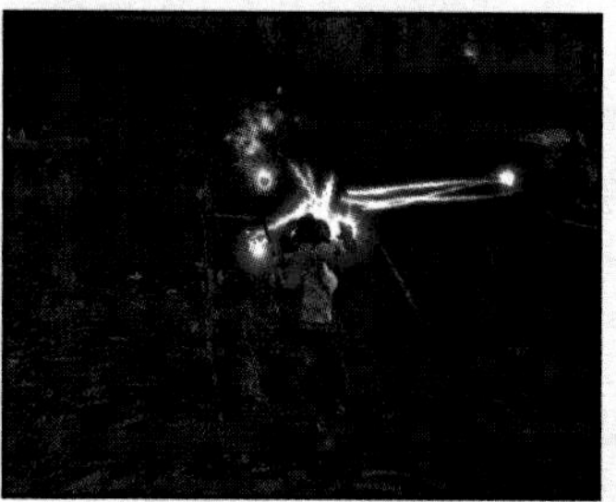

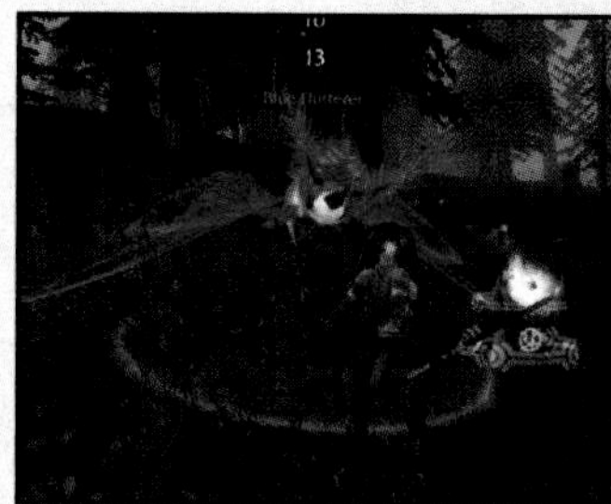

These Furbolg are stronger than most of the enemies you've fought before. They hit harder and take more damage to bring down. Use ranged attacks against the enemies without mana (they have to close the distance before they can hurt you) and have abilities that interrupt casting ready for the shamans.

The Bristlelimb Shamans also cast a Searing Totem. This can't be interrupted and the totem will use fire attacks against you constantly. Finish the shaman and then destroy the totem. Don't destroy the totem first as the shaman can cast another one instantly.

Saving Princess Stillpine is easier said than done. Her cage is locked and only *High Chief Bristlelimb's Key* can open it. The chief is a coward and won't show his face unless absolutely necessary. Kill the Furbolg on your way northeast. They won't be killing the princess any time soon and you have other things to take care of.

Saving Princess Stillpine	
Faction	Alliance
Location	Bristlelimb Enclave
Quest Giver	Princess Stillpine
Quest Completion	Ambassador Frasaboo at Blood Watch
Reward	Choice of Stillpine Shocker (Wand, 9.4 DPS) or The Thumper (Main-hand Mace, 6.9 DPS, +1 STR)

Head to the northeast corner of this smaller island. Naga patrol around a small hill topped with ruins. Watch the patrols and pull single targets when the patrols are away. Once you have a clear spot, pull the patrols to get them out of the way so you can start making your way to the ramp on the west side.

The Naga are your level or higher and are quite damaging. Be ready to rest more often as you shouldn't start a fight with less than 75% health and never fight two at once. If the fighting is more difficult that you want to engage in, take some time to kill the Furbolg and other life around Kessel's Crossing. A level and gear upgrades can make the difference.

Make your way to the top of the ramp and clear the immediate area. *Lord Xiz* patrols inside the ruins. Watch his movement patterns and pull any Naga near him. You don't want to fight him with another enemy. If you pull both, turn and run for it. Fighting two is certain death. Run and return to try again.

When you have the area clear of nearby enemies, pull Lord Xiz. Have potions and Gift of the Naaru ready. He hits like an Elekk and is almost as pretty. If you cleared the area quickly, you can snare him and retreat to heal or use ranged attacks. Be careful about retreating into other enemies, though.

Once he's dead, stand over his corpse and plant the banner in his body. With this quest done, descend and return to the woods. Watch for *Bloodmyst Hatchlings* and *Sand Pears* to finish those quests.

Fight your way into the northern Furbolg camp. Continue killing the Furbolg until *High Chief Bristlelimb* yells "Face the wrath of Bristlelimb!" This will show up as red text (unless you've altered your interface) in the chat window. This signals the spawn of High Chief Bristlelimb in the northern camp.

Take the time to clear some of the Furbolg from around him before you pull him. Have a potion ready as he also hits fairly hard, but he isn't as dangerous as Lord Xiz. Pry the *High Chief's Key* from his dead hands and return to Princess Stillpine.

Release the princess and make your way back to Kessel's Crossing. If you haven't finished **A Favorite Treat** and **Alien Predators**, linger in the woods a bit longer before you head in.

Kessel is quite pleased with your progress and asks you to **Report to Exarch Admetius**. There isn't anything left for you at Kessel's Crossing. Follow the road north to Blood Watch and the front lines of the restoration effort.

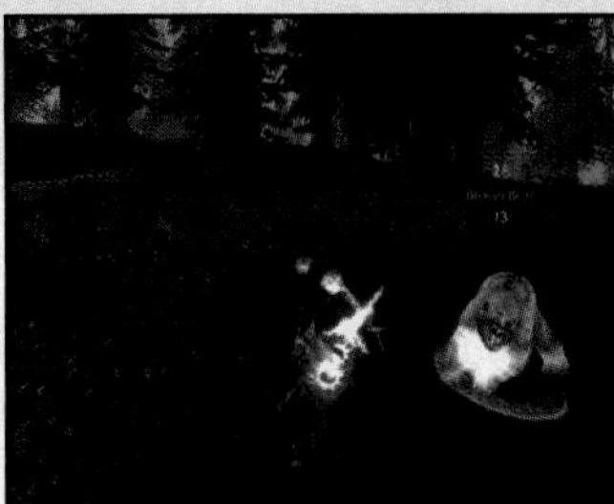

Report to Exarch Admetius	
Faction	Alliance
Location	Kessel's Crossing
Quest Giver	Kessel
Quest Completion	Exarch Admetius
Reward	Experience

Blood Watch

There are quite a few people in Blood Watch and many of them want to speak with you. Ignore most of them for now and turn in your quest to Exarch Admetius. Speak with Caregiver Topher Loaal about **Beds, Bandages, and Beyond**. This is a quest chain that shows you how to using the hippogryphs for faster travel.

Speak with Laando at the northeast part of camp on the highest ride. He'll explain about transport **On the Wings of a Hippogryph**. With the screen open, select the landing you want to be taken to (in this case, the Exodar). The hippogryph takes you to your destination faster than an Elekk.

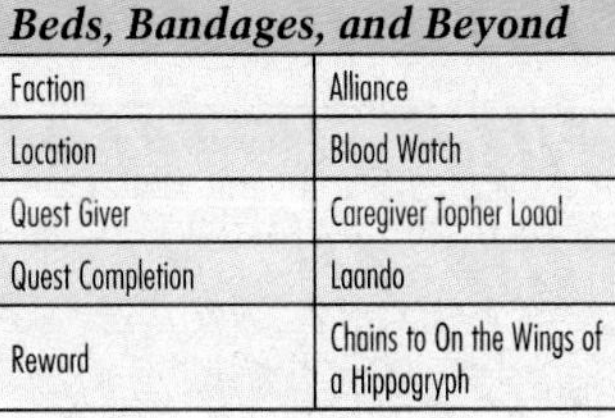

Beds, Bandages, and Beyond	
Faction	Alliance
Location	Blood Watch
Quest Giver	Caregiver Topher Loaal
Quest Completion	Laando
Reward	Chains to On the Wings of a Hippogryph

On the Wings of a Hippogryph	
Faction	Alliance
Location	Blood Watch
Quest Giver	Laando
Quest Completion	Nurguni
Reward	Chains to Hippogryph Master Stephanos

Make a quick trip into the Exodar to speak with Nurguni and train. Nurguni takes the supply order and gives you everything that can fit on a hippogryph. She'll send the heavier items by wagon, but sends you to **Hippogryph Master Stephanos**.

Hippogryph Master Stephanos	
Faction	Alliance
Location	The Exodar
Quest Giver	Nurguni
Quest Completion	Stephanos
Reward	Chains to Return to Topher Loaal

Return to Topher Loaal	
Faction	Alliance
Location	The Exodar
Quest Giver	Stephanos
Quest Completion	Caregiver Topher Loaal
Reward	Experience

After your **Return to Topher Loaal**, there is much to do in Blood Watch. Reset your Hearthstone by speaking with Topher. Move around and collect all the quests. This is the largest group of quests you've gotten at once. There is plenty to do and plenty of time to do it in.

There are a few quests that can be done in town. **What Argus Means to Me** sends you to speak with Vindicator Boros. With all the killing you've already done, you may have the **Irradiated Crystal Shards** Tracker Lyceon is asking for.

What Argus Means to Me	
Faction	Alliance
Location	Blood Watch
Quest Giver	Exarch Admetius
Quest Completion	Vindicator Boros
Reward	Chains to Blood Watch

Irradiated Crystal Shards	
Faction	Alliance
Location	Blood Watch
Quest Giver	Tracker Lyceon
Quest Completion	Tracker Lyceon
Reward	Choice of Crystal of Vitality (Use Increases Stamina by 5. Lasts 30 mins.) or Crystal of Insight (Use Increases Intellect by 5. Lasts 30 mins.) or Crystal of Ferocity (Use Increases Attack Power by 10. Lasts 30 mins.)

Turning in **Irradiated Crystal Shards** causes a blue "?" to appear above Tracker Lyceon. This shows he has a repeatable quest available. Speak with him again and **More Irradiated Crystal Shards** is an option you can choose, but it doesn't let you accept the quest. From now on, any time you bring him 10 *Irradiated Crystal Shards*, he will give you the reward for the quest. He doesn't give you money or experience after the first time, but the buffs from the items are quite nice.

South of Blood Watch

Check the General Goods merchant and see if you can afford another bag if you don't have all slots used. The questing in Bloodmyst will fill your bags quickly, and it's time to head out. The first quests you'll be doing are **Learning from the Crystals**, **Victims of Corruption**, **Catch and Release**, **Mac'Aree Mushroom Menagerie**, and **Know Thine Enemy**.

Learning from the Crystals	
Faction	Alliance
Location	Blood Watch
Quest Giver	Harbinger Mikolaas
Quest Completion	Harbinger Mikolaas
Reward	Choice of Crystal-Flecked Pants (Cloth Legs, 20 Armor, +2 INT) or Crystal-Studded Legguards (Mail Legs, 107 Armor, +1 STR, +1 STA), or Shard-Covered Leggings (Leather Legs, 54 Armor, +2 AGI)

Victims of Corruption	
Faction	Alliance
Location	Blood Watch
Quest Giver	Morae
Quest Completion	Morae
Reward	Experience

Catch and Release	
Faction	Alliance
Location	Blood Watch
Quest Giver	Morae
Quest Completion	Morae
Reward	Choice of Protective Field Gloves (Mail Hands, 72 Armor, +1 STA) or Researcher's Gloves (Leather Hands, 39 Armor) or Scholar's Gloves (Cloth Hands, 15 Armor, +1 INT, +1 SPI)

Mac'Aree Mushroom Menagerie	
Faction	Alliance
Location	Blood Watch
Quest Giver	Jessera of Mac'Aree
Quest Completion	Jessera of Mac'Aree
Reward	Choice of Jessera's Fungus Lined Cuffs (Cloth Wrist, 11 Armor, +1 INT) or Jessera's Fungus Lined Bands (Leather Wrist, 28 Armor, +1 STA) or Jessera's Fungus Lined Bracers (Mail Wrist, 57 Armor, +1 STA)

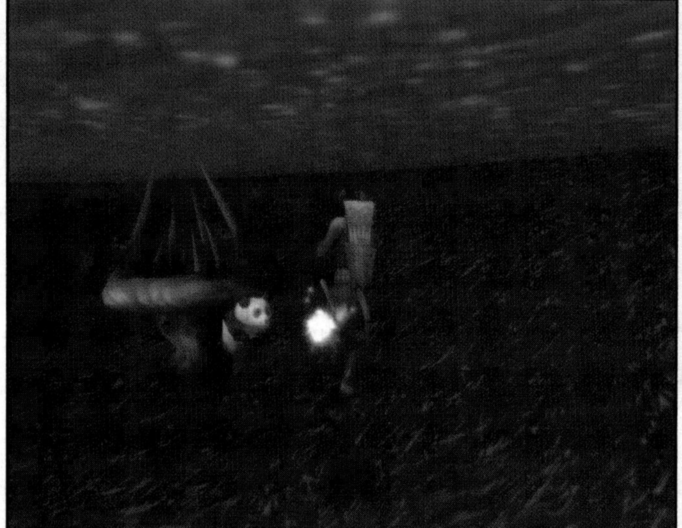

Know Thine Enemy	
Faction	Alliance
Location	Blood Watch
Quest Giver	Vindicator Aalesia
Quest Completion	Vindicator Aalesia
Reward	Chains to Containing the Threat

Strike out in a southerly direction. Don't bother following the road as you have quests for nearly every enemy out here but take care moving about as the enemies wander a great deal and are aggressive. Even when resting or fighting, watch for other enemies that are getting too close. Move your fight away from potential adds if necessary.

The Corrupted Treants wander this area are drop the *Crystallized Bark* you need. Watch for them as you cut your way toward the river. The *Blood Mushroom* also grows in this area. Its glowing top makes it easier to see by those looking. Crossing the river is a painless affair. The red water won't hurt you, but the *Aquatic Stinkhorn* might draw your attention.

Look for the wreckage patrolled by Bloodmyst Hatchlings. You've fought these before. Make your way to the red crystal at the center of the wreckage and use your *Crystal Mining Pick* to get the sample you need.

The next quest on the list is a bit different. Make your way to Blacksilt Shore. The scouts you need are purple in color, but you don't need to kill them; in fact, you can't kill them if you want to complete the quest. Put the *Murloc Tagger* on a quick-bar slot and kill the other murlocs to clear a path to the scouts.

When you're in range of the *Blacksilt Scout*, use the *Murloc Tagger*. The scout will walk around a moment longer before vanishing. Continue along the shoreline tagging scouts and killing everything else until the quest is complete. If there aren't any scouts (or not enough), kill everything in the area and wait a short while. This will force some scouts to respawn.

Your next target is Nazzivian. Approach the northern most portion of Nazzivian from the west side. This should be a short walk as you've been following the coastline looking for murlocs. Keep an eye out for the *Fel Cone Fungus* that grows around the satyrs tainted energies. It's harder to see than the other mushrooms as it's dull in color and short.

Fight your way into the ruins. The satyrs won't run, but some use ranged spells, and all of them are mean. They will attack you in groups if you're careless in your pulling. Watch your text window as you fight your way toward the monument. If you see Tzerak say anything, then watch your back. This demon is tougher than the satyr, travels with friends, and wanders the length of the camp.

Grab the *Nazzivus Monument Glyph* and use your Hearthstone to get back to Blood Watch in a hurry. Don't worry if you haven't completed **Victims of Corruption** or **Mac'Aree Mushroom Menagerie**. There will be more time in the future.

West of Blood Watch

Take care of your in-town errands (selling, repairing, and turning in quests). Make sure to grab **Blood Watch** and **The Second Sample** before leaving camp to the west.

The Second Sample	
Faction	Alliance
Location	Blood Watch
Quest Giver	Harbinger Mikolaas
Quest Completion	Harbinger Mikolaas
Reward	Leads to The Final Sample

Blood Watch	
Faction	Alliance
Location	Blood Watch
Quest Giver	Vindicator Boros
Quest Completion	Vindicator Boros
Reward	Choice of Fist of Argus (Main-hand Mace, 8.2 DPS, +1 STA, +1 INT) or Blade of Argus (Main-hand Sword, 8.1 DPS, +1 AGI, +1 STA) or Hand of Argus Crossbow (Crossbow, 9.1 DPS, +1 AGI, +1 STA)

Watch for *Corrupted Treats* as you make your way toward Bladewood. The *Sunhawk Spies* won't appreciate your approach, so be ready for any hiding near the trees or in the bushes. They have Demoralizing Shout, which reduces attack power, and Mark of the Sunhawk, which increases the damage you take. Use ranged attacks when possible as they have no way of countering these. Casters should be wary as the spies can also interrupt spellcasts. Use spells with shorter cast times to avoid this.

Make your way to the westernmost of the three camps. At the center of the magical device is a short red crystal. Use your *Crystal Mining Pick* on this to obtain the crystal sample. You have to be very close to get the sample, so clear the camp before approaching. Finish killing Sunhawk Spies on your way back to Blood Watch. Not all quest groups are long and involved.

East of Blood Watch

Turn in your quests, repair your gear, sell your excess loot, and pick up any quests you didn't have before. The next quests are **Victims of Corruption**, **Mac'Aree Mushroom Menagerie**, and **The Missing Survey Team**.

The Missing Survey Team	
Faction	Alliance
Location	Blood Watch
Quest Giver	Harbinger Mikolaas
Quest Completion	Draenei Cartographer
Reward	Chains to Salvaging the Data

Exit Blood Watch to the east and pick off a few more treants (if you haven't finished the quest) on your way to the Ruins of Loreth'Aman. The Naga patrol the ruins. Watch the patrols to avoid fighting more than one at a time. The female Naga are casters and use Frost Bolt, while the males are melee opponents. Don't try to run from the casters as the movement-slowing ability of Frost Bolt will spell your doom.

Climb the hill to the ruins and find what's left of the survey team. The Draenei Cartographer is quite dead, but there is still hope. **Salvaging the Data** will keep them from dying in vain. Kill the Naga in the area until you find the *Survey Data Crystal* and keep an eye out for the *Ruinous Polyspore* while you're here. As its name implies, it grows near the ruins.

Salvaging the Data	
Faction	Alliance
Location	Ruins of Loreth'Aran
Quest Giver	Draenei Cartographer
Quest Completion	Harbinger Mikolaas
Reward	Surveyor's Mantle (Cloak, 12 Armor, +1 STA)

With three quests done, make your way back to Blood Watch and prepare for a much longer quest group. Repair, sell anything you can, and stock up on recover items if you need them.

Northern Bloodmyst

Before heading out, take a trip to the Exodar to train. When you return to Blood Watch, check your quest log. Make sure you have **WANTED: Deathclaw**, **Culling the Aggression**, **Constrictor Vines**, **The Bear Necessities**, **The Final Sample**, **Containing the Threat**, and **Explorers' League, Is That Something for Gnomes?**

WANTED: Deathclaw	
Faction	Alliance
Location	Blood Watch
Quest Giver	Wanted Poster
Quest Completion	Tracker Lyceon
Reward	Choice of Carved Crystalline Orb (Off-hand, +2 STA, +2 INT) or Peacekeeper's Buckler (Shield, 361 Armor, 6 Block, +2 STR, +2 STA)

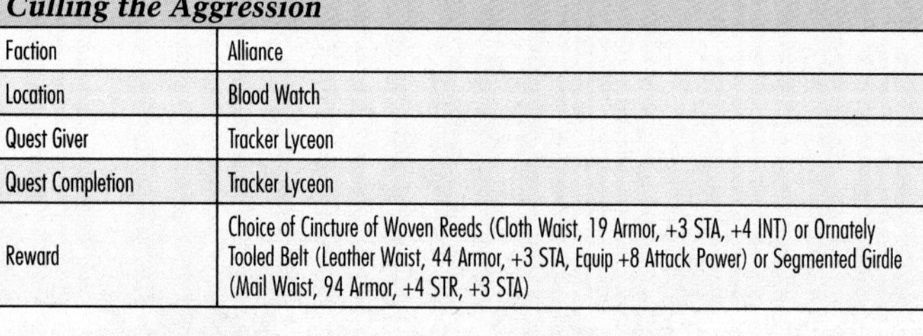

Culling the Aggression	
Faction	Alliance
Location	Blood Watch
Quest Giver	Tracker Lyceon
Quest Completion	Tracker Lyceon
Reward	Choice of Cincture of Woven Reeds (Cloth Waist, 19 Armor, +3 STA, +4 INT) or Ornately Tooled Belt (Leather Waist, 44 Armor, +3 STA, Equip +8 Attack Power) or Segmented Girdle (Mail Waist, 94 Armor, +4 STR, +3 STA)

Constrictor Vines	
Faction	Alliance
Location	Blood Watch
Quest Giver	Tracker Lyceon
Quest Completion	Tracker Lyceon
Reward	Experience

The Bear Necessities	
Faction	Alliance
Location	Blood Watch
Quest Giver	Tracker Lyceon
Quest Completion	Tracker Lyceon
Reward	Experience

The Final Sample	
Faction	Alliance
Location	Blood Watch
Quest Giver	Harbinger Mikolaas
Quest Completion	Harbinger Mikolaas
Reward	Experience

Containing the Threat	
Faction	Alliance
Location	Blood Watch
Quest Giver	Vindicator Aalesia
Quest Completion	Vindicator Aalesia
Reward	Choice of Huntsman's Crossbow (Crossbow, 9.5 DPS, +1 AGI) or Lightspark (Wand, 12.8 DPS, +1 INT)

Explorers' League, Is That Something for Gnomes?	
Faction	Alliance
Location	Blood Watch
Quest Giver	Prospector Nachlan
Quest Completion	Clopper Wizbang
Reward	Experience

This seems like quite a bit...and it is! Follow the road north out of Blood Watch. When the road splits, follow the northern fork toward the Warp Piston. Wander off the left side of the road and start killing the Elder Brown Bears for the *Elder Brown Bear Flanks*, the Mutated Constrictors for the *Thorny Constrictor Vines*, and the *Royal Blue Flutterers* for being there.

The Mutated Constrictors can cast Entangling Roots and can't be run from. The Elder Brown Bears and Royal Blue Flutterers both do decent melee damage and are best fought at range when possible. All the enemies in this area are aggressive and move around a great deal. Keep watch around you at all times and be ready to move a fight if more enemies are wandering too close.

Continue moving north until you reach The Coastline. Keep killing everything as you move west. On the beach is a large turtle skeleton. As you get closer to it, make your way down to the beach. Kill the murlocs that are wandering about the skeleton and peak inside to find *Clopper Wizbang*.

The crazy little man has been living inside the turtle shell! He'll buy excess loot from you and he has a couple quests for you. Offer to help him collect **Artifacts of the Blacksilt** and find his **Pilfered Equipment**.

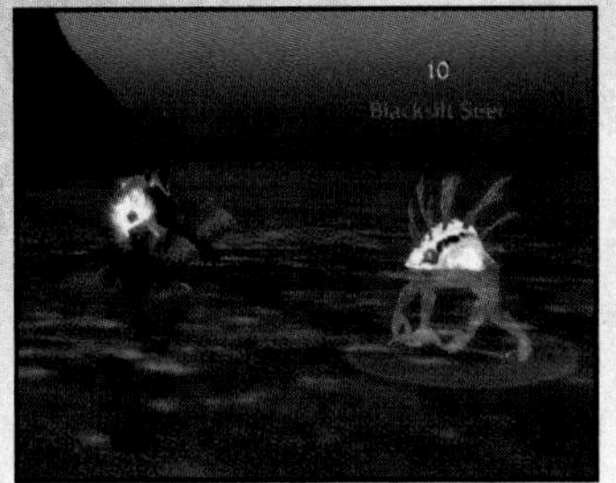

Artifacts of the Blacksilt	
Faction	Alliance
Location	Blacksilt Shore
Quest Giver	Clopper Wizbang
Quest Completion	Clopper Wizbang
Reward	Weathered Treasure Map (This Item Begins a Quest)

Pilfered Equipment	
Faction	Alliance
Location	Blacksilt Shore
Quest Giver	Clopper Wizbang
Quest Completion	Clopper Wizbang
Reward	Experience

Now you have quests to kill *everything!* Take your time to get used to the area. The Blacksilt Seers are casters and drop the *Crude Murloc Idols*, while the Blacksilt Shorestrikers and Warriors are melee enemies and drop the *Crude Murloc Knives*.

The murlocs function much better in the water than you do, so fight them on land whenever possible. To pull the Blacksilt Seers to land, shoot them and run away until they follow you onto firmer ground. You need a good bit of room behind you for this to work, but it's possible.

Kill your way along the shoreline west. Look in each of the camps for *Clopper's Equipment*; it's in a small crate and easy to miss if you aren't looking. When the shoreline meets the river, follow the river to the waterfall and get ready for a tough fight.

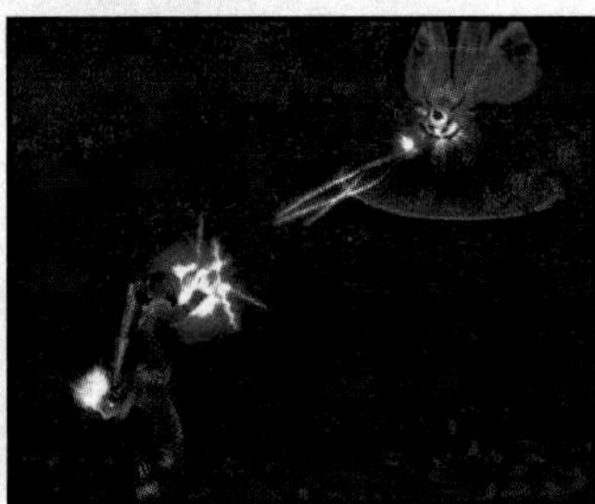

Deathclaw lives down here. Kill the enemies near Deathclaw in preparation. She doesn't have as much health as you might think, but she hits very hard. Have a potion ready and lay on the damage as quickly as possible.

With *Deathclaw's Paw* in your possession, return to killing everything around you. Alternate between killing murlocs on the shoreline to killing bears, plants, and moths inland. Switch between the two any time one has been cleared completely.

When both **Pilfered Equipment** and **Artifacts of the Blacksilt** are complete, return to Clopper. Sell your excess loot as you still have a while before you return to town. Use the *Weathered Treasure Map*. It's a map, but **A Map to Where?**

A Map to Where?	
Faction	Alliance
Location	Blacksilt Shore
Quest Giver	Weathered Treasure Map
Quest Completion	Battered Ancient Book
Reward	Leads to Deciphering the Book

The map is pretty vague, so we'll stick with what we know first. Follow the cliff east and south as you continue killing bears, plants, and moths for your quests. Before long, you begin climbing toward Axxarien and satyrs begin appearing.

The *Axxarien Shadowstalkers* have a mean damage-over-time curse, while the *Axxarien Hellcallers* can blanket an entire area in a rain of fire. Have abilities that interrupt their spellcasting ready. The fights up here will be tough, so recruit help from others if you need it.

Slowly kill your way into the east side of Axxarien. The *Corrupted Crystals* are scattered throughout the camp, but make sure each one is clear of enemies before you approach. None of the satyrs stealth, but they tend to hide in the huts, so be watchful.

At the north edge of Axxarien stands a monument guarded by *Zevrax*. Without any special abilities (aside from those the other satyrs have), he's a straightforward fight. Throw damage at him until he stops twitching. Nearby is a short red crystal that looks familiar. Use your *Crystal Mining Pick* to acquire the sample before moving on.

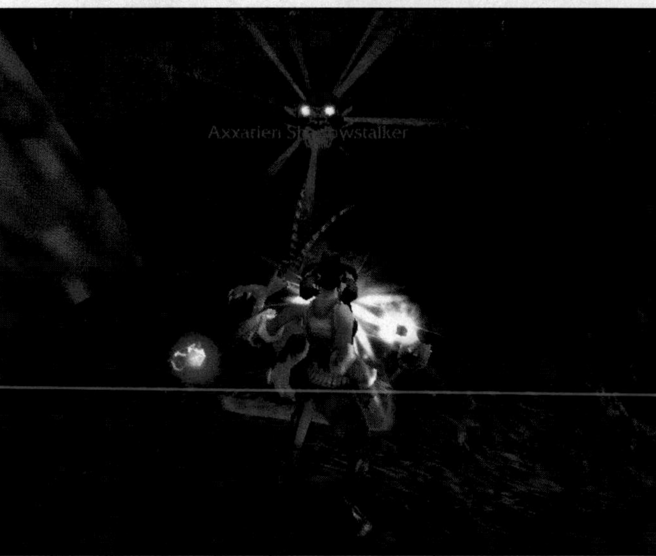

Finish killing satyrs and collecting crystals as you move south. Kill any bears, plants, and moths that get in your path to Blood Watch. Don't worry about completing every quest as you'll be back this way and you've already done quite a bit. Turn in all your quests, clear your inventory, and make a trip to the Exodar if you've gain an even level since you last trained.

Wyrmscar Island and the Bloodcursed Reef

Back at Blood Watch, there are a great many quests to grab. The section you'll do next has a few difficult fights, so you may want to partner with another adventurer; this isn't necessary, but it does make it much safer.

Speak with Messenger Hermesius, who has an **Urgent Delivery** for you. Accepting his quest doesn't add anything to your log. That's because he dropped a piece of mail in your mailbox. Right click on the mailbox to open it and click the *Letter from the Admiral* to put it in your inventory. Once in you inventory, right-click on the letter to get **Bloodcurse Legacy**. Make sure you also have **A Map to Where?** and **Ysera's Tears** before you head out.

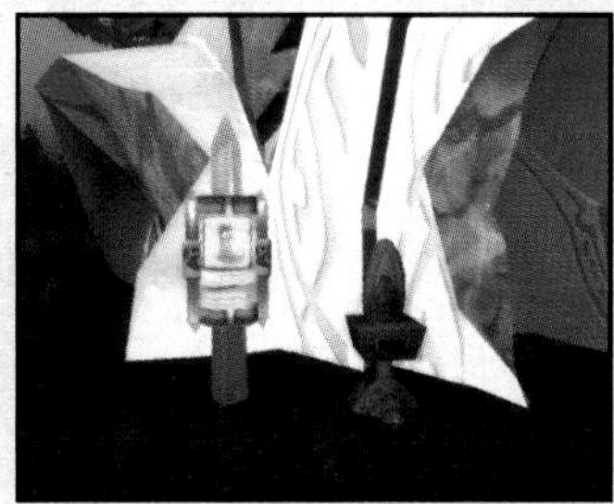

Urgent Delivery	
Faction	Alliance
Location	Blood Watch
Quest Giver	Messenger Hermesius
Quest Completion	Messenger Hermesius
Reward	Chains to The Bloodcurse Legacy

The Bloodcurse Legacy	
Faction	Alliance
Location	Blood Watch
Quest Giver	A Letter from the Admiral
Quest Completion	Captain Edward Hanes
Reward	Chains to The Bloodcursed Naga

Ysera's Tears	
Faction	Alliance
Location	Blood Watch
Quest Giver	Jessera of Mac'Aree
Quest Completion	Jessera of Mac'Aree
Reward	Free Choice of Jessera's Fungus Lined Tunic (Cloth Chest, 28 Armor, +2 STA, +3 INT) or Jessera's Fungus Lined Vest (Leather Chest, 68 Armor, +2 STA, Equip +6 Attack Power) or Jessera's Fungus Lined Hauberk (Mail Chest, 174 Armor, +2 STR, +2 STA)

Your first stop is the Ruins of Loreth'Aman. The Naga are much easier to deal with now that you are a couple levels higher than them, but don't try to run past them. Kill them for easy experience and to relieve stress on your way to the northern part of the ruins. Climb the crumbled stone to get atop the small gazebo. A book lies on the ground. Pick up the book and gain the quest **Deciphering the Book**.

Deciphering the Book	
Faction	Alliance
Location	Ruins of Loreth'Aman
Quest Giver	Battered Ancient Book
Quest Completion	Anchorite Paetheus
Reward	Chains to Nolkai's Words

Swim out to Wyrmscar Island, which is inhabited by undead Veridian Whelps and Broodlings. The Veridian Whelps can put you to sleep (until they hit you again), but the real danger is their brethren. The Veridian Broodlings have a ranged spit attack that poisons you. This is made worse when they hit you with multiple spits since the spits stack. More than a couple of these on you and you're in trouble. The good news is that the spit can be interrupted.

Stick to the beach for now unless you see the bright blue *Ysera's Tears* near trees or bones. You only need two of these, so grab them when you can, but don't wander around the dragonkin if you don't have to.

Another thing to watch for is Prince Toreth. He has a quest and wanders the island. It's easiest to find him on the east side and you have other business over there. Follow the shore east and north until you find Captain Edward Hanes. The Captain wants you to help him get revenge against **The Bloodcursed Naga**.

The Bloodcursed Naga	
Faction	Alliance
Location	Wyrmscale Island
Quest Giver	Captain Edward Hanes
Quest Completion	Captain Edward Hanes
Reward	Chains to The Hopeless Ones...

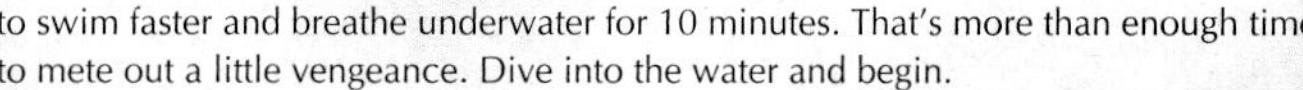

The Naga swim along the Bloodcursed Reef nearby, but Hanes gives you something to make the hunt easier: the ability to swim faster and breathe underwater for 10 minutes. That's more than enough time to mete out a little vengeance. Dive into the water and begin.

The *Bloodcursed Naga* cast ranged Frost Bolts. Although it's good to keep them interrupted if possible, it's not terribly dangerous for you if you fight them one at a time. They rarely swim near each other, so careful pulling will keep you more than safe. Slay the creatures and return to the Captain.

Each time you are near the Captain, take a look inland for Prince Toreth. Edward's next mission is to help **The Hopeless Ones...**

The Hopeless Ones...	
Faction	Alliance
Location	Wyrmscar Island
Quest Giver	Captain Edward Hanes
Quest Completion	Captain Edward Hanes
Reward	Chains to Ending the Bloodcurse

The Bloodcursed Voyagers wander further away from shore and deeper in the reef. It's a good thing the Captain restores the buff he gave you. Swim out and down to the voyagers. They are neutral and will not attack you unless attacked first. They also won't group up against you, so the fighting is a bit easier, but don't get careless.

You only need four *Bloodcursed Souls*. With 10 minutes of buff duration, you have plenty of time. You can't eat or drink while swimming, so you'll need to just tread water to regenerate mana and health. Take the fights one at a time and avoid dying as that cancels the beautiful buff the Captain gave you.

If At First You Don't Succeed...

Should you die while trying to collect the *Bloodcursed Souls*, you're resurrected without the buff Captain Edward Hanes gave you. Without it, it's very difficult to fight the Bloodcursed Voyagers.

Open your quest log and select the quest. Press the "Abandon quest" button. The quest is removed from your log and any *Bloodcursed Souls* you've already collected are removed from your inventory.

Return to Captain Edward Hanes to restart the quest. He'll recast the buff on you, and you can try again.

Return to the Captain when you have the souls he asked for. Now he wants you help with **Ending the Bloodcurse**. Before you leave the island, however, find Prince Toreth. He's working on **Restoring Sanctity** and could use your help.

Ending the Bloodcurse	
Faction	Alliance
Location	Wyrmscar Island
Quest Giver	Captain Edward Hanes
Quest Completion	Captain Edward Hanes
Reward	Wheel of the Lost Hope (Shield, 395 Armor, 7 Block, +3 STA)

Restoring Sanctity	
Faction	Alliance
Location	Wyrmscale Island
Quest Giver	Prince Toreth
Quest Completion	Prince Toreth
Reward	Chains to Into the Dream

Head south to Bloodcurse Isle. It's a long swim, but any time left on Edward's buff makes it much faster. The Bloodcurse Naga on the isle are the same as the ones you fought earlier with only one exception: they're on land now. Kill them as you ascend the island, and watch for any patrollers that might make your life difficult.

At the top of the ramp is a small plateau with the statue of Queen Azshara. Clear the entire plateau before attacking the statue. You have to climb onto the statue before you're close enough to break it. Have full mana and health before you do this as *Atoph* will attack.

Atoph has high health and high armor and deals high damage. Casters attempting this alone should blast him with everything they have before dropping down to the ramp to the east. This will cause some falling damage, but Atoph will take the long way around and be back at maximum range for another volley.

Have a potion ready or a friend with you and Atoph will die like every other Naga on this island. With the leader destroyed, you are free to rest and descend to the water. There are some respawns, but nothing you can't handle. Swim west and return to Blood Watch.

Take a quick detour after speaking with Anchorite Paetheus about **Nolkai's Words**. In Wrathscale Lair, there is a *Mound of Dirt* that Nolkai hid his belongings in. The Naga are much lower level than you now and pose almost no threat. Grab the box and open it for your reward. Return to Blood Watch and prepare for another extended trip.

Nolkai's Words	
Faction	Alliance
Location	Blood Watch
Quest Giver	Anchorite Paetheus
Quest Completion	Mound of Dirt
Reward	Nolkai's Box (25 silver, Nolkai's Band, Nolkai's Lantern (Off-hand, +3 INT), and Nolkai's Bag (8-slot bag))

Ragefeather Ridge and Wyrmscar Island

It's time to deal with the Wildkin north of Blood Watch. Take care of any errands in town and head out. The Wildkin have taken the bones of the fallen dragons and you need to get them back.

The bones stick out of the ground in the Wildkin camps. The Wildkin aren't particularly dangerous alone, but the camps are fairly close together. Getting more than one enemy doesn't guarantee death, but it makes the fight much harder.

Collect the bones as you head north through the camps. Wyrmscar Island is your next stop when you have all eight bones. Finding Toreth is easier now that he shows up on your mini-map, and he asks for help sending the dragons **Into the Dream**.

Into The Dream	
Faction	Alliance
Location	Wyrmscar Island
Quest Giver	Prince Toreth
Quest Completion	Prince Toreth
Reward	Chains to Razormaw

There's no avoiding the dragonkin now. Travel the island in the direction that Toreth was patrolling, killing dragonkin along the way. This keeps Toreth as close to you as possible. Rest when you need it as the *Veridian Broodlings* and *Veridian Whelps* are still very dangerous. Return to the Prince when you've killed enough dragonkin.

Toreth tells you that with most of the dragonkin restful once again, only **Razormaw** needs to be dealt with. The great beast flies above the island and will only descend if the bone bundle is burned at the fire atop the hill. He is far too powerful for you now.

Razormaw	
Faction	Alliance
Location	Wyrmscar Island
Quest Giver	Prince Toreth
Quest Completion	Prince Toreth
Reward	Choice of Robe of the Dragon Slayer (Cloth Chest, 30 Armor, +3 STA, +3 INT, Equip Improves spell hit rating by 2), Tunic of the Dragon Slayer (Mail Chest, +3 STR, +3 STA, Equip Improves hit rating by 2), or Vest of the Dragon Slayer (Leather Chest, +3 AGI, +3 STA, Equip Improves hit rating by 2)

Speak with Captain Edward Hanes before leaving the island. Walk back to Blood Watch or use your hearthstone.

Amberweb Pass and The Cryo-Core

Empty your bags of excess loot and stock up on restoration items. Remember to turn in your *Irradiated Crystal Shards*. Check your quest log and make sure you have **Talk to the Hand**, **The Missing Expedition**, and **Searching for Galaen.**

Follow the road to Vindicator's Rest. Watch for Elder Brown Bears as you likely still need to kill a few. Matis the Cruel wanders the road near Vindicator's Rest; he's an elite enemy and more powerful than you, so avoid him.

Speak with everyone at Vindicator's Rest and collect a new back of quests. After adding **Cutting a Path**, **Treant Transformation**, and **Oh, What Tangled Webs They Weave** you quest log is looking pretty full again. Grab all of the quests. You won't be doing all of them yet, but you don't want to travel all the way out here just to get a quest again.

Cutting a Path	
Faction	Alliance
Location	Vindicator's Rest
Quest Giver	Scout Jorli
Quest Completion	Scout Jorli
Reward	Experience

Treant Transformation

Treant Transformation	
Faction	Alliance
Location	Vindicator's Rest
Quest Giver	Vindicator Corin
Quest Completion	Vindicator Corin
Reward	Experience

Oh, the Tangled Webs They Weave

Oh, the Tangled Webs They Weave	
Faction	Alliance
Location	Vindicator's Rest
Quest Giver	Vindicator Corin
Quest Completion	Vindicator Corin
Reward	Experience

Strike out northwest toward Amberweb Pass. *Mutated Tanglers, Corrupted Stompers,* and *Enraged Ravagers* are between you and your goal. It's a good thing you have quests to kill all of them!

The tanglers can root you, while the stompers and Ravagers do a good bit of damage. At half health, the Ravagers become enraged. This increases their damage significantly. Save your instant attacks and spells until they enrage and then blow them down. This keeps the damage you take to a minimum.

As all the quests up here are kill quests, grab a partner if you want more safety or go it alone if you want more of a challenge.

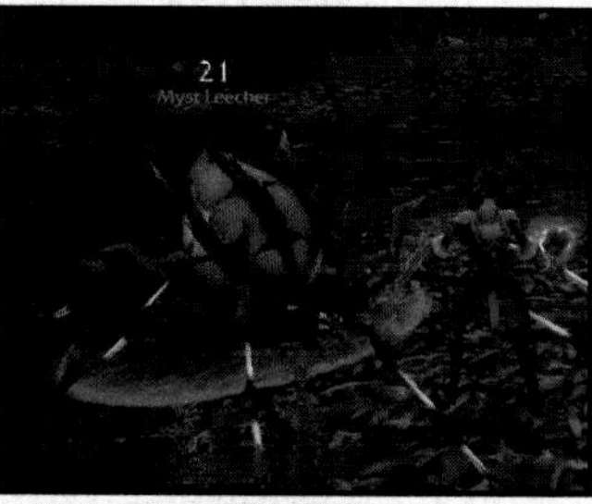

When you've killed all the enemies along the southern river bank, cross the river and engage the spiders. The Myst Spinners can web you and the Myst Leechers can poison you. Being able to cure poison or knowing someone who can is be quite useful, but it isn't necessary.

Avoid using area-of-effect abilities near the Webbed Creatures. This will either pop them out of the web or just annoy them. If they're annoyed, you will be stuck in combat (and unable to regain mana or health quickly) until they are dead. Released creatures tend to attack the first thing they see.

Clear the spiders as you climb the pass. Atop is *Zarakh.* She is massive and mean. Clear the spiders in an area so you have a bit of room to fight her, and pull her alone. Zarakh attacks very quickly and hits reasonably hard. Casters may have a difficult time casting any spells with all the interruption.

Use Gift of the Naaru before she closes so she can't increase the casting time and have a potion ready (if you have one). If you can survive the first several seconds of the fight, you're in good shape as her health isn't as high as her damage. Blow her down and retreat down the pass.

You're a good way up, so don't jump down. Take the slow way and walk. Finish the quest by killing the spiders on your way out. Cross the river and return to killing tanglers, stompers, and Ravagers.

Turn southeast and head to the Cryo-Core. There are quest targets all along the route there and you should be finished by time you get there. If you aren't, spend a little longer hunting before engaging the *Sunhawk Reclaimers.*

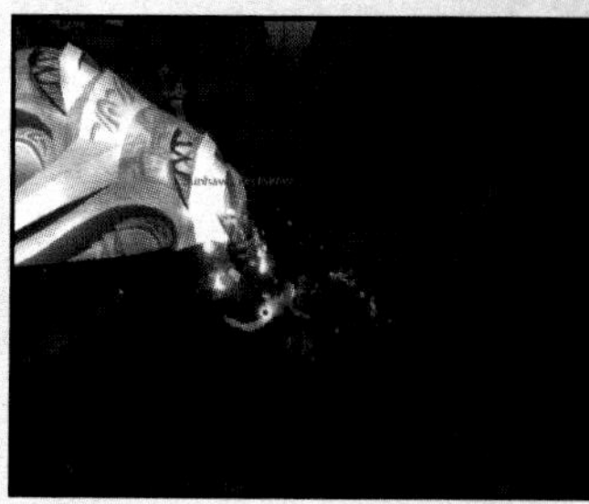

The Sunhawk Reclaimers use fire magic. Have interrupt abilities ready and keep them from making use of these attacks. They wander close to each other at times, so watch before you attack. They have low health and die quickly.

Make your way into the crater from the west side and move to the opening in the Cryo-Core. There are two enemies immediately inside. Peek in and use a ranged attack against one of them. Quickly move around the doorway so the enemy can't see you. Without line of sight, the Sunhawk Reclaimer is forced to come to you and away from possible reinforcements. Kill it when it turns the corner, then kill its friend.

Just inside is Galaen's Corpse. The spirit of Galaen remains long enough to ask you to notify Morae of **Galaen's Fate**. Examine the book on the ground. It is **Galaen's Journal-The Fate of Vindicator Sarvan**. Exit the wreck the way you entered.

Galaen's Fate

Galaen's Fate	
Faction	Alliance
Location	The Cryo-Core
Quest Giver	Galaen's Corpse
Quest Completion	Morae
Reward	Choice of Cryo-Core Attendant's Boots (Cloth Feet, 21 Armor, +3 STA, +2 INT), Lightweight Mesh Boots (Mail Feet, 107 Armor +2 STR, +3 STA) or Technician's Boots (Leather Feet, 50 Armor, +3 AGI, Equip +4 Attack Power)

Galaen's Journal-The Fate of Vindicator Sarvan

Galaen's Journal-The Fate of Vindicator Sarvan	
Faction	Alliance
Location	The Cryo-Core
Quest Giver	Galaen's Journal
Quest Completion	Vindicator Kuros
Reward	Experience

Kill the reclaimers in the area as you move east. Watch for the *Sunhawk Missive* and *Galaen's Amulet.* Be sure you have both before returning to Blood Watch with the bad news for Morae.

Your bags are quite full, so visit a merchant before you turn in any quests. Sell your ill-gotten goods and speak with everyone for your rewards. Vindicator Boros asks you to speak with Interrogator Elysia as she is skilled in **Translations...** She translates the missive for you and gives you orders to make an **Audience with the Prophet**.

Translations...	
Faction	Alliance
Location	Blood Watch
Quest Giver	Vindicator Boros
Quest Completion	Interrogator Elysia
Reward	Chains to Audience with the Prophet

Audience with the Prophet	
Faction	Alliance
Location	Blood Watch
Quest Giver	Interrogator Elysia
Quest Completion	Prophet of Velen
Reward	Chains to Truth of Fiction

Don't fly to the Exodar yet. Vindicator Aesom speaks about **What We Know...** and has you talk to Exarch Admetius. The Exarch wants to know **What We Don't Know...** and enlists your aid. He gives you a disguise that lets you pass for a Blood Elf. It's a good thing the guards are in on this!

What We Know...	
Faction	Alliance
Location	Blood Watch
Quest Giver	Vindicator Aesom
Quest Completion	Exarch Admetius
Reward	Chains to What We Don't Know...

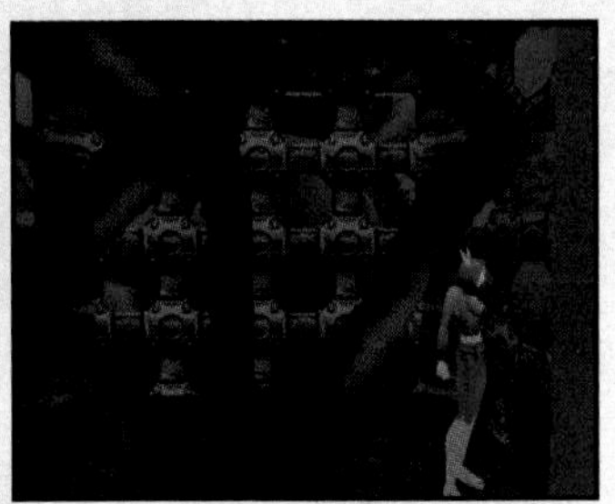

What We Don't Know...	
Faction	Alliance
Location	Blood Watch
Quest Giver	Exarch Admetius
Quest Completion	Exarch Admetius
Reward	Chains to Vindicator's Rest

Speak with the Captive Sunhawk Agent. Continue speaking with her until you've acquired all the information you need. When you return to the Exarch, he orders you to **Vindicator's Rest**. You have business in the Exodar, though.

Vindicator's Rest	
Faction	Alliance
Location	Blood Watch
Quest Giver	Exarch Admetius
Quest Completion	Vindicator Corin
Reward	Chains to Clearing the Way

Take a hippogryph to the Exodar and seek out Prophet Velen. He needs to know if everything is **Truth or Fiction** and sends you back to Blood Watch. Take the time to train while you're here, then make your way to Blood Watch.

Truth of Fiction	
Faction	Alliance
Location	The Exodar
Quest Giver	Prophet Velen
Quest Completion	Vindicator Boros
Reward	Chains to I Shoot Magic Into the Darkness

Finding the Sun Portal

Speak with Vindicator Boros before heading to the Warp Piston (**I Shoot Magic Into the Darkness**). This is a quick trip, but stray off the road and finish off any enemies you still have quests for (the Elder Brown Bears for Bear Necessities for example).

I Shoot Magic Into the Darkness	
Faction	Alliance
Location	Blood Watch
Quest Giver	Vindicator Boros
Quest Completion	Vindicator Boros
Reward	Choice of Vindicator's Soft Sole Slippers (Cloth Feet, 17 Armor, +1 STA, +1 INT), Vindicator's Leather Moccasins (Leather Feet, 45 Armor, +1 AGI, +1 STA), or Vindicator's Stompers (Mail Feet, 89 Armor, +2 STA)

Void Anomalies guard the Warp Piston, but you need to kill these anyway. Use ranged attacks to pull them one at a time as they like to team up. Approach the Warp Piston and verify that the Sun Portal isn't there.

With evidence of a portal at the Warp Piston recently, return to Blood Watch. Cut through Ragefeather Ridge for some easy fighting if you want some quick experience. Vindicator Boros is done for you now, but Vindicator Kuros wants you to take a trip to **The Cryo-Core**.

The Cryo-Core	
Faction	Alliance
Location	Blood Watch
Quest Giver	Vindicator Kuros
Quest Completion	Vindicator Kuros
Reward	Choice of Vindicator's Smasher (Two-hand Mace, 10.7 DPS, +3 STR, +2 STA), Vindicator's Walking Stick (Staff, 10.5 DPS, +2 STA, +3 INT), or Vindicator's Letter Opener (Two-hand Sword, 10.5 DPS, +3 STR, +2 AGI)

Head west to the Cryo-Core and collect the *Medical Supplies*. There are boxes on the ground and the Sunhawk Reclaimers carry them also. Take back what belongs to your people. When you have all 12, return to Blood Watch.

Pushing to the Vector Coil

With the medical supplies retrieved, Vindicator Aesom has a good bit of work for you. He wants you to destroy **The Sun Gate**. This may push you to the **Limits of Physical Exhaustion**, but **Don't Drink the Water**.

The Sun Gate	
Faction	Alliance
Location	Blood Watch
Quest Giver	Vindicator Aesom
Quest Completion	The Sun Gate
Reward	Experience

Limits of Physical Exhaustion	
Faction	Alliance
Location	Blood Watch
Quest Giver	Vindicator Aesom
Quest Completion	Vindicator Aesom
Reward	Experience

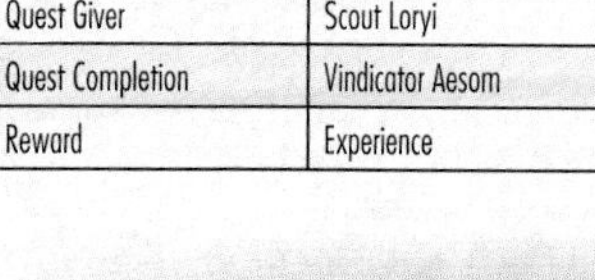

Don't Drink the Water	
Faction	Alliance
Location	Blood Watch
Quest Giver	Vindicator Aesom
Quest Completion	Vindicator Aesom
Reward	Experience

Repair, sell loot, and check your quest log before heading out. Make sure you also have **Vindicator's Rest**, **Matis the Cruel**, and **Critters of the Void**.

Critters of the Void	
Faction	Alliance
Location	Vindicator's Rest
Quest Giver	Scout Loryi
Quest Completion	Vindicator Aesom
Reward	Experience

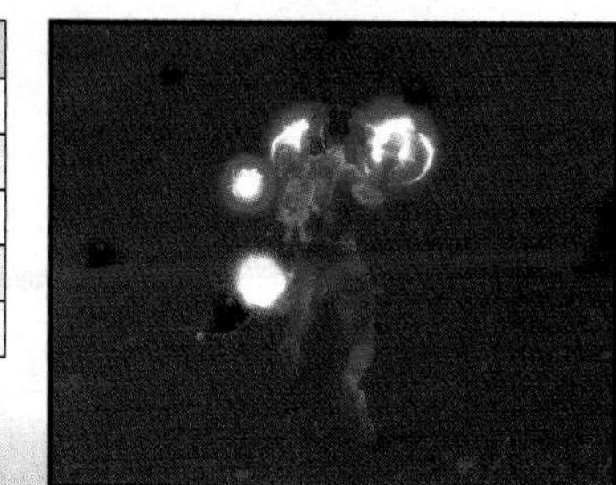

Matis the Cruel	
Faction	Alliance
Location	Blood Watch
Quest Giver	Vindicator Kuros
Quest Completion	Vindicator Kuros
Reward	Choice of Vindicator's Woolies (Cloth Legs, 25 Armor, +4 STA, +3 INT), Vindicator's Leather Chaps (Leather Legs, 60 Armor, +4 AGI, +3 STA), or Vindicator's Iron Legguards (Mail Legs, 132 Armor, +4 STR, +3 STA)

With a number of quests to be completed, head west past the Cryo-Core. South of the Vector Coil is the Sun Gate and one of the Sunhawks' most important camps. Defeating the *Sunhawk Pyromancers* and *Defenders* won't be easy, but that's why you were sent.

Fight your way through the camp. *Void Critters* litter the camp and the bottom of the lake. Kill these as you make your way through the Sunhawk forces.

At the lake, several Sunhawk Portal Controllers hold the *Sun Gate* open. Their entire attention is on the Sun Gate (it has to be), so you can murder them at your leisure. Once all the portal controllers are dead, swim to the Sun Gate and attack it. You have to be right under it to be in range. While you're already wet, kill a few Void Critters to finish the quest.

With the Sun Gate destroyed and the Void Critters decimated, make your way to the road and look for *Matis*. Avoid getting too close to the Vector Coil at this time as the enemies are too powerful for you.

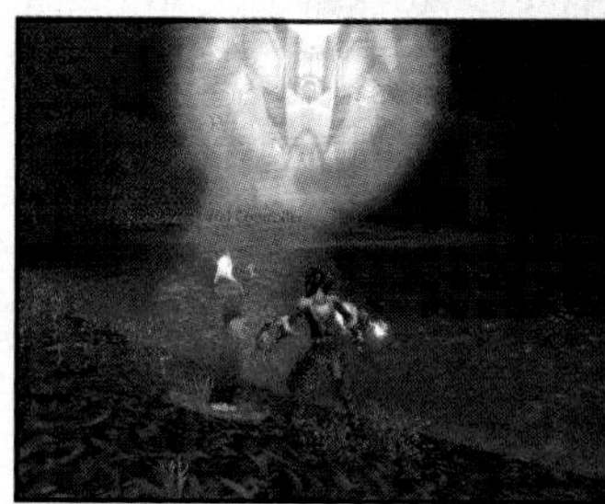

While you look for Matis, make a quick trip to Vindicator's Rest to turn in your quests. When Matis appears, get just in range to use the *Flare Gun* to summon aid. When aid arrives, help bring Matis down.

Head west again and finish killing the Sunhawk Pyromancers and Defenders. Follow the river past the elementals and jump off the waterfall next. The elementals will attack you. Once at the bottom of the waterfall, use the container to get the *Bloodmyst Water Sample*. Use your Hearthstone for a quick return to Blood Watch to turn in your quests.

Watch the exchange between the Image of Velen and Matis to learn more about the Sunhawk.

Razormaw and the Vector Coil

There is very little left to do on Bloodmyst Isle, and none of it that you can do alone. Find a friend or few and make your way to Wyrmscar Island.

Cut your way to the top of Talon's Stand and clear the entire summit. Rest to full health and/or mana and place the *Bundle of Dragon Bones* on the fire to call *Razormaw* to you.

He's very big and not happy. Keep your health high as he will cast fear on you during the fight and you don't want him to get free hits when you're low on health. With friends, this fight is more fun than challenge. Drop down and turn in the quest with Toreth and *Razormaw's Head* to Vindicator's Rest next.

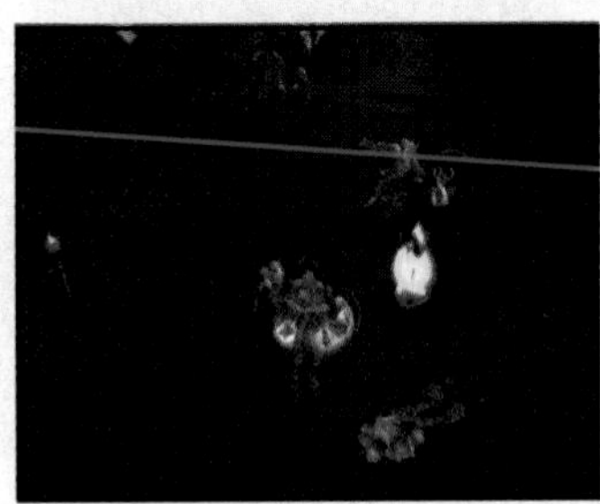

Speak with Vindicator Corin about **Clearing the** Way and Demolitionist Legoso about **Ending Their World**. Legoso wastes no time and sets off at a brisk pace so be ready to follow him.

Clearing the Way	
Faction	Alliance
Location	Vindicator's Rest
Quest Giver	Vindicator Corin
Quest Completion	Vindicator Corin
Reward	Choice of Flutterer Silk Handwraps (Cloth Hands, 20 Armor, +3 INT, +3 SPI), Ravager Hide Gloves (Leather Hands, 46 Armor, +3 AGI, +3 STA), or Corin's Handguards (Mail Hands, 100 Armor, +3 STR, +3 STA)

Ending Their World	
Faction	Alliance
Location	Vindicator's Rest
Quest Giver	Demolitionist Legoso
Quest Completion	Demolitionist Legoso
Reward	Choice of Blade of the Hand (Two-hand Sword, 13.1 DPS, +6 STA, Equip +8 Attack Power), Crossbow of the Hand (Crossbow, 10.9 DPS), Mace of the Hand (One-hand Mace, 10.0 DPS, +3 STR, +3 STA), or Staff of the Hand (Staff, 13.0 DPS, +4 STA, +3 INT, Equip Increases damage and healing done by magical spells and effects by up to 4)

Stick near Legoso, but let him lead. He's much tougher than you so let him take the hits. Melee classes should wait for Legoso to engage an enemy and only attack an enemy that he has already damaged. Classes with heavier armor (Warriors and Paladins) might consider pulling a single enemy off of Legoso if he has more than 2 enemies on him. Be warned that while he will heal himself, he will not heal you.

Casters should plan on staying back as you follow Legoso. Wait for him to engage an enemy before you cast offensive spells and don't heal him until he gets to half health. This will keep most of the enemies beating on him instead of on you.

Follow him to the large red crystal at the base of the Vector Coil. With his help, killing the *Sunhawk Saboteurs* and *Agents* is much easier. He'll plant the charge and set the coil aflame before climbing to the final rise.

Standing in the center of arcing energy is *Sironas*. This Eredar demon is siphoning energy straight from the Vector Coil. Legoso stops this, but Sironas immediately attacks.

Keep her attention on Legoso as she hits very hard and uses Curse of Blood to increase all damage her target takes by 10. All Draenei can use Gift of the Naaru to help keep Legoso healed. Keep pouring on the damage and destroy this abomination.

Return to Vindicator's Rest and then to Blood Watch to turn in your quests. Many people have come to congratulate you on your success. Your friends from Stillpine Hold and Odesyus' Landing have pledged their aid to the Draenei because of your efforts, and Prophet Velen has traveled all the way from the Exodar to tell you of **The Unwritten Prophecy**.

The Unwritten Prophecy	
Faction	Alliance
Location	Blood Watch
Quest Giver	Prophet Velen
Quest Completion	Prophet Velen
Reward	Tabard of the Hand and a choice of Signet Ring of the Hand (Ring, +2 INT, Equip Increases spell critical strike rating by 2) or Signet Ring of the Hand (Ring, Equip Improves critical strike rating by 2, +4 Attack Power)

Choose which gift to accept from the Prophet and return to the Exodar to train and prepare yourself for the journey into Azeroth!

WHERE FEW DARE TO TREAD

The maps and legends within provide a wealth of information on the many new zones for the expansion. In earlier chapters, we revealed the zones for the incoming Blood Elves and Draenei. Here, we'll show you a list of the people and places in this re-discovered world.

Hellfire Peninsula

Legend

Herbs

- Dreamfoil
- Felweed
- Dreaming Glory

Minerals

- Rich Thorium
- Fel Iron
- Khorium

Reputation Information

- Thrallmar (Horde)
- Mag'Har (Horde)
- Honor Hold (Alliance)
- Exodar (Alliance)

Hellfire
Zangarmarsh
Terokkar Forrest
Shattrath City
Nagrand
Blade's Edge
Netherstorm

Map Legend

(A) Thrallmar

Angela "The Claw" Kestrel	
Anvil	
Apothecary Antonivich	Grand Master Alchemist
Barim Spilthoof	Grand Master Leatherwork
Barley	Wind Rider Master
Battlecryer Blackeye	
Baxter	Chef
Blood Elf Pilgrim	57-59
Caza'rez	
Cookie One-Eye	Food & Drink Vendor
Dalinna	Grand Master Tailor
Falcon Watch Sentinel	59
Far Seer Regulkut	
Felannia	Grand Master Enchanter
Floyd Pinkus	Innkeeper
Forge	
General Krakork	
Huntsman Torf Angerhoof	Stable Master
Injured Thrallmar Grunt	57
Jir'see	
Kalaen	Grand Master Jewelcrafter
Krugosh	Mining Trainer
Mailbox	
Martik Tor'seldori	
Moorutu	Skinning Trainer
Nazgrel	
Quartermaster Urgronn	
Rohok	Grand Master Blacksmith
Ruak Stronghorn	Herbalism Trainer
Shadow Hunter Ty'jin	
Stone Guard Stok'ton	
Thrallmar Grunt	60
Thrallmar Marksman	60
Thrallmar Peon	51
Thrallmar Riding Wolf	56
Thrallmar Wolf Rider	60
Zebig	Grand Master Engineer

(B) Thrallmar Mine

Dagz	
Foreman Razelcraz	
Gan'arg Sapper	60-61
Maiden of Pain	59
Urga'zz	60

(C) Stonescythe Canyon

Deranged Helboar	60-61
Marauding Curst Burster	59-60

(D) Northern Rampart

Shattered Hand Acolyte	62
Shattered Hand Berserker	61
Shattered Hand Guard	62
Shattered Hand Mage	61

(E) The Dark Portal

Amish Wildhammer	Gryphon Master
Brother Daniels	
Commander Duron	
Dark Cleric Malod	Healing & Sustenance
Lieutenant General Orion	
Nurse Judith	
Quartermaster	Gunman
Rations Vendor	
Supply Master Broog	Supplies
Vlagga Freyfeather	Wind Rider Master

(F) Supply Caravan

Arcanist Torseldori	
Bloodmage	64-65 Elite
Sergeant Shatterskull	

(G) Forge Camp: Spite

Forge Camp Legionnaire	60-61 Elite
Gan'arg Servant	60-61
Mo'arg Forgefiend	62 Elite
Sister of Grief	60-61 Elite

(H) Felspark Ravine

Fel Reaver	70 Elite
Flamewaker Imp	58
Heckling Fel Sprite	58-59
Infernal Warbringer	58-59

(I) Forge Camp: Rage

Forge Camp Legionnaire	60-61 Elite
Gan'arg Servant	60-61
Mo'arg Forgefiend	62 Elite
Sister of Grief	60-61 Elite

(J) Forge Camp: Mageddon

Arix'malidash	62 Elite
Forge Camp Legionnaire	60-61 Elite
Gan'arg Servant	60-61
Mo'arg Forgefiend	62 Elite
Sister of Grief	60-61 Elite

(K) Hellfire Citadel

Drillmaster Zurok	62
Entrance to Citadel Wings	
Force-Copmmander Gorax	63 Elite
Shattered Hand Captain	62-63
Shattered Hand Grunt	62-63
Shattered Hand Neophyte	62
Shattered Hand Warlock	63

(L) Path of Glory

Shattered Hand Captain	62-63
Shattered Hand Grunt	62-63
Shattered Hand Neophyte	62
Shattered Hand Warlock	63

(M) Gryphons

Gryphoneer Leafbeard	Gryphon Master
Honor Hold Scout	65 Elite

(N) The Abyssal Shelf

Fel Reaver Sentry	70 Elite
Gan'arg Peon	68-70 Elite
Mo'arg Overseer	70 Elite

(O) Reaver's Fall

Armored Wyvern Destroyer	70
Bonechewer Evoker	59-60
Bonechewer Scavenger	59-60
Forward Commander To'arch	65 Elite
Supply Officer Isable	General Goods & Repairs
Wing Commander Brack	Wind Rider Master

(P) The Legion Front

Doom Whisperer	59-60
Fel Handler	59-60
Legion Antenna: Mageddon	
Netherhound	59-60
Subjugator Yalqiz	62
Wrathguard	59-60

(Q) The Stair of Destiny

Deathwhisperer	70 Elite
Dread Tactician	70 Elite
Fel Soldier	70 Elite
Pit Commander	70 Elite
Wrath Master	70 Elite

(R) Void Ridge

Collapsing Voidwalker	61-62
Vacillating Voidwalker	61-62

(S) Zeth'Gor

Bleeding Hollow Dark Shaman	61
Bleeding Hollow Grunt	60-61
Bleeding Hollow Necrolyte	60
Bleeding Hollow Peon	59-60
Bleeding Hollow Skeleton	60
Bleeding Hollow Tormentor	61
Bleeding Hollow Worg	60
Eye of Grillok	60
Feng	60
Grillok	60
Ripp	58
Starving Helboar	59-60
Warlord Morkh	60
Worg Master Kruush	60

(T) Spinebreaker Post

Althen the Historian	
Amilya Airheart	Wind Rider Master
Emissary Modiba	
Grelag	
Hagash the Blind	Bowyer
Lukra	General Goods
Mondul	Food & Drink Vendor
Ogath the Mad	
Peon Bolgar	Trade Goods
Stone Guard Ambelan	
Thrallmar Grunt	60
Thrallmar Peon	50

(U) Expedition Armory

Arch Mage Xintor	61
Commander Hogarth	
Lieutenant Commander Thalvos	
Unyielding Footman	59-60
Unyielding Knight	59-60
Unyielding Sorcerer	59-60

(V) The Warp Fields

Rogue Voidwalker	60-61
Uncontrolled Voidwalker	60-61

(W) Razorthorn Trail

Razorfang Hatchling	59-60
Razorfang	Ravager
61	

(X) Southern Rampart

Hulking Helboar	61
Shattered Hand Berserker	61-62
Shattered Hand Grenadier	61-62
Shattered Hand Guard	61-62

(Y) Gor'gaz Outpost

Shattered Hand Berserker	61-62

(Z) Zepplin Crash

Legassi	
"Screaming" Screed Luckheed	

Map Legend

AA The Great Fissure

Blacktalon the Savage	63 Elite
Stonescythe Alpha	61-62
Stonescythe Ambusher	61-62
Stonescythe Whelp	60-61
Tunneler	61-62

AB Falcon Watch

Apothecary Azethen	
Arcanist Calesthris Dawnstar	
Aresella	Medic
Cookpot	
Falcon Watch Ranger	68
Falconer Drenna Riverwind	
Fallesh Sunfallow	Weapon Merchant
Innalia	Wind Rider Master
Innkeeper Bazil Olof'tazun	Innkeeper
Lursa Sunfallow	Reagent Vendor
Magistrix Carinda	
Mailbox	
Orb of Translocation	
Pilgrim Gal'ressa	
Provisioner Valine	Food & Drink Vendor
Ranger Captain Venn'ren	
Recovering Pilgrim	58-60
Ryathen the Somber	
Wanted Poster	

AC Dwarf Camp

Gremni Longbeard	
Mirren Longbeard	

AD Den of Haal'esh

Haal'eshi Talonguard	62-63
Haal'eshi Windwalker	62
Kaliri Matriarch	63
Kaliri Nest	
Kaliri Swooper	60
Wounded Blood Elf Pilgrim	

AE Dustquill Ravine

Quilfang Ravager	62-63
Quilfang Skitterer	61-62

AF Cenarion Post

Amythiel Mistwalker	
Earthbinder Galandria Nightbreeze	
Mahuram Stouthoof	
Thiah Redmane	
Tola'thion	

AG Ruins of Sha'naar

Akoru the Firecaller	
Arzeth the Merciless	63 Elite
Arzeth the Powerless	63
Aylaan the Waterwaker	
Dreghood Brute	57
Dreghood Geomancer	56-57
Illadari Taskmaster	63
Morod the Windstirrer	
Naladu	

AH Thornpoint Hill

Thornfang Ravager	62-63
Thornfang Venomspitter	62-63

AI Fallen Sky Ridge

Raging Colossus	62-63 Elite
Raging Shardling	62-63

AJ Mag'har Post

Debilitated Mag'har Grunt	58
Earthcaller Ryga	
Gorkan Bloodfist	68 Elite
Mag'har Grunt	61
Mag'har Hunter	62-63
Mag'har Watcher	62-63
Provisioner Braknar	

AK Pools of Aggonar

Arazzius the Cruel	63 Elite
Blistering Oozeling	61-62
Blistering Rot	61-62
Mistress of Doom	62
Terrorfiend	61-62

AL Honor Hold

Anvil	
Caretaker Dilandrus	
Explorers' League Archaeologist	54-56
Father Malgor Devidicus	
Field Commander Romus	
Flightmaster Krill Bitterhue	Gryphon Master
Force Commander Danath Trollbane	
Forge	
Gaston	Chef
Gunny	
Hama	Grand Master Tailor
Honor Guard Greyn	
Honor Hold Archer	59-60
Honor Hold Defender	59-60
Humphry	Grand Master Blacksmith
Hurnak Grimmord	Mining Trainer
Injured Nethergarde Infantry	57-58
Injured Stormwind Infantry	57-58
Jelena Nightsky	Skinning Trainer
Lieutenant Chadwick	
Logistics Officer Ulrike	Honor Hold Quartermaster
Magus Filinthus	
Mailbox	
Marshal Isildor	
Master Sergeant Lorin Thalmerok	Stable Master
Nethergarde Infantry	58-60
Prospector Murantus	
Seargent Dalton	
Seer Kryv	
Sid Limbardi	Innkeeper
Stormwind Infantry	57
Tatiana	Grand Master Jewelcrafter
War Horse	56
Warrant Officer Tracy Proudwell	

AM Honor Hold Mine

Foreman Biggums	
Gan'arg Sapper	60-61
Honor Hold Miner	53-54
Maiden of Pain	59

AN Temple of Telhamat

Amaan the Wise	
Anchorite Alendar	
Anchorite Obadei	
Anvil	
Burko	Medic
Caregiver Ophera Windfury	Innkeeper
Elsaana	
Escaped Dreghood	58
Forge	
Ikan	
Kuma	Hippogryph Master
Mailbox	
Provisioner Anir	Food & Drink Vendor
Rumatu	
Scout Vanura	
Talaara	Weapon Merchant
Telhamat Protector	59-60
Vodesiin	Reagent Vendor
Yaluu	

AP Throne of Kil'jaeden

Greater Fel-Spark	70-71
Throne-Guard Champion	72 Elite
Throne-Guard Highlord	72 Elite
Doomforge Automaton	71 Elite
Throne-Guard Sentinel	71 Elite
Throne Hound	71 Elite
Doom Lord Kazzak	World Boss

AD Shatter Point

1 Hulking Helboar	**62-63**
2 Bonestripper Vulture	**61-62**
3 Magister Aledis	
4 The Overlook	
5 The Stadium	
6 Broken Hill	

Zangarmarsh

Right Click On Map To Zoom Out
BLADE'S EDGE
ANGO'ROSH GROUNDS
OREBOR HARBORAGE
COILFANG RESERVOIR
MARSHLIGHT LAKE
SERPENT LAKE
THE DEAD MIRE
TELREDOR
SPOREGGAR
ZABRA'JIN
TWIN SPIRE RUINS
SWAMPRAT POST
THE SPAWNING GLEN
THE LAGOON
CENARION REFUGE
UMBRAFEN LAKE
NAGRAND
TEROKKAR

Legend

Herbs

- Blindweed
- Golden Sansam
- Felweed
- Ragveil
- Dreaming Glory
- Flame Cap
- Withered Giant Corpse
- Withered Bog Lord Corpse
- Starving Fungal Giant Corpse

Minerals

- Fel Iron
- Adamantite

Reputation Information

- Cenarion Expedition (Both Factions)
- Sporeggar (Both Factions)

Map Legend

Ⓐ Telredor

Anchorite Ahuurn	
Anvil	
Caregiver Abidaar	Innkeeper
Cookpot	
Elevator	
Forge	
Joraal	Stable Master
K. Lee Smallfry	Grand Master Engineer
Mailbox	
Prospector Conall	
Ruam	
Telredor Guard	65 Elite
Vindicator Idaar	

Ⓑ Zabra'jin

Anvil	
Captured Gnome	Item Repair
Du'ga	Wind Rider Master
Farbosi	
Forge	
Gambarinka	Tradesman
Guard Untula	
Khalan	Stable Master
Mailbox	
Merajit	Innkeeper
Messenger Gazgrigg	
Seer Janidi	Reagent Vendor
Shadow Hunter Denjai	
Tayemba	
Wanted Poster	
Witch Doctor Tor'gash	
Zabra'jin Guard	65 Elite
Zurjaya	Fishing Trainer

Ⓒ Cenarion Refuge

Anvil	
Campfire	
Expedition Warden	70
Fedryen Swiftspear	Cenarion Expedition Quartermaster
Forge	
Ikeyen	
Innkeeper Coryth Stoktron	
Juno Dufrain	Fishing Supplies
Kameel Longstride	Stable Master
Keleth	
Lauranna Thar'well	
Lethyn Moonfire	
Mailbox	
Naka	Cooking Supplier
Talut	
Wanted Poster	
Warden Hamoot	
Windcaller Blackhoof	
Ysiel Windsinger	

Ⓓ East Zangarmarsh

Fen Strider	61-62
Marshfang Ripper	60-61
Umbraglow Stinger	60-61
Young Spore Bat	60-61

Ⓔ Umbrafen Lake/The Lagoon

Mire Hydra	61-62
Umbrafen Eel	61-62

Ⓕ Umbrafen Village

Boglash	61 Elite
Umbrafen Oracle	60-61
Umbrafen Seer	60-61
Umbrafen Witchdoctor	60-61

Ⓖ Funggor Cavern

Lord Klaq	62
Marsh Dredger	62
Marsh Lurker	61
Sporelok	61-62

Ⓗ Darkcrest Shore

Darkcrest Sentry	61
Darkcrest Siren	62-63
Darkcrest Taskmaster	62-63
Dreghood Drudge	62-63

Ⓘ Darkcrest Enclave

Darkcrest Sentry	61
Darkcrest Siren	62-63
Darkcrest Taskmaster	62-63
Dreghood Drudge	62-63
Steampump Overseer	63

Ⓙ The Dead Mire

Marshfang Ripper	60
Parched Hydra	62
Sporewing	61
Withered Bog Lord	62
Withered Giant	61

Ⓚ Swamprat Post

Lorti	Reagent Merchant
Magasha	
Reavij	
Swamprat Guard	65 Elite
Zurai	General Merchant

Ⓛ Bloodscale Grounds

Bloodscale Overseer	63-64
Bloodscale Sentry	62
Bloodscale Wavecaller	64
Wrekt Slave	63-64

Ⓜ Northern Zangarmarsh

Bogflare Needler	62-63
Greater Spore Bat	61-62

Ⓝ Central Zangarmarsh

Bloodthirsty Marshfang	60-61
Fen Strider	61
Spore Bat	60-61

Ⓞ Feralfen Village

Blacksting	62
Feralfen Druid	61-62
Feralfen Hunter	61-62
Tamed Spore Bat	56-57

Ⓟ Boha'mu Ruins

Elder Kuruti	62 Elite
Feralfen Druid	61-62
Feralfen Mystic	61-62

Ⓠ Southern Zangarmarsh

Fen Strider	61
Marshfang Slicer	62-63
Spore Bat	60-61

Ⓡ Serpent Lake

Entrance to Coilfang Instances	
Fenclaw Thrasher	64
Mragesh	64
Mudfin Frenzy	62-63
Watcher Jhang	

Ⓢ Orebor Harborage

Aktu	Armor Merchant
Cookpot	
Doba	Cooking Supplies
Ikuti	
Innkeeper Kerp	Innkeeper
Mailbox	
Muheru the Weaver	Tailoring Supplies
Orebor Harborage Defender	65 Elite
Puluu	
Timothy Daniels	
Wanted Poster	

Ⓣ Hewn Bog

Ango'rosh Ogre	62-63
Ango'rosh Shaman	62-63

Ⓤ Bloodscale Enclave

Bloodscale Enchantress	64
Bloodscale Sentry	62-63
Bloodscale Slavedriver	63-64
Marsh Walker	63-64
Wrekt Slave	63-64

Ⓥ The Edge

Greater Spore Bat	61-62
Ironspine Gazer	63-64
Ironspine Threshalisk	63

Ⓦ Daggerfen Village

Daggerfen Assassin	62-63
Daggerfen Muckdweller	62-63

Ⓧ Ango'rosh Grounds

Ango'rosh Brute	62-63
Ango'rosh Sentry	63-64
Ango'rosh Warlock	63-64

Ⓨ Ango'rosh Stronghold

Ango'rosh Mauler	63-64
Ango'rosh Souleater	63-64
Overlord Gorefist	63

Ⓩ Eastern Zangarmarsh

Greater Spore Bat	61-62
Marsh Walker	63-64
Marshlight Bleeder	63-64

(AA) Marshlight Lake

Bogstrok Crusher	62
Bogstrok Razorclaw	62

(AB) Sporeggar

Fhwoor	
Gshaff	
Gzhun'tt	
Khn'nix	
Msshi'fn	
Sporeggar Harvester	63-64
Sporeggar Preserver	63-64
T'shu	

(AC) Blade's Run

Map Legend

		Level
AC	**Quagg Ridge**	
	Bog Lord	64
	Fungal Giant	64
	Starving Bog Lord	63
	Starving Fungal Giant	63
AD	**The Spawning Glen**	
	Mature Spore Sac	
	Sporeggar Spawn	
	Starving Bog Lord	63
	Starving Fungal Giant	62
1	**Coosh'coosh**	**68 Elite**
2	**Portal Clearing**	
3	**Leesa'oh**	
4	**Fahssn**	
5	**West Beacon**	
6	**Twinspire Graveyard**	
7	**East Beacon**	
8	**Horde Field Scout**	
9	**Alliance Field Scout**	
10	**Count Ungula**	**62**

Terokkar Forest

Legend

Herbs

Felweed
Dreaming Glory
Terocone

Minerals

Fel Iron
Adamantite
Khorium

Reputation Information

No specific Reputations, but control of the region in PvP allows characters to collect Spirit Shards from the bosses for all Instances in the zone. These items are handed in to NPCs in Stonebreaker Hold and Allerian Stronghold for various items!

Map Legend

(A) Razorthorn Shelf

(B) Veil Shienor

Ayit	63
Shienor Sorcerer	62-63
Shienor Talonite	62-63

(C) Open Forest (Northeast)

Dampscale Devourer	63-64
Ironjaw	63-64
Royal Teromoth	63-64 Pacify (No Attack for Several Seconds)
Timber Worg Alpha	64
Stonegazer	64 Elite
Warp Stalker	63 Sprint, Movement/Attack Speed Debuff

(D) Firewing Point

Firewing Bloodwarder	63-64
Firewing Defender	63-64
Firewing Warlock	63-64
Isla Starmane	
Sharth Voldoun	65 Elite

(E) Tuurem

Tuuren Hunter	62-63
Tuuren Scavenger	62-63
Wrekt Seer	63

(F) Cenarion Thicket

Dreadfang Lurker	63-64 Very nasty poison attacks
Empoor	64
Empoor's Bodyguard	64
Teromoth	62-63
Timber Worg	62-63
Vicious Teromoth	62-63

(G) Grangol'var Village

Shadowy Advisor	63
Shadowy Executioner	63-64
Shadowy Hunter	65
Shadowy Initiate	62
Shadowy Laborer	60
Shadowy Leader	64
Shadowy Summoner	63-64

(H) Veil Skith

Skithian Dreadhawk	63-64
Skithian Windripper	63-64
Urdak	63

(I) The Bone Wastes

Bonelasher	64-65
Deathskitter	64 Elite Loot Mob
Der'izu Arcanist	64-65
Der'izu Bandit	64-65
Draenei Skeleton	64-65
Dreadfang Widow	63-64
Floon	
Lost Spirit	64-65

(J) Auchindoun

Clarissa	
Draenei Pilgrim	
Ha'lei	
Isfar	
Provisioner Tsaalt	Sha'tar Merchant
Ramdor the Mad	

(K) Veil Lithic

Kokorek	
Mug'gok	Wandering 65
Shalassi Oracle	64-65
Shalassi Talonguard	63-64

(L) Bleeding Hollow Ruins

Boulderfist Invader	64-65
Kilrath	68 Horde Elite
Unkor the Ruthless	65

(M) Stonebreaker Hold

Advisor Faila	
Anvil	
Bar Talet	Bowyer
Forge	
Gardok Ripjaw	
Grek	
Grek's Riding Wolf	
Grenk	General Goods
Innkeeper Grilka	Innkeeper
Kerna	Wind Rider Master
Kurgatok	
Mailbox	
Malukaz	
Mawg Grimshot	
Mokasa	
Rakoria	
Rokag	
Rungor	Trade Goods
Smoker	
Spirit Sage Gartok	
Stonebreaker Grunt	65
Stonebreaker Peon	50-51
Tooki	
Trag	Stable Master
Wanted Poster	

(N) Allerian Stronghold

Allerian Defender	64-66
Allerian Horseman	60
Allerian Peasant	55
Andarl	
Anvil	
Bertelm	
Captain Auric Sunchaser	
Cecil Meyers	Blacksmithing Supplies
Fabian Lanzonelli	General Goods and Bags
Forge	
Furnan Skysoar	Gryphon Master
High Elf Ranger	65
Innkeeper Biribi	Innkeeper
Jenai Starwhisper	
Lady Dena Kennedy	60 Elite
Leeli Longhaggle	Trade Goods
Lemla Hopewing	Apprentice Gryphon Master
Lieutenant Gravelhammer	
Mailbox	
Ros'eleth	
Spirit Sage Zran	
Supply Officer Mills	Rations
Taela Everstride	
Thander	
Wanted Poster	

(O) Bonechewer Ruins

Bonechewer Backbreaker	63-64
Bonechewer Devastator	63-64
Lisaile Fireweaver	64
Timber Worg Alpha	63-64
Warped Peon	64

(P) Skethyl Mountains (Flying Mount Required)

(Q) Veil Shalas

Dugar	63 Horde
Deirom	63 Alliance
Luanga	65 Elite
Shalassi Oracle	64-65
Shalassi Talonguard	63-64

(R) Veil Reskk

Ashkaz	62
Shienor Sorcerer	63
Shienor Talonite	62-63
Shienor Wing Guard	63

(S) The Barrier Hills

(T) Skettis

Skettis Talonite	70
Greater Kaliri	66-68
Skettis Surger	71
Skettis Wing Guard	70
Skettis Windwalker	71
Blackwind Sabrecat	70
Mountain Colossus	72 Elite
Skettis Eviscerator	72
Skettis Time-Shifter	71
Skettis Sentinel	72

(U) Netherweb Ridge

Dreadfang Widow	63-64

(V) Blackwind Lake/W Blackwind Valley

Skettis Talonite	70
Greater Kaliri	66-68
Skettis Surger	71
Skettis Wing Guard	70
Skettis Windwalker	71
Blackwind Sabrecat	70
Mountain Colossus	72 Elite

(1) Auchenai Crypts	**Instance Entrance**
(2) Mana-Tombs	**Instance Entrance**
(3) Sethekk Halls	**Instance Entrance**
(4) The Shadow Labyrinth	**Shadow Labyrinth Key Required**
(5) Spirit Towers	
(6) Silmyr Lake	
Dampscale Basilisk	62-63
(7) Shattrath City	
(8) Carrion Hill	
(9) Refugee Caravan	
(10) Sethekk Tomb	
(11) Tomb of Lights	
(12) Shadowstalker Kaide	**Horde 64**
(13) Theloria Shadecloak	**Alliance 64**
(14) Prospector Balmoral	**Alliance 65**
(15) Lookout Nodak	**Horde 65**
(16) Levixus the Soul Caller	**66 Elite Demon**

Shattrath City

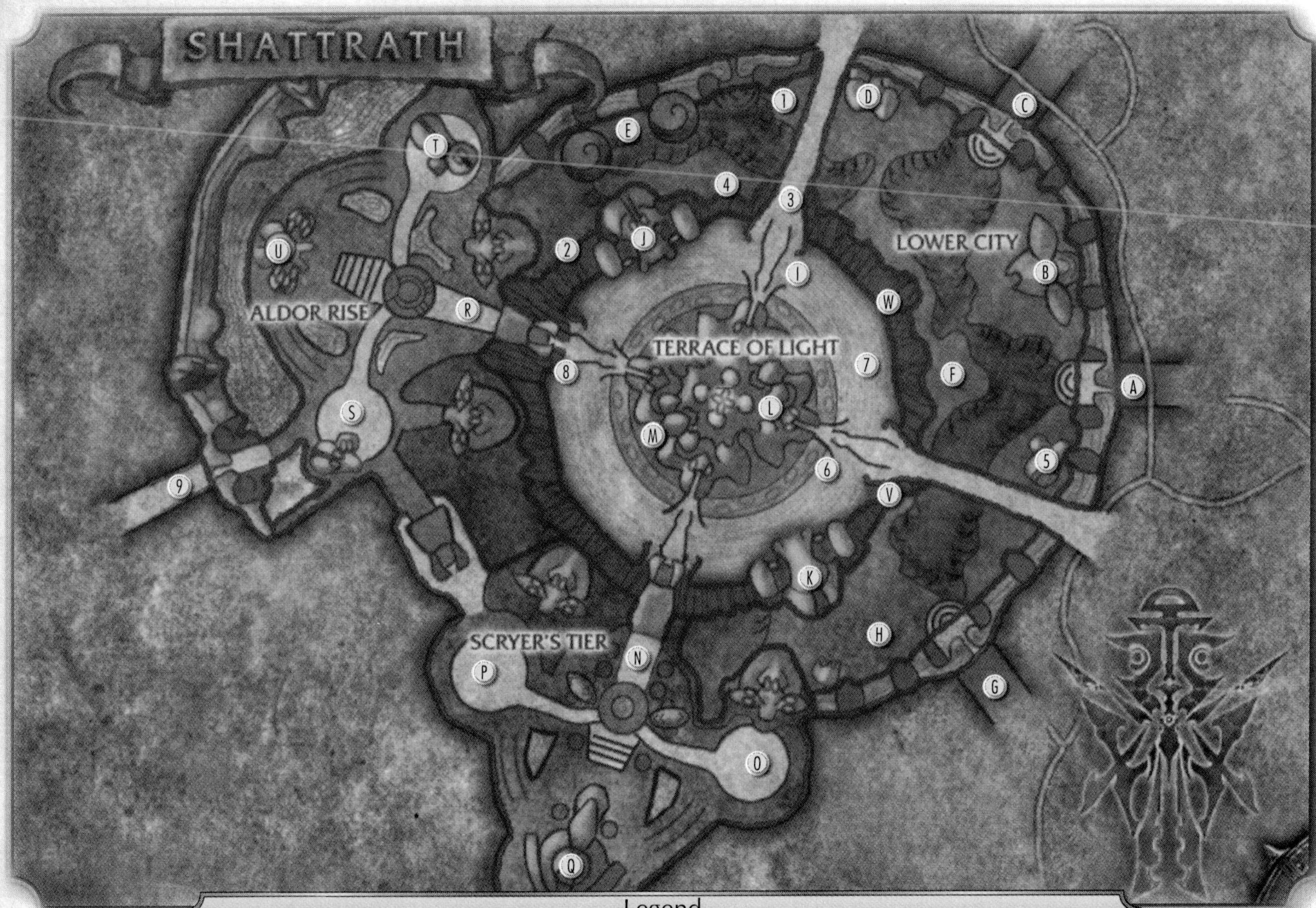

Legend

Herbs	Minerals	Reputation Information
None	None	Scryers (Both Factions)
		The Aldor (Both Factions)
		The Sha'tar (Both Faction)
		Lower City (Both Factions)

Map Legend

A Eastern City Entrance

Broken Refugee	
Dwarf Refugee	
Haggard War Veteran	
Vagabond	
Vagrant	

B World's End Tavern

Albert Quarksprocket	
Haris Pilton	Socialite
Kylene	Barmaid
Leatei	
Mailbox	
Raliq the Drunk	
Sal'salabim	68 Elite
Shaarubo	Bartender
Shattrath Saul	
Tinkerbell	Haris Pilton's Pet

C Northern City Entrance

Haggard War Veteran	

D Mildred's Clinic

Injured Refugee	
Mildred Fletcher	Physician
Refugee Kid	
Seth	
Sha'nir	The Aldor
Zahila	

E Skettis Rise

Araac	Underneath the Rise
Karokka	Poison Supplies
Lissaf	Blade Merchant
Skettis Outcast	

F Crafter's Cubby

Kradu Grimblade	Weapon Crafter
Zula Slagfury	Armor Crafter

G Southern Entrance

Vagabond	
Vagrant	

H Crafter's Market

Aaron Hollman	Blacksmithing Supplies
Cro Threadstrong	Leatherworking Supplies
Darmari	Grand Master Leatherworker
Elin	Tailoring Supplies
Eral	General Goods
Ernie Packwell	Trade Goods
Fantei	Reagent Vendor
Granny Smith	Fruit Seller
Griftah	Amazing Amulets
Jack Trapper	Cook
Jim Saltit	Cooking Supplier
Madame Ruby	Enchanting Supplies
Muffin Man Moser	Bread Merchant
Peasant Refugee	
Seymour	Grand Master Skinner
Viggz Shinesparked	Engineering Supplies

I Aldor Training Area

Aldor Neophyte	70
Aldor Vindicator	70 Elite
Emissary Mordin	63 Elite
Ezekiel	
Grand Anchorite Almonen	70
Harbinger Argomen	
High Exarch Commodus	70
Veteran Vindicator	70

J Aldor Bank

Gromden	Banker
Mailbox	
Mendorn	Banker
Quartermaster Endarin	

K Scryer Bank

Berudan Keysworn	Banker
Inscriber Veredis	Scryer Inscriptions
L'lura Goldspun	Banker
Mailbox	
Quartermaster Enuril	
Scryer Vault Guardian	70

L A'dal's Chamber (East Side)

A'dal	The Sha'tar
Aldor Anchorite	70
Aldor Marksman	70
Aldor Neophyte	70
Harbinger Argomen	
Khadgar	Sons of Lothar
Oric Coe	Alliance 70 Elite
Portal to Darnassus	Alliance Only
Portal to Ironforge	Alliance Only
Portal to Silvermoon City	Horde Only
Portal to Stormwind	Alliance Only
Portal to The Exodar	Alliance Only

M A'Dal's Chamber (West Side)

Aldor Anchorite	70
Aldor Neophyte	70
G'eras Vindicator	70 Elite
G'eras	Dungeon Hard Mode Rewards
Portal to Orgrimmar	Horde Only
Portal to Thunder Bluff	Horde Only
Portal to Undercity	Horde Only
Spymistress Mehlisah Suncrown	

N Scryer's Tier

Scryer Arcane Guardian	70
Scryer Arcanist	60-61
Scryer Retainer	64-66

O East Wing

Dathris Sunstriker	
Innkeeper Haelthol	Innkeeper
Lisrythe Bloodwatch	Fence/Gem Merchant
Mahir Redstroke	Dagger Vendor
Mailbox	
Nalama the Merchant	General Goods
Trader Endernor	Trade Goods
Urumir Stavebright	Staff Vendor

P West Wing

Quelama Greenroad	Wand Vendor
Scryer Arcanist	60-61
Scryer Retainer	64-66
Selanam the Blade	Sword Vendor

Q The Library

Arodis Sunblade	Keeper of Shattari Artifacts
Enchanter Aeldron	Expert Enchanter
Enchanter Salias	Apprentice Enchanter
Enchantress Metura	Journeyman Enchanter
Enchantress Volali	Artisan Enchanter
High Enchanter Bardolan	Master Enchanter
Magister Falris	
Magistrix Fyalenn	
Mi'irku Farstep	Portal Trainer
Olodam Farhollow	
Scryer Arcane Guardian	70
Scryer Arcanist	60-61
Scryer Retainer	64-66
Vinemster Alamaro	Wine Vendor
Voren'thal the Seer	
Yurial Soulwater	Enchanting Supplies

R Aldor Rise

Adyen the Lightwarden	72 Elite
Aldor Anchorite	
Harbinger Erothem	70

S South Rise

Aldor Vindicator	70 Elite
Garul	Food and Drink Vendor
Mailbox	
Minalei	Innkeeper
Neophyte Combatant	70

T North Rise

Ahamen	Staff Vendor
Aldor Anchorite	70
Aldor Vindicator	70 Elite
Hamanar	Grand Master Jewelcrafter
Inessera	Jewelcrafting Supplies Vendor

U Temple of the Aldor

Aldor Anchorite	70
Anchorite Attendant	19
Anchorite Lyteera	
Asuur	Keeper of Shattari Artifacts
Ishanah	High Priestess of the Aldor

V Horde Battlemasters

Keldor the Lost	Horde Arathi Basin Battlemaster
Montok Redhands	Horde Warsgon Gulch Battlemaster
Wolf-Sister Maka	Horde Alterac Valley Battlemaster
Yula the Fair	Horde Eye of the Storm Battlemaster

W Alliance Battlemasters

Adam Eternum	Alliance Arathi Basin Battlemaster
Haelga Slatefist	Alliance Alterac Valley Battlemaster
Iravar	Alliance Eye of the Storm Battlemaster
Lylandor	Alliance Warsong Gulch Battlemaster
Battle-Tiger	Adam Eternum's Pet

1	**Oloraak**	**Fish Merchant**
2	**"Dirty" Larry and "Epic" Malone**	
3	**Farmer Griffith and Ewe**	
4	**Arcanist Adyria and Iz'zard**	
5	**Nicole Bartlett's Boarding House and Mailbox**	
6	**Harbinger Haronem**	**The Aldor**
7	**Nutral**	**Flight Master**
8	**Lathrai**	
9	**Exit to Nagrand**	

Nagrand

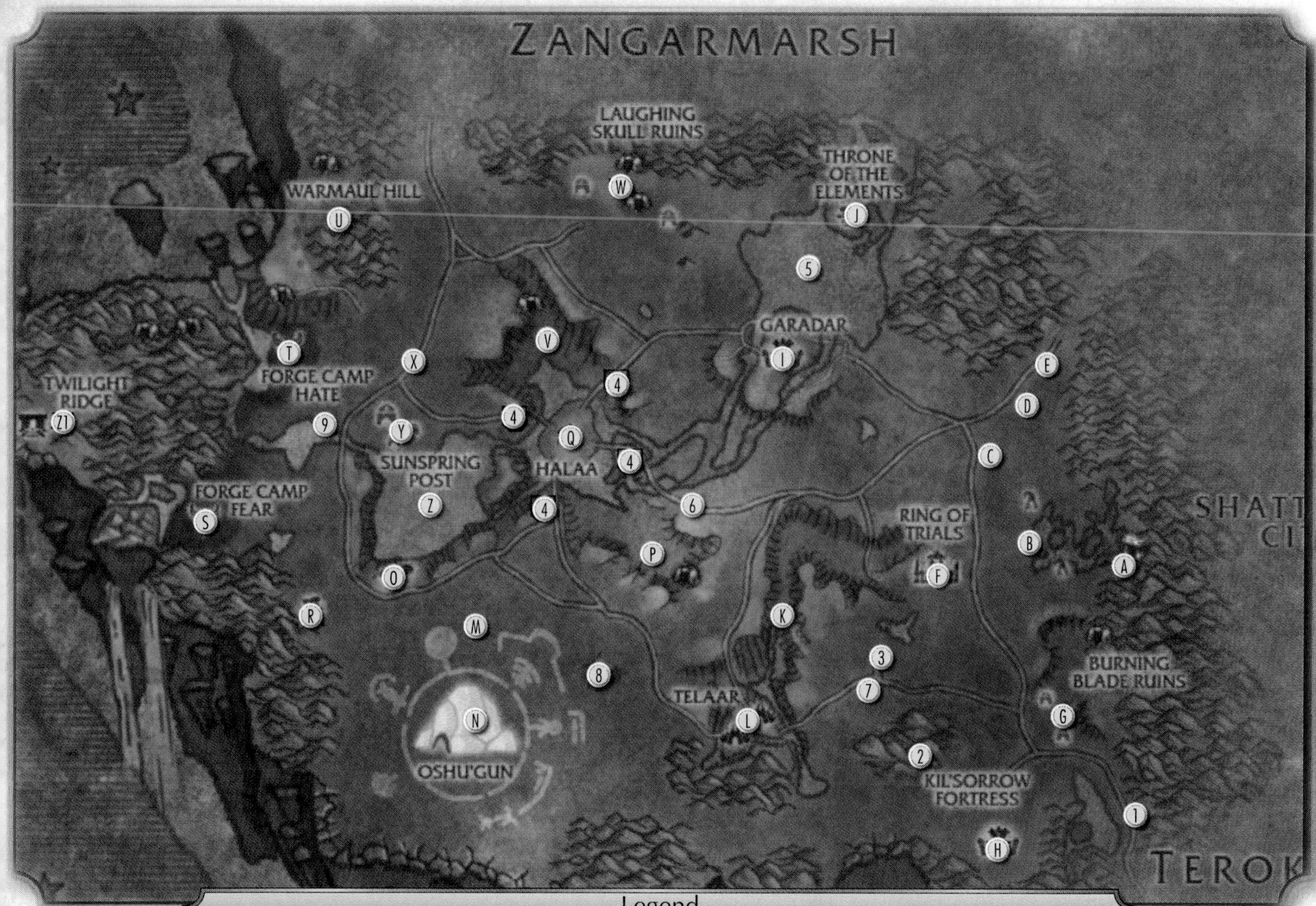

ZANGARMARSH
LAUGHING SKULL RUINS
THRONE OF THE ELEMENTS
WARMAUL HILL
GARADAR
TWILIGHT RIDGE
FORGE CAMP HATE
SUNSPRING POST
HALAA
FORGE CAMP FEAR
RING OF TRIALS
SHATT CI
BURNING BLADE RUINS
TELAAR
OSHU'GUN
KIL'SORROW FORTRESS
TEROK

Legend

Herbs

- Felweed
- Dreaming Glory

Minerals

- Fel Iron
- Adamantite
- Rich Adamantite
- Khorium

Reputation Information

- The Consortium (Both Factions)
- Mag'har (Horde)
- Kurenai (Alliance)

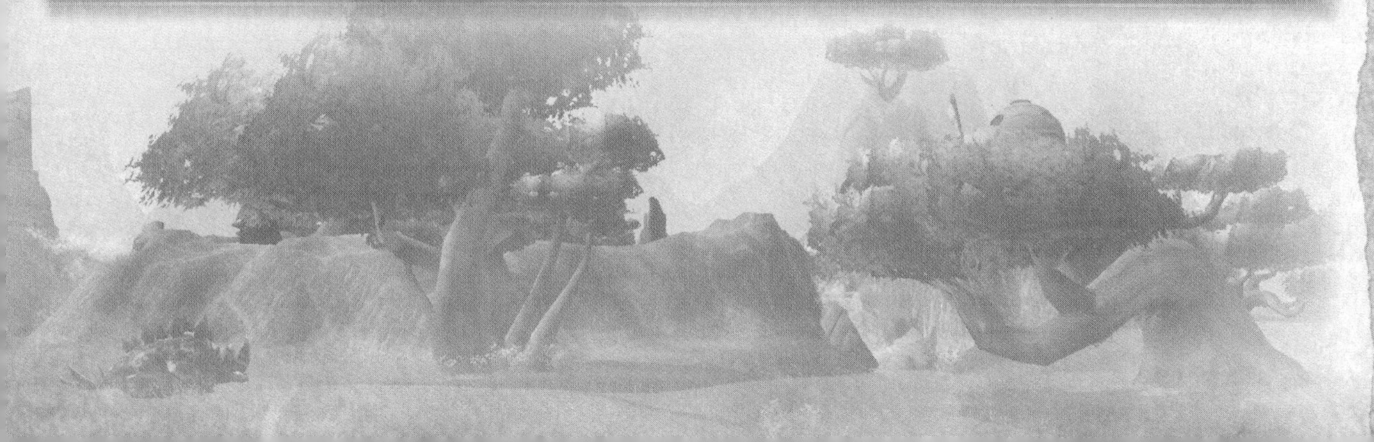

Map Legend

A The High Path
Entrance to Shattrath

B Windyreed Village

Windyreed Scavenger	64-65
Windyreed Wretch	64

C The Barrier Hills

Clefthoof	64-65
Dust Howler	64
Talbuk Stag	64-65
Tortured Earth Spirit	65

D Nesingwary Safari

Campfire	
Harold Lane	
Hemet Nesingwary	
Pilot Marsha	Engineering Goods
Shado "Fitz" Farstrider	

E Windyreed Pass

F Ring of Trials
Free-for-All Combat Area

G Burning Blade Ruins

Anvil	
Boulderfist Crusher	64-65
Boulderfist Mystic	65
Corki	60 Alliance
Burning Blade Pyres (3)	
Forge	
Lantresor of the Blade	70 Elite

H Kil'sorrow Fortress

Dark Worg	64-65
Giselda the Crone	67
Shadow Council Cultist	65
Shadow Council Deathsworn	65-66
Shadow Council Spellbinder	66-67
Warmaul Ogre Banner	

I Garadar

Bleeding Hollow Orphan	
Bleeding Hollow Refugee	
Captain Kroghan	
Captured Halaani Vindicator	
Consortium Recruiter	The Consortium
Elementalist Yal'hah	
Elkay'gan the Mystic	
Farseer Corhuk	The Lightning Sons
Farseer Kurkush	The Lightning Sons
Farseer Margadesh	The Lightning Sons
Garadar Bulletin Board	
Garadar Defender	65
Garadar Mailbox	
Garadar Wolf Rider	66-67
Garrosh	Son of Hellscream (Boss)
Greatmother Geyah	Boss
Gursha	Wind Rider Master
Jorin Deadeye	
Mag'har Pitfighter	
Mathar G'ochar	Trade Supplies
Matron Celestine	
Matron Tikkit	Innkeeper
Nula the Butcher	Cooking Supplies
Ohlorn Farstrider	Nesingwary Safari
Osrok the Immovable	Armorsmith and Blacksmithing Supplies
Provisioner Nasela	Mag'har Quartermaster
Stabled Bear	
Stabled Boar	
Stabled Panther	
Stabled Raptor	
Stabled Tallstrider	
Sunspring Post Orphan	
Sunspring Post Refugee	
Thrall	Boss
Vanteg	Reagents and Poisons
Warden Bullrok	

J Throne of the Elements

Aborius	Fury of Water
Elementalist Lo'ap	The Earthen Ring
Elementalist Morgh	The Earthen Ring
Elementalist Sharvak	The Earthen Ring
Elementalist Untrag	The Earthen Ring
Gordawg	Fury of Earth
Incineratus	Fury of Fire
Kalandrios	Fury of Air

K Telaari Basin

Enraged Crusher	66
Tortured Earth Spirit	64-65

L Telaar

"Shotgun" Jones	Nesingwary Safari
Arechron	
Borto	Trade Supplies
Caregiver Isel	Innkeeper
Elementalist Loki	The Earthen Ring
Furgu	Hippogryph Master
Huntress Bintook	
Huntress Kima	
Kurenai Pitfighter	
Luftasia	Stable Master
Mailbox	
Mo'mor the Breaker	
Nahuud	
Nancila	General Goods
Ogir	Reagents and Poisons
Otonbu the Sage	
Poli'lukluk the Wiser	
Sparik	Armorsmith and Blacksmithing Supplies
Stabled Kurenai Lion	
Stabled Kurenai Panther	
Talaari Watcher	65
Telaar Bulletin Board	
Telaari Citizen	
Telaari Elekk Rider	65
Trader Narasu	Kurenai Quartermaster
Warden Iolol	

M Spirit Fields

Aged Clefthood	67
Banthar	67 Elite
Bull Elekk	67
Clefthoof Bull	65-66
Clefthoof Calf	62
Clefthoof	64-65
Durn the Hungerer	67 Elite
Gava'xi	67
Living Cyclone	66
Oshu'gun Crystal Fragment	
Storm Rager	66
Vir'aani Arcanist	66-67
Vir'aani Raider	66
Voidspawn	65-66
Wild Elekk	66

N Oshu'gun

K'ure	Naaru
Orc Ancestor	
Shadow Council Ritualist	67-68
Subjugator Vaz'shir	68
Terrorguard	67-68

O Aeris Landing

Consortium Claviger	
Consortium Gemcutter	
Consortium Overseer	
Gezhe	
Zerid	

P Southwind Cleft

Boulderfist Mage	66
Boulderfist Warrior	65-66

Q Halaa

Chief Researcher Kartos	
Halaani Guard	65
Quartermaster Davian Vaclav	Halaa Faction Merchant

R Ancestral Grounds

Agitated Orc Spirit	66-67

S Forge Camp: Fear

Felguard Legionnaire	67-68 Elite
Gan'arg Tinkerer	66-68
Mo'arg Engineer	67-68 Elite
Xirkis, Overseer of Fear	68 Elite

T Forge Camp: Hate

Demos, Overseer of Hate	68 Elite
Fel Cannon: Hate	70
Felguard Legionnaire	67-68 Elite
Gan'arg Tinkerer	66-68
Mo'arg Engineer	67-68 Elite
Mo'arg Master Planner	68 Elite

U Warmaul Hill

Cho'war the Pillager	67 Elite
Earthen Brand	Gurok the Usurper Summoned Here
Mag'har Prisoners	Locked in Cages/Requires Warmaul Prisoner Key
Mountain Gronn	67 Elite
Warmaul Brute	66-67
Warmaul Chef Bufferlo	66 Elite
Warmaul Warlock	66-67

V Northwind Cleft

Boulderfist Mage	65-66
Boulderfist Warrior	65-66
Muck Spawn	65-66

W Laughing Skull Ruins

Blazing Warmaul Pyre	
Gurgthock	
Mogor	67 Elite (Chain Combat Event)
Warmaul Reaver	65-66
Warmaul Shaman	65-66
Zorbo the Advisor	66

X Mag'hari Procession

Elder Ungriz	Horde 68

Map Legend

	Elder Yorley	Horde 67
	Saurfang the Younger	Horde 70 Elite
Y	**Sunspring Post**	
	Kurenai Captive	Alliance 62
	Mag'har Captive	Horde 62
	Murkblood Brute	67
	Murkblood Putrifier	65-66
	Murkblood Raiders	66-67
	Murkblood Scavenger	64
	Ortor of Murkblood	67
	Sunspring Vilager	Corpses
Z	**Lake Sunspring**	
	Lake Surger	65-66
	Watoosun's Polluted Essence	66
1	**The Twilight Ridge**	
	Deathshadow Archon	70
	Deathshadow Spellbinder	70
	Deathshadow Overlord	71
	Deathshadow Warlock	70
	Deathshadow Imp	70
	Deathshadow Acolyte	70
	Deathshadow Hound	70
	Reth'hedron the Subduer	73 Elite
2	**The Low Path**	
3	**Lump**	**65 Sleeping, Charge**
4	**Clan Watch**	
5	**Wyvern Camps**	**Used to Start Bombing Runs**
6	**Skysong Lake**	
7	**Abandoned Armory**	
8	**Wazat**	
	Tusker	**68 Elite**
9	**Altrius the Sufferer**	**Quest Giver for Forge Camps**

Blade's Edge Mountains

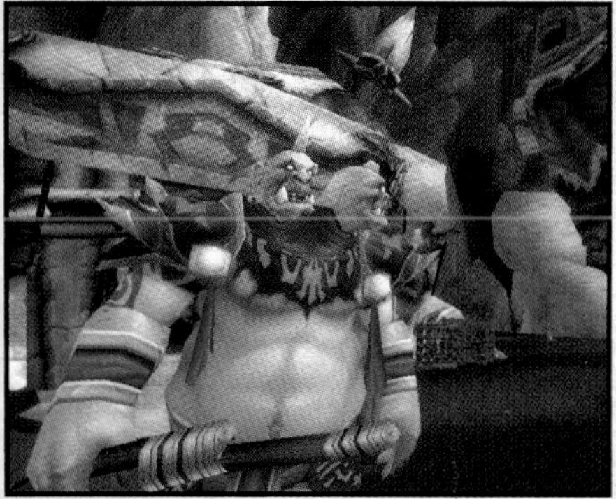

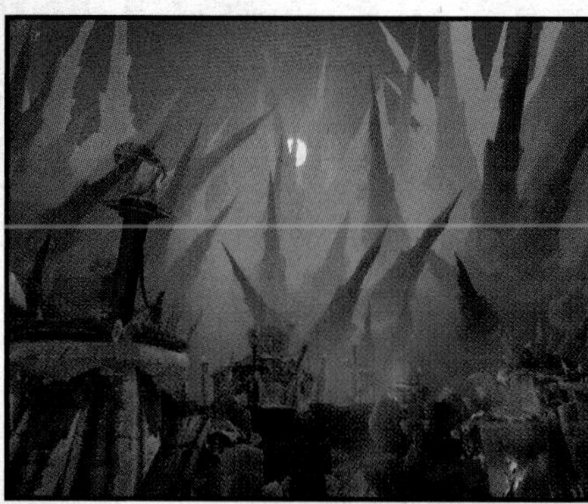

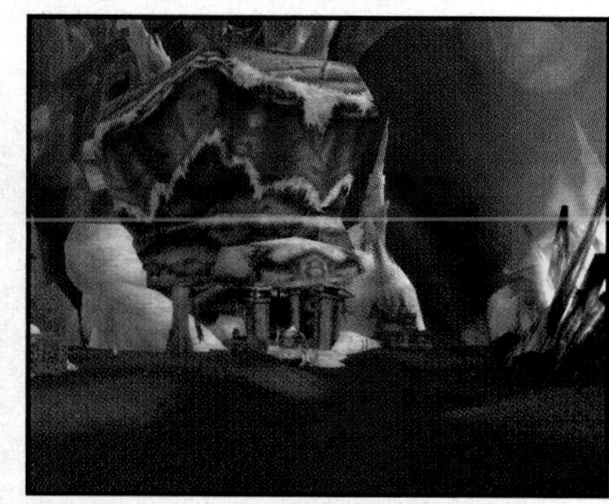

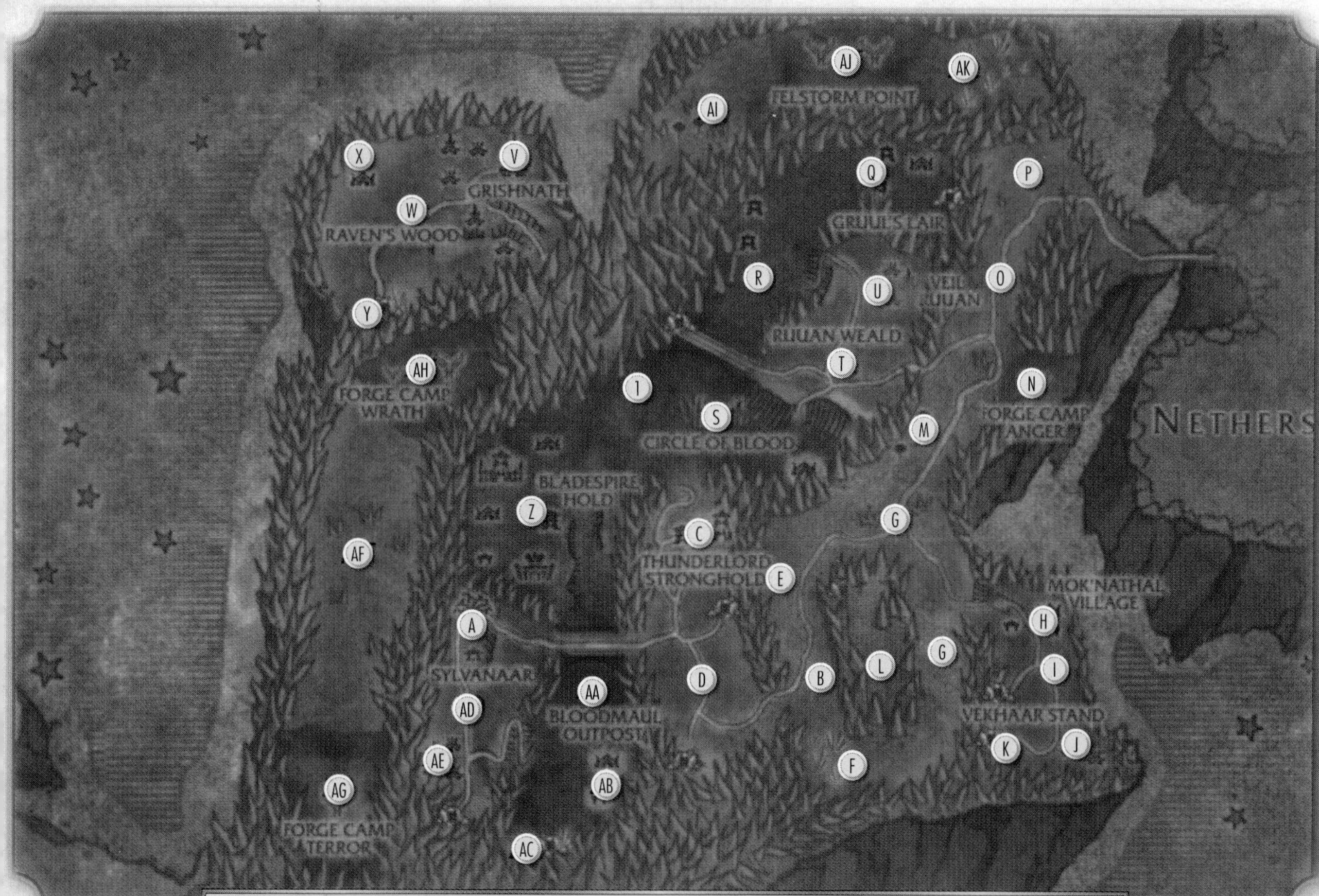

AJ
AK
FELSTORM POINT
AI
X
V
GRISHNATH
W
RAVEN'S WOOD
Q
P
GRUUL'S LAIR
R
U
VEIL RUUAN
O
Y
RUUAN WEALD
T
AH
FORGE CAMP WRATH
1
S
N
CIRCLE OF BLOOD
M
FORGE CAMP ANGER
NETHERS
BLADESPIRE HOLD
Z
C
G
AF
THUNDERLORD STRONGHOLD
E
MOK'NATHAL VILLAGE
A
H
G
L
B
D
I
SYLVANAAR
AA
AD
BLOODMAUL OUTPOST
VEKHAAR STAND
K
J
AE
F
AB
AG
FORGE CAMP TERROR
AC

Legend

Mining

Adamantite
Fel Iron

Herbalism

Felweed
Dreaming Glory

Reputation Information

Cenarion Expedition (Both Factions)

Map Legend

	Location / Name	Info
A	**Sylvanaar**	
	Amerun Leafshade	Hippogryph Master
	Borgrim Stouthammer	Quest Giver
	Bronwyn Stouthammer	Quest Giver
	Cahill	Weaponsmith
	Caoileann	Trade Goods
	Commander Skyshadow	Quest Giver
	Innkeeper Shaunessy	Innkeeper
	Kialon Nightblade	Quest Giver
	Mailbox	
	Moonwell	
	Rina Moonspring	Quest Giver
	Sylvanaar Sentinel	65
	Syvanaar Ancient Protector	70
	Tanaide	General Goods
	Trayana	Quest Giver
B	**Toshley's Station**	
	Bembil Knockhammer	General Goods
	Bossi Pentapiston	Engineering Supplies
	Razak Ironsides	70 Elite
	Rip Pedalslam	Gryphon Master
	Sassa Weldwell	Trade Goods
	Station Bot-Jock	67
	Station Guard	70
	Station Technician	67
	Tally Zapnabber	Quest Giver
	Tally's Twin	Quest Giver
C	**Thunderlord Stronghold**	
	Anvil	
	Daga Ramba	Potions
	Forge	
	Gholah	Innkeeper
	Gor'drek	Quest Giver
	Karnaze	General Goods
	Lor	Stable Master
	Mailbox	
	Nekthar	Quest Giver
	Old Orok	Fruit and Fungus
	Orgatha	Axesmith
	Pol Snowhoof	Trade Goods
	Raiza	Throwing Weapons
	Rexxar	72 Elite
	Rokgah Bloodgrip	Quest Giver
	Threlc	Fishmonger
	Thunderlord Grunt	65
	Tor'chunk Twoclaws	Quest Giver
	Unoke Tenderhoof	Wind Rider Master
	Wanted Poster	
D	**Jagged Ridge**	
	Bladewing Bloodletter	65-66
	Thunderlord Dire Wolf	65-66
E	**Bladespire Outpost**	
	Bladespire Crusher	67
	Bladespire Mystic	67
F	**Singing Ridge**	
	Blade's Edge Rock Flayer	66-67
	Lesser Nether Drake	66-67
G	**Razor Ridge**	
	Daggermaw Lashtail	66-67
	Ridgespine Stalker	67
	Scalewing Serpent	66
	Maggoc	66 Elite
H	**Mok'Nathal Village**	
	Braagor	Butcher
	Erool	Trade Goods
	Grikka	Grand Master Leatherworker
	Krugash	General Goods
	Matron Varah	Innkeeper
	Mok'Nathal Hunter	65
	Ragar	Leatherworking Supplies
	Ruka	Smashing Weapons
	Spiritcaller Grakosh	Quest Giver
	Spiritcaller Roxnar	Quest Giver
	Spiritcaller Skrash	Quest Giver
I	**Vekhaar Stand**	
	Tawny Silkwing	65-66
	Tawny Silkwing Larva	65-66
J	**Veil Vekh**	
	Angry Arakkoa Pet	61
	Vekh'nir Dreadhawk	65-66
	Vekh'nir Keeneye	65-66
	Vekh'nir Matriarch	66
	Vekh'nir Stormcaller	65-66
K	**Trogma's Claim**	
	Arakkoa Ogre Slave	65-66
	Vekh'nir Dreadhawk	65-66
	Vekh'nir Stormcaller	65-66
L	**Death's Door**	
	Deathforge Over-Smith	68
	Deathforge Technician	67-68
	Eredar Highlord	68 Elite
	Maiden of Nightmares	69
	Void Terror	68
M	**Razaani Camp**	
	Fiendling Flest Beast	67
	Razaani Nexus Stalker	67-68
	Razaani Raider	67-68
	Razaani Spell-Thief	67-68
	Ridgespine Horror	67
N	**Forge Camp: Anger**	
	Anger Guard	67-68
	Doomcryer	68 Elite
	Doomforge Attendant	69
	Doomforge Engineer	69
	Fel Corrupter	67
O	**Bladed Gulch**	
	Fel Corrupter	66-67
	Felsworn Daggermaw	67
	Felsworn Scalewing	67
P	**Skald**	
	Scalded Basilisk	67-68
	Searing Elemental	67-68
	Skald Imp	67-68
Q	**Gruul's Lair**	
	Bladespire Battlemage	67 Elite
	Bladespire Chef	67 Elite
	Bladespire Enforcer	67 Elite
	Bladespire Ravager	67 Elite
	Fingrom	67 Elite
	Goc	70 Elite
R	**Bloodmaul Camp**	
	Bloodmaul Battle Worg	66-67
	Bloodmaul Bremaster	66
	Bloodmaul Mauler	65-66
	Bloodmaul Warlock	65-66
	Dorgok	66
S	**Circle of Blood**	
	"Lefty" Puddemup	Arena Battlemaster
	Meminine	
	Steamwheedle Sam	Arena Promoter
T	**Ruuan Weald**	
	Expedition Warden	70
	Moonwell	
	Noko Moonwhisper	Reagent Vendor
	Rashere Pridehoof	Trade Goods
	Xerintha Ravenoak	Food and Drink
	Zenyen Swiftstrider	Trade Goods
U	**Veil Ruuan**	
	Beryl Silkwing Larva	66-67
	Beryl Silkwing	66-67
	Ruuan Weald Basilisk	66
	Ruuan'ok Cloudgazer	66-67
	Ruuan'ok Matriarch	67
	Ruuan'ok Ravenguard	66-67
	Ruuan'ok Skyfury	66-67
V	**Grishnath**	
	Grishna Basilisk	67
	Grishna Falconwing	67-68
	Grishna Harbinger	67-88
	Grishna Matriarch	68
	Grishna Raven	63-64
	Grishna Scorncrow	67-68
W	**Raven's Wood**	
	Dire Raven	67-68
	Raven's Wood Leafbeard	67-68
	Raven's Wood Stonebark	68 Elite
X	**Boulder'mok**	
	Plumpcheek Brute	67-68
	Plumpcheek Chieftain	68
	Plumpcheek Shaman	67-68
Y	**Blackwing Coven**	
	Wyrmcult Adept	68
	Wyrmcult Blackwhelp	67-68
	Wyrmcult Dragon Egg	65
	Wyrmcult Zealot	67-68
Z	**Bladespire Hold**	
	Anvil	
	Bladespire Brute	65-66
	Bladespire Champion	66
	Bladespire Cook	65-66
	Bladespire Raptor	65-66
	Bladespire Shaman	65-66
	Droggam	66
	Forge	
	Gorr'Dim	67
	Grulloc	66 Elite
	Korgaah	65
	Mugdorg	66
	Thunderlord Clan Arrow	
	Thunderlord Clan Drum	
	Thunderlord Clan Tablet	
AA	**Bloodmaul Ravine**	
	Bloodmaul Brew Keg	
	Bloodmaul Brewmaster	65
	Bloodmaul Dire Wolf	65
	Bloodmaul Geomancer	65-66
	Bloodmaul Skirmisher	65-66
	T'chali the Witch Doctor	Quest Giver
AB	**Bloodmaul Outpost**	
	Bloodmaul Brew Keg	
	Bloodmaul Brewmaster	65
	Bloodmaul Dire Wolf	65
	Bloodmaul Geomancer	65-66
	Bloodmaul Skirmisher	65-66
	Grimnok Battleborn	67
AC	**Draenethyst Mine**	
	Bloodmaul Brew Keg	
	Bloodmaul Brewmaster	65
	Bloodmaul Brute	65-66
	Bloodmaul Dire Wolf	65
	Bloodmaul Drudger	65-66
	Bloodmaul Geomancer	65-66

Map Legend

	Name	Level
	Bloodmaul Skirmisher	65-66
	T'chali's Hookah	
AD	**The Living Grove**	
	Fey Drake	65-66
	Grovestalker Lynx	65-66
	Living Grove Defender	65-66
	Stronglimb Deeproot	66 Elite
AE	**Veil Lashh**	
	Lashh'an Kaliri	61-62
	Lashh'an Talonite	65-66
	Lashh'an Windwalker	65-66
	Lashh'an Wing Guard	65-66
AF	**Vortex Pinnacle**	
	Deathlash Stinger	71
	Spire Needler	71-72
	Daggertail Lizard	73 Elite
	Wrath Corrupter	70-72
	Bladespine Basilisk	72
	Vortex Walker	71 Elite
AG	**Forge Camp: Terror**	
	Fear Fiend	70
	Legion Fel Cannon MKII	70
	Wrath Speaker	70
	Vile Fire-Soul	70
	Abyssal Flamebringer	71
	Terror-Fire Guardian	71
	Nightmare Imp	70
	Nightmare Weaver	70 Elite
	Terrordar the Tormentor	70 Elite
AH	**Forge Camp: Wrath**	
	Wrath Hound	69
	Wrath Reaver	72 Elite
	Wrath Fiend	70
	Fel Rager	70
	Furnace Guard	70
	Wrath Speaker	70
	Galvanoth	71 Elite
AI	**Bash'ir Landing**	
	Bash'ir Arcanist	71
	Lightning Wasp	70
	Unbound Ethereal	70
	Bash'ir Raider	70
	Bash'ir Spell-Thief	71
	Bash'ir Arcanist	72
	Deathlash Stinger	72-73
	Amberpelt Clefthoff	71
	Daggertail Lizard	72
AJ	**Felstorm Point**	
	Darkflame Infernal	70
	Felstorm Corruptor	71
	Insidious Familiar	71
	Witness of Doom	70
	Felstorm Overseer	71
AK	**Crystal Spine**	
	Shard-Hide Boar	70-71
	Warp-Mane Chimaera	72
	Shard Stalker	72
	Trigul	72 Elite
1	**Young Crust Burster**	**66-67**

NETHERSTORM

Legend

Mining		*Herbalism*	*Reputation Information*
Apex	67 Elite	Netherbloom	Aldor (Both Factions)
Farahlon Breaker	69-70	Felweed	Scryers (Both Factions)
Cragskaar	69 Elite	Golden Sansam	Consortium (Both Factions)
Adamantite		Dreaming Glory	
Rich Adamantite			

Map Legend

A Area 52

Anchorite Karja	Quest Giver
Area 52 Big Bruiser	70 Elite
Area 52 Bruiser	65
Bill	Quest Giver
Chief Engineer Trep	Quest Giver
Dash	Trade Supplies
Doc	
Exarch Orelis	Quest Giver
Gant	Food & Drink
Innkeeper Remi Dodoso	Innkeeper
Irradiated Worker	61
Kalynna Lathred	
Kizzie	General Supplies
Krexcil	Flight Master
Lee Sparks	The Taskmaster
Magistrix Larynna	Quest Giver
Mailbox	
Nether-Stalker Khay'ji	Quest Giver
Netherstorm Agent	65
Off-Duty Engineer	
Papa Wheeler	Quest Giver
Qiff	Engineering Supplies
Ravandwyr	Quest Giver
Rocket-Chief Fuselage	Quest Giver
Scryer Retainer	65
Seasoned Vindicator	70 Elite
Spymaster Thalodien	Quest Giver
Veronia	Quest Giver
Vixton Pinchwhistle	Arena Vendor
Wanted Poster	
Xyrol	Grand Master Engineer

B B'naar Balista Camp

Captain Arathyn	68
Sunfury Bloodwarder	67-68

C Manaforge B'naar

Arcane Annihilator	68 Elite
B'naar Control Console	
Sunfury Astromancer	67-68
Sunfury Bloodwarder	67-68
Sunfury Captain	68
Sunfury Geologist	67-68
Sunfury Magister	67-68
Sunfury Warp-Engineer	67-68
Sunfury Warp-Master	68

D Southwest Netherstorm

Mana Wraith	67-68
Nether Ray	67-68
Netherrock	68
Shaleskin Flayer	67-68
Sundered Rumbler	67-68
Warp Aberration	67-68

E Ruins of Enkaat

Bot-Specialist Alley	Quest Giver
Disembodied Protector	67-68
Disembodied Vindicator	67-68
Etherlithium Matrix Crystal	Quest Target
Maxx A. Million Mk. I	63
Maxx A. Million Mk. II	65
Maxx A. Million Mk. V	67

F Southwest Cliffs

Nether Ray	67-68
Phase Hunter	67-68

G Camp of Boom

Boom Bot	67-68
Dr. Boom	68

H Arklonis Ridge

Farahlon Giant	67-68

I Arklon Ruins

Artifact Seeker	67-68
Felblade Doomguard	67-68
Pentatharon	69

J The Heap

Ethereal Technology	Quest Target
N. D. Meancamp	Quest Giver
Scrapped Fel Reaver	70 Elite
Warp-Raider Nesaad	69
Zaxxis Raider	67-68
Zaxxis Stalker	67-68

K Manaforge Coruu

Arcane Annihilator	68 Elite
Arch Mage Adonis	68
Caledis Brightdawn	Quest Giver
Commander Dawnforge	68
Coruu Control Console	
Lariel Sunrunner	Quest Giver
Overseer Seylanna	68
Sunfury Arcanist	67-68
Sunfury Arch Mage	68
Sunfury Guardsman	67-68
Sunfury Guardsman	68
Sunfury Researcher	67-68

L Sunfury Hold

Sunfury Archer	67-68
Sunfury Flamekeeper	68
Sunfury Arch Mage	68
Sunfury Researcher	67-68

M Kirin'Var Village

Abjurist Belmara	68
Battle-Mage Dathric	68
Bessy	Quest Giver
Cohlien Frostweaver	68
Conjurer Luminrath	68
Kirin'Var Apprentice	69
Kirin'Var Ghost	68
Kirin'Var Rune	
Kirin'Var Spectre	68
Rhonsus	69
Severed Defender	68
Severed Spirit	68
Skeletal Stallion	68
Spectral Bovine	5
Tormented Soul	68

M1 Western Kirin'Var Village

Book Shelf	
Dresser	
Foot Locker	
Mageslayer	68-69
Mana Bomb Fragment	
Mana Seeker	68-69
Weapon Rack	

N The Violet Tower

Apprentice Andrethan	Quest Giver
Ar'kelos	68
Archmage Vargoth	Quest Giver
Custodian Dieworth	Quest Giver
Lieutenant-Sorcerer Morran	Quest Giver
Thadell	Quest Giver

O Chapel Yard

Kirin'Var Ghost	68
Naberius	69 Elite
Tormented Citizen	68
Tormented Soul	68

P The Vortex Fields

Apex	67 Elite
Mana Snapper	67
Swiftwing Shredder	69
Warp Chaser	67-68

Q Invasion Point: Destroyer

Drijya	Quest Giver
Warp-Gate Engineer	68-69

R Manaforge Duro

Duro Control Console	
Glacius	67
Nether Anomaly	68
Nether Beast	68
Summoner Kanthin	69
Sunfury Bowman	68-69
Sunfury Centurion	68-69
Sunfury Conjurer	68-69
Sunfury Technician	68

S The Scrap Field

Doomclaw	69
Gan'arg Engineer	68-69
Mo'arg Doomsmith	69

T Midrealm Post

Dealer Dunar	General Provisioner
Gahruj	Quest Giver
Mama Wheeler	Quest Giver
Mehrdad	Quest Giver
Shauly Pore	Quest Giver

U Eco-Dome Midrealm

Barbscale Crocolisk	68-69
Ivory Bell	Quest Target
Ripfang Lynx	68-69
Shimmerwing Moth	68-69

V Central Cliffs

Mana Snapper	67-68
Nether Ray	67-68

W Voidwind Plateau

Craghide Basilisk	68-69
Seeping Sludge	69-70
Shaleskin Ripper	68-69

X Celestial Ridge

Ethereal Teleport Pad	
Jorad Mace	Quest Giver
Nether Dragon	70
Nether Drake	68-69
Shrouded Figure	Quest Giver
Tyri	Quest Giver

Y Protectorate Watch Post

Captain Saeed	71

Map Legend

Y
Commander Ameer — Quest Giver
Dealer Hazzin — General Provisioner
Flesh Handler Viridius — Quest Giver
Professor Dabiri — Quest Giver
Protectorate Avenger — 69-70
Protectorate Nether Drake — 70
Protectorate Vanguard — 70
Researcher Navuud — Quest Giver
Subservient Flest Beast — 61
Wind Trader Marid — Quest Giver

Z Etherium Staging Grounds
Captured Protectorate Vanguard — Quest Giver
Congealed Void Horror — 70 Elite
Ethereum Archon — 69
Ethereum Assassin — 69
Ethereum Gladiator — 70
Ethereum Nexus-Stalker — 70
Ethereum Overlord — 69-70
Ethereum Prison
Ethereum Researcher — 69-70
Ethereum Shocktrooper — 69-70
Ethereum Sparring Dummy — 68
Ethereum Transponder Zeta
Void Waste — 69
Warden Icoshock — 70

AA Access Shaft Zeon
Agent Ya-six — Quest Giver
Arconus the Insatiable — 70
Fleshfiend — 69-70
Parasitic Fleshbeast — 69-70
Withered Corpse — 69-70

AB Manaforge Ultris
Dimensius the All-Devouring — 70 Elite
Seeping Ooze — 70
Seeping Sludge — 68-69
Unstable Voidwraith — 68-69
Voidshrieker — 68-69

AC Ruins of Farahlon
Culuthas — 70 Elite
Eye of Culuthas — 69-70
Hound of Culuthas — 69-70

AD Netherstone
Cragskaar — 69 Elite
Farahlon Breaker — 69-70

AE Eco-Dome Farfield
Scythetooth Raptor — 68-69

Tashar — Quest Giver
Tyrantus — 71

AF Forge Base: Gehenna
Fel Imp — 68-69
Forgemaster Sil'harad — 68 Elite
Gan'arg Technomancer — 68-69
Ironspine Forgelord — 68
Legion Fel Cannon — 70
Wrath Priestess — 68-69
Wrathbringer — 68-69

AG Forge Base: Oblivion
Cyber-Rage Foregelord — 69
Fel Imp — 68-69
Forgemaster Morug — 68 Elite
Gan'arg Mekgineer — 68-69
Legion Fel Cannon — 70
Wrath Priestess — 68-69
Wrathbringer — 68-69

AH Northern Netherstorm
Sundered Thunderer — 68-69
Warp Monstrosity — 68-69

AI Tuluman's Landing
Kaylaan — Quest Giver
Nether-Stalker Oazul — Quest Giver
Wind Trader Tuluman — Weapon Merchant

AJ Eco-Dome Sutheron
Farahlon Lasher — 68-69
Markaru — 68
Talbuk Doe — 68-69
Talbuk Sire — 68-69

AK Eco-Dome Skyperch
Farahlon Lasher — 68-69
Talbuk Doe — 68-69
Talbuk Sire — 68-69

AL The Stormspire
Action Jaxon — Quest Giver
Asarnan — Grand Master Enchanter
Audi the Needle — Quest Giver
Aurine Moonblaze — Quest Giver
Cookpot
Dealer Aljaan — Trade Goods
Dealer Digriz — General Goods
Dealer Jadyan — Exotic Weapons
Dealer Malij — Enchanting Supplies
Dealer Najeeb — Spare Parts
Dealer Rashaad — Exotic Creatures
Dealer Sadaqat — Potent Potables
Dealer Senzik — Gems and Jewelcrafting
Dealer Zijaad — Arcane Goods
Eyonix — Innkeeper
Ghabar — Quest Giver
Grennik — Flight Master
Image of Nexus-Prince Haramad — Quest Giver
Jazdalaad — Grand Master Jewelcrafter
Karaaz — Consortium Vendor
Mailbox
Nether-Stalker Nauthis — Quest Giver
Stormspire Nexus-Guard — 71 Elite
Zephyrion — Quest Giver
Zuben Elgenubi — Quest Giver
Zuben Eschamali — Quest Giver

AM Manaforge Ara
Ara Control Console
Daughter of Destiny — 70
Mana Beast — 69-70
Mo'arg Warp-Master — 70
Overseer Azarad — 70
Phase Hunter — 67-68
Sunfury Blood Knight — 70
Sunfury Nethermancer — 69-70

AN Socrethar's Seat
Adyen the Lightwarden — 71 Elite
Anchorite Karja — 71
Exarch Orelis — 69
Hatecryer — 70
Socrethar — 72 Elite
Wrath Lord — 70

1 Doctor Vomisa, Ph. T. — Quest Giver
2 Harpax — Flight Master
3 Tempest Keep
4 Agent Araxes — Quest Giver

The Blood Furnace

DUNGEON INFORMATION

Name:	The Blood Furnace
Location:	Hellfire Peninsula
Faction:	Both
Suggested Levels:	60-63 (group of 5)
Primary Enemies:	Humanoids, Demons
Damage Types:	Physical, Shadow, Nature
Time to Complete:	2 Hours

WHO TO BRING

No class is without use in the Blood Furnace. The Fel Orcs spare no expense at repelling your entry and you should be ready to bring the courageous with you. Below is a table of suggestions based on what each class can do.

Jobs	
Class	Abilities
Druid	Healing, Backup Tanking, DPS, In-fight Recovery, Abolish Poison
Hunter	Ranged DPS, Backup Tanking (Pet), In-combat CC (Freezing Trap), Aspect of the Wild
Mage	Ranged DPS, Burst DPS, In-combat CC (Polymorph), In-combat CC (Frost Nova), Counterspell
Paladin	Healing, Tanking, Mana Recovery, Cleanse, Shadow Resistance Aura
Priest	Healing, Shadow Protection, In-combat CC (Mind Control), Dispel Magic
Rogue	DPS, Burst DPS, Out-of-combat CC (Sap), In-combat CC (Blind), Stuns
Shaman	Healing, Wipe Protection, Poison Cleansing Totem, Nature Resistance Totem
Warlock	Ranged DPS, Devour Magic (Felhunter), In-combat CC (Succubus), In-combat CC (Banish), Wipe Protection, Enslave Demon
Warrior	Tanking, DPS

GETTING TO THE BLOOD FURNACE

As part of Hellfire Citadel, The Blood Furnace stands almost equidistant from either flight point. This is misleading however. The Blood Furnace can only be entered by the highest part of the wall and must be reached via a siege ladder in the southern part of Hellfire.

Alliance parties need only climb the wall on the southern side of the ravine and enter the instance. Horde parties must travel across the Path of Glory to the southern part of the wall and make their way to the instance.

A Quick In and Out!

The Blood Furnace, much like Hellfire Ramparts, is a very short instance. This allows players with more time to run it multiple times in the same evening, while also allowing players with less time access to this dungeon.

THE ENEMY GARRISON

Enemy	Level
Broggok	***63 Elite***
Notes: Poison Bolt (Randomly hits two targets), Poison Cloud (Leaves poison trail), Slime Spray (Poison front cone AoE)	
Fel Orc Neophyte	***62 Elite***
Notes: Intercept, Enrage (physical damage increased by 122, attack speed increased by 60%)	
Felguard Brute	***61 Elite***
Notes: Knockback	
Felguard Annihilator	***62 Elite***
Notes: Intercept, Knockback	
Hellfire Imp	***61***
Notes: Fire Bolt	
Keli'dan the Breaker	***63 Elite***
Notes: Burning Nova, Shadow Bolt Volley, Corruption	
Laughing Skull Enforcer	***61 Elite***
Notes: Shield Bash	
Laughing Skull Legionnaire	***61 Elite***
Notes: Enrages at 25% health	
Laughing Skull Rogue	***61 Elite***
Notes: Poison, Stealth, Kidney Shot, Backstab	
Laughing Skull Warden	***62 Elite***
Notes: Fast attack speed	
Nascent Fel Orc	***62***
Notes: Thunderclap	
Shadowmoon Adept	***61 Elite***
Notes: Shadow Bolt	
Shadowmoon Summoner	***61 Elite***
Notes: Shadow Bolt, Inferno, Summons Succubus	
Shadowmoon Technician	***62 Elite***
Notes: Proximity Bombs (1800 damage to all in range), Silence	
Shadowmoon Warlock	***62 Elite***
Notes: Shadow Bolt, Corruption, Curse of Tongues	
The Maker	***62 Elite***
Notes: Throw Beaker (Throws beaker at target dealing 1000-1200 nature damage and knocks target into air), Domination	
Shadowmoon Channeler	***62 Elite***
Notes: Shadow Bolt, Mark of Shadow (Magic, All Shadow damage taken is increased by 1,100. 2 minute duration)	

OUT OF THE FIRE AND INTO THE FURNACE

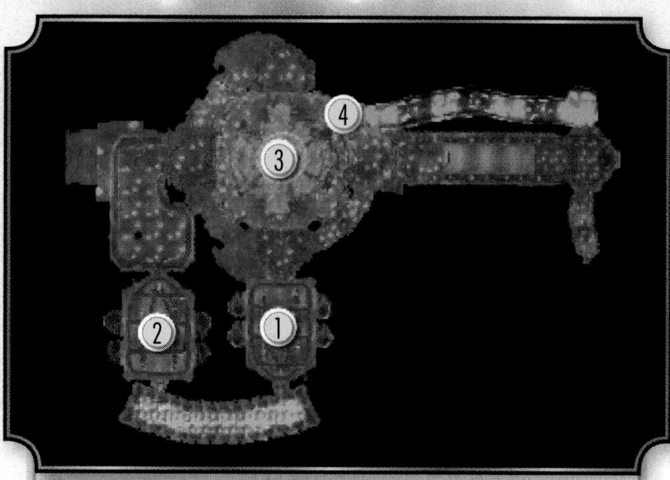

Map Legend	
1	The Maker
2	Broggok
3	Keli'dan the Breaker
4	Exit

The Stairs

The Fel Orcs of Hellfire Citadel have been warped and corrupted. They are far stronger and more resilient than normal Orcs and they are multiplying. Intelligence indicates that the Blood Furnace is an essential part of this operation.

Two Laughing Skull Enforcers guard the entrance. While this fight is simple, take the opportunity to discuss battle plans with the party. Use the party symbols to indicate who is targeting what to avoid confusion. Also discuss the attack order so you can keep your party's attacks focused and avoid breaking CC early.

Sample Explanation		
Symbol	**Designation**	**Attack Order**
Skull	Tank & DPS	1
Star	Seduce	2
Moon	Polymorph	3

The above example assumes three enemies and a party with a Warlock and Mage. Your party will most likely be different, so take the time to work out the battle strategy before you need it.

There are several groups guarding the bottom of the stairs. Each group consists of two Shadowmoon Adepts and one Hellfire Imp. The Adepts are elite and seem to be the real threat, but they are not. The Imp does immense damage, will not advance on you, and has relatively low health.

If you have a Warlock, keep the Imp banished until the Adepts are killed. Use interrupts to keep the Adepts from using their more powerful attacks. Another option is to have your Warlock enslave the first Imp. This gives your party a rather powerful ally. Be sure the Warlock warns you before he or she releases the Imp though.

If you are without a Warlock, CC as many of the Adepts as you can and kill the Imp quickly. At 1,000 Shadow damage a cast, you can't leave it alive and casting long.

Another pair of Laughing Skull Enforcers guard the stairs. Pull them away from the stairs and kill them as you did the first pair. Ascend the stairs slowly and together. Stealthing enemies wander the stairs and can do decent damage to a caster before the party can react. Alternatively, Hunters can use Flares and humans can use Perception to try to find these stealthed enemies. It's also a good idea to have a tank or another plate-wearer up the stairs first to draw the initial strike.

The enemy groups at the top of the stairs are packed fairly close together and have a wanderer with them. Each group has three Shadowmoon Adepts and one Hellfire Imp. Wait until the Shadowmoon Summoner wanders off to the left side before pulling the right group.

Use a ranged attack then duck into the previous room. By hiding behind a wall you break their line of sight and force them to come to you. Have CC ready when the enemies join you in the previous room. As with the battles at the bottom of the stairs, if you have a Warlock, banish the Imp and kill the Adepts. If you are without a Warlock, CC the Adepts and kill the Imp first.

Wait for the Summoner to wander to the right side once he is clear, pull the front left group into the previous room. Dispatch them as you did the first group. The Summoner is your next target. Use a ranged attack to get his attention and interrupts to keep him from casting. When he joins you, kill him.

The final group is now very much alone. Descend on them and show them the power of Azeroth. Proceed down the hall on your left.

There are two groups of guards. Each has a Laughing Skull Enforcer and Laughing Skull Legionnaire. Kill the Enforcer first as the Legionnaire enrages at low health. Be ready for the Legionnaire and crush it before it can capitalize on the damage increase.

The next set of guards can be dealt with in exactly the same manner. Proceed along the hallway until it connects with a larger room. As with the previous room, there are several groups and a wandering Shadowmoon Warlock. The groups here are much more dangerous than the previous room however.

Each group consists of Shadowmoon Adepts and Summoners. The Adepts aren't nearly as dangerous as the Summoners. In pulls with more than one Summoner, CC one and interrupt the other until its dead. If allowed time, the Summoners call a Succubus to their aid. This may not seem like much, but it can seduce your healer (or someone else) unless killed. If a Summoner calls a Succubus, kill the pet first. You can't afford to have 20% of your party CC'd by a pet.

Pull the first group when the Shadowmoon Warlock is away. Have crowd control and interrupts ready. The fighting is simple as long as the Summoner is locked down or killed quickly.

The wandering Warlock is your next target. Wait for it to move away from the far group and pull it around a wall. Kill it and engage the far group like you did the first. It's more likely than not that this group will have two Summoners, kill one quickly while the other is CC'd.

With the room cleared, only the two guards at the next doorway block your way forward. The Laughing Skull Enforcers aren't anything you haven't fought before. Dispatch them and rest to full as the next area requires more finesse.

The Prisons

While there are fewer enemies in each group, they are much more dangerous. Shadowmoon Summoners and Technicians are in pairs throughout the room, while a Laughing Skull Warden and Shadowmoon Technician patrol. The Technicians will be a nuisance through the next several rooms, so you need to learn how to deal with them.

The Shadowmoon Technicians can cast silence. This lasts for several seconds and makes your life much more difficult as tanks won't be able to taunt, healers can't heal, and casters can't bring the hammer. Kill the Technicians quickly to avoid a much more troubling fight.

They also drop Proximity Bombs. Once armed, these will explode and do 1,800 fire damage to any party members nearby when triggered. They are very visible, and should be avoided at all costs. Once the immediate fight is finished, have a Rogue disarm them or a high health party member set them off (after being healed to full). This keeps them from hindering the next fight.

Pull the first group on the left when the patrollers are away and duck around the doorway. Have an interrupt ready to force the Shadowmoon Summoner to come to you. When the enemies reach the doorway, CC the Shadowmoon Technician and kill the Summoner.

If you don't have any ranged interrupts, or if the Summoner resisted the interrupt, the fight is more challenging. CC the Technician as soon as it gets to the doorway. Kill the Succubus first. This leaves the Summoner free to cast, but you need the Succubus down before you engage the Summoner. Once the pet is dead, focus on the Summoner then the Technician.

The group on the right is your next target. Wait for the patrol to wander away before pulling the same way you did before. Continue this until the room is clear of all enemies except the Maker.

There are two doors on each side of the room with captured Orcs within, but they are too far gone for you to help. Rest to full and prepare for a fast and frantic fight.

The Maker has high Health, deals high damage, and has a couple tricks up his sleeve just to make your life more difficult. He can throw beakers at party members that toss them into the air. This effectively CC's the characters for a couple seconds and interrupts any spellcasts. If the tank is thrown into the air, stop attacks until the tank can regain aggro. His Domination ability actually resets aggro, so watch out for it.

The second ability can be just as devastating. The Maker can force a party member to join him for several seconds. This means the fight changes from five on one to four on two. Ignore the controlled character and keep focusing on the Maker.

Kill the Maker and the door forward opens. More of the Blood Furnace's function is revealed by a peak inside the next area. Shadowmoon Technicians stand around pods of some sort where Nascent Fel Orcs are being corrupted.

Pull the group of two Technicians and one Fel Orc into the previous room when the patrolling Laughing Skull Enforcers are away. As the Nascent Fel Orcs are not elite, they should be killed first while the Technicians are CC'd or kept busy. Once the Fel Orc is killed, dispatch the Technicians one at a time. Be watchful of the Proximity Bombs during the fight.

Wait for the Laughing Skull Enforcers patrol to return, then pull them into the previous room. This is another fight that is more to slow you down than to kill you. Slay the Enforcers as you have before.

Send your tank into the hallway and to the left side. It's a dead end, but a Laughing Skull Rogue waits there to ambush an unsuspecting caster. Destroy this Orc with extreme prejudice.

Now that it's safe for the softer party members, move into the hallway. The groups lining the hallway vary in composition, but you've fought all of them before. Watch the two patrolling Laughing Skull Enforcers further down. Don't let these join an existing fight.

Shadowmoon Technicians, Nascent Fel Orcs and various Shadowmoon casters will comprise the groups. The Fel Orcs can be slain quickly and should be your first targets. The Technicians should be controlled until you're ready to deal with them. The casters should be interrupted when possible. To pull the casters to you, hide behind the recessed areas of the walls to break line of sight.

Move through the corridor slowly and rest to regain Health and Mana after each fight. You want to be at your best if something goes wrong. Be sure to uncover and kill the Laughing Skull Rogue at the very end of the hallway before he can jump one of your casters.

Another large room with prison doors on both sides greets you. Shadowmoon Summoners and Technicians fill the room. The entire room needs to be cleared before you can advance, so start pulling the groups.

Pull the groups into the previous hallway. If you have a ranged interrupt, use it to keep the Summoners from calling their pets. Crowd control the Technicians as soon as they get to the hallway and kill the Summoner. The Technicians are easy prey when taken one at a time. Be watchful of the Proximity Bombs they leave.

If you do not have a ranged interrupt, pull the group around the corner. CC the Technicians as soon as they get there and kill any pets the Summoners have called. It's important to keep the Technicians CC'd so they don't silence your party members and the Succubae dead so they don't CC characters.

Fel Orc Neophytes are part of the final groups. Even with an obstructed view, you can now see Broggok. He isn't pretty. Don't get anxious, you'll be fighting him before long.

The Fel Orc Neophytes are fully corrupted and very dangerous. Unlike their Nascent cousins, they are elite. They also enrage themselves on occasion. This burning hatred increases their attack power and attack speed immensely. They can also intercept to stun and damage casters in your party without warning

CC the Neophytes and kill the other enemy first. These fights are more to give you a taste of what you're about to face then to kill you. Don't let anyone touch the lever on the floor until you've rested fully and are ready for a very difficult fight.

Pulling the lever begins an event that will test your group's ability to survive against overwhelming odds. Rather than opening the door to Broggok, it opens one of the prison doors. These prisoners are much more aware than the previous ones, and they aren't your friends.

The enemies will engage you and fight to the death. When they fall, the next door opens and another group charges you. The fights get progressively more difficult as more elite enemies are in each batch. Only after all four of the groups are dead will Broggok come forward. You won't have any time to rest between the Orc battles, so any class that can restore Mana or Health during the fighting will be worth its weight in gold.

Orc Groups		
Order	Nascent Fel Orcs	Fel Orc Neophytes
1	4	0
2	3	1
3	2	2
4	1	3

Take stock and make sure you're using all your characters to their fullest. Mages should Conjure Mana Rubies for themselves. Warlocks should provide a Healthstone to each party member. Blessing of Wisdom and Mana Spring Totem are going to be essential in keeping your casters in the fight. Consider passing out potions as well to keep some of the strain from the healers.

The first fight is against four Nascent Fel Orcs. While none of them are elite, avoid using AoE attacks as you need to conserve your Mana. CC some to lessen damage taken by the party, but let melee and wand attacks do the bulk of the damage.

When the last Orc falls, the second fight begins. This fight has one elite enemy and three non-elites. CC the Fel Orc Neophyte. If you have more in-combat CC, then CC the Nascent Fel Orcs, but the Neophyte needs to be CC'd until the party is ready. Kill the weaker Orcs, then the Neophyte.

The third group is more dangerous then the second. With two Fel Orc Neophytes, two Nascent Fel Orcs, and no rest since the last two fights. The fighting is probably getting a bit chaotic. Watch your Mana and use any timed abilities that regenerate it if you get low. Mana Tide Totem, Innervate, and Evocation are all abilities that can make a huge difference in this event. Using Mana potions is another option to keep you casting.

CC both the Fel Orc Neophytes if you can. With no possibility of additional mobs, use fear spells if you need to. Kill both the Nascent Fel Orcs then focus on the Neophytes one at a time.

The final fight is treacherous. You're low on Mana, low on Health, and the enemy has three Fel Orc Neophytes and a Nascent Fel Orc. Use any AoE CC you have to keep the enemies from dealing any substantial damage. Kill the Nascent Fel Orc and take the Neophytes one at a time. Once you engage the final enemy, pull the fight to the previous hallway. Killing the last Orc releases Broggok and he's not happy.

The Price of Failure

This is one of the 'wipe' fights for players new to the instance. The run from the graveyard is short so don't despair and don't destroy a group by blaming the wipe on a specific person.

Wiping on any of the Orc battles resets the entire event. Discuss what you can do better this time and come at it with a fresh mind and a little bit of petty vengeance.

Dying to Broggok does not reset the Orc encounters however. Once you kill the final Orc, they stay dead.

Broggok engages the party immediately and you won't have time to recover Mana or Health. He uses a variety of abilities that revolve around his use of poisons. His Poison Bolt randomly hits two targets, the Poison Cloud he trails forces players to pay attention so as not to stray into it, and his Slime Spray is a frontal cone, poison AoE. Avoid standing in the green rings and keep Broggok as far from the ranged members as possible. This limits the damage his AoE poison attacks do.

The tank should grab Broggok early and keep him facing away from the party. An easy way to do this is to constantly rotate around his lair. Move whenever Broggok puts a green circle at your feet, but keep Broggok away from the softer party members. Anything that can cure poison will be used heavily in this fight. Use Aspect of the Wild and Nature Resistance Totem if you have them to reduce the damage each attack does. Try to keep the poison off as many party members as possible.

DPS classes should burn any cooldowns they have that increase damage. This is a make or break fight. Throw everything you have at this disgusting creature. When Broggok crashes to the ground, collect your loot, pat yourselves on the back, and regain Health and Mana...you're not done yet.

The Blood Furnace

The room beyond is fairly large. Shadowmoon Warlocks with Felguard Brutes patrol. To the left is a large group of three Hellfire Imps and three Shadowmoon Warlocks. When the patrols are away, pull the group and duck around the corner. This forces them to approach you. CC as many as you can when they come around the corner. Kill any Imps that aren't CC'd first. You haven't fought these since the beginning, but their damage is still impressive.

Once the active Imps are dead, kill any active Warlocks before breaking CC. Wait for a patrol to wander near the door and pull it toward you. Kill the Shadowmoon Warlock first as it buffs the Felguard Brute. Move the party to where the Hellfire Imps were and look for the Laughing Skull Rogue. It's better to kill this treacherous snake on your terms.

The remaining patrol should be getting to your party soon. Engage and destroy it much the way you did the first patrol. Only two Felguard Brutes guard the door that blocks your advance. CC one if you have a Warlock and kill the other. If you are without a Warlock, use ranged snares or a Freezing Trap to keep one ineffective while you kill the other. Finish the final enemy and get your AoEs ready.

The next room contains only one group of enemies, but it's a large group. One Shadowmoon Warlock is surrounded by six Hellfire Imps. These aren't nearly as dangerous as the Imps before. They do less damage and have lower Health, but there are more of them. Pull the group around the corner to clump them all together and use AoE attacks to destroy the Imps. With his helpers dead, the Warlock is doomed.

If you are without sufficient AoE attacks, charge into the room and use burst DPS to kill the Imps as quickly as possible. Once the tank takes the first blast from all the enemies, the healer should use his or her largest heal and duck around the corner. Using a large heal like that will pull aggro from all the enemies that aren't engaged. This is good as they have to run around the corner to attack the healer. The time they spend running is time they don't spend casting.

Once the enemies close with the healer, he or she should run around the corner again (into the room with the party). This will disrupt the enemies again and bring them back to the party. Many of the Imps should be dead at this point and the tank needs to grab the remaining aggro before this little game of tag turns deadly. Handle the remainders as a standard fight.

Take the ramp to the right and start down to the main level. Two Felguard Annihilators guard the ramp. These are stronger than the Felguard Brutes, but can be dealt with in the same fashion. CC one and kill the other. Having a Warlock to Enslave and Banish is ideal, but Frost Nova or other rooting effects work just as well. Having the primary tank hold one while the rest of the party kills the other is the least ideal option, but it is still effective.

The bottom of the ramp leads to much tougher enemies. Groups of one Shadowmoon Warlock and two Felguard Annihilators stand guard. If you can CC an Annihilator do so and kill the Warlock first and the active Annihilator second. The Warlocks can buff the Annihilators just as they could buff the Brutes.

You can also use humanoid based CC on the Warlock and kill the Annihilators first. Be extremely careful using Sap as the second group is very close and you don't want to fight both at once.

With the first group dead, pull the second in the same fashion and rest to full Health and Mana. Through the doorway you can see the goal of your quest. Keli'dan the Breaker stands in the center of five Shadowmoon Channelers.

So Far From the Light

Consider equipping any items that increase your Shadow Protection. Both the Shadowmoon Channelers and Keli'dan use Shadow-based attacks. Any abilities that increase Shadow Protection should be cast or renewed if their duration is getting short. Shadow Protection and Shadow Resistance Aura are great for this.

The Channelers also cast Mark of Shadow. This magic debuff increases Shadow damage taken by 1,100 and lasts for two minutes. Characters with Cleanse, Dispel Magic, or Devour Magic (Felhunter) should be ready to keep this debuff from destroying your party.

Take the time to restore buffs, pass out Shadow Protection Potions, Healthstones, etc. while you discuss the plan ahead. With five elite enemies, you'll need to use every ounce of CC you have.

The Shadowmoon Channelers attack at the same time and cannot be pulled individually. Start the fight with Sap or Mind Control. If your Rogue has Improved Sap, let him or her CC one before you Mind Control. Let the Mind Controlled enemy die before the rest of the party engages. You don't get experience or loot from that enemy, but victory is more important.

Polymorph any you can and have interrupts ready for the enemies that aren't CC'd. If a caster or healer gains aggro, they should duck into the previous room to break los. This gives the rest of the party time to pull the enemy off the endangered.

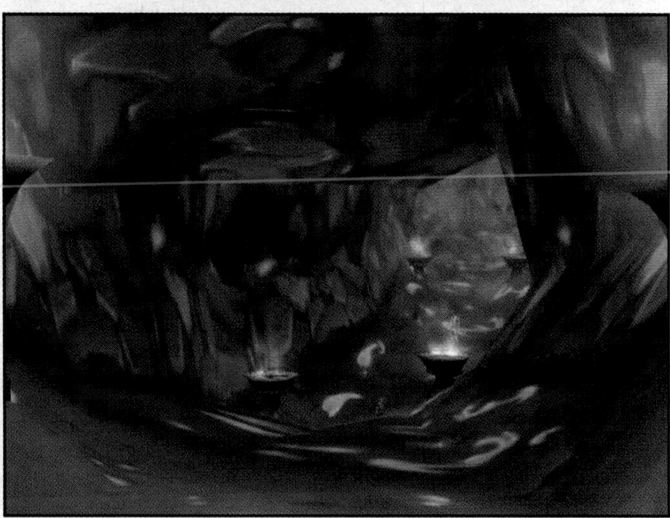

While Frost Nova won't do much to CC the enemies when used in the large room, pulling the enemies into the previous room before using it is much more useful. This roots the enemies where they can't cast on the party. Other CC abilities that work well are Intimidating Shout, Psychic Scream, and other fear attacks. Keli'dan won't attack until all the Channelers are dead, so fear away!

Use any abilities that regenerate Mana or Health once you get down to the final Channeler. If Innervate, Evocation, or Mana Tide Totem has recycled since you last used them, now is a good time to use them again. Having full Health and Mana when you engage Keli'dan makes the fight much easier.

As soon as the last Shadowmoon Channeler dies, Keli'dan the Breaker attacks. Don't stand near him unless you must. His primary attack is a Shadow Bolt Volley, so it doesn't matter which way he faces, but he also uses Burning Nova. If you have Mark of Shadow on more than a couple party members, this fight quickly devolves into a mad dash of kill before being killed.

Several times during the fight, Keli'dan will stop attacking for a moment and taunt you, "Come closer". Get out of melee range as quickly as you can. Keli'dan casts Burning Nova (5-second cast) followed by his Shadow Bolt Volley. Any characters hit by both of these takes a great deal of damage and may even be killed before the healer can restore their Health. To make matters worse, he becomes invulnerable when he begins casting Burning Nova. Run away as soon as you notice he's stopped taking damage to limit the damage done to your party.

This is the final fight of the instance. Any timed abilities or trinkets that increase your damage or reduces the damage you take should be used. Don't hold anything back as Keli'dan surely isn't. When his corpse is finally beneath your feet, collect your loot and follow the door that opened for a shortcut to the entrance and daylight.

Hellfire Ramparts

DUNGEON INFORMATION

Name	Hellfire Ramparts
Location	Hellfire Peninsula
Faction	Both
Suggested Levels	59-62 (group of 5)
Primary Enemies	Humanoids, Beasts
Damage Types	Physical, Shadow, Fire
Time to Complete	1-2 Hours

WHO TO BRING

Every class brings something to a group heading into Hellfire Ramparts. Below is a table of suggestions based on what each class can do.

Jobs	
Class	**Abilities**
Druid	Healing, Backup Tanking, DPS, In-combat CC (Hibernate), Remove Curse
Hunter	Ranged DPS, Backup Tanking (Pet), In-combat CC (Freezing Trap)
Mage	Ranged DPS, Burst DPS, In-combat CC (Polymorph), Remove Curse
Paladin	Healing, Tanking, Mana Recovery, Cleanse, Shadow Resistance Aura, Fire Resistance Aura
Priest	Healing, Shadow Protection, In-combat CC (Mind Control)
Rogue	DPS, Burst DPS, Out-of-combat CC (Sap), In-combat CC (Blind), Stuns
Shaman	Healing, Fire Resistance Totem, Wipe Protection
Warlock	Ranged DPS, Devour Magic (Felhunter), In-combat CC (Succubus), Wipe Protection
Warrior	Tanking, DPS

GETTING TO HELLFIRE RAMPARTS

Hellfire Ramparts is one wing of Hellfire Citadel. Situated neatly in the center of Hellfire Peninsula, it's close to both Horde and Alliance flight points and graveyards.

Alliance parties can climb the wall on the southern side of the ravine and drop down to the instance entrance. Horde parties should climb the wall on the northern side of the ravine and take the ramp down to the instance entrance.

A Quick In and Out!

One of the greatest parts of the Hellfire Ramparts is the shortness of the instance. It can be done multiple times in a day or during a shorter window of play for the more casual players.

THE ENEMY GARRISON

Bleeding Hollow Archer	***60 Elite***
Notes: Ranged Attacks	
Bleeding Hollow Darkcaster	***60 Elite***
Notes: Shadow bolt	
Bleeding Hollow Scryer	***61-62 Elite***
Notes: Shadow bolt, Fear, Life Drain	
Bleeding Hollow Seer	***60 Elite***
Notes: Shadow bolt, Fear	
Bonechewer Beastmaster	***60 Elite***
Notes: Summons 3 Shattered Hand Warhounds, Stealth Detection	
Bonechewer Destroyer	***60 Elite***
Notes: Cleave, Mortal Strike, Knockback	
Bonechewer Hungerer	***60-61 Elite***
Notes: Demoralizing Shout, Disarm	
Bonechewer Ravener	***60 Elite***
Notes: Kidney Shot	
Bonechewer Ripper	***60 Elite***
Notes: Enrage	
Felhound	***59-60***
Notes: Summoned by Omar the Unscarred	
Hellfire Sentry	***58 Elite***
Note: Kidney Shot, Heightened Stealth Detection	
Hellfire Watcher	***60 Elite***
Notes: Heal Watchkeeper Gargolmar	
Nazan	***62 Elite Boss***
Notes: Cone of Fire, Liquid Flame, Fireball	
Omor the Unscarred	***62 Elite Boss***
Notes: Summons Felhounds (these have the Spell Lock ability which can silence a caster), Treacherous Aura (360-440 damage every second), Shadow Bolt, Orbital Strike (Knocks a target into the air and bounces them around), Shadow Whip (Pulls an airborne target down to the ground), Demonic Shield (Casts when low on health, Reduces all damage by 75% for a short duration)	
Shattered Hand Warhounds	***50-60***
Notes: Stealth Detection	
Vazruden	***62 Elite Boss***
Notes: Revenge	
Watchkeeper Gargolmar	***62 Elite Boss***
Notes: Surge (Works like Intercept, but knocks down all nearby targets), Mortal Wound (Like a stacking Mortal Strike), Overpower, Gains Retaliation at low health	

ATOP THE WALLS

The Ramparts

While the trip in is uneventful, that ends at the instance portal. The rest of the trip is a hard fight through legions of enemies.

Guarding the first bridge is a pair of Bonechewer Hungerers. Wait for the patrolling Bonechewer Ravener to be on the other side of the bridge before pulling the two. The fight is fairly straight-forward.

Take this opportunity to practice the group's crowd control. The fight is small enough that failed crowd control isn't a death sentence and the instance portal is right behind you if anything goes wrong. The party leader should designate a symbol for each type of target and explain the attack order.

Sample Explanation

Symbol	Designation	Attack Order
Star	Sap	1
Moon	Polymorph	2
Skull	Tank & DPS	3

This example assumes three enemies and a group with a Rogue and Mage. Your group will be different, so take the time to find what everyone is comfortable with.

With the first two guards out of the way, grab the Bonechewer Ravener next time he wanders to this side of the bridge. Destroy him and dispatch the far two Bonechewer Hungerers in the same way you did the first two.

Cross the bridge and prepare for slightly more difficult fights. There are three enemies in each group and all of them are elite. The Bleeding Hollow Darkcasters and Archers attack from range, so they are good candidates for CC. The Bonechewer Destroyer has a number of melee attacks that make him quite dangerous. Kill him first to keep him from making the life of the caster(s) too difficult.

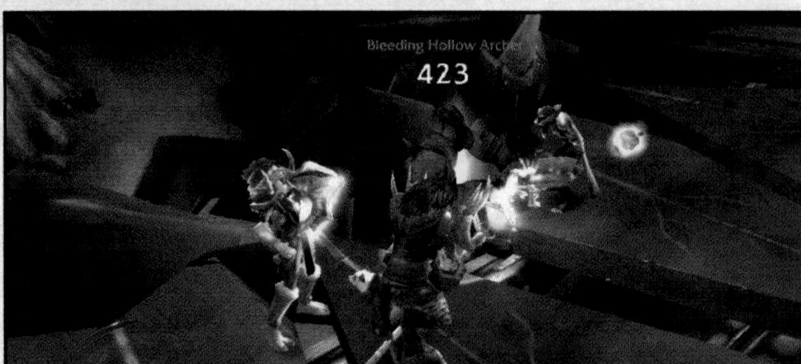

Keep your backs facing the bridge (or other areas you've cleared) while fighting the Bonechewer Destroyer. He can knock you off the ramparts if you are unlucky. A fall from the ramparts is death no matter who you are. He also has a cleave attack, so keep the Destroyer facing away from melee DPS characters and other soft target party members.

The Bleeding Hollow Darkcaster should be your next target as he can be interrupted and pulled to the group. Without use of his spells, he's little more than a glorified bookworm. With only one enemy left, the Bleeding Hollow Archer won't last long.

Move to the next group and handle it much the same. Continue along the rampart until you reach the group of two Bonechewer Hungerers and two Shattered Hand Warhounds. The Warhounds are not elite and can be killed quickly. CC the Hungerers until the Warhounds have been dispatched. Avoid using AoE attacks on the Warhounds; breaking CC on either or both of the Hungerers will prove to be deadly to the character who cast the AoE.

Do not attempt to use Sap on enemies near the Warhounds. The Warhounds can smell through stealth and alert others to your presence. If the only in-combat CC you have in the party is Hibernate, the tactics should change slightly. Hibernate one of the Warhounds; kill the other Warhound, then the two Hungerers. Kill the final Warhound last.

Once again, the enemies have upped the ante. There is a group of three Bleeding Hollow Seers surrounding a Bonechewer Ripper. This fight is going to test your CC capabilities as well as your pulling. All four enemies are elite and the Seers can cast fear.

CC as many of the Seers as possible and pull the fight back. As the Seers can fear, you don't want to fight near another group. One bad fear and you'll be fighting far more than you can handle.

Kill the active Seers first. If you have an off-tank, they should hold the Ripper away from the rest of the party until all non CC'd Seers are dead. Focus on the Ripper next, then the remaining Seers one at a time.

The Corridor

A Bonechewer Beastmaster and two Bonechewer Destroyers stand before you. Don't pull this group yet. Wait for the patrolling Bonechewer Hungerer with his two Shattered Hand Warhounds. When they are closest to you, pull them away from the Destroyers and Beastmaster.

Pulling these prior to the Beastmaster fight keeps them from joining when you least want them to. CC the Hungerer well away from the Beastmaster and kill the two Warhounds. Once the Warhounds are dead, finish the Hungerer and rest to full.

The next fight looks much easier than it is. Rest to full Mana and Health before beginning the fight. Two Bonechewer Destroyers stand near a Bonechewer Beastmaster. Do not attempt to Sap any of the targets as the Beastmaster can smell through stealth. CC one of the Destroyers as soon as the fight starts.

If you have spare CC, use it on the Beastmaster while you kill the second Destroyer. Keep the first Destroyer CC'd as you move to the Beastmaster. During the fight, he will summon several Shattered Hand Warhounds.

Hold the Beastmaster while you destroy all the Warhounds he summoned. They aren't elite, but will do incredible damage if allowed to chew on a caster. With all his friends dead, finish off the Beastmaster and the last Destroyer.

Learning the Ropes

This is one of the 'wipe' fights for players new to the instance. The run from the graveyard is short so don't despair and don't destroy a group by blaming the wipe on a specific person. Examine what you could have done better and note it for future runs as you make your way back to the instance.

The next fight is against another group of four elite enemies. One Bonechewer Ravener and one Bonechewer Destroyer are guarding two Bleeding Hollow Darkcasters. If you have enough in-combat CC, keep the Darkcasters from participating in the fight while you kill the Ravener and Destroyer. The Destroyer does more damage than the Ravener, but the Ravener will stun your tank repeatedly. A stunned tank can't control aggro, so kill the Ravener first. The rest of the fight is simple. Kill the Destroyer, than the Darkcasters one at a time.

If you are short on in-combat CC, kill the Darkcasters first, while the tank holds the Ravener and Destroyer away from the party. With stuns and knockbacks on the tank, losing aggro is expected. Kill the Darkcasters quickly and move on to the Ravener and Destroyer.

Many of the next fights involve both elite enemies and the Shattered Hand Warhounds. CC the elite enemies and kill the Warhounds. This tactic is extremely useful and keep you safe until you see Watchkeeper Gargolmar and his Hellfire Watchers patrolling.

This is the first boss and should not be taken lightly. Wait for him to patrol away and pull the enemy groups on each side of the corridor. The fights are similar to what you've done before and the enemies need to be cleared before you engage Gargolmar. Take a moment to regain Health and Mana before pulling Gargolmar's group.

Gargolmar inflicts high melee damage and can surge to intercept the party member furthest from him knocking all nearby targets down. The tank should hold Gargolmar while the rest of the group kills the two Hellfire Watchers. The Watchers heal Gargolmar if allowed to live. CC one if you have in-combat CC and kill the other. If you don't have any in-combat CC, have someone with interrupts keep the second Hellfire Watcher ineffective while the party kills the first.

Pet classes can leave their pet at range to take the brunt of Gargolmar's surges. This keeps the more fragile party members safe from his attention. With both the Watchers dead, show Gargolmar the power of Azeroth! Gargolmar's abilities can wreak havoc on your party, so watch out! His Mortal Wound stacks, but is like Mortal Strike in all other ways. This prevents healing and inflicts a considerable amount of damage. His Overpower and Retaliation (which counters melee attacks) are just like the Warrior abilities and can inflict serious damage to all members, especially non-plate wearers.

Jumping Ahead

If your party is experienced with Hellfire Ramparts and in a hurry, the next few groups on the right side of the corridor can be skipped by sticking to the left side. This should only be done by experienced parties as most characters can benefit from the practice, the reputation, and the item drops.

On the right are two more groups very similar to what you've already fought. With all the patrollers removed, these are straightforward fights. CC the casters, kill any non-elites, and then kill the elites one at a time.

The doorway at the end of the corridor is guarded by two Bonechewer Hungerers. You've fought these before and they aren't a threat if your party has made it this far. Kill them and enter the staircase. Approach the top of the staircase carefully as a large and challenging fight awaits you in the next corridor.

Four Bleeding Hollow Scryers surround one Bonechewer Ripper in the next hallway. The Scryers cast Shadow bolt and Fear and can be quite dangerous with so many of them. The Ripper can enrage as well.

Pull them with a ranged attack and wait for the Scryers to start casting. As soon as they begin casting, duck around the corner and back onto the stairs. This gives you time as they will try to complete their castings before they realize you are out of line of sight. Once they realize this, they will run to the stairs to start casting again.

Jump on the Ripper and kill him quickly. Use AoE CC abilities to keep the Scryers from doing anything useful. Psychic Scream and Intimidating Shout are good examples of these. If you are without AoE CC, use what CC you can and burn through the enemies at maximum speed. The less CC you have, the more damage you have, so use it.

Once the Ripper and a couple of the Scryers are down, the battle becomes much easier. It's far harder to die in a couple seconds when there are only two enemies. Once the encounter is done, rest to regain lost Mana and Health.

The doorway at the end of the corridor is guarded by two Bonechewer Destroyers. When your party is ready, pull and kill these two overmatched guards. The open area beyond is of much more concern.

The Platforms

There are groups on the left, on the right, in the center, and roaming the area. Wait for the roaming group to be away before pulling the group to the right back into the hallway.

If you fight them at the edge of the open area, the patrolling group will join. Have someone who isn't the tank pull this group and run back to the staircase and around the corner. This forces the two Bleeding Hollow Archers to run down the hallway and to their doom. Use in-combat CC to hold the Archers while you dispatch the Destroyer then the Archers.

The roaming Bonechewer Ravener and two Shattered Hand Warhounds are your next targets. Wait for them to patrol away from the other groups and pull them into the hallway. Kill the dogs first and the Ravener won't stand a chance.

The area is much manageable now. The group to the left consists of one Bleeding Hollow Darkcaster, one Bonechewer Hungerer, and two Bonechewer Destroyers. CC the Destroyers and rush the group. Kill the Darkcaster first as it won't have time to be effective before you're finished with it. The Hungerer is your second target and finish with the Destroyers.

The final group on the platform should be very scared. Charge them and kill the Darkcaster, then the Warhound before engaging the melee enemies. Both the Darkcaster and Warhound have lower Health and neither last long.

After exiting the platform area, take the entrance guarded by two Bonechewer Hungerers. Kill the Hungerers and proceed to Omor the Unscarred.

Two Darkcasters guard access to Omor. These can be kill without angering Omor, but don't charge them. Use any ranged interrupts you have and get CC ready. Pull one and interrupt the first to force it to come to you; CC the other. Bring the other Darkcaster to clear the way to Omor.

Omor's Treacherous Aura

Omor casts a rather damaging curse. Anyone able to remove curses should be prepared to do so. The curse causes massive Shadow damage to all members near the afflicted.

Equipping items that increase your Shadow Resistance can make this less painful, but nothing beats removal.

Omor isn't someone to be taken lightly. He has reasonable Health, summons friends, and casts a curse that can affect an entire party if you aren't careful. Your tank should charge in and hold Omor as close to the center of the platform as possible. Ranged DPS should spread out while still being in healing range.

This keeps your party out of range of the curse without reducing their effectiveness. If anyone gets cursed near you, move away from them to avoid taking damage. The Shadow damage can easily cause a wipe if you don't keep track of it.

Several times throughout the fight, Omor will summon Felhounds to aid him. These Felhounds have the Spell Lock ability that can destroy a party since it prevents casters from casting. Omor also has the Orbital Whip ability (which launches a target into the air and bounces them around) and the Shadow Whip ability (that pulls the target back to the ground). This can effectively keep a member of the party out of the fight. Burst DPS classes should destroy these before they can cause a problem for your healer. Casters should watch their Health as Omor casts Demonic Shield when he reaches low Health. Avoid using any of your large spells during the last few moments of his life.

With all of this in mind, the fight will go smoothly. Keep your party healed and Omor falls. Collect your booty and return to the central platform for the final few fights.

Vazruden the Herald flies over the final platform. There is a small group of enemies guarding the bridge, but they are of little consequence. Kill them, but don't pull the Hellfire Sentries. Rest to full Health and Mana and prepare for a frantic fight.

The Fires From Above

Vazruden the Herald employs a number of fire attacks throughout the fight. Consider using Fire Protection Potions and equipping items that increase your Fire Resistance to make the fight less stressful.

Pulling the Hellfire Sentries begins the final fight. While they aren't of consequence, Vazruden jumps off his dragon and engages you as soon as you kill the Sentries. Vazruden does high physical damage, but he's not your primary concern. Nazan breathes fire from the sky and small areas burn with dragonfire for a short time as a result. Do not stand in these flaming circles. The damage they do is immense.

Slowly kill Vazruden while dodging the breath attacks of Nazan. Hold as much of your Mana as you can as things get much worse later. When Vazruden gets low on Health, he'll summon his dragon to land and fight with him. Finish Vazruden quickly and turn your attention to Nazan.

Even on the ground, Nazan is terribly dangerous. His physical attacks aren't that strong, but he still uses a Fireball attack that leaves Liquid Flame on the ground. Be careful! While his physical attacks aren't strong, Vazruden's spells can alter the tide of battle in a second!

The tank needs to keep Nazan facing away from the party without standing in a circle of fire. Use all your Mana on your fastest damaging spells. Use any timers you have to increase your damage output. Keep the tank up as best you can with rapid fire healing. This is a race to see who can kill who first.

If your party stays out of the circles of fire, the healer should have enough Mana to keep the tank alive long enough for the party to kill the dragon. If the tank goes down, abandon all hope of healing people and switch to all out DPS. The only way to win is to kill the beast before it kills you.

Resurrect any party members that died in the engagement, collect your loot and head home.

Slave Pens

DUNGEON INFORMATION

Name:	Slave Pens
Location:	Zangarmarsh
Faction:	Both
Suggested Levels:	61-65 (group of 5)
Primary Enemies:	Humanoids
Damage Types:	Physical, Frost, Nature
Time to Complete:	2 Hours

WHO TO BRING

No one is without a place or use in Slave Pens. While avoiding redundancy is important, so many classes bring multiple abilities to a group that it's very easy to have two of the same class performing very different roles.

Jobs	
Class	Abilities
Druid	Healing, Backup Tanking, DPS
Hunter	Ranged DPS, Backup Tanking (Pet), In-combat CC (Freezing Trap), Aspect of the Wild
Mage	Ranged DPS, Burst DPS, In-combat CC (Polymorph)
Paladin	Healing, Tanking, Mana Recovery, Cleanse, Frost Resistance Aura
Priest	Healing, In-combat CC (Mind Control)
Rogue	DPS, Burst DPS, Out-of-combat CC (Sap), In-combat CC (Blind), Stuns
Shaman	Healing, Frost Resistance Totem, Wipe Protection
Warlock	Ranged DPS, In-combat CC (Succubus), Wipe Protection
Warrior	Tanking, DPS

GETTING TO THE SLAVE PENS

The Slave Pens is one of the many wings of Coilfang Reservoir. Horde parties can fly into Zabra'jin while Alliance parties fly into Telredor.

At the center of Serpent Lake is the Coilfang Reservoir. Dive beneath the water at the center of the pumping station and look for the drain. Swim through the drain and surface within the Reservoir. The Slave Pens are the western most instance portal.

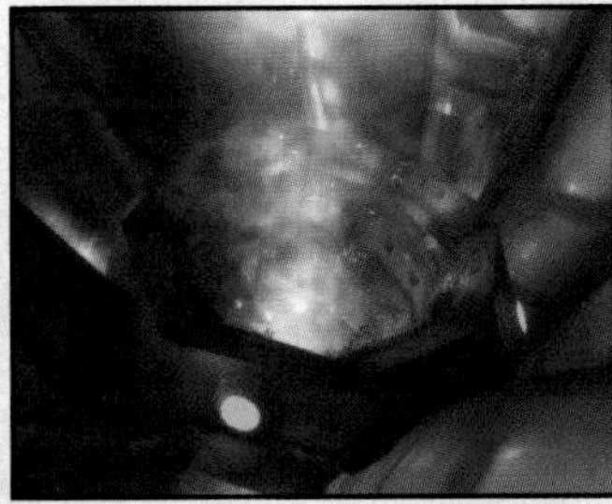

Part of a Larger Whole

The Slave Pens, while a stand alone instance, is meant to be part of the larger Coilfang Reservoir. The level difference between each wing is substantial enough that parties aren't likely to run one wing after another, but each wing is fairly short.

THE SLAVES AND THEIR KEEPERS

Bogstrok	***62 Elite***
Notes: Piercing Jab (139-161% weapon damage and reduces target's armor by 15% for 20 sec.)	
Coilfang Champion	***62 Elite***
Notes: Intimidating Shout, Cleave	
Coilfang Collaborator	***62 Elite***
Notes: Cripple (Reduces movement speed by 50%, increases swing time by 100%), Enrage	
Coilfang Defender	***63 Elite***
Notes: Spell Shield (reflects magic attacks when active)	
Coilfang Enchantress	***62-63 Elite***
Notes: Frost Bolt, Entangling Roots, Lightning Storm	
Coilfang Observer	***62 Elite***
Notes: Immolate, Accompanied by Coilfang Ray	
Coilfang Ray	***64 Elite***
Notes: Psychic Horror (6 second Horror)	
Coilfang Scale-Healer	***63 Elite***
Notes: Heal, Holy Nova	
Coilfang Slavehandler	***63 Elite***
Notes: Rend, Hamstring	
Coilfang Soothsayer	***62 Elite***
Notes: Decayed Intelligence (Magic, Intellect reduced by 25%, Area of Effect, Lasts 15 seconds)	
Coilfang Technician	***62-63 Elite***
Notes: Rain of Fire	
Greater Bogstrok	***62 Elite***
Notes: Decayed Strength (Disease, Strength reduced by 25)	
Mennu the Betrayer	***64 Elite Boss***
Notes: Lightning Bolt	
Quagmirran	***64 Elite Boss***
Notes: Poison Bolt Volley (AoE), Cleave, Uppercut (Damage & Knock back), Acid Geyser (AoE nature damage)	
Rokmar the Clacker	***64 Elite Boss***
Notes: Water Spit (AoE), Grievous Wounds (Bleed for 685-815 until they're healed)	
Wastewalker Slave	***63 Elite***
Notes: Amplify Magic, Fireball, Frost Bolt	
Wastewalker Taskmaster	***63 Elite***
Notes: Cripple (Reduces movement speed by 50%, increases swing time by 100%)	
Wastewalker Worker	***62 Elite***

DOWN THE DRAIN

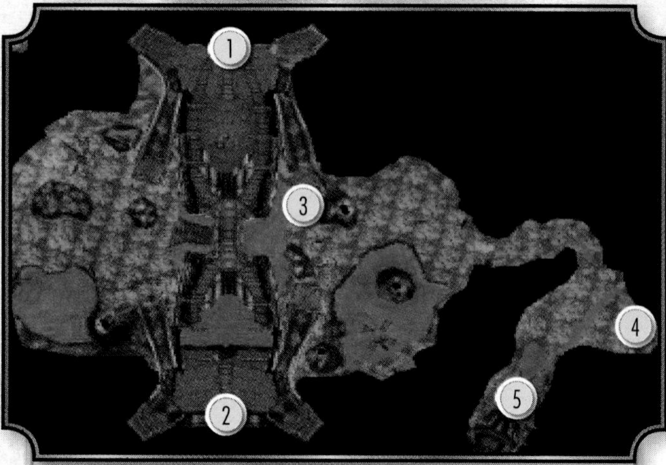

Map Legend	
1	Mennu the Betrayer
2	Weeder Greenthumb
3	Rokmar the Clacker
4	Naturalist Bite
5	Quagmirran

A Damp Beginning

At first, there is little sign of Naga presence in the Slave Pens. Bogstrok and Greater Bogstrok patrol the area in groups of three. These patrols move very quickly and cannot be safely bypassed.

Though quite monstrous looking, the Bogstrok are considered humanoid. This opens a variety of CC options including Polymorph, Freezing Trap, Blind, and Fear. Avoid using Fear as you don't need the fight to be any larger.

Gather aggro on the tank and slug away at the chitin-covered foes one at a time. While they aren't terribly dangerous, they present ideal practice for your party's fire control. Use the raid symbols to let everyone know what is getting CC'd and what order to kill the enemies in. No enemy will last long with your entire party firing at them.

Sample Explanation		
Symbol	Designation	Attack Order
Star	Sap	2
Skull	Tank & DPS	1
Moon	Polymorph	3

The first group was probably a little rough. The second group has the same composition and presents another try at perfection. Keep your tank's health high and all aggro on the tank as the Bogstroks do a good bit of damage.

Continue down the tunnel until it widens. Several Naga guard are watching over Broken slaves. This can be used to your advantage. The slaves only fight you while the Naga stands. Concentrate all your fire on the Coilfang Slavehandler and kill him quickly. When the Naga falls, the Wastewalker Workers will thank you for their freedom and run away.

Use a ranged attack to pull the enemies to you. This keeps you from fighting both groups at once. The first group consists of one Coilfang Slavehandler and three Wastewalker Workers.

As the Slavehandler is elite, he won't drop fast. Use CC to keep the Workers from dealing significant damage or have your tank hold the attention of all four enemies. Avoid using area of effect attacks as the Workers will continue attacking you if you do too much damage to them.

The next group is similar to the first with only minor differences. Instead of three Wastewalker Workers, there are two Wastewalker Slaves. The Slaves cast spells from range. This can be a problem as they do not realize they are free if the Slavehandler dies too far away. Drag the fight to the Slaves and kill the Naga first. Should they continue attacking you when the Naga falls, you have no choice but to kill them.

A pair of Coilfang Champions patrols ahead. Pull these back to your party as you don't want to fight them near the room ahead. CC one and pull the other to you. The tank should hold the target away from as much of the party as possible as Coilfang Champions use Intimidating Shout. This single ability can cause your entire party to run in fear if used close enough. Kill the Champions one at a time before proceeding.

Further down, the tunnel opens into a large cavern. Several groups of Naga and Bogstrok patrol. The enemy has established forces in the entire cavern, but you only have a few objectives. You can skip many of the enemies without endangering your mission. Should you want the additional experience or treasure, kill any mobs not mentioned in this walkthrough.

Hold your party at the entrance of the cavern for the time being. To the right are four Naga and a pet; a Coilfang Observer, two Coilfang Champions, a Coilfang Scale-Healer, and a Coilfang Ray. Remember that the Champions can fear several members of your party at once.

Pull the group and CC as many of the Champions as possible. Use the tunnel wall to break line of sight and force the enemies to close the distance. The Scale-Healer uses Holy Nova and does damage to any of your party in range and heal its companions. Keep it away from the bulk of the party and kill it first. The Coilfang Ray can fear one person at a time, but only uses it on a party member that doesn't have aggro. This means that the Ray won't fear your tank.

Once the Scale-Healer is dead, turn your focus to the Coilfang Ray. Renew the CC on the Champions as needed. If either breaks free, an off-tank or pet should grab them and keep them away from the party. This ensures they can't fear everyone. Kill the Observer next and the Champions last.

The patrol is next. Rest while you wait for it to patrol near your group. Use a ranged attack to pull the Coilfang Enchantresses and Champion. As before, CC the Champion until the softer targets are dealt with. The Enchantresses use area of effect attacks and should be kept away from as many party members as possible. If you have extra CC, keep one of the Enchantresses held while the party kills the other. Clean the mobs up one at a time and prepare to pull the Bogstrok on the bridge.

You've fought groups of Bogstrok before and these are no different. Use the same tactics of CC and focused firing that you used at the beginning of the instance.

Jumping Ahead

Many of the enemies within Slave Pens can be avoided. If your party is in need of practice, experience, or loot, take the time to clear any groups not mentioned here.

The Coilfang Stronghold

The Coilfang Defenders are fairly sturdy, but don't deal much damage unless you cast at them while they have a spell shield up. When the shield is up, all spells are reflected back at the caster. Stop casting when the shield goes up and kill the two annoyances.

Move into the passage and engage the two wander Coilfang Technicians. Have interrupts ready as the Technicians can cast AoE fire spells. These are channeled spells, so any interruption stops the rest of the spell.

To the right, Mennu the Betrayer paces up and down a ramp. There are groups of Coilfang Collaborators and Technicians at the bottom of the ramp. When Mennu is at the top of the ramp, pull the first group into the corridor. The Broken here are different. These have chosen to join forces with the Naga and will fight to the death. Deal with the Technician first while keeping the Collaborators CCd. The Collaborators enrage at low health, so keep your fire focused.

When they have been killed, rest to full Health and Mana and prepare to pull Mennu into the corridor. Mennu uses many of the same abilities Shamans do. He has a number of totems with various effects ranging from healing to AoE damage. Have a Hunter, or melee member (who isn't the tank) keep the totems destroyed during the fight.

Keep the tank's Health well above half as Mennu has a number of instant spells that can inflict a great bit of damage quickly. Hold your interrupts for his heals. When green energy surrounds his hands, use your interrupts. With his heals disabled and his totems destroyed, Mennu doesn't have much to rely on and won't survive your group's attack.

Remain at the bottom of the ramp and have your puller grab the group of two Coilfang Collaborators and one Technician. As before, CC the Collaborators until the Technician is dead. The Broken enrage at low Health, so be ready for the burst damage increase. Keep your tank's Health high and kill them one at a time to avoid two enraged enemies.

Ascend the ramp and be ready for another fight. A pair of Coilfang Technicians patrol along each bridge above. There are only two so the fights are fairly easy. Immediately rest after the first fight and prepare for the second. Though you only need to clear one bridge, clearing both will save you headache and a possible wipe ahead.

Follow a bridge to the center of the area and several more groups of enemies. Where the bridges connect, there is a group of two Coilfang Defenders and one Coilfang Collaborator.

Pull the fight to you as another group patrols on the other side of the walkway. CC the Defenders and kill the Collaborator first. With their spell shield, the Defenders take longer to kill while the Collaborator is less defensive.

Charge the next group now that the path is clear. The Coilfang Technician is flanked by two Coilfang Collaborators. CC the Collaborators first and kill the Technician. Have interrupts ready to keep it from using its Rain of Fire. Once the Coilfang is dead, focus on the kill the Collaborators one at a time.

Both of the bridges have been destroyed and there is no way to proceed except jumping into the water below. It's deep enough that you won't take damage from the fall. Do not jump toward the ledges below. Jump toward the center of the water instead.

Keep most of your party in the water and have your highest level member creep onto the broken portion of wall. There are three patrols nearby; one on each side and one on the ramp ahead. When all three are away, signal the party to ascend the broken wall and climb onto the wall to the left. Follow the wall as far as you can and wait. This gives the entire party a chance to see the Coilfang Enchantress and two Coilfang Technicians patrolling below. Decide CC and attack order before dropping down and engaging the enemy group.

The Enchantress is a high priority target. She can deal decent damage and turn your party members against you. Keep her spells interrupted and destroy her quickly while keeping the Technicians CCd. Once the Enchantress is dead, kill the Technicians one at a time and look around. There is a passage to the left, but you need to get to the top of the ramp before taking it.

One Coilfang Technician and two Collaborators patrol the ramp. When your party is ready, pull them into the passage. Breaking line of sight forces the enemy to come to you and keeps them from getting help from the other patrol. CC the Collaborators and kill the Technician first. Watch the last patrol and make your way up the ramp when it's clear.

Weeder Greenthumb isn't in the best shape, but now you know. Examine the body if you have the quest. With one Druid found, it's time to exit the Naga Stronghold and head into the deepest part of the dungeon. Take the passage out. Only two Coilfang Champions are guarding it.

Keep in mind the fear Coilfang Champions use when you engage them. CC one and kill the other to keep them from fearing your entire group for long periods. When both enemies are dead, rest to full Health and Mana while you look around.

The Deeper Tunnels

Don't get too used to the expansive cavern. You'll be back in cramped quarters soon. For now, there is a group of four Bogstrok that need to be killed. This is a simple and straight forward fight. CC as many as you can and kill them one at a time. Avoid using AoE attacks as your tank may not be able to keep the entire group from eating your casters.

Another fight that will truly test your party's CC and focus fire capability is ahead. A Coilfang Tempest, a Scale-Healer, an Observer, and a Ray stand guard near the center of the area. As before, the Scale-Healer should be your first target. CC as many of the others as you can starting with the Tempest.

Keep the fight away from as many party members as possible. The Scale-Healer uses Holy Nova and the Ray uses Psychic Horror. These abilities can make a fight very chaotic. Once the Scale-Healer is dead, turn to the Ray and destroy it. Kill the Observer and Tempest last.

When the bodies of your enemies litter the floor around you, rest to full Health and Mana before engaging Rokmar.

A Cold Reception

Rokmar is physically impressive. He deals high physical damage and has high Health. He also casts spells that can't be interrupted! He has a powerful bleed attack that can only be removed by healing the afflicted to 90% or better.

He uses a Water Spit. This Frost attack hits your entire party for moderate damage. Consider using any Frost Resistant abilities or gear you have and keep your member's Health high during the engagement.

Rokmar doesn't have any abilities that incapacitate your tank, so aggro shouldn't be a problem. Give the tank a few seconds to build aggro, and then start doing damage. Keep Entangling Roots dispelled from your tank. It doesn't CC your tank, but makes it more difficult to hold aggro.

Rokmar's Water Spit isn't a cone effect. It doesn't matter which way Rokmar is facing. As long as you are within range and line of sight, you will get hit by this. Be ready to use Potions, Bandages, or Healthstones if your healer falls behind. He or she will have enough work to do just keeping the tank alive against this giant crustacean.

This fight will give your healer a taste of what's in store. Use more Mana-efficient heals on the tank when he or she needs it. Cast faster heals on each party member after a Water Spit. It's important to get the weakest party members first as Rokmar will occasionally cast a second volley quickly after the first. Rokmar's Grievous Wounds ability is also one to pay attention to. It causes a bleed effect of 685-815 until the target is healed.

When the Clacker falls, resurrect the fallen, collect your loot and continue your journey. The next group of Naga is similar to the previous; one Coilfang Scale-Healer, one Observer, one Ray, and two Tempests.

Wait for the two patrolling Coilfang Defenders to move away before using a ranged attack to pull the larger group. As before, CC the Tempests and focus all fire on the Scale-Healer. If you are short on CC, have an off-tank or pet hold the two Tempests away from the party. When the Scale-Healer falls, engage the Ray and Observer. Leave the Tempests for last and kill them one at a time.

Engage the Defenders when they patrol back toward you. There are only two and you've fought them before. Keep your fire focuses and eliminate the Naga. The group on the left side of the ramp is your next target.

Two Coilfang Champions stand with an Enchantress and a Soothsayer. CC the Champions to keep them from fearing your group around and kill the casters first. Pull the fight back if the Champions break CC as you don't want to be feared into the next group.

Another large group stands on the right side of the ramp. Two Coilfang Tempests, an Observer, a Ray, and a Scale-Healer comprise the group. Start the fight by CCing as many Naga as possible. The Tempests make great CC targets followed by the Observer and the Ray. Kill the Scale-Healer first as it can draw the fight out significantly. If you are short on CC, have a pet or off-tank hold the two Tempests away from the party while you kill the first three. When the enemies are dead, rest while waiting for the patrol to come to the top of the ramp.

When the two Coilfang Champions, one Soothsayer, and one Enchantress stop at the top of the ramp, pull them. As before, CC the Champions and kill the casters first. This fight is marginally safer than the previous, but don't relax too much.

With the patrol dead, the passage is much safer for a short while. Ahead are two pair of Wastewalkers. Ignore these entirely as they will not attack unless you strike first.

There are four Bogstrok in the group ahead and all look very similar. When you begin the fight, pull the non-CC'd enemies away from the CC'd enemies. This keeps focusing fire simple and avoids accidentally breaking CC with AoE abilities. Use this same tactic on the next group of three Bogstrok.

Take a moment to rest. You want full Health and Mana for the next fight. Two Coilfang Defenders and two Coilfang Observers guard a cage. The Defenders take a lot of punishment before going down, so CC these first. Have an off-tank or pet hold the second Observer while the party kills the first. Use interrupts to keep the damage your party takes to a minimum. Kill the second Observer once the first is dead. Finish the fight by killing the Defenders one at a time. *Do not* let anyone speak with the Naturalist Bite in the cage until the party has a chance to rest.

Once again, take a moment to rest to full Health and Mana. Speak with the Druid when your party is ready. This triggers a fight against a Coilfang Enchantress, a Soothsayer and a Champion.

As the enemy forces you into combat, out of combat CC isn't an option. CC the Champion immediately as it can use its AoE fear to disrupt your party. With the Champion dealt with for now, CC the Soothsayer or have someone with interrupts keep it from casting. Focus all your fire on the Enchantress. It's very important to keep it from casting as they can turn your party members against you!

Focus all your DPS on the Enchantress and then the Soothsayer. Keep the Champion CC'd until both casters are dead. Once he is alone, kill the Champion and rest for the fight against Quagmirran.

A Sticky Situation

Quagmirran is a mountain of mold that submerges itself in slime. Perhaps it's no wonder that his most damaging attacks are Nature-based.

Several times during the fight, Quagmirran uses an AoE Poison Bolt. This does significant Nature damage immediately and even more Nature damage over time. Be ready to use Cure Poison, Abolish Poison, or Poison Cleansing Totem to counter this. He also has a severe acid spit attack that harms those in front of him.

Equipping items and trinkets that increase your Nature Resistance is highly recommended. Abilities such as Nature Resist Totem and Aspect of the Wild make the fight much easier.

Once the Naga ambush is dealt with, Quagmirran comes out of the water at the end of the tunnel. This keeps you from having to engage him while holding your breath. Send your tank in and blast away. Use your highest damage attacks and any trinkets that increase your damage output.

This entire fight is a race. Quagmirran hits very hard and uses Cleave. Any melee DPS should stand behind Quagmirran or risk taking damage very quickly. As the tank will have priority for heals, have potions and Healthstones (if you have a Warlock) ready. Quagmirran's final two abilities are Uppercut and Acid Geyser. His Uppercut damages the target and has a knock back and the Acid Geyser is a channeled ability which rains poison on nearby targets and inflicts nature damage the entire time.

There are no fights after Quagmirran. If you've been holding any timed abilities or trinkets for a rainy day, now's the time to use them. With Quagmirran's damage output, your healer *will* run out of Mana. Kill Quagmirran as quickly as possible. If your tank or healer goes down, keep blasting away. The only way to win the fight is for Quagmirran to die.

With the hulking mass of Quagmirran decaying, resurrect the fallen, collect your loot and make your way out of the instance. If you want to walk out, follow the tunnel back to Rokmar's room and jump into the water on the left. There is a ramp across the water that leads you to the front of the dungeon.

UNDERBOG

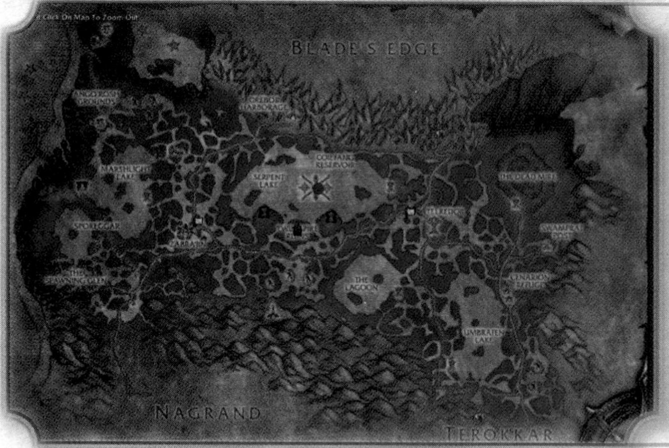

DUNGEON INFORMATION

Name:	Underbog
Location:	Zangarmarsh
Faction:	Both
Suggested Levels:	62-65 (group of 5)
Primary Enemies:	Humanoids, Elementals
Damage Types:	Physical, Nature
Time to Complete:	2-3 Hours

WHO TO BRING

Every class has something to do in the Underbog. In fact, most classes have several things to do.

Jobs	
Class	**Abilities**
Druid	Healing, Backup Tanking, DPS, Abolish Disease
Hunter	Ranged DPS, Backup Tanking (Pet), In-combat CC (Freezing Trap), Aspect of the Wild
Mage	Ranged DPS, Burst DPS, In-combat CC (Polymorph)
Paladin	Healing, Tanking, Mana Recovery, Cleanse
Priest	Healing, In-combat CC (Mind Control)
Rogue	DPS, Burst DPS, Out-of-combat CC (Sap), In-combat CC (Blind), Stuns
Shaman	Healing, Nature Resistance Totem, Poison Cleansing Totem, Wipe Protection
Warlock	Ranged DPS, In-combat CC (Succubus, Banish), Wipe Protection
Warrior	Tanking, DPS

GETTING TO UNDERBOG

Underbog is one of the many wings of Coilfang Reservoir. Horde parties can fly into Zabra'jin while Alliance parties fly into Telredor.

At the center of Serpent Lake is the Coilfang Reservoir. Dive beneath the water at the center of the pumping station and look for the drain. Swim through the drain and surface within the Reservoir. Underbog is the eastern most instance portal.

Bite-sized Pieces

The size and level deviance of Coilfang Reservoir is immense. To make the instance friendlier, it's been broken into several wings. This allows groups with more time to run it several times in an evening, or groups with less time to still run it.

THE ENEMY GARRISON

Bog Giant	63 Elite
Notes: Enrage, Fungal Decay (Disease. Nature damage every 3 seconds. Movement speed reduced by 40%)	
Claw	65 Elite Boss
Notes: Echoing Roar (Reduces nearby targets armor by 75% for 20 sec.), Maul	
Fen Ray	64 Elite
Notes: Horror	
Ghaz'an	65 Elite Boss
Notes: Tail Sweep (Damage and knock back), Acid Spit (AoE frontal cone poison attack)	
Hungarfen	65 Elite Boss
Notes: Foul Spores (Drains health from nearby targets while Hungarfen channels)	
Lykul Stinger	64 Elite
Notes: Frenzy	
Lykul Wasp	63-64 Elite
Notes: Ranged poison attack	
Murkblood Healer	64 Elite
Notes: Healer	
Murkblood Oracle	63-64 Elite
Notes: Fireball	
Murkblood Tribesman	63-64 Elite
Notes: Enrages	
Swamplord Musel'ek	65 Elite Boss
Notes: Multishot, Freeze trap, Raptor Strike, Deterrence	
The Black Stalker	65 Elite Boss
Notes: Chain lightning, Static Charge, Levitate, Suspend	
Underbat	62-63 Elite
Notes: Knockdown	
Underbog Frenzy	63-64 Elite
Notes: Aquatic	
Underbog Lord	64 Elite
Notes: Fungal Rot	
Underbog Lurker	62 Elite
Notes: Fungal Decay (Disease. Nature damage every 3 seconds. Movement speed reduced by 40%)	
Underbog Shambler	62-63 Elite
Notes: Fungal Decay (Disease. Nature damage every 3 seconds. Movement speed reduced by 40%)	
Wrathfin Myrmidon	63-64 Elite
Notes: Coral Cut (Physical damage every 3 sec. for 15 sec.)	
Wrathfin Sentry	64 Elite
Notes: Stealth Detection	
Wrathfin Warrior	64 Elite
Notes: Enrages at low health, Heroic Strike, Shield Bash	

CLOGGING THE DRAINS

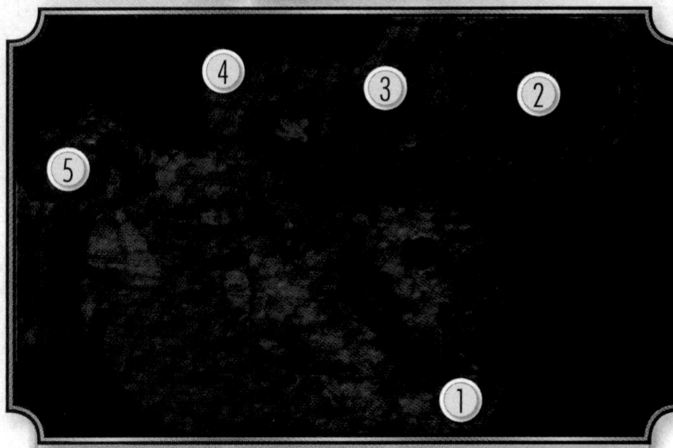

Map Legend	
1	Hungarfen
2	Ghaz'an
3	Earthbinder Rayge
4	Swamplord Musel'ek and Claw
5	The Black Stalker

CLIMBING THE RAMPS

You start in a tunnel with enemies patrolling nearby. The Underbats can be pulled singly or as a group. The first couple of fights are very easy. The Underbats have only a knockdown as a special ability. If your group includes a Warlock, use these to grab a couple easy Soul Shards.

The easy fights don't last long. As the passage opens into an immense cavern, a group of Underbog Lurkers and an Underbog Shambler patrol ahead. These creatures are immune to many forms of CC. Only Freezing Trap, Fear, and Banish are effective and using Fear with other enemies close by is begging for problems.

Use the raid symbols to designate which enemies to CC and what order to kill them in. This keeps your party from breaking CC and allow you to kill each enemy much quicker.

Sample Explanation		
Symbol	Designation	Attack Order
Skull	Tank & DPS	1
Blue Box	Freezing Trap	2
Moon	Banish	3

This example assumes three enemies and a group with both a Hunter and a Warlock. Your group will be different so take the time to get comfortable with the raid symbols. Time spent now will more than make up for itself by the end of the instance.

Follow the wall to the left as you move ahead. To the right is a group very similar in makeup to the previous fight. If your party had trouble with the previous fight, pull the group to the right for a little more practice before you get to the tougher opponents.

Pull the group of three Underbats ahead. While only having a knockdown and not doing much damage, having three of the Underbats on your tank can be very frustrating. A tank that is knocked down can't hold aggro, so use Polymorph or Freezing Trap to CC what you can. If you are short on CC, use other Warriors, Paladins, Hunter Pets, or Warlock Pets to hold aggro from the other Underbats until the first is

Using off-tanks increases the damage the party takes over all, but having a tank that is unable to hold aggro because he or she is constantly knocked down is even worse. Kill the Underbats one at a time.

Near the water and to the left is a group of three Underbog Lurkers. Pull and CC these just as you did earlier. If you are short on CC, have your tank hold all the active enemies and bring them down one at a time. Don't use AoE's unless your tank feels comfortable holding aggro against an AoE.

With the path clear, move to the edge of the water. Don't enter the water as Underbog Frenzies are waiting for a taste of your flesh. Watch the patrolling Underbats and Bog Giant. Pull the Bog Giant when the Underbats are away. The Bog Giant hits fairly hard and can disease your party members. Have abilities to cure disease ready and kill the Giant.

The patrolling Underbats are your next target. Pull them to you and kill them one at a time. Remember that they have a knockdown and the tank has a harder time holding aggro. Focusing your fire makes the tank's job much easier.

Practice Makes Perfect

The groups of enemies along the right walls can be skipped entirely if you follow the waterline. If your party needs the CC practice or is in the mood to kill everything, take the groups one at a time.

The groups are mixed. Two Underbats and one Underbog Lurker make up each group. These mixed groups make CC easier. Warlocks or Hunters can CC the Underbog Lurker, while Mages, Druids, or Hunters can CC the Underbats.

Follow the waterline until you get to the ramp. Underbog Lurkers and Shamblers guard the bottom of the ramp while several enemies patrol the length of the ramp. When the patrols are away, pull the Underbogs to you and destroy them one at a time. Avoid falling into the water nearby as the Underbog Frenzies are still looking to take a nibble out of you.

Wait for the patrollers to come down the ramp before you pull them. Take the Bog Giant first. Keep your tank's Health high as the Giant can inflict some troubling hits and you don't want to lose your tank due to an untimely critical.

Pull the group of Underbats next. You've fought them before so use the techniques that have worked for you. CC them if you have the classes to do so. Use off-tanks if you don't have the abilities to CC them. Ascend the ramp when the way is clear.

Two Bog Giants stand in front of Hungarfen. The good news is that these two can be pulled before you engage Hungarfen. The bad news is that you will get both and neither is vulnerable to many forms of CC. If you have a Hunter, use Freezing Trap for one while the party focuses on the other. Using an off-tank for the second Bog Giant is also feasible.

Keep your damage focused on one Giant at a time. Their high Health means they won't go down fast and your healer will run out of Mana keeping two tanks at high Health. When both Giants are dead, rest to full Mana and Health. Hungarfen will the first true test of your party.

All Mucked Up

This is one of the 'wipe' fights for players new to the instance. The run from the graveyard is short so don't despair and don't destroy a group by blaming the wipe on a specific person. Examine what you could have done better and note it for future runs as you make your way back to the instance.

Hungarfen has immense Health and does incredible physical damage. These aspects alone are major trouble but they are not the true power of this beast. Throughout much of the fight, Hungarfen drops mushrooms on the group. These will increase in size until they pop and infect any party members near them with Spore Cloud that deals 360 to 450 damage every 2 sec. for 20 sec..

That means this has to be a moving battle. Everyone in the party must be constant aware of their surrounds and move away from any mushrooms growing near them. Keeping Hungarfen's attention on the tank won't be difficult as long as the tank is kept alive.

When Hungarfen reaches 10% Health, he casts Fungal Spores. It drains health from all nearby targets and heals Hungarfen for a few seconds. To negate this ability, run away until he stops using the ability and resumes combat as before. Take this time to heal the party up to full and be ready for when Hungarfen reengages.

Once Hungarfen throws the vines away and comes at you again, finish the awful creature. Collect the **Underspore Frond** nearby if you have the quest for it. Rest at the next bridge and prepare for the pulls to resume.

A group of four Underbats patrols on the next rise. Pull them across the bridge when the patrolling Bog Giant is away. As all of the Underbats can knock your tank down, be very careful to focus fire. The tank won't be able to run around gathering loose aggro. Polymorph, Hibernate, and Freezing Trap and work against the Underbats. As you're pulling them across the bridge, Fear is a relatively safe option as well.

When the Underbats are dead, pull the Bog Giant. Being alone, he won't pose any significant threat. Keep your tank's health high and the enemy away from the softer party members and you'll be fine. Repeat this several times as you move across the bridge and left around the pillar.

Watch for the Sanquine Hibiscus as you move. They are groundspawns and quest items. There are only two more Bog Giants before the enemies greatly change. Pull the final Bog Giant when the Wrathfin Myrmidons are at the top of the ramp to avoid a much larger engagement.

The Tank

With the Bog Giant out of the way, move your party to the bottom of the ramp and against the wall. The enemies in this section are primarily humanoid. Polymorph, Mind Control, Seduce, Sap, and Freezing Trap are all valid forms of CC.

When the two wandering Wrathfin Myrmidons are at the bottom of the ramp, pull them. This engages only the two and leaves the Naga at the top of the ramp for next pull. The Myrmidons are melee enemies and will engage your tank directly. Kill them one at a time, but don't move up the ramp yet.

Have your puller move to the top of the ramp and watch for the patrol in the corridor ahead. When you see the patrol move away from the doorway, pull the two Wrathfin Sentries to the bottom of the ramp. Don't CC them until they get to the ramp as the patrol can add if it encounters a CC'd target.

Ascend the bridge and prepare for a much larger fight. Wait for the patrol to move away again before pulling the group to the right, just inside the doorway. There are four enemies in this group so CC and raid symbols will make your lives much easier.

Murkblood Healers are Too Good to Live

The Murkblood Healers are very powerful. They have both a single target heal and an AoE heal that is far more powerful than anything you have access to. They are so powerful that your entire attack plan hinges upon how to deal with them.

If you have a Priest, use Mind Control. You can either let the other enemies kill the Healer for you, or use the Healer to keep your party alive while the other enemies are dispatched.

If you do not have a Priest in your party, kill the Murkblood Healer first. Do not attempt any other form of CC. If the CC is broken early, the Healer can restore the Health of all other enemies very quickly.

The group consists of two Murkblood Spearmen, one Murkblood Healer, and one Wrathfin Warrior. Use the wall to break line of sight and force the enemies to come out of the corridor. Allow them to join you on the platform before you CC any. This is important as you don't want the patrol to join the fight.

CC the Spearmen and deal with the Healer and Warrior first. Once the Healer and Warrior are dead (or controlled), kill the Spearmen one at a time and watch the patrol again. As the patrol moves down the corridor, pull the group just inside and to the left of the doorway.

There are only three enemies in this group; one Murkblood Healer and two Murkblood Spearmen. Deal with this group much the same way you did with the previous group. CC the Spearmen as they join you on the platform and deal with the Healer first. When the Healer is taken care of, kill the Spearmen one at a time. Pull the patrol next time you see it.

Kill the Myrmidons and move your party into the corridor and to the right. This is a dead end, but gives you a better view of the next few pulls. The hallway continues west and there are several groups of enemies along the walls.

Rest up and prepare for the next couple fights. Wait for the larger patrol to move away before pulling the group of three. One is a Murkblood Oracle and casts at you from range. Use a ranged interrupt or duck out the door to force it to close with you. If you leave it at range, the patrol will add and overwhelm your party.

Deal with the Healer first, then the Oracle, then the Tribesman. This drops the enemies very quickly and opens your party to the least amount of damage. Grab the patrol as it comes back your direction. As the group is very large, CC will be important.

The Murkblood Healer must be dealt with first. CC the Murkblood Tribesman and Spearman. The Wrathfin Warrior can be CC'd until the Healer is dead if you have extra CC. Kill the Warrior, then the Spearman, and finally the Tribesman. Avoid using Fear as there are many enemies close by.

When the group is dead, move down the hall to the bottom of the ramp. Rest here while your puller ascends the ramp to get the next group. There are four enemies in this group just as there were in the last. Deal with them in the same fashion.

Move up the ramp and take a moment to look around. Groups of Naga stand along the path to the right and Ghaz'an swims in the water below.

Pull the groups along the walkway to the right one at a time. You've fought them all before and ducking down the stairs will force them to close with you. This keeps them well away from the other groups and avoids potential wipe situations.

Deal with the Healers first, then the casters, then the melee enemies to kill as quickly as possible. Watch the center of the room as you kill the groups. Ghaz'an climbs the pipes and perches atop the central platform.

Charge Ghaz'an and immediately face it away from the party; non-tank members should remain on Ghaz'an's flank and not stand right behind him to avoid the Tail Sweep!. It has a cone effect poison attack. If only the tank is in front of it, only the tank gets hit. Ghaz'an is fairly simple if you keep it facing away from the party. Its melee hits aren't terrible and its Health isn't as high as Hungarfen's. Party members behind Ghaz'an should avoid being too close to the edge as Ghaz'an's tail has a knockback effect.

When the water is calm again, jump out of the hole in the northern side of the tank. Make sure you have at least half your Health before jumping as it's embarrassing to die when no enemies are in sight. Recover from the fall before continuing.

The Druids and Getting Out

Follow the tunnel until it forks. On the left path is Earthbinder Rayge. Speak with him briefly for **Lost in Action** before moving your party back to the fork. Only the puller should descend down the right path for now. The next two pulls have three Fen Rays in each.

Each Fen Ray has an AoE Horror effect. It lasts only a couple seconds, but cannot be broken and they can use it several times in the fight. Focus fire and destroy the Rays one at a time. The fight can be fairly chaotic, but keep your cool and maintain aggro on the tank to get through it.

Pull the Fen Rays all the way back up the ramp to the group. As they have a horror ability, you don't want them sending a party member into another group. This extra room gives you more CC options against the Fen Rays. While Hibernate, Polymorph, and Freezing Trap would be the standard options against them, Fear and Scare Beast are safe to use with the added room.

CC as many as you can to keep the fight from becoming a nightmare and kill them one at a time. When the first group is dead, grab the second. The party should remain at the fork until both Fen Ray groups have been dispatched.

Move your group to the bottom of the ramp and engage the flying bugs. One Lykul Wasp and two Lykul Stingers make up the group. Destroy the Wasp first as its ranged poison attack can make the life of a caster very difficult. Be ready to use a shield or throw heals a bit faster when the Stingers glow red. This signals their Frenzy and the increase in attack speed and overall damage. Keep a close eye on your tank's Health during this.

Hold your party at the bottom of the ramp and send your puller forward. There is another group of Fen Rays that needs to be pulled back. Destroy these as you have the others but don't move forward yet. Once again, send your puller ahead.

Bring the group of two Fen Rays and one Lykul Wasp back to the group. Kill the Rays first as they interfere with standard group procedure by fearing your members around. Once the Rays are dealt with, kill the Wasp.

A group of two Fen Rays is next. It's a smaller group, so you can handle it without worry if you've gotten this far. Once this group is dead, move forward until you can see the last group of Fen Rays.

Two Fen Rays and a Lykul Wasp hover just before a boss encounter. Pull the fight well back as you don't want to be feared into either of the bosses or the patrolling Bog Giant. As before, kill the Rays first and the Wasp last.

Have your party rest while your puller hugs the left wall. Do not engage Swamplord Musel'ek or Claw yet. A Bog Giant patrols on the left and will make the boss fight much more difficult if it's allowed to join. Wait for it to patrol close to you and pull it back to the group. Kill it as you have in the past and rest to full in preparation of the next encounter.

Musel'ek and Claw attack as a pair and are both immune to CC. Both do incredible damage and Claw has immense Health. This means that Musel'ek needs to die first. If you have an off-tank as well as your primary tank, have the off-tank hold Claw. The primary tank will need to hold Musel'ek as he hits pretty hard. Voidwalkers and Hunter Pets can off-tank Claw if you need, but Druids, Warriors, and Paladins are better suited for it.

Use your most powerful attacks to bring Musel'ek down quickly, but don't use abilities that have substantial timers as there is a more difficult encounter shortly. Your healer will be strained at the start of the fight keeping two tanks alive. Casters shouldn't worry about conserving Mana in the beginning. Blow everything your have to kill Musel'ek.

Once Musel'ek is dead, the fight gets much simpler. Keep you tank above half Health in case Claw gets a couple critical strikes in a row. Lay into him with everything you have left. When Claw is defeated, he reverts to become Windcaller Claw. Speak with him before continuing

Move along the path to the south. An Underbog Lord stands guard over the way forward. While not a full boss, the Underbog Lord is pretty nasty. He can instantly stack five Fungal Rots on a target, so keep him looking at the same target as much as possible. Bring the Lord down as quickly as you can without using your timed abilities. Once again, rest to full Health.

When you see the bodies of the Fen Rays littering the floor, you're close. Around the corner, the passage opens into a large room. Engage the Black Stalker when you party is ready.

A Shocking Good Time

The Black Stalker uses a multitude of lightning-based attacks. While it isn't as pertinent for the casters of the group to have high Nature Resistance, it's quite useful for the tank.

Consider using items, potions, and abilities to increase your party's Nature Resistance with special attention to your tank as he or she is likely to get hit with many of the attacks. Nature Resistance Totem and Aspect of the Wild are both very potent.

Spread your ranged attackers about the room so none are close to each other, but all are in healing range. The tank should hold the Stalker at the southern portion to the room. Dismiss any pets as they are a liability to your survival.

The Black Stalker doesn't have as much Health as Hungarfen did, but it is far more damaging. It deals physical damage and has Chain Lightning (instant multiple target Nature damage), and Static Charge (debuff that damages all party members near the afflicted). As the Chain Lightning can bounce from your tank, to a pet, back to your tank, it's important that no pets join the tank in melee.

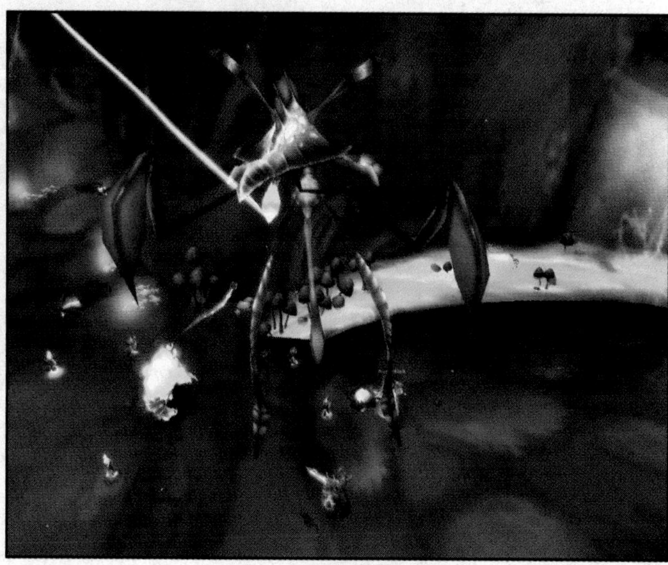

Keeping your party spread out will reduce the damage done by Static Field. This debuff can not by dispelled, so reducing the damage is the best you can do. The Black Stalker can also throw members into the air and hold them there. This is devastating to melee characters, but casters can still use spells when held in the air. Don't panic and keep being as useful as possible. If a healer is pulled into the air make sure the tank moves into healing range. Melee party members should switch to a ranged weapon until they fall back to the ground.

As soon as the fight starts, use all your timed abilities. This is the final fight of the dungeon and The Black Stalker is quite lethal. There is little rhyme or reason to which attack it uses when. Positioning is the best defense you have so blast away with everything in your arsenal.

When the smoldering corpse of the Stalker falls, take its head if you have the quest. Resurrect any members who fell and take the path further to leave the dungeon.

CRAFTING AND SKILL ITEMS

Alchemy

Created Item	Skill Lvl	Source	Reagent(s)
Minor Healing Potion	N/A	Special	1 Peacebloom, 1 Silverleaf, 1 Empty Vial
Elixir of Lion's Strength	N/A	Special	1 Earthroot, 1 Silverleaf, 1 Empty Vial
Elixir of Minor Defense	N/A	Special	2 Silverleaf, 1 Empty Vial
Weak Troll's Blood Potion	15	Trained	1 Peacebloom, 2 Earthroot, 1 Empty Vial
Minor Mana Potion	25	Trained	1 Mageroyal, 1 Silverleaf, 1 Empty Vial
Minor Rejuvenation Potion	40	Trained	2 Mageroyal, 1 Peacebloom, 1 Empty Vial
Elixir of Minor Fortitude	50	Trained	2 Earthroot, 1 Peacebloom, 1 Empty Vial
Elixir of Minor Agility	50	Found	1 Swiftthistle, 1 Silverleaf, 1 Empty Vial
Discolored Healing Potion	50	Found	1 Discolored Worg Heart, 1 Peacebloom, 1 Empty Vial
Lesser Healing Potion	55	Trained	1 Minor Healing Potion, 1 Briarthorn
Swiftness Potion	60	Found	1 Swiftthistle, 1 Briarthorn, 1 Empty Vial
Rage Potion	60	Found	1 Sharp Claw, 1 Briarthorn, 1 Empty Vial
Elixir of Tongues	70	Found	2 Earthroot, 2 Mageroyal, 1 Empty Vial
Blackmouth Oil	80	Trained	2 Oily Blackmouth, 1 Empty Vial
Elixir of Wisdom	90	Trained	1 Mageroyal, 2 Briarthorn, 1 Empty Vial
Elixir of Water Breathing	90	Trained	1 Stranglekelp, 2 Blackmouth Oil, 1 Empty Vial
Elixir of Giant Growth	90	Found	1 Deviate Fish, 1 Earthroot, 1 Empty Vial
Holy Protection Potion	100	Found	1 Bruiseweed, 1 Swiftthistle, 1 Empty Vial
Swim Speed Potion	100	Trained	1 Swiftthistle, 1 Blackmouth Oil, 1 Empty Vial
Minor Magic Resistance Potion	110	Found	3 Mageroyal, 1 Wild Steelbloom, 1 Empty Vial
Healing Potion	110	Trained	1 Bruiseweed, 1 Briarthorn, 1 Leaded Vial
Lesser Mana Potion	120	Trained	1 Mageroyal, 1 Stranglekelp, 1 Empty Vial
Elixir of Poison Resistance	120	Found	1 Large Venom Sac, 1 Bruiseweed, 1 Leaded Vial
Strong Troll's Blood Potion	125	Trained	2 Bruiseweed, 2 Briarthorn, 1 Leaded Vial
Cowardly Flight Potion	125	Found	1 Delicate Feather, 1 Kingsblood, 1 Leaded Vial
Elixir of Defense	130	Trained	1 Wild Steelbloom, 1 Stranglekelp, 1 Leaded Vial
Fire Oil	130	Trained	2 Firefin Snapper, 1 Empty Vial

Alchemy

Created Item	Skill Lvl	Source	Reagent(s)
Shadow Protection Potion	135	Found	1 Grave Moss, 1 Kingsblood, 1 Leaded Vial
Elixir of Lesser Agility	140	Found	1 Wild Steelbloom, 1 Swiftthistle, 1 Leaded Vial
Elixir of Firepower	140	Trained	2 Fire Oil, 1 Kingsblood, 1 Leaded Vial
Elixir of Ogre's Strength	150	Found	1 Earthroot, 1 Kingsblood, 1 Leaded Vial
Free Action Potion	150	Found	2 Blackmouth Oil, 1 Stranglekelp, 1 Leaded Vial
Greater Healing Potion	155	Trained	1 Liferoot, 1 Kingsblood, 1 Leaded Vial
Mana Potion	160	Trained	1 Stranglekelp, 1 Kingsblood, 1 Leaded Vial
Lesser Invisibility Potion	165	Trained	1 Fadeleaf, 1 Wild Steelbloom, 1 Leaded Vial
Shadow Oil	165	Found	4 Fadeleaf, 4 Grave Moss, 1 Leaded Vial
Fire Protection Potion	165	Found	1 Small Flame Sac, 1 Fire Oil, 1 Leaded Vial
Elixir of Fortitude	175	Trained	1 Wild Steelbloom, 1 Goldthorn, 1 Leaded Vial
Great Rage Potion	175	Found	1 Large Fang, 1 Kingsblood, 1 Leaded Vial
Mighty Troll's Blood Potion	180	Found	1 Liferoot, 1 Bruiseweed, 1 Leaded Vial
Elixir of Agility	185	Trained	1 Stranglekelp, 1 Goldthorn, 1 Leaded Vial
Frost Protection Potion	190	Found	1 Wintersbite, 1 Goldthorn, 1 Leaded Vial
Nature Protection Potion	190	Found	1 Liferoot, 1 Stranglekelp, 1 Leaded Vial
Elixir of Frost Power	190	Found	2 Wintersbite, 1 Khadgar's Whisker, 1 Leaded Vial
Elixir of Detect Lesser Invisibility	195	Found	1 Khadgar's Whisker, 1 Fadeleaf, 1 Leaded Vial
Elixir of Greater Defense	195	Trained	1 Wild Steelbloom, 1 Goldthorn, 1 Leaded Vial
Frost Oil	200	Found	4 Khadgar's Whisker, 2 Wintersbite, 1 Leaded Vial
Catseye Elixir	200	Trained	1 Goldthorn, 1 Fadeleaf, 1 Leaded Vial
Oil of Immolation	205	Trained	1 Firebloom, 1 Goldthorn, 1 Crystal Vial
Greater Mana Potion	205	Trained	1 Khadgar's Whisker, 1 Goldthorn, 1 Leaded Vial
Magic Resistance Potion	210	Found	1 Khadgar's Whisker, 1 Purple Lotus, 1 Crystal Vial
Goblin Rocket Fuel	210	Found	1 Firebloom, 1 Volatile Rum, 1 Leaded Vial
Lesser Stoneshield Potion	215	Found	1 Mithril Ore, 1 Goldthorn, 1 Leaded Vial

Alchemy

Created Item	Skill Lvl	Source	Reagent(s)
Superior Healing Potion	215	Trained	1 Sungrass, 1 Khadgar's Whisker, 1 Crystal Vial
Elixir of Greater Water Breathing	215	Trained	1 Ichor of Undeath, 2 Purple Lotus, 1 Crystal Vial
Gurubashi Mojo Madness	300	Special	1 Blood of Heroes, 1 Massive Mojo, 6 Powerful Mojo, 1 Black Lotus
Wildvine Potion	225	Found	1 Wildvine, 1 Purple Lotus, 1 Crystal Vial
Philosopher's Stone	225	Found	4 Iron Bar, 1 Black Vitriol, 4 Purple Lotus, 4 Firebloom
Transmute: Iron to Gold	225	Found	1 Iron Bar
Transmute: Mithril to Truesilver	225	Found	1 Mithril Bar
Elixir of Detect Undead	230	Trained	1 Arthas' Tears, 1 Crystal Vial
Dreamless Sleep Potion	230	Trained	3 Purple Lotus, 1 Crystal Vial
Arcane Elixir	235	Trained	1 Blindweed, 1 Goldthorn, 1 Crystal Vial
Invisibility Potion	235	Found	1 Ghost Mushroom, 1 Sungrass, 1 Crystal Vial
Elixir of Greater Intellect	235	Trained	1 Blindweed, 1 Khadgar's Whisker, 1 Crystal Vial
Gift of Arthas	240	Found	1 Arthas' Tears, 1 Blindweed, 1 Crystal Vial
Elixir of Greater Agility	240	Trained	1 Sungrass, 1 Goldthorn, 1 Crystal Vial
Elixir of Dream Vision	240	Found	3 Purple Lotus, 1 Crystal Vial
Elixir of Giants	245	Found	1 Sungrass, 1 Gromsblood, 1 Crystal Vial
Ghost Dye	245	Found	2 Ghost Mushroom, 1 Purple Dye, 1 Crystal Vial
Elixir of Shadow Power	250	Found	3 Ghost Mushroom, 1 Crystal Vial
Elixir of Demonslaying	250	Found	1 Gromsblood, 1 Ghost Mushroom, 1 Crystal Vial
Elixir of Detect Demon	250	Trained	2 Gromsblood, 1 Crystal Vial
Stonescale Oil	250	Trained	1 Stonescale Eel, 1 Leaded Vial
Limited Invulnerability Potion	250	Found	2 Blindweed, 1 Ghost Mushroom, 1 Crystal Vial
Elixir of Greater Firepower	250	Found	3 Fire Oil, 3 Firebloom, 1 Crystal Vial
Mighty Rage Potion	255	Found	3 Gromsblood, 1 Crystal Vial
Superior Mana Potion	260	Found	2 Sungrass, 2 Blindweed, 1 Crystal Vial
Elixir of Superior Defense	265	Found	2 Stonescale Oil, 1 Sungrass, 1 Crystal Vial
Elixir of the Sages	270	Found	1 Dreamfoil, 2 Plaguebloom, 1 Crystal Vial
Transmute: Arcanite	275	Found	1 Thorium Bar, 1 Arcane Crystal
Major Healing Potion	275	Found	2 Golden Sansam, 1 Mountain Silversage, 1 Crystal Vial
Elixir of Brute Force	275	Found	2 Gromsblood, 2 Plaguebloom, 1 Crystal Vial
Transmute: Air to Fire	275	Found	1 Essence of Air
Transmute: Earth to Water	275	Found	1 Essence of Earth
Transmute: Earth to Life	275	Found	1 Essence of Earth
Transmute: Fire to Earth	275	Found	1 Essence of Fire
Transmute: Undeath to Water	275	Found	1 Essence of Undeath
Transmute: Water to Air	275	Found	1 Essence of Water
Transmute: Water to Undeath	275	Found	1 Essence of Water
Transmute: Life to Earth	275	Found	1 Living Essence
Mageblood Potion	275	Found	1 Dreamfoil, 2 Plaguebloom, 1 Crystal Vial
Greater Dreamless Sleep Potion	275	Found	2 Dreamfoil, 1 Golden Sansam, 1 Crystal Vial
Greater Stoneshield Potion	280	Found	3 Stonescale Oil, 1 Thorium Ore, 1 Crystal Vial
Elixir of the Mongoose	280	Found	2 Mountain Silversage, 2 Plaguebloom, 1 Crystal Vial
Purification Potion	285	Found	2 Icecap, 2 Plaguebloom, 1 Crystal Vial
Greater Arcane Elixir	285	Found	3 Dreamfoil, 1 Mountain Silversage, 1 Crystal Vial
Living Action Potion	285	Found	2 Icecap, 2 Mountain Silversage, 2 Heart of the Wild, 1 Crystal Vial
Greater Fire Protection Potion	290	Found	1 Elemental Fire, 1 Dreamfoil, 1 Crystal Vial
Greater Frost Protection Potion	290	Found	1 Elemental Water, 1 Dreamfoil, 1 Crystal Vial
Greater Nature Protection Potion	290	Found	1 Elemental Earth, 1 Dreamfoil, 1 Crystal Vial
Greater Arcane Protection Potion	290	Found	1 Dream Dust, 1 Dreamfoil, 1 Crystal Vial
Greater Shadow Protection Potion	290	Found	1 Shadow Oil, 1 Dreamfoil, 1 Crystal Vial
Major Troll's Blood Potion	290	Found	1 Gromsblood, 2 Plaguebloom, 1 Crystal Vial
Major Mana Potion	295	Found	3 Dreamfoil, 2 Icecap, 1 Crystal Vial
Flask of the Titans	300	Found	30 Gromsblood, 10 Stonescale Oil, 1 Black Lotus, 1 Crystal Vial
Flask of Distilled Wisdom	300	Found	30 Dreamfoil, 10 Icecap, 1 Black Lotus, 1 Crystal Vial
Flask of Supreme Power	300	Found	30 Dreamfoil, 10 Mountain Silversage, 1 Black Lotus, 1 Crystal Vial
Flask of Chromatic Resistance	300	Found	30 Icecap, 10 Mountain Silversage, 1 Black Lotus, 1 Crystal Vial
Major Rejuvenation Potion	300	Found	1 Heart of the Wild, 4 Golden Sansam, 4 Dreamfoil, 1 Imbued Vial
Transmute: Elemental Fire	300	Found	1 Heart of Fire
Volatile Healing Potion	300	Trained	1 Golden Sansam, 1 Felweed, 1 Imbued Vial
Onslaught Elixir	300	Trained	1 Mountain Silversage, 1 Felweed, 1 Imbued Vial
Adept's Elixir	300	Trained	1 Dreamfoil, 1 Felweed, 1 Imbued Vial
Elixir of Camouflage	305	Found	1 Ragveil, 1 Felweed, 1 Imbued Vial
Elixir of Major Strength	305	Trained	1 Mountain Silversage, 1 Felweed, 1 Imbued Vial
Elixir of Healing Power	310	Trained	1 Golden Sansam, 1 Dreaming Glory, 1 Imbued Vial
Unstable Mana Potion	310	Trained	2 Ragveil, 1 Felweed, 1 Imbued Vial
Sneaking Potion	315	Found	2 Ragveil, 1 Felweed, 1 Imbued Vial
Elixir of Mastery	315	Trained	3 Terocone, 1 Felweed, 1 Imbued Vial
Elixir of Major Frost Power	320	Found	2 Mote of Water, 1 Ancient Lichen, 1 Imbued Vial
Insane Strength Potion	320	Found	3 Terocone, 1 Imbued Vial
Elixir of the Searching Eye	325	Found	2 Ragveil, 1 Terocone, 1 Imbued Vial
Super Healing Potion	325	Trained	2 Dreaming Glory, 1 Felweed, 1 Imbued Vial
Mercurial Stone	325	Trained	1 Primal Earth, 1 Primal Life, 1 Primal Mana
Elixir of Major Agility	330	Found	1 Terocone, 2 Felweed, 1 Imbued Vial
Shrouding Potion	335	Found	3 Ragveil, 1 Netherbloom, 1 Imbued Vial
Fel Strength Elixir	335	Found	2 Terocone, 2 Nightmare Vine, 1 Imbued Vial
Super Mana Potion	340	Found	2 Netherbloom, 1 Felweed, 1 Imbued Vial
Elixir of Major Firepower	345	Found	3 Mote of Fire, 1 Ancient Lichen, 1 Imbued Vial
Elixir of Major Defense	345	Found	3 Ancient Lichen, 1 Terocone, 1 Imbued Vial
Fel Regeneration Potion	345	Found	2 Felweed, 3 Nightmare Vine, 1 Imbued Vial
Alchemist's Stone	350	Found	1 Philosopher's Stone, 1 Earthstorm Diamond, 1 Skyfire Diamond, 2 Fel Lotus, 5 Primal Might
Elixir of Major Shadow Power	350	Found	1 Ancient Lichen, 1 Nightmare Vine, 1 Imbued Vial
Major Dreamless Sleep Potion	350	Found	1 Dreaming Glory, 1 Nightmare Vine, 1 Imbued Vial
Heroic Potion	350	Found	2 Terocone, 1 Ancient Lichen, 1 Imbued Vial
Haste Potion	350	Found	2 Terocone, 1 Netherbloom, 1 Imbued Vial
Destruction Potion	350	Found	2 Nightmare Vine, 1 Netherbloom, 1 Imbued Vial
Transmute: Primal Air to Fire	350	Found	1 Primal Air
Transmute: Primal Earth to Water	350	Found	1 Primal Earth
Transmute: Primal Fire to Earth	350	Found	1 Primal Fire
Transmute: Primal Water to Air	350	Found	1 Primal Water
Transmute: Primal Might	350	Found	1 Primal Earth, 1 Primal Water, 1 Primal Air, 1 Primal Fire, 1 Primal Mana
Transmute: Earthstorm Diamond	350	Found	3 Deep Peridot, 3 Shadow Draenite, 3 Golden Draenite, 2 Primal Earth, 2 Primal Water
Transmute: Skyfire Diamond	350	Found	3 Blood Garnet, 3 Flame Spessarite, 3 Azure Moonstone, 2 Primal Fire, 2 Primal Air
Elixir of Major Mageblood	355	Found	1 Ancient Lichen, 1 Netherbloom, 1 Imbued Vial
Major Arcane Protection Potion	360	Found	1 Primal Mana, 1 Mana Thistle, 1 Imbued Vial
Major Fire Protection Potion	360	Found	1 Primal Fire, 1 Mana Thistle, 1 Imbued Vial
Major Frost Protection Potion	360	Found	1 Primal Water, 1 Mana Thistle, 1 Imbued Vial
Major Holy Protection Potion	360	Found	1 Primal Life, 1 Primal Water, 1 Imbued Vial
Major Nature Protection Potion	360	Found	1 Primal Life, 1 Mana Thistle, 1 Imbued Vial

Alchemy

Created Item	Skill Lvl	Source	Reagent(s)
Major Shadow Protection Potion	360	Found	1 Primal Shadow, 1 Mana Thistle, 1 Imbued Vial
Fel Mana Potion	360	Found	1 Mana Thistle, 2 Nightmare Vine, 1 Imbued Vial
Elixir of Empowerment	365	Found	1 Netherbloom, 1 Mana Thistle, 1 Imbued Vial
Ironshield Potion	365	Found	2 Ancient Lichen, 1 Primal Earth, 1 Imbued Vial
Transmute: Primal Earth to Life	N/A	Special	1 Primal Earth
Transmute: Primal Fire to Mana	N/A	Special	1 Primal Fire
Transmute: Primal Life to Earth	N/A	Special	1 Primal Life
Transmute: Primal Mana to Fire	N/A	Special	1 Primal Mana
Transmute: Primal Shadow to Water	N/A	Special	1 Primal Shadow
Transmute: Primal Water to Shadow	N/A	Special	1 Primal Water
Super Rejuvination Potion	N/A	Special	2 Mana Thistle, 1 Dreaming Glory, 1 Netherbloom, 1 Imbued Vial
Flask of Arcane Fortification	N/A	Special	1 Fel Lotus, 10 Mana Thistle, 20 Netherbloom, 1 Imbued Vial
Flask of the Fortification	N/A	Special	1 Fel Lotus, 10 Mana Thistle, 20 Ancient Lichen, 1 Imbued Vial
Flask of Mighty Restoration	N/A	Special	1 Fel Lotus, 10 Mana Thistle, 20 Dreaming Glory, 1 Imbued Vial
Flask of Relentless Assault	N/A	Special	1 Fel Lotus, 10 Mana Thistle, 20 Terocone, 1 Imbued Vial
Flask of Shadow Fortification	N/A	Special	1 Fel Lotus, 10 Mana Thistle, 20 Nightmare Vine, 1 Imbued Vial

Blacksmithing

Created Item	Skill Lvl	Source	Reagent(s)
Copper Chain Pants	1	Trained	4 Copper Bar
Rough Sharpening Stone	N/A	Special	1 Rough Stone
Rough Weightstone	N/A	Special	1 Rough Stone, 1 Linen Cloth
Copper Bracers	N/A	Special	2 Copper Bar
Rough Copper Vest	N/A	Special	4 Copper Bar
Copper Mace	15	Trained	6 Copper Bar, 1 Weak Flux, 2 Linen Cloth
Copper Axe	20	Trained	6 Copper Bar, 1 Weak Flux, 2 Linen Cloth
Copper Chain Boots	20	Trained	8 Copper Bar
Copper Shortsword	25	Trained	6 Copper Bar, 1 Weak Flux, 2 Linen Cloth
Rough Grinding Stone	25	Trained	2 Rough Stone
Copper Dagger	30	Trained	6 Copper Bar, 1 Weak Flux, 1 Rough Grinding Stone, 1 Light Leather
Copper Claymore	30	Trained	10 Copper Bar, 2 Weak Flux, 1 Rough Grinding Stone, 1 Light Leather
Copper Chain Belt	35	Trained	6 Copper Bar
Copper Battle Axe	35	Trained	12 Copper Bar, 2 Weak Flux, 2 Malachite, 2 Rough Grinding Stone, 2 Light Leather
Copper Chain Vest	35	Found	8 Copper Bar, 2 Rough Grinding Stone
Runed Copper Gauntlets	40	Trained	8 Copper Bar, 2 Rough Grinding Stone
Runed Copper Pants	45	Trained	8 Copper Bar, 2 Fine Thread, 3 Rough Grinding Stone
Gemmed Copper Gauntlets	60	Found	8 Copper Bar, 1 Tigerseye, 1 Malachite
Coarse Sharpening Stone	65	Trained	1 Coarse Stone
Coarse Weightstone	65	Trained	1 Coarse Stone, 1 Wool Cloth
Heavy Copper Maul	65	Trained	12 Copper Bar, 2 Weak Flux, 2 Light Leather
Runed Copper Belt	70	Trained	10 Copper Bar
Thick War Axe	70	Trained	10 Copper Bar, 2 Weak Flux, 2 Silver Bar, 2 Rough Grinding Stone, 2 Light Leather
Ironforge Chain	70	Found	12 Copper Bar, 2 Malachite, 2 Rough Grinding Stone
Coarse Grinding Stone	75	Trained	2 Coarse Stone
Runed Copper Breastplate	80	Found	12 Copper Bar, 1 Shadowgem, 2 Rough Grinding Stone
Runed Copper Bracers	90	Trained	10 Copper Bar, 3 Rough Grinding Stone

Blacksmithing

Created Item	Skill Lvl	Source	Reagent(s)
Heavy Copper Broadsword	95	Trained	14 Copper Bar, 2 Weak Flux, 2 Tigerseye, 2 Medium Leather
Rough Bronze Boots	95	Trained	6 Bronze Bar, 6 Rough Grinding Stone
Rough Bronze Bracers	100	Found	4 Bronze Bar
Silver Rod	100	Trained	1 Silver Bar, 2 Rough Grinding Stone
Ironforge Breastplate	100	Found	16 Copper Bar, 2 Tigerseye, 3 Rough Grinding Stone
Silver Skeleton Key	100	Trained	1 Silver Bar, 1 Rough Grinding Stone
Thick Bronze Darts	100	Trained	6 Bronze Bar, 2 Rough Grinding Stone, 1 Medium Leather
Rough Bronze Leggings	105	Trained	6 Bronze Bar
Rough Bronze Cuirass	105	Trained	7 Bronze Bar
Big Bronze Knife	105	Trained	6 Bronze Bar, 4 Weak Flux, 2 Rough Grinding Stone, 1 Tigerseye, 1 Medium Leather
Bronze Mace	110	Trained	6 Bronze Bar, 4 Weak Flux, 1 Medium Leather
Rough Bronze Shoulders	110	Trained	5 Bronze Bar, 1 Coarse Grinding Stone
Pearl-handled Dagger	110	Trained	6 Bronze Bar, 1 Strong Flux, 2 Small Lustrous Pearl, 2 Coarse Grinding Stone
Bronze Axe	115	Trained	7 Bronze Bar, 4 Weak Flux, 1 Medium Leather
Patterned Bronze Bracers	120	Trained	5 Bronze Bar, 2 Coarse Grinding Stone
Bronze Shortsword	120	Trained	5 Bronze Bar, 4 Weak Flux, 2 Medium Leather
Heavy Sharpening Stone	125	Trained	1 Heavy Stone
Heavy Weightstone	125	Trained	1 Heavy Stone, 1 Wool Cloth
Deadly Bronze Poniard	125	Found	4 Bronze Bar, 1 Strong Flux, 1 Swiftness Potion, 2 Shadowgem, 2 Coarse Grinding Stone, 2 Medium Leather
Silvered Bronze Shoulders	125	Found	8 Bronze Bar, 2 Silver Bar, 2 Coarse Grinding Stone
Heavy Grinding Stone	125	Trained	3 Heavy Stone
Bronze Warhammer	125	Trained	8 Bronze Bar, 1 Strong Flux, 1 Medium Leather
Heavy Bronze Mace	130	Trained	8 Bronze Bar, 1 Strong Flux, 1 Moss Agate, 1 Shadowgem, 2 Coarse Grinding Stone, 2 Medium Leather
Silvered Bronze Boots	130	Trained	6 Bronze Bar, 1 Silver Bar, 2 Coarse Grinding Stone
Silvered Bronze Breastplate	130	Found	10 Bronze Bar, 2 Silver Bar, 2 Coarse Grinding Stone
Bronze Greatsword	130	Trained	12 Bronze Bar, 2 Strong Flux, 2 Medium Leather
Silvered Bronze Gauntlets	135	Trained	8 Bronze Bar, 1 Silver Bar, 2 Coarse Grinding Stone
Bronze Battle Axe	135	Trained	14 Bronze Bar, 1 Strong Flux, 2 Medium Leather
Iridescent Hammer	140	Found	10 Bronze Bar, 1 Strong Flux, 1 Iridescent Pearl, 2 Coarse Grinding Stone, 2 Medium Leather
Ironforge Gauntlets	140	Found	8 Bronze Bar, 3 Shadowgem, 4 Coarse Grinding Stone
Shining Silver Breastplate	145	Trained	20 Bronze Bar, 2 Moss Agate, 2 Lesser Moonstone, 2 Iridescent Pearl, 4 Silver Bar
Mighty Iron Hammer	145	Found	6 Iron Bar, 2 Strong Flux, 1 Elixir of Ogre's Strength, 2 Lesser Moonstone, 2 Coarse Grinding Stone, 2 Medium Leather
Green Iron Boots	145	Found	6 Iron Bar, 2 Coarse Grinding Stone, 1 Green Dye
Green Iron Gauntlets	150	Found	4 Iron Bar, 2 Small Lustrous Pearl, 2 Coarse Grinding Stone, 1 Green Dye
Iron Shield Spike	150	Found	6 Iron Bar, 4 Coarse Grinding Stone
Iron Buckle	150	Trained	1 Iron Bar
Golden Rod	150	Trained	1 Gold Bar, 2 Coarse Grinding Stone
Golden Skeleton Key	150	Trained	1 Gold Bar, 1 Heavy Grinding Stone
Solid Iron Maul	155	Found	8 Iron Bar, 2 Strong Flux, 1 Heavy Grinding Stone, 4 Silver Bar, 2 Heavy Leather
Green Iron Leggings	155	Trained	8 Iron Bar, 1 Heavy Grinding Stone, 1 Green Dye

Blacksmithing			
Created Item	Skill Lvl	Source	Reagent(s)
Silvered Bronze Leggings	155	Found	12 Bronze Bar, 4 Silver Bar, 2 Coarse Grinding Stone
Hardened Iron Shortsword	160	Found	6 Iron Bar, 2 Strong Flux, 1 Heavy Grinding Stone, 2 Lesser Moonstone, 3 Heavy Leather
Green Iron Shoulders	160	Found	7 Iron Bar, 1 Heavy Grinding Stone, 1 Green Dye
Barbaric Iron Shoulders	160	Found	8 Iron Bar, 4 Sharp Claw, 2 Heavy Grinding Stone
Barbaric Iron Breastplate	160	Found	20 Iron Bar, 4 Heavy Grinding Stone
Green Iron Bracers	165	Trained	6 Iron Bar, 1 Green Dye
Iron Counterweight	165	Found	4 Iron Bar, 2 Coarse Grinding Stone, 1 Lesser Moonstone
Golden Iron Destroyer	170	Found	10 Iron Bar, 4 Gold Bar, 2 Lesser Moonstone, 2 Strong Flux, 2 Heavy Leather, 2 Heavy Grinding Stone
Green Iron Helm	170	Trained	12 Iron Bar, 1 Citrine, 1 Green Dye
Golden Scale Leggings	170	Found	10 Iron Bar, 2 Gold Bar, 1 Heavy Grinding Stone
Jade Serpentblade	175	Found	8 Iron Bar, 2 Strong Flux, 2 Heavy Grinding Stone, 2 Jade, 3 Heavy Leather
Golden Scale Shoulders	175	Found	6 Steel Bar, 2 Gold Bar, 1 Heavy Grinding Stone
Barbaric Iron Helm	175	Found	10 Iron Bar, 2 Large Fang, 2 Sharp Claw
Moonsteel Broadsword	180	Found	8 Steel Bar, 2 Strong Flux, 2 Heavy Grinding Stone, 3 Lesser Moonstone, 3 Heavy Leather
Green Iron Hauberk	180	Trained	20 Iron Bar, 4 Heavy Grinding Stone, 2 Jade, 2 Moss Agate, 1 Green Leather Armor
Barbaric Iron Boots	180	Found	12 Iron Bar, 4 Large Fang, 2 Heavy Grinding Stone
Glinting Steel Dagger	180	Trained	10 Steel Bar, 2 Strong Flux, 1 Moss Agate, 1 Elemental Earth, 1 Heavy Leather
Massive Iron Axe	185	Found	14 Iron Bar, 2 Strong Flux, 2 Heavy Grinding Stone, 4 Gold Bar, 2 Heavy Leather
Polished Steel Boots	185	Found	8 Steel Bar, 1 Citrine, 1 Lesser Moonstone, 2 Heavy Grinding Stone
Golden Scale Bracers	185	Trained	5 Steel Bar, 2 Heavy Grinding Stone
Barbaric Iron Gloves	185	Found	14 Iron Bar, 3 Heavy Grinding Stone, 2 Large Fang
Golden Scale Coif	190	Found	8 Steel Bar, 2 Gold Bar, 2 Heavy Grinding Stone
Steel Weapon Chain	190	Found	8 Steel Bar, 2 Heavy Grinding Stone, 4 Heavy Leather
Searing Golden Blade	190	Found	10 Steel Bar, 4 Gold Bar, 2 Elemental Fire, 2 Heavy Leather
Edge of Winter	190	Found	10 Steel Bar, 1 Frost Oil, 2 Elemental Water, 2 Elemental Air, 2 Heavy Leather
Golden Scale Cuirass	195	Found	12 Steel Bar, 2 Gold Bar, 4 Heavy Grinding Stone
Frost Tiger Blade	200	Found	8 Steel Bar, 2 Strong Flux, 2 Heavy Grinding Stone, 2 Jade, 1 Frost Oil, 4 Heavy Leather
Shadow Crescent Axe	200	Found	10 Steel Bar, 2 Strong Flux, 3 Heavy Grinding Stone, 2 Citrine, 1 Shadow Oil, 3 Heavy Leather
Golden Scale Boots	200	Found	10 Steel Bar, 4 Gold Bar, 4 Heavy Grinding Stone
Steel Breastplate	200	Trained	16 Steel Bar, 3 Heavy Grinding Stone
Solid Sharpening Stone	200	Trained	1 Solid Stone
Solid Weightstone	200	Trained	1 Solid Stone, 1 Silk Cloth
Solid Grinding Stone	200	Trained	4 Solid Stone
Inlaid Mithril Cylinder	200	Found	5 Mithril Bar, 1 Gold Bar, 1 Truesilver Bar
Truesilver Rod	200	Trained	1 Truesilver Bar, 1 Heavy Grinding Stone
Truesilver Skeleton Key	200	Trained	1 Truesilver Bar, 1 Solid Grinding Stone
Whirling Steel Axes	200	Trained	5 Steel Bar, 2 Elemental Air, 2 Heavy Grinding Stone, 1 Heavy Leather
Heavy Mithril Shoulder	205	Trained	8 Mithril Bar, 6 Heavy Leather
Heavy Mithril Gauntlet	205	Trained	6 Mithril Bar, 4 Mageweave Cloth

Blacksmithing			
Created Item	Skill Lvl	Source	Reagent(s)
Golden Scale Gauntlets	205	Found	10 Steel Bar, 4 Gold Bar, 4 Heavy Grinding Stone
Mithril Scale Pants	210	Trained	12 Mithril Bar
Heavy Mithril Pants	210	Found	10 Mithril Bar
Heavy Mithril Axe	210	Trained	12 Mithril Bar, 2 Citrine, 1 Solid Grinding Stone, 4 Heavy Leather
Steel Plate Helm	215	Trained	14 Steel Bar, 1 Solid Grinding Stone
Mithril Scale Bracers	215	Found	8 Mithril Bar
Mithril Shield Spike	215	Found	4 Mithril Bar, 2 Truesilver Bar, 4 Solid Grinding Stone
Mithril Scale Gloves	220	Found	8 Mithril Bar, 6 Heavy Leather, 4 Mageweave Cloth
Ornate Mithril Pants	220	Found	12 Mithril Bar, 1 Truesilver Bar, 1 Solid Grinding Stone
Ornate Mithril Gloves	220	Found	10 Mithril Bar, 6 Mageweave Cloth, 1 Truesilver Bar, 1 Solid Grinding Stone
Blue Glittering Axe	220	Found	16 Mithril Bar, 2 Aquamarine, 1 Solid Grinding Stone, 4 Thick Leather
Ornate Mithril Shoulder	225	Found	12 Mithril Bar, 1 Truesilver Bar, 6 Thick Leather
Truesilver Gauntlets	225	Trained	10 Mithril Bar, 8 Truesilver Bar, 3 Aquamarine, 3 Citrine, 1 Guardian Gloves, 2 Solid Grinding Stone
Wicked Mithril Blade	225	Found	14 Mithril Bar, 4 Truesilver Bar, 1 Solid Grinding Stone, 2 Thick Leather
Orcish War Leggings	230	Found	12 Mithril Bar, 1 Elemental Earth
Heavy Mithril Breastplate	230	Trained	16 Mithril Bar
Mithril Coif	230	Trained	10 Mithril Bar, 6 Mageweave Cloth
Big Black Mace	230	Trained	16 Mithril Bar, 1 Black Pearl, 4 Shadowgem, 1 Solid Grinding Stone, 2 Thick Leather
Mithril Spurs	235	Found	4 Mithril Bar, 3 Solid Grinding Stone
Mithril Scale Shoulders	235	Found	14 Mithril Bar, 4 Thick Leather
Heavy Mithril Boots	235	Trained	14 Mithril Bar, 4 Thick Leather
The Shatterer	235	Trained	24 Mithril Bar, 4 Core of Earth, 6 Truesilver Bar, 5 Citrine, 5 Jade, 4 Solid Grinding Stone, 4 Thick Leather
Ornate Mithril Breastplate	240	Found	16 Mithril Bar, 6 Truesilver Bar, 1 Heart of Fire, 1 Solid Grinding Stone
Dazzling Mithril Rapier	240	Found	14 Mithril Bar, 1 Aquamarine, 2 Lesser Moonstone, 2 Moss Agate, 1 Solid Grinding Stone, 2 Mageweave Cloth
Heavy Mithril Helm	245	Found	14 Mithril Bar, 1 Aquamarine
Truesilver Breastplate	245	Trained	12 Mithril Bar, 12 Truesilver Bar, 2 Star Ruby, 2 Black Pearl, 2 Solid Grinding Stone
Ornate Mithril Boots	245	Found	14 Mithril Bar, 2 Truesilver Bar, 4 Thick Leather, 1 Solid Grinding Stone, 1 Aquamarine
Ornate Mithril Helm	245	Found	16 Mithril Bar, 2 Truesilver Bar, 1 Solid Grinding Stone
Phantom Blade	245	Trained	28 Mithril Bar, 6 Breath of Wind, 8 Truesilver Bar, 2 Lesser Invisibility Potion, 6 Aquamarine, 4 Solid Grinding Stone, 2 Thick Leather
Runed Mithril Hammer	245	Found	18 Mithril Bar, 2 Core of Earth, 1 Solid Grinding Stone, 4 Thick Leather
Blight	250	Trained	28 Mithril Bar, 10 Ichor of Undeath, 10 Truesilver Bar, 6 Solid Grinding Stone, 6 Thick Leather
Dense Sharpening Stone	250	Trained	1 Dense Stone
Dense Weightstone	250	Trained	1 Dense Stone, 1 Runecloth
Dense Grinding Stone	250	Trained	4 Dense Stone
Thorium Armor	250	Found	16 Thorium Bar, 1 Blue Sapphire, 4 Yellow Power Crystal
Thorium Belt	250	Found	12 Thorium Bar, 4 Red Power Crystal
Ebon Shiv	255	Found	12 Mithril Bar, 6 Truesilver Bar, 2 Star Ruby, 1 Solid Grinding Stone, 2 Thick Leather
Thorium Bracers	255	Found	12 Thorium Bar, 4 Blue Power Crystal
Truesilver Champion	260	Trained	30 Mithril Bar, 16 Truesilver Bar, 6 Star Ruby, 4 Breath of Wind, 8 Solid Grinding Stone, 6 Thick Leather

Blacksmithing

Created Item	Skill Lvl	Source	Reagent(s)
Radiant Belt	260	Found	10 Thorium Bar, 2 Heart of Fire
Thorium Greatsword	260	Found	16 Thorium Bar, 2 Dense Grinding Stone, 4 Rugged Leather
Earthforged Leggings	260	Trained	16 Mithril Bar, 2 Core of Earth
Light Earthforged Blade	260	Trained	12 Mithril Bar, 4 Core of Earth
Light Emberforged Hammer	260	Trained	12 Mithril Bar, 4 Heart of Fire
Light Skyforged Axe	260	Trained	12 Mithril Bar, 4 Breath of Wind
Windforged Leggings	260	Trained	16 Mithril Bar, 2 Breath of Wind
Dark Iron Pulverizer	265	Found	18 Dark Iron Bar, 4 Heart of Fire
Imperial Plate Shoulders	265	Found	12 Thorium Bar, 6 Rugged Leather
Imperial Plate Belt	265	Found	10 Thorium Bar, 6 Rugged Leather
Dark Iron Mail	270	Found	10 Dark Iron Bar, 2 Heart of Fire
Radiant Breastplate	270	Found	18 Thorium Bar, 2 Heart of Fire, 1 Star Ruby
Imperial Plate Bracers	270	Found	12 Thorium Bar
Wildthorn Mail	270	Found	40 Thorium Bar, 2 Enchanted Thorium Bar, 4 Living Essence, 4 Wildvine, 1 Huge Emerald
Bleakwood Hew	270	Found	30 Thorium Bar, 6 Living Essence, 6 Wildvine, 6 Large Opal, 2 Dense Grinding Stone, 8 Rugged Leather
Inlaid Thorium Hammer	270	Found	30 Thorium Bar, 4 Gold Bar, 2 Truesilver Bar, 2 Blue Sapphire, 4 Rugged Leather
Dark Iron Sunderer	275	Found	26 Dark Iron Bar, 4 Heart of Fire
Thorium Shield Spike	275	Found	4 Thorium Bar, 4 Dense Grinding Stone, 2 Essence of Earth
Ornate Thorium Handaxe	275	Found	20 Thorium Bar, 2 Large Opal, 2 Dense Grinding Stone, 4 Rugged Leather
Dawn's Edge	275	Found	30 Thorium Bar, 4 Enchanted Thorium Bar, 4 Star Ruby, 4 Blue Sapphire, 2 Dense Grinding Stone, 4 Rugged Leather
Arcanite Skeleton Key	275	Trained	1 Arcanite Bar, 1 Dense Grinding Stone
Arcanite Rod	275	Trained	3 Arcanite Bar, 1 Dense Grinding Stone
Dark Iron Shoulders	280	Found	6 Dark Iron Bar, 1 Heart of Fire
Thorium Boots	280	Found	20 Thorium Bar, 8 Rugged Leather, 4 Green Power Crystal
Thorium Helm	280	Found	24 Thorium Bar, 1 Star Ruby, 4 Yellow Power Crystal
Huge Thorium Battleaxe	280	Found	40 Thorium Bar, 6 Dense Grinding Stone, 6 Rugged Leather
Enchanted Battlehammer	280	Found	20 Thorium Bar, 6 Enchanted Thorium Bar, 2 Huge Emerald, 4 Powerful Mojo, 4 Rugged Leather
Blazing Rapier	280	Found	10 Enchanted Thorium Bar, 4 Essence of Fire, 4 Heart of Fire, 2 Azerothian Diamond, 2 Dense Grinding Stone
Dark Iron Plate	285	Found	20 Dark Iron Bar, 8 Heart of Fire
Radiant Gloves	285	Found	18 Thorium Bar, 4 Heart of Fire
Demon Forged Breastplate	285	Found	40 Thorium Bar, 10 Demonic Rune, 4 Blue Sapphire, 4 Star Ruby
Rune Edge	285	Found	30 Thorium Bar, 2 Large Opal, 2 Dense Grinding Stone, 4 Rugged Leather
Serenity	285	Found	6 Enchanted Thorium Bar, 2 Arcanite Bar, 4 Powerful Mojo, 2 Large Opal, 2 Blue Sapphire, 1 Huge Emerald
Radiant Boots	290	Found	14 Thorium Bar, 4 Heart of Fire
Dawnbringer Shoulders	290	Found	20 Thorium Bar, 4 Arcanite Bar, 2 Huge Emerald, 2 Essence of Water
Fiery Plate Gauntlets	290	Found	20 Thorium Bar, 6 Enchanted Thorium Bar, 2 Essence of Fire, 4 Star Ruby
Volcanic Hammer	290	Found	30 Thorium Bar, 4 Heart of Fire, 4 Star Ruby, 4 Rugged Leather
Corruption	290	Found	40 Thorium Bar, 2 Arcanite Bar, 16 Demonic Rune, 8 Essence of Undeath, 2 Blue Sapphire, 2 Dense Grinding Stone, 4 Rugged Leather
Heavy Timbermaw Belt	290	Found	12 Thorium Bar, 3 Essence of Earth, 3 Living Essence
Girdle of the Dawn	290	Found	8 Thorium Bar, 6 Truesilver Bar, 1 Righteous Orb

Blacksmithing

Created Item	Skill Lvl	Source	Reagent(s)
Imperial Plate Boots	295	Found	18 Thorium Bar
Imperial Plate Helm	295	Found	18 Thorium Bar, 1 Star Ruby
Radiant Circlet	295	Found	18 Thorium Bar, 4 Heart of Fire
Storm Gauntlets	295	Found	20 Thorium Bar, 4 Enchanted Thorium Bar, 4 Essence of Water, 4 Blue Sapphire
Dark Iron Bracers	295	Found	4 Dark Iron Bar, 2 Fiery Core, 2 Lava Core
Fiery Chain Girdle	295	Found	6 Dark Iron Bar, 3 Fiery Core, 3 Lava Core
Thorium Leggings	300	Found	26 Thorium Bar, 4 Red Power Crystal
Imperial Plate Chest	300	Found	20 Thorium Bar
Runic Plate Shoulders	300	Found	20 Thorium Bar, 2 Arcanite Bar, 6 Gold Bar
Runic Plate Boots	300	Found	20 Thorium Bar, 2 Arcanite Bar, 10 Silver Bar
Whitesoul Helm	300	Found	20 Thorium Bar, 4 Enchanted Thorium Bar, 6 Truesilver Bar, 6 Gold Bar, 2 Azerothian Diamond
Radiant Leggings	300	Found	20 Thorium Bar, 4 Heart of Fire
Runic Plate Helm	300	Found	30 Thorium Bar, 2 Arcanite Bar, 2 Truesilver Bar, 1 Huge Emerald
Imperial Plate Leggings	300	Found	24 Thorium Bar
Helm of the Great Chief	300	Found	40 Thorium Bar, 4 Enchanted Thorium Bar, 60 Jet Black Feather, 6 Large Opal, 2 Huge Emerald
Lionheart Helm	300	Found	80 Thorium Bar, 12 Arcanite Bar, 40 Wicked Claw, 10 Blue Sapphire, 4 Azerothian Diamond
Runic Breastplate	300	Found	40 Thorium Bar, 2 Arcanite Bar, 1 Star Ruby
Runic Plate Leggings	300	Found	40 Thorium Bar, 2 Arcanite Bar, 1 Star Ruby
Stronghold Gauntlets	300	Found	15 Arcanite Bar, 20 Enchanted Thorium Bar, 10 Essence of Earth, 4 Blue Sapphire, 4 Large Opal
Enchanted Thorium Helm	300	Found	6 Arcanite Bar, 16 Enchanted Thorium Bar, 6 Essence of Earth, 2 Large Opal, 1 Azerothian Diamond
Enchanted Thorium Leggings	300	Found	10 Arcanite Bar, 20 Enchanted Thorium Bar, 6 Essence of Water, 2 Blue Sapphire, 1 Huge Emerald
Enchanted Thorium Breastplate	300	Found	8 Arcanite Bar, 24 Enchanted Thorium Bar, 4 Essence of Earth, 4 Essence of Water, 2 Huge Emerald, 2 Azerothian Diamond
Invulnerable Mail	300	Found	30 Arcanite Bar, 30 Enchanted Thorium Bar, 6 Huge Emerald, 6 Azerothian Diamond
Blood Talon	300	Found	10 Enchanted Thorium Bar, 10 Arcanite Bar, 8 Demonic Rune, 10 Star Ruby, 2 Dense Grinding Stone
Darkspear	300	Found	20 Enchanted Thorium Bar, 20 Powerful Mojo, 2 Huge Emerald, 2 Azerothian Diamond, 2 Dense Grinding Stone
Hammer of the Titans	300	Found	50 Thorium Bar, 15 Arcanite Bar, 4 Guardian Stone, 6 Enchanted Leather, 10 Essence of Earth
Arcanite Champion	300	Found	15 Arcanite Bar, 8 Azerothian Diamond, 1 Righteous Orb, 4 Large Opal, 8 Enchanted Leather, 2 Dense Grinding Stone
Annihilator	300	Found	40 Thorium Bar, 12 Arcanite Bar, 10 Essence of Undeath, 8 Huge Emerald, 2 Dense Grinding Stone, 4 Enchanted Leather
Frostguard	300	Found	18 Arcanite Bar, 8 Blue Sapphire, 8 Azerothian Diamond, 4 Essence of Water, 2 Dense Grinding Stone, 4 Enchanted Leather
Masterwork Stormhammer	300	Found	20 Enchanted Thorium Bar, 8 Huge Emerald, 8 Large Opal, 6 Essence of Earth, 4 Enchanted Leather
Arcanite Reaper	300	Found	20 Arcanite Bar, 6 Enchanted Leather, 2 Dense Grinding Stone
Heartseeker	300	Found	10 Arcanite Bar, 10 Enchanted Thorium Bar, 2 Enchanted Leather, 6 Star Ruby, 6 Azerothian Diamond, 6 Large Opal, 4 Dense Grinding Stone
Dark Iron Leggings	300	Found	16 Dark Iron Bar, 4 Fiery Core, 6 Lava Core
Fiery Chain Shoulders	300	Found	16 Dark Iron Bar, 4 Fiery Core, 5 Lava Core

Alchemy

Blacksmithing

Cooking

Enchanting

Engineering

First Aid

Jewelcrafting

Leatherworking

Poisons

Tailoring

Blacksmithing

Created Item	Skill Lvl	Source	Reagent(s)
Dark Iron Destroyer	300	Found	18 Dark Iron Bar, 12 Lava Core, 2 Blood of the Mountain, 2 Enchanted Leather
Dark Iron Reaver	300	Found	16 Dark Iron Bar, 12 Fiery Core, 2 Blood of the Mountain, 2 Enchanted Leather
Sulfuron Hammer	300	Found	8 Sulfuron Ingot, 20 Dark Iron Bar, 50 Arcanite Bar, 25 Essence of Fire, 10 Blood of the Mountain, 10 Lava Core, 10 Fiery Core
Elemental Sharpening Stone	300	Found	2 Elemental Earth, 3 Dense Stone
Heavy Timbermaw Boots	300	Found	4 Arcanite Bar, 6 Essence of Earth, 6 Living Essence
Gloves of the Dawn	300	Found	2 Arcanite Bar, 10 Truesilver Bar, 1 Righteous Orb
Dark Iron Helm	300	Found	4 Lava Core, 2 Fiery Core, 4 Dark Iron Bar
Dark Iron Gauntlets	300	Found	3 Lava Core, 5 Fiery Core, 4 Core Leather, 4 Dark Iron Bar, 2 Blood of the Mountain
Black Amnesty	300	Found	3 Lava Core, 6 Fiery Core, 12 Arcanite Bar, 1 Blood of the Mountain, 4 Dark Iron Bar
Blackfury	300	Found	5 Lava Core, 2 Fiery Core, 16 Arcanite Bar, 6 Dark Iron Bar
Ebon Hand	300	Found	4 Lava Core, 7 Fiery Core, 12 Arcanite Bar, 8 Dark Iron Bar, 4 Azerothian Diamond
Blackguard	300	Found	6 Lava Core, 6 Fiery Core, 10 Arcanite Bar, 6 Dark Iron Bar, 12 Guardian Stone
Nightfall	300	Found	8 Lava Core, 5 Fiery Core, 10 Arcanite Bar, 12 Dark Iron Bar, 4 Huge Emerald
Bloodsoul Breastplate	300	Found	20 Thorium Bar, 10 Souldarite, 2 Bloodvine, 2 Star Ruby
Bloodsoul Gauntlets	300	Found	12 Thorium Bar, 6 Souldarite, 2 Bloodvine, 4 Enchanted Leather
Bloodsoul Shoulders	300	Found	16 Thorium Bar, 8 Souldarite, 2 Bloodvine, 1 Star Ruby
Darksoul Breastplate	300	Found	20 Thorium Bar, 14 Souldarite, 2 Large Opal
Darksoul Leggings	300	Found	18 Thorium Bar, 12 Souldarite, 2 Large Opal
Darksoul Shoulders	300	Found	16 Thorium Bar, 10 Souldarite, 1 Large Opal
Dark Iron Boots	300	Found	3 Lava Core, 3 Fiery Core, 4 Core Leather, 6 Dark Iron Bar
Darkrune Breastplate	300	Found	20 Thorium Bar, 10 Dark Rune, 10 Truesilver Bar
Darkrune Gauntlets	300	Found	12 Thorium Bar, 6 Dark Rune, 6 Truesilver Bar, 2 Enchanted Leather
Darkrune Helm	300	Found	16 Thorium Bar, 8 Dark Rune, 8 Truesilver Bar, 1 Black Diamond
Heavy Obsidian Belt	300	Found	14 Small Obsidian Shard, 4 Enchanted Thorium Bar, 2 Essence of Earth
Light Obsidian Belt	300	Found	14 Small Obsidian Shard, 4 Enchanted Leather
Jagged Obsidian Shield	300	Found	8 Large Obsidian Shard, 24 Small Obsidian Shard, 8 Enchanted Thorium Bar, 4 Essence of Earth
Black Grasp of the Destroyer	300	Found	8 Large Obsidian Shard, 24 Small Obsidian Shard, 8 Enchanted Leather, 1 Flask of Supreme Power
Obsidian Mail Tunic	300	Found	15 Large Obsidian Shard, 36 Small Obsidian Shard, 12 Enchanted Leather, 10 Guardian Stone, 4 Azerothian Diamond
Thick Obsidian Breastplate	300	Found	18 Large Obsidian Shard, 40 Small Obsidian Shard, 12 Enchanted Thorium Bar, 10 Essence of Earth, 4 Huge Emerald
Persuader	300	Found	15 Arcanite Bar, 10 Dark Iron Bar, 20 Essence of Undeath, 20 Dark Rune, 10 Devilsaur Leather, 2 Skin of Shadow
Titanic Leggings	300	Found	12 Arcanite Bar, 20 Enchanted Thorium Bar, 10 Essence of Earth, 2 Flask of the Titans
Sageblade	300	Found	12 Arcanite Bar, 2 Nexus Crystal, 2 Flask of Supreme Power, 4 Enchanted Leather
Icebane Bracers	300	Found	4 Frozen Rune, 12 Thorium Bar, 2 Arcanite Bar, 2 Essence of Water
Icebane Breastplate	300	Found	7 Frozen Rune, 16 Thorium Bar, 2 Arcanite Bar, 4 Essence of Water

Blacksmithing

Created Item	Skill Lvl	Source	Reagent(s)
Icebane Gauntlets	300	Found	5 Frozen Rune, 12 Thorium Bar, 2 Arcanite Bar, 2 Essence of Water
Ironvine Breastplate	300	Found	12 Enchanted Thorium Bar, 2 Bloodvine, 2 Arcanite Bar, 2 Living Essence
Ironvine Gloves	300	Found	8 Enchanted Thorium Bar, 1 Bloodvine, 2 Living Essence
Ironvine Belt	300	Found	6 Enchanted Thorium Bar, 2 Living Essence
Fel Iron Plate Gloves	300	Trained	4 Fel Iron Bar
Fel Iron Chain Coif	300	Trained	4 Fel Iron Bar
Fel Sharpening Stone	300	Trained	1 Fel Iron Bar, 1 Mote of Earth
Fel Iron Rod	300	Trained	6 Fel Iron Bar
Fel Weightstone	300	Trained	1 Fel Iron Bar, 1 Netherweave Cloth
Enchanted Thorium Blades	300	Trained	2 Enchanted Thorium Bar, 6 Thorium Bar, 1 Rugged Leather
Fel Iron Plate Belt	305	Trained	4 Fel Iron Bar
Fel Iron Chain Gloves	310	Trained	5 Fel Iron Bar
Fel Iron Hatchet	310	Trained	9 Fel Iron Bar
Fel Iron Plate Boots	315	Trained	6 Fel Iron Bar
Fel Iron Plate Pants	315	Trained	8 Fel Iron Bar
Fel Iron Chain Bracers	315	Trained	6 Fel Iron Bar
Fel Iron Hammer	315	Trained	10 Fel Iron Bar
Fel Iron Chain Tunic	320	Trained	9 Fel Iron Bar
Fel Iron Greatsword	320	Trained	12 Fel Iron Bar
Fel Iron Breastplate	325	Trained	10 Fel Iron Bar
Adamantite Maul	325	Found	8 Adamantite Bar
Lesser Rune of Warding	325	Trained	1 Adamantite Bar
Adamantite Cleaver	330	Found	8 Adamantite Bar
Adamantite Dagger	330	Found	7 Adamantite Bar, 2 Knothide Leather
Great Earthforged Hammer	330	Trained	12 Adamantite Bar, 6 Primal Earth
Heavy Earthforged Breastplate	330	Trained	8 Adamantite Bar, 4 Primal Earth
Lavaforged Warhammer	330	Trained	8 Adamantite Bar, 6 Primal Fire
Skyforged Great Axe	330	Trained	10 Adamantite Bar, 6 Primal Air
Stoneforged Claymore	330	Trained	10 Adamantite Bar, 6 Primal Earth
Stormforged Axe	330	Trained	8 Adamantite Bar, 3 Primal Water, 3 Primal Air
Stormforged Hauberk	330	Trained	8 Adamantite Bar, 2 Primal Water, 2 Primal Air
Windforged Rapier	330	Trained	6 Adamantite Bar, 6 Primal Air
Adamantite Rapier	335	Found	12 Adamantite Bar
Adamantite Plate Bracers	335	Found	8 Adamantite Bar, 2 Primal Earth, 6 Primal Fire
Adamantite Plate Gloves	335	Found	12 Adamantite Bar, 2 Knothide Leather, 4 Primal Earth, 4 Primal Fire
Adamantite Breastplate	340	Found	20 Adamantite Bar, 6 Primal Earth, 6 Primal Fire
Lesser Rune of Shielding	340	Found	1 Adamantite Bar
Flamebane Bracers	350	Found	6 Fel Iron Bar, 3 Primal Water, 2 Primal Fire
Adamantite Sharpening Stone	350	Found	1 Adamantite Bar, 2 Mote of Earth
Greater Rune of Warding	350	Found	1 Khorium Bar
Adamantite Rod	350	Found	10 Adamantite Bar
Breastplate of Kings	350	Trained	8 Primal Might, 6 Hardened Adamantite Bar, 6 Eternium Bar, 8 Khorium Bar
Drakefist Hammer	350	Trained	20 Primal Fire, 20 Primal Earth, 12 Eternium Bar, 8 Khorium Bar
Lionheart Blade	350	Trained	10 Primal Might, 14 Khorium Bar, 6 Hardened Adamantite Bar
Nether Chain Shirt	350	Trained	20 Primal Shadow, 20 Primal Air, 6 Hardened Adamantite Bar, 4 Felsteel Bar, 8 Khorium Bar
Fireguard	350	Trained	20 Primal Shadow, 20 Primal Mana, 14 Felsteel Bar
The Planar Edge	350	Trained	5 Primal Might, 20 Primal Shadow, 2 Hardened Adamantite Bar, 12 Felsteel Bar
Thunder	350	Trained	20 Primal Air, 20 Primal Water, 6 Hardened Adamantite Bar, 12 Khorium Bar
Lunar Crescent	350	Trained	12 Primal Air, 12 Primal Earth, 4 Primal Might, 22 Eternium Bar
Adamantite Weightstone	350	Found	1 Adamantite Bar, 2 Netherweave Cloth

Blacksmithing

Created Item	Skill Lvl	Source	Reagent(s)
Felsteel Whisper Knives	350	Trained	6 Felsteel Bar, 2 Primal Air, 2 Primal Fire, 1 Heavy Knothide Leather
Enchanted Adamantite Belt	355	Found	2 Hardened Adamantite Bar, 8 Arcane Dust, 2 Large Prismatic Shard
Enchanted Adamantite Boots	355	Found	3 Hardened Adamantite Bar, 12 Arcane Dust, 2 Large Prismatic Shard
Flamebane Helm	355	Found	12 Fel Iron Bar, 5 Primal Water, 3 Primal Fire
Enchanted Adamantite Breastplate	360	Found	4 Hardened Adamantite Bar, 20 Arcane Dust, 4 Large Prismatic Shard
Flamebane Gloves	360	Found	8 Fel Iron Bar, 4 Primal Water, 4 Primal Fire
Felsteel Gloves	360	Found	6 Felsteel Bar
Felsteel Leggings	360	Found	8 Felsteel Bar
Khorium Belt	360	Found	3 Khorium Bar, 2 Primal Water, 2 Primal Mana
Khorium Pants	360	Found	6 Khorium Bar, 4 Primal Water, 4 Primal Mana
Felsteel Shield Spike	360	Found	4 Felsteel Bar, 4 Primal Fire, 4 Primal Earth
Enchanted Adamantite Leggings	365	Found	4 Hardened Adamantite Bar, 24 Arcane Dust, 4 Large Prismatic Shard
Flamebane Breastplate	365	Found	16 Fel Iron Bar, 6 Primal Water, 4 Primal Fire
Felsteel Helm	365	Found	8 Felsteel Bar
Khorium Boots	365	Found	4 Khorium Bar, 3 Primal Water, 3 Primal Mana
Ragesteel Gloves	365	Found	8 Fel Iron Bar, 6 Primal Fire, 3 Khorium Bar, 2 Elixir of Major Strength
Ragesteel Helm	365	Found	10 Fel Iron Bar, 10 Primal Fire, 4 Khorium Bar, 4 Elixir of Major Strength
Felfury Gauntlets	365	Found	10 Felsteel Bar, 3 Primal Might, 1 Primal Nether
Gauntlets of the Iron Tower	365	Found	10 Hardened Adamantite Bar, 2 Primal Might, 15 Primal Earth, 1 Primal Nether
Steelgrip Gauntlets	365	Found	10 Felsteel Bar, 5 Primal Might, 1 Primal Nether
Storm Helm	365	Found	8 Hardened Adamantite Bar, 16 Primal Air, 16 Primal Water, 1 Primal Nether
Helm of the Stalwart Defender	365	Found	8 Hardened Adamantite Bar, 22 Primal Earth, 12 Primal Mana, 1 Primal Nether
Oathkeeper's Helm	365	Found	8 Hardened Adamantite Bar, 3 Primal Might, 18 Primal Life, 1 Primal Nether
Black Felsteel Bracers	365	Found	6 Felsteel Bar, 15 Primal Shadow, 1 Primal Nether
Bracers of the Green Fortress	365	Found	6 Hardened Adamantite Bar, 20 Primal Life, 1 Primal Nether
Blessed Bracers	365	Found	6 Hardened Adamantite Bar, 2 Primal Might, 15 Primal Water, 1 Primal Nether
Felsteel Longblade	365	Found	10 Felsteel Bar, 8 Primal Might, 2 Primal Nether
Khorium Champion	365	Found	20 Khorium Bar, 2 Hardened Adamantite Bar, 6 Primal Might, 2 Primal Nether
Fel Edged Battleaxe	365	Found	10 Felsteel Bar, 8 Primal Might, 2 Primal Nether
Felsteel Reaper	365	Found	10 Felsteel Bar, 8 Primal Might, 2 Primal Nether
Runic Hammer	365	Found	5 Hardened Adamantite Bar, 8 Primal Might, 2 Primal Nether
Fel Hardened Maul	365	Found	10 Felsteel Bar, 8 Primal Might, 2 Primal Nether
Eternium Runed Blade	365	Found	4 Felsteel Bar, 10 Eternium Bar, 8 Primal Might, 2 Primal Nether
Dirge	365	Found	10 Felsteel Bar, 8 Primal Might, 2 Primal Nether
Hand of Eternity	365	Found	4 Hardened Adamantite Bar, 10 Eternium Bar, 8 Primal Might, 2 Primal Nether
Ragesteel Breastplate	370	Found	12 Fel Iron Bar, 10 Primal Fire, 6 Khorium Bar, 4 Elixir of Major Strength
Swiftsteel Gloves	370	Found	6 Felsteel Bar, 2 Large Prismatic Shard, 4 Elixir of Major Agility, 4 Primal Air
Earthpeace Breastplate	370	Found	4 Hardened Adamantite Bar, 6 Primal Life, 4 Primal Earth
Greater Rune of Shielding	375	Found	1 Eternium Bar

Blacksmithing

Created Item	Skill Lvl	Source	Reagent(s)
Eternium Rod	375	Found	4 Eternium Bar
Black Planar Edge	375	Trained	1 The Planar Edge, 12 Primal Nether, 6 Felsteel Bar
Bulwark of Kings	375	Trained	1 Breastplate of Kings, 10 Primal Nether, 10 Primal Mana
Deep Thunder	375	Trained	1 Thunder, 12 Primal Nether, 10 Primal Mana
Dragonmaw	375	Trained	1 Drakefist Hammer, 12 Primal Nether, 2 Primal Might
Lionheart Champion	375	Trained	1 Lionheart Blade, 12 Primal Nether, 2 Primal Might
Mooncleaver	375	Trained	1 Lunar Crescent, 12 Primal Nether, 10 Primal Mana
Blazeguard	375	Trained	1 Fireguard, 12 Primal Nether, 10 Primal Air
Twisting Nether Chain Shirt	375	Trained	1 Nether Chain Shirt, 10 Primal Nether, 10 Primal Mana
Embrace of the Twisting Nether	375	Trained	1 Twisting Nether Chain Shirt, 5 Nether Vortex
Bulwark of the Ancient Kings	375	Trained	1 Bulwark of Kings, 5 Nether Vortex
Blazefury	375	Trained	1 Blazeguard, 20 Nether Vortex
Lionheart Executioner	375	Trained	1 Lionheart Champion, 20 Nether Vortex
Wicked Edge of the Planes	375	Trained	1 Black Planar Edge, 20 Nether Vortex
Bloodmoon	375	Trained	1 Mooncleaver, 20 Nether Vortex
Dragonstrike	375	Trained	1 Dragonmaw, 20 Nether Vortex
Stormherald	375	Trained	1 Deep Thunder, 20 Nether Vortex
Belt of the Guardian	375	Found	5 Nether Vortex, 2 Hardened Adamantite Bar, 4 Primal Water
Red Belt of Battle	375	Found	5 Nether Vortex, 2 Hardened Adamantite Bar, 4 Primal Fire
Boots of the Protector	375	Found	2 Primal Nether, 4 Hardened Adamantite Bar, 12 Primal Water
Red Havoc Boots	375	Found	2 Primal Nether, 4 Hardened Adamantite Bar, 12 Primal Fire
Wildguard Breastplate	375	Found	8 Felsteel Bar, 12 Primal Life, 12 Primal Shadow, 1 Primal Nether
Wildguard Leggings	375	Found	8 Felsteel Bar, 12 Primal Life, 12 Primal Shadow, 1 Primal Nether
Wildguard Helm	375	Found	8 Felsteel Bar, 12 Primal Life, 12 Primal Shadow, 1 Primal Nether
Iceguard Breastplate	375	Found	8 Khorium Bar, 12 Primal Water, 12 Primal Fire, 1 Primal Nether
Iceguard Leggings	375	Found	8 Khorium Bar, 12 Primal Water, 12 Primal Fire, 1 Primal Nether
Iceguard Helm	375	Found	8 Khorium Bar, 12 Primal Water, 12 Primal Fire, 1 Primal Nether

Cooking

Created Item	Skill Lvl	Source	Reagent(s)
Basic Campfire	N/A	Special	1 Simple Wood
Charred Wolf Meat	N/A	Special	1 Stringy Wolf Meat
Brilliant Smallfish	1	Found	1 Raw Brilliant Smallfish
Slitherskin Mackerel	1	Found	1 Raw Slitherskin Mackerel
Herb Baked Egg	1	Found	1 Small Egg, 1 Mild Spices
Crispy Bat Wing	1	Found	1 Meaty Bat Wing, 1 Mild Spices
Gingerbread Cookie	1	Found	1 Small Egg, 1 Holiday Spices
Lynx Steak	1	Found	1 Lynx Meat
Roasted Moongraze Tenderloin	1	Found	1 Moongraze Stag Tenderloin
Spice Bread	1	Trained	1 Simple Flour, 1 Mild Spices
Spiced Wolf Meat	10	Trained	1 Stringy Wolf Meat, 1 Mild Spices
Beer Basted Boar Ribs	10	Found	1 Crag Boar Rib, 1 Rhapsody Malt
Kaldorei Spider Kabob	10	Found	1 Small Spider Leg
Scorpid Surprise	20	Found	1 Scorpid Stinger
Roasted Kodo Meat	35	Found	1 Kodo Meat, 1 Mild Spices

Cooking			
Created Item	Skill Lvl	Source	Reagent(s)
Egg Nog	35	Found	1 Small Egg, 1 Ice Cold Milk, 1 Holiday Spirits, 1 Holiday Spices
Smoked Bear Meat	40	Found	1 Bear Meat
Coyote Steak	50	Trained	1 Coyote Meat
Goretusk Liver Pie	50	Found	1 Goretusk Liver, 1 Mild Spices
Fillet of Frenzy	50	Found	1 Soft Frenzy Flesh, 1 Mild Spices
Strider Stew	50	Found	1 Strider Meat, 1 Shiny Red Apple
Boiled Clams	50	Trained	1 Clam Meat, 1 Refreshing Spring Water
Longjaw Mud Snapper	50	Found	1 Raw Longjaw Mud Snapper
Loch Frenzy Delight	50	Found	1 Raw Loch Frenzy, 1 Mild Spices
Rainbow Fin Albacore	50	Found	1 Raw Rainbow Fin Albacore
Bat Bites	50	Found	1 Bat Flesh
Blood Sausage	60	Found	1 Bear Meat, 1 Boar Intestines, 1 Spider Ichor
Thistle Tea	60	Found	1 Swiftthistle, 1 Refreshing Spring Water
Goldthorn Tea	N/A	Special	1 Goldthorn, 1 Refreshing Spring Water
Crunchy Spider Surprise	60	Found	1 Crunchy Spider Leg
Westfall Stew	75	Found	1 Stringy Vulture Meat, 1 Murloc Eye, 1 Goretusk Snout
Crab Cake	75	Trained	1 Crawler Meat, 1 Mild Spices
Dry Pork Ribs	80	Trained	1 Boar Ribs, 1 Mild Spices
Crocolisk Steak	80	Found	1 Crocolisk Meat, 1 Mild Spices
Smoked Sagefish	80	Found	1 Raw Sagefish, 1 Mild Spices
Cooked Crab Claw	85	Found	1 Crawler Claw, 1 Mild Spices
Savory Deviate Delight	85	Found	1 Deviate Fish, 1 Mild Spices
Murloc Fin Soup	90	Found	2 Murloc Fin, 1 Hot Spices
Dig Rat Stew	90	Found	1 Dig Rat
Clam Chowder	90	Found	1 Clam Meat, 1 Ice Cold Milk, 1 Mild Spices
Redridge Goulash	100	Found	1 Crisp Spider Meat, 1 Tough Condor Meat
Seasoned Wolf Kabob	100	Found	2 Lean Wolf Flank, 1 Stormwind Seasoning Herbs
Crispy Lizard Tail	100	Found	1 Thunder Lizard Tail, 1 Hot Spices
Bristle Whisker Catfish	100	Found	1 Raw Bristle Whisker Catfish
Succulent Pork Ribs	110	Found	2 Boar Ribs, 1 Hot Spices
Gooey Spider Cake	110	Found	2 Gooey Spider Leg, 1 Hot Spices
Big Bear Steak	110	Found	1 Big Bear Meat, 1 Hot Spices
Lean Venison	110	Found	1 Stag Meat, 4 Mild Spices
Crocolisk Gumbo	120	Found	1 Tender Crocolisk Meat, 1 Hot Spices
Hot Lion Chops	125	Found	1 Lion Meat, 1 Hot Spices
Goblin Deviled Clams	125	Trained	1 Tangy Clam Meat, 1 Hot Spices
Lean Wolf Steak	125	Found	1 Lean Wolf Flank, 1 Mild Spices
Curiously Tasty Omelet	130	Found	1 Raptor Egg, 1 Hot Spices
Tasty Lion Steak	150	Found	2 Lion Meat, 1 Soothing Spices
Heavy Crocolisk Stew	150	Found	2 Tender Crocolisk Meat, 1 Soothing Spices
Soothing Turtle Bisque	175	Found	1 Turtle Meat, 1 Soothing Spices
Barbecued Buzzard Wing	175	Found	1 Buzzard Wing, 1 Hot Spices
Giant Clam Scorcho	175	Found	1 Giant Clam Meat, 1 Hot Spices
Rockscale Cod	175	Found	1 Raw Rockscale Cod
Roast Raptor	175	Found	1 Raptor Flesh, 1 Hot Spices
Hot Wolf Ribs	175	Found	1 Red Wolf Meat, 1 Hot Spices
Jungle Stew	175	Found	1 Tiger Meat, 1 Refreshing Spring Water, 2 Shiny Red Apple
Carrion Surprise	175	Found	1 Mystery Meat, 1 Hot Spices
Mystery Stew	175	Found	1 Mystery Meat, 1 Skin of Dwarven Stout
Mithril Headed Trout	175	Found	1 Raw Mithril Head Trout
Sagefish Delight	175	Found	1 Raw Greater Sagefish, 1 Hot Spices
Dragonbreath Chili	200	Found	1 Mystery Meat, 1 Small Flame Sac, 1 Hot Spices

Cooking			
Created Item	Skill Lvl	Source	Reagent(s)
Heavy Kodo Stew	200	Found	2 Heavy Kodo Meat, 1 Soothing Spices, 1 Refreshing Spring Water
Spider Sausage	200	Trained	2 White Spider Meat
Spiced Chili Crab	225	Found	1 Tender Crab Meat, 2 Hot Spices
Monster Omelet	225	Found	1 Giant Egg, 2 Soothing Spices
Cooked Glossy Mightfish	225	Found	1 Raw Glossy Mightfish, 1 Soothing Spices
Spotted Yellowtail	225	Found	1 Raw Spotted Yellowtail
Filet of Redgill	225	Found	1 Raw Redgill
Undermine Clam Chowder	225	Found	2 Zesty Clam Meat, 1 Hot Spices, 1 Ice Cold Milk
Tender Wolf Steak	225	Found	1 Tender Wolf Meat, 1 Soothing Spices
Grilled Squid	240	Found	1 Winter Squid, 1 Soothing Spices
Hot Smoked Bass	240	Found	1 Raw Summer Bass, 2 Hot Spices
Nightfin Soup	250	Found	1 Raw Nightfin Snapper, 1 Refreshing Spring Water
Poached Sunscale Salmon	250	Found	1 Raw Sunscale Salmon
Lobster Stew	275	Found	1 Darkclaw Lobster, 1 Refreshing Spring Water
Mightfish Steak	275	Found	1 Large Raw Mightfish, 1 Hot Spices, 1 Soothing Spices
Baked Salmon	275	Found	1 Raw Whitescale Salmon, 1 Soothing Spices
Runn Tum Tuber Surprise	275	Found	1 Runn Tum Tuber, 1 Soothing Spices
Smoked Desert Dumplings	285	Special	1 Sandworm Meat, 1 Soothing Spices
Dirge's Kickin' Chimaerok Chops	300	Found	1 Hot Spices, 1 Goblin Rocket Fuel, 1 Deeprock Salt, 1 Chimaerok Tenderloin
Buzzard Bites	300	Found	1 Buzzard Meat
Ravager Dog	300	Found	1 Ravager Flesh
Blackened Trout	300	Found	1 Barbed Gill Trout
Feltail Delight	300	Found	1 Spotted Feltail
Clam Bar	300	Found	2 Jaggal Clam Meat, 1 Soothing Spices
Sporeling Snack	310	Found	1 Strange Spores
Blackened Sporefish	310	Found	1 Zangarian Sporefish
Blackened Basilisk	315	Found	1 Chunk o' Basilisk
Grilled Mudfish	320	Found	1 Figluster's Mudfish
Poached Bluefish	320	Found	1 Icefin Bluefish
Roasted Clefthoof	325	Found	1 Clefthoof Meat
Warp Burger	325	Found	1 Warped Flesh
Talbuk Steak	325	Found	1 Talbuk Venison
Golden Fish Sticks	325	Found	1 Golden Darter
Crunchy Serpent	335	Found	1 Serpent Flesh
Mok'Nathal Shortribs	335	Found	1 Raptor Ribs
Spicy Crawdad	350	Found	1 Furious Crawdad

Enchanting			
Created Item	Skill Lvl	Source	Reagent(s)
Enchant Bracer - Minor Health	N/A	Special	1 Strange Dust
Runed Copper Rod	N/A	Special	1 Copper Rod, 1 Strange Dust, 1 Lesser Magic Essence
Enchant Bracer - Minor Deflection	N/A	Special	1 Lesser Magic Essence, 1 Strange Dust
Lesser Magic Wand	10	Trained	1 Simple Wood, 1 Lesser Magic Essence
Enchant Chest - Minor Health	15	Trained	1 Strange Dust
Enchant Chest - Minor Absorption	40	Trained	2 Strange Dust, 1 Lesser Magic Essence
Enchant Chest - Minor Mana	40	Found	1 Lesser Magic Essence
Enchant Cloak - Minor Resistance	45	Trained	1 Strange Dust, 2 Lesser Magic Essence
Minor Wizard Oil	45	Found	2 Strange Dust, 1 Maple Seed, 1 Empty Vial
Enchant Bracer - Minor Stamina	50	Trained	3 Strange Dust
Enchant Chest - Lesser Health	60	Trained	2 Strange Dust, 2 Lesser Magic Essence
Enchant Bracer - Minor Spirit	60	Found	2 Lesser Magic Essence

Enchanting			
Created Item	Skill Lvl	Source	Reagent(s)
Enchant Cloak - Minor Protection	70	Trained	3 Strange Dust, 1 Greater Magic Essence
Greater Magic Wand	70	Trained	1 Simple Wood, 1 Greater Magic Essence
Enchant Chest - Lesser Mana	80	Found	1 Greater Magic Essence, 1 Lesser Magic Essence
Enchant Bracer - Minor Agility	80	Trained	2 Strange Dust, 1 Greater Magic Essence
Enchant Bracer - Minor Strength	80	Found	5 Strange Dust
Enchant Weapon - Minor Beastslayer	90	Found	4 Strange Dust, 2 Greater Magic Essence
Enchant Weapon - Minor Striking	90	Trained	2 Strange Dust, 1 Greater Magic Essence, 1 Small Glimmering Shard
Enchant 2H Weapon - Minor Impact	100	Trained	4 Strange Dust, 1 Small Glimmering Shard
Enchant 2H Weapon - Lesser Intellect	100	Found	3 Greater Magic Essence
Runed Silver Rod	100	Trained	1 Silver Rod, 6 Strange Dust, 3 Greater Magic Essence, 1 Runed Copper Rod
Enchant Shield - Minor Stamina	105	Trained	1 Lesser Astral Essence, 2 Strange Dust
Enchant 2H Weapon - Lesser Spirit	110	Found	1 Lesser Astral Essence, 6 Strange Dust
Enchant Cloak - Minor Agility	110	Found	1 Lesser Astral Essence
Enchant Cloak - Lesser Protection	115	Trained	6 Strange Dust, 1 Small Glimmering Shard
Enchant Shield - Lesser Protection	115	Found	1 Lesser Astral Essence, 1 Strange Dust, 1 Small Glimmering Shard
Enchant Chest - Health	120	Trained	4 Strange Dust, 1 Lesser Astral Essence
Enchant Bracer - Lesser Spirit	120	Found	2 Lesser Astral Essence
Enchant Cloak - Lesser Fire Resistance	125	Trained	1 Fire Oil, 1 Lesser Astral Essence
Enchant Boots - Minor Stamina	125	Found	8 Strange Dust
Enchant Boots - Minor Agility	125	Found	6 Strange Dust, 2 Lesser Astral Essence
Enchant Shield - Lesser Spirit	130	Trained	2 Lesser Astral Essence, 4 Strange Dust
Enchant Bracer - Lesser Stamina	130	Trained	2 Soul Dust
Enchant Cloak - Lesser Shadow Resistance	135	Found	1 Greater Astral Essence, 1 Shadow Protection Potion
Enchant Weapon - Lesser Striking	140	Trained	2 Soul Dust, 1 Large Glimmering Shard
Enchant Bracer - Lesser Strength	140	Found	2 Soul Dust
Enchant Chest - Lesser Absorption	140	Trained	2 Strange Dust, 1 Greater Astral Essence, 1 Large Glimmering Shard
Enchant 2H Weapon - Lesser Impact	145	Trained	3 Soul Dust, 1 Large Glimmering Shard
Enchant Chest - Mana	145	Trained	1 Greater Astral Essence, 2 Lesser Astral Essence
Enchant Gloves - Mining	145	Found	1 Soul Dust, 3 Iron Ore
Enchant Gloves - Herbalism	145	Found	1 Soul Dust, 3 Kingsblood
Enchant Gloves - Fishing	145	Found	1 Soul Dust, 3 Blackmouth Oil
Enchant Bracer - Lesser Intellect	150	Trained	2 Greater Astral Essence
Enchant Chest - Minor Stats	150	Trained	1 Greater Astral Essence, 1 Soul Dust, 1 Large Glimmering Shard
Runed Golden Rod	150	Trained	1 Golden Rod, 1 Iridescent Pearl, 2 Greater Astral Essence, 2 Soul Dust, 1 Runed Silver Rod
Minor Mana Oil	150	Found	3 Soul Dust, 2 Maple Seed, 1 Leaded Vial
Enchant Shield - Lesser Stamina	155	Trained	1 Lesser Mystic Essence, 1 Soul Dust
Enchant Cloak - Defense	155	Trained	1 Small Glowing Shard, 3 Soul Dust
Lesser Mystic Wand	155	Trained	1 Star Wood, 1 Lesser Mystic Essence, 1 Soul Dust
Enchant Boots - Lesser Agility	160	Trained	1 Soul Dust, 1 Lesser Mystic Essence
Enchant Chest - Greater Health	160	Trained	3 Soul Dust
Enchant Bracer - Spirit	165	Trained	1 Lesser Mystic Essence
Enchant Boots - Lesser Stamina	170	Trained	4 Soul Dust
Enchant Bracer - Lesser Deflection	170	Found	1 Lesser Mystic Essence, 2 Soul Dust
Enchant Bracer - Stamina	170	Trained	6 Soul Dust
Enchant Weapon - Lesser Beastslayer	175	Found	1 Lesser Mystic Essence, 2 Large Fang, 1 Small Glowing Shard

Enchanting			
Created Item	Skill Lvl	Source	Reagent(s)
Enchant Weapon - Lesser Elemental Slayer	175	Found	1 Lesser Mystic Essence, 1 Elemental Earth, 1 Small Glowing Shard
Enchant Cloak - Fire Resistance	175	Trained	1 Lesser Mystic Essence, 1 Elemental Fire
Greater Mystic Wand	175	Trained	1 Star Wood, 1 Greater Mystic Essence, 1 Vision Dust
Enchant Shield - Spirit	180	Trained	1 Greater Mystic Essence, 1 Vision Dust
Enchant Bracer - Strength	180	Trained	1 Vision Dust
Enchant Chest - Greater Mana	185	Trained	1 Greater Mystic Essence
Enchant Boots - Lesser Spirit	190	Found	1 Greater Mystic Essence, 2 Lesser Mystic Essence
Enchant Weapon - Winter's Might	190	Found	3 Greater Mystic Essence, 3 Vision Dust, 1 Large Glowing Shard, 2 Wintersbite
Enchant Shield - Lesser Block	195	Found	2 Greater Mystic Essence, 2 Vision Dust, 1 Large Glowing Shard
Enchant Weapon - Striking	195	Trained	2 Greater Mystic Essence, 1 Large Glowing Shard
Enchant 2H Weapon - Impact	200	Trained	4 Vision Dust, 1 Large Glowing Shard
Enchant Gloves - Skinning	200	Found	1 Vision Dust, 3 Green Whelp Scale
Enchant Chest - Lesser Stats	200	Trained	2 Greater Mystic Essence, 2 Vision Dust, 1 Large Glowing Shard
Runed Truesilver Rod	200	Trained	1 Truesilver Rod, 1 Black Pearl, 2 Greater Mystic Essence, 2 Vision Dust, 1 Runed Golden Rod
Lesser Wizard Oil	200	Found	3 Vision Dust, 2 Stranglethorn Seed, 1 Leaded Vial
Enchant Cloak - Greater Defense	205	Trained	3 Vision Dust
Enchant Cloak - Resistance	205	Trained	1 Lesser Nether Essence
Enchant Gloves - Agility	210	Trained	1 Lesser Nether Essence, 1 Vision Dust
Enchant Shield - Stamina	210	Found	5 Vision Dust
Enchant Bracer - Intellect	210	Trained	2 Lesser Nether Essence
Enchant Boots - Stamina	215	Trained	5 Vision Dust
Enchant Gloves - Advanced Mining	215	Found	3 Vision Dust, 3 Truesilver Bar
Enchant Bracer - Greater Spirit	220	Found	3 Lesser Nether Essence, 1 Vision Dust
Enchant Chest - Superior Health	220	Trained	6 Vision Dust
Enchant Gloves - Advanced Herbalism	225	Found	3 Vision Dust, 3 Sungrass
Enchant Cloak - Lesser Agility	225	Found	2 Lesser Nether Essence
Enchant Gloves - Strength	225	Trained	2 Lesser Nether Essence, 3 Vision Dust
Enchant Boots - Minor Speed	225	Trained	1 Small Radiant Shard, 1 Aquamarine, 1 Lesser Nether Essence
Enchant Shield - Greater Spirit	230	Trained	1 Greater Nether Essence, 2 Dream Dust
Enchant Weapon - Demonslaying	230	Found	1 Small Radiant Shard, 2 Dream Dust, 1 Elixir of Demonslaying
Enchant Chest - Superior Mana	230	Trained	1 Greater Nether Essence, 2 Lesser Nether Essence
Enchant Bracer - Deflection	235	Found	1 Greater Nether Essence, 2 Dream Dust
Enchant Shield - Frost Resistance	235	Found	1 Large Radiant Shard, 1 Frost Oil
Enchant Boots - Agility	235	Trained	2 Greater Nether Essence
Enchant 2H Weapon - Greater Impact	240	Trained	2 Large Radiant Shard, 2 Dream Dust
Enchant Bracer - Greater Strength	240	Trained	2 Dream Dust, 1 Greater Nether Essence
Enchant Chest - Stats	245	Trained	1 Large Radiant Shard, 3 Dream Dust, 2 Greater Nether Essence
Enchant Weapon - Greater Striking	245	Trained	2 Large Radiant Shard, 2 Greater Nether Essence
Enchant Bracer - Greater Stamina	245	Found	5 Dream Dust
Enchant Gloves - Riding Skill	250	Found	2 Large Radiant Shard, 3 Dream Dust
Enchant Gloves - Minor Haste	250	Trained	2 Large Radiant Shard, 2 Wildvine
Enchanted Leather	250	Trained	1 Rugged Leather, 1 Lesser Eternal Essence
Enchanted Thorium	250	Trained	1 Thorium Bar, 3 Dream Dust
Lesser Mana Oil	250	Found	3 Dream Dust, 2 Purple Lotus, 1 Crystal Vial

Enchanting

Created Item	Skill Lvl	Source	Reagent(s)
Enchant Bracer - Greater Intellect	255	Found	3 Lesser Eternal Essence
Enchant Boots - Greater Stamina	260	Found	10 Dream Dust
Enchant Weapon - Fiery Weapon	265	Found	4 Small Radiant Shard, 1 Essence of Fire
Smoking Heart of the Mountain	265	Found	1 Blood of the Mountain, 1 Essence of Fire, 3 Small Brilliant Shard
Enchant Cloak - Greater Resistance	265	Found	2 Lesser Eternal Essence, 1 Heart of Fire, 1 Core of Earth, 1 Globe of Water, 1 Breath of Wind, 1 Ichor of Undeath
Enchant Shield - Greater Stamina	265	Found	10 Dream Dust
Enchant Bracer - Superior Spirit	270	Found	3 Lesser Eternal Essence, 10 Dream Dust
Enchant Gloves - Greater Agility	270	Found	3 Lesser Eternal Essence, 3 Illusion Dust
Enchant Boots - Spirit	275	Found	2 Greater Eternal Essence, 1 Lesser Eternal Essence
Enchant Chest - Major Health	275	Found	6 Illusion Dust, 1 Small Brilliant Shard
Wizard Oil	275	Found	3 Illusion Dust, 2 Firebloom, 1 Crystal Vial
Enchant Shield - Superior Spirit	280	Found	2 Greater Eternal Essence, 4 Illusion Dust
Enchant Weapon - Icy Chill	285	Found	4 Small Brilliant Shard, 1 Essence of Water, 1 Essence of Air, 1 Icecap
Enchant Cloak - Superior Defense	285	Found	8 Illusion Dust
Enchant Chest - Major Mana	290	Found	3 Greater Eternal Essence, 1 Small Brilliant Shard
Runed Arcanite Rod	290	Found	1 Arcanite Rod, 1 Golden Pearl, 10 Illusion Dust, 4 Greater Eternal Essence, 1 Runed Truesilver Rod, 2 Large Brilliant Shard
Enchant Weapon - Strength	290	Found	6 Large Brilliant Shard, 6 Greater Eternal Essence, 4 Illusion Dust, 2 Essence of Earth
Enchant Weapon - Agility	290	Found	6 Large Brilliant Shard, 6 Greater Eternal Essence, 4 Illusion Dust, 2 Essence of Air
Enchant Bracer - Mana Regeneration	290	Found	16 Illusion Dust, 4 Greater Eternal Essence, 2 Essence of Water
Enchant 2H Weapon - Agility	290	Found	10 Large Brilliant Shard, 6 Greater Eternal Essence, 14 Illusion Dust, 4 Essence of Air
Enchant Gloves - Greater Strength	295	Found	4 Greater Eternal Essence, 4 Illusion Dust
Enchant Boots - Greater Agility	295	Found	8 Greater Eternal Essence
Enchant Bracer - Superior Strength	295	Found	6 Illusion Dust, 6 Greater Eternal Essence
Enchant 2H Weapon - Superior Impact	295	Found	4 Large Brilliant Shard, 10 Illusion Dust
Enchant Weapon - Unholy Weapon	295	Found	4 Large Brilliant Shard, 4 Essence of Undeath
Enchant 2H Weapon - Major Intellect	300	Found	12 Greater Eternal Essence, 2 Large Brilliant Shard
Enchant Weapon - Superior Striking	300	Found	2 Large Brilliant Shard, 10 Greater Eternal Essence
Enchant Bracer - Superior Stamina	300	Found	15 Illusion Dust
Enchant Weapon - Crusader	300	Found	4 Large Brilliant Shard, 2 Righteous Orb
Enchant Chest - Greater Stats	300	Found	4 Large Brilliant Shard, 15 Illusion Dust, 10 Greater Eternal Essence
Enchant Weapon - Lifestealing	300	Found	6 Large Brilliant Shard, 6 Essence of Undeath, 6 Living Essence
Enchant 2H Weapon - Major Spirit	300	Found	12 Greater Eternal Essence, 2 Large Brilliant Shard
Enchant Weapon - Spell Power	300	Found	4 Large Brilliant Shard, 12 Greater Eternal Essence, 4 Essence of Fire, 4 Essence of Water, 4 Essence of Air, 2 Golden Pearl
Enchant Weapon - Healing Power	300	Found	4 Large Brilliant Shard, 8 Greater Eternal Essence, 6 Living Essence, 6 Essence of Water, 1 Righteous Orb
Enchant Bracer - Healing Power	300	Found	2 Large Brilliant Shard, 20 Illusion Dust, 4 Greater Eternal Essence, 6 Living Essence
Enchant Weapon - Mighty Spirit	300	Found	10 Large Brilliant Shard, 8 Greater Eternal Essence, 15 Illusion Dust

Enchanting

Created Item	Skill Lvl	Source	Reagent(s)
Enchant Weapon - Mighty Intellect	300	Found	15 Large Brilliant Shard, 12 Greater Eternal Essence, 20 Illusion Dust
Enchant Gloves - Threat	300	Found	4 Nexus Crystal, 6 Large Brilliant Shard, 8 Larval Acid
Enchant Gloves - Shadow Power	300	Found	3 Nexus Crystal, 10 Large Brilliant Shard, 6 Essence of Undeath
Enchant Gloves - Frost Power	300	Found	3 Nexus Crystal, 10 Large Brilliant Shard, 4 Essence of Water
Enchant Gloves - Fire Power	300	Found	2 Nexus Crystal, 10 Large Brilliant Shard, 4 Essence of Fire
Enchant Gloves - Healing Power	300	Found	3 Nexus Crystal, 8 Large Brilliant Shard, 1 Righteous Orb
Enchant Gloves - Superior Agility	300	Found	3 Nexus Crystal, 8 Large Brilliant Shard, 4 Essence of Air
Enchant Cloak - Greater Fire Resistance	300	Found	3 Nexus Crystal, 8 Large Brilliant Shard, 4 Essence of Fire
Enchant Cloak - Greater Nature Resistance	300	Found	2 Nexus Crystal, 8 Large Brilliant Shard, 4 Living Essence
Enchant Cloak - Stealth	300	Found	3 Nexus Crystal, 8 Large Brilliant Shard, 2 Black Lotus
Enchant Cloak - Subtlety	300	Found	4 Nexus Crystal, 6 Large Brilliant Shard, 2 Black Diamond
Enchant Cloak - Dodge	300	Found	3 Nexus Crystal, 8 Large Brilliant Shard, 8 Guardian Stone
Brilliant Wizard Oil	300	Found	2 Large Brilliant Shard, 3 Firebloom, 1 Imbued Vial
Brilliant Mana Oil	300	Found	2 Large Brilliant Shard, 3 Purple Lotus, 1 Imbued Vial
Runed Fel Iron Rod	300	Trained	1 Fel Iron Rod, 4 Greater Eternal Essence, 6 Large Brilliant Shard, 1 Runed Arcanite Rod
Enchant Chest - Restore Mana Prime	300	Trained	2 Lesser Planar Essence, 2 Arcane Dust
Enchant Bracer - Assault	300	Trained	6 Arcane Dust
Enchant Bracer - Brawn	305	Trained	6 Arcane Dust
Enchant Boots - Vitality	305	Found	6 Arcane Dust, 4 Major Healing Potion, 4 Major Mana Potion
Enchant Gloves - Blasting	305	Trained	1 Lesser Planar Essence, 4 Arcane Dust
Enchant Bracer - Major Intellect	305	Trained	3 Lesser Planar Essence
Enchant Shield - Tough Shield	310	Trained	6 Arcane Dust, 10 Primal Earth
Enchant Cloak - Major Armor	310	Trained	8 Arcane Dust
Superior Mana Oil	310	Found	3 Arcane Dust, 1 Netherbloom, 1 Imbued Vial
Enchant Gloves - Assault	310	Trained	8 Arcane Dust
Enchant Cloak - Greater Agility	310	Trained	1 Greater Planar Essence, 4 Arcane Dust, 1 Primal Air
Enchant Bracer - Stats	315	Trained	6 Arcane Dust, 6 Lesser Planar Essence
Enchant Chest - Exceptional Health	315	Trained	8 Arcane Dust, 4 Major Healing Potion, 2 Large Brilliant Shard
Enchant Bracer - Major Defense	320	Found	2 Small Prismatic Shard, 10 Arcane Dust
Enchant Boots - Fortitude	320	Found	12 Arcane Dust
Enchant Chest - Major Spirit	320	Trained	2 Greater Planar Essence
Enchant Bracer - Superior Healing	325	Found	4 Greater Planar Essence, 4 Primal Life
Enchant Shield - Intellect	325	Found	4 Greater Planar Essence
Enchant Chest - Exceptional Mana	325	Found	1 Large Prismatic Shard, 4 Major Mana Potion, 3 Greater Planar Essence
Arcane Dust	325	Found	1 Arcane Crystal
Enchant Cloak - Spell Penetration	325	Found	2 Greater Planar Essence, 6 Arcane Dust, 2 Primal Mana
Enchant Shield - Major Stamina	325	Found	15 Arcane Dust
Prismatic Sphere	325	Trained	4 Large Prismatic Shard
Enchant Cloak - Major Resistance	330	Found	4 Greater Planar Essence, 4 Primal Fire, 4 Primal Air, 4 Primal Earth, 4 Primal Water
Enchant Bracer - Restore Mana Prime	335	Found	8 Greater Planar Essence
Large Prismatic Shard	335	Found	3 Small Prismatic Shard

Enchanting

Created Item	Skill Lvl	Source	Reagent(s)
Enchant Shield - Shield Block	340	Found	12 Arcane Dust, 4 Greater Planar Essence, 10 Primal Earth
Enchant Boots - Dexterity	340	Found	8 Greater Planar Essence, 8 Arcane Dust
Enchant Weapon - Major Striking	340	Found	2 Large Prismatic Shard, 6 Greater Planar Essence, 6 Arcane Dust
Enchant Weapon - Major Intellect	340	Found	2 Large Prismatic Shard, 10 Greater Planar Essence
Superior Wizard Oil	340	Found	3 Arcane Dust, 1 Nightmare Vine, 1 Imbued Vial
Enchant Gloves - Major Strength	340	Trained	12 Arcane Dust, 1 Greater Planar Essence
Enchant Chest - Exceptional Stats	345	Found	4 Large Prismatic Shard, 4 Arcane Dust, 4 Greater Planar Essence
Enchant Chest - Major Resilience	345	Found	4 Greater Planar Essence, 10 Arcane Dust
Enchant Bracer - Fortitude	350	Found	1 Large Prismatic Shard, 10 Greater Planar Essence, 20 Arcane Dust
Enchant Weapon - Potency	350	Found	4 Large Prismatic Shard, 5 Greater Planar Essence, 20 Arcane Dust
Enchant 2H Weapon - Savagery	350	Found	4 Large Prismatic Shard, 40 Arcane Dust
Enchant Weapon - Major Spellpower	350	Found	8 Large Prismatic Shard, 8 Greater Planar Essence
Runed Adamantite Rod	350	Found	1 Adamantite Rod, 8 Greater Planar Essence, 8 Large Prismatic Shard, 1 Primal Might, 1 Runed Fel Iron Rod
Enchant Gloves - Major Healing	350	Found	6 Greater Planar Essence, 6 Large Prismatic Shard, 6 Primal Life
Enchant Cloak - Greater Arcane Resistance	350	Found	4 Large Prismatic Shard, 8 Primal Mana
Enchant Cloak - Greater Shadow Resistance	350	Found	4 Large Prismatic Shard, 8 Primal Shadow
Enchant Weapon - Major Healing	350	Found	8 Large Prismatic Shard, 8 Primal Water, 8 Primal Life
Void Sphere	350	Trained	2 Void Crystal
Enchant Bracer - Spellpower	360	Found	6 Large Prismatic Shard, 8 Primal Fire, 8 Primal Water
Enchant Ring - Striking	360	Found	8 Large Prismatic Shard, 24 Arcane Dust
Enchant Ring - Spellpower	360	Found	8 Large Prismatic Shard, 8 Greater Planar Essence
Enchant Shield - Resistance	360	Found	6 Large Prismatic Shard, 3 Primal Earth, 3 Primal Fire, 3 Primal Air, 3 Primal Water
Enchant 2H Weapon - Major Agility	360	Found	8 Large Prismatic Shard, 6 Greater Planar Essence, 20 Arcane Dust
Enchant Weapon - Battlemaster	360	Found	2 Void Crystal, 8 Large Prismatic Shard, 8 Primal Water
Enchant Weapon - Spellsurge	360	Found	12 Large Prismatic Shard, 10 Greater Planar Essence, 20 Arcane Dust
Enchant Gloves - Spell Strike	360	Found	8 Greater Planar Essence, 2 Arcane Dust, 2 Large Prismatic Shard
Enchant Gloves - Major Spellpower	360	Found	6 Greater Planar Essence, 6 Large Prismatic Shard, 6 Primal Mana
Enchant Boots - Cat's Swiftness	360	Found	8 Large Prismatic Shard, 8 Primal Air
Enchant Boots - Boar's Speed	360	Found	8 Large Prismatic Shard, 8 Primal Earth
Enchant Ring - Healing Power	370	Found	8 Large Prismatic Shard, 10 Greater Planar Essence, 20 Arcane Dust
Enchant Boots - Surefooted	370	Found	2 Void Crystal, 4 Large Prismatic Shard, 1 Primal Nether
Enchant Ring - Stats	375	Found	6 Void Crystal, 6 Large Prismatic Shard
Enchant Weapon - Mongoose	375	Found	6 Void Crystal, 10 Large Prismatic Shard, 8 Greater Planar Essence, 40 Arcane Dust
Enchant Weapon - Sunfire	375	Found	6 Void Crystal, 10 Large Prismatic Shard, 8 Greater Planar Essence, 10 Primal Fire, 2 Primal Might
Enchant Weapon - Soulfrost	375	Found	6 Void Crystal, 10 Large Prismatic Shard, 8 Greater Planar Essence, 10 Primal Water, 10 Primal Shadow
Runed Eternium Rod	375	Found	1 Eternium Rod, 12 Greater Planar Essence, 2 Void Crystal, 4 Primal Might, 1 Runed Adamantite Rod

Engineering

Created Item	Skill Lvl	Source	Reagent(s)
Rough Blasting Powder	N/A	Special	1 Rough Stone
Rough Dynamite	N/A	Special	2 Rough Blasting Powder, 1 Linen Cloth
Crafted Light Shot	N/A	Special	1 Rough Blasting Powder, 1 Copper Bar
Handful of Copper Bolts	30	Trained	1 Copper Bar
Rough Copper Bomb	30	Trained	1 Copper Bar, 1 Handful of Copper Bolts, 2 Rough Blasting Powder, 1 Linen Cloth
Copper Tube	50	Trained	2 Copper Bar, 1 Weak Flux
Rough Boomstick	50	Trained	1 Copper Tube, 1 Handful of Copper Bolts, 1 Wooden Stock
Arclight Spanner	50	Trained	6 Copper Bar
Crude Scope	60	Trained	1 Copper Tube, 1 Malachite, 1 Handful of Copper Bolts
Copper Modulator	65	Trained	2 Handful of Copper Bolts, 1 Copper Bar, 2 Linen Cloth
Mechanical Squirrel	75	Found	1 Copper Modulator, 1 Handful of Copper Bolts, 1 Copper Bar, 2 Malachite
Coarse Blasting Powder	75	Trained	1 Coarse Stone
Crafted Heavy Shot	75	Trained	1 Coarse Blasting Powder, 1 Copper Bar
Coarse Dynamite	75	Trained	3 Coarse Blasting Powder, 1 Linen Cloth
Target Dummy	85	Trained	1 Copper Modulator, 2 Handful of Copper Bolts, 1 Bronze Bar, 1 Wool Cloth
Silver Contact	90	Trained	1 Silver Bar
Small Seaforium Charge	100	Found	2 Coarse Blasting Powder, 1 Copper Modulator, 1 Light Leather, 1 Refreshing Spring Water
Flying Tiger Goggles	100	Trained	6 Light Leather, 2 Tigerseye
Practice Lock	100	Trained	1 Bronze Bar, 2 Handful of Copper Bolts, 1 Weak Flux
EZ-Thro Dynamite	100	Found	4 Coarse Blasting Powder, 1 Wool Cloth
Deadly Blunderbuss	105	Trained	2 Copper Tube, 4 Handful of Copper Bolts, 1 Wooden Stock, 2 Medium Leather
Large Copper Bomb	105	Trained	3 Copper Bar, 4 Coarse Blasting Powder, 1 Silver Contact
Bronze Tube	105	Trained	2 Bronze Bar, 1 Weak Flux
Standard Scope	110	Trained	1 Bronze Tube, 1 Moss Agate
Lovingly Crafted Boomstick	120	Found	2 Bronze Tube, 2 Handful of Copper Bolts, 1 Heavy Stock, 3 Moss Agate
Shadow Goggles	120	Found	4 Medium Leather, 2 Shadowgem
Small Bronze Bomb	120	Trained	4 Coarse Blasting Powder, 2 Bronze Bar, 1 Silver Contact, 1 Wool Cloth
Whirring Bronze Gizmo	125	Trained	2 Bronze Bar, 1 Wool Cloth
Flame Deflector	125	Found	1 Whirring Bronze Gizmo, 1 Small Flame Sac
Heavy Blasting Powder	125	Trained	1 Heavy Stone
Heavy Dynamite	125	Trained	2 Heavy Blasting Powder, 1 Wool Cloth
Crafted Solid Shot	125	Trained	1 Heavy Blasting Powder, 1 Bronze Bar
Gnomish Universal Remote	125	Found	6 Bronze Bar, 1 Whirring Bronze Gizmo, 2 Flask of Oil, 1 Tigerseye, 1 Malachite
Small Blue Rocket	125	Found	1 Coarse Blasting Powder, 1 Medium Leather
Small Green Rocket	125	Found	1 Coarse Blasting Powder, 1 Medium Leather
Small Red Rocket	125	Found	1 Coarse Blasting Powder, 1 Medium Leather
Silver-plated Shotgun	130	Trained	2 Bronze Tube, 2 Whirring Bronze Gizmo, 1 Heavy Stock, 3 Silver Bar
Goblin Rocket Boots	130	Found	1 Black Mageweave Boots, 2 Mithril Tube, 4 Heavy Leather, 2 Goblin Rocket Fuel, 1 Unstable Trigger
Ornate Spyglass	135	Trained	2 Bronze Tube, 2 Whirring Bronze Gizmo, 1 Copper Modulator, 1 Moss Agate
Big Bronze Bomb	140	Trained	2 Heavy Blasting Powder, 3 Bronze Bar, 1 Silver Contact
Minor Recombobulator	140	Found	1 Bronze Tube, 2 Whirring Bronze Gizmo, 2 Medium Leather, 1 Moss Agate
Bronze Framework	145	Trained	2 Bronze Bar, 1 Medium Leather, 1 Wool Cloth
Moonsight Rifle	145	Found	3 Bronze Tube, 3 Whirring Bronze Gizmo, 1 Heavy Stock, 2 Lesser Moonstone
Explosive Sheep	150	Trained	1 Bronze Framework, 1 Whirring Bronze Gizmo, 2 Heavy Blasting Powder, 2 Wool Cloth

Engineering

Created Item	Skill Lvl	Source	Reagent(s)
Green Tinted Goggles	150	Trained	4 Medium Leather, 2 Moss Agate, 1 Flying Tiger Goggles
Aquadynamic Fish Attractor	150	Trained	2 Bronze Bar, 1 Nightcrawlers, 1 Coarse Blasting Powder
Gold Power Core	150	Trained	1 Gold Bar
Red Firework	150	Found	1 Heavy Blasting Powder, 1 Heavy Leather
Green Firework	150	Found	1 Heavy Blasting Powder, 1 Heavy Leather
Blue Firework	150	Found	1 Heavy Blasting Powder, 1 Heavy Leather
Ice Deflector	155	Found	1 Whirring Bronze Gizmo, 1 Frost Oil
Iron Strut	160	Trained	2 Iron Bar
Discombobulator Ray	160	Found	3 Whirring Bronze Gizmo, 2 Silk Cloth, 1 Jade, 1 Bronze Tube
Portable Bronze Mortar	165	Found	4 Bronze Tube, 1 Iron Strut, 4 Heavy Blasting Powder, 4 Medium Leather
Goblin Jumper Cables	165	Found	6 Iron Bar, 2 Whirring Bronze Gizmo, 2 Flask of Oil, 2 Silk Cloth, 2 Shadowgem, 1 Fused Wiring
Gyrochronatom	170	Trained	1 Iron Bar, 1 Gold Power Core
Iron Grenade	175	Trained	1 Iron Bar, 1 Heavy Blasting Powder, 1 Silk Cloth
Compact Harvest Reaper Kit	175	Trained	2 Iron Strut, 1 Bronze Framework, 2 Gyrochronatom, 4 Heavy Leather
Solid Blasting Powder	175	Trained	2 Solid Stone
Solid Dynamite	175	Trained	1 Solid Blasting Powder, 1 Silk Cloth
Bright-Eye Goggles	175	Found	6 Heavy Leather, 2 Citrine
Gyromatic Micro-Adjustor	175	Trained	4 Steel Bar
Large Blue Rocket	175	Found	1 Heavy Blasting Powder, 1 Heavy Leather
Large Green Rocket	175	Found	1 Heavy Blasting Powder, 1 Heavy Leather
Large Red Rocket	175	Found	1 Heavy Blasting Powder, 1 Heavy Leather
Accurate Scope	180	Found	1 Bronze Tube, 1 Jade, 1 Citrine
Advanced Target Dummy	185	Trained	1 Iron Strut, 1 Bronze Framework, 1 Gyrochronatom, 4 Heavy Leather
Craftsman's Monocle	185	Found	6 Heavy Leather, 2 Citrine
Flash Bomb	185	Found	1 Blue Pearl, 1 Heavy Blasting Powder, 1 Silk Cloth
Big Iron Bomb	190	Trained	3 Iron Bar, 3 Heavy Blasting Powder, 1 Silver Contact
SnowMaster 9000	190	Found	8 Mithril Bar, 4 Gyrochronatom, 4 Snowball, 1 Frost Oil
Goblin Land Mine	195	Found	3 Heavy Blasting Powder, 2 Iron Bar, 1 Gyrochronatom
Mithril Tube	195	Trained	3 Mithril Bar
Mechanical Dragonling	200	Found	1 Bronze Framework, 4 Iron Strut, 4 Gyrochronatom, 2 Citrine, 1 Fused Wiring
Gnomish Cloaking Device	200	Found	4 Gyrochronatom, 2 Jade, 2 Lesser Moonstone, 2 Citrine, 1 Fused Wiring
Large Seaforium Charge	200	Found	2 Solid Blasting Powder, 2 Heavy Leather, 1 Refreshing Spring Water
Unstable Trigger	200	Trained	1 Mithril Bar, 1 Mageweave Cloth, 1 Solid Blasting Powder
Mechanical Repair Kit	200	Trained	1 Mithril Bar, 1 Mageweave Cloth, 1 Solid Blasting Powder
EZ-Thro Dynamite II	200	Found	1 Solid Blasting Powder, 2 Mageweave Cloth
Fire Goggles	205	Trained	1 Green Tinted Goggles, 2 Citrine, 2 Elemental Fire, 4 Heavy Leather
Mithril Blunderbuss	205	Trained	1 Mithril Tube, 1 Unstable Trigger, 1 Heavy Stock, 4 Mithril Bar, 2 Elemental Fire
Goblin Rocket Fuel Recipe	205	Trained	1 Blank Parchment, 1 Engineer's Ink
Goblin Mortar	205	Trained	2 Mithril Tube, 4 Mithril Bar, 5 Solid Blasting Powder, 1 Gold Power Core, 1 Elemental Fire
Goblin Mining Helmet	205	Trained	8 Mithril Bar, 1 Citrine, 4 Elemental Earth
Goblin Construction Helmet	205	Trained	8 Mithril Bar, 1 Citrine, 4 Elemental Fire
Goblin Sapper Charge	205	Trained	1 Mageweave Cloth, 3 Solid Blasting Powder, 1 Unstable Trigger
Inlaid Mithril Cylinder Plans	205	Trained	1 Blank Parchment, 1 Engineer's Ink

Engineering

Created Item	Skill Lvl	Source	Reagent(s)
Gnomish Shrink Ray	205	Trained	1 Mithril Tube, 1 Unstable Trigger, 4 Mithril Bar, 4 Flask of Mojo, 2 Jade
Lil' Smoky	205	Found	1 Core of Earth, 2 Gyrochronatom, 1 Fused Wiring, 2 Mithril Bar, 1 Truesilver Bar
Pet Bombling	205	Found	1 Big Iron Bomb, 1 Heart of Fire, 1 Fused Wiring, 6 Mithril Bar
Hi-Impact Mithril Slugs	210	Trained	1 Mithril Bar, 1 Solid Blasting Powder
Deadly Scope	210	Found	1 Mithril Tube, 2 Aquamarine, 2 Thick Leather
Gnomish Goggles	210	Trained	1 Fire Goggles, 1 Mithril Tube, 2 Gold Power Core, 2 Flask of Mojo, 2 Heavy Leather
Gnomish Net-o-Matic Projector	210	Trained	1 Mithril Tube, 2 Shadow Silk, 4 Thick Spider's Silk, 2 Solid Blasting Powder, 4 Mithril Bar
Mithril Casing	215	Trained	3 Mithril Bar
Mithril Frag Bomb	215	Trained	1 Mithril Casing, 1 Unstable Trigger, 1 Solid Blasting Powder
Gnomish Harm Prevention Belt	215	Trained	1 Dusky Belt, 4 Mithril Bar, 2 Truesilver Bar, 1 Unstable Trigger, 2 Aquamarine
Catseye Ultra Goggles	220	Found	4 Thick Leather, 2 Aquamarine, 1 Catseye Elixir
Mithril Heavy-bore Rifle	220	Found	2 Mithril Tube, 1 Unstable Trigger, 1 Heavy Stock, 6 Mithril Bar, 2 Citrine
Spellpower Goggles Xtreme	225	Found	4 Thick Leather, 2 Star Ruby
Parachute Cloak	225	Found	4 Bolt of Mageweave, 2 Shadow Silk, 1 Unstable Trigger, 4 Solid Blasting Powder
Gnomish Rocket Boots	225	Trained	1 Black Mageweave Boots, 2 Mithril Tube, 4 Heavy Leather, 8 Solid Blasting Powder, 4 Gyrochronatom
Blue Rocket Cluster	225	Found	1 Solid Blasting Powder, 1 Thick Leather
Green Rocket Cluster	225	Found	1 Solid Blasting Powder, 1 Thick Leather
Red Rocket Cluster	225	Found	1 Solid Blasting Powder, 1 Thick Leather
Firework Launcher	225	Found	1 Inlaid Mithril Cylinder, 1 Goblin Rocket Fuel, 1 Unstable Trigger, 1 Mithril Casing
Deepdive Helmet	230	Found	8 Mithril Bar, 1 Mithril Casing, 1 Truesilver Bar, 4 Tigerseye, 4 Malachite
Rose Colored Goggles	230	Trained	6 Thick Leather, 2 Star Ruby
Goblin Bomb Dispenser	230	Trained	2 Mithril Casing, 4 Solid Blasting Powder, 6 Truesilver Bar, 1 Unstable Trigger, 2 Accurate Scope
Gnomish Battle Chicken	230	Trained	1 Mithril Casing, 6 Truesilver Bar, 6 Mithril Bar, 2 Inlaid Mithril Cylinder, 1 Gold Power Core, 2 Jade
Hi-Explosive Bomb	235	Trained	2 Mithril Casing, 1 Unstable Trigger, 2 Solid Blasting Powder
The Big One	235	Trained	1 Mithril Casing, 1 Goblin Rocket Fuel, 6 Solid Dynamite, 1 Unstable Trigger
Gnomish Mind Control Cap	235	Trained	10 Mithril Bar, 4 Truesilver Bar, 1 Gold Power Core, 2 Star Ruby, 4 Mageweave Cloth
Sniper Scope	240	Found	1 Mithril Tube, 1 Star Ruby, 2 Truesilver Bar
Gnomish Death Ray	240	Trained	2 Mithril Tube, 1 Unstable Trigger, 1 Essence of Undeath, 4 Ichor of Undeath, 1 Inlaid Mithril Cylinder
Goblin Dragon Gun	240	Trained	2 Mithril Tube, 4 Goblin Rocket Fuel, 6 Mithril Bar, 6 Truesilver Bar, 1 Unstable Trigger
The Mortar: Reloaded	N/A	Special	1 Goblin Mortar, 1 Mithril Bar, 3 Solid Blasting Powder
Mithril Gyro-Shot	245	Trained	2 Mithril Bar, 2 Solid Blasting Powder
Green Lens	245	Trained	8 Thick Leather, 3 Jade, 3 Aquamarine, 2 Heart of the Wild, 2 Wildvine
Goblin Rocket Helmet	245	Trained	1 Goblin Construction Helmet, 4 Goblin Rocket Fuel, 4 Mithril Bar, 1 Unstable Trigger
Mithril Mechanical Dragonling	250	Found	14 Mithril Bar, 4 Heart of Fire, 4 Truesilver Bar, 2 Inlaid Mithril Cylinder, 2 Goblin Rocket Fuel, 2 Star Ruby
Salt Shaker	250	Trained	1 Mithril Casing, 6 Thorium Bar, 1 Gold Power Core, 4 Unstable Trigger
Dense Blasting Powder	250	Trained	2 Dense Stone
Dense Dynamite	250	Trained	2 Dense Blasting Powder, 3 Runecloth
Snake Burst Firework	250	Found	2 Dense Blasting Powder, 2 Runecloth, 1 Deeprock Salt

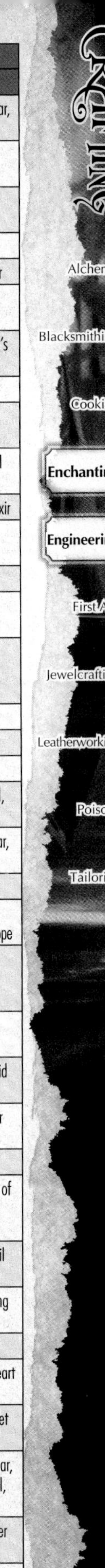

Engineering

Created Item	Skill Lvl	Source	Reagent(s)
Thorium Grenade	260	Found	1 Thorium Widget, 3 Thorium Bar, 3 Dense Blasting Powder, 3 Runecloth
Thorium Rifle	260	Found	2 Mithril Tube, 2 Mithril Casing, 2 Thorium Widget, 4 Thorium Bar, 1 Deadly Scope
Thorium Widget	260	Found	3 Thorium Bar, 1 Runecloth
Truesilver Transformer	260	Found	2 Truesilver Bar, 2 Elemental Earth, 1 Elemental Air
Gyrofreeze Ice Reflector	260	Found	6 Thorium Widget, 2 Truesilver Transformer, 2 Blue Sapphire, 4 Essence of Fire, 2 Frost Oil, 4 Icecap
World Enlarger	260	Found	1 Mithril Casing, 2 Thorium Widget, 1 Gold Power Core, 1 Unstable Trigger, 1 Citrine
Ultrasafe Transporter - Gadgetzan	N/A	Special	12 Mithril Bar, 2 Truesilver Transformer, 4 Core of Earth, 2 Globe of Water, 4 Aquamarine, 1 Inlaid Mithril Cylinder
Dimensional Ripper - Everlook	N/A	Special	10 Mithril Bar, 1 Truesilver Transformer, 4 Heart of Fire, 2 Star Ruby, 1 The Big One
Lifelike Mechanical Toad	265	Found	1 Living Essence, 4 Thorium Widget, 1 Gold Power Core, 1 Rugged Leather
Goblin Jumper Cables XL	265	Found	2 Thorium Widget, 2 Truesilver Transformer, 2 Fused Wiring, 2 Ironweb Spider Silk, 2 Star Ruby
Alarm-O-Bot	265	Found	4 Thorium Bar, 2 Thorium Widget, 4 Rugged Leather, 1 Star Ruby, 1 Fused Wiring
Spellpower Goggles Xtreme Plus	270	Found	1 Spellpower Goggles Xtreme, 4 Star Ruby, 2 Enchanted Leather, 8 Runecloth
Dark Iron Rifle	275	Found	2 Thorium Tube, 6 Dark Iron Bar, 2 Deadly Scope, 2 Blue Sapphire, 2 Large Opal, 4 Rugged Leather
Masterwork Target Dummy	275	Found	1 Mithril Casing, 1 Thorium Tube, 2 Thorium Widget, 1 Truesilver Bar, 2 Rugged Leather, 4 Runecloth
Thorium Tube	275	Found	6 Thorium Bar
Major Recombobulator	275	Found	2 Thorium Tube, 1 Truesilver Transformer, 2 Runecloth
Powerful Seaforium Charge	275	Found	2 Thorium Widget, 3 Dense Blasting Powder, 2 Rugged Leather, 1 Refreshing Spring Water
Large Blue Rocket Cluster	275	Found	1 Dense Blasting Powder, 1 Rugged Leather
Large Green Rocket Cluster	275	Found	1 Dense Blasting Powder, 1 Rugged Leather
Large Red Rocket Cluster	275	Found	1 Dense Blasting Powder, 1 Rugged Leather
Firework Cluster Launcher	275	Found	4 Inlaid Mithril Cylinder, 4 Goblin Rocket Fuel, 2 Truesilver Transformer, 1 Mithril Casing
Steam Tonk Controller	275	Found	2 Thorium Widget, 1 Mithril Casing, 1 Gold Power Core
Delicate Arcanite Converter	285	Found	1 Arcanite Bar, 1 Ironweb Spider Silk
Dark Iron Bomb	285	Found	2 Thorium Widget, 1 Dark Iron Bar, 3 Dense Blasting Powder, 3 Runecloth
Thorium Shells	285	Found	2 Thorium Bar, 1 Dense Blasting Powder
Voice Amplification Modulator	290	Found	2 Delicate Arcanite Converter, 1 Gold Power Core, 1 Thorium Widget, 1 Large Opal
Master Engineer's Goggles	290	Found	1 Fire Goggles, 2 Huge Emerald, 4 Enchanted Leather
Hyper-Radiant Flame Reflector	290	Found	4 Dark Iron Bar, 3 Truesilver Transformer, 6 Essence of Water, 4 Star Ruby, 2 Azerothian Diamond
Arcane Bomb	300	Found	1 Delicate Arcanite Converter, 3 Thorium Bar, 1 Runecloth
Arcanite Dragonling	300	Found	1 Mithril Mechanical Dragonling, 8 Delicate Arcanite Converter, 10 Enchanted Thorium Bar, 6 Thorium Widget, 4 Gold Power Core, 6 Enchanted Leather
Flawless Arcanite Rifle	300	Found	10 Arcanite Bar, 2 Thorium Tube, 2 Essence of Fire, 2 Essence of Earth, 2 Azerothian Diamond, 2 Enchanted Leather
Field Repair Bot 74A	300	Found	12 Thorium Bar, 4 Rugged Leather, 1 Fused Wiring, 2 Elemental Earth, 1 Elemental Fire
Biznicks 247x128 Accurascope	300	Found	2 Lava Core, 2 Essence of Earth, 4 Delicate Arcanite Converter, 6 Dark Iron Bar, 1 Thorium Tube
Core Marksman Rifle	300	Found	4 Fiery Core, 2 Lava Core, 6 Arcanite Bar, 2 Delicate Arcanite Converter, 2 Thorium Tube
Force Reactive Disk	300	Found	6 Arcanite Bar, 2 Delicate Arcanite Converter, 8 Essence of Air, 12 Living Essence, 8 Essence of Earth

Engineering

Created Item	Skill Lvl	Source	Reagent(s)
Ultra-Flash Shadow Reflector	300	Found	8 Dark Iron Bar, 4 Truesilver Transformer, 6 Living Essence, 4 Essence of Undeath, 2 Azerothian Diamond, 2 Large Opal
Bloodvine Goggles	300	Found	4 Bloodvine, 5 Souldarite, 2 Delicate Arcanite Converter, 8 Powerful Mojo, 4 Enchanted Leather
Bloodvine Lens	300	Found	5 Bloodvine, 5 Souldarite, 1 Delicate Arcanite Converter, 8 Powerful Mojo, 4 Enchanted Leather
Tranquil Mechanical Yeti	N/A	Special	1 Cured Rugged Hide, 4 Thorium Widget, 2 Globe of Water, 2 Truesilver Transformer, 1 Gold Power Core
Elemental Blasting Powder	300	Trained	1 Mote of Fire, 1 Mote of Earth
Fel Iron Casing	300	Trained	3 Fel Iron Bar
Handful of Fel Iron Bolts	300	Trained	1 Fel Iron Bar
Fel Iron Bomb	305	Trained	1 Fel Iron Casing, 2 Handful of Fel Iron Bolts, 1 Elemental Blasting Powder
Zapthrottle Mote Extractor	305	Found	2 Fel Iron Casing, 2 Handful of Fel Iron Bolts, 4 Primal Life, 1 Delicate Arcanite Converter
Fel Iron Shells	310	Trained	2 Fel Iron Bar, 1 Elemental Blasting Powder
Fel Iron Musket	320	Trained	2 Thorium Tube, 3 Fel Iron Casing, 4 Handful of Fel Iron Bolts
Adamantite Grenade	325	Trained	4 Adamantite Bar, 2 Handful of Fel Iron Bolts, 1 Elemental Blasting Powder
Crashin' Thrashin' Robot	325	Found	1 Adamantite Frame, 2 Fel Iron Casing, 1 Gold Power Core, 2 Handful of Fel Iron Bolts
Fel Iron Toolbox	325	Found	1 Fel Iron Casing, 5 Fel Iron Bar, 2 Handful of Fel Iron Bolts
Adamantite Frame	325	Trained	4 Adamantite Bar, 1 Primal Earth
Critter Enlarger	325	Found	1 Adamantite Frame, 2 Handful of Fel Iron Bolts, 1 Gold Power Core
The Bigger One	325	Trained	3 Fel Iron Casing, 6 Elemental Blasting Powder, 3 Arcane Powder, 2 Handful of Fel Iron Bolts
Gnomish Flame Turret	325	Trained	1 Adamantite Frame, 2 Handful of Fel Iron Bolts, 1 Primal Fire, 1 Thorium Tube
Healing Potion Injector	330	Found	1 Fel Iron Casing, 1 Handful of Fel Iron Bolts, 2 Knothide Leather, 20 Super Healing Potion
Adamantite Scope	335	Found	1 Thorium Tube, 8 Adamantite Bar, 2 Golden Draenite
White Smoke Flare	335	Found	1 Elemental Blasting Powder, 1 Netherweave Cloth
Red Smoke Flare	335	Found	1 Elemental Blasting Powder, 1 Netherweave Cloth, 1 Red Dye
Blue Smoke Flare	335	Found	1 Elemental Blasting Powder, 1 Netherweave Cloth, 1 Blue Dye
Green Smoke Flare	335	Found	1 Elemental Blasting Powder, 1 Netherweave Cloth, 1 Green Dye
Adamantite Shells	335	Found	2 Adamantite Bar, 1 Elemental Blasting Powder
Purple Smoke Flare	335	Found	1 Elemental Blasting Powder, 1 Netherweave Cloth, 1 Purple Dye
Dimensional Ripper - Area 52	N/A	Special	1 Adamantite Frame, 2 Primal Fire, 2 The Bigger One, 4 Handful of Fel Iron Bolts, 1 Khorium Power Core
Ultrasafe Transporter - Toshley's Station	N/A	Special	1 Adamantite Frame, 2 Primal Air, 2 Felsteel Stabilizer, 4 Handful of Fel Iron Bolts, 1 Khorium Power Core
Cogspinner Goggles	340	Found	4 Heavy Knothide Leather, 2 Blood Garnet, 8 Arcane Dust
Power Amplification Goggles	340	Found	4 Heavy Knothide Leather, 2 Flame Spessarite, 8 Arcane Dust
Super Sapper Charge	340	Trained	4 Netherweave Cloth, 4 Elemental Blasting Powder, 1 Primal Mana
Gnomish Poultryizer	340	Trained	2 Hardened Adamantite Tube, 2 Khorium Power Core, 10 Arcane Dust, 2 Large Prismatic Shard
Mana Potion Injector	345	Found	1 Fel Iron Casing, 1 Handful of Fel Iron Bolts, 2 Knothide Leather, 20 Super Mana Potion
Adamantite Rifle	350	Found	2 Thorium Tube, 2 Adamantite Frame, 4 Handful of Fel Iron Bolts
Ultra-Spectropic Detection Goggles	350	Found	4 Heavy Knothide Leather, 2 Khorium Bar, 2 Deep Peridot, 2 Small Prismatic Shard
Khorium Toolbox	350	Found	1 Fel Iron Casing, 5 Khorium Bar, 2 Handful of Fel Iron Bolts

Engineering			
Created Item	Skill Lvl	Source	Reagent(s)
Hardened Adamantite Tube	350	Trained	3 Hardened Adamantite Bar
Khorium Power Core	350	Trained	3 Khorium Bar, 1 Primal Fire
Felsteel Stabilizer	350	Trained	2 Felsteel Bar
Elemental Seaforium Charge	350	Found	2 Elemental Blasting Powder, 1 Fel Iron Casing, 1 Handful of Fel Iron Bolts
Goblin Rocket Launcher	350	Trained	2 Hardened Adamantite Tube, 1 Khorium Power Core, 2 Felsteel Stabilizer, 6 Primal Fire, 6 Primal Earth, 2 Delicate Arcanite Converter
Nigh Invulnerability Belt	350	Trained	8 Heavy Knothide Leather, 4 Khorium Power Core, 10 Primal Life, 10 Primal Shadow, 2 Delicate Arcanite Converter
Rocket Boots Xtreme	355	Found	8 Heavy Knothide Leather, 2 Khorium Power Core, 2 Hardened Adamantite Tube, 4 Felsteel Stabilizer
Felsteel Boomstick	360	Found	1 Hardened Adamantite Tube, 4 Felsteel Stabilizer, 4 Handful of Fel Iron Bolts
Hyper-Vision Goggles	360	Found	4 Heavy Knothide Leather, 2 Khorium Bar, 2 Nightseye, 2 Large Prismatic Shard
Khorium Scope	360	Found	1 Hardened Adamantite Tube, 4 Khorium Bar, 2 Dawnstone
Ornate Khorium Rifle	375	Found	2 Hardened Adamantite Tube, 12 Khorium Bar, 4 Handful of Fel Iron Bolts, 2 Noble Topaz
Stabilized Eternium Scope	375	Found	2 Hardened Adamantite Tube, 6 Felsteel Stabilizer, 2 Star of Elune
Foreman's Enchanted Helmet	375	Trained	4 Shadoweave Cloth, 12 Primal Mana, 12 Primal Air
Foreman's Reinforced Helmet	375	Trained	8 Hardened Adamantite Bar, 12 Primal Earth, 12 Primal Fire
Gnomish Power Goggles	375	Trained	4 Spellfire Cloth, 8 Primal Fire, 8 Primal Air, 8 Primal Earth, 8 Primal Water, 2 Talasite
Gnomish Battle Goggles	375	Trained	8 Heavy Knothide Leather, 12 Primal Shadow, 12 Primal Earth, 12 Primal Fire, 2 Living Ruby

First Aid			
Created Item	Skill Lvl	Source	Reagent(s)
Linen Bandage	N/A	Special	1 Linen Cloth
Heavy Linen Bandage	40	Trained	2 Linen Cloth
Wool Bandage	80	Trained	1 Wool Cloth
Anti-Venom	80	Trained	1 Small Venom Sac
Heavy Wool Bandage	115	Trained	2 Wool Cloth
Strong Anti-Venom	130	Found	1 Large Venom Sac
Silk Bandage	150	Trained	1 Silk Cloth
Heavy Silk Bandage	180	Found	2 Silk Cloth
Mageweave Bandage	210	Found	1 Mageweave Cloth
Heavy Mageweave Bandage	240	Special	2 Mageweave Cloth
Runecloth Bandage	260	Special	1 Runecloth
Heavy Runecloth Bandage	290	Special	2 Runecloth
Powerful Anti-Venom	300	Found	1 Huge Venom Sac
Netherweave Bandage	330	Found	1 Netherweave Cloth
Heavy Netherweave Bandage	360	Found	2 Netherweave Cloth

Jewelcrafting			
Created Item	Skill Lvl	Source	Reagent(s)
Delicate Copper Wire	N/A	Special	2 Copper Bar
Braided Copper Ring	N/A	Special	2 Delicate Copper Wire
Woven Copper Ring	N/A	Special	2 Delicate Copper Wire, 1 Copper Bar
Rough Stone Statue	N/A	Special	8 Rough Stone
Heavy Copper Ring	5	Trained	4 Copper Bar, 2 Delicate Copper Wire
Malachite Pendant	20	Trained	1 Malachite, 1 Delicate Copper Wire
Tigerseye Band	20	Trained	1 Tigerseye, 1 Delicate Copper Wire
Inlaid Malachite Ring	30	Trained	2 Malachite, 2 Copper Bar
Ornate Tigerseye Necklace	30	Trained	2 Tigerseye, 2 Copper Bar, 1 Delicate Copper Wire
Bronze Setting	50	Trained	2 Bronze Bar
Elegant Silver Ring	50	Trained	1 Silver Bar
Solid Bronze Ring	50	Trained	4 Bronze Bar
Thick Bronze Necklace	50	Trained	2 Bronze Bar, 1 Shadowgem, 1 Delicate Copper Wire
Coarse Stone Statue	50	Trained	8 Coarse Stone
Simple Pearl Ring	60	Trained	1 Small Lustrous Pearl, 1 Bronze Setting, 2 Copper Bar
Bronze Band of Force	65	Trained	2 Bronze Bar, 1 Bronze Setting, 3 Malachite, 3 Tigerseye, 2 Shadowgem
Gloom Band	70	Trained	2 Shadowgem, 1 Bronze Setting, 2 Delicate Copper Wire
Brilliant Necklace	75	Trained	4 Bronze Bar, 1 Bronze Setting, 1 Moss Agate
Ring of Silver Might	80	Trained	2 Silver Bar
Bronze Torc	80	Trained	6 Bronze Bar, 1 Bronze Setting, 1 Lesser Moonstone
Heavy Silver Ring	90	Trained	2 Silver Bar, 1 Bronze Setting, 1 Moss Agate, 1 Lesser Moonstone
Ring of Twilight Shadows	100	Trained	2 Shadowgem, 2 Bronze Bar
Heavy Jade Ring	105	Trained	1 Jade, 1 Bronze Setting, 2 Iron Bar
Amulet of the Moon	110	Found	2 Lesser Moonstone, 1 Bronze Setting
Barbaric Iron Collar	110	Trained	8 Iron Bar, 2 Large Fang, 2 Bronze Setting
Heavy Stone Statue	110	Trained	8 Heavy Stone
Moonsoul Crown	120	Trained	3 Lesser Moonstone, 3 Small Lustrous Pearl, 4 Soul Dust, 4 Silver Bar, 2 Mana Potion
Pendant of the Agate Shield	120	Found	1 Moss Agate, 1 Bronze Setting
Wicked Moonstone Ring	125	Found	1 Lesser Moonstone, 1 Shadow Oil, 4 Iron Bar
Heavy Iron Knuckles	125	Found	8 Iron Bar, 2 Elixir of Ogre's Strength
Golden Dragon Ring	135	Trained	1 Jade, 2 Gold Bar, 2 Delicate Copper Wire
Silver Rose Pendant	145	Found	1 Moss Agate, 1 Jade, 2 Silver Bar, 2 Bronze Setting
Heavy Golden Necklace of Battle	150	Found	1 Gold Bar, 2 Moss Agate, 1 Elixir of Ogre's Strength
Mithril Filigree	150	Trained	2 Mithril Bar
Blazing Citrine Ring	150	Found	1 Citrine, 4 Mithril Bar
Jade Pendant of Blasting	160	Found	1 Jade, 3 Mithril Filigree
The Jade Eye	170	Found	1 Jade, 2 Elemental Earth
Engraved Truesilver Ring	170	Trained	1 Truesilver Bar, 2 Gold Bar
Solid Stone Statue	175	Trained	10 Solid Stone
Citrine Ring of Rapid Healing	180	Trained	1 Citrine, 2 Elemental Water, 2 Mithril Bar
Golden Ring of Power	180	Trained	4 Gold Bar, 1 Lesser Moonstone, 1 Jade, 1 Citrine
Citrine Pendant of Golden Healing	190	Found	1 Citrine, 2 Elemental Water, 2 Gold Bar, 1 Bronze Setting
Figurine - Jade Owl	200	Trained	4 Jade, 2 Truesilver Bar, 4 Vision Dust, 4 Mithril Filigree

Jewelcrafting

Created Item	Skill Lvl	Source	Reagent(s)
Figurine - Golden Hare	200	Found	6 Gold Bar, 2 Cut Citrine
Truesilver Commander's Ring	200	Trained	3 Truesilver Bar, 2 Star Ruby, 2 Citrine
Aquamarine Signet	210	Trained	3 Aquamarine, 4 Flask of Mojo
Figurine - Black Pearl Panther	215	Found	4 Black Pearl, 4 Flask of Mojo
Aquamarine Pendant of the Warrior	220	Trained	1 Aquamarine, 2 Flask of Mojo, 3 Mithril Filigree
Ruby Crown of Restoration	225	Found	2 Star Ruby, 2 Black Pearl, 4 Truesilver Bar, 4 Thorium Setting, 4 Greater Mana Potion
Thorium Setting	225	Trained	3 Thorium Bar
Figurine - Truesilver Crab	225	Found	2 Aquamarine, 4 Truesilver Bar, 2 Core of Earth, 2 Globe of Water, 4 Flask of Mojo
Dense Stone Statue	225	Trained	10 Dense Stone
Red Ring of Destruction	230	Trained	1 Star Ruby, 1 Citrine, 1 Thorium Setting
Figurine - Truesilver Boar	235	Found	2 Star Ruby, 4 Truesilver Bar, 2 Heart of Fire, 2 Breath of Wind, 4 Flask of Mojo
Ruby Pendant of Fire	235	Trained	1 Star Ruby, 1 Thorium Setting
Truesilver Healing Ring	240	Trained	2 Truesilver Bar, 4 Heart of the Wild
The Aquamarine Ward	245	Found	1 Aquamarine, 2 Truesilver Bar, 1 Thorium Setting, 2 Mithril Bar
Gem Studded Band	250	Found	2 Aquamarine, 2 Citrine, 4 Thorium Setting, 2 Truesilver Bar
Opal Necklace of Impact	250	Found	2 Large Opal, 2 Thorium Setting, 4 Truesilver Bar, 2 Large Radiant Shard, 2 Mithril Filigree
Figurine - Ruby Serpent	260	Found	2 Star Ruby, 2 Essence of Fire, 4 Flask of Big Mojo, 2 Truesilver Bar
Simple Opal Ring	260	Trained	2 Large Opal, 1 Thorium Setting, 2 Thorium Bar
Diamond Focus Ring	265	Trained	1 Azerothian Diamond, 1 Thorium Setting
Sapphire Signet	275	Trained	4 Blue Sapphire, 2 Truesilver Bar, 1 Thorium Setting
Emerald Crown of Destruction	275	Found	2 Huge Emerald, 2 Large Opal, 2 Blue Sapphire, 2 Arcanite Bar, 6 Thorium Bar
Onslaught Ring	280	Trained	8 Thorium Bar, 2 Powerful Mojo, 2 Essence of Earth
Sapphire Pendant of Winter Night	280	Trained	1 Blue Sapphire, 2 Essence of Undeath, 1 Essence of Water, 1 Thorium Setting
Glowing Thorium Band	280	Trained	2 Azerothian Diamond, 1 Thorium Bar, 1 Thorium Setting
Figurine - Emerald Owl	285	Found	2 Huge Emerald, 2 Arcanite Bar, 2 Thorium Bar, 4 Powerful Mojo
Ring of Bitter Shadows	285	Found	1 Arcanite Bar, 4 Essence of Undeath, 2 Demonic Rune
Living Emerald Pendant	290	Trained	2 Huge Emerald, 4 Living Essence, 4 Powerful Mojo
Emerald Lion Ring	290	Trained	2 Huge Emerald, 1 Thorium Bar, 1 Thorium Setting
Figurine - Black Diamond Crab	300	Found	4 Pristine Black Diamond, 4 Black Diamond, 2 Azerothian Diamond, 2 Arcanite Bar, 4 Thorium Bar
Figurine - Dark Iron Scorpid	300	Found	4 Dark Iron Bar, 2 Arcanite Bar, 2 Star Ruby
Teardrop Blood Garnet	300	Found	1 Blood Garnet
Inscribed Flame Spessarite	300	Found	1 Flame Spessarite
Radiant Deep Peridot	300	Found	1 Deep Peridot
Glowing Shadow Draenite	300	Found	1 Shadow Draenite
Brilliant Golden Draenite	300	Found	1 Golden Draenite
Solid Azure Moonstone	300	Found	1 Azure Moonstone
Primal Stone Statue	300	Found	1 Primal Earth
Necklace of the Diamond Tower	305	Found	2 Azerothian Diamond, 2 Thorium Setting, 2 Arcanite Bar

Jewelcrafting

Created Item	Skill Lvl	Source	Reagent(s)
Bold Blood Garnet	305	Found	1 Blood Garnet
Luminous Flame Spessarite	305	Found	1 Flame Spessarite
Jagged Deep Peridot	305	Found	1 Deep Peridot
Royal Shadow Draenite	305	Found	1 Shadow Draenite
Gleaming Golden Draenite	305	Found	1 Golden Draenite
Sparkling Azure Moonstone	305	Found	1 Azure Moonstone
Bright Blood Garnet	305	Found	1 Blood Garnet
Band of Natural Fire	310	Trained	1 Flame Spessarite, 4 Essence of Fire, 4 Living Essence
Fel Iron Blood Ring	310	Trained	1 Fel Iron Bar, 2 Blood Garnet
Golden Draenite Ring	310	Trained	1 Fel Iron Bar, 2 Golden Draenite
Arcanite Sword Pendant	315	Found	4 Arcanite Bar, 4 Essence of Earth, 4 Essence of Air
Runed Blood Garnet	315	Found	1 Blood Garnet
Glinting Flame Spessarite	315	Found	1 Flame Spessarite
Enduring Deep Peridot	315	Found	1 Deep Peridot
Shifting Shadow Draenite	315	Found	1 Shadow Draenite
Thick Golden Draenite	315	Found	1 Golden Draenite
Stormy Azure Moonstone	315	Found	1 Azure Moonstone
Azure Moonstone Ring	320	Trained	1 Fel Iron Bar, 2 Azure Moonstone, 1 Deep Peridot
Blood Crown	325	Found	8 Thorium Bar, 2 Blood of the Mountain, 4 Star Ruby, 2 Blood of Heroes
Delicate Blood Garnet	325	Found	1 Blood Garnet
Potent Flame Spessarite	325	Found	1 Flame Spessarite
Dazzling Deep Peridot	325	Found	1 Deep Peridot
Soveriegn Shadow Draenite	325	Found	1 Shadow Draenite
Rigid Golden Draenite	325	Found	1 Golden Draenite
Lustrous Azure Moonstone	325	Found	1 Azure Moonstone
Smooth Golden Draenite	325	Found	1 Golden Draenite
Mercurial Adamantite	325	Trained	4 Adamantite Powder, 1 Primal Earth
Thick Adamantite Necklace	335	Trained	2 Adamantite Bar, 1 Mercurial Adamantite
Heavy Adamantite Ring	335	Trained	1 Adamantite Bar, 1 Mercurial Adamantite
Heavy Felsteel Ring	345	Found	2 Felsteel Bar, 4 Mercurial Adamantite
Bright Living Ruby	350	Found	1 Living Ruby
Brilliant Dawnstone	350	Found	1 Dawnstone
Dazzling Talasite	350	Found	1 Talasite
Delicate Living Ruby	350	Found	1 Living Ruby
Enduring Talasite	350	Found	1 Talasite
Inscribed Noble Topaz	350	Found	1 Noble Topaz
Flashing Living Ruby	350	Found	1 Living Ruby
Gleaming Dawnstone	350	Found	1 Dawnstone
Glinting Noble Topaz	350	Found	1 Noble Topaz
Glowing Nightseye	350	Found	1 Nightseye
Jagged Talasite	350	Found	1 Talasite
Luminous Noble Topaz	350	Found	1 Noble Topaz
Lustrous Star of Elune	350	Found	1 Star of Elune
Mystic Dawnstone	350	Found	1 Dawnstone
Potent Noble Topaz	350	Found	1 Noble Topaz
Radiant Talasite	350	Found	1 Talasite
Rigid Dawnstone	350	Found	1 Dawnstone
Royal Nightseye	350	Found	1 Nightseye
Runed Living Ruby	350	Found	1 Living Ruby
Shifting Nightseye	350	Found	1 Nightseye
Smooth Dawnstone	350	Found	1 Dawnstone
Sovereign Nightseye	350	Found	1 Nightseye
Solid Star of Elune	350	Found	1 Star of Elune
Sparkling Star of Elune	350	Found	1 Star of Elune

Jewelcrafting			
Created Item	Skill Lvl	Source	Reagent(s)
Stormy Star of Elune	350	Found	1 Star of Elune
Subtle Living Ruby	350	Found	1 Living Ruby
Teardrop Living Ruby	350	Found	1 Living Ruby
Thick Dawnstone	350	Found	1 Dawnstone
Bold Living Ruby	350	Found	1 Living Ruby
Khorium Band of Shadows	350	Found	2 Khorium Bar, 3 Mercurial Adamantite, 3 Primal Shadow
Khorium Band of Frost	355	Found	2 Khorium Bar, 4 Mercurial Adamantite, 3 Primal Water
Khorium Inferno Band	355	Found	2 Khorium Bar, 4 Mercurial Adamantite, 3 Primal Fire
Delicate Eternium Ring	355	Found	1 Eternium Bar, 5 Mercurial Adamantite
Thick Felsteel Necklace	355	Found	2 Felsteel Bar, 3 Mercurial Adamantite
Living Ruby Pendant	355	Found	4 Khorium Bar, 1 Mercurial Adamantite, 1 Living Ruby
Khorium Band of Leaves	360	Found	2 Khorium Bar, 4 Mercurial Adamantite, 3 Primal Life
Pendant of Frozen Flame	360	Found	2 Felsteel Bar, 6 Primal Water, 4 Primal Fire, 1 Mercurial Adamantite
Pendant of Thawing	360	Found	2 Felsteel Bar, 6 Primal Fire, 4 Primal Water, 1 Mercurial Adamantite
Pendant of Withering	360	Found	2 Felsteel Bar, 6 Primal Shadow, 4 Primal Life, 1 Mercurial Adamantite
Pendant of Shadow's End	360	Found	2 Felsteel Bar, 6 Primal Life, 4 Primal Shadow, 1 Mercurial Adamantite
Pendant of the Null Rune	360	Found	2 Felsteel Bar, 8 Primal Mana, 1 Mercurial Adamantite
Braided Eternium Chain	360	Found	2 Eternium Bar, 3 Mercurial Adamantite
Eye of the Night	360	Found	2 Hardened Adamantite Bar, 2 Mercurial Adamantite, 1 Nightseye
Ring of Arcane Shielding	360	Found	2 Eternium Bar, 8 Primal Mana
Arcane Khorium Band	365	Found	2 Khorium Bar, 4 Mercurial Adamantite, 3 Primal Mana
Blazing Eternium Band	365	Found	2 Eternium Bar, 4 Mercurial Adamantite, 4 Primal Fire
Embrace of the Dawn	365	Found	2 Eternium Bar, 4 Mercurial Adamantite, 2 Golden Draenite
Chain of the Twilight Owl	365	Found	2 Khorium Bar, 4 Mercurial Adamantite, 2 Azure Moonstone
Bracing Earthstorm Diamond	365	Found	1 Earthstorm Diamond
Brutal Earthstorm Diamond	365	Found	1 Earthstorm Diamond
Insightful Earthstorm Diamond	365	Found	1 Earthstorm Diamond
Powerful Earthstorm Diamond	365	Found	1 Earthstorm Diamond
Tenacious Earthstorm Diamond	365	Found	1 Earthstorm Diamond
Destructive Skyfire Diamond	365	Found	1 Skyfire Diamond
Enigmatic Skyfire Diamond	365	Found	1 Skyfire Diamond
Mystical Skyfire Diamond	365	Found	1 Skyfire Diamond
Swift Skyfire Diamond	365	Found	1 Skyfire Diamond
Coronet of the Verdant Flame	370	Found	20 Khorium Bar, 20 Primal Life, 2 Talasite, 5 Mercurial Adamantite
Circlet of Arcane Might	370	Found	20 Felsteel Bar, 20 Primal Mana, 2 Star of Elune, 5 Mercurial Adamantite
Figurine - Felsteel Boar	370	Found	8 Felsteel Bar, 2 Blood Garnet, 4 Primal Earth
Figurine - Dawnstone Crab	370	Found	4 Khorium Bar, 2 Dawnstone, 4 Golden Draenite
Figurine - Living Ruby Serpent	370	Found	2 Felsteel Bar, 2 Living Ruby, 4 Primal Fire
Figurine - Talasite Owl	370	Found	2 Eternium Bar, 2 Talasite, 4 Primal Mana
Figurine - Nightseye Panther	370	Found	6 Hardened Adamantite Bar, 2 Nightseye, 2 Primal Shadow

Jewelcrafting			
Created Item	Skill Lvl	Source	Reagent(s)
The Frozen Eye	375	Found	4 Mercurial Adamantite, 2 Khorium Bar, 6 Primal Water, 6 Primal Fire
The Natural Ward	375	Found	4 Mercurial Adamantite, 2 Felsteel Bar, 6 Primal Life, 6 Primal Shadow

Leatherworking			
Created Item	Skill Lvl	Source	Reagent(s)
Handstitched Leather Boots	N/A	Special	2 Light Leather, 1 Coarse Thread
Light Armor Kit	N/A	Special	1 Light Leather
Light Leather	N/A	Special	3 Ruined Leather Scraps
Handstitched Leather Vest	N/A	Special	3 Light Leather, 1 Coarse Thread
Handstitched Leather Cloak	N/A	Special	2 Light Leather, 1 Coarse Thread
Handstitched Leather Bracers	N/A	Special	2 Light Leather, 3 Coarse Thread
Handstitched Leather Pants	15	Trained	4 Light Leather, 1 Coarse Thread
Handstitched Leather Belt	25	Trained	6 Light Leather, 1 Coarse Thread
Light Leather Quiver	30	Trained	4 Light Leather, 2 Coarse Thread
Small Leather Ammo Pouch	30	Trained	3 Light Leather, 4 Coarse Thread
Cured Light Hide	35	Trained	1 Light Hide, 1 Salt
Rugged Leather Pants	35	Found	5 Light Leather, 5 Coarse Thread
Embossed Leather Vest	40	Trained	8 Light Leather, 4 Coarse Thread
Kodo Hide Bag	40	Found	3 Thin Kodo Leather, 4 Light Leather, 1 Coarse Thread
Embossed Leather Boots	55	Trained	8 Light Leather, 5 Coarse Thread
Embossed Leather Gloves	55	Trained	3 Light Leather, 2 Coarse Thread
Embossed Leather Cloak	60	Trained	5 Light Leather, 2 Coarse Thread
White Leather Jerkin	60	Found	8 Light Leather, 2 Coarse Thread, 1 Bleach
Light Leather Bracers	70	Trained	6 Light Leather, 4 Coarse Thread
Fine Leather Gloves	75	Found	1 Cured Light Hide, 4 Light Leather, 2 Coarse Thread
Embossed Leather Pants	75	Trained	1 Cured Light Hide, 6 Light Leather, 2 Coarse Thread
Fine Leather Belt	80	Trained	6 Light Leather, 2 Coarse Thread
Fine Leather Cloak	85	Trained	10 Light Leather, 2 Fine Thread
Fine Leather Tunic	85	Trained	3 Cured Light Hide, 6 Light Leather, 4 Coarse Thread
Fine Leather Boots	90	Found	7 Light Leather, 2 Coarse Thread
Murloc Scale Belt	90	Found	8 Slimy Murloc Scale, 6 Light Leather, 1 Fine Thread
Deviate Scale Cloak	90	Found	4 Deviate Scale, 1 Cured Light Hide, 1 Fine Thread
Moonglow Vest	90	Found	6 Light Leather, 1 Cured Light Hide, 4 Coarse Thread, 1 Small Lustrous Pearl

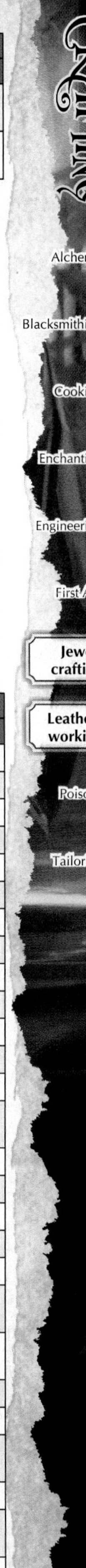

Leatherworking

Created Item	Skill Lvl	Source	Reagent(s)
Murloc Scale Breastplate	95	Found	12 Slimy Murloc Scale, 1 Cured Light Hide, 8 Light Leather, 1 Fine Thread
Light Leather Pants	95	Trained	10 Light Leather, 1 Cured Light Hide, 1 Fine Thread
Medium Armor Kit	100	Trained	4 Medium Leather, 1 Coarse Thread
Dark Leather Boots	100	Trained	4 Medium Leather, 2 Fine Thread, 1 Gray Dye
Dark Leather Tunic	100	Found	6 Medium Leather, 1 Fine Thread, 1 Gray Dye
Hillman's Leather Vest	100	Found	1 Fine Leather Tunic, 2 Cured Light Hide, 2 Coarse Thread
Cured Medium Hide	100	Trained	1 Medium Hide, 1 Salt
Black Whelp Cloak	100	Found	12 Black Whelp Scale, 4 Medium Leather, 1 Fine Thread
Medium Leather	100	Trained	4 Light Leather
Black Whelp Tunic	100	Found	8 Medium Leather, 8 Black Whelp Scale, 1 Cured Light Hide, 2 Fine Thread
Fine Leather Pants	105	Found	8 Medium Leather, 1 Bolt of Woolen Cloth, 1 Fine Thread
Deviate Scale Gloves	105	Found	5 Deviate Scale, 2 Fine Thread
Dark Leather Cloak	110	Trained	8 Medium Leather, 1 Fine Thread, 1 Gray Dye
Dark Leather Pants	115	Trained	12 Medium Leather, 1 Gray Dye, 1 Fine Thread
Deviate Scale Belt	115	Found	6 Perfect Deviate Scale, 4 Deviate Scale, 2 Fine Thread
Toughened Leather Armor	120	Trained	10 Medium Leather, 2 Cured Light Hide, 2 Fine Thread
Dark Leather Gloves	120	Found	1 Fine Leather Gloves, 1 Cured Medium Hide, 1 Fine Thread, 1 Gray Dye
Hillman's Belt	120	Found	8 Medium Leather, 1 Elixir of Wisdom, 2 Fine Thread
Red Whelp Gloves	120	Found	6 Red Whelp Scale, 4 Medium Leather, 1 Fine Thread
Nimble Leather Gloves	120	Trained	1 Elixir of Minor Agility, 6 Medium Leather, 1 Fine Thread
Dark Leather Belt	125	Trained	1 Fine Leather Belt, 1 Cured Medium Hide, 2 Fine Thread, 1 Gray Dye
Guardian Cloak	125	Found	14 Heavy Leather, 2 Bolt of Silk Cloth, 2 Silken Thread
Fletcher's Gloves	125	Trained	8 Medium Leather, 4 Long Tail Feather, 2 Fine Thread
Hillman's Shoulders	130	Trained	1 Cured Medium Hide, 4 Medium Leather, 1 Fine Thread
Toughened Leather Gloves	135	Trained	4 Medium Leather, 2 Cured Medium Hide, 2 Elixir of Defense, 2 Spider's Silk, 2 Fine Thread
Herbalist's Gloves	135	Found	8 Medium Leather, 4 Kingsblood, 2 Fine Thread
Earthen Leather Shoulders	135	Found	6 Medium Leather, 1 Elemental Earth, 2 Fine Thread
Dark Leather Shoulders	140	Found	12 Medium Leather, 1 Elixir of Lesser Agility, 1 Gray Dye, 2 Fine Thread
Pilferer's Gloves	140	Found	10 Medium Leather, 2 Lucky Charm, 2 Fine Thread
Hillman's Leather Gloves	145	Trained	14 Medium Leather, 4 Fine Thread
Heavy Earthen Gloves	145	Found	12 Medium Leather, 2 Elemental Earth, 2 Bolt of Woolen Cloth, 2 Fine Thread
Hillman's Cloak	150	Trained	5 Heavy Leather, 2 Fine Thread
Barbaric Gloves	150	Found	6 Heavy Leather, 2 Large Fang, 1 Fine Thread
Cured Heavy Hide	150	Trained	1 Heavy Hide, 3 Salt
Heavy Armor Kit	150	Trained	5 Heavy Leather, 1 Fine Thread
Heavy Quiver	150	Trained	8 Heavy Leather, 2 Fine Thread

Leatherworking

Created Item	Skill Lvl	Source	Reagent(s)
Heavy Leather Ammo Pouch	150	Trained	8 Heavy Leather, 2 Fine Thread
Heavy Leather	150	Trained	5 Medium Leather
Heavy Leather Ball	150	Found	2 Heavy Leather, 1 Fine Thread
Green Leather Armor	155	Found	9 Heavy Leather, 2 Green Dye, 4 Fine Thread
Barbaric Bracers	155	Found	8 Heavy Leather, 2 Cured Heavy Hide, 4 Small Lustrous Pearl, 1 Raptor Hide, 4 Large Fang
Green Leather Belt	160	Trained	1 Cured Heavy Hide, 5 Heavy Leather, 1 Fine Thread, 1 Green Dye, 1 Iron Buckle
Guardian Pants	160	Trained	12 Heavy Leather, 2 Bolt of Silk Cloth, 2 Fine Thread
Raptor Hide Belt	165	Found	4 Raptor Hide, 4 Heavy Leather, 2 Fine Thread
Raptor Hide Harness	165	Found	6 Raptor Hide, 4 Heavy Leather, 2 Fine Thread
Dusky Leather Leggings	165	Found	10 Heavy Leather, 1 Black Dye, 2 Fine Thread
Guardian Belt	170	Found	2 Cured Heavy Hide, 4 Heavy Leather, 1 Fine Thread, 1 Iron Buckle
Thick Murloc Armor	170	Found	12 Thick Murloc Scale, 1 Cured Heavy Hide, 10 Heavy Leather, 3 Fine Thread
Barbaric Leggings	170	Found	10 Heavy Leather, 2 Fine Thread, 1 Moss Agate
Guardian Armor	175	Found	2 Cured Heavy Hide, 12 Heavy Leather, 1 Shadow Oil, 2 Fine Thread
Barbaric Shoulders	175	Trained	8 Heavy Leather, 1 Cured Heavy Hide, 2 Fine Thread
Dusky Leather Armor	175	Trained	10 Heavy Leather, 1 Shadow Oil, 2 Fine Thread
Green Whelp Armor	175	Found	4 Green Whelp Scale, 10 Heavy Leather, 2 Fine Thread
Green Leather Bracers	180	Trained	2 Cured Heavy Hide, 6 Heavy Leather, 1 Green Dye, 1 Fine Thread
Frost Leather Cloak	180	Trained	6 Heavy Leather, 2 Elemental Earth, 2 Elemental Water, 2 Fine Thread
Gem-studded Leather Belt	185	Found	4 Cured Heavy Hide, 2 Iridescent Pearl, 2 Jade, 1 Citrine, 1 Fine Thread
Dusky Bracers	185	Trained	16 Heavy Leather, 1 Black Dye, 2 Silken Thread
Barbaric Harness	190	Trained	14 Heavy Leather, 2 Fine Thread, 1 Iron Buckle
Murloc Scale Bracers	190	Found	16 Thick Murloc Scale, 1 Cured Heavy Hide, 14 Heavy Leather, 1 Silken Thread
Guardian Gloves	190	Trained	4 Heavy Leather, 1 Cured Heavy Hide, 1 Silken Thread
Green Whelp Bracers	190	Found	6 Green Whelp Scale, 8 Heavy Leather, 2 Silken Thread
Gloves of the Greatfather	190	Found	8 Heavy Leather, 4 Elemental Earth, 1 Silken Thread
Guardian Leather Bracers	195	Found	6 Heavy Leather, 2 Cured Heavy Hide, 1 Silken Thread
Dusky Belt	195	Trained	10 Heavy Leather, 2 Bolt of Silk Cloth, 2 Black Dye, 1 Iron Buckle
Barbaric Belt	200	Found	6 Heavy Leather, 2 Cured Heavy Hide, 2 Coarse Gorilla Hair, 1 Great Rage Potion, 1 Silken Thread, 1 Iron Buckle
Dusky Boots	200	Found	8 Heavy Leather, 2 Shadowcat Hide, 1 Shadow Oil, 2 Silken Thread
Swift Boots	200	Found	10 Heavy Leather, 2 Swiftness Potion, 2 Thick Spider's Silk, 1 Silken Thread
Cured Thick Hide	200	Trained	1 Thick Hide, 1 Deeprock Salt
Thick Armor Kit	200	Trained	5 Thick Leather, 1 Silken Thread
Comfortable Leather Hat	200	Found	12 Heavy Leather, 2 Cured Heavy Hide, 2 Silken Thread

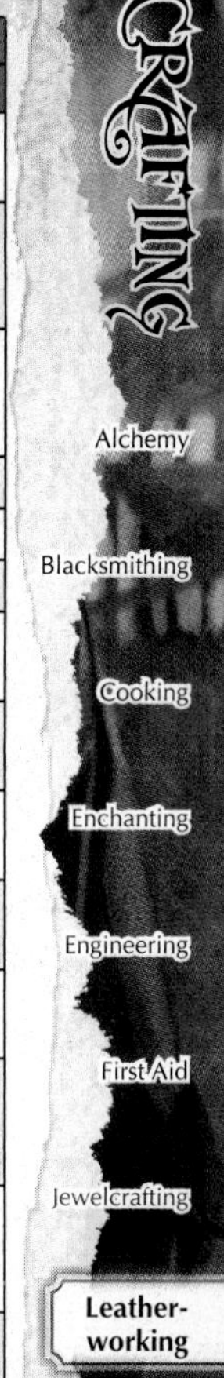

Leatherworking			
Created Item	Skill Lvl	Source	Reagent(s)
Thick Leather	200	Trained	6 Heavy Leather
Shadowskin Gloves	200	Found	6 Thick Leather, 8 Shadowcat Hide, 2 Black Pearl, 2 Cured Heavy Hide, 4 Shadowgem, 1 Heavy Silken Thread
Nightscape Tunic	205	Trained	7 Thick Leather, 2 Silken Thread
Nightscape Headband	205	Trained	5 Thick Leather, 2 Silken Thread
Turtle Scale Gloves	205	Found	6 Thick Leather, 8 Turtle Scale, 1 Heavy Silken Thread
Turtle Scale Breastplate	210	Trained	6 Thick Leather, 12 Turtle Scale, 1 Heavy Silken Thread
Nightscape Shoulders	210	Found	8 Thick Leather, 6 Mageweave Cloth, 3 Silken Thread
Turtle Scale Bracers	210	Trained	8 Thick Leather, 12 Turtle Scale, 1 Heavy Silken Thread
Big Voodoo Robe	215	Found	10 Thick Leather, 4 Flask of Mojo, 1 Heavy Silken Thread
Tough Scorpid Breastplate	220	Found	12 Thick Leather, 12 Scorpid Scale, 4 Silken Thread
Wild Leather Shoulders	220	Found	10 Thick Leather, 1 Wildvine, 1 Cured Thick Hide
Big Voodoo Mask	220	Found	8 Thick Leather, 6 Flask of Mojo, 1 Heavy Silken Thread
Tough Scorpid Bracers	220	Found	10 Thick Leather, 4 Scorpid Scale, 2 Silken Thread
Tough Scorpid Gloves	225	Found	6 Thick Leather, 8 Scorpid Scale, 2 Silken Thread
Wild Leather Vest	225	Found	12 Thick Leather, 2 Wildvine, 1 Cured Thick Hide
Wild Leather Helmet	225	Found	10 Thick Leather, 2 Wildvine, 1 Cured Thick Hide
Dragonscale Gauntlets	225	Trained	24 Thick Leather, 12 Worn Dragonscale, 4 Heavy Silken Thread, 2 Cured Thick Hide
Wolfshead Helm	225	Trained	18 Thick Leather, 2 Thick Wolfhide, 8 Wicked Claw, 4 Heavy Silken Thread, 2 Cured Thick Hide
Quickdraw Quiver	225	Trained	12 Thick Leather, 1 Cured Thick Hide, 1 Elixir of Agility, 4 Silken Thread
Thick Leather Ammo Pouch	225	Trained	10 Thick Leather, 1 Cured Thick Hide, 1 Elixir of Greater Defense, 6 Silken Thread
Nightscape Pants	230	Trained	14 Thick Leather, 4 Silken Thread
Nightscape Cloak	230	Found	12 Thick Leather, 4 Silken Thread
Turtle Scale Helm	230	Trained	14 Thick Leather, 24 Turtle Scale, 1 Heavy Silken Thread
Gauntlets of the Sea	230	Trained	20 Thick Leather, 8 Globe of Water, 2 Core of Earth, 1 Cured Thick Hide, 4 Heavy Silken Thread
Tough Scorpid Boots	235	Found	12 Thick Leather, 12 Scorpid Scale, 6 Silken Thread
Turtle Scale Leggings	235	Trained	14 Thick Leather, 28 Turtle Scale, 1 Heavy Silken Thread
Nightscape Boots	235	Trained	16 Thick Leather, 2 Heavy Silken Thread
Big Voodoo Pants	240	Found	10 Thick Leather, 6 Flask of Big Mojo, 2 Heavy Silken Thread
Big Voodoo Cloak	240	Found	14 Thick Leather, 4 Flask of Big Mojo, 2 Heavy Silken Thread
Tough Scorpid Shoulders	240	Found	12 Thick Leather, 16 Scorpid Scale, 2 Heavy Silken Thread
Wild Leather Boots	245	Found	14 Thick Leather, 4 Wildvine, 2 Cured Thick Hide
Tough Scorpid Leggings	245	Found	14 Thick Leather, 8 Scorpid Scale, 2 Heavy Silken Thread
Tough Scorpid Helm	250	Found	10 Thick Leather, 20 Scorpid Scale, 2 Heavy Silken Thread
Wild Leather Leggings	250	Found	16 Thick Leather, 6 Wildvine, 2 Cured Thick Hide

Leatherworking			
Created Item	Skill Lvl	Source	Reagent(s)
Wild Leather Cloak	250	Found	16 Thick Leather, 6 Wildvine, 2 Cured Thick Hide
Helm of Fire	250	Trained	40 Thick Leather, 8 Heart of Fire, 4 Core of Earth, 2 Cured Thick Hide, 4 Heavy Silken Thread
Feathered Breastplate	250	Trained	40 Thick Leather, 40 Jet Black Feather, 2 Black Pearl, 4 Cured Thick Hide, 4 Heavy Silken Thread
Cured Rugged Hide	250	Trained	1 Rugged Hide, 1 Refined Deeprock Salt
Rugged Armor Kit	250	Trained	5 Rugged Leather
Rugged Leather	250	Trained	6 Thick Leather
Dragonscale Breastplate	255	Trained	40 Thick Leather, 30 Worn Dragonscale, 4 Heavy Silken Thread, 4 Cured Thick Hide
Heavy Scorpid Bracers	255	Found	4 Rugged Leather, 4 Heavy Scorpid Scale, 1 Rune Thread
Wicked Leather Gauntlets	260	Found	8 Rugged Leather, 1 Black Dye, 1 Rune Thread
Green Dragonscale Breastplate	260	Found	20 Rugged Leather, 25 Green Dragonscale, 2 Rune Thread
Blackstorm Leggings	260	Trained	10 Rugged Leather, 8 Breath of Wind, 2 Cured Thick Hide, 1 Rune Thread
Dragonstrike Leggings	260	Trained	10 Rugged Leather, 10 Worn Dragonscale, 2 Heart of Fire, 2 Cured Thick Hide, 1 Rune Thread
Wildfeather Leggings	260	Trained	10 Rugged Leather, 40 Jet Black Feather, 4 Wildvine, 2 Cured Thick Hide, 1 Rune Thread
Heavy Scorpid Vest	265	Found	6 Rugged Leather, 6 Heavy Scorpid Scale, 1 Rune Thread
Wicked Leather Bracers	265	Found	8 Rugged Leather, 1 Black Dye, 1 Rune Thread
Chimeric Gloves	265	Found	6 Rugged Leather, 6 Chimera Leather, 1 Rune Thread
Runic Leather Gauntlets	270	Found	10 Rugged Leather, 6 Runecloth, 1 Rune Thread
Volcanic Leggings	270	Found	6 Rugged Leather, 1 Essence of Fire, 1 Core of Earth, 1 Rune Thread
Green Dragonscale Leggings	270	Found	20 Rugged Leather, 25 Green Dragonscale, 1 Rune Thread
Living Shoulders	270	Found	12 Rugged Leather, 4 Living Essence, 1 Rune Thread
Ironfeather Shoulders	270	Found	24 Rugged Leather, 80 Ironfeather, 2 Jade, 1 Rune Thread
Chimeric Boots	275	Found	4 Rugged Leather, 8 Chimera Leather, 1 Rune Thread
Heavy Scorpid Gauntlets	275	Found	6 Rugged Leather, 8 Heavy Scorpid Scale, 1 Rune Thread
Runic Leather Bracers	275	Found	6 Rugged Leather, 1 Black Pearl, 6 Runecloth, 1 Rune Thread
Frostsaber Boots	275	Found	4 Rugged Leather, 6 Frostsaber Leather, 1 Rune Thread
Stormshroud Pants	275	Found	16 Rugged Leather, 2 Essence of Water, 2 Essence of Air, 1 Rune Thread
Warbear Harness	275	Found	28 Rugged Leather, 12 Warbear Leather, 1 Rune Thread
Heavy Scorpid Belt	280	Found	6 Rugged Leather, 8 Heavy Scorpid Scale, 1 Rune Thread
Wicked Leather Headband	280	Found	12 Rugged Leather, 1 Black Dye, 1 Rune Thread
Runic Leather Belt	280	Found	12 Rugged Leather, 10 Runecloth, 1 Rune Thread
Chimeric Leggings	280	Found	8 Rugged Leather, 8 Chimera Leather, 1 Rune Thread
Green Dragonscale Gauntlets	280	Trained	20 Rugged Leather, 30 Green Dragonscale, 1 Cured Rugged Hide, 2 Rune Thread

Leatherworking			
Created Item	Skill Lvl	Source	Reagent(s)
Frostsaber Leggings	285	Found	6 Rugged Leather, 8 Frostsaber Leather, 1 Rune Thread
Heavy Scorpid Leggings	285	Found	8 Rugged Leather, 12 Heavy Scorpid Scale, 1 Rune Thread
Volcanic Breastplate	285	Found	8 Rugged Leather, 1 Essence of Fire, 1 Essence of Earth, 1 Rune Thread
Blue Dragonscale Breastplate	285	Found	28 Rugged Leather, 30 Blue Dragonscale, 1 Cured Rugged Hide, 1 Rune Thread
Living Leggings	285	Found	16 Rugged Leather, 6 Living Essence, 1 Cured Rugged Hide, 1 Rune Thread
Stormshroud Armor	285	Found	16 Rugged Leather, 3 Essence of Water, 3 Essence of Air, 1 Cured Rugged Hide, 1 Rune Thread
Warbear Woolies	285	Found	24 Rugged Leather, 14 Warbear Leather, 1 Rune Thread
Chimeric Vest	290	Found	10 Rugged Leather, 10 Chimera Leather, 1 Rune Thread
Black Dragonscale Breastplate	290	Found	40 Rugged Leather, 60 Black Dragonscale, 1 Cured Rugged Hide, 2 Rune Thread
Devilsaur Gauntlets	290	Found	30 Rugged Leather, 8 Devilsaur Leather, 1 Rune Thread
Ironfeather Breastplate	290	Found	40 Rugged Leather, 120 Ironfeather, 1 Jade, 1 Cured Rugged Hide, 1 Rune Thread
Runic Leather Headband	290	Found	14 Rugged Leather, 10 Runecloth, 1 Rune Thread
Wicked Leather Pants	290	Found	16 Rugged Leather, 1 Cured Rugged Hide, 3 Black Dye, 1 Rune Thread
Might of the Timbermaw	290	Found	30 Rugged Leather, 2 Powerful Mojo, 4 Living Essence, 2 Cured Rugged Hide, 2 Rune Thread
Dawn Treaders	290	Found	30 Rugged Leather, 2 Guardian Stone, 4 Essence of Water, 2 Cured Rugged Hide, 2 Rune Thread
Blue Dragonscale Shoulders	295	Found	28 Rugged Leather, 30 Blue Dragonscale, 2 Enchanted Leather, 1 Cured Rugged Hide, 1 Rune Thread
Frostsaber Gloves	295	Found	6 Rugged Leather, 10 Frostsaber Leather, 1 Rune Thread
Heavy Scorpid Helm	295	Found	8 Rugged Leather, 12 Heavy Scorpid Scale, 1 Cured Rugged Hide, 1 Rune Thread
Stormshroud Shoulders	295	Found	12 Rugged Leather, 3 Essence of Water, 3 Essence of Air, 2 Enchanted Leather, 1 Rune Thread
Corehound Boots	295	Found	20 Core Leather, 6 Fiery Core, 2 Lava Core, 2 Rune Thread
Red Dragonscale Breastplate	300	Found	40 Rugged Leather, 30 Red Dragonscale, 1 Rune Thread
Black Dragonscale Shoulders	300	Found	44 Rugged Leather, 45 Black Dragonscale, 2 Enchanted Leather, 1 Cured Rugged Hide, 1 Rune Thread
Devilsaur Leggings	300	Found	30 Rugged Leather, 14 Devilsaur Leather, 1 Cured Rugged Hide, 1 Rune Thread
Living Breastplate	300	Found	16 Rugged Leather, 8 Living Essence, 2 Mooncloth, 1 Cured Rugged Hide, 2 Rune Thread
Onyxia Scale Cloak	300	Found	1 Scale of Onyxia, 1 Cindercloth Cloak, 1 Rune Thread
Runic Leather Pants	300	Found	18 Rugged Leather, 12 Runecloth, 2 Enchanted Leather, 1 Rune Thread
Wicked Leather Belt	300	Found	14 Rugged Leather, 2 Black Dye, 2 Rune Thread
Heavy Scorpid Shoulders	300	Found	14 Rugged Leather, 14 Heavy Scorpid Scale, 1 Cured Rugged Hide, 2 Rune Thread

Leatherworking			
Created Item	Skill Lvl	Source	Reagent(s)
Runic Leather Armor	300	Found	22 Rugged Leather, 4 Enchanted Leather, 16 Runecloth, 1 Cured Rugged Hide, 2 Rune Thread
Volcanic Shoulders	300	Found	10 Rugged Leather, 1 Essence of Fire, 1 Essence of Earth, 2 Rune Thread
Wicked Leather Armor	300	Found	20 Rugged Leather, 2 Cured Rugged Hide, 2 Felcloth, 4 Black Dye, 2 Rune Thread
Black Dragonscale Leggings	300	Found	40 Rugged Leather, 60 Black Dragonscale, 4 Enchanted Leather, 1 Cured Rugged Hide, 2 Rune Thread
Frostsaber Tunic	300	Found	12 Rugged Leather, 12 Frostsaber Leather, 1 Cured Rugged Hide, 2 Rune Thread
Onyxia Scale Breastplate	300	Found	40 Rugged Leather, 12 Scale of Onyxia, 60 Black Dragonscale, 2 Rune Thread
Runic Leather Shoulders	300	Found	16 Rugged Leather, 4 Enchanted Leather, 18 Runecloth, 1 Cured Rugged Hide, 2 Rune Thread
Molten Helm	300	Found	15 Core Leather, 3 Fiery Core, 6 Lava Core, 2 Rune Thread
Black Dragonscale Boots	300	Found	6 Enchanted Leather, 30 Black Dragonscale, 4 Fiery Core, 3 Lava Core, 2 Rune Thread
Core Armor Kit	300	Found	3 Core Leather, 2 Rune Thread
Girdle of Insight	300	Found	12 Rugged Leather, 12 Powerful Mojo, 2 Cured Rugged Hide, 4 Rune Thread
Mongoose Boots	300	Found	12 Rugged Leather, 6 Essence of Air, 4 Black Diamond, 2 Cured Rugged Hide, 4 Rune Thread
Swift Flight Bracers	300	Found	12 Rugged Leather, 8 Larval Acid, 60 Ironfeather, 4 Cured Rugged Hide, 4 Rune Thread
Chromatic Cloak	300	Found	30 Rugged Leather, 12 Brilliant Chromatic Scale, 30 Black Dragonscale, 30 Red Dragonscale, 5 Cured Rugged Hide, 8 Rune Thread
Hide of the Wild	300	Found	30 Rugged Leather, 12 Living Essence, 10 Essence of Water, 8 Larval Acid, 3 Cured Rugged Hide, 8 Rune Thread
Shifting Cloak	300	Found	30 Rugged Leather, 12 Essence of Air, 4 Skin of Shadow, 8 Guardian Stone, 4 Cured Rugged Hide, 8 Rune Thread
Timbermaw Brawlers	300	Found	8 Enchanted Leather, 6 Powerful Mojo, 6 Living Essence, 2 Cured Rugged Hide, 2 Ironweb Spider Silk
Golden Mantle of the Dawn	300	Found	8 Enchanted Leather, 4 Living Essence, 4 Guardian Stone, 2 Cured Rugged Hide, 2 Rune Thread
Lava Belt	300	Found	5 Lava Core, 4 Cured Rugged Hide, 4 Ironweb Spider Silk
Chromatic Gauntlets	300	Found	5 Fiery Core, 2 Lava Core, 4 Core Leather, 4 Brilliant Chromatic Scale, 4 Cured Rugged Hide, 4 Ironweb Spider Silk
Corehound Belt	300	Found	8 Fiery Core, 12 Core Leather, 10 Enchanted Leather, 4 Cured Rugged Hide, 4 Ironweb Spider Silk
Molten Belt	300	Found	2 Fiery Core, 7 Lava Core, 6 Essence of Earth, 4 Cured Rugged Hide, 4 Ironweb Spider Silk
Blood Tiger Breastplate	300	Found	35 Primal Tiger Leather, 2 Bloodvine, 3 Cured Rugged Hide, 3 Rune Thread
Blood Tiger Shoulders	300	Found	25 Primal Tiger Leather, 2 Bloodvine, 3 Cured Rugged Hide, 3 Rune Thread
Primal Batskin Bracers	300	Found	8 Primal Bat Leather, 3 Cured Rugged Hide, 4 Living Essence, 3 Rune Thread
Primal Batskin Gloves	300	Found	10 Primal Bat Leather, 4 Cured Rugged Hide, 4 Living Essence, 3 Rune Thread

Leatherworking

Created Item	Skill Lvl	Source	Reagent(s)
Primal Batskin Jerkin	300	Found	14 Primal Bat Leather, 5 Cured Rugged Hide, 4 Living Essence, 4 Rune Thread
Blue Dragonscale Leggings	300	Trained	28 Rugged Leather, 36 Blue Dragonscale, 2 Cured Rugged Hide, 2 Rune Thread
Spitfire Bracers	300	Found	1 Light Silithid Carapace, 20 Silithid Chitin, 2 Essence of Fire
Spitfire Gauntlets	300	Found	2 Light Silithid Carapace, 30 Silithid Chitin, 2 Essence of Fire, 1 Cured Rugged Hide
Spitfire Breastplate	300	Found	3 Light Silithid Carapace, 40 Silithid Chitin, 2 Essence of Fire, 2 Cured Rugged Hide
Sandstalker Bracers	300	Found	1 Heavy Silithid Carapace, 20 Silithid Chitin, 2 Larval Acid
Sandstalker Gauntlets	300	Found	2 Heavy Silithid Carapace, 30 Silithid Chitin, 2 Larval Acid, 1 Cured Rugged Hide
Sandstalker Breastplate	300	Found	3 Heavy Silithid Carapace, 40 Silithid Chitin, 2 Larval Acid, 2 Cured Rugged Hide
Dreamscale Breastplate	300	Found	12 Enchanted Leather, 6 Dreamscale, 4 Living Essence, 4 Cured Rugged Hide, 6 Ironweb Spider Silk
Stormshroud Gloves	300	Found	6 Enchanted Leather, 4 Essence of Water, 4 Essence of Air, 2 Cured Rugged Hide, 2 Ironweb Spider Silk
Icy Scale Bracers	300	Found	4 Frozen Rune, 16 Heavy Scorpid Scale, 2 Essence of Water, 2 Cured Rugged Hide, 4 Ironweb Spider Silk
Icy Scale Breastplate	300	Found	7 Frozen Rune, 24 Heavy Scorpid Scale, 2 Essence of Water, 4 Cured Rugged Hide, 4 Ironweb Spider Silk
Icy Scale Gauntlets	300	Found	5 Frozen Rune, 16 Heavy Scorpid Scale, 2 Essence of Water, 3 Cured Rugged Hide, 4 Ironweb Spider Silk
Polar Bracers	300	Found	4 Frozen Rune, 12 Enchanted Leather, 2 Essence of Water, 2 Cured Rugged Hide, 4 Ironweb Spider Silk
Polar Gloves	300	Found	5 Frozen Rune, 12 Enchanted Leather, 2 Essence of Water, 3 Cured Rugged Hide, 4 Ironweb Spider Silk
Polar Tunic	300	Found	7 Frozen Rune, 16 Enchanted Leather, 2 Essence of Water, 4 Cured Rugged Hide, 4 Ironweb Spider Silk
Bramblewood Belt	300	Found	4 Enchanted Leather, 2 Living Essence, 1 Cured Rugged Hide
Bramblewood Boots	300	Found	6 Enchanted Leather, 2 Larval Acid, 2 Living Essence, 2 Cured Rugged Hide
Bramblewood Helm	300	Found	12 Enchanted Leather, 2 Bloodvine, 2 Living Essence, 2 Cured Rugged Hide
Knothide Leather	300	Trained	5 Knothide Leather Scraps
Knothide Armor Kit	300	Trained	6 Knothide Leather
Felscale Gloves	300	Trained	5 Knothide Leather, 1 Fel Scales, 2 Rune Thread
Scaled Draenic Pants	300	Trained	6 Knothide Leather, 3 Fel Scales, 2 Rune Thread
Thick Draenic Gloves	300	Trained	6 Knothide Leather, 2 Rune Thread
Wild Draenish Boots	300	Trained	6 Knothide Leather, 3 Rune Thread
Comfortable Insoles	300	Found	2 Knothide Leather
Gordok Ogre Suit	N/A	Special	4 Rugged Leather, 2 Bolt of Runecloth, 1 Ogre Tannin, 1 Rune Thread
Felscale Boots	310	Trained	8 Knothide Leather, 1 Fel Scales, 2 Rune Thread
Scaled Draenic Gloves	310	Trained	8 Knothide Leather, 1 Fel Scales, 2 Rune Thread
Wild Draenish Gloves	310	Trained	9 Knothide Leather, 3 Rune Thread
Thick Draenic Pants	315	Trained	10 Knothide Leather, 2 Rune Thread
Felscale Pants	320	Trained	10 Knothide Leather, 3 Fel Scales, 3 Rune Thread
Thick Draenic Boots	320	Trained	10 Knothide Leather, 3 Rune Thread
Wild Draenish Leggings	320	Trained	13 Knothide Leather, 3 Rune Thread
Heavy Knothide Leather	325	Found	5 Knothide Leather
Vindicator's Armor Kit	325	Found	3 Heavy Knothide Leather, 1 Primal Earth
Magister's Armor Kit	325	Found	3 Heavy Knothide Leather, 1 Primal Mana
Scaled Draenic Vest	325	Trained	12 Knothide Leather, 3 Fel Scales, 3 Rune Thread
Reinforced Mining Bag	325	Found	6 Heavy Knothide Leather, 4 Primal Earth
Thick Draenic Vest	330	Trained	14 Knothide Leather, 3 Rune Thread
Wild Draenish Vest	330	Trained	15 Knothide Leather, 3 Rune Thread
Golden Dragonstrike Breastplate	330	Trained	20 Knothide Leather, 8 Black Dragonscale, 3 Primal Fire, 2 Rune Thread
Living Crystal Breastplate	330	Trained	20 Knothide Leather, 12 Crystal Infused Leather, 3 Primal Life, 2 Rune Thread
Primalstorm Breastplate	330	Trained	20 Knothide Leather, 2 Primal Air, 2 Primal Earth, 2 Rune Thread
Felscale Breastplate	335	Trained	14 Knothide Leather, 3 Fel Scales, 3 Rune Thread
Scaled Draenic Boots	335	Trained	12 Knothide Leather, 2 Fel Scales, 3 Rune Thread
Cobrahide Leg Armor	335	Found	4 Heavy Knothide Leather, 2 Cobra Scales, 4 Primal Air
Clefthide Leg Armor	335	Found	4 Heavy Knothide Leather, 8 Thick Clefthoof Leather, 4 Primal Earth
Fel Leather Gloves	340	Found	6 Heavy Knothide Leather, 6 Fel Hide, 6 Primal Shadow, 3 Rune Thread
Netherfury Belt	340	Found	4 Heavy Knothide Leather, 8 Crystal Infused Leather, 3 Primal Water, 3 Primal Mana, 2 Rune Thread
Netherfury Leggings	340	Found	8 Heavy Knothide Leather, 12 Crystal Infused Leather, 5 Primal Water, 5 Primal Mana, 2 Rune Thread
Shadow Armor Kit	340	Found	4 Heavy Knothide Leather, 4 Primal Life
Flame Armor Kit	340	Found	4 Heavy Knothide Leather, 4 Primal Water
Frost Armor Kit	340	Found	4 Heavy Knothide Leather, 4 Primal Fire
Nature Armor Kit	340	Found	4 Heavy Knothide Leather, 4 Primal Shadow
Arcane Armor Kit	340	Found	4 Heavy Knothide Leather, 4 Primal Mana
Drums of War	340	Trained	2 Heavy Knothide Leather, 1 Primal Fire, 2 Thick Clefthoof Leather
Drums of Speed	345	Found	2 Heavy Knothide Leather, 1 Primal Air
Riding Crop	350	Found	4 Heavy Knothide Leather, 1 Primal Might, 6 Arcane Dust, 1 Small Prismatic Shard
Stylin' Purple Hat	350	Found	6 Heavy Knothide Leather, 2 Cobra Scales, 8 Primal Shadow, 4 Zhevra Leather, 3 Rune Thread
Stylin' Adventure Hat	350	Found	6 Heavy Knothide Leather, 2 Cobra Scales, 8 Primal Life, 4 Zhevra Leather, 3 Rune Thread
Stylin' Jungle Hat	350	Found	6 Heavy Knothide Leather, 2 Cobra Scales, 8 Primal Earth, 3 Rune Thread
Stylin' Crimson Hat	350	Found	6 Heavy Knothide Leather, 2 Cobra Scales, 8 Primal Fire, 4 Zhevra Leather, 3 Rune Thread
Fel Leather Boots	350	Found	10 Heavy Knothide Leather, 8 Fel Hide, 8 Primal Shadow, 3 Rune Thread
Fel Leather Leggings	350	Found	10 Heavy Knothide Leather, 10 Fel Hide, 10 Primal Shadow, 3 Rune Thread
Felstalker Belt	350	Found	6 Heavy Knothide Leather, 4 Fel Hide, 8 Crystal Infused Leather, 6 Primal Air, 2 Rune Thread
Netherfury Boots	350	Found	6 Heavy Knothide Leather, 10 Crystal Infused Leather, 4 Primal Water, 4 Primal Mana, 2 Rune Thread

Leatherworking			
Created Item	Skill Lvl	Source	Reagent(s)
Enchanted Felscale Boots	350	Found	4 Heavy Knothide Leather, 10 Fel Scales, 6 Primal Mana
Enchanted Felscale Gloves	350	Found	4 Heavy Knothide Leather, 10 Fel Scales, 6 Primal Mana
Enchanted Felscale Leggings	350	Found	6 Heavy Knothide Leather, 12 Fel Scales, 8 Primal Mana
Flamescale Belt	350	Found	4 Heavy Knothide Leather, 8 Crystal Infused Leather, 3 Primal Fire, 3 Primal Water
Flamescale Boots	350	Found	4 Heavy Knothide Leather, 8 Crystal Infused Leather, 3 Primal Fire, 3 Primal Water
Flamescale Leggings	350	Found	6 Heavy Knothide Leather, 12 Crystal Infused Leather, 4 Primal Fire, 4 Primal Water
Enchanted Clefthoof Boots	350	Found	4 Heavy Knothide Leather, 16 Thick Clefthoof Leather, 6 Primal Mana
Enchanted Clefthoof Gloves	350	Found	4 Heavy Knothide Leather, 16 Thick Clefthoof Leather, 6 Primal Mana
Enchanted Clefthoof Leggings	350	Found	6 Heavy Knothide Leather, 24 Thick Clefthoof Leather, 8 Primal Mana
Blastguard Belt	350	Found	4 Heavy Knothide Leather, 6 Fel Hide, 3 Primal Fire, 3 Primal Water
Blastguard Boots	350	Found	4 Heavy Knothide Leather, 8 Fel Hide, 3 Primal Fire, 3 Primal Water
Blastguard Pants	350	Found	6 Heavy Knothide Leather, 10 Fel Hide, 4 Primal Fire, 4 Primal Water
Drums of Restoration	350	Found	2 Heavy Knothide Leather, 2 Primal Life
Heavy Clefthoof Leggings	355	Found	6 Heavy Knothide Leather, 34 Thick Clefthoof Leather, 4 Primal Earth, 2 Rune Thread
Heavy Clefthoof Boots	355	Found	4 Heavy Knothide Leather, 20 Thick Clefthoof Leather, 4 Primal Earth, 2 Rune Thread
Heavy Clefthoof Vest	360	Found	6 Heavy Knothide Leather, 40 Thick Clefthoof Leather, 4 Primal Earth, 2 Rune Thread
Felstalker Bracer	360	Found	6 Heavy Knothide Leather, 6 Fel Hide, 6 Crystal Infused Leather, 4 Primal Air, 2 Rune Thread
Felstalker Breastplate	360	Found	10 Heavy Knothide Leather, 4 Fel Hide, 8 Crystal Infused Leather, 8 Primal Air, 2 Rune Thread
Drums of Battle	365	Found	2 Heavy Knothide Leather, 1 Primal Fire, 1 Primal Earth
Nethercobra Leg Armor	365	Found	4 Heavy Knothide Leather, 4 Cobra Scales, 8 Primal Air, 1 Primal Nether
Nethercleft Leg Armor	365	Found	4 Heavy Knothide Leather, 16 Thick Clefthoof Leather, 8 Primal Earth, 1 Primal Nether
Cobrascale Gloves	365	Found	4 Heavy Knothide Leather, 8 Cobra Scales, 12 Primal Air, 12 Primal Shadow, 1 Primal Nether
Cobrascale Hood	365	Found	6 Heavy Knothide Leather, 10 Cobra Scales, 15 Primal Air, 15 Primal Shadow, 1 Primal Nether
Earthen Netherscale Boots	365	Found	4 Heavy Knothide Leather, 24 Nether Dragonscales, 22 Primal Earth, 4 Primal Mana, 1 Primal Nether
Gloves of the Living Touch	365	Found	4 Heavy Knothide Leather, 16 Primal Life, 12 Primal Earth, 1 Primal Nether
Hood of Primal Life	365	Found	6 Heavy Knothide Leather, 20 Primal Life, 8 Primal Water, 1 Primal Nether
Living Dragonscale Helm	365	Found	6 Heavy Knothide Leather, 28 Nether Dragonscales, 12 Primal Life, 12 Primal Mana, 1 Primal Nether
Netherdrake Gloves	365	Found	4 Heavy Knothide Leather, 24 Nether Dragonscales, 14 Primal Fire, 10 Primal Mana, 1 Primal Nether

Leatherworking			
Created Item	Skill Lvl	Source	Reagent(s)
Netherdrake Helm	365	Found	6 Heavy Knothide Leather, 28 Nether Dragonscales, 18 Primal Fire, 12 Primal Mana, 1 Primal Nether
Thick Netherscale Breastplate	365	Found	8 Heavy Knothide Leather, 32 Nether Dragonscales, 20 Primal Earth, 8 Primal Air, 1 Primal Nether
Windslayer Wraps	365	Found	4 Heavy Knothide Leather, 12 Wind Scales, 18 Primal Earth, 8 Primal Air, 1 Primal Nether
Windscale Hood	365	Found	6 Heavy Knothide Leather, 20 Wind Scales, 18 Primal Air, 10 Primal Mana, 1 Primal Nether
Windstrike Gloves	365	Found	4 Heavy Knothide Leather, 14 Wind Scales, 14 Primal Air, 10 Primal Fire, 1 Primal Nether
Drums of Panic	370	Found	2 Heavy Knothide Leather, 2 Primal Shadow
Ebon Netherscale Belt	375	Trained	6 Heavy Knothide Leather, 24 Nether Dragonscales, 12 Primal Fire, 12 Primal Shadow, 1 Primal Nether
Ebon Netherscale Bracers	375	Trained	4 Heavy Knothide Leather, 18 Nether Dragonscales, 8 Primal Fire, 8 Primal Shadow
Ebon Netherscale Breastplate	375	Trained	8 Heavy Knothide Leather, 30 Nether Dragonscales, 16 Primal Fire, 16 Primal Shadow, 2 Primal Nether
Netherstrike Belt	375	Trained	6 Heavy Knothide Leather, 24 Nether Dragonscales, 12 Primal Mana, 12 Primal Air, 1 Primal Nether
Netherstrike Bracers	375	Trained	4 Heavy Knothide Leather, 18 Nether Dragonscales, 8 Primal Mana, 8 Primal Air
Netherstrike Breastplate	375	Trained	8 Heavy Knothide Leather, 30 Nether Dragonscales, 16 Primal Mana, 16 Primal Air, 2 Primal Nether
Primalstrike Belt	375	Trained	6 Heavy Knothide Leather, 5 Primal Might, 1 Primal Nether
Primalstrike Bracers	375	Trained	4 Heavy Knothide Leather, 3 Primal Might
Primalstrike Vest	375	Trained	8 Heavy Knothide Leather, 6 Primal Might, 2 Primal Nether
Windhawk Belt	375	Trained	6 Heavy Knothide Leather, 16 Wind Scales, 12 Primal Air, 2 Primal Might, 1 Primal Nether
Windhawk Bracers	375	Trained	4 Heavy Knothide Leather, 12 Wind Scales, 8 Primal Air, 1 Primal Might
Windhawk Hauberk	375	Trained	8 Heavy Knothide Leather, 20 Wind Scales, 16 Primal Air, 3 Primal Might, 2 Primal Nether
Belt of Natural Power	375	Found	5 Nether Vortex, 4 Heavy Knothide Leather, 4 Primal Life, 2 Rune Thread
Belt of Deep Shadow	375	Found	5 Nether Vortex, 4 Heavy Knothide Leather, 4 Primal Shadow, 2 Rune Thread
Belt of the Black Eagle	375	Found	4 Nether Vortex, 4 Heavy Knothide Leather, 4 Primal Air, 6 Wind Scales, 2 Rune Thread
Monsoon Belt	375	Found	4 Nether Vortex, 4 Heavy Knothide Leather, 4 Primal Water, 6 Wind Scales, 2 Rune Thread
Boots of Natural Grace	375	Found	2 Primal Nether, 4 Heavy Knothide Leather, 12 Primal Life, 2 Rune Thread
Boots of Utter Darkness	375	Found	2 Primal Nether, 4 Heavy Knothide Leather, 12 Primal Shadow, 2 Rune Thread
Boots of the Crimson Hawk	375	Found	2 Primal Nether, 4 Heavy Knothide Leather, 10 Primal Air, 6 Wind Scales, 2 Rune Thread
Hurricane Boots	375	Found	2 Primal Nether, 4 Heavy Knothide Leather, 10 Primal Water, 6 Wind Scales, 2 Rune Thread

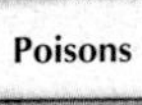

Poisons

Created Item	Skill Lvl	Source	Reagent(s)
Instant Poison	N/A	Special	1 Dust of Decay, 1 Empty Vial
Crippling Poison	1	Trained	1 Essence of Pain, 1 Empty Vial
Mind-numbing Poison	100	Trained	1 Dust of Decay, 1 Essence of Pain, 1 Empty Vial
Instant Poison II	120	Trained	3 Dust of Decay, 1 Leaded Vial
Deadly Poison	130	Trained	1 Deathweed, 1 Leaded Vial
Wound Poison	140	Trained	1 Essence of Pain, 1 Deathweed, 1 Leaded Vial
Blinding Powder	150	Trained	1 Fadeleaf
Instant Poison III	160	Trained	1 Dust of Deterioration, 1 Leaded Vial
Deadly Poison II	170	Trained	2 Deathweed, 1 Leaded Vial
Mind-numbing Poison II	170	Trained	4 Dust of Decay, 4 Essence of Pain, 1 Leaded Vial
Wound Poison II	180	Trained	1 Essence of Pain, 2 Deathweed, 1 Leaded Vial
Instant Poison IV	200	Trained	2 Dust of Deterioration, 1 Crystal Vial
Deadly Poison III	210	Trained	3 Deathweed, 1 Crystal Vial
Wound Poison III	220	Trained	1 Essence of Agony, 2 Deathweed, 1 Crystal Vial
Crippling Poison II	230	Trained	3 Essence of Agony, 1 Crystal Vial
Instant Poison V	240	Trained	3 Dust of Deterioration, 1 Crystal Vial
Mind-numbing Poison III	240	Trained	2 Dust of Deterioration, 2 Essence of Agony, 1 Crystal Vial
Deadly Poison IV	250	Trained	5 Deathweed, 1 Crystal Vial
Wound Poison IV	260	Trained	2 Essence of Agony, 2 Deathweed, 1 Crystal Vial
Instant Poison VI	280	Trained	4 Dust of Deterioration, 1 Crystal Vial
Deadly Poison V	280	Trained	7 Deathweed, 1 Crystal Vial
Deadly Poison VI	290	Trained	1 Maiden's Anguish, 1 Crystal Vial
Wound Poison V	300	Trained	3 Essence of Agony, 3 Deathweed, 1 Crystal Vial
Instant Poison VII	320	Trained	1 Maiden's Anguish, 1 Dust of Deterioration, 1 Crystal Vial
Deadly Poison VII	330	Trained	1 Maiden's Anguish, 1 Deathweed, 1 Crystal Vial
Anesthetic Poison	340	Trained	4 Lethargy Root, 1 Deathweed, 1 Crystal Vial

Tailoring

Created Item	Skill Lvl	Source	Reagent(s)
Bolt of Linen Cloth	N/A	Special	2 Linen Cloth
Linen Cloak	N/A	Special	1 Bolt of Linen Cloth, 1 Coarse Thread
Brown Linen Shirt	N/A	Special	1 Bolt of Linen Cloth, 1 Coarse Thread
Simple Linen Pants	N/A	Special	1 Bolt of Linen Cloth, 1 Coarse Thread
White Linen Shirt	1	Trained	1 Bolt of Linen Cloth, 1 Coarse Thread, 1 Bleach
Brown Linen Vest	10	Trained	1 Bolt of Linen Cloth, 1 Coarse Thread
Linen Belt	15	Trained	1 Bolt of Linen Cloth, 1 Coarse Thread
Simple Linen Boots	20	Trained	2 Bolt of Linen Cloth, 1 Light Leather, 1 Coarse Thread
Brown Linen Pants	30	Trained	2 Bolt of Linen Cloth, 1 Coarse Thread
Brown Linen Robe	30	Trained	3 Bolt of Linen Cloth, 1 Coarse Thread
White Linen Robe	30	Trained	3 Bolt of Linen Cloth, 1 Coarse Thread, 1 Bleach
Heavy Linen Gloves	35	Trained	2 Bolt of Linen Cloth, 1 Coarse Thread
Red Linen Robe	40	Found	3 Bolt of Linen Cloth, 2 Coarse Thread, 2 Red Dye
Red Linen Shirt	40	Trained	2 Bolt of Linen Cloth, 1 Coarse Thread, 1 Red Dye
Blue Linen Shirt	40	Trained	2 Bolt of Linen Cloth, 1 Coarse Thread, 1 Blue Dye

Tailoring

Created Item	Skill Lvl	Source	Reagent(s)
Simple Dress	40	Trained	2 Bolt of Linen Cloth, 1 Coarse Thread, 1 Blue Dye, 1 Bleach
Linen Bag	45	Trained	3 Bolt of Linen Cloth, 3 Coarse Thread
Blue Linen Vest	55	Found	3 Bolt of Linen Cloth, 1 Coarse Thread, 1 Blue Dye
Red Linen Vest	55	Found	3 Bolt of Linen Cloth, 1 Coarse Thread, 1 Red Dye
Reinforced Linen Cape	60	Trained	2 Bolt of Linen Cloth, 3 Coarse Thread
Green Linen Bracers	60	Trained	3 Bolt of Linen Cloth, 2 Coarse Thread, 1 Green Dye
Linen Boots	65	Trained	3 Bolt of Linen Cloth, 1 Coarse Thread, 1 Light Leather
Barbaric Linen Vest	70	Trained	4 Bolt of Linen Cloth, 1 Light Leather, 1 Fine Thread
Green Linen Shirt	70	Trained	3 Bolt of Linen Cloth, 1 Fine Thread, 1 Green Dye
Handstitched Linen Britches	70	Trained	4 Bolt of Linen Cloth, 2 Fine Thread
Red Linen Bag	70	Found	4 Bolt of Linen Cloth, 1 Fine Thread, 1 Red Dye
Blue Linen Robe	70	Found	4 Bolt of Linen Cloth, 2 Coarse Thread, 2 Blue Dye
Bolt of Woolen Cloth	75	Trained	3 Wool Cloth
Woolen Cape	75	Trained	1 Bolt of Woolen Cloth, 1 Fine Thread
Simple Kilt	75	Trained	4 Bolt of Linen Cloth, 1 Fine Thread
Soft-soled Linen Boots	80	Trained	5 Bolt of Linen Cloth, 2 Light Leather, 1 Fine Thread
Woolen Bag	80	Trained	3 Bolt of Woolen Cloth, 1 Fine Thread
Green Woolen Vest	85	Trained	2 Bolt of Woolen Cloth, 2 Fine Thread, 1 Green Dye
Heavy Woolen Gloves	85	Trained	3 Bolt of Woolen Cloth, 1 Fine Thread
Pearl-clasped Cloak	90	Trained	3 Bolt of Woolen Cloth, 2 Fine Thread, 1 Small Lustrous Pearl
Green Woolen Robe	90	Found	3 Bolt of Woolen Cloth, 2 Fine Thread, 1 Green Dye
Woolen Boots	95	Trained	4 Bolt of Woolen Cloth, 2 Fine Thread, 2 Light Leather
Red Woolen Boots	95	Found	4 Bolt of Woolen Cloth, 2 Light Leather, 1 Fine Thread, 2 Red Dye
Green Woolen Bag	95	Found	4 Bolt of Woolen Cloth, 1 Green Dye, 1 Fine Thread
Gray Woolen Shirt	100	Trained	2 Bolt of Woolen Cloth, 1 Fine Thread, 1 Gray Dye
Heavy Woolen Cloak	100	Found	3 Bolt of Woolen Cloth, 2 Fine Thread, 2 Small Lustrous Pearl
Blue Overalls	100	Found	4 Bolt of Woolen Cloth, 2 Fine Thread, 2 Blue Dye
Gray Woolen Robe	105	Found	4 Bolt of Woolen Cloth, 3 Fine Thread, 1 Gray Dye
Double-stitched Woolen Shoulders	110	Trained	3 Bolt of Woolen Cloth, 2 Fine Thread
Heavy Woolen Pants	110	Trained	5 Bolt of Woolen Cloth, 4 Fine Thread
Stylish Red Shirt	110	Trained	3 Bolt of Woolen Cloth, 2 Red Dye, 1 Fine Thread
White Woolen Dress	110	Trained	3 Bolt of Woolen Cloth, 4 Bleach, 1 Fine Thread
Red Woolen Bag	115	Found	4 Bolt of Woolen Cloth, 1 Red Dye, 1 Fine Thread
Greater Adept's Robe	115	Found	5 Bolt of Woolen Cloth, 3 Fine Thread, 3 Red Dye
Reinforced Woolen Shoulders	120	Found	6 Bolt of Woolen Cloth, 2 Medium Leather, 2 Fine Thread
Stylish Blue Shirt	120	Found	4 Bolt of Woolen Cloth, 2 Blue Dye, 1 Gray Dye, 1 Fine Thread

Tailoring			
Created Item	Skill Lvl	Source	Reagent(s)
Stylish Green Shirt	120	Found	4 Bolt of Woolen Cloth, 2 Green Dye, 1 Gray Dye, 1 Fine Thread
Colorful Kilt	120	Found	5 Bolt of Woolen Cloth, 3 Red Dye, 1 Fine Thread
Bolt of Silk Cloth	125	Trained	4 Silk Cloth
Phoenix Pants	125	Found	6 Bolt of Woolen Cloth, 1 Iridescent Pearl, 3 Fine Thread
Spidersilk Boots	125	Trained	2 Bolt of Silk Cloth, 4 Medium Leather, 4 Spider's Silk, 2 Iridescent Pearl
Phoenix Gloves	125	Found	4 Bolt of Woolen Cloth, 1 Iridescent Pearl, 4 Fine Thread, 2 Bleach
Gloves of Meditation	130	Trained	4 Bolt of Woolen Cloth, 3 Fine Thread, 1 Elixir of Wisdom
Bright Yellow Shirt	135	Found	1 Bolt of Silk Cloth, 1 Yellow Dye, 1 Fine Thread
Lesser Wizard's Robe	135	Trained	2 Bolt of Silk Cloth, 2 Fine Thread, 2 Spider's Silk
Spider Silk Slippers	140	Found	3 Bolt of Silk Cloth, 1 Spider's Silk, 2 Fine Thread
Azure Silk Pants	140	Trained	4 Bolt of Silk Cloth, 2 Blue Dye, 3 Fine Thread
Boots of Darkness	140	Found	3 Bolt of Silk Cloth, 2 Medium Leather, 1 Shadow Protection Potion, 2 Fine Thread
Azure Silk Gloves	145	Found	3 Bolt of Silk Cloth, 2 Heavy Leather, 2 Blue Dye, 2 Fine Thread
Azure Silk Hood	145	Trained	2 Bolt of Silk Cloth, 2 Blue Dye, 1 Fine Thread
Hands of Darkness	145	Found	3 Bolt of Silk Cloth, 2 Heavy Leather, 2 Shadow Protection Potion, 2 Fine Thread
Azure Silk Vest	150	Trained	5 Bolt of Silk Cloth, 4 Blue Dye
Small Silk Pack	150	Trained	3 Bolt of Silk Cloth, 2 Heavy Leather, 3 Fine Thread
Robes of Arcana	150	Found	4 Bolt of Silk Cloth, 2 Fine Thread, 2 Spider's Silk
Truefaith Gloves	150	Found	3 Bolt of Silk Cloth, 2 Heavy Leather, 4 Healing Potion, 1 Fine Thread
Dark Silk Shirt	155	Found	2 Bolt of Silk Cloth, 2 Gray Dye, 1 Fine Thread
White Swashbuckler's Shirt	160	Trained	3 Bolt of Silk Cloth, 2 Bleach, 1 Silken Thread
Silk Headband	160	Trained	3 Bolt of Silk Cloth, 2 Fine Thread
Enchanter's Cowl	165	Found	3 Bolt of Silk Cloth, 2 Fine Thread, 2 Thick Spider's Silk
Green Silk Armor	165	Found	5 Bolt of Silk Cloth, 2 Green Dye, 1 Silken Thread
Shadow Hood	170	Found	4 Bolt of Silk Cloth, 1 Silken Thread, 1 Shadow Oil
Formal White Shirt	170	Trained	3 Bolt of Silk Cloth, 2 Bleach, 1 Fine Thread
Earthen Vest	170	Trained	3 Bolt of Silk Cloth, 1 Elemental Earth, 2 Fine Thread
Bolt of Mageweave	175	Trained	5 Mageweave Cloth
Boots of the Enchanter	175	Found	4 Bolt of Silk Cloth, 1 Silken Thread, 2 Thick Spider's Silk
Green Silk Pack	175	Found	4 Bolt of Silk Cloth, 3 Heavy Leather, 3 Fine Thread, 1 Green Dye
Red Swashbuckler's Shirt	175	Trained	3 Bolt of Silk Cloth, 2 Red Dye, 1 Silken Thread
Azure Silk Belt	175	Trained	4 Bolt of Silk Cloth, 1 Elemental Water, 2 Blue Dye, 2 Fine Thread, 1 Iron Buckle
Crimson Silk Belt	175	Trained	4 Bolt of Silk Cloth, 1 Iron Buckle, 2 Red Dye, 1 Silken Thread
Azure Silk Cloak	175	Found	3 Bolt of Silk Cloth, 2 Blue Dye, 2 Fine Thread

Tailoring			
Created Item	Skill Lvl	Source	Reagent(s)
Spider Belt	180	Found	4 Bolt of Silk Cloth, 2 Thick Spider's Silk, 1 Iron Buckle
Green Silken Shoulders	180	Trained	5 Bolt of Silk Cloth, 2 Silken Thread
Crimson Silk Cloak	180	Found	5 Bolt of Silk Cloth, 2 Red Dye, 2 Fire Oil, 1 Silken Thread
Long Silken Cloak	185	Trained	4 Bolt of Silk Cloth, 1 Mana Potion, 1 Silken Thread
Rich Purple Silk Shirt	185	Found	4 Bolt of Silk Cloth, 1 Purple Dye, 1 Silken Thread
Black Silk Pack	185	Found	5 Bolt of Silk Cloth, 1 Black Dye, 4 Fine Thread
Crimson Silk Vest	185	Trained	4 Bolt of Silk Cloth, 2 Red Dye, 2 Fine Thread
Robe of Power	190	Trained	2 Bolt of Mageweave, 2 Elemental Earth, 2 Elemental Water, 2 Elemental Fire, 2 Elemental Air, 2 Silken Thread
Crimson Silk Shoulders	190	Found	5 Bolt of Silk Cloth, 2 Fire Oil, 2 Red Dye, 2 Silken Thread
Azure Shoulders	190	Found	6 Bolt of Silk Cloth, 2 Naga Scale, 2 Blue Dye, 2 Silken Thread
Green Holiday Shirt	190	Found	5 Bolt of Silk Cloth, 4 Green Dye, 1 Silken Thread
Earthen Silk Belt	195	Found	5 Bolt of Silk Cloth, 4 Elemental Earth, 4 Heavy Leather, 1 Iron Buckle, 2 Silken Thread
Crimson Silk Pantaloons	195	Trained	4 Bolt of Silk Cloth, 2 Red Dye, 2 Silken Thread
Icy Cloak	200	Found	3 Bolt of Mageweave, 2 Silken Thread, 1 Frost Oil, 2 Thick Spider's Silk
Star Belt	200	Found	4 Bolt of Mageweave, 4 Heavy Leather, 1 Citrine, 1 Iron Buckle, 1 Silken Thread
Black Swashbuckler's Shirt	200	Found	5 Bolt of Silk Cloth, 1 Black Dye, 1 Silken Thread
Crimson Silk Robe	205	Found	8 Bolt of Silk Cloth, 4 Elemental Fire, 2 Mana Potion, 4 Red Dye, 1 Silken Thread
Black Mageweave Vest	205	Trained	2 Bolt of Mageweave, 3 Silken Thread
Black Mageweave Leggings	205	Trained	2 Bolt of Mageweave, 3 Silken Thread
Crimson Silk Gloves	210	Trained	6 Bolt of Silk Cloth, 2 Elemental Fire, 2 Fire Oil, 2 Thick Leather, 4 Red Dye, 2 Silken Thread
Black Mageweave Robe	210	Trained	3 Bolt of Mageweave, 1 Heavy Silken Thread
Black Mageweave Gloves	215	Trained	2 Bolt of Mageweave, 2 Heavy Silken Thread
Red Mageweave Vest	215	Found	3 Bolt of Mageweave, 2 Red Dye, 1 Heavy Silken Thread
White Bandit Mask	215	Found	1 Bolt of Mageweave, 1 Bleach, 1 Heavy Silken Thread
Red Mageweave Pants	215	Found	3 Bolt of Mageweave, 2 Red Dye, 1 Heavy Silken Thread
Orange Mageweave Shirt	215	Trained	1 Bolt of Mageweave, 1 Orange Dye, 1 Heavy Silken Thread
Stormcloth Pants	220	Found	4 Bolt of Mageweave, 2 Globe of Water, 2 Heavy Silken Thread
Stormcloth Gloves	220	Found	3 Bolt of Mageweave, 2 Globe of Water, 2 Heavy Silken Thread
Orange Martial Shirt	220	Found	2 Bolt of Mageweave, 2 Orange Dye, 1 Heavy Silken Thread
Mageweave Bag	225	Trained	4 Bolt of Mageweave, 2 Silken Thread
Red Mageweave Gloves	225	Found	3 Bolt of Mageweave, 2 Red Dye, 2 Heavy Silken Thread
Dreamweave Gloves	225	Trained	4 Bolt of Mageweave, 4 Wildvine, 2 Heart of the Wild, 2 Heavy Silken Thread
Stormcloth Vest	225	Found	5 Bolt of Mageweave, 3 Globe of Water, 2 Heavy Silken Thread

Tailoring

Created Item	Skill Lvl	Source	Reagent(s)
Cindercloth Robe	225	Trained	5 Bolt of Mageweave, 2 Heart of Fire, 2 Heavy Silken Thread
Dreamweave Vest	225	Trained	6 Bolt of Mageweave, 6 Wildvine, 2 Heart of the Wild, 2 Heavy Silken Thread
Enchanted Mageweave Pouch	225	Found	4 Bolt of Mageweave, 4 Vision Dust, 2 Heavy Silken Thread
Black Mageweave Headband	230	Trained	3 Bolt of Mageweave, 2 Heavy Silken Thread
Black Mageweave Boots	230	Trained	3 Bolt of Mageweave, 2 Heavy Silken Thread, 2 Thick Leather
Black Mageweave Shoulders	230	Trained	3 Bolt of Mageweave, 2 Heavy Silken Thread
Lavender Mageweave Shirt	230	Found	2 Bolt of Mageweave, 2 Purple Dye, 2 Heavy Silken Thread
Simple Black Dress	235	Trained	3 Bolt of Mageweave, 1 Black Dye, 1 Heavy Silken Thread, 1 Bleach
Red Mageweave Shoulders	235	Found	4 Bolt of Mageweave, 2 Red Dye, 3 Heavy Silken Thread
Red Mageweave Bag	235	Trained	4 Bolt of Mageweave, 2 Red Dye, 2 Heavy Silken Thread
Pink Mageweave Shirt	235	Found	3 Bolt of Mageweave, 1 Pink Dye, 1 Heavy Silken Thread
Admiral's Hat	240	Found	3 Bolt of Mageweave, 6 Long Elegant Feather, 2 Heavy Silken Thread
Stormcloth Headband	240	Found	4 Bolt of Mageweave, 4 Globe of Water, 2 Heavy Silken Thread
Red Mageweave Headband	240	Found	4 Bolt of Mageweave, 2 Red Dye, 2 Heavy Silken Thread
Tuxedo Shirt	240	Found	4 Bolt of Mageweave, 2 Heavy Silken Thread
Shadoweave Pants	N/A	Special	3 Bolt of Mageweave, 2 Shadow Silk, 1 Heavy Silken Thread
Shadoweave Robe	N/A	Special	3 Bolt of Mageweave, 2 Shadow Silk, 1 Heavy Silken Thread
Shadoweave Gloves	N/A	Special	5 Bolt of Mageweave, 5 Shadow Silk, 2 Heavy Silken Thread
Shadoweave Shoulders	N/A	Special	5 Bolt of Mageweave, 4 Shadow Silk, 2 Heavy Silken Thread
Shadoweave Boots	N/A	Special	6 Bolt of Mageweave, 6 Shadow Silk, 3 Heavy Silken Thread, 2 Thick Leather
Shadoweave Mask	245	Found	2 Bolt of Mageweave, 8 Shadow Silk, 2 Heavy Silken Thread
Stormcloth Shoulders	245	Found	5 Bolt of Mageweave, 6 Globe of Water, 3 Heavy Silken Thread
Cindercloth Boots	245	Trained	5 Bolt of Mageweave, 1 Heart of Fire, 3 Heavy Silken Thread, 2 Thick Leather
Tuxedo Pants	245	Found	4 Bolt of Mageweave, 3 Heavy Silken Thread
Stormcloth Boots	250	Found	6 Bolt of Mageweave, 6 Globe of Water, 3 Heavy Silken Thread, 2 Thick Leather
White Wedding Dress	250	Found	5 Bolt of Mageweave, 3 Heavy Silken Thread
Dreamweave Circlet	250	Trained	8 Bolt of Mageweave, 4 Wildvine, 2 Heart of the Wild, 3 Heavy Silken Thread, 1 Truesilver Bar, 1 Jade
Tuxedo Jacket	250	Found	5 Bolt of Mageweave, 3 Heavy Silken Thread
Bolt of Runecloth	250	Trained	5 Runecloth
Mooncloth	250	Found	2 Felcloth
Mooncloth Boots	N/A	Special	6 Bolt of Runecloth, 4 Mooncloth, 2 Black Pearl, 1 Rune Thread
Festival Dress	250	Found	4 Bolt of Runecloth, 2 Firebloom, 2 Red Dye, 1 Rune Thread
Festive Red Pant Suit	250	Found	4 Bolt of Runecloth, 2 Firebloom, 2 Red Dye, 1 Rune Thread
Runecloth Belt	255	Trained	3 Bolt of Runecloth, 1 Rune Thread

Tailoring

Created Item	Skill Lvl	Source	Reagent(s)
Frostweave Tunic	255	Found	5 Bolt of Runecloth, 2 Globe of Water, 1 Rune Thread
Frostweave Robe	255	Found	5 Bolt of Runecloth, 2 Globe of Water, 1 Rune Thread
Runecloth Robe	260	Found	5 Bolt of Runecloth, 1 Ironweb Spider Silk, 1 Rune Thread
Runecloth Bag	260	Found	5 Bolt of Runecloth, 2 Rugged Leather, 1 Rune Thread
Runecloth Tunic	260	Found	5 Bolt of Runecloth, 1 Ironweb Spider Silk, 1 Rune Thread
Cindercloth Vest	260	Found	5 Bolt of Runecloth, 2 Heart of Fire, 1 Rune Thread
Soul Pouch	260	Found	6 Bolt of Runecloth, 4 Rugged Leather, 2 Ichor of Undeath, 1 Rune Thread
Runecloth Cloak	265	Found	4 Bolt of Runecloth, 1 Ironweb Spider Silk, 1 Rune Thread
Ghostweave Belt	265	Found	3 Bolt of Runecloth, 2 Ghost Dye, 1 Ironweb Spider Silk, 1 Rune Thread
Frostweave Gloves	265	Found	3 Bolt of Runecloth, 1 Essence of Water, 1 Rune Thread
Cindercloth Gloves	270	Found	4 Bolt of Runecloth, 2 Heart of Fire, 1 Rune Thread
Brightcloth Gloves	270	Found	4 Bolt of Runecloth, 2 Gold Bar, 1 Rune Thread
Ghostweave Gloves	270	Found	4 Bolt of Runecloth, 2 Ghost Dye, 1 Ironweb Spider Silk, 1 Rune Thread
Brightcloth Robe	270	Found	5 Bolt of Runecloth, 2 Gold Bar, 1 Rune Thread
Ghostweave Vest	275	Found	6 Bolt of Runecloth, 4 Ghost Dye, 1 Ironweb Spider Silk, 1 Rune Thread
Runecloth Gloves	275	Found	4 Bolt of Runecloth, 4 Rugged Leather, 1 Rune Thread
Cindercloth Cloak	275	Found	5 Bolt of Runecloth, 1 Essence of Fire, 1 Rune Thread
Felcloth Pants	275	Found	5 Bolt of Runecloth, 2 Felcloth, 1 Rune Thread
Brightcloth Cloak	275	Found	4 Bolt of Runecloth, 2 Gold Bar, 1 Rune Thread
Wizardweave Leggings	275	Found	6 Bolt of Runecloth, 1 Dream Dust, 1 Rune Thread
Cloak of Fire	275	Found	6 Bolt of Runecloth, 4 Essence of Fire, 4 Heart of Fire, 4 Elemental Fire, 1 Rune Thread
Enchanted Runecloth Bag	275	Found	5 Bolt of Runecloth, 2 Greater Eternal Essence, 2 Rune Thread
Cenarion Herb Bag	275	Found	5 Bolt of Runecloth, 10 Purple Lotus, 8 Morrowgrain, 2 Rune Thread
Runecloth Boots	280	Found	4 Bolt of Runecloth, 2 Ironweb Spider Silk, 4 Rugged Leather, 1 Rune Thread
Frostweave Pants	280	Found	6 Bolt of Runecloth, 1 Essence of Water, 1 Rune Thread
Cindercloth Pants	280	Found	6 Bolt of Runecloth, 1 Essence of Fire, 1 Rune Thread
Robe of Winter Night	285	Found	10 Bolt of Runecloth, 12 Felcloth, 4 Essence of Undeath, 4 Essence of Water, 1 Rune Thread
Felcloth Boots	285	Found	6 Bolt of Runecloth, 2 Felcloth, 4 Rugged Leather, 1 Rune Thread
Runecloth Pants	285	Found	6 Bolt of Runecloth, 2 Ironweb Spider Silk, 1 Rune Thread
Felcloth Bag	285	Found	12 Felcloth, 6 Enchanted Leather, 2 Dark Rune, 4 Ironweb Spider Silk
Brightcloth Pants	290	Found	6 Bolt of Runecloth, 4 Gold Bar, 1 Ironweb Spider Silk, 1 Rune Thread
Mooncloth Leggings	290	Found	6 Bolt of Runecloth, 4 Mooncloth, 1 Rune Thread

Tailoring

Created Item	Skill Lvl	Source	Reagent(s)
Ghostweave Pants	290	Found	6 Bolt of Runecloth, 4 Ghost Dye, 1 Rune Thread
Felcloth Hood	290	Found	5 Bolt of Runecloth, 2 Felcloth, 1 Rune Thread
Wisdom of the Timbermaw	290	Found	8 Bolt of Runecloth, 3 Essence of Earth, 3 Living Essence, 2 Ironweb Spider Silk
Argent Boots	290	Found	6 Bolt of Runecloth, 4 Enchanted Leather, 2 Golden Pearl, 2 Guardian Stone, 2 Ironweb Spider Silk
Runecloth Headband	295	Found	4 Bolt of Runecloth, 2 Ironweb Spider Silk, 1 Rune Thread
Gordok Ogre Suit	N/A	Special	2 Bolt of Runecloth, 4 Rugged Leather, 1 Ogre Tannin, 1 Rune Thread
Mooncloth Bag	300	Found	4 Bolt of Runecloth, 1 Mooncloth, 1 Rune Thread
Wizardweave Robe	300	Found	8 Bolt of Runecloth, 2 Dream Dust, 1 Rune Thread
Mooncloth Vest	300	Found	6 Bolt of Runecloth, 4 Mooncloth, 1 Rune Thread
Mooncloth Shoulders	300	Found	5 Bolt of Runecloth, 5 Mooncloth, 1 Rune Thread
Runecloth Shoulders	300	Found	7 Bolt of Runecloth, 2 Ironweb Spider Silk, 4 Rugged Leather, 1 Rune Thread
Wizardweave Turban	300	Found	6 Bolt of Runecloth, 4 Dream Dust, 1 Star Ruby, 1 Rune Thread
Felcloth Robe	300	Found	8 Bolt of Runecloth, 3 Felcloth, 2 Demonic Rune, 2 Rune Thread
Mooncloth Circlet	300	Found	4 Bolt of Runecloth, 6 Mooncloth, 1 Azerothian Diamond, 2 Enchanted Leather, 2 Rune Thread
Felcloth Shoulders	300	Found	7 Bolt of Runecloth, 3 Felcloth, 2 Demonic Rune, 4 Rugged Leather, 2 Rune Thread
Gloves of Spell Mastery	300	Found	10 Bolt of Runecloth, 10 Mooncloth, 10 Ghost Dye, 6 Golden Pearl, 6 Huge Emerald, 8 Enchanted Leather, 2 Rune Thread
Bottomless Bag	300	Found	8 Bolt of Runecloth, 12 Mooncloth, 2 Large Brilliant Shard, 2 Core Leather, 2 Rune Thread
Truefaith Vestments	300	Found	12 Bolt of Runecloth, 10 Mooncloth, 4 Righteous Orb, 4 Golden Pearl, 10 Ghost Dye, 2 Rune Thread
Robe of the Archmage	300	Found	12 Bolt of Runecloth, 10 Essence of Fire, 10 Essence of Air, 10 Essence of Earth, 10 Essence of Water, 2 Rune Thread
Robe of the Void	300	Found	12 Bolt of Runecloth, 20 Demonic Rune, 40 Felcloth, 12 Essence of Fire, 12 Essence of Undeath, 2 Rune Thread
Flarecore Mantle	300	Found	12 Bolt of Runecloth, 4 Fiery Core, 4 Lava Core, 6 Enchanted Leather, 2 Rune Thread
Flarecore Gloves	300	Found	8 Bolt of Runecloth, 6 Fiery Core, 4 Essence of Fire, 2 Enchanted Leather, 2 Rune Thread
Flarecore Wraps	300	Found	6 Mooncloth, 8 Fiery Core, 2 Essence of Fire, 6 Enchanted Leather, 4 Rune Thread
Belt of the Archmage	300	Found	16 Bolt of Runecloth, 10 Ghost Dye, 10 Mooncloth, 12 Essence of Water, 12 Essence of Fire, 6 Large Brilliant Shard, 6 Rune Thread
Felcloth Gloves	300	Found	12 Bolt of Runecloth, 20 Felcloth, 6 Demonic Rune, 8 Essence of Undeath, 2 Rune Thread
Inferno Gloves	300	Found	12 Bolt of Runecloth, 10 Essence of Fire, 2 Star Ruby, 2 Rune Thread
Mooncloth Gloves	300	Found	12 Bolt of Runecloth, 6 Mooncloth, 2 Golden Pearl, 2 Rune Thread

Tailoring

Created Item	Skill Lvl	Source	Reagent(s)
Cloak of Warding	300	Found	12 Bolt of Runecloth, 4 Guardian Stone, 1 Arcanite Bar, 2 Rune Thread
Mooncloth Robe	300	Found	6 Bolt of Runecloth, 4 Mooncloth, 2 Golden Pearl, 2 Rune Thread
Mantle of the Timbermaw	300	Found	5 Mooncloth, 5 Essence of Earth, 5 Living Essence, 2 Ironweb Spider Silk
Argent Shoulders	300	Found	5 Mooncloth, 2 Guardian Stone, 2 Ironweb Spider Silk
Flarecore Robe	300	Found	10 Mooncloth, 2 Fiery Core, 3 Lava Core, 6 Essence of Fire, 4 Ironweb Spider Silk
Flarecore Leggings	300	Found	8 Mooncloth, 5 Fiery Core, 3 Lava Core, 10 Essence of Fire, 4 Ironweb Spider Silk
Bloodvine Boots	300	Found	3 Mooncloth, 3 Bloodvine, 4 Enchanted Leather, 4 Bolt of Runecloth, 4 Ironweb Spider Silk
Bloodvine Leggings	300	Found	4 Mooncloth, 4 Bloodvine, 4 Powerful Mojo, 4 Bolt of Runecloth, 2 Ironweb Spider Silk
Bloodvine Vest	300	Found	3 Mooncloth, 5 Bloodvine, 4 Powerful Mojo, 4 Bolt of Runecloth, 2 Ironweb Spider Silk
Runed Stygian Belt	300	Found	2 Bolt of Runecloth, 6 Dark Rune, 2 Felcloth, 2 Enchanted Leather, 2 Ironweb Spider Silk
Runed Stygian Boots	300	Found	4 Bolt of Runecloth, 6 Dark Rune, 4 Felcloth, 2 Enchanted Leather, 2 Ironweb Spider Silk
Runed Stygian Leggings	300	Found	6 Bolt of Runecloth, 8 Dark Rune, 6 Felcloth, 2 Ironweb Spider Silk
Core Felcloth Bag	300	Found	20 Felcloth, 16 Core Leather, 8 Bloodvine, 4 Essence of Fire, 4 Ironweb Spider Silk
Bolt of Netherweave	300	Trained	6 Netherweave Cloth
Big Bag of Enchantment	300	Found	6 Bolt of Runecloth, 4 Large Brilliant Shard, 4 Enchanted Leather, 4 Ironweb Spider Silk
Satchel of Cenarius	300	Found	6 Bolt of Runecloth, 2 Mooncloth, 1 Black Lotus, 4 Ironweb Spider Silk
Gaea's Embrace	300	Found	1 Bloodvine, 2 Mooncloth, 4 Living Essence, 4 Ironweb Spider Silk
Glacial Cloak	300	Found	5 Frozen Rune, 4 Bolt of Runecloth, 2 Essence of Water, 4 Ironweb Spider Silk
Glacial Gloves	300	Found	5 Frozen Rune, 4 Bolt of Runecloth, 4 Essence of Water, 4 Ironweb Spider Silk
Glacial Vest	300	Found	7 Frozen Rune, 8 Bolt of Runecloth, 6 Essence of Water, 8 Ironweb Spider Silk
Glacial Wrists	300	Found	4 Frozen Rune, 2 Bolt of Runecloth, 2 Essence of Water, 4 Ironweb Spider Silk
Sylvan Crown	300	Found	4 Bolt of Runecloth, 2 Mooncloth, 2 Living Essence, 2 Ironweb Spider Silk
Sylvan Shoulders	300	Found	2 Bolt of Runecloth, 4 Living Essence, 2 Ironweb Spider Silk
Sylvan Vest	300	Found	4 Bolt of Runecloth, 2 Bloodvine, 2 Living Essence, 2 Ironweb Spider Silk
Netherweave Net	300	Trained	3 Netherweave Cloth
Netherweave Bracers	310	Trained	3 Bolt of Netherweave, 1 Rune Thread
Netherweave Belt	310	Trained	3 Bolt of Netherweave, 1 Rune Thread
Netherweave Bag	315	Trained	4 Bolt of Netherweave, 1 Rune Thread
Netherweave Gloves	320	Trained	4 Bolt of Netherweave, 2 Knothide Leather, 1 Rune Thread
Bolt of Imbued Netherweave	325	Found	3 Bolt of Netherweave, 2 Arcane Dust
Netherweave Pants	325	Trained	6 Bolt of Netherweave, 1 Rune Thread
Heavy Netherweave Net	325	Found	6 Netherweave Cloth
Netherweave Boots	335	Trained	6 Bolt of Netherweave, 2 Knothide Leather, 1 Rune Thread
Mystic Spellthread	335	Found	1 Rune Thread, 5 Primal Mana
Silver Spellthread	335	Found	1 Rune Thread, 5 Primal Life

Tailoring			
Created Item	Skill Lvl	Source	Reagent(s)
Imbued Netherweave Bag	340	Found	4 Bolt of Imbued Netherweave, 2 Netherweb Spider Silk, 1 Greater Planar Essence
Netherweave Robe	340	Found	8 Bolt of Netherweave, 2 Rune Thread
Imbued Netherweave Pants	340	Found	5 Bolt of Imbued Netherweave, 2 Netherweb Spider Silk, 1 Rune Thread
Bag of Jewels	340	Found	6 Bolt of Imbued Netherweave, 4 Knothide Leather
Bolt of Soulcloth	345	Found	1 Bolt of Netherweave, 8 Soul Essence
Netherweave Tunic	345	Found	8 Bolt of Netherweave, 2 Rune Thread
Primal Mooncloth	350	Found	1 Bolt of Imbued Netherweave, 1 Primal Life, 1 Primal Water
Imbued Netherweave Boots	350	Found	4 Bolt of Imbued Netherweave, 6 Knothide Leather, 2 Netherweb Spider Silk, 1 Rune Thread
Arcanoweave Bracers	350	Found	6 Bolt of Netherweave, 12 Arcane Dust, 2 Rune Thread
Unyielding Bracers	350	Found	4 Bolt of Imbued Netherweave, 8 Primal Earth
Bracers of Havok	350	Found	4 Bolt of Imbued Netherweave, 4 Primal Earth, 4 Primal Shadow
Blackstrike Bracers	350	Found	4 Bolt of Imbued Netherweave, 8 Primal Fire
Cloak of the Black Void	350	Found	6 Bolt of Imbued Netherweave, 3 Primal Mana, 3 Primal Shadow
Cloak of Eternity	350	Found	6 Bolt of Imbued Netherweave, 6 Primal Earth
White Remedy Cape	350	Found	6 Bolt of Imbued Netherweave, 6 Primal Life
Spellcloth	350	Found	1 Bolt of Imbued Netherweave, 1 Primal Mana, 1 Primal Fire
Shadowcloth	350	Found	1 Bolt of Imbued Netherweave, 1 Primal Shadow, 1 Primal Fire
Cloak of Arcane Evasion	350	Found	4 Bolt of Imbued Netherweave, 3 Primal Mana, 3 Primal Life, 2 Netherweb Spider Silk
Flameheart Bracers	350	Found	5 Bolt of Netherweave, 5 Primal Fire, 2 Rune Thread
Spellfire Belt	355	Found	4 Spellcloth, 10 Primal Fire, 2 Netherweb Spider Silk
Frozen Shadoweave Shoulders	355	Found	4 Shadowcloth, 10 Primal Water, 2 Netherweb Spider Silk
Primal Mooncloth Belt	355	Found	6 Primal Mooncloth, 2 Netherweb Spider Silk
Soulcloth Gloves	355	Found	5 Bolt of Soulcloth, 6 Knothide Leather, 4 Rune Thread
Lifeblood Belt	355	Found	6 Bolt of Netherweave, 4 Knothide Leather, 3 Primal Water, 3 Primal Life, 2 Netherweb Spider Silk
Lifeblood Bracers	355	Found	4 Bolt of Netherweave, 4 Knothide Leather, 2 Primal Water, 2 Primal Life, 2 Netherweb Spider Silk
Lifeblood Leggings	355	Found	10 Bolt of Netherweave, 5 Primal Water, 5 Primal Life, 2 Netherweb Spider Silk
Netherflame Belt	355	Found	6 Bolt of Netherweave, 4 Knothide Leather, 3 Primal Fire, 4 Primal Shadow, 2 Netherweb Spider Silk
Netherflame Boots	355	Found	6 Bolt of Netherweave, 4 Knothide Leather, 2 Primal Fire, 6 Primal Shadow, 2 Netherweb Spider Silk
Netherflame Robe	355	Found	10 Bolt of Netherweave, 5 Primal Fire, 6 Primal Shadow, 2 Netherweb Spider Silk
Imbued Netherweave Robe	360	Found	6 Bolt of Imbued Netherweave, 2 Netherweb Spider Silk, 1 Rune Thread
Imbued Netherweave Tunic	360	Found	6 Bolt of Imbued Netherweave, 2 Netherweb Spider Silk, 1 Rune Thread

Tailoring			
Created Item	Skill Lvl	Source	Reagent(s)
Arcanoweave Boots	360	Found	8 Bolt of Netherweave, 16 Arcane Dust, 2 Rune Thread
Flameheart Gloves	360	Found	7 Bolt of Netherweave, 7 Primal Fire, 2 Rune Thread
Spellfire Gloves	365	Found	8 Spellcloth, 12 Primal Fire, 4 Netherweb Spider Silk
Frozen Shadoweave Boots	365	Found	8 Shadowcloth, 12 Primal Water, 2 Netherweb Spider Silk
Primal Mooncloth Shoulders	365	Found	12 Primal Mooncloth, 2 Netherweb Spider Silk
Soulcloth Shoulders	365	Found	6 Bolt of Soulcloth, 4 Rune Thread
Unyielding Girdle	365	Found	8 Primal Mooncloth, 16 Primal Earth, 1 Primal Nether
Girdle of Ruination	365	Found	10 Shadowcloth, 16 Primal Fire, 1 Primal Nether
Black Belt of Knowledge	365	Found	6 Bolt of Imbued Netherweave, 14 Primal Mana, 1 Primal Nether
Resolute Cape	365	Found	10 Primal Mooncloth, 12 Primal Earth, 1 Primal Nether
Vengeance Wrap	365	Found	10 Shadowcloth, 14 Primal Air, 1 Primal Nether
Manaweave Cloak	365	Found	10 Spellcloth, 12 Primal Mana, 1 Primal Nether
Arcanoweave Robe	370	Found	12 Bolt of Netherweave, 20 Arcane Dust, 2 Rune Thread
Flameheart Vest	370	Found	9 Bolt of Netherweave, 9 Primal Fire, 2 Rune Thread
Spellfire Vest	375	Found	14 Spellcloth, 16 Primal Fire, 4 Netherweb Spider Silk
Spellfire Bag	375	Found	6 Spellcloth, 4 Greater Planar Essence, 4 Netherweb Spider Silk
Frozen Shadoweave Vest	375	Found	14 Shadowcloth, 16 Primal Water, 4 Netherweb Spider Silk
Ebon Shadowbag	375	Found	6 Shadowcloth, 4 Netherweb Spider Silk
Primal Mooncloth Robe	375	Found	20 Primal Mooncloth, 10 Primal Mana, 4 Netherweb Spider Silk
Primal Mooncloth Bag	375	Found	8 Primal Mooncloth, 4 Netherweb Spider Silk
Soulcloth Vest	375	Found	8 Bolt of Soulcloth, 4 Rune Thread
Runic Spellthread	375	Found	1 Rune Thread, 10 Primal Mana, 1 Primal Nether
Golden Spellthread	375	Found	1 Rune Thread, 10 Primal Life, 1 Primal Nether
Whitemend Pants	375	Found	10 Primal Mooncloth, 5 Primal Might, 1 Primal Nether
Spellstrike Pants	375	Found	10 Spellcloth, 5 Primal Might, 1 Primal Nether
Battlecast Pants	375	Found	12 Bolt of Imbued Netherweave, 8 Primal Might, 1 Primal Nether
Whitemend Hood	375	Found	10 Primal Mooncloth, 5 Primal Might, 1 Primal Nether
Spellstrike Hood	375	Found	10 Spellcloth, 5 Primal Might, 1 Primal Nether
Battlecast Hood	375	Found	12 Bolt of Imbued Netherweave, 8 Primal Might, 1 Primal Nether
Belt of Blasting	375	Found	5 Nether Vortex, 4 Bolt of Imbued Netherweave, 2 Primal Fire, 2 Rune Thread
Boots of Blasting	375	Found	2 Primal Nether, 4 Shadowcloth, 4 Spellcloth, 2 Rune Thread
Belt of the Long Road	375	Found	5 Nether Vortex, 4 Bolt of Imbued Netherweave, 2 Primal Life, 2 Rune Thread
Boots of the Long Road	375	Found	2 Primal Nether, 4 Primal Mooncloth, 4 Spellcloth, 2 Rune Thread

QUESTS

Ammen Vale

Title	Location	Faction	Race & Class	Group #	Starter	Finisher	Prerequisite	Reputation	Tradeskill	XP	Money
Welcome!	Ammen Vale	Alliance	All		Ammen Vale Gift Voucher	Jaeleil					
CHOICE OF: 1 Diablo Stone, or 1 Panda Collar, or 1 Zergling Leash											
You Survived!	Ammen Vale	Alliance	Draenei		Megelon	Proenitus				40	
Replenishing the Healing Crystals	Ammen Vale	Alliance	Draenei		Proenitus	Proenitus				80	15●
CHOICE OF: 1 Salvaged Leather Belt, or 1 Slightly Rusted Bracers, or 1 Worn Slippers											
Rescue the Survivors!	Ammen Vale	Alliance	All		Zalduun	Zalduun	Urgent Delivery!			220	65●
REWARD: 1 Empty Draenei Supply Pouch											
Paladin Training	Ammen Vale	Alliance	Draenei Paladin			Aurelon	Replenishing the Healing Crystals			85	
Hunter Training	Ammen Vale	Alliance	Draenei Hunter			Keilnei	Replenishing the Healing Crystals			85	
Warrior Training	Ammen Vale	Alliance	Draenei Warrior			Kore	Replenishing the Healing Crystals			85	
Mage Training	Ammen Vale	Alliance	Draenei Mage			Valaatu	Replenishing the Healing Crystals			85	
Priest Training	Ammen Vale	Alliance	Draenei Priest			Zalduun	Replenishing the Healing Crystals			85	
What Must Be Done...	Ammen Vale	Alliance	All		Botanist Taerix	Botanist Taerix	Volatile Mutations			170	35●
Healing the Lake	Ammen Vale	Alliance	All		Botanist Taerix	Botanist Taerix	What Must Be Done...			250	
Inoculation	Ammen Vale	Alliance	All		Vindicator Aldar	Vindicator Aldar				450	1●50●
CHOICE OF: 3 Elixir of Minor Defense, or 3 Elixir of Lion's Strength											
REWARD: 3 Minor Healing Potion											
Spare Parts	Ammen Vale	Alliance	All		Technician Zhanaa	Technician Zhanaa				360	
CHOICE OF: 1 Beaten Chain Leggings, or 1 Rough Leather Leggings, or 1 Hand Sewn Pants											
The Missing Scout	Ammen Vale	Alliance	All		Vindicator Aldar	Tolaan	Inoculation			110	
Blood Elf Spy	Ammen Vale	Alliance	All		Tolaan	Vindicator Aldar	The Blood Elves			675	3●
CHOICE OF: 1 Exodar Bastard Sword, or 1 Exodar Dagger, or 1 Exodar Maul, or 1 Exodar Shortsword, or 1 Exodar Crossbow, or 1 Exodar Staff											
The Emitter	Ammen Vale	Alliance	All		Vindicator Aldar	Technician Zhanaa	Blood Elf Spy			110	
Travel to Azure Watch	Ammen Vale	Alliance	All		Technician Zhanaa	Technician Dyvuun	The Emitter			550	
Word from Azure Watch	Ammen Vale	Alliance	All		Aeun	Caregiver Chellan				110	
CHOICE OF: 5 Brilliant Smallfish, or 5 Refreshing Spring Water											
Replenishing the Healing Crystals	Ammen Vale	Alliance	Non-Draenei		Proenitus	Proenitus				80	15●
CHOICE OF: 1 Salvaged Leather Belt, or 1 Slightly Rusted Bracers, or 1 Worn Slippers											
Botanist Taerix	Ammen Vale	Alliance	All		Proenitus	Botanist Taerix	Urgent Delivery!			45	
Urgent Delivery!	Ammen Vale	Alliance	All		Proenitus	Zalduun	Replenishing the Healing Crystals			45	
Shaman Training	Ammen Vale	Alliance	Draenei Shaman			Firmanvaar	Replenishing the Healing Crystals			85	
Call of Earth	Ammen Vale	Alliance	Draenei Shaman		Firmanvaar	Spirit of the Vale				270	
Call of Earth	Ammen Vale	All	Draenei Shaman		Spirit of the Vale	Spirit of the Vale	Call of Earth			360	
Call of Earth	Ammen Vale	Alliance	Draenei Shaman		Spirit of the Vale	Firmanvaar	Call of Earth			450	
REWARD: 1 Earth Totem											
Blood Elf Plans	Ammen Vale	Alliance	All		Blood Elf Plans	Vindicator Aldar	The Missing Scout			450	1●
Botanical Legwork	Ammen Vale	Alliance	All		Apprentice Vishael	Apprentice Vishael	Volatile Mutations			250	50●
Volatile Mutations	Ammen Vale	Alliance	All		Botanist Taerix	Botanist Taerix				170	35●
The Blood Elves	Ammen Vale	Alliance	All		Tolaan	Tolaan	The Missing Scout			360	
CHOICE OF: 1 Weathered Cloth Armor, or 1 Weathered Leather Vest, or 1 Weathered Mail Tunic											
Vindicator Aldar	Ammen Vale	Alliance	All		Botanist Taerix	Vindicator Aldar	Healing the Lake			180	

Ashenvale

Title	Location	Faction	Race & Class	Group #	Starter	Finisher	Prerequisite	Reputation	Tradeskill	XP	Money
Destroy the Legion	Ashenvale	Alliance	All		Vindicator Vedaar	Vindicator Vedaar				2450	
A Shameful Waste	Ashenvale	Alliance	All		Architect Nemos	Gnarl				2300	
Agents of Destruction	Ashenvale	Alliance	All		Sentinel Luciel Starwhisper	Sentinel Luciel Starwhisper				2300	25●
The Lost Chalice	Ashenvale	Alliance	All		Kayneth Stillwind	Kayneth Stillwind				2200	22●
Diabolical Plans	Ashenvale	Alliance	All		Diabolical Plans	Vindicator Vedaar				1200	
Report from the Northern Front	Ashenvale	Alliance	All		Sentinel Luciel Starwhisper	Sentinel Farsong				500	
Never Again!	Ashenvale	Alliance	All		Vindicator Vedaar	Vindicator Vedaar	Diabolical Plans			3200	65●
CHOICE OF: 1 Band of Argas, or 1 Seal of Argas, or 1 Signet of Argas											
Reclaiming Felfire Hill	Ashenvale	Alliance	All		Gnarl	Gnarl				2450	
A Helping Hand	Ashenvale	Alliance	All		Vindicator Palanaar	Architect Nemos				1000	
Destroy the Legion	Ashenvale	Horde	All		Valusha	Valusha				2450	
Diabolical Plans	Ashenvale	Horde	All		Diabolical Plans	Valusha				1200	

Title	Location	Faction	Race & Class	Group #	Starter	Finisher	Prerequisite	Reputation	Tradeskill	XP	Money
Never Again!	Ashenvale	Horde	All		Valusha	Valusha	Diabolical Plans			3200	65
CHOICE OF: 1 Band of Argas, or 1 Seal of Argas, or 1 Signet of Argas											
Onward to Ashenvale	Ashenvale	Alliance	All		Thundris Windweaver	Raene Wolfrunner				1150	9
The Soul Devices	Auchindoun	All	All	5	Spy To'gun	Spymistress Mehlisah Highcrown	Find Spy To'gun			16650	10
CHOICE OF: 1 Shattrath Wraps, or 1 Spymistress's Wristguards, or 1 Auchenai Bracers, or 1 Sha'tari Wrought Armguards											
The Codex of Blood	Auchindoun	All	All	5	Field Commander Mahfuun	The Codex of Blood				16650	
Into the Heart of the Labyrinth	Auchindoun	All	All	5	The Codex of Blood	Spymistress Mehlisah Highcrown	The Codex of Blood			20000	15
CHOICE OF: 1 Shattrath Jumpers, or 1 Spymistress's Boots, or 1 Auchenai Boots, or 1 Sha'tari Wrought Greaves											
Brother Against Brother	Auchindoun	All	All	5	Isfar	Isfar				15400	8 20
CHOICE OF: 1 Torc of the Sethekk Prophet, or 1 Sethekk Oracle's Focus, or 1 Talon Lord's Collar, or 1 Mark of the Ravenguard											
Terokk's Legacy	Auchindoun	All	All	5	Isfar	Isfar				15400	8 20
CHOICE OF: 1 The Saga of Terokk, or 1 Terokk's Mask, or 1 Terokk's Quill											
Everything Will Be Alright	Auchindoun	All	All	5	Greatfather Aldrimus	Greatfather Aldrimus	Levixus the Soul Caller			17450	
CHOICE OF: 1 Auchenai Anchorite's Robe, or 1 Auchenai Monk's Tunic, or 1 Auchenai Tracker's Hauberk, or 1 The Exarch's Protector											
Undercutting the Competition	Auchindoun	All	All	5	Nexus-Prince Haramad	Nexus-Prince Haramad				17000	10 50
CHOICE OF: 1 Haramad's Leggings of the Third Coin, or 1 Consortium Plated Legguards, or 1 Haramad's Leg Wraps, or 1 Haramad's Linked Chain Pantaloons											
Trouble at Auchindoun	Auchindoun	All	All	5	Spymistress Mehlisah Highcrown	Field Commander Mahfuun				10000	
Find Spy To'gun	Auchindoun	All	All	5	Spy Grik'tha	Spy To'gun				13350	
Can't Stay Away	Auchindoun	All	All	5	Oloraak	Isfar				3100	
Safety Is Job One	Auchindoun	All	All	5	Artificer Morphalius	Ethereal Transporter Control Panel				14150	
Someone Else's Hard Work Pays Off	Auchindoun	All	All	5		Nexus-Prince Haramad	Safety Is Job One			17000	10 50
CHOICE OF: 1 Consortium Prince's Wrap, or 1 Cryo-mitts, or 1 Consortium Mantle of Phasing, or 1 Flesh Beast's Metal Greaves											
I See Dead Draenei	Auchindoun	All	All	5	Ha'lei	Ramdor the Mad				1150	
Ezekiel	Auchindoun	All	All	5	Ramdor the Mad	Ezekiel	I See Dead Draenei			2900	
What Book? I Don't See Any Book.	Auchindoun	All	All	3	Ezekiel	"Dirty" Larry	Ezekiel			11650	
The Master's Grand Design?	Auchindoun	All	All	5	"Dirty" Larry	Nitrin the Learned	What Book? I Don't See Any Book.			5800	
Vision of the Dead	Auchindoun	All	All	3	Nitrin the Learned	Nitrin the Learned	The Master's Grand Design?			11650	
Levixus the Soul Caller	Auchindoun	All	All	3	Nitrin the Learned	Ramdor the Mad	Vision of the Dead			17450	
CHOICE OF: 1 Cover of Righteous Fury, or 1 Earthbreaker's Greaves, or 1 Gloves of Penitence, or 1 Leggings of the Third Coin											
The Book of Fel Names	Auchindoun	All	All		Altruis the Sufferer	Altruis the Sufferer	Illidan's Pupil			15800	
Red Snapper - Very Tasty!	Azuremyst Isle	Alliance	All		Diktynna	Diktynna				550	
REWARD: 1 Fishing Pole and 1 Shiny Bauble											
Find Acteon!	Azuremyst Isle	Alliance	All		Diktynna	Acteon	Red Snapper - Very Tasty!			55	
The Great Moongraze Hunt	Azuremyst Isle	Alliance	All		Acteon	Acteon				410	1
REWARD: 5 Roasted Moongraze Tenderloin and 1 Recipe: Roasted Moongraze Tenderloin											
Strange Findings	Azuremyst Isle	Alliance	All		Faintly Glowing Crystal	Exarch Menelaous				480	
Nightstalker Clean Up, Isle 2...	Azuremyst Isle	Alliance	All		Exarch Menelaous	Exarch Menelaous	Strange Findings			700	2 25
CHOICE OF: 1 Huntsman's Bracers, or 1 Reinforced Mail Boots, or 1 Slightly Worn Bracer											
Call of Fire	Azuremyst Isle	Alliance	Draenei Shaman		Tuluun	Prophet Velen	Call of Fire			210	
Call of Fire	Azuremyst Isle	Alliance	Draenei Shaman		Sulaa	Tuluun				210	
Medicinal Purpose	Azuremyst Isle	Alliance	Draenei		Anchorite Fateema	Anchorite Fateema				550	
Call of Fire	Azuremyst Isle	Alliance	Draenei Shaman		Tuluun	Temper				850	
Call of Fire	Azuremyst Isle	All	Draenei Shaman		Temper	Temper	Call of Fire			850	
Call of Fire	Azuremyst Isle	All	Draenei Shaman		Temper	Temper	Call of Fire			850	
Call of Fire	Azuremyst Isle	Alliance	Draenei Shaman		Temper	Tuluun	Call of Fire			1050	
An Alternative Alternative	Azuremyst Isle	Alliance	All		Daedal	Daedal	Medicinal Purpose			700	
The Prophecy of Velen	Azuremyst Isle	Alliance	All		Daedal	Admiral Odesyus	An Alternative Alternative			525	
A Small Start	Azuremyst Isle	Alliance	All		Admiral Odesyus	Admiral Odesyus				625	
Cookie's Jumbo Gumbo	Azuremyst Isle	Alliance	All		"Cookie" McWeaksauce	"Cookie" McWeaksauce				480	
REWARD: 10 Cookie's Jumbo Gumbo											
Reclaiming the Ruins	Azuremyst Isle	Alliance	All		Priestess Kyleen Il'dinare	Priestess Kyleen Il'dinare	A Small Start			700	
Rune Covered Tablet	Azuremyst Isle	Alliance	All		Rune Covered Tablet	Priestess Kyleen Il'dinare				70	
Warlord Sriss'tiz	Azuremyst Isle	Alliance	All		Priestess Kyleen Il'dinare	Priestess Kyleen Il'dinare	Rune Covered Tablet			850	10
CHOICE OF: 1 Battle Tested Blade, or 1 Naga Scale Boots											
Precious and Fragile Things Need Special Handling	Azuremyst Isle	Alliance	All		Archaeologist Adamant Ironheart	Archaeologist Adamant Ironheart	A Small Start			700	2 25
All That Remains	Azuremyst Isle	Alliance	All		Cowlen	Cowlen				850	
A Cry For Help	Azuremyst Isle	Alliance	All	2	Magwin	Cowlen				850	
REWARD: 1 Cowlen's Bracers of Kinship											

Azuremyst Isle

Title	Location	Faction	Race & Class	Group #	Starter	Finisher	Prerequisite	Reputation	Tradeskill	XP	Money
I've Got a Plant	Azuremyst Isle	Alliance	All		Admiral Odesyus	Admiral Odesyus	A Small Start			200	
Tree's Company	Azuremyst Isle	Alliance	All		Admiral Odesyus	Admiral Odesyus	I've Got a Plant			600	9
Show Gnomercy	Azuremyst Isle	Alliance	All		Admiral Odesyus	Admiral Odesyus	Tree's Company			775	
CHOICE OF: 1 Crossbow of the Albatross, or 1 McWeaksauce's Meat Tenderizer, or 1 Seafarer's Blade, or 1 The Discipline Stick, or 1 The Shell Cracker											
Learning the Language	Azuremyst Isle	Alliance	All		Cryptographer Aurren	Totem of Akida				70	
Totem of Coo	Azuremyst Isle	All	All		Totem of Akida	Totem of Coo	Learning the Language			85	
Totem of Tikti	Azuremyst Isle	All	All		Totem of Coo	Totem of Tikti	Totem of Coo			85	
Totem of Yor	Azuremyst Isle	All	All		Totem of Tikti	Totem of Yor	Totem of Tikti			85	
Totem of Vark	Azuremyst Isle	All	All		Totem of Yor	Totem of Vark	Totem of Yor			85	
The Prophecy of Akida	Azuremyst Isle	Alliance	All		Totem of Vark	Arugoo of the Stillpine	Totem of Vark			1250	
CHOICE OF: 1 Stillpine Defender, or 1 Stillpine Stinger, or 1 Arugoo's Crossbow of Destruction											
Call of Air	Azuremyst Isle	Alliance	Draenei Shaman		Tuluun	Farseer Nobundo				600	
Call of Air	Azuremyst Isle	Alliance	Draenei Shaman		Sulaa	Farseer Nobundo				600	
Call of Air	Azuremyst Isle	Alliance	Draenei Shaman		Farseer Nobundo	Velaada				2450	
Call of Air	Azuremyst Isle	Alliance	Draenei Shaman		Velaada	Susurrus	Call of Air			600	
Call of Air	Azuremyst Isle	Alliance	Draenei Shaman		Susurrus	Farseer Nobundo	Call of Air			3050	
REWARD: 1 Air Totem											
Call of Fire	Azuremyst Isle	Alliance	Draenei Shaman		Prophet Velen	Farseer Nobundo	Call of Fire			210	
REWARD: 1 Fire Totem											
Stillpine Hold	Azuremyst Isle	Alliance	All		Arugoo of the Stillpine	High Chief Stillpine	The Prophecy of Akida			210	
Beasts of the Apocalypse!	Azuremyst Isle	Alliance	All		Moordo	Moordo	The Prophecy of Akida			850	
CHOICE OF: 1 Ravager Hide Leggings, or 1 Ravager Chitin Tunic, or 1 Thick Ravager Belt											
Murlocs... Why Here? Why Now?	Azuremyst Isle	Alliance	All		Gurf	Gurf	The Prophecy of Akida			850	3 50
Gurf's Dignity	Azuremyst Isle	Alliance	All		Gurf's Dignity	Gurf	The Prophecy of Akida			875	
CHOICE OF: 1 Heavy Chain Leggings, or 1 Savage Leggings, or 1 Fur Covered Robe											
Search Stillpine Hold	Azuremyst Isle	Alliance	All		High Chief Stillpine	Blood Crystal	Murlocs... Why Here? Why Now?			625	
Blood Crystals	Azuremyst Isle	Alliance	All		Blood Crystal	High Chief Stillpine	Search Stillpine Hold			625	
The Kurken is Lurkin'	Azuremyst Isle	Alliance	All		Kurz the Revelator	Kurz the Revelator	Search Stillpine Hold			1150	
The Kurken's Hide	Azuremyst Isle	Alliance	All		Kurz the Revelator	Moordo	The Kurken is Lurkin'			85	
CHOICE OF: 1 Kurkenstoks, or 1 Kurken Hide Jerkin											
Chieftain Oomooroo	Azuremyst Isle	Alliance	All		Stillpine the Younger	Stillpine the Younger	Murlocs... Why Here? Why Now?			875	
CHOICE OF: 1 Sturdy Leather Belt, or 1 Fortified Wristguards											
Strength of One	Azuremyst Isle	Alliance	All Warrior		Ruada	Ruada				850	
Help Tavara	Azuremyst Isle	Alliance	All Priest		Guvan	Guvan				450	
REWARD: 1 Azure Watch Robes											
Taming the Beast	Azuremyst Isle	Alliance	Draenei Hunter		Huntress Kella Nightbow	Huntress Kella Nightbow				850	
Taming the Beast	Azuremyst Isle	Alliance	Draenei Hunter		Huntress Kella Nightbow	Huntress Kella Nightbow	Taming the Beast			850	
Taming the Beast	Azuremyst Isle	Alliance	Draenei Hunter		Huntress Kella Nightbow	Huntress Kella Nightbow	Taming the Beast			850	
Control	Azuremyst Isle	Alliance	Draenei Mage		Semid	Bati				875	
CHOICE OF: 1 Ley Staff, or 1 Ley Orb											
Deliver Them From Evil...	Azuremyst Isle	Alliance	All		Admiral Odesyus	Exarch Menelaous	Show Gnomercy			200	
A Hearty Thanks!	Azuremyst Isle	Alliance	All			Exarch Menelaous				525	4 50
Bandits!	Azuremyst Isle	Alliance	All		Blood Elf Communication	Exarch Menelaous				625	
CHOICE OF: 1 Battle Worn Gauntlets, or 1 Battle Worn Gloves, or 1 Battle Worn Handguards											
Warn Your People	Azuremyst Isle	Alliance	All		High Chief Stillpine	Exarch Menelaous	Chieftain Oomooroo			650	
Coming of Age	Azuremyst Isle	Alliance	All		Exarch Menelaous	Torallius the Pack Handler				90	
Elekks Are Serious Business	Azuremyst Isle	Alliance	All		Torallius the Pack Handler	Vorkhan the Elekk Herder	Coming of Age			220	1
Beast Training	Azuremyst Isle	Alliance	Draenei Hunter		Huntress Kella Nightbow	Ganaar	Taming the Beast			420	
REWARD: 1 Silver Crossbow											
The Great Moongraze Hunt	Azuremyst Isle	Alliance	All		Acteon	Acteon	The Great Moongraze Hunt			525	1 75
CHOICE OF: 1 Moongraze Fur Cloak, or 1 Moongraze Hide Boots											
Behomat	Azuremyst Isle	Alliance	All		Ruada	Behomat	Strength of One			420	
CHOICE OF: 1 Mercenary Clout, or 1 Mercenary Greatsword, or 1 Mercenary Stiletto, or 1 Mercenary Sword											
Caedmos	Azuremyst Isle	Alliance	All			Caedmos				85	
Jol	Azuremyst Isle	Alliance	All		Tullas	Jol				90	
The Missing Fisherman	Azuremyst Isle	Alliance	All		Dulvi	Cowlen				420	
Call of Air	Azuremyst Isle	Alliance	All		Farseer Umbrua	Farseer Nobundo				600	
Unclaimed Baggage	Badlands	Horde	All		Advisor Sarophas	Advisor Sarophas				3150	50
The Encroaching Wilderness	Blade's Edge	Alliance	All		Rina Moonspring	Rina Moonspring				11300	3 50
Marauding Wolves	Blade's Edge	Alliance	All		Rina Moonspring	Rina Moonspring	The Encroaching Wilderness			11300	3 50

Badlands

Title	Location	Faction	Race & Class	Group #	Starter	Finisher	Prerequisite	Reputation	Tradeskill	XP	Money
Protecting Our Own	Blade's Edge	Alliance	All		Rina Moonspring	Rina Moonspring	Marauding Wolves			11300	3 50
CHOICE OF: 1 Sylvanaar Gloves, or 1 Living Grove Shoulderpads, or 1 Protector's Boots, or 1 Sentinel Armbands											
The Encroaching Wilderness	Blade's Edge	Horde	All		Gor'drek	Gor'drek				11300	3 50
Dust from the Drakes	Blade's Edge	Horde	All		Gor'drek	Gor'drek	The Encroaching Wilderness			11300	3 50
Protecting Our Own	Blade's Edge	Horde	All		Gor'drek	Gor'drek	Dust from the Drakes			11300	3 50
CHOICE OF: 1 Thunderlord Armbands, or 1 Dire Wolf Handler Gloves, or 1 Gor'drek's Pauldrons, or 1 Wolf Chaps											
Felling an Ancient Tree	Blade's Edge	Horde	All		Wanted Poster	Tor'chunk Twoclaws				11300	3 50
CHOICE OF: 1 Bear-Strength Harness, or 1 Wild Horned Helm, or 1 Boots of the Ancient-Killer, or 1 Dark Deed Leggings											
The Bloodmaul Ogres	Blade's Edge	Alliance	All		Commander Skyshadow	Commander Skyshadow				11300	3 50
The Bladespire Threat	Blade's Edge	Horde	All		Tor'chunk Twoclaws	Tor'chunk Twoclaws				14150	7
The Bladespire Ogres	Blade's Edge	Alliance	All		Commander Skyshadow	Commander Skyshadow	The Bloodmaul Ogres			11300	3 50
CHOICE OF: 1 Ogre Vanquisher's Belt, or 1 Agile Mountain Bracers, or 1 Sylvanaar Defender's Pauldrons, or 1 Commander Skyshadow's Gloves											
The Bloodmaul Ogres	Blade's Edge	Horde	All		Tor'chunk Twoclaws	Tor'chunk Twoclaws	The Bladespire Threat			11300	3 50
CHOICE OF: 1 Red Hands of the Thunderlord, or 1 Rugged Mountain Bracers, or 1 Tor'chunk's Foot Covers, or 1 Ogre Beater's Belt											
A Dire Situation	Blade's Edge	Alliance	All		Rina Moonspring	Rina Moonspring	Protecting Our Own			11300	3 50
Into the Draenethyst Mine	Blade's Edge	Alliance	All		Bronwyn Stouthammer	Bronwyn Stouthammer				11300	3 50
CHOICE OF: 1 Spelunker's Mantle, or 1 All-Weather Armguards, or 1 Miner's Gloves, or 1 Explorer's Boots											
Strange Brew	Blade's Edge	Alliance	All		Borgrim Stouthammer	Borgrim Stouthammer				11300	3 50
Getting the Bladespire Tanked	Blade's Edge	Alliance	All		Borgrim Stouthammer	Borgrim Stouthammer	Strange Brew			11300	3 50
The Trappings of a Vindicator	Blade's Edge	Alliance	All		Vindicator Vuuleen	Vindicator Vuuleen				11300	3 50
Gorr'Dim, Your Time Has Come...	Blade's Edge	Alliance	All		Vindicator Vuuleen	Vindicator Vuuleen	The Trappings of a Vindicator			11650	3 70
Planting the Banner	Blade's Edge	Alliance	All	3	Vindicator Vuuleen	Commander Skyshadow	Gorr'Dim, Your Time Has Come...			14600	7 40
CHOICE OF: 1 Sylvanaar Elite Caster's Armor, or 1 Ogre Assassin's Britches, or 1 Gurn's Horned Helmet, or 1 Sylvanaar Champion's Shoulders											
Thunderlord Clan Artifacts	Blade's Edge	Horde	All		Thunderlord Clan Artifact	Rokgah Bloodgrip				11300	3 50
Vision Guide	Blade's Edge	Horde	All		Rokgah Bloodgrip	Rokgah Bloodgrip	Thunderlord Clan Artifacts			8550	
The Thunderspike	Blade's Edge	Horde	All		Rokgah Bloodgrip	Rokgah Bloodgrip	Vision Guide			14600	7 40
CHOICE OF: 1 Thunderlord Scalpel, or 1 Slow Death Dirk, or 1 Wand of the Ancestors											
They Stole Me Hookah and Me Brews!	Blade's Edge	Horde	All		T'chali the Witch Doctor	T'chali the Witch Doctor				11300	3 50
Grimnok and Korgaah, I Am For You!	Blade's Edge	Horde	All		T'chali the Witch Doctor	T'chali the Witch Doctor	Bladespire Kegger			11650	3 70
A Curse Upon Both of Your Clans!	Blade's Edge	Horde	All		T'chali the Witch Doctor	T'chali the Witch Doctor	Grimnok and Korgaah, I Am For You!			14150	7
CHOICE OF: 1 Witch Doctor's Beads, or 1 T'chali's Kilt, or 1 Hexxer's Belt, or 1 Ogre Defiler's Handguards											
Bladespire Kegger	Blade's Edge	Horde	All		T'chali the Witch Doctor	T'chali the Witch Doctor	They Stole Me Hookah and Me Brews!			11300	3 50
Malaise	Blade's Edge	Alliance	All		Daranelle	Lashh'an Tome				11300	
Scratches	Blade's Edge	Alliance	All		Lashh'an Tome	Daranelle	Malaise			8550	3 50
Test Flight: The Zephyrium Capacitorium	Blade's Edge	Alliance	All		Tally Zapnabber	Tally Zapnabber				2650	80
The Stones of Vekh'nir	Blade's Edge	Horde	All		Dertrok	Dertrok				5650	
Trial and Error	Blade's Edge	Horde	All		Dertrok	Dertrok	The Stones of Vekh'nir			11300	3 70
Creating the Pendant	Blade's Edge	All	All		Timeon	Timeon				11300	
Where Did Those Darn Gnomes Go?	Blade's Edge	Alliance	All		Commander Skyshadow	R-3DO	Planting the Banner			2900	
Follow the Breadcrumbs	Blade's Edge	Alliance	All		R-3DO	Toshley	Where Did Those Darn Gnomes Go?			2900	
Picking Up Some Power Converters	Blade's Edge	Alliance	All		Toshley	Toshley				11650	3 70
Gauging the Resonant Frequency	Blade's Edge	Alliance	All		Nickwinkle the Metro-Gnome	Nickwinkle the Metro-Gnome	Crystal Clear			11650	3 70
CHOICE OF: 1 Party Hat Mistake, or 1 Nickwinkle's Harness Experiment, or 1 Last Year's "In" Belt, or 1 Metro's Slimming Legs											
Whispers of the Raven God	Blade's Edge	All	All		Timeon	Timeon	Creating the Pendant			12000	
CHOICE OF: 1 Wraithcloth Bindings, or 1 Supple Leather Boots, or 1 Diluvian Spaulders, or 1 Whiteknuckle Gauntlets											
Crystal Clear	Blade's Edge	Alliance	All		Nickwinkle the Metro-Gnome	Nickwinkle the Metro-Gnome				11650	3 70
What Came First, the Drake or the Egg?	Blade's Edge	Alliance	All		Fizit "Doc" Clocktock	Fizit "Doc" Clocktock				11650	3 70
CHOICE OF: 1 Fizit's Mantle of Drake Hunting, or 1 Precise Gloves of the Physician, or 1 Devolved Drake Girdle, or 1 Clocktock's Jumpers											
REWARD: 5 Medicinal Drake Essence											
Whispers on the Wind	Blade's Edge	Horde	All		Rexxar	Leoroxx	The Spirits Have Voices			1150	
Ruuan Weald	Blade's Edge	Horde	All		Dertrok	Timeon	Trial and Error			2650	
Silkwing Cocoons	Blade's Edge	Horde	All		Taerek	Taerek				11300	3 50
The Softest Wings	Blade's Edge	Horde	All		Silmara	Silmara				11000	3 30

Title	Location	Faction	Race & Class	Group #	Starter	Finisher	Prerequisite	Reputation	Tradeskill	XP	Money
Ridgespine Menace	Blade's Edge	Alliance	All		Dizzy Dina	Dizzy Dina	Picking Up Some Power Converters			11650	3 70
CHOICE OF: 5 Distilled Stalker Sight, or 5 Stealth of the Stalker											
Cutting Your Teeth	Blade's Edge	Alliance	All		Razak Ironsides	Razak Ironsides	Picking Up Some Power Converters			11650	3 70
CHOICE OF: 1 Vibro Shanker, or 1 Vibro Dagger, or 1 Vibro Sword											
Ride the Lightning	Blade's Edge	Alliance	All		Toshley	Toshley	Picking Up Some Power Converters			11650	3 70
CHOICE OF: 1 Energized Wristwraps, or 1 Charged Footwear, or 1 Scalewing Gloves, or 1 Muscle Toning Belt											
REWARD: 5 Pure Energy											
More than a Pound of Flesh	Blade's Edge	Alliance	All		Dizzy Dina	Dizzy Dina	Ridgespine Menace			11650	3 70
Trapping the Light Fantastic	Blade's Edge	Alliance	All		Toshley	Toshley	Ride the Lightning			11650	3 70
Show Them Gnome Mercy!	Blade's Edge	Alliance	All		Toshley	Toshley	Trapping the Light Fantastic			14950	7 80
CHOICE OF: 1 Gnomish Casting Boots, or 1 Toshley's Station Hero's Hat, or 1 Razaani-Buster Leggings, or 1 Soul Saver's Chest Plate											
REWARD: 1 Power Converter											
A Time for Negotiation...	Blade's Edge	All	All		Tree Warden Chawn	Tree Warden Chawn				11650	3 70
The Den Mother	Blade's Edge	Alliance	All		Wanted Poster	Commander Skyshadow				11300	3 50
CHOICE OF: 1 Wolf Hewer's Axe, or 1 Heavy Elven Dirk, or 1 Arcane Wand of Sylvanaar											
Reunion	Blade's Edge	Horde	All		Leoroxx	Rexxar	Whispers on the Wind			2900	
Test Flight: The Singing Ridge	Blade's Edge	Alliance	All		Tally Zapnabber	Tally Zapnabber	Test Flight: The Zephyrium Capacitorium			5400	1 60
Test Flight: Razaan's Landing	Blade's Edge	Alliance	All		Tally Zapnabber	Tally Zapnabber	Ride the Lightning			5400	2 40
Test Flight: Ruuan Weald	Blade's Edge	Alliance	All		Tally Zapnabber	O'Mally Zapnabber	Show Them Gnome Mercy!			5400	3 10
...and a Time for Action	Blade's Edge	All	All		Tree Warden Chawn	Tree Warden Chawn	A Time for Negotiation...			11650	3 70
CHOICE OF: 1 Hewing Gloves, or 1 Tree Warden's Belt, or 1 Bracers of the Weald, or 1 Expedition Defender's Shoulders											
On Spirit's Wings	Blade's Edge	Horde	All		Rexxar	Rexxar	Reunion			11650	3 70
Into the Churning Gulch	Blade's Edge	Horde	All		Baron Sablemane	Baron Sablemane	Baron Sablemane			11650	3 70
REWARD: 5 Bloodboil Poison											
Poaching from Poachers	Blade's Edge	All	All		Samia Inkling	Samia Inkling	A Time for Negotiation...			11650	3 70
The Spirits Have Voices	Blade's Edge	Horde	All		Garm Wolfbrother	Rexxar				1150	
Did You Get The Note?	Blade's Edge	All	All		Meeting Note	Tree Warden Chawn	A Time for Negotiation...			1150	
The Smallest Creatures	Blade's Edge	Horde	All		Rexxar	Rexxar	Baron Sablemane's Poison			11650	3 70
A Boaring Time for Grulloc	Blade's Edge	Horde	All		Rexxar	Baron Sablemane	The Smallest Creatures			11650	3 70
Meeting at the Blackwing Coven	Blade's Edge	All	All		Watcher Moonshade	Tree Warden Chawn	Longtail is the Lynchpin			12000	3 90
Gorgrom the Dragon-Eater	Blade's Edge	Horde	All		Rexxar	Rexxar	It's a Trap!			12000	
CHOICE OF: 1 Fanged Axe, or 1 Whistling Sword, or 1 Adjudicator's Staff											
Prisoner of the Bladespire	Blade's Edge	Horde	All	3	Rexxar	Rexxar	Gorgrom the Dragon-Eater			11650	3 70
Showdown	Blade's Edge	Horde	All	3	Rexxar	Rexxar	Prisoner of the Bladespire			19000	13 20
CHOICE OF: 1 Tourmaline Crown, or 1 Clefthoof Hide Leggings, or 1 Oilcloth Breeches, or 1 Malefactor's Eyepatch, or 1 Leonine Breastplate, or 1 Blackened Chestplate											
Whelps of the Wyrmcult	Blade's Edge	All	All		Samia Inkling	Samia Inkling	Poaching from Poachers			12000	3 90
CHOICE OF: 1 Wyrmcultist's Hood, or 1 Blackwhelp Belt, or 1 Whelpscale Gauntlets, or 1 Inkling's Leggings											
Maxnar Must Die!	Blade's Edge	All	All		Tree Warden Chawn	Tree Warden Chawn	Meeting at the Blackwing Coven			14950	7 80
CHOICE OF: 1 Coven Britches, or 1 Chest of the Wyrmcult, or 1 Dragonkin Shirt, or 1 Blackwing Helm											
Baron Sablemane's Poison	Blade's Edge	Horde	All		Baron Sablemane	Rexxar	Into the Churning Gulch			1150	
Culling the Wild	Blade's Edge	All	All		Faradrella	Faradrella				8750	2 90
Little Embers	Blade's Edge	All	All		Mosswood the Ancient	Mosswood the Ancient				11650	3 70
From the Ashes	Blade's Edge	All	All		Mosswood the Ancient	Mosswood the Ancient				11650	3 70
CHOICE OF: 1 Wild Wood Staff, or 1 Scorch Wood Bow, or 1 Iron Oak Shield											
Crush the Bloodmaul Camp	Blade's Edge	Horde	All		Tor'chunk Twoclaws	Tor'chunk Twoclaws	Baron Sablemane's Poison			11650	3 70
CHOICE OF: 1 Darktread Boots, or 1 Twin Moon Shoulderguards, or 1 Chaintwine Cinch, or 1 Fairweather's Wristguards											
It's a Trap!	Blade's Edge	Horde	All		Baron Sablemane	Rexxar	A Boaring Time for Grulloc			1150	
Slaughter at Boulder'mok	Blade's Edge	Horde	All		Tor'chunk Twoclaws	Tor'chunk Twoclaws	It's a Trap!			14950	7 80
A Date with Dorgok	Blade's Edge	Alliance	All		Commander Haephus Stonewall	Commander Haephus Stonewall				11650	3 70
Crush the Bloodmaul Camp!	Blade's Edge	Alliance	All		Lieutenant Fairweather	Lieutenant Fairweather				11650	3 70
CHOICE OF: 1 Darktread Boots, or 1 Twin Moon Shoulderguards, or 1 Chaintwine Cinch, or 1 Fairweather's Wristguards											

Title	Location	Faction	Race & Class	Group #	Starter	Finisher	Prerequisite	Reputation	Tradeskill	XP	Money
Favor of the Gronn	Blade's Edge	Alliance	All		Gorgrom's Favor	Commander Haephus Stonewall				1150	
Pay the Baron a Visit	Blade's Edge	Alliance	All		Commander Haephus Stonewall	Baron Sablemane	Favor of the Gronn			1150	
Into the Churning Gulch	Blade's Edge	Alliance	All		Baron Sablemane	Baron Sablemane	Pay the Baron a Visit			11650	3g 70s
REWARD: 5 Bloodboil Poison											
Goodnight, Gronn	Blade's Edge	Alliance	All		Baron Sablemane	Baron Sablemane	Into the Churning Gulch			11650	3g 70s
It's a Trap!	Blade's Edge	Alliance	All		Baron Sablemane	Commander Haephus Stonewall	Goodnight, Gronn			1150	
Gorgrom the Dragon-Eater	Blade's Edge	Alliance	All		Commander Haephus Stonewall	Commander Haephus Stonewall	It's a Trap!			14950	7g 80s
CHOICE OF: 1 Fanged Axe, or 1 Whistling Sword, or 1 Adjudicator's Staff											
Slaughter at Boulder'mok	Blade's Edge	Alliance	All		Lieutenant Fairweather	Lieutenant Fairweather	It's a Trap!			12000	3g 80s
Massacre at Gruul's Lair	Blade's Edge	Alliance	All	3	Baron Sablemane	Baron Sablemane	Baron Sablemane Has Requested Your Presence			14600	7g 40s
Showdown	Blade's Edge	Alliance	All	3	Baron Sablemane	Baron Sablemane	Massacre at Gruul's Lair			19000	13g 20s
CHOICE OF: 1 Tourmaline Crown, or 1 Clefthoof Hide Leggings, or 1 Oilcloth Breeches, or 1 Malefactor's Eyepatch, or 1 Leonine Breastplate, or 1 Blackened Chestplate											
Damaged Mask	Blade's Edge	Alliance	All		Damaged Mask	O'Mally Zapnabber				3050	1g
Mystery Mask	Blade's Edge	Alliance	All		O'Mally Zapnabber	Wildlord Antelarion	Damaged Mask			3050	1g
Baron Sablemane Has Requested Your Presence	Blade's Edge	Alliance	All		Commander Haephus Stonewall	Baron Sablemane	Gorgrom the Dragon-Eater			1150	
Felsworn Gas Mask	Blade's Edge	All	All		Wildlord Antelarion	Legion Communicator	Mystery Mask			12000	
Deceive thy Enemy	Blade's Edge	All	All		pnagle's test dude	Legion Communicator	Felsworn Gas Mask			9000	
You're Fired!	Blade's Edge	All	All	2	pnagle's test dude	Wildlord Antelarion	Deceive thy Enemy			12000	7g 80s
CHOICE OF: 1 Ruuan Weald Wristguards, or 1 Evergrove Ranger's Cloak, or 1 Expedition Pendant, or 1 Wildlord's Band											
The Truth Unorbed	Blade's Edge	All	All		Orb of the Grishna	Tree Warden Chawn				1200	
Treebole Must Know	Blade's Edge	All	All		Tree Warden Chawn	Treebole	The Truth Unorbed			1200	
Exorcising the Trees	Blade's Edge	All	All		Treebole	Treebole	Treebole Must Know			14950	7g 80s
CHOICE OF: 1 Raven's Wood Exorciser's Band, or 1 Leafbeard Ring, or 1 Treebole's Hoop, or 1 Ring of the Stonebark											
Since Time Forgotten...	Blade's Edge	Horde	All		Leoroxx	Leoroxx	Understanding the Mok'Nathal			12000	3g 90s
Slay the Brood Mother	Blade's Edge	Horde	All		Leoroxx	Leoroxx	Since Time Forgotten...			12000	3g 90s
CHOICE OF: 1 Dreadwing Skin Belt, or 1 Brood Mother Leggings, or 1 Netherhide Gloves, or 1 Nether Protector's Chest											
Understanding the Mok'Nathal	Blade's Edge	Horde	All		Leoroxx	Leoroxx	The Stones of Vekh'nir			11650	3g 70s
The Totems of My Enemy	Blade's Edge	Horde	All		Spiritcaller Dohgar	Spiritcaller Dohgar	Understanding the Mok'Nathal			11650	3g 70s
Spirit Calling	Blade's Edge	Horde	All		Spiritcaller Dohgar	Spiritcaller Dohgar	The Totems of My Enemy			11650	3g 70s
CHOICE OF: 1 Nether-Empowered Footgear, or 1 Ritualist's Helm, or 1 Mok'Nathal Champion's Shoulderguards, or 1 Nether Drake Wristguards											
REWARD: 5 Medicinal Drake Essence											
Gather the Orbs	Blade's Edge	Horde	All		Spiritcaller Dohgar	Spiritcaller Dohgar	Spirit Calling			11650	3g 70s
Mok'Nathal Treats	Blade's Edge	Horde	All		Matron Varah	Matron Varah				11650	3g 70s
REWARD: 3 Mok'Nathal Shortribs and 3 Crunchy Serpent and 1 Recipe: Mok'Nathal Shortribs and 1 Recipe: Crunchy Serpent											
Inform Leoroxx!	Blade's Edge	Horde	All		Spiritcaller Dohgar	Leoroxx	Gather the Orbs			1200	
There Can Be Only One Response	Blade's Edge	Horde	All		Leoroxx	Spiritcaller Dohgar	Inform Leoroxx!			14950	7g 80s
CHOICE OF: 1 Mok'Nathal Mantle, or 1 Spiritcaller's Mask, or 1 Mok'Nathal Hero's Pantaloons, or 1 Belt of the Soul Saver											
Longtail is the Lynchpin	Blade's Edge	All	All		Watcher Moonshade	Watcher Moonshade	Wyrmskull Watcher			11650	3g 70s
Wyrmskull Watcher	Blade's Edge	All	All		Tree Warden Chawn	Watcher Moonshade	Did You Get The Note?			1150	
Harvesting the Fel Ammunition	Blade's Edge	All	All			Evergrove Druid	Death's Door			12000	3g 90s
Death's Door	Blade's Edge	All	All		Wildlord Antelarion	Evergrove Druid	You're Fired!			12000	3g 90s
Fire At Will!	Blade's Edge	All	All			Evergrove Druid	Harvesting the Fel Ammunition			12000	3g 90s
The Hound-Master	Blade's Edge	All	All			Wildlord Antelarion	Fire At Will!			17950	11g 70s
CHOICE OF: 1 Natasha's Arcane Filament, or 1 Natasha's Battle Chain, or 1 Natasha's Choker, or 1 Natasha's Ember Necklace, or 1 Natasha's Guardian Cord, or 1 Natasha's Pack Collar											
Killing the Crawlers	Blade's Edge	Alliance	All		Sentinel Moonwhisper	Commander Skyshadow				11000	3g 30s
Killing the Crawlers	Blade's Edge	Horde	All		Grunt Grahk	Tor'chunk Twoclaws				11000	3g 30s
Through the Dark Portal	Blasted Lands	Horde	All		Warlord Dar'toon	Lieutenant General Orion				2400	
Through the Dark Portal	Blasted Lands	Alliance	All		Watch Commander Relthorn Netherwane	Commander Duron				2400	
Call of Water	Bloodmyst Isle	Alliance	Draenei Shaman		Tuluun	Farseer Nobundo				390	
Call of Water	Bloodmyst Isle	Alliance	Draenei Shaman		Farseer Nobundo	Aqueous				1550	
Call of Water	Bloodmyst Isle	Alliance	Draenei Shaman		Sulaa	Farseer Nobundo				390	
Call of Water	Bloodmyst Isle	All	Draenei Shaman		Aqueous	Aqueous	Call of Water			1550	
Call of Water	Bloodmyst Isle	All	Draenei Shaman		Aqueous	Aqueous	Call of Water			1950	
Call of Water	Bloodmyst Isle	All	Draenei Shaman		Aqueous	Aqueous	Call of Water			1850	
Call of Water	Bloodmyst Isle	Alliance	Draenei Shaman		Aqueous	Farseer Nobundo	Call of Water			2350	
REWARD: 1 Water Totem											

Title	Location	Faction	Race & Class	Group #	Starter	Finisher	Prerequisite	Reputation	Tradeskill	XP	Money
Pilfered Equipment	Bloodmyst Isle	Alliance	All		Clopper Wizbang	Clopper Wizbang				1250	9
Artifacts of the Blacksilt	Bloodmyst Isle	Alliance	All		Clopper Wizbang	Clopper Wizbang				1250	9
REWARD: 1 Weathered Treasure Map											
A Map to Where?	Bloodmyst Isle	Alliance	All		Weathered Treasure Map	Battered Ancient Book				1150	
Deciphering the Book	Bloodmyst Isle	Alliance	All		Battered Ancient Book	Anchorite Paetheus	A Map to Where?			1150	
Nolkai's Words	Bloodmyst Isle	Alliance	All		Anchorite Paetheus	Mound of Dirt	Deciphering the Book			1150	
REWARD: 1 Nolkai's Box											
Know Thine Enemy	Bloodmyst Isle	Alliance	All		Vindicator Aalesia	Vindicator Aalesia				975	6
Containing the Threat	Bloodmyst Isle	Alliance	All		Vindicator Aalesia	Vindicator Aalesia	Know Thine Enemy			1350	10
CHOICE OF: 1 Huntsman's Crossbow, or 1 Lightspark											
Victims of Corruption	Bloodmyst Isle	Alliance	All		Morae	Morae	Catch and Release			975	6
Cruelfin's Necklace	Bloodmyst Isle	Alliance	All		Red Crystal Pendant	Morae				900	5
Searching for Galaen	Bloodmyst Isle	Alliance	All		Morae	Galaen's Corpse				1350	
Galaen's Fate	Bloodmyst Isle	Alliance	All		Galaen's Corpse	Morae	Searching for Galaen			1350	10
CHOICE OF: 1 Cryo-Core Attendant's Boots, or 1 Lightweight Mesh Boots, or 1 Technician's Boots											
The Bear Necessities	Bloodmyst Isle	Alliance	All		Tracker Lyceon	Tracker Lyceon				1150	8
Learning from the Crystals	Bloodmyst Isle	Alliance	All		Harbinger Mikolaas	Harbinger Mikolaas				875	4
CHOICE OF: 1 Crystal-Flecked Pants, or 1 Crystal-Studded Legguards, or 1 Shard-Covered Leggings											
The Second Sample	Bloodmyst Isle	Alliance	All		Harbinger Mikolaas	Harbinger Mikolaas	Salvaging the Data			975	6
The Final Sample	Bloodmyst Isle	Alliance	All		Harbinger Mikolaas	Harbinger Mikolaas	The Second Sample			1350	10
Signs of the Legion	Bloodmyst Isle	Alliance	All		Tzerak's Armor Plate	Vindicator Aalesia				975	6
Redemption	Bloodmyst Isle	Alliance	Draenei Paladin		Jol	Jol				460	
Redemption	Bloodmyst Isle	Alliance	Draenei Paladin		Jol	Jol	Redemption			900	
Beds, Bandages, and Beyond	Bloodmyst Isle	Alliance	All		Caregiver Topher Loaal	Laando				420	
On the Wings of a Hippogryph	Bloodmyst Isle	Alliance	All		Laando	Nurguni	Beds, Bandages, and Beyond			420	
Hippogryph Master Stephanos	Bloodmyst Isle	Alliance	All		Nurguni	Stephanos	On the Wings of a Hippogryph			420	
Return to Topher Loaal	Bloodmyst Isle	Alliance	All		Stephanos	Caregiver Topher Loaal	Hippogryph Master Stephanos			850	7
The Missing Survey Team	Bloodmyst Isle	Alliance	All		Harbinger Mikolaas	Draenei Cartographer	Learning from the Crystals			975	
A Favorite Treat	Bloodmyst Isle	Alliance	All		Aonar	Aonar				900	5
CHOICE OF: 1 Elekk Handler's Leathers, or 1 Farmhand's Vest, or 1 Elekk Rider's Mail											
REWARD: 20 Sand Pear Pie											
Salvaging the Data	Bloodmyst Isle	Alliance	All			Harbinger Mikolaas	The Missing Survey Team			975	6
REWARD: 1 Surveyor's Mantle											
Catch and Release	Bloodmyst Isle	Alliance	All		Morae	Morae				900	6
CHOICE OF: 1 Protective Field Gloves, or 1 Researcher's Gloves, or 1 Scholar's Gloves											
Newfound Allies	Bloodmyst Isle	Alliance	All		Anchorite Paetheus	Huntress Kella Nightbow				800	
The Way to Auberdine	Bloodmyst Isle	Alliance	All		Huntress Kella Nightbow	Thundris Windweaver	Newfound Allies			1050	
Alien Predators	Bloodmyst Isle	Alliance	All		Vorkhan the Elekk Herder	Vorkhan the Elekk Herder				875	4
CHOICE OF: 1 2 Stone Sledgehammer, or 1 Elekk Handler's Blade, or 1 Old Elekk Prod, or 1 Surplus Bastard Sword											
Irradiated Crystal Shards	Bloodmyst Isle	Alliance	All		Vindicator Boros	Vindicator Boros				1050	
CHOICE OF: 1 Crystal of Vitality, or 1 Crystal of Insight, or 1 Crystal of Ferocity											
More Irradiated Crystal Shards	Bloodmyst Isle	Alliance	All			Vindicator Boros	Irradiated Crystal Shards				
CHOICE OF: 1 Crystal of Vitality, or 1 Crystal of Insight, or 1 Crystal of Ferocity											
Constrictor Vines	Bloodmyst Isle	Alliance	All		Tracker Lyceon	Tracker Lyceon				1050	7
WANTED: Deathclaw	Bloodmyst Isle	Alliance	All		Wanted Poster	Harbinger Mikolaas				1250	18
CHOICE OF: 1 Carved Cystalline Orb, or 1 Peacekeeper's Buckler											
Culling the Flutterers	Bloodmyst Isle	Alliance	All		Tracker Lyceon	Tracker Lyceon	Constrictor Vines			1150	8
CHOICE OF: 1 Cincture of Woven Reeds, or 1 Ornately Tooled Belt, or 1 Segmented Girdle											
Mac'Aree Mushroom Menagerie	Bloodmyst Isle	Alliance	All		Jessera of Mac'Aree	Jessera of Mac'Aree				975	13
CHOICE OF: 1 Jessera's Fungus Lined Cuffs, or 1 Jessera's Fungus Lined Bands, or 1 Jessera's Fungus Lined Bracers											
Ysera's Tears	Bloodmyst Isle	Alliance	All		Jessera of Mac'Aree	Jessera of Mac'Aree	Mac'Aree Mushroom Menagerie			1350	30
CHOICE OF: 1 Jessera's Fungus Lined Tunic, or 1 Jessera's Fungus Lined Vest, or 1 Jessera's Fungus Lined Hauberk											
The Kessel Run	Bloodmyst Isle	Alliance	All		Kessel	Kessel				900	
Declaration of Power	Bloodmyst Isle	Alliance	All		Kessel	Kessel	The Kessel Run			900	6
CHOICE OF: 1 Kessel's Cinch Wrap, or 1 Kessel's Sweat Stained Elekk Leash, or 1 Kessel's Sturdy Riding Handle											
Saving Princess Stillpine	Bloodmyst Isle	Alliance	All		Princess Stillpine	Stillpine Ambassador Frasaboo	Stillpine Hold			1150	
CHOICE OF: 1 Stillpine Shocker, or 1 The Thumper											
Report to Exarch Admetius	Bloodmyst Isle	Alliance	All		Kessel	Exarch Admetius	Declaration of Power			90	
The Missing Expedition	Bloodmyst Isle	Alliance	All		Achelus	Achelus				1450	30
They're Alive! Maybe...	Bloodmyst Isle	Alliance	All		Researcher Cornelius	Researcher Cornelius				1450	
REWARD: 1 Venomous Silk Cover											
Urgent Delivery	Bloodmyst Isle	Alliance	All			Messenger Hermesius	A Small Start				

Title	Location	Faction	Race & Class	Group #	Starter	Finisher	Prerequisite	Reputation	Tradeskill	XP	Money
The Bloodcurse Legacy	Bloodmyst Isle	Alliance	All		A Letter from the Admiral	Captain Edward Hanes	Urgent Delivery			340	
The Bloodcursed Naga	Bloodmyst Isle	Alliance	All		Captain Edward Hanes	Captain Edward Hanes	The Bloodcurse Legacy			1350	
The Hopeless Ones...	Bloodmyst Isle	Alliance	All		Captain Edward Hanes	Captain Edward Hanes	The Bloodcursed Naga			1350	
Ending the Bloodcurse	Bloodmyst Isle	Alliance	All		Captain Edward Hanes	Captain Edward Hanes	The Hopeless Ones...			1450	
REWARD: 1 Wheel of the Lost Hope											
Restoring Sanctity	Bloodmyst Isle	Alliance	All		Prince Toreth	Prince Toreth				1350	
Into the Dream	Bloodmyst Isle	Alliance	All		Prince Toreth	Prince Toreth	Restoring Sanctity			1450	
Razormaw	Bloodmyst Isle	Alliance	All	2	Prince Toreth	Prince Toreth	Into the Dream			1650	
CHOICE OF: 1 Robe of the Dragon Slayer, or 1 Tunic of the Dragon Slayer, or 1 Vest of the Dragon Slayer											
What Argus Means to Me	Bloodmyst Isle	Alliance	All		Exarch Admetius	Vindicator Boros				110	
Blood Watch	Bloodmyst Isle	Alliance	All		Vindicator Boros	Vindicator Boros	What Argus Means to Me			1050	
CHOICE OF: 1 Fist of Argus, or 1 Blade of Argus, or 1 Hand of Argus Crossfire											
Translations...	Bloodmyst Isle	Alliance	All		Vindicator Boros	Interrogator Elysia	Intercepting the Message			120	
Audience with the Prophet	Bloodmyst Isle	Alliance	All		Interrogator Elysia	Prophet Velen	Translations...			1150	
Truth or Fiction	Bloodmyst Isle	Alliance	All		Prophet Velen	Vindicator Boros	Audience with the Prophet			290	
I Shoot Magic Into the Darkness	Bloodmyst Isle	Alliance	All		Vindicator Boros	Vindicator Boros	Truth or Fiction			1150	
CHOICE OF: 1 Vindicator's Soft Sole Slippers, or 1 Vindicator's Leather Moccasins, or 1 Vindicator's Stompers											
The Cryo-Core	Bloodmyst Isle	Alliance	All		Vindicator Kuros	Vindicator Kuros	I Shoot Magic Into the Darkness			1250	
CHOICE OF: 1 Vindicator's Smasher, or 1 Vindicator's Walking Stick, or 1 Vindicator's Letter Opener											
Galaen's Journal - The Fate of Vindicator Saruan	Bloodmyst Isle	Alliance	All		Galaen's Journal	Vindicator Kuros	Blood Watch			1000	
Matis the Cruel	Bloodmyst Isle	Alliance	All	2	Vindicator Kuros	Vindicator Kuros	Galaen's Journal - The Fate of Vindicator Saruan			1350	
CHOICE OF: 1 Vindicator's Woolies, or 1 Vindicator's Leather Chaps, or 1 Vindicator's Iron Legguards											
The Sun Gate	Bloodmyst Isle	Alliance	All		Vindicator Aesom	Vindicator Aesom	Limits of Physical Exhaustion			1350	
Critters of the Void	Bloodmyst Isle	Alliance	All		Scout Loryi	Vindicator Aesom				1000	
Limits of Physical Exhaustion	Bloodmyst Isle	Alliance	All		Vindicator Aesom	Vindicator Aesom	Don't Drink the Water			1350	
Don't Drink the Water	Bloodmyst Isle	Alliance	All		Vindicator Aesom	Vindicator Aesom	The Cryo-Core			1350	
The Bloodcurse Legacy	Bloodmyst Isle	Alliance	All		Admiral Odesyus	Captain Edward Hanes	Urgent Delivery			340	
What We Know...	Bloodmyst Isle	Alliance	Draenei	2	Vindicator Aesom	Exarch Admetius				160	
What We Don't Know...	Bloodmyst Isle	Alliance	Draenei	2	Exarch Admetius	Exarch Admetius	What We Know...			1150	
Ending Their World	Bloodmyst Isle	Alliance	Draenei	2	Demolitionist Legoso	Exarch Admetius	What We Don't Know...			2350	35
CHOICE OF: 1 Blade of the Hand, or 1 Crossbow of the Hand, or 1 Mace of the Hand, or 1 Staff of the Hand											
Vindicator's Rest	Bloodmyst Isle	Alliance	Draenei	2	Exarch Admetius	Vindicator Corin	What We Don't Know...			390	
Clearing the Way	Bloodmyst Isle	Alliance	Draenei	2	Vindicator Corin	Vindicator Corin	Vindicator's Rest			1950	
CHOICE OF: 1 Flutterer Silk Handwraps, or 1 Ravager Hide Gloves, or 1 Corin's Handguards											
The Unwritten Prophecy	Bloodmyst Isle	Alliance	Draenei			Prophet Velen	Ending Their World				
CHOICE OF: 1 Signet Ring of the Hand, or 1 Signet Ring of the Hand											
REWARD: 1 Tabard of the Hand											
Intercepting the Message	Bloodmyst Isle	Alliance	All		Vindicator Boros	Vindicator Boros	Blood Watch			1150	
Explorers' League, Is That Something for Gnomes?	Bloodmyst Isle	Alliance	All		Prospector Nachlan	Clopper Wizbang				320	
Talk to the Hand	Bloodmyst Isle	Alliance	All		Harbinger Mikolaas	Scout Jorli				140	
Cutting a Path	Bloodmyst Isle	Alliance	All		Scout Jorli	Scout Jorli				1250	
Oh, the Tangled Webs They Weave	Bloodmyst Isle	Alliance	All		Vindicator Corin	Vindicator Corin				1700	10
Fouled Water Spirits	Bloodmyst Isle	Alliance	All		Vindicator Corin	Vindicator Corin				1450	11
Call of Water	Bloodmyst Isle	Alliance	All		Farseer Umbrua	Farseer Nobundo				390	
The Master's Touch	Caverns of Time	All	All		Khadgar	Medivh	The Second and Third Fragments			15800	
The Caverns of Time	Caverns of Time	All	All		Andormu	Andormu				1200	
To The Master's Lair	Caverns of Time	All	All		Steward of Time	Andormu				1150	
Old Hillsbrad	Caverns of Time	All	All	5	Andormu	Erozion	The Caverns of Time			1200	
Taretha's Diversion	Caverns of Time	All	All	5	Erozion	Thrall	Old Hillsbrad			17950	
Escape from Durnholde	Caverns of Time	All	All	5	Thrall	Erozion	Taretha's Diversion			17950	
Return to Andormu	Caverns of Time	All	All		Erozion	Andormu	Escape from Durnholde			1200	
CHOICE OF: 1 Tempest's Touch, or 1 Southshore Sneakers, or 1 Tarren Mill Defender's Cinch, or 1 Warchief's Mantle											
The Black Morass	Caverns of Time	All	All	5	Andormu	Sa'at	Return to Andormu			1250	
The Opening of the Dark Portal	Caverns of Time	All	All	5	Sa'at	Sa'at	The Black Morass			19000	

Title	Location	Faction	Race & Class	Group #	Starter	Finisher	Prerequisite	Reputation	Tradeskill	XP	Money
Caverns of Time											
Hero of the Brood	Caverns of Time	All	All		Sa'at	Andormu	The Opening of the Dark Portal			1250	
CHOICE OF: 1 Band of the Guardian, or 1 Keeper's Ring of Piety, or 1 Time-bending Gem, or 1 Andormu's Tear											
The Vials of Eternity	Caverns of Time	All	All	Raid	Soridormi	Soridormi				19000	13 20
Defender's Pledge	Caverns of Time	All	All			Soridormi		3000 with The Scale of the Sands		12650	
REWARD: 1 Band of Eternity											
Restorer's Pledge	Caverns of Time	All	All			Soridormi		3000 with The Scale of the Sands		12650	
REWARD: 1 Band of Eternity											
Champion's Pledge	Caverns of Time	All	All			Soridormi		3000 with The Scale of the Sands		12650	
REWARD: 1 Band of Eternity											
Sage's Pledge	Caverns of Time	All	All			Soridormi		3000 with The Scale of the Sands		12650	
REWARD: 1 Band of Eternity											
Sage's Vow	Caverns of Time	All	All		Soridormi	Soridormi	Sage's Pledge			15800	
REWARD: 1 Band of Eternity											
Restorer's Vow	Caverns of Time	All	All		Soridormi	Soridormi	Restorer's Pledge			15800	
REWARD: 1 Band of Eternity											
Champion's Vow	Caverns of Time	All	All		Soridormi	Soridormi	Champion's Pledge			15800	
REWARD: 1 Band of Eternity											
Defender's Vow	Caverns of Time	All	All		Soridormi	Soridormi	Defender's Pledge			15800	
REWARD: 1 Band of Eternity											
Sage's Oath	Caverns of Time	All	All		Soridormi	Soridormi	Sage's Vow			15800	
REWARD: 1 Band of Eternity											
Restorer's Oath	Caverns of Time	All	All		Soridormi	Soridormi	Restorer's Vow			15800	
REWARD: 1 Band of Eternity											
Champion's Oath	Caverns of Time	All	All		Soridormi	Soridormi	Champion's Vow			15800	
REWARD: 1 Band of Eternity											
Defender's Oath	Caverns of Time	All	All		Soridormi	Soridormi	Defender's Vow			15800	
REWARD: 1 Band of Eternity											
Sage's Covenant	Caverns of Time	All	All		Soridormi	Soridormi	Sage's Oath			15800	
REWARD: 1 Band of the Eternal Sage											
Restorer's Covenant	Caverns of Time	All	All		Soridormi	Soridormi	Restorer's Oath			15800	
REWARD: 1 Band of the Eternal Restorer											
Champion's Covenant	Caverns of Time	All	All		Soridormi	Soridormi	Champion's Oath			15800	
REWARD: 1 Band of the Eternal Champion											
Defender's Covenant	Caverns of Time	All	All		Soridormi	Soridormi	Defender's Oath			15800	
REWARD: 1 Band of the Eternal Defender											
Coilfang Reservoir											
Lost in Action	Coilfang Reservoir	All	All	5	Watcher Jhang	Watcher Jhang				16500	
CHOICE OF: 1 Cenarion Ring of Casting, or 1 Goldenvine Wraps, or 1 Dark Cloak of the Marsh											
The Warlord's Hideout	Coilfang Reservoir	All	All	5	Watcher Jhang	Watcher Jhang				19000	13 20
CHOICE OF: 1 Hydromancer's Headwrap, or 1 Helm of the Claw, or 1 Earthwarden's Coif, or 1 Myrmidon's Headdress											
Orders from Lady Vashj	Coilfang Reservoir	All	All		Orders from Lady Vashj	Ysiel Windsinger				12650	
Preparing for War	Coilfang Reservoir	All	All	5	Ysiel Windsinger	Ysiel Windsinger	Orders from Lady Vashj			12650	
Coilfang Armaments	Coilfang Reservoir	All	All			Ysiel Windsinger	Preparing for War				
The Mark of Vashj	Coilfang Reservoir	All	All	Raid		Skar'this the Heretic					
The Cudgel of Kar'desh	Coilfang Reservoir	All	All	Raid	Skar'this the Heretic	Skar'this the Heretic	The Mark of Vashj			19000	
Eversong Woods											
Twilight of the Dawn Runner	Dustwallow Marsh	Horde	All		Balandar Brightstar	Balandar Brightstar				2850	40
Unstable Mana Crystals	Eversong Woods	Horde	All		Aeldon Sunbrand	Aeldon Sunbrand				450	1
Wanted: Thaelis the Hungerer	Eversong Woods	Horde	All		Wanted: Thaelis the Hungerer	Sergeant Kan'ren				550	2 50
Major Malfunction	Eversong Woods	Horde	All		Magister Jaronis	Magister Jaronis				450	1
CHOICE OF: 1 Green Chain Belt, or 1 Light Silk Robe, or 1 Soft Leather Vest											
A Somber Task	Eversong Woods	Horde	All		Larianna Riverwind	Larianna Riverwind				775	3
Old Whitebark's Pendant	Eversong Woods	Horde	All		Old Whitebark's Pendant	Larianna Riverwind				850	3 50
The Dead Scar	Eversong Woods	Horde	All		Ranger Jaela	Ranger Jaela				550	
CHOICE OF: 1 Black Leather Vest, or 1 Gatewatcher's Chain Gloves, or 1 Guard's Leggings											
Amani Encroachment	Eversong Woods	Horde	All		Lieutenant Dawnrunner	Lieutenant Dawnrunner				850	3 50
The Spearcrafter's Hammer	Eversong Woods	Horde	All		Arathel Sunforge	Arathel Sunforge				850	3 50
CHOICE OF: 1 Farstrider Sword, or 1 Smooth Metal Staff, or 1 Ranger's Pocketknife											

Title	Location	Faction	Race & Class	Group #	Starter	Finisher	Prerequisite	Reputation	Tradeskill	XP	Money
Zul'Marosh	Eversong Woods	Horde	All		Ven'jashi	Ven'jashi				875	
CHOICE OF: 1 Ven'jashi's Bow, or 1 Hoodoo Wand											
Lost Armaments	Eversong Woods	Horde	All		Velendris Whitemorn	Velendris Whitemorn				625	1● 75●
CHOICE OF: 1 Rusty Sin'dorei Sword, or 1 Rusty Mace											
Incriminating Documents	Eversong Woods	Horde	All		Incriminating Documents	Aeldon Sunbrand				675	2● 50●
The Dwarven Spy	Eversong Woods	Horde	All		Aeldon Sunbrand	Aeldon Sunbrand	Incriminating Documents			800	
CHOICE OF: 1 Bloodhawk Claymore, or 1 Long Knife											
Arcane Instability	Eversong Woods	Horde	All		Ley-Keeper Velania	Ley-Keeper Velania	Malfunction at the West Sanctum			550	
CHOICE OF: 1 Ley-Keeper's Blade, or 1 Velania's Walking Stick											
Corrupted Soil	Eversong Woods	Horde	All		Apprentice Mirveda	Apprentice Mirveda				775	3●
Unexpected Results	Eversong Woods	Horde	All		Apprentice Mirveda	Apprentice Mirveda	Corrupted Soil			775	3●
Powering our Defenses	Eversong Woods	Horde	All		Runewarden Deryan	Runewarden Deryan				850	3● 50●
Pelt Collection	Eversong Woods	Horde	All		Velan Brightoak	Velan Brightoak				625	1● 75●
CHOICE OF: 1 Springpaw Hide Leggings, or 1 Fur Lined Chain Shirt, or 1 Springpaw Hide Cloak											
Fish Heads, Fish Heads...	Eversong Woods	Horde	All		Hathvelion Sungaze	Hathvelion Sungaze				625	
The Ring of Mmmrrrggglll	Eversong Woods	Horde	All		Hathvelion Sungaze	Hathvelion Sungaze	Fish Heads, Fish Heads...			975	6●
CHOICE OF: 1 Worn Ranger's Bow, or 1 Farstrider's Buckler, or 1 Satin Lined Gloves, or 1 Slightly Used Ranger's Blade											
Grimscale Pirates!	Eversong Woods	Horde	All		Captain Kelisendra	Captain Kelisendra				700	2● 25●
Captain Kelisendra's Lost Rudders	Eversong Woods	Horde	All		Captain Kelisendra's Lost Rudders	Captain Kelisendra				700	2● 25●
The Magister's Apprentice	Eversong Woods	Horde	All		Magister Duskwither	Apprentice Loralthalis				85	
Deactivating the Spire	Eversong Woods	Horde	All		Apprentice Loralthalis	Apprentice Loralthalis				625	
Word from the Spire	Eversong Woods	Horde	All		Apprentice Loralthalis	Magister Duskwither	Deactivating the Spire			850	
REWARD: 1 Fallen Apprentice's Robe											
Abandoned Investigations	Eversong Woods	Horde	All		Magister Duskwither's Journal	Magister Duskwither				850	3● 50●
Situation at Sunsail Anchorage	Eversong Woods	Horde	All		Ranger Degolien	Ranger Degolien				625	1● 75●
Cleaning up the Grounds	Eversong Woods	Horde	All		Groundskeeper Wyllithen	Groundskeeper Wyllithen				850	3● 50●
Delivery to the North Sanctum	Eversong Woods	Horde	All		Magister Jaronis	Ley-Keeper Caidanis	Major Malfunction			140	35●
Roadside Ambush	Eversong Woods	Horde	All		Apprentice Ralen	Apprentice Meledor				55	
Soaked Pages	Eversong Woods	Horde	All		Apprentice Meledor	Apprentice Meledor				270	2● 50●
Taking the Fall	Eversong Woods	Horde	All		Apprentice Meledor	Instructor Antheol	Soaked Pages			140	1● 25●
Swift Discipline	Eversong Woods	Horde	All		Instructor Antheol	Instructor Antheol	Taking the Fall			550	1● 25●
REWARD: 1 Magister's Pouch											
The Party Never Ends	Eversong Woods	Horde	All		Lord Saltheril	Lord Saltheril				775	9●
REWARD: 1 Saltheril's Haven Party Invitation											
Wretched Ringleader	Eversong Woods	Horde	All		Velendris Whitemorn	Velendris Whitemorn	Lost Armaments			700	2● 25●
CHOICE OF: 1 Sunsail Bracers, or 1 Longshoreman's Bindings, or 1 Silk Wristbands											
Malfunction at the West Sanctum	Eversong Woods	Horde	All		Ley-Keeper Caidanis	Ley-Keeper Velania	Delivery to the North Sanctum			450	1●
Missing in the Ghostlands	Eversong Woods	Horde	All		Magistrix Landra Dawnstrider	Courier Dawnstrider				420	
Defending Fairbreeze Village	Eversong Woods	Horde	All		Ranger Sareyn	Ranger Sareyn				775	3●
Runewarden Deryan	Eversong Woods	Horde	All		Ranger Sareyn	Runewarden Deryan	Defending Fairbreeze Village			210	85●
The Wayward Apprentice	Eversong Woods	Horde	All		Magistrix Landra Dawnstrider	Apprentice Mirveda				390	70●
Research Notes	Eversong Woods	Horde	All		Apprentice Mirveda	Magistrix Landra Dawnstrider	Unexpected Results			390	70●
Fairbreeze Village	Eversong Woods	Horde	All		Aeldon Sunbrand	Ranger Degolien	The Dwarven Spy			320	85●
The Scorched Grove	Eversong Woods	Horde	All		Ardeyn Riverwind	Larianna Riverwind				210	85●

Eversong Woods

Title	Location	Faction	Race & Class	Group #	Starter	Finisher	Prerequisite	Reputation	Tradeskill	XP	Money
Darnassian Intrusions	Eversong Woods	Horde	All		Aeldon Sunbrand	Ley-Keeper Velania	Unstable Mana Crystals			550	1● 25●
Ranger Sareyn	Eversong Woods	Horde	All		Marniel Amberlight	Ranger Sareyn				80	
Farstrider Retreat	Eversong Woods	Horde	All		Ranger Degolien	Lieutenant Dawnrunner	Situation at Sunsail Anchorage			85	
Amani Invasion	Eversong Woods	Horde	All		Amani Invasion Plans	Lieutenant Dawnrunner				875	4●
Warning Fairbreeze Village	Eversong Woods	Horde	All		Lieutenant Dawnrunner	Ranger Degolien	Amani Invasion			440	2●
CHOICE OF: 1 Blackened Chain Girdle, or 1 Ranger's Vest, or 1 Satin Lined Boots											
Where's Wyllithen?	Eversong Woods	Horde	All		Apprentice Loralthalis	Groundskeeper Wyllithen				85	
Saltheril's Haven	Eversong Woods	Horde	All		Magistrix Landra Dawnstrider	Lord Saltheril				80	
Fetch!	Eversong Woods	Horde	All Mage		Instructor Antheol	Instructor Antheol				210	
The Purest Water	Eversong Woods	Horde	All Mage		Instructor Antheol	Instructor Antheol	Fetch!			850	
Recently Living	Eversong Woods	Horde	All Mage		Instructor Antheol	Instructor Antheol	The Purest Water			850	
CHOICE OF: 1 Ley Staff, or 1 Ley Orb											
Combining Forces	Eversong Woods	Horde	Blood Elf Rogue		Keltus Darkleaf	Keltus Darkleaf	Find Keltus Darkleaf			900	
REWARD: 1 Stack of Reports											
Taming the Beast	Eversong Woods	Horde	Blood Elf Hunter		Lieutenant Dawnrunner	Lieutenant Dawnrunner				850	
Taming the Beast	Eversong Woods	Horde	Blood Elf Hunter		Lieutenant Dawnrunner	Lieutenant Dawnrunner	Taming the Beast			850	
Taming the Beast	Eversong Woods	Horde	Blood Elf Hunter		Lieutenant Dawnrunner	Lieutenant Dawnrunner	Taming the Beast			850	
Cleansing the Scar	Eversong Woods	Horde	Blood Elf Priest		Ponaris	Ponaris				450	
REWARD: 1 Robes of Silvermoon											
The Stone	Eversong Woods	Horde	Blood Elf Warlock		Talionia	Voidstone				850	
Find Keltus Darkleaf	Eversong Woods	Horde	Blood Elf Rogue		Zelanis	Keltus Darkleaf				850	
Seek the Farstriders	Eversong Woods	Horde	Blood Elf Hunter		Oninath	Lieutenant Dawnrunner				85	
Return the Reports	Eversong Woods	Horde	Blood Elf Rogue		Keltus Darkleaf	Zelanis	Combining Forces			850	
REWARD: 1 Blade of Cunning											
The Rune of Summoning	Eversong Woods	Horde	Blood Elf Warlock		Voidstone	Talionia	The Stone			850	
Summons from Knight-Lord Bloodvalor	Eversong Woods	Horde	Blood Elf Paladin		Noellene	Knight-Lord Bloodvalor				90	
Whitebark's Memory	Eversong Woods	Horde	All		Larianna Riverwind	Whitebark's Spirit	Old Whitebark's Pendant			850	

Exodar

Title	Location	Faction	Race & Class	Group #	Starter	Finisher	Prerequisite	Reputation	Tradeskill	XP	Money
Seek Huntress Kella Nightbow	Exodar	Alliance	Draenei Hunter		Killac	Huntress Kella Nightbow				85	
A Donation of Mageweave	Exodar	Alliance	All			Dugiru				3300	
A Donation of Runecloth	Exodar	Alliance	All			Dugiru	A Donation of Wool			6600	
Additional Runecloth	Exodar	Alliance	All			Dugiru	A Donation of Runecloth				
Yorus Barleybrew	Exodar	Alliance	All		Ahonan	Yorus Barleybrew				160	
A Call to Arms: The Plaguelands!	Exodar	Alliance	All		Herald Bran'daan	Commander Ashlam Valorfist				470	
Assisting Arch Druid Staghelm	Exodar	Alliance	All		Caregiver Breel	Arch Druid Fandral Staghelm				470	

Ghostlands

Title	Location	Faction	Race & Class	Group #	Starter	Finisher	Prerequisite	Reputation	Tradeskill	XP	Money
Goods from Silvermoon City	Ghostlands	Horde	Blood Elf		Quartermaster Lymel	Skymaster Sunwing	The Forsaken			210	
Fly to Silvermoon City	Ghostlands	Horde	Blood Elf		Skymaster Sunwing	Sathren Azuredawn	Goods from Silvermoon City			420	1● 75●
Skymistress Gloaming	Ghostlands	Horde	Blood Elf		Sathren Azuredawn	Skymistress Gloaming	Fly to Silvermoon City			210	
Return to Quartermaster Lymel	Ghostlands	Horde	Blood Elf		Skymistress Gloaming	Quartermaster Lymel	Skymistress Gloaming			1050	3● 50●
Suncrown Village	Ghostlands	Horde	All		Arcanist Vandril	Arcanist Vandril	Return to Arcanist Vandril			850	3● 50●
Goldenmist Village	Ghostlands	Horde	All		Arcanist Vandril	Arcanist Vandril	Suncrown Village			875	4●
REWARD: 5 Goldenmist Special Brew and 1 Quel'Thalas Recurve											
Windrunner Village	Ghostlands	Horde	All		Arcanist Vandril	Arcanist Vandril	Goldenmist Village			1250	13●
CHOICE OF: 1 Arcanist's Dagger, or 1 Salvaged Mail Leggings, or 1 Padded Running Shoes, or 1 Arcanist's Wand											
Dealing with Zeb'Sora	Ghostlands	Horde	All		Ranger Valanna	Ranger Valanna				900	
Help Ranger Valanna!	Ghostlands	Horde	All		Ranger Lethvalin	Ranger Valanna	The Forsaken	3000 with Tranquillien		230	
Report to Captain Helios	Ghostlands	Horde	All		Ranger Valanna	Captain Helios	Dealing with Zeb'Sora			230	5●
CHOICE OF: 1 Farstrider's Tunic, or 1 Troll Handler Gloves, or 1 Farstrider's Shield											

Title	Location	Faction	Race & Class	Group #	Starter	Finisher	Prerequisite	Reputation	Tradeskill	XP	Money
The Fallen Courier	Ghostlands	Horde	All		Apothecary Thedra	Apothecary Thedra				850	
Delivery to Tranquillien	Ghostlands	Horde	All		Courier Dawnstrider	Arcanist Vandril	The Fallen Courier			420	1● 75●
CHOICE OF: 1 Courier's Wraps, or 1 Tranquillien Scout's Bracers, or 1 Bronze Mail Bracers											
REWARD: 1 Courier's Bag											
The Plagued Coast	Ghostlands	Horde	All		Apothecary Renzithen	Apothecary Renzithen	The Forsaken			900	6●
REWARD: 2 Swim Speed Potion and 1 Renzithen's Dusty Cloak											
Salvaging the Past	Ghostlands	Horde	All		Magister Darenis	Magister Darenis	The Forsaken	3000 with Tranquillien		900	5●
The Sanctum of the Sun	Ghostlands	Horde	All		Magister Darenis	Magister Idonis				775	6●
Tomber's Supplies	Ghostlands	Horde	All		Rathis Tomber	Rathis Tomber	The Forsaken			875	4●
Down the Dead Scar	Ghostlands	Horde	All		Deathstalker Rathiel	Deathstalker Rathiel	The Forsaken	3000 with Tranquillien		975	6●
Wanted: Knucklerot and Luzran	Ghostlands	Horde	All	3	Wanted Poster	Deathstalker Rathiel				2500	40●
CHOICE OF: 1 Invoker's Signet, or 1 Slayer's Band											
Forgotten Rituals	Ghostlands	Horde	All		Geranis Whitemorn	Geranis Whitemorn				900	5●
Bearers of the Plague	Ghostlands	Horde	All		Farstrider Sedina	Farstrider Sedina				975	6●
Curbing the Plague	Ghostlands	Horde	All		Farstrider Sedina	Farstrider Sedina	Bearers of the Plague			1050	7●
CHOICE OF: 1 Ranger's Sash, or 1 Farstrider's Belt, or 1 Rusted Chain Girdle											
REWARD: 1 Survival Knife											
Investigate An'daroth	Ghostlands	Horde	All		Dame Auriferous	Dame Auriferous	The Forsaken	3000 with Tranquillien		875	4●
REWARD: 2 Lesser Healing Potion											
The Traitor's Shadow	Ghostlands	Horde	All		Ranger Vynna	Dusty Journal				1150	
Hints of the Past	Ghostlands	Horde	All		Dusty Journal	Ranger Vynna	The Traitor's Shadow			1150	8●
Into Occupied Territory	Ghostlands	Horde	All		Dame Auriferous	Dame Auriferous	Investigate An'daroth	3000 with Tranquillien		975	6●
Captives at Deatholme	Ghostlands	Horde	All		Apothecary Renzithen	Arcanist Janeda	A Restorative Draught			1950	25●
Deliver the Plans to An'telas	Ghostlands	Horde	All		Dame Auriferous	Magister Sylastor	Into Occupied Territory	3000 with Tranquillien		290	
The Traitor's Destruction	Ghostlands	Horde	All	5	Magister Kaendris	Magister Kaendris	The Twin Ziggurats			2500	40●
CHOICE OF: 1 Staff of the Sun, or 1 Farstrider's Longbow, or 1 Dawnblade, or 1 Sin'dorei Warblade											
Deactivate An'owyn	Ghostlands	Horde	All		Magister Sylastor	Magister Sylastor	Deliver the Plans to An'telas	3000 with Tranquillien		1450	16●
CHOICE OF: 1 Sylastor's Cloak, or 1 Divining Crystal, or 1 An'telas Scale Shirt											
Dar'Khan's Lieutenants	Ghostlands	Horde	All		Magister Idonis	Magister Idonis	War on Deatholme			1950	25●
CHOICE OF: 1 Reforged Quel'dorei Crest, or 1 Ley-Keeper's Wand, or 1 Ghostclaw Leggings											
Culinary Crunch	Ghostlands	Horde	All		Master Chef Mouldier	Master Chef Mouldier	The Forsaken	3000 with Tranquillien		1050	
REWARD: 5 Crunchy Spider Surprise and 1 Recipe: Crunchy Spider Surprise											
Report to Magister Kaendris	Ghostlands	Horde	All		Ranger Vynna	Magister Kaendris	Hints of the Past			1150	8●
CHOICE OF: 1 Red Silk Trousers, or 1 Black Leather Jerkin, or 1 Tranquillien Scale Leggings											
Retaking Windrunner Spire	Ghostlands	Horde	All		High Executor Mavren	High Executor Mavren	The Forsaken	9000 with Tranquillien		1050	7●
Vanquishing Aquantion	Ghostlands	Horde	All		Geranis Whitemorn	Geranis Whitemorn	Forgotten Rituals			1150	11●
The Lady's Necklace	Ghostlands	Horde	All		The Lady's Necklace	High Executor Mavren				1050	14●
The Twin Ziggurats	Ghostlands	Horde	All		Magister Kaendris	Magister Kaendris	Report to Magister Kaendris			1900	9●
CHOICE OF: 1 Sunwell Blade, or 1 Sunwell Orb											
Journey to Undercity	Ghostlands	Horde	Non-Blood Elf		High Executor Mavren	Lady Sylvanas Windrunner	The Lady's Necklace			1350	
Journey to Undercity	Ghostlands	Horde	Blood Elf		High Executor Mavren	Lady Sylvanas Windrunner	The Lady's Necklace			1350	
Trouble at the Underlight Mines	Ghostlands	Horde	All		Deathstalker Maltendis	Deathstalker Maltendis	The Forsaken	3000 with Tranquillien		975	6●
Investigate the Amani Catacombs	Ghostlands	Horde	All		Advisor Valwyn	Advisor Valwyn				1250	9●
Troll Juju	Ghostlands	Horde	All		Deathstalker Maltendis	Deathstalker Maltendis				1250	9●
CHOICE OF: 1 Rotting Handwraps, or 1 Undertaker's Gloves, or 1 Maltendis's Handguards											
Underlight Ore Samples	Ghostlands	Horde	All		Apprentice Shatharia	Magister Quallestis		3000 with Tranquillien		975	6●
Escape from the Catacombs	Ghostlands	Horde	All		Ranger Lilatha	Captain Helios				1250	9●
CHOICE OF: 1 Troll Kickers, or 1 Troll Kickers, or 1 Troll Kickers											
Shadowpine Weaponry	Ghostlands	Horde	All		Captain Helios	Captain Helios				1350	10●
Bring Me Kel'gash's Head!	Ghostlands	Horde	All	2	Wanted Poster: Kel'gash the Wicked	Captain Helios				1950	25●
CHOICE OF: 1 Well Crafted Long Bow, or 1 Well Crafted Sword, or 1 Well Crafted Staff											
Rotting Hearts	Ghostlands	Horde	All		Magistrix Aminel	Magistrix Aminel				1150	
REWARD: 1 Scourgebane Draught											
More Rotting Hearts	Ghostlands	Horde	All			Magistrix Aminel	Rotting Hearts				
REWARD: 1 Scourgebane Draught											
Spinal Dust	Ghostlands	Horde	All		Magistrix Aminel	Magistrix Aminel				1350	
REWARD: 1 Scourgebane Infusion											

Ghostlands

Title	Location	Faction	Race & Class	Group #	Starter	Finisher	Prerequisite	Reputation	Tradeskill	XP	Money
More Spinal Dust	Ghostlands	Horde	All			Magistrix Aminel	Spinal Dust				
REWARD: 1 Scourgebane Infusion											
War on Deatholme	Ghostlands	Horde	All		Magister Idonis	Magister Idonis				1950	25
Spirits of the Drowned	Ghostlands	Horde	All		Ranger Krenn'an	Ranger Krenn'an				900	5
A Little Dash of Seasoning	Ghostlands	Horde	All		Apothecary Venustus	Apothecary Venustus				1450	11
Attack on Zeb'Tela	Ghostlands	Horde	All		Farstrider Solanna	Farstrider Solanna				1350	10
Assault on Zeb'Nowa	Ghostlands	Horde	All		Farstrider Solanna	Farstrider Solanna	Attack on Zeb'Tela			1450	11
CHOICE OF: 1 Sentry Bracers, or 1 Supple Cotton Bracer, or 1 Farstrider's Bracers											
Clearing the Way	Ghostlands	Horde	All		Apprentice Vor'el	Apprentice Vor'el				1350	20
The Farstrider Enclave	Ghostlands	Horde	All		Magister Kaendris	Ranger Vynna				575	
Anok'suten	Ghostlands	Horde	All	2	Dying Blood Elf	Arcanist Vandril	The Forsaken			875	4
CHOICE OF: 1 Fortified Oven Mitts, or 1 Stung, or 1 Vandril's Hand Me Down Pants, or 1 Tranquillien Breeches											
The Forsaken	Ghostlands	Horde	Blood Elf		Arcanist Vandril	High Executor Mavren				85	
The Forsaken	Ghostlands	Horde	Non-Blood Elf		Arcanist Vandril	High Executor Mavren				85	
Arcane Reavers	Ghostlands	Horde	Blood Elf Mage		Arcanist Vandril	Arcanist Vandril				1150	
A Simple Robe	Ghostlands	Horde	Blood Elf Mage		Arcanist Vandril	Arcanist Vandril	Arcane Reavers			1150	
REWARD: 1 Manaweave Robe											
Greed	Ghostlands	Horde	All Rogue		Eralan	Eralan				1350	
REWARD: 1 Bulging Sack of Silver											
Return to Arcanist Vandril	Ghostlands	Horde	All		High Executor Mavren	Arcanist Vandril	The Forsaken			85	
A Restorative Draught	Ghostlands	Horde	All		Arcanist Janeda	Apothecary Renzithen	War on Deatholme			390	
The Sad Truth	Ghostlands	Horde	All		Eralan	Eralan	Greed			1350	
CHOICE OF: 1 Leafblade Dagger, or 1 Ghostclaw Tunic											

Hellfire Citadel

Title	Location	Faction	Race & Class	Group #	Starter	Finisher	Prerequisite	Reputation	Tradeskill	XP	Money
Turning the Tide	Hellfire Citadel	Alliance	All	5	Force Commander Danath Trollbane	Force Commander Danath Trollbane				12650	4 40
CHOICE OF: 1 Nethekurse's Rod of Torment, or 1 Mantle of Vivification, or 1 Naliko's Revenge, or 1 Medallion of the Valiant Guardian											
Pride of the Fel Horde	Hellfire Citadel	Alliance	All	5	Field Commander Romus	Field Commander Romus				12650	4 40
Fel Embers	Hellfire Citadel	Alliance	All	5	Magus Zabraxis	Magus Zabraxis				12650	4 40
CHOICE OF: 1 Curate's Boots, or 1 Rune-Engraved Belt, or 1 Gloves of Preservation, or 1 Expedition Scout's Epaulets, or 1 Dauntless Handguards											
The Will of the Warchief	Hellfire Citadel	Horde	All	5	Nazgrel	Nazgrel				12650	4 40
CHOICE OF: 1 Rod of Dire Shadows, or 1 Vicar's Cloak, or 1 Conquerer's Band, or 1 Maimfist's Choker											
Pride of the Fel Horde	Hellfire Citadel	Horde	All	5	Shadow Hunter Ty'jin	Shadow Hunter Ty'jin				12650	4 40
Weaken the Ramparts	Hellfire Citadel	Horde	All	5	Stone Guard Stok'ton	Caza'rez	Apothecary Zelana			12600	5 40
CHOICE OF: 1 Handguards of Precison, or 1 Jade Warrior Pauldrons, or 1 Mantle of Magical Might, or 1 Sure-Step Boots											
Weaken the Ramparts	Hellfire Citadel	Alliance	All	5	Lieutenant Chadwick	Gunny	Ill Omens			12600	5 40
CHOICE OF: 1 Handguards of Precison, or 1 Jade Warrior Pauldrons, or 1 Mantle of Magical Might, or 1 Sure-Step Boots											
Dark Tidings	Hellfire Citadel	Alliance	All	5		Force Commander Danath Trollbane				10050	2 70
Dark Tidings	Hellfire Citadel	Horde	All	5		Nazgrel				10050	2 70
The Blood is Life	Hellfire Citadel	Alliance	All	5	Gunny	Gunny	Dark Tidings			12950	5 80
CHOICE OF: 1 Breastplate of Retribution, or 1 Deadly Borer Leggings, or 1 Moonkin Headdress, or 1 Scaled Legs of Ruination											
The Blood is Life	Hellfire Citadel	Horde	All	5	Caza'rez	Caza'rez	Dark Tidings			12950	5 80
CHOICE OF: 1 Breastplate of Retribution, or 1 Deadly Borer Leggings, or 1 Moonkin Headdress, or 1 Scaled Legs of Ruination											
Heart of Rage	Hellfire Citadel	Alliance	All	5	Gunny	Force Commander Danath Trollbane	Weaken the Ramparts			12950	5 80
CHOICE OF: 1 Crimson Pendant of Clarity, or 1 Holy Healing Band, or 1 Perfectly Balanced Cape											
Heart of Rage	Hellfire Citadel	Horde	All	5	Caza'rez	Nazgrel	Weaken the Ramparts			12950	5 80
CHOICE OF: 1 Crimson Pendant of Clarity, or 1 Holy Healing Band, or 1 Perfectly Balanced Cape											

Hellfire Peninsula

Title	Location	Faction	Race & Class	Group #	Starter	Finisher	Prerequisite	Reputation	Tradeskill	XP	Money
The Great Fissure	Hellfire Peninsula	Horde	All		Ranger Captain Venn'ren	Ranger Captain Venn'ren				10050	
Preparing the Salve	Hellfire Peninsula	Horde	All		Grelag	Grelag				9800	
REWARD: 20 Hellfire Spineleaf											
Ravager Egg Roundup	Hellfire Peninsula	All	All		Legassi	Legassi				9800	
REWARD: 5 Ravager Egg Omelet											
Voidwalkers Gone Wild	Hellfire Peninsula	All	All		"Screaming" Screed Luckheed	"Screaming" Screed Luckheed	In Case of Emergency...			9800	2
CHOICE OF: 1 Hypnotist's Watch, or 1 Charm of Alacrity											
A Job for an Intelligent Man	Hellfire Peninsula	Alliance	All		Foreman Biggums	Foreman Biggums	Ill Omens			9800	2
CHOICE OF: 1 Adept's Band, or 1 Imbued Chain											
Smooth as Butter	Hellfire Peninsula	All	All		Legassi	Legassi	Helboar, the Other White Meat			9800	2
REWARD: 5 Buzzard Bites and 1 Recipe: Buzzard Bites											
Helboar, the Other White Meat	Hellfire Peninsula	All	All		Legassi	Legassi	Ravager Egg Roundup			9800	2
REWARD: 5 Helboar Bacon											
In Need of Felblood	Hellfire Peninsula	Horde	All		Ryathen the Somber	Ryathen the Somber				10050	2 70

Title	Location	Faction	Race & Class	Group #	Starter	Finisher	Prerequisite	Reputation	Tradeskill	XP	Money
The Cleansing Must Be Stopped	Hellfire Peninsula	Horde	All		Ryathen the Somber	Ryathen the Somber	In Need of Felblood			10050	2● 70●
CHOICE OF: 1 Felforce Medallion, or 1 Lost Anchorite's Cloak, or 1 Felblood Band											
Demonic Contamination	Hellfire Peninsula	All	All		Thiah Redmane	Thiah Redmane				10400	2● 90●
Missing Missive	Hellfire Peninsula	All	All		Eroded Leather Case	Thiah Redmane				9800	2●
Arelion's Journal	Hellfire Peninsula	Horde	All		Magistrix Carinda	Magistrix Carinda				10050	2● 70●
The Road to Falcon Watch	Hellfire Peninsula	Horde	All	2	Wounded Blood Elf Pilgrim	Taleris Dawngazer				10400	2● 90●
A Pilgrim's Plight	Hellfire Peninsula	Horde	All		Taleris Dawngazer	Taleris Dawngazer	The Road to Falcon Watch			10400	2● 90●
CHOICE OF: 1 Pilgrim's Cover, or 1 Sunstrider Legguards, or 1 Segmented Breastplate											
Trueflight Arrows	Hellfire Peninsula	Horde	All		Falconer Drenna Riverwind	Falconer Drenna Riverwind				10400	2● 90●
An Ambitious Plan	Hellfire Peninsula	Alliance	All		Elsaana	Elsaana				10400	2● 90●
Rampaging Ravagers	Hellfire Peninsula	Alliance	All		Gremni Longbeard	Gremni Longbeard				10400	2● 90●
Source of the Corruption	Hellfire Peninsula	Horde	All		Apothecary Azethen	Apothecary Azethen				10400	2● 90●
CHOICE OF: 1 Broken Choker, or 1 Fallen Vindicator's Blade, or 1 Ring of the Slain Anchorite											
In Search of Sedai	Hellfire Peninsula	Alliance	All		Anchorite Obadei	Sedai's Corpse				2550	
Marking the Path	Hellfire Peninsula	Horde	All		Ranger Captain Venn'ren	Ranger Captain Venn'ren	The Great Fissure			10050	2● 70●
CHOICE OF: 1 Flamehandler's Gloves, or 1 Lightbearer's Gauntlets, or 1 Pilgrim's Belt											
Magic of the Arakkoa	Hellfire Peninsula	Horde	All		Arcanist Calesthris Dawnstar	Arcanist Calesthris Dawnstar				10050	2● 70●
Birds of a Feather	Hellfire Peninsula	Horde	All		Falconer Drenna Riverwind	Falconer Drenna Riverwind				10050	2● 70●
Deadly Predators	Hellfire Peninsula	Alliance	All		Scout Vanura	Scout Vanura				10050	2● 70●
Cruel Taskmasters	Hellfire Peninsula	Alliance	All		Ikan	Ikan				10400	2● 90●
The Assassin	Hellfire Peninsula	Horde	All		Nazgrel	Fel Orc Corpse	Apothecary Zelana			10050	
A Strange Weapon	Hellfire Peninsula	Horde	All		Fel Orc Corpse	Nazgrel	The Assassin			10050	2● 70●
The Warchief's Mandate	Hellfire Peninsula	Horde	All		Nazgrel	Far Seer Regulkut	A Strange Weapon			5000	
The Mag'har	Hellfire Peninsula	Horde	All		Gorkan Bloodfist	Nazgrel	A Spirit Guide			10050	
A Spirit Guide	Hellfire Peninsula	Horde	All		Far Seer Regulkut	Gorkan Bloodfist	The Warchief's Mandate			10050	
The Arakkoa Threat	Hellfire Peninsula	Alliance	All		Gremni Longbeard	Gremni Longbeard				10400	5● 80●
Avruu's Orb	Hellfire Peninsula	All	All		Avruu's Orb	Aeranas				10400	
CHOICE OF: 1 Windtalker's Cloak, or 1 Signet of Aeranas, or 1 Wind Dancer's Pendant											
The Finest Down	Hellfire Peninsula	Alliance	All		Mirren Longbeard	Mirren Longbeard	Gaining Mirren's Trust			10050	2● 70●
REWARD: 1 Mirren's Drinking Hat											
Return to Obadei	Hellfire Peninsula	Alliance	All		Sedai's Corpse	Anchorite Obadei	In Search of Sedai			2550	
Makuru's Vengeance	Hellfire Peninsula	Alliance	All		Makuru	Makuru	Return to Obadei			10400	
CHOICE OF: 1 Sedai's Blade, or 1 Sedai's Necklace, or 1 Sedai's Ring											
The Pools of Aggonar	Hellfire Peninsula	Alliance	All		Amaan the Wise	Amaan the Wise				10050	
Cleansing the Waters	Hellfire Peninsula	Alliance	All		Amaan the Wise	Amaan the Wise	The Pools of Aggonar			10050	
CHOICE OF: 1 Telhamat Pendant, or 1 Demonslayer's Wristguards, or 1 Amaan's Signet											
Sha'naar Relics	Hellfire Peninsula	Alliance	All		Amaan the Wise	Amaan the Wise	Atonement			10400	
Messenger to Thrall	Hellfire Peninsula	Horde	All		Nazgrel	Thrall	The Mag'har			10050	
A Debilitating Sickness	Hellfire Peninsula	Horde	All		Earthcaller Ryga	Earthcaller Ryga	Envoy to the Mag'har	0 with The Mag'har		10400	
Administering the Salve	Hellfire Peninsula	Horde	All		Earthcaller Ryga	Earthcaller Ryga	A Debilitating Sickness			10400	2● 90●
CHOICE OF: 1 Mag'har Bow, or 1 Earthcaller's Mace, or 1 Wolfrider's Dagger, or 1 Totemic Staff, or 1 Balanced Stone Dirk											
Wanted: Blacktalon the Savage	Hellfire Peninsula	Horde	All	2	Wanted Poster	Ranger Captain Venn'ren				12950	5● 80●
CHOICE OF: 1 Fine Sash, or 1 Venn'ren's Boots, or 1 Suntrider's Gauntlets											
Arelion's Mistress	Hellfire Peninsula	Horde	All		Magistrix Carinda	Magistrix Carinda	The Mistress Revealed			12600	5● 40●
REWARD: 1 Carinda's Wedding Band											

Title	Location	Faction	Race & Class	Group #	Starter	Finisher	Prerequisite	Reputation	Tradeskill	XP	Money
Life's Finer Pleasures	Hellfire Peninsula	Horde	All			Viera Sunwhisper					
The Rock Flayer Matriarch	Hellfire Peninsula	Alliance	All	2	Ikan	Ikan				12950	5● 80●
CHOICE OF: 1 Wastewalker's Sash, or 1 Boots of the Earthcaller, or 1 Defender's Gauntlets											
Falcon Watch	Hellfire Peninsula	Horde	Non-Blood Elf		Martik Tor'seldori	Ranger Captain Venn'ren	Felspark Ravine			1000	
Falcon Watch	Hellfire Peninsula	Horde	Blood Elf		Martik Tor'seldori	Ranger Captain Venn'ren	Apothecary Zelana			1000	
Atonement	Hellfire Peninsula	Alliance	All		Anchorite Obadei	Amaan the Wise	Makuru's Vengeance			1050	
The Seer's Relic	Hellfire Peninsula	Alliance	All		Amaan the Wise	Amaan the Wise	Sha'naar Relics			12950	
CHOICE OF: 1 Omenai Vest, or 1 Vindicator's Chain Helm, or 1 Leggings of Telhamat											
The Longbeards	Hellfire Peninsula	Alliance	All		Sid Limbardi	Gremni Longbeard	Ill Omens			1000	
Gaining Mirren's Trust	Hellfire Peninsula	Alliance	All		Mirren Longbeard	Mirren Longbeard				10050	
The Path of Glory	Hellfire Peninsula	Alliance	All		Warp-Scryer Kryv	Warp-Scryer Kryv	Ill Omens			9800	
Unyielding Souls	Hellfire Peninsula	Alliance	All		Honor Guard Wesilow	Honor Guard Wesilow	Ill Omens			9800	2●
Waste Not, Want Not	Hellfire Peninsula	Alliance	All		Dumphry	Dumphry				9800	2●
CHOICE OF: 1 Phantasmal Headdress, or 1 Battle Seeker Chestguard, or 1 Legionnaire's Studded Helm, or 1 Magistrate's Greaves											
An Old Gift	Hellfire Peninsula	Alliance	All		Father Malgor Devidicus	Father Malgor Devidicus	Ill Omens			9800	2●
Laying Waste to the Unwanted	Hellfire Peninsula	Alliance	All		Dumphry	Dumphry	Waste Not, Want Not			9800	2●
CHOICE OF: 1 Wanderer's Stitched Trousers, or 1 Nature-Stitched Kilt, or 1 Helm of Affinity, or 1 Scale Brand Breastplate											
When This Mine's a-Rockin'	Hellfire Peninsula	Alliance	All		Foreman Biggums	Foreman Biggums	Ill Omens			9800	2●
I Work... For the Horde!	Hellfire Peninsula	Horde	All		Megzeg Nukklebust	Megzeg Nukklebust				9800	2●
CHOICE OF: 1 Phantasmal Headdress, or 1 Battle Seeker Chestguard, or 1 Legionnaire's Studded Helm, or 1 Magistrate's Greaves											
Burn It Up... For the Horde!	Hellfire Peninsula	Horde	All		Megzeg Nukklebust	Megzeg Nukklebust	I Work... For the Horde!			9800	2●
CHOICE OF: 1 Wanderer's Stitched Trousers, or 1 Nature-Stitched Kilt, or 1 Helm of Affinity, or 1 Scale Brand Breastplate											
The Temple of Telhamat	Hellfire Peninsula	Alliance	All		Warp-Scryer Kryv	Amaan the Wise	The Path of Glory			2600	
The Mastermind	Hellfire Peninsula	Alliance	All		Foreman Biggums	Foreman Biggums	When This Mine's a-Rockin'			9800	2●
CHOICE OF: 1 Miner's Brace, or 1 Foreman's Sash, or 1 Heavy Miner's Belt											
Report to Zurai	Hellfire Peninsula	Horde	All		Ranger Captain Venn'ren	Zurai				2400	
Hellfire Fortifications	Hellfire Peninsula	Alliance	All		Warrant Officer Tracy Proudwell	Warrant Officer Tracy Proudwell	Ill Omens			6600	90●
REWARD: 3 Mark of Honor Hold											
Hellfire Fortifications	Hellfire Peninsula	Horde	All		Battlecryer Blackeye	Battlecryer Blackeye	Apothecary Zelana			6600	90●
REWARD: 3 Mark of Thrallmar											
Arrival in Outland	Hellfire Peninsula	Horde	All		Lieutenant General Orion	Vlagga Freyfeather				2400	
Eradicate the Burning Legion	Hellfire Peninsula	Horde	All		Nazgrel	Sergeant Shatterskull				975	
Felspark Ravine	Hellfire Peninsula	Horde	All		Sergeant Shatterskull	Sergeant Shatterskull	Eradicate the Burning Legion			9800	
CHOICE OF: 1 Rage Reaver, or 1 Screaming Dagger, or 1 The Staff of Twin Worlds, or 1 Agamaggan's Quill, or 1 Foe Reaver											
Forward Base: Reaver's Fall	Hellfire Peninsula	Horde	All		Sergeant Shatterskull	Forward Commander To'arch	Felspark Ravine			975	
Mission: Gateways Murketh and Shaadraz	Hellfire Peninsula	Horde	All		Forward Commander To'arch	Forward Commander To'arch	Disrupt Their Reinforcements			12600	
CHOICE OF: 1 Battle Scarred Leggings, or 1 Helm of Infinite Visions, or 1 Raging Spirit Harness, or 1 Protectorate Breastplate											
Colossal Menace	Hellfire Peninsula	All	All	2	Tola'thion	Tola'thion				12950	5● 80●
CHOICE OF: 1 Idol of the Wild, or 1 Expedition Repeater, or 1 Libram of Wracking, or 1 Totem of Lightning, or 1 Survivalist's Wand											
Crimson Crystal Clue	Hellfire Peninsula	All	All	2	Crimson Crystal Shard	Tola'thion				5250	1● 50●
Cruel's Intentions	Hellfire Peninsula	Horde	All	3	Nazgrel	Nazgrel	Doorway to the Abyss			15550	8● 70●
CHOICE OF: 1 Vengeance of the Illidari, or 1 Bladefist's Breadth, or 1 Regal Protectorate											
Journey to Honor Hold	Hellfire Peninsula	Alliance	All		Amish Wildhammer	Marshal Isildor	Arrival in Outland			2400	
The Legion Reborn	Hellfire Peninsula	Alliance	All		Force Commander Danath Trollbane	Sergeant Altumus				975	
The Path of Anguish	Hellfire Peninsula	Alliance	All		Sergeant Altumus	Sergeant Altumus	The Legion Reborn			9800	
CHOICE OF: 1 Rage Reaver, or 1 Screaming Dagger, or 1 The Staff of Twin Worlds, or 1 Agamaggan's Quill, or 1 Foe Reaver											

Title	Location	Faction	Race & Class	Group #	Starter	Finisher	Prerequisite	Reputation	Tradeskill	XP	Money
Expedition Point	Hellfire Peninsula	Alliance	All		Sergeant Altumus	Forward Commander Kingston	The Path of Anguish			975	
Disrupt Their Reinforcements	Hellfire Peninsula	Alliance	All		Forward Commander Kingston	Forward Commander Kingston	Expedition Point			10050	
CHOICE OF: 1 Shadowbrim Travel Hat, or 1 Flayer-Hide Leggings, or 1 Arcane Ringed Tunic, or 1 Invader's Greathelm, or 1 Fire Scarred Breastplate											
Mission: The Murketh and Shaadraz Gateways	Hellfire Peninsula	Alliance	All		Forward Commander Kingston	Forward Commander Kingston	Disrupt Their Reinforcements			12600	
CHOICE OF: 1 Battle Scarred Leggings, or 1 Helm of Infinite Visions, or 1 Raging Spirit Harness, or 1 Protectorate Breastplate											
Keep Thornfang Hill Clear!	Hellfire Peninsula	All	All		Mahuram Stouthoof	Mahuram Stouthoof				10400	2 90
Know your Enemy	Hellfire Peninsula	Alliance	All		Force Commander Danath Trollbane	Lieutenant Amadi				2400	
In Case of Emergency...	Hellfire Peninsula	All	All		"Screaming" Screed Luckheed	"Screaming" Screed Luckheed				9800	2 90
CHOICE OF: 1 Dirigible Crash Helmet, or 1 Aerodynamic Scaled Vest, or 1 Flintlocke's Piloting Pants											
Mission: The Abyssal Shelf	Hellfire Peninsula	Horde	All		Forward Commander To'arch	Forward Commander To'arch	Mission: Gateways Murketh and Shaadraz			10050	
CHOICE OF: 1 Whispering Tunic, or 1 Veteran's Skullcap, or 1 Arcane Ringed Greaves, or 1 Skyfire Greaves											
Mission: The Abyssal Shelf	Hellfire Peninsula	Alliance	All		Wing Commander Gryphongar	Wing Commander Gryphongar	Mission: The Murketh and Shaadraz Gateways			10050	
CHOICE OF: 1 Whispering Tunic, or 1 Veteran's Skullcap, or 1 Arcane Ringed Greaves, or 1 Skyfire Greaves											
Disrupt Their Reinforcements	Hellfire Peninsula	Horde	All		Forward Commander To'arch	Forward Commander To'arch	Forward Base: Reaver's Fall			10050	2 70
CHOICE OF: 1 Shadowbrim Travel Hat, or 1 Flayer-Hide Leggings, or 1 Arcane Ringed Tunic, or 1 Invader's Greathelm, or 1 Fire Scarred Breastplate											
Investigate the Crash	Hellfire Peninsula	Horde	All		Grelag	"Screaming" Screed Luckheed	Preparing the Salve			2400	
Make Them Listen	Hellfire Peninsula	Horde	All		Emissary Mordiba	Emissary Mordiba				9800	2
Decipher the Tome	Hellfire Peninsula	Horde	All		A Mysterious Tome	Althen the Historian				975	
The Battle Horn	Hellfire Peninsula	Horde	All		Althen the Historian	Althen the Historian	Decipher the Tome			9800	
Outland Sucks!	Hellfire Peninsula	All	All		Foreman Razelcraz	Foreman Razelcraz				9800	2
REWARD: 5 Fel Iron Ore											
How to Serve Goblins	Hellfire Peninsula	All	All		Foreman Razelcraz	Foreman Razelcraz	Outland Sucks!			9800	2
REWARD: 5 Peon Sleep Potion											
Spinebreaker Post	Hellfire Peninsula	Horde	All		Apothecary Zelana	Apothecary Albreck	Apothecary Zelana			1650	2 3
Bloody Vengeance	Hellfire Peninsula	Horde	All		Althen the Historian	Althen the Historian	The Battle Horn			9800	
Force Commander Danath	Hellfire Peninsula	Alliance	All		Marshal Isildor	Force Commander Danath Trollbane	Journey to Honor Hold			650	
Testing the Antidote	Hellfire Peninsula	All	All		Thiah Redmane	Thiah Redmane	Demonic Contamination			10400	2 90
CHOICE OF: 1 Dreadtusk's Fury, or 1 Helboar Carving Blade, or 1 Cenarion Naturalist's Staff											
Honor the Fallen	Hellfire Peninsula	Horde	All		Althen the Historian	Commander Hogarth	Bloody Vengeance			9800	
CHOICE OF: 1 Blade of the Unyielding, or 1 Rod of the Unyielding											
The Warp Rifts	Hellfire Peninsula	Horde	All		Ogath the Mad	Ogath the Mad				9800	2
Arelion's Secret	Hellfire Peninsula	Horde	All		Magistrix Carinda	Magister Aledis	Arelion's Journal			7600	
The Mistress Revealed	Hellfire Peninsula	Horde	All			Magistrix Carinda	Arelion's Secret			5000	1 40
Arrival in Outland	Hellfire Peninsula	Alliance	All		Commander Duron	Amish Wildhammer				2400	
Journey to Thrallmar	Hellfire Peninsula	Horde	All		Vlagga Freyfeather	General Krakork	Arrival in Outland			2400	
Report to Nazgrel	Hellfire Peninsula	Horde	All		General Krakork	Nazgrel				3300	
Void Ridge	Hellfire Peninsula	Horde	All		Ogath the Mad	Ogath the Mad	The Warp Rifts			9800	2
From the Abyss	Hellfire Peninsula	Horde	All		Ogath the Mad	Ogath the Mad	Void Ridge			10400	2 90
CHOICE OF: 1 Rod of the Void Caller, or 1 Circle of Banishing, or 1 Abyssal Shroud											
Shatter Point	Hellfire Peninsula	Alliance	All		Forward Commander Kingston	Runetog Wildhammer	Mission: The Murketh and Shaadraz Gateways			650	
Wing Commander Gryphongar	Hellfire Peninsula	Alliance	All		Runetog Wildhammer	Wing Commander Gryphongar	Shatter Point			650	
Return to the Abyssal Shelf	Hellfire Peninsula	Alliance	All		Gryphoneer Windbellow	Gryphoneer Windbellow	Mission: The Abyssal Shelf				
Return to the Abyssal Shelf	Hellfire Peninsula	Horde	All		Wing Commander Brack	Wing Commander Brack	Mission: The Abyssal Shelf				
The Earthbinder	Hellfire Peninsula	All	All	2	Tola'thion	Earthbinder Galandria Nightbreeze	Crimson Crystal Clue			1050	30

Title	Location	Faction	Race & Class	Group #	Starter	Finisher	Prerequisite	Reputation	Tradeskill	XP	Money
Natural Remedies	Hellfire Peninsula	All	All	2	Earthbinder Galandria Nightbreeze	Earthbinder Galandria Nightbreeze	The Earthbinder			13350	6 20
CHOICE OF: 1 Studded Green Anklewraps, or 1 Destroyers' Mantle, or 1 Golden Cenarion Greaves, or 1 Verdant Handwraps											
A Traitor Among Us	Hellfire Peninsula	All	All		Naladu	Naladu				10050	
The Dreghood Elders	Hellfire Peninsula	All	All		Naladu	Naladu	A Traitor Among Us			10050	
Arzeth's Demise	Hellfire Peninsula	All	All		Naladu	Naladu	The Dreghood Elders			12600	5 40
Go to the Front	Hellfire Peninsula	Alliance	All		Wing Commander Gryphongar	Field Marshal Brock	Mission: The Abyssal Shelf			975	
Return to Thrallmar	Hellfire Peninsula	Horde	All		Overlord Hun Maimfist	Nazgrel	Mission: Gateways Murketh and Shaadraz			975	
The Agony and the Darkness	Hellfire Peninsula	Horde	All		Magister Bloodhawk	Magister Bloodhawk	Doorway to the Abyss			9800	2
Forge Camp: Mageddon	Hellfire Peninsula	Horde	All		Nazgrel	Nazgrel	Return to Thrallmar			9800	2
Cannons of Rage	Hellfire Peninsula	Horde	All		Nazgrel	Nazgrel	Forge Camp: Mageddon			9800	2
Doorway to the Abyss	Hellfire Peninsula	Horde	All		Nazgrel	Nazgrel	Cannons of Rage			9800	2
Vile Plans	Hellfire Peninsula	Horde	All		Burning Legion Missive	Magister Bloodhawk				4850	
Disruption - Forge Camp: Mageddon	Hellfire Peninsula	Alliance	All		Field Marshal Brock	Field Marshal Brock	Go to the Front			9800	2
The Dark Missive	Hellfire Peninsula	Alliance	All		Burning Legion Missive	Warp-Scryer Kryv				4850	
Enemy of my Enemy...	Hellfire Peninsula	Alliance	All		Field Marshal Brock	Field Marshal Brock	Disruption - Forge Camp: Mageddon			9800	2
Invasion Point: Annihilator	Hellfire Peninsula	Alliance	All		Field Marshal Brock	Field Marshal Brock	Enemy of my Enemy...			9800	2
The Heart of Darkness	Hellfire Peninsula	Alliance	All		Warp-Scryer Kryv	Warp-Scryer Kryv	The Dark Missive			9800	2
Overlord	Hellfire Peninsula	Alliance	All	3	Force Commander Danath Trollbane	Force Commander Danath Trollbane	The Dark Missive			15550	8 70
CHOICE OF: 1 Vengeance of the Illidari, or 1 Bladefist's Breadth, or 1 Regal Protectorate											
Naladu	Hellfire Peninsula	All	All		Morod the Windstirrer	Naladu				2550	
Helping the Cenarion Post	Hellfire Peninsula	Horde	All		Falconer Drenna Riverwind	Thiah Redmane				975	
Helping the Cenarion Post	Hellfire Peninsula	Alliance	Quest		Amaan the Wise	Thiah Redmane				975	
Apothecary Zelana	Hellfire Peninsula	Horde	All		Vurtok Axebreaker	Apothecary Zelana	Bonechewer Blood			1650	23
Bonechewer Blood	Hellfire Peninsula	Horde	All		Vurtok Axebreaker	Vurtok Axebreaker				6600	90
CHOICE OF: 1 Desolation Rod, or 1 Adamantine Kite Shield, or 1 Landslide Buckler, or 1 Hellfire Skiver, or 1 Ironstar Repeater											
Fel Orc Scavengers	Hellfire Peninsula	Alliance	All		Lieutenant Amadi	Lieutenant Amadi				6200	90
CHOICE OF: 1 Desolation Rod, or 1 Adamantine Kite Shield, or 1 Landslide Buckler, or 1 Hellfire Skiver, or 1 Ironstar Repeater											
Ill Omens	Hellfire Peninsula	Alliance	All		Lieutenant Amadi	Corporal Ironridge	Fel Orc Scavengers			1550	
Cursed Talismans	Hellfire Peninsula	Alliance	All		Corporal Ironridge	Corporal Ironridge	Ill Omens			6200	90
Warlord of the Bleeding Hollow	Hellfire Peninsula	Alliance	All		Corporal Ironridge	Corporal Ironridge	Cursed Talismans			6600	90
Boiling Blood	Hellfire Peninsula	Horde	All		Apothecary Albreck	Apothecary Albreck	Spinebreaker Post			6600	90
Shizz Work	Hellfire Peninsula	All	All		Foreman Razelcraz	Foreman Razelcraz	How to Serve Goblins			9800	4
REWARD: 5 Ez-Thro Dynamite II											
Beneath Thrallmar	Hellfire Peninsula	All	All		Foreman Razelcraz	Foreman Razelcraz	Shizz Work			9800	2
CHOICE OF: 1 Underworld Helm, or 1 Shatterstone Pick, or 1 Deep Core Lantern											
Grand Master Rohok	Hellfire Peninsula	Horde	All		Nazgrel	Rohok	Entry Into the Citadel			3150	
Rohok's Request	Hellfire Peninsula	Horde	All		Rohok	Rohok	Grand Master Rohok			12650	
Hotter than Hell	Hellfire Peninsula	Horde	All	3	Rohok	Rohok	Rohok's Request			15800	
REWARD: 1 Shattered Halls Key											
Grand Master Dumphry	Hellfire Peninsula	Alliance	All		Force Commander Danath Trollbane	Dumphry	Entry Into the Citadel			3150	
Dumphry's Request	Hellfire Peninsula	Alliance	All		Dumphry	Dumphry	Grand Master Dumphry			12650	
Hotter than Hell	Hellfire Peninsula	Alliance	All	3	Dumphry	Dumphry	Rohok's Request			15800	
REWARD: 1 Shattered Halls Key											

Title	Location	Faction	Race & Class	Group #	Starter	Finisher	Prerequisite	Reputation	Tradeskill	XP	Money
Zeth'Gor Must Burn!	Hellfire Peninsula	Horde	All		Captain Darkhowl	Captain Darkhowl	Wanted: Worg Master Kruush			9800	2
CHOICE OF: 1 Infiltrator's Cloak, or 1 Vindicator's Cloak											
Wanted: Worg Master Kruush	Hellfire Peninsula	Horde	All		Wanted Poster	Captain Darkhowl				6600	1 80
The Eyes of Grillok	Hellfire Peninsula	Horde	All		Zezzak	Zezzak	Wanted: Worg Master Kruush			5000	1 40
Grillok "Darkeye"	Hellfire Peninsula	Horde	All	2	Zezzak	Zezzak	The Eyes of Grillok			12600	5 40
CHOICE OF: 1 Bonechewer Berserker's Vest, or 1 Goldweave Tunic, or 1 Sacred Feather Vest, or 1 Gilded Crimson Chestplate, or 1 Jerkin of the Untamed Spirit											
Apothecary Antonivich	Hellfire Peninsula	Horde	All		Apothecary Albreck	Apothecary Antonivich	Boiling Blood			2400	52
The Demoniac Scryer	Hellfire Peninsula	Horde	All	2	Apothecary Antonivich	Apothecary Antonivich	A Burden of Souls			12200	4
REWARD: 1 Demoniac Soul Prison											
A Burden of Souls	Hellfire Peninsula	Horde	All		Apothecary Antonivich	Apothecary Antonivich	Apothecary Antonivich			9800	2
Report to Nazgrel	Hellfire Peninsula	Horde	All		Apothecary Antonivich	Nazgrel				2400	
The Foot of the Citadel	Hellfire Peninsula	Horde	All	3	Nazgrel	Nazgrel	Report to Nazgrel			12950	5 80
CHOICE OF: 1 Stormstrike Vest, or 1 Shadowcast Tunic, or 1 Darkstorm Tunic, or 1 Battlemaster's Breastplate											
Zeth'Gor Must Burn!	Hellfire Peninsula	Alliance	All		Wing Commander Dabir'ee	Wing Commander Dabir'ee				8300	1 80
CHOICE OF: 1 Bonechewer Berserker's Vest, or 1 Goldweave Tunic, or 1 Sacred Feather Vest, or 1 Gilded Crimson Chestplate, or 1 Jerkin of the Untamed Spirit											
Return to Honor Hold	Hellfire Peninsula	Alliance	All		Corporal Ironridge	Assistant Klatu	Warlord of the Bleeding Hollow			4850	
Fel Spirits	Hellfire Peninsula	Alliance	All		Assistant Klatu	Assistant Klatu	Return to Honor Hold			9800	2
Digging for Prayer Beads	Hellfire Peninsula	Alliance	All		Assistant Klatu	Assistant Klatu	Return to Honor Hold			4850	
Fei Fei's Treat	Hellfire Peninsula	Alliance	All			Fei Fei					
The Exorcism of Colonel Jules	Hellfire Peninsula	Alliance	All		Assistant Klatu	Assistant Klatu	Fel Spirits			12200	4
Trollbane is Looking for You	Hellfire Peninsula	Alliance	All		Assistant Klatu	Force Commander Danath Trollbane	The Exorcism of Colonel Jules			975	
Drill the Drillmaster	Hellfire Peninsula	Alliance	All	2	Force Commander Danath Trollbane	Force Commander Danath Trollbane	Trollbane is Looking for You			12600	5 40
CHOICE OF: 1 Stormstrike Vest, or 1 Darkstorm Tunic, or 1 Shadowcast Tunic, or 1 Battlemaster's Breastplate											
Missing Crystals	Hillsbrad Foothills	Alliance	All		Huraan	Huraan				2350	25
Featherbeard's Endorsement	Hinterlands	Alliance	All		Ambassador Rualeth	Featherbeard's Journal				3050	
A Gesture of Goodwill	Hinterlands	Alliance	All		Ambassador Rualeth	Ambassador Rualeth				4050	65
Preying on the Predators	Hinterlands	Alliance	All		Ambassador Rualeth	Ambassador Rualeth				3750	65
Reclaiming the Eggs	Hinterlands	Alliance	All		Featherbeard's Remains	Ambassador Rualeth	In Pursuit of Featherbeard			5050	1 30
In Pursuit of Featherbeard	Hinterlands	Alliance	All		Featherbeard's Journal	Featherbeard's Remains	Featherbeard's Endorsement			4050	
Imperial Plate Armor	Ironforge	Alliance	All		Myolor Sunderfury	Derotain Mudsipper			265 skill in Blacksmithing	3550	
Medivh's Journal	Karazhan	All	All	Raid	Archmage Alturus	Wravien		9000 with The Violet Eye			
A Colleague's Aid	Karazhan	All	All		Archmage Alturus	Kalynna Lathred	Digging Up the Past			6250	
Kalynna's Request	Karazhan	All	All		Kalynna Lathred	Kalynna Lathred	A Colleague's Aid			12650	
In Good Hands	Karazhan	All	All		Wravien	Gradav	Medivh's Journal	9000 with The Violet Eye		1250	
Kamsis	Karazhan	All	All		Gradav	Kamsis	In Good Hands			1250	
The Shade of Aran	Karazhan	All	All	Raid	Kamsis	Kamsis	Kamsis			12650	
Nightbane	Karazhan	All	All	Raid	Kalynna Lathred	Archmage Alturus	Kalynna's Request	9000 with The Violet Eye		12650	
CHOICE OF: 1 Pulsing Amethyst, or 1 Soothing Amethyst, or 1 Infused Amethyst											
The Master's Terrace	Karazhan	All	All	Raid	Kamsis	Archmage Alturus	The Shade of Aran			12650	
Digging Up the Past	Karazhan	All	All		Archmage Alturus	Archmage Alturus	The Master's Terrace			12650	
Arcane Disturbances	Karazhan	All	All		Archmage Alturus	Archmage Alturus				12650	4 40
Restless Activity	Karazhan	All	All		Archmage Alturus	Archmage Alturus				12650	4 40
Contact from Dalaran	Karazhan	All	All		Archmage Alturus	Archmage Cedric	Arcane Disturbances			6250	
Return to Khadgar	Karazhan	All	All		Medivh	Khadgar	The Master's Touch			19000	
REWARD: 1 The Master's Key											
The Violet Eye	Karazhan	All	All		Khadgar	Archmage Alturus	Return to Khadgar			6250	
Assessing the Situation	Karazhan	All	All	Raid	Archmage Alturus	Koren	The Violet Eye			12650	
Keanna's Log	Karazhan	All	All	Raid	Koren	Archmage Alturus	Assessing the Situation			12650	
A Demonic Presence	Karazhan	All	All	Raid	Archmage Alturus	Archmage Alturus	Keanna's Log			12650	4 40
The New Directive	Karazhan	All	All		Archmage Alturus	Archmage Cedric	A Demonic Presence			19000	13 20
REWARD: 1 Violet Badge											

Title	Location	Faction	Race & Class	Group #	Starter	Finisher	Prerequisite	Reputation	Tradeskill	XP	Money
Eminence Among the Violet Eye	Karazhan	All	All		Archmage Leryda	Archmage Leryda	Distinguished Service			15800	
REWARD: 1 Violet Signet of the Archmage											
Eminence Among the Violet Eye	Karazhan	All	All		Archmage Leryda	Archmage Leryda	Distinguished Service			15800	
REWARD: 1 Violet Signet of the Grand Restorer											
Eminence Among the Violet Eye	Karazhan	All	All		Archmage Leryda	Archmage Leryda	Distinguished Service			15800	
REWARD: 1 Violet Signet of the Master Assassin											
Eminence Among the Violet Eye	Karazhan	All	All		Archmage Leryda	Archmage Leryda	Distinguished Service			15800	
REWARD: 1 Violet Signet of the Great Protector											
Path of the Violet Mage	Karazhan	All	All			Archmage Leryda		3000 with The Violet Eye		12650	
REWARD: 1 Violet Signet											
Path of the Violet Restorer	Karazhan	All	All			Archmage Leryda		3000 with The Violet Eye		12650	
REWARD: 1 Violet Signet											
Path of the Violet Assassin	Karazhan	All	All			Archmage Leryda		3000 with The Violet Eye		12650	
REWARD: 1 Violet Signet											
Path of the Violet Protector	Karazhan	All	All			Archmage Leryda		3000 with The Violet Eye		12650	
REWARD: 1 Violet Signet											
Down the Violet Path	Karazhan	All	All		Archmage Leryda	Archmage Leryda	Path of the Violet Mage			15800	
REWARD: 1 Violet Signet											
Down the Violet Path	Karazhan	All	All		Archmage Leryda	Archmage Leryda	Path of the Violet Restorer			15800	
REWARD: 1 Violet Signet											
Down the Violet Path	Karazhan	All	All		Archmage Leryda	Archmage Leryda	Path of the Violet Assassin			15800	
REWARD: 1 Violet Signet											
Down the Violet Path	Karazhan	All	All		Archmage Leryda	Archmage Leryda	Path of the Violet Protector			15800	
REWARD: 1 Violet Signet											
Distinguished Service	Karazhan	All	All		Archmage Leryda	Archmage Leryda	Down the Violet Path			15800	
REWARD: 1 Violet Signet											
Distinguished Service	Karazhan	All	All		Archmage Leryda	Archmage Leryda	Down the Violet Path			15800	
REWARD: 1 Violet Signet											
Distinguished Service	Karazhan	All	All		Archmage Leryda	Archmage Leryda	Down the Violet Path			15800	
REWARD: 1 Violet Signet											
Distinguished Service	Karazhan	All	All		Archmage Leryda	Archmage Leryda	Down the Violet Path			15800	
REWARD: 1 Violet Signet											
The Hunter's Path	Mulgore	Horde	All		Yaw Sharpmane	Lieutenant Downrunner				85	
Clefthoof Mastery	Nagrand	All	All		Hemet Nesingwary	Hemet Nesingwary				11300	3● 50●
A Rare Bean	Nagrand	All	All		Elementalist Lo'ap	Elementalist Lo'ap				11000	
REWARD: 20 Nagrand Cherry											
Agitated Spirits of Skysong	Nagrand	All	All		Elementalist Lo'ap	Elementalist Lo'ap	A Rare Bean			11000	
Blessing of Incineratus	Nagrand	All	All		Elementalist Lo'ap	Elementalist Lo'ap	Agitated Spirits of Skysong			11000	
The Spirit Polluted	Nagrand	All	All		Elementalist Lo'ap	Elementalist Lo'ap	Blessing of Incineratus			11300	7●
CHOICE OF: 1 Ango'rosh Souleater's Cowl, or 1 Salvaged Ango'rosh Pauldrons, or 1 Oversized Ogre Hauberk											
Muck Diving	Nagrand	All	All		Elementalist Lo'ap	Elementalist Lo'ap				11300	
CHOICE OF: 1 Lo'ap's Muck Diving Pads, or 1 Muck-ridden Galoshes, or 1 Lo'ap's Tunic of Muck Diving											
The Underneath	Nagrand	All	All		Elementalist Untrag	Gordawg					
The Tortured Earth	Nagrand	All	All		Gordawg	Gordawg	The Underneath			11000	
Eating Damnation	Nagrand	All	All		Gordawg	Gordawg	The Tortured Earth			11300	
Shattering the Veil	Nagrand	All	All		Gordawg	Gordawg	Eating Damnation			17450	
Clefthoof Mastery	Nagrand	All	All		Hemet Nesingwary	Hemet Nesingwary	Clefthoof Mastery			11650	3● 70●
Clefthoof Mastery	Nagrand	All	All	2	Hemet Nesingwary	Hemet Nesingwary	Clefthoof Mastery			14600	7● 40●
CHOICE OF: 1 Clefthoof Gloves, or 1 Clefthoof Wristguards, or 1 Clefthoof Helm											
The Ultimate Bloodsport	Nagrand	All	All	2	Hemet Nesingwary	Hemet Nesingwary	Clefthoof Mastery			17950	11● 70●
CHOICE OF: 1 Nesingwary Safari Stick, or 1 Fitz's Throwing Axe, or 1 Hemet's Elekk Gun, or 1 Harold's Rejuvenating Broach, or 1 Blessed Book of Nagrand, or 1 Totem of the Plains											
Gurok the Usurper	Nagrand	All	All	3	Gordawg	Gordawg	Shattering the Veil			17450	
CHOICE OF: 1 Earthen Mark of Power, or 1 Earthen Mark of Health, or 1 Earthen Mark of Razing											
Windroc Mastery	Nagrand	All	All		Shado 'Fitz' Farstrider	Shado 'Fitz' Farstrider				11000	3● 30●
Windroc Mastery	Nagrand	All	All		Shado 'Fitz' Farstrider	Shado 'Fitz' Farstrider	Windroc Mastery			11650	3● 70●
Windroc Mastery	Nagrand	All	All	2	Shado 'Fitz' Farstrider	Shado 'Fitz' Farstrider	Windroc Mastery			14600	7● 40●
CHOICE OF: 1 Windroc Shroud, or 1 Windroc Boots, or 1 Windroc Greaves											
Talbuk Mastery	Nagrand	All	All		Harold Lane	Harold Lane				11000	3● 30●

Title	Location	Faction	Race & Class	Group #	Starter	Finisher	Prerequisite	Reputation	Tradeskill	XP	Money
Talbuk Mastery	Nagrand	All	All		Harold Lane	Harold Lane	Talbuk Mastery			11300	3g 50s
Talbuk Mastery	Nagrand	All	All	2	Harold Lane	Harold Lane	Talbuk Mastery			14150	7g
CHOICE OF: 1 Talbuk Sticker, or 1 Talbuk Cape, or 1 Talbuk Dirk											
The Howling Wind	Nagrand	All	All		Howling Wind	Elementalist Morgh				11650	
Murkblood Corrupters	Nagrand	All	All		Elementalist Morgh	Elementalist Morgh	The Howling Wind			11650	
CHOICE OF: 1 Judicator's Gauntlets, or 1 Spaulders of the Ring, or 1 Cord of the Ring											
Vile Idolatry	Nagrand	Horde	All		Farseer Kurkush	Farseer Kurkush		0 with The Mag'har		11300	
CHOICE OF: 1 Melia's Lustrous Crown, or 1 Warcaster's Scaled Leggings, or 1 Murkblood Avenger's Chestplate											
The Missing War Party	Nagrand	Horde	All		Farseer Corhuk	Saurfang the Younger		0 with The Mag'har		2900	
Once Were Warriors	Nagrand	Horde	All		Saurfang the Younger	Saurfang the Younger	The Missing War Party			11650	
He Will Walk The Earth...	Nagrand	Horde	All		Saurfang the Younger	Farseer Corhuk	Once Were Warriors			5800	
CHOICE OF: 1 Greenkeeper's Pantaloons, or 1 Smuggler's Mitts, or 1 Thunderbringer's Guard											
Murkblood Leaders...	Nagrand	Horde	All		Farseer Margadesh	Farseer Margadesh		0 with The Mag'har		11650	
CHOICE OF: 1 Eighty Silver Links, or 1 Murkblood Avenger's Legplates, or 1 Murkblood Oven Mitts											
The Totem of Kar'dash	Nagrand	Horde	All	2		Garrosh		0 with The Mag'har		14600	
The Throne of the Elements	Nagrand	All	All		Elementalist Ioki	Elementalist Sharvak		0 with Kurenai		2850	3g 50s
The Throne of the Elements	Nagrand	All	All		Elementalist Yal'hah	Elementalist Sharvak		0 with The Mag'har		2850	3g 50s
Murkblood Invaders	Nagrand	Alliance	All		Murkblood Invasion Plans	Arechron				11650	
Murkblood Invaders	Nagrand	Horde	All		Murkblood Invasion Plans	Garrosh				11650	
Ortor My Old Friend...	Nagrand	Alliance	All		Arechron	Arechron	Murkblood Invaders			11650	
CHOICE OF: 1 Eighty Silver Links, or 1 Murkblood Oven Mitts, or 1 Murkblood Avenger's Legplates											
Stopping the Spread	Nagrand	Alliance	All		Otonbu the Sage	Otonbu the Sage		0 with Kurenai		11650	
CHOICE OF: 1 Melia's Lustrous Crown, or 1 Warcaster's Scaled Leggings, or 1 Murkblood Avenger's Chestplate											
Solving the Problem	Nagrand	Alliance	All		Poli'lukluk the Wiser	Poli'lukluk the Wiser		0 with Kurenai		11650	
CHOICE OF: 1 Greenblood Pantaloons, or 1 Caustic Feelers, or 1 Dark Shaman's Cover											
The Totem of Kar'dash	Nagrand	Alliance	All	2		Arechron		0 with Kurenai		14600	
Stealing from Thieves	Nagrand	All	All		Gezhe	Gezhe		-3000 to 2999 with The Consortium		11300	3g 50s
More Crystal Fragments	Nagrand	All	All			Gezhe	Stealing from Thieves	-3000 to 2999 with The Consortium			
Membership Benefits	Nagrand	All	All			Gezhe		9000 to 20999 with The Consortium			
REWARD: 1 Unmarked Bag of Gems											
Membership Benefits	Nagrand	All	All			Gezhe		21000 to 41999 with The Consortium			
REWARD: 1 Bulging Sack of Gems											
Membership Benefits	Nagrand	All	All			Gezhe		3000 to 8999 with The Consortium			
REWARD: 1 Gem-Stuffed Envelope											
Membership Benefits	Nagrand	All	All			Gezhe		42000 to 42999 with The Consortium			
REWARD: 1 Bag of Premium Gems											
The Impotent Leader	Nagrand	Horde	All		Jorin Deadeye	Kilrath				2700	
Don't Kill the Fat One	Nagrand	Horde	All		Kilrath	Unkor the Ruthless	The Impotent Leader			11000	
Success!	Nagrand	Horde	All		Unkor the Ruthless	Kilrath	Don't Kill the Fat One			1100	
Because Kilrath is a Coward	Nagrand	Horde	All		Kilrath	Jorin Deadeye	Success!			2700	
More Obsidian Warbeads	Nagrand	All	All			Gezhe	Obsidian Warbeads	3000 with The Consortium			38s
Obsidian Warbeads	Nagrand	All	All		Gezhe	Gezhe		3000 with The Consortium		11650	3g 70s
I'm Saved!	Nagrand	All	All			Harold Lane				11000	3g 30s
Gava'xi	Nagrand	All	All		Zerid	Zerid				11650	3g 70s
CHOICE OF: 1 Ethereal Sash, or 1 Oshu'gun Relic, or 1 Zerid's Vintage Musket											
Message in a Battle	Nagrand	Horde	All		Jorin Deadeye	Jorin Deadeye	Because Kilrath is a Coward			11000	
An Audacious Advance	Nagrand	Horde	All		Jorin Deadeye	Jorin Deadeye	Message in a Battle			14150	
CHOICE OF: 1 Staff of the Four Golden Coins, or 1 Bracers of the Battle Cleric, or 1 King's Bulwark											
Standards and Practices	Nagrand	Horde	All		Elkay'gan the Mystic	Elkay'gan the Mystic	Because Kilrath is a Coward			11000	
The Consortium Needs You!	Nagrand	All	All		Consortium Recruiter	Gezhe				1150	
A Head Full of Ivory	Nagrand	All	All		Shadrek	Shadrek		0 to 2999 with The Consortium		11300	3g 50s

Title	Location	Faction	Race & Class	Group #	Starter	Finisher	Prerequisite	Reputation	Tradeskill	XP	Money
More Heads Full of Ivory	Nagrand	All	All			Shadrek	A Head Full of Ivory	0 to 2999 with The Consortium			
Bleeding Hollow Supply Crates	Nagrand	Horde	All		Elkay'gan the Mystic	Elkay'gan the Mystic	Standards and Practices			11300	
CHOICE OF: 1 Ogre Basher's Slippers, or 1 Ogre Handler's Shooter, or 1 Ogre Mauler's Badge											
Do My Eyes Deceive Me	Nagrand	Alliance	All		Huntress Bintook	Huntress Bintook				11000	
Not On My Watch!	Nagrand	Alliance	All		Huntress Bintook	Huntress Bintook	Do My Eyes Deceive Me			11000	
Mo'mor the Breaker	Nagrand	Alliance	All		Huntress Bintook	Mo'mor the Breaker	Not On My Watch!				
The Ruins of Burning Blade	Nagrand	Alliance	All		Mo'mor the Breaker	Mo'mor the Breaker	Mo'mor the Breaker			11000	
The Twin Clefts of Nagrand	Nagrand	Alliance	All		Mo'mor the Breaker	Mo'mor the Breaker	The Ruins of Burning Blade			14150	
CHOICE OF: 1 Bracers of the Battle Cleric, or 1 King's Bulwark, or 1 Staff of the Four Golden Coins											
HELP!	Nagrand	Alliance	All		Corki	Arechron				11000	9 90
Corki's Gone Missing Again!	Nagrand	Alliance	All		Arechron	Arechron	HELP!			11300	
CHOICE OF: 1 Boots of the Specialist, or 1 Wand of Happiness, or 1 Uniting Charm											
Matters of Security	Nagrand	All	All		Zerid	Zerid				11300	3 50
Ruthless Cunning	Nagrand	All	All		Lantresor of the Blade	Lantresor of the Blade	Diplomatic Measures			11300	3 50
Armaments for Deception	Nagrand	All	All		Lantresor of the Blade	Lantresor of the Blade	Diplomatic Measures			11300	3 50
Returning the Favor	Nagrand	All	All		Lantresor of the Blade	Lantresor of the Blade	Armaments for Deception			11300	7
Body of Evidence	Nagrand	All	All		Lantresor of the Blade	Lantresor of the Blade	Ruthless Cunning			11300	7
Message to Telaar	Nagrand	Alliance	All		Lantresor of the Blade	Arechron	Returning the Favor			14150	10 50
CHOICE OF: 1 Burning Blade Cultist Band, or 1 Lantresor's Warblade, or 1 Burning Blade Devotee's Cinch											
Message to Garadar	Nagrand	Horde	All		Lantresor of the Blade	Garrosh	Returning the Favor			14150	10 50
CHOICE OF: 1 Burning Blade Cultist Band, or 1 Lantresor's Warblade, or 1 Burning Blade Devotee's Cinch											
Wanted: Giselda the Crone	Nagrand	Horde	All		Garadar Bulletin Board	Warden Bullrok		0 with The Mag'har		11300	10 50
Wanted: Giselda the Crone	Nagrand	Alliance	All		Telaar Bulletin Board	Warden Iolol		0 with Kurenai		11300	10 50
Wanted: Durn the Hungerer	Nagrand	Horde	All	5	Warden Bullrok	Warden Bullrok	Wanted: Giselda the Crone	0 with The Mag'har		14600	11 10
CHOICE OF: 1 Azure Lightblade, or 1 Hungering Bone Cudgel, or 1 Crystalline Kopesh											
Wanted: Durn the Hungerer	Nagrand	Alliance	All	5	Warden Iolol	Warden Iolol	Wanted: Giselda the Crone	0 with Kurenai		14600	11 10
CHOICE OF: 1 Azure Lightblade, or 1 Hungering Bone Cudgel, or 1 Crystalline Kopesh											
Wanted: Zorbo the Advisor	Nagrand	Horde	All		Garadar Bulletin Board	Warden Bullrok		0 with The Mag'har		11300	7
Wanted: Zorbo the Advisor	Nagrand	Alliance	All		Telaar Bulletin Board	Warden Iolol		0 with Kurenai		11300	7
Missing Mag'hari Procession	Nagrand	Horde	All		Matron Drakia	Elder Yorley		0 with The Mag'har		1150	
War on the Warmaul	Nagrand	Horde	All		Elder Yorley	Elder Yorley		0 with The Mag'har		11650	3 70
Cho'war the Pillager	Nagrand	Horde	All	3	Elder Yorley	Elder Yorley	War on the Warmaul			14600	7 40
CHOICE OF: 1 Ogre Slayer's Cover, or 1 Ogre Slayer's Pendant, or 1 Ogre Slayer's Band											
Finding the Survivors	Nagrand	Horde	All		Elder Ungriz	Elder Ungriz		0 with The Mag'har		11650	3 70
CHOICE OF: 1 Manacles of Remembrance, or 1 Warmaul Slayer's Band, or 1 Warmaul Defender's Cloak											
Corki's Ransom	Nagrand	Alliance	All	3	Arechron	Corki	Corki's Gone Missing Again!			11650	
Cho'war the Pillager	Nagrand	Alliance	All	3	Corki	Arechron	Corki's Ransom			14600	7 40
CHOICE OF: 1 Ogre Slayer's Cover, or 1 Ogre Slayer's Pendant, or 1 Ogre Slayer's Band											
The Ravaged Caravan	Nagrand	Alliance	All		Huntress Kima	Huntress Kima		0 with Kurenai		11650	3 70
CHOICE OF: 1 Manacles of Remembrance, or 1 Warmaul Slayer's Band, or 1 Warmaul Defender's Cloak											
The Ring of Blood: Brokentoe	Nagrand	All	All	5	Gurgthock	Gurgthock				11650	11 10
The Ring of Blood: The Blue Brothers	Nagrand	All	All	5	Gurgthock	Gurgthock	The Ring of Blood: Brokentoe			11650	11 10
The Ring of Blood: Rokdar the Sundered Lord	Nagrand	All	All	5	Gurgthock	Gurgthock	The Ring of Blood: The Blue Brothers			14600	11 10
REWARD: 5 Super Healing Potion and 5 Super Mana Potion											
The Ring of Blood: Skra'gath	Nagrand	All	All	5	Gurgthock	Gurgthock	The Ring of Blood: Rokdar the Sundered Lord			14600	11 10
REWARD: 5 Super Healing Potion and 5 Super Mana Potion and 20 Netherweave Bandage											
The Ring of Blood: The Warmaul Champion	Nagrand	All	All	5	Gurgthock	Gurgthock	The Ring of Blood: Skra'gath			14600	11 10
The Ring of Blood: The Final Challenge	Nagrand	All	All	5	Gurgthock	Gurgthock	The Ring of Blood: The Warmaul Champion			17950	11 70
CHOICE OF: 1 Honed Voidaxe, or 1 Battle Mage's Baton, or 1 Ceremonial Warmaul Blood-blade, or 1 Staff of Beasts, or 1 Mag'hari Fury Brand, or 1 Mogor's Anointing Club											
He Called Himself Altruis...	Nagrand	Alliance	All		Huntress Kima	Altruis the Sufferer				1200	
He Called Himself Altruis...	Nagrand	Horde	All		Matron Celestine	Altruis the Sufferer				1200	
Survey the Land	Nagrand	All	All	3	Altruis the Sufferer	Altruis the Sufferer				3050	
Buying Time	Nagrand	All	All	3	Altruis the Sufferer	Altruis the Sufferer	Survey the Land			12000	

Title	Location	Faction	Race & Class	Group #	Starter	Finisher	Prerequisite	Reputation	Tradeskill	XP	Money
The Master Planner	Nagrand	All	All	3	Altruis the Sufferer	Altruis the Sufferer	Buying Time			12000	
Patience and Understanding	Nagrand	All	All	3	Altruis the Sufferer	Sal'salabim	The Master Planner			12000	
Crackin' Some Skulls	Nagrand	All	All	3	Sal'salabim	Sal'salabim	Patience and Understanding			12000	3● 90●
It's Just That Easy?	Nagrand	All	All	3	Sal'salabim	Altruis the Sufferer	Crackin' Some Skulls			6000	
Forge Camp: Annihilated	Nagrand	All	All	3	Altruis the Sufferer	Altruis the Sufferer	It's Just That Easy?			17950	11● 70●
CHOICE OF: 1 Watcher's Tunic, or 1 Leggings of Unending Assault, or 1 Metallic Headband of Simm'onz, or 1 Breastplate of the Warbringer											
A Visit With the Greatmother	Nagrand	Horde	All		Garrosh	Greatmother Geyah	The Totem of Kar'dash			1200	
Material Components	Nagrand	Horde	All		Greatmother Geyah	Greatmother Geyah	A Visit With the Greatmother			14950	
Oshu'gun Crystal Powder	Nagrand	Horde	All		Chief Researcher Amereldine	Chief Researcher Amereldine				11650	3● 70●
REWARD: 1 Halaa Research Token											
Oshu'gun Crystal Powder	Nagrand	Horde	All			Chief Researcher Amereldine	Oshu'gun Crystal Powder			8750	2● 90●
REWARD: 1 Halaa Research Token											
Oshu'gun Crystal Powder	Nagrand	Alliance	All		Chief Researcher Kartos	Chief Researcher Kartos				11650	3● 70●
REWARD: 1 Halaa Research Token											
Oshu'gun Crystal Powder	Nagrand	Alliance	All			Chief Researcher Kartos	Oshu'gun Crystal Powder			8750	2● 90●
REWARD: 1 Halaa Research Token											
To Meet Mother Kashur	Nagrand	Horde	All		Greatmother Geyah	Mother Kashur	Material Components			1200	
The Agitated Ancestors	Nagrand	Horde	All		Mother Kashur	Mother Kashur	To Meet Mother Kashur			12000	
A Visit With The Ancestors	Nagrand	Horde	All		Mother Kashur	Mother Kashur	The Agitated Ancestors			12000	
When Spirits Speak	Nagrand	Horde	All		Mother Kashur	K'ure	A Visit With The Ancestors			12000	
A Secret Revealed	Nagrand	All	All			A'dal	When Spirits Speak			12000	
Diplomatic Measures	Nagrand	Horde	All		Jorin Deadeye	Lantresor of the Blade	An Audacious Advance			8550	
Diplomatic Measures	Nagrand	Alliance	All		Mo'mor the Breaker	Lantresor of the Blade	The Twin Clefts of Nagrand			8550	
I Must Have Them!	Nagrand	All	All		Wazat	Wazat				11300	3● 50●
REWARD: 1 Jump-a-tron 4000 Key											
Bring Me The Egg!	Nagrand	All	All	2	Wazat	Wazat	I Must Have Them!			14150	7●
CHOICE OF: 1 Spell-slinger's Protector, or 1 Delicate Green Poncho, or 1 Nomad's Woven Cloak											
The Nesingwary Safari	Nagrand	Alliance	All		"Shotgun" Jones	Hemet Nesingwary				1100	
The Nesingwary Safari	Nagrand	Horde	All		Ohlorn Farstrider	Shado 'Fitz' Farstrider				1100	
Auchindoun...	Nagrand	All	All	Raid	A'dal	D'ore	A Secret Revealed			14950	
What the Soul Sees	Nagrand	Horde	All	3		Mother Kashur	Auchindoun...			14950	
Return to the Greatmother	Nagrand	Horde	All		Mother Kashur	Greatmother Geyah	What the Soul Sees			1200	
The Inconsolable Chieftain	Nagrand	Horde	All		Greatmother Geyah	Garrosh	Return to the Greatmother			1200	
There Is No Hope	Nagrand	Horde	All		Garrosh	Greatmother Geyah	The Inconsolable Chieftain			3050	
Thrall, Son of Durotan	Nagrand	Horde	All		Greatmother Geyah	Thrall	There Is No Hope			12000	
Hero of the Mag'har	Nagrand	Horde	All		Thrall	Greatmother Geyah	Thrall, Son of Durotan			17950	
CHOICE OF: 1 Mag'hari Huntsman's Leggings, or 1 Mag'hari Ritualist's Horns, or 1 Mag'hari Scout's Tunic, or 1 Mag'hari Warlord's Legplates											
REWARD: 1 Insignia of the Mag'hari Hero											
Fierce Enemies	Nagrand	Alliance	All		Warden Iolol	Warden Iolol		0 with Kurenai		11650	
More Warbeads	Nagrand	Alliance	All			Warden Iolol	Fierce Enemies				
More Warbeads!	Nagrand	Horde	All			Warden Bullrok	Proving Your Strength				
Proving Your Strength	Nagrand	Horde	All		Warden Bullrok	Warden Bullrok		0 with The Mag'har		11650	
Illidan's Pupil	Nagrand	All	All		Altruis the Sufferer	Altruis the Sufferer	Against the Legion			6250	
The Archmage's Staff	Netherstorm	All	All		Ravandwyr	Ravandwyr				12000	3● 90●
Curse of the Violet Tower	Netherstorm	All	All		Ravandwyr	Image of Archmage Vargoth	Rebuilding the Staff			3050	
Ar'kelos the Guardian	Netherstorm	All	All			Archmage Vargoth	Summoner Kanthin's Prize			12000	3● 90●
CHOICE OF: 1 Pendant of the Battle-Mage, or 1 Core of Ar'kelos, or 1 Cloak of the Valiant Defender, or 1 Rejuvenating Scepter											
Battle-Mage Dathric	Netherstorm	All	All		Dathric's Blade	Custodian Dieworth				12000	
Off To Area 52	Netherstorm	All	All		Netherologist Coppernickels	Rocket-Chief Fuselage				3050	1●
Malevolent Remnants	Netherstorm	All	All		Custodian Dieworth	Custodian Dieworth	Rebuilding the Staff			12000	3● 90●
A Fate Worse Than Death	Netherstorm	All	All		Custodian Dieworth	Custodian Dieworth	Curse of the Violet Tower			12000	3● 90●
CHOICE OF: 1 Mana Infused Wristguards, or 1 Spiritbinder's Mantle, or 1 Farahlite Studded Boots, or 1 Spiritualist's Gauntlets											
You're Hired!	Netherstorm	All	All		Rocket-Chief Fuselage	Rocket-Chief Fuselage				12000	3● 90●
CHOICE OF: 1 Junior Technician 3rd Grade Bracers, or 1 Junior Technician 3rd Grade Gloves, or 1 Junior Technician 3rd Grade Shoulders, or 1 Junior Technician 3rd Grade Goggles											

Title	Location	Faction	Race & Class	Group #	Starter	Finisher	Prerequisite	Reputation	Tradeskill	XP	Money
The Sigil of Krasus	Netherstorm	All	All		Image of Archmage Vargoth	Image of Archmage Vargoth	Curse of the Violet Tower			12300	4g 10s
CHOICE OF: 1 Kirin'Var Journeyman's Belt, or 1 Kirin'Var Scout's Belt, or 1 Battle-Mage's Helmet, or 1 Kirin'Var Defender's Chausses											
Manaforge B'naar	Netherstorm	All	All		Spymaster Thalodien	Spymaster Thalodien	Allegiance to the Scryers	0 with The Scryers		12000	3g 90s
Recharging the Batteries	Netherstorm	All	All		Bot-Specialist Alley	Bot-Specialist Alley				12000	3g 90s
Mark V is Alive!	Netherstorm	All	All	2	Maxx A. Million Mk. V	Bot-Specialist Alley				14950	7g 80s
CHOICE OF: 1 Alley's Recurve, or 1 Mark V's Throwing Star, or 1 Unearthed Enkaat Wand											
Krasus's Compendium	Netherstorm	All	All		Image of Archmage Vargoth	Image of Archmage Vargoth	The Sigil of Krasus			12300	4g 10s
High Value Targets	Netherstorm	All	All		Spymaster Thalodien	Spymaster Thalodien	Manaforge B'naar	0 with The Scryers		12000	3g 90s
Stealth Flight	Netherstorm	All	All		Spymaster Thalodien	Veronia	Shutting Down Manaforge B'naar	0 with The Scryers		1200	
A Convincing Disguise	Netherstorm	All	All		Caledis Brightdawn	Caledis Brightdawn	Behind Enemy Lines	0 with The Scryers		12000	3g 90s
Information Gathering	Netherstorm	All	All		Caledis Brightdawn	Caledis Brightdawn	A Convincing Disguise	0 with The Scryers		9000	
CHOICE OF: 1 Spymaster's Crossbow, or 1 Belt of the Sage, or 1 Brightdawn Bracers, or 1 Bloodguard's Greaves											
That Little Extra Kick	Netherstorm	All	All		Boots	Boots	Securing the Shaleskin Shale			12000	3g 90s
CHOICE OF: 1 After Hours Pauldrons, or 1 Boot's Boots, or 1 Doc's Belt, or 1 Mixologist's Gloves											
Return to Thalodien	Netherstorm	All	All		Caledis Brightdawn	Spymaster Thalodien	Shutting Down Manaforge Coruu	0 with The Scryers		1200	
A Defector	Netherstorm	All	All		Magistrix Larynna	Magister Theledorn	Kick Them While They're Down	0 with The Scryers		6250	
Invaluable Asset Zapping	Netherstorm	All	All		Rocket-Chief Fuselage	Lead Sapper Blastfizzle	You're Hired!			12300	4g 10s
Bloodgem Crystals	Netherstorm	All	All		Magistrix Larynna	Magistrix Larynna	Manaforge B'naar	0 with The Scryers		12000	3g 90s
Warp-Raider Nesaad	Netherstorm	All	All		Nether-Stalker Khay'ji	Nether-Stalker Khay'ji	A Heap of Ethereals			12300	4g 10s
CHOICE OF: 1 Zaxxis Boots, or 1 Zaxxis Bracers, or 1 Zaxxis Gloves											
Pick Your Part	Netherstorm	All	All		Papa Wheeler	Papa Wheeler	Consortium Crystal Collection			12000	3g 90s
CHOICE OF: 1 Mech Tech Shoulders, or 1 Papa's Armbands, or 1 Wheeler Family Heirloom											
Summoner Kanthin's Prize	Netherstorm	All	All		Image of Archmage Vargoth	Image of Archmage Vargoth	Unlocking the Compendium			12300	4g 10s
Dr. Boom!	Netherstorm	All	All		Lead Sapper Blastfizzle	Lead Sapper Blastfizzle	Invaluable Asset Zapping			12000	3g 90s
CHOICE OF: 1 Sparky's Discarded Helmet, or 1 Nether Leggings, or 1 Nether Vest, or 1 Nether Guards											
The Sunfury Garrison	Netherstorm	All	All		Custodian Dieworth	Custodian Dieworth	The Sigil of Krasus			12300	4g 10s
Down With Daellis	Netherstorm	All	All		Custodian Dieworth	Custodian Dieworth	The Sunfury Garrison			12300	4g 10s
CHOICE OF: 1 Dawnstrike's Cloak, or 1 Signet of the Violet Tower, or 1 Nightstalker's Wristguards, or 1 Strength of the Violet Tower											
Essence for the Engines	Netherstorm	All	All		Chief Engineer Trep	Chief Engineer Trep	Report to Engineering			12000	3g 90s
Report to Engineering	Netherstorm	All	All		Rocket-Chief Fuselage	Chief Engineer Trep	You're Hired!			1200	
Elemental Power Extraction	Netherstorm	All	All		Chief Engineer Trep	Chief Engineer Trep	Essence for the Engines			12000	3g 90s
CHOICE OF: 1 Area 52 Engineering Gloves, or 1 Heavy-Duty Engineering Boots, or 1 Trepp's Shoulderguards, or 1 Chief Engineer's Belt											
In A Scrap With The Legion	Netherstorm	All	All		Papa Wheeler	Papa Wheeler	Pick Your Part			12300	4g 10s
Torching Sunfury Hold	Netherstorm	All	All		Lieutenant-Sorcerer Morran	Lieutenant-Sorcerer Morran	Krasus's Compendium			12300	4g 10s
One Demon's Trash...	Netherstorm	All	All		Mama Wheeler	Mama Wheeler	Pick Your Part			12300	4g 10s
Declawing Doomclaw	Netherstorm	All	All		Mama Wheeler	Mama Wheeler	One Demon's Trash...			12300	4g 10s
CHOICE OF: 1 Mama's Insurance, or 1 Pilfered Ethereal Blade, or 1 Ripfang Paw											
Warn Area 52!	Netherstorm	All	All		Mama Wheeler	Rocket-Chief Fuselage	Declawing Doomclaw			3100	
Potential Energy Source	Netherstorm	All	All		Lieutenant-Sorcerer Morran	Lieutenant-Sorcerer Morran	The Unending Invasion			12300	4g 10s
Building a Perimeter	Netherstorm	All	All		Lieutenant-Sorcerer Morran	Lieutenant-Sorcerer Morran	Potential Energy Source			12300	4g 10s
CHOICE OF: 1 Crimson Mail Bracers, or 1 Harmony's Touch, or 1 Kirin'Var Defender's Greaves, or 1 Boots of the Beneficent											
Distraction at Manaforge B'naar	Netherstorm	All	All		Exarch Orelis	Exarch Orelis	Allegiance to the Aldor	0 with The Aldor		12000	3g 90s
Naaru Technology	Netherstorm	All	All		Anchorite Karja	B'naar Control Console	Distraction at Manaforge B'naar	0 with The Aldor		12000	
B'naar Console Transcription	Netherstorm	All	All		B'naar Control Console	Anchorite Karja	Naaru Technology	0 with The Aldor		12000	3g 90s
Attack on Manaforge Coruu	Netherstorm	All	All		Exarch Orelis	Exarch Orelis	Shutting Down Manaforge B'naar	0 with The Aldor		12000	
Doctor Vomisa, Ph.T.	Netherstorm	All	All	3	Rocket-Chief Fuselage	Doctor Vomisa, Ph.T.	Warn Area 52!			1250	
You, Robot	Netherstorm	All	All	3	Doctor Vomisa, Ph.T.	Doctor Vomisa, Ph.T.	Doctor Vomisa, Ph.T.			12300	4g 10s
Back to the Chief!	Netherstorm	All	All		Doctor Vomisa, Ph.T.	Rocket-Chief Fuselage	You, Robot			18450	12g 30s
CHOICE OF: 1 Area 52 Defender's Pants, or 1 X-52 Technician's Helm, or 1 X-52 Pilot's Leggings											
REWARD: 1 X-52 Rocket Helmet											
Finding the Keymaster	Netherstorm	All	All	2	Archmage Vargoth	Archmage Vargoth	Ar'kelos the Guardian			12300	4g 10s
Capturing the Keystone	Netherstorm	All	All	5	Archmage Vargoth	Archmage Vargoth	Finding the Keymaster			19000	13g 20s
Wanted: Annihilator Servo!	Netherstorm	All	All	2	Wanted Poster	Papa Wheeler				12000	7g 80s
CHOICE OF: 1 Exotic Spiked Shoulders, or 1 Lost Chestplate of the Reverent, or 1 Red Pointy Hat											

Title	Location	Faction	Race & Class	Group #	Starter	Finisher	Prerequisite	Reputation	Tradeskill	XP	Money
A Heap of Ethereals	Netherstorm	All	All		Nether-Stalker Khay'ji	Nether-Stalker Khay'ji	Consortium Crystal Collection			12000	3● 90●
Assisting the Consortium	Netherstorm	All	All		Anchorite Karja	Nether-Stalker Khay'ji	You're Hired!			1200	
Assisting the Consortium	Netherstorm	All	All		Spymaster Thalodien	Nether-Stalker Khay'ji	You're Hired!			1200	
Consortium Crystal Collection	Netherstorm	All	All		Nether-Stalker Khay'ji	Nether-Stalker Khay'ji				12300	4● 10●
Request for Assistance	Netherstorm	All	All		Nether-Stalker Khay'ji	Gahruj	Warp-Raider Nesaad			3100	
Rightful Repossession	Netherstorm	All	All		Gahruj	Gahruj	Request for Assistance			12300	4● 10●
CHOICE OF: 1 Duro Footgear, or 1 Eco-Dome Leggings, or 1 Midrealm Hat											
An Audience with the Prince	Netherstorm	All	All		Gahruj	Image of Nexus-Prince Haramad	Rightful Repossession			6150	2● 10●
Triangulation Point One	Netherstorm	All	All		Image of Nexus-Prince Haramad	Dealer Hazzin	An Audience with the Prince			12300	4● 10●
A Not-So-Modest Proposal	Netherstorm	All	All		Wind Trader Marid	Image of Wind Trader Marid				12650	4● 40●
Getting Down to Business	Netherstorm	All	All		Image of Wind Trader Marid	Shrouded Figure	A Not-So-Modest Proposal			12650	4● 40●
A Promising Start	Netherstorm	All	All		Tyri	Tyri	Formal Introductions			12650	4● 40●
Troublesome Distractions	Netherstorm	All	All		Tyri	Tyri	A Promising Start			12650	4● 40●
Securing the Celestial Ridge	Netherstorm	All	All	3	Tyri	Tyri	Troublesome Distractions			15800	8● 80●
CHOICE OF: 1 Shimmering Azure Boots, or 1 Dragon Crested Epaulets, or 1 Goldenlink Bracers, or 1 Blued Steel Gauntlets											
Triangulation Point Two	Netherstorm	All	All		Dealer Hazzin	Wind Trader Tuluman	Triangulation Point One			12650	4● 40●
Full Triangle	Netherstorm	All	All	2	Wind Trader Tuluman	Image of Nexus-Prince Haramad	Triangulation Point Two			12650	4● 40●
Special Delivery to Shattrath City	Netherstorm	All	All		Image of Nexus-Prince Haramad	A'dal	Full Triangle			19000	13● 20●
CHOICE OF: 1 Chestplate of A'dal, or 1 Pants of the Naaru, or 1 Shattrath Leggings											
Formal Introductions	Netherstorm	All	All		Shrouded Figure	Tyri	Getting Down to Business			3150	
In Search of Farahlite	Netherstorm	All	All	2	Zuben Elgenubi	Zuben Elgenubi				12650	4● 40●
Hitting the Motherlode	Netherstorm	All	All	2	Zuben Elgenubi	Zuben Elgenubi	In Search of Farahlite			12300	4● 10●
CHOICE OF: 1 Cloak of Woven Energy, or 1 Celestial Jewel Ring, or 1 Chain of Glowing Tendrils											
Shutting Down Manaforge B'naar	Netherstorm	All	All		Anchorite Karja	Anchorite Karja	B'naar Console Transcription	0 with The Aldor		12000	3● 90●
Rebuilding the Staff	Netherstorm	All	All		Ravandwyr	Ravandwyr	The Archmage's Staff			12300	4● 10●
Unlocking the Compendium	Netherstorm	All	All		Image of Archmage Vargoth	Image of Archmage Vargoth	Krasus's Compendium			12300	4● 10●
Abjurist Belmara	Netherstorm	All	All		Belmara's Tome	Custodian Dieworth				12300	
Conjurer Luminrath	Netherstorm	All	All		Luminrath's Mantle	Custodian Dieworth				12300	
Cohlien Frostweaver	Netherstorm	All	All		Cohlien's Cap	Custodian Dieworth				12300	
Another Heap of Ethereals	Netherstorm	All	All			Nether-Stalker Khay'ji	A Heap of Ethereals				
It's a Fel Reaver, But with Heart	Netherstorm	All	All	3	N. D. Meancamp	N. D. Meancamp				12000	3● 90●
CHOICE OF: 1 Heap Leggings, or 1 Scavenged Breastplate, or 1 Warp-Raider's Eyepatch											
Sabotage the Warp-Gate!	Netherstorm	All	All	3	Drijya	Gahruj				15800	8● 80●
CHOICE OF: 1 Consortium Combatant's Robes, or 1 Midrealm Leggings, or 1 Netherstorm Eyepatch											
Drijya Needs Your Help	Netherstorm	All	All		Gahruj	Drijya				1250	
The Annals of Kirin'Var	Netherstorm	All	All		Custodian Dieworth	Custodian Dieworth	Malevolent Remnants			12300	4● 10●
Measuring Warp Energies	Netherstorm	All	All		Exarch Orelis	Exarch Orelis	Distraction at Manaforge B'naar	0 with The Aldor		12000	
CHOICE OF: 1 Energized Helm, or 1 Warp-Shielded Hauberk, or 1 Resonating Axe, or 1 Warpweaver's Gloves											
A Lingering Suspicion	Netherstorm	All	All		Necromantic Focus	Custodian Dieworth	Searching for Evidence			12300	4● 10●
Neutralizing the Nethermancers	Netherstorm	All	All		Nether-Stalker Oazul	Nether-Stalker Oazul				12650	4● 40●
Searching for Evidence	Netherstorm	All	All		Custodian Dieworth	Necromantic Focus	The Annals of Kirin'Var			12300	
Dealing with the Foreman	Netherstorm	All	All		Wind Trader Tuluman	Foreman Sundown				12650	
Dealing with the Overmaster	Netherstorm	All	All		Foreman Sundown	Wind Trader Tuluman	Dealing with the Foreman			12650	4● 40●
CHOICE OF: 1 Gloves of the Nether-Stalker, or 1 Landing Boots, or 1 Overmaster's Shoulders, or 1 Wind Trader's Band											
Capturing the Phylactery	Netherstorm	All	All		Custodian Dieworth	Custodian Dieworth	A Lingering Suspicion			12300	4● 10●
Destroy Naberius!	Netherstorm	All	All	3	Custodian Dieworth	Custodian Dieworth	Capturing the Phylactery			15400	4● 10●
CHOICE OF: 1 Kirin Tor Apprentice's Robes, or 1 Lifewarden's Breastplate, or 1 Coif of the Wicked, or 1 Legguards of the Resolute Defender											
Shutting Down Manaforge Coruu	Netherstorm	All	All		Anchorite Karja	Anchorite Karja	Shutting Down Manaforge B'naar	0 with The Aldor		12300	4● 10●
Shutting Down Manaforge Duro	Netherstorm	All	All		Anchorite Karja	Anchorite Karja	Shutting Down Manaforge Coruu	0 with The Aldor		12650	
Shutting Down Manaforge Ara	Netherstorm	All	All	3	Anchorite Karja	Anchorite Karja	Shutting Down Manaforge Duro	0 with The Aldor		12650	4● 40●
CHOICE OF: 1 Karja's Medallion, or 1 Overseer's Signet											

Title	Location	Faction	Race & Class	Group #	Starter	Finisher	Prerequisite	Reputation	Tradeskill	XP	Money
Sunfury Briefings	Netherstorm	All	All		Exarch Orelis	Exarch Orelis	Shutting Down Manaforge Coruu	0 with The Aldor		12650	
Shutting Down Manaforge B'naar	Netherstorm	All	All		Spymaster Thalodien	Spymaster Thalodien	High Value Targets	0 with The Scryers		12000	3● 90●
Shutting Down Manaforge Coruu	Netherstorm	All	All		Caledis Brightdawn	Caledis Brightdawn	Information Gathering	0 with The Scryers		12300	4● 10●
Indispensable Tools	Netherstorm	All	All		Apprentice Andrethan	Apprentice Andrethan				12300	4● 10●
Master Smith Rhonsus	Netherstorm	All	All		Apprentice Andrethan	Apprentice Andrethan	Indispensable Tools			12300	4● 10●
CHOICE OF: 1 Master Smith's Hammer, or 1 Finely Wrought Scale Leggings, or 1 Andrethan's Masterwork, or 1 Reinforced Heaume											
Help Mama Wheeler	Netherstorm	All	All		Papa Wheeler	Mama Wheeler	Pick Your Part			1250	
Needs More Cowbell	Netherstorm	All	All		Thadell	Bessy				9250	4● 10●
Surveying the Ruins	Netherstorm	All	All		Zephyrion	Zephyrion				12650	4● 40●
CHOICE OF: 1 Chestguard of the Stormspire, or 1 Ethereal Gloves, or 1 Zephyrion's Belt											
The Minions of Culuthas	Netherstorm	All	All		Nether-Stalker Nauthis	Nether-Stalker Nauthis				12650	4● 40●
When the Cows Come Home	Netherstorm	All	All	2	Bessy	Thadell	Needs More Cowbell			12300	4● 10●
CHOICE OF: 1 Wrangler's Boots, or 1 Cowpoke's Riding Gloves, or 1 Engraved Cattleman's Buckle, or 1 Thadell's Bracers, or 1 Hotshot Cattle Prod											
Shutting Down Manaforge Duro	Netherstorm	All	All		Spymaster Thalodien	Spymaster Thalodien	Return to Thalodien	0 with The Scryers		12650	
The Ethereum	Netherstorm	All	All		Commander Ameer	Image of Commander Ameer				12650	
Kick Them While They're Down	Netherstorm	All	All		Magistrix Larynna	Magistrix Larynna	Shutting Down Manaforge Coruu	0 with The Scryers		12650	
CHOICE OF: 1 Warp-Master's Maul, or 1 Sunfury Blade, or 1 Jeweled Halberd, or 1 Conjurer's Staff											
Securing the Shaleskin Shale	Netherstorm	All	All		Boots	Boots				12000	3● 90●
The Unending Invasion	Netherstorm	All	All		Lieutenant-Sorcerer Morran	Lieutenant-Sorcerer Morran	Curse of the Violet Tower			3100	
The Flesh Lies...	Netherstorm	All	All		Agent Araxes	Agent Araxes				12650	
CHOICE OF: 1 Demolisher's Bracers, or 1 Flesh Handler's Gauntlets, or 1 Protectorate Waistband, or 1 Boots of the Nexus Warden											
New Opportunities	Netherstorm	All	All		Mehrdad	Mehrdad				12300	4● 10●
Arconus the Insatiable	Netherstorm	All	All		Agent Ya-six	Commander Ameer				12650	4● 40●
CHOICE OF: 1 Flesh Handler's Headpiece, or 1 Protectorate Assassin's Tunic, or 1 Starcaller's Plated Belt, or 1 Netherfarer's Leggings											
Shutting Down Manaforge Ara	Netherstorm	All	All	3	Spymaster Thalodien	Spymaster Thalodien	Shutting Down Manaforge Duro	0 with The Scryers		12650	4● 40●
CHOICE OF: 1 Manastorm Band, or 1 Thalodien's Charm											
A Dark Pact	Netherstorm	All	All		Kaylaan	Kaylaan	Outside Assistance	0 with The Aldor		12650	
Aldor No More	Netherstorm	All	All		Kaylaan	Exarch Orelis	A Dark Pact	0 with The Aldor		9500	
CHOICE OF: 1 Aldor Ceremonial Wraps, or 1 Vindicator's Light Vest, or 1 Kaylaan's Spaulders, or 1 Girdle of the Lost Vindicator											
Ethereum Data	Netherstorm	All	All		Image of Commander Ameer	Image of Commander Ameer	The Ethereum			6250	
Potential for Brain Damage = High	Netherstorm	All	All		Image of Commander Ameer	Image of Commander Ameer	Ethereum Data			12650	
S-A-B-O-T-A-G-E	Netherstorm	All	All		Image of Commander Ameer	Image of Commander Ameer	Potential for Brain Damage = High			12650	
Delivering the Message	Netherstorm	All	All		Image of Commander Ameer	Image of Commander Ameer	S-A-B-O-T-A-G-E			12650	
CHOICE OF: 1 Druidic Force Boots, or 1 Protectorate Headplate, or 1 Surger's Hand Wraps, or 1 Warpthread Vest											
Socrethar's Shadow	Netherstorm	All	All	2	Anchorite Karja	Anchorite Karja	Aldor No More	0 with The Aldor		15800	4● 40●
Nexus-King Salhadaar	Netherstorm	All	All	5	Image of Commander Ameer	Image of Commander Ameer	Delivering the Message			19000	13● 20●
CHOICE OF: 1 Ameer's Impulse Taser, or 1 Ameer's Judgement, or 1 Fleshling Simulation Staff, or 1 Twin-Bladed Ripper, or 1 The Burning Crusader											
Deathblow to the Legion	Netherstorm	All	All	5	Ishanah	Ishanah	Ishanah's Help	0 with The Aldor		19000	13● 20●
CHOICE OF: 1 Slippers of the High Priestess, or 1 Cleansed Fel Pauldrons, or 1 Gauntlets of the Redeemed Vindicator, or 1 Lightwarden's Girdle, or 1 Kaylaan's Signet											
Ishanah's Help	Netherstorm	All	All		Anchorite Karja	Ishanah	Socrethar's Shadow	0 with The Aldor		9500	
Electro-Shock Goodness!	Netherstorm	All	All		Researcher Navuud	Researcher Navuud				12650	13● 20●
The Horrors of Pollution	Netherstorm	All	All		Vial of Void Horror Ooze	Researcher Navuud				15800	8● 80●
CHOICE OF: 1 Diviner's Cloak, or 1 Protectorate Assassin's Ring, or 1 Starkiller's Bauble											
Run a Diagnostic!	Netherstorm	All	All		Mehrdad	Mehrdad				6000	3● 90●
Deal With the Saboteurs	Netherstorm	All	All		Mehrdad	Mehrdad	Run a Diagnostic!			12000	3● 90●
Captain Tyralius	Netherstorm	All	All		Flesh Handler Viridius	Flesh Handler Viridius				12650	13● 20●
To the Stormspire	Netherstorm	All	All		Mehrdad	Ghabar	Deal With the Saboteurs			1250	
Diagnosis: Critical	Netherstorm	All	All		Ghabar	Ghabar	To the Stormspire			9250	2● 10●
Escape from the Staging Grounds	Netherstorm	All	All			Commander Ameer				12650	
CHOICE OF: 1 Diviner's Cinch, or 1 Ferocious Bands, or 1 Spaulders of the Protectorate, or 1 Starcaller's Plated Stompers											
Flora of the Eco-Domes	Netherstorm	All	All		Aurine Moonblaze	Aurine Moonblaze				12300	4● 10●
Creatures of the Eco-Domes	Netherstorm	All	All		Aurine Moonblaze	Aurine Moonblaze	Flora of the Eco-Domes			12300	4● 10●
When Nature Goes Too Far	Netherstorm	All	All		Aurine Moonblaze	Aurine Moonblaze	Creatures of the Eco-Domes			12300	4● 10●
Testing the Prototype	Netherstorm	All	All		Ghabar	Tashar	Diagnosis: Critical			1250	
Outside Assistance	Netherstorm	All	All		Exarch Orelis	Kaylaan	Sunfury Briefings			3150	
Damning Evidence	Netherstorm	All	All		Magister Theledorn	Spymaster Thalodien	A Defector	0 with The Scryers		12650	
Keeping Up Appearances	Netherstorm	All	All		Shauly Pore	Shauly Pore				12300	4● 10●

Title	Location	Faction	Race & Class	Group #	Starter	Finisher	Prerequisite	Reputation	Tradeskill	XP	Money
The Dynamic Duo	Netherstorm	All	All		Shauly Pore	Audi the Needle	Keeping Up Appearances			1250	
Retrieving the Goods	Netherstorm	All	All		Audi the Needle	Audi the Needle	The Dynamic Duo			12300	4g 10s
CHOICE OF: 1 Audi's Embroidered Boots, or 1 Field Agent's Bracers, or 1 B.O.O.M. Operative's Belt, or 1 Otherwordly Pauldrons											
All Clear!	Netherstorm	All	All		Tashar	Tashar	Testing the Prototype			12300	4g 10s
Recipe for Destruction	Netherstorm	All	All		Professor Dabiri	Professor Dabiri				12650	
On Nethery Wings	Netherstorm	All	All		Professor Dabiri	Professor Dabiri	Recipe for Destruction			12650	
Dimensius the All-Devouring	Netherstorm	All	All	5	Professor Dabiri	Professor Dabiri	On Nethery Wings			19000	13g 20s
CHOICE OF: 1 Circlet of the Starcaller, or 1 Dabiri's Enigma, or 1 Starcaller's Plated Legguards, or 1 Void Slayer's Tunic											
Success!	Netherstorm	All	All		Tashar	Ghabar	All Clear!			3100	
CHOICE OF: 1 Heavenly Inspiration, or 1 Leggings of Concentrated Power, or 1 Nexus-Guard's Pauldrons, or 1 Gold-Trimmed Cuffs											
Turning Point	Netherstorm	All	All	5	Voren'thal the Seer	Voren'thal the Seer	Bound for Glory	0 with The Scryers		19000	13g 20s
CHOICE OF: 1 Gauntlets of the Vanquisher, or 1 Socrethar's Girdle, or 1 Netherfused Pauldrons, or 1 Greaves of Spellpower, or 1 Wand of the Seer											
A Gift for Voren'thal	Netherstorm	All	All	2	Spymaster Thalodien	Spymaster Thalodien	Damning Evidence	0 with The Scryers		15800	4g 40s
Bound for Glory	Netherstorm	All	All		Spymaster Thalodien	Voren'thal the Seer	A Gift for Voren'thal	0 with The Scryers		9500	
Behind Enemy Lines	Netherstorm	All	All		Veronia	Caledis Brightdawn	Stealth Flight	0 with The Scryers		1250	
Breaking Down Netherock	Netherstorm	All	All	2	Wanted Poster	Rocket-Chief Fuselage				12000	7g 80s
CHOICE OF: 1 Rocket-Chief Pauldrons, or 1 Nether-Rocket Gloves, or 1 Goblin Girdle, or 1 Sinister Area 52 Boots											
Nether Gas In a Fel Fire Engine	Netherstorm	All	All			Inactive Fel Reaver					
Fel Reavers, No Thanks!	Netherstorm	All	All		Nether-Stalker Nauthis	Nether-Stalker Nauthis				12300	4g 10s
The Best Defense	Netherstorm	All	All		Nether-Stalker Nauthis	Nether-Stalker Nauthis	Fel Reavers, No Thanks!			12300	
Teleport This!	Netherstorm	All	All		Nether-Stalker Nauthis	Nether-Stalker Nauthis	The Best Defense			15400	
CHOICE OF: 1 Saboteur's Axe, or 1 Runed Silver Staff, or 1 Nether-Stalker's Blade, or 1 Imbued Draenethyst Crystal											
Master of Transmutation	Netherstorm	All	All		Zarevhi	Zarevhi			325 skill in Alchemy	12650	
Bloody Imp-ossible!	Netherstorm	All	All		Sab'aoth	Sab'aoth				12300	4g 10s
Report to Splintertree Post	Orgrimmar	Horde	Blood Elf		Ambassador Dawnsinger	Advisor Sunsworn				775	
Envoy to the Mag'har	Orgrimmar	Horde	All		Thrall	Gorkan Bloodfist	Messenger to Thrall			10400	
CHOICE OF: 1 Ceremonial Robes, or 1 Tribal Hauberk, or 1 Thunderforge Leggings, or 1 Clefthoof Hide Mask											
Meeting the Warchief	Orgrimmar	Horde	Blood Elf		Lady Sylvanas Windrunner	Thrall	Envoy to the Horde			1650	
Meeting the Warchief	Orgrimmar	Horde	Non-Blood Elf		Lady Sylvanas Windrunner	Thrall	Envoy to the Horde			1650	
Imperial Plate Armor	Orgrimmar	Horde	All		Krathok Moltenfist	Derotain Mudsipper			265 skill in Blacksmithing	3550	
Escape from Coilskar Cistern	Shadowmoon Valley	All	All	2		Earthmender Torlok				15800	13g 20s
CHOICE OF: 1 Earthmender's Bracer of Shattering, or 1 Earthmender's Crimson Spaulders, or 1 Earthmender's Fists of Undoing, or 1 Earthmender's Plated Boots											
Enraged Spirits of Fire and Earth	Shadowmoon Valley	All	All		Earthmender Torlok	Earthmender Torlok				12650	
Enraged Spirits of Water	Shadowmoon Valley	All	All		Earthmender Torlok	Earthmender Torlok	Enraged Spirits of Fire and Earth			12650	
Enraged Spirits of Air	Shadowmoon Valley	All	All		Earthmender Torlok	Earthmender Torlok	Enraged Spirits of Water			12650	
CHOICE OF: 1 Boots of the Skybreaker, or 1 Grips of the Void, or 1 Manimal's Cinch, or 1 Skybreaker's Pauldrons											
Oronok Torn-heart	Shadowmoon Valley	All	All		Earthmender Torlok	Oronok Torn-heart	Enraged Spirits of Air			1250	
I Was A Lot Of Things...	Shadowmoon Valley	All	All		Oronok Torn-heart	Oronok Torn-heart	Oronok Torn-heart			12650	
CHOICE OF: 20 Oronok's Tuber of Healing, or 20 Oronok's Tuber of Agility, or 20 Oronok's Tuber of Strength, or 20 Oronok's Tuber of Spell Power											
A Lesson Learned	Shadowmoon Valley	All	All		Oronok Torn-heart	Oronok Torn-heart	I Was A Lot Of Things...			12650	
The Cipher of Damnation - Truth and History	Shadowmoon Valley	All	All		Oronok Torn-heart	Oronok Torn-heart	A Lesson Learned			1250	
Grom'tor, Son of Oronok	Shadowmoon Valley	All	All		Oronok Torn-heart	Grom'tor, Son of Oronok	The Cipher of Damnation - Truth and History			1250	
The Cipher of Damnation - Grom'tor's Charge	Shadowmoon Valley	All	All		Grom'tor, Son of Oronok	Grom'tor, Son of Oronok	Grom'tor, Son of Oronok			15800	
The Cipher of Damnation - The First Fragment Recovered	Shadowmoon Valley	All	All		Grom'tor, Son of Oronok	Oronok Torn-heart	The Cipher of Damnation - Grom'tor's Charge			3150	
CHOICE OF: 1 Grom'tor's Friend's Cousin's Tunic, or 1 Grom'tor's Bloodied Bandage, or 1 Grom'tor's Pendant of Conquest, or 1 Oronok's Old Bracers											
Ar'tor, Son of Oronok	Shadowmoon Valley	All	All		Oronok Torn-heart	Ar'tor, Son of Oronok	The Cipher of Damnation - Truth and History			6250	
Demonic Crystal Prisons	Shadowmoon Valley	All	All		Ar'tor, Son of Oronok	Ar'tor, Son of Oronok	Ar'tor, Son of Oronok			9500	
Lohn'goron, Bow of the Torn-heart	Shadowmoon Valley	All	All		Spirit of Ar'tor	Spirit of Ar'tor	Demonic Crystal Prisons			12650	
The Cipher of Damnation - Ar'tor's Charge	Shadowmoon Valley	All	All		Spirit of Ar'tor	Spirit of Ar'tor	Lohn'goron, Bow of the Torn-heart			15800	

Title	Location	Faction	Race & Class	Group #	Starter	Finisher	Prerequisite	Reputation	Tradeskill	XP	Money
The Cipher of Damnation - The Second Fragment Recovered	Shadowmoon Valley	All	All		Spirit of Ar'tor	Oronok Torn-heart	The Cipher of Damnation - Ar'tor's Charge			6250	
CHOICE OF: 1 Eva's Strap, or 1 Ghostly Headwrap, or 1 Oronok's Old Leggings, or 1 Torn-heart Cloak, or 1 Torn-heart Family Tunic											
Borak, Son of Oronok	Shadowmoon Valley	All	All		Oronok Torn-heart	Borak, Son of Oronok	The Cipher of Damnation - Truth and History			3150	
Of Thistleheads and Eggs...	Shadowmoon Valley	All	All		Borak, Son of Oronok	Tobias the Filth Gorger	Borak, Son of Oronok			12650	
The Bundle of Bloodthistle	Shadowmoon Valley	All	All		Tobias the Filth Gorger	Borak, Son of Oronok	Of Thistleheads and Eggs...			3150	
Besieged!	Shadowmoon Valley	Alliance	All		Wing Commander Nuainn	Wing Commander Nuainn				12300	4● 10●
To Legion Hold	Shadowmoon Valley	Alliance	All		Wing Commander Nuainn	Wing Commander Nuainn	Besieged!			12300	4● 10●
Blast the Infernals!	Shadowmoon Valley	Alliance	All		Wing Commander Nuainn	Wing Commander Nuainn	Setting Up the Bomb			12300	4● 10●
CHOICE OF: 1 Bloodforged Guard, or 1 Crimson Mail Hauberk, or 1 Mooncrest Headdress, or 1 Soothsayer's Kilt											
Tablets of Baa'ri	Shadowmoon Valley	All	All		Anchorite Ceyla	Anchorite Ceyla	Allegiance to the Aldor	0 with The Aldor		12650	
The Sketh'lon Wreckage	Shadowmoon Valley	Alliance	All		Gryphonrider Kieran	Gryphonrider Kieran				12300	4● 10●
To Catch A Thistlehead	Shadowmoon Valley	All	All		Borak, Son of Oronok	Borak, Son of Oronok	The Bundle of Bloodthistle			9500	
Oronu the Elder	Shadowmoon Valley	All	All		Anchorite Ceyla	Anchorite Ceyla	Tablets of Baa'ri	0 with The Aldor		12650	
Setting Up the Bomb	Shadowmoon Valley	Alliance	All		Wing Commander Nuainn	Wing Commander Nuainn	To Legion Hold			12300	4● 10●
The Deathforge	Shadowmoon Valley	Alliance	All		Wing Commander Nuainn	Stormer Ewan Wildwing	Blast the Infernals!			1250	
The Ashtongue Corruptors	Shadowmoon Valley	All	All		Anchorite Ceyla	Anchorite Ceyla	Oronu the Elder	0 with The Aldor		12650	
The Warden's Cage	Shadowmoon Valley	All	All		Anchorite Ceyla	Sanoru	The Ashtongue Corruptors	0 with The Aldor		6250	
The Shadowmoon Shuffle	Shadowmoon Valley	All	All		Borak, Son of Oronok	Borak, Son of Oronok	To Catch A Thistlehead			12650	
What Illidan Wants, Illidan Gets...	Shadowmoon Valley	All	All		Borak, Son of Oronok	Borak, Son of Oronok	The Shadowmoon Shuffle			9500	
The Cipher of Damnation - Borak's Charge	Shadowmoon Valley	All	All	3	Borak, Son of Oronok	Borak, Son of Oronok	What Illidan Wants, Illidan Gets...			12650	
The Cipher of Damnation - The Third Fragment Recovered	Shadowmoon Valley	All	All		Borak, Son of Oronok	Oronok Torn-heart	The Cipher of Damnation - Borak's Charge			6250	
CHOICE OF: 1 Ar'tor's Mainstay, or 1 Borak's Belt of Bravery, or 1 Felboar Hide Shoes, or 1 Spaulders of the Torn-heart, or 1 The Hands of Fate, or 1 Umberhowl's Collar											
Minions of the Shadow Council	Shadowmoon Valley	Alliance	All		Stormer Ewan Wildwing	Stormer Ewan Wildwing	The Deathforge			12300	4● 10●
The Fate of Flanis	Shadowmoon Valley	Alliance	All		Stormer Ewan Wildwing	Stormer Ewan Wildwing	Minions of the Shadow Council			12300	4● 10●
The Summoning Chamber	Shadowmoon Valley	Alliance	All		Stormer Ewan Wildwing	Stormer Ewan Wildwing	Minions of the Shadow Council			12300	4● 10●
Bring Down the Warbringer!	Shadowmoon Valley	Alliance	All		Stormer Ewan Wildwing	Wing Commander Nuainn	The Fate of Flanis			12300	4● 10●
Karabor Training Grounds	Shadowmoon Valley	All	All		Exarch Onaala	Exarch Onaala	Allegiance to the Aldor	0 with The Aldor		12650	
The Cipher of Damnation	Shadowmoon Valley	All	All	5	Oronok Torn-heart	Earthmender Torlok	The Cipher of Damnation - The First Fragment Recovered			19000	13● 20●
CHOICE OF: 1 Borak's Reminder, or 1 Grom'tor's Charge, or 1 Lohn'goron, or Bow of the Torn-heart, or 1 Oronok's Ancient Scepter, or 1 Torn-heart Axe of Battle, or 1 Staff of the Redeemer											
REWARD: 1 Amulet of the Torn-heart											
Gaining Access	Shadowmoon Valley	Alliance	All		Wing Commander Nuainn	Wing Commander Nuainn	Bring Down the Warbringer!			12300	4● 10●
Besieged!	Shadowmoon Valley	Horde	All		Blood Guard Gulmok	Blood Guard Gulmok				12300	4● 10●
To Legion Hold	Shadowmoon Valley	Horde	All		Blood Guard Gulmok	Blood Guard Gulmok	Besieged!			12300	4● 10●
Setting Up the Bomb	Shadowmoon Valley	Horde	All		Blood Guard Gulmok	Blood Guard Gulmok	To Legion Hold			12300	4● 10●
Blast the Infernals!	Shadowmoon Valley	Horde	All		Blood Guard Gulmok	Blood Guard Gulmok	Setting Up the Bomb			12300	4● 10●
CHOICE OF: 1 Bloodforged Guard, or 1 Crimson Mail Hauberk, or 1 Mooncrest Headdress, or 1 Soothsayer's Kilt											
The Deathforge	Shadowmoon Valley	Horde	All		Blood Guard Gulmok	Scout Zagran	Blast the Infernals!			1250	
Minions of the Shadow Council	Shadowmoon Valley	Horde	All		Scout Zagran	Scout Zagran	The Deathforge			12300	4● 10●
The Fate of Kagrosh	Shadowmoon Valley	Horde	All		Scout Zagran	Scout Zagran	Minions of the Shadow Council			12300	4● 10●
The Summoning Chamber	Shadowmoon Valley	Horde	All		Scout Zagran	Scout Zagran	Minions of the Shadow Council			12300	4● 10●
Bring Down the Warbringer!	Shadowmoon Valley	Horde	All		Scout Zagran	Blood Guard Gulmok	The Fate of Kagrosh			12300	4● 10●

Title	Location	Faction	Race & Class	Group #	Starter	Finisher	Prerequisite	Reputation	Tradeskill	XP	Money
Gaining Access	Shadowmoon Valley	Horde	All		Blood Guard Gulmok	Blood Guard Gulmok	Bring Down the Warbringer!			12300	4 10
The Art of Fel Reaver Maintenance	Shadowmoon Valley	Alliance	All		Plexi	Plexi	Invasion Point: Cataclysm			12300	4 10
The Art of Fel Reaver Maintenance	Shadowmoon Valley	Horde	All		Nakansi	Nakansi	Invasion Point: Cataclysm			12300	4 10
The Fel and the Furious	Shadowmoon Valley	Alliance	All		Plexi	Plexi	The Art of Fel Reaver Maintenance			15400	4 10
The Fel and the Furious	Shadowmoon Valley	Horde	All		Nakansi	Nakansi	The Art of Fel Reaver Maintenance			15400	4 10
The Ashtongue Tribe	Shadowmoon Valley	All	All		Vindicator Aluumen	Vindicator Aluumen	Allegiance to the Aldor	0 with The Aldor		12650	
Illidari-Bane Shard	Shadowmoon Valley	Alliance	All		Illidari-Bane Shard	Ordinn Thunderfist				9250	4 10
Proof of Allegiance	Shadowmoon Valley	All	All		Sanoru	Sanoru	The Warden's Cage				
Illidari-Bane Shard	Shadowmoon Valley	Horde	All		Illidari-Bane Shard	Grokom Deatheye				9250	4 10
A Haunted History	Shadowmoon Valley	Horde	All		Chief Apothecary Hildagard	Chief Apothecary Hildagard				12300	4 10
Spectrecles	Shadowmoon Valley	Horde	All		Chief Apothecary Hildagard	Chief Apothecary Hildagard	A Haunted History			12300	4 10
Capture the Weapons	Shadowmoon Valley	Alliance	All	3	Ordinn Thunderfist	Ordinn Thunderfist	Illidari-Bane Shard			12300	4 10
CHOICE OF: 1 Ashwalker's Footwraps, or 1 Azurestrike Shoulders, or 1 Darkhunter's Cinch, or 1 Singed Vambraces											
Capture the Weapons	Shadowmoon Valley	Horde	All	3	Grokom Deatheye	Grokom Deatheye	Illidari-Bane Shard			12300	4 10
CHOICE OF: 1 Ashwalker's Footwraps, or 1 Azurestrike Shoulders, or 1 Darkhunter's Cinch, or 1 Singed Vambraces											
Akama	Shadowmoon Valley	All	All		Sanoru	Akama	Proof of Allegiance			3150	
Teron Gorefiend - Lore and Legend	Shadowmoon Valley	Horde	All		Chief Apothecary Hildagard	Ancient Shadowmoon Spirit	Spectrecles			6250	
Divination: Gorefiend's Armor	Shadowmoon Valley	All	All	5	Ancient Shadowmoon Spirit	Ancient Shadowmoon Spirit	Teron Gorefiend - Lore and Legend			15800	
Divination: Gorefiend's Cloak	Shadowmoon Valley	All	All		Ancient Shadowmoon Spirit	Ancient Shadowmoon Spirit	Teron Gorefiend - Lore and Legend			12650	
Divination: Gorefiend's Truncheon	Shadowmoon Valley	All	All	2	Ancient Shadowmoon Spirit	Ancient Shadowmoon Spirit	Teron Gorefiend - Lore and Legend			12650	
A Necessary Distraction	Shadowmoon Valley	All	All		Exarch Onaala	Exarch Onaala	Karabor Training Grounds	0 with The Aldor		12650	
Teron Gorefiend, I am...	Shadowmoon Valley	Horde	All		Ancient Shadowmoon Spirit	Chief Apothecary Hildagard	Divination: Gorefiend's Cloak			19000	
CHOICE OF: 1 Druidic Helmet of of Second Sight, or 1 Evoker's Helmet of Second Sight, or 1 Overlord's Helmet of Second Sight, or 1 Stalker's Helmet of Second Sight, or 1 Shamanistic Helmet of Second Sight, or 1 Stealther's Helmet of Second Sight											
Altruis	Shadowmoon Valley	All	All		Exarch Onaala	Altruis the Sufferer	A Necessary Distraction	0 with The Aldor		6250	
Against the Legion	Shadowmoon Valley	All	All		Altruis the Sufferer	Altruis the Sufferer	Altruis			12650	
A Ghost in the Machine	Shadowmoon Valley	Alliance	All		Zorus the Judicator	Zorus the Judicator				12300	4 10
Harbingers of Shadowmoon	Shadowmoon Valley	Alliance	All		Zorus the Judicator	Zorus the Judicator	A Ghost in the Machine			12300	4 10
Teron Gorefiend - Lore and Legend	Shadowmoon Valley	Alliance	All		Zorus the Judicator	Ancient Shadowmoon Spirit	Harbingers of Shadowmoon			6250	
Teron Gorefiend, I am...	Shadowmoon Valley	Alliance	All		Ancient Shadowmoon Spirit	Zorus the Judicator	Divination: Gorefiend's Armor			19000	
CHOICE OF: 1 Druidic Helmet of of Second Sight, or 1 Evoker's Helmet of Second Sight, or 1 Overlord's Helmet of Second Sight, or 1 Stalker's Helmet of Second Sight, or 1 Shamanistic Helmet of Second Sight, or 1 Stealther's Helmet of Second Sight											
Wanted: Uvuros, Scourge of Shadowmoon	Shadowmoon Valley	Horde	All	4	Wanted Poster	Warcaller Sardon Truslice				15800	13 20
CHOICE OF: 1 Uvuros Hide Boots, or 1 Uvuros Hide Cinch, or 1 Uvuros Hide Gloves, or 1 Uvuros Plated Spaulders											
Wanted: Uvuros, Scourge of Shadowmoon	Shadowmoon Valley	Alliance	All	4	Wanted Poster	Warcaller Beersnout				15800	13 20
CHOICE OF: 1 Uvuros Hide Boots, or 1 Uvuros Hide Cinch, or 1 Uvuros Hide Gloves, or 1 Uvuros Plated Spaulders											
Return to the Aldor	Shadowmoon Valley	All	All		Altruis the Sufferer	Exarch Onaala	The Book of Fel Names	0 with The Aldor		6250	
Varedis Must Be Stopped	Shadowmoon Valley	All	All	5	Exarch Onaala	Exarch Onaala	Return to the Aldor	0 with The Aldor		19000	
CHOICE OF: 1 Ceremonial Kris, or 1 Hauberk of Karabor, or 1 Slayer's Axe, or 1 Summoner's Blade, or 1 Sunfury Legguards, or 1 Wildcaller											
What Strange Creatures...	Shadowmoon Valley	Horde	All		Researcher Tiorus	Researcher Tiorus				12300	4 10
Spleendid!	Shadowmoon Valley	Alliance	All		Gnomus	Gnomus				12300	4 10
The Hermit Smith	Shadowmoon Valley	Alliance	All		Ordinn Thunderfist	David Wayne	Capture the Weapons			1250	
The Hermit Smith	Shadowmoon Valley	Horde	All		Grokom Deatheye	David Wayne	Capture the Weapons			1250	
Additional Materials	Shadowmoon Valley	All	All		David Wayne	David Wayne	The Hermit Smith			9250	4 10
Fresh From the Mechanar	Shadowmoon Valley	All	All	5	David Wayne	David Wayne	Additional Materials			12300	

Title	Location	Faction	Race & Class	Group #	Starter	Finisher	Prerequisite	Reputation	Tradeskill	XP	Money
The Lexicon Demonica	Shadowmoon Valley	All	All	5	David Wayne	David Wayne	Additional Materials			12300	4● 10●
Underworld Loam	Shadowmoon Valley	All	All	5	David Wayne	David Wayne	Fresh From the Mechanar			12650	4● 40●
Against the Illidari	Shadowmoon Valley	All	All		Altruis the Sufferer	Altruis the Sufferer	Altruis			12650	
Against All Odds	Shadowmoon Valley	All	All		Altruis the Sufferer	Altruis the Sufferer	Altruis			12650	
Tear of the Earthmother	Shadowmoon Valley	All	All	5	David Wayne	David Wayne	Fresh From the Mechanar			12650	4● 40●
Frankly, It Makes No Sense...	Shadowmoon Valley	Horde	All		Researcher Tiorus	Researcher Tiorus	What Strange Creatures...			12300	4● 10●
Felspine the Greater	Shadowmoon Valley	Horde	All		Researcher Tiorus	Researcher Tiorus	Frankly, It Makes No Sense...			12650	8● 80●
Bane of the Illidari	Shadowmoon Valley	All	All		David Wayne	David Wayne	Underworld Loam			1250	
The Second Course...	Shadowmoon Valley	Alliance	All		Gnomus	Gnomus	Spleendid!			12300	4● 10●
The Main Course!	Shadowmoon Valley	Alliance	All		Gnomus	Gnomus	The Second Course...			12650	8● 80●
Quenching the Blade	Shadowmoon Valley	All	All		David Wayne	David Wayne	Bane of the Illidari			15800	4● 40●
CHOICE OF: 1 Illidari-Bane Broadsword, or 1 Illidari-Bane Claymore, or 1 Illidari-Bane Mageblade, or 1 Illidari-Bane Dagger											
The Hand of Gul'dan	Shadowmoon Valley	Alliance	All		Earthmender Sophurus	Earthmender Torlok				3150	
The Hand of Gul'dan	Shadowmoon Valley	Horde	All		Earthmender Splinthoof	Earthmender Torlok				3150	
Tablets of Baa'ri	Shadowmoon Valley	All	All		Arcanist Thelis	Arcanist Thelis	Allegiance to the Scryers	0 with The Scryers		12650	
Oronu the Elder	Shadowmoon Valley	All	All		Arcanist Thelis	Arcanist Thelis	Tablets of Baa'ri	0 with The Scryers		12650	
The Ashtongue Corruptors	Shadowmoon Valley	All	All		Arcanist Thelis	Arcanist Thelis	Oronu the Elder	0 with The Scryers		12650	
The Warden's Cage	Shadowmoon Valley	All	All		Arcanist Thelis	Sanoru	The Ashtongue Corruptors	0 with The Scryers		6250	
Karabor Training Grounds	Shadowmoon Valley	All	All		Larissa Sunstrike	Larissa Sunstrike	Allegiance to the Scryers	0 with The Scryers		12650	
A Necessary Distraction	Shadowmoon Valley	All	All		Larissa Sunstrike	Larissa Sunstrike	Karabor Training Grounds	0 with The Scryers		12650	
Altruis	Shadowmoon Valley	All	All		Larissa Sunstrike	Altruis the Sufferer	A Necessary Distraction	0 with The Scryers		6250	
Return to the Scryers	Shadowmoon Valley	All	All		Altruis the Sufferer	Larissa Sunstrike	The Book of Fel Names	0 with The Scryers		6250	
Varedis Must Be Stopped	Shadowmoon Valley	All	All	5	Larissa Sunstrike	Larissa Sunstrike	Return to the Aldor	0 with The Scryers		19000	
CHOICE OF: 1 Ceremonial Kris, or 1 Hauberk of Karabor, or 1 Slayer's Axe, or 1 Summoner's Blade, or 1 Sunfury Legguards, or 1 Wildcaller											
A Grunt's Work...	Shadowmoon Valley	Horde	All		Overlord Or'barokh	Overlord Or'barokh				12300	12● 30●
Put On Yer Kneepads...	Shadowmoon Valley	Alliance	All		Thane Yoregar	Thane Yoregar				12300	12● 30●
A Mysterious Portent	Shadowmoon Valley	All	All		Udalo	Akama	Seer Udalo			9500	
The Ata'mal Terrace	Shadowmoon Valley	All	All	5	Akama	Akama	A Mysterious Portent			12650	
Akama's Promise	Shadowmoon Valley	All	All		Akama	A'dal	The Ata'mal Terrace			19000	
CHOICE OF: 1 Akama's Sash, or 1 Ashtongue Blade, or 1 Bloodwarder's Rifle, or 1 Verdant Gloves, or 1 Spellbreaker's Buckler, or 1 Staff of the Ashtongue Deathsworn											
News of Victory	Shadowmoon Valley	Alliance	All		Plexi	Kurdran Wildhammer	The Fel and the Furious			15800	4● 40●
CHOICE OF: 1 Band of Anguish, or 1 Gloves of the High Magus, or 1 Idol of the Avenger, or 1 Libram of Righteous Power, or 1 Stormfury Totem											
News of Victory	Shadowmoon Valley	Horde	All		Nakansi	Overlord Or'barokh	The Fel and the Furious			15800	4● 40●
CHOICE OF: 1 Band of Anguish, or 1 Gloves of the High Magus, or 1 Idol of the Avenger, or 1 Libram of Righteous Power, or 1 Stormfury Totem											
The Path of Conquest	Shadowmoon Valley	Horde	All	3	Overlord Or'barokh	Kor'kron Wind Rider				9500	
Breaching the Path	Shadowmoon Valley	Horde	All	3	Kor'kron Wind Rider	Kor'kron Wind Rider	The Path of Conquest			15800	
Entry Into the Citadel	Shadowmoon Valley	Alliance	All		Primed Key Mold	Force Commander Danath Trollbane				12650	
Entry Into the Citadel	Shadowmoon Valley	Horde	All		Primed Key Mold	Nazgrel				12650	
Find the Deserter	Shadowmoon Valley	Alliance	All		Gryphonrider Kieran	Parshah	The Sketh'lon Wreckage			1250	
The Sketh'lon Wreckage	Shadowmoon Valley	Horde	All		Bahat	Sergeant Kargrul				12300	4● 10●
Find the Deserter	Shadowmoon Valley	Horde	All		Bahat	Parshah	The Sketh'lon Wreckage			1250	
When Worlds Collide...	Shadowmoon Valley	Horde	All	3	Kor'kron Wind Rider	Kor'kron Wind Rider	Breaching the Path			15800	

Title	Location	Faction	Race & Class	Group #	Starter	Finisher	Prerequisite	Reputation	Tradeskill	XP	Money
Invasion Point: Cataclysm	Shadowmoon Valley	Alliance	All		Wing Commander Nuainn	Plexi	Gaining Access			1250	
Invasion Point: Cataclysm	Shadowmoon Valley	Horde	All		Blood Guard Gulmok	Nakansi	Gaining Access			1250	
Tabards of the Illidari	Shadowmoon Valley	Horde	All	3	Kor'kron Wind Rider	Kor'kron Wind Rider	When Worlds Collide...			15800	
Dissention Amongst the Ranks...	Shadowmoon Valley	Horde	All	3	Kor'kron Wind Rider	Overlord Or'barokh	Tabards of the Illidari			19000	13● 20●
CHOICE OF: 1 Evoker's Mark of the Redemption, or 1 Slayer's Mark of the Redemption, or 1 Spellsword's Mark of the Redemption, or 1 Protector's Mark of the Redemption											
The Path of Conquest	Shadowmoon Valley	Alliance	All	3	Thane Yoregar	Wildhammer Gryphon Rider				9500	
Breaching the Path	Shadowmoon Valley	Alliance	All	3	Wildhammer Gryphon Rider	Wildhammer Gryphon Rider	The Path of Conquest			15800	
Blood Elf + Giant = ???	Shadowmoon Valley	Alliance	All	3	Wildhammer Gryphon Rider	Wildhammer Gryphon Rider	Breaching the Path			15800	
Tabards of the Illidari	Shadowmoon Valley	Alliance	All	3	Wildhammer Gryphon Rider	Wildhammer Gryphon Rider	Blood Elf + Giant = ???			15800	
Dissention Amongst the Ranks...	Shadowmoon Valley	Alliance	All	3	Wildhammer Gryphon Rider	Thane Yoregar	Tabards of the Illidari			19000	13● 20●
CHOICE OF: 1 Evoker's Mark of the Redemption, or 1 Slayer's Mark of the Redemption, or 1 Spellsword's Mark of the Redemption, or 1 Protector's Mark of the Redemption											
Asghar's Totem	Shadowmoon Valley	All	All		Parshah	Parshah	Find the Deserter			12300	4● 10●
The Rod of Lianthe	Shadowmoon Valley	All	All		Parshah	Parshah	Asghar's Totem			12300	4● 10●
Sketh'lon Feathers	Shadowmoon Valley	All	All		Parshah	Parshah	The Rod of Lianthe			12300	4● 10●
Battle of the Crimson Watch	Shadowmoon Valley	All	All	4	Marcus Auralion	A'dal	The Journal of Val'zareq: Portends of War			19000	13● 20●
CHOICE OF: 1 Acrobat's Mark of the Sha'tar, or 1 Aggressor's Mark of the Sha'tar, or 1 Mage's Mark of the Sha'tar, or 1 Spiritualist's Mark of the Sha'tar											
REWARD: 1 Offering of the Sha'tar											
Imbuing the Headpiece	Shadowmoon Valley	All	All		Parshah	Parshah	Sketh'lon Feathers			12300	4● 10●
The Journal of Val'zareq: Portends of War	Shadowmoon Valley	All	All	4	The Journal of Val'zareq	Crystal Prison				9500	
Kindness	Shadowmoon Valley	All	All		Mordenai	Mordenai				12650	
The Ashtongue Broken	Shadowmoon Valley	All	All		Varen the Reclaimer	Varen the Reclaimer	Allegiance to the Scryers	0 with The Scryers		12650	
Thwart the Dark Conclave	Shadowmoon Valley	All	All		Parshah	Parshah	Imbuing the Headpiece			15400	4● 10●
CHOICE OF: 1 Ash Tempered Legguards, or 1 Crown of Cinders, or 1 Runed Sketh'lon Legplates, or 1 Sketh'lon Survivor's Tunic											
Seek Out Neltharaku	Shadowmoon Valley	All	All		Mordenai	Neltharaku	Kindness			3150	
Neltharaku's Tale	Shadowmoon Valley	All	All		Neltharaku	Neltharaku	Seek Out Neltharaku			3150	
Reclaiming Holy Grounds	Shadowmoon Valley	All	All		Vindicator Aluumen	Vindicator Aluumen	The Ashtongue Tribe	0 with The Aldor		12650	4● 40●
CHOICE OF: 1 Aged Leather Bindings, or 1 Ash-Covered Helm, or 1 Ata'mal Crown, or 1 Blackened Chain Greaves											
The Great Retribution	Shadowmoon Valley	All	All		Varen the Reclaimer	Varen the Reclaimer	The Ashtongue Tribe	0 with The Scryers		12650	4● 40●
CHOICE OF: 1 Aged Leather Bindings, or 1 Ash-Covered Helm, or 1 Ata'mal Crown, or 1 Blackened Chain Greaves											
Single Sunfury Signet	Shadowmoon Valley	All	All			Battlemage Vyara	Sunfury Signets	0 with The Scryers			
More Sunfury Signets	Shadowmoon Valley	All	All			Battlemage Vyara	Sunfury Signets	0 with The Scryers			
Sunfury Signets	Shadowmoon Valley	All	All		Battlemage Vyara	Battlemage Vyara	Allegiance to the Scryers	0 with The Scryers		12650	
Marks of Sargeras	Shadowmoon Valley	All	All		Harbinger Saronen	Harbinger Saronen	Allegiance to the Aldor	0 with The Aldor		12650	
More Marks of Sargeras	Shadowmoon Valley	All	All			Harbinger Saronen	Marks of Sargeras	0 with The Aldor			
Single Mark of Sargeras	Shadowmoon Valley	All	All			Harbinger Saronen	Marks of Sargeras				
Infiltrating Dragonmaw Fortress	Shadowmoon Valley	All	All		Neltharaku	Neltharaku	Neltharaku's Tale			12650	
To Netherwing Ledge!	Shadowmoon Valley	All	All		Neltharaku	Neltharaku	Infiltrating Dragonmaw Fortress			12650	
The Force of Neltharaku	Shadowmoon Valley	All	All		Neltharaku	Neltharaku	To Netherwing Ledge!			12650	
Karynaku	Shadowmoon Valley	All	All	5	Neltharaku	Karynaku	The Force of Neltharaku			3150	
Zuluhed the Whacked	Shadowmoon Valley	Horde	Non-Human	5	Karynaku	Karynaku	Karynaku			12650	
Ally of the Netherwing	Shadowmoon Valley	All	Non-Human		Karynaku	Mordenai	Zuluhed the Whacked			19000	13● 20●
CHOICE OF: 1 Claw of the Netherwing Flight, or 1 Netherwing Defender's Shield, or 1 Netherwing Protector's Shield, or 1 Netherwing Sorceror's Charm, or 1 Netherwing Spiritualist's Charm											
Ally of the Netherwing	Shadowmoon Valley	All	Human		Karynaku	Mordenai	Zuluhed the Whacked			19000	13● 20●
CHOICE OF: 1 Claw of the Netherwing Flight, or 1 Netherwing Defender's Shield, or 1 Netherwing Protector's Shield, or 1 Netherwing Sorceror's Charm, or 1 Netherwing Spiritualist's Charm											

Title	Location	Faction	Race & Class	Group #	Starter	Finisher	Prerequisite	Reputation	Tradeskill	XP	Money
Zuluhed the Whacked	Shadowmoon Valley	All	Human	5	Karynaku	Karynaku	Karynaku			12650	
Khadgar	Shattrath City	All	All		Archmage Cedric	Khadgar	Contact from Dalaran			6250	
Entry Into Karazhan	Shattrath City	All	All	5	Khadgar	Khadgar	Khadgar			12650	
The Second and Third Fragments	Shattrath City	All	All	5	Khadgar	Khadgar	Entry Into Karazhan			15800	
Strained Supplies	Shattrath City	All	All		Sha'nir	Sha'nir	Allegiance to the Aldor	Less than 0 with the Aldor		10750	
More Venom Sacs	Shattrath City	All	All			Sha'nir	Strained Supplies	Less than 0 with the Aldor			
A Cure for Zahlia	Shattrath City	All	All	2	Sha'nir	Sha'nir	Allegiance to the Aldor	Less than 0 with the Aldor		13350	6 20
Restoring the Light	Shattrath City	All	All		Ishanah	Ishanah	Allegiance to the Aldor	Less than 0 with the Aldor		10750	
Voren'thal's Visions	Shattrath City	All	All		Arcanist Adyria	Arcanist Adyria	Allegiance to the Scryers	Less than 0 with the Scryers		11000	
More Basilisk Eyes	Shattrath City	All	All			Arcanist Adyria	Voren'thal's Visions	Less than 0 with the Scryers			
Losing Gracefully	Shattrath City	All	All		Magister Falris	Marksman Regiment's Cooking Pot	Allegiance to the Scryers	Less than 0 with the Scryers		5500	
A'dal	Shattrath City	All	All		Haggard War Veteran	A'dal				5500	
City of Light	Shattrath City	All	All		Khadgar	Khadgar	A'dal			5500	
Marks of Kil'jaeden	Shattrath City	All	All		Adyen the Lightwarden	Adyen the Lightwarden	Allegiance to the Aldor	0 with The Aldor		11000	
More Marks of Kil'jaeden	Shattrath City	All	All			Adyen the Lightwarden	Marks of Kil'jaeden	0 to 8999 with The Aldor			
Single Mark of Kil'jaeden	Shattrath City	All	All			Adyen the Lightwarden	Marks of Kil'jaeden	0 to 8999 with The Aldor			
Firewing Signets	Shattrath City	All	All		Magistrix Fyalenn	Magistrix Fyalenn	Allegiance to the Scryers	0 with The Scryers		11000	
Single Firewing Signet	Shattrath City	All	All			Magistrix Fyalenn	Firewing Signets	0 to 8999 with The Scryers			
More Firewing Signets	Shattrath City	All	All			Magistrix Fyalenn	Firewing Signets	0 to 8999 with The Scryers			
Synthesis of Power	Shattrath City	All	All		Voren'thal the Seer	Voren'thal the Seer		0 with The Scryers		15800	
REWARD: 1 Arcane Rune											
Arcane Tomes	Shattrath City	All	All			Voren'thal the Seer	Synthesis of Power	0 with The Scryers			
REWARD: 1 Arcane Rune											
A Cleansing Light	Shattrath City	All	All		Ishanah	Ishanah		0 with The Aldor		15800	
REWARD: 1 Holy Dust											
Fel Armaments	Shattrath City	All	All			Ishanah	A Cleansing Light	0 with The Aldor			
REWARD: 1 Holy Dust											
Allegiance to the Aldor	Shattrath City	All	All			Khadgar	City of Light				
Allegiance to the Scryers	Shattrath City	All	All			Khadgar	City of Light				
Voren'thal the Seer	Shattrath City	All	All		Khadgar	Voren'thal the Seer	Allegiance to the Scryers			1100	
Ishanah	Shattrath City	All	All		Khadgar	Ishanah	Allegiance to the Aldor			1100	
Marks of Sargeras	Shattrath City	All	All		Adyen the Lightwarden	Adyen the Lightwarden	Allegiance to the Aldor	0 with The Aldor		12650	
More Marks of Sargeras	Shattrath City	All	All			Adyen the Lightwarden	Marks of Sargeras	0 with The Aldor			
Single Mark of Sargeras	Shattrath City	All	All			Adyen the Lightwarden	Marks of Sargeras	0 with The Aldor			
Sunfury Signets	Shattrath City	All	All		Magistrix Fyalenn	Magistrix Fyalenn	Allegiance to the Scryers	0 with The Scryers		12650	
More Sunfury Signets	Shattrath City	All	All			Magistrix Fyalenn	Sunfury Signets	0 with The Scryers			
Single Sunfury Signet	Shattrath City	All	All			Magistrix Fyalenn	Sunfury Signets	0 to 8999 with The Scryers			
How to Break Into the Arcatraz	Shattrath City	All	All	5	A'dal	A'dal	Special Delivery to Shattrath City			19000	13 20
CHOICE OF: 1 Sha'tari Anchorite's Cloak, or 1 A'dal's Gift, or 1 Naaru Belt of Precision, or 1 Shattrath's Champion Belt, or 1 Sha'tari Vindicator's Waistguard											
REWARD: 1 Key to the Arcatraz											
Becoming a Mooncloth Tailor	Shattrath City	All	All		Nasmara Moonsong	Nasmara Moonsong			350 skill in Tailoring	9500	
Becoming a Spellfire Tailor	Shattrath City	All	All		Gidge Spellweaver	Gidge Spellweaver			350 skill in Tailoring	9500	
Becoming a Shadoweave Tailor	Shattrath City	All	All		Andrion Darkspinner	Andrion Darkspinner			350 skill in Tailoring	9500	
Harbinger of Doom	Shattrath City	All	All	5	A'dal	A'dal	How to Break Into the Arcatraz			19000	13 20
CHOICE OF: 1 Potent Sha'tari Pendant, or 1 A'dal's Recovery Necklace, or 1 Shattrath Choker of Power											
The Tempest Key	Shattrath City	All	All		Khadgar	A'dal	The Cipher of Damnation			1250	
Trial of the Naaru: Mercy	Shattrath City	All	All		A'dal	A'dal	The Tempest Key			19000	
Trial of the Naaru: Strength	Shattrath City	All	All		A'dal	A'dal	The Tempest Key			19000	
Trial of the Naaru: Tenacity	Shattrath City	All	All		A'dal	A'dal	The Tempest Key			19000	

Title	Location	Faction	Race & Class	Group #	Starter	Finisher	Prerequisite	Reputation	Tradeskill	XP	Money
Trial of the Naaru: Magtheridon	Shattrath City	All	All	Raid	A'dal	A'dal	Trial of the Naaru: Mercy			19000	13 20
REWARD: 1 The Tempest Key and 1 Phoenix-fire Band											
Master of Elixirs	Shattrath City	All	All	5	Lorokeem	Lorokeem			325 skill in Alchemy	12650	
Hero of the Sin'dorei	Silvermoon City	Horde	Blood Elf		Magister Kaendris	Lor'themar Theron	The Traitor's Destruction			825	
Allegiance to the Horde	Silvermoon City	Horde	Blood Elf		Thrall	Lor'themar Theron	Meeting the Warchief			2500	
Beast Training	Silvermoon City	Horde	Blood Elf Hunter		Lieutenant Dawnrunner	Halthenis	Taming the Beast			420	
REWARD: 1 Farstrider's Bow											
The First Trial	Silvermoon City	Horde	Blood Elf Paladin		Knight-Lord Bloodvalor	Knight-Lord Bloodvalor				900	
A Study in Power	Silvermoon City	Horde	Blood Elf Paladin		Knight-Lord Bloodvalor	Magister Astalor Bloodsworn	The First Trial			460	
Claiming the Light	Silvermoon City	Horde	Blood Elf Paladin		Magister Astalor Bloodsworn	Knight-Lord Bloodvalor	A Study in Power			460	
Redeeming the Dead	Silvermoon City	Horde	Blood Elf Paladin		Knight-Lord Bloodvalor	Knight-Lord Bloodvalor	Claiming the Light			1150	
The Second Trial	Silvermoon City	Horde	Blood Elf Paladin		Master Kelerun Bloodmourn	Master Kelerun Bloodmourn	The Second Trial			1550	
The Second Trial	Silvermoon City	Horde	Blood Elf Paladin		Knight-Lord Bloodvalor	Master Kelerun Bloodmourn				390	
Return to Silvermoon	Silvermoon City	Horde	Blood Elf Paladin		Master Kelerun Bloodmourn	Knight-Lord Bloodvalor	The Second Trial			925	
The Path of the Adept	Silvermoon City	Horde	Blood Elf Paladin	5	Knight-Lord Bloodvalor	Knight-Lord Bloodvalor	Return to Silvermoon			2300	
Forging the Weapon	Silvermoon City	Horde	Blood Elf Paladin		Knight-Lord Bloodvalor	Bemarrin	The Path of the Adept			925	
The Blood-Tempered Ranseur	Silvermoon City	Horde	Blood Elf Paladin		Bemarrin	Bemarrin	Forging the Weapon				
REWARD: 1 Blood-Tempered Ranseur											
The Thalassian Warhorse	Silvermoon City	Horde	Blood Elf Paladin			Knight-Lord Bloodvalor					
A Summons from Lady Liadrin	Silvermoon City	Horde	Blood Elf Paladin		Knight-Lord Bloodvalor	Lady Liadrin				650	
The Master's Path	Silvermoon City	Horde	Blood Elf Paladin		Lady Liadrin	Lady Liadrin	A Summons from Lady Liadrin				
A Gesture of Commitment	Silvermoon City	Horde	Blood Elf Paladin	5	Lady Liadrin	Lady Liadrin	The Master's Path			3300	
A Demonstration of Loyalty	Silvermoon City	Horde	Blood Elf Paladin		Lady Liadrin	Lady Liadrin	A Gesture of Commitment			8300	
True Masters of the Light	Silvermoon City	Horde	Blood Elf Paladin	5	Lady Liadrin	Lady Liadrin	A Demonstration of Loyalty			8300	
True Masters of the Light	Silvermoon City	Horde	Blood Elf Paladin	5	Lady Liadrin	Lady Liadrin	True Masters of the Light			4950	
True Masters of the Light	Silvermoon City	Horde	Blood Elf Paladin	5	Lady Liadrin	Lady Liadrin	True Masters of the Light			8300	
REWARD: 1 Blood Knight Tabard											
Friend of the Sin'dorei	Silvermoon City	Horde	Non-Blood Elf		Magister Kaendris	Lor'themar Theron	The Traitor's Destruction			825	
A Donation of Wool	Silvermoon City	Horde	All			Sorim Lightsong				650	
A Donation of Silk	Silvermoon City	Horde	All			Sorim Lightsong				1650	
A Donation of Mageweave	Silvermoon City	Horde	All			Sorim Lightsong				3300	
A Donation of Runecloth	Silvermoon City	Horde	All			Sorim Lightsong	A Donation of Wool			6600	
Additional Runecloth	Silvermoon City	Horde	All			Sorim Lightsong	A Donation of Runecloth				
A Discreet Inquiry	Silvermoon City	Horde	All Rogue		Zelanis	Eralan				120	
A Call to Arms: The Plaguelands!	Silvermoon City	Horde	All		Herald Amorlin	High Executor Derrington				470	
Carendin Summons	Silvermoon City	Horde	All		Alamma	Carendin Halgar				160	
Rogues of the Shattered Hand	Silvermoon City	Horde	All		Zelanis	Shenthul				200	
Travel to Darkshire	Stormwind	Alliance	Draenei		Emissary Taluun	Anchorite Delan				775	
Travel to Astranaar	Stormwind	Alliance	Draenei		Emissary Valustraa	Vindicator Palanaar				775	
Bloodscalp Insight	Stranglethorn Vale	Horde	All		Nemeth Hawkeye	Nemeth Hawkeye				2700	35
An Unusual Patron	Stranglethorn Vale	Horde	All		Nemeth Hawkeye	Nemeth Hawkeye	Bloodscalp Insight			3500	75
Reclaiming Sunstrider Isle	Sunstrider Isle	Horde	Blood Elf		Magistrix Erona	Magistrix Erona				100	30
CHOICE OF: 1 Green Chain Boots, or 1 Wyrm Sash											
Unfortunate Measures	Sunstrider Isle	Horde	Blood Elf		Magistrix Erona	Magistrix Erona	Reclaiming Sunstrider Isle			250	50
CHOICE OF: 1 Green Chain Vest, or 1 Lynxskin Gloves, or 1 Sunrise Bracers											
Report to Lanthan Perilon	Sunstrider Isle	Horde	Blood Elf		Magistrix Erona	Lanthan Perilon	Unfortunate Measures			25	
Mage Training	Sunstrider Isle	Horde	Blood Elf Mage		Magistrix Erona	Julia Sunstriker	Reclaiming Sunstrider Isle			40	

Sunstrider Isle

Title	Location	Faction	Race & Class	Group #	Starter	Finisher	Prerequisite	Reputation	Tradeskill	XP	Money
Solanian's Belongings	Sunstrider Isle	Horde	Blood Elf		Well Watcher Solanian	Well Watcher Solanian				360	75
CHOICE OF: 1 Sunspire Cord, or 1 Well Watcher Gloves											
Aggression	Sunstrider Isle	Horde	Blood Elf		Lanthan Perilon	Lanthan Perilon	Unfortunate Measures			360	75
CHOICE OF: 1 Sunstrider Axe, or 1 Sunstrider Dagger, or 1 Sunstrider Mace, or 1 Sunstrider Staff, or 1 Sunstrider Sword											
Felendren the Banished	Sunstrider Isle	Horde	Blood Elf		Lanthan Perilon	Lanthan Perilon	Aggression			550	2
CHOICE OF: 1 Sunstrider Bow, or 1 Sunstrider Shield											
A Fistful of Slivers	Sunstrider Isle	Horde	Blood Elf		Arcanist Ithanas	Arcanist Ithanas				360	
REWARD: 1 Daylight Cloak											
Tainted Arcane Sliver	Sunstrider Isle	Horde	Blood Elf		Tainted Arcane Sliver	Arcanist Helion				360	1 50
Windows to the Source	Sunstrider Isle	Horde	Blood Elf Warlock		Summoner Teli'Larien	Summoner Teli'Larien				360	
The Shrine of Dath'Remar	Sunstrider Isle	Horde	Blood Elf		Well Watcher Solanian	Well Watcher Solanian				360	1 50
Thirst Unending	Sunstrider Isle	Horde	Blood Elf		Arcanist Helion	Arcanist Helion				250	
CHOICE OF: 1 Green Chain Gauntlets, or 1 Vigorous Bracers, or 1 Striding Pants											
Aiding the Outrunners	Sunstrider Isle	Horde	Blood Elf		Lanthan Perilon	Outrunner Alarion	Felendren the Banished			45	
Completing the Delivery	Sunstrider Isle	Horde	Blood Elf		Outrunner Alarion	Innkeeper Delaniel	Package Recovery			110	
CHOICE OF: 5 Refreshing Spring Water, or 5 Shiny Red Apple											
Welcome!	Sunstrider Isle	Horde	Blood Elf		Sunstrider Isle Gift Voucher	Marsilla Dawnstar					
CHOICE OF: 1 Diablo Stone, or 1 Panda Collar, or 1 Zergling Leash											
Warlock Training	Sunstrider Isle	Horde	Blood Elf Warlock		Magistrix Erona	Summoner Teli'Larien	Reclaiming Sunstrider Isle			40	
Priest Training	Sunstrider Isle	Horde	Blood Elf Priest		Magistrix Erona	Matron Arena	Reclaiming Sunstrider Isle			40	
Rogue Training	Sunstrider Isle	Horde	Blood Elf Rogue		Magistrix Erona	Pathstalker Kariel	Reclaiming Sunstrider Isle			40	
Hunter Training	Sunstrider Isle	Horde	Blood Elf Hunter		Magistrix Erona	Ranger Sallina	Reclaiming Sunstrider Isle			40	
Paladin Training	Sunstrider Isle	Horde	Blood Elf Paladin		Magistrix Erona	Jesthenis Sunstriker	Reclaiming Sunstrider Isle			40	
Slain by the Wretched	Sunstrider Isle	Horde	Blood Elf		Outrunner Alarion	Slain Outrunner				110	
Package Recovery	Sunstrider Isle	Horde	Blood Elf		Slain Outrunner	Outrunner Alarion	Slain by the Wretched			230	50
Well Watcher Solanian	Sunstrider Isle	Horde	Blood Elf		Julia Sunstriker	Well Watcher Solanian	Mage Training			15	
Well Watcher Solanian	Sunstrider Isle	Horde	Blood Elf		Jesthenis Sunstriker	Well Watcher Solanian	Paladin Training			15	
Well Watcher Solanian	Sunstrider Isle	Horde	Blood Elf		Ranger Sallina	Well Watcher Solanian	Hunter Training			15	
Well Watcher Solanian	Sunstrider Isle	Horde	Blood Elf		Pathstalker Kariel	Well Watcher Solanian	Rogue Training			15	
Well Watcher Solanian	Sunstrider Isle	Horde	Blood Elf		Matron Arena	Well Watcher Solanian	Priest Training			15	
Well Watcher Solanian	Sunstrider Isle	Horde	Blood Elf		Summoner Teli'Larien	Well Watcher Solanian	Warlock Training			15	

Swamp of Sorrows

Title	Location	Faction	Race & Class	Group #	Starter	Finisher	Prerequisite	Reputation	Tradeskill	XP	Money
Little Morsels	Swamp of Sorrows	Horde	All		Cersei Dusksinger	Cersei Dusksinger				2850	45
Mercy for the Cursed	Swamp of Sorrows	Alliance	All		Anchorite Avuun	Anchorite Avuun				2850	45
Help Watcher Biggs	Swamp of Sorrows	Alliance	All		Anchorite Avuun	Watcher Biggs				700	
Pool of Tears	Swamp of Sorrows	Alliance	All		Holaaru	Holaaru				4450	1 20

Tempest Keep

Title	Location	Faction	Race & Class	Group #	Starter	Finisher	Prerequisite	Reputation	Tradeskill	XP	Money
Seer Udalo	Tempest Keep	All	All	5	Akama	Udalo	Akama			12650	

Terokkar Forest

Title	Location	Faction	Race & Class	Group #	Starter	Finisher	Prerequisite	Reputation	Tradeskill	XP	Money
It's Watching You!	Terokkar Forest	All	All		Warden Treelos	Warden Treelos				13350	
CHOICE OF: 1 Lucky Circle of the Fool, or 1 Moonstruck Bands, or 1 Crazy Cenarion Cloak, or 1 Lunatic's Choker, or 1 Madman's Blade											
What's Wrong at Cenarion Thicket?	Terokkar Forest	All	All		Lethyn Moonfire	Earthbinder Tavgren		3000 with Cenarion Expedition		2600	
What's Wrong at Cenarion Thicket?	Terokkar Forest	Horde	All		Tooki	Earthbinder Tavgren				2600	
What's Wrong at Cenarion Thicket?	Terokkar Forest	Alliance	All		Jenai Starwhisper	Earthbinder Tavgren				2600	
Strange Energy	Terokkar Forest	All	All		Earthbinder Tavgren	Earthbinder Tavgren				10400	2 90
Clues in the Thicket	Terokkar Forest	All	All		Earthbinder Tavgren	Earthbinder Tavgren				10400	2 90
By Any Means Necessary	Terokkar Forest	All	All		Earthbinder Tavgren	Empoor	Strange Energy			10400	
Wind Trader Lathrai	Terokkar Forest	All	All		Empoor	Wind Trader Lathrai	By Any Means Necessary			5250	
Stymying the Arakkoa	Terokkar Forest	Alliance	All		Thander	Thander				10750	3 10
CHOICE OF: 5 Super Healing Potion, or 5 Super Mana Potion											
Stymying the Arakkoa	Terokkar Forest	Horde	All		Rokag	Rokag				10750	3 10
CHOICE OF: 5 Super Healing Potion, or 5 Super Mana Potion											
Investigate Tuurem	Terokkar Forest	All	All		Wind Trader Lathrai	Earthbinder Tavgren	A Personal Favor			10750	3 10
Olemba Seeds	Terokkar Forest	Alliance	All		Ros'eleth	Ros'eleth				10400	2 90
Olemba Seed Oil	Terokkar Forest	Horde	All		Rakoria	Rakoria				10400	2 90

Title	Location	Faction	Race & Class	Group #	Starter	Finisher	Prerequisite	Reputation	Tradeskill	XP	Money
What Are These Things?	Terokkar Forest	Alliance	All		Earthbinder Tavgren	Jenai Starwhisper	Investigate Tuurem			5400	1 60
What Are These Things?	Terokkar Forest	Horde	All		Earthbinder Tavgren	Tooki	Investigate Tuurem			5400	1 60
Attack on Firewing Point	Terokkar Forest	Alliance	All		Lieutenant Meridian	Lieutenant Meridian	Report to the Allerian Post			10750	3 10
Attack on Firewing Point	Terokkar Forest	Horde	All		Sergeant Chawni	Sergeant Chawni	Report to Stonebreaker Camp			10750	3 10
Unruly Neighbors	Terokkar Forest	Alliance	All		Bertelm	Theloria Shadecloak				10400	2 90
An Unwelcome Presence	Terokkar Forest	Horde	All		Kurgatok	Shadowstalker Kaide				10400	2 90
The Firewing Liaison	Terokkar Forest	Alliance	All		Theloria Shadecloak	Theloria Shadecloak	Unruly Neighbors			10750	3 10
The Firewing Liaison	Terokkar Forest	Horde	All		Shadowstalker Kaide	Shadowstalker Kaide	An Unwelcome Presence			10750	3 10
Letting Earthbinder Tavgren Know	Terokkar Forest	Alliance	All		Jenai Starwhisper	Earthbinder Tavgren	The Final Code			15550	8 70
CHOICE OF: 1 Cenarion Thicket Circlet, or 1 Cenarion Thicket Helm, or 1 Cenarion Thicket Jerkin, or 1 Cenarion Thicket Legplates											
Letting Earthbinder Tavgren Know	Terokkar Forest	Horde	All		Tooki	Earthbinder Tavgren	The Final Code			15550	8 70
CHOICE OF: 1 Cenarion Thicket Circlet, or 1 Cenarion Thicket Helm, or 1 Cenarion Thicket Jerkin, or 1 Cenarion Thicket Legplates											
Thinning the Ranks	Terokkar Forest	Alliance	All		Theloria Shadecloak	Theloria Shadecloak	Unruly Neighbors			10750	3 10
CHOICE OF: 1 Deadeye's Piece, or 1 Stout Oak Longbow, or 1 Dark Augur's Wand											
What Happens in Terokkar Stays in Terokkar	Terokkar Forest	Horde	All		Shadowstalker Kaide	Shadowstalker Kaide				10750	3 10
CHOICE OF: 1 Dark Augur's Wand, or 1 Deadeye's Piece, or 1 Stout Oak Longbow											
Fel Orc Plans	Terokkar Forest	Alliance	All		Fel Orc Plans	Bertelm	Unruly Neighbors			10750	3 10
An Unseen Hand	Terokkar Forest	Horde	All		Fel Orc Plans	Rokag	An Unwelcome Presence			10750	3 10
Timber Worg Tails	Terokkar Forest	Alliance	All		Bertelm	Bertelm				10750	3 10
Vestments of the Wolf Spirit	Terokkar Forest	Horde	All		Malukaz	Malukaz				10750	3 10
The Elusive Ironjaw	Terokkar Forest	Alliance	All		Bertelm	Bertelm	Timber Worg Tails			13350	3 10
CHOICE OF: 1 Helm of Lupine Cunning, or 1 Helm of Lupine Grace, or 1 Helm of Lupine Ferocity, or 1 Wolf Hunter's Guise											
Patriarch Ironjaw	Terokkar Forest	Horde	All		Malukaz	Malukaz	Vestments of the Wolf Spirit			13350	3 10
Magical Disturbances	Terokkar Forest	Alliance	All		Andarl	Andarl				10750	3 10
Magical Disturbances	Terokkar Forest	Horde	All		Kurgatok	Kurgatok				10750	3 10
Vessels of Power	Terokkar Forest	Alliance	All		Ros'eleth	Ros'eleth	Olemba Seeds			10400	2 90
Recover the Bones	Terokkar Forest	All	All		Soolaveen	Ramdor the Mad	The Tomb of Lights			11000	3 30
Helping the Lost Find Their Way	Terokkar Forest	All	All		Ramdor the Mad	Soolaveen	Recover the Bones			11000	3 30
CHOICE OF: 1 Girdle of the Penitent, or 1 Gloves of the Afterlife, or 1 Fleet Refugee's Boots, or 1 Cilice of Suffering											
Wanted: Bonelashers Dead!	Terokkar Forest	Alliance	All		Wanted Poster	Taela Everstride				11000	3 30
Wanted: Bonelashers Dead!	Terokkar Forest	Horde	All		Wanted Poster	Mawg Grimshot				11000	3 30
Torgos!	Terokkar Forest	Alliance	All	2	Taela Everstride	Taela Everstride	Wanted: Bonelashers Dead!			13750	6 60
CHOICE OF: 1 Terokkar Tablet of Precision, or 1 Terokkar Tablet of Vim											
Torgos!	Terokkar Forest	Horde	All	2	Mawg Grimshot	Mawg Grimshot	Wanted: Bonelashers Dead!			13750	6 60
CHOICE OF: 1 Terokkar Tablet of Precision, or 1 Terokkar Tablet of Vim											
Rather Be Fishin'	Terokkar Forest	All	All		Seth	Seth				10750	
REWARD: 1 Seth's Graphite Fishing Pole											
Speak with Private Weeks	Terokkar Forest	Alliance	All		Lieutenant Gravelhammer	Private Weeks				2650	
Speak with Scout Neftis	Terokkar Forest	Horde	All		Advisor Faila	Scout Neftis				2650	
Who Are They?	Terokkar Forest	Alliance	All		Private Weeks	Private Weeks	Speak with Private Weeks			11000	3 30
Who Are They?	Terokkar Forest	Horde	All		Scout Neftis	Scout Neftis	Speak with Scout Neftis			11000	3 30
Kill the Shadow Council!	Terokkar Forest	Alliance	All		Private Weeks	Lieutenant Gravelhammer	Who Are They?			13750	6 60
CHOICE OF: 1 Extra Sharp Blade, or 1 Invincible Stave, or 1 Spiked Destroyer											
Kill the Shadow Council!	Terokkar Forest	Horde	All		Scout Neftis	Advisor Faila	Who Are They?			13750	6 60
CHOICE OF: 1 Extra Sharp Blade, or 1 Invincible Stave, or 1 Spiked Destroyer											
Escape from Firewing Point!	Terokkar Forest	Alliance	All	2	Isla Starmane	Captain Auric Sunchaser				13350	6 20
CHOICE OF: 1 Blood-Guided Knife, or 1 Healer's Staff of the Forest, or 1 Terokkar Axe											
Escape from Firewing Point!	Terokkar Forest	Horde	All	2	Isla Starmane	Advisor Faila				13350	6 20
CHOICE OF: 1 Blood-Guided Knife, or 1 Healer's Staff of the Forest, or 1 Terokkar Axe											
A Personal Favor	Terokkar Forest	All	All		Wind Trader Lathrai	Wind Trader Lathrai	Wind Trader Lathrai			10750	3 10
CHOICE OF: 1 Consortium Cloak of the Quick, or 1 Nexus-Stalker's Band, or 1 Ethereal Healing Pendant, or 1 Arakkoa Divining Rod											
And Now, the Moment of Truth	Terokkar Forest	Horde	All		Rakoria	Rakoria	Olemba Seed Oil			8250	
CHOICE OF: 1 Brilliant Mana Oil, or 1 Brilliant Wizard Oil											
Report to the Allerian Post	Terokkar Forest	Alliance	All		Jenai Starwhisper	Lieutenant Meridian	What Are These Things?			1100	
The Final Code	Terokkar Forest	Alliance	All		Lieutenant Meridian	Jenai Starwhisper	Attack on Firewing Point			13750	6 60
CHOICE OF: 1 Edge of Inevitability, or 1 Warpstalker Breastplate, or 1 Ancient Terokkar Hood, or 1 Bloodfire Leggings											
The Final Code	Terokkar Forest	Horde	All		Sergeant Chawni	Tooki	Attack on Firewing Point			13750	6 60
CHOICE OF: 1 Edge of Inevitability, or 1 Warpstalker Breastplate, or 1 Ancient Terokkar Hood, or 1 Bloodfire Leggings											

Title	Location	Faction	Race & Class	Group #	Starter	Finisher	Prerequisite	Reputation	Tradeskill	XP	Money
TEROKKAR FOREST											
Report to Stonebreaker Camp	Terokkar Forest	Horde	All		Tooki	Sergeant Chawni	What Are These Things?			1100	
Welcoming the Wolf Spirit	Terokkar Forest	Horde	All		Malukaz	Malukaz	Patriarch Ironjaw			1100	
CHOICE OF: 1 Helm of Lupine Cunning, or 1 Helm of Lupine Ferocity, or 1 Helm of Lupine Grace, or 1 Wolf Hunter's Guise											
Veil Skith: Darkstone of Terokk	Terokkar Forest	All	All		Kirrik the Awakened	Kirrik the Awakened	Seek Out Kirrik			10750	3● 10●
The Tomb of Lights	Terokkar Forest	All	All		High Priest Orglum	High Priest Orglum	Taken in the Night			11000	3● 30●
The Vengeful Harbinger	Terokkar Forest	All	All	3	High Priest Orglum	Draenei Ascendant	Taken in the Night			13750	
CHOICE OF: 1 Ancient Draenei War Talisman, or 1 Ancient Draenei Arcane Relic											
The Eyes of Skettis	Terokkar Forest	All	All		Rilak the Redeemed	Rilak the Redeemed				10050	2● 70●
CHOICE OF: 1 Super Healing Potion, or 1 Super Mana Potion											
Veil Rhaze: Unliving Evil	Terokkar Forest	All	All		Kirrik the Awakened	Kirrik the Awakened	Veil Skith: Darkstone of Terokk			10750	3● 10●
CHOICE OF: 1 Talonbranch Wand, or 1 Feather-Wrapped Bow											
Seek Out Kirrik	Terokkar Forest	All	All		Rilak the Redeemed	Kirrik the Awakened	The Eyes of Skettis			2600	74●
Missing Friends	Terokkar Forest	All	All		Ethan	Ethan	Seek Out Kirrik			10750	
REWARD: 1 Battered Steam Tonk Controller											
Veil Lithic: Preemptive Strike	Terokkar Forest	All	All		Kirrik the Awakened	Kirrik the Awakened	Veil Rhaze: Unliving Evil			10750	3● 10●
CHOICE OF: 1 Feathered Armbands, or 1 Feathered Wrist Cuffs, or 1 Eagle Engraved Bracers, or 1 Talonstalker Bracers											
Surrender to the Horde	Terokkar Forest	Horde	All		Rokag	Rilak the Redeemed				10400	2● 30●
Secrets of the Arakkoa	Terokkar Forest	Alliance	All		Lady Dena Kennedy	Rilak the Redeemed				10400	2● 30●
Arakkoa War Path	Terokkar Forest	Horde	All		Advisor Faila	Advisor Faila				10050	2● 70●
Thin the Flock	Terokkar Forest	Alliance	All		Lieutenant Gravelhammer	Lieutenant Gravelhammer				10050	2● 70●
Taken in the Night	Terokkar Forest	All	All		Scout Navrin	Scout Navrin				11000	3● 30●
Veil Shalas: Signal Fires	Terokkar Forest	All	All		Kirrik the Awakened	Kirrik the Awakened	Veil Lithic: Preemptive Strike			11000	3● 30●
CHOICE OF: 1 Arakkoa Sage's Shawl, or 1 Cloak of Grasping Talons, or 1 Kokorek's Signet											
The Dread Relic	Terokkar Forest	All	All		Oakun	Oakun				11300	3● 50●
Before Darkness Falls	Terokkar Forest	All	All		Mekeda	Mekeda				10400	
The Skettis Offensive	Terokkar Forest	All	All	2	Defender Grashna	Rilak the Redeemed	Return to Shattrath			16500	9● 90●
CHOICE OF: 1 Choker of Bloodied Feathers, or 1 Necklace of Bloodied Feathers											
Cabal Orders	Terokkar Forest	All	All		Cabal Orders	Mekeda				5400	
The Shadow Tomb	Terokkar Forest	All	All		Mekeda	Mekeda	Cabal Orders			13350	
CHOICE OF: 1 Heirloom Signet of Convalescence, or 1 Heirloom Signet of Valor, or 1 Heirloom Signet of Willpower											
Escaping the Tomb	Terokkar Forest	All	All		Akuno	Mekeda				10750	
CHOICE OF: 1 Akuno's Blade, or 1 Ancient Draenei Crest, or 1 Mekeda's Gift, or 1 Unearthed Orb											
Return to Shattrath	Terokkar Forest	All	All		Kirrik the Awakened	Rilak the Redeemed	Veil Shalas: Signal Fires			8250	2● 60●
The Infested Protectors	Terokkar Forest	All	All		Lakotae	Lakotae				11000	3● 30●
Skywing	Terokkar Forest	All	All	2	Skywing	Rilak the Redeemed				13750	6● 60●
CHOICE OF: 1 Skywitch Hat, or 1 Redeemer's Plate, or 1 Stillfire Leggings											
REWARD: 1 Miniwing											
Speak with Rilak the Redeemed	Terokkar Forest	All	All		Kirrik the Awakened	Rilak the Redeemed				1050	3●
An Improper Burial	Terokkar Forest	All	All		Commander Ra'vaj	Commander Ra'vaj				11000	
A Hero Is Needed	Terokkar Forest	All	All		Commander Ra'vaj	Commander Ra'vaj	An Improper Burial			11000	
The Fallen Exarch	Terokkar Forest	All	All		Commander Ra'vaj	Commander Ra'vaj	A Hero Is Needed			11000	
CHOICE OF: 1 Death-speaker's Tunic, or 1 Elekk Hide Spaulders, or 1 Sha'tari Marskman's Gloves, or 1 Sha'tari Vindicator's Legplates											
The Outcast's Plight	Terokkar Forest	All	All		Vekax	Vekax				11000	3● 30●
REWARD: 1 Outcast's Cache											
More Feathers	Terokkar Forest	All	All			Vekax	The Outcast's Plight	8999 with Lower City			
REWARD: 1 Outcast's Cache											
For the Fallen	Terokkar Forest	All	All		Vindicator Haylen	Vindicator Haylen				11000	
Terokkarantula	Terokkar Forest	All	All	3	Vindicator Haylen	Vindicator Haylen	For the Fallen			11000	
CHOICE OF: 1 Blade of Retribution, or 1 Blessed Signet Ring, or 1 Noble Plate Pauldrons, or 1 Book of Many Blessings											
Digging Through Bones	Terokkar Forest	All	All	2	Chief Archaelogist Letoll	Dwarfowitz				11000	
Evil Draws Near	Terokkar Forest	All	All	3	Oakun	Oakun	The Dread Relic			11000	
CHOICE OF: 1 Dragonbone Greatsword, or 1 Dragonbone Shoulders, or 1 Dragonbone Talisman											
Return to the Sha'tari Base Camp	Terokkar Forest	All	All		Vindicator Haylen	Scout Navrin	Terokkarantula			8250	
Fumping	Terokkar Forest	All	All	2	Dwarfowitz	Dwarfowitz	Digging Through Bones			11000	
The Big Bone Worm	Terokkar Forest	All	All	3	Dwarfowitz	Dwarfowitz	Fumping			13750	
CHOICE OF: 1 Dib'Muad's Crysknife, or 1 Revered Mother's Crysknife, or 1 Shani's Crysknife											
THOUSAND NEEDLES											
A Different Approach	Thousand Needles	Horde	All		Magistrix Elosai	Wizlo Bearingshiner				2300	2●5●
A Dip in the Moonwell	Thousand Needles	Horde	All		Wizlo Bearingshiner	Wizlo Bearingshiner	A Different Approach			2300	
Testing the Tonic	Thousand Needles	Horde	All		Wizlo Bearingshiner	Magistrix Elosai	A Dip in the Moonwell			2300	2●5●
Delivery to the Sepulcher	Undercity	Horde	Blood Elf		Ambassador Sunsorrow	Advisor Sorrelon	Journey to Undercity			550	3●50●
Report to Tarren Mill	Undercity	Horde	Blood Elf		Ambassador Sunsorrow	Advisor Duskingdawn				775	

Title	Location	Faction	Race & Class	Group #	Starter	Finisher	Prerequisite	Reputation	Tradeskill	XP	Money
Envoy to the Horde	Undercity	Horde	Blood Elf		Lor'themar Theron	Lady Sylvanas Windrunner	Hero of the Sin'dorei			825	
Envoy to the Horde	Undercity	Horde	Non-Blood Elf		Lor'themar Theron	Lady Sylvanas Windrunner	Hero of the Sin'dorei			825	
The So-Called Mark of the Lightbringer	Western Plaguelands	Horde	All		Mehlar Dawnblade	Mehlar Dawnblade				6200	
Defiling Uther's Tomb	Western Plaguelands	Horde	All		Mehlar Dawnblade	Mehlar Dawnblade	The So-Called Mark of the Lightbringer			7750	
Tomb of the Lightbringer	Western Plaguelands	Alliance	All	2	Anchorite Truuen	High Priestess MacDonnell	The Mark of the Lightbringer			7750	
The Mark of the Lightbringer	Western Plaguelands	Alliance	All		Anchorite Truuen	Anchorite Truuen				6200	
Prove Your Hatred	Western Plaguelands	Horde	Blood Elf Paladin		Mehlar Dawnblade	Mehlar Dawnblade				5100	
Wisdom of the Banshee Queen	Western Plaguelands	Horde	Blood Elf Paladin		Mehlar Dawnblade	Lady Sylvanas Windrunner	Prove Your Hatred			2550	
Ancient Evil	Western Plaguelands	Horde	Blood Elf Paladin	5	Lady Sylvanas Windrunner	Mehlar Dawnblade	Wisdom of the Banshee Queen			6350	
REWARD: 1 Scourgebane											
The Zapthrottle Mote Extractor!	Zangarmarsh	Horde	All		Mack Diver	Mack Diver			305 skill in Engineering	6600	
REWARD: 1 Schematic: Zapthrottle Mote Extractor											
The Zapthrottle Mote Extractor!	Zangarmarsh	Alliance	All		K. Lee Smallfry	K. Lee Smallfry			305 skill in Engineering	6600	
REWARD: 1 Schematic: Zapthrottle Mote Extractor											
Watcher Leesa'oh	Zangarmarsh	All	All		Lethyn Moonfire	Watcher Leesa'oh		3000 with Cenarion Expedition		5250	
Observing the Sporelings	Zangarmarsh	All	All		Watcher Leesa'oh	Watcher Leesa'oh				10400	2 90
A Question of Gluttony	Zangarmarsh	All	All		Watcher Leesa'oh	Watcher Leesa'oh	Observing the Sporelings			10750	3 10
Familiar Fungi	Zangarmarsh	All	All		Watcher Leesa'oh	Watcher Leesa'oh	A Question of Gluttony			10400	2 90
Stealing Back the Mushrooms	Zangarmarsh	All	All		Watcher Leesa'oh	Watcher Leesa'oh	Familiar Fungi			13350	6 20
CHOICE OF: 1 Zangar Epaulets, or 1 Marsh Survivalist's Belt, or 1 Helm of Natural Purity, or 1 Leesa'oh's Wristbands											
Bring Me Another Shrubbery!	Zangarmarsh	All	All	5		Gzhun'tt	Bring Me A Shrubbery!	3000 with Sporeggar			
Bring Me A Shrubbery!	Zangarmarsh	All	All	5	Gzhun'tt	Gzhun'tt		3000 with Sporeggar		11000	
Disturbance at Umbrafen Lake	Zangarmarsh	All	All		Ysiel Windsinger	Ysiel Windsinger				10400	2 90
Oh, It's On!	Zangarmarsh	All	All	5	T'shu	T'shu		0 with Sporeggar		13750	
REWARD: 1 Everlasting Underspore Frond											
As the Crow Flies	Zangarmarsh	All	All		Ysiel Windsinger	Ysiel Windsinger	Disturbance at Umbrafen Lake			7800	
Stalk the Stalker	Zangarmarsh	All	All	5	Khn'nix	Khn'nix		0 with Sporeggar		13750	
CHOICE OF: 1 Essence Infused Mushroom, or 1 Power Infused Mushroom											
Balance Must Be Preserved	Zangarmarsh	All	All		Ysiel Windsinger	Ysiel Windsinger	As the Crow Flies			13350	3 10
Warning the Cenarion Circle	Zangarmarsh	All	All		Ysiel Windsinger	Amythiel Mistwalker	Drain Schematics			5400	1 60
Now That We're Friends...	Zangarmarsh	All	All		Gzhun'tt	Gzhun'tt		3000 with Sporeggar		10750	
CHOICE OF: 1 Staff of the Wild, or 1 Survivalist's Pike, or 1 Hammer of the Sporelings, or 1 Zangarmarsh Claymore											
Now That We're Still Friends...	Zangarmarsh	All	All		Gzhun'tt	Gzhun'tt	Now That We're Friends...	3000 with Sporeggar			
A Warm Welcome	Zangarmarsh	All	All		Warden Hamoot	Warden Hamoot				13350	3 10
REWARD: 5 Volatile Healing Potion											
Fhwoor Smash!	Zangarmarsh	All	All	3	Fhwoor	Gzhun'tt		42000 with Sporeggar		13750	
CHOICE OF: 1 Hewing Axe of the Marsh, or 1 Sporeling Claw, or 1 Sporeggar Smasher											
Leader of the Darkcrest	Zangarmarsh	All	All	2	Wanted Poster	Warden Hamoot				13350	6 20
CHOICE OF: 1 Cushy Cenarion Walkers, or 1 Expedition Mantle, or 1 Swift Cenarion Footwear, or 1 Hearty Cenarion Cincture											
Drain Schematics	Zangarmarsh	All	All		Drain Schematics	Ysiel Windsinger				10400	2 90
CHOICE OF: 1 Expedition Caster's Band, or 1 Pendant of the Marsh, or 1 Warden's Ring of Precision, or 1 Watcher's Cloak of Vigilance											
Return to the Marsh	Zangarmarsh	All	All		Amythiel Mistwalker	Ysiel Windsinger	Warning the Cenarion Circle			10400	
CHOICE OF: 1 Cenarion Expedition Boots, or 1 Windcaller's Gauntlets, or 1 Marshstrider's Spaulders											
The Sporelings' Plight	Zangarmarsh	All	All		Fahssn	Fahssn				10400	
More Spore Sacs	Zangarmarsh	All	All			Fahssn	The Sporelings' Plight	-42999 with Sporeggar-2999 with Sporeggar			
Natural Enemies	Zangarmarsh	All	All		Fahssn	Fahssn		-42000 with Sporeggar		10750	
More Tendrils!	Zangarmarsh	All	All			Fahssn	Natural Enemies	-42999 with Sporeggar-2999 with Sporeggar			
The Umbrafen Tribe	Zangarmarsh	All	All		Ikeyen	Ikeyen				10050	2 70
Escape from Umbrafen	Zangarmarsh	All	All		Kayra Longmane	Ysiel Windsinger				10400	2 90
CHOICE OF: 1 Explorer's Leggings, or 1 Preserver's Medallion, or 1 Warden's Hammer											

Title	Location	Faction	Race & Class	Group #	Starter	Finisher	Prerequisite	Reputation	Tradeskill	XP	Money
There's No Explanation for Fashion	Zangarmarsh	Horde	All		Magasha	Magasha				10050	2 70
Menacing Marshfangs	Zangarmarsh	Horde	All		Reavij	Reavij				10050	2 70
Searching for Scout Jyoba	Zangarmarsh	Horde	All		Zurai	Scout Jyoba	Thick Hydra Scales			10050	
Jyoba's Report	Zangarmarsh	Horde	All		Scout Jyoba	Zurai	Searching for Scout Jyoba			10050	2 70
CHOICE OF: 1 Bog Walker's Bands, or 1 Murk-Darkened Bracers, or 1 Bog Walker's Belt, or 1 Deep Mire Cloak											
No More Mushrooms!	Zangarmarsh	Horde	All		Magasha	Magasha				9800	2
Thick Hydra Scales	Zangarmarsh	Horde	All		Zurai	Zurai				10050	2 70
Report to Shadow Hunter Denjai	Zangarmarsh	Horde	All		Zurai	Shadow Hunter Denjai				2550	
The Orebor Harborage	Zangarmarsh	Alliance	All		Anchorite Ahuurn	Ikuti				2650	
Fulgor Spores	Zangarmarsh	Alliance	All		Ruam	Ruam				10050	2 70
Warden Hamoot	Zangarmarsh	All	All		Ysiel Windsinger	Warden Hamoot				1100	
Umbrafen Eel Filets	Zangarmarsh	Alliance	All		Noraani	Noraani	Menacing Marshfangs			10050	2 70
Too Many Mouths to Feed	Zangarmarsh	Alliance	All		Haalrun	Haalrun				10050	2 70
The Dead Mire	Zangarmarsh	Alliance	All		Vindicator Idaar	Vindicator Idaar				10050	2 70
An Unnatural Drought	Zangarmarsh	Alliance	All		Vindicator Idaar	Vindicator Idaar	The Dead Mire			10050	2 70
CHOICE OF: 1 Explorer's Bands, or 1 Fen Strider's Bracer, or 1 Vindicator's Cinch, or 1 Researcher's Mantle											
Identify Plant Parts	Zangarmarsh	All	All			Lauranna Thar'well	Plants of Zangarmarsh	8999 with Cenarion Expedition			
REWARD: 1 Package of Identified Plants											
Blessings of the Ancients	Zangarmarsh	All	All		Windcaller Blackhoof	Windcaller Blackhoof		3000 with Cenarion Expedition		5400	
The Boha'mu Ruins	Zangarmarsh	Alliance	All		Anchorite Ahuurn	Anchorite Ahuurn				10050	2 70
Idols of the Feralfen	Zangarmarsh	Alliance	All		Anchorite Ahuurn	Anchorite Ahuurn	The Boha'mu Ruins			10050	2 70
A Damp, Dark Place	Zangarmarsh	All	All		Ikeyen	Ikeyen	The Umbrafen Tribe			10050	2 70
CHOICE OF: 1 Ikeyen's Boots, or 1 Mud Encrusted Boots, or 1 Ikeyen's Pauldrons, or 1 Refuge Armor											
Diaphanous Wings	Zangarmarsh	Alliance	All		Haalrun	Haalrun	Too Many Mouths to Feed			10050	2 70
Menacing Marshfangs	Zangarmarsh	Alliance	All		Noraani	Noraani				10050	2 70
A Message to Telaar	Zangarmarsh	Alliance	All		Ikuti	Nahuud		0 with Kurenai		2650	
The Fate of Tuurem	Zangarmarsh	Alliance	All		Vindicator Idaar	Andarl				2550	
No Time for Curiosity	Zangarmarsh	Alliance	All		Timothy Daniels	Kialon Nightblade				2700	
The Ogre Threat	Zangarmarsh	Horde	All		Shadow Hunter Denjai	Nekthar				2700	
News from Zangarmarsh	Zangarmarsh	Horde	All		Zurai	Mokasa				2550	
Reinforcements for Garadar	Zangarmarsh	Horde	All		Messenger Gazgrigg	Captain Kroghan				2650	
Gathering the Reagents	Zangarmarsh	Alliance	All		Anchorite Ahuurn	Anchorite Ahuurn	Idols of the Feralfen			10050	2 70
Plants of Zangarmarsh	Zangarmarsh	All	All		Lauranna Thar'well	Lauranna Thar'well				10400	
REWARD: 1 Package of Identified Plants											
Messenger to the Feralfen	Zangarmarsh	Alliance	All		Anchorite Ahuurn	Anchorite Ahuurn	Gathering the Reagents			12600	2 70
CHOICE OF: 1 Feralfen Mystic's Handwraps, or 1 Feralfen Beastmaster's Hauberk, or 1 Feralfen Champion's Boots, or 1 Feralfen Skulker's Belt											
Fertile Spores	Zangarmarsh	All	All		Gshaff	Gshaff		0 with Sporeggar		10750	
REWARD: 1 Glowcap											
More Fertile Spores	Zangarmarsh	All	All			Gshaff	Fertile Spores	0 with Sporeggar			
REWARD: 1 Glowcap											
Glowcap Mushrooms	Zangarmarsh	All	All		Msshi'fn	Msshi'fn		0 with Sporeggar-2999 with Sporeggar		10750	
More Glowcaps	Zangarmarsh	All	All			Msshi'fn	Glowcap Mushrooms	0 with Sporeggar-2999 with Sporeggar			
Burstcap Mushrooms, Mon!	Zangarmarsh	Horde	All		Witch Doctor Tor'gash	Witch Doctor Tor'gash				10750	3 10
Have You Ever Seen One of These?	Zangarmarsh	Horde	All		Witch Doctor Tor'gash	Witch Doctor Tor'gash	Burstcap Mushrooms, Mon!			10750	3 10
CHOICE OF: 1 The Witch Doctor's Wraps, or 1 Daggerfen Mail, or 1 Fen Strider's Footguards											
Leader of the Bloodscale	Zangarmarsh	All	All	2	Wanted Poster	Warden Hamoot				12950	5 80
CHOICE OF: 1 Wild Shoulderpads, or 1 Gloves of Marshmanship, or 1 Belt of the Moonkin, or 1 Expedition Footgear											
WANTED: Boss Grog'ak	Zangarmarsh	Horde	All		Wanted Poster	Shadow Hunter Denjai				13350	3 10
Impending Attack	Zangarmarsh	Horde	All		Shadow Hunter Denjai	Shadow Hunter Denjai	WANTED: Boss Grog'ak			10750	3 10
Us or Them	Zangarmarsh	Horde	All		Shadow Hunter Denjai	Shadow Hunter Denjai	Impending Attack			13350	6 20
REWARD: 1 Captain Krosh's Crash Helmet and 5 Crimson Steer Energy Drink											
Withered Basidium	Zangarmarsh	Alliance	All		Withered Basidium	Ruam				10050	2 70
Withered Basidium	Zangarmarsh	Horde	All		Withered Basidium	Reavij				10050	2 70
Stinger Venom	Zangarmarsh	Alliance	All		Puluu	Puluu		0 with Kurenai		10750	3 10
Lines of Communication	Zangarmarsh	Alliance	All		Puluu	Puluu		0 with Kurenai		10750	3 10
CHOICE OF: 1 Ensorcelled Marshfang Blade, or 1 Keen Marshfang Slicer, or 1 Marshfang Blade Axe											
Natural Armor	Zangarmarsh	Alliance	All		Maktu	Maktu		0 with Kurenai		10750	3 10
Ango'rosh Encroachment	Zangarmarsh	Alliance	All		Ikuti	Ikuti				10750	3 10

Title	Location	Faction	Race & Class	Group #	Starter	Finisher	Prerequisite	Reputation	Tradeskill	XP	Money
Overlord Gorefist	Zangarmarsh	Alliance	All		Ikuti	Ikuti	Ango'rosh Encroachment	3000 with Kurenai		13350	3 10
CHOICE OF: 1 Glowing Crystal Insignia, or 1 Telaar Courier's Cloak, or 1 Marsh Bracers											
Stinging the Stingers	Zangarmarsh	Horde	All		Gambarinka	Gambarinka				10750	3 10
The Sharpest Blades	Zangarmarsh	Horde	All		Gambarinka	Gambarinka	Stinging the Stingers			10750	3 10
CHOICE OF: 1 Marshfang Blade Axe, or 1 Ensorcelled Marshfang Blade, or 1 Keen Marshfang Slicer											
Angling to Beat the Competition	Zangarmarsh	Horde	All		Zurjaya	Zurjaya				10750	3 10
Spirits of the Feralfen	Zangarmarsh	Horde	All		Seer Janidi	Seer Janidi				10050	2 70
A Spirit Ally?	Zangarmarsh	Horde	All		Seer Janidi	Seer Janidi	Spirits of the Feralfen			10750	3 10
CHOICE OF: 1 Ancient Crystal Talisman, or 1 Serpent Spirit's Drape, or 1 Marsh Bracers											
Secrets of the Daggerfen	Zangarmarsh	Alliance	All		Timothy Daniels	Timothy Daniels				10750	3 10
REWARD: 1 Tim's Trusty Helmet and 5 Crimson Steer Energy Drink											
Uncatalogued Species	Zangarmarsh	All	All		Uncatalogued Species	Lauranna Thar'well					
Failed Incursion	Zangarmarsh	All	All		Ysiel Windsinger	Watcher Jhang	Return to the Marsh			1100	
Safeguarding the Watchers	Zangarmarsh	All	All	2	Windcaller Blackhoof	Windcaller Blackhoof	The Umbrafen Tribe			10050	2 70
The Dying Balance	Zangarmarsh	All	All	2	Lethyn Moonfire	Lethyn Moonfire				12600	2 70
Blacksting's Bane	Zangarmarsh	Alliance	All		Prospector Conall	Prospector Conall	Unfinished Business			10050	2 70
CHOICE OF: 1 Blacksting Shoulders, or 1 Stalwart Girdle, or 1 Blacksting Gloves, or 1 Marshfang Boots											
Nothin' Says Lovin' Like a Big Stinger	Zangarmarsh	Horde	All		Reavij	Reavij	Menacing Marshfangs			10050	2 70
CHOICE OF: 1 Blacksting Shoulders, or 1 Stalwart Girdle, or 1 Blacksting Gloves, or 1 Marshfang Boots											
A Job Undone	Zangarmarsh	Horde	All		Magasha	Magasha	No More Mushrooms!			10050	2 70
CHOICE OF: 5 Scroll of Agility V, or 5 Scroll of Strength V, or 5 Scroll of Stamina V, or 5 Scroll of Intellect V, or 5 Scroll of Spirit V, or 5 Scroll of Protection V											
Unfinished Business	Zangarmarsh	Alliance	All		Prospector Conall	Prospector Conall				10050	2 70
CHOICE OF: 5 Scroll of Strength V, or 5 Scroll of Spirit V, or 5 Scroll of Stamina V, or 5 Scroll of Intellect V, or 5 Scroll of Agility V, or 5 Scroll of Protection V											
The Terror of Marshlight Lake	Zangarmarsh	Alliance	All		Puluu	Puluu		0 with Kurenai		10750	3 10
CHOICE OF: 1 Swamprunner's Boots, or 1 Fierce Mantle, or 1 Fearless Girdle, or 1 Terrorcloth Mantle											
The Biggest of Them All	Zangarmarsh	Horde	All		Zurjaya	Zurjaya	Angling to Beat the Competition			10750	3 10
CHOICE OF: 5 Adept's Elixir, or 5 Onslaught Elixir											
Pursuing Terrorclaw	Zangarmarsh	Horde	All		Zurjaya	Zurjaya	Angling to Beat the Competition			10750	3 10
CHOICE OF: 1 Swamprunner's Boots, or 1 Fierce Mantle, or 1 Fearless Girdle, or 1 Terrorcloth Mantle											
Maktu's Revenge	Zangarmarsh	Alliance	All		Maktu	Maktu	Natural Armor	0 with Kurenai		10750	3 10
CHOICE OF: 5 Adept's Elixir, or 5 Onslaught Elixir											
The Count of the Marshes	Zangarmarsh	All	All		"Count" Ungula's Mandible	Watcher Leesa'oh				10750	3 10
The Cenarion Expedition	Zangarmarsh	All	All		Amythiel Mistwalker	Ysiel Windsinger				1000	
Sporeggar	Zangarmarsh	All	All		Fahssn	Msshi'fn		0 with Sporeggar		10750	
Saving the Sporeloks	Zangarmarsh	All	All		Lauranna Thar'well	Lauranna Thar'well	The Umbrafen Tribe			10050	2 70
CHOICE OF: 1 Expedition Forager Leggings, or 1 Chemise of Rebirth, or 1 Circle's Stalwart Helmet, or 1 Scout's Hood											
Concerns About Tuurem	Zangarmarsh	Alliance	All		Ikuti	Andarl				2550	
News for Rakoria	Zangarmarsh	Horde	All		Shadow Hunter Denjai	Rakoria				2550	
Daggerfen Deviance	Zangarmarsh	Alliance	All		Ikuti	Ikuti				10750	3 10
Wanted: Chieftain Mummaki	Zangarmarsh	Alliance	All	2	Wanted Poster	Ikuti				10750	6 20
Wanted: Chieftain Mummaki	Zangarmarsh	Horde	All	2	Wanted Poster	Shadow Hunter Denjai				10750	6 20
Message to the Daggerfen	Zangarmarsh	Horde	All		Shadow Hunter Denjai	Shadow Hunter Denjai	Impending Attack			10750	3 10
Withered Flesh	Zangarmarsh	Alliance	All		Ruam	Ruam	Withered Basidium			10050	2 70
Master of Potions	Zangarmarsh	All	All	5	Lauranna Thar'well	Lauranna Thar'well			325 skill in Alchemy	12650	

EQUIPMENT

ARMOR

CLOTH

Level	Name	Binding Info	Armor
42	Robes of Insight	Bind on Equip	84
PROPERTIES: Reduces the cost of your next spell cast within 10 sec by up to 500 mana.			
50	Embrace of the Wind Serpent	Bind on Pickup	98
PROPERTIES: Nature Resistance Resistance Resistance +12			
57	Alanna's Embrace	Bind on Pickup	109
PROPERTIES: Increases damage and healing done by magical spells and effects by up to 20.			
57	Robe of the Archmage	Bind on Pickup	109
PROPERTIES: Increases damage and healing done by magical spells and effects by up to 40, Increases your spell critical strike rating by 14, Restores 375 to 625 mana.			
57	Robe of the Void	Bind on Pickup	109
PROPERTIES: Increases damage and healing done by magical spells and effects by up to 46, Heal your pet for 450 to 750.			
57	Truefaith Vestments	Bind on Pickup	109
PROPERTIES: Increases healing done by spells and effects by up to 73, Restores 6 mana per 5 sec, Reduces the cooldown of your Fade ability by 2 sec.			
60	Field Marshal's Silk Vestments	Bind on Pickup	129
PROPERTIES: Increases your spell critical strike rating by 14, Increases damage and healing done by magical spells and effects by up to 33.			
60	Warlord's Silk Raiment	Bind on Pickup	129
PROPERTIES: Increases your spell critical strike rating by 14, Increases damage and healing done by magical spells and effects by up to 33.			
60	Arcanist Robes	Bind on Pickup	116
PROPERTIES: Increases damage and healing done by magical spells and effects by up to 23. Fire Resistance Resistance +10			
60	Felheart Robes	Bind on Pickup	116
PROPERTIES: Increases damage and healing done by magical spells and effects by up to 13, Increases your spell hit rating by 8, Fire Resistance Resistance +10			
60	Robes of Prophecy	Bind on Pickup	116
PROPERTIES: Increases healing done by spells and effects by up to 22. Fire Resistance Resistance +10			
60	Netherwind Robes	Bind on Pickup	132
PROPERTIES: Increases your spell critical strike rating by 14, Increases damage and healing done by magical spells and effects by up to 32, Fire Resistance Resistance +10, Nature Resistance Resistance +10			
60	Robes of Transcendence	Bind on Pickup	132
PROPERTIES: Increases healing done by spells and effects by up to 57. Fire Resistance Resistance +10, Nature Resistance Resistance +10			
60	Nemesis Robes	Bind on Pickup	132
PROPERTIES: Increases your spell critical strike rating by 14, Increases damage and healing done by magical spells and effects by up to 32, Fire Resistance Resistance +10, Nature Resistance Resistance +10			
60	Field Marshal's Dreadweave Robe	Bind on Pickup	129
PROPERTIES: Increases damage and healing done by magical spells and effects by up to 32.			
60	Warlord's Dreadweave Robe	Bind on Pickup	129
PROPERTIES: Increases damage and healing done by magical spells and effects by up to 32.			
60	Field Marshal's Satin Vestments	Bind on Pickup	129
PROPERTIES: Increases damage and healing done by magical spells and effects by up to 33, Restores 4 mana per 5 sec.			
60	Warlord's Satin Robes	Bind on Pickup	129
PROPERTIES: Increases damage and healing done by magical spells and effects by up to 33, Restores 4 mana per 5 sec.			
60	Robe of Volatile Power	Bind on Pickup	116
PROPERTIES: Increases your spell critical strike rating by 28, Increases damage and healing done by magical spells and effects by up to 23.			
60	Flarecore Robe	Bind on Equip	116
PROPERTIES: Increases damage and healing done by magical spells and effects by up to 23. Fire Resistance Resistance +15			
60	Black Ash Robe	Bind on Pickup	131
PROPERTIES: Fire Resistance Resistance +30			
60	Flowing Ritual Robes	Bind on Pickup	114
PROPERTIES: Increases damage and healing done by magical spells and effects by up to 22.			
60	Jade Inlaid Vestments	Bind on Pickup	124
PROPERTIES: Increases damage and healing done by magical spells and effects by up to 44.			
60	Doomcaller's Robes	Bind on Pickup	151
PROPERTIES: Increases damage and healing done by magical spells and effects by up to 41, Increases your spell critical strike rating by 14, Increases your spell penetration by 20.			
60	Enigma Robes	Bind on Pickup	151
PROPERTIES: Increases damage and healing done by magical spells and effects by up to 39, Increases your spell critical strike rating by 14, Increases your spell penetration by 20.			
60	Vestments of the Oracle	Bind on Pickup	151
PROPERTIES: Increases damage and healing done by magical spells and effects by up to 36, Increases your spell critical strike rating by 14, Increases your spell penetration by 10.			
60	Vestments of the Shifting Sands	Bind on Pickup	116
PROPERTIES: Increases damage and healing done by magical spells and effects by up to 32, Increases your spell critical strike rating by 14.			
60	Darkwater Robes	Bind on Pickup	134
PROPERTIES: Increases damage done by Frost spells and effects by up to 39. Fire Resistance Resistance +30			
60	Robes of the Guardian Saint	Bind on Pickup	134
PROPERTIES: Increases healing done by spells and effects by up to 70, Restores 7 mana per 5 sec.			
60	Robes of the Battleguard	Bind on Pickup	132
PROPERTIES: Increases damage and healing done by magical spells and effects by up to 36, Increases your spell penetration by 20.			
60	Robes of the Triumvirate	Bind on Pickup	131
PROPERTIES: Restores 7 mana per 5 sec. Nature Resistance Resistance +30			
60	Garb of Royal Ascension	Bind on Pickup	124
PROPERTIES: Increases damage and healing done by magical spells and effects by up to 30, Increases your spell hit rating by 16, Shadow Resistance Resistance +25			

Epic Cloth Chest

Level	Name	Binding Info	Armor
60	Frostfire Robe	Bind on Pickup	158
PROPERTIES: Increases damage and healing done by magical spells and effects by up to 47, Increases your spell hit rating by 8, Increases your spell critical strike rating by 14, Increases your spell penetration by 15.			
60	Plagueheart Robe	Bind on Pickup	158
PROPERTIES: Increases your spell hit rating by 8, Increases damage and healing done by magical spells and effects by up to 51, Increases your spell critical strike rating by 14.			
60	Robe of Faith	Bind on Pickup	158
PROPERTIES: Increases healing done by spells and effects by up to 64, Restores 5 mana per 5 sec.			
60	Necro-Knight's Garb	Bind on Pickup	147
PROPERTIES: Increases damage and healing done by magical spells and effects by up to 37.			
60	Crystal Webbed Robe	Bind on Pickup	147
PROPERTIES: Increases damage and healing done by magical spells and effects by up to 53.			
60	Glacial Vest	Bind on Equip	139
PROPERTIES: Increases damage and healing done by magical spells and effects by up to 21. Frost Resistance Resistance +40			
70	Primal Mooncloth Robe	Bind on Pickup	178
PROPERTIES: Increases healing done by spells and effects by up to 121, Restores 8 mana per 5 sec.			
70	Gladiator's Dreadweave Robe	Bind on Pickup	194
PROPERTIES: Increases damage and healing done by magical spells and effects by up to 30.			
70	Gladiator's Silk Raiment	Bind on Pickup	194
PROPERTIES: Increases damage and healing done by magical spells and effects by up to 26.			
70	Gladiator's Satin Robe	Bind on Pickup	194
PROPERTIES: Increases damage and healing done by magical spells and effects by up to 26.			
70	Masquerade Gown	Bind on Pickup	170
PROPERTIES: Increases healing done by spells and effects by up to 77, Chance on spell cast to increase your Spirit by 145 for 15 secs.			
70	Robe of Elder Scribes	Bind on Pickup	170
PROPERTIES: Increases damage and healing done by magical spells and effects by up to 27, Gives a chance when your harmful spells land to increase the damage of your spells and effects by up to 130 for 10 sec.			
70	Voidheart Robe	Bind on Pickup	143
PROPERTIES: Increases damage and healing done by magical spells and effects by up to 36.			
70	Robes of the Incarnate	Bind on Pickup	178
PROPERTIES: Increases healing done by spells and effects by up to 77.			
70	Shroud of the Incarnate	Bind on Pickup	178
PROPERTIES: Increases damage and healing done by magical spells and effects by up to 41.			
70	Vestments of the Aldor	Bind on Pickup	178
PROPERTIES: Increases damage and healing done by magical spells and effects by up to 43, Increases your spell penetration by 15.			
70	Robe of Hateful Echoes	Bind on Pickup	194
PROPERTIES: Increases damage and healing done by magical spells and effects by up to 46.			
70	Vestments of the Sza-Witch	Bind on Pickup	210
PROPERTIES: Increases damage and healing done by magical spells and effects by up to 50, Increases your spell penetration by 25.			
70	Vestments of the Avatar	Bind on Pickup	202
PROPERTIES: Increases healing done by spells and effects by up to 88.			
70	Shroud of the Avatar	Bind on Pickup	202
PROPERTIES: Increases damage and healing done by magical spells and effects by up to 47.			
70	Robes of Tirisfal	Bind on Pickup	202
PROPERTIES: Increases damage and healing done by magical spells and effects by up to 35.			
70	Gladiator's Felweave Raiment	Bind on Pickup	194
PROPERTIES: Increases damage and healing done by magical spells and effects by up to 26.			
70	Robe of the Corruptor	Bind on Pickup	202

Epic Cloth Chest

Level	Name	Binding Info	Armor
PROPERTIES: Increases damage and healing done by magical spells and effects by up to 40.			
70	Infernoweave Robe	Bind on Pickup	162
PROPERTIES: Fire Resistance Resistance +60			
70	Spellfire Vest	Bind on Pickup	178
PROPERTIES: Increases damage done by Fire spells and effects by up to 86, Increases damage done by Arcane spells and effects by up to 86.			
70	Soulcloth Vest	Bind on Equip	170
PROPERTIES: Arcane Resistance Resistance +45			
70	Frozen Shadoweave Vest	Bind on Pickup	178
PROPERTIES: Increases damage done by Shadow spells and effects by up to 78, Increases damage done by Frost spells and effects by up to 78.			
	Zandalar Demoniac's Robe	Bind on Pickup	114
PROPERTIES: Increases your spell hit rating by 8, Increases damage and healing done by magical spells and effects by up to 27.			
	Zandalar Illusionist's Robe	Bind on Pickup	114
PROPERTIES: Increases your spell hit rating by 8, Increases damage and healing done by magical spells and effects by up to 27.			
	Sorcerer's Robes	Bind on Pickup	106
PROPERTIES: Increases damage and healing done by magical spells and effects by up to 16, Increases your spell penetration by 20.			
	Deathmist Robe	Bind on Pickup	106
PROPERTIES: Increases damage and healing done by magical spells and effects by up to 12, Increases your spell critical strike rating by 14.			
	Virtuous Robe	Bind on Pickup	106
PROPERTIES: Increases damage and healing done by magical spells and effects by up to 14, Restores 6 mana per 5 sec.			

Superior Cloth Chest

Level	Name	Binding Info	Armor
19	Tree Bark Jacket	Bind on Equip	42
19	Corsair's Overshirt	Bind on Pickup	42
20	Necrology Robes	Bind on Equip	43
PROPERTIES: Shadow Resistance Resistance +5			
21	Black Velvet Robes	Bind on Equip	44
24	Robes of Arugal	Bind on Pickup	46
26	Mechbuilder's Overalls	Bind on Equip	48
PROPERTIES: Arcane Resistance Resistance +5			
29	Beguiler Robes	Bind on Equip	50
33	Robe of Power	Bind on Pickup	55
PROPERTIES: Increases damage and healing done by magical spells and effects by up to 14.			
35	Robe of the Magi	Bind on Equip	58
PROPERTIES: Increases damage and healing done by magical spells and effects by up to 22.			
35	Death's Head Vestment	Bind on Equip	58
36	Elemental Raiment	Bind on Equip	59
PROPERTIES: Increases damage and healing done by magical spells and effects by up to 21. Fire Resistance Resistance +5, Nature Resistance Resistance +5, Frost Resistance Resistance +5, Shadow Resistance Resistance +5, Arcane Resistance Resistance +5			
39	Robes of the Lich	Bind on Pickup	64
40	Dreamweave Vest	Bind on Equip	65
PROPERTIES: Increases damage and healing done by magical spells and effects by up to 18.			
42	Grimlok's Tribal Vestments	Bind on Pickup	68
46	Funeral Pyre Vestment	Bind on Equip	73
PROPERTIES: Fire Resistance Resistance +10			
46	Nature's Embrace	Bind on Pickup	73
PROPERTIES: Increases damage done by Holy spells and effects by up to 29, Restores 8 mana per 5 sec.			

Superior Cloth Chest

Level	Name	Binding Info	Armor
47	Chan's Imperial Robes	Bind on Equip	75
PROPERTIES: Nature Resistance Resistance +5			
50	Vestments of the Atal'ai Prophet	Bind on Pickup	78
52	Robe of Winter Night	Bind on Equip	81
PROPERTIES: Increases damage done by Shadow spells and effects by up to 40, Increases damage done by Frost spells and effects by up to 40.			
55	Robes of the Royal Crown	Bind on Pickup	85
PROPERTIES: Increases damage and healing done by magical spells and effects by up to 18.			
55	Mooncloth Vest	Bind on Equip	85
56	Necropile Robe	Bind on Pickup	87
PROPERTIES: Increases damage and healing done by magical spells and effects by up to 8.			
56	Mooncloth Robe	Bind on Equip	87
56	Polychromatic Visionwrap	Bind on Pickup	87
PROPERTIES: Fire Resistance Resistance +20, Nature Resistance Resistance +20, Frost Resistance Resistance +20, Shadow Resistance Resistance +20, Arcane Resistance Resistance +20			
56	The Postmaster's Tunic	Bind on Pickup	87
PROPERTIES: Increases damage and healing done by magical spells and effects by up to 15.			
57	Freezing Lich Robes	Bind on Pickup	88
PROPERTIES: Increases damage done by Frost spells and effects by up to 43.			
57	Robe of Everlasting Night	Bind on Pickup	88
PROPERTIES: Increases damage and healing done by magical spells and effects by up to 27.			
57	Mindsurge Robe	Bind on Pickup	88
PROPERTIES: Restores 10 mana per 5 sec.			
58	Widow's Clutch	Bind on Pickup	89
PROPERTIES: Arcane Resistance Resistance +13			
58	Robes of the Exalted	Bind on Pickup	89
PROPERTIES: Increases healing done by spells and effects by up to 68.			
58	Knight-Captain's Silk Raiment	Bind on Pickup	89
PROPERTIES: Increases your spell critical strike rating by 14.			
58	Legionnaire's Silk Robes	Bind on Pickup	89
PROPERTIES: Increases your spell critical strike rating by 14.			
58	Magister's Robes	Bind on Pickup	89
58	Devout Robe	Bind on Pickup	89
58	Dreadmist Robe	Bind on Pickup	89
58	Knight-Captain's Dreadweave Robe	Bind on Pickup	89
PROPERTIES: Increases damage and healing done by magical spells and effects by up to 16.			
58	Legionnaire's Dreadweave Robe	Bind on Pickup	89
PROPERTIES: Increases damage and healing done by magical spells and effects by up to 16.			
58	Knight-Captain's Satin Robes	Bind on Pickup	89
PROPERTIES: Increases damage and healing done by magical spells and effects by up to 16.			
58	Legionnaire's Satin Vestments	Bind on Pickup	89
PROPERTIES: Increases damage and healing done by magical spells and effects by up to 16.			
58	Robe of Undead Cleansing	Bind on Pickup	89
PROPERTIES: Increases damage done to Undead by magical spells and effects by up to 48.			
60	Legionnaire's Dreadweave Tunic	Bind on Pickup	96
PROPERTIES: Increases damage and healing done by magical spells and effects by up to 25.			
60	Legionnaire's Satin Tunic	Bind on Pickup	96
PROPERTIES: Increases damage and healing done by magical spells and effects by up to 21, Restores 6 mana per 5 sec.			
60	Legionnaire's Silk Tunic	Bind on Pickup	96
PROPERTIES: Increases your spell critical strike rating by 14, Increases damage and healing done by magical spells and effects by up to 21.			

Superior Cloth Chest

Level	Name	Binding Info	Armor
60	Knight-Captain's Dreadweave Tunic	Bind on Pickup	96
PROPERTIES: Increases damage and healing done by magical spells and effects by up to 25.			
60	Knight-Captain's Satin Tunic	Bind on Pickup	96
PROPERTIES: Increases damage and healing done by magical spells and effects by up to 21, Restores 6 mana per 5 sec.			
60	Knight-Captain's Silk Tunic	Bind on Pickup	96
PROPERTIES: Increases your spell critical strike rating by 14, Increases damage and healing done by magical spells and effects by up to 21.			
60	Bloodvine Vest	Bind on Equip	92
PROPERTIES: Increases your spell hit rating by 16, Increases damage and healing done by magical spells and effects by up to 27.			
60	Sylvan Vest	Bind on Equip	98
PROPERTIES: Increases damage and healing done by magical spells and effects by up to 12. Nature Resistance Resistance +30			
61	Sun-Touched Raiments	Bind on Pickup	122
PROPERTIES: Increases healing done by spells and effects by up to 46.			
63	Robes of the Augurer	Bind on Pickup	129
PROPERTIES: Increases damage and healing done by magical spells and effects by up to 28.			
68	Robe of the Great Dark Beyond	Bind on Pickup	152
PROPERTIES: Increases damage and healing done by magical spells and effects by up to 39.			
68	Bloodfyre Robes of Annihilation	Bind on Pickup	152
PROPERTIES: Increases damage and healing done by magical spells and effects by up to 54.			
70	Imbued Netherweave Robe	Bind on Equip	155
PROPERTIES: Increases damage and healing done by magical spells and effects by up to 33, Restores 11 mana per 5 sec.			
70	Arcanoweave Robe	Bind on Equip	156
PROPERTIES: Restores 9 mana per 5 sec. Arcane Resistance Resistance +50			
70	Shattra Ceremonial Gown	Bind on Pickup	156
PROPERTIES: Increases healing done by spells and effects by up to 73, Restores 7 mana per 5 sec.			
70	Vermillion Robes of the Dominant	Bind on Pickup	156
PROPERTIES: Increases damage and healing done by magical spells and effects by up to 42.			
70	Mana-Etched Robe	Bind on Pickup	156
PROPERTIES: Increases damage and healing done by magical spells and effects by up to 29.			
70	Incanter's Robe	Bind on Pickup	156
PROPERTIES: Increases damage and healing done by magical spells and effects by up to 30.			
70	Hallowed Garments	Bind on Pickup	156
PROPERTIES: Increases healing done by spells and effects by up to 57.			
70	Robe of Oblivion	Bind on Pickup	156
PROPERTIES: Increases damage and healing done by magical spells and effects by up to 33.			
70	Warp Infused Drape	Bind on Pickup	156
PROPERTIES: Increases damage and healing done by magical spells and effects by up to 30.			
70	Grand Marshal's Dreadweave Robe	Bind on Pickup	156
PROPERTIES: Increases damage and healing done by magical spells and effects by up to 29.			
70	Grand Marshal's Satin Robe	Bind on Pickup	156
PROPERTIES: Increases damage and healing done by magical spells and effects by up to 27.			
70	Grand Marshal's Silk Raiment	Bind on Pickup	156
PROPERTIES: Increases damage and healing done by magical spells and effects by up to 23.			
70	High Warlord's Dreadweave Robe	Bind on Pickup	156
PROPERTIES: Increases damage and healing done by magical spells and effects by up to 29.			
70	High Warlord's Satin Robe	Bind on Pickup	156
PROPERTIES: Increases damage and healing done by magical spells and effects by up to 27.			
70	High Warlord's Silk Raiment	Bind on Pickup	156
PROPERTIES: Increases damage and healing done by magical spells and effects by up to 23.			

Superior Cloth Chest

Level	Name	Binding Info	Armor
70	Anchorite's Robes	Bind on Pickup	156
PROPERTIES: Increases damage and healing done by magical spells and effects by up to 29.			
70	Netherflame Robe	Bind on Equip	149
PROPERTIES: Increases damage and healing done by magical spells and effects by up to 41.			
70	Imbued Netherweave Tunic	Bind on Equip	155
PROPERTIES: Increases damage and healing done by magical spells and effects by up to 50, Restores 11 mana per 5 sec.			
70	Stormspire Vest	Bind on Equip	156
PROPERTIES: Increases damage and healing done by magical spells and effects by up to 39, Restores 13 mana per 5 sec.			
70	Flameheart Vest	Bind on Equip	156
PROPERTIES: Fire Resistance Resistance +50			
	Enchanted Gold Bloodrobe	Bind on Pickup	55
	Civinad Robes	Bind on Pickup	54
	Robes of Servitude	Bind on Pickup	75
PROPERTIES: Increases damage done by Fire spells and effects by up to 23, Increases damage done by Shadow spells and effects by up to 23.			
	Auchenai Anchorite's Robe	Bind on Pickup	136
PROPERTIES: Increases damage and healing done by magical spells and effects by up to 28.			
	Kirin Tor Apprentice's Robes	Bind on Pickup	148
PROPERTIES: Increases damage and healing done by magical spells and effects by up to 40.			
	Robes of Servitude	Bind on Pickup	75
	Earthpower Vest	Bind on Pickup	93
PROPERTIES: Increases your spell critical strike rating by 14, Increases damage and healing done by magical spells and effects by up to 25.			
	Watcher's Tunic	Bind on Pickup	140
PROPERTIES: Increases healing done by spells and effects by up to 68.			
	Goldweave Tunic	Bind on Pickup	118
PROPERTIES: Increases damage and healing done by magical spells and effects by up to 42.			

Epic Cloth Feet

Level	Name	Binding Info	
60	Marshal's Silk Footwraps	Bind on Pickup	85
PROPERTIES: Increases damage and healing done by magical spells and effects by up to 21, Increases your spell hit rating by 8.			
60	General's Silk Boots	Bind on Pickup	85
PROPERTIES: Increases damage and healing done by magical spells and effects by up to 21, Increases your spell hit rating by 8.			
60	Arcanist Boots	Bind on Pickup	80
PROPERTIES: Increases your spell critical strike rating by 14, Increases damage and healing done by magical spells and effects by up to 11. Shadow Resistance Resistance +10			
60	Felheart Slippers	Bind on Pickup	80
PROPERTIES: Increases damage and healing done by magical spells and effects by up to 18. Shadow Resistance Resistance +7			
60	Boots of Prophecy	Bind on Pickup	80
PROPERTIES: Increases healing done by spells and effects by up to 18. Shadow Resistance Resistance +7			
60	Netherwind Boots	Bind on Pickup	91
PROPERTIES: Increases damage and healing done by magical spells and effects by up to 27. Fire Resistance Resistance +10			
60	Boots of Transcendence	Bind on Pickup	91
PROPERTIES: Increases healing done by spells and effects by up to 35. Fire Resistance Resistance +10			
60	Nemesis Boots	Bind on Pickup	91
PROPERTIES: Increases damage and healing done by magical spells and effects by up to 23. Fire Resistance Resistance +10			

Epic Cloth Feet

Level	Name	Binding Info	
60	Marshal's Dreadweave Boots	Bind on Pickup	85
PROPERTIES: Increases damage and healing done by magical spells and effects by up to 26.			
60	General's Dreadweave Boots	Bind on Pickup	85
PROPERTIES: Increases damage and healing done by magical spells and effects by up to 26.			
60	Marshal's Satin Sandals	Bind on Pickup	85
PROPERTIES: Increases damage and healing done by magical spells and effects by up to 23.			
60	General's Satin Boots	Bind on Pickup	85
PROPERTIES: Increases damage and healing done by magical spells and effects by up to 23.			
60	Snowblind Shoes	Bind on Pickup	83
PROPERTIES: Increases damage and healing done by magical spells and effects by up to 32, Restores 5 mana per 5 sec.			
60	Shimmering Geta	Bind on Pickup	92
PROPERTIES: Restores 12 mana per 5 sec.			
60	Boots of Pure Thought	Bind on Pickup	84
PROPERTIES: Increases healing done by spells and effects by up to 62.			
60	Ringo's Blizzard Boots	Bind on Pickup	85
PROPERTIES: Increases damage done by Frost spells and effects by up to 40, Increases your spell hit rating by 8.			
60	Betrayer's Boots	Bind on Pickup	79
PROPERTIES: Increases damage and healing done by magical spells and effects by up to 30.			
60	Mendicant's Slippers	Bind on Pickup	85
PROPERTIES: Restores 10 mana per 5 sec.			
60	Doomcaller's Footwraps	Bind on Pickup	93
PROPERTIES: Increases damage and healing done by magical spells and effects by up to 28, Increases your spell penetration by 10.			
60	Enigma Boots	Bind on Pickup	93
PROPERTIES: Increases damage and healing done by magical spells and effects by up to 28, Increases your spell hit rating by 8, Restores 4 mana per 5 sec.			
60	Footwraps of the Oracle	Bind on Pickup	93
PROPERTIES: Increases damage and healing done by magical spells and effects by up to 21, Restores 3 mana per 5 sec.			
60	Boots of Epiphany	Bind on Pickup	96
PROPERTIES: Increases damage and healing done by magical spells and effects by up to 34.			
60	Recomposed Boots	Bind on Pickup	91
PROPERTIES: Increases damage and healing done by magical spells and effects by up to 20. Nature Resistance Resistance +20			
60	Frostfire Sandals	Bind on Pickup	102
PROPERTIES: Increases your spell critical strike rating by 14, Increases damage and healing done by magical spells and effects by up to 28.			
60	Plagueheart Sandals	Bind on Pickup	102
PROPERTIES: Increases damage and healing done by magical spells and effects by up to 32, Increases your spell critical strike rating by 14.			
60	Sandals of Faith	Bind on Pickup	102
PROPERTIES: Restores 6 mana per 5 sec, Increases healing done by spells and effects by up to 44.			
70	Frozen Shadoweave Boots	Bind on Pickup	122
PROPERTIES: Increases damage done by Shadow spells and effects by up to 57, Increases damage done by Frost spells and effects by up to 57.			
70	General's Dreadweave Stalkers	Bind on Pickup	128
PROPERTIES: Increases damage and healing done by magical spells and effects by up to 28.			
70	General's Silk Footguards	Bind on Pickup	128
PROPERTIES: Increases damage and healing done by magical spells and effects by up to 25.			
70	Boots of Foretelling	Bind on Pickup	117
PROPERTIES: Increases damage and healing done by magical spells and effects by up to 23.			

Epic Cloth Feet

Level	Name	Binding Info	
70	Ruby Slippers	Bind on Pickup	117
PROPERTIES: Increases damage and healing done by magical spells and effects by up to 32, Returns you to Bind Location. Speak to an Innkeeper in a different place to change your home location.			
70	Boots of the Incorrupt	Bind on Pickup	117
PROPERTIES: Restores 7 mana per 5 sec, Increases healing done by spells and effects by up to 53.			
70	Boots of the Infernal Coven	Bind on Pickup	117
PROPERTIES: Increases damage and healing done by magical spells and effects by up to 30.			
70	Marshal's Dreadweave Stalkers	Bind on Pickup	128
PROPERTIES: Increases damage and healing done by magical spells and effects by up to 28.			
70	Marshal's Silk Footguards	Bind on Pickup	128
PROPERTIES: Increases damage and healing done by magical spells and effects by up to 25.			
70	Boots of Blasphemy	Bind on Pickup	112
PROPERTIES: Increases damage and healing done by magical spells and effects by up to 34.			
70	Boots of the Pious	Bind on Pickup	112
PROPERTIES: Increases healing done by spells and effects by up to 57.			
70	Boots of Ethereal Manipulation	Bind on Pickup	112
PROPERTIES: Increases damage and healing done by magical spells and effects by up to 30.			
70	Boots of the Long Road	Bind on Pickup	134
PROPERTIES: Increases healing done by spells and effects by up to 64, Restores 6 mana per 5 sec.			
70	Boots of Blasting	Bind on Pickup	134
PROPERTIES: Increases damage and healing done by magical spells and effects by up to 34.			
70	Boots of the Shifting Nightmare	Bind on Pickup	134
PROPERTIES: Increases damage done by Shadow spells and effects by up to 51.			
70	Velvet Boots of the Guardian	Bind on Pickup	134
PROPERTIES: Increases damage and healing done by magical spells and effects by up to 42.			
70	Soul-Strider Boots	Bind on Pickup	134
PROPERTIES: Increases healing done by spells and effects by up to 31.			
70	Glider's Foot-Wraps	Bind on Pickup	112
70	Infernoweave Boots	Bind on Pickup	112
PROPERTIES: Fire Resistance Resistance +45			
	Sorcerer's Boots	Bind on Pickup	73
PROPERTIES: Increases damage and healing done by magical spells and effects by up to 21.			
	Deathmist Sandals	Bind on Pickup	73
PROPERTIES: Increases damage and healing done by magical spells and effects by up to 12.			
	Virtuous Sandals	Bind on Pickup	73
PROPERTIES: Increases damage and healing done by magical spells and effects by up to 12, Restores 7 mana per 5 sec.			

Superior Cloth Feet

Level	Name	Binding Info	Armor
20	Spidersilk Boots	Bind on Equip	29
24	Moccasins of the White Hare	Bind on Equip	32
27	Acidic Walkers	Bind on Pickup	34
PROPERTIES: Increases damage and healing done by magical spells and effects by up to 5, Nature Resistance Resistance +5			
28	Highlander's Cloth Boots	Bind on Pickup	34
PROPERTIES: Run speed increased slightly, Increases damage and healing done by magical spells and effects by up to 7.			
28	Defiler's Cloth Boots	Bind on Pickup	34
PROPERTIES: Run speed increased slightly, Increases damage and healing done by magical spells and effects by up to 7.			

Superior Cloth Feet

Level	Name	Binding Info	Armor
33	Thoughtcast Boots	Bind on Equip	38
38	Highlander's Cloth Boots	Bind on Pickup	43
PROPERTIES: Run speed increased slightly, Increases damage and healing done by magical spells and effects by up to 8.			
38	Defiler's Cloth Boots	Bind on Pickup	43
PROPERTIES: Run speed increased slightly, Increases damage and healing done by magical spells and effects by up to 8.			
39	Furen's Boots	Bind on Equip	44
45	Mistwalker Boots	Bind on Equip	49
46	Vinerot Sandals	Bind on Pickup	50
PROPERTIES: Nature Resistance Resistance +12,			
48	Highlander's Cloth Boots	Bind on Pickup	52
PROPERTIES: Run speed increased slightly, Increases damage and healing done by magical spells and effects by up to 9.			
48	Defiler's Cloth Boots	Bind on Pickup	52
PROPERTIES: Run speed increased slightly, Increases damage and healing done by magical spells and effects by up to 9.			
50	Phasing Boots	Bind on Equip	54
50	Coldstone Slippers	Bind on Equip	54
PROPERTIES: Restores 4 mana per 5 sec.			
51	Mooncloth Boots	Bind on Equip	55
51	Soot Encrusted Footwear	Bind on Pickup	55
PROPERTIES: Increases healing done by spells and effects by up to 20.			
53	Argent Boots	Bind on Equip	57
PROPERTIES: Shadow Resistance Resistance +4			
54	Omnicast Boots	Bind on Pickup	58
PROPERTIES: Increases damage and healing done by magical spells and effects by up to 22.			
54	High Priestess Boots	Bind on Pickup	58
PROPERTIES: Shadow Resistance Resistance +10			
54	Wolfrunner Shoes	Bind on Equip	58
PROPERTIES: Increases damage and healing done by magical spells and effects by up to 13.			
54	Ogreseer Tower Boots	Bind on Pickup	58
54	Magister's Boots	Bind on Pickup	58
54	Devout Sandals	Bind on Pickup	58
54	Dreadmist Sandals	Bind on Pickup	58
56	The Postmaster's Treads	Bind on Pickup	60
PROPERTIES: Increases damage and healing done by magical spells and effects by up to 7.			
56	Necropile Boots	Bind on Pickup	60
PROPERTIES: Increases damage and healing done by magical spells and effects by up to 11.			
56	Kayser's Boots of Precision	Bind on Pickup	60
PROPERTIES: Increases your spell hit rating by 8.			
56	Ironweave Boots	Bind on Pickup	60
57	Boots of the Full Moon	Bind on Pickup	60
PROPERTIES: Increases healing done by spells and effects by up to 26.			
57	Maleki's Footwraps	Bind on Pickup	60
PROPERTIES: Increases damage done by Shadow spells and effects by up to 27.			
58	Fire Striders	Bind on Pickup	61
PROPERTIES: Increases damage done by Fire spells and effects by up to 29, Fire Resistance Resistance +15			
58	Knight-Lieutenant's Silk Boots	Bind on Pickup	61
PROPERTIES: Increases damage and healing done by magical spells and effects by up to 12.			
58	Blood Guard's Silk Footwraps	Bind on Pickup	61
PROPERTIES: Increases damage and healing done by magical spells and effects by up to 12.			

Superior Cloth Feet

Level	Name	Binding Info	Armor
58	Knight-Lieutenant's Dreadweave Boots	Bind on Pickup	61
PROPERTIES: Increases damage and healing done by magical spells and effects by up to 19.			
58	Blood Guard's Dreadweave Boots	Bind on Pickup	61
PROPERTIES: Increases damage and healing done by magical spells and effects by up to 12.			
58	Knight-Lieutenant's Satin Boots	Bind on Pickup	61
PROPERTIES: Increases damage and healing done by magical spells and effects by up to 12.			
58	Blood Guard's Satin Boots	Bind on Pickup	61
PROPERTIES: Increases damage and healing done by magical spells and effects by up to 12.			
58	Dragonrider Boots	Bind on Pickup	61
PROPERTIES: Increases damage and healing done by magical spells and effects by up to 18, Fire Resistance Resistance +10			
58	Highlander's Cloth Boots	Bind on Pickup	61
PROPERTIES: Run speed increased slightly, Increases damage and healing done by magical spells and effects by up to 12.			
58	Defiler's Cloth Boots	Bind on Pickup	61
PROPERTIES: Run speed increased slightly, Increases damage and healing done by magical spells and effects by up to 12.			
58	Runed Stygian Boots	Bind on Equip	61
PROPERTIES: Restores 4 mana per 5 sec. Shadow Resistance Resistance +20,			
58	Faith Healer's Boots	Bind on Pickup	61
PROPERTIES: Increases healing done by spells and effects by up to 26.			
60	Bloodvine Boots	Bind on Equip	63
PROPERTIES: Increases your spell hit rating by 8, Increases damage and healing done by magical spells and effects by up to 19.			
60	Quicksand Waders	Bind on Pickup	70
PROPERTIES: Increases damage and healing done by magical spells and effects by up to 16.			
60	Treads of the Wandering Nomad	Bind on Pickup	69
PROPERTIES: Increases healing done by spells and effects by up to 37.			
60	Blood Guard's Dreadweave Walkers	Bind on Pickup	64
PROPERTIES: Increases damage and healing done by magical spells and effects by up to 18.			
60	Blood Guard's Satin Walkers	Bind on Pickup	64
PROPERTIES: Increases damage and healing done by magical spells and effects by up to 14.			
60	Blood Guard's Silk Walkers	Bind on Pickup	64
PROPERTIES: Increases damage and healing done by magical spells and effects by up to 15, Increases your spell hit rating by 8.			
60	Knight-Lieutenant's Dreadweave Walkers	Bind on Pickup	64
PROPERTIES: Increases damage and healing done by magical spells and effects by up to 18.			
60	Knight-Lieutenant's Satin Walkers	Bind on Pickup	64
PROPERTIES: Increases damage and healing done by magical spells and effects by up to 14.			
60	Knight-Lieutenant's Silk Walkers	Bind on Pickup	64
PROPERTIES: Increases damage and healing done by magical spells and effects by up to 15, Increases your spell hit rating by 8.			
63	Windwalker's Footwraps	Bind on Equip	89
64	Ethereal Boots of Arcanistry	Bind on Pickup	91
PROPERTIES: Increases damage and healing done by magical spells and effects by up to 26.			
65	Boots of Maladaar	Bind on Pickup	94
PROPERTIES: Increases healing done by spells and effects by up to 35.			
68	Boots of the Darkwalker	Bind on Pickup	105
PROPERTIES: Increases damage done by Shadow spells and effects by up to 36.			
68	Jeweled Sandals of Sanctification	Bind on Pickup	105
PROPERTIES: Increases healing done by spells and effects by up to 55, Restores 6 mana per 5 sec.			
68	Extravagant Boots of Malice	Bind on Pickup	105
PROPERTIES: Increases damage and healing done by magical spells and effects by up to 30.			
68	Embroidered Boots of Ferocity	Bind on Pickup	105

Superior Cloth Feet

Level	Name	Binding Info	Armor
PROPERTIES: Increases damage and healing done by magical spells and effects by up to 41.			
68	Boots of the Darkweaver	Bind on Pickup	105
PROPERTIES: Increases healing done by spells and effects by up to 29, Restores 10 mana per 5 sec.			
69	Imbued Netherweave Boots	Bind on Equip	102
PROPERTIES: Increases damage and healing done by magical spells and effects by up to 23, Restores 8 mana per 5 sec.			
70	Arcanoweave Boots	Bind on Equip	106
PROPERTIES: Arcane Resistance Resistance +35			
70	Silent Slippers of Meditation	Bind on Pickup	107
PROPERTIES: Increases damage and healing done by magical spells and effects by up to 26.			
70	Sigil-Laced Boots	Bind on Pickup	107
PROPERTIES: Increases damage and healing done by magical spells and effects by up to 20.			
70	Netherflame Boots	Bind on Equip	103
PROPERTIES: Increases damage and healing done by magical spells and effects by up to 29.			
	Shalassi Oracle's Sandals	Bind on Pickup	86
PROPERTIES: Increases damage and healing done by magical spells and effects by up to 18.			
	Shattrath Jumpers	Bind on Pickup	107
PROPERTIES: Increases damage and healing done by magical spells and effects by up to 29.			
	Slippers of the High Priestess	Bind on Pickup	102
PROPERTIES: Increases damage and healing done by magical spells and effects by up to 28.			

Epic Cloth Hands

Level	Name	Binding Info	Armor
57	Gloves of Spell Mastery	Bind on Equip	68
PROPERTIES: Increases your spell critical strike rating by 28.			
57	Flarecore Gloves	Bind on Equip	68
PROPERTIES: Fire Resistance Resistance +25			
60	Marshal's Silk Gloves	Bind on Pickup	78
PROPERTIES: Increases damage and healing done by magical spells and effects by up to 27, Increases the damage absorbed by your Mana Shield by 285.			
60	General's Silk Handguards	Bind on Pickup	78
PROPERTIES: Increases the damage absorbed by your Mana Shield by 285, Increases damage and healing done by magical spells and effects by up to 27.			
60	Arcanist Gloves	Bind on Pickup	72
PROPERTIES: Restores 4 mana per 5 sec, Increases damage and healing done by magical spells and effects by up to 14. Fire Resistance Resistance +7			
60	Felheart Gloves	Bind on Pickup	72
PROPERTIES: Increases your spell critical strike rating by 14, Increases damage and healing done by magical spells and effects by up to 9. Fire Resistance Resistance +7			
60	Gloves of Prophecy	Bind on Pickup	72
PROPERTIES: Restores 6 mana per 5 sec, Increases healing done by spells and effects by up to 18. Fire Resistance Resistance +7			
60	Netherwind Gloves	Bind on Pickup	83
PROPERTIES: Increases your spell critical strike rating by 14, Increases damage and healing done by magical spells and effects by up to 20. Shadow Resistance Resistance +10			
60	Handguards of Transcendence	Bind on Pickup	83
PROPERTIES: Increases your spell critical strike rating by 14, Increases healing done by spells and effects by up to 29. Shadow Resistance Resistance +10			
60	Nemesis Gloves	Bind on Pickup	83
PROPERTIES: Restores 4 health per 5 sec, Increases damage and healing done by magical spells and effects by up to 15, Increases your spell critical strike rating by 14. Shadow Resistance Resistance +10			
60	Marshal's Dreadweave Gloves	Bind on Pickup	78
PROPERTIES: Gives you a 50% chance to avoid interruption caused by damage while casting Searing Pain, Increases damage and healing done by magical spells and effects by up to 30.			

Epic Cloth Hands

Level	Name	Binding Info	Armor
60	General's Dreadweave Gloves	Bind on Pickup	78
PROPERTIES: Gives you a 50% chance to avoid interruption caused by damage while casting Searing Pain, Increases damage and healing done by magical spells and effects by up to 30.			
60	Marshal's Satin Gloves	Bind on Pickup	78
PROPERTIES: Increases damage and healing done by magical spells and effects by up to 23, Gives you a 50% chance to avoid interruption caused by damage while casting Mind Blast.			
60	General's Satin Gloves	Bind on Pickup	78
PROPERTIES: Gives you a 50% chance to avoid interruption caused by damage while casting Mind Blast, Increases damage and healing done by magical spells and effects by up to 23.			
60	Gloves of the Hypnotic Flame	Bind on Pickup	77
PROPERTIES: Increases damage done by Fire spells and effects by up to 23, Increases damage and healing done by magical spells and effects by up to 9.			
60	Gloves of Rapid Evolution	Bind on Pickup	80
60	Ebony Flame Gloves	Bind on Pickup	82
PROPERTIES: Increases damage done by Shadow spells and effects by up to 43.			
60	Gloves of Delusional Power	Bind on Pickup	79
PROPERTIES: Restores 5 mana per 5 sec, Increases damage and healing done by magical spells and effects by up to 27.			
60	Doomcaller's Handwraps	Bind on Pickup	85
60	Gloves of Dark Wisdom	Bind on Pickup	79
PROPERTIES: Increases healing done by spells and effects by up to 35, Restores 5 mana per 5 sec.			
60	Dark Storm Gauntlets	Bind on Pickup	95
PROPERTIES: Increases damage and healing done by magical spells and effects by up to 37, Increases your spell hit rating by 8.			
60	Gloves of the Messiah	Bind on Pickup	85
PROPERTIES: Increases healing done by spells and effects by up to 26, Restores 10 mana per 5 sec.			
60	Gloves of the Immortal	Bind on Pickup	78
60	Frostfire Gloves	Bind on Pickup	95
PROPERTIES: Increases damage and healing done by magical spells and effects by up to 36.			
60	Plagueheart Gloves	Bind on Pickup	95
PROPERTIES: Increases your spell critical strike rating by 14, Increases damage and healing done by magical spells and effects by up to 26.			
60	Gloves of Faith	Bind on Pickup	95
PROPERTIES: Increases healing done by spells and effects by up to 40, Restores 4 mana per 5 sec.			
60	Glacial Gloves	Bind on Equip	87
PROPERTIES: Increases damage and healing done by magical spells and effects by up to 15. Frost Resistance Resistance +30			
70	Spellfire Gloves	Bind on Pickup	111
PROPERTIES: Increases damage done by Fire spells and effects by up to 57, Increases damage done by Arcane spells and effects by up to 57.			
70	Soulcloth Gloves	Bind on Equip	106
PROPERTIES: Arcane Resistance Resistance +35			
70	Gladiator's Dreadweave Gloves	Bind on Pickup	116
PROPERTIES: Gives you a 50% chance to avoid interruption caused by damage while casting Fear, Increases damage and healing done by magical spells and effects by up to 28.			
70	Gladiator's Silk Handguards	Bind on Pickup	116
PROPERTIES: Improves the range of your Fire Blast spell by 5 yards, Increases damage and healing done by magical spells and effects by up to 28.			
70	Gladiator's Satin Gloves	Bind on Pickup	116
PROPERTIES: Increases the duration of your Psychic Scream spell by 1 sec, Increases damage and healing done by magical spells and effects by up to 25.			
70	Handwraps of Flowing Thought	Bind on Pickup	106
PROPERTIES: Increases damage and healing done by magical spells and effects by up to 32.			

Epic Cloth Hands

Level	Name	Binding Info	Armor
70	Gloves of Saintly Blessings	Bind on Pickup	106
PROPERTIES: Increases healing done by spells and effects by up to 33.			
70	Magtheridon Loot 2 Cloth Gloves	Bind on Pickup	116
PROPERTIES: Increases damage and healing done by magical spells and effects by up to 34.			
70	Voidheart Gloves	Bind on Pickup	89
PROPERTIES: Increases damage and healing done by magical spells and effects by up to 30.			
70	Soul-Eater's Handwraps	Bind on Pickup	111
PROPERTIES: Increases healing done by spells and effects by up to 51, Restores 9 mana per 5 sec.			
70	Gloves of the Incarnate	Bind on Pickup	111
PROPERTIES: Increases damage and healing done by magical spells and effects by up to 27.			
70	Gloves of the Aldor	Bind on Pickup	111
PROPERTIES: Increases damage and healing done by magical spells and effects by up to 32.			
70	Gauntlets of the Sun-King	Bind on Pickup	132
PROPERTIES: Increases damage and healing done by magical spells and effects by up to 34.			
70	Gloves of the Avatar	Bind on Pickup	126
PROPERTIES: Increases healing done by spells and effects by up to 64.			
70	Handguards of the Avatar	Bind on Pickup	126
PROPERTIES: Increases damage and healing done by magical spells and effects by up to 34.			
70	Gladiator's Felweave Handguards	Bind on Pickup	116
PROPERTIES: Gives you a 50% chance to avoid interruption caused by damage while casting Searing Pain, Increases damage and healing done by magical spells and effects by up to 28.			
70	Gloves of Tirisfal	Bind on Pickup	126
PROPERTIES: Increases damage and healing done by magical spells and effects by up to 35.			
70	Gloves of the Corruptor	Bind on Pickup	126
PROPERTIES: Increases damage and healing done by magical spells and effects by up to 35.			
70	Grasp of the Dead	Bind on Pickup	106
PROPERTIES: Increases damage done by Frost spells and effects by up to 41.			
70	Anger-Spark Gloves	Bind on Pickup	111
PROPERTIES: Increases damage and healing done by magical spells and effects by up to 26.			
70	Infernoweave Gloves	Bind on Pickup	101
PROPERTIES: Fire Resistance Resistance +40			
	Sorcerer's Gloves	Bind on Pickup	61
PROPERTIES: Increases damage and healing done by magical spells and effects by up to 12, Increases your spell hit rating by 8.			
	Deathmist Wraps	Bind on Pickup	61
PROPERTIES: Increases damage and healing done by magical spells and effects by up to 13. Increases your spell hit rating by 8.			
	Virtuous Gloves	Bind on Pickup	61
PROPERTIES: Increases damage and healing done by magical spells and effects by up to 11.			

Superior Cloth Hands

Level	Name	Binding Info	Armor
15	Magefist Gloves	Bind on Equip	23
27	Hotshot Pilot's Gloves	Bind on Equip	31
29	Gloves of Old	Bind on Equip	32
40	Dreamweave Gloves	Bind on Equip	41
PROPERTIES: Increases damage and healing done by magical spells and effects by up to 18.			
42	Jumanza Grips	Bind on Pickup	42
47	Atal'ai Gloves	Bind on Pickup	47
PROPERTIES: Increases damage and healing done by magical spells and effects by up to 9.			
49	Silkweb Gloves	Bind on Pickup	48
PROPERTIES: Restores 3 mana per 5 sec.			

Superior Cloth Hands

Level	Name	Binding Info	Armor
50	Gloves of the Atal'ai Prophet	Bind on Pickup	49
52	Demonskin Gloves	Bind on Pickup	51
52	Mana Shaping Handwraps	Bind on Pickup	51
PROPERTIES: Increases damage and healing done by magical spells and effects by up to 16.			
54	Hands of the Exalted Herald	Bind on Pickup	52
PROPERTIES: Increases healing done by spells and effects by up to 33.			
54	Magister's Gloves	Bind on Equip	52
54	Devout Gloves	Bind on Equip	52
54	Dreadmist Wraps	Bind on Equip	52
55	Hands of Power	Bind on Pickup	53
PROPERTIES: Increases damage and healing done by magical spells and effects by up to 26.			
55	Brightspark Gloves	Bind on Pickup	53
PROPERTIES: Increases your spell critical strike rating by 14.			
55	Shadowy Laced Handwraps	Bind on Pickup	53
PROPERTIES: Restores 5 mana per 5 sec. Shadow Resistance Resistance +12			
56	Ironweave Gloves	Bind on Pickup	54
57	Darkshade Gloves	Bind on Pickup	55
PROPERTIES: Shadow Resistance Resistance +10, Arcane Resistance Resistance +15			
57	Felcloth Gloves	Bind on Equip	55
PROPERTIES: Increases damage done by Shadow spells and effects by up to 33.			
57	Inferno Gloves	Bind on Equip	55
PROPERTIES: Increases damage done by Fire spells and effects by up to 33.			
57	Mooncloth Gloves	Bind on Equip	55
57	Shivery Handwraps	Bind on Pickup	55
PROPERTIES: Increases damage done by Frost spells and effects by up to 17.			
57	The Shadow's Grasp	Bind on Pickup	55
PROPERTIES: Increases damage done by Shadow spells and effects by up to 20.			
58	Knight-Lieutenant's Silk Gloves	Bind on Pickup	56
PROPERTIES: Increases the damage absorbed by your Mana Shield by 285, Increases damage and healing done by magical spells and effects by up to 21.			
58	Blood Guard's Silk Gloves	Bind on Pickup	56
PROPERTIES: Increases the damage absorbed by your Mana Shield by 285, Increases damage and healing done by magical spells and effects by up to 21.			
58	Knight-Lieutenant's Dreadweave Gloves	Bind on Pickup	56
PROPERTIES: Gives you a 50% chance to avoid interruption caused by damage while casting Searing Pain.			
58	Blood Guard's Dreadweave Gloves	Bind on Pickup	56
PROPERTIES: Gives you a 50% chance to avoid interruption caused by damage while casting Searing Pain, Increases damage and healing done by magical spells and effects by up to 21.			
58	Knight-Lieutenant's Satin Gloves	Bind on Pickup	56
PROPERTIES: Gives you a 50% chance to avoid interruption caused by damage while casting Mind Blast, Increases damage and healing done by magical spells and effects by up to 21.			
58	Blood Guard's Satin Gloves	Bind on Pickup	56
PROPERTIES: Gives you a 50% chance to avoid interruption caused by damage while casting Mind Blast, Increases damage and healing done by magical spells and effects by up to 21.			
60	Bloodtinged Gloves	Bind on Pickup	62
PROPERTIES: Increases damage and healing done by magical spells and effects by up to 19, Increases your spell hit rating by 8.			
60	Blood Guard's Dreadweave Handwraps	Bind on Pickup	58
PROPERTIES: Gives you a 50% chance to avoid interruption caused by damage while casting Searing Pain, Increases damage and healing done by magical spells and effects by up to 21.			
60	Blood Guard's Satin Handwraps	Bind on Pickup	58
PROPERTIES: Gives you a 50% chance to avoid interruption caused by damage while casting Mind Blast, Increases damage and healing done by magical spells and effects by up to 21.			

Superior Cloth Hands

Level	Name	Binding Info	Armor
60	Blood Guard's Silk Handwraps	Bind on Pickup	58
PROPERTIES: Increases the damage absorbed by your Mana Shield by 285, Increases damage and healing done by magical spells and effects by up to 18,			
60	Knight-Lieutenant's Dreadweave Handwraps	Bind on Pickup	58
PROPERTIES: Gives you a 50% chance to avoid interruption caused by damage while casting Searing Pain, Increases damage and healing done by magical spells and effects by up to 21.			
60	Knight-Lieutenant's Satin Handwraps	Bind on Pickup	58
PROPERTIES: Gives you a 50% chance to avoid interruption caused by damage while casting Mind Blast, Increases damage and healing done by magical spells and effects by up to 21.			
60	Knight-Lieutenant's Silk Handwraps	Bind on Pickup	58
PROPERTIES: Increases the damage absorbed by your Mana Shield by 285, Increases damage and healing done by magical spells and effects by up to 18.			
61	Bloody Surgeon's Mitts	Bind on Pickup	76
PROPERTIES: Increases healing done by spells and effects by up to 31.			
63	Manaspark Gloves	Bind on Pickup	81
PROPERTIES: Increases damage and healing done by magical spells and effects by up to 16.			
68	Gloves of the Deadwatcher	Bind on Pickup	95
PROPERTIES: Increases damage and healing done by magical spells and effects by up to 29.			
68	Hands of the Sun	Bind on Pickup	95
PROPERTIES: Increases damage done by Fire spells and effects by up to 34.			
68	Jaedenfire Gloves of Annihilation	Bind on Pickup	95
PROPERTIES: Increases damage done by Shadow spells and effects by up to 39.			
68	Prismatic Mittens of Mending	Bind on Pickup	95
PROPERTIES: Increases healing done by spells and effects by up to 55, Restores 7 mana per 5 sec.			
68	Energis Armwraps	Bind on Pickup	95
PROPERTIES: Increases damage and healing done by magical spells and effects by up to 34.			
70	Mana-Etched Gloves	Bind on Pickup	97
PROPERTIES: Increases damage and healing done by magical spells and effects by up to 20.			
70	Incanter's Gloves	Bind on Pickup	97
PROPERTIES: Increases damage and healing done by magical spells and effects by up to 29.			
70	Hallowed Handwraps	Bind on Pickup	97
PROPERTIES: Increases healing done by spells and effects by up to 51.			
70	Gloves of Oblivion	Bind on Pickup	97
PROPERTIES: Increases damage and healing done by magical spells and effects by up to 26.			
70	Grand Marshal's Dreadweave Gloves	Bind on Pickup	97
PROPERTIES: Gives you a 50% chance to avoid interruption caused by damage while casting Fear, Increases damage and healing done by magical spells and effects by up to 26.			
70	Grand Marshal's Satin Gloves	Bind on Pickup	97
PROPERTIES: Increases the duration of your Psychic Scream spell by 1 sec, Increases damage and healing done by magical spells and effects by up to 25.			
70	Grand Marshal's Silk Handguards	Bind on Pickup	97
PROPERTIES: Improves the range of your Fire Blast spell by 5 yards, Increases damage and healing done by magical spells and effects by up to 19.			
70	High Warlord's Dreadweave Gloves	Bind on Pickup	97
PROPERTIES: Gives you a 50% chance to avoid interruption caused by damage while casting Fear, Increases damage and healing done by magical spells and effects by up to 26.			
70	High Warlord's Satin Gloves	Bind on Pickup	97
PROPERTIES: Increases the duration of your Psychic Scream spell by 1 sec, Increases damage and healing done by magical spells and effects by up to 25.			
70	High Warlord's Silk Handguards	Bind on Pickup	97
PROPERTIES: Improves the range of your Fire Blast spell by 5 yards, Increases damage and healing done by magical spells and effects by up to 19.			
70	Flameheart Gloves	Bind on Equip	97
PROPERTIES: Fire Resistance Resistance +40			

Superior Cloth Hands

Level	Name	Binding Info	Armor
	Gordok's Handwraps	Bind on Pickup	53
PROPERTIES: Increases your spell critical strike rating by 14.			
	Sandworm Skin Gloves	Bind on Pickup	56
PROPERTIES: Increases damage and healing done by magical spells and effects by up to 27.			
	Desert Bloom Gloves	Bind on Pickup	56
PROPERTIES: Increases healing done by spells and effects by up to 51.			
	Gloves of Undead Cleansing	Bind on Pickup	56
PROPERTIES: Increases damage done to Undead by magical spells and effects by up to 35.			
	Gloves of Penitence	Bind on Pickup	83
PROPERTIES: Increases healing done by spells and effects by up to 46.			
	Tempest's Touch	Bind on Pickup	88
PROPERTIES: Increases damage and healing done by magical spells and effects by up to 27, Increases your spell penetration by 10.			

Epic Cloth Head

Level	Name	Binding Info	Armor
49	Eye of Flame	Bind on Equip	79
PROPERTIES: Increases damage done by Fire spells and effects by up to 43. Fire Resistance Resistance +15			
54	Circle of Flame	Bind on Pickup	85
PROPERTIES: Channels 75 health into mana every 1 sec for 10 sec. Fire Resistance Resistance +15			
60	Field Marshal's Coronet	Bind on Pickup	105
PROPERTIES: Increases your spell critical strike rating by 14, Increases damage and healing done by magical spells and effects by up to 33.			
60	Warlord's Silk Cowl	Bind on Pickup	105
PROPERTIES: Increases your spell critical strike rating by 14, Increases damage and healing done by magical spells and effects by up to 33.			
60	Arcanist Crown	Bind on Pickup	94
PROPERTIES: Increases damage and healing done by magical spells and effects by up to 20. Increases your spell hit rating by 8. Fire Resistance Resistance +10			
60	Felheart Horns	Bind on Pickup	94
PROPERTIES: Increases damage and healing done by magical spells and effects by up to 20. Fire Resistance Resistance +10			
60	Circlet of Prophecy	Bind on Pickup	94
PROPERTIES: Increases damage and healing done by magical spells and effects by up to 12. Fire Resistance Resistance +10			
60	Netherwind Crown	Bind on Pickup	107
PROPERTIES: Restores 4 mana per 5 sec, Increases damage and healing done by magical spells and effects by up to 32. Frost Resistance Resistance +10, Shadow Resistance Resistance +10			
60	Halo of Transcendence	Bind on Pickup	107
PROPERTIES: Increases healing done by spells and effects by up to 48. Fire Resistance Resistance +10, Frost Resistance Resistance +10			
60	Nemesis Skullcap	Bind on Pickup	107
PROPERTIES: Restores 4 health per 5 sec, Increases damage and healing done by magical spells and effects by up to 32. Frost Resistance Resistance +10, Shadow Resistance Resistance +10			
60	Field Marshal's Coronal	Bind on Pickup	105
PROPERTIES: Increases damage and healing done by magical spells and effects by up to 32.			
60	Warlord's Dreadweave Hood	Bind on Pickup	105
PROPERTIES: Increases damage and healing done by magical spells and effects by up to 32.			
60	Field Marshal's Headdress	Bind on Pickup	105
PROPERTIES: Increases damage and healing done by magical spells and effects by up to 33, Restores 4 mana per 5 sec.			
60	Warlord's Satin Cowl	Bind on Pickup	105
PROPERTIES: Increases damage and healing done by magical spells and effects by up to 33, Restores 4 mana per 5 sec.			

Epic Cloth Head

Level	Name	Binding Info	Armor
60	Crystal Adorned Crown	Bind on Pickup	97
PROPERTIES: Increases healing done by spells and effects by up to 92.			
60	Mish'undare, Circlet of the Mind Flayer	Bind on Pickup	117
PROPERTIES: Increases damage and healing done by magical spells and effects by up to 35, Increases your spell critical strike rating by 28.			
60	Doomcaller's Circlet	Bind on Pickup	114
PROPERTIES: Increases damage and healing done by magical spells and effects by up to 33, Increases your spell critical strike rating by 14, Increases your spell hit rating by 8.			
60	Enigma Circlet	Bind on Pickup	114
PROPERTIES: Increases damage and healing done by magical spells and effects by up to 33, Increases your spell critical strike rating by 14, Increases your spell hit rating by 8.			
60	Tiara of the Oracle	Bind on Pickup	114
PROPERTIES: Increases damage and healing done by magical spells and effects by up to 28, Restores 7 mana per 5 sec, Increases your spell hit rating by 8.			
60	Dustwind Turban	Bind on Pickup	98
PROPERTIES: Increases healing done by spells and effects by up to 31, Increases your spell critical strike rating by 14.			
60	Gnomish Turban of Psychic Might	Bind on Pickup	106
PROPERTIES: Restores 9 mana per 5 sec, Increases your resistance to silence effects by 10%.			
60	Don Rigoberto's Lost Hat	Bind on Pickup	114
PROPERTIES: Increases healing done by spells and effects by up to 64, Restores 11 mana per 5 sec.			
60	Frostfire Circlet	Bind on Pickup	123
PROPERTIES: Increases damage and healing done by magical spells and effects by up to 35, Increases your spell hit rating by 8, Increases your spell critical strike rating by 28.			
60	Plagueheart Circlet	Bind on Pickup	123
PROPERTIES: Increases damage and healing done by magical spells and effects by up to 33, Increases your spell critical strike rating by 28, Increases your spell hit rating by 8.			
60	Circlet of Faith	Bind on Pickup	123
PROPERTIES: Increases healing done by spells and effects by up to 75, Restores 5 mana per 5 sec.			
60	Glacial Headdress	Bind on Pickup	117
PROPERTIES: Increases damage and healing done by magical spells and effects by up to 18. Frost Resistance Resistance +40			
60	Preceptor's Hat	Bind on Pickup	117
PROPERTIES: Increases damage and healing done by magical spells and effects by up to 51.			
70	Whitemend Hood	Bind on Equip	138
PROPERTIES: Increases healing done by spells and effects by up to 79, Restores 11 mana per 5 sec.			
70	Old Spellstrike Hood	Bind on Pickup	145
70	Spellstrike Hood	Bind on Equip	145
PROPERTIES: Increases damage and healing done by magical spells and effects by up to 42.			
70	Battlecast Hood	Bind on Equip	138
PROPERTIES: Increases damage and healing done by magical spells and effects by up to 41.			
70	Gladiator's Dreadweave Hood	Bind on Pickup	151
PROPERTIES: Increases damage and healing done by magical spells and effects by up to 19.			
70	Gladiator's Silk Cowl	Bind on Pickup	151
PROPERTIES: Increases damage and healing done by magical spells and effects by up to 26.			
70	Gladiator's Satin Hood	Bind on Pickup	151
PROPERTIES: Increases damage and healing done by magical spells and effects by up to 19.			
70	Wicked Witch's Hat	Bind on Pickup	138
PROPERTIES: Increases damage and healing done by magical spells and effects by up to 39.			
70	Uni-mind Headdress	Bind on Pickup	138
PROPERTIES: Increases damage and healing done by magical spells and effects by up to 41.			
70	Headdress of the High Potentate	Bind on Pickup	138
PROPERTIES: Increases healing done by spells and effects by up to 73.			

Epic Cloth Head

Level	Name	Binding Info	Armor
70	Collar of Cho'gall	Bind on Pickup	151
PROPERTIES: Increases damage and healing done by magical spells and effects by up to 62.			
70	Voidheart Crown	Bind on Pickup	145
PROPERTIES: Increases damage and healing done by magical spells and effects by up to 34.			
70	Light-Collar of the Incarnate	Bind on Pickup	145
PROPERTIES: Increases healing done by spells and effects by up to 64, Restores 5 mana per 5 sec.			
70	Soul-Collar of the Incarnate	Bind on Pickup	145
PROPERTIES: Increases damage and healing done by magical spells and effects by up to 34.			
70	Collar of the Aldor	Bind on Pickup	145
PROPERTIES: Increases damage and healing done by magical spells and effects by up to 36.			
70	Nether Runner's Cowl	Bind on Pickup	132
70	Collar of the Grand Engineer	Bind on Pickup	158
PROPERTIES: Increases damage and healing done by magical spells and effects by up to 41.			
70	Crown of the Sun	Bind on Pickup	171
PROPERTIES: Increases healing done by spells and effects by up to 79.			
70	Cowl of the Avatar	Bind on Pickup	164
PROPERTIES: Increases healing done by spells and effects by up to 62.			
70	Hood of the Avatar	Bind on Pickup	164
PROPERTIES: Increases damage and healing done by magical spells and effects by up to 40.			
70	Gladiator's Felweave Cowl	Bind on Pickup	151
PROPERTIES: Increases damage and healing done by magical spells and effects by up to 26.			
70	Cowl of Tirisfal	Bind on Pickup	164
PROPERTIES: Increases damage and healing done by magical spells and effects by up to 40.			
70	Hood of the Corruptor	Bind on Pickup	164
PROPERTIES: Increases damage and healing done by magical spells and effects by up to 47.			
	Cap of the Scarlet Savant	Bind on Pickup	89
PROPERTIES: Increases your spell critical strike rating by 28.			
	Sorcerer's Crown	Bind on Pickup	86
PROPERTIES: Increases damage and healing done by magical spells and effects by up to 11, Increases your spell critical strike rating by 14.			
	Deathmist Mask	Bind on Pickup	86
PROPERTIES: Increases damage and healing done by magical spells and effects by up to 16, Increases your spell hit rating by 8.			
	Virtuous Crown	Bind on Pickup	86
PROPERTIES: Increases damage and healing done by magical spells and effects by up to 11, Restores 6 mana per 5 sec, Increases your spell critical strike rating by 14.			
	Gnomish Power Goggles	Bind on Pickup	132
PROPERTIES: Increases damage and healing done by magical spells and effects by up to 59, Increases your spell critical strike rating by 28.			
	Foreman's Enchanted Helmet	Bind on Pickup	132
PROPERTIES: Increases your chance to resist Silence and Interrupt effects by 10%.			

Superior Cloth Head

Level	Name	Binding Info	Armor
27	Holy Shroud	Bind on Equip	40
PROPERTIES: Increases healing done by spells and effects by up to 33.			
30	Embalmed Shroud	Bind on Pickup	42
32	Electromagnetic Gigaflux Reactivator	Bind on Pickup	44
PROPERTIES: Channels a bolt of lightning and hurls it towards all enemies in front of the caster causing 147 to 167 Nature damage. The caster is then surrounded by a barrier of electricity for 10 min.			
35	Corpseshroud	Bind on Equip	47

Superior Cloth Head

Level	Name	Binding Info	Armor
38	Papal Fez	Bind on Equip	51
PROPERTIES: Increases healing done by spells and effects by up to 22.			
39	Whitemane's Chapeau	Bind on Pickup	52
39	Miner's Hat of the Deep	Bind on Equip	52
42	Cassandra's Grace	Bind on Equip	55
PROPERTIES: Increases healing done by spells and effects by up to 44.			
44	Bad Mojo Mask	Bind on Pickup	57
PROPERTIES: Increases damage done by Shadow spells and effects by up to 14.			
45	Dreamweave Circlet	Bind on Equip	58
PROPERTIES: Increases damage and healing done by magical spells and effects by up to 21.			
46	Soulcatcher Halo	Bind on Equip	59
49	Eye of Theradras	Bind on Pickup	63
50	Chief Architect's Monocle	Bind on Pickup	64
54	Crimson Felt Hat	Bind on Pickup	68
PROPERTIES: Increases damage and healing done by magical spells and effects by up to 30.			
55	Starfire Tiara	Bind on Pickup	69
PROPERTIES: Fire Resistance Resistance +10			
55	Dragonskin Cowl	Bind on Pickup	69
PROPERTIES: Increases damage and healing done by magical spells and effects by up to 18.			
56	The Postmaster's Band	Bind on Pickup	70
PROPERTIES: Increases damage and healing done by magical spells and effects by up to 14.			
57	Mooncloth Circlet	Bind on Equip	71
57	Magister's Crown	Bind on Pickup	71
57	Devout Crown	Bind on Pickup	71
57	Dreadmist Mask	Bind on Pickup	71
58	Lieutenant Commander's Crown	Bind on Pickup	73
PROPERTIES: Increases your spell critical strike rating by 14.			
58	Champion's Silk Hood	Bind on Pickup	73
PROPERTIES: Increases your spell critical strike rating by 14.			
58	Lieutenant Commander's Headguard	Bind on Pickup	73
PROPERTIES: Increases damage and healing done by magical spells and effects by up to 16.			
58	Champion's Dreadweave Hood	Bind on Pickup	73
PROPERTIES: Increases damage and healing done by magical spells and effects by up to 16.			
58	Lieutenant Commander's Diadem	Bind on Pickup	73
PROPERTIES: Increases damage and healing done by magical spells and effects by up to 16.			
58	Champion's Satin Cowl	Bind on Pickup	73
PROPERTIES: Increases damage and healing done by magical spells and effects by up to 16.			
58	Crown of the Ogre King	Bind on Pickup	73
PROPERTIES: Increases your spell critical strike rating by 14.			
58	Frost Runed Headdress	Bind on Pickup	73
PROPERTIES: Increases damage done by Frost spells and effects by up to 41.			
58	Fire Crown	Bind on Pickup	73
PROPERTIES: Increases damage done by Fire spells and effects by up to 20.			
58	Shadow Crown	Bind on Pickup	73
PROPERTIES: Increases damage done by Shadow spells and effects by up to 20.			
58	Ironweave Cowl	Bind on Pickup	73
60	The Hexxer's Cover	Bind on Pickup	81
PROPERTIES: Increases damage and healing done by magical spells and effects by up to 41.			
60	Bloodvine Goggles	Bind on Equip	75
PROPERTIES: Increases your spell hit rating by 16, Increases your spell critical strike rating by 14, Restores 9 mana per 5 sec.			

Superior Cloth Head

Level	Name	Binding Info	Armor
60	Spellweaver's Turban	Bind on Pickup	73
PROPERTIES: Increases damage and healing done by magical spells and effects by up to 36, Increases your spell hit rating by 8.			
60	Zulian Headdress	Bind on Pickup	78
PROPERTIES: Increases healing done by spells and effects by up to 55.			
60	Sylvan Crown	Bind on Equip	80
PROPERTIES: Increases damage and healing done by magical spells and effects by up to 18. Nature Resistance Resistance +30			
60	Champion's Dreadweave Cowl	Bind on Pickup	81
PROPERTIES: Increases damage and healing done by magical spells and effects by up to 21, Increases your spell critical strike rating by 14.			
60	Champion's Satin Hood	Bind on Pickup	81
PROPERTIES: Increases damage and healing done by magical spells and effects by up to 21, Restores 6 mana per 5 sec.			
60	Champion's Silk Cowl	Bind on Pickup	81
PROPERTIES: Increases your spell critical strike rating by 14, Increases damage and healing done by magical spells and effects by up to 21.			
60	Lieutenant Commander's Dreadweave Cowl	Bind on Pickup	81
PROPERTIES: Increases damage and healing done by magical spells and effects by up to 21, Increases your spell critical strike rating by 14.			
60	Lieutenant Commander's Satin Hood	Bind on Pickup	81
PROPERTIES: Increases damage and healing done by magical spells and effects by up to 21, Restores 6 mana per 5 sec.			
60	Lieutenant Commander's Silk Cowl	Bind on Pickup	81
PROPERTIES: Increases your spell critical strike rating by 14, Increases damage and healing done by magical spells and effects by up to 21.			
65	Deadwatcher Headdress	Bind on Pickup	111
PROPERTIES: Increases healing done by spells and effects by up to 66.			
66	Exorcist's Dreadweave Hood	Bind on Pickup	111
PROPERTIES: Increases damage and healing done by magical spells and effects by up to 29.			
66	Exorcist's Silk Hood	Bind on Pickup	111
PROPERTIES: Increases damage and healing done by magical spells and effects by up to 29.			
68	Embroidered Hood of Abjuration	Bind on Pickup	124
PROPERTIES: Increases damage and healing done by magical spells and effects by up to 39.			
68	Helm of the All-Seeing	Bind on Pickup	124
PROPERTIES: Increases healing done by spells and effects by up to 73.			
70	Headdress of Alacrity	Bind on Pickup	127
PROPERTIES: Increases damage and healing done by magical spells and effects by up to 33.			
70	Demonfang Ritual Helm	Bind on Pickup	127
PROPERTIES: Increases damage and healing done by magical spells and effects by up to 36.			
70	Mana-Etched Crown	Bind on Pickup	127
PROPERTIES: Increases your spell penetration by 15, Increases damage and healing done by magical spells and effects by up to 34.			
70	Incanter's Cowl	Bind on Pickup	127
PROPERTIES: Increases damage and healing done by magical spells and effects by up to 29.			
70	Hallowed Crown	Bind on Pickup	127
PROPERTIES: Increases healing done by spells and effects by up to 57.			
70	Hood of Oblivion	Bind on Pickup	127
PROPERTIES: Increases damage and healing done by magical spells and effects by up to 40.			
70	Grand Marshal's Dreadweave Hood	Bind on Pickup	127
PROPERTIES: Increases damage and healing done by magical spells and effects by up to 29.			
70	Grand Marshal's Satin Hood	Bind on Pickup	127
PROPERTIES: Increases damage and healing done by magical spells and effects by up to 18.			
70	Grand Marshal's Silk Cowl	Bind on Pickup	127
PROPERTIES: Increases damage and healing done by magical spells and effects by up to 23.			

Superior Cloth Head

Level	Name	Binding Info	Armor
70	High Warlord's Dreadweave Hood	Bind on Pickup	127
PROPERTIES: Increases damage and healing done by magical spells and effects by up to 29.			
70	High Warlord's Satin Hood	Bind on Pickup	127
PROPERTIES: Increases damage and healing done by magical spells and effects by up to 18.			
70	High Warlord's Silk Cowl	Bind on Pickup	127
PROPERTIES: Increases damage and healing done by magical spells and effects by up to 23.			
70	Watcher's Cowl	Bind on Pickup	127
PROPERTIES: Increases healing done by spells and effects by up to 79.			
	Green Lens	Bind on Equip	57
	Gemburst Circlet	Bind on Pickup	63
	Crown of Caer Darrow	Bind on Pickup	73
PROPERTIES: Frost Resistance Resistance +15			
	Power Amplification Goggles	Bind on Equip	100
PROPERTIES: Increases damage and healing done by magical spells and effects by up to 36.			
	Ultra-Spectropic Detection Goggles	Bind on Equip	124
PROPERTIES: Allows detection of objects that are slightly out of phase such as the arcane vortexes of netherstorm, Allows you to look far into the distance.			
	Mag'hari Ritualist's Horns	Bind on Pickup	114
PROPERTIES: Increases damage and healing done by magical spells and effects by up to 50.			
	Hydromancer's Headwrap	Bind on Pickup	127
PROPERTIES: Increases damage and healing done by magical spells and effects by up to 33.			

Epic Cloth Legs

Level	Name	Binding Info	Armor
58	Manastorm Leggings	Bind on Pickup	97
PROPERTIES: Restores 14 mana per 5 sec.			
60	Marshal's Silk Leggings	Bind on Pickup	109
PROPERTIES: Increases damage and healing done by magical spells and effects by up to 30, Increases your spell critical strike rating by 14.			
60	General's Silk Trousers	Bind on Pickup	109
PROPERTIES: Increases damage and healing done by magical spells and effects by up to 30, Increases your spell critical strike rating by 14.			
60	Arcanist Leggings	Bind on Pickup	101
PROPERTIES: Increases your spell critical strike rating by 14, Increases damage and healing done by magical spells and effects by up to 20. Shadow Resistance Resistance +10			
60	Felheart Pants	Bind on Pickup	101
PROPERTIES: Increases damage and healing done by magical spells and effects by up to 30. Shadow Resistance Resistance +10			
60	Pants of Prophecy	Bind on Pickup	101
PROPERTIES: Restores 6 mana per 5 sec, Increases healing done by spells and effects by up to 22. Shadow Resistance Resistance +10			
60	Netherwind Pants	Bind on Pickup	116
PROPERTIES: Increases damage and healing done by magical spells and effects by up to 30, Increases your spell critical strike rating by 14. Fire Resistance Resistance +10, Arcane Resistance Resistance +10			
60	Leggings of Transcendence	Bind on Pickup	116
PROPERTIES: Increases healing done by spells and effects by up to 46, Restores 7 mana per 5 sec. Shadow Resistance Resistance +10, Arcane Resistance Resistance +10			
60	Nemesis Leggings	Bind on Pickup	116
PROPERTIES: Increases damage and healing done by magical spells and effects by up to 39. Fire Resistance Resistance +10, Arcane Resistance Resistance +10			
60	Marshal's Dreadweave Leggings	Bind on Pickup	109
PROPERTIES: Increases damage and healing done by magical spells and effects by up to 37.			
60	General's Dreadweave Pants	Bind on Pickup	109
PROPERTIES: Increases damage and healing done by magical spells and effects by up to 37.			

Epic Cloth Legs

Level	Name	Binding Info	Armor
60	Marshal's Satin Pants	Bind on Pickup	109
PROPERTIES: Increases damage and healing done by magical spells and effects by up to 32, Restores 4 mana per 5 sec.			
60	General's Satin Leggings	Bind on Pickup	109
PROPERTIES: Increases damage and healing done by magical spells and effects by up to 32, Restores 4 mana per 5 sec.			
60	Leggings of Arcane Supremacy	Bind on Pickup	106
PROPERTIES: Increases damage done by Arcane spells and effects by up to 36. Frost Resistance Resistance +10, Arcane Resistance Resistance +10			
60	Fel Infused Leggings	Bind on Pickup	109
PROPERTIES: Increases damage done by Shadow spells and effects by up to 64.			
60	Flarecore Leggings	Bind on Equip	107
PROPERTIES: Increases damage and healing done by magical spells and effects by up to 43. Fire Resistance Resistance +16			
60	Empowered Leggings	Bind on Pickup	117
PROPERTIES: Increases healing done by spells and effects by up to 77, Increases your spell critical strike rating by 14.			
60	Doomcaller's Trousers	Bind on Pickup	123
PROPERTIES: Increases damage and healing done by magical spells and effects by up to 34, Increases your spell critical strike rating by 14.			
60	Enigma Leggings	Bind on Pickup	123
PROPERTIES: Increases damage and healing done by magical spells and effects by up to 34, Increases your spell critical strike rating by 14, Restores 5 mana per 5 sec.			
60	Trousers of the Oracle	Bind on Pickup	123
PROPERTIES: Increases damage and healing done by magical spells and effects by up to 33, Restores 6 mana per 5 sec.			
60	Leggings of the Black Blizzard	Bind on Pickup	110
PROPERTIES: Increases damage and healing done by magical spells and effects by up to 41, Increases your spell critical strike rating by 14.			
60	Leggings of the Festering Swarm	Bind on Pickup	116
PROPERTIES: Increases damage done by Fire spells and effects by up to 57.			
60	Frostfire Leggings	Bind on Pickup	133
PROPERTIES: Increases your spell hit rating by 8, Increases damage and healing done by magical spells and effects by up to 46.			
60	Plagueheart Leggings	Bind on Pickup	133
PROPERTIES: Increases your spell critical strike rating by 14, Increases damage and healing done by magical spells and effects by up to 37, Increases your spell penetration by 10.			
60	Leggings of Faith	Bind on Pickup	133
PROPERTIES: Increases healing done by spells and effects by up to 66.			
60	Outrider's Silk Leggings	Bind on Pickup	100
PROPERTIES: Increases damage and healing done by magical spells and effects by up to 28.			
60	Sentinel's Silk Leggings	Bind on Pickup	100
PROPERTIES: Increases damage and healing done by magical spells and effects by up to 28.			
60	Leggings of Polarity	Bind on Pickup	128
PROPERTIES: Increases damage and healing done by magical spells and effects by up to 44, Increases your spell critical strike rating by 28.			
70	Whitemend Pants	Bind on Equip	149
PROPERTIES: Increases healing done by spells and effects by up to 62, Restores 11 mana per 5 sec.			
70	Spellstrike Pants	Bind on Equip	149
PROPERTIES: Increases damage and healing done by magical spells and effects by up to 33.			
70	Battlecast Pants	Bind on Equip	149
PROPERTIES: Increases damage and healing done by magical spells and effects by up to 43.			
70	Gladiator's Dreadweave Leggings	Bind on Pickup	163
PROPERTIES: Increases damage and healing done by magical spells and effects by up to 42.			
70	Gladiator's Silk Trousers	Bind on Pickup	163
PROPERTIES: Increases damage and healing done by magical spells and effects by up to 37.			

Epic Cloth Legs

Level	Name	Binding Info	Armor
70	Gladiator's Satin Leggings	Bind on Pickup	163
PROPERTIES: Increases damage and healing done by magical spells and effects by up to 42.			
70	Trial-Fire Trousers	Bind on Pickup	149
PROPERTIES: Increases damage and healing done by magical spells and effects by up to 42.			
70	Pantaloons of Repentance	Bind on Pickup	149
PROPERTIES: Increases healing done by spells and effects by up to 59.			
70	Voidheart Leggings	Bind on Pickup	125
PROPERTIES: Increases damage and healing done by magical spells and effects by up to 43.			
70	Trousers of the Incarnate	Bind on Pickup	156
PROPERTIES: Increases healing done by spells and effects by up to 77.			
70	Leggings of the Incarnate	Bind on Pickup	156
PROPERTIES: Increases damage and healing done by magical spells and effects by up to 39.			
70	Legwraps of the Aldor	Bind on Pickup	156
PROPERTIES: Increases damage and healing done by magical spells and effects by up to 43.			
70	Trousers of the Astromancer	Bind on Pickup	170
PROPERTIES: Increases damage and healing done by magical spells and effects by up to 35.			
70	Star-soul Breeches	Bind on Pickup	170
PROPERTIES: Increases healing done by spells and effects by up to 66.			
70	Breeches of the Avatar	Bind on Pickup	177
PROPERTIES: Increases healing done by spells and effects by up to 73, Restores 10 mana per 5 sec.			
70	Leggings of the Avatar	Bind on Pickup	177
PROPERTIES: Increases damage and healing done by magical spells and effects by up to 39.			
70	Gladiator's Felweave Trousers	Bind on Pickup	163
PROPERTIES: Increases damage and healing done by magical spells and effects by up to 37.			
70	Leggings of Tirisfal	Bind on Pickup	177
PROPERTIES: Increases damage and healing done by magical spells and effects by up to 43.			
70	Leggings of the Corruptor	Bind on Pickup	177
PROPERTIES: Increases damage and healing done by magical spells and effects by up to 47, Increases your spell penetration by 13.			
70	Breeches of the Occultist	Bind on Pickup	142
PROPERTIES: Increases damage and healing done by magical spells and effects by up to 35.			
70	Kirin Tor Master's Trousers	Bind on Pickup	142
PROPERTIES: Increases damage and healing done by magical spells and effects by up to 32.			
70	Hallowed Trousers	Bind on Pickup	142
PROPERTIES: Increases healing done by spells and effects by up to 59.			
70	Pontifex Leggings	Bind on Pickup	142
PROPERTIES: Increases healing done by spells and effects by up to 59.			
70	Leggings of the Seventh Circle	Bind on Pickup	156
PROPERTIES: Increases healing done by spells and effects by up to 101, Restores 11 mana per 5 sec.			
70	Gilded Trousers of Benediction	Bind on Pickup	156
PROPERTIES: Increases damage and healing done by magical spells and effects by up to 44.			
70	Infernoweave Leggings	Bind on Pickup	142
PROPERTIES: Fire Resistance Resistance +55			
	Glacial Leggings	Bind on Pickup	121
PROPERTIES: Increases damage and healing done by magical spells and effects by up to 18. Frost Resistance Resistance +40			

Superior Cloth Legs

Level	Name	Binding Info	Armor
17	Darkweave Breeches	Bind on Equip	35
20	Abomination Skin Leggings	Bind on Pickup	37
PROPERTIES: Increases damage and healing done by magical spells and effects by up to 9.			
26	Leech Pants	Bind on Pickup	42
30	Necromancer Leggings	Bind on Equip	45
PROPERTIES: Increases damage done by Shadow spells and effects by up to 10.			
30	Blighted Leggings	Bind on Pickup	45
PROPERTIES: Increases damage done by Shadow spells and effects by up to 10.			
35	Stoneweaver Leggings	Bind on Pickup	51
45	Spellshock Leggings	Bind on Equip	63
PROPERTIES: Increases damage and healing done by magical spells and effects by up to 23.			
47	Dalewind Trousers	Bind on Equip	65
50	Kilt of the Atal'ai Prophet	Bind on Pickup	69
50	Senior Designer's Pantaloons	Bind on Pickup	69
PROPERTIES: Increases healing done by spells and effects by up to 40.			
52	Haunting Specter Leggings	Bind on Pickup	71
52	Sacred Cloth Leggings	Bind on Equip	71
PROPERTIES: Increases damage and healing done by magical spells and effects by up to 14.			
53	Mooncloth Leggings	Bind on Equip	72
55	Skyshroud Leggings	Bind on Pickup	75
PROPERTIES: Increases damage and healing done by magical spells and effects by up to 34.			
56	Wolfshear Leggings	Bind on Pickup	76
PROPERTIES: Increases healing done by spells and effects by up to 26. Nature Resistance Resistance +10			
56	The Postmaster's Trousers	Bind on Pickup	76
56	Skullsmoke Pants	Bind on Pickup	76
PROPERTIES: Fire Resistance Resistance +10, Shadow Resistance Resistance +5			
56	Necropile Leggings	Bind on Pickup	76
56	Magister's Leggings	Bind on Pickup	76
56	Devout Skirt	Bind on Pickup	76
56	Dreadmist Leggings	Bind on Pickup	76
56	Padre's Trousers	Bind on Pickup	76
PROPERTIES: Restores 6 mana per 5 sec, Increases healing done by spells and effects by up to 42.			
57	Abyssal Cloth Pants	Bind on Equip	77
PROPERTIES: Increases your spell critical strike rating by 14.			
57	Ironweave Pants	Bind on Pickup	77
58	Spiritshroud Leggings	Bind on Pickup	78
PROPERTIES: Increases damage and healing done by magical spells and effects by up to 19.			
58	Knight-Captain's Silk Leggings	Bind on Pickup	78
PROPERTIES: Increases damage and healing done by magical spells and effects by up to 19.			
58	Legionnaire's Silk Pants	Bind on Pickup	78
PROPERTIES: Increases damage and healing done by magical spells and effects by up to 19.			
58	Knight-Captain's Dreadweave Leggings	Bind on Pickup	78
PROPERTIES: Increases damage and healing done by magical spells and effects by up to 16.			
58	Legionnaire's Dreadweave Leggings	Bind on Pickup	78
PROPERTIES: Increases damage and healing done by magical spells and effects by up to 28.			
58	Knight-Captain's Satin Leggings	Bind on Pickup	78
PROPERTIES: Increases damage and healing done by magical spells and effects by up to 19.			
58	Legionnaire's Satin Trousers	Bind on Pickup	78
PROPERTIES: Increases damage and healing done by magical spells and effects by up to 19.			
58	Runed Stygian Leggings	Bind on Equip	78
PROPERTIES: Restores 6 mana per 5 sec. Shadow Resistance Resistance +25			

Superior Cloth Legs

Level	Name	Binding Info	Armor
58	Leggings of Torment	Bind on Pickup	78
PROPERTIES: Increases damage done by Shadow spells and effects by up to 34.			
60	Bloodvine Leggings	Bind on Equip	80
PROPERTIES: Increases your spell hit rating by 8, Increases damage and healing done by magical spells and effects by up to 37.			
60	Bloodtinged Kilt	Bind on Pickup	87
PROPERTIES: Increases damage and healing done by magical spells and effects by up to 28.			
60	Ritualistic Legguards	Bind on Pickup	84
PROPERTIES: Increases healing done by spells and effects by up to 37.			
60	Legionnaire's Dreadweave Legguards	Bind on Pickup	84
PROPERTIES: Increases damage and healing done by magical spells and effects by up to 28.			
60	Legionnaire's Satin Legguards	Bind on Pickup	84
PROPERTIES: Increases damage and healing done by magical spells and effects by up to 21, Restores 6 mana per 5 sec.			
60	Legionnaire's Silk Legguards	Bind on Pickup	84
PROPERTIES: Increases damage and healing done by magical spells and effects by up to 21, Increases your spell critical strike rating by 14.			
60	Knight-Captain's Dreadweave Legguards	Bind on Pickup	84
PROPERTIES: Increases damage and healing done by magical spells and effects by up to 28.			
60	Knight-Captain's Satin Legguards	Bind on Pickup	84
PROPERTIES: Increases damage and healing done by magical spells and effects by up to 21, Restores 6 mana per 5 sec.			
60	Knight-Captain's Silk Legguards	Bind on Pickup	84
PROPERTIES: Increases damage and healing done by magical spells and effects by up to 21, Increases your spell critical strike rating by 14.			
60	Lifegiver Britches	Bind on Pickup	103
PROPERTIES: Increases healing done by spells and effects by up to 44.			
62	Skethyl Legwraps	Bind on Pickup	110
PROPERTIES: Increases damage and healing done by magical spells and effects by up to 33.			
66	Stormreaver Apron	Bind on Pickup	123
PROPERTIES: Increases damage and healing done by magical spells and effects by up to 30.			
66	Hierophant's Leggings	Bind on Pickup	119
PROPERTIES: Increases damage and healing done by magical spells and effects by up to 29.			
67	Imbued Netherweave Pants	Bind on Equip	126
PROPERTIES: Increases damage and healing done by magical spells and effects by up to 30, Restores 10 mana per 5 sec.			
67	Lifeblood Leggings	Bind on Equip	126
PROPERTIES: Increases healing done by spells and effects by up to 77, Restores 14 mana per 5 sec.			
68	Trousers of Oblivion	Bind on Pickup	136
PROPERTIES: Increases damage and healing done by magical spells and effects by up to 39.			
68	Khadgar's Kilt of Abjuration	Bind on Pickup	133
PROPERTIES: Increases damage and healing done by magical spells and effects by up to 36.			
68	Aran's Sorceress Slacks	Bind on Pickup	133
PROPERTIES: Increases damage and healing done by magical spells and effects by up to 23.			
68	Pontiff's Pantaloons of Prophecy	Bind on Pickup	133
PROPERTIES: Increases healing done by spells and effects by up to 55.			
68	Devil-Stitched Leggings	Bind on Pickup	133
PROPERTIES: Increases damage and healing done by magical spells and effects by up to 29.			
70	Incanter's Trousers	Bind on Pickup	136
PROPERTIES: Increases damage and healing done by magical spells and effects by up to 42.			
70	Hallowed Trousers	Bind on Pickup	136
PROPERTIES: Increases healing done by spells and effects by up to 73, Restores 7 mana per 5 sec.			

Superior Cloth Legs

Level	Name	Binding Info	Armor
70	Mana-Etched Leggings	Bind on Pickup	136
PROPERTIES: Increases damage and healing done by magical spells and effects by up to 33, Increases your spell penetration by 18.			
70	Grand Marshal's Dreadweave Leggings	Bind on Pickup	136
PROPERTIES: Increases damage and healing done by magical spells and effects by up to 39.			
70	Grand Marshal's Satin Leggings	Bind on Pickup	136
PROPERTIES: Increases damage and healing done by magical spells and effects by up to 36.			
70	Grand Marshal's Silk Trousers	Bind on Pickup	136
PROPERTIES: Increases damage and healing done by magical spells and effects by up to 33.			
70	High Warlord's Dreadweave Leggings	Bind on Pickup	136
PROPERTIES: Increases damage and healing done by magical spells and effects by up to 39.			
70	High Warlord's Satin Leggings	Bind on Pickup	136
PROPERTIES: Increases damage and healing done by magical spells and effects by up to 36.			
70	High Warlord's Silk Trousers	Bind on Pickup	136
PROPERTIES: Increases damage and healing done by magical spells and effects by up to 33.			
70	Pantaloons of Flaming Wrath	Bind on Pickup	136
PROPERTIES: Increases damage and healing done by magical spells and effects by up to 33.			
70	Leggings of the Skettis Exile	Bind on Pickup	136
PROPERTIES: Increases damage and healing done by magical spells and effects by up to 39.			
	Rainstrider Leggings	Bind on Pickup	69
	Cenarion Reservist's Pants	Bind on Pickup	78
PROPERTIES: Increases damage and healing done by magical spells and effects by up to 15. Nature Resistance Resistance +25			
	Cenarion Reservist's Pants	Bind on Pickup	78
PROPERTIES: Increases damage and healing done by magical spells and effects by up to 15. Nature Resistance Resistance +25			
	Cenarion Reservist's Pants	Bind on Pickup	78
PROPERTIES: Increases healing done by spells and effects by up to 29. Nature Resistance Resistance +25			
	Sorcerer's Leggings	Bind on Pickup	81
PROPERTIES: Increases damage and healing done by magical spells and effects by up to 16.			
	Deathmist Leggings	Bind on Pickup	81
PROPERTIES: Increases damage and healing done by magical spells and effects by up to 16.			
	Virtuous Skirt	Bind on Pickup	81
PROPERTIES: Increases damage and healing done by magical spells and effects by up to 16, Restores 6 mana per 5 sec.			
	Deadly Borer Leggings	Bind on Pickup	106
PROPERTIES: Increases damage and healing done by magical spells and effects by up to 27.			
	Haramad's Leg Wraps	Bind on Pickup	116
PROPERTIES: Increases healing done by spells and effects by up to 24, Restores 11 mana per 5 sec.			
	Pants of the Naaru	Bind on Pickup	130
PROPERTIES: Increases healing done by spells and effects by up to 77.			

Epic Cloth Shoulders

Level	Name	Binding Info	Armor
56	Flarecore Mantle	Bind on Equip	81
PROPERTIES: Fire Resistance Resistance +24			
60	Field Marshal's Silk Spaulders	Bind on Pickup	97
PROPERTIES: Increases damage and healing done by magical spells and effects by up to 25, Increases your spell penetration by 10.			
60	Warlord's Silk Amice	Bind on Pickup	97
PROPERTIES: Increases damage and healing done by magical spells and effects by up to 25, Increases your spell penetration by 10.			

Epic Cloth Shoulders

Level	Name	Binding Info	Armor
60	Arcanist Mantle	Bind on Pickup	87
PROPERTIES: Restores 4 mana per 5 sec, Increases damage and healing done by magical spells and effects by up to 14, Shadow Resistance Resistance +7			
60	Felheart Shoulder Pads	Bind on Pickup	87
PROPERTIES: Increases damage and healing done by magical spells and effects by up to 9. Shadow Resistance Resistance +7			
60	Mantle of Prophecy	Bind on Pickup	87
PROPERTIES: Increases damage and healing done by magical spells and effects by up to 9. Shadow Resistance Resistance +7			
60	Netherwind Mantle	Bind on Pickup	99
PROPERTIES: Restores 4 mana per 5 sec, Increases damage and healing done by magical spells and effects by up to 21, Fire Resistance Resistance +10			
60	Pauldrons of Transcendence	Bind on Pickup	99
PROPERTIES: Increases healing done by spells and effects by up to 26. Fire Resistance Resistance +10			
60	Nemesis Spaulders	Bind on Pickup	99
PROPERTIES: Restores 4 health per 5 sec, Increases damage and healing done by magical spells and effects by up to 23, Fire Resistance Resistance +10			
60	Field Marshal's Dreadweave Shoulders	Bind on Pickup	97
PROPERTIES: Increases damage and healing done by magical spells and effects by up to 25.			
60	Warlord's Dreadweave Mantle	Bind on Pickup	97
PROPERTIES: Increases damage and healing done by magical spells and effects by up to 25.			
60	Field Marshal's Satin Mantle	Bind on Pickup	97
PROPERTIES: Increases damage and healing done by magical spells and effects by up to 25.			
60	Warlord's Satin Mantle	Bind on Pickup	97
PROPERTIES: Increases damage and healing done by magical spells and effects by up to 25.			
60	Mantle of the Blackwing Cabal	Bind on Pickup	96
PROPERTIES: Increases damage and healing done by magical spells and effects by up to 34.			
60	Highlander's Epaulets	Bind on Pickup	86
PROPERTIES: Increases damage and healing done by magical spells and effects by up to 12, Restores 4 mana per 5 sec.			
60	Defiler's Epaulets	Bind on Pickup	86
PROPERTIES: Increases damage and healing done by magical spells and effects by up to 12, Restores 4 mana per 5 sec.			
60	Doomcaller's Mantle	Bind on Pickup	102
PROPERTIES: Increases damage and healing done by magical spells and effects by up to 28, Increases your spell penetration by 10, Increases your spell hit rating by 8.			
60	Enigma Shoulderpads	Bind on Pickup	102
PROPERTIES: Increases damage and healing done by magical spells and effects by up to 30, Increases your spell penetration by 10, Restores 4 mana per 5 sec.			
60	Mantle of the Oracle	Bind on Pickup	102
PROPERTIES: Increases damage and healing done by magical spells and effects by up to 20, Restores 3 mana per 5 sec, Increases your spell penetration by 10.			
60	Mantle of Phrenic Power	Bind on Pickup	99
PROPERTIES: Increases damage done by Fire spells and effects by up to 33.			
60	Ternary Mantle	Bind on Pickup	98
PROPERTIES: Increases healing done by spells and effects by up to 44.			
60	Frostfire Shoulderpads	Bind on Pickup	111
PROPERTIES: Increases damage and healing done by magical spells and effects by up to 36.			
60	Plagueheart Shoulderpads	Bind on Pickup	111
PROPERTIES: Increases your spell hit rating by 8, Increases damage and healing done by magical spells and effects by up to 36.			
60	Shoulderpads of Faith	Bind on Pickup	111
PROPERTIES: Increases healing done by spells and effects by up to 51, Restores 3 mana per 5 sec.			

Epic Cloth Shoulders

Level	Name	Binding Info	Armor
60	Rime Covered Mantle	Bind on Pickup	108
PROPERTIES: Increases damage and healing done by magical spells and effects by up to 39, Increases your spell critical strike rating by 14.			
70	Soulcloth Shoulders	Bind on Equip	127
PROPERTIES: Arcane Resistance Resistance +30			
70	Frozen Shadoweave Shoulders	Bind on Pickup	133
PROPERTIES: Increases damage done by Shadow spells and effects by up to 49, Increases damage done by Frost spells and effects by up to 49.			
70	Primal Mooncloth Shoulders	Bind on Pickup	133
PROPERTIES: Increases healing done by spells and effects by up to 88, Restores 6 mana per 5 sec.			
70	Gladiator's Dreadweave Mantle	Bind on Pickup	140
PROPERTIES: Increases damage and healing done by magical spells and effects by up to 28.			
70	Gladiator's Silk Amice	Bind on Pickup	140
PROPERTIES: Increases damage and healing done by magical spells and effects by up to 28.			
70	Gladiator's Satin Mantle	Bind on Pickup	140
PROPERTIES: Increases damage and healing done by magical spells and effects by up to 16.			
70	Pauldrons of the Solace-Giver	Bind on Pickup	127
PROPERTIES: Increases healing done by spells and effects by up to 51, Restores 9 mana per 5 sec.			
70	Mantle of the Mind Flayer	Bind on Pickup	127
PROPERTIES: Increases damage and healing done by magical spells and effects by up to 32, Increases your spell penetration by 20.			
70	Voidheart Mantle	Bind on Pickup	133
PROPERTIES: Increases damage and healing done by magical spells and effects by up to 33.			
70	Light-Mantle of the Incarnate	Bind on Pickup	133
PROPERTIES: Increases healing done by spells and effects by up to 44.			
70	Soul-Mantle of the Incarnate	Bind on Pickup	133
PROPERTIES: Increases damage and healing done by magical spells and effects by up to 26.			
70	Pauldrons of the Aldor	Bind on Pickup	133
PROPERTIES: Increases damage and healing done by magical spells and effects by up to 23.			
70	Mantle of Elven Kings	Bind on Pickup	146
PROPERTIES: Increases damage and healing done by magical spells and effects by up to 34.			
70	Illidari Shoulderpads	Bind on Pickup	146
PROPERTIES: Increases damage and healing done by magical spells and effects by up to 34.			
70	Mantle of the Avatar	Bind on Pickup	152
PROPERTIES: Increases healing done by spells and effects by up to 55, Restores 10 mana per 5 sec.			
70	Wings of the Avatar	Bind on Pickup	152
PROPERTIES: Increases healing done by spells and effects by up to 55.			
70	Gladiator's Felweave Amice	Bind on Pickup	140
PROPERTIES: Increases damage and healing done by magical spells and effects by up to 28.			
70	Mantle of Tirisfal	Bind on Pickup	152
PROPERTIES: Increases damage and healing done by magical spells and effects by up to 35, Increases your spell penetration by 18.			
70	Mantle of the Corruptor	Bind on Pickup	152
PROPERTIES: Increases damage and healing done by magical spells and effects by up to 23.			
	Zandalar Confessor's Mantle	Bind on Pickup	90
PROPERTIES: Increases healing done by spells and effects by up to 22.			
	Zandalar Illusionist's Mantle	Bind on Pickup	81
PROPERTIES: Increases damage and healing done by magical spells and effects by up to 12.			
	Zandalar Demoniac's Mantle	Bind on Pickup	81
PROPERTIES: Increases damage and healing done by magical spells and effects by up to 12.			
	Glacial Mantle	Bind on Pickup	108
PROPERTIES: Increases damage and healing done by magical spells and effects by up to 16. Frost Resistance Resistance +33			

Superior Cloth Shoulders

Level	Name	Binding Info	Armor
20	Magician's Mantle	Bind on Equip	32
PROPERTIES: Increases damage and healing done by magical spells and effects by up to 5.			
22	Slime-encrusted Pads	Bind on Pickup	34
PROPERTIES: Restores 3 health every 4 sec.			
23	Feline Mantle	Bind on Pickup	34
27	Batwing Mantle	Bind on Pickup	37
33	Pads of the Venom Spider	Bind on Equip	41
PROPERTIES: Nature Resistance Resistance +5			
42	Flameseer Mantle	Bind on Pickup	51
PROPERTIES: Increases damage done by Fire spells and effects by up to 14.			
47	Kentic Amice	Bind on Pickup	56
PROPERTIES: Increases damage and healing done by magical spells and effects by up to 14.			
48	Rotgrip Mantle	Bind on Pickup	57
48	Mantle of Lost Hope	Bind on Pickup	57
PROPERTIES: Increases healing done by spells and effects by up to 26, Restores 3 mana per 5 sec.			
51	Elder Wizard's Mantle	Bind on Equip	60
PROPERTIES: Increases damage and healing done by magical spells and effects by up to 11.			
52	Boreal Mantle	Bind on Pickup	61
PROPERTIES: Increases damage done by Frost spells and effects by up to 29.			
55	Soulstealer Mantle	Bind on Pickup	64
55	Magister's Mantle	Bind on Pickup	64
55	Devout Mantle	Bind on Pickup	64
55	Dreadmist Mantle	Bind on Pickup	64
56	Sunderseer Mantle	Bind on Pickup	65
PROPERTIES: Increases damage and healing done by magical spells and effects by up to 8.			
56	Mooncloth Shoulders	Bind on Equip	65
56	Necropile Mantle	Bind on Pickup	65
56	Burial Shawl	Bind on Pickup	65
PROPERTIES: Increases damage and healing done by magical spells and effects by up to 20.			
56	Ironweave Mantle	Bind on Pickup	65
56	Mantle of the Scarlet Crusade	Bind on Pickup	65
PROPERTIES: Increases healing done by spells and effects by up to 20.			
57	Deadwalker Mantle	Bind on Pickup	66
PROPERTIES: Increases damage done by Shadow spells and effects by up to 13.			
57	Diabolic Mantle	Bind on Pickup	66
PROPERTIES: Restores 8 mana per 5 sec.			
58	Lieutenant Commander's Silk Spaulders	Bind on Pickup	67
PROPERTIES: Increases damage and healing done by magical spells and effects by up to 12.			
58	Champion's Silk Shoulderpads	Bind on Pickup	67
PROPERTIES: Increases damage and healing done by magical spells and effects by up to 12.			
58	Lieutenant Commander's Dreadweave Mantle	Bind on Pickup	67
PROPERTIES: Increases damage and healing done by magical spells and effects by up to 12.			
58	Champion's Dreadweave Shoulders	Bind on Pickup	67
PROPERTIES: Increases damage and healing done by magical spells and effects by up to 12.			
58	Lieutenant Commander's Satin Amice	Bind on Pickup	67
PROPERTIES: Increases damage and healing done by magical spells and effects by up to 12.			
58	Champion's Satin Shoulderpads	Bind on Pickup	67
PROPERTIES: Increases damage and healing done by magical spells and effects by up to 12.			
58	Shroud of the Nathrezim	Bind on Pickup	67
PROPERTIES: Increases your spell critical strike rating by 14.			
58	Thuzadin Mantle	Bind on Pickup	67
PROPERTIES: Increases damage and healing done by magical spells and effects by up to 12.			

Superior Cloth Shoulders

Level	Name	Binding Info	Armor
59	Mantle of the Timbermaw	Bind on Equip	68
PROPERTIES: Restores 6 mana per 5 sec.			
59	Argent Shoulders	Bind on Equip	68
PROPERTIES: Shadow Resistance Resistance +5			
60	Abyssal Cloth Amice	Bind on Pickup	72
PROPERTIES: Increases your spell hit rating by 8.			
60	Mantle of Maz'Nadir	Bind on Pickup	78
PROPERTIES: Increases damage and healing done by magical spells and effects by up to 21.			
60	Sylvan Shoulders	Bind on Equip	74
PROPERTIES: Increases damage and healing done by magical spells and effects by up to 7. Nature Resistance Resistance +20			
60	Champion's Dreadweave Spaulders	Bind on Pickup	75
PROPERTIES: Increases damage and healing done by magical spells and effects by up to 12, Increases your spell critical strike rating by 14.			
60	Champion's Satin Mantle	Bind on Pickup	75
PROPERTIES: Increases damage and healing done by magical spells and effects by up to 16, Restores 6 mana per 5 sec.			
60	Champion's Silk Mantle	Bind on Pickup	75
PROPERTIES: Increases damage and healing done by magical spells and effects by up to 15, Increases your spell critical strike rating by 14.			
60	Lieutenant Commander's Dreadweave Spaulders	Bind on Pickup	75
PROPERTIES: Increases damage and healing done by magical spells and effects by up to 12, Increases your spell critical strike rating by 14.			
60	Lieutenant Commander's Satin Mantle	Bind on Pickup	75
PROPERTIES: Increases damage and healing done by magical spells and effects by up to 16, Restores 6 mana per 5 sec.			
60	Lieutenant Commander's Silk Mantle	Bind on Pickup	75
PROPERTIES: Increases damage and healing done by magical spells and effects by up to 15, Increases your spell critical strike rating by 14.			
60	Pauldrons of Arcane Rage	Bind on Pickup	88
PROPERTIES: Increases damage and healing done by magical spells and effects by up to 27.			
66	Pauldrons of Sufferance	Bind on Pickup	105
PROPERTIES: Increases healing done by spells and effects by up to 35.			
68	Shoulderpads of the Intrepid	Bind on Pickup	114
PROPERTIES: Increases damage and healing done by magical spells and effects by up to 34, Increases your spell penetration by 10.			
68	Mantle of Three Terrors	Bind on Pickup	114
PROPERTIES: Increases damage and healing done by magical spells and effects by up to 29.			
68	Vestia's Pauldrons of Inner Grace	Bind on Pickup	114
PROPERTIES: Increases healing done by spells and effects by up to 48, Restores 8 mana per 5 sec.			
68	Mana-Sphere Shoulderguards	Bind on Pickup	114
PROPERTIES: Increases damage and healing done by magical spells and effects by up to 29.			
70	Incanter's Pauldrons	Bind on Pickup	117
PROPERTIES: Increases damage and healing done by magical spells and effects by up to 20.			
70	Hallowed Pauldrons	Bind on Pickup	117
PROPERTIES: Increases healing done by spells and effects by up to 42.			
70	Spaulders of Oblivion	Bind on Pickup	117
PROPERTIES: Increases damage and healing done by magical spells and effects by up to 29.			
70	Mana-Etched Spaulders	Bind on Pickup	117
PROPERTIES: Increases damage and healing done by magical spells and effects by up to 20.			
70	Grand Marshal's Dreadweave Mantle	Bind on Pickup	117
PROPERTIES: Increases damage and healing done by magical spells and effects by up to 26.			
70	Grand Marshal's Satin Mantle	Bind on Pickup	117
PROPERTIES: Increases damage and healing done by magical spells and effects by up to 15.			

Superior Cloth Shoulders

Level	Name	Binding Info	Armor
70	Grand Marshal's Silk Amice	Bind on Pickup	117
PROPERTIES: Increases damage and healing done by magical spells and effects by up to 25.			
70	High Warlord's Dreadweave Mantle	Bind on Pickup	117
PROPERTIES: Increases damage and healing done by magical spells and effects by up to 26.			
70	High Warlord's Satin Mantle	Bind on Pickup	117
PROPERTIES: Increases damage and healing done by magical spells and effects by up to 15.			
70	High Warlord's Silk Amice	Bind on Pickup	117
PROPERTIES: Increases damage and healing done by magical spells and effects by up to 25.			
	Berylline Pads	Bind on Pickup	39
	Durability Shoulderpads	Not Bound	2
	Sorcerer's Mantle	Bind on Pickup	69
PROPERTIES: Increases damage and healing done by magical spells and effects by up to 9.			
	Deathmist Mantle	Bind on Pickup	69
PROPERTIES: Increases damage and healing done by magical spells and effects by up to 12.			
	Virtuous Mantle	Bind on Pickup	69
PROPERTIES: Increases damage and healing done by magical spells and effects by up to 12.			
	Mantle of Magical Might	Bind on Pickup	88
PROPERTIES: Increases damage and healing done by magical spells and effects by up to 19.			
	Destroyers' Mantle	Bind on Pickup	94
PROPERTIES: Increases damage and healing done by magical spells and effects by up to 35.			

Epic Cloth Waist

Level	Name	Binding Info	Armor
57	Belt of the Archmage	Bind on Equip	62
PROPERTIES: Increases your spell critical strike rating by 14.			
60	Marshal's Silk Sash	Bind on Pickup	64
60	General's Silk Sash	Bind on Pickup	64
60	Arcanist Belt	Bind on Equip	65
PROPERTIES: Increases damage and healing done by magical spells and effects by up to 14. Fire Resistance Resistance +10			
60	Felheart Belt	Bind on Equip	65
PROPERTIES: Increases damage and healing done by magical spells and effects by up to 20. Fire Resistance Resistance +7			
60	Girdle of Prophecy	Bind on Equip	65
PROPERTIES: Restores 4 mana per 5 sec, Increases damage and healing done by magical spells and effects by up to 9, Fire Resistance Resistance +7			
60	Netherwind Belt	Bind on Pickup	74
PROPERTIES: Increases damage and healing done by magical spells and effects by up to 23. Shadow Resistance Resistance +10			
60	Belt of Transcendence	Bind on Pickup	74
PROPERTIES: Increases healing done by spells and effects by up to 26. Shadow Resistance Resistance +10			
60	Nemesis Belt	Bind on Pickup	74
PROPERTIES: Increases your spell critical strike rating by 14, Increases damage and healing done by magical spells and effects by up to 25, Shadow Resistance Resistance +10			
60	Marshal's Dreadweave Sash	Bind on Pickup	64
60	General's Dreadweave Belt	Bind on Pickup	64
60	Marshal's Satin Sash	Bind on Pickup	64
60	General's Satin Cinch	Bind on Pickup	64
60	Sash of Whispered Secrets	Bind on Pickup	70
PROPERTIES: Increases damage done by Shadow spells and effects by up to 33, Restores 6 health per 5 sec.			
60	Mana Igniting Cord	Bind on Pickup	70
PROPERTIES: Increases damage and healing done by magical spells and effects by up to 25, Increases your spell critical strike rating by 14.			

Epic Cloth Waist

Level	Name	Binding Info	Armor
60	Angelista's Grasp	Bind on Pickup	75
PROPERTIES: Increases your spell hit rating by 16.			
60	Firemaw's Clutch	Bind on Pickup	74
PROPERTIES: Increases damage and healing done by magical spells and effects by up to 35, Restores 5 mana per 5 sec.			
60	Belt of the Dark Bog	Bind on Pickup	70
PROPERTIES: Increases damage and healing done by magical spells and effects by up to 14. Nature Resistance Resistance +25			
60	Grasp of the Old God	Bind on Pickup	85
PROPERTIES: Increases healing done by spells and effects by up to 59, Restores 7 mana per 5 sec.			
60	Frostfire Belt	Bind on Pickup	85
PROPERTIES: Increases damage and healing done by magical spells and effects by up to 28, Increases your spell hit rating by 8.			
60	Plagueheart Belt	Bind on Pickup	85
PROPERTIES: Increases damage and healing done by magical spells and effects by up to 34, Increases your spell critical strike rating by 14.			
60	Belt of Faith	Bind on Pickup	85
PROPERTIES: Increases healing done by spells and effects by up to 48.			
60	Eyestalk Waist Cord	Bind on Pickup	85
PROPERTIES: Increases your spell critical strike rating by 14, Increases damage and healing done by magical spells and effects by up to 41.			
70	Spellfire Belt	Bind on Pickup	100
PROPERTIES: Increases damage done by Fire spells and effects by up to 50, Increases damage done by Arcane spells and effects by up to 50.			
70	Primal Mooncloth Belt	Bind on Pickup	100
PROPERTIES: Increases healing done by spells and effects by up to 77, Restores 9 mana per 5 sec.			
70	Unyielding Girdle	Bind on Equip	96
70	Girdle of Ruination	Bind on Equip	96
PROPERTIES: Increases damage and healing done by magical spells and effects by up to 30.			
70	Black Belt of Knowledge	Bind on Equip	96
70	General's Dreadweave Belt	Bind on Pickup	105
PROPERTIES: Increases damage and healing done by magical spells and effects by up to 28.			
70	General's Silk Belt	Bind on Pickup	105
PROPERTIES: Increases damage and healing done by magical spells and effects by up to 25.			
70	Nethershard Girdle	Bind on Pickup	96
PROPERTIES: Increases damage and healing done by magical spells and effects by up to 32.			
70	Cincture of Will	Bind on Pickup	96
PROPERTIES: Increases healing done by spells and effects by up to 55.			
70	Malefic Girdle	Bind on Pickup	96
PROPERTIES: Increases damage and healing done by magical spells and effects by up to 34.			
70	Belt of Divine Inspiration	Bind on Pickup	105
PROPERTIES: Increases damage and healing done by magical spells and effects by up to 37.			
70	Marshal's Dreadweave Belt	Bind on Pickup	105
PROPERTIES: Increases damage and healing done by magical spells and effects by up to 28.			
70	Marshal's Silk Belt	Bind on Pickup	105
PROPERTIES: Increases damage and healing done by magical spells and effects by up to 25.			
70	Belt of Depravity	Bind on Pickup	91
PROPERTIES: Increases damage and healing done by magical spells and effects by up to 30.			
70	Cord of Sanctification	Bind on Pickup	91
PROPERTIES: Increases healing done by spells and effects by up to 48, Restores 6 mana per 5 sec.			
70	Sash of Arcane Visions	Bind on Pickup	91
PROPERTIES: Increases damage and healing done by magical spells and effects by up to 26.			
70	Fire-Cord of the Magus	Bind on Pickup	109
PROPERTIES: Increases damage done by Fire spells and effects by up to 43.			

Epic Cloth Waist

Level	Name	Binding Info	Armor
70	Belt of the Long Road	Bind on Equip	109
PROPERTIES: Increases healing done by spells and effects by up to 62.			
70	Belt of Blasting	Bind on Equip	109
PROPERTIES: Increases damage and healing done by magical spells and effects by up to 33.			
70	Cord of Screaming Terrors	Bind on Pickup	109
PROPERTIES: Increases damage and healing done by magical spells and effects by up to 43.			
70	Inferno Waist Cord	Bind on Pickup	96
PROPERTIES: Increases damage done by Fire spells and effects by up to 54.			
70	Lurker's Cord	Bind on Pickup	91
	Zandalar Confessor's Bindings	Bind on Pickup	61
PROPERTIES: Increases healing done by spells and effects by up to 26.			

Superior Cloth Waist

Level	Name	Binding Info	Armor
18	Keller's Girdle	Bind on Equip	23
24	Belt of Arugal	Bind on Pickup	26
28	Highlander's Cloth Girdle	Bind on Pickup	28
PROPERTIES: Increases damage and healing done by magical spells and effects by up to 11.			
28	Defiler's Cloth Girdle	Bind on Pickup	28
PROPERTIES: Increases damage and healing done by magical spells and effects by up to 11.			
32	Sutarn's Ring	Bind on Equip	30
36	Deathmage Sash	Bind on Pickup	33
38	Highlander's Cloth Girdle	Bind on Pickup	35
PROPERTIES: Increases damage and healing done by magical spells and effects by up to 14.			
38	Defiler's Cloth Girdle	Bind on Pickup	35
PROPERTIES: Increases damage and healing done by magical spells and effects by up to 14.			
45	Satyrmane Sash	Bind on Pickup	40
PROPERTIES: Shadow Resistance Resistance +10			
48	Dawnspire Cord	Bind on Pickup	43
48	Serenity Belt	Bind on Equip	43
48	Highlander's Cloth Girdle	Bind on Pickup	43
PROPERTIES: Increases your spell critical strike rating by 14, Increases damage and healing done by magical spells and effects by up to 9.			
48	Defiler's Cloth Girdle	Bind on Pickup	43
PROPERTIES: Increases your spell critical strike rating by 14, Increases damage and healing done by magical spells and effects by up to 9.			
49	Ban'thok Sash	Bind on Pickup	43
PROPERTIES: Increases your spell hit rating by 8, Increases damage and healing done by magical spells and effects by up to 12.			
53	Sash of the Burning Heart	Bind on Pickup	46
PROPERTIES: Increases damage done by Fire spells and effects by up to 14.			
53	Magister's Belt	Bind on Equip	46
53	Devout Belt	Bind on Equip	46
53	Dreadmist Belt	Bind on Equip	46
53	Wisdom of the Timbermaw	Bind on Equip	46
PROPERTIES: Restores 4 mana per 5 sec.			
54	Grimgore Noose	Bind on Pickup	47
54	Whipvine Cord	Bind on Pickup	47
PROPERTIES: Restores 6 mana per 5 sec, Increases healing done by spells and effects by up to 31.			
55	Knight-Captain's Silk Sash	Bind on Pickup	48
55	Legionnaire's Silk Belt	Bind on Pickup	48
55	Knight-Captain's Dreadweave Belt	Bind on Pickup	48
55	Legionnaire's Dreadweave Belt	Bind on Pickup	48

Superior Cloth Waist

Level	Name	Binding Info	Armor
55	Knight-Captain's Satin Cord	Bind on Pickup	48
55	Legionnaire's Satin Sash	Bind on Pickup	48
55	Frostwolf Cloth Belt	Bind on Pickup	48
PROPERTIES: Increases damage and healing done by magical spells and effects by up to 18. Frost Resistance Resistance +5			
55	Stormpike Cloth Girdle	Bind on Pickup	48
PROPERTIES: Increases damage and healing done by magical spells and effects by up to 18. Frost Resistance Resistance +5			
55	Waistband of Balzaphon	Bind on Pickup	48
PROPERTIES: Increases damage done by Frost spells and effects by up to 20.			
56	Dustfeather Sash	Bind on Pickup	49
PROPERTIES: Increases damage and healing done by magical spells and effects by up to 9.			
56	Clutch of Andros	Bind on Pickup	49
PROPERTIES: Increases your spell hit rating by 8.			
56	Thuzadin Sash	Bind on Pickup	49
PROPERTIES: Increases damage and healing done by magical spells and effects by up to 11.			
56	Ironweave Belt	Bind on Pickup	49
58	Highlander's Cloth Girdle	Bind on Pickup	50
PROPERTIES: Increases your spell critical strike rating by 14, Increases damage and healing done by magical spells and effects by up to 14.			
58	Defiler's Cloth Girdle	Bind on Pickup	50
PROPERTIES: Increases your spell critical strike rating by 14, Increases damage and healing done by magical spells and effects by up to 14.			
58	Runed Stygian Belt	Bind on Equip	50
PROPERTIES: Restores 3 mana per 5 sec. Shadow Resistance Resistance +20			
60	Belt of the Inquisition	Bind on Pickup	56
PROPERTIES: Increases healing done by spells and effects by up to 24, Restores 4 mana per 5 sec.			
60	Belt of Untapped Power	Bind on Pickup	54
PROPERTIES: Increases damage and healing done by magical spells and effects by up to 29.			
61	Waistband of Alacrity	Bind on Pickup	68
PROPERTIES: Increases damage and healing done by magical spells and effects by up to 21.			
66	Hierophant's Sash	Bind on Pickup	77
PROPERTIES: Increases damage and healing done by magical spells and effects by up to 22.			
68	Cord of Belief	Bind on Pickup	86
PROPERTIES: Increases healing done by spells and effects by up to 46, Restores 8 mana per 5 sec.			
68	Coldwhisper Cord	Bind on Pickup	86
PROPERTIES: Increases damage done by Frost spells and effects by up to 36.			
70	Mosswoven Waistguard of the Arcanum	Bind on Pickup	88
PROPERTIES: Increases damage and healing done by magical spells and effects by up to 28.			
70	Oracle Belt of Timeless Mystery	Bind on Pickup	88
PROPERTIES: Increases damage and healing done by magical spells and effects by up to 29.			
70	Sash of Serpentra	Bind on Pickup	88
PROPERTIES: Increases damage and healing done by magical spells and effects by up to 25.			
70	Mana-Etched Sash	Bind on Pickup	88
PROPERTIES: Increases damage and healing done by magical spells and effects by up to 30.			
70	Netherflame Belt	Bind on Equip	84
PROPERTIES: Increases damage and healing done by magical spells and effects by up to 29.			
70	Lifeblood Belt	Bind on Equip	84
PROPERTIES: Increases healing done by spells and effects by up to 55, Restores 10 mana per 5 sec.			
	Warsong Sash	Bind on Pickup	25
	Belt of Tiny Heads	Bind on Pickup	55
PROPERTIES: Restores 7 mana per 5 sec.			

Superior Cloth Waist

Level	Name	Binding Info	Armor
	Sorcerer's Belt	Bind on Pickup	52
PROPERTIES: Increases damage and healing done by magical spells and effects by up to 14.			
	Deathmist Belt	Bind on Pickup	52
PROPERTIES: Increases damage and healing done by magical spells and effects by up to 12.			
	Virtuous Belt	Bind on Pickup	52
PROPERTIES: Increases damage and healing done by magical spells and effects by up to 12.			
	Nigh Invulnerability Belt	Bind on Equip	55
PROPERTIES: Protects you with a shield of force that stops 4000 damage for 8 sec.			
	Consortium Prince's Wrap	Bind on Pickup	75
PROPERTIES: Increases damage and healing done by magical spells and effects by up to 30, Increases your spell penetration by 20.			

Epic Cloth Wrist

Level	Name	Binding Info	Armor
40	Dryad's Wrist Bindings	Bind on Pickup	35
PROPERTIES: Increases damage and healing done by magical spells and effects by up to 16.			
50	Dryad's Wrist Bindings	Bind on Pickup	43
PROPERTIES: Increases damage and healing done by magical spells and effects by up to 20.			
60	Marshal's Silk Bracers	Bind on Pickup	50
60	General's Silk Cuffs	Bind on Pickup	50
60	Arcanist Bindings	Bind on Equip	51
PROPERTIES: Increases damage and healing done by magical spells and effects by up to 12, Restores 3 mana per 5 sec.			
60	Felheart Bracers	Bind on Equip	51
PROPERTIES: Increases damage and healing done by magical spells and effects by up to 13.			
60	Vambraces of Prophecy	Bind on Equip	51
PROPERTIES: Restores 2 mana per 5 sec, Increases healing done by spells and effects by up to 24.			
60	Netherwind Bindings	Bind on Pickup	58
PROPERTIES: Increases damage and healing done by magical spells and effects by up to 19, Restores 4 mana per 5 sec.			
60	Bindings of Transcendence	Bind on Pickup	58
PROPERTIES: Increases healing done by spells and effects by up to 33.			
60	Nemesis Bracers	Bind on Pickup	58
PROPERTIES: Increases damage and healing done by magical spells and effects by up to 15.			
60	Marshal's Dreadweave Cuffs	Bind on Pickup	50
60	General's Dreadweave Bracers	Bind on Pickup	50
60	Marshal's Satin Bracers	Bind on Pickup	50
60	General's Satin Bracers	Bind on Pickup	50
60	Flarecore Wraps	Bind on Equip	49
PROPERTIES: Restores 9 mana per 5 sec. Fire Resistance Resistance +7			
60	Blacklight Bracer	Bind on Pickup	51
PROPERTIES: Increases your spell critical strike rating by 14.			
60	Bracers of Arcane Accuracy	Bind on Pickup	57
PROPERTIES: Increases your spell hit rating by 8, Increases damage and healing done by magical spells and effects by up to 21.			
60	Dryad's Wrist Bindings	Bind on Pickup	50
PROPERTIES: Increases damage and healing done by magical spells and effects by up to 22.			
60	Black Bark Wristbands	Bind on Pickup	54
PROPERTIES: Increases damage and healing done by magical spells and effects by up to 25.			
60	Shackles of the Unscarred	Bind on Pickup	55
PROPERTIES: Increases damage and healing done by magical spells and effects by up to 21, Increases your spell penetration by 10.			
60	Bracelets of Royal Redemption	Bind on Pickup	61
PROPERTIES: Increases healing done by spells and effects by up to 53.			

Epic Cloth Wrist

Level	Name	Binding Info	Armor
60	Burrower Bracers	Bind on Pickup	61
PROPERTIES: Increases damage and healing done by magical spells and effects by up to 28.			
60	Frostfire Bindings	Bind on Pickup	66
PROPERTIES: Increases your spell penetration by 10, Increases damage and healing done by magical spells and effects by up to 27.			
60	Plagueheart Bindings	Bind on Pickup	66
PROPERTIES: Increases damage and healing done by magical spells and effects by up to 23.			
60	Bindings of Faith	Bind on Pickup	66
PROPERTIES: Increases healing done by spells and effects by up to 40.			
60	Glacial Wrists	Bind on Equip	61
PROPERTIES: Increases damage and healing done by magical spells and effects by up to 12. Frost Resistance Resistance +20,			
60	The Soul Harvester's Bindings	Bind on Pickup	63
PROPERTIES: Increases your spell critical strike rating by 14, Increases damage and healing done by magical spells and effects by up to 21.			
70	General's Dreadweave Cuffs	Bind on Pickup	74
PROPERTIES: Increases damage and healing done by magical spells and effects by up to 20.			
70	General's Silk Cuffs	Bind on Pickup	74
PROPERTIES: Increases damage and healing done by magical spells and effects by up to 18.			
70	Harbinger Bands	Bind on Pickup	74
PROPERTIES: Increases damage and healing done by magical spells and effects by up to 23.			
70	Bands of Indwelling	Bind on Pickup	74
PROPERTIES: Increases healing done by spells and effects by up to 42.			
70	Band of Rarefield Magic	Bind on Pickup	91
PROPERTIES: Increases damage and healing done by magical spells and effects by up to 21.			
70	Bands of Nefarious Deeds	Bind on Pickup	74
PROPERTIES: Increases damage and healing done by magical spells and effects by up to 28.			
70	Marshal's Dreadweave Cuffs	Bind on Pickup	74
PROPERTIES: Increases damage and healing done by magical spells and effects by up to 20.			
70	Marshal's Silk Cuffs	Bind on Pickup	74
PROPERTIES: Increases damage and healing done by magical spells and effects by up to 18.			
70	Bindings of the Timewalker	Bind on Pickup	71
PROPERTIES: Increases healing done by spells and effects by up to 62.			
70	Bands of Negation	Bind on Pickup	71
PROPERTIES: Increases damage and healing done by magical spells and effects by up to 27.			
70	Bands of the Benevolent	Bind on Pickup	71
PROPERTIES: Increases healing done by spells and effects by up to 40.			
70	Bands of Rarefied Magic	Bind on Pickup	71
PROPERTIES: Increases damage and healing done by magical spells and effects by up to 21.			
70	Mindstorm Wristbands	Bind on Pickup	85
PROPERTIES: Increases damage and healing done by magical spells and effects by up to 15.			
70	Ravager's Cuffs	Bind on Pickup	71
	Zandalar Confessor's Wraps	Bind on Pickup	47
PROPERTIES: Increases healing done by spells and effects by up to 24.			
	Zandalar Illusionist's Wraps	Bind on Pickup	47
PROPERTIES: Increases damage and healing done by magical spells and effects by up to 14.			
	Zandalar Demoniac's Wraps	Bind on Pickup	47
PROPERTIES: Increases damage and healing done by magical spells and effects by up to 16.			
	Rockfury Bracers	Bind on Pickup	48
PROPERTIES: Increases damage and healing done by magical spells and effects by up to 27, Increases your spell hit rating by 8.			
	Bracers of Hope	Bind on Pickup	46
PROPERTIES: Increases healing done by spells and effects by up to 18.			

Superior Cloth Wrist

Level	Name	Binding Info	Armor
17	Mindthrust Bracers	Bind on Equip	17
26	Glowing Magical Bracelets	Bind on Equip	21
41	Forgotten Wraps	Bind on Equip	29
45	First Sergeant's Silk Cuffs	Bind on Pickup	31
45	Sergeant Major's Silk Cuffs	Bind on Pickup	31
45	Arena Wristguards	Bind on Equip	31
PROPERTIES: Increases your spell critical strike rating by 14.			
49	Aristocratic Cuffs	Bind on Equip	34
52	Flameweave Cuffs	Bind on Pickup	35
PROPERTIES: Fire Resistance Resistance +10			
52	Tearfall Bracers	Bind on Pickup	35
52	Magister's Bindings	Bind on Equip	35
52	Devout Bracers	Bind on Equip	35
52	Dreadmist Bracers	Bind on Equip	35
54	Funeral Cuffs	Bind on Pickup	37
PROPERTIES: Shadow Resistance Resistance +10			
55	Knight-Captain's Silk Cuffs	Bind on Pickup	37
55	Knight-Captain's Dreadweave Bracers	Bind on Pickup	37
55	Legionnaire's Dreadweave Bracers	Bind on Pickup	37
55	Knight-Captain's Satin Cuffs	Bind on Pickup	37
55	Legionnaire's Satin Cuffs	Bind on Pickup	37
55	Sublime Wristguards	Bind on Pickup	37
PROPERTIES: Increases damage and healing done by magical spells and effects by up to 12.			
56	Necropile Cuffs	Bind on Pickup	38
56	Ironweave Bracers	Bind on Pickup	38
57	Magiskull Cuffs	Bind on Equip	38
57	Bracers of Mending	Bind on Pickup	38
PROPERTIES: Increases healing done by spells and effects by up to 18.			
58	First Sergeant's Silk Cuffs	Bind on Pickup	39
58	Sergeant Major's Silk Cuffs	Bind on Pickup	39
58	Bracers of Undead Cleansing	Bind on Equip	39
PROPERTIES: Increases damage done to Undead by magical spells and effects by up to 26.			
60	Abyssal Cloth Wristbands	Bind on Pickup	42
60	Bracers of Qiraji Command	Bind on Pickup	44
PROPERTIES: Restores 4 mana per 5 sec.			
61	Arcing Bracers	Bind on Pickup	53
PROPERTIES: Increases damage and healing done by magical spells and effects by up to 18.			
68	Light Scribe Bands	Bind on Pickup	67
PROPERTIES: Increases healing done by spells and effects by up to 29.			
68	Bands of Nethekurse	Bind on Pickup	67
PROPERTIES: Increases damage and healing done by magical spells and effects by up to 21, Increases your spell penetration by 15.			
69	Arcanoweave Bracers	Bind on Equip	67
PROPERTIES: Arcane Resistance Resistance +25			
69	Unyielding Bracers	Bind on Equip	67
69	Bracers of Havok	Bind on Equip	67
PROPERTIES: Increases damage and healing done by magical spells and effects by up to 30.			
69	Blackstrike Bracers	Bind on Equip	67
PROPERTIES: Restores 5 mana per 5 sec.			
69	Lifeblood Bracers	Bind on Equip	67
PROPERTIES: Increases healing done by spells and effects by up to 42, Restores 8 mana per 5 sec.			
69	Flameheart Bracers	Bind on Equip	67
PROPERTIES: Fire Resistance Resistance +30			

Superior Cloth Wrist

Level	Name	Binding Info	Armor
70	Crimson Bracers of Gloom	Bind on Pickup	68
PROPERTIES: Increases damage and healing done by magical spells and effects by up to 22.			
70	Aldor'l Signet Bands	Bind on Pickup	68
PROPERTIES: Increases damage and healing done by magical spells and effects by up to 30.			
	Manacle Cuffs	Bind on Pickup	34
	Wyrmthalak's Shackles	Bind on Pickup	37
	Sorcerer's Bindings	Bind on Pickup	40
PROPERTIES: Increases damage and healing done by magical spells and effects by up to 8.			
	Deathmist Bracers	Bind on Pickup	40
PROPERTIES: Increases damage and healing done by magical spells and effects by up to 8.			
	Virtuous Bracers	Bind on Pickup	40
PROPERTIES: Increases damage and healing done by magical spells and effects by up to 9, Restores 2 mana per 5 sec.			
	Goldenvine Wraps	Bind on Pickup	56
PROPERTIES: Increases healing done by spells and effects by up to 29.			
	Shattrath Wraps	Bind on Pickup	68
PROPERTIES: Increases damage and healing done by magical spells and effects by up to 21.			

LEATHER

Epic Leather Chest

Level	Name	Binding Info	Armor
60	Field Marshal's Dragonhide Breastplate	Bind on Pickup	251
PROPERTIES: Increases damage and healing done by magical spells and effects by up to 21, Improves critical strike rating by 14.			
60	Field Marshal's Leather Chestpiece	Bind on Pickup	251
PROPERTIES: Improves critical strike rating by 14, Increases your hit rating by 10.			
60	Warlord's Dragonhide Hauberk	Bind on Pickup	251
PROPERTIES: Increases damage and healing done by magical spells and effects by up to 21, Improves critical strike rating by 14.			
60	Warlord's Leather Breastplate	Bind on Pickup	251
PROPERTIES: Increases your hit rating by 10, Improves critical strike rating by 14.			
60	Nightslayer Chestpiece	Bind on Pickup	228
PROPERTIES: Improves critical strike rating by 14. Fire Resistance Resistance +10			
60	Stormrage Chestguard	Bind on Pickup	257
PROPERTIES: Increases your spell critical strike rating by 14, Increases healing done by spells and effects by up to 42. Fire Resistance Resistance +10, Nature Resistance Resistance +10			
60	Bloodfang Chestpiece	Bind on Pickup	257
PROPERTIES: Improves critical strike rating by 14, Increases your hit rating by 20. Fire Resistance Resistance +10, Nature Resistance Resistance +10			
60	Malfurion's Blessed Bulwark	Bind on Pickup	254
60	Interlaced Shadow Jerkin	Bind on Pickup	243
PROPERTIES: Increases attack power by 28. Shadow Resistance Resistance +30			
60	Genesis Vest	Bind on Pickup	289
PROPERTIES: Increases damage and healing done by magical spells and effects by up to 28, Increases your spell critical strike rating by 14, Improves critical strike rating by 14.			
60	Deathdealer's Vest	Bind on Pickup	289
PROPERTIES: Improves critical strike rating by 14, Increases your hit rating by 10.			
60	Thick Silithid Chestguard	Bind on Pickup	237
PROPERTIES: Fire Resistance Resistance +5, Nature Resistance Resistance +5, Frost Resistance Resistance +5, Shadow Resistance Resistance +5, Arcane Resistance Resistance +5			
60	Vest of Swift Execution	Bind on Pickup	262
60	Bonescythe Breastplate	Bind on Pickup	299
PROPERTIES: Improves critical strike rating by 28, Increases attack power by 80, Increases your hit rating by 10.			

Epic Leather Chest

Level	Name	Binding Info	Armor
60	Dreamwalker Tunic	Bind on Pickup	299
PROPERTIES: Increases healing done by spells and effects by up to 66, Restores 8 mana per 5 sec.			
60	Polar Tunic	Bind on Equip	267
PROPERTIES: Frost Resistance Resistance +40			
60	Ghoul Skin Tunic	Bind on Pickup	276
PROPERTIES: Improves critical strike rating by 28.			
60	Cenarion Vestments	Bind on Pickup	228
PROPERTIES: Restores 3 mana per 5 sec, Increases healing done by spells and effects by up to 22. Fire Resistance Resistance +10			
70	Gladiator's Leather Tunic	Bind on Pickup	364
PROPERTIES: Increases attack power by 20.			
70	Gladiator's Dragonhide Tunic	Bind on Pickup	364
PROPERTIES: Increases healing done by spells and effects by up to 20.			
70	Gladiator's Wyrmhide Tunic	Bind on Pickup	364
PROPERTIES: Increases damage and healing done by magical spells and effects by up to 37, Restores 6 mana per 5 sec.			
70	Stonebough Jerkin	Bind on Pickup	318
PROPERTIES: Increases healing done by spells and effects by up to 68, Restores 8 mana per 5 sec.			
70	Chest of the Conniver	Bind on Pickup	318
PROPERTIES: Increases attack power by 82.			
70	Netherblade Chestpiece	Bind on Pickup	333
PROPERTIES: Increases attack power by 86.			
70	Chestguard of Malorne	Bind on Pickup	333
PROPERTIES: Increases healing done by spells and effects by up to 77.			
70	Chestpiece of Malorne	Bind on Pickup	333
PROPERTIES: Increases damage and healing done by magical spells and effects by up to 41.			
70	Breastplate of Malorne	Bind on Pickup	333
70	Windhawk Hauberk	Bind on Pickup	268
PROPERTIES: Increases damage and healing done by magical spells and effects by up to 28, Increases healing done by spells and effects by up to 35.			
70	Primalstrike Vest	Bind on Pickup	268
PROPERTIES: Increases attack power by 100.			
70	Gnarled Chestpiece of the Ancients	Bind on Pickup	364
PROPERTIES: Increases healing done by spells and effects by up to 99.			
70	Bloodsea Brigand's Vest	Bind on Pickup	364
PROPERTIES: Increases attack power by 76.			
70	Deathmantle Chestguard	Bind on Pickup	379
PROPERTIES: Increases attack power by 100.			
70	Nordrassil Chestguard	Bind on Pickup	379
PROPERTIES: Increases healing done by spells and effects by up to 66, Restores 6 mana per 5 sec.			
70	Nordrassil Chestplate	Bind on Pickup	379
70	Nordrassil Chestpiece	Bind on Pickup	379
PROPERTIES: Increases damage and healing done by magical spells and effects by up to 35.			
70	Fel Reaver Loot Rogue Chest	Bind on Pickup	333
PROPERTIES: Increases attack power by 86.			
70	Inferno Hardened Chestguard	Bind on Pickup	306
PROPERTIES: Fire Resistance Resistance +60			
	Breastplate of Bloodthirst	Bind on Pickup	217
PROPERTIES: Improves critical strike rating by 28, Increases your dodge rating by 12.			
	Zandalar Madcap's Tunic	Bind on Pickup	225
PROPERTIES: Improves critical strike rating by 28, Increases attack power by 44.			
	Zandalar Haruspex's Tunic	Bind on Pickup	225
PROPERTIES: Increases healing done by spells and effects by up to 33.			

Epic Leather Chest

Level	Name	Binding Info	Armor
	Darkmantle Tunic	Bind on Pickup	211
PROPERTIES: Increases your hit rating by 20.			
	Feralheart Vest	Bind on Pickup	211
PROPERTIES: Increases damage and healing done by magical spells and effects by up to 12, Restores 4 mana per 5 sec.			

Superior Leather Chest

Level	Name	Binding Info	Armor
17	Starsight Tunic	Bind on Equip	89
19	Blackened Defias Armor	Bind on Pickup	92
20	Gloomshroud Armor	Bind on Equip	94
30	Spirewind Fetter	Bind on Equip	112
31	Wolffear Harness	Bind on Equip	113
34	Quillward Harness	Bind on Equip	120
44	Jinxed Hoodoo Skin	Bind on Pickup	144
45	Feathered Breastplate	Bind on Equip	146
46	Cow King's Hide	Bind on Equip	148
PROPERTIES: Fire Resistance Resistance +10, Nature Resistance Resistance +10, Frost Resistance Resistance +10, Shadow Resistance Resistance +10, Arcane Resistance Resistance +10			
46	Fungus Shroud Armor	Bind on Pickup	148
48	Flamestrider Robes	Bind on Pickup	153
PROPERTIES: Increases damage and healing done by magical spells and effects by up to 20. Fire Resistance Resistance +10			
50	Mixologist's Tunic	Bind on Pickup	158
50	Warbear Harness	Bind on Equip	158
52	Stormshroud Armor	Bind on Equip	163
PROPERTIES: Improves critical strike rating by 28, Increases your dodge rating by 12.			
53	Songbird Blouse	Bind on Pickup	165
53	Ironfeather Breastplate	Bind on Equip	165
55	Living Breastplate	Bind on Equip	169
PROPERTIES: Increases healing done by spells and effects by up to 26. Nature Resistance Resistance +5			
56	Nightbrace Tunic	Bind on Pickup	172
PROPERTIES: Increases attack power by 50. Fire Resistance Resistance +10, Shadow Resistance Resistance +10			
56	Cadaverous Armor	Bind on Pickup	172
PROPERTIES: Increases attack power by 60.			
57	Tombstone Breastplate	Bind on Pickup	174
PROPERTIES: Improves critical strike rating by 28.			
57	Chestplate of Tranquility	Bind on Pickup	174
PROPERTIES: Increases damage and healing done by magical spells and effects by up to 23.			
58	Knight-Captain's Leather Armor	Bind on Pickup	176
PROPERTIES: Improves critical strike rating by 14.			
58	Knight-Captain's Dragonhide Tunic	Bind on Pickup	176
PROPERTIES: Increases damage and healing done by magical spells and effects by up to 16, Improves critical strike rating by 14.			
58	Legionnaire's Dragonhide Breastplate	Bind on Pickup	176
PROPERTIES: Improves critical strike rating by 14, Increases damage and healing done by magical spells and effects by up to 16.			
58	Legionnaire's Leather Hauberk	Bind on Pickup	176
PROPERTIES: Improves critical strike rating by 14.			
58	Wildheart Vest	Bind on Pickup	176
58	Shadowcraft Tunic	Bind on Pickup	176

Superior Leather Chest

Level	Name	Binding Info	Armor
58	Tunic of the Crescent Moon	Bind on Pickup	176
PROPERTIES: Increases damage and healing done by magical spells and effects by up to 15, Increases your spell critical strike rating by 14.			
58	Tunic of Undead Slaying	Bind on Pickup	176
PROPERTIES: Increases attack power by 81 when fighting Undead.			
60	Primal Batskin Jerkin	Bind on Equip	181
PROPERTIES: Increases your hit rating by 10.			
60	Blood Tiger Breastplate	Bind on Equip	181
60	Legionnaire's Dragonhide Chestpiece	Bind on Pickup	188
PROPERTIES: Improves critical strike rating by 14, Increases damage and healing done by magical spells and effects by up to 15.			
60	Legionnaire's Leather Chestpiece	Bind on Pickup	188
PROPERTIES: Improves critical strike rating by 14, Increases your hit rating by 10, Increases attack power by 34.			
60	Knight-Captain's Dragonhide Chestpiece	Bind on Pickup	188
PROPERTIES: Improves critical strike rating by 14, Increases damage and healing done by magical spells and effects by up to 15.			
60	Knight-Captain's Leather Chestpiece	Bind on Pickup	188
PROPERTIES: Improves critical strike rating by 14, Increases your hit rating by 10, Increases attack power by 34.			
61	Vest of Vengeance	Bind on Pickup	232
PROPERTIES: Increases attack power by 42.			
62	Warden's Hauberk	Bind on Pickup	238
63	Underbog Moss-Tunic	Bind on Pickup	244
PROPERTIES: Increases damage and healing done by magical spells and effects by up to 26.			
65	Primalstorm Breastplate	Bind on Pickup	255
PROPERTIES: Increases attack power by 60.			
65	Living Crystal Breastplate	Bind on Pickup	255
PROPERTIES: Increases damage and healing done by magical spells and effects by up to 29, Increases healing done by spells and effects by up to 55.			
68	Drakeskin Chestguard	Bind on Pickup	285
PROPERTIES: Increases attack power by 70.			
68	Chestguard of No Remorse	Bind on Pickup	285
PROPERTIES: Increases attack power by 92.			
68	Raiments of Nature's Breath	Bind on Pickup	285
PROPERTIES: Restores 7 mana per 5 sec, Increases healing done by spells and effects by up to 73.			
68	Starry Robes of the Crescent	Bind on Pickup	285
PROPERTIES: Increases damage and healing done by magical spells and effects by up to 39.			
70	Heavy Clefthoof Vest	Bind on Equip	290
70	Tunic of Assassination	Bind on Pickup	292
PROPERTIES: Increases attack power by 54.			
70	Wastewalker Chestpiece	Bind on Pickup	292
PROPERTIES: Increases attack power by 56.			
70	Grand Marshal's Dragonhide Tunic	Bind on Pickup	292
PROPERTIES: Increases healing done by spells and effects by up to 31.			
70	Grand Marshal's Leather Tunic	Bind on Pickup	292
PROPERTIES: Increases attack power by 12.			
70	Grand Marshal's Wyrmhide Tunic	Bind on Pickup	292
PROPERTIES: Increases damage and healing done by magical spells and effects by up to 22, Restores 5 mana per 5 sec.			
70	High Warlord's Dragonhide Tunic	Bind on Pickup	292
PROPERTIES: Increases healing done by spells and effects by up to 31.			
70	High Warlord's Leather Tunic	Bind on Pickup	292
PROPERTIES: Increases attack power by 12.			

Superior Leather Chest

Level	Name	Binding Info	Armor
70	High Warlord's Wyrmhide Tunic	Bind on Pickup	292
PROPERTIES: Increases damage and healing done by magical spells and effects by up to 22, Restores 5 mana per 5 sec.			
70	Moonglade Robe	Bind on Pickup	292
PROPERTIES: Increases healing done by spells and effects by up to 55.			
	Tunic of Westfall	Bind on Pickup	92
	Forest's Embrace	Bind on Pickup	151
PROPERTIES: Increases healing done by spells and effects by up to 55.			
	Grizzled Pelt	Bind on Pickup	151
	Sacred Feather Vest	Bind on Pickup	225
PROPERTIES: Increases damage and healing done by magical spells and effects by up to 42.			
	Jerkin of the Untamed Spirit	Bind on Pickup	225
	Mag'hari Scout's Tunic	Bind on Pickup	263
PROPERTIES: Increases attack power by 86.			
	Auchenai Monk's Tunic	Bind on Pickup	255
PROPERTIES: Increases attack power by 18.			
	Lifewarden's Breastplate	Bind on Pickup	270
PROPERTIES: Increases healing done by spells and effects by up to 64.			

Epic Leather Feet

Level	Name	Binding Info	Armor
54	Corehound Boots	Bind on Equip	144
PROPERTIES: Fire Resistance Resistance +24			
60	Marshal's Leather Footguards	Bind on Pickup	167
PROPERTIES: Increases the duration of your Sprint ability by 3 sec.			
60	Marshal's Dragonhide Boots	Bind on Pickup	167
PROPERTIES: Increases damage and healing done by magical spells and effects by up to 16.			
60	General's Dragonhide Boots	Bind on Pickup	167
PROPERTIES: Increases damage and healing done by magical spells and effects by up to 16.			
60	General's Leather Treads	Bind on Pickup	167
PROPERTIES: Increases the duration of your Sprint ability by 3 sec.			
60	Nightslayer Boots	Bind on Pickup	157
PROPERTIES: Shadow Resistance Resistance +7			
60	Cenarion Boots	Bind on Pickup	157
PROPERTIES: Restores 3 mana per 5 sec, Increases healing done by spells and effects by up to 18. Shadow Resistance Resistance +7			
60	Stormrage Boots	Bind on Pickup	176
PROPERTIES: Increases your spell critical strike rating by 14, Increases healing done by spells and effects by up to 26. Fire Resistance Resistance +10			
60	Bloodfang Boots	Bind on Pickup	176
PROPERTIES: Increases your dodge rating by 12. Fire Resistance Resistance +10			
60	Boots of the Shadow Flame	Bind on Pickup	190
PROPERTIES: Increases attack power by 44, Increases your hit rating by 20.			
60	Rogue Boots	Bind on Pickup	202
PROPERTIES: Improves critical strike rating by 14, Resistance Resistance +200 Armor.			
60	Boots of Fright	Bind on Pickup	169
PROPERTIES: Increases damage and healing done by magical spells and effects by up to 34.			
60	Genesis Boots	Bind on Pickup	180
PROPERTIES: Increases damage and healing done by magical spells and effects by up to 20, Restores 4 mana per 5 sec, Increases your spell penetration by 10.			
60	Deathdealer's Boots	Bind on Pickup	180
PROPERTIES: Increases your hit rating by 10.			
60	Boots of the Vanguard	Bind on Pickup	157

Epic Leather Feet

Level	Name	Binding Info	Armor
60	Drudge Boots	Bind on Pickup	178
PROPERTIES: Nature Resistance Resistance +20			
60	Wormhide Boots	Bind on Pickup	186
60	Hive Tunneler's Boots	Bind on Pickup	178
60	Bonescythe Sabatons	Bind on Pickup	195
PROPERTIES: Increases your hit rating by 10, Improves critical strike rating by 14, Increases attack power by 64.			
60	Dreamwalker Boots	Bind on Pickup	195
PROPERTIES: Increases healing done by spells and effects by up to 46, Restores 5 mana per 5 sec.			
60	Boots of Displacement	Bind on Pickup	190
PROPERTIES: Increases your effective stealth level.			
70	General's Leather Boots	Bind on Pickup	240
PROPERTIES: Increases attack power by 22.			
70	General's Dragonhide Boots	Bind on Pickup	240
PROPERTIES: Increases healing done by spells and effects by up to 33.			
70	General's Wyrmhide Boots	Bind on Pickup	240
PROPERTIES: Increases damage and healing done by magical spells and effects by up to 29, Restores 6 mana per 5 sec.			
70	Karazhan Moroes Loot 1 Socketed Rogue Boots	Bind on Pickup	219
PROPERTIES: Increases attack power by 38.			
70	Rapscallion Boots	Bind on Pickup	219
PROPERTIES: Increases attack power by 76.			
70	Forestlord Striders	Bind on Pickup	219
PROPERTIES: Increases healing done by spells and effects by up to 48.			
70	Marshal's Dragonhide Boots	Bind on Pickup	240
PROPERTIES: Increases healing done by spells and effects by up to 33.			
70	Marshal's Leather Boots	Bind on Pickup	240
PROPERTIES: Increases attack power by 24.			
70	Marshal's Wyrmhide Boots	Bind on Pickup	240
PROPERTIES: Increases damage and healing done by magical spells and effects by up to 29, Restores 6 mana per 5 sec.			
70	Shadowstep Striders	Bind on Pickup	210
PROPERTIES: Increases attack power by 52.			
70	Barkchip Boots	Bind on Pickup	210
PROPERTIES: Increases healing done by spells and effects by up to 48.			
70	Boots of Utter Darkness	Bind on Pickup	250
PROPERTIES: Increases attack power by 58.			
70	Boots of Natural Grace	Bind on Pickup	250
PROPERTIES: Increases healing done by spells and effects by up to 53.			
70	Boots of Effortless Striking	Bind on Pickup	250
PROPERTIES: Increases attack power by 40.			
70	Coilfang - Raid - Boss 4 Loot 1 Druid Boots	Bind on Pickup	250
PROPERTIES: Increases healing done by spells and effects by up to 62.			
70	Zierhut's Lost Treads	Bind on Pickup	219
70	Glider's Boots	Bind on Pickup	210
70	Doomlord Kazzak Loot Druid Boots	Bind on Pickup	229
PROPERTIES: Increases healing done by spells and effects by up to 77.			
70	Inferno Hardened Boots	Bind on Pickup	210
PROPERTIES: Fire Resistance Resistance +45			
	Darkmantle Boots	Bind on Pickup	145
PROPERTIES: Increases your effective stealth level.			
	Feralheart Boots	Bind on Pickup	145
PROPERTIES: Increases damage and healing done by magical spells and effects by up to 11, Restores 2 mana per 5 sec.			

Superior Leather Feet

Level	Name	Binding Info	Armor
19	Feet of the Lynx	Bind on Equip	63
25	Harbinger Boots	Bind on Equip	71
28	Highlander's Chain Greaves	Bind on Pickup	74
PROPERTIES: Run speed increased slightly.			
28	Highlander's Lizardhide Boots	Bind on Pickup	74
PROPERTIES: Run speed increased slightly.			
28	Highlander's Leather Boots	Bind on Pickup	74
PROPERTIES: Run speed increased slightly.			
28	Highlander's Mail Greaves	Bind on Pickup	74
PROPERTIES: Run speed increased slightly.			
28	Defiler's Chain Greaves	Bind on Pickup	74
PROPERTIES: Run speed increased slightly.			
28	Defiler's Lizardhide Boots	Bind on Pickup	74
PROPERTIES: Run speed increased slightly.			
28	Defiler's Leather Boots	Bind on Pickup	74
PROPERTIES: Run speed increased slightly.			
28	Defiler's Mail Greaves	Bind on Pickup	74
PROPERTIES: Run speed increased slightly.			
31	Briar Tredders	Bind on Equip	78
32	Swampwalker Boots	Bind on Equip	79
38	Highlander's Lizardhide Boots	Bind on Pickup	89
PROPERTIES: Run speed increased slightly, Increases attack power by 6.			
38	Highlander's Leather Boots	Bind on Pickup	89
PROPERTIES: Run speed increased slightly, Increases attack power by 6.			
38	Defiler's Lizardhide Boots	Bind on Pickup	89
PROPERTIES: Run speed increased slightly, Increases attack power by 6.			
38	Defiler's Leather Boots	Bind on Pickup	89
PROPERTIES: Run speed increased slightly, Increases attack power by 6.			
42	Sandstalker Ankleguards	Bind on Pickup	95
47	Slitherscale Boots	Bind on Pickup	104
48	Albino Crocscale Boots	Bind on Pickup	105
PROPERTIES: Nature Resistance +5			
48	Highlander's Lizardhide Boots	Bind on Pickup	105
PROPERTIES: Run speed increased slightly, Increases attack power by 12.			
48	Highlander's Leather Boots	Bind on Pickup	105
PROPERTIES: Run speed increased slightly, Increases attack power by 12.			
48	Defiler's Lizardhide Boots	Bind on Pickup	105
PROPERTIES: Run speed increased slightly, Increases attack power by 12.			
48	Defiler's Leather Boots	Bind on Pickup	105
PROPERTIES: Run speed increased slightly, Increases attack power by 12.			
49	Sandals of the Insurgent	Bind on Equip	107
50	Shadefiend Boots	Bind on Pickup	109
52	Coal Miner Boots	Bind on Pickup	112
PROPERTIES: Fire Resistance +10			
52	Firemoss Boots	Bind on Pickup	112
PROPERTIES: Increases healing done by spells and effects by up to 20.			
53	Waterspout Boots	Bind on Pickup	114
PROPERTIES: Increases damage and healing done by magical spells and effects by up to 25.			
53	Dawn Treaders	Bind on Equip	114
PROPERTIES: Increases your dodge rating by 12.			
54	Swiftwalker Boots	Bind on Pickup	115
54	Shadowcraft Boots	Bind on Pickup	115

Superior Leather Feet

Level	Name	Binding Info	Armor
54	Wildheart Boots	Bind on Pickup	115
54	Rogue Boots	Bind on Pickup	115
55	Pads of the Dread Wolf	Bind on Pickup	116
PROPERTIES: Increases attack power by 40.			
56	Verdant Footpads	Bind on Pickup	118
PROPERTIES: Increases healing done by spells and effects by up to 37, Increases damage done by Nature spells and effects by up to 24.			
56	Cadaverous Walkers	Bind on Pickup	118
PROPERTIES: Increases attack power by 24.			
56	Ash Covered Boots	Bind on Pickup	118
PROPERTIES: Increases your dodge rating by 12.			
56	Boots of Ferocity	Bind on Pickup	118
57	Boots of the Shrieker	Bind on Pickup	120
PROPERTIES: Increases damage and healing done by magical spells and effects by up to 12. Shadow Resistance +10			
57	Mongoose Boots	Bind on Equip	120
58	Knight-Lieutenant's Leather Boots	Bind on Pickup	121
PROPERTIES: Increases the duration of your Sprint ability by 3 sec.			
58	Knight-Lieutenant's Dragonhide Footwraps	Bind on Pickup	121
PROPERTIES: Increases damage and healing done by magical spells and effects by up to 14.			
58	Blood Guard's Dragonhide Boots	Bind on Pickup	121
PROPERTIES: Increases damage and healing done by magical spells and effects by up to 14.			
58	Blood Guard's Leather Treads	Bind on Pickup	121
PROPERTIES: Increases the duration of your Sprint ability by 3 sec.			
58	Highlander's Leather Boots	Bind on Pickup	121
PROPERTIES: Run speed increased slightly, Increases attack power by 16.			
58	Highlander's Lizardhide Boots	Bind on Pickup	121
PROPERTIES: Run speed increased slightly, Increases attack power by 16.			
58	Defiler's Lizardhide Boots	Bind on Pickup	121
PROPERTIES: Run speed increased slightly, Increases attack power by 16.			
58	Defiler's Leather Boots	Bind on Pickup	121
PROPERTIES: Run speed increased slightly, Increases attack power by 16.			
60	Animist's Boots	Bind on Pickup	134
PROPERTIES: Increases healing done by spells and effects by up to 29.			
60	Blooddrenched Footpads	Bind on Pickup	129
PROPERTIES: Increases your hit rating by 10.			
60	Bramblewood Boots	Bind on Equip	132
PROPERTIES: Nature Resistance +25			
60	Blood Guard's Dragonhide Treads	Bind on Pickup	126
PROPERTIES: Increases damage and healing done by magical spells and effects by up to 14.			
60	Blood Guard's Leather Walkers	Bind on Pickup	126
PROPERTIES: Increases the duration of your Sprint ability by 3 sec, Increases attack power by 28.			
60	Knight-Lieutenant's Dragonhide Treads	Bind on Pickup	126
PROPERTIES: Increases damage and healing done by magical spells and effects by up to 14.			
60	Knight-Lieutenant's Leather Walkers	Bind on Pickup	126
PROPERTIES: Increases the duration of your Sprint ability by 3 sec, Increases attack power by 28.			
63	Talonite's Boots	Bind on Equip	168
64	Netherwalker Boots	Bind on Pickup	172
PROPERTIES: Increases attack power by 44.			
68	Moonstrider Boots	Bind on Pickup	196
PROPERTIES: Increases damage and healing done by magical spells and effects by up to 25, Restores 6 mana per 5 sec.			

Superior Leather Feet

Level	Name	Binding Info	Armor
68	Boots of the Glade-Keeper	Bind on Pickup	196
PROPERTIES: Increases healing done by spells and effects by up to 53.			
69	Fel Leather Boots	Bind on Equip	196
PROPERTIES: Increases attack power by 36.			
69	Heavy Clefthoof Boots	Bind on Equip	198
69	Enchanted Clefthoof Boots	Bind on Equip	196
PROPERTIES: Arcane Resistance +30			
69	Blastguard Boots	Bind on Equip	196
PROPERTIES: Fire Resistance +30			
70	Terror Guard Greaves	Bind on Pickup	201
PROPERTIES: Increases attack power by 50, Increases your effective stealth level by 1.			
70	Boots of the Unjust	Bind on Pickup	201
PROPERTIES: Increases attack power by 64.			
70	Boots of Shifting Sands	Bind on Pickup	201
PROPERTIES: Increases attack power by 40.			
70	Nimble-foot Treads	Bind on Pickup	201
	Warsong Boots	Bind on Pickup	67
	Sedge Boots	Bind on Pickup	121
PROPERTIES: Nature Resistance +5, Shadow Resistance +5			
	Whisperwalk Boots	Bind on Pickup	104
PROPERTIES: Increases your effective stealth level by 1.			
	Sandstorm Boots	Bind on Pickup	121
PROPERTIES: Increases damage and healing done by magical spells and effects by up to 14, Restores 4 mana per 5 sec.			
	Dunestalker's Boots	Bind on Pickup	121
	Rocket Boots Xtreme	Bind on Equip	196
PROPERTIES: Increases attack power by 50, Engage the rocket boots to greatly increase your speed. You probably wont be still standing when you get there though.			
	Sure-Step Boots	Bind on Pickup	155
PROPERTIES: Increases attack power by 38.			
	Studded Green Anklewraps	Bind on Pickup	163
	Spymistress's Boots	Bind on Pickup	201
PROPERTIES: Increases attack power by 36.			
	Southshore Sneakers	Bind on Pickup	181
PROPERTIES: Increases attack power by 42.			

Epic Leather Hands

Level	Name	Binding Info	Armor
37	Gloves of Holy Might	Bind on Equip	99
PROPERTIES: Improves critical strike rating by 14, Increases attack power by 20, Increases attack power by 30 when fighting Undead.			
60	Marshal's Dragonhide Gauntlets	Bind on Pickup	152
PROPERTIES: Slightly increases your stealth detection, Increases damage and healing done by magical spells and effects by up to 12.			
60	Marshal's Leather Handgrips	Bind on Pickup	152
PROPERTIES: Improves critical strike rating by 14.			
60	General's Dragonhide Gloves	Bind on Pickup	152
PROPERTIES: Slightly increases your stealth detection, Increases damage and healing done by magical spells and effects by up to 12.			
60	General's Leather Mitts	Bind on Pickup	152
PROPERTIES: Improves critical strike rating by 14.			
60	Nightslayer Gloves	Bind on Pickup	143
PROPERTIES: Increases your hit rating by 10. Fire Resistance Resistance +7			

Epic Leather Hands

Level	Name	Binding Info	Armor
60	Cenarion Gloves	Bind on Pickup	143
PROPERTIES: Increases healing done by spells and effects by up to 18. Fire Resistance +7			
60	Stormrage Handguards	Bind on Pickup	160
PROPERTIES: Increases healing done by spells and effects by up to 42. Shadow Resistance +10			
60	Bloodfang Gloves	Bind on Pickup	160
PROPERTIES: Immune to Disarm. Shadow Resistance +10			
60	Doomhide Gauntlets	Bind on Pickup	152
PROPERTIES: Increases attack power by 42. Fire Resistance +8, Shadow Resistance +8			
60	Aged Core Leather Gloves	Bind on Pickup	148
PROPERTIES: Improves critical strike rating by 14, Increases dagger skill rating by 12. Fire Resistance +8, Shadow Resistance +5			
60	Taut Dragonhide Gloves	Bind on Pickup	162
PROPERTIES: Increases your spell critical strike rating by 14, Restores 6 mana per 5 sec.			
60	Rogue Gloves	Bind on Pickup	184
PROPERTIES: Resistance +200 Armor, Improves critical strike rating by 14.			
60	Gauntlets of New Life	Bind on Pickup	153
PROPERTIES: Increases healing done by spells and effects by up to 26, Restores 4 mana per 5 sec.			
60	Gloves of the Hidden Temple	Bind on Pickup	169
PROPERTIES: Shadow Resistance +6			
60	Wasphide Gauntlets	Bind on Pickup	164
PROPERTIES: Increases healing done by spells and effects by up to 53.			
60	Gloves of Enforcement	Bind on Pickup	160
PROPERTIES: Increases your hit rating by 10.			
60	Bile-Covered Gauntlets	Bind on Pickup	164
PROPERTIES: Nature Resistance +20			
60	Gloves of Ebru	Bind on Pickup	158
PROPERTIES: Increases damage and healing done by magical spells and effects by up to 27, Increases your spell critical strike rating by 14.			
60	Bonescythe Gauntlets	Bind on Pickup	180
PROPERTIES: Increases your hit rating by 10, Increases attack power by 66, Improves critical strike rating by 14.			
60	Dreamwalker Handguards	Bind on Pickup	180
PROPERTIES: Increases healing done by spells and effects by up to 53.			
60	Polar Gloves	Bind on Equip	167
PROPERTIES: Frost Resistance +30			
70	Gladiator's Leather Gloves	Bind on Pickup	218
PROPERTIES: Increases attack power by 24, Causes your Deadly Throw ability to interrupt spellcasting and prevent any spell in that school from being cast for 3 sec.			
70	Gladiator's Dragonhide Gloves	Bind on Pickup	218
PROPERTIES: Increases healing done by spells and effects by up to 9, Reduces the cast time of your Cyclone spell by 0.1 sec.			
70	Gladiator's Wyrmhide Gloves	Bind on Pickup	218
PROPERTIES: Increases damage and healing done by magical spells and effects by up to 34, Reduces the cast time of your Cyclone spell by 0.1 sec, Restores 5 mana per 5 sec.			
70	Gloves of Dexterous Manipulation	Bind on Pickup	199
PROPERTIES: Increases attack power by 36.			
70	Mitts of the Treemender	Bind on Pickup	199
PROPERTIES: Increases healing done by spells and effects by up to 57.			
70	Magtheridon Loot 1 Rogue Gloves	Bind on Pickup	218
PROPERTIES: Increases attack power by 64.			
70	Netherblade Gloves	Bind on Pickup	208
PROPERTIES: Increases attack power by 64.			
70	Handguards of Malorne	Bind on Pickup	208
PROPERTIES: Increases healing done by spells and effects by up to 55, Restores 6 mana per 5 sec.			

Epic Leather Hands

Level	Name	Binding Info	Armor
70	Gloves of Malorne	Bind on Pickup	208
PROPERTIES: Increases damage and healing done by magical spells and effects by up to 29.			
70	Gauntlets of Malorne	Bind on Pickup	208
70	Master Thief's Gloves	Bind on Pickup	191
PROPERTIES: Increases attack power by 56, Immune to Disarm.			
70	Cobrascale Gloves	Bind on Equip	191
PROPERTIES: Increases attack power by 44.			
70	Gloves of the Living Touch	Bind on Equip	191
PROPERTIES: Increases healing done by spells and effects by up to 79.			
70	Windslayer Wraps	Bind on Equip	191
70	Gloves of the Searing Grip	Bind on Pickup	228
PROPERTIES: Increases attack power by 58, Increases sword skill rating by 9, Increases fist skill rating by 8, Increases mace skill rating by 9, Increases dagger skill rating by 8.			
70	Bark-Gloves of Ancient Wisdom	Bind on Pickup	228
PROPERTIES: Increases healing done by spells and effects by up to 51.			
70	Deathmantle Handguards	Bind on Pickup	237
PROPERTIES: Increases attack power by 58.			
70	Nordrassil Gloves	Bind on Pickup	237
PROPERTIES: Increases healing done by spells and effects by up to 62.			
70	Nordrassil Handgrips	Bind on Pickup	237
70	Nordrassil Gauntlets	Bind on Pickup	237
PROPERTIES: Increases damage and healing done by magical spells and effects by up to 33.			
70	Grips of the Deftness	Bind on Pickup	199
PROPERTIES: Increases attack power by 46, Increases sword skill rating by 12, Increases mace skill rating by 12, Increases dagger skill rating by 12,			
70	Inferno Hardened Gloves	Bind on Pickup	191
PROPERTIES: Fire Resistance +40			
	Darkmantle Gloves	Bind on Pickup	123
	Feralheart Gloves	Bind on Pickup	123
PROPERTIES: Increases damage and healing done by magical spells and effects by up to 11.			

Superior Leather Hands

Level	Name	Binding Info	Armor
22	Naga Battle Gloves	Bind on Pickup	61
22	Wolfclaw Gloves	Bind on Equip	61
22	Toughened Leather Gloves	Bind on Equip	61
23	Brawler Gloves	Bind on Equip	62
30	Ebon Vise	Bind on Pickup	70
35	Shadowskin Gloves	Bind on Equip	76
PROPERTIES: Improves critical strike rating by 14.			
37	Arachnid Gloves	Bind on Pickup	79
PROPERTIES: Nature Resistance +10			
41	Gauntlets of the Sea	Bind on Equip	85
PROPERTIES: Heal friendly target for 300 to 500.			
45	Elven Spirit Claws	Bind on Equip	91
PROPERTIES: Increases damage done by Nature spells and effects by up to 21.			
48	Bloodfire Talons	Bind on Pickup	96
PROPERTIES: Increases damage and healing done by magical spells and effects by up to 18. Fire Resistance +10			
49	Ogreseer Fists	Bind on Pickup	97
PROPERTIES: Increases damage and healing done by magical spells and effects by up to 13.			
51	Mar Alom's Grip	Bind on Equip	100
PROPERTIES: Increases healing done by spells and effects by up to 22.			

Superior Leather Hands

Level	Name	Binding Info	Armor
53	Devilsaur Gauntlets	Bind on Equip	103
PROPERTIES: Increases attack power by 28, Improves critical strike rating by 14.			
53	Plaguebat Fur Gloves	Bind on Equip	103
PROPERTIES: Shadow Resistance +10			
54	Skul's Fingerbone Claws	Bind on Pickup	105
PROPERTIES: Increases attack power by 40.			
54	Shadowcraft Gloves	Bind on Equip	105
54	Wildheart Gloves	Bind on Equip	105
54	Gloves of Restoration	Bind on Pickup	105
PROPERTIES: Increases healing done by spells and effects by up to 37.			
54	Stonebark Gauntlets	Bind on Equip	105
PROPERTIES: Nature Resistance +16			
56	Fallbrush Handgrips	Bind on Pickup	107
PROPERTIES: Increases healing done by spells and effects by up to 20.			
56	Slaghide Gauntlets	Bind on Pickup	107
56	Gargoyle Slashers	Bind on Pickup	107
PROPERTIES: Improves critical strike rating by 14.			
56	Cadaverous Gloves	Bind on Pickup	107
PROPERTIES: Increases attack power by 44.			
57	Quickdraw Gloves	Bind on Pickup	109
PROPERTIES: Increases your dodge rating by 12.			
57	Stormshroud Gloves	Bind on Equip	109
PROPERTIES: Improves critical strike rating by 14, Increases your hit rating by 10.			
58	Knight-Lieutenant's Leather Gauntlets	Bind on Pickup	110
PROPERTIES: Increases attack power by 32.			
58	Knight-Lieutenant's Dragonhide Gloves	Bind on Pickup	110
PROPERTIES: Slightly increases your stealth detection.			
58	Blood Guard's Dragonhide Gauntlets	Bind on Pickup	110
PROPERTIES: Slightly increases your stealth detection.			
58	Blood Guard's Leather Vices	Bind on Pickup	110
PROPERTIES: Increases attack power by 32.			
59	Timbermaw Brawlers	Bind on Equip	112
60	Primal Batskin Gloves	Bind on Equip	113
PROPERTIES: Increases your hit rating by 20.			
60	Blooddrenched Grips	Bind on Pickup	122
PROPERTIES: Increases attack power by 34, Improves critical strike rating by 14.			
60	Shadow Panther Hide Gloves	Bind on Equip	113
PROPERTIES: Improves critical strike rating by 14.			
60	Gauntlets of Southwind	Bind on Pickup	126
PROPERTIES: Increases damage and healing done by magical spells and effects by up to 25.			
60	Toughened Silithid Hide Gloves	Bind on Pickup	122
60	Blood Guard's Dragonhide Grips	Bind on Pickup	115
PROPERTIES: Slightly increases your stealth detection.			
60	Blood Guard's Leather Grips	Bind on Pickup	115
PROPERTIES: Increases attack power by 20, Improves critical strike rating by 14.			
60	Knight-Lieutenant's Dragonhide Grips	Bind on Pickup	115
PROPERTIES: Slightly increases your stealth detection.			
60	Knight-Lieutenant's Leather Grips	Bind on Pickup	115
PROPERTIES: Increases attack power by 20, Improves critical strike rating by 14.			
62	Deft Handguards	Bind on Pickup	149
PROPERTIES: Increases attack power by 52.			

Superior Leather Hands

Level	Name	Binding Info	Armor
63	Marshlight Gloves	Bind on Pickup	153
PROPERTIES: Increases damage and healing done by magical spells and effects by up to 25.			
67	Fel Leather Gloves	Bind on Equip	169
PROPERTIES: Increases attack power by 36.			
68	Gauntlets of the Void	Bind on Pickup	178
PROPERTIES: Increases attack power by 48.			
68	Grips of the Lunar Eclipse	Bind on Pickup	178
PROPERTIES: Increases damage and healing done by magical spells and effects by up to 28.			
68	Gloves of the Unbound	Bind on Pickup	178
PROPERTIES: Increases attack power by 38.			
69	Enchanted Clefthoof Gloves	Bind on Equip	178
PROPERTIES: Arcane Resistance +30			
70	Moonglade Handwraps	Bind on Pickup	183
PROPERTIES: Increases healing done by spells and effects by up to 40.			
70	Handgrips of Assassination	Bind on Pickup	183
PROPERTIES: Increases attack power by 50.			
70	Wastewalker Gloves	Bind on Pickup	183
PROPERTIES: Increases attack power by 16.			
70	Natural Mender's Wraps	Bind on Pickup	183
PROPERTIES: Increases healing done by spells and effects by up to 55.			
70	Grand Marshal's Dragonhide Gloves	Bind on Pickup	183
PROPERTIES: Increases healing done by spells and effects by up to 35, Reduces the cast time of your Cyclone spell by 0.1 sec.			
70	Grand Marshal's Leather Gloves	Bind on Pickup	183
PROPERTIES: Increases attack power by 22, Causes your Deadly Throw ability to interrupt spellcasting and prevent any spell in that school from being cast for 3 sec.			
70	Grand Marshal's Wyrmhide Gloves	Bind on Pickup	183
PROPERTIES: Increases damage and healing done by magical spells and effects by up to 32, Reduces the cast time of your Cyclone spell by 0.1 sec, Restores 4 mana per 5 sec.			
70	High Warlord's Dragonhide Gloves	Bind on Pickup	183
PROPERTIES: Increases healing done by spells and effects by up to 35, Reduces the cast time of your Cyclone spell by 0.1 sec.			
70	High Warlord's Leather Gloves	Bind on Pickup	183
PROPERTIES: Increases attack power by 22, Causes your Deadly Throw ability to interrupt spellcasting and prevent any spell in that school from being cast for 3 sec.			
70	High Warlord's Wyrmhide Gloves	Bind on Pickup	183
PROPERTIES: Increases damage and healing done by magical spells and effects by up to 32, Reduces the cast time of your Cyclone spell by 0.1 sec, Restores 4 mana per 5 sec.			
	Gordok's Gloves	Bind on Pickup	106
PROPERTIES: Increases your spell critical strike rating by 14.			
	Gloves of Earthen Power	Bind on Pickup	109
PROPERTIES: Increases damage and healing done by magical spells and effects by up to 27.			
	Handwraps of Undead Slaying	Bind on Pickup	110
PROPERTIES: Increases attack power by 60 when fighting Undead.			
	Rapscallion's Touch	Bind on Pickup	149
	Cryo-mitts	Bind on Pickup	156
PROPERTIES: Increases healing done by spells and effects by up to 57.			

Epic Leather Head

Level	Name	Binding Info	Armor
55	Molten Helm	Bind on Equip	171
PROPERTIES: Increases your dodge rating by 12. Fire Resistance +29			
60	Field Marshal's Dragonhide Helmet	Bind on Pickup	204
PROPERTIES: Improves critical strike rating by 14, Increases damage and healing done by magical spells and effects by up to 18.			

Epic Leather Head

Level	Name	Binding Info	Armor
60	Field Marshal's Leather Mask	Bind on Pickup	204
PROPERTIES: Improves critical strike rating by 14, Increases your hit rating by 10.			
60	Warlord's Dragonhide Helmet	Bind on Pickup	204
PROPERTIES: Increases damage and healing done by magical spells and effects by up to 18, Improves critical strike rating by 14.			
60	Warlord's Leather Helm	Bind on Pickup	204
PROPERTIES: Increases your hit rating by 10, Improves critical strike rating by 14.			
60	Nightslayer Cover	Bind on Pickup	186
PROPERTIES: Improves critical strike rating by 28. Fire Resistance +10			
60	Cenarion Helm	Bind on Pickup	186
PROPERTIES: Increases damage and healing done by magical spells and effects by up to 12. Fire Resistance +10			
60	Stormrage Cover	Bind on Pickup	208
PROPERTIES: Restores 6 mana per 5 sec, Increases healing done by spells and effects by up to 29. Frost Resistance +10, Shadow Resistance +10			
60	Bloodfang Hood	Bind on Pickup	208
PROPERTIES: Improves critical strike rating by 14. Frost Resistance +10, Shadow Resistance +10			
60	Foror's Eyepatch	Bind on Pickup	183
PROPERTIES: Improves critical strike rating by 28, Increases attack power by 44.			
60	Rogue Cap	Bind on Pickup	239
PROPERTIES: Increases your dodge rating by 24, Resistance +200 Armor.			
60	Circlet of Restless Dreams	Bind on Pickup	199
PROPERTIES: Increases dagger skill rating by 14.			
60	Deviate Growth Cap	Bind on Pickup	199
PROPERTIES: Increases healing done by spells and effects by up to 64, Restores 8 mana per 5 sec, Increases your spell critical strike rating by 14.			
60	Genesis Helm	Bind on Pickup	219
PROPERTIES: Increases damage and healing done by magical spells and effects by up to 27, Improves critical strike rating by 14.			
60	Deathdealer's Helm	Bind on Pickup	219
PROPERTIES: Improves critical strike rating by 14, Increases your hit rating by 10.			
60	Wormhide Protector	Bind on Pickup	219
PROPERTIES: Nature Resistance +30			
60	Creeping Vine Helm	Bind on Pickup	208
PROPERTIES: Increases healing done by spells and effects by up to 59.			
60	Guise of the Devourer	Bind on Pickup	206
PROPERTIES: Increases your dodge rating by 12.			
60	Bonescythe Helmet	Bind on Pickup	235
PROPERTIES: Increases your hit rating by 10, Improves critical strike rating by 28.			
60	Dreamwalker Headpiece	Bind on Pickup	235
PROPERTIES: Increases healing done by spells and effects by up to 66.			
60	Polar Helmet	Bind on Pickup	224
PROPERTIES: Frost Resistance +44			
70	Gladiator's Leather Helm	Bind on Pickup	283
PROPERTIES: Increases attack power by 20.			
70	Gladiator's Dragonhide Helm	Bind on Pickup	283
PROPERTIES: Increases healing done by spells and effects by up to 35.			
70	Gladiator's Wyrmhide Helm	Bind on Pickup	283
PROPERTIES: Increases damage and healing done by magical spells and effects by up to 39, Restores 5 mana per 5 sec.			
70	Cowl of Defiance	Bind on Pickup	259
PROPERTIES: Increases attack power by 92.			
70	Malefic Mask of the Shadows	Bind on Pickup	283
PROPERTIES: Increases attack power by 76.			

Epic Leather Head

Level	Name	Binding Info	Armor
70	Cowl of Nature's Breath	Bind on Pickup	283
PROPERTIES: Increases healing done by spells and effects by up to 84.			
70	Netherblade Facemask	Bind on Pickup	271
PROPERTIES: Increases attack power by 74.			
70	Crown of Malorne	Bind on Pickup	271
PROPERTIES: Increases healing done by spells and effects by up to 59, Restores 8 mana per 5 sec.			
70	Antlers of Malorne	Bind on Pickup	271
PROPERTIES: Increases damage and healing done by magical spells and effects by up to 32.			
70	Stag-Helm of Malorne	Bind on Pickup	271
70	Cobrascale Hood	Bind on Equip	249
PROPERTIES: Increases attack power by 70.			
70	Windscale Hood	Bind on Equip	249
PROPERTIES: Increases damage and healing done by magical spells and effects by up to 41, Restores 14 mana per 5 sec.			
70	Hood of Primal Life	Bind on Equip	249
PROPERTIES: Increases healing done by spells and effects by up to 66.			
70	Deathmantle Helm	Bind on Pickup	308
PROPERTIES: Increases attack power by 72.			
70	Nordrassil Headdress	Bind on Pickup	308
PROPERTIES: Increases healing done by spells and effects by up to 88.			
70	Nordrassil Headguard	Bind on Pickup	308
70	Nordrassil Headpiece	Bind on Pickup	308
PROPERTIES: Increases damage and healing done by magical spells and effects by up to 47.			
	Darkmantle Cap	Bind on Pickup	171
PROPERTIES: Improves critical strike rating by 14.			
	Feralheart Cowl	Bind on Pickup	171
PROPERTIES: Increases damage and healing done by magical spells and effects by up to 16.			
	Gnomish Battle Goggles	Bind on Pickup	249
PROPERTIES: Increases attack power by 100, Improves critical strike rating by 28.			

Superior Leather Head

Level	Name	Binding Info	Armor
28	Enduring Cap	Bind on Equip	88
32	Adventurer's Pith Helmet	Bind on Equip	94
33	Expert Goldminer's Helmet	Bind on Equip	95
PROPERTIES: Increases axe skill rating by 17.			
40	Wolfshead Helm	Bind on Equip	109
PROPERTIES: When shapeshifting into Cat form the Druid gains 20 energy, when shapeshifting into Bear form the Druid gains 5 rage.			
43	Winged Helm	Bind on Equip	115
45	Helm of Fire	Bind on Equip	118
PROPERTIES: Hurls a fiery ball that causes 286 to 376 Fire damage and an additional 40 damage over 8 sec. Fire Resistance +5			
45	Embrace of the Lycan	Bind on Pickup	118
PROPERTIES: Increases attack power by 32.			
47	Soothsayer's Headdress	Bind on Pickup	122
51	Tattered Leather Hood	Bind on Equip	130
PROPERTIES: Increases your hit rating by 10.			
52	Ragefury Eyepatch	Bind on Pickup	132
PROPERTIES: Improves critical strike rating by 28.			
52	Ghostshroud	Bind on Pickup	132
PROPERTIES: Shadow Resistance +5			

Superior Leather Head

Level	Name	Binding Info	Armor
52	Mask of the Unforgiven	Bind on Pickup	132
PROPERTIES: Increases your hit rating by 20, Improves critical strike rating by 14.			
53	Felhide Cap	Bind on Pickup	134
PROPERTIES: Fire Resistance +8, Shadow Resistance +8			
55	Tribal War Feathers	Bind on Pickup	137
PROPERTIES: Increases healing done by spells and effects by up to 33.			
56	Insightful Hood	Bind on Pickup	139
PROPERTIES: Increases your spell critical strike rating by 14, Increases healing done by spells and effects by up to 33.			
56	Helm of the New Moon	Bind on Pickup	139
PROPERTIES: Increases damage and healing done by magical spells and effects by up to 23.			
57	Bone Ring Helm	Bind on Pickup	141
57	Shadowcraft Cap	Bind on Pickup	141
57	Wildheart Cowl	Bind on Pickup	141
58	Eye of Rend	Bind on Pickup	143
PROPERTIES: Improves critical strike rating by 28.			
58	Feathermoon Headdress	Bind on Equip	143
58	Lieutenant Commander's Leather Veil	Bind on Pickup	143
PROPERTIES: Increases your dodge rating by 12, Increases attack power by 12, Increases your hit rating by 10.			
58	Lieutenant Commander's Dragonhide Shroud	Bind on Pickup	143
PROPERTIES: Increases attack power by 16, Increases damage and healing done by magical spells and effects by up to 13.			
58	Champion's Dragonhide Helm	Bind on Pickup	143
PROPERTIES: Increases attack power by 16, Increases damage and healing done by magical spells and effects by up to 13.			
58	Champion's Leather Headguard	Bind on Pickup	143
PROPERTIES: Increases your dodge rating by 12, Increases your hit rating by 10, Increases attack power by 12.			
60	Bloodvine Lens	Bind on Equip	147
PROPERTIES: Improves critical strike rating by 28, Slightly increases your stealth detection.			
60	Southwind Helm	Bind on Pickup	164
PROPERTIES: Increases your hit rating by 10.			
60	Helm of Regrowth	Bind on Pickup	162
PROPERTIES: Increases healing done by spells and effects by up to 22.			
60	Blooddrenched Mask	Bind on Pickup	153
PROPERTIES: Increases your hit rating by 20.			
60	Bramblewood Helm	Bind on Equip	156
PROPERTIES: Nature Resistance +30			
60	Champion's Dragonhide Headguard	Bind on Pickup	158
PROPERTIES: Increases damage and healing done by magical spells and effects by up to 18.			
60	Champion's Leather Helm	Bind on Pickup	158
PROPERTIES: Improves critical strike rating by 14, Increases your hit rating by 10, Increases attack power by 36.			
60	Lieutenant Commander's Dragonhide Headguard	Bind on Pickup	158
PROPERTIES: Increases damage and healing done by magical spells and effects by up to 18.			
60	Lieutenant Commander's Leather Helm	Bind on Pickup	158
PROPERTIES: Improves critical strike rating by 14, Increases your hit rating by 10, Increases attack power by 36.			
65	Cowl of Many Eyes	Bind on Pickup	208
PROPERTIES: Increases healing done by spells and effects by up to 35.			
65	Darkguard Face Mask	Bind on Pickup	208
PROPERTIES: Increases attack power by 60.			
66	Exorcist's Leather Helm	Bind on Pickup	208
PROPERTIES: Increases attack power by 20.			

Superior Leather Head

Level	Name	Binding Info	Armor
66	Exorcist's Dragonhide Helm	Bind on Pickup	208
PROPERTIES: Increases healing done by spells and effects by up to 37.			
66	Exorcist's Wyrmhide Helm	Bind on Pickup	208
PROPERTIES: Increases damage and healing done by magical spells and effects by up to 34.			
68	Crown of the Forest Lord	Bind on Pickup	232
PROPERTIES: Increases healing done by spells and effects by up to 68.			
68	Sethekk Headdress	Bind on Pickup	237
PROPERTIES: Increases attack power by 58.			
68	Moon-Crown Antlers	Bind on Pickup	232
PROPERTIES: Increases damage and healing done by magical spells and effects by up to 40.			
69	Stylin' Jungle Hat	Bind on Equip	232
PROPERTIES: Restores 10 mana per 5 sec, Increases damage and healing done by magical spells and effects by up to 19.			
70	Cowl of the Guiltless	Bind on Pickup	237
PROPERTIES: Increases attack power by 52.			
70	Wastewalker Helm	Bind on Pickup	237
PROPERTIES: Increases attack power by 56.			
70	Moonglade Cowl	Bind on Pickup	237
PROPERTIES: Increases healing done by spells and effects by up to 53.			
70	Helm of Assassination	Bind on Pickup	237
PROPERTIES: Increases attack power by 66.			
70	Grand Marshal's Dragonhide Helm	Bind on Pickup	237
PROPERTIES: Increases healing done by spells and effects by up to 31.			
70	Grand Marshal's Leather Helm	Bind on Pickup	237
PROPERTIES: Increases attack power by 20.			
70	Grand Marshal's Wyrmhide Helm	Bind on Pickup	237
PROPERTIES: Increases damage and healing done by magical spells and effects by up to 34, Restores 5 mana per 5 sec.			
70	High Warlord's Dragonhide Helm	Bind on Pickup	237
PROPERTIES: Increases healing done by spells and effects by up to 31.			
70	High Warlord's Leather Helm	Bind on Pickup	237
PROPERTIES: Increases attack power by 20.			
70	High Warlord's Wyrmhide Helm	Bind on Pickup	237
PROPERTIES: Increases damage and healing done by magical spells and effects by up to 34, Restores 5 mana per 5 sec.			
	Engineer's Guild Headpiece	Bind on Pickup	113
	Ebon Mask	Bind on Pickup	122
PROPERTIES: Improves critical strike rating by 14, Increases attack power by 36.			
	Pirate's Eye Patch	Bind on Pickup	122
PROPERTIES: Increases your chance to resist Fear effects by 4%.			
	Moonshadow Hood	Bind on Pickup	122
PROPERTIES: Increases damage and healing done by magical spells and effects by up to 18, Increases your spell critical strike rating by 14.			
	Sanctified Leather Helm	Bind on Pickup	149
PROPERTIES: Increases healing done by spells and effects by up to 40.			
	Cogspinner Goggles	Bind on Equip	220
	Hyper-Vision Goggles	Bind on Equip	232
PROPERTIES: Increases attack power by 84, Increases your stealth detection for 15 sec.			
	Moonkin Headdress	Bind on Pickup	188
PROPERTIES: Increases damage and healing done by magical spells and effects by up to 23.			
	Helm of the Claw	Bind on Pickup	237
PROPERTIES: Increases attack power by 66.			

Superior Leather Head

Level	Name	Binding Info	Armor
	Terokk's Mask	Bind on Pickup	237
PROPERTIES: Increases attack power by 66.			
	Circlet of the Starcaller	Bind on Pickup	226
PROPERTIES: Increases damage and healing done by magical spells and effects by up to 47.			

Epic Leather Legs

Level	Name	Binding Info	Armor
59	Salamander Scale Pants	Bind on Pickup	195
PROPERTIES: Increases healing done by spells and effects by up to 51, Restores 9 mana per 5 sec. Fire Resistance +10			
60	Marshal's Dragonhide Legguards	Bind on Pickup	212
PROPERTIES: Improves critical strike rating by 14.			
60	Marshal's Leather Leggings	Bind on Pickup	212
PROPERTIES: Increases your hit rating by 20, Improves critical strike rating by 14.			
60	General's Dragonhide Leggings	Bind on Pickup	212
PROPERTIES: Improves critical strike rating by 14.			
60	General's Leather Legguards	Bind on Pickup	212
PROPERTIES: Increases your hit rating by 20, Improves critical strike rating by 14.			
60	Nightslayer Pants	Bind on Pickup	200
PROPERTIES: Improves critical strike rating by 14. Shadow Resistance +10			
60	Cenarion Leggings	Bind on Pickup	200
PROPERTIES: Increases your spell critical strike rating by 14, Restores 4 mana per 5 sec, Increases healing done by spells and effects by up to 22. Shadow Resistance +10			
60	Stormrage Legguards	Bind on Pickup	224
PROPERTIES: Increases healing done by spells and effects by up to 48, Restores 6 mana per 5 sec. Fire Resistance +10, Arcane Resistance +10			
60	Bloodfang Pants	Bind on Pickup	224
PROPERTIES: Improves critical strike rating by 14. Fire Resistance +10, Arcane Resistance +10			
60	Rogue Pants	Bind on Pickup	257
PROPERTIES: Increases your parry rating by 20, Resistance +250 Armor.			
60	Dark Heart Pants	Bind on Pickup	212
PROPERTIES: Improves critical strike rating by 28, Increases attack power by 48.			
60	Genesis Trousers	Bind on Pickup	236
PROPERTIES: Increases damage and healing done by magical spells and effects by up to 27, Improves critical strike rating by 14, Restores 4 mana per 5 sec.			
60	Deathdealer's Leggings	Bind on Pickup	236
PROPERTIES: Improves critical strike rating by 14.			
60	Leggings of Immersion	Bind on Pickup	217
PROPERTIES: Increases damage and healing done by magical spells and effects by up to 39, Restores 6 mana per 5 sec.			
60	Bonescythe Legplates	Bind on Pickup	253
PROPERTIES: Improves critical strike rating by 14, Increases your hit rating by 10.			
60	Dreamwalker Legguards	Bind on Pickup	253
PROPERTIES: Increases healing done by spells and effects by up to 66, Restores 8 mana per 5 sec.			
60	Outrider's Leather Pants	Bind on Pickup	197
PROPERTIES: Improves critical strike rating by 14.			
60	Outrider's Lizardhide Pants	Bind on Pickup	197
PROPERTIES: Increases damage and healing done by magical spells and effects by up to 11.			
60	Sentinel's Leather Pants	Bind on Pickup	197
PROPERTIES: Improves critical strike rating by 14.			
60	Sentinel's Lizardhide Pants	Bind on Pickup	197
PROPERTIES: Increases damage and healing done by magical spells and effects by up to 11.			
60	Leggings of Apocalypse	Bind on Pickup	241
PROPERTIES: Improves critical strike rating by 28.			

Epic Leather Legs

Level	Name	Binding Info	Armor
70	Gladiator's Leather Legguards	Bind on Pickup	305
PROPERTIES: Increases attack power by 34.			
70	Gladiator's Dragonhide Legguards	Bind on Pickup	305
PROPERTIES: Increases healing done by spells and effects by up to 13.			
70	Gladiator's Wyrmhide Legguards	Bind on Pickup	305
PROPERTIES: Increases damage and healing done by magical spells and effects by up to 44, Restores 9 mana per 5 sec.			
70	Karazhan Opera House Shared Loot Druid Legs	Bind on Pickup	278
PROPERTIES: Increases healing done by spells and effects by up to 73.			
70	Karazhan Netherspite Loot 2 Rogue Legs	Bind on Pickup	278
PROPERTIES: Increases attack power by 56.			
70	Netherblade Breeches	Bind on Pickup	292
PROPERTIES: Increases attack power by 76.			
70	Legguards of Malorne	Bind on Pickup	292
PROPERTIES: Increases healing done by spells and effects by up to 75, Restores 8 mana per 5 sec.			
70	Britches of Malorne	Bind on Pickup	292
PROPERTIES: Increases damage and healing done by magical spells and effects by up to 40, Restores 6 mana per 5 sec.			
70	Greaves of Malorne	Bind on Pickup	292
70	Leggings of the Murderous Intent	Bind on Pickup	345
PROPERTIES: Increases attack power by 112.			
70	Deathmantle Legguards	Bind on Pickup	332
PROPERTIES: Increases attack power by 110.			
70	Nordrassil Feral-Kilt	Bind on Pickup	332
PROPERTIES: Increases healing done by spells and effects by up to 86.			
70	Nordrassil Wrath-Kilt	Bind on Pickup	332
70	Nordrassil Life-Kilt	Bind on Pickup	332
PROPERTIES: Increases damage and healing done by magical spells and effects by up to 46.			
70	Forestwalker Kilt	Bind on Pickup	268
PROPERTIES: Increases healing done by spells and effects by up to 57.			
70	Midnight Legguards	Bind on Pickup	268
PROPERTIES: Increases attack power by 60.			
70	Inferno Hardened Leggings	Bind on Pickup	268
PROPERTIES: Fire Resistance +55			
	Leggings of Arcana	Bind on Pickup	190
PROPERTIES: Increases damage and healing done by magical spells and effects by up to 18.			
	Shadowhide Leggings	Bind on Pickup	164
PROPERTIES: Increases your spell critical strike rating by 14, Increases damage done by Frost spells and effects by up to 14.			
	Polar Leggings	Bind on Pickup	234
PROPERTIES: Frost Resistance +40			

Superior Leather Legs

Level	Name	Binding Info	Armor
18	Leggings of the Fang	Bind on Pickup	79
25	Petrolspill Leggings	Bind on Equip	90
PROPERTIES: Fire Resistance +10			
25	Troll's Bane Leggings	Bind on Equip	90
34	Warchief Kilt	Bind on Equip	105
38	Basilisk Hide Pants	Bind on Equip	113
44	Jinxed Hoodoo Kilt	Bind on Pickup	126
45	Blackstorm Leggings	Bind on Pickup	132
PROPERTIES: Increases attack power by 32.			

Superior Leather Legs

Level	Name	Binding Info	Armor
45	Wildfeather Leggings	Bind on Pickup	132
PROPERTIES: Increases damage and healing done by magical spells and effects by up to 14, Increases healing done by spells and effects by up to 26.			
49	Windscale Sarong	Bind on Pickup	136
50	Stormshroud Pants	Bind on Equip	138
PROPERTIES: Improves critical strike rating by 28, Increases your dodge rating by 12.			
51	Unbridled Leggings	Bind on Equip	140
PROPERTIES: Restores 7 health per 5 sec.			
52	Living Leggings	Bind on Equip	142
PROPERTIES: Increases healing done by spells and effects by up to 26. Nature Resistance +5			
52	Warbear Woolies	Bind on Equip	142
52	Leggings of Frenzied Magic	Bind on Pickup	142
PROPERTIES: Increases damage and healing done by magical spells and effects by up to 16, Restores 5 mana per 5 sec.			
53	Warstrife Leggings	Bind on Pickup	144
PROPERTIES: Increases your dodge rating by 24.			
54	Luminary Kilt	Bind on Pickup	147
PROPERTIES: Increases damage and healing done by magical spells and effects by up to 22.			
55	Earthborn Kilt	Bind on Equip	148
55	Tressermane Leggings	Bind on Pickup	148
PROPERTIES: Increases damage and healing done by magical spells and effects by up to 19.			
55	Devilsaur Leggings	Bind on Equip	148
PROPERTIES: Increases attack power by 46, Improves critical strike rating by 14.			
56	Cadaverous Leggings	Bind on Pickup	150
PROPERTIES: Increases attack power by 52.			
56	Shadowcraft Pants	Bind on Pickup	150
56	Wildheart Kilt	Bind on Pickup	150
56	Ghoul Skin Leggings	Bind on Pickup	150
PROPERTIES: Increases healing done by spells and effects by up to 44.			
57	Ghostloom Leggings	Bind on Pickup	152
PROPERTIES: Restores 6 mana per 5 sec.			
57	Tanglemoss Leggings	Bind on Pickup	150
PROPERTIES: Increases your spell critical strike rating by 14.			
57	Plaguehound Leggings	Bind on Equip	152
PROPERTIES: Increases your hit rating by 10.			
57	Abyssal Leather Leggings	Bind on Equip	152
PROPERTIES: Improves critical strike rating by 14.			
58	Blademaster Leggings	Bind on Pickup	154
PROPERTIES: Increases your hit rating by 10, Improves critical strike rating by 14, Increases your dodge rating by 24.			
58	Knight-Captain's Leather Legguards	Bind on Pickup	154
PROPERTIES: Improves critical strike rating by 28.			
58	Knight-Captain's Dragonhide Leggings	Bind on Pickup	154
PROPERTIES: Increases your dodge rating by 12, Increases attack power by 18.			
58	Legionnaire's Dragonhide Trousers	Bind on Pickup	154
PROPERTIES: Increases your dodge rating by 12, Increases attack power by 18.			
58	Legionnaire's Leather Leggings	Bind on Pickup	154
PROPERTIES: Improves critical strike rating by 28.			
60	Animist's Leggings	Bind on Pickup	170
PROPERTIES: Increases healing done by spells and effects by up to 35.			
60	Blooddrenched Leggings	Bind on Pickup	170
60	Legionnaire's Dragonhide Leggings	Bind on Pickup	165
PROPERTIES: Increases your spell critical strike rating by 14, Increases damage and healing done by magical spells and effects by up to 14.			

Superior Leather Legs

Level	Name	Binding Info	Armor
60	Legionnaire's Leather Legguards	Bind on Pickup	165
PROPERTIES: Improves critical strike rating by 14, Increases your hit rating by 10, Increases attack power by 34.			
60	Knight-Captain's Dragonhide Leggings	Bind on Pickup	165
PROPERTIES: Increases your spell critical strike rating by 14, Increases damage and healing done by magical spells and effects by up to 14.			
60	Knight-Captain's Leather Legguards	Bind on Pickup	165
PROPERTIES: Improves critical strike rating by 14, Increases your hit rating by 10, Increases attack power by 34.			
61	Kilt of Leaves	Bind on Pickup	203
PROPERTIES: Restores 6 mana per 5 sec, Increases healing done by spells and effects by up to 33.			
63	Skulldugger's Breeches	Bind on Pickup	214
PROPERTIES: Increases attack power by 40.			
66	Dreamstalker Leggings	Bind on Pickup	224
PROPERTIES: Increases healing done by spells and effects by up to 44.			
66	Shadowstalker's Leggings	Bind on Pickup	224
PROPERTIES: Increases attack power by 30.			
68	Moonchild Leggings	Bind on Pickup	249
PROPERTIES: Increases damage and healing done by magical spells and effects by up to 23.			
68	Mennu's Patchwork Leggings	Bind on Pickup	249
PROPERTIES: Increases attack power by 44.			
69	Fel Leather Leggings	Bind on Equip	249
PROPERTIES: Increases attack power by 52.			
69	Enchanted Clefthoof Leggings	Bind on Equip	249
PROPERTIES: Arcane Resistance +40			
69	Blastguard Pants	Bind on Equip	249
PROPERTIES: Fire Resistance +40			
70	Heavy Clefthoof Leggings	Bind on Equip	251
70	Leggings of the Unrepentant	Bind on Pickup	256
PROPERTIES: Increases attack power by 60.			
70	Earthsoul Britches	Bind on Pickup	256
PROPERTIES: Increases healing done by spells and effects by up to 73.			
70	Wastewalker Leggings	Bind on Pickup	256
PROPERTIES: Increases attack power by 28.			
70	Moonglade Pants	Bind on Pickup	256
PROPERTIES: Increases healing done by spells and effects by up to 55.			
70	Leggings of Assassination	Bind on Pickup	256
PROPERTIES: Increases attack power by 44.			
70	Warpscale Leggings	Bind on Pickup	256
PROPERTIES: Increases attack power by 56.			
70	Grand Marshal's Dragonhide Legguards	Bind on Pickup	256
PROPERTIES: Increases healing done by spells and effects by up to 48.			
70	Grand Marshal's Leather Legguards	Bind on Pickup	256
PROPERTIES: Increases attack power by 28.			
70	Grand Marshal's Wyrmhide Legguards	Bind on Pickup	256
PROPERTIES: Increases damage and healing done by magical spells and effects by up to 39, Restores 8 mana per 5 sec.			
70	High Warlord's Dragonhide Legguards	Bind on Pickup	256
PROPERTIES: Increases healing done by spells and effects by up to 48.			
70	High Warlord's Leather Legguards	Bind on Pickup	256
PROPERTIES: Increases attack power by 28.			
70	High Warlord's Wyrmhide Legguards	Bind on Pickup	256
PROPERTIES: Increases damage and healing done by magical spells and effects by up to 39, Restores 8 mana per 5 sec.			

Superior Leather Legs

Level	Name	Binding Info	Armor
70	Nomad's Leggings	Bind on Pickup	256
PROPERTIES: Increases attack power by 66.			
70	Retainer's Leggings	Bind on Pickup	256
PROPERTIES: Increases attack power by 92.			
70	Tempest Leggings	Bind on Pickup	256
PROPERTIES: Increases damage and healing done by magical spells and effects by up to 44.			
70	Kurenai Kilt	Bind on Pickup	256
PROPERTIES: Increases damage and healing done by magical spells and effects by up to 44.			
	Triprunner Dungarees	Bind on Pickup	101
	Shadowhide Leggings	Bind on Pickup	132
PROPERTIES: Shadow Resistance +6			
	Cenarion Reservist's Leggings	Bind on Pickup	154
PROPERTIES: Increases attack power by 26. Nature Resistance +25			
	Cenarion Reservist's Leggings	Bind on Pickup	154
PROPERTIES: Increases healing done by spells and effects by up to 29. Nature Resistance +25			
	Darkmantle Pants	Bind on Pickup	160
	Feralheart Kilt	Bind on Pickup	160
PROPERTIES: Increases damage and healing done by magical spells and effects by up to 9.			
	Leggings of Unending Assault	Bind on Pickup	230
PROPERTIES: Increases attack power by 62.			
	Leggings of the Third Coin	Bind on Pickup	219
PROPERTIES: Increases damage and healing done by magical spells and effects by up to 32, Restores 4 mana per 5 sec.			
	Haramad's Leggings of the Third Coin	Bind on Pickup	219
PROPERTIES: Increases damage and healing done by magical spells and effects by up to 27.			
	X-52 Pilot's Leggings	Bind on Pickup	236
PROPERTIES: Increases attack power by 62.			
	Shattrath Leggings	Bind on Pickup	243
PROPERTIES: Increases feral combat skill rating by 22.			

Epic Leather Shoulders

Level	Name	Binding Info	Armor
60	Field Marshal's Dragonhide Spaulders	Bind on Pickup	188
PROPERTIES: Increases damage and healing done by magical spells and effects by up to 18.			
60	Field Marshal's Leather Epaulets	Bind on Pickup	188
PROPERTIES: Increases your hit rating by 10.			
60	Warlord's Dragonhide Epaulets	Bind on Pickup	188
PROPERTIES: Increases damage and healing done by magical spells and effects by up to 18.			
60	Warlord's Leather Spaulders	Bind on Pickup	188
PROPERTIES: Increases your hit rating by 10.			
60	Nightslayer Shoulder Pads	Bind on Pickup	171
PROPERTIES: Increases your hit rating by 10. Shadow Resistance +7			
60	Bloodfang Spaulders	Bind on Pickup	192
PROPERTIES: Increases your dodge rating by 12. Fire Resistance +10			
60	Cenarion Spaulders	Bind on Pickup	171
PROPERTIES: Restores 4 mana per 5 sec, Increases healing done by spells and effects by up to 18. Shadow Resistance +7			
60	Stormrage Pauldrons	Bind on Pickup	192
PROPERTIES: Increases healing done by spells and effects by up to 29, Restores 4 mana per 5 sec. Fire Resistance +10			
60	Wild Growth Spaulders	Bind on Pickup	182
PROPERTIES: Increases healing done by spells and effects by up to 62.			

Epic Leather Shoulders

Level	Name	Binding Info	Armor
60	Fireguard Shoulders	Bind on Pickup	182
PROPERTIES: Fire Resistance +22			
60	Taut Dragonhide Shoulderpads	Bind on Pickup	195
PROPERTIES: Increases attack power by 46.			
60	Highlander's Leather Shoulders	Bind on Pickup	169
PROPERTIES: Increases attack power by 30.			
60	Highlander's Lizardhide Shoulders	Bind on Pickup	169
PROPERTIES: Increases attack power by 30.			
60	Defiler's Lizardhide Shoulders	Bind on Pickup	169
PROPERTIES: Increases attack power by 30.			
60	Defiler's Leather Shoulders	Bind on Pickup	169
PROPERTIES: Increases attack power by 30.			
60	Rogue Spaulders	Bind on Pickup	220
PROPERTIES: Resistance +200 Armor, Improves critical strike rating by 14.			
60	Unnatural Leather Spaulders	Bind on Pickup	184
PROPERTIES: Increases attack power by 18. Nature Resistance +25			
60	Genesis Shoulderpads	Bind on Pickup	196
PROPERTIES: Increases damage and healing done by magical spells and effects by up to 20, Restores 3 mana per 5 sec.			
60	Deathdealer's Spaulders	Bind on Pickup	196
PROPERTIES: Increases your hit rating by 10.			
60	Mantle of Wicked Revenge	Bind on Pickup	195
60	Bonescythe Pauldrons	Bind on Pickup	212
PROPERTIES: Improves critical strike rating by 14, Increases your hit rating by 10.			
60	Dreamwalker Spaulders	Bind on Pickup	212
PROPERTIES: Restores 5 mana per 5 sec, Increases healing done by spells and effects by up to 48.			
60	Polar Shoulder Pads	Bind on Pickup	207
PROPERTIES: Frost Resistance +33			
70	Gladiator's Leather Spaulders	Bind on Pickup	262
PROPERTIES: Increases attack power by 12.			
70	Gladiator's Dragonhide Spaulders	Bind on Pickup	262
PROPERTIES: Increases healing done by spells and effects by up to 22.			
70	Gladiator's Wyrmhide Spaulders	Bind on Pickup	262
PROPERTIES: Increases damage and healing done by magical spells and effects by up to 22, Restores 3 mana per 5 sec.			
70	Forest Wind Shoulderpads	Bind on Pickup	239
PROPERTIES: Increases healing done by spells and effects by up to 59.			
70	Bladed Shoulderpads of the Merciless	Bind on Pickup	239
PROPERTIES: Increases attack power by 54.			
70	Netherblade Shoulderpads	Bind on Pickup	250
PROPERTIES: Increases attack power by 44.			
70	Shoulderguards of Malorne	Bind on Pickup	250
PROPERTIES: Increases healing done by spells and effects by up to 62, Restores 4 mana per 5 sec.			
70	Pauldrons of Malorne	Bind on Pickup	250
PROPERTIES: Increases damage and healing done by magical spells and effects by up to 33, Restores 4 mana per 5 sec.			
70	Mantle of Malorne	Bind on Pickup	250
70	Shoulderpads of the Stranger	Bind on Pickup	273
PROPERTIES: Increases attack power by 54, Increases dagger skill rating by 8.			
70	Runetotem's Mantle	Bind on Pickup	296
PROPERTIES: Increases healing done by spells and effects by up to 84.			
70	Deathmantle Shoulderpads	Bind on Pickup	284
PROPERTIES: Increases attack power by 40.			

Epic Leather Shoulders

Level	Name	Binding Info	Armor
70	Nordrassil Feral-Mantle	Bind on Pickup	284
PROPERTIES: Increases healing done by spells and effects by up to 44, Restores 8 mana per 5 sec.			
70	Nordrassil Wrath-Mantle	Bind on Pickup	284
70	Nordrassil Life-Mantle	Bind on Pickup	284
PROPERTIES: Increases damage and healing done by magical spells and effects by up to 23.			
	Zandalar Madcap's Mantle	Bind on Pickup	160
PROPERTIES: Increases your hit rating by 10.			

Superior Leather Shoulders

Level	Name	Binding Info	Armor
25	Mantle of Thieves	Bind on Equip	77
25	Feathered Mantle	Bind on Equip	77
26	Forest Tracker Epaulets	Bind on Equip	78
27	Watchman Pauldrons	Bind on Equip	80
33	Flintrock Shoulders	Bind on Equip	88
37	Fleshhide Shoulders	Bind on Pickup	95
40	Sheepshear Mantle	Bind on Equip	100
46	Phytoskin Spaulders	Bind on Pickup	111
PROPERTIES: Nature Resistance +10			
47	Atal'ai Spaulders	Bind on Pickup	113
49	Living Shoulders	Bind on Equip	117
PROPERTIES: Increases healing done by spells and effects by up to 31. Nature Resistance +3			
49	Ironfeather Shoulders	Bind on Equip	117
50	Splinthide Shoulders	Bind on Pickup	118
PROPERTIES: Increases damage and healing done by magical spells and effects by up to 9.			
52	Icy Tomb Spaulders	Bind on Equip	122
PROPERTIES: Frost Resistance +10, Shadow Resistance +10			
52	Dark Warder's Pauldrons	Bind on Pickup	122
54	Demonic Runed Spaulders	Bind on Pickup	126
54	Stormshroud Shoulders	Bind on Equip	126
PROPERTIES: Improves critical strike rating by 14, Increases your dodge rating by 12.			
55	Shadowcraft Spaulders	Bind on Pickup	127
55	Wildheart Spaulders	Bind on Pickup	127
56	Truestrike Shoulders	Bind on Pickup	129
PROPERTIES: Increases your hit rating by 20, Increases attack power by 24.			
56	Spaulders of the Unseen	Bind on Equip	129
56	Cyclone Spaulders	Bind on Pickup	129
PROPERTIES: Increases damage and healing done by magical spells and effects by up to 14.			
57	Death's Clutch	Bind on Pickup	131
57	Flamescarred Shoulders	Bind on Pickup	131
PROPERTIES: Fire Resistance +10			
58	Wyrmtongue Shoulders	Bind on Pickup	132
58	Lieutenant Commander's Leather Spaulders	Bind on Pickup	132
PROPERTIES: Increases attack power by 12.			
58	Lieutenant Commander's Dragonhide Epaulets	Bind on Pickup	132
PROPERTIES: Increases damage and healing done by magical spells and effects by up to 8.			
58	Champion's Dragonhide Spaulders	Bind on Pickup	132
PROPERTIES: Increases damage and healing done by magical spells and effects by up to 8.			
58	Champion's Leather Mantle	Bind on Pickup	132
PROPERTIES: Increases attack power by 12.			
59	Golden Mantle of the Dawn	Bind on Equip	134
PROPERTIES: Increases your dodge rating by 12.			

Superior Leather Shoulders

Level	Name	Binding Info	Armor
60	Blood Tiger Shoulders	Bind on Equip	136
60	Animist's Spaulders	Bind on Pickup	141
PROPERTIES: Increases healing done by spells and effects by up to 37.			
60	Abyssal Leather Shoulders	Bind on Pickup	141
PROPERTIES: Increases your hit rating by 10.			
60	Chitinous Shoulderguards	Bind on Pickup	151
60	Champion's Dragonhide Shoulders	Bind on Pickup	146
PROPERTIES: Increases damage and healing done by magical spells and effects by up to 14.			
60	Champion's Leather Shoulders	Bind on Pickup	146
PROPERTIES: Increases attack power by 22, Improves critical strike rating by 14, Increases your hit rating by 10.			
60	Lieutenant Commander's Dragonhide Shoulders	Bind on Pickup	146
PROPERTIES: Increases damage and healing done by magical spells and effects by up to 14.			
60	Lieutenant Commander's Leather Shoulders	Bind on Pickup	146
PROPERTIES: Increases attack power by 22, Improves critical strike rating by 14, Increases your hit rating by 10.			
61	Blood Etched Shoulders	Bind on Pickup	174
PROPERTIES: Increases attack power by 40.			
66	Dream Walker's Shoulderpads	Bind on Pickup	197
PROPERTIES: Increases healing done by spells and effects by up to 26.			
66	Mantle of Perenolde	Bind on Pickup	197
PROPERTIES: Increases attack power by 20.			
68	Sun-Gilded Shouldercaps	Bind on Pickup	214
PROPERTIES: Increases attack power by 48.			
68	Lunar-Claw Pauldrons	Bind on Pickup	214
PROPERTIES: Increases damage and healing done by magical spells and effects by up to 29.			
68	Mantle of Autumn	Bind on Pickup	214
PROPERTIES: Increases healing done by spells and effects by up to 68.			
70	Moonglade Shoulders	Bind on Pickup	219
PROPERTIES: Increases healing done by spells and effects by up to 29.			
70	Shoulderpads of Assassination	Bind on Pickup	219
PROPERTIES: Increases attack power by 42.			
70	Wastewalker Shoulderpads	Bind on Pickup	219
PROPERTIES: Increases attack power by 34.			
70	Mantle of the Unforgiven	Bind on Pickup	219
PROPERTIES: Increases attack power by 52.			
70	Grand Marshal's Dragonhide Spaulders	Bind on Pickup	219
PROPERTIES: Increases healing done by spells and effects by up to 18.			
70	Grand Marshal's Leather Spaulders	Bind on Pickup	219
PROPERTIES: Increases attack power by 22.			
70	Grand Marshal's Wyrmhide Spaulders	Bind on Pickup	219
PROPERTIES: Increases damage and healing done by magical spells and effects by up to 13, Restores 2 mana per 5 sec.			
70	High Warlord's Dragonhide Spaulders	Bind on Pickup	219
PROPERTIES: Increases healing done by spells and effects by up to 18.			
70	High Warlord's Leather Spaulders	Bind on Pickup	219
PROPERTIES: Increases attack power by 22.			
70	High Warlord's Wyrmhide Spaulders	Bind on Pickup	219
PROPERTIES: Increases damage and healing done by magical spells and effects by up to 13, Restores 2 mana per 5 sec.			
70	Talbuk Hide Spaulders	Bind on Pickup	219
PROPERTIES: Increases attack power by 70.			
70	Blackened Leather Spaulders	Bind on Pickup	219
PROPERTIES: Increases attack power by 70.			

Superior Leather Shoulders

Level	Name	Binding Info	Armor
	Halycon's Muzzle	Bind on Pickup	127
PROPERTIES: Arcane Resistance +10			
	Darkmantle Spaulders	Bind on Pickup	136
	Feralheart Spaulders	Bind on Pickup	136
PROPERTIES: Increases damage and healing done by magical spells and effects by up to 6, Restores 2 mana per 5 sec.			
	Cleansed Fel Pauldrons	Bind on Pickup	208
PROPERTIES: Increases attack power by 20.			
	Netherfused Pauldrons	Bind on Pickup	208
PROPERTIES: Increases damage and healing done by magical spells and effects by up to 28.			

Epic Leather Waist

Level	Name	Binding Info	Armor
56	Sash of Mercy	Bind on Equip	120
PROPERTIES: Increases healing done by spells and effects by up to 53.			
60	Marshal's Dragonhide Waistguard	Bind on Pickup	127
60	Marshal's Leather Cinch	Bind on Pickup	127
60	General's Dragonhide Belt	Bind on Pickup	127
60	General's Leather Girdle	Bind on Pickup	127
60	Nightslayer Belt	Bind on Equip	128
PROPERTIES: Improves critical strike rating by 14. Fire Resistance +7			
60	Cenarion Belt	Bind on Equip	128
PROPERTIES: Restores 4 mana per 5 sec, Increases damage and healing done by magical spells and effects by up to 9. Fire Resistance +7			
60	Stormrage Belt	Bind on Pickup	144
PROPERTIES: Increases healing done by spells and effects by up to 26, Restores 4 mana per 5 sec. Shadow Resistance +10			
60	Bloodfang Belt	Bind on Pickup	144
PROPERTIES: Improves critical strike rating by 14. Shadow Resistance +10			
60	Flayed Doomguard Belt	Bind on Pickup	132
PROPERTIES: Increases your spell critical strike rating by 14, Increases damage and healing done by magical spells and effects by up to 14.			
60	Lava Belt	Bind on Equip	128
PROPERTIES: Fire Resistance +26			
60	Corehound Belt	Bind on Equip	135
PROPERTIES: Increases healing done by spells and effects by up to 62. Fire Resistance +12			
60	Molten Belt	Bind on Equip	135
PROPERTIES: Fire Resistance +12			
60	Taut Dragonhide Belt	Bind on Pickup	143
PROPERTIES: Increases attack power by 60, Increases your dodge rating by 12.			
60	Rogue Belt	Bind on Equip	165
PROPERTIES: Improves critical strike rating by 14. Fire Resistance +8, Nature Resistance +8, Frost Resistance +8, Shadow Resistance +8, Arcane Resistance +7			
60	Belt of Never-ending Agony	Bind on Pickup	162
PROPERTIES: Increases attack power by 64, Improves critical strike rating by 14, Increases your hit rating by 10.			
60	Regenerating Belt of Vek'nilash	Bind on Pickup	152
PROPERTIES: Increases healing done by spells and effects by up to 55.			
60	Thick Qirajihide Belt	Bind on Pickup	144
PROPERTIES: Increases your parry rating by 20.			
60	Bonescythe Waistguard	Bind on Pickup	162
PROPERTIES: Improves critical strike rating by 14.			
60	Dreamwalker Girdle	Bind on Pickup	162
PROPERTIES: Increases healing done by spells and effects by up to 51, Restores 4 mana per 5 sec.			

Epic Leather Waist

Level	Name	Binding Info	Armor
70	General's Leather Belt	Bind on Pickup	196
PROPERTIES: Increases attack power by 24.			
70	General's Dragonhide Belt	Bind on Pickup	196
PROPERTIES: Increases healing done by spells and effects by up to 33.			
70	General's Wyrmhide Belt	Bind on Pickup	196
PROPERTIES: Increases damage and healing done by magical spells and effects by up to 29, Restores 6 mana per 5 sec.			
70	Cord of Nature's Sustenance	Bind on Pickup	179
PROPERTIES: Increases healing done by spells and effects by up to 59, Restores 5 mana per 5 sec.			
70	Girdle of Treachery	Bind on Pickup	179
PROPERTIES: Increases attack power by 52.			
70	Gronn-Stitched Girdle	Bind on Pickup	196
PROPERTIES: Increases attack power by 64.			
70	Marshal's Dragonhide Belt	Bind on Pickup	196
PROPERTIES: Increases healing done by spells and effects by up to 33.			
70	Marshal's Leather Belt	Bind on Pickup	196
PROPERTIES: Increases attack power by 24.			
70	Marshal's Wyrmhide Belt	Bind on Pickup	196
PROPERTIES: Increases damage and healing done by magical spells and effects by up to 29, Restores 6 mana per 5 sec.			
70	Girdle of the Deathdealer	Bind on Pickup	172
PROPERTIES: Increases attack power by 54.			
70	Tree-Mender's Belt	Bind on Pickup	172
PROPERTIES: Increases healing done by spells and effects by up to 44.			
70	Windhawk Belt	Bind on Pickup	151
PROPERTIES: Increases damage and healing done by magical spells and effects by up to 21, Increases healing done by spells and effects by up to 37.			
70	Primalstrike Belt	Bind on Pickup	151
PROPERTIES: Increases attack power by 80.			
70	Girdle of Zaetar	Bind on Pickup	205
PROPERTIES: Increases healing done by spells and effects by up to 62.			
70	Belt of Deep Shadow	Bind on Equip	205
PROPERTIES: Increases attack power by 48.			
70	Belt of Natural Power	Bind on Equip	205
PROPERTIES: Increases healing done by spells and effects by up to 46.			
70	Belt of One-Hundred Deaths	Bind on Pickup	222
PROPERTIES: Increases attack power by 40, Increases dagger skill rating by 22.			
70	Lurker's Grasp	Bind on Pickup	172
	Zandalar Haruspex's Belt	Bind on Pickup	120
PROPERTIES: Increases healing done by spells and effects by up to 15.			

Superior Leather Waist

Level	Name	Binding Info	Armor
18	Deviate Scale Belt	Bind on Equip	51
22	Silver-lined Belt	Bind on Equip	55
26	Moss Cinch	Bind on Pickup	59
28	Highlander's Chain Girdle	Bind on Pickup	61
PROPERTIES: Increases attack power by 24.			
28	Highlander's Lizardhide Girdle	Bind on Pickup	61
28	Highlander's Leather Girdle	Bind on Pickup	61
PROPERTIES: Increases attack power by 24.			
28	Highlander's Mail Girdle	Bind on Pickup	61

Superior Leather Waist

Level	Name	Binding Info	Armor
28	Defiler's Chain Girdle	Bind on Pickup	61
PROPERTIES: Increases attack power by 24.			
28	Defiler's Lizardhide Girdle	Bind on Pickup	61
28	Defiler's Leather Girdle	Bind on Pickup	61
PROPERTIES: Increases attack power by 24.			
28	Defiler's Mail Girdle	Bind on Pickup	61
32	Gem-studded Leather Belt	Bind on Equip	65
PROPERTIES: Heal yourself for 225 to 375.			
37	Ogron's Sash	Bind on Equip	71
38	Highlander's Lizardhide Girdle	Bind on Pickup	73
38	Highlander's Leather Girdle	Bind on Pickup	73
PROPERTIES: Increases attack power by 30.			
38	Defiler's Lizardhide Girdle	Bind on Pickup	73
38	Defiler's Leather Girdle	Bind on Pickup	73
PROPERTIES: Increases attack power by 30.			
48	Highlander's Lizardhide Girdle	Bind on Pickup	86
PROPERTIES: Increases your spell critical strike rating by 14.			
48	Highlander's Leather Girdle	Bind on Pickup	86
PROPERTIES: Improves critical strike rating by 14, Increases attack power by 20.			
48	Defiler's Lizardhide Girdle	Bind on Pickup	86
PROPERTIES: Increases your spell critical strike rating by 14.			
48	Defiler's Leather Girdle	Bind on Pickup	86
PROPERTIES: Improves critical strike rating by 14, Increases attack power by 20.			
50	Girdle of Beastial Fury	Bind on Pickup	89
PROPERTIES: Increases attack power by 30.			
52	Serpentine Sash	Bind on Equip	92
53	Shadowcraft Belt	Bind on Equip	93
53	Wildheart Belt	Bind on Equip	93
53	Might of the Timbermaw	Bind on Equip	93
55	Cloudrunner Girdle	Bind on Pickup	95
55	Knight-Captain's Leather Belt	Bind on Pickup	95
55	Knight-Captain's Dragonhide Girdle	Bind on Pickup	95
55	Legionnaire's Dragonhide Waistband	Bind on Pickup	95
55	Legionnaire's Leather Girdle	Bind on Pickup	95
55	Frostwolf Leather Belt	Bind on Pickup	95
PROPERTIES: Frost Resistance +5			
55	Stormpike Leather Girdle	Bind on Pickup	95
PROPERTIES: Frost Resistance +5			
56	Crystallized Girdle	Bind on Pickup	97
PROPERTIES: Increases damage and healing done by magical spells and effects by up to 9.			
56	Cadaverous Belt	Bind on Pickup	97
PROPERTIES: Increases attack power by 40.			
56	Belt of the Trickster	Bind on Pickup	97
57	Frostbite Girdle	Bind on Pickup	98
PROPERTIES: Frost Resistance +10			
57	Eyestalk Cord	Bind on Pickup	98
PROPERTIES: Increases healing done by spells and effects by up to 35.			
57	Girdle of Insight	Bind on Equip	98
57	Mugger's Belt	Bind on Pickup	98
PROPERTIES: Improves critical strike rating by 14, Increases dagger skill rating by 12.			
58	Highlander's Leather Girdle	Bind on Pickup	99
PROPERTIES: Improves critical strike rating by 14, Increases attack power by 34.			

Superior Leather Waist

Level	Name	Binding Info	Armor
58	Highlander's Lizardhide Girdle	Bind on Pickup	99
PROPERTIES: Increases your spell critical strike rating by 14.			
58	Defiler's Lizardhide Girdle	Bind on Pickup	99
PROPERTIES: Increases your spell critical strike rating by 14.			
58	Defiler's Leather Girdle	Bind on Pickup	99
PROPERTIES: Improves critical strike rating by 14, Increases attack power by 34.			
60	Shadow Panther Hide Belt	Bind on Equip	102
PROPERTIES: Increases your dodge rating by 12.			
60	Southwind's Grasp	Bind on Pickup	110
PROPERTIES: Increases damage and healing done by magical spells and effects by up to 16, Increases your spell critical strike rating by 14.			
60	Bramblewood Belt	Bind on Equip	108
PROPERTIES: Nature Resistance +15			
60	Shifting Sash	Bind on Pickup	127
PROPERTIES: Increases attack power by 28.			
66	Shadowstalker's Sash	Bind on Pickup	144
PROPERTIES: Increases attack power by 26.			
66	Dreamstalker Sash	Bind on Pickup	144
PROPERTIES: Increases healing done by spells and effects by up to 31.			
68	Moonrage Girdle	Bind on Pickup	160
PROPERTIES: Increases damage and healing done by magical spells and effects by up to 25.			
68	Liar's Cord	Bind on Pickup	160
PROPERTIES: Increases attack power by 34.			
68	The Sleeper's Cord	Bind on Pickup	160
PROPERTIES: Increases healing done by spells and effects by up to 53.			
69	Blastguard Belt	Bind on Equip	160
PROPERTIES: Fire Resistance +30			
70	Wastewalker Belt	Bind on Pickup	164
PROPERTIES: Increases attack power by 50.			
70	Murmuring Girdle	Bind on Pickup	164
PROPERTIES: Increases attack power by 40.			
	Nagmara's Whipping Belt	Bind on Pickup	89
	Vosh'gajin's Strand	Bind on Pickup	95
PROPERTIES: Improves critical strike rating by 14, Increases your dodge rating by 12.			
	Belt of Preserved Heads	Bind on Pickup	108
PROPERTIES: Increases your hit rating by 10.			
	Darkmantle Belt	Bind on Pickup	102
	Feralheart Belt	Bind on Pickup	102
PROPERTIES: Increases damage and healing done by magical spells and effects by up to 7.			
	Burning Blade Devotee's Cinch	Bind on Pickup	141
	Socrethar's Girdle	Bind on Pickup	156
PROPERTIES: Increases attack power by 48.			

Epic Leather Wrist

Level	Name	Binding Info	Armor
40	Forest Stalker's Bracers	Bind on Pickup	73
44	Bladebane Armguards	Bind on Equip	78
50	Forest Stalker's Bracers	Bind on Pickup	86
60	Marshal's Dragonhide Bracers	Bind on Pickup	99
60	Marshal's Leather Armsplints	Bind on Pickup	99
60	General's Dragonhide Bracers	Bind on Pickup	99
60	General's Leather Armsplints	Bind on Pickup	99

Epic Leather Wrist

Level	Name	Binding Info	Armor
60	Nightslayer Bracelets	Bind on Equip	100
60	Cenarion Bracers	Bind on Equip	100
PROPERTIES: Increases damage and healing done by magical spells and effects by up to 6.			
60	Stormrage Bracers	Bind on Pickup	112
PROPERTIES: Increases healing done by spells and effects by up to 33.			
60	Bloodfang Bracers	Bind on Pickup	112
PROPERTIES: Increases your hit rating by 10.			
60	Wristguards of Stability	Bind on Pickup	99
60	Forest Stalker's Bracers	Bind on Pickup	99
60	Rogue Bracers	Bind on Equip	128
PROPERTIES: Improves critical strike rating by 14. Fire Resistance +4, Nature Resistance +4, Frost Resistance +4, Shadow Resistance +4, Arcane Resistance +5			
60	Dragonspur Wraps	Bind on Pickup	106
PROPERTIES: Increases attack power by 32. Fire Resistance +4, Nature Resistance +4, Frost Resistance +4, Shadow Resistance +4, Arcane Resistance +4			
60	Bracers of the Fallen Son	Bind on Pickup	126
PROPERTIES: Increases damage and healing done by magical spells and effects by up to 27, Increases your spell hit rating by 8.			
60	Qiraji Execution Bracers	Bind on Pickup	118
PROPERTIES: Increases your hit rating by 10.			
60	Beetle Scaled Wristguards	Bind on Pickup	109
PROPERTIES: Increases attack power by 18. Nature Resistance +15			
60	Bonescythe Bracers	Bind on Pickup	126
PROPERTIES: Improves critical strike rating by 14.			
60	Dreamwalker Wristguards	Bind on Pickup	126
PROPERTIES: Increases healing done by spells and effects by up to 40, Restores 5 mana per 5 sec.			
60	Polar Bracers	Bind on Equip	117
PROPERTIES: Frost Resistance +20			
70	General's Leather Bracers	Bind on Pickup	139
PROPERTIES: Increases attack power by 12.			
70	General's Dragonhide Bracers	Bind on Pickup	139
PROPERTIES: Increases healing done by spells and effects by up to 11.			
70	General's Wyrmhide Bracers	Bind on Pickup	139
PROPERTIES: Increases damage and healing done by magical spells and effects by up to 9, Restores 4 mana per 5 sec.			
70	Bracers of the White Stag	Bind on Pickup	139
PROPERTIES: Increases damage and healing done by magical spells and effects by up to 23.			
70	Bracers of Maliciousness	Bind on Pickup	139
PROPERTIES: Increases attack power by 46.			
70	Marshal's Dragonhide Bracers	Bind on Pickup	139
PROPERTIES: Increases healing done by spells and effects by up to 11.			
70	Marshal's Leather Bracers	Bind on Pickup	139
PROPERTIES: Increases attack power by 12.			
70	Marshal's Wyrmhide Bracers	Bind on Pickup	139
PROPERTIES: Increases damage and healing done by magical spells and effects by up to 9, Restores 4 mana per 5 sec.			
70	Nightfall Wristguards	Bind on Pickup	134
PROPERTIES: Increases attack power by 40.			
70	Forestheart Bracers	Bind on Pickup	134
PROPERTIES: Increases healing done by spells and effects by up to 31.			
70	Windhawk Bracers	Bind on Pickup	146
PROPERTIES: Increases damage and healing done by magical spells and effects by up to 15, Increases healing done by spells and effects by up to 29.			

Epic Leather Wrist

Level	Name	Binding Info	Armor
70	Primalstrike Bracers	Bind on Pickup	117
PROPERTIES: Increases attack power by 60.			
70	Vambraces of Ending	Bind on Pickup	159
PROPERTIES: Increases attack power by 44.			
70	Grove-Bands of Remulos	Bind on Pickup	159
PROPERTIES: Increases healing done by spells and effects by up to 62.			
70	Ravager's Wrist-Wraps	Bind on Pickup	134
	Zandalar Madcap's Bracers	Bind on Pickup	93
	Zandalar Haruspex's Bracers	Bind on Pickup	93
PROPERTIES: Increases healing done by spells and effects by up to 24.			
	Bracers of Subterfuge	Bind on Pickup	92

Superior Leather Wrist

Level	Name	Binding Info	Armor
20	Drakewing Bands	Bind on Equip	41
27	Barbaric Bracers	Bind on Equip	47
28	Emissary Cuffs	Bind on Pickup	47
PROPERTIES: Arcane Resistance +5			
30	Unearthed Bands	Bind on Equip	49
PROPERTIES: Increases attack power by 8.			
34	Enchanted Kodo Bracers	Bind on Equip	52
45	First Sergeant's Leather Armguards	Bind on Pickup	64
45	First Sergeant's Dragonhide Armguards	Bind on Pickup	64
45	Sergeant Major's Leather Armsplints	Bind on Pickup	64
45	Sergeant Major's Dragonhide Armsplints	Bind on Pickup	64
45	Arena Bracers	Bind on Equip	64
47	Darkwater Bracers	Bind on Pickup	66
PROPERTIES: Shadow Resistance +7			
50	Deepfury Bracers	Bind on Equip	69
52	Cinderhide Armsplints	Bind on Pickup	71
PROPERTIES: Fire Resistance +10			
52	Shadowcraft Bracers	Bind on Equip	71
52	Wildheart Bracers	Bind on Equip	71
53	Malefic Bracers	Bind on Equip	72
54	Magistrate's Cuffs	Bind on Pickup	73
PROPERTIES: Restores 4 mana per 5 sec.			
55	Knight-Captain's Leather Bracers	Bind on Pickup	74
55	Knight-Captain's Dragonhide Armsplints	Bind on Pickup	74
55	Legionnaire's Dragonhide Armguards	Bind on Pickup	74
55	Wristguards of Renown	Bind on Pickup	74
56	Bleak Howler Armguards	Bind on Pickup	75
PROPERTIES: Increases healing done by spells and effects by up to 15.			
57	Bracers of the Eclipse	Bind on Pickup	76
PROPERTIES: Increases attack power by 24.			
58	Blackmist Armguards	Bind on Pickup	77
PROPERTIES: Increases your hit rating by 10. Shadow Resistance +10			
58	First Sergeant's Leather Armguards	Bind on Pickup	77
58	First Sergeant's Dragonhide Armguards	Bind on Pickup	77
58	Sergeant Major's Leather Armsplints	Bind on Pickup	77
58	Sergeant Major's Dragonhide Armsplints	Bind on Pickup	77
58	Bracers of Prosperity	Bind on Pickup	77
PROPERTIES: Increases healing done by spells and effects by up to 22.			

Superior Leather Wrist

Level	Name	Binding Info	Armor
58	Yeti Hide Bracers	Bind on Pickup	77
58	Wristwraps of Undead Slaying	Bind on Equip	77
PROPERTIES: Increases attack power by 45 when fighting Undead.			
60	Primal Batskin Bracers	Bind on Equip	79
PROPERTIES: Increases your hit rating by 10.			
60	Abyssal Leather Bracers	Bind on Pickup	82
60	Scaled Bracers of the Gorger	Bind on Pickup	87
60	Bracers of Finesse	Bind on Pickup	99
PROPERTIES: Increases attack power by 28.			
68	Moon-Touched Bands	Bind on Pickup	125
PROPERTIES: Increases damage and healing done by magical spells and effects by up to 21.			
68	Armwraps of Disdain	Bind on Pickup	125
PROPERTIES: Increases attack power by 38.			
70	Bracers of the Bog King	Bind on Pickup	128
PROPERTIES: Increases attack power by 40.			
70	Lucid Dream Bracers	Bind on Pickup	128
PROPERTIES: Increases healing done by spells and effects by up to 37.			
	Darkmantle Bracers	Bind on Pickup	79
	Feralheart Bracers	Bind on Pickup	79
PROPERTIES: Increases damage and healing done by magical spells and effects by up to 5.			
	Spymistress's Wristguards	Bind on Pickup	128

MAIL

Epic Mail Chest

Level	Name	Binding Info	Armor
39	Icemail Jerkin	Bind on Equip	336
PROPERTIES: Frost Resistance +10			
52	Savage Gladiator Chain	Bind on Pickup	421
PROPERTIES: Improves critical strike rating by 28.			
57	Invulnerable Mail	Bind on Equip	461
PROPERTIES: When struck in combat has a 5% chance to make you invulnerable to melee damage for 3 sec. This effect can only occur once every 30 sec, Increases defense rating by 20.			
57	Onyxia Scale Breastplate	Bind on Equip	455
PROPERTIES: Improves critical strike rating by 14. Fire Resistance +9			
60	Field Marshal's Chain Breastplate	Bind on Pickup	537
PROPERTIES: Increases attack power by 44, Improves critical strike rating by 14.			
60	Warlord's Chain Chestpiece	Bind on Pickup	537
PROPERTIES: Increases attack power by 44, Improves critical strike rating by 14.			
60	Warlord's Mail Armor	Bind on Pickup	537
PROPERTIES: Improves critical strike rating by 14, Increases your spell critical strike rating by 14, Increases damage and healing done by magical spells and effects by up to 9.			
60	Giantstalker's Breastplate	Bind on Pickup	482
PROPERTIES: Improves critical strike rating by 14, Increases attack power by 34. Fire Resistance +10			
60	Dragonstalker's Breastplate	Bind on Pickup	551
PROPERTIES: Improves critical strike rating by 14, Increases attack power by 44. Fire Resistance +10, Nature Resistance +10			
60	Breastplate of Ten Storms	Bind on Pickup	551
PROPERTIES: Increases damage and healing done by magical spells and effects by up to 23. Fire Resistance +10, Nature Resistance +10			
60	Runed Bloodstained Hauberk	Bind on Pickup	475
PROPERTIES: Increases attack power by 58, Improves critical strike rating by 14.			

Epic Mail Chest

Level	Name	Binding Info	Armor
60	Dreamscale Breastplate	Bind on Equip	496
PROPERTIES: Restores 4 mana per 5 sec. Nature Resistance +30			
60	Striker's Hauberk	Bind on Pickup	631
PROPERTIES: Improves critical strike rating by 14, Increases damage and healing done by magical spells and effects by up to 9, Increases attack power by 52.			
60	Stormcaller's Hauberk	Bind on Pickup	631
PROPERTIES: Increases damage and healing done by magical spells and effects by up to 32, Improves critical strike rating by 14, Increases your spell critical strike rating by 14.			
60	Obsidian Mail Tunic	Bind on Equip	523
PROPERTIES: Increases attack power by 76, Improves critical strike rating by 14, Spell Damage received is reduced by 10.			
60	Cryptstalker Tunic	Bind on Pickup	658
PROPERTIES: Increases your hit rating by 10, Improves critical strike rating by 14, Restores 4 mana per 5 sec, Increases attack power by 60,			
60	Earthshatter Tunic	Bind on Pickup	658
PROPERTIES: Increases healing done by spells and effects by up to 59, Restores 12 mana per 5 sec.			
60	Icy Scale Breastplate	Bind on Equip	578
PROPERTIES: Increases attack power by 40. Frost Resistance +40			
60	Field Marshal's Mail Armor	Bind on Pickup	537
PROPERTIES: Improves critical strike rating by 14, Increases your spell critical strike rating by 14, Increases damage and healing done by magical spells and effects by up to 9.			
70	Nether Chain Shirt	Bind on Pickup	744
PROPERTIES: Increases attack power by 40, Restores 7 mana per 5 sec.			
70	Twisting Nether Chain Shirt	Bind on Pickup	846
PROPERTIES: Increases attack power by 58, Restores 8 mana per 5 sec, You are protected from all physical attacks for 6 sec, but cannot attack or use physical abilities.			
70	Embrace of the Twisting Nether	Bind on Pickup	981
PROPERTIES: Increases attack power by 48, Restores 9 mana per 5 sec, You are protected from all physical attacks for 6 sec, but cannot attack or use physical abilities.			
70	Gladiator's Linked Armor	Bind on Pickup	812
PROPERTIES: Restores 8 mana per 5 sec.			
70	Gladiator's Mail Armor	Bind on Pickup	812
PROPERTIES: Restores 6 mana per 5 sec, Increases damage and healing done by magical spells and effects by up to 19.			
70	Gladiator's Chain Armor	Bind on Pickup	812
PROPERTIES: Restores 8 mana per 5 sec.			
70	Gladiator's Chain Armor	Bind on Pickup	812
PROPERTIES: Increases attack power by 20.			
70	Breastplate of Carnage	Bind on Pickup	710
PROPERTIES: Increases attack power by 72, Restores 7 mana per 5 sec.			
70	Earthblood Chestguard	Bind on Pickup	710
PROPERTIES: Increases healing done by spells and effects by up to 77, Restores 10 mana per 5 sec.			
70	Cyclone Hauberk	Bind on Pickup	744
PROPERTIES: Increases healing done by spells and effects by up to 57, Restores 9 mana per 5 sec.			
70	Cyclone Chestguard	Bind on Pickup	744
PROPERTIES: Increases damage and healing done by magical spells and effects by up to 30.			
70	Cyclone Breastplate	Bind on Pickup	744
PROPERTIES: Increases damage and healing done by magical spells and effects by up to 27.			
70	Demon Stalker Harness	Bind on Pickup	744
PROPERTIES: Increases attack power by 62, Restores 5 mana per 5 sec.			
70	Thick Netherscale Breastplate	Bind on Equip	677
PROPERTIES: Increases attack power by 60.			

Epic Mail Chest

Level	Name	Binding Info	Armor
70	Ebon Netherscale Breastplate	Bind on Pickup	744
PROPERTIES: Increases attack power by 72, Restores 8 mana per 5 sec.			
70	Netherstrike Breastplate	Bind on Pickup	597
PROPERTIES: Increases damage and healing done by magical spells and effects by up to 33, Restores 8 mana per 5 sec.			
70	Fire Crest Breastplate	Bind on Pickup	812
PROPERTIES: Increases healing done by spells and effects by up to 73, Restores 8 mana per 5 sec.			
70	Ranger-General's Chestguard	Bind on Pickup	812
PROPERTIES: Increases attack power by 40.			
70	Rift Stalker Hauberk	Bind on Pickup	846
PROPERTIES: Increases attack power by 46, Restores 8 mana per 5 sec.			
70	Cataclysm Chestplate	Bind on Pickup	846
PROPERTIES: Increases healing done by spells and effects by up to 57, Restores 9 mana per 5 sec.			
70	Cataclysm Chestguard	Bind on Pickup	846
PROPERTIES: Increases damage and healing done by magical spells and effects by up to 30, Restores 5 mana per 5 sec.			
70	Cataclysm Chestpiece	Bind on Pickup	846
PROPERTIES: Increases damage and healing done by magical spells and effects by up to 22.			
70	Inferno Forged Hauberk	Bind on Pickup	677
PROPERTIES: Fire Resistance +60			
	Zandalar Augur's Hauberk	Bind on Pickup	475
PROPERTIES: Increases damage and healing done by magical spells and effects by up to 34, Increases your spell critical strike rating by 14.			
	Beastmaster's Tunic	Bind on Pickup	441
PROPERTIES: Increases your pet's armor by 10%, Improves critical strike rating by 14, Increases attack power by 32.			
	Vest of The Five Thunders	Bind on Pickup	441
PROPERTIES: Increases your spell critical strike rating by 14, Increases damage and healing done by magical spells and effects by up to 14.			

Superior Mail Chest

Level	Name	Binding Info	Armor
20	Phantom Armor	Bind on Pickup	201
20	Tortoise Armor	Bind on Pickup	201
21	Martyr's Chain	Bind on Equip	204
23	Mutant Scale Breastplate	Bind on Pickup	211
24	Shining Silver Breastplate	Bind on Equip	214
25	Double Link Tunic	Bind on Equip	218
PROPERTIES: Increases defense rating by 14.			
26	Avenger's Armor	Bind on Equip	221
30	Ironspine's Ribcage	Bind on Pickup	235
31	Green Iron Hauberk	Bind on Equip	238
33	Archon Chestpiece	Bind on Equip	245
34	Scarlet Chestpiece	Bind on Equip	250
39	Polished Jazeraint Armor	Bind on Equip	270
39	Deathchill Armor	Bind on Pickup	270
43	Gahz'rilla Scale Armor	Bind on Pickup	290
46	Dragonscale Breastplate	Bind on Equip	306
PROPERTIES: Absorbs 600 magical damage. Lasts 2 min Buff. Fire Resistance +13, Frost Resistance +13, Shadow Resistance +12			
47	Atal'ai Breastplate	Bind on Pickup	311
PROPERTIES: Increases attack power by 22.			

Superior Mail Chest

Level	Name	Binding Info	Armor
47	Green Dragonscale Breastplate	Bind on Equip	311
PROPERTIES: Nature Resistance +11			
49	Wildthorn Mail	Bind on Equip	322
PROPERTIES: Increases damage done by Nature spells and effects by up to 34.			
52	Deathdealer Breastplate	Bind on Pickup	338
PROPERTIES: Improves critical strike rating by 28.			
52	Blue Dragonscale Breastplate	Bind on Equip	338
PROPERTIES: Arcane Resistance +8			
53	Royal Decorated Armor	Bind on Pickup	344
53	Black Dragonscale Breastplate	Bind on Equip	344
PROPERTIES: Increases attack power by 50. Fire Resistance +12			
56	Bonebrace Hauberk	Bind on Equip	360
PROPERTIES: Increases attack power by 56.			
56	Bloodmail Hauberk	Bind on Pickup	360
PROPERTIES: Increases your dodge rating by 12.			
56	Red Dragonscale Breastplate	Bind on Equip	360
PROPERTIES: Increases healing done by spells and effects by up to 66. Fire Resistance +12			
57	Dreamwalker Armor	Bind on Equip	365
57	Ogre Forged Hauberk	Bind on Pickup	365
PROPERTIES: Improves critical strike rating by 14.			
57	Sandstalker Breastplate	Bind on Equip	365
PROPERTIES: Nature Resistance +25			
57	Spitfire Breastplate	Bind on Equip	365
PROPERTIES: Restores 6 mana per 5 sec, Increases damage and healing done by magical spells and effects by up to 15.			
58	Breastplate of the Chosen	Bind on Pickup	370
58	Knight-Captain's Chain Hauberk	Bind on Pickup	370
PROPERTIES: Increases attack power by 46, Improves critical strike rating by 14.			
58	Legionnaire's Mail Chestpiece	Bind on Pickup	370
PROPERTIES: Improves critical strike rating by 14.			
58	Legionnaire's Chain Breastplate	Bind on Pickup	370
PROPERTIES: Increases attack power by 46, Improves critical strike rating by 14.			
58	Vest of Elements	Bind on Pickup	370
58	Beaststalker's Tunic	Bind on Pickup	370
PROPERTIES: Increases attack power by 28.			
58	Chestguard of Undead Slaying	Bind on Pickup	370
PROPERTIES: Increases attack power by 81 when fighting Undead.			
60	Bloodsoul Breastplate	Bind on Equip	381
PROPERTIES: Improves critical strike rating by 28.			
60	Legionnaire's Chain Hauberk	Bind on Pickup	398
PROPERTIES: Improves critical strike rating by 28, Increases attack power by 20.			
60	Legionnaire's Mail Hauberk	Bind on Pickup	398
PROPERTIES: Improves critical strike rating by 14.			
60	Knight-Captain's Chain Hauberk	Bind on Pickup	398
PROPERTIES: Improves critical strike rating by 28, Increases attack power by 20.			
60	Knight-Captain's Mail Hauberk	Bind on Pickup	398
PROPERTIES: Improves critical strike rating by 14.			
62	Fenrage Chestguard	Bind on Pickup	523
PROPERTIES: Increases damage and healing done by magical spells and effects by up to 18, Restores 6 mana per 5 sec.			
63	Shamblehide Doublet	Bind on Pickup	539
PROPERTIES: Increases attack power by 44.			

Superior Mail Chest

Level	Name	Binding Info	Armor
65	Golden Dragonstrike Breastplate	Bind on Pickup	570
PROPERTIES: Increases attack power by 50, Restores 9 mana per 5 sec.			
65	Stormforged Hauberk	Bind on Pickup	570
PROPERTIES: Increases attack power by 50, Restores 7 mana per 5 sec.			
68	Shard Encrusted Breastplate	Bind on Pickup	635
PROPERTIES: Increases attack power by 70, Restores 3 mana per 5 sec.			
68	Laughing Skull Battle-Harness	Bind on Pickup	635
PROPERTIES: Increases attack power by 40.			
68	Worldfire Chestguard	Bind on Pickup	635
PROPERTIES: Increases damage and healing done by magical spells and effects by up to 40.			
70	Earthpeace Breastplate	Bind on Equip	652
PROPERTIES: Restores 16 mana per 5 sec, Increases healing done by spells and effects by up to 92.			
70	Felstalker Breastplate	Bind on Equip	646
PROPERTIES: Increases attack power by 52, Restores 10 mana per 5 sec.			
70	Harness of the Deep Currents	Bind on Pickup	652
PROPERTIES: Increases healing done by spells and effects by up to 68, Restores 10 mana per 5 sec.			
70	Beast Lord Curiass	Bind on Pickup	652
PROPERTIES: Increases attack power by 40, Restores 4 mana per 5 sec.			
70	Tidefury Chestpiece	Bind on Pickup	652
PROPERTIES: Increases damage and healing done by magical spells and effects by up to 36, Restores 4 mana per 5 sec.			
70	Hellfire Chestpiece	Bind on Pickup	652
PROPERTIES: Increases attack power by 50.			
70	Grand Marshal's Chain Armor	Bind on Pickup	652
PROPERTIES: Increases attack power by 12.			
70	Grand Marshal's Linked Armor	Bind on Pickup	652
PROPERTIES: Restores 9 mana per 5 sec.			
70	Grand Marshal's Mail Armor	Bind on Pickup	652
PROPERTIES: Restores 5 mana per 5 sec, Increases damage and healing done by magical spells and effects by up to 16.			
70	High Warlord's Chain Armor	Bind on Pickup	652
PROPERTIES: Increases attack power by 12.			
70	High Warlord's Linked Armor	Bind on Pickup	652
PROPERTIES: Restores 9 mana per 5 sec.			
70	High Warlord's Mail Armor	Bind on Pickup	652
PROPERTIES: Restores 5 mana per 5 sec, Increases damage and healing done by magical spells and effects by up to 16.			
70	Salvager's Hauberk	Bind on Pickup	652
PROPERTIES: Increases attack power by 66.			
	Fire Hardened Hauberk	Bind on Pickup	218
PROPERTIES: Increase Rage by 30.			
	Brutal Hauberk	Bind on Pickup	218
PROPERTIES: Increase Rage by 30.			
	Bonechewer Berserker's Vest	Bind on Pickup	491
PROPERTIES: Restores 4 mana per 5 sec, Increases attack power by 72.			
	Auchenai Tracker's Hauberk	Bind on Pickup	570
PROPERTIES: Increases attack power by 60, Restores 5 mana per 5 sec.			
	Void Slayer's Tunic	Bind on Pickup	619
PROPERTIES: Increases healing done by spells and effects by up to 88, Restores 8 mana per 5 sec.			

Epic Mail Feet

Level	Name	Binding Info	Armor
56	Black Dragonscale Boots	Bind on Equip	308
PROPERTIES: Increases attack power by 28. Fire Resistance +24			
60	Marshal's Chain Boots	Bind on Pickup	355
PROPERTIES: Increases your hit rating by 10, Increases attack power by 34.			
60	General's Chain Boots	Bind on Pickup	355
PROPERTIES: Increases your hit rating by 10, Increases attack power by 34.			
60	General's Mail Boots	Bind on Pickup	355
PROPERTIES: Increases the speed of your Ghost Wolf ability by 15%, Increases damage and healing done by magical spells and effects by up to 20, Restores 5 mana per 5 sec.			
60	Earthfury Boots	Bind on Pickup	331
PROPERTIES: Increases healing done by spells and effects by up to 18. Shadow Resistance +7			
60	Giantstalker's Boots	Bind on Pickup	331
PROPERTIES: Increases attack power by 36. Shadow Resistance +7			
60	Dragonstalker's Greaves	Bind on Pickup	379
PROPERTIES: Increases attack power by 40. Fire Resistance +10			
60	Greaves of Ten Storms	Bind on Pickup	379
PROPERTIES: Increases damage and healing done by magical spells and effects by up to 20. Fire Resistance +10			
60	Sabatons of the Flamewalker	Bind on Pickup	341
PROPERTIES: Increases attack power by 30.			
60	Boots of the Endless Moor	Bind on Pickup	355
PROPERTIES: Restores 3 mana per 5 sec. Nature Resistance +25			
60	Malignant Footguards	Bind on Pickup	360
PROPERTIES: Increases damage and healing done by magical spells and effects by up to 27.			
60	Striker's Footguards	Bind on Pickup	388
PROPERTIES: Increases damage and healing done by magical spells and effects by up to 6, Increases attack power by 40.			
60	Stormcaller's Footguards	Bind on Pickup	388
PROPERTIES: Increases damage and healing done by magical spells and effects by up to 22, Increases your spell penetration by 10, Restores 4 mana per 5 sec.			
60	Wormscale Stompers	Bind on Pickup	402
PROPERTIES: Increases damage and healing done by magical spells and effects by up to 15, Restores 5 mana per 5 sec.			
60	Boots of the Fallen Prophet	Bind on Pickup	364
PROPERTIES: Increases damage and healing done by magical spells and effects by up to 20.			
60	Cryptstalker Boots	Bind on Pickup	425
PROPERTIES: Increases your hit rating by 10, Increases attack power by 44.			
60	Earthshatter Boots	Bind on Pickup	425
PROPERTIES: Increases healing done by spells and effects by up to 37, Restores 6 mana per 5 sec.			
60	Marshal's Mail Boots	Bind on Pickup	355
PROPERTIES: Increases the speed of your Ghost Wolf ability by 15%, Increases damage and healing done by magical spells and effects by up to 20, Restores 5 mana per 5 sec.			
70	General's Chain Sabatons	Bind on Pickup	535
PROPERTIES: Increases attack power by 24.			
70	Ferocious Swift-Kickers	Bind on Pickup	488
PROPERTIES: Increases attack power by 52.			
70	General's Linked Sabatons	Bind on Pickup	535
70	General's Mail Sabatons	Bind on Pickup	535
PROPERTIES: Increases damage and healing done by magical spells and effects by up to 25.			
70	Fiend Slayer Boots	Bind on Pickup	488
PROPERTIES: Increases attack power by 52.			
70	Windshear Boots	Bind on Pickup	535
PROPERTIES: Increases damage and healing done by magical spells and effects by up to 34.			

Epic Mail Feet

Level	Name	Binding Info	Armor
70	Marshal's Chain Sabatons	Bind on Pickup	535
PROPERTIES: Increases attack power by 24.			
70	Marshal's Linked Sabatons	Bind on Pickup	535
70	Marshal's Mail Sabatons	Bind on Pickup	535
PROPERTIES: Increases damage and healing done by magical spells and effects by up to 25.			
70	Wave-Crest Striders	Bind on Pickup	466
PROPERTIES: Increases damage and healing done by magical spells and effects by up to 30, Restores 7 mana per 5 sec.			
70	Boots of the Endless Hunt	Bind on Pickup	466
PROPERTIES: Increases attack power by 44, Restores 6 mana per 5 sec.			
70	Earthen Netherscale Boots	Bind on Equip	466
PROPERTIES: Run speed increased slightly, Restores 9 mana per 5 sec.			
70	Star-Strider Boots	Bind on Pickup	558
PROPERTIES: Increases attack power by 40, Restores 6 mana per 5 sec.			
70	Hurricane Boots	Bind on Pickup	558
PROPERTIES: Increases damage and healing done by magical spells and effects by up to 29, Restores 7 mana per 5 sec.			
70	Boots of the Crimson Hawk	Bind on Pickup	558
PROPERTIES: Increases attack power by 48, Restores 7 mana per 5 sec.			
70	Tempest-Strider Boots	Bind on Pickup	558
PROPERTIES: Increases healing done by spells and effects by up to 44, Restores 14 mana per 5 sec.			
70	Cobra-Lash Boots	Bind on Pickup	605
PROPERTIES: Increases attack power by 52, Restores 6 mana per 5 sec.			
70	Glider's Sabatons	Bind on Pickup	466
70	Inferno Forged Boots	Bind on Pickup	466
PROPERTIES: Fire Resistance +45			
	Beastmaster's Boots	Bind on Pickup	303
PROPERTIES: Increases damage dealt by your pet by 3%, Increases attack power by 32.			
	Boots of The Five Thunders	Bind on Pickup	303
PROPERTIES: Increases damage and healing done by magical spells and effects by up to 12, Restores 4 mana per 5 sec.			

Superior Mail Feet

Level	Name	Binding Info	Armor
16	Silver-linked Footguards	Bind on Equip	129
27	Caverndeep Trudgers	Bind on Equip	154
28	Highlander's Lamellar Greaves	Bind on Pickup	157
PROPERTIES: Run speed increased slightly.			
28	Highlander's Plate Greaves	Bind on Pickup	157
PROPERTIES: Run speed increased slightly.			
28	Defiler's Lamellar Greaves	Bind on Pickup	157
PROPERTIES: Run speed increased slightly.			
28	Defiler's Plate Greaves	Bind on Pickup	157
PROPERTIES: Run speed increased slightly.			
30	Scarlet Boots	Bind on Equip	161
30	Ravasaur Scale Boots	Bind on Equip	161
32	Black Ogre Kickers	Bind on Equip	166
40	Highlander's Chain Greaves	Bind on Pickup	183
PROPERTIES: Run speed increased slightly, Increases attack power by 12.			
40	Highlander's Mail Greaves	Bind on Pickup	183
PROPERTIES: Run speed increased slightly, Increases attack power by 12.			

Superior Mail Feet

Level	Name	Binding Info	Armor
40	Defiler's Chain Greaves	Bind on Pickup	183
PROPERTIES: Run speed increased slightly, Increases attack power by 12.			
40	Defiler's Mail Greaves	Bind on Pickup	183
PROPERTIES: Run speed increased slightly, Increases attack power by 12.			
45	Elven Chain Boots	Bind on Equip	206
48	Fleetfoot Greaves	Bind on Pickup	218
48	Highlander's Chain Greaves	Bind on Pickup	218
PROPERTIES: Run speed increased slightly, Increases attack power by 16.			
48	Highlander's Mail Greaves	Bind on Pickup	218
PROPERTIES: Run speed increased slightly, Increases attack power by 16.			
48	Defiler's Chain Greaves	Bind on Pickup	218
PROPERTIES: Run speed increased slightly, Increases attack power by 16.			
48	Defiler's Mail Greaves	Bind on Pickup	218
PROPERTIES: Run speed increased slightly, Increases attack power by 16.			
48	Greaves of Withering Despair	Bind on Pickup	218
PROPERTIES: Increases damage and healing done by magical spells and effects by up to 11, Increases your spell hit rating by 8.			
49	Bloodshot Greaves	Bind on Pickup	221
52	Savage Gladiator Greaves	Bind on Pickup	233
53	Swiftdart Battleboots	Bind on Pickup	236
54	Timmy's Galoshes	Bind on Pickup	240
54	Boots of Elements	Bind on Pickup	240
54	Beaststalker's Boots	Bind on Pickup	240
PROPERTIES: Increases attack power by 28.			
54	Merciful Greaves	Bind on Pickup	240
PROPERTIES: Increases healing done by spells and effects by up to 20.			
56	Wind Dancer Boots	Bind on Equip	247
PROPERTIES: Increases your dodge rating by 12.			
56	Windreaver Greaves	Bind on Pickup	247
PROPERTIES: Increases your hit rating by 10.			
56	Bloodmail Boots	Bind on Pickup	247
PROPERTIES: Increases your hit rating by 10.			
57	Flame Walkers	Bind on Pickup	251
PROPERTIES: Increases your dodge rating by 12. Fire Resistance +18			
57	Odious Greaves	Bind on Pickup	251
PROPERTIES: Increases attack power by 22.			
57	Shadowy Mail Greaves	Bind on Pickup	251
PROPERTIES: Shadow Resistance +10			
58	Knight-Lieutenant's Chain Boots	Bind on Pickup	255
PROPERTIES: Increases your dodge rating by 12, Increases attack power by 12.			
58	Blood Guard's Mail Walkers	Bind on Pickup	255
PROPERTIES: Increases damage and healing done by magical spells and effects by up to 14, Increases the speed of your Ghost Wolf ability by 15%.			
58	Blood Guard's Chain Boots	Bind on Pickup	255
PROPERTIES: Increases your dodge rating by 12, Increases attack power by 12.			
58	Highlander's Chain Greaves	Bind on Pickup	255
PROPERTIES: Run speed increased slightly, Increases attack power by 20.			
58	Highlander's Mail Greaves	Bind on Pickup	255
PROPERTIES: Run speed increased slightly, Increases attack power by 20.			
58	Defiler's Chain Greaves	Bind on Pickup	255
PROPERTIES: Run speed increased slightly, Increases attack power by 20.			
58	Defiler's Mail Greaves	Bind on Pickup	255
PROPERTIES: Run speed increased slightly, Increases attack power by 20.			
59	Heavy Timbermaw Boots	Bind on Equip	258
PROPERTIES: Increases attack power by 20.			
60	Bloodstained Greaves	Bind on Pickup	274
60	Seafury Boots	Bind on Pickup	274
PROPERTIES: Increases damage and healing done by magical spells and effects by up to 12, Restores 5 mana per 5 sec.			
60	Boots of the Fiery Sands	Bind on Pickup	293
PROPERTIES: Restores 4 mana per 5 sec, Increases damage and healing done by magical spells and effects by up to 12.			
60	Boots of the Qiraji General	Bind on Pickup	285
60	Blood Guard's Chain Greaves	Bind on Pickup	266
PROPERTIES: Increases attack power by 26.			
60	Blood Guard's Mail Greaves	Bind on Pickup	266
PROPERTIES: Increases the speed of your Ghost Wolf ability by 15%.			
60	Knight-Lieutenant's Chain Greaves	Bind on Pickup	266
PROPERTIES: Increases attack power by 26.			
60	Knight-Lieutenant's Mail Greaves	Bind on Pickup	266
PROPERTIES: Increases the speed of your Ghost Wolf ability by 15%.			
63	Dreadhawk's Schynbald	Bind on Equip	370
64	Boots of the Skystrider	Bind on Pickup	381
PROPERTIES: Increases attack power by 44.			
68	Boots of Living Metal	Bind on Pickup	437
PROPERTIES: Increases attack power by 64.			
68	Wavefury Boots	Bind on Pickup	437
PROPERTIES: Increases healing done by spells and effects by up to 55, Restores 8 mana per 5 sec.			
68	Magma Plume Boots	Bind on Pickup	437
PROPERTIES: Increases damage and healing done by magical spells and effects by up to 29.			
68	Sky-Hunter Swift Boots	Bind on Pickup	437
PROPERTIES: Increases attack power by 26, Restores 5 mana per 5 sec.			
69	Netherfury Boots	Bind on Equip	392
PROPERTIES: Increases damage and healing done by magical spells and effects by up to 21, Restores 7 mana per 5 sec.			
69	Enchanted Felscale Boots	Bind on Equip	437
PROPERTIES: Arcane Resistance +30			
69	Flamescale Boots	Bind on Equip	437
PROPERTIES: Fire Resistance +30			
70	Outland Striders	Bind on Pickup	448
PROPERTIES: Increases attack power by 50.			
	Auchenai Boots	Bind on Pickup	448
PROPERTIES: Restores 10 mana per 5 sec.			
	Earthbreaker's Greaves	Bind on Pickup	381
PROPERTIES: Restores 3 mana per 5 sec, Increases damage and healing done by magical spells and effects by up to 25.			
	Greaves of Spellpower	Bind on Pickup	426
PROPERTIES: Increases damage and healing done by magical spells and effects by up to 28, Restores 8 mana per 5 sec.			

Epic Mail Hands

Level	Name	Binding Info	Armor
44	Edgemaster's Handguards	Bind on Equip	230
PROPERTIES: Increases axe skill rating by 17, Increases dagger skill rating by 17, Increases sword skill rating by 17.			
60	Marshal's Chain Grips	Bind on Pickup	323
PROPERTIES: Increases the damage done by your Multi-Shot by 4%, Improves critical strike rating by 14, Increases attack power by 28.			
60	General's Chain Gloves	Bind on Pickup	323
PROPERTIES: Increases the damage done by your Multi-Shot by 4%, Improves critical strike rating by 14, Increases attack power by 28.			
60	General's Mail Gauntlets	Bind on Pickup	323
PROPERTIES: Improves critical strike rating by 14.			
60	Earthfury Gauntlets	Bind on Pickup	301
PROPERTIES: Increases your spell critical strike rating by 14, Increases damage and healing done by magical spells and effects by up to 9. Fire Resistance +7			
60	Giantstalker's Gloves	Bind on Pickup	301
PROPERTIES: Increases your hit rating by 20, Increases attack power by 24. Fire Resistance +7			
60	Dragonstalker's Gauntlets	Bind on Pickup	344
PROPERTIES: Improves critical strike rating by 14, Increases attack power by 26. Shadow Resistance +10			
60	Gauntlets of Ten Storms	Bind on Pickup	344
PROPERTIES: Restores 6 mana per 5 sec, Increases damage and healing done by magical spells and effects by up to 8, Increases healing done by spells and effects by up to 15. Shadow Resistance +10			
46	Stonerender Gauntlets	Bind on Equip	238
PROPERTIES: Nature Resistance +10			
60	Chromatic Gauntlets	Bind on Equip	318
PROPERTIES: Increases attack power by 44, Improves critical strike rating by 14, Increases your spell critical strike rating by 14. Fire Resistance +5, Nature Resistance +5, Frost Resistance +5, Shadow Resistance +5			
	Skyfury Gauntlets	Bind on Pickup	288
PROPERTIES: Increases your spell critical strike rating by 14, Improves critical strike rating by 14, Increases your spell hit rating by 8.			
60	Seafury Gauntlets	Bind on Pickup	310
PROPERTIES: Improves critical strike rating by 14, Increases your spell critical strike rating by 14, Restores 7 mana per 5 sec.			
60	Slimy Scaled Gauntlets	Bind on Pickup	310
PROPERTIES: Increases damage and healing done by magical spells and effects by up to 12, Increases your spell critical strike rating by 14.			
60	Vek'lor's Gloves of Devastation	Bind on Pickup	365
PROPERTIES: Improves critical strike rating by 14.			
60	Gauntlets of Kalimdor	Bind on Pickup	353
PROPERTIES: Increases damage and healing done by magical spells and effects by up to 20, Increases your spell critical strike rating by 14.			
60	Gloves of the Fallen Prophet	Bind on Pickup	340
PROPERTIES: Increases healing done by spells and effects by up to 44.			
	Beastmaster's Gloves	Bind on Pickup	255
PROPERTIES: Increases attack power by 18, Increases your pet's critical strike chance by 2%.			
	Gauntlets of The Five Thunders	Bind on Pickup	255
PROPERTIES: Restores 4 mana per 5 sec, Increases damage and healing done by magical spells and effects by up to 12.			
60	Black Grasp of the Destroyer	Bind on Equip	318
PROPERTIES: Increases attack power by 28, Improves critical strike rating by 14, On successful melee or ranged attack gain 8 mana and if possible drain 8 mana from the target.			
60	Cryptstalker Handguards	Bind on Pickup	395
PROPERTIES: Improves critical strike rating by 14, Restores 4 mana per 5 sec, Increases attack power by 32.			
60	Earthshatter Handguards	Bind on Pickup	395
PROPERTIES: Increases healing done by spells and effects by up to 35, Restores 6 mana per 5 sec.			

Epic Mail Hands

Level	Name	Binding Info	Armor
60	Icy Scale Gauntlets	Bind on Equip	361
PROPERTIES: Increases attack power by 22. Frost Resistance +30			
70	Felfury Gauntlets	Bind on Equip	444
PROPERTIES: Increases attack power by 38.			
70	Gladiator's Linked Gauntlets	Bind on Pickup	486
PROPERTIES: Increases the damage done by your Lightning Shield by 8%.			
70	Gladiator's Mail Gauntlets	Bind on Pickup	486
PROPERTIES: Improves the range of all Shock spells by 5 yards, Increases damage and healing done by magical spells and effects by up to 28.			
70	Gladiator's Chain Gauntlets	Bind on Pickup	486
PROPERTIES: Increases the damage done by your Lightning Shield by 8%.			
70	Gladiator's Chain Gauntlets	Bind on Pickup	486
PROPERTIES: Increases attack power by 24, Increases the damage done by your Multi-Shot by 4%.			
70	Gloves of Quickening	Bind on Pickup	444
PROPERTIES: Increases attack power by 46, Restores 4 mana per 5 sec.			
70	Gloves of Centering	Bind on Pickup	444
PROPERTIES: Increases healing done by spells and effects by up to 55, Restores 5 mana per 5 sec.			
70	Gauntlets of the Dragonslayer	Bind on Pickup	486
PROPERTIES: Increases attack power by 38.			
70	Cyclone Gloves	Bind on Pickup	465
PROPERTIES: Increases healing done by spells and effects by up to 59, Restores 8 mana per 5 sec.			
70	Cyclone Handguards	Bind on Pickup	465
PROPERTIES: Increases damage and healing done by magical spells and effects by up to 30, Restores 4 mana per 5 sec.			
70	Cyclone Gauntlets	Bind on Pickup	465
PROPERTIES: Increases damage and healing done by magical spells and effects by up to 21, Restores 4 mana per 5 sec.			
70	Demon Stalker Gauntlets	Bind on Pickup	465
PROPERTIES: Increases attack power by 52, Restores 5 mana per 5 sec.			
70	Windstrike Gloves	Bind on Equip	423
70	Netherdrake Gloves	Bind on Equip	423
PROPERTIES: Increases attack power by 50, Restores 7 mana per 5 sec.			
60	Marshal's Mail Gauntlets	Bind on Pickup	323
PROPERTIES: Improves critical strike rating by 14.			
70	Tempest Keep - Raid - Boss 2 Loot 2 Shaman Healer Gloves	Bind on Pickup	507
PROPERTIES: Increases healing done by spells and effects by up to 55, Restores 6 mana per 5 sec.			
70	Rift Stalker Gauntlets	Bind on Pickup	528
PROPERTIES: Increases attack power by 58.			
70	Cataclysm Gloves	Bind on Pickup	528
PROPERTIES: Increases healing done by spells and effects by up to 73, Restores 7 mana per 5 sec.			
70	Cataclysm Handgrips	Bind on Pickup	528
PROPERTIES: Increases damage and healing done by magical spells and effects by up to 39.			
70	Cataclysm Gauntlets	Bind on Pickup	528
PROPERTIES: Increases damage and healing done by magical spells and effects by up to 26, Restores 6 mana per 5 sec.			
70	Inferno Forged Gloves	Bind on Pickup	423
PROPERTIES: Fire Resistance +40			

Superior Mail Hands

Level	Name	Binding Info	Armor
18	Thorbia's Gauntlets	Bind on Equip	122
23	Algae Fists	Bind on Pickup	132
29	Grubbis Paws	Bind on Pickup	144
30	The Frozen Clutch	Bind on Pickup	147
PROPERTIES: Increases attack power by 20.			
31	Reticulated Bone Gauntlets	Bind on Equip	149
31	Stormgale Fists	Bind on Equip	149
39	Gauntlets of Divinity	Bind on Pickup	168
PROPERTIES: Increases attack power by 32.			
40	Dragonscale Gauntlets	Bind on Equip	171
PROPERTIES: Improves critical strike rating by 14.			
41	Murkwater Gauntlets	Bind on Equip	174
48	Battlecaller Gauntlets	Bind on Equip	198
48	Rockgrip Gauntlets	Bind on Pickup	198
PROPERTIES: Increases attack power by 28.			
51	Green Dragonscale Gauntlets	Bind on Equip	208
PROPERTIES: Nature Resistance +9			
52	Savage Gladiator Grips	Bind on Pickup	211
53	Molten Fists	Bind on Pickup	215
PROPERTIES: Fire Resistance +10			
54	Storm Gauntlets	Bind on Equip	218
PROPERTIES: Adds 3 Lightning damage to your melee attacks, Increases damage done by Nature spells and effects by up to 21. Fire Resistance +10			
54	Trueaim Gauntlets	Bind on Pickup	218
PROPERTIES: Increases Bow skill rating by 19, Increases your hit rating by 10, Increases gun skill rating by 19, Increases Crossbow skill rating by 19.			
54	Gauntlets of Elements	Bind on Equip	218
54	Beaststalker's Gloves	Bind on Equip	218
PROPERTIES: Increases attack power by 18.			
55	Gilded Gauntlets	Bind on Pickup	221
PROPERTIES: Restores 4 mana per 5 sec.			
56	Bloodmail Gauntlets	Bind on Pickup	225
PROPERTIES: Improves critical strike rating by 14.			
57	Sandstalker Gauntlets	Bind on Equip	228
PROPERTIES: Nature Resistance +20			
57	Spitfire Gauntlets	Bind on Equip	228
PROPERTIES: Restores 5 mana per 5 sec, Increases damage and healing done by magical spells and effects by up to 11.			
58	Dracorian Gauntlets	Bind on Pickup	231
PROPERTIES: Increases damage and healing done by magical spells and effects by up to 16.			
58	Knight-Lieutenant's Chain Gauntlets	Bind on Pickup	231
PROPERTIES: Reduces the mana cost of your Arcane Shot by 15, Increases attack power by 14.			
58	Blood Guard's Mail Grips	Bind on Pickup	231
PROPERTIES: Increases damage and healing done by magical spells and effects by up to 19.			
58	Blood Guard's Chain Gauntlets	Bind on Pickup	231
PROPERTIES: Reduces the mana cost of your Arcane Shot by 15, Increases attack power by 14.			
58	Harmonious Gauntlets	Bind on Pickup	231
PROPERTIES: Increases healing done by spells and effects by up to 51.			
58	Handguards of Savagery	Bind on Pickup	231
PROPERTIES: Increases attack power by 38.			
58	Gauntlets of Deftness	Bind on Pickup	231
60	Bloodsoul Gauntlets	Bind on Equip	238
PROPERTIES: Improves critical strike rating by 14.			

Superior Mail Hands

Level	Name	Binding Info	Armor
60	Scaled Silithid Gauntlets	Bind on Pickup	266
60	Gloves of the Tormented	Bind on Pickup	249
PROPERTIES: Improves critical strike rating by 14.			
60	Blood Guard's Chain Vices	Bind on Pickup	242
PROPERTIES: Increases the damage done by your Multi-Shot by 4%, Increases attack power by 24.			
60	Blood Guard's Mail Vices	Bind on Pickup	242
PROPERTIES: Increases your spell critical strike rating by 14, Increases damage and healing done by magical spells and effects by up to 13.			
60	Knight-Lieutenant's Chain Vices	Bind on Pickup	242
PROPERTIES: Increases the damage done by your Multi-Shot by 4%, Increases attack power by 24.			
60	Bloodstained Ravager Gauntlets	Bind on Pickup	307
PROPERTIES: Increases attack power by 26.			
60	Knight-Lieutenant's Mail Vices	Bind on Pickup	242
PROPERTIES: Increases your spell critical strike rating by 14, Increases damage and healing done by magical spells and effects by up to 13.			
66	Weathered Gloves of the Ancients	Bind on Pickup	367
PROPERTIES: Increases damage and healing done by magical spells and effects by up to 19, Restores 6 mana per 5 sec.			
68	Hungarhide Gauntlets	Bind on Pickup	397
PROPERTIES: Increases attack power by 44.			
68	Earth Mantle Handwraps	Bind on Pickup	397
PROPERTIES: Increases damage and healing done by magical spells and effects by up to 20.			
69	Enchanted Felscale Gloves	Bind on Equip	397
PROPERTIES: Arcane Resistance +30			
70	Swiftsteel Gloves	Bind on Equip	407
PROPERTIES: Restores 10 mana per 5 sec, Increases attack power by 50.			
70	Beast Lord Handguards	Bind on Pickup	407
PROPERTIES: Increases attack power by 34.			
70	Tidefury Gauntlets	Bind on Pickup	407
PROPERTIES: Increases damage and healing done by magical spells and effects by up to 29, Restores 7 mana per 5 sec.			
70	Hellfire Gauntlets	Bind on Pickup	407
PROPERTIES: Increases attack power by 32.			
70	Fathomheart Gauntlets	Bind on Pickup	407
PROPERTIES: Restores 7 mana per 5 sec, Increases healing done by spells and effects by up to 55.			
70	Grand Marshal's Chain Gauntlets	Bind on Pickup	407
PROPERTIES: Increases attack power by 20, Increases the damage done by your Multi-Shot by 4%.			
70	Grand Marshal's Linked Gauntlets	Bind on Pickup	407
PROPERTIES: Increases the damage done by your Lightning Shield by 8%.			
70	Grand Marshal's Mail Gauntlets	Bind on Pickup	407
PROPERTIES: Improves the range of all Shock spells by 5 yards, Increases damage and healing done by magical spells and effects by up to 25.			
70	High Warlord's Chain Gauntlets	Bind on Pickup	407
PROPERTIES: Increases attack power by 20, Increases the damage done by your Multi-Shot by 4%.			
70	High Warlord's Linked Gauntlets	Bind on Pickup	407
PROPERTIES: Increases the damage done by your Lightning Shield by 8%.			
70	High Warlord's Mail Gauntlets	Bind on Pickup	407
PROPERTIES: Improves the range of all Shock spells by 5 yards, Increases damage and healing done by magical spells and effects by up to 25.			
	Voone's Vice Grips	Bind on Pickup	221
PROPERTIES: Increases your hit rating by 20.			
	Warsong Gauntlets	Bind on Pickup	130
	Gordok's Gauntlets	Bind on Pickup	221
PROPERTIES: Increases your spell critical strike rating by 14.			

Superior Mail Hands

Level	Name	Binding Info	Armor
	Azurite Fists	Bind on Pickup	195
PROPERTIES: Increases your spell critical strike rating by 14.			
	Wastewalker's Gauntlets	Bind on Pickup	231
	Desertstalkers's Gauntlets	Bind on Pickup	231
	Handguards of Undead Slaying	Bind on Pickup	231
PROPERTIES: Increases attack power by 60 when fighting Undead.			
	Handguards of Precison	Bind on Pickup	307
PROPERTIES: Increases attack power by 38.			
	Verdant Handwraps	Bind on Pickup	327
PROPERTIES: Increases damage and healing done by magical spells and effects by up to 35, Restores 3 mana per 5 sec.			
	Gauntlets of the Redeemed Vindicator	Bind on Pickup	387
PROPERTIES: Increases attack power by 48.			

Epic Mail Head

Level	Name	Binding Info	Armor
54	Helm of Narv	Bind on Equip	353
57	Helm of the Lifegiver	Bind on Pickup	370
PROPERTIES: Increases healing done by spells and effects by up to 42.			
60	Field Marshal's Chain Helm	Bind on Pickup	436
PROPERTIES: Improves critical strike rating by 14, Increases attack power by 44.			
60	Warlord's Chain Helmet	Bind on Pickup	436
PROPERTIES: Improves critical strike rating by 14, Increases attack power by 44.			
60	Warlord's Mail Helm	Bind on Pickup	436
PROPERTIES: Improves critical strike rating by 14, Increases your spell critical strike rating by 14, Increases damage and healing done by magical spells and effects by up to 9.			
60	Earthfury Helmet	Bind on Pickup	392
PROPERTIES: Restores 6 mana per 5 sec, Increases healing done by spells and effects by up to 22. Fire Resistance +10			
60	Giantstalker's Helmet	Bind on Pickup	392
PROPERTIES: Improves critical strike rating by 14, Increases attack power by 30. Fire Resistance +10			
60	Dragonstalker's Helm	Bind on Pickup	447
PROPERTIES: Improves critical strike rating by 14, Increases attack power by 36. Frost Resistance +10, Shadow Resistance +10			
60	Helmet of Ten Storms	Bind on Pickup	447
PROPERTIES: Increases your spell critical strike rating by 14, Increases damage and healing done by magical spells and effects by up to 9, Increases healing done by spells and effects by up to 18. Frost Resistance +10, Shadow Resistance +10			
60	Infernal Headcage	Bind on Pickup	408
PROPERTIES: Increases damage and healing done by magical spells and effects by up to 16. Fire Resistance +10, Shadow Resistance +10			
60	Crown of Destruction	Bind on Pickup	447
PROPERTIES: Improves critical strike rating by 28, Increases attack power by 44. Fire Resistance +10			
60	Striker's Diadem	Bind on Pickup	475
PROPERTIES: Improves critical strike rating by 14, Increases damage and healing done by magical spells and effects by up to 12, Increases attack power by 38.			
60	Stormcaller's Diadem	Bind on Pickup	475
PROPERTIES: Increases damage and healing done by magical spells and effects by up to 32, Increases your spell critical strike rating by 14.			
60	Cryptstalker Headpiece	Bind on Pickup	513
PROPERTIES: Improves critical strike rating by 28, Restores 3 mana per 5 sec, Increases attack power by 40.			
60	Earthshatter Headpiece	Bind on Pickup	513
PROPERTIES: Increases healing done by spells and effects by up to 68, Restores 8 mana per 5 sec.			

Epic Mail Head

Level	Name	Binding Info	Armor
60	Icy Scale Coif	Bind on Pickup	486
PROPERTIES: Frost Resistance +44			
60	Field Marshal's Mail Helm	Bind on Pickup	436
PROPERTIES: Improves critical strike rating by 14, Increases your spell critical strike rating by 14, Increases damage and healing done by magical spells and effects by up to 9.			
70	Storm Helm	Bind on Equip	577
PROPERTIES: Increases attack power by 44, Restores 9 mana per 5 sec.			
70	Gladiator's Linked Helm	Bind on Pickup	632
70	Gladiator's Mail Helm	Bind on Pickup	632
PROPERTIES: Increases damage and healing done by magical spells and effects by up to 26.			
70	Gladiator's Chain Helm	Bind on Pickup	632
PROPERTIES: Increases attack power by 30.			
70	Big Bad Wolf's Head	Bind on Pickup	577
PROPERTIES: Increases damage and healing done by magical spells and effects by up to 32.			
70	Steelspine Faceguard	Bind on Pickup	577
PROPERTIES: Increases attack power by 54, Restores 8 mana per 5 sec.			
70	Maulgar's Warhelm	Bind on Pickup	632
PROPERTIES: Increases attack power by 76.			
70	Cyclone Headdress	Bind on Pickup	604
PROPERTIES: Increases healing done by spells and effects by up to 64, Restores 6 mana per 5 sec.			
70	Cyclone Faceguard	Bind on Pickup	604
PROPERTIES: Increases damage and healing done by magical spells and effects by up to 34, Restores 6 mana per 5 sec.			
70	Cyclone Helm	Bind on Pickup	604
PROPERTIES: Increases damage and healing done by magical spells and effects by up to 27.			
70	Demon Stalker Greathelm	Bind on Pickup	604
PROPERTIES: Increases attack power by 56.			
70	Living Dragonscale Helm	Bind on Equip	550
PROPERTIES: Increases healing done by spells and effects by up to 77, Restores 14 mana per 5 sec.			
70	Netherdrake Helm	Bind on Equip	550
PROPERTIES: Increases attack power by 60, Restores 12 mana per 5 sec.			
70	Rift Stalker Helm	Bind on Pickup	687
PROPERTIES: Increases attack power by 58, Restores 5 mana per 5 sec.			
70	Cataclysm Headguard	Bind on Pickup	687
PROPERTIES: Increases healing done by spells and effects by up to 90.			
70	Cataclysm Headpiece	Bind on Pickup	687
PROPERTIES: Increases damage and healing done by magical spells and effects by up to 49.			
70	Cataclysm Helm	Bind on Pickup	687
PROPERTIES: Increases damage and healing done by magical spells and effects by up to 39.			
70	Fathom-Helm of th Deeps	Bind on Pickup	604
PROPERTIES: Increases healing done by spells and effects by up to 95, Restores 7 mana per 5 sec.			
	Skyfury Helm	Bind on Pickup	370
PROPERTIES: Increases your spell critical strike rating by 28, Improves critical strike rating by 14.			
	Beastmaster's Cap	Bind on Pickup	359
PROPERTIES: Increases your hit rating by 10, Increases your pet's maximum health by 3%, Increases attack power by 28.			
	Coif of The Five Thunders	Bind on Pickup	359
PROPERTIES: Increases damage and healing done by magical spells and effects by up to 14, Increases your spell critical strike rating by 14.			
	Foreman's Reinforced Helmet	Bind on Pickup	550
PROPERTIES: Increases attack power by 56, Increases your chance to resist Stun and Disorient effects by 10%.			

Superior Mail Head

Level	Name	Binding Info	Armor
27	Frostreaver Crown	Bind on Equip	182
28	Sunblaze Coif	Bind on Equip	185
PROPERTIES: Fire Resistance +10			
37	Raging Berserker's Helm	Bind on Pickup	213
PROPERTIES: Improves critical strike rating by 14.			
42	High Bergg Helm	Bind on Equip	231
46	Bloomsprout Headpiece	Bind on Pickup	249
PROPERTIES: Increases attack power by 36. Nature Resistance +10			
47	Braincage	Bind on Equip	253
51	Horns of Eranikus	Bind on Pickup	271
52	Savage Gladiator Helm	Bind on Pickup	275
53	Fervent Helm	Bind on Pickup	279
PROPERTIES: Restores 7 health per 5 sec.			
55	Dragoneye Coif	Bind on Pickup	288
PROPERTIES: Increases attack power by 38.			
56	Helm of the Great Chief	Bind on Equip	292
57	Coif of Elements	Bind on Pickup	297
57	Beaststalker's Cap	Bind on Pickup	297
PROPERTIES: Increases attack power by 26.			
58	Crown of Tyranny	Bind on Pickup	301
PROPERTIES: Increases attack power by 40, Improves critical strike rating by 14.			
58	Lieutenant Commander's Chain Helmet	Bind on Pickup	301
PROPERTIES: Increases attack power by 32.			
58	Champion's Mail Helm	Bind on Pickup	301
PROPERTIES: Improves critical strike rating by 14.			
58	Champion's Chain Headguard	Bind on Pickup	301
PROPERTIES: Increases attack power by 32.			
60	Bloodstained Coif	Bind on Pickup	337
PROPERTIES: Improves critical strike rating by 28, Increases attack power by 28.			
60	Coif of Elemental Fury	Bind on Equip	323
PROPERTIES: Increases your spell critical strike rating by 14, Increases damage and healing done by magical spells and effects by up to 20.			
60	Champion's Chain Helm	Bind on Pickup	337
PROPERTIES: Improves critical strike rating by 28, Increases attack power by 24.			
60	Champion's Mail Headguard	Bind on Pickup	337
PROPERTIES: Improves critical strike rating by 14, Increases your spell critical strike rating by 14.			
60	Lieutenant Commander's Chain Helm	Bind on Pickup	337
PROPERTIES: Improves critical strike rating by 28, Increases attack power by 24.			
60	Lieutenant Commander's Mail Headguard	Bind on Pickup	337
PROPERTIES: Improves critical strike rating by 14, Increases your spell critical strike rating by 14.			
64	Veil of Spirits	Bind on Pickup	451
PROPERTIES: Increases damage and healing done by magical spells and effects by up to 18.			
65	Veil of the Departed	Bind on Pickup	463
PROPERTIES: Increases attack power by 44.			
66	Exorcist's Chain Helm	Bind on Pickup	463
PROPERTIES: Increases attack power by 20.			
66	Exorcist's Linked Helm	Bind on Pickup	463
66	Exorcist's Mail Helm	Bind on Pickup	463
PROPERTIES: Increases damage and healing done by magical spells and effects by up to 29.			
68	Headdress of the Tides	Bind on Pickup	516
PROPERTIES: Increases healing done by spells and effects by up to 73, Restores 9 mana per 5 sec.			
68	Dream-Wing Helm	Bind on Pickup	516
PROPERTIES: Restores 6 mana per 5 sec, Increases attack power by 66.			

Superior Mail Head

Level	Name	Binding Info	Armor
68	Mask of Inner FIre	Bind on Pickup	516
PROPERTIES: Increases damage and healing done by magical spells and effects by up to 39.			
68	Mok'Nathal Mask of Battle	Bind on Pickup	516
PROPERTIES: Increases attack power by 30.			
69	Stylin' Adventure Hat	Bind on Equip	516
PROPERTIES: Increases damage and healing done by magical spells and effects by up to 50, Restores 16 mana per 5 sec.			
69	Stylin' Crimson Hat	Bind on Equip	516
PROPERTIES: Increases attack power by 96, Restores 12 mana per 5 sec.			
70	Hellfire Helm	Bind on Pickup	530
PROPERTIES: Increases attack power by 66.			
70	Beast Lord Helm	Bind on Pickup	530
PROPERTIES: Increases attack power by 50.			
70	Tidefury Helm	Bind on Pickup	530
PROPERTIES: Increases damage and healing done by magical spells and effects by up to 32, Restores 6 mana per 5 sec.			
70	Grand Marshal's Chain Helm	Bind on Pickup	530
PROPERTIES: Increases attack power by 28.			
70	Grand Marshal's Linked Helm	Bind on Pickup	530
70	Grand Marshal's Mail Helm	Bind on Pickup	530
PROPERTIES: Increases damage and healing done by magical spells and effects by up to 23.			
70	High Warlord's Chain Helm	Bind on Pickup	530
PROPERTIES: Increases attack power by 28.			
70	High Warlord's Linked Helm	Bind on Pickup	530
70	High Warlord's Mail Helm	Bind on Pickup	530
PROPERTIES: Increases damage and healing done by magical spells and effects by up to 23.			
70	Earthcaller's Headdress	Bind on Pickup	530
PROPERTIES: Increases attack power by 50.			
70	Far Seer's Helm	Bind on Pickup	530
PROPERTIES: Increases attack power by 50.			
	Helm of Exile	Bind on Pickup	266
	Backwood Helm	Bind on Pickup	301
PROPERTIES: Improves critical strike rating by 14.			
	Helm of Latent Power	Bind on Pickup	297
PROPERTIES: Increases your spell critical strike rating by 14, Increases damage and healing done by magical spells and effects by up to 14.			
	Metallic Headband of Simm'onz	Bind on Pickup	476
PROPERTIES: Increases healing done by spells and effects by up to 68, Restores 12 mana per 5 sec.			
	Earthwarden's Coif	Bind on Pickup	530
PROPERTIES: Increases attack power by 34, Restores 7 mana per 5 sec.			
	Coif of the Wicked	Bind on Pickup	490
PROPERTIES: Increases attack power by 52, Restores 10 mana per 5 sec.			

Epic Mail Legs

Level	Name	Binding Info	Armor
60	Marshal's Chain Legguards	Bind on Pickup	452
PROPERTIES: Improves critical strike rating by 14, Increases attack power by 44.			
60	General's Chain Legguards	Bind on Pickup	452
PROPERTIES: Improves critical strike rating by 14, Increases attack power by 44.			
60	General's Mail Leggings	Bind on Pickup	452
PROPERTIES: Increases damage and healing done by magical spells and effects by up to 27, Increases your spell critical strike rating by 14, Improves critical strike rating by 14.			

Epic Mail Legs

Level	Name	Binding Info	Armor
60	Earthfury Legguards	Bind on Pickup	422
PROPERTIES: Restores 6 mana per 5 sec, Increases damage and healing done by magical spells and effects by up to 12. Shadow Resistance +10			
60	Giantstalker's Leggings	Bind on Pickup	422
PROPERTIES: Improves critical strike rating by 14, Increases attack power by 42. Shadow Resistance +10			
60	Dragonstalker's Legguards	Bind on Pickup	482
PROPERTIES: Increases your hit rating by 10, Improves critical strike rating by 14, Increases attack power by 40. Fire Resistance +10, Arcane Resistance +10			
60	Legplates of Ten Storms	Bind on Pickup	482
PROPERTIES: Increases your spell critical strike rating by 14, Increases damage and healing done by magical spells and effects by up to 29. Fire Resistance +10, Arcane Resistance +10			
60	Primalist's Linked Legguards	Bind on Pickup	476
PROPERTIES: Increases your spell critical strike rating by 28, Increases your spell hit rating by 8.			
60	Emberweave Leggings	Bind on Pickup	476
PROPERTIES: Fire Resistance +35			
60	Ancient Corroded Leggings	Bind on Pickup	458
60	Leggings of the Demented Mind	Bind on Pickup	458
PROPERTIES: Increases healing done by spells and effects by up to 40.			
60	Striker's Leggings	Bind on Pickup	511
PROPERTIES: Improves critical strike rating by 14, Increases damage and healing done by magical spells and effects by up to 9, Increases attack power by 48.			
60	Stormcaller's Leggings	Bind on Pickup	511
PROPERTIES: Increases damage and healing done by magical spells and effects by up to 29, Increases your spell critical strike rating by 14, Restores 4 mana per 5 sec.			
60	Onyx Embedded Leggings	Bind on Pickup	488
PROPERTIES: Shadow Resistance +30			
60	Slime-coated Leggings	Bind on Pickup	494
PROPERTIES: Increases damage and healing done by magical spells and effects by up to 11, Increases attack power by 40. Nature Resistance +28			
60	Scaled Sand Reaver Leggings	Bind on Pickup	488
PROPERTIES: Increases attack power by 62, Improves critical strike rating by 28.			
60	Scaled Leggings of Qiraji Fury	Bind on Pickup	482
PROPERTIES: Increases damage and healing done by magical spells and effects by up to 36, Increases your spell critical strike rating by 14.			
60	Cryptstalker Legguards	Bind on Pickup	552
PROPERTIES: Improves critical strike rating by 14, Restores 6 mana per 5 sec, Increases attack power by 56.			
60	Earthshatter Legguards	Bind on Pickup	552
PROPERTIES: Increases healing done by spells and effects by up to 59, Restores 9 mana per 5 sec.			
60	Outrider's Chain Leggings	Bind on Pickup	415
PROPERTIES: Improves critical strike rating by 14, Increases your hit rating by 10.			
60	Outrider's Mail Leggings	Bind on Pickup	415
PROPERTIES: Improves critical strike rating by 14, Increases your spell critical strike rating by 14, Restores 6 mana per 5 sec.			
60	Sentinel's Chain Leggings	Bind on Pickup	415
PROPERTIES: Improves critical strike rating by 14, Increases your hit rating by 10.			
60	Leggings of Elemental Fury	Bind on Pickup	535
PROPERTIES: Increases damage and healing done by magical spells and effects by up to 32, Increases your spell critical strike rating by 28.			
60	Marshal's Mail Leggings	Bind on Pickup	452
PROPERTIES: Increases damage and healing done by magical spells and effects by up to 27, Increases your spell critical strike rating by 14, Improves critical strike rating by 14.			
60	Sentinel's Mail Leggings	Bind on Pickup	415
PROPERTIES: Improves critical strike rating by 14, Increases your spell critical strike rating by 14, Restores 6 mana per 5 sec.			

Epic Mail Legs

Level	Name	Binding Info	Armor
70	Gladiator's Linked Leggings	Bind on Pickup	681
70	Gladiator's Mail Leggings	Bind on Pickup	681
PROPERTIES: Increases damage and healing done by magical spells and effects by up to 37, Restores 5 mana per 5 sec.			
70	Gladiator's Chain Leggings	Bind on Pickup	681
PROPERTIES: Increases attack power by 34.			
70	Rip-flayer Leggings	Bind on Pickup	621
PROPERTIES: Increases attack power by 44, Restores 8 mana per 5 sec.			
70	Heart-flame Leggings	Bind on Pickup	621
PROPERTIES: Increases healing done by spells and effects by up to 79.			
70	Cyclone Kilt	Bind on Pickup	651
PROPERTIES: Increases healing done by spells and effects by up to 84, Restores 10 mana per 5 sec.			
70	Cyclone Legguards	Bind on Pickup	651
PROPERTIES: Increases damage and healing done by magical spells and effects by up to 44, Restores 7 mana per 5 sec.			
70	Cyclone War-Kilt	Bind on Pickup	651
PROPERTIES: Increases damage and healing done by magical spells and effects by up to 28, Restores 6 mana per 5 sec.			
70	Demon Stalker Greaves	Bind on Pickup	651
PROPERTIES: Increases attack power by 74.			
70	Void Reaver Greaves	Bind on Pickup	710
PROPERTIES: Increases attack power by 40.			
70	Sunhawk Leggings	Bind on Pickup	769
PROPERTIES: Increases healing done by spells and effects by up to 68, Restores 10 mana per 5 sec.			
70	Rift Stalker Leggings	Bind on Pickup	740
PROPERTIES: Increases attack power by 78, Restores 6 mana per 5 sec.			
70	Cataclysm Legguards	Bind on Pickup	740
PROPERTIES: Increases healing done by spells and effects by up to 88, Restores 12 mana per 5 sec.			
70	Cataclysm Leggings	Bind on Pickup	740
PROPERTIES: Increases damage and healing done by magical spells and effects by up to 47, Restores 8 mana per 5 sec.			
70	Cataclysm Legplates	Bind on Pickup	740
PROPERTIES: Increases damage and healing done by magical spells and effects by up to 18.			
70	Wyrmscale Greaves	Bind on Pickup	593
PROPERTIES: Increases attack power by 60, Restores 6 mana per 5 sec.			
70	Stormsong Kilt	Bind on Pickup	593
PROPERTIES: Increases damage and healing done by magical spells and effects by up to 32.			
70	Sealed Greaves of the Marksman	Bind on Pickup	651
PROPERTIES: Increases attack power by 62, Increases Bow skill rating by 16, Increases gun skill rating by 16, Increases Crossbow skill rating by 16,			
70	Inferno Forged Leggings	Bind on Pickup	593
PROPERTIES: Fire Resistance +55			
	Legguards of the Chromatic Defier	Bind on Pickup	398
PROPERTIES: Fire Resistance +5, Nature Resistance +5, Frost Resistance +5, Shadow Resistance +5, Arcane Resistance +5			
	Legplates of the Chromatic Defier	Bind on Pickup	398
PROPERTIES: Fire Resistance +5, Nature Resistance +5, Frost Resistance +5, Shadow Resistance +5, Arcane Resistance +5			
	Icy Scale Leggings	Bind on Pickup	505
PROPERTIES: Frost Resistance +40			

Superior Mail Legs

Level	Name	Binding Info	Armor
21	Dreamsinger Legguards	Bind on Equip	179
34	Legguards of the Vault	Bind on Equip	218
34	Firemane Leggings	Bind on Equip	218
PROPERTIES: Fire Resistance +10			
38	Scarlet Leggings	Bind on Pickup	233
45	Infernal Trickster Leggings	Bind on Pickup	263
PROPERTIES: Increases Bow skill rating by 9.			
45	Dragonstrike Leggings	Bind on Pickup	272
PROPERTIES: Increases attack power by 24, Restores 4 mana per 5 sec.			
47	Windforged Leggings	Bind on Pickup	272
PROPERTIES: Increases attack power by 28, Restores 5 mana per 5 sec.			
48	Searingscale Leggings	Bind on Pickup	277
PROPERTIES: Fire Resistance +10			
49	Green Dragonscale Leggings	Bind on Equip	282
PROPERTIES: Nature Resistance +11			
51	Windrunner Legguards	Bind on Equip	291
52	Savage Gladiator Leggings	Bind on Pickup	296
53	Woollies of the Prancing Minstrel	Bind on Pickup	301
PROPERTIES: Restores 10 mana per 5 sec.			
55	Blue Dragonscale Leggings	Bind on Equip	310
PROPERTIES: Arcane Resistance +12			
56	Bloodmail Legguards	Bind on Pickup	315
56	Kilt of Elements	Bind on Pickup	315
56	Beaststalker's Pants	Bind on Pickup	315
PROPERTIES: Increases attack power by 34.			
57	Maelstrom Leggings	Bind on Pickup	320
PROPERTIES: Increases healing done by spells and effects by up to 13.			
57	Black Dragonscale Leggings	Bind on Equip	320
PROPERTIES: Increases attack power by 54. Fire Resistance +13			
57	Silvermoon Leggings	Bind on Pickup	320
PROPERTIES: Increases damage and healing done by magical spells and effects by up to 18.			
57	Abyssal Mail Legguards	Bind on Equip	320
PROPERTIES: Improves critical strike rating by 14.			
58	Tristam Legguards	Bind on Pickup	324
PROPERTIES: Increases attack power by 34, Increases your dodge rating by 24.			
58	Knight-Captain's Chain Leggings	Bind on Pickup	324
PROPERTIES: Improves critical strike rating by 14, Increases your dodge rating by 12, Increases attack power by 24.			
58	Legionnaire's Mail Leggings	Bind on Pickup	324
PROPERTIES: Increases damage and healing done by magical spells and effects by up to 25.			
58	Legionnaire's Chain Leggings	Bind on Pickup	324
PROPERTIES: Improves critical strike rating by 14, Increases your dodge rating by 12, Increases attack power by 24.			
58	Leggings of Destruction	Bind on Pickup	324
PROPERTIES: Improves critical strike rating by 14.			
60	Bloodstained Legplates	Bind on Pickup	363
PROPERTIES: Improves critical strike rating by 14.			
60	Seafury Leggings	Bind on Pickup	348
PROPERTIES: Increases damage and healing done by magical spells and effects by up to 16.			
60	Obsidian Scaled Leggings	Bind on Pickup	377
PROPERTIES: Increases damage and healing done by magical spells and effects by up to 19.			
60	Legionnaire's Chain Legguards	Bind on Pickup	348
PROPERTIES: Improves critical strike rating by 28, Increases attack power by 20.			

Superior Mail Legs

Level	Name	Binding Info	Armor
60	Legionnaire's Mail Legguards	Bind on Pickup	348
PROPERTIES: Increases damage and healing done by magical spells and effects by up to 21, Increases your spell critical strike rating by 14.			
60	Knight-Captain's Chain Legguards	Bind on Pickup	348
PROPERTIES: Improves critical strike rating by 28, Increases attack power by 20.			
60	Wasteland Stitched Leggings	Bind on Pickup	429
PROPERTIES: Increases attack power by 32.			
60	Splitrock Kilt	Bind on Pickup	429
PROPERTIES: Restores 7 mana per 5 sec, Increases damage and healing done by magical spells and effects by up to 16.			
60	Knight-Captain's Mail Legguards	Bind on Pickup	348
PROPERTIES: Increases damage and healing done by magical spells and effects by up to 21, Increases your spell critical strike rating by 14.			
66	Marksman's Greaves of Patience	Bind on Pickup	513
PROPERTIES: Increases attack power by 46, Restores 4 mana per 5 sec.			
66	Marksman's Legguards	Bind on Pickup	499
PROPERTIES: Increases attack power by 22.			
66	Stormbreaker's Leggings	Bind on Pickup	499
PROPERTIES: Increases damage and healing done by magical spells and effects by up to 27.			
67	Netherfury Leggings	Bind on Equip	527
PROPERTIES: Increases damage and healing done by magical spells and effects by up to 29, Restores 10 mana per 5 sec.			
68	Oceansong Kilt	Bind on Pickup	556
PROPERTIES: Increases healing done by spells and effects by up to 84.			
68	Hellfire Britches	Bind on Pickup	570
PROPERTIES: Increases attack power by 66.			
68	Emerald-Scale Greaves	Bind on Pickup	556
PROPERTIES: Increases attack power by 56, Restores 5 mana per 5 sec.			
69	Enchanted Felscale Leggings	Bind on Equip	556
PROPERTIES: Arcane Resistance +40			
69	Flamescale Leggings	Bind on Equip	556
PROPERTIES: Fire Resistance +40			
70	Blackstalker Legplates	Bind on Pickup	570
PROPERTIES: Increases attack power by 56, Restores 7 mana per 5 sec.			
70	Beast Lord Leggings	Bind on Pickup	570
PROPERTIES: Increases attack power by 52, Restores 7 mana per 5 sec.			
70	Tidefury Kilt	Bind on Pickup	570
PROPERTIES: Increases damage and healing done by magical spells and effects by up to 35.			
70	Molten Earth Kilt	Bind on Pickup	570
PROPERTIES: Increases damage and healing done by magical spells and effects by up to 40, Restores 10 mana per 5 sec.			
70	Grand Marshal's Chain Leggings	Bind on Pickup	570
PROPERTIES: Increases attack power by 28.			
70	Grand Marshal's Linked Leggings	Bind on Pickup	570
70	Grand Marshal's Mail Leggings	Bind on Pickup	570
PROPERTIES: Increases damage and healing done by magical spells and effects by up to 33, Restores 4 mana per 5 sec.			
70	High Warlord's Chain Leggings	Bind on Pickup	570
PROPERTIES: Increases attack power by 28.			
70	High Warlord's Linked Leggings	Bind on Pickup	570
70	High Warlord's Mail Leggings	Bind on Pickup	570
PROPERTIES: Increases damage and healing done by magical spells and effects by up to 33, Restores 4 mana per 5 sec.			
	Chausses of Westfall	Bind on Pickup	173

Superior Mail Legs

Level	Name	Binding Info	Armor
	Dual Reinforced Leggings	Bind on Pickup	211
PROPERTIES: Increases defense rating by 7.			
	Cenarion Reservist's Legguards	Bind on Pickup	324
PROPERTIES: Nature Resistance +25			
	Cenarion Reservist's Legguards	Bind on Pickup	324
PROPERTIES: Nature Resistance +25			
	Beastmaster's Pants	Bind on Pickup	339
PROPERTIES: Increases attack power by 36.			
	Kilt of The Five Thunders	Bind on Pickup	339
PROPERTIES: Increases damage and healing done by magical spells and effects by up to 11.			
	Leggings of the Plague Hunter	Bind on Pickup	339
PROPERTIES: Improves critical strike rating by 14.			
	Scaled Legs of Ruination	Bind on Pickup	444
PROPERTIES: Increases damage and healing done by magical spells and effects by up to 27.			
	Mag'hari Huntsman's Leggings	Bind on Pickup	513
PROPERTIES: Increases attack power by 86.			
	Haramad's Linked Chain Pantaloons	Bind on Pickup	485
PROPERTIES: Increases damage and healing done by magical spells and effects by up to 34, Restores 12 mana per 5 sec.			
	Area 52 Defender's Pants	Bind on Pickup	527
PROPERTIES: Increases damage and healing done by magical spells and effects by up to 36, Restores 6 mana per 5 sec. Arcane Resistance +12			

Epic Mail Shoulders

Level	Name	Binding Info	Armor
57	Fiery Chain Shoulders	Bind on Equip	341
PROPERTIES: Fire Resistance +25			
60	Field Marshal's Chain Spaulders	Bind on Pickup	403
PROPERTIES: Increases your hit rating by 10, Increases attack power by 34.			
60	Warlord's Chain Shoulders	Bind on Pickup	403
PROPERTIES: Increases your hit rating by 10, Increases attack power by 34.			
60	Warlord's Mail Spaulders	Bind on Pickup	403
PROPERTIES: Increases damage and healing done by magical spells and effects by up to 16.			
60	Earthfury Epaulets	Bind on Pickup	362
PROPERTIES: Restores 4 mana per 5 sec, Increases healing done by spells and effects by up to 18. Shadow Resistance +7			
60	Giantstalker's Epaulets	Bind on Pickup	362
PROPERTIES: Increases your hit rating by 10, Increases attack power by 32. Shadow Resistance +7			
60	Dragonstalker's Spaulders	Bind on Pickup	413
PROPERTIES: Increases your hit rating by 10, Increases attack power by 30. Fire Resistance +10			
60	Epaulets of Ten Storms	Bind on Pickup	413
PROPERTIES: Increases your spell critical strike rating by 14. Fire Resistance +10			
60	Deep Earth Spaulders	Bind on Pickup	387
PROPERTIES: Increases damage done by Nature spells and effects by up to 40.			
60	Black Brood Pauldrons	Bind on Pickup	408
PROPERTIES: Restores 9 mana per 5 sec.			
60	Highlander's Chain Pauldrons	Bind on Pickup	356
PROPERTIES: Increases attack power by 26.			
60	Highlander's Mail Pauldrons	Bind on Pickup	356
PROPERTIES: Restores 4 mana per 5 sec.			
60	Defiler's Chain Pauldrons	Bind on Pickup	356
PROPERTIES: Increases attack power by 26.			

Epic Mail Shoulders

Level	Name	Binding Info	Armor
60	Defiler's Mail Pauldrons	Bind on Pickup	356
PROPERTIES: Restores 4 mana per 5 sec.			
60	Striker's Pauldrons	Bind on Pickup	438
PROPERTIES: Increases damage and healing done by magical spells and effects by up to 6, Increases attack power by 34.			
60	Stormcaller's Pauldrons	Bind on Pickup	423
PROPERTIES: Increases damage and healing done by magical spells and effects by up to 28, Restores 3 mana per 5 sec.			
60	Runic Stone Shoulders	Bind on Pickup	392
PROPERTIES: Increases damage and healing done by magical spells and effects by up to 14.			
60	Mantle of the Desert's Fury	Bind on Pickup	413
PROPERTIES: Increases damage and healing done by magical spells and effects by up to 28.			
60	Barrage Shoulders	Bind on Pickup	398
60	Cryptstalker Spaulders	Bind on Pickup	464
PROPERTIES: Improves critical strike rating by 14, Increases attack power by 38.			
60	Earthshatter Spaulders	Bind on Pickup	464
PROPERTIES: Increases healing done by spells and effects by up to 42, Restores 6 mana per 5 sec.			
60	Pauldrons of Elemental Fury	Bind on Pickup	458
PROPERTIES: Increases damage and healing done by magical spells and effects by up to 26, Increases your spell critical strike rating by 14, Increases your spell hit rating by 8.			
60	Field Marshal's Mail Spaulders	Bind on Pickup	403
PROPERTIES: Increases damage and healing done by magical spells and effects by up to 16.			
70	Gladiator's Linked Spaulders	Bind on Pickup	583
PROPERTIES: Restores 4 mana per 5 sec.			
70	Gladiator's Mail Spaulders	Bind on Pickup	583
PROPERTIES: Restores 5 mana per 5 sec, Increases damage and healing done by magical spells and effects by up to 16.			
70	Gladiator's Chain Spaulders	Bind on Pickup	583
PROPERTIES: Increases attack power by 14.			
70	Beastman Pauldrons	Bind on Pickup	533
PROPERTIES: Increases attack power by 40, Restores 7 mana per 5 sec.			
70	Dragon-Quake Shoulderguards	Bind on Pickup	533
PROPERTIES: Restores 7 mana per 5 sec, Increases healing done by spells and effects by up to 59.			
70	Cyclone Shoulderpads	Bind on Pickup	558
PROPERTIES: Increases healing done by spells and effects by up to 59.			
70	Cyclone Shoulderguards	Bind on Pickup	558
PROPERTIES: Increases damage and healing done by magical spells and effects by up to 32.			
70	Cyclone Shoulderplates	Bind on Pickup	558
PROPERTIES: Increases damage and healing done by magical spells and effects by up to 18.			
70	Demon Stalker Shoulderguards	Bind on Pickup	558
PROPERTIES: Increases attack power by 38, Restores 4 mana per 5 sec.			
70	Mantle of the Tireless Tracker	Bind on Pickup	609
PROPERTIES: Increases attack power by 40.			
70	Coral-barbed Shoulderpads	Bind on Pickup	533
PROPERTIES: Restores 4 mana per 5 sec, Increases healing done by spells and effects by up to 62.			
70	Rift Stalker Mantle	Bind on Pickup	634
PROPERTIES: Increases attack power by 38.			
70	Cataclysm Shoulderpads	Bind on Pickup	634
PROPERTIES: Increases healing done by spells and effects by up to 64, Restores 6 mana per 5 sec.			
70	Cataclysm Shoulderguards	Bind on Pickup	634
PROPERTIES: Increases damage and healing done by magical spells and effects by up to 34.			
70	Cataclysm Shoulderplates	Bind on Pickup	634
PROPERTIES: Restores 6 mana per 5 sec.			

Epic Mail Shoulders

Level	Name	Binding Info	Armor
	Zandalar Predator's Mantle	Bind on Pickup	372
PROPERTIES: Restores 4 mana per 5 sec, Increases attack power by 28.			
	Icy Scale Spaulders	Bind on Pickup	448
PROPERTIES: Frost Resistance +33			

Superior Mail Shoulders

Level	Name	Binding Info	Armor
24	Sparkleshell Mantle	Bind on Equip	161
37	Herod's Shoulder	Bind on Pickup	196
38	Skeletal Shoulders	Bind on Equip	199
40	Spaulders of a Lost Age	Bind on Equip	205
50	Dregmetal Spaulders	Bind on Pickup	246
50	Lead Surveyor's Mantle	Bind on Pickup	246
PROPERTIES: Increases damage and healing done by magical spells and effects by up to 15.			
51	Golem Fitted Pauldrons	Bind on Pickup	250
53	Demonheart Spaulders	Bind on Pickup	258
54	Blue Dragonscale Shoulders	Bind on Equip	262
PROPERTIES: Arcane Resistance +6			
55	Black Dragonscale Shoulders	Bind on Equip	266
PROPERTIES: Increases attack power by 40. Fire Resistance +6			
55	Pauldrons of Elements	Bind on Pickup	266
55	Beaststalker's Mantle	Bind on Pickup	266
PROPERTIES: Increases attack power by 14.			
55	Denwatcher's Shoulders	Bind on Pickup	266
PROPERTIES: Increases damage and healing done by magical spells and effects by up to 18.			
55	Stratholme Militia Shoulderguard	Bind on Equip	266
56	Drakesfire Epaulets	Bind on Equip	270
PROPERTIES: Fire Resistance +10			
57	Royal Cap Spaulders	Bind on Pickup	274
PROPERTIES: Increases healing done by spells and effects by up to 26.			
57	Bone Golem Shoulders	Bind on Pickup	274
58	Bonespike Shoulder	Bind on Pickup	278
PROPERTIES: Deals 60 to 90 damage when you are the victim of a critical melee strike.			
58	Lieutenant Commander's Chain Pauldrons	Bind on Pickup	278
PROPERTIES: Increases attack power by 24.			
58	Champion's Mail Shoulders	Bind on Pickup	278
PROPERTIES: Increases damage and healing done by magical spells and effects by up to 6.			
58	Champion's Chain Pauldrons	Bind on Pickup	278
PROPERTIES: Increases attack power by 24.			
58	Winteraxe Epaulets	Bind on Pickup	278
60	Bloodsoul Shoulders	Bind on Equip	286
60	Abyssal Mail Pauldrons	Bind on Pickup	298
PROPERTIES: Increases your hit rating by 10.			
60	Champion's Chain Shoulders	Bind on Pickup	311
PROPERTIES: Improves critical strike rating by 14, Increases attack power by 24.			
60	Champion's Mail Pauldrons	Bind on Pickup	311
PROPERTIES: Increases damage and healing done by magical spells and effects by up to 15, Increases your spell critical strike rating by 14.			
60	Lieutenant Commander's Chain Shoulders	Bind on Pickup	311
PROPERTIES: Improves critical strike rating by 14, Increases attack power by 24.			
60	Lieutenant Commander's Mail Pauldrons	Bind on Pickup	311
PROPERTIES: Increases damage and healing done by magical spells and effects by up to 15, Increases your spell critical strike rating by 14.			

Superior Mail Shoulders

Level	Name	Binding Info	Armor
62	Mantid Shoulders	Bind on Pickup	392
PROPERTIES: Increases attack power by 30, Restores 6 mana per 5 sec.			
64	Lightningshard Pauldrons	Bind on Pickup	416
PROPERTIES: Restores 5 mana per 5 sec, Increases damage and healing done by magical spells and effects by up to 22.			
68	Volcanic Pauldrons	Bind on Pickup	477
PROPERTIES: Increases damage and healing done by magical spells and effects by up to 29.			
68	Mantle of the Sea Wolf	Bind on Pickup	477
PROPERTIES: Increases healing done by spells and effects by up to 51, Restores 8 mana per 5 sec.			
68	Towering Mantle of the Hunt	Bind on Pickup	477
PROPERTIES: Increases attack power by 48.			
70	Hellfire Pauldrons	Bind on Pickup	489
70	Beast Lord Mantle	Bind on Pickup	489
PROPERTIES: Increases attack power by 34, Restores 5 mana per 5 sec.			
70	Tidefury Shoulderguards	Bind on Pickup	489
PROPERTIES: Increases damage and healing done by magical spells and effects by up to 19, Restores 6 mana per 5 sec.			
70	Wyrmfury Pauldrons	Bind on Pickup	489
PROPERTIES: Increases attack power by 50.			
70	Grand Marshal's Chain Spaulders	Bind on Pickup	489
PROPERTIES: Increases attack power by 22.			
70	Grand Marshal's Linked Spaulders	Bind on Pickup	489
PROPERTIES: Restores 3 mana per 5 sec.			
70	Grand Marshal's Mail Spaulders	Bind on Pickup	489
PROPERTIES: Restores 4 mana per 5 sec, Increases damage and healing done by magical spells and effects by up to 15.			
70	High Warlord's Chain Spaulders	Bind on Pickup	489
PROPERTIES: Increases attack power by 22.			
70	High Warlord's Linked Spaulders	Bind on Pickup	489
PROPERTIES: Restores 3 mana per 5 sec.			
70	High Warlord's Mail Spaulders	Bind on Pickup	489
PROPERTIES: Restores 4 mana per 5 sec, Increases damage and healing done by magical spells and effects by up to 15.			
	Beastmaster's Mantle	Bind on Pickup	286
PROPERTIES: Increases attack power by 16.			
	Pauldrons of The Five Thunders	Bind on Pickup	286
PROPERTIES: Increases damage and healing done by magical spells and effects by up to 12.			
	Shalassi Sentry's Epaulets	Bind on Pickup	392
PROPERTIES: Increases attack power by 42.			
	Consortium Mantle of Phasing	Bind on Pickup	416
PROPERTIES: Increases attack power by 46, Restores 9 mana per 5 sec.			

Epic Mail Waist

Level	Name	Binding Info	Armor
54	Fiery Chain Girdle	Bind on Equip	245
PROPERTIES: Fire Resistance +24			
60	Marshal's Chain Girdle	Bind on Pickup	267
60	General's Chain Girdle	Bind on Pickup	267
60	General's Mail Waistband	Bind on Pickup	267
60	Earthfury Belt	Bind on Equip	271
PROPERTIES: Restores 4 mana per 5 sec, Increases healing done by spells and effects by up to 18. Fire Resistance +7			
60	Giantstalker's Belt	Bind on Equip	271
PROPERTIES: Improves critical strike rating by 14, Increases attack power by 24. Fire Resistance +7			

Epic Mail Waist

Level	Name	Binding Info	Armor
60	Dragonstalker's Belt	Bind on Pickup	310
PROPERTIES: Improves critical strike rating by 14, Increases attack power by 26. Shadow Resistance +10			
60	Belt of Ten Storms	Bind on Pickup	310
PROPERTIES: Increases your spell critical strike rating by 14, Increases healing done by spells and effects by up to 26. Shadow Resistance +10			
60	Therazane's Link	Bind on Pickup	336
PROPERTIES: Increases attack power by 44, Improves critical strike rating by 14.			
60	Primalist's Linked Waistguard	Bind on Pickup	314
PROPERTIES: Increases damage and healing done by magical spells and effects by up to 20.			
60	Ossirian's Binding	Bind on Pickup	294
PROPERTIES: Improves critical strike rating by 14, Increases your hit rating by 10.			
60	Grasp of the Fallen Emperor	Bind on Pickup	329
PROPERTIES: Increases damage and healing done by magical spells and effects by up to 19, Restores 5 mana per 5 sec.			
60	Cryptstalker Girdle	Bind on Pickup	355
PROPERTIES: Increases your hit rating by 10, Improves critical strike rating by 14, Restores 3 mana per 5 sec, Increases attack power by 30,			
60	Earthshatter Girdle	Bind on Pickup	355
PROPERTIES: Restores 7 mana per 5 sec, Increases healing done by spells and effects by up to 42.			
60	Girdle of Elemental Fury	Bind on Pickup	344
PROPERTIES: Increases damage and healing done by magical spells and effects by up to 29, Restores 5 mana per 5 sec.			
70	General's Chain Girdle	Bind on Pickup	438
PROPERTIES: Increases attack power by 24.			
70	Belt of Gale Force	Bind on Pickup	399
PROPERTIES: Restores 8 mana per 5 sec, Increases healing done by spells and effects by up to 55.			
70	General's Linked Girdle	Bind on Pickup	438
70	General's Mail Girdle	Bind on Pickup	438
PROPERTIES: Increases damage and healing done by magical spells and effects by up to 25.			
70	Girdle of the Prowler	Bind on Pickup	399
PROPERTIES: Increases attack power by 44, Restores 5 mana per 5 sec.			
70	Magtheridon Loot 1 Hunter Belt	Bind on Pickup	438
PROPERTIES: Increases attack power by 38, Restores 7 mana per 5 sec.			
70	Marshal's Chain Girdle	Bind on Pickup	438
PROPERTIES: Increases attack power by 24.			
70	Marshal's Linked Girdle	Bind on Pickup	438
70	Marshal's Mail Girdle	Bind on Pickup	438
PROPERTIES: Increases damage and healing done by magical spells and effects by up to 25.			
70	Wave-Song Girdle	Bind on Pickup	381
PROPERTIES: Increases damage and healing done by magical spells and effects by up to 30.			
70	Girdle of Ferocity	Bind on Pickup	381
PROPERTIES: Increases attack power by 40.			
70	Ebon Netherscale Belt	Bind on Pickup	418
PROPERTIES: Increases attack power by 44, Restores 7 mana per 5 sec.			
70	Netherstrike Belt	Bind on Pickup	336
PROPERTIES: Increases damage and healing done by magical spells and effects by up to 25, Restores 8 mana per 5 sec.			
70	Girdle of Fallen Stars	Bind on Pickup	457
PROPERTIES: Increases healing done by spells and effects by up to 44.			
70	Monsoon Belt	Bind on Equip	457
PROPERTIES: Increases damage and healing done by magical spells and effects by up to 34.			
70	Belt of the Black Eagle	Bind on Equip	457
PROPERTIES: Increases attack power by 56.			

Epic Mail Waist

Level	Name	Binding Info	Armor
70	Girdle of the Tidal Call	Bind on Pickup	457
PROPERTIES: Restores 6 mana per 5 sec.			
70	Belt of the Tracker	Bind on Pickup	399
PROPERTIES: Restores 15 mana per 5 sec, Increases attack power by 30.			
70	Lurker's Belt	Bind on Pickup	381
	Zandalar Augur's Belt	Bind on Pickup	252
PROPERTIES: Increases damage and healing done by magical spells and effects by up to 12, Restores 4 mana per 5 sec.			
	Zandalar Predator's Belt	Bind on Pickup	252
PROPERTIES: Increases your hit rating by 10, Increases attack power by 26.			

Superior Mail Waist

Level	Name	Binding Info	Armor
15	Stormbringer Belt	Bind on Equip	104
19	Cobrahn's Grasp	Bind on Pickup	111
28	Girdle of Golem Strength	Bind on Equip	128
PROPERTIES: Increases defense rating by 5.			
28	Highlander's Lamellar Girdle	Bind on Pickup	128
28	Highlander's Plate Girdle	Bind on Pickup	128
28	Defiler's Lamellar Girdle	Bind on Pickup	128
28	Defiler's Plate Girdle	Bind on Pickup	128
28	Defiler's Lamellar Girdle	Bind on Pickup	128
37	Boar Champion's Belt	Bind on Pickup	147
40	Highlander's Chain Girdle	Bind on Pickup	149
PROPERTIES: Improves critical strike rating by 14, Increases attack power by 8.			
40	Highlander's Mail Girdle	Bind on Pickup	149
40	Defiler's Chain Girdle	Bind on Pickup	149
PROPERTIES: Improves critical strike rating by 14, Increases attack power by 8.			
40	Defiler's Mail Girdle	Bind on Pickup	149
44	Belt of the Gladiator	Bind on Equip	166
48	Highlander's Chain Girdle	Bind on Pickup	178
PROPERTIES: Improves critical strike rating by 14, Increases attack power by 20.			
48	Highlander's Mail Girdle	Bind on Pickup	178
PROPERTIES: Increases your spell critical strike rating by 14.			
48	Defiler's Chain Girdle	Bind on Pickup	178
PROPERTIES: Improves critical strike rating by 14, Increases attack power by 20.			
48	Defiler's Mail Girdle	Bind on Pickup	178
PROPERTIES: Increases your spell critical strike rating by 14.			
51	Verek's Leash	Bind on Pickup	187
PROPERTIES: Increases damage and healing done by magical spells and effects by up to 11.			
52	Chillsteel Girdle	Bind on Pickup	190
PROPERTIES: Frost Resistance +10			
53	Cord of Elements	Bind on Equip	193
53	Beaststalker's Belt	Bind on Equip	193
PROPERTIES: Increases attack power by 12.			
53	Heavy Timbermaw Belt	Bind on Equip	193
PROPERTIES: Increases attack power by 42.			
55	Chiselbrand Girdle	Bind on Pickup	199
PROPERTIES: Increases attack power by 44.			
55	Knight-Captain's Chain Girdle	Bind on Pickup	199
55	Legionnaire's Mail Cinch	Bind on Pickup	199
55	Legionnaire's Chain Girdle	Bind on Pickup	199

Superior Mail Waist

Level	Name	Binding Info	Armor
55	Frostwolf Mail Belt	Bind on Pickup	199
PROPERTIES: Frost Resistance +5			
55	Stormpike Mail Girdle	Bind on Pickup	199
PROPERTIES: Frost Resistance +5			
55	Sash of the Grand Hunt	Bind on Pickup	199
PROPERTIES: Increases Bow skill rating by 4, Increases Gun skill rating by 4, Increases Crossbow skill rating by 4.			
56	Foresight Girdle	Bind on Pickup	202
PROPERTIES: Restores 5 health per 5 sec.			
56	Bloodmail Belt	Bind on Pickup	202
56	Warpwood Binding	Bind on Pickup	202
PROPERTIES: Improves critical strike rating by 14.			
56	Sash of the Windreaver	Bind on Equip	202
PROPERTIES: Increases damage done by Nature spells and effects by up to 29.			
56	Barrage Girdle	Bind on Pickup	202
PROPERTIES: Increases damage and healing done by magical spells and effects by up to 23.			
56	Marksman's Girdle	Bind on Pickup	202
PROPERTIES: Increases your hit rating by 10.			
57	Detention Strap	Bind on Pickup	205
58	Feralsurge Girdle	Bind on Pickup	208
PROPERTIES: Restores 8 mana per 5 sec.			
58	Highlander's Chain Girdle	Bind on Pickup	208
PROPERTIES: Improves critical strike rating by 14, Increases attack power by 34.			
58	Highlander's Mail Girdle	Bind on Pickup	208
PROPERTIES: Increases your spell critical strike rating by 14.			
58	Defiler's Chain Girdle	Bind on Pickup	208
PROPERTIES: Improves critical strike rating by 14, Increases attack power by 34.			
58	Defiler's Mail Girdle	Bind on Pickup	208
PROPERTIES: Increases your spell critical strike rating by 14.			
60	Light Obsidian Belt	Bind on Equip	224
PROPERTIES: Increases attack power by 32, Improves critical strike rating by 14, Resistance +5 All Resistances.			
61	Spiritfire Girdle	Bind on Pickup	285
PROPERTIES: Restores 6 mana per 5 sec, Increases healing done by spells and effects by up to 18.			
62	Tracker's Cord	Bind on Pickup	294
PROPERTIES: Increases attack power by 42.			
66	Dusktracker's Girdle	Bind on Pickup	351
PROPERTIES: Increases attack power by 38.			
66	Stormbreaker's Girdle	Bind on Pickup	321
66	Marksman's Belt	Bind on Pickup	321
PROPERTIES: Increases attack power by 20.			
67	Netherfury Belt	Bind on Equip	339
PROPERTIES: Increases damage and healing done by magical spells and effects by up to 21, Restores 9 mana per 5 sec.			
68	Archery Belt of the Broken	Bind on Pickup	357
PROPERTIES: Increases attack power by 58.			
68	Girdle of Living Flame	Bind on Pickup	357
PROPERTIES: Increases damage and healing done by magical spells and effects by up to 29.			
69	Felstalker Belt	Bind on Equip	357
PROPERTIES: Increases attack power by 50, Restores 7 mana per 5 sec.			
69	Flamescale Belt	Bind on Equip	357
PROPERTIES: Fire Resistance +30			
70	Hellfire Girdle	Bind on Pickup	367
PROPERTIES: Increases attack power by 30.			

Superior Mail Waist

Level	Name	Binding Info	Armor
70	Telaari War Girdle	Bind on Pickup	367
PROPERTIES: Increases attack power by 50, Restores 6 mana per 5 sec.			
70	Stillwater Girdle	Bind on Pickup	367
PROPERTIES: Restores 8 mana per 5 sec, Increases healing done by spells and effects by up to 53.			
70	Blessed Scale Girdle	Bind on Pickup	367
PROPERTIES: Increases attack power by 70.			
70	Belt of Flowing Thought	Bind on Pickup	367
PROPERTIES: Restores 13 mana per 5 sec.			
	Stonefist Girdle	Bind on Pickup	134
	Belt of Shriveled Heads	Bind on Pickup	230
	Beastmaster's Belt	Bind on Pickup	214
PROPERTIES: Increases attack power by 20.			
	Cord of The Five Thunders	Bind on Pickup	214
PROPERTIES: Increases damage and healing done by magical spells and effects by up to 12, Restores 4 mana per 5 sec.			
	Tarren Mill Defender's Cinch	Bind on Pickup	330
PROPERTIES: Restores 12 mana per 5 sec.			

Epic Mail Wrists

Level	Name	Binding Info	Armor
40	Windtalker's Wristguards	Bind on Pickup	149
PROPERTIES: Increases attack power by 28.			
50	Windtalker's Wristguards	Bind on Pickup	178
PROPERTIES: Increases attack power by 34.			
60	Marshal's Chain Bracers	Bind on Pickup	208
60	General's Chain Wristguards	Bind on Pickup	208
60	General's Mail Bracers	Bind on Pickup	208
60	Earthfury Bracers	Bind on Equip	211
PROPERTIES: Increases damage and healing done by magical spells and effects by up to 6.			
60	Giantstalker's Bracers	Bind on Equip	211
PROPERTIES: Increases attack power by 26.			
60	Dragonstalker's Bracers	Bind on Pickup	241
PROPERTIES: Increases attack power by 30.			
60	Bracers of Ten Storms	Bind on Pickup	241
PROPERTIES: Restores 6 mana per 5 sec.			
60	Wristguards of True Flight	Bind on Pickup	226
PROPERTIES: Increases your hit rating by 10.			
60	Windtalker's Wristguards	Bind on Pickup	208
PROPERTIES: Increases attack power by 38.			
60	Bracers of Eternal Reckoning	Bind on Pickup	276
60	Wristguards of Elemental Fury	Bind on Pickup	276
PROPERTIES: Increases damage and healing done by magical spells and effects by up to 25, Restores 6 mana per 5 sec.			
60	Cryptstalker Wristguards	Bind on Pickup	276
PROPERTIES: Increases your hit rating by 10, Increases attack power by 34.			
60	Earthshatter Wristguards	Bind on Pickup	276
PROPERTIES: Increases healing done by spells and effects by up to 33, Restores 4 mana per 5 sec.			
60	Icy Scale Bracers	Bind on Equip	253
PROPERTIES: Increases attack power by 32. Frost Resistance +20			
70	General's Chain Bracers	Bind on Pickup	311
PROPERTIES: Increases attack power by 12.			
70	Stalker's War Bands	Bind on Pickup	311
PROPERTIES: Increases attack power by 40.			

Epic Mail Wrists

Level	Name	Binding Info	Armor
70	Whirlwind Bracers	Bind on Pickup	311
PROPERTIES: Increases healing done by spells and effects by up to 42, Restores 6 mana per 5 sec.			
70	General's Linked Bracers	Bind on Pickup	311
70	General's Mail Bracers	Bind on Pickup	311
PROPERTIES: Increases damage and healing done by magical spells and effects by up to 18.			
70	Marshal's Chain Bracers	Bind on Pickup	311
PROPERTIES: Increases attack power by 12.			
70	Marshal's Linked Bracers	Bind on Pickup	311
70	Marshal's Mail Bracers	Bind on Pickup	311
PROPERTIES: Increases damage and healing done by magical spells and effects by up to 18.			
70	Wave-Fury Vambraces	Bind on Pickup	296
PROPERTIES: Increases damage and healing done by magical spells and effects by up to 19, Restores 5 mana per 5 sec.			
70	Bracers of the Hunt	Bind on Pickup	296
PROPERTIES: Increases attack power by 28, Restores 4 mana per 5 sec.			
70	Ebon Netherscale Bracers	Bind on Pickup	325
PROPERTIES: Increases attack power by 34, Restores 5 mana per 5 sec.			
70	Netherstrike Bracers	Bind on Pickup	261
PROPERTIES: Increases damage and healing done by magical spells and effects by up to 18, Restores 6 mana per 5 sec.			
70	Bands of the Celestial Archer	Bind on Pickup	355
PROPERTIES: Increases attack power by 36, Restores 6 mana per 5 sec.			
70	Blakfathom Warbands	Bind on Pickup	355
PROPERTIES: Increases healing done by spells and effects by up to 55.			
70	True-aim Stalker Bands	Bind on Pickup	355
PROPERTIES: Increases attack power by 40, Restores 5 mana per 5 sec.			
70	Ravager's Bands	Bind on Pickup	296
	Zandalar Augur's Bracers	Bind on Pickup	196
PROPERTIES: Increases damage and healing done by magical spells and effects by up to 13, Restores 4 mana per 5 sec.			
	Zandalar Predator's Bracers	Bind on Pickup	196
PROPERTIES: Increases ranged attack power by 34, Restores 4 mana per 5 sec.			

Superior Mail Wrist

Level	Name	Binding Info	Armor
21	Jimmied Handcuffs	Bind on Pickup	89
22	Yorgen Bracers	Bind on Equip	91
25	Pugilist Bracers	Bind on Equip	95
30	First Sergeant's Mail Wristguards	Bind on Pickup	103
36	Crushridge Bindings	Bind on Equip	113
37	Ironaya's Bracers	Bind on Pickup	115
44	Slimescale Bracers	Bind on Equip	129
45	First Sergeant's Mail Wristguards	Bind on Pickup	131
45	Sergeant Major's Chain Armguards	Bind on Pickup	131
45	Arena Bands	Bind on Equip	131
PROPERTIES: Increases attack power by 28.			
49	Bracers of the Stone Princess	Bind on Pickup	141
PROPERTIES: Increases attack power by 30.			
50	Rubicund Armguards	Bind on Pickup	143
51	Marksman Bands	Bind on Equip	146
PROPERTIES: Increases Bow skill rating by 4, Increases Crossbow skill rating by 4, Increases Gun skill rating by 4.			

Superior Mail Wrist

Level	Name	Binding Info	Armor
52	Pyremail Wristguards	Bind on Pickup	148
PROPERTIES: Fire Resistance +10			
52	Bindings of Elements	Bind on Equip	148
52	Beaststalker's Bindings	Bind on Equip	148
PROPERTIES: Increases attack power by 20.			
54	Lordly Armguards	Bind on Equip	153
55	Brazecore Armguards	Bind on Pickup	155
PROPERTIES: Restores 3 mana per 5 sec.			
55	Slashclaw Bracers	Bind on Pickup	155
PROPERTIES: Increases your hit rating by 10.			
55	Knight-Captain's Chain Armguards	Bind on Pickup	155
55	Legionnaire's Chain Bracers	Bind on Pickup	155
56	Loomguard Armbraces	Bind on Pickup	157
PROPERTIES: Increases healing done by spells and effects by up to 33.			
57	Demon Howl Wristguards	Bind on Pickup	160
PROPERTIES: Increases attack power by 14.			
57	Swift Flight Bracers	Bind on Equip	160
PROPERTIES: Increases ranged attack power by 41.			
57	Sandstalker Bracers	Bind on Equip	160
PROPERTIES: Nature Resistance +15			
57	Spitfire Bracers	Bind on Equip	160
PROPERTIES: Restores 4 mana per 5 sec, Increases damage and healing done by magical spells and effects by up to 8.			
58	First Sergeant's Mail Wristguards	Bind on Pickup	162
58	Sergeant Major's Chain Armguards	Bind on Pickup	162
58	Wristguards of Undead Slaying	Bind on Equip	162
PROPERTIES: Increases attack power by 45 when fighting Undead.			
60	Abyssal Mail Armguards	Bind on Pickup	174
60	Sand Reaver Wristguards	Bind on Pickup	181
63	Lykul Bloodbands	Bind on Pickup	236
PROPERTIES: Increases attack power by 30.			
68	World's End Bracers	Bind on Pickup	278
PROPERTIES: Increases damage and healing done by magical spells and effects by up to 21.			
68	Bracers of Shirrak	Bind on Pickup	278
PROPERTIES: Increases attack power by 48, Restores 5 mana per 5 sec.			
70	Felstalker Bracers	Bind on Equip	283
PROPERTIES: Increases attack power by 38, Restores 4 mana per 5 sec.			
70	Emerald Eye Bracer	Bind on Pickup	285
PROPERTIES: Restores 5 mana per 5 sec, Increases attack power by 46.			
70	Primal Surge Bracers	Bind on Pickup	285
PROPERTIES: Increases healing done by spells and effects by up to 37, Restores 6 mana per 5 sec.			
	Beastmaster's Bindings	Bind on Pickup	167
PROPERTIES: Increases attack power by 20.			
	Bindings of The Five Thunders	Bind on Pickup	167
PROPERTIES: Increases damage and healing done by magical spells and effects by up to 8.			
	Auchenai Bracers	Bind on Pickup	285
PROPERTIES: Increases attack power by 36, Restores 4 mana per 5 sec.			

PLATE

Epic Plate Chest

Level	Name	Binding Info	Armor
60	Field Marshal's Lamellar Chestplate	Bind on Pickup	954
PROPERTIES: Improves critical strike rating by 14, Increases damage and healing done by magical spells and effects by up to 25, Restores 5 mana per 5 sec.			
60	Field Marshal's Plate Armor	Bind on Pickup	954
PROPERTIES: Improves critical strike rating by 14.			
60	Warlord's Plate Armor	Bind on Pickup	954
PROPERTIES: Improves critical strike rating by 14.			
60	Lawbringer Chestguard	Bind on Pickup	855
PROPERTIES: Increases healing done by spells and effects by up to 22. Fire Resistance +10			
60	Breastplate of Might	Bind on Pickup	855
PROPERTIES: Increases your block rating by 15, Increases defense rating by 10. Fire Resistance +10			
60	Judgement Breastplate	Bind on Pickup	978
PROPERTIES: Restores 5 mana per 5 sec, Increases damage and healing done by magical spells and effects by up to 25. Fire Resistance +10, Nature Resistance +10			
60	Breastplate of Wrath	Bind on Pickup	978
PROPERTIES: Increases defense rating by 16. Fire Resistance +10, Nature Resistance +10			
60	Warrior Breastplate	Bind on Pickup	1148
PROPERTIES: Increases your hit rating by 20. Fire Resistance +10, Nature Resistance +10, Frost Resistance +10, Shadow Resistance +10, Arcane Resistance +10			
60	Conqueror's Breastplate	Bind on Pickup	1124
PROPERTIES: Increases defense rating by 9.			
60	Avenger's Breastplate	Bind on Pickup	1124
PROPERTIES: Increases damage and healing done by magical spells and effects by up to 18, Increases your spell critical strike rating by 14, Improves critical strike rating by 14.			
60	Silithid Carapace Chestguard	Bind on Pickup	990
PROPERTIES: Nature Resistance +35			
60	Breastplate of Annihilation	Bind on Pickup	941
PROPERTIES: Improves critical strike rating by 14, Increases your hit rating by 10.			
60	Thick Obsidian Breastplate	Bind on Equip	929
PROPERTIES: When struck by a non-periodic damage spell you have a 30% chance of getting a 6 sec spell shield that absorbs 300 to 500 of that school of damage.			
60	Dreadnaught Breastplate	Bind on Pickup	1172
PROPERTIES: Increases defense rating by 20, Increases your dodge rating by 12, Increases your hit rating by 20.			
60	Redemption Tunic	Bind on Pickup	1172
PROPERTIES: Increases healing done by spells and effects by up to 59, Increases your spell critical strike rating by 14, Restores 10 mana per 5 sec.			
60	Icebane Breastplate	Bind on Equip	1027
PROPERTIES: Increases defense rating by 12. Frost Resistance +42			
60	Plated Abomination Ribcage	Bind on Pickup	1087
PROPERTIES: Improves critical strike rating by 14, Increases your hit rating by 10.			
60	Titanic Breastplate	Not Bound	1148
PROPERTIES: Improves critical strike rating by 14, Increases defense rating by 15. Nature Resistance +10, Arcane Resistance +10			
60	Warlord's Lamellar Chestplate	Bind on Pickup	954
PROPERTIES: Improves critical strike rating by 14, Increases damage and healing done by magical spells and effects by up to 25, Restores 5 mana per 5 sec.			
70	Warrior Breastplate	Bind on Pickup	1632
70	Gladiator's Plate Chestpiece	Bind on Pickup	1450
70	Gladiator's Lamellar Chestpiece	Bind on Pickup	1450
PROPERTIES: Increases damage and healing done by magical spells and effects by up to 12.			
70	Gladiator's Scaled Chestpiece	Bind on Pickup	1450
PROPERTIES: Increases damage and healing done by magical spells and effects by up to 12.			

Epic Plate Chest

Level	Name	Binding Info	Armor
70	Breastplate of Kings	Bind on Pickup	1268
70	Bulwark of Kings	Bind on Pickup	1510
PROPERTIES: Temporarily Increases Health by 1500 and Strength by 150 for 15 sec.			
70	Bulwark of the Ancient Kings	Bind on Pickup	1753
PROPERTIES: Temporarily Increases Health by 1500 and Strength by 150 for 15 sec.			
70	Panzar'Thar Breastplate	Bind on Pickup	1268
PROPERTIES: Increases the block value of your shield by 33.			
70	Breastplate of the Lightbinder	Bind on Pickup	1268
PROPERTIES: Increases healing done by spells and effects by up to 73, Restores 11 mana per 5 sec.			
70	Warbringer Chestguard	Bind on Pickup	1329
PROPERTIES: Increases the block value of your shield by 39.			
70	Warbringer Breastplate	Bind on Pickup	1329
70	Justicar Chestpiece	Bind on Pickup	1329
PROPERTIES: Increases healing done by spells and effects by up to 81, Restores 5 mana per 5 sec.			
70	Justicar Chestguard	Bind on Pickup	1329
PROPERTIES: Increases damage and healing done by magical spells and effects by up to 22, Restores 5 mana per 5 sec.			
70	Justicar Breastplate	Bind on Pickup	1329
PROPERTIES: Increases damage and healing done by magical spells and effects by up to 26.			
70	Glowing Breastplate of Truth	Bind on Pickup	1450
PROPERTIES: Restores 9 mana per 5 sec.			
70	Krakken-Heart Breastplate	Bind on Pickup	1571
70	Destroyer Chestguard	Bind on Pickup	1510
70	Destroyer Breastplate	Bind on Pickup	1510
70	Crystalforge Chestguard	Bind on Pickup	1510
PROPERTIES: Increases damage and healing done by magical spells and effects by up to 14, Increases the block value of your shield by 33.			
70	Crystalforge Breastplate	Bind on Pickup	1510
PROPERTIES: Increases damage and healing done by magical spells and effects by up to 39, Restores 6 mana per 5 sec.			
70	Crystalforge Chestpiece	Bind on Pickup	1510
PROPERTIES: Increases healing done by spells and effects by up to 81.			
70	Gladiator's Plate Chestpiece Tier 2	Bind on Pickup	1450
70	Inferno Tempered Chestguard	Bind on Pickup	1208
PROPERTIES: Fire Resistance +60			
	Breastplate of the Chromatic Flight	Bind on Pickup	806
PROPERTIES: Fire Resistance +15			
	Zandalar Vindicator's Breastplate	Bind on Pickup	842
PROPERTIES: Increases defense rating by 6.			
	Zandalar Freethinker's Breastplate	Bind on Pickup	842
PROPERTIES: Improves critical strike rating by 14.			
	Breastplate of Heroism	Bind on Pickup	781
PROPERTIES: Increases your hit rating by 10.			
	Soulforge Breastplate	Bind on Pickup	781
PROPERTIES: Increases damage and healing done by magical spells and effects by up to 14, Improves critical strike rating by 14.			

Superior Plate Chest

Level	Name	Binding Info	Armor
40	Carapace of Tuten'kash	Bind on Pickup	373
44	Truesilver Breastplate	Bind on Equip	519
PROPERTIES: When struck in combat has a 3% chance to heal you for 60 to 100.			
49	Warrior's Embrace	Bind on Pickup	567
PROPERTIES: Increases your dodge rating by 24.			

Armor

Weapons

Superior Plate Chest

Level	Name	Binding Info	Armor
49	Spiderfang Carapace	Bind on Pickup	567
PROPERTIES: Increases damage and healing done by magical spells and effects by up to 13.			
49	Hydralick Armor	Bind on Equip	567
PROPERTIES: Fire Resistance +10			
50	Carapace of Anub'shiah	Bind on Pickup	577
52	Demon Forged Breastplate	Bind on Equip	597
PROPERTIES: When struck has a 3% chance of stealing 120 life from the attacker over 4 sec.			
54	Dark Iron Plate	Bind on Pickup	617
PROPERTIES: Fire Resistance +19			
54	Skul's Cold Embrace	Bind on Pickup	617
PROPERTIES: Increases defense rating by 9. Frost Resistance +10			
54	Energized Chestplate	Bind on Pickup	617
PROPERTIES: Restores 5 mana per 5 sec.			
55	Plate of the Shaman King	Bind on Pickup	627
PROPERTIES: Increases damage and healing done by magical spells and effects by up to 18.			
56	Deathbone Chestplate	Bind on Pickup	637
PROPERTIES: Increases defense rating by 25, Restores 5 mana per 5 sec.			
57	Kromcrush's Chestplate	Bind on Pickup	647
PROPERTIES: Increases defense rating by 15.			
58	Enchanted Thorium Breastplate	Bind on Equip	657
PROPERTIES: Increases defense rating by 13.			
58	General's Ceremonial Plate	Bind on Pickup	657
58	Knight-Captain's Plate Chestguard	Bind on Pickup	657
PROPERTIES: Improves critical strike rating by 14.			
58	Knight-Captain's Lamellar Breastplate	Bind on Pickup	657
PROPERTIES: Improves critical strike rating by 14.			
58	Legionnaire's Plate Armor	Bind on Pickup	657
PROPERTIES: Improves critical strike rating by 14.			
58	Lightforge Breastplate	Bind on Pickup	657
58	Breastplate of Valor	Bind on Pickup	657
58	Darkrune Breastplate	Bind on Equip	657
PROPERTIES: Increases your dodge rating by 12. Shadow Resistance +25			
58	Breastplate of Undead Slaying	Bind on Pickup	657
PROPERTIES: Increases attack power by 81 when fighting Undead.			
60	Darksoul Breastplate	Bind on Equip	676
PROPERTIES: Increases your hit rating by 10.			
60	Ironvine Breastplate	Bind on Equip	726
PROPERTIES: Increases defense rating by 10. Nature Resistance +30			
60	Legionnaire's Plate Hauberk	Bind on Pickup	706
PROPERTIES: Improves critical strike rating by 14.			
60	Knight-Captain's Lamellar Breastplate	Bind on Pickup	706
PROPERTIES: Increases damage and healing done by magical spells and effects by up to 25.			
60	Knight-Captain's Plate Hauberk	Bind on Pickup	706
PROPERTIES: Improves critical strike rating by 14.			
60	Light-Touched Breastplate	Bind on Pickup	873
PROPERTIES: Restores 5 mana per 5 sec.			
60	Legionnaire's Lamellar Breastplate	Bind on Pickup	706
PROPERTIES: Increases damage and healing done by magical spells and effects by up to 25.			
62	Unscarred Breastplate	Bind on Pickup	932
65	Heavy Earthforged Breastplate	Bind on Pickup	1018
66	Durotan's Battle Harness	Bind on Pickup	1048
67	Adamantite Breastplate	Bind on Equip	1077
68	Breastplate of Many Graces	Bind on Pickup	1135
PROPERTIES: Increases healing done by spells and effects by up to 75, Restores 10 mana per 5 sec.			
68	Jade-Skull Breastplate	Bind on Pickup	1135
68	Breastplate of Righteous Fury	Bind on Pickup	1135
PROPERTIES: Increases damage and healing done by magical spells and effects by up to 23.			
70	Enchanted Adamantite Breastplate	Bind on Equip	1154
PROPERTIES: Arcane Resistance +40			
70	Flamebane Breastplate	Bind on Equip	1164
PROPERTIES: Fire Resistance +40			
70	Ragesteel Breastplate	Bind on Equip	1164
70	Crimsonforge Breastplate	Bind on Pickup	1164
70	Breastplate of the Righteous	Bind on Pickup	1164
PROPERTIES: Increases damage and healing done by magical spells and effects by up to 23.			
70	Breastplate of the Bold	Bind on Pickup	1164
70	Doomplate Chestpiece	Bind on Pickup	1164
70	Grand Marshal's Lamellar Chestpiece	Bind on Pickup	1164
PROPERTIES: Increases damage and healing done by magical spells and effects by up to 9.			
70	Grand Marshal's Plate Chestpiece	Bind on Pickup	1164
70	Grand Marshal's Scaled Chestpiece	Bind on Pickup	1164
PROPERTIES: Increases damage and healing done by magical spells and effects by up to 9.			
70	High Warlord's Lamellar Chestpiece	Bind on Pickup	1164
PROPERTIES: Increases damage and healing done by magical spells and effects by up to 9.			
70	High Warlord's Plate Chestpiece	Bind on Pickup	1164
70	High Warlord's Scaled Chestpiece	Bind on Pickup	1164
PROPERTIES: Increases damage and healing done by magical spells and effects by up to 9.			
70	Vindicator's Hauberk	Bind on Pickup	1164
	Ornate Adamantium Breastplate	Bind on Pickup	657
PROPERTIES: Increases defense rating by 15.			
	Breastplate of Retribution	Bind on Pickup	902
PROPERTIES: Increases damage and healing done by magical spells and effects by up to 27.			
	Breastplate of the Warbringer	Bind on Pickup	1048
	Fleshripper's Bladed Chestplate	Bind on Pickup	873
	Gilded Crimson Chestplate	Bind on Pickup	873
PROPERTIES: Increases damage and healing done by magical spells and effects by up to 42, Restores 4 mana per 5 sec.			
	The Exarch's Protector	Bind on Pickup	1018
	Chestplate of A'dal	Bind on Pickup	1106

Epic Plate Feet

Level	Name	Binding Info	Armor
40	Boots of Avoidance	Bind on Equip	411
PROPERTIES: Increases your dodge rating by 24.			
60	Marshal's Lamellar Boots	Bind on Pickup	630
PROPERTIES: Increases damage and healing done by magical spells and effects by up to 18, Restores 6 mana per 5 sec.			
60	Marshal's Plate Boots	Bind on Pickup	630
PROPERTIES: Increases your hit rating by 10.			
60	General's Plate Boots	Bind on Pickup	630
PROPERTIES: Increases your hit rating by 10.			
60	Lawbringer Boots	Bind on Pickup	588
PROPERTIES: Restores 2 mana per 5 sec, Increases healing done by spells and effects by up to 18. Shadow Resistance +7			

Epic Plate Feet

Level	Name	Binding Info	Armor
60	Sabatons of Might	Bind on Pickup	588
PROPERTIES: Increases defense rating by 8. Shadow Resistance +7			
60	Judgement Sabatons	Bind on Pickup	672
PROPERTIES: Increases damage and healing done by magical spells and effects by up to 18. Fire Resistance +10			
60	Sabatons of Wrath	Bind on Pickup	672
PROPERTIES: Increases the block value of your shield by 14, Increases defense rating by 10. Fire Resistance +10			
60	Core Forged Greaves	Bind on Pickup	621
PROPERTIES: Increases defense rating by 6. Fire Resistance +12, Shadow Resistance +8			
60	Magma Tempered Boots	Bind on Pickup	621
PROPERTIES: Increases healing done by spells and effects by up to 18. Fire Resistance +8			
60	Chromatic Boots	Bind on Pickup	681
PROPERTIES: Increases your hit rating by 10.			
60	Dark Iron Boots	Bind on Equip	621
PROPERTIES: Fire Resistance +28			
60	Warrior Sabatons	Bind on Pickup	789
PROPERTIES: Improves critical strike rating by 14. Fire Resistance +8, Nature Resistance +8, Frost Resistance +8, Shadow Resistance +8, Arcane Resistance +7			
60	Acid Inscribed Greaves	Bind on Pickup	639
PROPERTIES: Increases defense rating by 9. Nature Resistance +25			
60	Conqueror's Greaves	Bind on Pickup	689
PROPERTIES: Increases defense rating by 6.			
60	Avenger's Greaves	Bind on Pickup	689
PROPERTIES: Increases damage and healing done by magical spells and effects by up to 14, Restores 4 mana per 5 sec.			
60	Boots of the Fallen Hero	Bind on Pickup	664
PROPERTIES: Increases your hit rating by 10.			
60	Boots of the Redeemed Prophecy	Bind on Pickup	647
PROPERTIES: Increases healing done by spells and effects by up to 33.			
60	Boots of the Unwavering Will	Bind on Pickup	647
PROPERTIES: Increases defense rating by 8.			
60	Dreadnaught Sabatons	Bind on Pickup	756
PROPERTIES: Increases defense rating by 13, Increases your dodge rating by 12.			
60	Redemption Boots	Bind on Pickup	756
PROPERTIES: Increases healing done by spells and effects by up to 42, Increases your spell critical strike rating by 14, Restores 5 mana per 5 sec.			
60	General's Lamellar Boots	Bind on Pickup	630
PROPERTIES: Increases damage and healing done by magical spells and effects by up to 18, Restores 6 mana per 5 sec.			
70	Warrior Sabatons	Bind on Pickup	1122
70	General's Plate Greaves	Bind on Pickup	955
70	Boots of Valiance	Bind on Pickup	872
PROPERTIES: Increases healing done by spells and effects by up to 48.			
70	Ironstriders of Urgency	Bind on Pickup	872
70	General's Lamellar Greaves	Bind on Pickup	955
PROPERTIES: Increases damage and healing done by magical spells and effects by up to 25.			
70	General's Scaled Greaves	Bind on Pickup	955
PROPERTIES: Increases damage and healing done by magical spells and effects by up to 25.			
70	Battlescar Boots	Bind on Pickup	872
70	Marshal's Lamellar Greaves	Bind on Pickup	955
PROPERTIES: Increases damage and healing done by magical spells and effects by up to 25.			
70	Marshal's Plate Greaves	Bind on Pickup	955

Epic Plate Feet

Level	Name	Binding Info	Armor
70	Marshal's Scaled Greaves	Bind on Pickup	955
PROPERTIES: Increases damage and healing done by magical spells and effects by up to 25.			
70	Eaglecrest Warboots	Bind on Pickup	831
70	Boots of the Righteous Path	Bind on Pickup	831
PROPERTIES: Increases damage and healing done by magical spells and effects by up to 26.			
70	Boots of Courage Unending	Bind on Pickup	997
PROPERTIES: Increases healing done by spells and effects by up to 81.			
70	Red Havoc Boots	Bind on Pickup	997
70	Boots of the Protector	Bind on Pickup	997
PROPERTIES: Increases damage and healing done by magical spells and effects by up to 25, Restores 8 mana per 5 sec.			
70	Warboots of Obliteration	Bind on Pickup	997
70	General's Plate Greaves Tier 2	Bind on Pickup	955
70	Boots of Elusion	Bind on Pickup	872
70	Glider's Greaves	Bind on Pickup	831
70	Inferno Tempered Boots	Bind on Pickup	831
PROPERTIES: Fire Resistance +45			
	Boots of Heroism	Bind on Pickup	537
PROPERTIES: Increases your hit rating by 10.			
	Soulforge Boots	Bind on Pickup	537
PROPERTIES: Increases damage and healing done by magical spells and effects by up to 12, Restores 4 mana per 5 sec.			

Superior Plate Feet

Level	Name	Binding Info	Armor
40	Obsidian Greaves	Bind on Equip	257
40	Highlander's Lamellar Greaves	Bind on Pickup	289
PROPERTIES: Run speed increased slightly.			
40	Highlander's Plate Greaves	Bind on Pickup	289
PROPERTIES: Run speed increased slightly.			
40	Defiler's Lamellar Greaves	Bind on Pickup	289
PROPERTIES: Run speed increased slightly.			
40	Defiler's Plate Greaves	Bind on Pickup	289
PROPERTIES: Run speed increased slightly.			
48	Highlander's Lamellar Greaves	Bind on Pickup	383
PROPERTIES: Run speed increased slightly.			
48	Highlander's Plate Greaves	Bind on Pickup	383
PROPERTIES: Run speed increased slightly.			
48	Defiler's Lamellar Greaves	Bind on Pickup	383
PROPERTIES: Run speed increased slightly.			
48	Defiler's Plate Greaves	Bind on Pickup	383
PROPERTIES: Run speed increased slightly.			
50	Battlechaser's Greaves	Bind on Equip	397
50	Entrenching Boots	Bind on Pickup	397
PROPERTIES: Increases damage and healing done by magical spells and effects by up to 7.			
53	Shalehusk Boots	Bind on Pickup	417
PROPERTIES: Increases your dodge rating by 24.			
53	Sapphiron's Scale Boots	Bind on Equip	417
54	Lightforge Boots	Bind on Pickup	424
54	Boots of Valor	Bind on Pickup	424
54	Death Knight Sabatons	Bind on Pickup	424
56	Ribsteel Footguards	Bind on Pickup	438
56	Master Cannoneer Boots	Bind on Pickup	438

Superior Plate Feet

Level	Name	Binding Info	Armor
56	Deathbone Sabatons	Bind on Pickup	438
PROPERTIES: Restores 6 mana per 5 sec, Increases defense rating by 15.			
57	Corpselight Greaves	Bind on Pickup	445
PROPERTIES: Shadow Resistance +10			
58	Knight-Lieutenant's Plate Boots	Bind on Pickup	452
58	Knight-Lieutenant's Lamellar Sabatons	Bind on Pickup	452
58	Blood Guard's Plate Boots	Bind on Pickup	452
58	Grimy Metal Boots	Bind on Pickup	452
PROPERTIES: Increases your dodge rating by 12.			
58	Highlander's Plate Greaves	Bind on Pickup	452
PROPERTIES: Run speed increased slightly.			
58	Highlander's Lamellar Greaves	Bind on Pickup	452
PROPERTIES: Run speed increased slightly.			
58	Defiler's Lamellar Greaves	Bind on Pickup	452
PROPERTIES: Run speed increased slightly.			
58	Defiler's Plate Greaves	Bind on Pickup	452
PROPERTIES: Run speed increased slightly.			
58	Defiler's Lamellar Greaves	Bind on Pickup	452
PROPERTIES: Run speed increased slightly.			
60	Bloodsoaked Greaves	Bind on Pickup	486
PROPERTIES: Increases defense rating by 7.			
60	Peacekeeper Boots	Bind on Pickup	486
PROPERTIES: Restores 6 mana per 5 sec, Increases healing done by spells and effects by up to 22.			
60	Boots of the Desert Protector	Bind on Pickup	519
PROPERTIES: Restores 4 mana per 5 sec.			
60	Slime Kickers	Bind on Pickup	519
PROPERTIES: Increases your hit rating by 10.			
60	Blood Guard's Plate Greaves	Bind on Pickup	472
60	Knight-Lieutenant's Lamellar Sabatons	Bind on Pickup	472
PROPERTIES: Increases damage and healing done by magical spells and effects by up to 15.			
60	Knight-Lieutenant's Plate Greaves	Bind on Pickup	472
60	Ironsole Clompers	Bind on Pickup	600
60	Blood Guard's Lamellar Sabatons	Bind on Pickup	472
PROPERTIES: Increases damage and healing done by magical spells and effects by up to 15.			
63	Ravenguard's Greaves	Bind on Equip	661
66	Uther's Ceremonial Boots	Bind on Pickup	720
PROPERTIES: Increases damage and healing done by magical spells and effects by up to 15, Restores 8 mana per 5 sec.			
68	Bloodsworn Warboots	Bind on Pickup	780
68	Boots of the Colossus	Bind on Pickup	780
68	Ornate Boots of the Sanctified	Bind on Pickup	780
PROPERTIES: Increases damage and healing done by magical spells and effects by up to 29.			
68	Boots of the Watchful Heart	Bind on Pickup	780
PROPERTIES: Increases healing done by spells and effects by up to 55, Restores 7 mana per 5 sec.			
70	Enchanted Adamantite Boots	Bind on Equip	787
PROPERTIES: Arcane Resistance +30			
70	Khorium Boots	Bind on Equip	800
PROPERTIES: Restores 8 mana per 5 sec, Increases damage and healing done by magical spells and effects by up to 26.			
70	Obsidian Clodstompers	Bind on Pickup	800
	Crystal Encrusted Greaves	Bind on Pickup	452
PROPERTIES: Increases defense rating by 7.			

Superior Plate Feet

Level	Name	Binding Info	Armor
	Crystal Lined Greaves	Bind on Pickup	452
PROPERTIES: Increases healing done by spells and effects by up to 15.			
	Golden Cenarion Greaves	Bind on Pickup	641
PROPERTIES: Restores 3 mana per 5 sec, Increases damage and healing done by magical spells and effects by up to 35.			
	Sha'tari Wrought Greaves	Bind on Pickup	800
	Flesh Beast's Metal Greaves	Bind on Pickup	680

Epic Plate Hands

Level	Name	Binding Info	Armor
57	Stronghold Gauntlets	Bind on Equip	504
PROPERTIES: Immune to Disarm, Increases your parry rating by 20, Improves critical strike rating by 14.			
60	Marshal's Lamellar Gloves	Bind on Pickup	573
PROPERTIES: Increases the Holy damage bonus of your Judgement of the Crusader by 20, Improves critical strike rating by 14.			
60	Marshal's Plate Gauntlets	Bind on Pickup	573
PROPERTIES: Hamstring Rage cost reduced by 3, Improves critical strike rating by 14.			
60	General's Plate Gauntlets	Bind on Pickup	573
PROPERTIES: Hamstring Rage cost reduced by 3, Improves critical strike rating by 14.			
60	Lawbringer Gauntlets	Bind on Pickup	534
PROPERTIES: Increases healing done by spells and effects by up to 18. Fire Resistance +7			
60	Gauntlets of Might	Bind on Pickup	534
PROPERTIES: Increases your hit rating by 10, Increases defense rating by 8. Fire Resistance +7			
60	Judgement Gauntlets	Bind on Pickup	611
PROPERTIES: Restores 6 mana per 5 sec, Increases damage and healing done by magical spells and effects by up to 15. Shadow Resistance +10			
60	Gauntlets of Wrath	Bind on Pickup	611
PROPERTIES: Increases your parry rating by 20, Increases defense rating by 10. Shadow Resistance +10			
60	Flameguard Gauntlets	Bind on Pickup	557
PROPERTIES: Improves critical strike rating by 14, Increases attack power by 54.			
60	Dark Iron Gauntlets	Bind on Equip	565
PROPERTIES: Fire Resistance +28			
60	Warrior Gauntlets	Bind on Pickup	718
PROPERTIES: Resistance +200 Armor, Improves critical strike rating by 14.			
60	Peacekeeper Gauntlets	Bind on Pickup	550
PROPERTIES: Increases healing done by spells and effects by up to 59, Restores 4 mana per 5 sec.			
60	Gauntlets of the Shining Light	Bind on Pickup	581
PROPERTIES: Increases healing done by spells and effects by up to 22.			
60	Gauntlets of the Immovable	Bind on Pickup	550
PROPERTIES: Increases your parry rating by 20, Increases defense rating by 7.			
60	Gloves of the Swarm	Bind on Pickup	550
PROPERTIES: Increases damage and healing done by magical spells and effects by up to 12.			
60	Gauntlets of Annihilation	Bind on Pickup	702
PROPERTIES: Improves critical strike rating by 14, Increases your hit rating by 10.			
60	Gauntlets of the Righteous Champion	Bind on Pickup	627
PROPERTIES: Increases damage and healing done by magical spells and effects by up to 16, Improves critical strike rating by 14.			
60	Gauntlets of Steadfast Determination	Bind on Pickup	611
PROPERTIES: Increases defense rating by 13.			
60	Ooze-ridden Gauntlets	Bind on Pickup	603
PROPERTIES: Nature Resistance +25			

Epic Plate Hands

Level	Name	Binding Info	Armor
60	Gloves of the Redeemed Prophecy	Bind on Pickup	603
PROPERTIES: Increases healing done by spells and effects by up to 37.			
60	Dreadnaught Gauntlets	Bind on Pickup	702
PROPERTIES: Increases defense rating by 13, Increases your block rating by 13, Increases the block value of your shield by 21.			
60	Redemption Handguards	Bind on Pickup	702
PROPERTIES: Restores 8 mana per 5 sec, Increases healing done by spells and effects by up to 33.			
60	Icebane Gauntlets	Bind on Equip	642
PROPERTIES: Increases defense rating by 8. Frost Resistance +32			
60	Fists of the Unrelenting	Bind on Pickup	718
PROPERTIES: Immune to Disarm, Improves critical strike rating by 14, Increases your hit rating by 10.			
60	General's Lamellar Gloves	Bind on Pickup	573
PROPERTIES: Increases the Holy damage bonus of your Judgement of the Crusader by 20, Improves critical strike rating by 14.			
70	Gauntlets of the Iron Tower	Bind on Equip	793
70	Steelgrip Gauntlets	Bind on Equip	793
PROPERTIES: Immune to Disarm.			
70	Warrior Gauntlets	Bind on Pickup	1020
PROPERTIES: Resistance +200 Armor, Improves critical strike rating by 14.			
70	Gladiator's Plate Gauntlets	Bind on Pickup	868
PROPERTIES: Hamstring Rage cost reduced by 3.			
70	Gladiator's Lamellar Gauntlets	Bind on Pickup	868
PROPERTIES: Increases damage and healing done by magical spells and effects by up to 25, Increases the Holy damage bonus of your Judgement of the Crusader by 20.			
70	Gladiator's Scaled Gauntlets	Bind on Pickup	868
PROPERTIES: Increases damage and healing done by magical spells and effects by up to 25, Increases the Holy damage bonus of your Judgement of the Crusader by 20.			
70	Gauntlets of Renewed Hope	Bind on Pickup	793
PROPERTIES: Restores 4 mana per 5 sec, Increases healing done by spells and effects by up to 55.			
70	Iron Gauntlets of the Maiden	Bind on Pickup	793
PROPERTIES: Increases the block value of your shield by 33.			
70	Gauntlets of Martial Perfections	Bind on Pickup	868
70	Warbringer Handguards	Bind on Pickup	831
70	Warbringer Gauntlets	Bind on Pickup	831
70	Justicar Gloves	Bind on Pickup	831
PROPERTIES: Increases healing done by spells and effects by up to 66.			
70	Justicar Handguards	Bind on Pickup	831
PROPERTIES: Increases damage and healing done by magical spells and effects by up to 23, Increases the block value of your shield by 30.			
70	Justicar Gauntlets	Bind on Pickup	831
PROPERTIES: Increases damage and healing done by magical spells and effects by up to 22.			
70	Royal Gauntlets of Silvermoon	Bind on Pickup	982
70	Glorious Gauntlets of Crestfall	Bind on Pickup	982
PROPERTIES: Increases healing done by spells and effects by up to 44.			
70	Destroyer Handguards	Bind on Pickup	944
PROPERTIES: Increases the block value of your shield by 33.			
70	Destroyer Gauntlets	Bind on Pickup	944
70	Crystalforge Handguards	Bind on Pickup	944
PROPERTIES: Increases damage and healing done by magical spells and effects by up to 26.			
70	Crystalforge Gauntlets	Bind on Pickup	944
PROPERTIES: Increases damage and healing done by magical spells and effects by up to 29, Restores 8 mana per 5 sec.			
70	Crystalforge Gloves	Bind on Pickup	944
PROPERTIES: Increases healing done by spells and effects by up to 66, Restores 8 mana per 5 sec.			

Epic Plate Hands

Level	Name	Binding Info	Armor
70	Gladiator's Plate Gauntlets Tier 2	Bind on Pickup	868
PROPERTIES: Hamstring Rage cost reduced by 3.			
70	Topaz-studded Battlegrips	Bind on Pickup	831
70	Inferno Tempered Gauntlets	Bind on Pickup	755
PROPERTIES: Fire Resistance +40			
	Gauntlets of Heroism	Bind on Pickup	449
PROPERTIES: Improves critical strike rating by 14.			
	Soulforge Gauntlets	Bind on Pickup	449
PROPERTIES: Increases damage and healing done by magical spells and effects by up to 11, Improves critical strike rating by 14.			

Superior Plate Hands

Level	Name	Binding Info	Armor
40	Truesilver Gauntlets	Bind on Equip	300
40	Cragfists	Bind on Pickup	300
PROPERTIES: Increases defense rating by 7.			
40	Plated Fist of Hakoo	Bind on Equip	300
43	Vice Grips	Bind on Pickup	318
PROPERTIES: Increases attack power by 14.			
51	Fists of Phalanx	Bind on Pickup	367
53	Fiery Plate Gauntlets	Bind on Equip	379
PROPERTIES: Adds 4 fire damage to your weapon attack. Fire Resistance +10			
54	Lightforge Gauntlets	Bind on Equip	386
54	Gauntlets of Valor	Bind on Equip	386
54	Razor Gauntlets	Bind on Pickup	386
PROPERTIES: When struck in combat inflicts 3 Arcane damage to the attacker.			
55	Backusarian Gauntlets	Bind on Pickup	392
PROPERTIES: Restores 4 mana per 5 sec.			
55	Stonegrip Gauntlets	Bind on Equip	392
PROPERTIES: Increases defense rating by 15.			
56	Reiver Claws	Bind on Pickup	398
PROPERTIES: Improves critical strike rating by 14.			
56	Deathbone Gauntlets	Bind on Pickup	398
PROPERTIES: Increases defense rating by 15, Restores 4 mana per 5 sec.			
56	Force Imbued Gauntlets	Bind on Pickup	398
PROPERTIES: Increases defense rating by 10.			
57	Boneclenched Gauntlets	Bind on Pickup	404
PROPERTIES: Increases defense rating by 10.			
57	Death Grips	Bind on Pickup	404
PROPERTIES: Immune to Disarm.			
58	Knight-Lieutenant's Plate Gauntlets	Bind on Pickup	410
PROPERTIES: Hamstring Rage cost reduced by 3.			
58	Knight-Lieutenant's Lamellar Gauntlets	Bind on Pickup	410
PROPERTIES: Increases the Holy damage bonus of your Judgement of the Crusader by 20.			
58	Blood Guard's Plate Gloves	Bind on Pickup	410
PROPERTIES: Hamstring Rage cost reduced by 3.			
58	Darkrune Gauntlets	Bind on Equip	410
PROPERTIES: Increases your block rating by 10. Shadow Resistance +20			
59	Gloves of the Dawn	Bind on Equip	417
60	Bloodsoaked Gauntlets	Bind on Pickup	460
PROPERTIES: Increases defense rating by 8, Increases your dodge rating by 12.			
60	Sacrificial Gauntlets	Bind on Pickup	441

Superior Plate Hands

Level	Name	Binding Info	Armor
PROPERTIES: Improves critical strike rating by 14, Increases your hit rating by 10.			
60	Ironvine Gloves	Bind on Equip	454
PROPERTIES: Increases defense rating by 15. Nature Resistance +20			
60	Blood Guard's Plate Gauntlets	Bind on Pickup	429
PROPERTIES: Hamstring Rage cost reduced by 3.			
60	Knight-Lieutenant's Lamellar Gauntlets	Bind on Pickup	429
PROPERTIES: Increases the Holy damage bonus of your Judgement of the Crusader by 20, Improves critical strike rating by 14.			
60	Knight-Lieutenant's Plate Gauntlets	Bind on Pickup	429
PROPERTIES: Hamstring Rage cost reduced by 3.			
60	Blood Guard's Lamellar Gauntlets	Bind on Pickup	429
PROPERTIES: Increases the Holy damage bonus of your Judgement of the Crusader by 20, Improves critical strike rating by 14.			
61	Ironblade Gauntlets	Bind on Pickup	564
64	Faith Bearer's Gauntlets	Bind on Pickup	619
PROPERTIES: Increases damage and healing done by magical spells and effects by up to 14, Restores 3 mana per 5 sec.			
66	Adamantite Plate Gloves	Bind on Equip	655
68	Life Bearer's Gauntlets	Bind on Pickup	709
PROPERTIES: Increases healing done by spells and effects by up to 55.			
68	Gauntlets of Cruel Intention	Bind on Pickup	709
68	Thatia's Self-Correcting Gauntlets	Bind on Equip	709
PROPERTIES: Increases the block value of your shield by 39.			
70	Flamebane Gloves	Bind on Equip	722
PROPERTIES: Fire Resistance +30			
70	Felsteel Gloves	Bind on Equip	722
70	Ragesteel Gloves	Bind on Equip	728
70	Gauntlets of the Bold	Bind on Pickup	728
70	Doomplate Gauntlets	Bind on Pickup	728
70	Gauntlets of the Righteous	Bind on Pickup	728
PROPERTIES: Increases damage and healing done by magical spells and effects by up to 21, Restores 7 mana per 5 sec.			
70	Gauntlets of Vindication	Bind on Pickup	728
PROPERTIES: Restores 7 mana per 5 sec, Increases damage and healing done by magical spells and effects by up to 11.			
70	Grand Marshal's Lamellar Gauntlets	Bind on Pickup	728
PROPERTIES: Increases damage and healing done by magical spells and effects by up to 21, Increases the Holy damage bonus of your Judgement of the Crusader by 20.			
70	Grand Marshal's Plate Gauntlets	Bind on Pickup	728
PROPERTIES: Hamstring Rage cost reduced by 3.			
70	Grand Marshal's Scaled Gauntlets	Bind on Pickup	728
PROPERTIES: Increases damage and healing done by magical spells and effects by up to 21, Increases the Holy damage bonus of your Judgement of the Crusader by 20.			
70	High Warlord's Lamellar Gauntlets	Bind on Pickup	728
PROPERTIES: Increases damage and healing done by magical spells and effects by up to 21, Increases the Holy damage bonus of your Judgement of the Crusader by 20.			
70	High Warlord's Plate Gauntlets	Bind on Pickup	728
PROPERTIES: Hamstring Rage cost reduced by 3.			
70	High Warlord's Scaled Gauntlets	Bind on Pickup	728
PROPERTIES: Increases damage and healing done by magical spells and effects by up to 21, Increases the Holy damage bonus of your Judgement of the Crusader by 20.			
70	Gauntlets of the Chosen	Bind on Pickup	728
	Gordok's Handguards	Bind on Pickup	392
PROPERTIES: Improves critical strike rating by 14.			

Superior Plate Hands

Level	Name	Binding Info	Armor
	Gauntlets of Undead Slaying	Bind on Pickup	410
PROPERTIES: Increases attack power by 60 when fighting Undead.			
	Gauntlets of the Vanquisher	Bind on Pickup	691

Epic Plate Head

Level	Name	Binding Info	Armor
56	Lionheart Helm	Bind on Equip	645
PROPERTIES: Improves critical strike rating by 28, Increases your hit rating by 20.			
60	Field Marshal's Lamellar Faceguard	Bind on Pickup	775
PROPERTIES: Improves critical strike rating by 14, Increases damage and healing done by magical spells and effects by up to 25, Restores 5 mana per 5 sec.			
60	Field Marshal's Plate Helm	Bind on Pickup	775
PROPERTIES: Improves critical strike rating by 14.			
60	Warlord's Plate Headpiece	Bind on Pickup	775
PROPERTIES: Improves critical strike rating by 14.			
60	Lawbringer Helm	Bind on Pickup	695
PROPERTIES: Restores 4 mana per 5 sec, Increases healing done by spells and effects by up to 22. Fire Resistance +10			
60	Helm of Might	Bind on Pickup	695
PROPERTIES: Increases your dodge rating by 12, Increases defense rating by 10. Fire Resistance +10			
60	Judgement Crown	Bind on Pickup	795
PROPERTIES: Increases damage and healing done by magical spells and effects by up to 32. Frost Resistance +10, Shadow Resistance +10			
60	Helm of Wrath	Bind on Pickup	795
PROPERTIES: Increases defense rating by 16. Frost Resistance +10, Shadow Resistance +10			
60	Dark Iron Helm	Bind on Equip	695
PROPERTIES: Fire Resistance +35			
60	Helm of Endless Rage	Bind on Pickup	775
60	Warrior Helm	Bind on Pickup	933
PROPERTIES: Increases your hit rating by 20, Restores 10 health per 5 sec.			
60	Conqueror's Crown	Bind on Pickup	844
PROPERTIES: Increases defense rating by 9.			
60	Avenger's Crown	Bind on Pickup	844
PROPERTIES: Increases damage and healing done by magical spells and effects by up to 23, Improves critical strike rating by 14.			
60	Helm of Domination	Bind on Pickup	755
PROPERTIES: Increases your parry rating by 20, Increases defense rating by 10.			
60	Dreadnaught Helmet	Bind on Pickup	913
PROPERTIES: Increases your dodge rating by 12, Increases defense rating by 21.			
60	Redemption Headpiece	Bind on Pickup	913
PROPERTIES: Increases healing done by spells and effects by up to 64, Increases your spell critical strike rating by 14, Restores 8 mana per 5 sec.			
60	Icebane Helmet	Bind on Pickup	864
PROPERTIES: Increases defense rating by 12. Frost Resistance +44			
60	Warlord's Lamellar Faceguard	Bind on Pickup	775
PROPERTIES: Improves critical strike rating by 14, Increases damage and healing done by magical spells and effects by up to 25, Restores 5 mana per 5 sec.			
70	Helm of the Stalwart Defender	Bind on Equip	1030
70	Oathkeeper's Helm	Bind on Equip	1030
PROPERTIES: Increases damage and healing done by magical spells and effects by up to 26, Restores 9 mana per 5 sec.			
70	Warrior Helm	Bind on Pickup	1326
70	Gladiator's Plate Helm	Bind on Pickup	1129
70	Gladiator's Lamellar Helm	Bind on Pickup	1129

Epic Plate Head

Level	Name	Binding Info	Armor
PROPERTIES: Increases damage and healing done by magical spells and effects by up to 21.			
70	Gladiator's Scaled Helm	Bind on Pickup	1129
PROPERTIES: Increases damage and healing done by magical spells and effects by up to 21.			
70	Eternium Greathelm	Bind on Pickup	1030
70	Thundering Greathelm	Bind on Pickup	1129
70	Warbringer Greathelm	Bind on Pickup	1080
PROPERTIES: Increases the block value of your shield by 33.			
70	Warbringer Battle-Helm	Bind on Pickup	1080
70	Justicar Diadem	Bind on Pickup	1080
PROPERTIES: Increases healing done by spells and effects by up to 64.			
70	Justicar Faceguard	Bind on Pickup	1080
PROPERTIES: Increases damage and healing done by magical spells and effects by up to 22.			
70	Justicar Crown	Bind on Pickup	1080
PROPERTIES: Increases damage and healing done by magical spells and effects by up to 32.			
70	Fel-Steel Warhelm	Bind on Pickup	1178
70	Brighthelm of Justice	Bind on Pickup	1178
PROPERTIES: Increases healing done by spells and effects by up to 86, Restores 12 mana per 5 sec.			
70	Destroyer Greathelm	Bind on Pickup	1227
70	Destroyer Battle-Helm	Bind on Pickup	1227
70	Crystalforge Faceguard	Bind on Pickup	1227
PROPERTIES: Increases damage and healing done by magical spells and effects by up to 27, Restores 6 mana per 5 sec.			
70	Crystalforge War-Helm	Bind on Pickup	1227
PROPERTIES: Increases damage and healing done by magical spells and effects by up to 27.			
70	Crystalforge Greathelm	Bind on Pickup	1227
PROPERTIES: Increases healing done by spells and effects by up to 86, Restores 8 mana per 5 sec.			
70	Gladiator's Plate Helm Tier 2	Bind on Pickup	1129
70	Faceguard of the Endless Watch	Bind on Pickup	1080
	Helm of Heroism	Bind on Pickup	634
PROPERTIES: Improves critical strike rating by 14.			
	Soulforge Helm	Bind on Pickup	634
PROPERTIES: Increases damage and healing done by magical spells and effects by up to 14, Increases your spell critical strike rating by 14.			

Superior Plate Head

Level	Name	Binding Info	Armor
40	Horned Viking Helmet	Bind on Pickup	303
PROPERTIES: Charge an enemy, knocking it silly for 30 seconds. Also knocks you down, stunning you for a short period of time. Any damage caused will revive the target.			
40	Icemetal Barbute	Bind on Pickup	383
PROPERTIES: Frost Resistance +10			
47	Mugthol's Helm	Bind on Equip	445
48	Helm of the Mountain	Bind on Pickup	453
PROPERTIES: Increases defense rating by 10. Nature Resistance +10			
50	Foreman's Head Protector	Bind on Pickup	469
PROPERTIES: Increases damage and healing done by magical spells and effects by up to 13.			
51	Golem Skull Helm	Bind on Pickup	477
PROPERTIES: Increases defense rating by 11.			
53	Helm of Awareness	Bind on Pickup	493
PROPERTIES: Increases your dodge rating by 24.			
55	Whitesoul Helm	Bind on Equip	509
PROPERTIES: Increases healing done by spells and effects by up to 35.			

Superior Plate Head

Level	Name	Binding Info	Armor
55	Gyth's Skull	Bind on Pickup	509
PROPERTIES: Increases defense rating by 14.			
57	Enchanted Thorium Helm	Bind on Equip	526
PROPERTIES: Increases defense rating by 13.			
57	Lightforge Helm	Bind on Pickup	526
57	Helm of Valor	Bind on Pickup	526
58	Lieutenant Commander's Plate Helm	Bind on Pickup	534
58	Lieutenant Commander's Lamellar Headguard	Bind on Pickup	534
58	Champion's Plate Headguard	Bind on Pickup	534
58	Grand Crusader's Helm	Bind on Pickup	534
PROPERTIES: Shadow Resistance +15			
58	Darkrune Helm	Bind on Equip	534
PROPERTIES: Improves critical strike rating by 14. Shadow Resistance +25			
58	Helm of the Executioner	Bind on Pickup	534
PROPERTIES: Increases your hit rating by 20.			
60	Gurubashi Helm	Bind on Equip	549
60	Helm of the Holy Avenger	Bind on Equip	574
PROPERTIES: Increases damage and healing done by magical spells and effects by up to 20, Improves critical strike rating by 14.			
60	Champion's Plate Helm	Bind on Pickup	598
PROPERTIES: Improves critical strike rating by 14, Increases your hit rating by 10.			
60	Lieutenant Commander's Lamellar Headguard	Bind on Pickup	598
PROPERTIES: Increases damage and healing done by magical spells and effects by up to 26.			
60	Lieutenant Commander's Plate Helmet	Bind on Pickup	598
PROPERTIES: Improves critical strike rating by 14, Increases your hit rating by 10.			
60	Champion's Lamellar Headguard	Bind on Pickup	598
PROPERTIES: Increases damage and healing done by magical spells and effects by up to 26.			
65	Hope Bearer Helm	Bind on Pickup	827
PROPERTIES: Improves hit rating by 13.			
66	Exorcist's Plate Helm	Bind on Pickup	827
PROPERTIES: Improves critical strike rating by 25, Improves resilience rating by 11.			
66	Exorcist's Lamellar Helm	Bind on Pickup	827
PROPERTIES: Increases damage and healing done by magical spells and effects by up to 29.			
66	Exorcist's Scaled Helm	Bind on Pickup	827
PROPERTIES: Increases damage and healing done by magical spells and effects by up to 22.			
68	Irondrake Faceguard	Bind on Pickup	922
68	Greathelm of the Unbreakable	Bind on Pickup	922
PROPERTIES: Increases defense rating by 30.			
68	Mask of Pennance	Bind on Pickup	922
PROPERTIES: Increases healing done by spells and effects by up to 66, Restores 10 mana per 5 sec.			
70	Flamebane Helm	Bind on Equip	930
PROPERTIES: Fire Resistance +40			
70	Felsteel Helm	Bind on Equip	946
PROPERTIES: Increases defense rating by 33.			
70	Ragesteel Helm	Bind on Equip	946
PROPERTIES: Improves critical strike rating by 37.			
70	Ruby Helm of the Just	Bind on Pickup	946
PROPERTIES: Increases damage and healing done by magical spells and effects by up to 28, Restores 10 mana per 5 sec.			
70	Doomplate Warhelm	Bind on Pickup	946

Superior Plate Head

Level	Name	Binding Info	Armor
70	Helm of the Righteous	Bind on Pickup	946
	PROPERTIES: Increases damage and healing done by magical spells and effects by up to 23, Restores 6 mana per 5 sec.		
70	Warhelm of the Bold	Bind on Pickup	946
	PROPERTIES: Increases defense rating by 20.		
70	Grand Marshal's Lamellar Helm	Bind on Pickup	946
	PROPERTIES: Increases damage and healing done by magical spells and effects by up to 19, Improves spell critical strike rating by 25, Improves your resilience by 20.		
70	Grand Marshal's Plate Helm	Bind on Pickup	946
	PROPERTIES: Improves critical strike rating by 24, Improves resilience by 19.		
70	Grand Marshal's Scaled Helm	Bind on Pickup	946
	PROPERTIES: Increases damage and healing done by magical spells and effects by up to 19, Improves critical strike rating by 20.		
70	High Warlord's Lamellar Helm	Bind on Pickup	946
	PROPERTIES: Increases damage and healing done by magical spells and effects by up to 19, Improves spell critical strike rating by 20, Improves resilience by 20.		
70	High Warlord's Plate Helm	Bind on Pickup	946
70	High Warlord's Scaled Helm	Bind on Pickup	946
	PROPERTIES: Increases damage and healing done by magical spells and effects by up to 19.		
	Avenguard Helm	Bind on Pickup	461
	Fury Visor	Bind on Pickup	445
	PROPERTIES: Improves critical strike rating by 14, Increases your hit rating by 10.		
	Myrmidon's Headdress	Bind on Pickup	946
	Cover of Righteous Fury	Bind on Pickup	804
	PROPERTIES: Increases damage and healing done by magical spells and effects by up to 30, Restores 4 mana per 5 sec., Increases defense rating by 16.		
	X-52 Pilot's Helmet	Bind on Pickup	875
	PROPERTIES: Increases damage and healing done by magical spells and effects by up to 36, Restores 6 mana per 5 sec.		

Epic Plate Legs

Level	Name	Binding Info	Armor
55	Dark Iron Leggings	Bind on Equip	683
	PROPERTIES: Fire Resistance +30		
55	Titanic Leggings	Bind on Equip	683
	PROPERTIES: Increases your hit rating by 20, Improves critical strike rating by 14.		
56	Flamewaker Legplates	Bind on Pickup	694
	PROPERTIES: Increases your dodge rating by 12. Fire Resistance +11, Shadow Resistance +11		
57	Cloudkeeper Legplates	Bind on Equip	705
	PROPERTIES: Increases attack power by 100 for 30 sec.		
60	Marshal's Lamellar Legplates	Bind on Pickup	802
	PROPERTIES: Increases damage and healing done by magical spells and effects by up to 27, Improves critical strike rating by 14.		
60	Marshal's Plate Legguards	Bind on Pickup	802
	PROPERTIES: Improves critical strike rating by 28, Increases your hit rating by 10.		
60	General's Plate Leggings	Bind on Pickup	802
	PROPERTIES: Improves critical strike rating by 28, Increases your hit rating by 10.		
60	Lawbringer Legplates	Bind on Pickup	748
	PROPERTIES: Restores 3 mana per 5 sec, Increases healing done by spells and effects by up to 22. Shadow Resistance +10		
60	Legplates of Might	Bind on Pickup	748
	PROPERTIES: Increases your parry rating by 20, Increases defense rating by 10. Shadow Resistance +10		

Epic Plate Legs

Level	Name	Binding Info	Armor
60	Judgement Legplates	Bind on Pickup	856
	PROPERTIES: Increases damage and healing done by magical spells and effects by up to 20, Restores 4 mana per 5 sec. Fire Resistance +10, Arcane Resistance +10		
60	Legplates of Wrath	Bind on Pickup	856
	PROPERTIES: Increases your dodge rating by 24, Increases defense rating by 16. Fire Resistance +10, Arcane Resistance +10		
60	Legguards of the Fallen Crusader	Bind on Pickup	845
60	Bloodsoaked Legplates	Bind on Pickup	770
	PROPERTIES: Increases defense rating by 15.		
60	Warrior Legplates	Bind on Pickup	1005
	PROPERTIES: Increases your parry rating by 20. Fire Resistance +10, Nature Resistance +10, Frost Resistance +10, Shadow Resistance +10, Arcane Resistance +10		
60	Strangely Glyphed Legplates	Bind on Pickup	813
	PROPERTIES: Increases healing done by spells and effects by up to 29.		
60	Conqueror's Legguards	Bind on Pickup	909
	PROPERTIES: Increases defense rating by 9, Increases your hit rating by 10.		
60	Avenger's Legguards	Bind on Pickup	909
	PROPERTIES: Increases damage and healing done by magical spells and effects by up to 16, Improves critical strike rating by 14, Restores 4 mana per 5 sec.		
60	Legplates of Blazing Light	Bind on Pickup	856
	PROPERTIES: Increases healing done by spells and effects by up to 68, Increases your spell critical strike rating by 14.		
60	Dreadnaught Legplates	Bind on Pickup	983
	PROPERTIES: Increases defense rating by 19, Increases your dodge rating by 12, Increases the block value of your shield by 32.		
60	Redemption Legguards	Bind on Pickup	983
	PROPERTIES: Increases your spell critical strike rating by 14, Increases healing done by spells and effects by up to 42, Restores 8 mana per 5 sec.		
60	Outrider's Plate Legguards	Bind on Pickup	737
	PROPERTIES: Improves critical strike rating by 14, Increases your hit rating by 10.		
60	Sentinel's Plate Legguards	Bind on Pickup	737
	PROPERTIES: Improves critical strike rating by 14, Increases your hit rating by 10.		
60	Sentinel's Plate Legguards	Bind on Pickup	737
	PROPERTIES: Improves critical strike rating by 14, Increases your hit rating by 10.		
60	Sentinel's Lamellar Legguards	Bind on Pickup	737
	PROPERTIES: Improves critical strike rating by 14, Increases your hit rating by 10, Increases damage and healing done by magical spells and effects by up to 25.		
60	Legplates of Carnage	Bind on Pickup	930
	PROPERTIES: Improves critical strike rating by 28.		
60	Leggings of the Grand Crusader	Bind on Pickup	952
	PROPERTIES: Increases damage and healing done by magical spells and effects by up to 26, Improves critical strike rating by 28.		
60	General's Lamellar Legplates	Bind on Pickup	802
	PROPERTIES: Increases damage and healing done by magical spells and effects by up to 27, Improves critical strike rating by 14.		
60	Outrider's Lamellar Legguards	Bind on Pickup	737
	PROPERTIES: Improves critical strike rating by 14, Increases your hit rating by 10, Increases damage and healing done by magical spells and effects by up to 25.		
70	Gladiator's Plate Legguards	Bind on Pickup	1216
	PROPERTIES: Improves critical strike rating by 32,Improves resilience by 26.		
70	Gladiator's Lamellar Legguards	Bind on Pickup	1216
	PROPERTIES: Increases damage and healing done by magical spells and effects by up to 33.		
70	Gladiator's Scaled Legguards	Bind on Pickup	1216
	PROPERTIES: Increases damage and healing done by magical spells and effects by up to 33, Improves spell critical rating by 28, Improves resilience by 28.		

Epic Plate Legs

Level	Name	Binding Info	Armor
70	Wrynn Dynasty Greaves	Bind on Pickup	1110
PROPERTIES: Increases defense rating by 23, Increases your dodge rating by 25.			
70	Legplates of the Innocent	Bind on Pickup	1110
PROPERTIES: Increases healing done by spells and effects by up to 57, Restores 7 mana per 5 sec., Improves spell critical strike rating by 18.			
70	Warbringer Legguards	Bind on Pickup	1163
70	Warbringer Greaves	Bind on Pickup	1163
PROPERTIES: Increases defense rating by 29, Increases your dodge rating by 31.			
70	Justicar Leggings	Bind on Pickup	1163
PROPERTIES: Increases healing done by spells and effects by up to 77, Restores 10 mana per 5 sec.			
70	Justicar Legguards	Bind on Pickup	1163
PROPERTIES: Increases damage and healing done by magical spells and effects by up to 25, Restores 8 mana per 5 sec.			
70	Justicar Greaves	Bind on Pickup	1163
PROPERTIES: Increases damage and healing done by magical spells and effects by up to 36, Restores 8 mana per 5 sec.			
70	Greaves of the Bloodwarder	Bind on Pickup	1269
PROPERTIES: Improves critical strike rating by 24.			
70	Destroyer Legguards	Bind on Pickup	1322
PROPERTIES: Increases the block value of your shield by 24, Increases defense rating by 33, Increases your shield block rating by 26.			
70	Destroyer Greaves	Bind on Pickup	1322
70	Crystalforge Legguards	Bind on Pickup	1322
PROPERTIES: Increases damage and healing done by magical spells and effects by up to 34.			
70	Crystalforge Greaves	Bind on Pickup	1322
PROPERTIES: Increases damage and healing done by magical spells and effects by up to 39.			
70	Crystalforge Leggings	Bind on Pickup	1322
PROPERTIES: Increases healing done by spells and effects by up to 86, Restores 10 mana per 5 sec.			
70	Vanquisher's Legplates	Bind on Pickup	1057
PROPERTIES: Improves critical strike rating by 20.			
70	Greaves of the Martyr	Bind on Pickup	1057
PROPERTIES: Increases damage and healing done by magical spells and effects by up to 26, Restores 7 mana per 5 sec.			
70	Inferno Tempered Leggings	Bind on Pickup	1057
PROPERTIES: Fire Resistance +55			
	Icebane Leggings	Bind on Pickup	898
PROPERTIES: Increases defense rating by 9. Frost Resistance +40			

Superior Plate Legs

Level	Name	Binding Info	Armor
41	Golem Shard Leggings	Bind on Equip	429
PROPERTIES: Increases defense rating by 9.			
46	Silvershell Leggings	Bind on Equip	470
47	Earthforged Leggings	Bind on Pickup	479
PROPERTIES: Increases defense rating by 10.			
49	Elemental Rockridge Leggings	Bind on Pickup	496
PROPERTIES: Nature Resistance +10			
52	Legplates of the Eternal Guardian	Bind on Pickup	522
PROPERTIES: Increases defense rating by 22.			
53	Lavacrest Leggings	Bind on Pickup	531
55	Handcrafted Mastersmith Leggings	Bind on Pickup	548
56	Deathbone Legguards	Bind on Pickup	557

Superior Plate Legs

Level	Name	Binding Info	Armor
PROPERTIES: Restores 5 mana per 5 sec, Increases defense rating by 20.			
56	Lightforge Legplates	Bind on Pickup	557
56	Legplates of Valor	Bind on Pickup	557
56	Chitinous Plate Legguards	Bind on Pickup	557
PROPERTIES: Restores 5 mana per 5 sec.			
57	Eldritch Reinforced Legplates	Bind on Pickup	566
PROPERTIES: Improves critical strike rating by 14.			
57	Wraithplate Leggings	Bind on Pickup	566
PROPERTIES: Increases your parry rating by 20.			
57	Abyssal Plate Legplates	Bind on Equip	566
PROPERTIES: Improves critical strike rating by 14.			
58	Enchanted Thorium Leggings	Bind on Equip	575
PROPERTIES: Increases defense rating by 12.			
58	Warmaster Legguards	Bind on Pickup	575
PROPERTIES: Increases your dodge rating by 24.			
58	Direwing Legguards	Bind on Equip	575
58	Knight-Captain's Plate Leggings	Bind on Pickup	575
PROPERTIES: Improves critical strike rating by 28.			
58	Knight-Captain's Lamellar Leggings	Bind on Pickup	575
PROPERTIES: Improves critical strike rating by 28.			
58	Legionnaire's Plate Legguards	Bind on Pickup	575
PROPERTIES: Improves critical strike rating by 28.			
58	Legplates of Vigilance	Bind on Pickup	575
PROPERTIES: Increases defense rating by 22.			
60	Darksoul Leggings	Bind on Equip	592
PROPERTIES: Increases your hit rating by 20.			
60	Peacekeeper Leggings	Bind on Pickup	618
PROPERTIES: Increases healing done by spells and effects by up to 37, Restores 7 mana per 5 sec.			
60	Legplates of the Destroyer	Bind on Pickup	670
PROPERTIES: Increases damage and healing done by magical spells and effects by up to 12.			
60	Legplates of the Qiraji Command	Bind on Pickup	644
PROPERTIES: Improves critical strike rating by 28.			
60	Legionnaire's Plate Leggings	Bind on Pickup	618
PROPERTIES: Improves critical strike rating by 28.			
60	Knight-Captain's Lamellar Leggings	Bind on Pickup	618
PROPERTIES: Increases damage and healing done by magical spells and effects by up to 25.			
60	Knight-Captain's Plate Leggings	Bind on Pickup	618
PROPERTIES: Improves critical strike rating by 28.			
60	Legionnaire's Lamellar Leggings	Bind on Pickup	618
PROPERTIES: Increases damage and healing done by magical spells and effects by up to 25.			
62	Rusty Lightgreaves	Bind on Pickup	815
PROPERTIES: Restores 6 mana per 5 sec, Increases damage and healing done by magical spells and effects by up to 16.			
63	Marshreaver Britches	Bind on Pickup	841
66	Slayer's Legguards	Bind on Pickup	891
PROPERTIES: Improves critical strike rating by 17, Improves resilience by 25.			
66	Avenger's Legguards	Bind on Pickup	891
PROPERTIES: Increases damage and healing done by magical spells and effects by up to 27.			
68	Bloodlord Legplates	Bind on Pickup	993
PROPERTIES: Improves critical strike rating by 11.			
68	Cassock of the Loyal	Bind on Pickup	993
PROPERTIES: Increases healing done by spells and effects by up to 68.			

Superior Plate Legs

Level	Name	Binding Info	Armor
68	Ornate Leggings of the Venerated	Bind on Pickup	993
PROPERTIES: Increases damage and healing done by magical spells and effects by up to 26.			
68	Legplates of the Bold	Bind on Pickup	1019
PROPERTIES: Increases defense rating by 26.			
70	Enchanted Adamantite Leggings	Bind on Equip	1019
PROPERTIES: Arcane Resistance +40			
70	Felsteel Leggings	Bind on Equip	1010
PROPERTIES: Increases defense rating by 33.			
70	Khorium Pants	Bind on Equip	1010
PROPERTIES: Restores 11 mana per 5 sec, Increases damage and healing done by magical spells and effects by up to 33.			
70	Greaves of the Shatterer	Bind on Pickup	1019
PROPERTIES: Increases defense rating by 25.			
70	Legplates of the Righteous	Bind on Pickup	1019
PROPERTIES: Restores 10 mana per 5 sec, Increases damage and healing done by magical spells and effects by up to 28.			
70	Doomplate Legguards	Bind on Pickup	1019
PROPERTIES: Improves hit rating by 17, Improves critical strike by 27.			
70	Grand Marshal's Plate Legguards	Bind on Pickup	1019
PROPERTIES: Improves critical strike rating by 28, Improves resilience by 23.			
70	Grand Marshal's Scaled Legguards	Bind on Pickup	1019
PROPERTIES: Increases damage and healing done by magical spells and effects by up to 28.			
70	Grand Marshal's Lamellar Legguards	Bind on Pickup	1019
PROPERTIES: Increases damage and healing done by magical spells and effects by up to 28.			
70	High Warlord's Lamellar Legguards	Bind on Pickup	1019
PROPERTIES: Increases damage and healing done by magical spells and effects by up to 28.			
70	High Warlord's Plate Legguards	Bind on Pickup	1019
PROPERTIES: Improves critical strike rating by 28, Improves resilience by 23.			
70	High Warlord's Scaled Legguards	Bind on Pickup	1019
PROPERTIES: Increases damage and healing done by magical spells and effects by up to 28.			
70	Timewarden's Leggings	Bind on Pickup	1019
PROPERTIES: Increases defense rating by 26, Increases your dodge rating by 19.			
	Cenarion Reservist's Legplates	Bind on Pickup	575
PROPERTIES: Increases defense rating by 13. Nature Resistance +25			
	Cenarion Reservist's Legplates	Bind on Pickup	575
PROPERTIES: Nature Resistance +25			
	Legplates of Heroism	Bind on Pickup	601
PROPERTIES: Increases defense rating by 8.			
	Soulforge Legplates	Bind on Pickup	601
PROPERTIES: Increases damage and healing done by magical spells and effects by up to 11.			
	Mag'hari Warlord's Legplates	Bind on Pickup	917
PROPERTIES: Increases defense rating by 16, Improves hit rating by 15, Improves critical strike rating by 12.			
	Consortium Plated Legguards	Bind on Pickup	866
PROPERTIES: Increases healing done by spells and effects by up to 51, Restores 9 mana per 5 sec.			
	Legguards of the Resolute Defender	Bind on Pickup	942
PROPERTIES: Increases your parry rating by 20.			
	Starcaller's Plated Legguards	Bind on Pickup	968
PROPERTIES: Increases healing done by spells and effects by up to 88, Restores 7 mana per 5 sec.			

Epic Plate Shoulders

Level	Name	Binding Info	Armor
50	Stockade Pauldrons	Bind on Equip	539
PROPERTIES: Increases defense rating by 15.			
60	Field Marshal's Lamellar Pauldrons	Bind on Pickup	715
PROPERTIES: Increases damage and healing done by magical spells and effects by up to 19, Restores 6 mana per 5 sec.			
60	Field Marshal's Plate Shoulderguards	Bind on Pickup	715
PROPERTIES: Increases your hit rating by 10.			
60	Warlord's Plate Shoulders	Bind on Pickup	715
PROPERTIES: Increases your hit rating by 10.			
60	Lawbringer Spaulders	Bind on Pickup	641
PROPERTIES: Increases healing done by spells and effects by up to 18. Shadow Resistance +7			
60	Pauldrons of Might	Bind on Pickup	641
PROPERTIES: Increases your block rating by 10, Increases defense rating by 8. Shadow Resistance +7			
60	Judgement Spaulders	Bind on Pickup	733
PROPERTIES: Restores 5 mana per 5 sec, Increases damage and healing done by magical spells and effects by up to 13. Fire Resistance +10			
60	Pauldrons of Wrath	Bind on Pickup	733
PROPERTIES: Increases the block value of your shield by 27, Increases defense rating by 10. Fire Resistance +10			
60	Drake Talon Pauldrons	Bind on Pickup	724
PROPERTIES: Increases your dodge rating by 12.			
60	Highlander's Plate Spaulders	Bind on Pickup	632
60	Highlander's Lamellar Spaulders	Bind on Pickup	632
60	Defiler's Lamellar Spaulders	Bind on Pickup	632
60	Defiler's Plate Spaulders	Bind on Pickup	632
60	Acid Inscribed Pauldrons	Bind on Pickup	697
PROPERTIES: Increases defense rating by 9. Nature Resistance +25			
60	Conqueror's Spaulders	Bind on Pickup	752
PROPERTIES: Increases defense rating by 6, Increases your hit rating by 10.			
60	Avenger's Pauldrons	Bind on Pickup	752
PROPERTIES: Increases damage and healing done by magical spells and effects by up to 14, Restores 3 mana per 5 sec.			
60	Mantle of the Horusath	Bind on Pickup	697
PROPERTIES: Increases damage and healing done by magical spells and effects by up to 14.			
60	Pauldrons of the Unrelenting	Bind on Pickup	743
PROPERTIES: Increases defense rating by 13, Increases your dodge rating by 12.			
60	Mantle of the Desert Crusade	Bind on Pickup	733
PROPERTIES: Increases healing done by spells and effects by up to 44.			
60	Dreadnaught Pauldrons	Bind on Pickup	825
PROPERTIES: Increases your hit rating by 10, Increases the block value of your shield by 21, Increases defense rating by 13.			
60	Redemption Spaulders	Bind on Pickup	825
PROPERTIES: Increases your spell critical strike rating by 14, Increases healing done by spells and effects by up to 40, Restores 4 mana per 5 sec.			
60	Icebane Pauldrons	Bind on Pickup	797
PROPERTIES: Increases defense rating by 10. Frost Resistance +33			
60	Spaulders of the Grand Crusader	Bind on Pickup	816
PROPERTIES: Restores 4 mana per 5 sec, Improves critical strike rating by 14, Increases damage and healing done by magical spells and effects by up to 20.			
60	Warlord's Lamellar Pauldrons	Bind on Pickup	715
PROPERTIES: Increases damage and healing done by magical spells and effects by up to 19, Restores 6 mana per 5 sec.			
70	Gladiator's Plate Shoulders	Bind on Pickup	1042
PROPERTIES: Improves critical strike rating by 17, Improves resilience rating by 18.			

Epic Plate Shoulders

Level	Name	Binding Info	Armor
70	Gladiator's Lamellar Shoulders	Bind on Pickup	1042
PROPERTIES: Increases damage and healing done by magical spells and effects by up to 13.			
70	Gladiator's Scaled Shoulders	Bind on Pickup	1042
PROPERTIES: Increases damage and healing done by magical spells and effects by up to 13.			
70	Pauldrons of the Justice-Seeker	Bind on Pickup	951
PROPERTIES: Increases healing done by spells and effects by up to 51, Restores 6 mana per 5 sec., Improves spell critical strike rating by 20.			
70	Mantle of Abrahmis	Bind on Pickup	951
PROPERTIES: Increases defense rating by 20.			
70	Warbringer Shoulderguards	Bind on Pickup	997
PROPERTIES: Increases defense rating by 14, Increases dodge rating by 23.			
70	Warbringer Shoulderplates	Bind on Pickup	997
PROPERTIES: Improves hit rating by 10.			
70	Justicar Pauldrons	Bind on Pickup	997
PROPERTIES: Increases healing done by spells and effects by up to 59, Restores 4 mana per 5 sec.			
70	Justicar Shoulderguards	Bind on Pickup	997
PROPERTIES: Increases damage and healing done by magical spells and effects by up to 22, Increases the block value of your shield by 23.			
70	Justicar Shoulderplates	Bind on Pickup	997
PROPERTIES: Increases damage and healing done by magical spells and effects by up to 23.			
70	Pauldrons of the Wardancer	Bind on Pickup	1087
PROPERTIES: Improves critical strike rating by 23.			
70	Pauldrons of the Argent Sentinel	Bind on Pickup	1087
PROPERTIES: Increases healing done by spells and effects by up to 64, Improves spell critical strike rating by 28.			
70	Destroyer Shoulderguards	Bind on Pickup	1133
PROPERTIES: Increases the block value of your shield by 38.			
70	Destroyer Shoulderblades	Bind on Pickup	1133
PROPERTIES: Improves critical strike rating by 30.			
70	Crystalforge Shoulderguards	Bind on Pickup	1133
PROPERTIES: Increases damage and healing done by magical spells and effects by up to 12, Restores 6 mana per 5 sec.			
70	Crystalforge Shoulderbraces	Bind on Pickup	1133
PROPERTIES: Increases damage and healing done by magical spells and effects by up to 29.			
70	Crystalforge Pauldrons	Bind on Pickup	1133
PROPERTIES: Increases healing done by spells and effects by up to 42.			
70	Ripfiend Shoulderplates	Bind on Pickup	997
PROPERTIES: Improves hit rating by 9, Improves critical strike rating by 18.			

Superior Plate Shoulders

Level	Name	Binding Info	Armor
45	Big Bad Pauldrons	Bind on Pickup	396
46	Wyrmslayer Spaulders	Bind on Equip	403
47	Earthslag Shoulders	Bind on Pickup	410
PROPERTIES: Increases damage and healing done by magical spells and effects by up to 9.			
52	Wailing Nightbane Pauldrons	Bind on Pickup	448
PROPERTIES: Increases defense rating by 5. Shadow Resistance +10			
53	Dawnbringer Shoulders	Bind on Equip	455
PROPERTIES: Increases healing done by spells and effects by up to 44.			
54	Ebonsteel Spaulders	Bind on Pickup	463
55	Slamshot Shoulders	Bind on Pickup	470
PROPERTIES: Increases attack power by 20.			

Superior Plate Shoulders

Level	Name	Binding Info	Armor
55	Lightforge Spaulders	Bind on Pickup	470
55	Spaulders of Valor	Bind on Pickup	470
55	Bulky Iron Spaulders	Bind on Pickup	470
PROPERTIES: Increases defense rating by 9.			
56	Stoneform Shoulders	Bind on Pickup	478
PROPERTIES: Increases defense rating by 10.			
57	Bile-etched Spaulders	Bind on Pickup	485
PROPERTIES: Increases defense rating by 10.			
58	Lieutenant Commander's Plate Pauldrons	Bind on Pickup	493
58	Lieutenant Commander's Lamellar Shoulders	Bind on Pickup	493
58	Champion's Plate Pauldrons	Bind on Pickup	493
60	Darksoul Shoulders	Bind on Equip	507
PROPERTIES: Increases your hit rating by 10.			
60	Bloodsoaked Pauldrons	Bind on Pickup	552
PROPERTIES: Increases defense rating by 5.			
60	Abyssal Plate Epaulets	Bind on Pickup	530
PROPERTIES: Increases your hit rating by 10.			
60	Polished Obsidian Pauldrons	Bind on Equip	530
PROPERTIES: Increases defense rating by 10.			
60	Champion's Plate Shoulders	Bind on Pickup	552
PROPERTIES: Improves critical strike rating by 14.			
60	Lieutenant Commander's Lamellar Shoulders	Bind on Pickup	552
PROPERTIES: Increases damage and healing done by magical spells and effects by up to 20.			
60	Lieutenant Commander's Plate Shoulders	Bind on Pickup	552
PROPERTIES: Improves critical strike rating by 14.			
60	Champion's Lamellar Shoulders	Bind on Pickup	552
PROPERTIES: Increases damage and healing done by magical spells and effects by up to 20.			
63	Truth Bearer Shoulderguards	Bind on Pickup	721
PROPERTIES: Increases damage and healing done by magical spells and effects by up to 8.			
68	Fanblade Pauldrons	Bind on Pickup	851
PROPERTIES: Increases defense rating by 20, Increases parry rating by 15.			
70	Justice Bearer's Pauldrons	Bind on Pickup	873
PROPERTIES: Restores 7 mana per 5 sec, Increases healing done by spells and effects by up to 55.			
70	Spaulders of the Righteous	Bind on Pickup	873
PROPERTIES: Increases damage and healing done by magical spells and effects by up to 15.			
70	Doomplate Shoulderguards	Bind on Pickup	873
70	Shoulderguards of the Bold	Bind on Pickup	873
PROPERTIES: Increases defense rating by 17.			
70	Pauldrons of Swift Retribution	Bind on Pickup	873
PROPERTIES: Increases damage and healing done by magical spells and effects by up to 22.			
70	Pauldrons of the Crimson Flight	Bind on Pickup	873
70	Grand Marshal's Lamellar Shoulders	Bind on Pickup	873
PROPERTIES: Increases damage and healing done by magical spells and effects by up to 12.			
70	Grand Marshal's Plate Shoulders	Bind on Pickup	873
PROPERTIES: Improves critical strike rating by 17, Improves resilience by 13.			
70	Grand Marshal's Scaled Shoulders	Bind on Pickup	873
PROPERTIES: Increases damage and healing done by magical spells and effects by up to 14.			
70	High Warlord's Lamellar Shoulders	Bind on Pickup	873
PROPERTIES: Increases damage and healing done by magical spells and effects by up to 12.			
70	High Warlord's Plate Shoulders	Bind on Pickup	873
PROPERTIES: Improves critical strike rating by 17, Improves resilience by 13.			

Superior Plate Shoulders

Level	Name	Binding Info	Armor
70	High Warlord's Scaled Shoulders	Bind on Pickup	873
PROPERTIES: Increases damage and healing done by magical spells and effects by up to 14.			
70	Spaulders of Slaughter	Bind on Pickup	873
PROPERTIES: Improves critical strike rating by 27.			
	Razorsteel Shoulders	Bind on Pickup	410
PROPERTIES: Increases your hit rating by 10.			
	Spaulders of Heroism	Bind on Pickup	507
	Soulforge Spaulders	Bind on Pickup	507
PROPERTIES: Increases damage and healing done by magical spells and effects by up to 12, Restores 4 mana per 5 sec.			
	Jade Warrior Pauldrons	Bind on Pickup	655
	Eagle Crested Pauldrons	Bind on Pickup	699
	Warchief's Mantle	Bind on Pickup	786
PROPERTIES: Increases parry rating by 18.			

Epic Plate Waist

Level	Name	Binding Info	Armor
60	Lawbringer Belt	Bind on Equip	481
PROPERTIES: Increases healing done by spells and effects by up to 18. Fire Resistance +7			
60	Belt of Might	Bind on Equip	481
PROPERTIES: Increases your dodge rating by 12, Increases defense rating by 8. Fire Resistance +7			
60	Judgement Belt	Bind on Pickup	550
PROPERTIES: Increases damage and healing done by magical spells and effects by up to 23. Shadow Resistance +10			
60	Waistband of Wrath	Bind on Pickup	550
PROPERTIES: Increases your block rating by 15, Increases defense rating by 10. Shadow Resistance +10			
60	Unmelting Ice Girdle	Bind on Pickup	516
PROPERTIES: Increases defense rating by 12. Frost Resistance +16			
60	Onslaught Girdle	Bind on Pickup	564
PROPERTIES: Improves critical strike rating by 14, Increases your hit rating by 10.			
60	Girdle of the Fallen Crusader	Bind on Pickup	557
60	Royal Qiraji Belt	Bind on Pickup	584
PROPERTIES: Increases your parry rating by 20, Increases defense rating by 12.			
60	Belt of the Fallen Emperor	Bind on Pickup	584
PROPERTIES: Increases healing done by spells and effects by up to 35.			
60	Triad Girdle	Bind on Pickup	543
60	Dreadnaught Waistguard	Bind on Pickup	632
PROPERTIES: Increases the block value of your shield by 18, Increases your block rating by 13, Increases defense rating by 13.			
60	Redemption Girdle	Bind on Pickup	632
PROPERTIES: Increases healing done by spells and effects by up to 40, Restores 5 mana per 5 sec.			
60	Girdle of the Mentor	Bind on Pickup	612
PROPERTIES: Improves critical strike rating by 14, Increases your hit rating by 10.			
60	Belt of the Grand Crusader	Bind on Pickup	612
PROPERTIES: Increases damage and healing done by magical spells and effects by up to 21, Restores 7 mana per 5 sec.			
70	General's Plate Belt	Bind on Pickup	782
PROPERTIES: Improves critical strike rating by 24, Improves resilience by 24.			
70	Crimson Girdle of the Indomitable	Bind on Pickup	713
PROPERTIES: Increases defense rating by 21, Increases your shield block rating by 17.			
70	General's Lamellar Belt	Bind on Pickup	782
PROPERTIES: Increases damage and healing done by magical spells and effects by up to 25.			

Epic Plate Waist

Level	Name	Binding Info	Armor
70	General's Scaled Belt	Bind on Pickup	782
PROPERTIES: Increases damage and healing done by magical spells and effects by up to 25.			
70	Girdle of Truth	Bind on Pickup	713
PROPERTIES: Increases healing done by spells and effects by up to 59, Restores 7 mana per 5 sec.			
70	Girdle of the Endless Pit	Bind on Pickup	782
PROPERTIES: Increases healing done by spells and effects by up to 40, Restores 5 mana per 5 sec., Improves critical strike rating by 21.			
70	Marshal's Lamellar Belt	Bind on Pickup	782
PROPERTIES: Increases damage and healing done by magical spells and effects by up to 25.			
70	Marshal's Plate Belt	Bind on Pickup	782
PROPERTIES: Improves critical strike rating by 24, Improves resilience by 24.			
70	Marshal's Scaled Belt	Bind on Pickup	782
PROPERTIES: Increases damage and healing done by magical spells and effects by up to 25.			
70	Lion's Heart Girdle	Bind on Pickup	680
PROPERTIES: Increases defense rating by 22, Improves critical strike rating by 21.			
70	Girdle of Valorous Deeds	Bind on Pickup	680
PROPERTIES: Increases damage and healing done by magical spells and effects by up to 22, Restores 6 mana per 5 sec.			
70	Girdle of the Righteous Path	Bind on Pickup	816
PROPERTIES: Increases healing done by spells and effects by up to 64.			
70	Red Belt of Battle	Bind on Equip	816
PROPERTIES: Increases defense rating by 25.			
70	Belt of the Guardian	Bind on Equip	816
PROPERTIES: Increases damage and healing done by magical spells and effects by up to 27, Increases the block value of your shield by 27.			
70	Girdle of the Invulnerable	Bind on Pickup	816
PROPERTIES: Increases defense rating by 19, Increases dodge rating by 20.			
70	Lurker's Girdle	Bind on Pickup	680
	Zandalar Vindicator's Belt	Bind on Pickup	446
PROPERTIES: Improves critical strike rating by 14.			
	Zandalar Freethinker's Belt	Bind on Pickup	446
PROPERTIES: Increases healing done by spells and effects by up to 26.			

Superior Plate Waist

Level	Name	Binding Info	Armor
40	Enormous Ogre Belt	Bind on Equip	164
40	Highlander's Lamellar Girdle	Bind on Pickup	236
40	Highlander's Plate Girdle	Bind on Pickup	236
40	Defiler's Lamellar Girdle	Bind on Pickup	236
40	Defiler's Plate Girdle	Bind on Pickup	236
40	Defiler's Lamellar Girdle	Bind on Pickup	236
46	Atal'alarion's Tusk Ring	Bind on Pickup	302
48	Highlander's Lamellar Girdle	Bind on Pickup	313
PROPERTIES: Improves critical strike rating by 14.			
48	Highlander's Plate Girdle	Bind on Pickup	313
PROPERTIES: Improves critical strike rating by 14.			
48	Defiler's Lamellar Girdle	Bind on Pickup	313
PROPERTIES: Improves critical strike rating by 14.			
48	Defiler's Plate Girdle	Bind on Pickup	313
PROPERTIES: Improves critical strike rating by 14.			
48	Defiler's Lamellar Girdle	Bind on Pickup	313
PROPERTIES: Improves critical strike rating by 14.			
50	Stonewall Girdle	Bind on Pickup	324

Superior Plate Waist

Level	Name	Binding Info	Armor
52	Girdle of Uther	Bind on Equip	336
53	Rainbow Girdle	Bind on Pickup	341
53	Lightforge Belt	Bind on Equip	341
53	Belt of Valor	Bind on Equip	341
53	Girdle of the Dawn	Bind on Equip	341
55	Knight-Captain's Plate Girdle	Bind on Pickup	353
55	Knight-Captain's Lamellar Cinch	Bind on Pickup	353
55	Legionnaire's Plate Cinch	Bind on Pickup	353
55	Belt of the Ordained	Bind on Equip	353
PROPERTIES: Increases healing done by spells and effects by up to 42.			
55	Frostwolf Plate Belt	Bind on Pickup	353
PROPERTIES: Frost Resistance +5			
55	Stormpike Plate Girdle	Bind on Pickup	353
PROPERTIES: Frost Resistance +5			
56	Deathbone Girdle	Bind on Pickup	358
PROPERTIES: Increases defense rating by 14, Restores 4 mana per 5 sec.			
56	Elemental Plate Girdle	Bind on Pickup	358
58	Brigam Girdle	Bind on Pickup	369
PROPERTIES: Increases your hit rating by 10.			
58	Handcrafted Mastersmith Girdle	Bind on Pickup	369
58	Highlander's Plate Girdle	Bind on Pickup	369
PROPERTIES: Improves critical strike rating by 14.			
58	Highlander's Plate Girdle	Bind on Pickup	369
PROPERTIES: Improves critical strike rating by 14.			
58	Highlander's Lamellar Girdle	Bind on Pickup	369
PROPERTIES: Improves critical strike rating by 14.			
58	Defiler's Lamellar Girdle	Bind on Pickup	369
PROPERTIES: Improves critical strike rating by 14.			
58	Defiler's Plate Girdle	Bind on Pickup	369
PROPERTIES: Improves critical strike rating by 14.			
58	Defiler's Lamellar Girdle	Bind on Pickup	369
PROPERTIES: Improves critical strike rating by 14.			
60	Belt of the Sand Reaver	Bind on Pickup	414
PROPERTIES: Increases defense rating by 7.			
60	Heavy Obsidian Belt	Bind on Equip	397
PROPERTIES: Resistance +5 All Resistances.			
60	Ironvine Belt	Bind on Equip	408
PROPERTIES: Increases defense rating by 5. Nature Resistance +15			
60	Tenacious Defender	Bind on Pickup	491
63	Studded Girdle of Virtue	Bind on Pickup	540
PROPERTIES: Increases damage and healing done by magical spells and effects by up to 13, Restores 4 mana per 5 sec.			
66	Slayer's Waistguard	Bind on Pickup	573
66	Avenger's Waistguard	Bind on Pickup	573
PROPERTIES: Increases damage and healing done by magical spells and effects by up to 20.			
68	Girdle of Many Blessings	Bind on Pickup	638
PROPERTIES: Increases healing done by spells and effects by up to 46.			
68	Girdle of Gallantry	Bind on Pickup	638
PROPERTIES: Increases damage and healing done by magical spells and effects by up to 15.			
68	Rubium War-Girdle	Bind on Pickup	638
PROPERTIES: Improves critical strike rating by 18.			

Superior Plate Waist

Level	Name	Binding Info	Armor
70	Enchanted Adamantite Belt	Bind on Equip	644
PROPERTIES: Arcane Resistance +30			
70	Khorium Belt	Bind on Equip	649
PROPERTIES: Restores 8 mana per 5 sec, Increases damage and healing done by magical spells and effects by up to 25.			
70	Girdle of the Immovable	Bind on Pickup	655
PROPERTIES: Increases defense rating by 18, Increases your shield block rating by 12.			
	Omokk's Girth Restrainer	Bind on Pickup	353
PROPERTIES: Improves critical strike rating by 14.			
	Belt of Shrunken Heads	Bind on Pickup	408
	Belt of Heroism	Bind on Pickup	380
PROPERTIES: Increases defense rating by 10.			
	Soulforge Belt	Bind on Pickup	380
PROPERTIES: Increases damage and healing done by magical spells and effects by up to 12, Restores 4 mana per 5 sec.			
	Lightwarden's Girdle	Bind on Pickup	622
PROPERTIES: Increases damage and healing done by magical spells and effects by up to 28.			

Epic Plate Wrist

Level	Name	Binding Info	Armor
40	Berserker Bracers	Bind on Pickup	262
50	Berserker Bracers	Bind on Pickup	314
54	Dark Iron Bracers	Bind on Equip	336
PROPERTIES: Fire Resistance +18			
60	Lawbringer Bracers	Bind on Equip	374
PROPERTIES: Restores 4 mana per 5 sec.			
60	Bracers of Might	Bind on Equip	374
60	Judgement Bindings	Bind on Pickup	428
PROPERTIES: Increases damage and healing done by magical spells and effects by up to 7.			
60	Bracelets of Wrath	Bind on Pickup	428
60	Berserker Bracers	Bind on Pickup	368
60	Dragonbone Wristguards	Bind on Pickup	401
PROPERTIES: Increases your parry rating by 20.			
60	Bracers of Brutality	Bind on Pickup	406
60	Wristguards of Castigation	Bind on Pickup	492
PROPERTIES: Increases healing done by spells and effects by up to 40, Restores 4 mana per 5 sec.			
60	Hive Defiler Wristguards	Bind on Pickup	439
60	Dreadnaught Bracers	Bind on Pickup	492
PROPERTIES: Increases defense rating by 7.			
60	Redemption Wristguards	Bind on Pickup	492
PROPERTIES: Increases healing done by spells and effects by up to 31, Restores 4 mana per 5 sec.			
60	Icebane Bracers	Bind on Equip	449
PROPERTIES: Increases defense rating by 7. Frost Resistance +24			
60	Wristguards of Vengeance	Bind on Pickup	465
PROPERTIES: Improves critical strike rating by 14.			
70	Black Felsteel Bracers	Bind on Equip	555
PROPERTIES: Improves critical strike rating by 17.			
70	Bracers of the Green Fortress	Bind on Equip	555
PROPERTIES: Increases defense rating by 14.			
70	Blessed Bracers	Bind on Equip	555
PROPERTIES: Increases damage and healing done by magical spells and effects by up to 35.			
70	General's Plate Bracers	Bind on Pickup	555
PROPERTIES: Improves critical strike rating by 12, Improves resilience rating by 12.			

Epic Plate Wrist

Level	Name	Binding Info	Armor
70	First Sergeant's Lamellar Bracers	Bind on Pickup	555
PROPERTIES: Increases damage and healing done by magical spells and effects by up to 18.			
70	Vambraces of Courage	Bind on Pickup	555
PROPERTIES: Increases the block value of your shield by 30.			
70	Bracers of Justice	Bind on Pickup	555
PROPERTIES: Increases healing done by spells and effects by up to 42.			
70	General's Lamellar Bracers	Bind on Pickup	555
PROPERTIES: Increases damage and healing done by magical spells and effects by up to 18.			
70	General's Scaled Bracers	Bind on Pickup	555
PROPERTIES: Increases damage and healing done by magical spells and effects by up to 18.			
70	Bladespire Warbands	Bind on Pickup	608
PROPERTIES: Improves critical strike rating by 21.			
70	Marshal's Lamellar Bracers	Bind on Pickup	555
PROPERTIES: Increases damage and healing done by magical spells and effects by up to 18.			
70	Marshal's Plate Bracers	Bind on Pickup	555
PROPERTIES: Improves critical strike rating by 12, Improves resilience rating by 12.			
70	Marshal's Scaled Bracers	Bind on Pickup	555
PROPERTIES: Increases damage and healing done by magical spells and effects by up to 18.			
70	Warpath Bracers	Bind on Pickup	529
PROPERTIES: Increases defense rating by 11.			
70	Bracers of Dignity	Bind on Pickup	529
PROPERTIES: Increases damage and healing done by magical spells and effects by up to 18.			
70	Amber Bands of the Aggressor	Bind on Pickup	529
PROPERTIES: Increases defense rating by 12.			
70	Bracers of Eradication	Bind on Pickup	634
PROPERTIES: Improves hit rating by 14, Improves critical strike rating by 21.			
70	Ravager's Bracers	Bind on Pickup	529
PROPERTIES: Nature Resistance +24.			
	Zandalar Vindicator's Armguards	Bind on Pickup	347
	Zandalar Freethinker's Armguards	Bind on Pickup	347
PROPERTIES: Increases healing done by spells and effects by up to 11.			
	Deeprock Bracers	Bind on Pickup	352

Superior Plate Wrist

Level	Name	Binding Info	Armor
30	First Sergeant's Plate Bracers	Bind on Pickup	114
30	Sergeant Major's Plate Bracers	Bind on Pickup	114
40	Skullplate Bracers	Bind on Equip	163
43	Giantslayer Bracers	Bind on Equip	223
45	First Sergeant's Plate Bracers	Bind on Pickup	231
45	Sergeant Major's Plate Wristguards	Bind on Pickup	231
45	Arena Vambraces	Bind on Equip	231
46	Noxxion's Shackles	Bind on Pickup	235
PROPERTIES: Nature Resistance +15			
48	Runed Golem Shackles	Bind on Equip	244
PROPERTIES: Increases defense rating by 6.			
52	Emberplate Armguards	Bind on Pickup	261
PROPERTIES: Fire Resistance +10			
52	Lightforge Bracers	Bind on Equip	261
52	Bracers of Valor	Bind on Equip	261
52	Black Steel Bindings	Bind on Pickup	261
54	Vambraces of the Sadist	Bind on Pickup	270
PROPERTIES: Improves critical strike rating by 14.			

Superior Plate Wrist

Level	Name	Binding Info	Armor
55	Knight-Captain's Plate Wristguards	Bind on Pickup	274
55	Knight-Captain's Lamellar Armsplints	Bind on Pickup	274
55	Legionnaire's Plate Bracers	Bind on Pickup	274
56	Morlune's Bracer	Bind on Equip	279
57	Vigorsteel Vambraces	Bind on Pickup	283
57	Fel Hardened Bracers	Bind on Pickup	283
PROPERTIES: Increases defense rating by 5.			
58	Battleborn Armbraces	Bind on Pickup	287
PROPERTIES: Increases your hit rating by 10, Improves critical strike rating by 14.			
58	First Sergeant's Plate Bracers	Bind on Pickup	287
58	Sergeant Major's Plate Wristguards	Bind on Pickup	287
58	Gordok Bracers of Power	Bind on Pickup	287
58	Frozen Steel Vambraces	Bind on Pickup	287
58	Bracers of Undead Slaying	Bind on Equip	287
PROPERTIES: Increases attack power by 45 when fighting Undead.			
60	Abyssal Plate Vambraces	Bind on Pickup	309
64	Bracers of the Nexus-Prince	Bind on Pickup	433
66	Adamantite Plate Bracers	Bind on Equip	458
68	Bracers of Just Rewards	Bind on Pickup	497
PROPERTIES: Restores 4 mana per 5 sec, Increases damage and healing done by magical spells and effects by up to 18.			
68	Vambraces of Daring	Bind on Pickup	497
PROPERTIES: Increases the block value of your shield by 23.			
68	Virtue Bearer's Vambraces	Bind on Pickup	497
PROPERTIES: Increases healing done by spells and effects by up to 35, Restores 6 mana per 5 sec.			
68	Bands of Syth	Bind on Pickup	497
69	Flamebane Bracers	Bind on Equip	497
PROPERTIES: Fire Resistance +28			
	Bracers of Heroism	Bind on Pickup	296
PROPERTIES: Increases defense rating by 4.			
	Soulforge Bracers	Bind on Pickup	296
PROPERTIES: Increases damage and healing done by magical spells and effects by up to 8.			
	Sha'tari Wrought Armguards	Bind on Pickup	509

SHIELDS

Epic Shields

Level	Name	Binding Info	Armor
36	The Green Tower	Bind on Equip	1507
PROPERTIES: When struck in combat has a 1% chance of raising a thorny shield that inflicts 3 Nature damage to attackers when hit and increases Nature resistance by 50 for 30 sec.			
41	Blackskull Shield	Bind on Equip	2063
PROPERTIES: Shadow Resistance +10			
45	Wall of the Dead	Bind on Equip	2226
PROPERTIES: When struck in combat has a 3% chance to encase the caster in bone, increasing armor by 150 for 20 sec.			
54	Skullflame Shield	Bind on Equip	2593
PROPERTIES: When struck in combat has a 3% chance of stealing 35 life from target enemy, When struck in combat has a 1% chance of dealing 75 to 125 Fire damage to all targets around you, Fire Resistance +10, Shadow Resistance +10			
60	Drillborer Disk	Bind on Pickup	2918
PROPERTIES: When struck in combat inflicts 3 Arcane damage to the attacker, Increases your block rating by 10, Increases the block value of your shield by 23.			

Epic Shields

Level	Name	Binding Info	Armor
60	Malistar's Defender	Bind on Pickup	3244
PROPERTIES: Restores 9 mana per 5 sec.			
60	Force Reactive Disk	Bind on Equip	2836
PROPERTIES: When the shield blocks it releases an electrical charge that damages all nearby enemies. This also has a chance of damaging the shield.			
60	Grand Marshal's Aegis	Bind on Pickup	3366
PROPERTIES: When struck in combat has a 5% chance of inflicting 35 to 65 Nature damage to the attacker.			
60	High Warlord's Shield Wall	Bind on Pickup	3366
PROPERTIES: When struck in combat has a 5% chance of inflicting 35 to 65 Nature damage to the attacker.			
60	The Immovable Object	Bind on Pickup	2836
PROPERTIES: Increases the block value of your shield by 27.			
60	Red Dragonscale Protector	Bind on Pickup	3204
PROPERTIES: Increases healing done by spells and effects by up to 37.			
60	Elementium Reinforced Bulwark	Bind on Pickup	3325
PROPERTIES: Increases the block value of your shield by 19, Increases defense rating by 10.			
60	Aegis of the Blood God	Bind on Pickup	2959
PROPERTIES: Increases the block value of your shield by 30, Increases defense rating by 10, Increases your block rating by 10.			
60	Earthen Guard	Bind on Pickup	2836
PROPERTIES: Increases defense rating by 11, Increases the block value of your shield by 12.			
60	Blessed Qiraji Bulwark	Bind on Pickup	3407
PROPERTIES: Increases your block rating by 13, Increases the block value of your shield by 15, Increases defense rating by 12.			
60	Buru's Skull Fragment	Bind on Pickup	2959
PROPERTIES: Increases defense rating by 9.			
60	Wormscale Blocker	Bind on Pickup	3488
PROPERTIES: Increases healing done by spells and effects by up to 35, Restores 6 mana per 5 sec.			
60	Jagged Obsidian Shield	Bind on Equip	3040
PROPERTIES: Increases your block rating by 9, Resistance +5 All Resistances, When struck by a harmful spell, the caster of that spell has a 5% chance to be silenced for 3 sec.			
60	The Plague Bearer	Bind on Pickup	3570
PROPERTIES: Increases defense rating by 14, Frost Resistance +15			
60	Shield of Condemnation	Bind on Pickup	3936
PROPERTIES: Restores 6 mana per 5 sec, Increases healing done by spells and effects by up to 59.			
60	The Face of Death	Bind on Pickup	3854
PROPERTIES: Increases your block rating by 12, Increases the block value of your shield by 21.			
60	Death's Bargain	Bind on Pickup	3570
PROPERTIES: Increases your spell critical strike rating by 14, Increases healing done by spells and effects by up to 29, Restores 4 mana per 5 sec.			
60	Stygian Buckler	Bind on Pickup	3570
PROPERTIES: When struck has a 15% chance of reducing the attacker's movement speed by 50% for 5 secs.			
70	Gladiator's Shield Wall	Bind on Pickup	4872
70	Shield of Impenetrable Darkness	Bind on Pickup	4261
PROPERTIES: Increases the block value of your shield by 30.			
70	Dragonheart Flameshield	Bind on Pickup	4261
PROPERTIES: Increases damage and healing done by magical spells and effects by up to 21, Restores 6 mana per 5 sec.			
70	Triptych Shield of the Ancients	Bind on Pickup	4261
PROPERTIES: Increases healing done by spells and effects by up to 37, Restores 7 mana per 5 sec.			
70	Aldori Legacy Defender	Bind on Pickup	4668
70	Crest of the Sha'tar	Bind on Pickup	4058
PROPERTIES: Increases the block value of your shield by 23.			

Epic Shields

Level	Name	Binding Info	Armor
70	Azure-Shield of Coldarra	Bind on Pickup	4058
PROPERTIES: Increases the block value of your shield by 30.			
70	Light-Bearer's Faith Shield	Bind on Pickup	4058
PROPERTIES: Increases healing done by spells and effects by up to 53.			
70	Mazthoril Honor Shield	Bind on Pickup	4058
PROPERTIES: Increases damage and healing done by magical spells and effects by up to 22.			
70	Legionnaire's Kite Shield	Bind on Pickup	4058
70	Aegis of the Vindicator	Bind on Pickup	4668
PROPERTIES: Increases healing done by spells and effects by up to 46, Restores 10 mana per 5 sec.			

Superior Shields

Level	Name	Binding Info	Armor
15	Gold-plated Buckler	Bind on Pickup	471
15	Kresh's Back	Bind on Pickup	471
PROPERTIES: Increases defense rating by 6.			
19	Redbeard Crest	Bind on Equip	547
20	Seedcloud Buckler	Bind on Pickup	566
23	Commander's Crest	Bind on Pickup	623
25	Shield of Thorsen	Bind on Equip	661
26	Resplendent Guardian	Bind on Equip	680
PROPERTIES: Increases your block rating by 5.			
31	Heart of Agamaggan	Bind on Pickup	776
32	Thermaplugg's Central Core	Bind on Pickup	795
PROPERTIES: When struck in combat has a 5% chance of inflicting 35 to 65 Nature damage to the attacker.			
33	Skullance Shield	Bind on Equip	814
37	Olaf's All Purpose Shield	Bind on Pickup	1287
PROPERTIES: Reduces your fall speed for 10 sec.			
37	Savage Boar's Guard	Bind on Pickup	1287
39	Aegis of the Scarlet Commander	Bind on Pickup	1548
41	Mountainside Buckler	Bind on Equip	1612
43	Troll Protector	Bind on Equip	1676
PROPERTIES: Increases your block rating by 10.			
47	Stoneshell Guard	Bind on Pickup	1803
48	Gizlock's Hypertech Buckler	Bind on Pickup	1835
PROPERTIES: Restores 4 mana per 5 sec.			
49	Aegis of Stormwind	Bind on Equip	1867
51	Crest of Supremacy	Bind on Pickup	1930
51	Astral Guard	Bind on Pickup	1930
53	Rock Golem Bulwark	Bind on Pickup	1994
PROPERTIES: Nature Resistance +10, Arcane Resistance +10			
54	Quel'dorai Guard	Bind on Equip	2026
PROPERTIES: Increases your dodge rating by 12. Arcane Resistance +11			
54	Avalanchion's Stony Hide	Bind on Equip	2026
PROPERTIES: Increases the block value of your shield by 10.			
55	Crest of Retribution	Bind on Pickup	2057
PROPERTIES: Deals 5 to 35 damage every time you block.			
56	Rhombeard Protector	Bind on Pickup	2089
56	Husk of Nerub'enkan	Bind on Pickup	2089
PROPERTIES: Nature Resistance +15,			
56	Observer's Shield	Bind on Pickup	2089
57	Garrett Family Crest	Bind on Equip	2121

Superior Shields

Level	Name	Binding Info	Armor
57	Rattlecage Buckler	Bind on Pickup	2121
57	Barrier Shield	Bind on Pickup	2121
PROPERTIES: Increases your block rating by 10, Increases the block value of your shield by 18.			
57	Intricately Runed Shield	Bind on Pickup	2121
PROPERTIES: Increases the block value of your shield by 24.			
57	Dreadguard's Protector	Bind on Pickup	2121
57	Lord Blackwood's Buckler	Bind on Pickup	2121
PROPERTIES: Increases the block value of your shield by 27.			
58	Draconian Deflector	Bind on Pickup	2153
PROPERTIES: Increases defense rating by 15. Fire Resistance +10,			
58	Draconian Aegis of the Legion	Bind on Pickup	2153
PROPERTIES: Increases damage and healing done by magical spells and effects by up to 20.			
60	Zulian Defender	Bind on Pickup	2312
62	Petrified Lichen Guard	Bind on Pickup	3043
PROPERTIES: Afflicts your attacker with deadly poison spores each time you block.			
64	Shield of the Void	Bind on Pickup	3234
PROPERTIES: Increases the block value of your shield by 24.			
68	Blood Knight Defender	Bind on Pickup	3711
PROPERTIES: Arcane Resistance +20			
68	Platinum Shield of the Valorous	Bind on Pickup	3711
68	Aegis of the Sunbird	Bind on Pickup	3711
PROPERTIES: Increases the block value of your shield by 29.			
70	Stormshield of Renewal	Bind on Pickup	3806
PROPERTIES: Increases healing done by spells and effects by up to 57.			
70	Silvermoon Crest Shield	Bind on Pickup	3806
PROPERTIES: Increases damage and healing done by magical spells and effects by up to 23, Restores 5 mana per 5 sec.			
70	High Warlord's Barricade	Bind on Pickup	3806
70	Grand Marshal's Barricade	Bind on Pickup	3806
70	Grand Marshal's Barricade	Bind on Pickup	3806
	Marbled Buckler	Bind on Pickup	776
	Arctic Buckler	Bind on Pickup	642
PROPERTIES: Frost Resistance +5,			
	Argent Defender	Bind on Pickup	2121
PROPERTIES: Has a 1% chance when struck in combat of increasing block rating by 250 for 10 sec.			
	Darrowshire Strongguard	Bind on Pickup	2153
PROPERTIES: Nature Resistance +10, Frost Resistance +10.			
	Sacred Protector	Bind on Pickup	2121
	Milli's Shield	Bind on Pickup	2026
PROPERTIES: Restores 4 health per 5 sec.			
	Ironbark Shield	Bind on Pickup	1803
PROPERTIES: Improves critical strike rating with Nature spells by 14.			

CLOAKS

Epic Cloaks

Level	Name	Binding Info	Armor
55	Onyxia Scale Cloak	Bind on Equip	53
57	Chromatic Cloak	Bind on Equip	55
PROPERTIES: Increases your spell critical strike rating by 14. Fire Resistance +9, Shadow Resistance +9			
57	Hide of the Wild	Bind on Equip	55
PROPERTIES: Increases healing done by spells and effects by up to 42.			

Epic Cloaks

Level	Name	Binding Info	Armor
57	Shifting Cloak	Bind on Equip	55
PROPERTIES: Increases your dodge rating by 12.			
60	Cloak of Flames	Bind on Equip	57
PROPERTIES: Deals 5 Fire damage to anyone who strikes you with a melee attack, Fire Resistance +15			
60	Sapphiron Drape	Bind on Pickup	63
PROPERTIES: Increases damage and healing done by magical spells and effects by up to 14. Frost Resistance +6, Arcane Resistance +6			
60	Cloak of the Shrouded Mists	Bind on Pickup	65
PROPERTIES: Fire Resistance +6, Nature Resistance +6			
60	Dragon's Blood Cape	Bind on Pickup	64
PROPERTIES: Fire Resistance +5, Shadow Resistance +5, Arcane Resistance +5			
60	Eskhandar's Pelt	Bind on Pickup	58
PROPERTIES: Improves critical strike rating by 14.			
60	Drape of Benediction	Bind on Pickup	59
PROPERTIES: Increases healing done by spells and effects by up to 31.			
60	Puissant Cape	Bind on Pickup	61
PROPERTIES: Increases attack power by 40, Increases your hit rating by 10.			
60	Fireproof Cloak	Bind on Pickup	62
PROPERTIES: Fire Resistance +18			
60	Cloak of the Brood Lord	Bind on Pickup	72
PROPERTIES: Increases damage and healing done by magical spells and effects by up to 28.			
60	Elementium Threaded Cloak	Bind on Pickup	67
PROPERTIES: Increases your dodge rating by 24.			
60	Cloak of Firemaw	Bind on Pickup	65
PROPERTIES: Increases attack power by 50.			
60	Shroud of Pure Thought	Bind on Pickup	65
PROPERTIES: Increases healing done by spells and effects by up to 33, Restores 6 mana per 5 sec.			
60	Cloak of Draconic Might	Bind on Pickup	61
60	Cloak of Consumption	Bind on Pickup	60
PROPERTIES: Increases damage and healing done by magical spells and effects by up to 23, Increases your spell hit rating by 8.			
60	Deathguard's Cloak	Bind on Pickup	57
PROPERTIES: Increases attack power by 34.			
60	Cloak of the Honor Guard	Bind on Pickup	57
PROPERTIES: Increases attack power by 34.			
60	Frost Shroud	Bind on Pickup	77
PROPERTIES: Increases damage done by Frost spells and effects by up to 21, Restores 4 mana per 5 sec.			
60	Green Dragonskin Cloak	Bind on Pickup	62
PROPERTIES: Restores 4 health per 5 sec. Nature Resistance +20			
60	Windshear Cape	Bind on Pickup	57
60	Fire Shroud	Bind on Pickup	58
PROPERTIES: Increases damage done by Fire spells and effects by up to 17.			
60	Shadow Shroud	Bind on Pickup	58
PROPERTIES: Increases damage done by Shadow spells and effects by up to 17.			
60	Drape of Unyielding Strength	Bind on Pickup	59
PROPERTIES: Increases your hit rating by 10.			
60	Cape of Eternal Justice	Bind on Pickup	59
PROPERTIES: Restores 5 mana per 5 sec.			
60	Cloak of the Gathering Storm	Bind on Pickup	59
PROPERTIES: Increases damage and healing done by magical spells and effects by up to 14.			

Epic Cloaks

Level	Name	Binding Info	Armor
60	Cloak of the Unseen Path	Bind on Pickup	59
PROPERTIES: Increases your hit rating by 10, Increases attack power by 22.			
60	Cloak of Veiled Shadows	Bind on Pickup	59
PROPERTIES: Increases your hit rating by 10.			
60	Cloak of Unending Life	Bind on Pickup	59
PROPERTIES: Increases damage and healing done by magical spells and effects by up to 11.			
60	Shroud of Infinite Wisdom	Bind on Pickup	59
PROPERTIES: Increases healing done by spells and effects by up to 24.			
60	Drape of Vaulted Secrets	Bind on Pickup	59
PROPERTIES: Increases damage and healing done by magical spells and effects by up to 18.			
60	Shroud of Unspoken Names	Bind on Pickup	59
PROPERTIES: Increases damage and healing done by magical spells and effects by up to 18.			
60	Sandstorm Cloak	Bind on Pickup	63
PROPERTIES: Increases your dodge rating by 12, Increases defense rating by 9.			
60	Cloak of Clarity	Bind on Pickup	76
PROPERTIES: Increases healing done by spells and effects by up to 40, Restores 8 mana per 5 sec.			
60	Cloak of the Golden Hive	Bind on Pickup	68
PROPERTIES: Increases defense rating by 9.			
60	Cloak of Untold Secrets	Bind on Pickup	67
PROPERTIES: Shadow Resistance +20			
60	Cape of the Trinity	Bind on Pickup	65
PROPERTIES: Increases damage and healing done by magical spells and effects by up to 21.			
60	Cloak of Concentrated Hatred	Bind on Pickup	64
PROPERTIES: Increases your hit rating by 10.			
60	Cloak of the Fallen God	Bind on Pickup	76
60	Glacial Cloak	Bind on Equip	69
PROPERTIES: Frost Resistance +24			
60	Cloak of the Devoured	Bind on Pickup	76
PROPERTIES: Increases damage and healing done by magical spells and effects by up to 30, Increases your spell hit rating by 8.			
60	Cryptfiend Silk Cloak	Bind on Pickup	72
PROPERTIES: Increases defense rating by 10, Increases your dodge rating by 12, Increases your hit rating by 10.			
60	Cloak of Suturing	Bind on Pickup	72
PROPERTIES: Increases healing done by spells and effects by up to 48, Restores 5 mana per 5 sec.			
60	Veil of Eclipse	Bind on Pickup	72
PROPERTIES: Increases damage and healing done by magical spells and effects by up to 28, Increases your spell penetration by 10.			
60	Cloak of the Scourge	Bind on Pickup	72
PROPERTIES: Increases attack power by 30, Increases your hit rating by 10.			
60	Shroud of Dominion	Bind on Pickup	77
PROPERTIES: Improves critical strike rating by 14, Increases attack power by 50.			
60	Cloak of the Necropolis	Bind on Pickup	77
PROPERTIES: Increases damage and healing done by magical spells and effects by up to 26, Increases your spell critical strike rating by 14, Increases your spell hit rating by 8.			
70	Resolute Cape	Bind on Equip	85
70	Vengeance Wrap	Bind on Equip	85
PROPERTIES: Increases attack power by 60.			
70	Manaweave Cloak	Bind on Equip	85
PROPERTIES: Restores 10 mana per 5 sec.			
70	Warrior Cloak	Bind on Pickup	109
70	Sergeant's Heavy Cloak	Bind on Pickup	93
PROPERTIES: Increases attack power by 34.			

Epic Cloaks

Level	Name	Binding Info	Armor
70	Sergeant's Heavy Cape	Bind on Pickup	93
PROPERTIES: Increases damage and healing done by magical spells and effects by up to 23.			
70	Sergeant's Heavy Cape	Bind on Pickup	93
PROPERTIES: Increases damage and healing done by magical spells and effects by up to 23.			
70	Sergeant's Heavy Cloak	Bind on Pickup	93
PROPERTIES: Increases attack power by 34.			
70	Royal Cloak of the Arathi Kings	Bind on Pickup	85
PROPERTIES: Improves hit rating by 14.			
70	Shadow-Cloak of Dalaran	Bind on Pickup	85
PROPERTIES: Increases damage and healing done by magical spells and effects by up to 33.			
70	Red Riding Hood's Cloak	Bind on Pickup	85
PROPERTIES: Increases healing done by spells and effects by up to 44, Restores 6 mana per 5 sec.			
70	Shadowvine Cloak of Infusion	Bind on Pickup	85
PROPERTIES: Restores 8 mana per 5 sec.			
70	Gilded Thorium Cloak	Bind on Pickup	85
70	Drape of Dark Reavers	Bind on Pickup	85
PROPERTIES: Increases attack power by 30.			
70	Farstrider Wildercloak	Bind on Pickup	93
PROPERTIES: Increases attack power by 62.			
70	Stainleses Cloak of the Pure Hearted	Bind on Pickup	93
PROPERTIES: Increases healing done by spells and effects by up to 46, Restores 6 mana per 5 sec.			
70	Ruby Drape of the Mysticant	Bind on Pickup	93
PROPERTIES: Increases damage and healing done by magical spells and effects by up to 27.			
70	Cloak of the Pit Stalker	Bind on Pickup	93
PROPERTIES: Increases attack power by 50.			
70	Brute Cloak of the Oger-Magi	Bind on Pickup	93
PROPERTIES: Increases damage and healing done by magical spells and effects by up to 25.			
70	Light-Touched Stole of Altruism	Bind on Pickup	81
PROPERTIES: Increases healing done by spells and effects by up to 51.			
70	Shawl of Shifting Probabilities	Bind on Pickup	81
PROPERTIES: Increases damage and healing done by magical spells and effects by up to 18.			
70	Bishop's Cloak	Bind on Pickup	81
PROPERTIES: Increases healing done by spells and effects by up to 40, Restores 8 mana per 5 sec.			
70	Blood Knight War Cloak	Bind on Pickup	81
PROPERTIES: Increases attack power by 46.			
70	Farstrider Defender's Cloak	Bind on Pickup	81
PROPERTIES: Increases the block value of your shield by 35.			
70	Phoenix-Wing Cloak	Bind on Pickup	97
70	Sunshower Light Cloak	Bind on Pickup	105
PROPERTIES: Increases healing done by spells and effects by up to 51.			
70	Royal Cloak of the Sunstriders	Bind on Pickup	105
PROPERTIES: Increases damage and healing done by magical spells and effects by up to 32.			
70	Thalassian Wildercloak	Bind on Pickup	105
PROPERTIES: Increases attack power by 58.			
70	Razor-Scale Battlecloak	Bind on Pickup	97
70	Drape of the Righteous	Bind on Pickup	85
PROPERTIES: Restores 6 mana per 5 sec, Increases the damage done by Holy spells and effects by up to 40.			
70	Black-Iron Battlecloak	Bind on Pickup	89
PROPERTIES: Increases attack power by 52.			
70	Ancient Spellcloak of the Highborne	Bind on Pickup	89
PROPERTIES: Increases damage and healing done by magical spells and effects by up to 33.			

Superior Cloaks

Level	Name	Binding Info	Armor
16	Firebane Cloak	Bind on Equip	19
PROPERTIES: Fire Resistance +5			
16	Tranquillien Champion's Cloak	Bind on Equip	19
17	Glowing Lizardscale Cloak	Bind on Pickup	20
18	Battle Healer's Cloak	Bind on Pickup	20
PROPERTIES: Increases healing done by spells and effects by up to 9.			
18	Caretaker's Cape	Bind on Pickup	20
PROPERTIES: Increases healing done by spells and effects by up to 9.			
19	Sentry Cloak	Bind on Equip	21
20	Cape of the Brotherhood	Bind on Pickup	21
23	Amy's Blanket	Bind on Equip	23
24	Glowing Thresher Cape	Bind on Pickup	23
25	Sergeant Major's Cape	Bind on Pickup	24
28	Battle Healer's Cloak	Bind on Pickup	25
PROPERTIES: Increases healing done by spells and effects by up to 13.			
28	Caretaker's Cape	Bind on Pickup	25
PROPERTIES: Increases healing done by spells and effects by up to 13.			
29	Tigerstrike Mantle	Bind on Equip	25
30	Sergeant's Cloak	Bind on Pickup	26
30	Sergeant's Cape	Bind on Pickup	26
32	Dark Hooded Cape	Bind on Equip	27
33	Wing of the Whelpling	Bind on Equip	28
34	Energy Cloak	Bind on Equip	28
PROPERTIES: Restores 375 to 425 mana.			
35	Icy Cloak	Bind on Equip	29
PROPERTIES: Frost Resistance +11			
35	Silky Spider Cape	Bind on Pickup	30
36	Mantle of Lady Falther'ess	Bind on Pickup	30
PROPERTIES: Increases damage and healing done by magical spells and effects by up to 9.			
38	Battle Healer's Cloak	Bind on Pickup	31
PROPERTIES: Increases healing done by spells and effects by up to 18.			
38	Caretaker's Cape	Bind on Pickup	31
PROPERTIES: Increases healing done by spells and effects by up to 18.			
40	Sergeant Major's Cape	Bind on Pickup	32
40	Grunt's Cloak	Bind on Pickup	32
41	Blackmetal Cape	Bind on Equip	33
44	Blackflame Cape	Bind on Equip	35
PROPERTIES: Fire Resistance +5, Shadow Resistance +5			
45	Sergeant's Cloak	Bind on Pickup	36
45	Sergeant's Cape	Bind on Pickup	36
47	Spritecaster Cape	Bind on Pickup	37
PROPERTIES: Increases damage and healing done by magical spells and effects by up to 14.			
47	Grovekeeper's Drape	Bind on Pickup	37
PROPERTIES: Nature Resistance +10			
48	Blackveil Cape	Bind on Pickup	38
48	Nightfall Drape	Bind on Pickup	38
48	Battle Healer's Cloak	Bind on Pickup	38
PROPERTIES: Increases healing done by spells and effects by up to 22.			
48	Caretaker's Cape	Bind on Pickup	38
PROPERTIES: Increases healing done by spells and effects by up to 22.			
49	Featherskin Cape	Bind on Pickup	39
50	Graverot Cape	Bind on Pickup	39

Superior Cloaks

Level	Name	Binding Info	Armor
50	Blisterbane Wrap	Bind on Equip	39
PROPERTIES: Shadow Resistance +6			
50	Dark Phantom Cape	Bind on Equip	39
50	Cloak of Fire	Bind on Equip	39
PROPERTIES: Deals 25 Fire damage every 5 sec to all nearby enemies for 15 sec. Fire Resistance +6			
51	Stoneshield Cloak	Bind on Equip	40
53	Cape of the Fire Salamander	Bind on Pickup	41
PROPERTIES: Fire Resistance +12			
53	Butcher's Apron	Bind on Pickup	41
53	Mageflame Cloak	Bind on Equip	41
PROPERTIES: Increases damage done by Fire spells and effects by up to 21. Fire Resistance +10			
53	Juno's Shadow	Bind on Equip	41
PROPERTIES: Shadow Resistance +15			
54	Royal Tribunal Cloak	Bind on Pickup	42
54	Shadewood Cloak	Bind on Pickup	42
PROPERTIES: Nature Resistance +7			
54	Gracious Cape	Bind on Equip	42
PROPERTIES: Restores 6 mana per 5 sec.			
55	The Emperor's New Cape	Bind on Pickup	43
55	Armswake Cloak	Bind on Pickup	43
PROPERTIES: Increases attack power by 16.			
55	Onyxia Scale Cloak	Bind on Equip	43
PROPERTIES: Protects the wearer from being fully engulfed by Shadow Flame. Fire Resistance +16			
55	Sergeant Major's Cape	Bind on Pickup	43
55	Heliotrope Cloak	Bind on Pickup	43
PROPERTIES: Increases your spell critical strike rating by 14			
55	Frostwolf Legionnaire's Cloak	Bind on Pickup	43
PROPERTIES: Increases attack power by 24. Frost Resistance +5			
55	Stormpike Soldier's Cloak	Bind on Pickup	43
PROPERTIES: Increases attack power by 24. Frost Resistance +5			
55	Frostwolf Advisor's Cloak	Bind on Pickup	43
PROPERTIES: Increases damage and healing done by magical spells and effects by up to 14. Frost Resistance +5			
55	Stormpike Sage's Cloak	Bind on Pickup	43
PROPERTIES: Increases damage and healing done by magical spells and effects by up to 14. Frost Resistance +5			
56	Wildfire Cape	Bind on Pickup	43
PROPERTIES: Fire Resistance +20			
56	Archivist Cape	Bind on Pickup	43
PROPERTIES: Restores 4 mana per 5 sec.			
56	Stoneskin Gargoyle Cape	Bind on Pickup	43
56	Shroud of Arcane Mastery	Bind on Pickup	43
PROPERTIES: Increases your spell hit rating by 8.			
57	Fluctuating Cloak	Bind on Pickup	44
PROPERTIES: Restores 4 health per 5 sec.			
57	Cloak of the Cosmos	Bind on Pickup	44
PROPERTIES: Increases healing done by spells and effects by up to 26.			
57	Cloak of Warding	Bind on Equip	44
PROPERTIES: Increases defense rating by 7.			
57	Phantasmal Cloak	Bind on Pickup	44
57	Pale Moon Cloak	Bind on Pickup	44
PROPERTIES: Shadow Resistance +10			

Superior Cloaks

Level	Name	Binding Info	Armor
58	Bloodmoon Cloak	Bind on Pickup	45
PROPERTIES: Arcane Resistance +7			
58	Frostweaver Cape	Bind on Pickup	45
PROPERTIES: Frost Resistance +10			
58	Cape of the Black Baron	Bind on Pickup	45
PROPERTIES: Increases attack power by 20.			
58	Sergeant's Cape	Bind on Pickup	45
58	Sergeant's Cloak	Bind on Pickup	45
58	Redoubt Cloak	Bind on Pickup	45
PROPERTIES: Increases defense rating by 10.			
58	Battle Healer's Cloak	Bind on Pickup	45
PROPERTIES: Increases healing done by spells and effects by up to 26.			
58	Caretaker's Cape	Bind on Pickup	45
PROPERTIES: Increases healing done by spells and effects by up to 26.			
58	Crystalline Threaded Cape	Bind on Equip	45
PROPERTIES: Increases damage and healing done by magical spells and effects by up to 20.			
58	Shadow Prowler's Cloak	Bind on Pickup	45
58	Shroud of Domination	Bind on Pickup	45
58	Cloak of Revanchion	Bind on Pickup	45
60	Corporal's Cloak	Bind on Pickup	46
60	Hakkari Loa Cloak	Bind on Pickup	50
PROPERTIES: Increases healing done by spells and effects by up to 33.			
60	Overlord's Embrace	Bind on Pickup	50
PROPERTIES: Increases defense rating by 10, Increases your block rating by 5.			
60	Zulian Tigerhide Cloak	Bind on Pickup	48
PROPERTIES: Increases your hit rating by 10.			
60	Cloak of the Savior	Bind on Pickup	52
PROPERTIES: Increases healing done by spells and effects by up to 22.			
60	Gaea's Embrace	Bind on Equip	49
PROPERTIES: Nature Resistance +20			
60	Cloak of the Hakkari Worshippers	Bind on Pickup	48
PROPERTIES: Increases damage and healing done by magical spells and effects by up to 23.			
60	Might of the Tribe	Bind on Pickup	48
PROPERTIES: Increases attack power by 28.			
60	Mok'Nathal Wildercloak	Bind on Pickup	59
62	Spore-Soaked Vaneer	Bind on Pickup	63
PROPERTIES: Increases damage and healing done by magical spells and effects by up to 19.			
62	Bogstrok Scale Cloak	Bind on Pickup	63
63	Cloak of Enduring Swiftness	Bind on Pickup	64
63	Cloak of Healing Rays	Bind on Pickup	64
PROPERTIES: Increases healing done by spells and effects by up to 33.			
64	Muck-Covered Drape	Bind on Pickup	66
PROPERTIES: Reduces your threat to enemy targets within 30 yards, making them less likely to attack you.			
64	Cloak of Revival	Bind on Pickup	66
PROPERTIES: Restores 4 mana per 5 sec, Increases healing done by spells and effects by up to 35.			
66	Cloak of Impulsiveness	Bind on Pickup	70
PROPERTIES: Increases attack power by 40.			
68	Cloak of the Everliving	Bind on Pickup	76
PROPERTIES: Restores 9 mana per 5 sec, Increases healing done by spells and effects by up to 51.			

Superior Cloaks

Level	Name	Binding Info	Armor
68	Embroidered Cape of Mysteries	Bind on Pickup	76
PROPERTIES: Increases damage and healing done by magical spells and effects by up to 25.			
68	Cloak of Malice	Bind on Pickup	76
PROPERTIES: Increases attack power by 38.			
68	Ironscale War Cloak	Bind on Pickup	76
PROPERTIES: Increases the block value of your shield by 29.			
68	Cloak of Whispering Shells	Bind on Pickup	76
PROPERTIES: Restores 4 mana per 5 sec, Increases healing done by spells and effects by up to 40.			
68	Mantle of the Inciter	Bind on Pickup	76
PROPERTIES: Increases attack power by 30.			
68	Avian Mantle of Feathers	Bind on Pickup	78
PROPERTIES: Restores 5 mana per 5 sec, Increases healing done by spells and effects by up to 42.			
68	Sethekk Oracle Cloak	Bind on Pickup	78
PROPERTIES: Increases damage and healing done by magical spells and effects by up to 22.			
68	Burnoose of the Shifting Ages	Bind on Pickup	76
PROPERTIES: Increases the block value of your shield by 29.			
68	Capacitus' Cloak of Calibration	Bind on Pickup	76
68	Thoriumweave Cloak	Bind on Pickup	76
68	Syrannis' Mystic Sheen	Bind on Pickup	76
PROPERTIES: Fire Resistance +12, Nature Resistance +12, Frost Resistance +12, Shadow Resistance +12, Arcane Resistance +12			
68	Mithril-Bark Cloak	Bind on Pickup	76
68	Tempest Keep Arcane Prison Lvl 70 The Pacifier Healer Cloak	Bind on Pickup	76
PROPERTIES: Increases healing done by spells and effects by up to 42.			
69	Cloak of the Black Void	Bind on Equip	76
PROPERTIES: Increases damage and healing done by magical spells and effects by up to 35.			
69	Cloak of Eternity	Bind on Equip	76
69	White Remedy Cape	Bind on Equip	76
PROPERTIES: Increases healing done by spells and effects by up to 59, Restores 7 mana per 5 sec.			
69	Cloak of Arcane Evasion	Bind on Equip	76
PROPERTIES: Arcane Resistance +32			
70	Devilshark Cape	Bind on Pickup	78
PROPERTIES: Increases the block value of your shield by 29.			
70	Auchenai Death Shroud	Bind on Pickup	78
PROPERTIES: Increases attack power by 36.			
70	Tempest Keep Factory Lvl 70 The Foreman Loot 1 Caster Cloak	Bind on Pickup	78
PROPERTIES: Increases damage and healing done by magical spells and effects by up to 22.			
70	Tempest Keep Atrium Lvl 70 Warp Splinter Loot 2 Warrior DPS Cloak	Bind on Pickup	78
70	Ceremonial Cover	Bind on Pickup	78
PROPERTIES: Restores 6 mana per 5 sec.			
70	Cloak of the Ancient Spirits	Bind on Pickup	78
PROPERTIES: Restores 6 mana per 5 sec.			
	Shroud of the Exile	Bind on Pickup	45
	Deep Woodlands Cloak	Bind on Pickup	37
PROPERTIES: Increases damage and healing done by magical spells and effects by up to 12.			
	Duskbat Drape	Bind on Pickup	37
PROPERTIES: Reduces damage from falling.			
	Faded Hakkari Cloak	Bind on Pickup	42
PROPERTIES: Restores 6 mana per 5 sec.			
	Tattered Hakkari Cape	Bind on Pickup	42
PROPERTIES: Restores 6 health per 5 sec.			

Superior Cloaks

Level	Name	Binding Info	Armor
	Earthweave Cloak	Bind on Pickup	44
PROPERTIES: Increases your hit rating by 10.			
	Frightmaw Hide	Bind on Pickup	37
	Dark Cloak of the Marsh	Bind on Pickup	64
PROPERTIES: Increases attack power by 30.			
	Perfectly Balanced Cape	Bind on Pickup	61
PROPERTIES: Increases attack power by 30.			
	Ogre Slayer's Cover	Bind on Pickup	68
PROPERTIES: Increases damage and healing done by magical spells and effects by up to 20.			
	Mantle of Vivification	Bind on Pickup	74
PROPERTIES: Restores 7 mana per 5 sec, Increases healing done by spells and effects by up to 40.			
	Vicar's Cloak	Bind on Pickup	74
PROPERTIES: Restores 7 mana per 5 sec, Increases healing done by spells and effects by up to 40.			
	Spell-slinger's Protector	Bind on Pickup	66
PROPERTIES: Increases damage and healing done by magical spells and effects by up to 16.			
	Nomad's Woven Cloak	Bind on Pickup	66
	Delicate Green Poncho	Bind on Pickup	66
PROPERTIES: Increases attack power by 28.			
	Cloak of Woven Energy	Bind on Pickup	72
PROPERTIES: Increases damage and healing done by magical spells and effects by up to 29.			

WEAPONS

AXES

Epic One Hand Axe

Lvl	Name	Binding Info	DPS	Damage	Speed
42	Flurry Axe	Bind on Equip	35.3	Physical 37-69	1.5
PROPERTIES: Grants 1 extra attack on your next swing.					
52	Axe of the Deep Woods	Bind on Equip	41.5	Physical 78-146	2.7
PROPERTIES: Blasts a target for 90 to 126 Nature damage, Main Hand Weapon					
60	Deathbringer	Bind on Pickup	56.4	Physical 114-213	2.9
PROPERTIES: Sends a shadowy bolt at the enemy causing 110 to 140 Shadow damage.					
60	Grand Marshal's Handaxe	Bind on Pickup	59.5	Physical 138-207	2.9
PROPERTIES: Improves critical strike rating by 14, Increases attack power by 28.					
60	High Warlord's Cleaver	Bind on Pickup	59.5	Physical 138-207	2.9
PROPERTIES: Improves critical strike rating by 14, Increases attack power by 28.					
60	Doom's Edge	Bind on Pickup	51.5	Physical 83-154	2.3
60	Crul'shorukh, Edge of Chaos	Bind on Pickup	62.8	Physical 101-188	2.3
PROPERTIES: Increases attack power by 36.					
60	Ancient Hakkari Manslayer	Bind on Pickup	49.8	Physical 69-130	2
PROPERTIES: Steals 48 to 54 life from target enemy.					
60	Blessed Qiraji War Axe	Bind on Pickup	60.6	Physical 110-205	2.6
PROPERTIES: Improves critical strike rating by 14, Increases attack power by 14.					
60	Sickle of Unyielding Strength	Bind on Pickup	51.4	Physical 75-141	2.1
PROPERTIES: Increases defense rating by 6.					
60	Scythe of the Unseen Path	Bind on Pickup	51.5	Physical 86-161	2.4
PROPERTIES: Restores 3 mana per 5 sec, Increases attack power by 20.					
60	Hatchet of Sundered Bone	Bind on Pickup	65.4	Physical 119-221	2.6
PROPERTIES: Increases attack power by 36, Improves critical strike rating by 14.					
70	Fel Edged Battleaxe	Bind on Equip	81.1	Physical 125-232	2.2
70	Warrior 1H Axe	Bind on Equip	95	Physical 146-272	2.2

Epic One Hand Axe

Lvl	Name	Binding Info	DPS	Damage	Speed
70	Gladiator's Cleaver	Bind on Pickup	88.1	Physical 183-275	2.6
PROPERTIES: Increases attack power by 28.					
70	Gladiator's Hacker	Bind on Pickup	88.3	Physical 127-191	1.8
PROPERTIES: Increases attack power by 28.					
70	Warbringer	Bind on Pickup	78.9	Physical 99-185	1.8
70	Netherbane	Bind on Pickup	88.1	Physical 160-298	2.6
PROPERTIES: Increases attack power by 30.					
70	The Planar Edge	Bind on Pickup	81.1	Physical 153-285	2.7
PROPERTIES: Increases attack power by 40, Main Hand Weapon					
70	Black Planar Edge	Bind on Pickup	88.1	Physical 166-310	2.7
PROPERTIES: Increases attack power by 42, Main Hand Weapon					
70	Wicked Edge of the Planes	Bind on Pickup	95	Physical 179-334	2.7
PROPERTIES: Increases attack power by 46, Main Hand Weapon					
70	The Decapitator	Bind on Pickup	85.8	Physical 156-290	2.6
PROPERTIES: Hurls your axe in an attempt to decapitate your target causing 513 to 567 damage, Main Hand Weapon					

Superior One Hand Axe

Lvl	Name	Binding Info	DPS	Damage	Speed
15	Serpent's Kiss	Bind on Equip	13.4	Physical 23-44	2.5
PROPERTIES: Poisons target for 7 Nature damage every 3 sec for 15 sec.					
18	Razor's Edge	Bind on Equip	15.2	Physical 25-48	2.4
18	Guillotine Axe	Bind on Equip	15	Physical 28-53	2.7
PROPERTIES: Main Hand Weapon					
20	Butcher's Cleaver	Bind on Pickup	16.2	Physical 23-32	1.7
20	Grimclaw	Bind on Equip	16	Physical 22-42	2
PROPERTIES: Sends a shadowy bolt at the enemy causing 30 Shadow damage.					
22	Axe of the Enforcer	Bind on Equip	17.1	Physical 31-58	2.6
25	Headsplitter	Bind on Equip	18.9	Physical 30-57	2.3
25	Vibroblade	Bind on Equip	19.1	Physical 21-40	1.6
PROPERTIES: Punctures target's armor lowering it by 100.					
25	Bearded Boneaxe	Bind on Equip	18.9	Physical 25-47	1.9
PROPERTIES: Main Hand Weapon					
31	Pronged Reaver	Bind on Pickup	24	Physical 40-75	2.4
32	Stalvan's Reaper	Bind on Equip	24.8	Physical 50-94	2.9
PROPERTIES: Lowers all attributes of target by 2 for 1 min.					
33	Shovelphlange's Mining Axe	Bind on Equip	25.7	Physical 50-94	2.8
PROPERTIES: Increases attack power by 10.					
33	Steelclaw Reaver	Bind on Equip	25.8	Physical 32-61	1.8
PROPERTIES: Main Hand Weapon					
34	Sickle Axe	Bind on Equip	26.5	Physical 48-90	2.6
40	Digmaster 5000	Bind on Equip	30.3	Physical 38-71	1.8
PROPERTIES: Punctures target's armor lowering it by 100.					
40	Curve-bladed Ripper	Bind on Equip	30.3	Physical 40-75	1.9
PROPERTIES: Main Hand Weapon					
43	Winter's Bite	Bind on Equip	32.1	Physical 47-88	2.1
PROPERTIES: Launches a bolt of frost at the enemy causing 20 to 30 Frost damage and slowing movement speed by 50% for 5 sec, Main Hand Weapon					
45	Ripsaw	Bind on Pickup	33.3	Physical 63-117	2.7
PROPERTIES: Wounds the target for 75 damage, Main Hand Weapon					
47	Light Skyforged Axe	Bind on Pickup	34.6	Physical 60-113	2.5
PROPERTIES: Main Hand Weapon					
48	Axe of Rin'ji	Bind on Equip	35	Physical 46-87	1.9

Superior One Hand Axe

Lvl	Name	Binding Info	DPS	Damage	Speed
48	Ribsplitter	Bind on Equip	35.2	Physical 66-124	2.7
PROPERTIES: Increases attack power by 10, Main Hand Weapon					
50	Dawn's Edge	Bind on Equip	36.4	Physical 53-100	2.1
PROPERTIES: Improves critical strike rating by 14.					
50	Grizzle's Skinner	Bind on Pickup	36.5	Physical 61-114	2.4
PROPERTIES: Main Hand Weapon					
51	Tooth of Eranikus	Bind on Pickup	37.1	Physical 62-116	2.4
PROPERTIES: Increases your hit rating by 10, Main Hand Weapon					
51	Wraith Scythe	Bind on Pickup	37	Physical 57-106	2.2
PROPERTIES: Steals 45 life from target enemy, Main Hand Weapon					
52	Soul Breaker	Bind on Pickup	37.5	Physical 42-78	1.6
PROPERTIES: Target enemy loses 12 health and mana every 3 sec for 30 sec, Main Hand Weapon					
53	Rivenspike	Bind on Pickup	38.1	Physical 77-144	2.9
PROPERTIES: Punctures target's armor lowering it by 200. Can be applied up to 3 times.					
54	Demonfork	Bind on Pickup	38.9	Physical 76-142	2.8
PROPERTIES: Transfers 10 health every 5 seconds from the target to the caster for 25 sec, Main Hand Weapon					
55	Hedgecutter	Bind on Pickup	39.5	Physical 60-90	1.9
56	Serathil	Bind on Equip	40	Physical 53-99	1.9
PROPERTIES: Resistance +100 Armor					
57	Bone Slicing Hatchet	Bind on Pickup	40.6	Physical 48-90	1.7
57	Soulrender	Bind on Pickup	40.8	Physical 71-133	2.5
PROPERTIES: Increases attack power by 28.					
57	Iceblade Hacker	Bind on Pickup	40.8	Physical 57-106, Frost +1-5	2
PROPERTIES: Main Hand Weapon					
58	Annihilator	Bind on Equip	41.5	Physical 49-92	1.7
PROPERTIES: Reduces an enemy's armor by 200. Stacks up to 3 times, Main Hand Weapon					
60	Frostbite	Bind on Pickup	42.6	Physical 80-150	2.7
60	Zulian Hacker	Bind on Equip	42.7	Physical 71-134	2.4
PROPERTIES: Increases axe skill rating by 4.					
60	Grunt's Waraxe	Bind on Pickup	52.9	Physical 70-131	1.9
PROPERTIES: Increases attack power by 22.					
60	Dark Iron Destroyer	Bind on Equip	42.7	Physical 71-134	2.4
PROPERTIES: Main Hand Weapon, Fire Resistance +6					
65	Stormforged Axe	Bind on Pickup	60.6	Physical 110-205	2.6
PROPERTIES: Main Hand Weapon					
66	Amani Venom Axe	Bind on Pickup	62.8	Physical 101-188	2.3
PROPERTIES: Increases attack power by 26.					
68	Firebrand Battlexe	Bind on Pickup	69.4	Physical 116-217	2.4
PROPERTIES: Increases axe skill rating by 14.					
68	Bogreaver	Bind on Pickup	69.4	Physical 82-154	1.7
PROPERTIES: Increases attack power by 28.					
68	Stellaris	Bind on Pickup	69.5	Physical 92-172	1.9
PROPERTIES: Increases attack power by 22.					
70	The Harvester of Souls	Bind on Pickup	71.7	Physical 130-243	2.6
70	High Warlord's Cleaver	Bind on Pickup	71.7	Physical 149-224	2.6
PROPERTIES: Increases attack power by 26.					
70	High Warlord's Hacker	Bind on Pickup	71.7	Physical 103-155	1.8
PROPERTIES: Increases attack power by 26.					
70	Grand Marshal's Cleaver	Bind on Pickup	71.7	Physical 149-224	2.6
PROPERTIES: Increases attack power by 26.					

Superior One Hand Axe

Lvl	Name	Binding Info	DPS	Damage	Speed
70	Grand Marshal's Hacker	Bind on Pickup	71.7	Physical 103-155	1.8
PROPERTIES: Increases attack power by 26.					
	Windreaper	Bind on Pickup	39.3	Physical 63-118	2.3
PROPERTIES: Inflicts Nature damage every 2 sec for 20 sec.					

Epic Two Hand Axe

Lvl	Name	Binding Info	DPS	Damage	Speed
35	Fiery War Axe	Bind on Equip	40.3	Physical 93-141	2.9
PROPERTIES: Hurls a fiery ball that causes 155 to 197 Fire damage and an additional 24 damage over 6 sec.					
55	Brain Hacker	Bind on Equip	56.7	Physical 95-143	2.1
PROPERTIES: Wounds the target for 200 to 300 damage and lowers Intellect of target by 25 for 30 sec.					
44	Kang the Decapitator	Bind on Equip	47.4	Physical 136-205	3.6
PROPERTIES: Wounds the target causing them to bleed for 559 damage over 30 sec.					
60	Spinal Reaper	Bind on Pickup	74.7	Physical 203-305	3.4
PROPERTIES: Restores 150 mana or 20 rage when you kill a target that gives experience; this effect cannot occur more than once every 10 seconds, Increases attack power by 34.					
58	Treant's Bane	Bind on Pickup	59.4	Physical 161-243	3.4
PROPERTIES: Improves critical strike rating by 28.					
60	Grand Marshal's Sunderer	Bind on Pickup	77.4	Physical 235-353	3.8
PROPERTIES: Improves critical strike rating by 14.					
60	High Warlord's Battle Axe	Bind on Pickup	77.4	Physical 235-353	3.8
PROPERTIES: Improves critical strike rating by 14.					
60	Nightfall	Bind on Equip	67	Physical 187-282	3.5
PROPERTIES: Spell damage taken by target increased by 15% for 5 sec.					
60	Drake Talon Cleaver	Bind on Pickup	73.4	Physical 199-300	3.4
PROPERTIES: Delivers a fatal wound for 240 damage.					
60	Draconic Avenger	Bind on Pickup	68.1	Physical 174-262	3.2
PROPERTIES: Increases your parry rating by 40.					
60	Warrior Axe	Not Bound	97	Physical 271-408	3.5
PROPERTIES: Restores 10 health per 5 sec, Increases your parry rating by 20.					
60	Dark Edge of Insanity	Bind on Pickup	86.6	Physical 242-364	3.5
PROPERTIES: Disorients the target, causing it to wander aimlessly for up to 3 sec.					
60	Neretzek, The Blood Drinker	Bind on Pickup	68.2	Physical 202-303	3.7
PROPERTIES: Steals 141 to 163 life from target enemy.					
60	Severance	Bind on Pickup	81.8	Physical 235-354	3.6
PROPERTIES: Improves critical strike rating by 28.					
70	Felsteel Reaper	Bind on Equip	105.6	Physical 287-431	3.4
PROPERTIES: Increases attack power by 108.					
70	Gladiator's Decapitator	Bind on Pickup	114.7	Physical 330-496	3.6
PROPERTIES: Increases attack power by 64.					
70	Lunar Crescent	Bind on Pickup	105.5	Physical 312-469	3.7
PROPERTIES: Increases attack power by 92.					
70	Mooncleaver	Bind on Pickup	114.6	Physical 339-509	3.7
PROPERTIES: Increases attack power by 98.					
70	Bloodmoon	Bind on Pickup	123.6	Physical 366-549	3.7
PROPERTIES: Increases attack power by 106.					
70	Legacy	Bind on Pickup	105.6	Physical 295-444	3.5
PROPERTIES: Increases attack power by 72, Restores 7 mana per 5 sec.					
70	Gorehowl	Bind on Pickup	111.7	Physical 321-483	3.6
70	Axe of the Gronn Lords	Not Bound	111.7	Physical 321-483	3.6
PROPERTIES: Increases attack power by 110.					
70	Ethereum Nexus-Reaver	Not Bound	108.5	Physical 295-443	3.4

Superior Two Hand Axe

Lvl	Name	Binding Info	DPS	Damage	Speed
15	Boahn's Fang	Bind on Equip	17.6	Physical 35-53	2.5
15	Prospector Axe	Bind on Equip	17.5	Physical 33-51	2.4
18	Night Reaver	Bind on Equip	19.7	Physical 52-78, Shadow +1-5	3.3
PROPERTIES: Sends a shadowy bolt at the enemy causing 60 to 90 Shadow damage.					
18	Taskmaster Axe	Bind on Pickup	19.6	Physical 42-64	2.7
20	The Axe of Severing	Bind on Pickup	21	Physical 50-76	3
21	Killmaim	Bind on Equip	21.7	Physical 55-84	3.2
PROPERTIES: Wounds the target causing them to bleed for 99 damage over 30 sec.					
23	Supercharger Battle Axe	Bind on Equip	23	Physical 51-78	2.8
PROPERTIES: Blasts a target for 80 to 100 Nature damage.					
27	Bloodspiller	Bind on Equip	26.7	Physical 57-87	2.7
PROPERTIES: Wounds the target causing them to bleed for 130 damage over 30 sec.					
28	Burning War Axe	Bind on Equip	27.7	Physical 73-110	3.3
PROPERTIES: Hurls a fiery ball that causes 86 to 110 Fire damage and an additional 18 damage over 6 sec.					
29	Corpsemaker	Bind on Pickup	28.9	Physical 88-132	3.8
32	Thermaplugg's Left Arm	Bind on Pickup	32.6	Physical 70-106	2.7
34	Manslayer	Bind on Equip	34.5	Physical 88-133	3.2
PROPERTIES: Increases attack power by 38.					
35	Obsidian Cleaver	Bind on Equip	35.6	Physical 94-141	3.3
35	Hellslayer Battle Axe	Bind on Equip	35.5	Physical 82-124	2.9
PROPERTIES: Increases attack power by 66 when fighting Undead.					
37	Ravager	Bind on Pickup	37.3	Physical 104-157	3.5
PROPERTIES: You attack all nearby enemies for 9 sec causing weapon damage plus an additional 5 every 3 sec.					
39	Pendulum of Doom	Bind on Equip	38.9	Physical 124-187	4
PROPERTIES: Delivers a fatal wound for 250 to 350 damage.					
43	Executioner's Cleaver	Bind on Equip	41.8	Physical 127-191	3.8
PROPERTIES: Increases your hit rating by 10.					
44	The Minotaur	Bind on Equip	42.7	Physical 109-164	3.2
48	Gatorbite Axe	Bind on Pickup	45.8	Physical 117-176	3.2
PROPERTIES: Wounds the target causing them to bleed for 229 damage over 30 sec.					
49	Bleakwood Hew	Bind on Equip	46.5	Physical 100-151	2.7
PROPERTIES: Enemy is inflicted with the Bleakwood Curse that reduces their magic resistances by 25. Can be applied up to 3 times.					
51	Angerforge's Battle Axe	Bind on Pickup	48.1	Physical 100-150	2.6
51	Lord Alexander's Battle Axe	Bind on Equip	48.1	Physical 123-185	3.2
52	Dark Iron Sunderer	Bind on Equip	48.8	Physical 101-153	2.6
PROPERTIES: Reduces targets armor by 300 for 20 sec.					
53	The Nicker	Bind on Pickup	49.8	Physical 159-239	4
PROPERTIES: Wounds the target for 50 to 150 damage and deals an additional 6 damage every 1 sec for 25 sec.					
53	Waveslicer	Bind on Pickup	49.7	Physical 123-185	3.1
PROPERTIES: Improves critical strike rating by 14.					
54	Dreadforge Retaliator	Bind on Pickup	50.5	Physical 149-225	3.7
PROPERTIES: Increases your parry rating by 20, Improves critical strike rating by 14, Increases attack power by 30.					
57	Gravestone War Axe	Bind on Pickup	53.1	Physical 144-217	3.4
PROPERTIES: Diseases target enemy for 55 Nature damage every 3 sec for 15 sec.					
57	Malicious Axe	Bind on Pickup	52.9	Physical 131-197	3.1
PROPERTIES: Increases attack power by 26.					
58	Arcanite Reaper	Bind on Equip	53.8	Physical 153-256	3.8
PROPERTIES: Increases attack power by 62.					

Superior Two Hand Axe

Lvl	Name	Binding Info	DPS	Damage	Speed
60	Zulian Stone Axe	Bind on Pickup	58.6	Physical 131-197	2.8
PROPERTIES: Increases attack power by 44, Improves critical strike rating by 14.					
60	Gri'lek's Carver	Bind on Pickup	58.5	Physical 182-274	3.9
PROPERTIES: Increases attack power by 117 when fighting Dragonkin.					
61	Warsong Howling Axe	Bind on Pickup	70.3	Physical 174-262	3.1
PROPERTIES: Increases attack power by 80.					
65	Skyforged Great Axe	Bind on Pickup	78.5	Physical 213-321	3.4
PROPERTIES: Increases attack power by 80.					
68	Crow Wing Reaper	Bind on Pickup	93.2	Physical 253-381	3.4
70	Axe of the Nexus-Kings	Bind on Pickup	93.2	Physical 253-381	3.4
PROPERTIES: Increases attack power by 72.					
70	Reaver of the Infinites	Bind on Pickup	93.2	Physical 268-403	3.6
PROPERTIES: Increases attack power by 50.					
70	High Warlord's Decapitator	Bind on Pickup	93.2	Physical 268-403	3.6
PROPERTIES: Increases attack power by 56.					
70	Grand Marshal's Decapitator	Bind on Pickup	93.2	Physical 268-403	3.6
PROPERTIES: Increases attack power by 56.					
70	Hellscream's Will	Bind on Pickup	93.3	Physical 261-392	3.5
PROPERTIES: Increases attack power by 84.					
	Bonebiter	Bind on Pickup	38.8	Physical 105-159	3.4
	Whirlwind Axe	Bind on Pickup	35.6	Physical 102-154	3.6
	Hewing Axe of the Marsh	Bind on Pickup	73.5	Physical 176-265	3
	Honed Voidaxe	Bind on Pickup	81.5	Physical 221-333	3.4
	The Burning Crusader	Bind on Pickup	87.4	Physical 251-378	3.6
PROPERTIES: Increases two-handed axes skill rating by 17.					

BOWS

Epic Bows

Lvl	Name	Binding Info	DPS	Damage	Speed
37	Bow of Searing Arrows	Bind on Equip	30.9	Physical 58-109	2.7
PROPERTIES: Chance to strike your ranged target with a Searing Arrow for 18 to 26 Fire damage.					
48	Hurricane	Bind on Equip	37.8	Physical 42-79	1.6
PROPERTIES: Chance to strike your target with a Frost Arrow for 31 to 45 Frost damage.					
60	Striker's Mark	Bind on Pickup	48.4	Physical 84-158	2.5
PROPERTIES: Increases attack power by 22, Increases your hit rating by 10.					
60	Rhok'delar, Longbow of the Ancient Keepers	Bind on Pickup	53.3	Physical 108-201	2.9
PROPERTIES: Improves critical strike rating by 14, Increases ranged attack power by 17.					
60	Grand Marshal's Bullseye	Bind on Pickup	55.8	Physical 80-121	1.8
PROPERTIES: Increases ranged attack power by 36.					
60	High Warlord's Recurve	Bind on Pickup	55.8	Physical 80-121	1.8
PROPERTIES: Increases ranged attack power by 36.					
60	Heartstriker	Bind on Pickup	53.3	Physical 97-180	2.6
PROPERTIES: Increases attack power by 24.					
60	Mandokir's Sting	Bind on Pickup	46.3	Physical 84-157	2.6
60	Rogue Bow	Bind on Pickup	68.6	Physical 120-223	2.5
PROPERTIES: Restores 2 energy per 5 sec, Fire Resistance +3, Nature Resistance +3, Frost Resistance +3, Shadow Resistance +3, Arcane Resistance +3					
60	Bow of Taut Sinew	Bind on Pickup	47.7	Physical 73-137	2.2
PROPERTIES: Increases attack power by 22, Nature Resistance +8					
60	Huhuran's Stinger	Bind on Pickup	55.7	Physical 105-196	2.7

Epic Bows

Lvl	Name	Binding Info	DPS	Damage	Speed
60	Soulstring	Bind on Pickup	60.7	Physical 123-229	2.9
PROPERTIES: Improves critical strike rating by 14, Increases attack power by 16.					
70	Sunfury Bow of the Phoenix	Bind on Pickup	77.4	Physical 157-292	2.9
PROPERTIES: Increases attack power by 30.					
70	Marksman's Bow	Bind on Pickup	73.8	Physical 206-207	2.8
PROPERTIES: Increases attack power by 22.					
70	Wrathtide Longbow	Bind on Pickup	72	Physical 151-281	3
PROPERTIES: Increases attack power by 28.					

Superior Bows

Lvl	Name	Binding Info	DPS	Damage	Speed
18	Outrider's Bow	Bind on Pickup	15.2	Physical 25-48	2.4
18	Outrunner's Bow	Bind on Pickup	15.2	Physical 25-48	2.4
19	Venomstrike	Bind on Pickup	15.8	Physical 26-50	2.4
PROPERTIES: Chance to strike your ranged target with a Venom Shot for 31 to 45 Nature damage.					
20	Ranger Bow	Bind on Equip	16.1	Physical 30-57	2.7
27	Nightstalker Bow	Bind on Pickup	20.3	Physical 24-45	1.7
27	Harpyclaw Short Bow	Bind on Equip	20.3	Physical 25-48	1.8
28	Outrider's Bow	Bind on Pickup	21.3	Physical 35-67	2.4
28	Outrunner's Bow	Bind on Pickup	21.3	Physical 35-67	2.4
33	Quillshooter	Bind on Equip	25.4	Physical 49-93	2.8
PROPERTIES: Chance to strike your ranged target with a Quill Shot for 66 to 98 Nature damage.					
34	Skystriker Bow	Bind on Equip	26.2	Physical 38-72	2.1
36	Monolithic Bow	Bind on Equip	27.6	Physical 52-97	2.7
38	Outrider's Bow	Bind on Pickup	28.8	Physical 48-90	2.4
38	Outrunner's Bow	Bind on Pickup	28.8	Physical 48-90	2.4
42	Stinging Bow	Bind on Equip	31	Physical 45-85	2.1
PROPERTIES: Increases attack power by 14.					
42	Needle Threader	Bind on Equip	31	Physical 43-81	2
48	Houndmaster's Bow	Bind on Pickup	35	Physical 44-82	1.8
PROPERTIES: Increases attack power by 24 when fighting Beasts.					
48	Outrider's Bow	Bind on Pickup	34.8	Physical 58-109	2.4
48	Outrunner's Bow	Bind on Pickup	34.8	Physical 58-109	2.4
50	Gryphonwing Long Bow	Bind on Equip	36.1	Physical 68-127	2.7
53	Satyr's Bow	Bind on Pickup	38.1	Physical 64-119	2.4
PROPERTIES: Increases your hit rating by 10.					
54	Riphook	Bind on Pickup	38.6	Physical 59-111	2.2
PROPERTIES: Increases attack power by 22.					
55	Screeching Bow	Bind on Pickup	39.1	Physical 90-90	2.3
PROPERTIES: Shadow Resistance +10					
55	Deep Strike Bow	Bind on Pickup	39.3	Physical 74-138	2.7
56	Ancient Bone Bow	Bind on Pickup	39.8	Physical 78-145	2.8
56	Malgen's Long Bow	Bind on Pickup	39.7	Physical 80-150	2.9
PROPERTIES: Increases attack power by 20.					
58	Eaglehorn Long Bow	Bind on Equip	40.8	Physical 51-96	1.8
58	Outrider's Bow	Bind on Pickup	40.8	Physical 68-128	2.4
58	Outrunner's Bow	Bind on Pickup	40.8	Physical 68-128	2.4
60	Hoodoo Hunting Bow	Bind on Pickup	43.9	Physical 86-160	2.8
60	Bland Bow of Steadiness	Bind on Pickup	39	Physical 58-59	1.5
62	Splintermark	Bind on Pickup	53.4	Physical 93-174	2.5
PROPERTIES: Increases attack power by 16.					
62	Splintermark	Bind on Pickup	53.4	Physical 93-174	2.5
PROPERTIES: Increases attack power by 16.					

Superior Bows

Lvl	Name	Binding Info	DPS	Damage	Speed
64	Ethereal Warp-Bow	Bind on Pickup	55.7	Physical 120-181	2.7
68	Skyfire Hawk-Bow	Bind on Pickup	64.6	Physical 108-202	2.4
PROPERTIES: Increases attack power by 26.					
68	Starbolt Longbow	Bind on Pickup	64.5	Physical 126-235	2.8
68	Melmorta's Twilight Longbow	Bind on Pickup	64.5	Physical 135-252	3
PROPERTIES: Increases attack power by 30.					
	Gorewood Bow	Bind on Pickup	40.2	Physical 70-131	2.5
	Verdant Keeper's Aim	Bind on Pickup	34.8	Physical 68-127	2.8
PROPERTIES: Chance to strike your ranged target with Keeper's Sting for 15 to 21 Nature damage.					
	Farstrider's Longbow	Bind on Pickup	14.4	Physical 17-32	1.7

CROSSBOWS

Epic Crossbows

Lvl	Name	Binding Info	DPS	Damage	Speed
60	Grand Marshal's Repeater	Bind on Pickup	55.9	Physical 129-195	2.9
PROPERTIES: Increases ranged attack power by 36.					
60	High Warlord's Crossbow	Bind on Pickup	55.9	Physical 129-195	2.9
PROPERTIES: Increases ranged attack power by 36.					
60	Ashjre'thul, Crossbow of Smiting	Bind on Pickup	55	Physical 149-225	3.4
PROPERTIES: Increases ranged attack power by 36.					
60	Polished Ironwood Crossbow	Bind on Pickup	50	Physical 124-186	3.1
PROPERTIES: Increases attack power by 24, Nature Resistance +7					
60	Crossbow of Imminent Doom	Bind on Pickup	50.8	Physical 126-189	3.1
PROPERTIES: Increases your hit rating by 10.					
60	Nerubian Slavemaker	Bind on Pickup	67.5	Physical 151-281	3.2
PROPERTIES: Increases attack power by 24, Improves critical strike rating by 14.					
70	Gladiator's Heavy Crossbow	Bind on Pickup	79.1	Physical 202-304	3.2
PROPERTIES: Increases ranged attack power by 24.					
70	Steelhawk Crossbow	Bind on Pickup	73.8	Physical 144-269	2.8
PROPERTIES: Increases attack power by 28.					
70	Serpent Spine Crossbow	Bind on Pickup	82.7	Physical 173-323	3
PROPERTIES: Increases attack power by 36.					

Superior Crossbows

Lvl	Name	Binding Info	DPS	Damage	Speed
27	Crystalpine Stinger	Bind on Equip	20.5	Physical 46-69	2.8
35	Swiftwind	Bind on Equip	27	Physical 43-65	2
43	Skull Splitting Crossbow	Bind on Equip	31.7	Physical 66-99	2.6
PROPERTIES: Increases attack power by 14.					
51	Heartseeking Crossbow	Bind on Equip	36.8	Physical 91-137	3.1
PROPERTIES: Chance to strike your ranged target with a Shadowbolt for 13 to 19 Shadow damage.					
54	Blackcrow	Bind on Pickup	38.8	Physical 99-149	3.2
PROPERTIES: Increases your hit rating by 10.					
56	Carapace Spine Crossbow	Bind on Pickup	39.8	Physical 105-158	3.3
57	Stoneshatter	Bind on Pickup	40.3	Physical 93-141	2.9
PROPERTIES: Increases Crossbow skill rating by 9.					
62	Coilfang Needler	Bind on Pickup	53.6	Physical 124-187	2.9
PROPERTIES: Increases attack power by 22.					
68	Emberhawk Crossbow	Bind on Pickup	64.7	Physical 155-233	3
PROPERTIES: Increases attack power by 14.					
70	Adamantine Repeater	Bind on Pickup	66.3	Physical 159-239	3

Superior Crossbows

Lvl	Name	Binding Info	DPS	Damage	Speed
70	High Warlord's Heavy Crossbow	Bind on Pickup	66.4	Physical 170-255	3.2
PROPERTIES: Increases ranged attack power by 22.					
70	Grand Marshal's Heavy Crossbow	Bind on Pickup	66.4	Physical 170-255	3.2
PROPERTIES: Increases ranged attack power by 22.					
	Bloodseeker	Bind on Pickup	40.9	Physical 108-162	3.3
	Fahrad's Reloading Repeater	Bind on Pickup	42	Physical 107-162	3.2
PROPERTIES: Increases your hit rating by 10.					

DAGGERS

Epic Daggers

Lvl	Name	Binding Info	DPS	Damage	Speed
40	Gut Ripper	Bind on Equip	33.9	Physical 42-80	1.8
PROPERTIES: Wounds the target for 95 to 121 damage.					
48	Shadowblade	Bind on Equip	38.9	Physical 38-71	1.4
PROPERTIES: Sends a shadowy bolt at the enemy causing 110 to 140 Shadow damage.					
49	Blade of Eternal Darkness	Bind on Pickup	39.3	Physical 41-77	1.5
PROPERTIES: Chance on landing a damaging spell to deal 100 Shadow damage and restore 100 mana to you, Main Hand Weapon					
58	Felstriker	Bind on Pickup	45.6	Physical 54-101	1.7
PROPERTIES: All attacks are guaranteed to land and will be critical strikes for the next 3 sec.					
58	Alcor's Sunrazor	Bind on Equip	45.4	Physical 41-77	1.3
PROPERTIES: Blasts a target for 75 to 105 Fire damage, Fire Resistance +10					
60	Fang of the Mystics	Bind on Pickup	51.7	Physical 54-101	1.5
PROPERTIES: Increases your spell critical strike rating by 14, Restores 4 mana per 5 sec, Increases damage and healing done by magical spells and effects by up to 40, Main Hand Weapon					
60	Gutgore Ripper	Bind on Pickup	50.6	Physical 63-119	1.8
PROPERTIES: Sends a shadowy bolt at the enemy causing 75 Shadow damage and lowering all stats by 25 for 30 sec.					
60	Core Hound Tooth	Bind on Pickup	51.3	Physical 57-107	1.6
PROPERTIES: Improves critical strike rating by 14, Increases attack power by 20.					
60	Perdition's Blade	Bind on Pickup	58.3	Physical 73-137	1.8
PROPERTIES: Blasts a target for 40 to 56 Fire damage.					
60	Grand Marshal's Dirk	Bind on Pickup	59.5	Physical 95-143	2
PROPERTIES: Improves critical strike rating by 14, Increases attack power by 28.					
60	High Warlord's Razor	Bind on Pickup	59.5	Physical 95-143	2
PROPERTIES: Improves critical strike rating by 14, Increases attack power by 28.					
60	Sorcerous Dagger	Bind on Pickup	47.1	Physical 46-86	1.4
PROPERTIES: Increases damage and healing done by magical spells and effects by up to 20, Main Hand Weapon					
60	Black Amnesty	Bind on Equip	47.8	Physical 53-100	1.6
PROPERTIES: Reduce your threat to the current target making them less likely to attack you.					
60	The Lobotomizer	Bind on Pickup	47.2	Physical 59-111	1.8
PROPERTIES: Wounds the target for 200 to 300 damage and lowers Intellect of target by 25 for 30 sec.					
60	Dragonfang Blade	Bind on Pickup	55.3	Physical 69-130	1.8
60	Claw of Chromaggus	Bind on Pickup	58.3	Physical 61-114	1.5
PROPERTIES: Increases damage and healing done by magical spells and effects by up to 64, Restores 4 mana per 5 sec. Main Hand Weapon					
60	Fang of the Faceless	Bind on Pickup	49.7	Physical 66-123	1.9
PROPERTIES: Improves critical strike rating by 14, Increases attack power by 28.					
60	Fang of Venoxis	Bind on Pickup	47.3	Physical 43-80	1.3
PROPERTIES: Increases damage and healing done by magical spells and effects by up to 24, Restores 6 mana per 5 sec. Main Hand Weapon					
60	Sageclaw	Bind on Pickup	47.4	Physical 56-105	1.7
PROPERTIES: Increases damage and healing done by magical spells and effects by up to 30, Increases your spell critical strike rating by 14. Armor 40. Main Hand Weapon					

Epic Daggers

Lvl	Name	Binding Info	DPS	Damage	Speed
60	Mindfang	Bind on Pickup	47.4	Physical 56-105	1.7
PROPERTIES: Increases damage and healing done by magical spells and effects by up to 30, Increases your spell critical strike rating by 14. Armor 40. Main Hand Weapon					
60	Emerald Dragonfang	Bind on Pickup	52.5	Physical 66-123	1.8
PROPERTIES: Blasts the enemy with acid for 87 to 105 Nature damage.					
60	Death's Sting	Bind on Pickup	66.4	Physical 95-144	1.8
PROPERTIES: Increases attack power by 38, Increases dagger skill rating by 7.					
60	Blessed Qiraji Pugio	Bind on Pickup	60.6	Physical 72-134	1.7
PROPERTIES: Improves critical strike rating by 14, Increases your hit rating by 10, Increases attack power by 18.					
60	Dagger of Veiled Shadows	Bind on Pickup	51.7	Physical 65-121	1.8
PROPERTIES: Increases your hit rating by 10.					
60	Kris of Unspoken Names	Bind on Pickup	51.7	Physical 54-101	1.5
PROPERTIES: Increases damage and healing done by magical spells and effects by up to 59, Main Hand Weapon					
60	Qiraji Sacrificial Dagger	Bind on Pickup	48.2	Physical 64-119	1.9
PROPERTIES: Increases attack power by 20.					
60	Shadowsong's Sorrow	Bind on Pickup	57.4	Physical 68-127	1.7
60	Fang of Korialstrasz	Bind on Pickup	57.5	Physical 72-135	1.8
PROPERTIES: Increases healing done by spells and effects by up to 121, Main Hand Weapon					
60	Kingsfall	Bind on Pickup	73.1	Physical 105-158	1.8
PROPERTIES: Improves critical strike rating by 14, Increases your hit rating by 10.					
60	Midnight Haze	Bind on Pickup	62.8	Physical 79-147	1.8
PROPERTIES: Increases damage and healing done by magical spells and effects by up to 85, Main Hand Weapon					
60	Maexxna's Fang	Bind on Pickup	65.3	Physical 94-141	1.8
PROPERTIES: Increases attack power by 36, Increases your hit rating by 10.					
60	Harbinger of Doom	Bind on Pickup	65.3	Physical 83-126	1.6
PROPERTIES: Improves critical strike rating by 14, Increases your hit rating by 10.					
60	Grand Marshal's Mageblade	Bind on Pickup	59.5	Physical 83-155	2
PROPERTIES: Increases damage and healing done by magical spells and effects by up to 72, Increases your spell critical strike rating by 14. Main Hand Weapon					
60	High Warlord's Spellblade	Bind on Pickup	59.5	Physical 83-155	2
PROPERTIES: Increases damage and healing done by magical spells and effects by up to 72, Increases your spell critical strike rating by 14. Main Hand Weapon					
60	High Warlord's Spellblade	Bind on Pickup	59.5	Physical 83-155	2
PROPERTIES: Increases damage and healing done by magical spells and effects by up to 72, Increases your spell critical strike rating by 14. Main Hand Weapon					
70	Eternium Runed Blade	Bind on Equip	74.4	Physical 88-165	1.7
PROPERTIES: Increases damage and healing done by magical spells and effects by up to 180, Main Hand Weapon					
70	Dirge	Bind on Equip	81.1	Physical 79-148	1.4
PROPERTIES: Increases attack power by 36.					
70	Gladiator's Spellblade	Bind on Pickup	88.1	Physical 98-184	1.6
PROPERTIES: Increases damage and healing done by magical spells and effects by up to 187, Main Hand Weapon					
70	Gladiator's Shiv	Bind on Pickup	87.9	Physical 98-148	1.4
PROPERTIES: Increases attack power by 28.					
70	Gladiator's Shanker	Bind on Pickup	88.3	Physical 127-191	1.8
PROPERTIES: Increases attack power by 28.					
70	Emerald Ripper	Bind on Pickup	81.4	Physical 117-176	1.8
PROPERTIES: Increases attack power by 32.					
70	Blade of the Unrequited	Bind on Pickup	81.3	Physical 104-156	1.6
PROPERTIES: Increases attack power by 14.					
70	Malchazeen	Bind on Pickup	85.8	Physical 123-186	1.8
PROPERTIES: Increases attack power by 46.					
70	Nathrezim Mindblade	Bind on Pickup	85.8	Physical 108-201	1.8

Epic Daggers

Lvl	Name	Binding Info	DPS	Damage	Speed
40	Gut Ripper	Bind on Equip	33.9	Physical 42-80	1.8
PROPERTIES: Wounds the target for 95 to 121 damage.					
48	Shadowblade	Bind on Equip	38.9	Physical 38-71	1.4
PROPERTIES: Sends a shadowy bolt at the enemy causing 110 to 140 Shadow damage.					
49	Blade of Eternal Darkness	Bind on Pickup	39.3	Physical 41-77	1.5
PROPERTIES: Chance on landing a damaging spell to deal 100 Shadow damage and restore 100 mana to you, Main Hand Weapon					
58	Felstriker	Bind on Pickup	45.6	Physical 54-101	1.7
PROPERTIES: All attacks are guaranteed to land and will be critical strikes for the next 3 sec.					
58	Alcor's Sunrazor	Bind on Equip	45.4	Physical 41-77	1.3
PROPERTIES: Blasts a target for 75 to 105 Fire damage, Fire Resistance +10					
60	Fang of the Mystics	Bind on Pickup	51.7	Physical 54-101	1.5
PROPERTIES: Increases your spell critical strike rating by 14, Restores 4 mana per 5 sec, Increases damage and healing done by magical spells and effects by up to 40, Main Hand Weapon					
60	Gutgore Ripper	Bind on Pickup	50.6	Physical 63-119	1.8
PROPERTIES: Sends a shadowy bolt at the enemy causing 75 Shadow damage and lowering all stats by 25 for 30 sec.					
60	Core Hound Tooth	Bind on Pickup	51.3	Physical 57-107	1.6
PROPERTIES: Improves your critical strike rating by 14, Increases attack power by 20.					
60	Perdition's Blade	Bind on Pickup	58.3	Physical 73-137	1.8
PROPERTIES: Blasts a target for 40 to 56 Fire damage.					
60	Grand Marshal's Dirk	Bind on Pickup	59.5	Physical 95-143	2
PROPERTIES: Improves your critical strike rating by 14, Increases attack power by 28.					
60	High Warlord's Razor	Bind on Pickup	59.5	Physical 95-143	2
PROPERTIES: Improves your critical strike rating by 14, Increases attack power by 28.					
60	Sorcerous Dagger	Bind on Pickup	47.1	Physical 46-86	1.4
PROPERTIES: Increases damage and healing done by magical spells and effects by up to 20, Main Hand Weapon					
60	Black Amnesty	Bind on Equip	47.8	Physical 53-100	1.6
PROPERTIES: Reduce your threat to the current target making them less likely to attack you.					
60	The Lobotomizer	Bind on Pickup	47.2	Physical 59-111	1.8
PROPERTIES: Wounds the target for 200 to 300 damage and lowers Intellect of target by 25 for 30 sec.					
60	Dragonfang Blade	Bind on Pickup	55.3	Physical 69-130	1.8
60	Claw of Chromaggus	Bind on Pickup	58.3	Physical 61-114	1.5
PROPERTIES: Increases damage and healing done by magical spells and effects by up to 64, Restores 4 mana per 5 sec. Main Hand Weapon					
60	Fang of the Faceless	Bind on Pickup	49.7	Physical 66-123	1.9
PROPERTIES: Improves your critical strike rating by 14, Increases attack power by 28.					
60	Fang of Venoxis	Bind on Pickup	47.3	Physical 43-80	1.3
PROPERTIES: Increases damage and healing done by magical spells and effects by up to 24, Restores 6 mana per 5 sec. Main Hand Weapon					
60	Sageclaw	Bind on Pickup	47.4	Physical 56-105	1.7
PROPERTIES: Increases damage and healing done by magical spells and effects by up to 30, Increases your spell critical strike rating by 14. Armor 40. Main Hand Weapon					
60	Mindfang	Bind on Pickup	47.4	Physical 56-105	1.7
PROPERTIES: Increases damage and healing done by magical spells and effects by up to 30, Increases your spell critical strike rating by 14. Armor 40. Main Hand Weapon					
60	Rogue Dagger	Bind on Pickup	74.5	Physical 104-194	2
PROPERTIES: Increases your Dodge rating by 12, Fire Resistance +2, Nature Resistance +2, Frost Resistance +2, Shadow Resistance +2, Arcane Resistance +3					
60	Emerald Dragonfang	Bind on Pickup	52.5	Physical 66-123	1.8
PROPERTIES: Blasts the enemy with acid for 87 to 105 Nature damage.					
60	Death's Sting	Bind on Pickup	66.4	Physical 95-144	1.8
PROPERTIES: Increases attack power by 38, Increases dagger skill rating by 7.					

Epic Daggers

Lvl	Name	Binding Info	DPS	Damage	Speed
60	Blessed Qiraji Pugio	Bind on Pickup	60.6	Physical 72-134	1.7
PROPERTIES: Improves your critical strike rating by 14, Increases your hit rating by 10, Increases attack power by 18.					
60	Dagger of Veiled Shadows	Bind on Pickup	51.7	Physical 65-121	1.8
PROPERTIES: Increases your hit rating by 10.					
60	Kris of Unspoken Names	Bind on Pickup	51.7	Physical 54-101	1.5
PROPERTIES: Increases damage and healing done by magical spells and effects by up to 59, Main Hand Weapon					
60	Qiraji Sacrificial Dagger	Bind on Pickup	48.2	Physical 64-119	1.9
PROPERTIES: Increases attack power by 20.					
60	Shadowsong's Sorrow	Bind on Pickup	57.4	Physical 68-127	1.7
60	Fang of Korialstrasz	Bind on Pickup	57.5	Physical 72-135	1.8
PROPERTIES: Increases healing done by spells and effects by up to 121, Main Hand Weapon					
60	Kingsfall	Bind on Pickup	73.1	Physical 105-158	1.8
PROPERTIES: Improves your critical strike rating by 14, Increases your hit rating by 10.					
60	Midnight Haze	Bind on Pickup	62.8	Physical 79-147	1.8
PROPERTIES: Increases damage and healing done by magical spells and effects by up to 85, Main Hand Weapon					
60	Maexxna's Fang	Bind on Pickup	65.3	Physical 94-141	1.8
PROPERTIES: Increases attack power by 36, Increases your hit rating by 10.					
60	Harbinger of Doom	Bind on Pickup	65.3	Physical 83-126	1.6
PROPERTIES: Improves your critical strike rating by 14, Increases your hit rating by 10.					
60	Grand Marshal's Mageblade	Bind on Pickup	59.5	Physical 83-155	2
PROPERTIES: Increases damage and healing done by magical spells and effects by up to 72, Increases your spell critical strike rating by 14. Main Hand Weapon					
60	High Warlord's Spellblade	Bind on Pickup	59.5	Physical 83-155	2
PROPERTIES: Increases damage and healing done by magical spells and effects by up to 72, Increases your spell critical strike rating by 14. Main Hand Weapon					
60	High Warlord's Spellblade	Bind on Pickup	59.5	Physical 83-155	2
PROPERTIES: Increases damage and healing done by magical spells and effects by up to 72, Increases your spell critical strike rating by 14. Main Hand Weapon					
70	Eternium Runed Blade	Bind on Equip	74.4	Physical 88-165	1.7
PROPERTIES: Increases damage and healing done by magical spells and effects by up to 180, Main Hand Weapon					
70	Dirge	Bind on Equip	81.1	Physical 79-148	1.4
PROPERTIES: Increases attack power by 36.					
70	Gladiator's Spellblade	Bind on Pickup	88.1	Physical 98-184	1.6
PROPERTIES: Increases damage and healing done by magical spells and effects by up to 187, Main Hand Weapon					
70	Gladiator's Shiv	Bind on Pickup	87.9	Physical 98-148	1.4
PROPERTIES: Increases attack power by 28.					
70	Gladiator's Shanker	Bind on Pickup	88.3	Physical 127-191	1.8
PROPERTIES: Increases attack power by 28.					
70	Emerald Ripper	Bind on Pickup	81.4	Physical 117-176	1.8
PROPERTIES: Increases attack power by 32.					
70	Blade of the Unrequited	Bind on Pickup	81.3	Physical 104-156	1.6
PROPERTIES: Increases attack power by 14.					
70	Malchazeen	Bind on Pickup	85.8	Physical 123-186	1.8
PROPERTIES: Increases attack power by 46.					
70	Nathrezim Mindblade	Bind on Pickup	85.8	Physical 108-201	1.8
PROPERTIES: Increases damage and healing done by magical spells and effects by up to 178, Main Hand Weapon					
70	Guile of Khoraazi	Bind on Pickup	79.1	Physical 101-152	1.6
PROPERTIES: Increases attack power by 50.					
70	Retainer's Blade	Bind on Pickup	78.7	Physical 94-142	1.5

Epic Daggers

Lvl	Name	Binding Info	DPS	Damage	Speed
70	Riftmaker	Bind on Pickup	78.9	Physical 120-180	1.9
PROPERTIES: Encloses enemy in a temporal rift, increasing the time between their attacks by 10% for 10 sec, Increases attack power by 20.					
70	Searing Sunblade	Bind on Pickup	78.5	Physical 71-133	1.3
PROPERTIES: Off Hand Weapon					
70	Feltooth Eviscerator	Bind on Pickup	78.9	Physical 77-144	1.4
PROPERTIES: Increases attack power by 32.					
70	Vileblade of the Betrayer	Bind on Pickup	78.9	Physical 113-171	1.8
PROPERTIES: Increases attack power by 56.					
70	Heartrazor	Bind on Pickup	88.1	Physical 111-206	1.8
PROPERTIES: Increases attack power by 250 for 10 sec.					
70	Fang of Vashj	Bind on Pickup	92.8	Physical 133-201	1.8
PROPERTIES: Increases attack power by 50, Increases dagger skill rating by 14.					
70	Talon of the Tempest	Bind on Pickup	83.6	Physical 105-196	1.8
PROPERTIES: Increases damage and healing done by magical spells and effects by up to 168, Main Hand Weapon					
	Keanna's Will	Bind on Pickup	51.7	Physical 65-121	1.8
PROPERTIES: Increases healing done by spells and effects by up to 31, Main Hand Weapon					

Superior Daggers

Lvl	Name	Binding Info	DPS	Damage	Speed
18	Evocator's Blade	Bind on Equip	15.3	Physical 17-32	1.6
18	Scout's Blade	Bind on Pickup	15.3	Physical 18-34	1.7
18	Sentinel's Blade	Bind on Pickup	15.3	Physical 18-34	1.7
19	Assassin's Blade	Bind on Equip	15.5	Physical 20-39	1.9
20	Blackfang	Bind on Equip	16.3	Physical 17-32	1.5
PROPERTIES: Shadow Resistance +5					
20	Doomspike	Bind on Equip	16.3	Physical 17-32	1.5
21	Prison Shank	Bind on Pickup	16.7	Physical 21-39	1.8
21	Blackvenom Blade	Bind on Equip	16.7	Physical 21-39, Shadow +1-7	1.8
PROPERTIES: Poisons target for 5 Nature damage every 3 sec for 15 sec.					
21	Talon of Vultros	Bind on Equip	16.8	Physical 23-44	2
23	Bite of Serra'kis	Bind on Pickup	17.7	Physical 16-30	1.3
PROPERTIES: Poisons target for 4 Nature damage every 2 sec for 20 sec.					
24	Meteor Shard	Bind on Pickup	18.3	Physical 23-43	1.8
PROPERTIES: Blasts a target for 35 Fire damage.					
26	Vendetta	Bind on Equip	19.2	Physical 17-33	1.3
27	Claw of the Shadowmancer	Bind on Equip	20.5	Physical 27-51	1.9
PROPERTIES: Sends a shadowy bolt at the enemy causing 35 Shadow damage.					
27	Toxic Revenger	Bind on Pickup	20.5	Physical 27-51	1.9
PROPERTIES: Deals 5 Nature damage every 5 sec to any enemy in an 8 yard radius around the caster for 15 sec.					
28	Scout's Blade	Bind on Pickup	21.2	Physical 25-47	1.7
28	Sentinel's Blade	Bind on Pickup	21.2	Physical 25-47	1.7
29	Torturing Poker	Bind on Pickup	22.1	Physical 26-49, Fire +5-7	1.7
30	Swinetusk Shank	Bind on Pickup	23	Physical 24-45	1.5
30	Scorn's Focal Dagger	Bind on Pickup	22.9	Physical 22-42	1.4
PROPERTIES: Increases damage and healing done by magical spells and effects by up to 9, Main Hand Weapon					
31	Howling Blade	Bind on Equip	23.9	Physical 23-44	1.4
PROPERTIES: Reduces target's attack power by 30 for 30 sec.					
31	Stonevault Shiv	Bind on Equip	24	Physical 25-47	1.5

Superior Daggers

Lvl	Name	Binding Info	DPS	Damage	Speed
32	Sliverblade	Bind on Equip	25	Physical 24-46	1.4
PROPERTIES: Blasts a target for 45 Frost damage.					
34	Hypnotic Blade	Bind on Pickup	26.8	Physical 26-49	1.4
PROPERTIES: Increases damage and healing done by magical spells and effects by up to 9, Main Hand Weapon					
34	The Ziggler	Bind on Equip	26.5	Physical 31-59	1.7
PROPERTIES: Blasts a target for 10 to 20 Nature damage.					
38	Scout's Blade	Bind on Pickup	29.1	Physical 34-65	1.7
38	Sentinel's Blade	Bind on Pickup	29.1	Physical 34-65	1.7
39	Coldrage Dagger	Bind on Pickup	29.7	Physical 31-58	1.5
PROPERTIES: Launches a bolt of frost at the enemy causing 20 to 30 Frost damage and slowing movement speed by 50% for 5 sec.					
42	Widowmaker	Bind on Equip	31.6	Physical 42-78	1.9
42	Gutwrencher	Bind on Equip	31.6	Physical 35-66	1.6
PROPERTIES: Wounds the target causing them to bleed for 80 damage over 30 sec.					
44	Stealthblade	Bind on Equip	32.9	Physical 32-60	1.4
PROPERTIES: Reduces threat level on all enemies by a small amount for 10 sec.					
45	Satyr's Lash	Bind on Pickup	33.2	Physical 39-74	1.7
PROPERTIES: Sends a shadowy bolt at the enemy causing 55 to 85 Shadow damage.					
46	Searing Needle	Bind on Equip	33.9	Physical 42-80	1.8
PROPERTIES: Blasts a target for 60 Fire damage and increases damage done to target by Fire damage by 10 for 30 sec, Main Hand Weapon					
48	Scout's Blade	Bind on Pickup	35	Physical 41-78	1.7
48	Sentinel's Blade	Bind on Pickup	35	Physical 41-78	1.7
49	Hookfang Shanker	Bind on Equip	35.7	Physical 35-65	1.4
PROPERTIES: Corrosive acid that deals 7 Nature damage every 3 sec and lowers target's armor by 50 for 30 sec.					
49	Charstone Dirk	Bind on Pickup	35.9	Physical 40-75	1.6
PROPERTIES: Restores 2 mana per 5 sec, Main Hand Weapon					
50	Julie's Dagger	Bind on Equip	36.5	Physical 33-62	1.3
PROPERTIES: Heals wielder of 78 damage over 12 sec.					
50	Barman Shanker	Bind on Pickup	36.5	Physical 51-95	2
PROPERTIES: Wounds the target causing them to bleed for 99 damage over 30 sec, Main Hand Weapon					
51	Dire Nail	Bind on Pickup	36.7	Physical 38-72	1.5
PROPERTIES: Shadow Resistance +5, Ramdom Property					
52	Blood-etched Blade	Bind on Pickup	37.7	Physical 39-74	1.5
PROPERTIES: Increases damage and healing done by magical spells and effects by up to 6, Main Hand Weapon					
52	Flarethorn	Bind on Pickup	37.5	Physical 47-88	1.8
PROPERTIES: Increases damage done by Fire spells and effects by up to 17, Main Hand Weapon					
52	The Shadowfoot Stabber	Bind on Equip	37.5	Physical 47-88	1.8
PROPERTIES: Increases attack power by 18.					
55	Keris of Zul'Serak	Bind on Pickup	39.4	Physical 49-93	1.8
PROPERTIES: Inflicts numbing pain that deals 10 Nature damage every 2 sec and increases time between target's attacks by 10% for 10 sec.					
55	Crystal Tipped Stiletto	Bind on Pickup	39.5	Physical 52-98	1.9
PROPERTIES: Increases attack power by 24.					
56	Fang of the Crystal Spider	Bind on Pickup	40.3	Physical 45-84	1.6
PROPERTIES: Slows target enemy's casting speed and increases the time between melee and ranged attacks by 10% for 10 sec.					
56	Frightalon	Bind on Pickup	40	Physical 39-73	1.4
PROPERTIES: Lowers all attributes of target by 10 for 1 min.					
57	Bonescraper	Bind on Pickup	40.7	Physical 40-74	1.4
PROPERTIES: Increases attack power by 30.					

Superior Daggers

Lvl	Name	Binding Info	DPS	Damage	Speed
57	Witchblade	Bind on Pickup	40.6	Physical 45-85	1.6
PROPERTIES: Increases damage and healing done by magical spells and effects by up to 14, Main Hand Weapon					
57	Blade of the New Moon	Bind on Pickup	40.7	Physical 40-74	1.4
PROPERTIES: Increases damage done by Shadow spells and effects by up to 19, Main Hand Weapon					
57	Distracting Dagger	Bind on Pickup	40.8	Physical 42-64	1.3
PROPERTIES: Increases dagger skill rating by 14, Off Hand Weapon					
57	Specter's Blade	Bind on Pickup	40.8	Physical 51-96	1.8
PROPERTIES: Increases attack power by 45 when fighting Undead.					
58	Scarlet Kris	Bind on Equip	41.3	Physical 43-81	1.5
58	Finkle's Skinner	Bind on Pickup	40.4	Physical 39-66	1.3
PROPERTIES: Skinning Resistance +10, Off Hand Weapon					
58	Finkle's Skinner	Bind on Pickup	41.2	Physical 37-70	1.3
PROPERTIES: Skinning Resistance +10, Increases attack power by 45 when fighting Beasts. Main Hand Weapon					
58	Heartseeker	Bind on Equip	41.5	Physical 49-92	1.7
PROPERTIES: Improves your critical strike rating by 14.					
58	Gift of the Elven Magi	Bind on Pickup	41.3	Physical 43-81	1.5
58	Scout's Blade	Bind on Pickup	41.5	Physical 49-92	1.7
58	Sentinel's Blade	Bind on Pickup	41.5	Physical 49-92	1.7
60	Glacial Blade	Bind on Pickup	42.5	Physical 53-100	1.8
PROPERTIES: Blasts a target for 45 Frost damage.					
60	Electrified Dagger	Bind on Pickup	42.5	Physical 53-100	1.8
PROPERTIES: Blasts a target for 45 Nature damage.					
60	Wushoolay's Poker	Bind on Pickup	45	Physical 50-94	1.6
PROPERTIES: Increases healing done by spells and effects by up to 31, Restores 6 mana per 5 sec. Main Hand Weapon					
60	Dark Whisper Blade	Bind on Equip	42.5	Physical 41-78	1.4
PROPERTIES: Increases damage and healing done by magical spells and effects by up to 19, Main Hand Weapon					
60	The Lost Kris of Zedd	Bind on Equip	45	Physical 47-88	1.5
PROPERTIES: Increases your spell critical strike rating by 14, Increases damage and healing done by magical spells and effects by up to 14. Main Hand Weapon					
62	Wastewalker Shiv	Bind on Pickup	55.3	Physical 69-130	1.8
PROPERTIES: Increases attack power by 28, Main Hand Weapon					
62	Hardened Stone Shard	Bind on Pickup	55.3	Physical 79-120	1.8
PROPERTIES: Increases attack power by 22.					
63	Zangartooth Shortblade	Bind on Pickup	56.7	Physical 59-111	1.5
PROPERTIES: Increases damage and healing done by magical spells and effects by up to 61, Main Hand Weapon					
63	The Stalker's Fang	Bind on Pickup	56.7	Physical 71-133	1.8
PROPERTIES: Increases attack power by 20.					
63	Nethershard	Bind on Pickup	56.5	Physical 67-125	1.7
PROPERTIES: Increases damage and healing done by magical spells and effects by up to 61.					
66	Chronoblade Dagger	Bind on Pickup	62.6	Physical 74-139	1.7
PROPERTIES: Increases damage and healing done by magical spells and effects by up to 85, Main Hand Weapon					
68	Starlight Dagger	Bind on Pickup	69.7	Physical 73-136	1.5
PROPERTIES: Increases damage and healing done by magical spells and effects by up to 121, Main Hand Weapon					
68	Twinblade of Mastery	Bind on Pickup	69.3	Physical 77-117	1.4
PROPERTIES: Increases dagger skill rating by 11.					
68	Runesong Dagger	Bind on Pickup	69.7	Physical 73-136	1.5
PROPERTIES: Increases damage and healing done by magical spells and effects by up to 121, Main Hand Weapon					

Superior Daggers

Lvl	Name	Binding Info	DPS	Damage	Speed
68	Runed Dagger of Solace	Bind on Pickup	69.7	Physical 73-136	1.5
PROPERTIES: Increases healing done by spells and effects by up to 227, Main Hand Weapon					
70	Terror Flame Dagger	Bind on Pickup	71.7	Physical 103-155	1.8
PROPERTIES: Increases attack power by 34.					
70	Whispering Blade of Slaying	Bind on Pickup	71.8	Physical 109-164	1.9
PROPERTIES: Increases attack power by 26, Increases dagger skill rating by 15.					
70	Timeslicer	Bind on Pickup	71.8	Physical 80-121	1.4
PROPERTIES: Increases attack power by 30, Increases dagger skill rating by 15.					
70	Warp Splinter's Thorn	Bind on Pickup	71.5	Physical 74-112	1.3
70	Backsplitter	Bind on Pickup	71.7	Physical 103-155	1.8
PROPERTIES: Increases attack power by 30.					
70	High Warlord's Shanker	Bind on Pickup	71.7	Physical 103-155	1.8
PROPERTIES: Increases attack power by 26.					
70	High Warlord's Shiv	Bind on Pickup	71.8	Physical 80-121	1.4
PROPERTIES: Increases attack power by 26.					
70	High Warlord's Spellblade	Bind on Pickup	71.6	Physical 80-149	1.6
PROPERTIES: Increases damage and healing done by magical spells and effects by up to 121, Main Hand Weapon					
70	Grand Marshal's Shanker	Bind on Pickup	71.7	Physical 103-155	1.8
PROPERTIES: Increases attack power by 26.					
70	Grand Marshal's Shiv	Bind on Pickup	71.8	Physical 80-121	1.4
PROPERTIES: Increases attack power by 26.					
70	Grand Marshal's Spellblade	Bind on Pickup	71.6	Physical 80-149	1.6
PROPERTIES: Increases damage and healing done by magical spells and effects by up to 121, Main Hand Weapon					
	Black Menace	Bind on Pickup	29.7	Physical 31-58	1.5
PROPERTIES: Sends a shadowy bolt at the enemy causing 30 Shadow damage.					
	Lifeforce Dirk	Bind on Pickup	35.9	Physical 40-75	1.6
	Darrowspike	Bind on Pickup	41.3	Physical 43-81	1.5
PROPERTIES: Blasts a target for 90 Frost damage.					
	Lorespinner	Bind on Pickup	37.7	Physical 45-68	1.5
PROPERTIES: Restores 3 mana per 5 sec, Main Hand Weapon					
	Glacial Spike	Bind on Pickup	34.6	Physical 31-59	1.3
PROPERTIES: Your Frostbolt spells have a 6% chance to restore 50 mana when cast.					
	The Thunderwood Poker	Bind on Pickup	42.5	Physical 53-100	1.8
	Shivsprocket's Shiv	Bind on Pickup	42.7	Physical 44-84	1.5
PROPERTIES: Increases damage and healing done by magical spells and effects by up to 13, Main Hand Weapon					
	Verimonde's Last Resort	Bind on Pickup	43.2	Physical 42-79	1.4
PROPERTIES: Increases damage and healing done by magical spells and effects by up to 19, Main Hand Weapon					
	Dawnblade	Bind on Pickup	13.8	Physical 15-29	1.6
	Ceremonial Warmaul Blood-blade	Bind on Pickup	62.6	Physical 74-139	1.7
PROPERTIES: Increases attack power by 26.					
	Azure Lightblade	Bind on Pickup	60.3	Physical 72-109	1.5
PROPERTIES: Increases healing done by spells and effects by up to 143, Main Hand Weapon					
	Twin-Bladed Ripper	Bind on Pickup	66.9	Physical 84-157	1.8
PROPERTIES: Increases attack power by 24, Increases dagger skill rating by 7.					

FIST

Epic Fist Weapons

Lvl	Name	Binding Info	DPS	Damage	Speed
60	Eskhandar's Left Claw	Bind on Pickup	48	Physical 50-94	1.5
PROPERTIES: Slows enemy's movement by 60% and causes them to bleed for 150 damage over 30 sec. Off Hand Weapon.					
60	Eskhandar's Right Claw	Bind on Pickup	48	Physical 50-94	1.5
PROPERTIES: Increases your haste rating by 300 for 5 sec. Main Hand Weapon.					
60	Grand Marshal's Right Hand Blade	Bind on Pickup	59.5	Physical 138-207	2.9
PROPERTIES: Improves your critical strike rating by 14, Increases attack power by 28. Main Hand Weapon.					
60	High Warlord's Right Claw	Bind on Pickup	59.5	Physical 138-207	2.9
PROPERTIES: Improves your critical strike rating by 14, Increases attack power by 28. Main Hand Weapon.					
60	Grand Marshal's Left Hand Blade	Bind on Pickup	59.5	Physical 138-207	2.9
PROPERTIES: Improves your critical strike rating by 14, Increases attack power by 28. Off Hand Weapon.					
60	High Warlord's Left Claw	Bind on Pickup	59.5	Physical 138-207	2.9
PROPERTIES: Improves your critical strike rating by 14, Increases attack power by 28. Off Hand Weapon.					
60	Claw of the Black Drake	Bind on Pickup	56.3	Physical 102-191	2.6
PROPERTIES: Improves your critical strike rating by 14. Main Hand Weapon.					
60	Thekal's Grasp	Bind on Pickup	47	Physical 72-135	2.2
PROPERTIES: Improves your critical strike rating by 14. Main Hand Weapon.					
60	Arlokk's Grasp	Bind on Pickup	47	Physical 49-92	1.5
PROPERTIES: Sends a shadowy bolt at the enemy causing 55 to 85 Shadow damage. Off Hand Weapon.					
60	Silithid Claw	Bind on Pickup	57.5	Physical 64-120	1.6
PROPERTIES: Improves your critical strike rating by 14, Increases attack power by 30. Main Hand Weapon.					
60	Claw of the Frost Wyrm	Bind on Pickup	71.7	Physical 75-140	1.5
PROPERTIES: Improves your critical strike rating by 14, Increases your hit rating by 10, Increases attack power by 22. Off Hand Weapon.					
70	Gladiator's Right Ripper	Bind on Pickup	88.1	Physical 160-298	2.6
PROPERTIES: Increases attack power by 28. Main Hand Weapon.					
70	Gladiator's Left Ripper	Bind on Pickup	88.1	Physical 111-206	1.8
PROPERTIES: Increases attack power by 28. Off Hand Weapon.					
70	Big Bad Wolf's Claw	Bind on Pickup	81.2	Physical 142-264	2.5
PROPERTIES: Main Hand Weapon.					
70	The Bladefist	Bind on Pickup	78.8	Physical 143-267	2.6
PROPERTIES: Increases your haste rating by 170 for 10 sec. Main Hand Weapon.					
70	Talon of the Phoenix	Bind on Pickup	88	Physical 92-172	1.5
PROPERTIES: Increases attack power by 32. Off Hand Weapon.					

Superior Fist Weapons

Lvl	Name	Binding Info	DPS	Damage	Speed
21	Iron Knuckles	Bind on Pickup	16.5	Physical 19-37	1.7
PROPERTIES: Pummel the target for 4 damage and interrupt the spell being cast for 5 sec.					
46	Vilerend Slicer	Bind on Equip	33.9	Physical 33-62	1.4
PROPERTIES: Wounds the target for 75 damage. Main Hand Weapon.					
47	Claw of Celebras	Bind on Pickup	34.4	Physical 43-81	1.8
PROPERTIES: Poisons target for 9 Nature damage every 2 sec for 20 sec. Off Hand Weapon.					
51	Bloodfist	Bind on Pickup	36.7	Physical 38-72	1.5
PROPERTIES: Wounds the target for 20 damage.					

Superior Fist Weapons

Lvl	Name	Binding Info	DPS	Damage	Speed
54	Gargoyle Shredder Talons	Bind on Pickup	38.9	Physical 49-91	1.8
PROPERTIES: Wounds the target causing them to bleed for 110 damage over 30 sec. Off Hand Weapon.					
55	Blood Talon	Bind on Pickup	39.2	Physical 35-67	1.3
PROPERTIES: Wounds the target causing them to bleed for 99 damage over 30 sec. Main Hand Weapon.					
55	Hurd Smasher	Bind on Pickup	39.4	Physical 49-93	1.8
PROPERTIES: Knocks target silly for 2 sec.					
56	Lefty's Brass Knuckle	Bind on Pickup	40	Physical 42-78	1.5
56	Willey's Back Scratcher	Bind on Pickup	40.2	Physical 73-136	2.6
PROPERTIES: Increases attack power by 10. Main Hand Weapon.					
64	Creepjacker	Bind on Pickup	58.3	Physical 106-197	2.6
PROPERTIES: Increases attack power by 28. Main Hand Weapon.					
68	Boggspine Knuckles	Bind on Pickup	69.4	Physical 126-235	2.6
PROPERTIES: Increases attack power by 10. Off Hand Weapon.					
68	Claw of the Watcher	Bind on Pickup	69.4	Physical 121-226	2.5
PROPERTIES: Increases attack power by 24. Main Hand Weapon.					
68	Stormreaver Warblades	Bind on Pickup	69.4	Physical 77-145	1.6
PROPERTIES: Increases attack power by 22. Off Hand Weapon.					
68	Reflex Blades	Bind on Pickup	69.4	Physical 131-244	2.7
PROPERTIES: Increases attack power by 32. Main Hand Weapon.					
70	Demonblood Eviscerator	Bind on Pickup	71.7	Physical 130-243	2.6
PROPERTIES: Increases attack power by 28, Increases fist weapons skill rating by 17. Main Hand Weapon.					
70	High Warlord's Left Ripper	Bind on Pickup	71.7	Physical 90-168	1.8
PROPERTIES: Increases attack power by 26. Off Hand Weapon.					
70	High Warlord's Right Ripper	Bind on Pickup	71.7	Physical 130-243	2.6
PROPERTIES: Increases attack power by 26. Main Hand Weapon.					
70	Grand Marshal's Left Ripper	Bind on Pickup	71.7	Physical 90-168	1.8
PROPERTIES: Increases attack power by 26. Off Hand Weapon.					
70	Grand Marshal's Right Ripper	Bind on Pickup	71.7	Physical 130-243	2.6
PROPERTIES: Increases attack power by 26. Main Hand Weapon.					
	Devilsaur Claws	Bind on Pickup	34.5	Physical 48-90	2
PROPERTIES: Increases your hit rating by 10. Main Hand Weapon.					
	Devilsaur Claws	Bind on Pickup	34.5	Physical 48-90	2
PROPERTIES: Increases fist weapons skill rating by 9. Off Hand Weapon.					
	Sporeling Claw	Bind on Pickup	56.6	Physical 99-184	2.5
PROPERTIES: Increases attack power by 24.					
	Mag'hari Fury Brand	Bind on Pickup	62.6	Physical 109-204	2.5
PROPERTIES: Increases attack power by 26.					

GUNS

Epic Guns

Lvl	Name	Binding Info	DPS	Damage	Speed
43	Precisely Calibrated Boomstick	Bind on Equip	34.7	Physical 48-56	1.5
53	Dwarven Hand Cannon	Bind on Equip	41	Physical 83-155	2.9
PROPERTIES: Chance to strike your ranged target with a Flaming Cannonball for 33 to 49 Fire damage.					
60	Blastershot Launcher	Bind on Pickup	49.2	Physical 89-167	2.6
PROPERTIES: Improves your critical strike rating by 14.					
60	Core Marksman Rifle	Bind on Equip	45.4	Physical 79-148	2.5
PROPERTIES: Increases ranged attack power by 22, Increases your hit rating by 10.					

Epic Guns

Lvl	Name	Binding Info	DPS	Damage	Speed
60	Grand Marshal's Hand Cannon	Bind on Pickup	55.9	Physical 129-195	2.9
PROPERTIES: Increases ranged attack power by 36.					
60	High Warlord's Street Sweeper	Bind on Pickup	55.9	Physical 129-195	2.9
PROPERTIES: Increases ranged attack power by 36.					
60	Dragonbreath Hand Cannon	Bind on Pickup	53.2	Physical 104-194	2.8
60	Gurubashi Dwarf Destroyer	Bind on Pickup	47.7	Physical 93-174	2.8
PROPERTIES: Increases attack power by 30.					
60	Warrior Gun	Bind on Equip	68.6	Physical 120-223	2.5
PROPERTIES: Improves your critical strike rating by 14, Fire Resistance +3, Nature Resistance +2, Frost Resistance +2, Shadow Resistance +2, Arcane Resistance +2					
60	Blessed Qiraji Musket	Bind on Pickup	56.7	Physical 103-192	2.6
PROPERTIES: Increases ranged attack power by 31.					
60	Toxin Injector	Bind on Pickup	58.8	Physical 82-153	2
PROPERTIES: Increases attack power by 28.					
60	Larvae of the Great Worm	Bind on Pickup	58.7	Physical 123-229	3
PROPERTIES: Improves your critical strike rating by 14, Increases attack power by 18.					
70	Warrior Gun	Bind on Equip	84.6	Physical 148-275	2.5
70	Wolfslayer Sniper Rifle	Bind on Pickup	73.7	Physical 139-259	2.7
PROPERTIES: Increases attack power by 30.					
70	Veteran's Musket	Bind on Pickup	72	Physical 136-253	2.7
PROPERTIES: Increases attack power by 22.					
70	Arcanite Steam-Pistol	Bind on Pickup	79.1	Physical 160-299	2.9
70	Barrel-Blade Long Rifle	Bind on Pickup	75.6	Physical 137-256	2.6
	The Purifier	Bind on Pickup	42.3	Physical 89-165	3
PROPERTIES: Improves your critical strike rating by 14.					

Superior Guns

Lvl	Name	Binding Info	DPS	Damage	Speed
16	Lil Timmy's Peashooter	Bind on Equip	14.2	Physical 26-48	2.6
22	Double-barreled Shotgun	Bind on Equip	17.2	Physical 27-52	2.3
24	Hi-tech Supergun	Bind on Equip	18.3	Physical 29-55	2.3
28	Chesterfall Musket	Bind on Equip	21.3	Physical 34-64	2.3
29	Ironweaver	Bind on Equip	22.1	Physical 40-75	2.6
30	Glass Shooter	Bind on Pickup	22.9	Physical 46-87	2.9
37	The Silencer	Bind on Equip	28.2	Physical 55-103	2.8
PROPERTIES: Increases attack power by 14.					
38	Shadowforge Bushmaster	Bind on Equip	28.8	Physical 58-109	2.9
PROPERTIES: Shadow Resistance +7					
42	Galgann's Fireblaster	Bind on Pickup	31.2	Physical 56-106	2.6
PROPERTIES: Chance to strike your ranged target with a Fire Blast for 12 to 18 Fire damage.					
45	Guttbuster	Bind on Equip	33	Physical 62-116	2.7
48	Houndmaster's Rifle	Bind on Pickup	34.8	Physical 56-104	2.3
PROPERTIES: Increases attack power by 24 when fighting Beasts.					
48	Megashot Rifle	Bind on Pickup	34.7	Physical 41-77	1.7
PROPERTIES: Increases ranged attack power by 19, Arcane Resistance +5					
50	Dark Iron Rifle	Bind on Equip	36.1	Physical 68-127	2.7
PROPERTIES: Chance to strike your ranged target with Shadow Shot for 18 to 26 Shadow damage.					
51	Burstshot Harquebus	Bind on Pickup	36.9	Physical 67-125	2.6
PROPERTIES: Increases attack power by 10.					
53	Shell Launcher Shotgun	Bind on Equip	38	Physical 61-114	2.3
PROPERTIES: Chance to strike your ranged target with a Flaming Shell for 18 to 26 Fire damage.					
56	Willey's Portable Howitzer	Bind on Pickup	39.7	Physical 80-150	2.9
PROPERTIES: Increases attack power by 8.					
56	Flawless Arcanite Rifle	Bind on Equip	39.7	Physical 83-155	3
PROPERTIES: Increases gun skill rating by 9, Increases ranged attack power by 10.					
57	Xorothian Firestick	Bind on Pickup	40.4	Physical 73-137	2.6
PROPERTIES: Shadow Resistance +6					
60	Crystal Slugthrower	Bind on Equip	42	Physical 82-153	2.8
PROPERTIES: Increases attack power by 20.					
60	Silithid Husked Launcher	Bind on Equip	43.9	Physical 86-160	2.8
61	Legion Blunderbuss	Bind on Pickup	52.5	Physical 110-205	3
PROPERTIES: Increases attack power by 24.					
68	Recoilless Rocket Ripper X-54	Bind on Pickup	64.7	Physical 131-244	2.9
68	Wrathfire Hand-Cannon	Bind on Pickup	64.5	Physical 90-168	2
PROPERTIES: Increases attack power by 40.					
70	Felsteel Boomstick	Bind on Equip	62.1	Physical 104-194	2.4
70	Ornate Khorium Rifle	Bind on Equip	66.5	Physical 144-268	3.1
70	Telescopic Sharprifle	Bind on Pickup	66.3	Physical 139-259	3
PROPERTIES: Increases attack power by 28.					
70	Consortium Blaster	Bind on Pickup	66.3	Physical 111-207	2.4
PROPERTIES: Increases attack power by 36.					
	Hemet's Elekk Gun	Bind on Pickup	59.2	Physical 103-193	2.5
PROPERTIES: Increases attack power by 24.					

MACES

Epic One Hand Maces

Lvl	Name	Binding Info	DPS	Damage	Speed
38	Ardent Custodian	Bind on Equip	32.9	Physical 48-90	2.1
PROPERTIES: Increases defense rating by 7, Armor 100, Main Hand Weapon					
40	Hammer of Expertise	Bind on Pickup	36.9	Physical 54-101	2.1
PROPERTIES: Main Hand Weapon					
49	Hammer of the Northern Wind	Bind on Equip	39.5	Physical 58-108	2.1
PROPERTIES: Launches a bolt of frost at the enemy causing 20 to 30 Frost damage and slowing movement speed by 50% for 5 sec, Main Hand Weapon					
55	Ironfoe	Bind on Pickup	43.5	Physical 73-136	2.4
PROPERTIES: Grants 2 extra attacks on your next swing, Main Hand Weapon					
57	Hand of Edward the Odd	Bind on Equip	45	Physical 50-94	1.6
PROPERTIES: Next spell cast within 4 sec will cast instantly, Main Hand Weapon					
58	Persuader	Bind on Equip	45.7	Physical 86-161	2.7
PROPERTIES: Increases your hit rating by 10, Improves your critical strike rating by 14. Main Hand Weapon					
60	Grand Marshal's Punisher	Bind on Pickup	59.5	Physical 138-207	2.9
PROPERTIES: Improves your critical strike rating by 14, Increases attack power by 28.					
60	High Warlord's Bludgeon	Bind on Pickup	59.5	Physical 138-207	2.9
PROPERTIES: Improves your critical strike rating by 14, Increases attack power by 28.					
60	Ebon Hand	Bind on Equip	51.6	Physical 90-168	2.5
PROPERTIES: Sends a shadowy bolt at the enemy causing 125 to 275 Shadow damage, Fire Resistance +7					
60	Blessed Qiraji War Hammer	Bind on Pickup	60.7	Physical 89-166	2.1
PROPERTIES: Increases attack power by 280 in Cat, Bear, Dire Bear, and Moonkin forms only, Increases defense rating by 12, Armor 70.					
60	Sand Polished Hammer	Bind on Pickup	53.5	Physical 97-181	2.6
PROPERTIES: Improves your critical strike rating by 14, Increases attack power by 20.					
60	Anubisath Warhammer	Bind on Pickup	52.5	Physical 66-123	1.8
PROPERTIES: Increases mace skill rating by 9, Increases attack power by 32.					

Epic One Hand Maces

Lvl	Name	Binding Info	DPS	Damage	Speed
60	The Castigator	Bind on Pickup	65.4	Physical 119-221	2.6
PROPERTIES: Improves your critical strike rating by 14, Increases your hit rating by 10, Increases attack power by 16.					
60	Misplaced Servo Arm	Bind on Pickup	65.4	Physical 128-238	2.8
PROPERTIES: Chance to discharge electricity causing 100 to 150 Nature damage to your target.					
60	Aurastone Hammer	Bind on Pickup	50.6	Physical 95-178	2.7
PROPERTIES: Restores 5 mana per 5 sec, Increases damage and healing done by magical spells and effects by up to 25. Main Hand Weapon					
60	Empyrean Demolisher	Bind on Pickup	48	Physical 94-175	2.8
PROPERTIES: Increases your haste rating by 200 for 10 sec, Main Hand Weapon					
60	Spineshatter	Bind on Pickup	54.4	Physical 99-184	2.6
PROPERTIES: Increases defense rating by 7, Main Hand Weapon					
60	Lok'amir il Romathis	Bind on Pickup	62.9	Physical 92-172	2.1
PROPERTIES: Increases damage and healing done by magical spells and effects by up to 84, Main Hand Weapon					
60	Jin'do's Hexxer	Bind on Pickup	47.9	Physical 80-150	2.4
PROPERTIES: Increases healing done by spells and effects by up to 51, Increases your spell critical strike rating by 14. Main Hand Weapon					
60	Hammer of Bestial Fury	Bind on Pickup	52.4	Physical 69-130	1.9
PROPERTIES: Increases attack power by 154 in Cat, Bear, Dire Bear, and Moonkin forms only, Armor 90, Main Hand Weapon.					
60	Hammer of the Gathering Storm	Bind on Pickup	51.5	Physical 86-161	2.4
PROPERTIES: Increases damage and healing done by magical spells and effects by up to 53, Main Hand Weapon					
60	Mace of Unending Life	Bind on Pickup	51.5	Physical 93-175	2.6
PROPERTIES: Increases damage and healing done by magical spells and effects by up to 40, Increases attack power by 140 in Cat, Bear, Dire Bear, and Moonkin forms only. Main Hand Weapon					
60	Gavel of Infinite Wisdom	Bind on Pickup	51.5	Physical 97-181	2.7
PROPERTIES: Restores 4 mana per 5 sec, Increases healing done by spells and effects by up to 90. Main Hand Weapon					
60	Stinger of Ayamiss	Bind on Pickup	50.6	Physical 85-158	2.4
PROPERTIES: Increases your spell critical strike rating by 14, Increases damage and healing done by magical spells and effects by up to 36. Main Hand Weapon					
60	Scepter of the False Prophet	Bind on Pickup	66.4	Physical 83-156	1.8
PROPERTIES: Increases healing done by spells and effects by up to 187, Restores 3 mana per 5 sec. Main Hand Weapon					
60	The Widow's Embrace	Bind on Pickup	62.9	Physical 83-156	1.9
PROPERTIES: Increases healing done by spells and effects by up to 161, Main Hand Weapon					
60	The End of Dreams	Bind on Pickup	65.3	Physical 86-162	1.9
PROPERTIES: Increases damage and healing done by magical spells and effects by up to 95, Increases attack power by 305 in Cat, Bear, Dire Bear, and Moonkin forms only, Restores 5 mana per 5 sec, Main Hand Weapon					
60	Hammer of the Twisting Nether	Bind on Pickup	73.2	Physical 97-181	1.9
PROPERTIES: Increases healing done by spells and effects by up to 238, Restores 8 mana per 5 sec. Main Hand Weapon					
60	Hammer of the Sun	Not Bound	74.5	Physical 104-194	2
PROPERTIES: Improves your critical strike rating by 14, Armor 80, Main Hand Weapon, Fire Resistance +10, Shadow Resistance +10					
60	Grand Marshal's Warhammer	Bind on Pickup	59.7	Physical 121-225	2.9
PROPERTIES: Increases healing done by spells and effects by up to 134, Restores 6 mana per 5 sec. Main Hand Weapon					
60	High Warlord's Battle Mace	Bind on Pickup	59.7	Physical 121-225	2.9
PROPERTIES: Increases healing done by spells and effects by up to 134, Restores 6 mana per 5 sec. Main Hand Weapon					
60	High Warlord's Battle Mace	Bind on Pickup	59.7	Physical 121-225	2.9
PROPERTIES: Increases healing done by spells and effects by up to 134, Restores 6 mana per 5 sec. Main Hand Weapon					

Epic One Hand Maces

Lvl	Name	Binding Info	DPS	Damage	Speed
70	Runic Hammer	Bind on Equip	81.3	Physical 136-254	2.4
PROPERTIES: Increases attack power by 50.					
70	Gladiator's Bonecracker	Bind on Pickup	88.3	Physical 127-191	1.8
PROPERTIES: Increases attack power by 28.					
70	Gladiator's Pummeler	Bind on Pickup	88.1	Physical 183-275	2.6
PROPERTIES: Increases attack power by 28.					
70	Hand of Eternity	Bind on Equip	81.3	Physical 108-201	1.9
PROPERTIES: Restores 7 mana per 5 sec, Increases healing done by spells and effects by up to 300. Main Hand Weapon					
70	Drakefist Hammer	Bind on Pickup	81.1	Physical 153-285	2.7
PROPERTIES: Increases your haste rating by 200 for 10 sec, Main Hand Weapon					
70	Dragonmaw	Bind on Pickup	88.1	Physical 166-310	2.7
PROPERTIES: Increases your haste rating by 200 for 10 sec, Main Hand Weapon					
70	Dragonstrike	Bind on Pickup	95	Physical 179-334	2.7
PROPERTIES: Increases your haste rating by 200 for 10 sec, Main Hand Weapon					
70	Shard of the Virtuous	Bind on Pickup	81.3	Physical 108-201	1.9
PROPERTIES: Increases healing done by spells and effects by up to 299, Restores 6 mana per 5 sec. Main Hand Weapon					
70	Fool's Bane	Bind on Pickup	81.2	Physical 147-275	2.6
PROPERTIES: Increases attack power by 26, Main Hand Weapon					
70	Light's Justice	Bind on Pickup	85.8	Physical 108-201	1.8
PROPERTIES: Increases healing done by spells and effects by up to 334, Main Hand Weapon					
70	Gavel of Pure Light	Bind on Pickup	78.9	Physical 105-195	1.9
PROPERTIES: Increases healing done by spells and effects by up to 282, Restores 8 mana per 5 sec. Main Hand Weapon					
70	Shockwave Truncheon	Bind on Pickup	78.9	Physical 105-195	1.9
PROPERTIES: Increases healing done by spells and effects by up to 282, Restores 8 mana per 5 sec. Main Hand Weapon					
70	Rod of the Sun King	Bind on Pickup	92.8	Physical 175-326	2.7
PROPERTIES: Chance on melee attack to gain 20 Energy or 10 Rage, Main Hand Weapon					
70	Mallet of the Tides	Bind on Pickup	88.2	Physical 105-195	1.7
PROPERTIES: Increases mace skill rating by 12, Main Hand Weapon					
70	Lightfathom Scepter	Bind on Pickup	92.6	Physical 123-229	1.9
PROPERTIES: Increases healing done by spells and effects by up to 386, Restores 9 mana per 5 sec. Main Hand Weapon					
70	Gavel of Unearthed Secrets	Bind on Pickup	78.9	Physical 149-277	2.7
PROPERTIES: Increases damage and healing done by magical spells and effects by up to 150, Main Hand Weapon					

Superior One Hand Maces

Lvl	Name	Binding Info	DPS	Damage	Speed
16	Face Smasher	Bind on Equip	14	Physical 25-48	2.6
19	Stinging Viper	Bind on Pickup	15.5	Physical 30-57	2.8
PROPERTIES: Poisons target for 7 Nature damage every 3 sec for 15 sec.					
19	Skeletal Club	Bind on Equip	15.6	Physical 28-53	2.6
PROPERTIES: Sends a shadowy bolt at the enemy causing 30 Shadow damage, Main Hand Weapon					
20	Diamond Hammer	Bind on Equip	16.2	Physical 28-53	2.5
22	Crested Scepter	Bind on Equip	17.1	Physical 31-58	2.6
PROPERTIES: Main Hand Weapon					
23	Oscillating Power Hammer	Bind on Equip	17.5	Physical 24-46	2
24	Beazel's Basher	Bind on Equip	18.4	Physical 32-60	2.5
PROPERTIES: Main Hand Weapon					
26	Looming Gavel	Bind on Equip	19.8	Physical 33-62	2.4
PROPERTIES: Main Hand Weapon					

Superior One Hand Maces

Lvl	Name	Binding Info	DPS	Damage	Speed
28	Death Speaker Scepter	Bind on Pickup	21.4	Physical 42-78	2.8
PROPERTIES: Increases healing done by spells and effects by up to 11, Increases damage done by Shadow spells and effects by up to 7. Main Hand Weapon					
28	Dreamslayer	Bind on Equip	21.4	Physical 31-59	2.1
PROPERTIES: Main Hand Weapon					
30	Ironspine's Fist	Bind on Pickup	22.9	Physical 38-72	2.4
30	Royal Diplomatic Scepter	Bind on Pickup	23	Physical 37-69	2.3
31	Excavator's Brand	Bind on Equip	24	Physical 43-82	2.6
PROPERTIES: Hurls a fiery ball that causes 40 Fire damage and an additional 9 damage over 6 sec.					
32	Ebony Boneclub	Bind on Equip	25	Physical 31-59	1.8
PROPERTIES: Shadow Resistance +5					
32	Deadwood Sledge	Bind on Equip	25	Physical 33-62	1.9
PROPERTIES: Main Hand Weapon					
33	Midnight Mace	Bind on Equip	25.8	Physical 45-84, Shadow +1-10	2.5
PROPERTIES: Shadow Resistance +10					
34	Fight Club	Bind on Equip	26.6	Physical 41-76	2.2
37	Stonevault Bonebreaker	Bind on Equip	28.7	Physical 54-101	2.7
39	Hand of Righteousness	Bind on Pickup	29.8	Physical 56-105	2.7
PROPERTIES: Increases healing done by spells and effects by up to 15, Main Hand Weapon					
40	Wirt's Third Leg	Bind on Equip	30.4	Physical 49-91	2.3
40	Heaven's Light	Bind on Equip	30.4	Physical 57-107	2.7
PROPERTIES: Main Hand Weapon					
41	Mug O' Hurt	Bind on Equip	31.2	Physical 37-69	1.7
PROPERTIES: Slows the target's movement by 50% for 10 sec.					
42	The Shatterer	Bind on Equip	31.7	Physical 53-99	2.4
PROPERTIES: Disarm target's weapon for 10 sec, Main Hand Weapon					
43	The Hand of Antu'sul	Bind on Pickup	32.2	Physical 61-113	2.7
PROPERTIES: Blasts nearby enemies with thunder increasing the time between their attacks by 11% for 10 sec and doing 7 Nature damage to them. Will affect up to 4 targets, Main Hand Weapon					
45	Changuk Smasher	Bind on Equip	33.4	Physical 44-83	1.9
47	Light Emberforged Hammer	Bind on Pickup	34.6	Physical 63-117	2.6
PROPERTIES: Increases attack power by 26, Main Hand Weapon					
48	Bonesnapper	Bind on Equip	35.2	Physical 66-124	2.7
PROPERTIES: Main Hand Weapon					
48	Fist of Stone	Bind on Pickup	35.3	Physical 44-83	1.8
PROPERTIES: Restores 50 mana, Main Hand Weapon					
49	Viking Warhammer	Bind on Equip	35.8	Physical 60-112	2.4
PROPERTIES: Main Hand Weapon					
49	Might of Hakkar	Bind on Pickup	35.8	Physical 60-112	2.4
PROPERTIES: Main Hand Weapon					
51	Rubidium Hammer	Bind on Pickup	36.8	Physical 51-96	2
PROPERTIES: Armor 120, Main Hand Weapon					
52	The Hammer of Grace	Bind on Pickup	37.6	Physical 71-132	2.7
PROPERTIES: Increases healing done by spells and effects by up to 31, Main Hand Weapon					
52	Serenity	Bind on Equip	37.5	Physical 52-98	2
PROPERTIES: Dispels a magic effect on the current foe, Main Hand Weapon					
52	Hurley's Tankard	Bind on Pickup	37.6	Physical 71-132	2.7
PROPERTIES: Main Hand Weapon					
54	Energetic Rod	Bind on Pickup	38.7	Physical 71-107	2.3
PROPERTIES: Increases damage and healing done by magical spells and effects by up to 14, Main Hand Weapon					
54	Baron Charr's Sceptre	Bind on Equip	38.8	Physical 70-132	2.6
PROPERTIES: Blasts a target for 35 Fire damage, Main Hand Weapon					

Superior One Hand Maces

Lvl	Name	Binding Info	DPS	Damage	Speed
55	Venomspitter	Bind on Pickup	39.5	Physical 52-98	1.9
PROPERTIES: Poisons target for 7 Nature damage every 2 sec for 30 sec.					
55	Bashguuder	Bind on Pickup	39.4	Physical 49-93	1.8
PROPERTIES: Punctures target's armor lowering it by 200. Can be applied up to 3 times.					
55	Mastersmith's Hammer	Bind on Pickup	39.4	Physical 66-123	2.4
PROPERTIES: Increases damage and healing done by magical spells and effects by up to 14, Main Hand Weapon					
56	The Cruel Hand of Timmy	Bind on Pickup	40	Physical 50-94	1.8
PROPERTIES: Lowers all attributes of target by 15 for 1 min.					
56	Hammer of the Vesper	Bind on Pickup	40.2	Physical 70-131	2.5
56	The Jaw Breaker	Bind on Pickup	40.3	Physical 45-84	1.6
PROPERTIES: Improves your critical strike rating by 14.					
56	Bludstone Hammer	Bind on Equip	40.2	Physical 59-110	2.1
PROPERTIES: Main Hand Weapon					
56	Hammer of Revitalization	Bind on Pickup	40	Physical 75-141	2.7
PROPERTIES: Increases healing done by spells and effects by up to 26, Main Hand Weapon					
57	Bonechill Hammer	Bind on Pickup	40.6	Physical 68-127	2.4
PROPERTIES: Blasts a target for 90 Frost damage.					
57	Timeworn Mace	Bind on Pickup	40.7	Physical 62-117	2.2
PROPERTIES: Armor 120					
57	Masterwork Stormhammer	Bind on Equip	41.5	Physical 58-108	2
PROPERTIES: Blasts up to 3 targets for 105 to 145 Nature damage, Main Hand Weapon					
57	Mass of McGowan	Bind on Equip	40.9	Physical 80-149	2.8
PROPERTIES: Main Hand Weapon					
57	Hardened Steel Warhammer	Bind on Pickup	40.8	Physical 74-138	2.6
PROPERTIES: Increases healing done by spells and effects by up to 11, Main Hand Weapon					
58	Scepter of the Unholy	Bind on Pickup	41.3	Physical 69-129	2.4
PROPERTIES: Increases damage done by Shadow spells and effects by up to 19, Main Hand Weapon					
60	Stormstrike Hammer	Bind on Pickup	42.6	Physical 80-150	2.7
60	Sceptre of Smiting	Bind on Pickup	42.7	Physical 77-145	2.6
PROPERTIES: Increases mace skill rating by 4, Blasts the enemy with poison for 63 to 93 Nature damage.					
60	Gri'lek's Grinder	Bind on Pickup	44.8	Physical 75-140	2.4
PROPERTIES: Increases attack power by 48 when fighting Dragonkin.					
60	Zulian Scepter of Rites	Bind on Pickup	44.8	Physical 81-152	2.6
PROPERTIES: Increases healing done by spells and effects by up to 26, Restores 4 mana per 5 sec. Main Hand Weapon					
61	Diamond Core Sledgemace	Bind on Pickup	54	Physical 94-176	2.5
PROPERTIES: Increases damage and healing done by magical spells and effects by up to 51, Restores 5 mana per 5 sec. Main Hand Weapon					
62	Scepter of the Exarchs	Bind on Pickup	55.4	Physical 93-173	2.4
PROPERTIES: Increases healing done by spells and effects by up to 106, Main Hand Weapon					
62	Preserver's Cudgel	Bind on Pickup	55.4	Physical 97-180	2.5
PROPERTIES: Increases healing done by spells and effects by up to 105, Restores 5 mana per 5 sec. Main Hand Weapon					
65	Lavaforged Warhammer	Bind on Pickup	60.4	Physical 105-197	2.5
PROPERTIES: Increases attack power by 48, Main Hand Weapon					
66	Northshire Battlemace	Bind on Pickup	62.6	Physical 118-220	2.7
PROPERTIES: Restores 5 mana per 5 sec, Increases healing done by spells and effects by up to 161. Main Hand Weapon					
68	Blackout Truncheon	Bind on Pickup	69.7	Physical 73-136	1.5
PROPERTIES: Increases your haste rating by 132 for 10 sec.					
68	Terokk's Nightmace	Bind on Pickup	71.8	Physical 100-187	2
PROPERTIES: Increases mace skill rating by 19.					

Superior One Hand Maces

Lvl	Name	Binding Info	DPS	Damage	Speed
68	Bloodskull Destroyer	Bind on Pickup	69.4	Physical 126-235	2.6
PROPERTIES: Increases attack power by 22.					
68	Sky Breaker	Bind on Pickup	71.7	Physical 90-168	1.8
PROPERTIES: Increases damage and healing done by magical spells and effects by up to 132, Main Hand Weapon					
68	Dathrohan's Ceremonial Hammer	Bind on Pickup	69.4	Physical 87-163	1.8
PROPERTIES: Increases healing done by spells and effects by up to 227, Main Hand Weapon					
68	Hammer of the Penitent	Bind on Pickup	69.4	Physical 87-163	1.8
PROPERTIES: Increases healing done by spells and effects by up to 227, Restores 6 mana per 5 sec. Main Hand Weapon					
70	Truncheon of Five Hells	Bind on Pickup	71.7	Physical 90-168	1.8
70	High Warlord's Bonecracker	Bind on Pickup	71.7	Physical 103-155	1.8
PROPERTIES: Increases attack power by 26.					
70	High Warlord's Pummeler	Bind on Pickup	71.7	Physical 149-224	2.6
PROPERTIES: Increases attack power by 26.					
70	Grand Marshal's Bonecracker	Bind on Pickup	71.7	Physical 103-155	1.8
PROPERTIES: Increases attack power by 26.					
70	Grand Marshal's Pummeler	Bind on Pickup	71.7	Physical 149-224	2.6
PROPERTIES: Increases attack power by 26.					
70	Lightsworn Hammer	Bind on Pickup	71.7	Physical 90-168	1.8
PROPERTIES: Increases healing done by spells and effects by up to 227, Restores 8 mana per 5 sec. Main Hand Weapon					
70	Bleeding Hollow Warhammer	Bind on Pickup	71.7	Physical 120-224	2.4
PROPERTIES: Increases damage and healing done by magical spells and effects by up to 121, Main Hand Weapon					
70	Will of the Fallen Exarch	Bind on Pickup	71.7	Physical 90-168	1.8
PROPERTIES: Increases healing done by spells and effects by up to 227, Main Hand Weapon					
	Hungering Bone Cudgel	Bind on Pickup	60.3	Physical 67-126	1.6
PROPERTIES: Increases attack power by 26.					
	Cold Forged Hammer	Bind on Pickup	41.4	Physical 72-135	2.5
PROPERTIES: Restores 3 mana per 5 sec, Main Hand Weapon					
	Simone's Cultivating Hammer	Bind on Pickup	42.5	Physical 53-100	1.8
PROPERTIES: Increases healing done by spells and effects by up to 37, Main Hand Weapon					
	Sporeggar Smasher	Bind on Pickup	56.7	Physical 83-155	2.1
PROPERTIES: Increases healing done by spells and effects by up to 61, Main Hand Weapon					
	Mogor's Anointing Club	Bind on Pickup	62.6	Physical 92-171	2.1
PROPERTIES: Restores 5 mana per 5 sec, Increases healing done by spells and effects by up to 160. Main Hand Weapon					

Legendary Two Hand Mace

Lvl	Name	Binding Info	DPS	Damage	Speed
60	Sulfuras, Hand of Ragnaros	Bind on Pickup	80.4	Physical 223-372	3.7
PROPERTIES: Hurls a fiery ball that causes 273 to 333 Fire damage and an additional 75 damage over 10 sec, Deals 5 Fire damage to anyone who strikes you with a melee attack, Fire Resistance +30					

Epic Two Hand Mace

Lvl	Name	Binding Info	DPS	Damage	Speed
47	Taran Icebreaker	Bind on Equip	49.6	Physical 91-137	2.3
PROPERTIES: Hurls a fiery ball that causes 180 to 220 Fire damage and an additional 36 damage over 8 sec.					
60	Earthshaker	Bind on Pickup	62.6	Physical 175-263	3.5

Epic Two Hand Mace

Lvl	Name	Binding Info	DPS	Damage	Speed
PROPERTIES: Knocks down all nearby enemies for 3 sec, Increases attack power by 22.					
60	Sulfuron Hammer	Bind on Equip	63.6	Physical 176-295	3.7
PROPERTIES: Hurls a fiery ball that causes 83 to 101 Fire damage and an additional 16 damage over 8 sec.					
60	Finkle's Lava Dredger	Bind on Pickup	67.1	Physical 155-234	2.9
PROPERTIES: Restores 9 mana per 5 sec, Fire Resistance +15					
60	Grand Marshal's Battle Hammer	Bind on Pickup	77.4	Physical 235-353	3.8
PROPERTIES: Improves your critical strike rating by 14.					
60	High Warlord's Pulverizer	Bind on Pickup	77.4	Physical 235-353	3.8
PROPERTIES: Improves your critical strike rating by 14.					
60	The Unstoppable Force	Bind on Pickup	61.4	Physical 175-292	3.8
PROPERTIES: Improves your critical strike rating by 28, Stuns target for 1 sec.					
60	Herald of Woe	Bind on Pickup	73.4	Physical 199-300	3.4
60	Draconic Maul	Bind on Pickup	67	Physical 187-282	3.5
PROPERTIES: Improves your critical strike rating by 28.					
60	Jeklik's Crusher	Bind on Pickup	61.5	Physical 177-266	3.6
PROPERTIES: Wounds the target for 200 to 220 damage.					
60	Fist of Cenarius	Bind on Pickup	62.6	Physical 175-263	3.5
PROPERTIES: Increases damage and healing done by magical spells and effects by up to 40, Increases your spell critical strike rating by 28.					
60	Hammer of Ji'zhi	Bind on Pickup	70.7	Physical 198-297	3.5
PROPERTIES: Increases damage and healing done by magical spells and effects by up to 30.					
60	Might of Menethil	Bind on Pickup	95.3	Physical 289-435	3.8
PROPERTIES: Improves your critical strike rating by 28.					
60	Maul of the Redeemed Crusader	Bind on Pickup	84.9	Physical 244-367	3.6
PROPERTIES: Restores 8 mana per 5 sec, Increases damage and healing done by magical spells and effects by up to 35.					
60	Grand Marshal's Demolisher	Bind on Pickup	77.4	Physical 235-353	3.8
PROPERTIES: Restores 7 mana per 5 sec, Increases damage and healing done by magical spells and effects by up to 27.					
60	High Warlord's Destroyer	Bind on Pickup	77.4	Physical 235-353	3.8
PROPERTIES: Restores 7 mana per 5 sec, Increases damage and healing done by magical spells and effects by up to 27.					
60	High Warlord's Destroyer	Bind on Pickup	77.4	Physical 235-353	3.8
PROPERTIES: Restores 7 mana per 5 sec, Increases damage and healing done by magical spells and effects by up to 27.					
70	Fel Hardened Maul	Bind on Equip	105.6	Physical 270-406	3.2
70	Gladiator's Bonegrinder	Bind on Pickup	114.7	Physical 330-496	3.6
70	Thunder	Bind on Pickup	105.7	Physical 321-482	3.8
70	Deep Thunder	Bind on Pickup	114.6	Physical 348-523	3.8
PROPERTIES: Stuns target for 4 sec.					
70	Stormherald	Bind on Pickup	123.7	Physical 376-564	3.8
PROPERTIES: Stuns target for 4 sec.					
70	Gladiator's Maul	Bind on Pickup	114.7	Physical 330-496	3.6
PROPERTIES: Increases attack power by 654 in Cat, Bear, Dire Bear, and Moonkin forms only.					
70	Hammer of the Naaru	Bind on Pickup	111.7	Physical 321-483	3.6
PROPERTIES: Increases damage and healing done by magical spells and effects by up to 27.					
70	Earthwarden	Bind on Pickup	102.5	Physical 262-394	3.2
PROPERTIES: Increases feral combat skill rating by 24, Increases attack power by 525 in Cat, Bear, Dire Bear, and Moonkin forms only. Armor 500.					
70	World Breaker	Bind on Pickup	114.6	Physical 339-509	3.7
PROPERTIES: Increases the critical strike rating of your next attack by 800.					

Superior Two Hand Maces

Lvl	Name	Binding Info	DPS	Damage	Speed
16	Black Malice	Bind on Equip	18.3	Physical 48-73, Shadow +1-6	3.3
PROPERTIES: Sends a shadowy bolt at the enemy causing 55 to 85 Shadow damage.					
16	Rakzur Club	Bind on Equip	18.3	Physical 38-57	2.6
18	Smite's Mighty Hammer	Bind on Pickup	19.7	Physical 55-83	3.5
23	Dense Triangle Mace	Bind on Equip	22.9	Physical 44-66	2.4
24	Slaghammer	Bind on Equip	23.8	Physical 53-80	2.8
29	Cobalt Crusher	Bind on Equip	28.9	Physical 74-111, Frost +5-5	3.2
PROPERTIES: Blasts a target for 110 to 120 Frost damage.					
29	Manual Crowd Pummeler	Bind on Pickup	29	Physical 46-70	2
PROPERTIES: Increases your haste rating by 500 for 30 sec.					
30	Viscous Hammer	Bind on Equip	30.2	Physical 70-105	2.9
PROPERTIES: Increases attack power by 34.					
32	The Pacifier	Bind on Equip	32.5	Physical 104-156	4
32	The Shoveler	Bind on Equip	32.5	Physical 88-133	3.4
PROPERTIES: Increases attack power by 20.					
37	Thornstone Sledgehammer	Bind on Equip	37.2	Physical 95-143	3.2
PROPERTIES: Nature Resistance +10					
39	Mograine's Might	Bind on Pickup	38.9	Physical 87-131	2.8
40	The Jackhammer	Bind on Equip	39.6	Physical 79-119	2.5
PROPERTIES: Increases your haste rating by 300 for 10 sec.					
44	The Rockpounder	Bind on Pickup	42.7	Physical 126-190	3.7
PROPERTIES: Improves your critical strike rating by 28.					
45	Ragehammer	Bind on Equip	43.4	Physical 128-193	3.7
PROPERTIES: Increases damage done by 20 and haste rating by 50 for 15 sec.					
45	Blanchard's Stout	Bind on Equip	43.4	Physical 107-162	3.1
PROPERTIES: Fire Resistance +5					
47	The Judge's Gavel	Bind on Equip	45	Physical 122-184	3.4
PROPERTIES: Stuns target for 3 sec.					
49	Princess Theradras' Scepter	Bind on Pickup	46.5	Physical 126-190	3.4
PROPERTIES: Wounds the target for 160 damage and lowers their armor by 100.					
50	Dark Iron Pulverizer	Bind on Equip	47.4	Physical 140-211	3.7
PROPERTIES: Stuns target for 8 sec.					
51	Force of Magma	Bind on Pickup	48.1	Physical 123-185	3.2
PROPERTIES: Blasts a target for 150 Fire damage.					
51	Enchanted Battlehammer	Bind on Equip	48.1	Physical 100-150	2.6
PROPERTIES: Increases your parry rating by 20, Increases your hit rating by 20.					
52	Impervious Giant	Bind on Pickup	48.9	Physical 105-159	2.7
PROPERTIES: Increases your hit rating by 10, Improves your critical strike rating by 28. Armor 30.					
53	Twig of the World Tree	Bind on Equip	49.7	Physical 147-221	3.7
53	Lavastone Hammer	Bind on Pickup	49.7	Physical 135-203	3.4
PROPERTIES: Increases damage and healing done by magical spells and effects by up to 20.					
54	Frightskull Shaft	Bind on Pickup	50.4	Physical 137-206	3.4
PROPERTIES: Deals 8 Shadow damage every 2 sec for 30 sec and lowers their Strength for the duration of the disease.					
55	Fist of Omokk	Bind on Pickup	51.4	Physical 135-204	3.3
56	Malown's Slam	Bind on Pickup	52.1	Physical 158-238	3.8
PROPERTIES: Knocks target silly for 2 sec and increases Strength by 50 for 30 sec.					
57	Unyielding Maul	Bind on Pickup	53	Physical 135-204	3.2
PROPERTIES: Increases defense rating by 12. Armor 250.					
57	Hammer of Divine Might	Bind on Pickup	53.1	Physical 89-134	2.1
PROPERTIES: Increases damage and healing done by magical spells and effects by up to 27.					

Superior Two Hand Maces

Lvl	Name	Binding Info	DPS	Damage	Speed
58	Hammer of the Titans	Bind on Equip	53.8	Physical 163-246	3.8
PROPERTIES: Stuns target for 3 sec.					
58	Seeping Willow	Bind on Pickup	53.9	Physical 155-233	3.6
PROPERTIES: Lowers all stats by 20 and deals 20 Nature damage every 3 sec to all enemies within an 8 yard radius of the caster for 30 sec.					
58	Hammer of the Grand Crusader	Bind on Pickup	53.9	Physical 116-175	2.7
PROPERTIES: Increases healing done by spells and effects by up to 22.					
58	Crystal Spiked Maul	Bind on Equip	53.8	Physical 168-252	3.9
PROPERTIES: Improves your critical strike rating by 28.					
60	Gavel of Qiraji Authority	Bind on Pickup	61.4	Physical 108-162	2.2
PROPERTIES: Increases damage and healing done by magical spells and effects by up to 19, Restores 6 mana per 5 sec.					
60	Heart Fire Warhammer	Bind on Pickup	68.9	Physical 121-182	2.2
PROPERTIES: Increases damage and healing done by magical spells and effects by up to 12, Restores 4 mana per 5 sec.					
63	Hatebringer	Bind on Pickup	73.6	Physical 212-318	3.6
65	Great Earthforged Hammer	Bind on Pickup	78.6	Physical 220-330	3.5
PROPERTIES: Increases attack power by 70.					
68	Firemaul of Destruction	Bind on Pickup	90.3	Physical 250-418	3.7
68	Warmaul of Infused Light	Bind on Pickup	90.4	Physical 237-396	3.5
70	Scepter of Sha'tar	Bind on Pickup	93.3	Physical 245-408	3.5
PROPERTIES: Increases damage and healing done by magical spells and effects by up to 35.					
70	High Warlord's Bonegrinder	Bind on Pickup	93.2	Physical 268-403	3.6
70	High Warlord's Maul	Bind on Pickup	93.2	Physical 268-403	3.6
PROPERTIES: Increases attack power by 423 in Cat, Bear, Dire Bear, and Moonkin forms only.					
70	Grand Marshal's Bonegrinder	Bind on Pickup	93.2	Physical 268-403	3.6
70	Grand Marshal's Maul	Bind on Pickup	93.2	Physical 268-403	3.6
PROPERTIES: Increases attack power by 423 in Cat, Bear, Dire Bear, and Moonkin forms only.					
70	Arechron's Gift	Bind on Pickup	93.3	Physical 261-392	3.5
PROPERTIES: Increases attack power by 84.					
	Verigan's Fist	Bind on Pickup	25.6	Physical 65-99	3.2
	Whirlwind Warhammer	Bind on Pickup	35.7	Physical 97-146	3.4
	Shimmering Platinum Warhammer	Bind on Pickup	53.9	Physical 142-192	3.1
PROPERTIES: Blasts a target for 180 to 250 Nature damage.					
	Bonecrusher	Bind on Pickup	53.8	Physical 129-194	3
PROPERTIES: Improves your critical strike rating by 14.					
	Doomulus Prime	Bind on Pickup	55.7	Physical 158-265	3.8
PROPERTIES: Increases your hit rating by 10.					

POLEARMS

Epic Polearms

Lvl	Name	Binding Info	DPS	Damage	Speed
58	Shadowstrike	Bind on Pickup	59.4	Physical 147-221	3.1
PROPERTIES: Steals 100 to 180 life from target enemy, Transforms Shadowstrike into Thunderstrike.					
58	Thunderstrike	Bind on Pickup	59.4	Physical 147-221	3.1
PROPERTIES: Blasts up to 3 targets for 150 to 250 Nature damage. Each target after the first takes less damage, Transforms Thunderstrike into Shadowstrike.					
60	Grand Marshal's Glaive	Bind on Pickup	77.4	Physical 235-353	3.8
PROPERTIES: Improves your critical strike rating by 14.					
60	High Warlord's Pig Sticker	Bind on Pickup	77.4	Physical 235-353	3.8
PROPERTIES: Improves your critical strike rating by 14.					

Epic Polearms

Lvl	Name	Binding Info	DPS	Damage	Speed
60	Blackfury	Bind on Equip	62.6	Physical 105-158	2.1
PROPERTIES: Improves your critical strike rating by 14, Fire Resistance +10					
60	Halberd of Smiting	Bind on Pickup	62.6	Physical 175-263	3.5
PROPERTIES: Chance to decapitate the target on a melee swing, causing 452 to 676 damage.					
60	Barb of the Sand Reaver	Bind on Pickup	76.1	Physical 225-338	3.7
PROPERTIES: Increases attack power by 40.					
60	The Eye of Nerub	Bind on Pickup	85	Physical 251-378	3.7
PROPERTIES: Increases Bow skill rating by 9, Increases Crossbow skill rating by 9, Increases gun skill rating by 9, Increases attack power by 60,					
70	Gladiator's Painsaw	Bind on Pickup	114.5	Physical 201-303	2.2
PROPERTIES: Increases attack power by 64.					
70	Glaive of the Pit	Bind on Pickup	111.6	Physical 330-496	3.7
PROPERTIES: Steals 238 to 262 life from target enemy.					
70	Trident of the Outcast Tribe	Bind on Pickup	102.5	Physical 262-394	3.2

Superior Polearms

Lvl	Name	Binding Info	DPS	Damage	Speed
20	Gargoyle's Bite	Bind on Equip	19	Physical 44-66	2.9
PROPERTIES: Armor 60.					
23	Bloodpike	Bind on Equip	23.1	Physical 59-89	3.2
PROPERTIES: Wounds the target causing them to bleed for 110 damage over 30 sec.					
31	Poison-tipped Bone Spear	Bind on Equip	31.3	Physical 57-87	2.3
PROPERTIES: Poisons target for 30 Nature damage every 6 sec for 30 sec.					
34	Ruthless Shiv	Bind on Equip	34.8	Physical 75-113	2.7
35	Grim Reaper	Bind on Equip	35.6	Physical 88-133	3.1
PROPERTIES: Wounds the target for 130 damage.					
39	Khoo's Point	Bind on Equip	38.8	Physical 77-117	2.5
42	Grimlok's Charge	Bind on Pickup	40.9	Physical 88-133	2.7
43	Eyegouger	Bind on Equip	41.8	Physical 100-151	3
43	Bonechewer	Bind on Equip	42	Physical 94-141	2.8
44	Diabolic Skiver	Bind on Pickup	42.8	Physical 99-149	2.9
PROPERTIES: Delivers a fatal wound for 160 to 180 damage.					
45	Blight	Bind on Equip	43.3	Physical 93-141	2.7
PROPERTIES: Diseases a target for 50 Nature damage and an additional 180 damage over 1 min.					
46	Headspike	Bind on Pickup	44.2	Physical 106-159	3
47	Stoneraven	Bind on Equip	44.8	Physical 118-178	3.3
49	Smoldering Claw	Bind on Pickup	46.6	Physical 108-162	2.9
PROPERTIES: Hurls a fiery ball that causes 135 Fire damage and an additional 15 damage over 6 sec, Fire Resistance +10					
51	Flame Wrath	Bind on Pickup	48.2	Physical 127-191	3.3
PROPERTIES: Envelops the caster with a Fire shield for 15 sec and shoots a ring of fire dealing 130 to 170 damage to all nearby enemies.					
51	Frenzied Striker	Bind on Equip	48.2	Physical 108-162	2.8
PROPERTIES: Increases your parry rating by 20, Increases your hit rating by 20.					
54	Peacemaker	Bind on Pickup	50.4	Physical 137-206	3.4
PROPERTIES: Improves your critical strike rating by 14, Increases attack power by 56.					
55	Darkspear	Bind on Equip	51.3	Physical 131-197	3.2
PROPERTIES: Party members have a chance to increase their critical strike rating by 56. Lasts for 20 sec.					
55	The Needler	Bind on Equip	51.4	Physical 90-136	2.2
PROPERTIES: Wounds the target for 75 damage.					
55	Stonecutting Glaive	Bind on Pickup	51.4	Physical 152-228	3.7
55	Darkspear (Purple Glow)	Bind on Equip	51.3	Physical 131-197	3.2
PROPERTIES: Party members have a chance to increase their critical strike rating by 56. Lasts for 20 sec.					

Superior Polearms

Lvl	Name	Binding Info	DPS	Damage	Speed
56	Chillpike	Bind on Pickup	52.3	Physical 117-176	2.8
PROPERTIES: Blasts a target for 160 to 250 Frost damage.					
56	Huntsman's Harpoon	Bind on Pickup	52.2	Physical 150-226	3.6
57	Monstrous Glaive	Bind on Pickup	53.1	Physical 123-185	2.9
PROPERTIES: Increases your parry rating by 20, Increases defense rating by 10.					
58	Blackhand Doomsaw	Bind on Pickup	54	Physical 151-227	3.5
PROPERTIES: Wounds the target for 324 to 540 damage.					
60	Tigule's Harpoon	Bind on Pickup	58.5	Physical 154-232	3.3
PROPERTIES: Increases your hit rating by 20, Increases attack power by 60 when fighting Beasts.					
60	Pitchfork of Madness	Bind on Pickup	58.4	Physical 163-246	3.5
PROPERTIES: Increases attack power by 117 when fighting Demons.					
60	Hellreaver	Bind on Pickup	68.8	Physical 187-281	3.4
68	Plasma Rat's Hyper-Scythe	Bind on Pickup	90.4	Physical 253-380	3.5
70	Sonic Spear	Bind on Pickup	93.3	Physical 261-392	3.5
PROPERTIES: Increases attack power by 62.					
70	High Warlord's Painsaw	Bind on Pickup	93.2	Physical 164-246	2.2
PROPERTIES: Increases attack power by 56.					
70	Grand Marshal's Painsaw	Bind on Pickup	93.2	Physical 164-246	2.2
PROPERTIES: Increases attack power by 56.					
70	Hellforged Halberd	Bind on Pickup	93.3	Physical 261-392	3.5
PROPERTIES: Increases attack power by 92.					
70	Blackened Spear	Bind on Pickup	93.3	Physical 261-392	3.5
PROPERTIES: Increases attack power by 92.					
	Ice Barbed Spear	Bind on Pickup	53.9	Physical 155-233	3.6
	Hunting Spear	Bind on Pickup	45	Physical 111-168	3.1
PROPERTIES: Improves your critical strike rating by 14, Restores 5 mana per 5 sec.					
	Blood-Tempered Ranseur	Bind on Pickup	19.7	Physical 45-69	2.9
	Lantresor's Warblade	Bind on Pickup	75.7	Physical 181-273	3
	Lantresor's Warblade	Bind on Pickup	75.7	Physical 181-273	3
	Terokk's Quill	Bind on Pickup	93.3	Physical 246-370	3.3

STAVES

Legendary Staves

Lvl	Name	Binding Info	DPS	Damage	Speed
60	Atiesh, Greatstaff of the Guardian	Bind on Pickup	97.1	Physical 225-338	2.9
PROPERTIES: Increases your spell hit rating by 16, Increases damage and healing done by magical spells and effects by up to 150, Increases the spell critical strike rating of all party members within 30 yards by 28, Creates a portal, teleporting group members that use it to Karazhan,					
60	Atiesh, Greatstaff of the Guardian	Bind on Pickup	97.1	Physical 225-338	2.9
PROPERTIES: Increases your spell critical strike rating by 28, Increases damage and healing done by magical spells and effects by up to 150, Increases damage and healing done by magical spells and effects of all party members within 30 yards by up to 33. Creates a portal, teleporting group members that use it to Karazhan,					
60	Atiesh, Greatstaff of the Guardian	Bind on Pickup	97.1	Physical 225-338	2.9
PROPERTIES: Increases healing done by magical spells and effects of all party members within 30 yards by up to 62. Increases your spell damage by up to 120 and your healing by up to 300. Creates a portal, teleporting group members that use it to Karazhan.					
60	Atiesh, Greatstaff of the Guardian	Bind on Pickup	97.1	Physical 225-338	2.9
PROPERTIES: Restores 11 mana per 5 seconds to all party members within 30 yards, Increases healing done by spells and effects by up to 300, Increases attack power by 420 in Cat, Bear, Dire Bear, and Moonkin forms only, Creates a portal, teleporting group members that use it to Karazhan,					

Epic Staves

Lvl	Name	Binding Info	DPS	Damage	Speed
35	Staff of Jordan	Bind on Equip	40.4	Physical 119-180	3.7
PROPERTIES: Increases damage and healing done by magical spells and effects by up to 26.					
43	Warden Staff	Bind on Equip	46.5	Physical 89-134	2.4
PROPERTIES: Increases defense rating by 15. Armor 260.					
49	Glowing Brightwood Staff	Bind on Equip	51.3	Physical 127-191	3.1
PROPERTIES: Nature Resistance +15					
56	Elemental Mage Staff	Bind on Equip	57.5	Physical 147-221	3.2
PROPERTIES: Increases damage done by Fire spells and effects by up to 36, Increases damage done by Frost spells and effects by up to 36. Fire Resistance +20, Frost Resistance +20					
57	Headmaster's Charge	Bind on Pickup	58.4	Physical 135-204	2.9
PROPERTIES: Gives 20 additional intellect to party members within 30 yards.					
60	Amberseal Keeper	Bind on Pickup	63.6	Physical 168-252	3.3
PROPERTIES: Restores 12 mana per 5 sec, Increases damage and healing done by magical spells and effects by up to 44. Fire Resistance +5, Nature Resistance +5, Frost Resistance +5, Shadow Resistance +5, Arcane Resistance +5					
60	Benediction	Bind on Pickup	73.3	Physical 176-264	3
PROPERTIES: Calls forth Anathema, Increases healing done by spells and effects by up to 106. Shadow Resistance +20					
60	Anathema	Bind on Pickup	73.3	Physical 176-264	3
PROPERTIES: Calls forth Benediction, Restores 7 mana per 5 sec, Increases damage done by Shadow spells and effects by up to 69, Shadow Resistance +20					
60	Lok'delar, Stave of the Ancient Keepers	Bind on Pickup	73.3	Physical 187-282	3.2
PROPERTIES: Improves your critical strike rating by 28, Increases attack power by 45 when fighting Demons. Nature Resistance +10					
60	Staff of Dominance	Bind on Pickup	67.1	Physical 155-234	2.9
PROPERTIES: Increases your spell critical strike rating by 14, Increases damage and healing done by magical spells and effects by up to 40.					
60	Grand Marshal's Stave	Bind on Pickup	77.3	Physical 185-279	3
PROPERTIES: Increases damage and healing done by magical spells and effects by up to 71.					
60	High Warlord's War Staff	Bind on Pickup	77.3	Physical 185-279	3
PROPERTIES: Increases damage and healing done by magical spells and effects by up to 71.					
60	Shadow Wing Focus Staff	Bind on Pickup	73.3	Physical 187-282	3.2
PROPERTIES: Increases damage and healing done by magical spells and effects by up to 56.					
60	Staff of the Shadow Flame	Bind on Pickup	81.9	Physical 209-315	3.2
PROPERTIES: Increases your spell critical strike rating by 28, Increases damage and healing done by magical spells and effects by up to 84.					
60	Jin'do's Judgement	Bind on Pickup	62.6	Physical 165-248	3.3
PROPERTIES: Increases your spell hit rating by 16, Restores 14 mana per 5 sec, Increases damage and healing done by magical spells and effects by up to 27.					
60	Will of Arlokk	Bind on Pickup	61.5	Physical 147-222	3
PROPERTIES: Increases healing done by spells and effects by up to 46.					
60	Nat Pagle's Fish Terminator	Bind on Pickup	61.4	Physical 172-258	3.5
60	Ironbark Staff	Bind on Pickup	61.5	Physical 156-262	3.4
PROPERTIES: Increases your spell critical strike rating by 28, Increases damage and healing done by magical spells and effects by up to 41. Armor 100.					
60	Frost Staff	Bind on Pickup	97	Physical 209-315	2.7
PROPERTIES: Increases your spell critical strike rating by 28, Increases damage done by Frost spells and effects by up to 132, Restores 5 mana per 5 sec.					
60	Staff of Rampant Growth	Bind on Pickup	68.3	Physical 142-213	2.6
PROPERTIES: Increases healing done by spells and effects by up to 84, Restores 11 mana per 5 sec. Nature Resistance +20					
60	Fire Staff	Bind on Pickup	48.1	Physical 91-169	2.7
PROPERTIES: Increases damage done by Fire spells and effects by up to 57.					
60	Shadow Staff	Bind on Pickup	48.1	Physical 91-169	2.7
PROPERTIES: Increases damage done by Shadow spells and effects by up to 57.					

Epic Staves

Lvl	Name	Binding Info	DPS	Damage	Speed
60	Staff of the Qiraji Prophets	Bind on Pickup	73.3	Physical 170-255	2.9
PROPERTIES: Increases damage and healing done by magical spells and effects by up to 56, Gives a chance when your harmful spells land to reduce the magical resistances of your spell targets by 50 for 8 sec. Fire Resistance +10, Nature Resistance +10, Frost Resistance +10, Shadow Resistance +10, Arcane Resistance +10					
60	Blessed Qiraji Acolyte Staff	Bind on Pickup	78.8	Physical 189-284	3
PROPERTIES: Increases damage and healing done by magical spells and effects by up to 76, Increases your spell hit rating by 16, Increases your spell critical strike rating by 14.					
60	Blessed Qiraji Augur Staff	Bind on Pickup	78.8	Physical 189-284	3
PROPERTIES: Increases healing done by spells and effects by up to 143, Restores 15 mana per 5 sec.					
60	Staff of the Ruins	Bind on Pickup	69.6	Physical 189-284	3.4
PROPERTIES: Increases damage and healing done by magical spells and effects by up to 60, Increases your spell critical strike rating by 14, Increases your spell hit rating by 8.					
60	Soulseeker	Bind on Pickup	95.2	Physical 243-366	3.2
PROPERTIES: Increases damage and healing done by magical spells and effects by up to 126, Increases your spell critical strike rating by 28, Increases your spell penetration by 25.					
60	Brimstone Staff	Bind on Pickup	85	Physical 217-327	3.2
PROPERTIES: Increases your spell hit rating by 16, Increases damage and healing done by magical spells and effects by up to 113, Increases your spell critical strike rating by 14.					
60	Spire of Twilight	Bind on Pickup	85	Physical 217-327	3.2
PROPERTIES: Restores 10 mana per 5 sec, Increases healing done by spells and effects by up to 178.					
60	Terokk's Shadowstaff	Bind on Pickup	102.5	Physical 262-394	3.2
PROPERTIES: Increases damage and healing done by magical spells and effects by up to 150.					
70	Gladiator's War Staff	Bind on Pickup	114.7	Physical 275-413	3
PROPERTIES: Increases damage and healing done by magical spells and effects by up to 187.					
70	Nightstaff of the Everliving	Bind on Pickup	105.6	Physical 270-406	3.2
PROPERTIES: Increases healing done by spells and effects by up to 300.					
70	Staff of Infinite Mysteries	Bind on Pickup	105.6	Physical 270-406	3.2
PROPERTIES: Increases damage and healing done by magical spells and effects by up to 159.					
70	Terestian's Stranglestaff	Bind on Pickup	105.5	Physical 253-380	3
PROPERTIES: Increases attack power by 556 in Cat, Bear, Dire Bear, and Moonkin forms only.					
70	Crystalheart Pulse-Staff	Bind on Pickup	111.6	Physical 285-429	3.2
PROPERTIES: Increases healing done by spells and effects by up to 334, Restores 15 mana per 5 sec.					
70	Feral Staff of Lashing	Bind on Pickup	102.7	Physical 246-370	3
PROPERTIES: Increases attack power by 525 in Cat, Bear, Dire Bear, and Moonkin forms only. Armor 300.					
70	Etherium Life-Staff	Bind on Pickup	114.5	Physical 293-440	3.2
PROPERTIES: Increases healing done by spells and effects by up to 352.					
70	The Nexus Key	Bind on Pickup	120.8	Physical 309-464	3.2
PROPERTIES: Increases damage and healing done by magical spells and effects by up to 205.					
70	Wildfury Greatstaff	Bind on Pickup	114.7	Physical 275-413	3
PROPERTIES: Increases attack power by 654 in Cat, Bear, Dire Bear, and Moonkin forms only. Armor 630.					
70	Exodar Life-Staff	Bind on Pickup	108.6	Physical 278-417	3.2
PROPERTIES: Increases healing done by spells and effects by up to 317, Restores 15 mana per 5 sec.					

Superior Staves

Lvl	Name	Binding Info	DPS	Damage	Speed
17	Witching Stave	Bind on Equip	19.2	Physical 55-83	3.6
PROPERTIES: Increases damage done by Shadow spells and effects by up to 11.					
18	Staff of the Blessed Seer	Bind on Equip	19.7	Physical 47-71	3
PROPERTIES: Increases healing done by spells and effects by up to 24.					
18	Emberstone Staff	Bind on Pickup	19.7	Physical 47-71	3
18	Advisor's Gnarled Staff	Bind on Pickup	19.7	Physical 45-69	2.9
PROPERTIES: Restores 3 mana per 5 sec.					

Superior Staves

Lvl	Name	Binding Info	DPS	Damage	Speed
18	Lorekeeper's Staff	Bind on Pickup	19.7	Physical 45-69	2.9
PROPERTIES: Restores 3 mana per 5 sec.					
19	Twisted Chanter's Staff	Bind on Equip	20.4	Physical 55-84	3.4
19	Staff of the Friar	Bind on Equip	20.4	Physical 42-64	2.6
20	Living Root	Bind on Pickup	21.2	Physical 49-74	2.9
PROPERTIES: Nature Resistance +5					
21	Odo's Ley Staff	Bind on Pickup	21.7	Physical 50-76	2.9
22	Staff of the Shade	Bind on Equip	22.3	Physical 46-70	2.6
PROPERTIES: Increases damage done by Shadow spells and effects by up to 21.					
24	Rod of the Sleepwalker	Bind on Pickup	23.8	Physical 53-80	2.8
26	Gnarled Ash Staff	Bind on Equip	25.6	Physical 65-99	3.2
27	Wind Spirit Staff	Bind on Pickup	26.7	Physical 70-106	3.3
27	Hydrocane	Bind on Pickup	26.6	Physical 59-90	2.8
PROPERTIES: Allows underwater breathing, Frost Resistance +15					
28	Advisor's Gnarled Staff	Bind on Pickup	27.8	Physical 64-97	2.9
PROPERTIES: Restores 4 mana per 5 sec.					
28	Lorekeeper's Staff	Bind on Pickup	27.8	Physical 64-97	2.9
PROPERTIES: Restores 4 mana per 5 sec.					
31	Loksey's Training Stick	Bind on Pickup	31.3	Physical 77-117	3.1
PROPERTIES: Increases attack power by 60 when fighting Beasts.					
32	Windweaver Staff	Bind on Equip	32.4	Physical 80-121	3.1
PROPERTIES: Increases damage done by Arcane spells and effects by up to 14.					
33	Black Duskwood Staff	Bind on Equip	33.6	Physical 75-113	2.8
PROPERTIES: Sends a shadowy bolt at the enemy causing 110 to 140 Shadow damage.					
34	Illusionary Rod	Bind on Pickup	34.7	Physical 94-142	3.4
37	Ironshod Bludgeon	Bind on Pickup	37.2	Physical 74-112	2.5
38	Advisor's Gnarled Staff	Bind on Pickup	38.1	Physical 88-133	2.9
PROPERTIES: Restores 6 mana per 5 sec.					
38	Lorekeeper's Staff	Bind on Pickup	38.1	Physical 88-133	2.9
PROPERTIES: Restores 6 mana per 5 sec.					
41	Tanglewood Staff	Bind on Equip	40.3	Physical 109-165	3.4
PROPERTIES: Increases damage done by Nature spells and effects by up to 14.					
42	Witch Doctor's Cane	Bind on Equip	41.1	Physical 75-114	2.3
PROPERTIES: Increases damage done by Nature spells and effects by up to 33.					
42	Bludgeon of the Grinning Dog	Bind on Equip	41.2	Physical 112-168	3.4
PROPERTIES: Stuns target for 3 sec.					
42	Zum'rah's Vexing Cane	Bind on Pickup	40.9	Physical 88-133	2.7
PROPERTIES: Increases damage and healing done by magical spells and effects by up to 21.					
45	The Chief's Enforcer	Bind on Pickup	43.5	Physical 118-178	3.4
PROPERTIES: Stuns target for 3 sec.					
48	Kindling Stave	Bind on Pickup	45.9	Physical 106-160	2.9
PROPERTIES: Increases your spell critical strike rating by 14, Fire Resistance +10					
48	Advisor's Gnarled Staff	Bind on Pickup	45.9	Physical 106-160	2.9
PROPERTIES: Restores 7 mana per 5 sec.					
48	Lorekeeper's Staff	Bind on Pickup	45.9	Physical 106-160	2.9
PROPERTIES: Restores 7 mana per 5 sec.					
49	Soulkeeper	Bind on Equip	46.6	Physical 141-213	3.8
49	Spire of Hakkar	Bind on Pickup	46.5	Physical 126-190	3.4
PROPERTIES: Increases damage and healing done by magical spells and effects by up to 18.					
51	Spire of the Stoneshaper	Bind on Equip	48.2	Physical 131-197	3.4
PROPERTIES: Increases armor by 1000 for 10 sec but cannot cast spells or attack for the duration of the spell.					

Superior Staves

Lvl	Name	Binding Info	DPS	Damage	Speed
53	Quel'dorai Channeling Rod	Bind on Pickup	49.6	Physical 111-167	2.8
PROPERTIES: Restores 8 mana per 5 sec.					
54	Guiding Stave of Wisdom	Bind on Pickup	50.5	Physical 133-200	3.3
PROPERTIES: Increases healing done by spells and effects by up to 53, Frost Resistance +10					
55	Slavedriver's Cane	Bind on Pickup	51.4	Physical 160-241	3.9
55	Amethyst War Staff	Bind on Pickup	51.4	Physical 119-179	2.9
PROPERTIES: Increases damage and healing done by magical spells and effects by up to 34.					
55	Staff of Balzaphon	Bind on Pickup	51.4	Physical 160-241	3.9
PROPERTIES: Increases damage and healing done by magical spells and effects by up to 29, Increases your spell critical strike rating by 14.					
56	Trindlehaven Staff	Bind on Pickup	52.1	Physical 87-132	2.1
PROPERTIES: Increases damage and healing done by magical spells and effects by up to 14.					
56	Redemption	Bind on Pickup	52.1	Physical 87-132	2.1
PROPERTIES: Increases healing done by spells and effects by up to 66.					
57	Staff of Hale Magefire	Bind on Equip	53	Physical 140-210	3.3
57	Staff of Metanoia	Bind on Pickup	53.1	Physical 89-134	2.1
PROPERTIES: Increases healing done by spells and effects by up to 35.					
58	Rod of the Ogre Magi	Bind on Pickup	53.9	Physical 116-175	2.7
PROPERTIES: Increases your spell critical strike rating by 14, Increases damage and healing done by magical spells and effects by up to 23.					
58	Advisor's Gnarled Staff	Bind on Pickup	54	Physical 125-188	2.9
PROPERTIES: Restores 8 mana per 5 sec.					
58	Lorekeeper's Staff	Bind on Pickup	54	Physical 125-188	2.9
PROPERTIES: Restores 8 mana per 5 sec.					
58	Lord Valthalak's Staff of Command	Bind on Pickup	53.8	Physical 90-136	2.1
PROPERTIES: Increases damage and healing done by magical spells and effects by up to 30, Increases your spell hit rating by 8.					
60	Whiteout Staff	Bind on Pickup	55.6	Physical 138-207	3.1
PROPERTIES: Increases damage and healing done by magical spells and effects by up to 15.					
60	Crackling Staff	Bind on Pickup	55.6	Physical 138-207	3.1
PROPERTIES: Increases damage and healing done by magical spells and effects by up to 15.					
60	Zulian Ceremonial Staff	Bind on Equip	55.6	Physical 115-174	2.6
PROPERTIES: Increases damage and healing done by magical spells and effects by up to 32.					
60	Crystalfire Staff	Bind on Pickup	68.8	Physical 115-174	2.1
PROPERTIES: Increases damage and healing done by magical spells and effects by up to 46.					
60	Ursol's Claw	Bind on Pickup	68.8	Physical 165-248	3
PROPERTIES: Increases attack power by 160 in Cat, Bear, Dire Bear, and Moonkin forms only.					
62	Explorer's Walking Stick	Bind on Pickup	72	Physical 132-199	2.3
PROPERTIES: Increases attack power by 68, Run speed increased slightly.					
64	Staff of Polarities	Bind on Pickup	75.7	Physical 127-191	2.1
PROPERTIES: Increases damage and healing done by magical spells and effects by up to 67.					
65	Ironstaff of Regeneration	Bind on Pickup	78.6	Physical 132-198	2.1
PROPERTIES: Increases healing done by spells and effects by up to 143.					
68	Greatstaff of the Leviathan	Bind on Pickup	90.2	Physical 173-260	2.4
PROPERTIES: Increases attack power by 423 in Cat, Bear, Dire Bear, and Moonkin forms only. Armor 360.					
68	Serpentcrest Life-Staff	Bind on Pickup	90.2	Physical 173-260	2.4
PROPERTIES: Increases healing done by spells and effects by up to 227.					
68	Epoch-Mender	Bind on Pickup	90.2	Physical 173-260	2.4
PROPERTIES: Increases healing done by spells and effects by up to 227, Restores 12 mana per 5 sec.					
68	Dreamer's Dragonstaff	Bind on Pickup	90.2	Physical 173-260	2.4
PROPERTIES: Increases attack power by 423 in Cat, Bear, Dire Bear, and Moonkin forms only.					

Superior Staves

Lvl	Name	Binding Info	DPS	Damage	Speed
70	Grand Scepter of the Nexus-Kings	Bind on Pickup	93.3	Physical 179-269	2.4
PROPERTIES: Increases damage and healing done by magical spells and effects by up to 121.					
70	Draenic Wildstaff	Bind on Pickup	93.3	Physical 179-269	2.4
PROPERTIES: Increases attack power by 423 in Cat, Bear, Dire Bear, and Moonkin forms only.					
70	Bloodfire Greatstaff	Bind on Pickup	93.3	Physical 179-269	2.4
PROPERTIES: Increases damage and healing done by magical spells and effects by up to 121.					
70	Warpstaff of Arcanum	Bind on Pickup	93.3	Physical 179-269	2.4
PROPERTIES: Increases damage and healing done by magical spells and effects by up to 121.					
70	High Warlord's War Staff	Bind on Pickup	93.3	Physical 224-336	3
PROPERTIES: Increases damage and healing done by magical spells and effects by up to 121.					
70	Grand Marshal's War Staff	Bind on Pickup	93.3	Physical 224-336	3
PROPERTIES: Increases damage and healing done by magical spells and effects by up to 121.					
70	Auchenai Staff	Bind on Pickup	93.1	Physical 156-235	2.1
PROPERTIES: Increases damage and healing done by magical spells and effects by up to 121.					
70	Seer's Cane	Bind on Pickup	93.1	Physical 156-235	2.1
PROPERTIES: Increases healing done by spells and effects by up to 228, Restores 10 mana per 5 sec.					
	Staff of Westfall	Bind on Pickup	20.5	Physical 49-74	3
	Crescent Staff	Bind on Pickup	20.3	Physical 47-71	2.9
	Celestial Stave	Bind on Pickup	35.7	Physical 85-129	3
PROPERTIES: Increases damage and healing done by magical spells and effects by up to 22.					
	Argent Crusader	Bind on Pickup	53	Physical 127-191	3
	Dancing Sliver	Bind on Pickup	51.3	Physical 98-148	2.4
	Resurgence Rod	Bind on Pickup	45.8	Physical 139-209	3.8
PROPERTIES: Restores 8 mana per 5 sec, Restores 5 health every 5 sec.					
	Feral Staff	Bind on Pickup	45	Physical 108-162	3
PROPERTIES: Armor 110.					
	Soul Harvester	Bind on Pickup	44.8	Physical 118-178	3.3
PROPERTIES: Increases your spell hit rating by 8, Increases damage done by Shadow spells and effects by up to 24.					
	Wildstaff	Bind on Pickup	45	Physical 90-135	2.5
PROPERTIES: Increases your hit rating by 10, Improves your critical strike rating by 14.					
	Moonshadow Stave	Bind on Pickup	45	Physical 133-200	3.7
PROPERTIES: Increases damage and healing done by magical spells and effects by up to 18, Restores 7 mana per 5 sec, Increases your spell critical strike rating by 14.					
	Staff of the Sun	Bind on Pickup	18.3	Physical 44-66	3
	Battle Mage's Baton	Bind on Pickup	81.7	Physical 137-206	2.1
PROPERTIES: Increases damage and healing done by magical spells and effects by up to 85.					
	Staff of Beasts	Bind on Pickup	81.5	Physical 215-323	3.3
PROPERTIES: Increases attack power by 298 in Cat, Bear, Dire Bear, and Moonkin forms only.					
	Fleshling Simulation Staff	Bind on Pickup	87.3	Physical 167-252	2.4
PROPERTIES: Increases attack power by 361 in Cat, Bear, Dire Bear, and Moonkin forms only, Increases feral combat skill rating by 17.					
	Ameer's Impulse Taser	Bind on Pickup	87.3	Physical 167-252	2.4
PROPERTIES: Increases damage and healing done by magical spells and effects by up to 103.					
	Ameer's Judgement	Bind on Pickup	87.3	Physical 167-252	2.4
PROPERTIES: Increases healing done by spells and effects by up to 194.					

SWORDS

Legendary One Hand Swords

Lvl	Name	Binding Info	DPS	Damage	Speed
60	Thunderfury, Blessed Blade of the Windseeker	Bind on Pickup	61.8	Physical 82-153, Nature +16-30	1.9
PROPERTIES: Blasts your enemy with lightning, dealing 300 Nature damage and then jumping to additional nearby enemies. Each jump reduces that victim's Nature resistance by 25. Affects 5 targets. Your primary target is also consumed by a cyclone, slowing. Fire Resistance +8, Nature Resistance +9					

Epic One Hand Swords

Lvl	Name	Binding Info	DPS	Damage	Speed
36	Dazzling Longsword	Bind on Equip	31.5	Physical 37-70	1.7
PROPERTIES: Decrease the armor of the target by 100 for 30 sec. While affected, the target cannot stealth or turn invisible. Main Hand Weapon.					
45	Bloodrazor	Bind on Equip	37	Physical 70-130	2.7
PROPERTIES: Wounds the target causing them to bleed for 120 damage over 30 sec. Main Hand Weapon.					
51	Krol Blade	Bind on Equip	40.9	Physical 80-149	2.8
PROPERTIES: Improves your critical strike rating by 14. Main Hand Weapon.					
52	Dragon's Call	Bind on Pickup	41.4	Physical 72-135	2.5
PROPERTIES: Calls forth an Emerald Dragon Whelp to protect you in battle for a short period of time.					
58	Elemental Attuned Blade	Bind on Equip	45.7	Physical 67-125	2.1
PROPERTIES: Increases damage and healing done by magical spells and effects by up to 32, Restores 3 mana per 5 sec. Main Hand Weapon.					
59	Sageblade	Bind on Equip	46.4	Physical 58-109	1.8
PROPERTIES: Increases damage and healing done by magical spells and effects by up to 20, Increases your spell penetration by 10. Main Hand Weapon.					
60	Grand Marshal's Longsword	Bind on Pickup	59.5	Physical 138-207	2.9
PROPERTIES: Improves your critical strike rating by 14, Increases attack power by 28.					
60	High Warlord's Blade	Bind on Pickup	59.5	Physical 138-207	2.9
PROPERTIES: Improves your critical strike rating by 14, Increases attack power by 28.					
60	Vis'kag the Bloodletter	Bind on Pickup	55.2	Physical 100-187	2.6
PROPERTIES: Delivers a fatal wound for 240 damage.					
60	Brutality Blade	Bind on Pickup	51.6	Physical 90-168	2.5
PROPERTIES: Improves your critical strike rating by 14.					
60	Blackguard	Bind on Equip	51.7	Physical 65-121	1.8
PROPERTIES: Increases your parry rating by 20.					
60	Maladath, Runed Blade of the Black Flight	Bind on Pickup	56.4	Physical 86-162	2.2
PROPERTIES: Increases your parry rating by 20, Increases sword skill rating by 9.					
60	Chromatically Tempered Sword	Bind on Pickup	58.5	Physical 106-198	2.6
60	Nightmare Blade	Bind on Pickup	52.6	Physical 99-185	2.7
PROPERTIES: Increases attack power by 32. Armor 70.					
60	Ravencrest's Legacy	Bind on Pickup	57.4	Physical 84-157	2.1
60	Ancient Qiraji Ripper	Bind on Pickup	58.4	Physical 114-213	2.8
PROPERTIES: Improves your critical strike rating by 14, Increases attack power by 20.					
60	Widow's Remorse	Bind on Pickup	62.8	Physical 70-131	1.6
PROPERTIES: Increases your hit rating by 10. Armor 100.					
60	Iblis, Blade of the Fallen Seraph	Bind on Pickup	62.8	Physical 70-131	1.6
PROPERTIES: Improves your critical strike rating by 14, Increases your hit rating by 10, Increases attack power by 26.					
60	Gressil, Dawn of Ruin	Bind on Pickup	73.1	Physical 138-257	2.7
PROPERTIES: Increases attack power by 40.					

Epic One Hand Swords

Lvl	Name	Binding Info	DPS	Damage	Speed
60	Grand Marshal's Swiftblade	Bind on Pickup	59.4	Physical 85-129	1.8
PROPERTIES: Improves your critical strike rating by 14, Increases attack power by 28.					
60	High Warlord's Quickblade	Bind on Pickup	59.4	Physical 85-129	1.8
PROPERTIES: Improves your critical strike rating by 14, Increases attack power by 28.					
60	High Warlord's Quickblade	Bind on Pickup	59.4	Physical 85-129	1.8
PROPERTIES: Improves your critical strike rating by 14, Increases attack power by 28.					
60	The Hungering Cold	Bind on Pickup	73	Physical 76-143	1.5
PROPERTIES: Increases sword skill rating by 14. Armor 140.					
60	Teebu's Blazing Longsword	Bind on Equip	47.2	Physical 96-178	2.9
PROPERTIES: Blasts a target for 150 Fire damage. Main Hand Weapon.					
60	Azuresong Mageblade	Bind on Pickup	52.5	Physical 88-164	2.4
PROPERTIES: Increases your spell critical strike rating by 14, Increases damage and healing done by magical spells and effects by up to 40. Main Hand Weapon.					
60	Quel'Serrar	Bind on Pickup	52.5	Physical 84-126	2
PROPERTIES: When active, grants the wielder 20 defense rating and 300 armor for 10 sec. Main Hand Weapon.					
60	Bloodcaller	Bind on Pickup	49.8	Physical 69-130	2
PROPERTIES: Increases damage and healing done by magical spells and effects by up to 33.					
60	Warblade of the Hakkari	Bind on Pickup	49.7	Physical 59-110	1.7
PROPERTIES: Increases attack power by 28, Improves your critical strike rating by 14. Main Hand Weapon.					
60	Bloodlord's Defender	Bind on Pickup	48.2	Physical 64-119	1.9
PROPERTIES: Increases defense rating by 6. Armor 80. Main Hand Weapon.					
60	Blade of Eternal Justice	Bind on Pickup	51.5	Physical 83-154	2.3
PROPERTIES: Restores 4 mana per 5 sec. Main Hand Weapon.					
60	Blade of Vaulted Secrets	Bind on Pickup	51.5	Physical 83-154	2.3
PROPERTIES: Increases your spell hit rating by 8, Increases damage and healing done by magical spells and effects by up to 40. Main Hand Weapon.					
60	Runesword of the Red	Bind on Pickup	57.3	Physical 88-164	2.2
PROPERTIES: Increases damage and healing done by magical spells and effects by up to 64. Main Hand Weapon.					
60	Sharpened Silithid Femur	Bind on Pickup	59.3	Physical 95-178	2.3
PROPERTIES: Increases damage and healing done by magical spells and effects by up to 72, Increases your spell critical strike rating by 14. Main Hand Weapon.					
60	Wraith Blade	Bind on Pickup	65.3	Physical 82-153	1.8
PROPERTIES: Increases damage and healing done by magical spells and effects by up to 95, Increases your spell hit rating by 8, Increases your spell critical strike rating by 14. Main Hand Weapon.					
60	Warblade of the Hakkari	Bind on Pickup	47.9	Physical 57-106	1.7
PROPERTIES: Increases attack power by 40. Off Hand Weapon.					
70	Felsteel Longblade	Bind on Equip	81.1	Physical 125-232	2.2
70	Gladiator's Slicer	Bind on Pickup	88.1	Physical 183-275	2.6
PROPERTIES: Increases attack power by 28.					
70	Gladiator's Quickblade	Bind on Pickup	88.3	Physical 127-191	1.8
PROPERTIES: Increases attack power by 28.					
70	Fireguard	Bind on Pickup	81.3	Physical 91-169	1.6
70	Blazeguard	Bind on Pickup	88.1	Physical 98-184	1.6
70	Blazefury	Bind on Pickup	95	Physical 106-198	1.6
70	Spiteblade	Bind on Pickup	81.1	Physical 153-285	2.7
PROPERTIES: Increases attack power by 42.					
70	King's Defender	Bind on Pickup	81.3	Physical 91-169	1.6
PROPERTIES: Armor 140.					
70	Vindicator's Brand	Bind on Pickup	78.8	Physical 143-267	2.6
PROPERTIES: Increases attack power by 38.					

Epic One Hand Swords

Lvl	Name	Binding Info	DPS	Damage	Speed
70	Honor's Call	Bind on Pickup	78.9	Physical 99-185	1.8
70	The Sun Eater	Bind on Pickup	78.8	Physical 88-164	1.6
70	Talon of Azshara	Bind on Pickup	88.1	Physical 166-310	2.7
PROPERTIES: Increases attack power by 36. Armor 140.					
70	Hope Ender	Bind on Pickup	83.7	Physical 152-283	2.6
PROPERTIES: Increases attack power by 60.					
70	Bloodmaw Magus-Blade	Bind on Pickup	85.8	Physical 108-201	1.8
PROPERTIES: Increases damage and healing done by magical spells and effects by up to 178. Main Hand Weapon.					
70	Blade of the Archmage	Bind on Pickup	78.9	Physical 99-185	1.8
PROPERTIES: Increases damage and healing done by magical spells and effects by up to 150. Main Hand Weapon.					
70	Stormcaller	Bind on Pickup	78.9	Physical 99-185	1.8
PROPERTIES: Increases damage and healing done by magical spells and effects by up to 150. Main Hand Weapon.					
70	Fang of the Leviathan	Bind on Pickup	88.1	Physical 111-206	1.8
PROPERTIES: Increases damage and healing done by magical spells and effects by up to 187. Main Hand Weapon.					
	Keanna's Will	Bind on Pickup	51.7	Physical 65-121	1.8
PROPERTIES: Increases healing done by spells and effects by up to 31. Main Hand Weapon.					

Superior One Hand Swords

Lvl	Name	Binding Info	DPS	Damage	Speed
15	Night Watch Shortsword	Bind on Equip	13.5	Physical 24-46	2.6
15	Ironpatch Blade	Bind on Equip	13.5	Physical 24-46	2.6
18	Legionnaire's Sword	Bind on Pickup	15	Physical 28-53	2.7
18	Protector's Sword	Bind on Pickup	15	Physical 28-53	2.7
19	Cruel Barb	Bind on Pickup	15.5	Physical 30-57	2.8
PROPERTIES: Increases attack power by 12.					
19	Shadowfang	Bind on Equip	15.6	Physical 29-55, Shadow +4-8	2.7
PROPERTIES: Sends a shadowy bolt at the enemy causing 30 Shadow damage. Main Hand Weapon.					
21	Twisted Sabre	Bind on Equip	16.7	Physical 21-39	1.8
PROPERTIES: Main Hand Weapon.					
22	Sword of Corruption	Bind on Equip	17.1	Physical 25-47	2.1
PROPERTIES: Corrupts the target, causing 30 damage over 3 sec.					
22	Heavy Marauder Scimitar	Bind on Equip	17.1	Physical 28-54	2.4
PROPERTIES: Main Hand Weapon.					
23	Sword of Decay	Bind on Equip	17.6	Physical 33-62	2.7
PROPERTIES: Reduces target's Strength by 10 for 30 sec. Main Hand Weapon.					
26	The Butcher	Bind on Equip	19.6	Physical 38-72	2.8
PROPERTIES: Main Hand Weapon.					
26	The Black Knight	Bind on Equip	19.7	Physical 26-49	1.9
PROPERTIES: Sends a shadowy bolt at the enemy causing 35 to 45 Shadow damage. Main Hand Weapon.					
28	Legionnaire's Sword	Bind on Pickup	21.3	Physical 40-75	2.7
28	Protector's Sword	Bind on Pickup	21.3	Physical 40-75	2.7
29	Zealot Blade	Bind on Equip	22.1	Physical 43-81	2.8
29	Electrocutioner Leg	Bind on Pickup	22.1	Physical 26-49	1.7
PROPERTIES: Blasts a target for 10 to 20 Nature damage. Main Hand Weapon.					
31	Tainted Pierce	Bind on Equip	24.2	Physical 32-60	1.9
PROPERTIES: Corrupts the target, causing 45 damage over 3 sec.					
32	Blade of the Basilisk	Bind on Equip	25	Physical 33-62	1.9
PROPERTIES: Increases defense rating by 50 for 5 sec.					

Superior One Hand Swords

Lvl	Name	Binding Info	DPS	Damage	Speed
33	Reforged Blade of Heroes	Bind on Equip	25.7	Physical 39-74, Fire +5-10	2.2
34	Scorpion Sting	Bind on Equip	26.5	Physical 44-83	2.4
PROPERTIES: Poisons target for 13 Nature damage every 5 sec for 25 sec.					
35	Annealed Blade	Bind on Equip	27.2	Physical 34-64	1.8
36	Ginn-su Sword	Bind on Equip	27.9	Physical 33-62	1.7
36	Speedsteel Rapier	Bind on Equip	28.1	Physical 35-66	1.8
38	Nordic Longshank	Bind on Pickup	29.3	Physical 45-84	2.2
38	Legionnaire's Sword	Bind on Pickup	29.3	Physical 55-103	2.7
38	Protector's Sword	Bind on Pickup	29.3	Physical 55-103	2.7
41	Bloodletter Scalpel	Bind on Equip	31.1	Physical 39-73	1.8
PROPERTIES: Wounds the target for 60 to 70 damage.					
42	Shortsword of Vengeance	Bind on Equip	31.7	Physical 53-99	2.4
PROPERTIES: Smites an enemy for 30 Holy damage.					
44	Sang'thraze the Deflector	Bind on Pickup	32.9	Physical 39-73	1.7
PROPERTIES: Increases your parry rating by 20.					
44	Serpent Slicer	Bind on Equip	32.8	Physical 57-107	2.5
PROPERTIES: Poisons target for 8 Nature damage every 2 sec for 20 sec.					
44	Phantom Blade	Bind on Equip	32.7	Physical 59-111	2.6
PROPERTIES: Decrease the armor of the target by 100 for 20 sec. While affected, the target cannot stealth or turn invisible. Main Hand Weapon.					
45	Jang'thraze the Protector	Bind on Pickup	33.4	Physical 44-83	1.9
PROPERTIES: Combines Jang'thraze and Sang'thraze to form the mighty sword, Sul'thraze, Shields the wielder from physical damage, absorbing 55 to 85 damage. Lasts 20 sec.					
45	Joonho's Mercy	Bind on Equip	33.3	Physical 49-91	2.1
PROPERTIES: Blasts a target for 70 Arcane damage.					
45	Jang'thraze the Protector	Bind on Pickup	33.4	Physical 44-83	1.9
PROPERTIES: Combines Jang'thraze and Sang'thraze to form the mighty sword, Sul'thraze, Shields the wielder from physical damage, absorbing 55 to 85 damage. Lasts 20 sec. Main Hand Weapon.					
47	Light Earthforged Blade	Bind on Pickup	34.6	Physical 58-108	2.4
PROPERTIES: Main Hand Weapon.					
48	Firebreather	Bind on Pickup	35.2	Physical 54-101	2.2
PROPERTIES: Hurls a fiery ball that causes 70 Fire damage and an additional 9 damage over 6 sec.					
48	Legionnaire's Sword	Bind on Pickup	35.2	Physical 66-124	2.7
48	Protector's Sword	Bind on Pickup	35.2	Physical 66-124	2.7
48	Arbiter's Blade	Bind on Pickup	35.2	Physical 59-110	2.4
PROPERTIES: Increases damage and healing done by magical spells and effects by up to 8. Main Hand Weapon.					
48	Inventor's Focal Sword	Bind on Pickup	35.2	Physical 54-101	2.2
PROPERTIES: Increases your spell critical strike rating by 14. Main Hand Weapon.					
49	Doomforged Straightedge	Bind on Equip	35.8	Physical 47-89	1.9
PROPERTIES: Increases attack power by 12.					
50	Hanzo Sword	Bind on Equip	36.3	Physical 38-71	1.5
PROPERTIES: Wounds the target for 75 damage.					
51	Blazing Rapier	Bind on Equip	37.1	Physical 44-82	1.7
PROPERTIES: Burns the enemy for 99 damage over 30 sec.					
51	Lord General's Sword	Bind on Pickup	36.9	Physical 67-125	2.6
PROPERTIES: Increases attack power by 50 for 30 sec. Main Hand Weapon.					
52	Assassination Blade	Bind on Equip	37.6	Physical 71-132	2.7
PROPERTIES: Improves your critical strike rating by 14.					
52	Phase Blade	Bind on Pickup	37.6	Physical 55-103	2.1
54	Fiendish Machete	Bind on Pickup	38.8	Physical 74-112	2.4
PROPERTIES: Increases attack power by 36 when fighting Elementals.					

Superior One Hand Swords

Lvl	Name	Binding Info	DPS	Damage	Speed
54	Ebon Hilt of Marduk	Bind on Pickup	38.9	Physical 73-137	2.7
PROPERTIES: Corrupts the target, causing 210 damage over 3 sec. Main Hand Weapon.					
56	Cho'Rush's Blade	Bind on Pickup	40	Physical 67-125	2.4
PROPERTIES: Increases attack power by 28.					
57	Lord Blackwood's Blade	Bind on Pickup	40.7	Physical 42-80	1.5
PROPERTIES: Armor 60.					
57	Silent Fang	Bind on Pickup	40.6	Physical 45-85	1.6
PROPERTIES: Silences an enemy preventing it from casting spells for 6 sec. Main Hand Weapon.					
57	Mind Carver	Bind on Pickup	40.8	Physical 57-106	2
PROPERTIES: Increases damage and healing done by magical spells and effects by up to 12. Main Hand Weapon.					
57	Blade of Necromancy	Bind on Pickup	40.7	Physical 42-80	1.5
PROPERTIES: Increases your spell critical strike rating by 14. Main Hand Weapon.					
58	Skullforge Reaver	Bind on Pickup	41.4	Physical 72-135	2.5
PROPERTIES: Drains target for 2 Shadow damage every 1 sec and transfers it to the caster. Lasts for 30 sec.					
58	Cold Forged Blade	Bind on Pickup	41.3	Physical 75-140	2.6
58	Legionnaire's Sword	Bind on Pickup	41.5	Physical 78-146	2.7
58	Protector's Sword	Bind on Pickup	41.5	Physical 78-146	2.7
58	Dal'Rend's Tribal Guardian	Bind on Pickup	41.4	Physical 52-97	1.8
PROPERTIES: Increases defense rating by 10. Armor 100. Off Hand Weapon.					
58	Sword of Zeal	Bind on Equip	41.4	Physical 81-151	2.8
PROPERTIES: A burst of energy fills the caster, increasing his damage by 10 and armor by 150 for 15 sec. Main Hand Weapon.					
58	Frostguard	Bind on Equip	41.3	Physical 66-124	2.3
PROPERTIES: Target's movement slowed by 30% and increasing the time between attacks by 25% for 5 sec. Main Hand Weapon.					
58	Dal'Rend's Sacred Charge	Bind on Pickup	41.4	Physical 81-151	2.8
PROPERTIES: Improves your critical strike rating by 14. Main Hand Weapon.					
60	Zulian Slicer	Bind on Pickup	44.8	Physical 78-146	2.5
PROPERTIES: Slices the enemy for 72 to 96 Nature damage, Increases attack power by 12, Skinning Resistance +10.					
60	Footman's Longsword	Bind on Pickup	52.9	Physical 77-145	2.1
PROPERTIES: Increases attack power by 22.					
60	Dark Iron Reaver	Bind on Equip	42.7	Physical 71-134	2.4
PROPERTIES: Main Hand Weapon. Fire Resistance +6					
60	Renataki's Soul Conduit	Bind on Pickup	45	Physical 66-123	2.1
PROPERTIES: Increases damage and healing done by magical spells and effects by up to 16, Restores 6 mana per 5 sec. Main Hand Weapon.					
60	Fiery Retributer	Bind on Pickup	44.7	Physical 56-105	1.8
PROPERTIES: Increases defense rating by 8, Adds 2 fire damage to your melee attacks. Armor 60. Main Hand Weapon.					
60	Shadowrend Longblade	Bind on Pickup	52.9	Physical 96-179	2.6
PROPERTIES: Increases attack power by 22. Main Hand Weapon.					
62	Spellfire Longsword	Bind on Pickup	55.5	Physical 85-159	2.2
PROPERTIES: Increases damage and healing done by magical spells and effects by up to 56. Main Hand Weapon.					
63	Gift of the Ethereal	Bind on Pickup	56.5	Physical 79-147	2
PROPERTIES: Increases attack power by 24. Main Hand Weapon.					
64	Scimitar of the Nexus Stalkers	Bind on Pickup	58.3	Physical 61-114	1.5
65	Windforged Rapier	Bind on Pickup	60.6	Physical 72-134	1.7
65	Shaarde the Lesser	Bind on Pickup	60.3	Physical 84-157	2
PROPERTIES: Increases sword skill rating by 14. Main Hand Weapon.					
68	Millennium Blade	Bind on Pickup	69.5	Physical 97-181	2

Superior One Hand Swords

Lvl	Name	Binding Info	DPS	Damage	Speed
68	Revenger	Bind on Pickup	69.7	Physical 73-136	1.5
PROPERTIES: Steals 105 to 125 life from target enemy.					
70	Phosphorescent Blade	Bind on Pickup	71.7	Physical 120-224	2.4
PROPERTIES: Increases attack power by 40.					
70	Latro's Shifting Sword	Bind on Pickup	71.8	Physical 70-131	1.4
PROPERTIES: Increases sword skill rating by 14, Increases attack power by 26.					
70	Edge of the Cosmos	Bind on Pickup	71.7	Physical 130-243	2.6
PROPERTIES: Increases attack power by 30.					
70	Warp-Storm Warblade	Bind on Pickup	71.8	Physical 85-159	1.7
70	High Warlord's Quickblade	Bind on Pickup	71.7	Physical 103-155	1.8
PROPERTIES: Increases attack power by 26.					
70	High Warlord's Slicer	Bind on Pickup	71.7	Physical 149-224	2.6
PROPERTIES: Increases attack power by 26.					
70	Grand Marshal's Quickblade	Bind on Pickup	71.7	Physical 103-155	1.8
PROPERTIES: Increases attack power by 26.					
70	Grand Marshal's Slicer	Bind on Pickup	71.7	Physical 149-224	2.6
PROPERTIES: Increases attack power by 26.					
70	The Willbreaker	Bind on Pickup	71.7	Physical 90-168	1.8
PROPERTIES: Increases damage and healing done by magical spells and effects by up to 121. Armor 60. Main Hand Weapon.					
70	Mana Wrath	Bind on Pickup	71.7	Physical 90-168	1.8
PROPERTIES: Increases damage and healing done by magical spells and effects by up to 126. Armor 60. Main Hand Weapon.					
70	Greatsword of Horrid Dreams	Bind on Pickup	71.7	Physical 90-168	1.8
PROPERTIES: Increases damage and healing done by magical spells and effects by up to 130. Armor 60. Main Hand Weapon.					
70	Continuum Blade	Bind on Pickup	71.7	Physical 90-168	1.8
PROPERTIES: Increases damage and healing done by magical spells and effects by up to 121. Main Hand Weapon.					
	Sword of Omen	Bind on Pickup	29.7	Physical 39-74	1.9
	Sword of Serenity	Bind on Pickup	30	Physical 46-86	2.2
	Vanquisher's Sword	Bind on Pickup	30	Physical 46-86	2.2
PROPERTIES: Increases attack power by 28.					
	Argent Avenger	Bind on Pickup	40.7	Physical 71-108	2.2
PROPERTIES: Increases attack power against Undead by 200 for 10 sec.					
	Mirah's Song	Bind on Pickup	40	Physical 57-87	1.8
	Outlaw Sabre	Bind on Pickup	18.9	Physical 35-67	2.7
PROPERTIES: Increases attack power by 15.					
	Thrash Blade	Bind on Pickup	35.2	Physical 66-124	2.7
PROPERTIES: Grants an extra attack on your next swing.					
	Ravenholdt Slicer	Bind on Pickup	42.7	Physical 83-156	2.8
PROPERTIES: Increases attack power by 26.					
	Crystalline Kopesh	Bind on Pickup	60.2	Physical 88-165	2.1
	Illidari-Bane Mageblade	Bind on Pickup	71.7	Physical 130-243	2.6
PROPERTIES: Increases damage done to Demons by magical spells and effects by up to 185.					
	Wingblade	Bind on Pickup	15.7	Physical 24-45	2.2
PROPERTIES: Main Hand Weapon.					
	Illidari-Bane Broadsword	Bind on Pickup	71.7	Physical 135-252	2.7
PROPERTIES: Increases attack power by 93 when fighting Demons. Main Hand Weapon.					

Epic Two Hand Swords

Lvl	Name	Binding Info	DPS	Damage	Speed
39	Nightblade	Bind on Equip	43.4	Physical 97-146	2.8
PROPERTIES: Sends a shadowy bolt at the enemy causing 125 to 275 Shadow damage.					
50	Sul'thraze the Lasher	Bind on Pickup	52.1	Physical 108-163	2.6
PROPERTIES: Strikes an enemy with the rage of Sul'thraze. Lowers target's strength by 15 and deals 90 to 210 Shadow damage with an additional 124 damage over 15 sec.					
52	Destiny	Bind on Equip	53.8	Physical 112-168	2.6
PROPERTIES: Increases Strength by 200 for 10 sec.					
58	Blackblade of Shahram	Bind on Pickup	59.4	Physical 166-250	3.5
PROPERTIES: Summons the infernal spirit of Shahram.					
58	Runeblade of Baron Rivendare	Bind on Pickup	59.4	Physical 171-257	3.6
PROPERTIES: Increases movement speed and life regeneration rate.					
59	Blade of Hanna	Bind on Equip	60.2	Physical 101-152	2.1
60	Bonereaver's Edge	Bind on Pickup	75.9	Physical 206-310	3.4
PROPERTIES: Your attacks ignore 700 of your enemies' armor for 10 sec. This effect stacks up to 3 times, Improves your critical strike rating by 14.					
60	Typhoon	Bind on Pickup	64.7	Physical 150-225	2.9
PROPERTIES: Increases your parry rating by 20.					
60	Obsidian Edged Blade	Bind on Pickup	64.7	Physical 176-264	3.4
PROPERTIES: Increases Two-Handed Swords skill rating by 19.					
60	Grand Marshal's Claymore	Bind on Pickup	77.4	Physical 235-353	3.8
PROPERTIES: Improves your critical strike rating by 14.					
60	High Warlord's Greatsword	Bind on Pickup	77.4	Physical 235-353	3.8
PROPERTIES: Improves your critical strike rating by 14.					
60	The Untamed Blade	Bind on Pickup	70.7	Physical 192-289	3.4
PROPERTIES: Increases Strength by 300 for 8 sec.					
60	Ashkandi, Greatsword of the Brotherhood	Bind on Pickup	81.9	Physical 229-344	3.5
PROPERTIES: Increases attack power by 86.					
60	Zin'rokh, Destroyer of Worlds	Bind on Pickup	64.6	Physical 196-295	3.8
PROPERTIES: Increases attack power by 72.					
60	Manslayer of the Qiraji	Bind on Pickup	62.5	Physical 180-270	3.6
60	Kalimdor's Revenge	Bind on Pickup	81.9	Physical 209-315	3.2
PROPERTIES: Instantly lightning shocks the target for 239 to 277 Nature damage.					
60	Corrupted Ashbringer	Bind on Pickup	90	Physical 259-389	3.6
PROPERTIES: Inflicts the will of the Ashbringer upon the wielder. Improves your critical strike rating by 28, Increases your hit rating by 10, Steals 185 to 215 life from target enemy.					
60	Claymore of Unholy Might	Bind on Pickup	81.8	Physical 235-354	3.6
PROPERTIES: Increases attack power by 98.					
70	Khorium Champion	Bind on Equip	105.5	Physical 278-418	3.3
PROPERTIES: Heal self for 270 to 450 and Increases Strength by 120 for 30 sec.					
70	Gladiator's Greatsword	Bind on Pickup	114.7	Physical 330-496	3.6
70	Lionheart Blade	Bind on Pickup	105.7	Physical 304-457	3.6
PROPERTIES: Increases your chance to resist Fear effects by 5%.					
70	Lionheart Champion	Bind on Pickup	114.7	Physical 330-496	3.6
PROPERTIES: Increases your chance to resist Fear effects by 5%, Increases Strength by 100 for 10 sec.					
70	Lionheart Executioner	Bind on Pickup	123.8	Physical 356-535	3.6
PROPERTIES: Increases your chance to resist Fear effects by 8%, Increases Strength by 100 for 10 sec.					
70	Despair	Bind on Pickup	105.6	Physical 295-444	3.5
PROPERTIES: Attempts to impale the target, causing 600 damage.					
70	Quantum Blade	Bind on Pickup	102.6	Physical 287-431	3.5
PROPERTIES: Increases attack power by 100.					
70	Twinblade of the Phoenix	Bind on Pickup	120.7	Physical 347-522	3.6
PROPERTIES: Increases attack power by 104.					

Superior Two Hand Swords

Lvl	Name	Binding Info	DPS	Damage	Speed
18	Searing Blade	Bind on Equip	19.6	Physical 39-59	2.5
PROPERTIES: Hurls a fiery ball that causes 70 Fire damage and an additional 9 damage over 6 sec.					
20	Duskbringer	Bind on Equip	21	Physical 57-86	3.4
PROPERTIES: Sends a shadowy bolt at the enemy causing 60 to 100 Shadow damage.					
21	Onyx Claymore	Bind on Equip	21.6	Physical 48-73	2.8
21	Guardian Blade	Bind on Equip	21.7	Physical 50-76	2.9
PROPERTIES: Increases defense rating by 13. Armor 40.					
23	Pysan's Old Greatsword	Bind on Equip	22.9	Physical 60-91	3.3
24	Gizmotron Megachopper	Bind on Equip	23.9	Physical 61-92	3.2
26	Strike of the Hydra	Bind on Pickup	25.6	Physical 67-102	3.3
PROPERTIES: Corrosive acid that deals 7 Nature damage every 3 sec and lowers target's armor by 50 for 30 sec.					
26	Deanship Claymore	Bind on Equip	23.8	Physical 53-80	2.8
PROPERTIES: Increases defense rating by 15.					
28	Combatant Claymore	Bind on Equip	27.8	Physical 64-97	2.9
30	Morbid Dawn	Bind on Pickup	30.2	Physical 70-105	2.9
31	Archaic Defender	Bind on Equip	31.3	Physical 77-117	3.1
PROPERTIES: Increases defense rating by 15. Armor 100.					
32	Boneslasher	Bind on Equip	32.6	Physical 70-106	2.7
35	X'caliboar	Bind on Pickup	37.3	Physical 98-148	3.3
36	Sword of the Magistrate	Bind on Equip	36.5	Physical 96-145	3.3
39	Witchfury	Bind on Equip	38.9	Physical 87-131	2.8
PROPERTIES: Sends a shadowy bolt at the enemy causing 150 Shadow damage.					
42	Mutilator	Bind on Pickup	41.2	Physical 82-124	2.5
PROPERTIES: Increases damage done to target by physical attacks by 5 for 1 min. Stacks up to 5 times.					
43	Deathblow	Bind on Equip	42	Physical 94-141	2.8
PROPERTIES: Delivers a fatal wound for 160 damage.					
44	Stoneslayer	Bind on Pickup	42.7	Physical 133-200	3.9
PROPERTIES: Increases damage by 10 for 8 sec.					
44	Blade of the Titans	Bind on Equip	42.6	Physical 112-169	3.3
47	Truesilver Champion	Bind on Equip	45	Physical 108-162	3
PROPERTIES: Protects the caster with a holy shield.					
47	Warmonger	Bind on Equip	45	Physical 108-162	3
PROPERTIES: Increases your hit rating by 30.					
47	Lightforged Blade	Bind on Pickup	44.8	Physical 118-178	3.3
PROPERTIES: Increases damage done by Holy spells and effects by up to 16, Fire Resistance Resistance +10, Frost Resistance Resistance +10, Shadow Resistance +10					
48	Drakefang Butcher	Bind on Pickup	45.9	Physical 99-149	2.7
PROPERTIES: Wounds the target causing them to bleed for 150 damage over 30 sec.					
51	Stone of the Earth	Bind on Pickup	48.1	Physical 123-185	3.2
PROPERTIES: Armor 280.					
52	Demonslayer	Bind on Equip	48.9	Physical 121-182	3.1
PROPERTIES: Increases attack power by 99 when fighting Demons.					
52	Ta'Kierthan Songblade	Bind on Equip	48.9	Physical 129-194, Arcane +1-20	3.3
53	Corruption	Bind on Pickup	49.7	Physical 119-179	3
55	Doombringer	Bind on Equip	51.4	Physical 115-173	2.8
PROPERTIES: Sends a shadowy bolt at the enemy causing 125 to 275 Shadow damage.					
56	Barovian Family Sword	Bind on Pickup	52.1	Physical 87-132	2.1
PROPERTIES: Deals 30 Shadow damage every 3 sec for 15 sec. All damage done is then transferred to the caster.					
57	Relentless Scythe	Bind on Pickup	53	Physical 140-210	3.3
PROPERTIES: Increases your parry rating by 20.					

Superior Two Hand Swords

Lvl	Name	Binding Info	DPS	Damage	Speed
57	Darkstone Claymore	Bind on Pickup	52.9	Physical 152-229	3.6
PROPERTIES: Increases attack power by 54.					
58	Arcanite Champion	Bind on Equip	53.8	Physical 129-194	3
PROPERTIES: Heal self for 270 to 450 and Increases Strength by 120 for 30 sec.					
58	Demonshear	Bind on Pickup	53.8	Physical 163-246	3.8
PROPERTIES: Sends a shadowy bolt at the enemy causing 150 Shadow damage and dealing 40 damage every 2 sec for 6 sec.					
58	Barbarous Blade	Bind on Pickup	53.9	Physical 138-207	3.2
PROPERTIES: Improves your critical strike rating by 14, Increases attack power by 60.					
64	Shaarde the Greater	Bind on Pickup	75.6	Physical 205-309	3.4
65	Stoneforged Claymore	Bind on Pickup	78.5	Physical 207-311	3.3
70	Endbringer	Bind on Pickup	93.2	Physical 253-381	3.4
PROPERTIES: Deals 30 Shadow damage every 3 sec for 15 sec. All damage done is then transferred to the caster.					
70	High Warlord's Claymore	Bind on Pickup	93.2	Physical 268-403	3.6
70	Greatsword of Forlorn Visions	Bind on Pickup	93.3	Physical 261-392	3.5
PROPERTIES: Protects the bearer against physical attacks, increasing Armor by Resistance +2750 for 10 sec.					
70	Grand Marshal's Warblade	Bind on Pickup	93.2	Physical 268-403	3.6
	Whirlwind Sword	Bind on Pickup	35.5	Physical 82-124	2.9
	Warblade of Caer Darrow	Bind on Pickup	53.9	Physical 142-214, Frost +1-22	3.3
	Sin'dorei Warblade	Bind on Pickup	18.2	Physical 49-75	3.4
	Illidari-Bane Claymore	Bind on Pickup	93.2	Physical 276-414	3.7
PROPERTIES: Increases attack power by 150 when fighting Demons.					

WEAPONS

Epic Thrown Weapons

Lvl	Name	Binding Info	DPS	Damage	Speed
70	Gladiator's War Edge	Bind on Pickup	79.2	Physical 82-124	1.3
PROPERTIES: Increases attack power by 22.					
70	Xavian Stilletto	Bind on Pickup	73.6	Physical 82-124	1.4
70	Shuriken of Negation	Bind on Pickup	73.3	Physical 70-106	1.2
PROPERTIES: Increases attack power by 36.					
70	Serpentshrine of Shuriken	Bind on Pickup	78.9	Physical 88-133	1.4

WANDS

Epic Wands

Lvl	Name	Binding Info	DPS	Damage	Speed
58	Crimson Shocker	Bind on Pickup	73.3	Fire 102-191	2
PROPERTIES: Fire Resistance Resistance +10					
60	Cold Snap	Bind on Pickup	85.3	Frost 101-189	1.7
PROPERTIES: Increases damage done by Frost spells and effects by up to 20.					
60	Dragon's Touch	Bind on Pickup	95.6	Fire 107-199	1.6
PROPERTIES: Increases damage and healing done by magical spells and effects by up to 6.					
60	Essence Gatherer	Bind on Pickup	85.4	Arcane 83-156	1.4
PROPERTIES: Restores 5 mana per 5 sec.					
60	Touch of Chaos	Bind on Pickup	82	Shadow 86-160	1.5
PROPERTIES: Increases damage and healing done by magical spells and effects by up to 18.					
60	Mar'li's Touch	Bind on Pickup	76.8	Nature 91-170	1.7

Epic Wands

Lvl	Name	Binding Info	DPS	Damage	Speed
60	Wand of Qiraji Nobility	Bind on Pickup	102.2	Shadow 114-213	1.6
PROPERTIES: Increases damage and healing done by magical spells and effects by up to 19.					
60	Wand of Fates	Bind on Pickup	113.7	Shadow 119-222	1.5
PROPERTIES: Increases damage and healing done by magical spells and effects by up to 12, Increases your spell hit rating by 8.					
60	Doomfinger	Bind on Pickup	139	Shadow 146-271	1.5
PROPERTIES: Increases your spell critical strike rating by 14, Increases damage and healing done by magical spells and effects by up to 16.					
60	Wand of the Whispering Dead	Bind on Pickup	113.7	Shadow 119-222	1.5
PROPERTIES: Increases healing done by spells and effects by up to 22.					
70	Touch of Defeat	Bind on Pickup	161.8	Fire 215-400	1.9
PROPERTIES: Increases damage and healing done by magical spells and effects by up to 13.					
70	Blackdiamond Witchwand	Bind on Pickup	149	Shadow 156-291	1.5
PROPERTIES: Increases healing done by spells and effects by up to 26.					
70	Tirisfal Wand of Ascendancy	Bind on Pickup	149	Shadow 156-291	1.5
PROPERTIES: Increases damage and healing done by magical spells and effects by up to 13.					
70	Eredar Wand of Obliteration	Bind on Pickup	157.7	Shadow 165-308	1.5
PROPERTIES: Increases damage and healing done by magical spells and effects by up to 14.					
70	The Black Stalk	Bind on Pickup	143	Shadow 150-279	1.5
PROPERTIES: Increases damage and healing done by magical spells and effects by up to 13.					
70	Wand of the Forgotten Star	Bind on Pickup	162	Shadow 170-316	1.5
PROPERTIES: Increases damage and healing done by magical spells and effects by up to 16.					
70	Luminescent Rod of the Naaru	Bind on Pickup	162	Shadow 170-316	1.5
PROPERTIES: Increases healing done by spells and effects by up to 29, Restores 5 mana per 5 sec.					

Superior Wands

Lvl	Name	Binding Info	DPS	Damage	Speed
15	Firebelcher	Bind on Pickup	20.3	Fire 24-45	1.7
16	Skycaller	Bind on Equip	21.6	Arcane 24-45	1.6
17	Cookie's Stirring Rod	Bind on Pickup	22.3	Arcane 20-38	1.3
22	Thunderwood	Bind on Equip	27.1	Nature 36-67	1.9
29	Starfaller	Bind on Equip	32.9	Arcane 32-60	1.4
30	Necrotic Wand	Bind on Pickup	33.2	Shadow 32-61	1.4
33	Earthen Rod	Bind on Equip	35.6	Nature 42-79	1.7
34	Freezing Shard	Bind on Equip	35.8	Frost 32-61	1.3
PROPERTIES: Increases damage done by Frost spells and effects by up to 10.					
35	Plaguerot Sprig	Bind on Pickup	37.2	Nature 41-78	1.6
PROPERTIES: Shadow Resistance Resistance +7					
36	Lady Falther'ess' Finger	Bind on Pickup	38.1	Shadow 34-65	1.3
PROPERTIES: Increases damage done by Shadow spells and effects by up to 10.					
37	Jaina's Firestarter	Bind on Equip	39.4	Fire 44-82	1.6
44	Flaming Incinerator	Bind on Equip	47.2	Fire 59-111	1.8
PROPERTIES: Fire Resistance Resistance +8					
45	Wand of Allistarj	Bind on Equip	48.4	Arcane 64-120	1.9
PROPERTIES: Arcane Resistance Resistance +9					
46	Noxious Shooter	Bind on Pickup	50	Nature 56-104	1.6
PROPERTIES: Nature Resistance Resistance +5					
48	Pyric Caduceus	Bind on Pickup	52.5	Fire 66-123	1.8
PROPERTIES: Increases damage done by Fire spells and effects by up to 13.					
51	Rod of Corrosion	Bind on Pickup	55	Nature 50-93	1.3
PROPERTIES: Nature Resistance Resistance +10					
51	Serpentine Skuller	Bind on Pickup	54.6	Shadow 53-100	1.4
PROPERTIES: Shadow Resistance Resistance +10					

Superior Wands

Lvl	Name	Binding Info	DPS	Damage	Speed
52	Skul's Ghastly Touch	Bind on Pickup	55.8	Shadow 70-131	1.8
PROPERTIES: Increases damage done by Shadow spells and effects by up to 14.					
52	Wand of Eternal Light	Bind on Pickup	55.7	Holy 58-109	1.5
PROPERTIES: Restores 2 mana per 5 sec, Increases healing done by spells and effects by up to 9.					
53	Torch of Austen	Bind on Equip	56.8	Fire 55-104	1.4
PROPERTIES: Fire Resistance Resistance +10					
54	Wand of Arcane Potency	Bind on Equip	58.4	Arcane 65-122	1.6
PROPERTIES: Increases damage done by Arcane spells and effects by up to 16.					
55	Banshee Finger	Bind on Pickup	59.7	Frost 79-148	1.9
PROPERTIES: Frost Resistance Resistance +10					
58	Ritssyn's Wand of Bad Mojo	Bind on Pickup	63.8	Shadow 58-108	1.3
PROPERTIES: Increases damage and healing done by magical spells and effects by up to 11.					
60	Thoughtblighter	Bind on Pickup	71.7	Shadow 90-168	1.8
PROPERTIES: Restores 5 mana per 5 sec.					
60	Antenna of Invigoration	Bind on Equip	71.6	Nature 80-149	1.6
PROPERTIES: Restores 3 mana per 5 sec, Increases healing done by spells and effects by up to 13.					
62	Calming Spore Reed	Bind on Pickup	96.9	Frost 108-202	1.6
PROPERTIES: Increases healing done by spells and effects by up to 20.					
62	Incendic Rod	Bind on Pickup	97.1	Fire 129-240	1.9
PROPERTIES: Increases damage and healing done by magical spells and effects by up to 14, Restores 3 mana per 5 sec.					
62	Incendic Rod	Bind on Pickup	97.1	Fire 129-240	1.9
PROPERTIES: Increases damage and healing done by magical spells and effects by up to 14, Restores 3 mana per 5 sec.					
62	Sporeling's Firestick	Bind on Pickup	96.9	Fire 88-164	1.3
PROPERTIES: Increases damage and healing done by magical spells and effects by up to 11.					
64	Voidfire Wand	Bind on Pickup	103.9	Frost 138-257	1.9
PROPERTIES: Increases damage and healing done by magical spells and effects by up to 11.					
68	Soul-Wand of the Aldor	Bind on Pickup	125.3	Shadow 158-293	1.8
PROPERTIES: Increases healing done by spells and effects by up to 22.					
68	Wand of the Netherwing	Bind on Pickup	125.3	Shadow 158-293	1.8
PROPERTIES: Increases damage and healing done by magical spells and effects by up to 16.					
68	Nether Core's Control Rod	Bind on Pickup	125.3	Shadow 158-293	1.8
PROPERTIES: Increases damage and healing done by magical spells and effects by up to 13.					
70	Nexus Torch	Bind on Pickup	129.4	Shadow 163-303	1.8
PROPERTIES: Increases damage and healing done by magical spells and effects by up to 8.					
	Gravestone Scepter	Bind on Pickup	29	Shadow 30-57	1.5
PROPERTIES: Shadow Resistance Resistance +5					
	Ragefire Wand	Bind on Pickup	37.1	Fire 36-68	1.4
PROPERTIES: Increases damage done by Fire spells and effects by up to 9.					
	Icefury Wand	Bind on Pickup	37.2	Frost 41-78	1.6
PROPERTIES: Increases damage done by Frost spells and effects by up to 9.					
	Nether Force Wand	Bind on Pickup	37.3	Arcane 39-73	1.5
PROPERTIES: Increases damage done by Arcane spells and effects by up to 9.					
	Stormrager	Bind on Pickup	62.7	Nature 57-106	1.3
	Wand of Biting Cold	Bind on Pickup	64	Frost 67-125	1.5
PROPERTIES: Increases damage done by Frost spells and effects by up to 16.					
	Woestave	Bind on Pickup	51.3	Shadow 68-127	1.9
PROPERTIES: Increases damage done by Shadow spells and effects by up to 11.					
	Nesingwary Safari Stick	Bind on Pickup	113.1	Shadow 142-265	1.8
PROPERTIES: Increases damage and healing done by magical spells and effects by up to 14.					
	Nethekurse's Rod of Torment	Bind on Pickup	121.1	Shadow 152-284	1.8
PROPERTIES: Increases damage and healing done by magical spells and effects by up to 11.					
	Rod of Dire Shadows	Bind on Pickup	121.1	Shadow 152-284	1.8
PROPERTIES: Increases damage and healing done by magical spells and effects by up to 11.					

STALKING NEW PREY

With new levels to gain and new areas to explore, you can expect there to be new foes to conquer as well. There are not only a huge number of new opponents, but there are entire races in Outland that have never before been seen in the WoW universe. Everything looks better than ever.

Arakkoa

PRIMARY LOCATIONS:
Hellfire Peninsula, Terokkar Forest, Shattrath City, Blade's Edge Mountains

TAMABLE:
No

The bird-like Skettis are found in several areas of Outland. It may seem at first like all of them are hostile and cruel; many of them are. However, they are pocket groups of these creatures that have renounced combat for the time and are seeking shelter in Shattrath City. Be wary of those you find out in the field, as they are most certainly not of that variety.

Arakkoa like to live both on the ground and higher up in the trees. They are able to create settlements with a fair degree of skill, and they are not shy about patrolling to keep these areas clear of vermin. In Terokkar Forest, home to many different groups of Arakkoa, friendly Arakkoa blessed by the Naaru are interested in fending off the hostile intentions of their former brethren.

Level	Name	Hit Points	Armor	Spells/Abilities
62-63	Shienor Talonite	5341-5527	4304-4599	Dual Wield
62-63	Shienor Sorcerer	3739-3870	2188-2338	Enveloping Winds, Lightning Bolt, Arakkoa Blast, Power of Kran'aish
62-63	Shienor Wing Guard	5341-5527	4304-4599	Shield Bash
63-64	Skithian Dreadhawk	5527-5715	4599-4894	Arakkoa Blast, Wing Clip, Throw
63-64	Skithian Windripper	3870-4002	2338-2489	Windfury, Regrowth, Arakkoa Blast, Power of Kran'aish
63-64	Shalassi Talonguard	5527-5715	4599-4894	Pierce Armor
64-65	Shalassi Oracle	4002-4140	2489-2639	Arakkoa Blast, Lightning Cloud, Chain Lightning, Shock, Power of Kran'aish
65-66	Lashh'an Talonite	5914-6116	5189-5484	Summon Lashh'an Kaliri, Backstab
65-66	Lashh'an Wing Guard	5914-6116	5189-5484	Debilitating Strike
65-66	Lashh'an Windwalker	4554-4709	2639-2789	Lightning Bolt, Lightning Shield
65-66	Vekh'nir Keeneye	5914-6116	5189-5484	Gushing Wound
65-66	Vekh'nir Stormcaller	4731-4892	4178-4416	Lightning Tether, Hurricane
65-66	Vekh'nir Dreadhawk	4731-4892	4178-4416	Heal, Whirlwind
66-67	Ruuan'ok Cloudgazer	4709-4872	2789-2939	Lightning Bolt, Lightning Shield
66-67	Ruuan'ok Skyfury	6116-6326	5484-5780	Lightning Fury
66	Lashh'an Matriarch	6360	4416	Shadow Bolt, Impending Doom, Shadow Mend
66	Vekh'nir Matriarch	6360	4416	Shadow Bolt, Impending Doom, Shadow Mend
67-68	Grishna Falconwing	4428-4579	5780-6075	Throw Scalable
67-68	Grishna Harbinger	4872-5038	2939-3089	Lightning Bolt
67-68	Grishna Scorncrow	6326-6542	5780-6075	Gushing Wound
67	Dark Conclave Talonite	6326	5780	
67	Ruuan'ok Matriarch	6578	4653	Shadow Bolt, Impending Doom, Shadow Mend
67-68	Dark Conclave Shadowmancer	4429-4580	2939-3089	Shadow Bolt, Fear, Dark Mending
68	Dark Conclave Ravenguard	6542	6075	Piercing Howl
68	Grishna Matriarch	6803	4891	Shadow Bolt, Impending Doom, Shadow Mend

The images used herein are concept drawings and in no way suggest final appearance.

Broken (The Broken)

Primary Locations:
Zangarmarsh, Coilfang Reservoir (Zangarmarsh), Nagrand, Shadowmoon Valley

Tamable:
No

The Orcs of Outland were not the only ones to suffer the Burning Legion's demonic corruption. The Broken, led by the great Akama, fell prey to the demons' sinister influence and were changed by the corruption. Though the Broken lost some of their former powers, they still present a clear danger to all of Illidan's enemies throughout Outland. It almost seems like a miracle that the Broken somehow managed to preserve their shamanistic heritage, yet no one can say for sure how many of their traditions are still intact. From the safety of the fortified villages the Broken hold in Outland, they lord over their lesser cousins, the wretched Lost Ones.

You can tell the difference between the Broken and the Lost by looking at the size. The Lost are small, spindly creatures, far removed from the strong and driven Draenei. Though the Broken look somewhat feral, they are still thick bodied and healthy, showing at least some of their ancestry.

Level	Name	Hit Points	Armor	Spells/Abilities
63	Wrekt Seer	4002-4140	2489-2639	Heal, Lightning Shield, Wrekt Visage
64	Murkblood Scavenger	1001	2489	
65	Wrekt Warrior	5715-5914	4894-5189	Whirlwind (2 sec),Strike,
65-66	Murkblood Putrifier	4140-4281	2639-2789	Tainted Chain Lightning Corrupted Earth
65	Nomad Lomen	4731	4178	
65	Murkblood Target Dummy	5914	5189	
65	Murkblood Twin	38441	5189	Sinister Strike, Eviscerate, Mutilate
66-67	Murkblood Raider	4281-4429	2789-2939	Cleave, Sunder Armor,
67	Murkblood Brute	4429	2939	Rushing Charge (Knockdown), Dual Wield,
67	Murkblood Invader	6326	5780	Cleave, Sunder Armor,

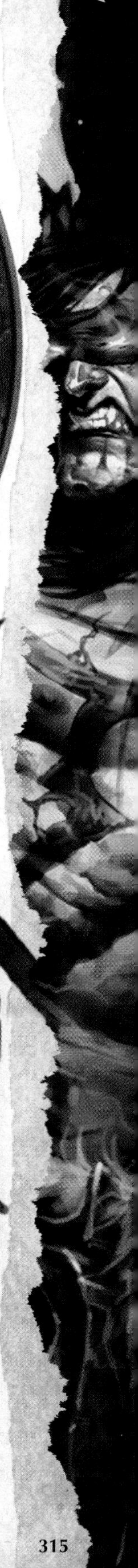

Burning Legion

Primary Locations:
Hellfire Peninsula, Nagrand, Netherstorm, Shadowmoon Valley, Blade's Edge Mountains

Tamable:
No

Many Demons of the Burning Legion are present in Outland. These evil foes attack settlements directly, but they also construct horrible Fel Cannons, Fel Reavers, and other cruel devices. To disrupt their efforts, adventurers from both factions must do their best to attack the Burning Legion wherever it is found.

There are several new types of Demons in this mix. Siege weapons, machines, various engineers, taskmasters, and so forth are all present. Only in the rarest cases will any of these things be allies in any remote sense; commonly, they are to be killed on sight (and you can expect the same treatment from them if you let your guard down).

The Aldor faction of Shattrath City has the greatest hatred of the Burning Legion. Many of the Demons drop Insignias that can be turned in for Reputation with the Aldor. Use this to your advantage if you wish to court these brave Draenei.

Level	Name	Hit Points	Armor	Spells/Abilities
58	Netherhound	1276	2706	Mana Burn Scalable
58-59	Wrathguard	3191-3313	2706-2749	Flame Wave,Dual Wield
58-59	Fel Handler	3191-3314	3361-3414	Mortal Strike,Cleave,Weapon Chain
62-63	Wrathguard Defender	4274-4422	3465-3703	Flame Wave,Uppercut
69-70	Deathwhisperer	33805-34930	6370-6665	Thrash,Flurry,Mind Flay
70	Dread Tactician	27945	5366	Sleep (20 sec),Carrion Swarm,Inferno
70	Fel Soldier	90818	6665	Cleave,Fel Fire,Cutdown
70	Infernal Siegebreaker	48902	6665	Immolation
71	Wrath Master	143620	6960	

Bursters

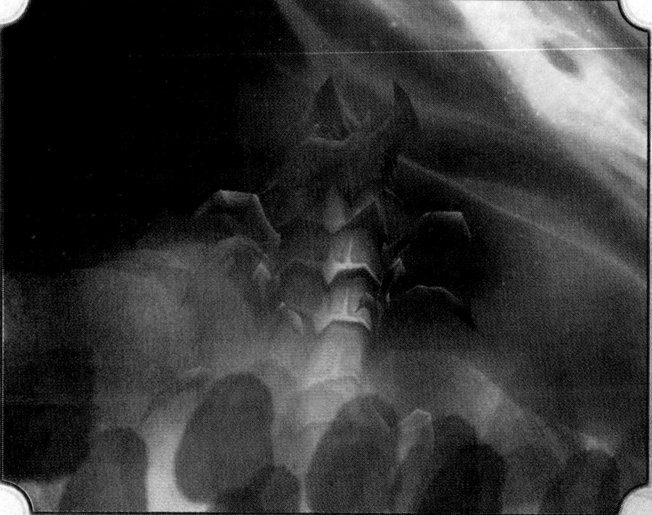

Primary Locations:
Hellfire Peninsula, Blade's Edge Mountains

Tamable:
No

These worm-like creatures are seen in areas of Outland that have loose soil that allow these burrowing creatures to hide themselves from danger. Then, when prey is close by and ready to pounce upon, they take their opportunity to strike. You know when one of them is near because of the breaking trail of earth that moves about.

Bursters cannot be attacked until they have emerged, thus ruining things like charge or early spellcasting. Then, even during the fight, these worms retreat into the earth and pop up behind your character. Be ready for this by either turning around and moving in (if you are a melee class), or by simply turning and preparing to cast (if you are a ranged class).

Level	Name	Hit Points	Armor	Spells/Abilities
59-60	Crust Burster	4142-4979	3414-3714	Poison Spit, Bore
59-60	Marauding Crust Burster	4142-4979	3414-3714	Crust Borer Inhale, Poison
66-67	Greater Crust Burster	18348-18978	5484-5780	Poison Spit, Bore

The images used herein are concept drawings and in no way suggest final appearance.

Dragonhawks

Primary Locations:
Eversong Woods, Tempest Keep (Netherstorm), Shadowmoon Valley

Tamable:
Yes

Dragonhawks are very rare indeed, and they are most often seen in Eversong Woods, home of the Blood Elves. Beautiful creatures, Dragonhawks are sought after by Hunters from around the world, even though their stats rarely outshine those of more savage beasts.

Level	Name	Hit Points	Armor	Spells/Abilities
5-6	Feral Dragonhawk Hatchling	98-115	83-127	Feather Burst
7-8	Crazed Dragonhawk	131-148	182-244	Feather Burst
67-68	Dragonhawk Protector	6326-6542	5780-6075	
67-68	Eclipsion Dragonhawk	6326-6542	5780-6075	Fire Breath
68-69	Unstable Dragonhawk	6542-6761	6075-6370	
69-69	Bloodfalcon	13522-13522	6370-6370	Swoop, Bloodburn

Elekks

Primary Locations:
Azuremyst Isle, Bloodmyst Isle, Nagrand, Blade's Edge Mountains

Tamable:
No

Elekks are hunted for their great tusks and for the thrill of engaging such powerful creatures. Seen heavily in Nagrand, Elekks are used as mounts by the Draenei and the Kurenai. If you thought that most cavalry was tough to face, imagine a lance of these bearing down on your position!

Elekks take a great deal of damage before collapsing, though they aren't an extremely high DPS foe to defeat. The best place to hunt Elekks in Outland is in southwestern Nagrand, where Wild Elekks are seen in moderate numbers. When trying to befriend the Consortium, this is a wise task because the Wild Elekk drop tusks that the Consortium is interested in acquiring.

Eredar

Primary Locations:
Bloodmyst Isle, Netherstorm, Blade's Edge Mountains

Tamable:
No

The Eredar are one of the oldest known races in the universe. They comprise the commanders and strategists of the Burning Legion. Exceptionally skilled in magic, their mastery of the arcane arts is renowned throughout the scattered worlds of the Great Dark Beyond. The likes of Archimonde and Kil'jaeden, feared and loathed for their unmatched cruelty and cunning, are among the more infamous members of the Eredar race, the vanguard of an unstoppable, demonic army bent on universal annihilation.

It is rare to face actual Eredar in combat, as they send their minions to do most of the dirty work.

Level	Name	Hit Points	Armor	Spells/Abilities
60-61	Eredar Fel-Lord	4979-5158	3714-4009	
68	Eredar Highlord	31398	4891	Cripple, Dominate Mind, Inferno
68-69	Eredar Tactician	6542-6761	6075-6370	
68-69	Legionlord	6542-6761	6075-6370	
70	Eredar Soul-Eater	33534	5366	Soul Steal, Entropic Aura, Soul Chill
70	Eredar Deathbringer	33534	5366	Unholy Aura, Forceful Cleave, Diminish Soul

Ethereals

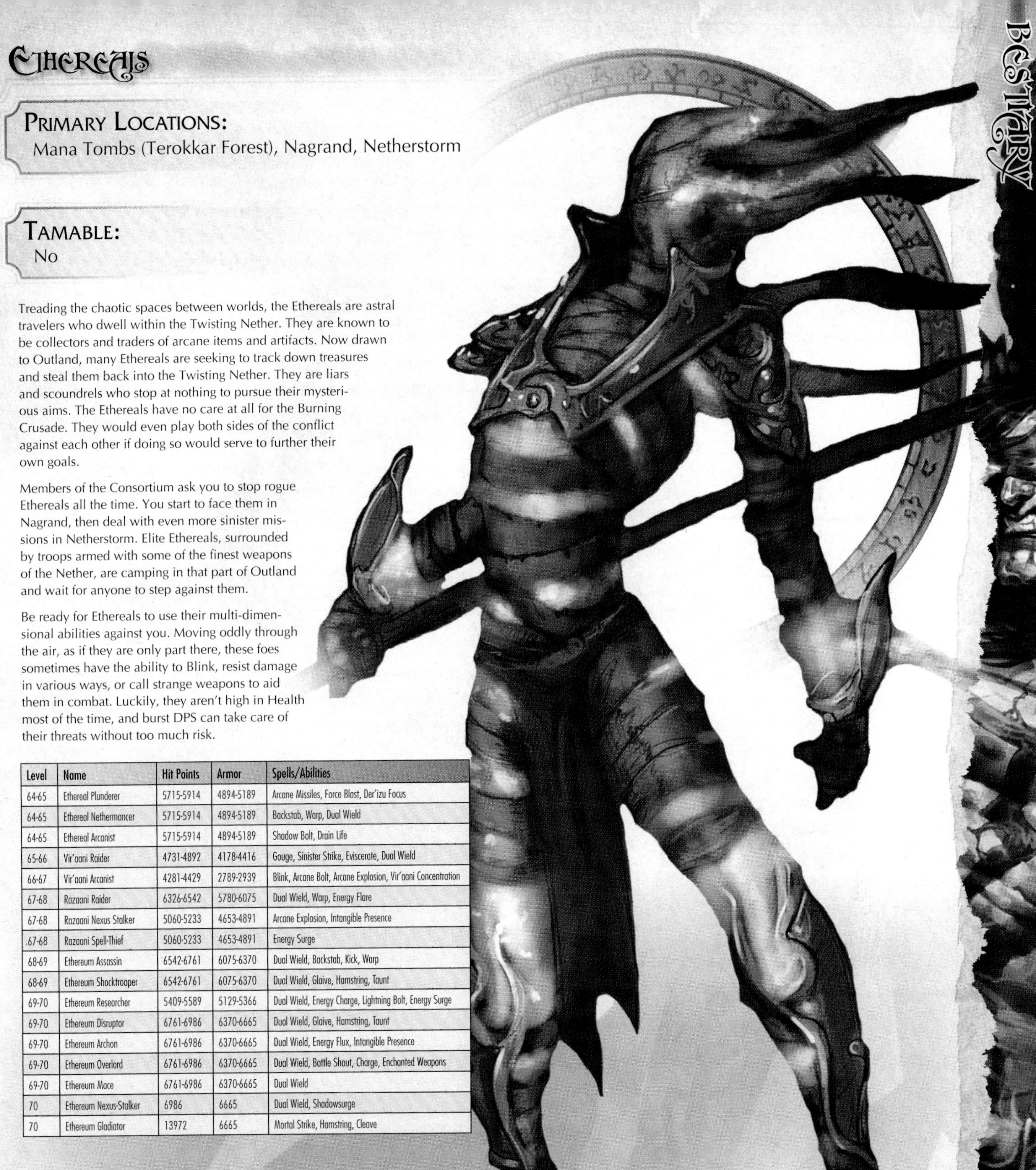

Primary Locations:

Mana Tombs (Terokkar Forest), Nagrand, Netherstorm

Tamable:

No

Treading the chaotic spaces between worlds, the Ethereals are astral travelers who dwell within the Twisting Nether. They are known to be collectors and traders of arcane items and artifacts. Now drawn to Outland, many Ethereals are seeking to track down treasures and steal them back into the Twisting Nether. They are liars and scoundrels who stop at nothing to pursue their mysterious aims. The Ethereals have no care at all for the Burning Crusade. They would even play both sides of the conflict against each other if doing so would serve to further their own goals.

Members of the Consortium ask you to stop rogue Ethereals all the time. You start to face them in Nagrand, then deal with even more sinister missions in Netherstorm. Elite Ethereals, surrounded by troops armed with some of the finest weapons of the Nether, are camping in that part of Outland and wait for anyone to step against them.

Be ready for Ethereals to use their multi-dimensional abilities against you. Moving oddly through the air, as if they are only part there, these foes sometimes have the ability to Blink, resist damage in various ways, or call strange weapons to aid them in combat. Luckily, they aren't high in Health most of the time, and burst DPS can take care of their threats without too much risk.

Level	Name	Hit Points	Armor	Spells/Abilities
64-65	Ethereal Plunderer	5715-5914	4894-5189	Arcane Missiles, Force Blast, Der'izu Focus
64-65	Ethereal Nethermancer	5715-5914	4894-5189	Backstab, Warp, Dual Wield
64-65	Ethereal Arcanist	5715-5914	4894-5189	Shadow Bolt, Drain Life
65-66	Vir'aani Raider	4731-4892	4178-4416	Gouge, Sinister Strike, Eviscerate, Dual Wield
66-67	Vir'aani Arcanist	4281-4429	2789-2939	Blink, Arcane Bolt, Arcane Explosion, Vir'aani Concentration
67-68	Razaani Raider	6326-6542	5780-6075	Dual Wield, Warp, Energy Flare
67-68	Razaani Nexus Stalker	5060-5233	4653-4891	Arcane Explosion, Intangible Presence
67-68	Razaani Spell-Thief	5060-5233	4653-4891	Energy Surge
68-69	Ethereum Assassin	6542-6761	6075-6370	Dual Wield, Backstab, Kick, Warp
68-69	Ethereum Shocktrooper	6542-6761	6075-6370	Dual Wield, Glaive, Hamstring, Taunt
69-70	Ethereum Researcher	5409-5589	5129-5366	Dual Wield, Energy Charge, Lightning Bolt, Energy Surge
69-70	Ethereum Disruptor	6761-6986	6370-6665	Dual Wield, Glaive, Hamstring, Taunt
69-70	Ethereum Archon	6761-6986	6370-6665	Dual Wield, Energy Flux, Intangible Presence
69-70	Ethereum Overlord	6761-6986	6370-6665	Dual Wield, Battle Shout, Charge, Enchanted Weapons
69-70	Ethereum Mace	6761-6986	6370-6665	Dual Wield
70	Ethereum Nexus-Stalker	6986	6665	Dual Wield, Shadowsurge
70	Ethereum Gladiator	13972	6665	Mortal Strike, Hamstring, Cleave

Fel Orcs

Primary Locations:
Hellfire Peninsula, Terokkar Forest, Nagrand, Blade's Edge Mountains

Tamable:
Hardly

Mystery and speculation surround the corrupted Fel Orcs who recently appeared in Outland. Though little is known about these savage warriors, the most disturbing revelation to come to light is that their numbers appear to be steadily increasing. Even more perplexing is the fact that the Orcs have discovered some alternate source of Fel energies to feed upon, despite the slaying of Mannoroth and the Horde's subsequent release from demonic corruption. Regardless of their connection to Fel energies, however, it is believed that this new breed is not working with the Burning Legion. What authority they do answer to remains a mystery.

The greatest concentration of Fel Orcs is in the area of Hellfire Citadel. There, divisions of the vicious Orcs are led by intelligent commanders who keep them busy with training and patrols. It is said that within Hellfire Citadel are several dungeons of the most powerful Fel Orcs, and what they are building, guarding, or using there is still unknown. What strange cries reverberate from beneath the fortress, and are they friend or foe?

Level	Name	Hit Points	Armor	Spells/Abilities
58-59	Bonechewer Mutant	3989-4142	3361-3414	Bonechewer Bite
58-59	Bonechewer Raider	3989-4142	3361-3414	Throw Net (5 sec), Ghost Visual
58-59	Bonechewer Evoker	2792-2899	1708-1735	Fireball, Immolation
60	Bleeding Hollow Worg	2490	3714	
60	Bleeding Hollow Skeleton	996	3714	
60	Bleeding Hollow Riding Worg	2490	3714	
60-61	Bleeding Hollow Warlock	3984-4126	2990-3228	Incinerate, Curse of Exhaustion
60-61	Bleeding Hollow Dark Shaman	3984-4126	2990-3228	Raise Soul, Shadow Bolt, Lightning Shield, Bloodlust, Fire Nova Totem
60-61	Bonechewer Cannibal	4979-5158	3714-4009	Bloodthirst, Dual Wield, Bonechewer Bite
60-61	Bleeding Hollow Vizier	3984-4126	2990-3228	Shadow Bolt, Death Coil, Shadow Nova
60-61	Bleeding Hollow Necrolyte	3484-3611	1888-2038	Fireball, Summon Skeletons, Raise Dead, Curse of the Bleeding Hollow

Level	Name	Hit Points	Armor	Spells/Abilities
60-61	Bleeding Hollow Tormentor	3984-4126	2990-3228	Mend Friend
61	Shattered Hand Grenadier	5158	4009	Throw Dynamite
61-62	Bleeding Hollow Shadowcaster	4126-4274	3228-3465	Shadow Bolt, Death Coil, Shadow Nova
61-62	Shattered Hand Berserker	5158-5341	4009-4304	Dual Wield, Charge
61-62	Hellfire Lieutenant	5158-5341	4009-4304	
61-62	Laughing Skull Berserker	5158-5341	4009-4304	Cleave, Mortal Strike
61-62	Shattered Hand Mage	3611-3739	2038-2188	Fireball, Frost Nova
61-62	Shattered Hand Guard	5158-5341	4009-4304	Strike, Counterstrike
61-62	Shattered Hand Acolyte	4126-4274	3228-3465	Heal, Mind Flay, Power Word: Fortitude
62-63	Shattered Hand Grunt	5341-5527	4304-4599	Strike, Kick
62-63	Shattered Hand Captain	5341-5527	4304-4599	Cleave, Mortal Strike
62-63	Shattered Hand Neophyte	4274-4422	3465-3703	Renew, Shadow Word: Pain, Bloodlust
62-63	Shattered Hand Warlock	4113-4257	2188-2338	Shadow Bolt, Immolate, Demon Armor

Fleshbeasts

Primary Locations:
Netherstorm, Karazhan

Tamable:
No

It is said that the sleep of reason produces monsters; that fantasy abandoned by sanity brings forth creatures of nightmare. For most, the horrors of their sleeping hours cannot follow them into the waking world; yet some are haunted by them even long after the veils of sleep have parted. The mindless Fleshbeasts were brought into this world by Medivh, summoned from some unspeakable place beyond. Once, the wizard used the Fleshbeasts in his clandestine experiments within the laboratories of Karazhan. Medivh is gone, but the slavering, hungering creatures of his twisted nightmares still remain, forever stalking the gloomy shadows of Karazhan.

A mine in eastern Netherstorm has become infested with Fleshbeasts as well. Consortium representatives are still baffled by this, and they nearly lost two of their soldiers while doing reconnaissance there; one of the agents is missing in action currently, though he is thought to be alive.

Level	Name	Hit Points	Armor	Spells/Abilities
1-2	Volatile Mutation	42-55	0	
61-65	Subservient Flesh Beast	5158-5914	4009-5189	Shadowform
67	Fiendling Flesh Beast	6326	5780	Rapid Pummel
67-68	Mutant Horror	6326-6542	5780-6075	Mutated Blood
69	Parasitic Fleshbeast	6761	6370	Rend, Parasite

Level	Name	Hit Points	Armor	Spells/Abilities
69	Parasitic Fleshling	676	6370	
69-70	Fleshfiend	6761-6986	6370-6665	Rapid Pummel
70	Mutated Fleshfiend	6986	6665	Dual Wield, Glaive, Hamstring, Taunt
72	Fleshbeast	73800	7255	Thrash, Gaping Maw, Infectious Poison
72	Greater Fleshbeast	118080	7255	Thrash, Gaping Maw, Infectious Poison

The images used herein are concept drawings and in no way suggest final appearance.

Floating Eye

Primary Locations:
Blood Furnace (Hellfire Peninsula), Netherstorm, Auchenai Crypts

Tamable:
No

Floating Eyes are only seen in specific locations, and that is probably a good thing; many adventurers are struck with fear at the sight of such odd and malevolent beings. One of the bosses inside the Blood Furnace, a wing of Hellfire Citadel, is said to be such a being. Other than that, only a few lesser Eyes have been located in Netherstorm. Whatever created these abominations is still unknown.

Level	Name	Hit Points	Armor	Spells/Abilities
69	Floating Eye	5409	5129	Tongue Lash, Mind Flay
69-70	Eye of Culuthas	5409-5589	5129-5366	Tongue Lash, Focused Bursts
70	Death Watcher	41916	6665	Tentacle Cleave, Drain Life
70	Entropic Eye	33534	5366	Chaos Breath, Tentacle Cleave

Forest Trolls

Primary Locations:
Eversong Woods, Ghostlands

Tamable:
No

Long before the rise and fall of humanity's kingdoms, the Amani Trolls of Lordaeron had built an enormous Troll empire. After centuries of war and hate, an alliance of elves and humans finally dealt a crushing blow to the Amani when they defeated a great Troll army at the foot of the Alterac Mountains. The empire did not recover from the defeat, and the Trolls never rose as one nation again. Yet some Forest Trolls survived, each generation nurturing their hatred of the elves in the dark forests of the north for thousands of years.

Level	Name	Hit Points	Armor	Spells/Abilities	Shadow Resistance
8-9	Amani Axe Thrower	156-176	297-386	Throw	
8-10	Amani Shadowpriest	148-186	244-401	Shadow Word: Pain	
9-10	Amani Berserker	176-198	386-492	Dual Wield	
10	Spearcrafter Otembe	186	401	Head Crack	
10-11	Shadowpine Ripper	198-222	492-518	Dual Wield, Pummel	
11-12	Shadowpine Witch	208-230	425-453	Lightning Shield	
15-16	Shadowpine Oracle	301-325	536-566	Dark Offering	
16-17	Mummified Headhunter	356-386	688-722		40
17-18	Shadowpine Headhunter	386-417	722-755	Throw	
17-19	Shadowpine Hexxer	350-404	594-651	Hex (Chicken, 3 sec.), Dispel Magic	
18-19	Shadowpine Catlord	377-404	620-651	Bloodlust (10 sec), Summon Ghostclaw Lynx	

Fungal Giants

Primary Locations:

Zangarmarsh, Coilfang Reservoir (Zangarmarsh)

Tamable:

No

The unique gases and nutrient-enriched soil of Zangarmarsh have given rise to a wondrous, diverse wetland ecology. The marsh's Fungal Giants stand as a prime example of the habitat's remarkable fauna. These lumbering behemoths are savagely efficient at dispatching their adversaries when provoked, though their low perception and only moderate speed prevent them from going after travelers with any frequency. Fungal Giants feed on other native swamp creatures as well as any Lost Ones unlucky enough to stray too close to the Giants' beloved hideaways.

The friendly creatures of Sporeggar are natural enemies of the Fungal Giants. In southwestern Zangarmarsh there is a constant feud between the two sides, and you can raise your Reputation with the Sporeggar considerably by slaying many of the Giants.

Be careful to avoid any fungus that is dropped by the Giants during combat. The reports of exploding fungal blooms are worrisome, but the Hunters involved stated that they were able to pull the Giants away from their deadly mushrooms before they detonated.

Level	Name	Hit Points	Armor	Spells/Abilities
61-62	Withered Giant	5158-5341	4009-4304	Osmosis, Absorb Vitality
61-62	Marsh Lurker	4126-4274	3228-3465	Wild Regeneration
61-62	Marsh Dredger	4126-4274	3228-3465	Strangling Roots
61-62	Lagoon Walker	5158-5341	4009-4304	Wild Regeneration, Moss Covered Feet
63-64	Starving Fungal Giant	5527-5715	4599-4894	Choking Vines, War Stomp, Consume
63-64	Fungal Giant	5527-5715	4599-4894	Fungal Decay, Boglord Bash, Unstable Mushroom
64	Bog Lord	5715	4894	Fungal Decay, Boglord Bash, Unstable Mushroom
64	Starving Bog Lord	5715	4894	Choking Vines, War Stomp, Consume

Giant Moths

Primary Locations:

Terokkar Forest, Blade's Edge Mountain

Tamable:

No

Giant Moths are usually peaceful, unless there is a major irritant in the area to provoke them. Though large in size, some of these Moths are kept safe more by their ability to emit some type of chemical that pacifies aggressors. Even under direct attack, enemies of the Moths are unable to strike for a modest time while these chemicals are emitted. During such occurrences, it is best to use non-damaging abilities to heal, avoid damage, or otherwise retreat from direct fighting until the effect wears off.

Level	Name	Hit Points	Armor	Spells/Abilities
1	Vale Moth	42	0	
9-11	Blue Flutterer	176-222	386-518	Rake, Screech
14-16	Royal Blue Flutterer	345-409	619-688	Rake, Screech
62-63	Vicious Teromoth	5341-5527	4304-4599	Dazzling Dust, Wing Buffet
62-63	Teromoth	5341-5527	4304-4599	Pacifying Dust
63-64	Royal Teromoth	5527-5715	4599-4894	Pacifying Dust, Wing Buffet
66-67	Grand Silkwing	6116-6326	5484-5780	

The images used herein are concept drawings and in no way suggest final appearance.

Gronn

Primary Locations:
Nagrand, Blade's Edge Mountains, Gruul's Lair (Blade's Edge Mountains)

Tamable:
There Isn't a Net Big Enough

Monstrous. Terror incarnate. Words cannot begin to describe the terrible Gronn of Outland, the immortal demigods of the Ogre race. Some say the Gronn gave rise to the lesser Ogres, yet if so, the Gronn show little love for their offspring, lording over the Ogre clans with an iron fist. There are said to be only seven Gronn in all of existence. Nonetheless, such rumors are cold comfort in light of the undeniable fact that the Gronn wield devastating power.

Two of the known Gronn are in Nagrand. One of these is powerful but still is likely to be felled by a smart assault for two or three heroes. The other, nicknamed The Hungerer, is an amazingly potent foe; many think that it would take five of the finest champions of Nagrand to stop such a monstrosity.

Farther north, in the Blade's Edge Mountains, more Gronn have been seen. Legends tell of a lair in that area where the greatest of these Gronn may be located. Whether this is true or not has yet to be confirmed...

Primary Locations:
Eversong Woods, Ghostlands, Terokkar Forest, Blade's Edge Mountains, Netherstorm

Tamable:
No

Lynxes are a new species of cats that have not been seen in quite some time. They exist in both Azeroth and Outland, but have been at the periphery.

They are consistently aggressive creatures, except in very unusual cases. Being territorial, they have a wide range of attack, so it is best to keep away from them while you are mounted and trying to pass through an area quickly.

Level	Name	Hit Points	Armor	Spells/Abilities
1	Springpaw Cub	42	0	
2-3	Springpaw Lynx	55-71	0-25	
6-7	Springpaw Stalker	120-137	156-221	
8-9	Elder Springpaw	156-176	297-386	
9-10	Springpaw Matriarch	194-218	386-492	
9-10	Starving Ghostclaw	176-198	386-492	
13-14	Ghostclaw Lynx	273-300	585-619	
16-17	Ghostclaw Ravager	356-386	688-722	Exploit Weakness
65-66	Grovestalker Lynx	5914-6116	5189-5484	
68-69	Darkmaw Cub	6542-6761	6075-6370	
68-69	Ripfang Lynx	6542-6761	6075-6370	Swipe

Mana Wyrm

Primary Locations:
Eversong Woods, Zangarmarsh, Netherstorm

Tamable:
No

With Mana Wyrms, there can be no doubt at all that they are drawn to Mana-rich areas. Found in Blood Elven territory and in sections of Outland that are heavy in Mana, these flying beasts are eager to drink from whatever source of power they find.

Level	Name	Hit Points	Armor	Spells/Abilities
1	Mana Wyrm	41	0	Faerie Fire
9-10	Mana Serpent	166-186	318-401	Faerie Fire
67-68	Phase Hunter	6326-6542	5780-6075	Phase Slip, Mana Burn
67-68	Mana Snapper	6326-6542	5780-6075	Phase Slip, Mana Burn
67-68	Mana Invader	5060-5233	4653-4891	

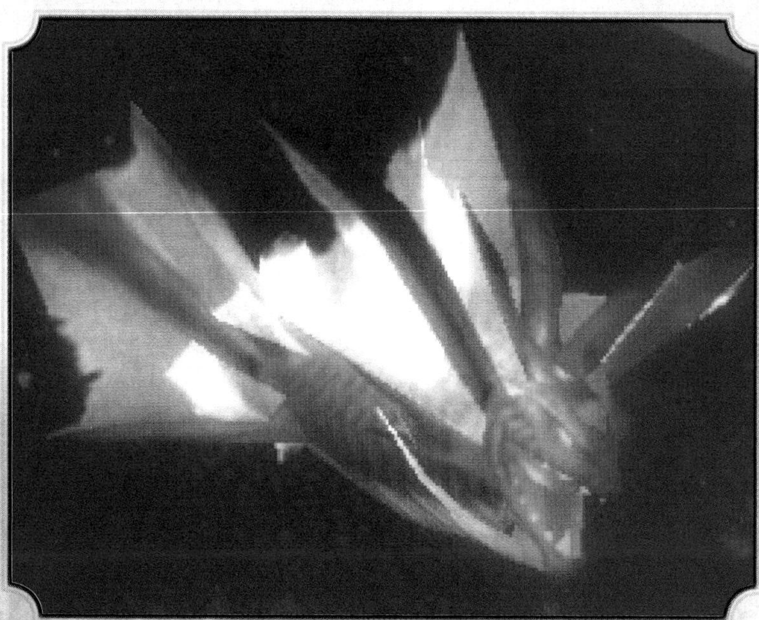

Naaru

Primary Locations:
Shattrath City

Tamable:
No

When Sargeras descended on the Eredar's homeworld, a race of sentient energy beings (the Naaru) helped some Eredar escape the corruption. Soon the Eredar refugees began calling themselves the Draenei, or "exiled ones." Moved by the Draenei's courage, the Naaru blessed them with Light-given knowledge and power. Ultimately, the benevolent Naaru hoped to unite all who opposed the Burning Legion and forge these heroes into a single unstoppable army of the Light.

In pursuit of that goal, the Naaru have recently traveled to Outland in a dimensional fortress known as Tempest Keep. Most of the Naaru disembarked to reconnoiter the ravaged land. In their absence, an army of Blood Elves led by Prince Kael'thas Sunstrider overran the keep and took its sole remaining guardian hostage. With Tempest Keep in Blood Elf hands, the Naaru find themselves stranded in Outland, facing a precarious future.

Anyone meeting the Naaru in Shattrath City will find that they are a benevolent race, clearly interested in helping those in need. These are not blind crusaders, struck on a path of violence. Indeed, whether man or woman, Human or Orc, you will be accepted and encouraged by the Naaru.

Disturbing scouting reports from Nagrand state that one of the Naaru may be captured there as well. The demons in Oshu'gun have displayed strange behavior, and the rituals performed in that place draw spirits from far and wide.

Nether Drakes

Primary Locations:
Blade's Edge Mountains, Netherstorm, Shadowmoon Valley

Tamable:
No

It is said that Nether Drakes can be broken of their aggressive tendencies and trained to become Flying Mounts. Though likely true, those who meet the Drakes will soon understand that only the bravest or luckiest explorers earn this right! Nether Drakes are naturally aggressive and are quite capable of defending themselves.

Level	Name	Hit Points	Armor	Spells/Abilities
66-67	Lesser Nether Drake	6116-6326	5484-5780	Intangible Presence
67	Adolescent Nether Drake	6326	5780	
67	Mature Nether Drake	6326	5780	
68-69	Nether Drake	6542-6761	6075-6370	Intangible Presence (Ethereal)
69	Netherwing Drake	6761	6370	Rapid Pummel
69	Mature Netherwing Drake	6761	6370	Intangible Presence (Ethereal), Netherbreath
69	Enslaved Netherdrake	6761	6370	

Nether Rays

Primary Locations:
Zangarmarsh, Netherstorm

Tamable:
Yes

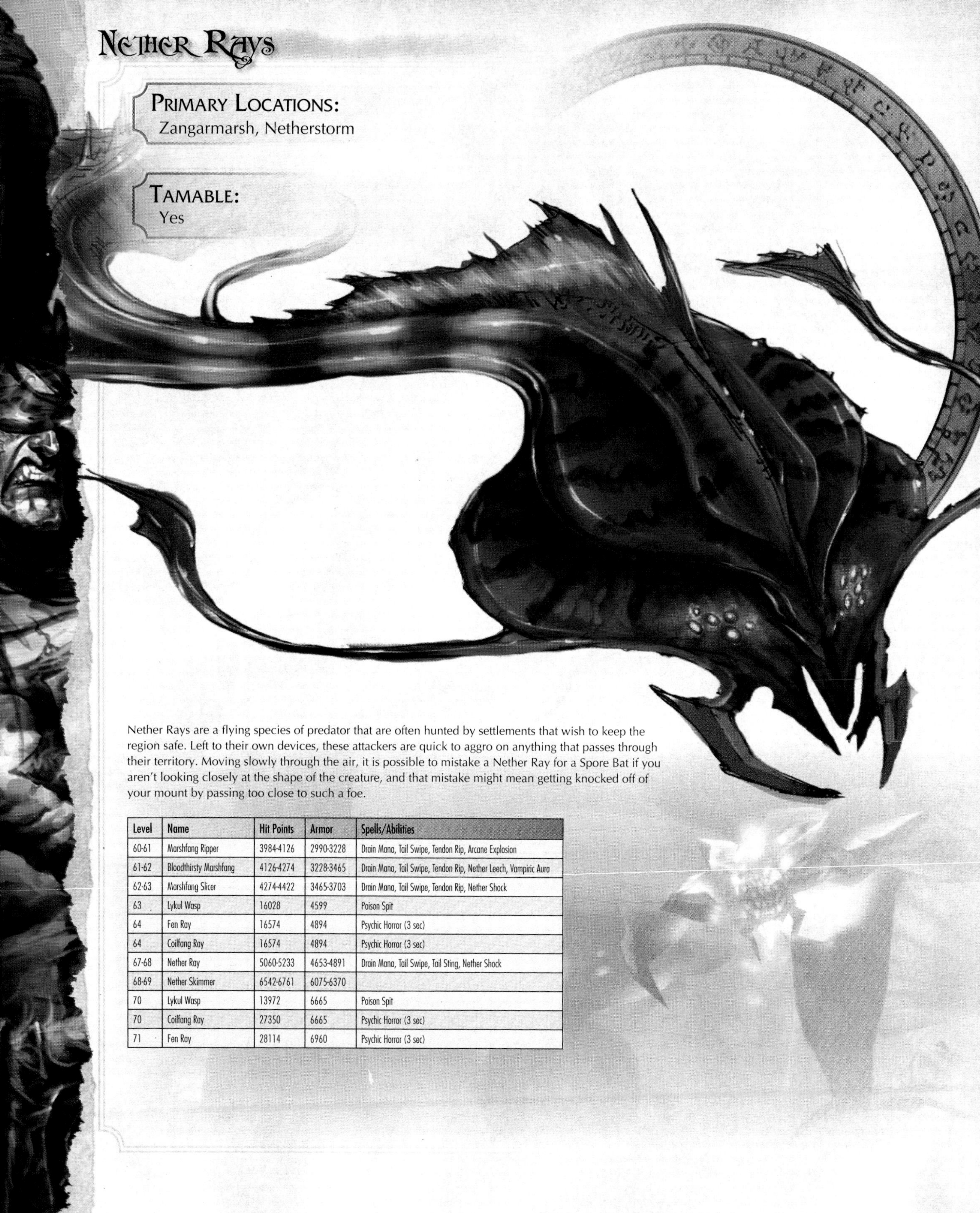

Nether Rays are a flying species of predator that are often hunted by settlements that wish to keep the region safe. Left to their own devices, these attackers are quick to aggro on anything that passes through their territory. Moving slowly through the air, it is possible to mistake a Nether Ray for a Spore Bat if you aren't looking closely at the shape of the creature, and that mistake might mean getting knocked off of your mount by passing too close to such a foe.

Level	Name	Hit Points	Armor	Spells/Abilities
60-61	Marshfang Ripper	3984-4126	2990-3228	Drain Mana, Tail Swipe, Tendon Rip, Arcane Explosion
61-62	Bloodthirsty Marshfang	4126-4274	3228-3465	Drain Mana, Tail Swipe, Tendon Rip, Nether Leech, Vampiric Aura
62-63	Marshfang Slicer	4274-4422	3465-3703	Drain Mana, Tail Swipe, Tendon Rip, Nether Shock
63	Lykul Wasp	16028	4599	Poison Spit
64	Fen Ray	16574	4894	Psychic Horror (3 sec)
64	Coilfang Ray	16574	4894	Psychic Horror (3 sec)
67-68	Nether Ray	5060-5233	4653-4891	Drain Mana, Tail Swipe, Tail Sting, Nether Shock
68-69	Nether Skimmer	6542-6761	6075-6370	
70	Lykul Wasp	13972	6665	Poison Spit
70	Coilfang Ray	27350	6665	Psychic Horror (3 sec)
71	Fen Ray	28114	6960	Psychic Horror (3 sec)

The images used herein are concept drawings and in no way suggest final appearance.

Ogre Lords

Primary Locations:
Nagrand, Blade's Edge Mountains

Tamable:
No

The Ogre Lords of Outland are the only Ogres known to retain some of the physical traits of their Gronn progenitors, such as the bony, calcified protrusions on their head and back, as well as a portion of the Gronn's immense size and strength. Other unique characteristics possessed by the Ogre Lords are their intelligence and reasoning abilities, which are more acute than those of their Ogre cousins. This combination of brute strength and increased intellect make the Ogre Lords worthy of both respect and fear.

For better and for worse, you won't see many of the Ogre Lords, even in Outland. It is rumored that one of the Lords leads some of the Ogres in northwestern Nagrand, perhaps ruling from the top of the rocky caves there. Perhaps there are even more in Blade's Edge Mountains, where the Ogres are some of the fiercest and strongest in either Azeroth or Outland!

Ravagers

Primary Locations:

Azuremyst Isle, Bloodmyst Isle, Hellfire Peninsula, Blade's Edge Mountains

Tamable:

Yes

These predatory beasts are found all across Outland, often lurking behind rocky clusters and towering escarpments, waiting to pounce on any prey foolhardy enough to wander within striking range of their blindingly fast, razor-sharp claws. Whether or not these creatures were mutated by the volatile energies unleashed when Ner'zhul's multiple portals ripped Outland apart is still a source of speculation. One thing, however, is for certain: these vicious carnivores are not to be trifled with. Interestingly, Ravagers are also found in Azeroth (accidentally brought here by the Draenei). Azuremyst and Bloodmyst Isles both have these alien foes.

Ravagers attack directly and go for the throat. Though rarely gifted with named leaders or Elite forms, Ravagers get their respect through sheer tenacity; they also like to group pretty closely together, making areas with Ravagers very dangerous!

Level	Name	Hit Points	Armor	Spells/Abilities
7-8	Ravager Hatchling	137-156	221-297	
8-9	Ravager Ambusher	156-176	297-386	
9-10	Ravager Specimen	176-198	386-492	Rend
10	Death Ravager	495	492	Enraging Bite, Intimidating Shout, Rend
13-14	Bloodmyst Ravager	273-300	585-619	Ravage
16-17	Enraged Ravager	356-386	688-722	Ravage

Level	Name	Hit Points	Armor	Spells/Abilities
59-60	Razorfang Hatchling	4142-4979	3414-3714	Ravage
61	Razorfang Ravager	5158	4009	Ravage
61-62	Quillfang Skitterer	5158-5341	4009-4304	Ravage, Corrosive Mist
62-63	Quillfang Ravager	5341-5527	4304-4599	Ravage, Corrosive Mist
62-63	Thornfang Ravager	5341-5527	4304-4599	Ravage, Thorns
62-63	Thornfang Venomspitter	5341-5527	4304-4599	Ravage, Venom Spit, Thorns

Rock Flayers

Primary Locations:

Blade's Edge Mountains, Netherstorm, Hellfire Peninsula

Tamable:

No

Rock flayers are one of Outland's indigenous species. Many careless wanderers have been killed by the primitive humanoids who roam the slopes and peaks of the Blade's Edge Mountains in murderous packs. Though they primarily hunt smaller mountain animals, they are not afraid of stalking potential prey that is much bigger than they are. There are accounts of packs of rock flayers taking down even mighty Elekk that had wandered into the Rock Flayers' territory. Their vicious blade scythes and climbing claws are so sharp they can even cut through sheer rock, enabling the rock flayers to climb the most difficult overhangs with ease. Even for a predatory species, they are extremely fast and very aggressive.

Rock Flayers are an awful target for experience grinding. High Health, considerable damage potential, and decent special abilities keep these from being even remotely soft targets. However, the Flayers look so cool that it's fun to fight them occasionally whether it is productive or not. The model is quite awesome to watch in battle, and it feels somewhat thrilling just to trash one even when they are non-Elite.

Level	Name	Hit Points	Armor	Spells/Abilities
60-61	Stonescythe Whelp	4979-5158	3714-4009	
60-61	Stonescythe Flayer	4979-5158	3714-4009	Flay, Rend, Charge, Rock Shell
60-61	Stonescythe Ripper	4979-5158	3714-4009	Rip, Tear Armor

Level	Name	Hit Points	Armor	Spells/Abilities
61	Stonescythe Ambusher	5158	4009	Flay, Cheap Shot, Sneak
61-62	Stonescythe Alpha	5158-5341	4009-4304	Flay, Tear Armor
68-69	Shaleskin Ripper	6542-6761	6075-6370	Rip, Shaleskin

The images used herein are concept drawings and in no way suggest final appearance.

Sporelings

Primary Locations:
Zangarmarsh

Tamable:
No, But They Like You

Sporelings are the nicer residents of Zangarmarsh; these indigenous people are a fungal race that try to carve out a niche for themselves between the vicious Naga and Fungal Giants of the region. Living off of Glowcaps and hard work, they stay moderately safe.

Sporelings are often in need of assistance, despite their best efforts! If you want to help them, kill off many of the Fungal Giants in the southwest, then collect Glowcaps to turn in to the Sporelings as payments for their Reputation rewards.

Level	Name	Hit Points	Armor	Spells/Abilities
60	Sporeggar Spawn	4979	3714	Sporeskin, Rend, Salvation
60	Sporeling Refugee	3662	3714	
63	Sporeggar Betrayer	5527	4599	
63-64	Sporeggar Preserver	4422-4572	3703-3941	Sporeskin, Healing Touch, Faerie Fire
63-64	Sporeggar Harvester	5527-5715	4599-4894	Sporeskin, Rend

Spore Bats

Primary Locations:
Zangarmarsh

Tamable:
Yes

The deadly Spore Bats are a sub-species of the Spore Walkers. Like their Walker cousins, the Spore Bats draw ingredients from the environment and combine them to form virulent toxins used in subduing the Spore Bats' prey. Unlike the walkers, however, the spore bats have the added advantage of flight in their arsenal. No corner of Zangarmarsh is safe as long as these silently gliding death-dealers are on the prowl.

In truth, most Spore Bats are not as hostile as some of the other creatures in Zangarmarsh, so their threat is limited to those who intentionally spark a fight. For further interest, these enemies release a series of spores when they collapse after battle. Such spores affect a variety of species and provide a short-term buff of considerable power. For this reason, it's pretty useful to slash down a Spore Bat from time to time while hunting.

Level	Name	Hit Points	Armor	Spells/Abilities
60-61	Young Spore Bat	4979-5158	3714-4009	Sporophyte Cloud
61-62	Spore Bat	5158-5341	4009-4304	Spore Cloud (Orange)
62	Sporewing	5341	4304	Spore Cloud (Orange)
62-63	Underbat	15489-16028	4304-4599	Blink, Tentacle Lash
62-63	Underbat Swarmer	1602-1658	4304-4599	Disarm, Diving Sweep

Spore Walkers

Primary Locations:
Zangarmarsh

Tamable:
No

It is believed that the Spore Walkers evolved over time from the simple organisms that dwell within the depths of Zangarmarsh into the more efficient hunting, killing, and eating machines that they are today. Utilizing their environment, the Spore Walkers are able to derive toxins from the spores and fungi of the marsh, which they in turn use to stun or immobilize their prey. When traveling through the marsh, adventurers would be wise to steer clear of these highly accomplished predators.

Though majestic to gaze upon, Spore Walkers can be quite a pain to fight. Many of these monsters have channeling abilities that are nasty if you let them get away with the spell. Health or Mana draining is certainly on the menu here, and anything that your character can do to disrupt those activities is worth the effort.

Level	Name	Hit Points	Armor	Spells/Abilities
61	Boglash	15474	4009	Corruption Cloud, Forked Lightning Tether, Thrash
61-62	Fen Strider	5158-5341	4009-4304	Lightning Tether, Thrash
63-64	Marsh Walker	5527-5715	4599-4894	Lightning Tether, Thrash

Talbuks

Primary Locations:
Nagrand, Netherstorm

Tamable:
No

You might not expect the Talbuks to be aggressive creatures, as they greatly resemble the types of prey animals that many see out in the Barrens and other such areas. However, there are indeed some stronger and more aggressive varieties of these beasts in Outland. Some are passive, but the males of the species are often wary and willing to fight at a moment's notice.

Many Talbuks have a Knockback ability, making it fairly dangerous to fight them near the edges of sudden drops. Keep your back to a wall or open space when engaging these beasts. Don't let their size fool you either; Talbuks can do damage with fair speed if you let them, so it is better to hurry and out-DPS them before this becomes a problem.

Talbuks are used as Mounts by some of the Nagrand factions. Reach Exalted with them to be able to purchase these Epic-speed Mounts.

Level	Name	Hit Points	Armor	Spells/Abilities
64	Injured Talbuk	3715	4894	
64-65	Talbuk Stag	5715-5914	4894-5189	Gore
65-66	Talbuk Thorngrazer	5914-6116	5189-5484	Gore, Talbuk Strike
66-67	Talbuk Patriarch	6116-6326	5484-5780	Gore, Talbuk Strike
68-69	Talbuk Doe	6542-6761	6075-6370	Gore
68-69	Talbuk Sire	6542-6761	6075-6370	Hoof Stomp

Warp Stalkers

Primary Locations:
Terokkar Forest, Netherstorm

Tamable:
Yes

Warp Stalkers are crafty, predatory hunters indigenous to Draenor that have been corrupted by the Burning Legion. Some reports even suggest that Legion officers employ the stalkers as mounts, utilizing the creatures' uncanny abilities to phase in and out of the physical and astral dimensions at will. Unbound by the constraints of physical reality, these powerful, mystical creatures often range far and wide, so that almost no realm is out of reach.

Warp Stalkers are the bane of travelers, for they possess keen senses. Don't expect to move near a Warp Stalker without catching their attention and aggression. Because some of the Warp Stalkers have the ability of Sprint and port about as well, it isn't easy to pass them even on a good mount.

Level	Name	Hit Points	Armor	Spells/Abilities
63-64	Warp Stalker	4422-4572	3703-3941	Phasing Invisibility (30 sec Pulse), Slow, Warp, Phase Burst
64-65	Warp Hunter	5715-5914	4894-5189	Phasing Invisibility (30 sec Pulse), Swipe, Warp, Phase Burst
67-68	Warp Beast	6326-6542	5780-6075	
67-68	Warp Chaser	6326-6542	5780-6075	Phasing Invisibility (30 sec Pulse), Warp Charge, Warp, Venomous Bite
68-69	Ravening Snap Dragon	6542-6761	6075-6370	
68-69	Greater Snap Dragon	6542-6761	6075-6370	

Old Enemies with New Threads

There are many new skins for the models that you have already seen in WoW. The new starting areas, dungeons, and outdoor zones of Outland are filled with creatures that look slightly different in color or style than they did before.

What adds to this greatly is that the use of equipment has been enabled for quite a few monster types. It is really exciting to see Voidwalkers that are draped in old, rotting cloth, or to face Ogres with a variety of armor types, or marvel at the wooly cousins of Kodo of Nagrand. This improvement is a great visual step.

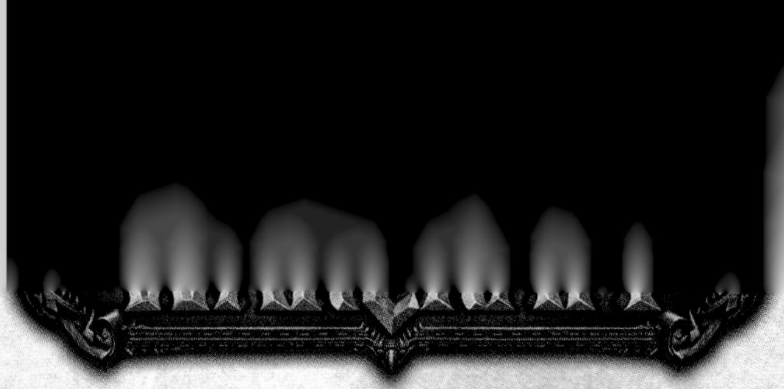

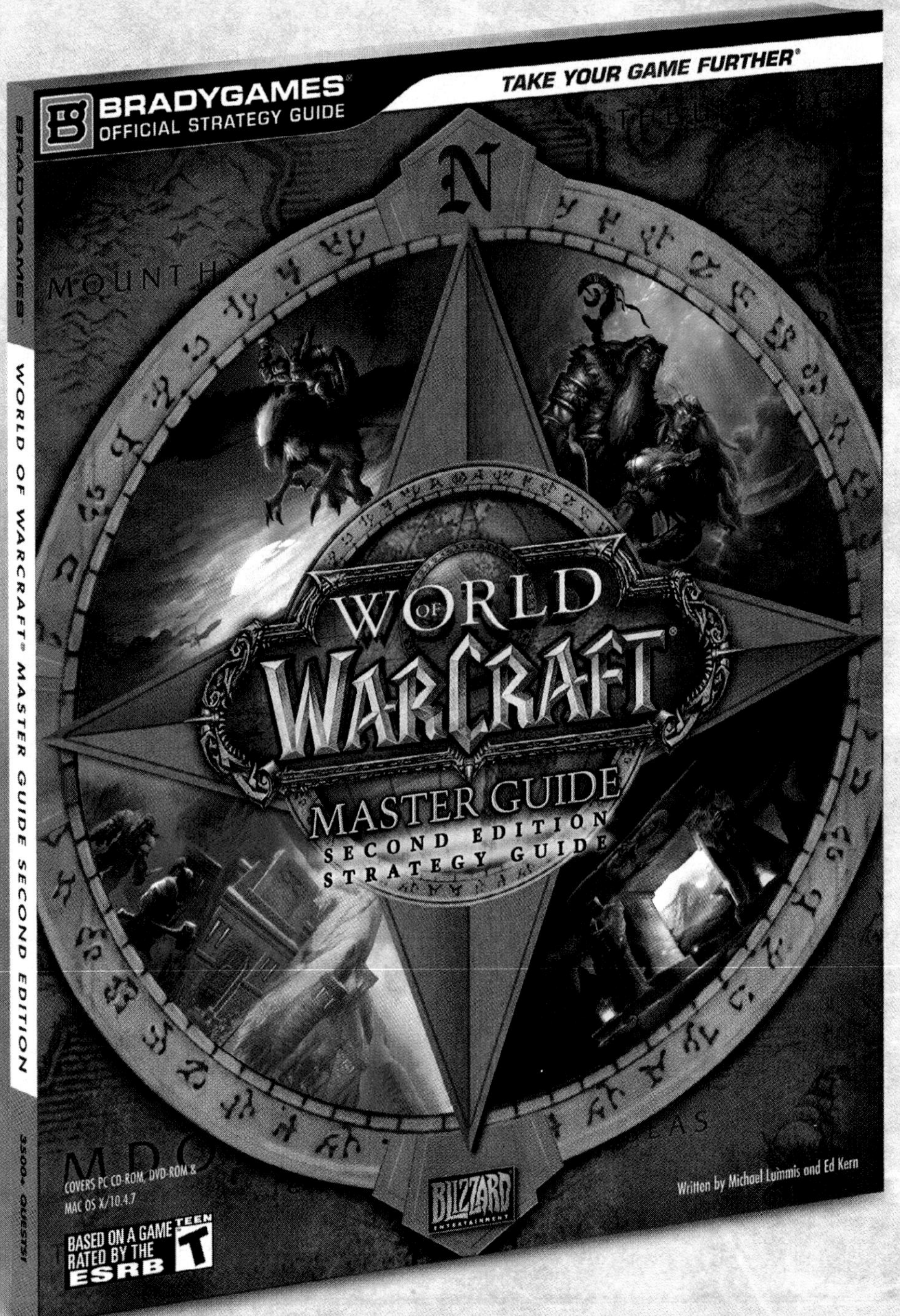

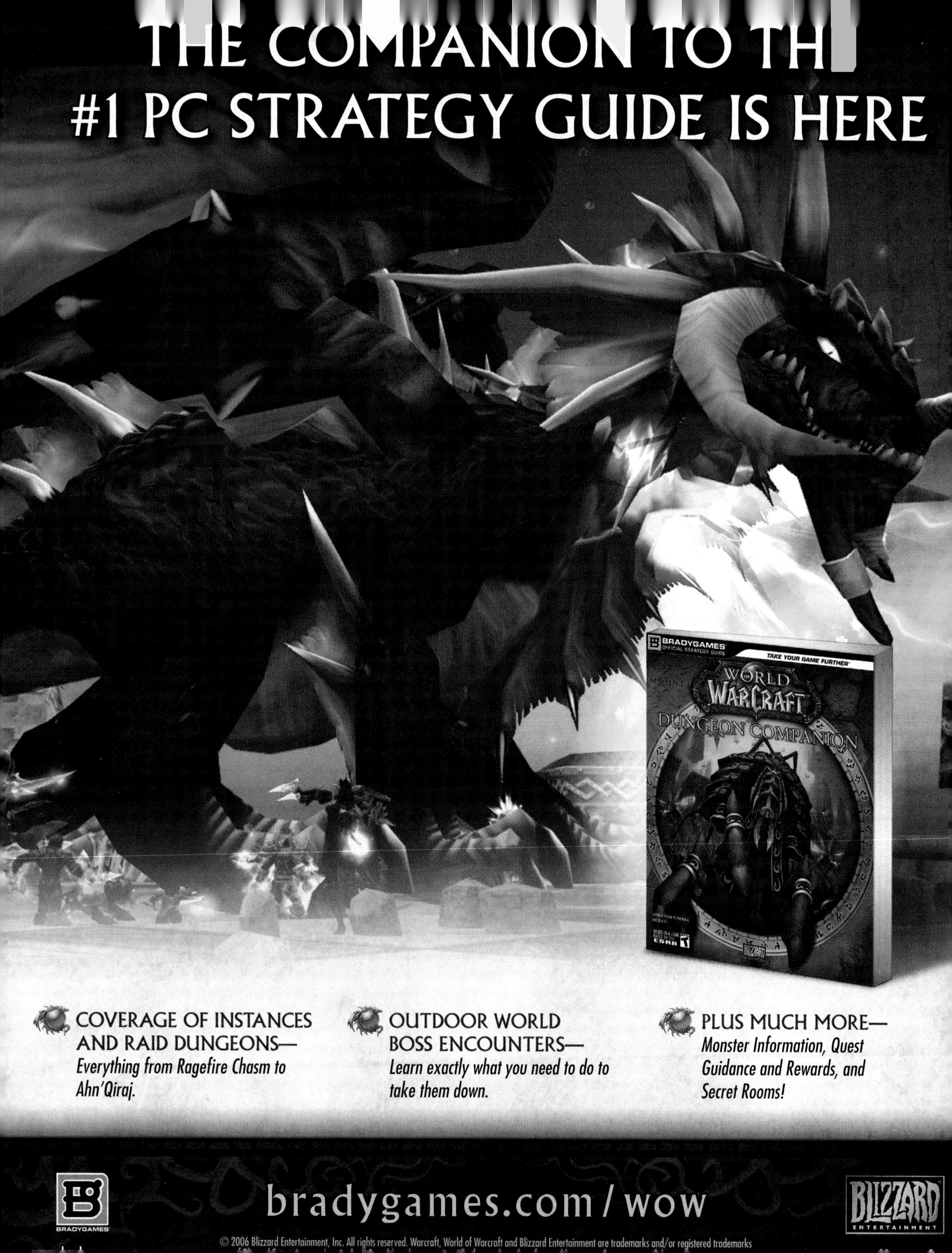
THE COMPANION TO TH
#1 PC STRATEGY GUIDE IS HERE
BRADYGAMES
OFFICIAL STRATEGY GUIDE
TAKE YOUR GAME FURTHER
WORLD OF WARCRAFT
DUNGEON COMPANION
COVERAGE OF INSTANCES AND RAID DUNGEONS—
Everything from Ragefire Chasm to Ahn'Qiraj.
OUTDOOR WORLD BOSS ENCOUNTERS—
Learn exactly what you need to do to take them down.
PLUS MUCH MORE—
Monster Information, Quest Guidance and Rewards, and Secret Rooms!
BRADYGAMES
bradygames.com/wow
BLIZZARD ENTERTAINMENT
© 2006 Blizzard Entertainment, Inc. All rights reserved. Warcraft, World of Warcraft and Blizzard Entertainment are trademarks and/or registered trademarks

BradyGAMES® Publishing

An Imprint of DK Publishing Inc.
800 East 96th Street, Third Floor
Indianapolis, Indiana 46240

ISBN: 0-7440-0833-6

Printing Code: The rightmost double-digit number is the year of the book's printing; the rightmost single-digit number is the number of the book's printing. For example, 07-1 shows that the first printing of the book occurred in 2007.

10 09 08 07 4 3 2 1

Manufactured in the United States of America.

BRADYGAMES STAFF

Publisher
David Waybright

Editor-In-Chief
H. Leigh Davis

Director of Marketing
Steve Escalante

Creative Director
Robin Lasek

Licensing Manager
Mike Degler

CREDITS

Development Editors
Brian Shotton
Ken Schmidt
& the entire editorial staff

Screenshot Editor
Michael Owen

Lead Designer
Brent Gann

Layout Designer
Tracy Wehmeyer

Cover Artist
Glenn Rane

LUMMIS' ACKNOWLEDGEMENTS

For my part, I would like to thank several groups of people for their support on the project. Starting at home plate, my thanks go to Edwin Kern and Kathleen Pleet for their considerable help, friendship, and fun during the creation of this guide. I wish that we could keep all of our loot (but we'll grab it again soon enough)!

At Brady, respect and thanks warmly go to Brian Shotton for his editing and guidance during our writing. It's fair to also thank Christian Sumner for being available at various times to contribute ideas and thoughts on the project (Miiiikkkkooooo). As always, Brady's design team is an amazement to me, so I'll reiterate that these books wouldn't be half of what they are without someone to bring it together and make it beautiful. For WoW guides, make that several someones over many days.

At Blizzard, my appreciation goes to Brian Hsieh, Carlos Guerrero, and John Hsieh for keeping us in the loop, getting us access to the Alpha and Beta and for trouble-shooting the minor bumps with us. I'm sure that I'm missing another half-a-dozen people, but being down in the trenches keeps me from shaking everyone's hand directly! To all of the others who helped, thanks again.

See you all in Outland. Don't let the Fel Reaver step on you.

BRIAN'S ACKNOWLEDGEMENTS

I would like to start by thanking my son, Orion. He has began to realize what Daddy does. His excitement and wonder at my job makes me try all the harder to merit his admiration and love.

I would like to thank all of Blizzard for a wonderful game, but special thanks go to Brian Hsieh, Cory Jones, Joanna Cleland, and Gloria Soto who work their collective rears off to get me the stuff I need to make a guide worthy of Blizzard and BradyGames.

Finally, to my co-workers: you guys are the best. You picked me up and helped me across the finish line. This book in many ways represents why BradyGames is the best. We love games and we truly care about what we put out to the public. So, to Trace, Arm-n-hammer, Dan-o, Mr. Cruz, my boss Leigh, macroMowen, Fitzy, the maestro Brent, my dear friend Haus, Bobby, Robin, K-Lowe, Schmidty, Carol, Areva, and my personal WoW savior Xian—thank you.

BLIZZARD ACKNOWLEDGEMENTS

Creative Development Manager
Shawn Carnes

Director of Global Licensing
Cory Jones

Producer
Gloria Soto

Licensing Manager
Brian Hsieh

Art Approvals
Joanna Cleland-Jolly

QA Approvals
Meghan Dawson, Drew Dobernecker, Joseph Magdalena, Andrew Rowe, Shawn Su, Rodney Tsing, Don Vu

Development Team Support
Luis Barriga, J. Allen Brack, Alexander Brazie, Tom Chilton, Jeff Kaplan, Jonathan LeCraft

Blizzard Special Thanks
Ben "But the minis…" Brode, Shane Cargilo, Tim Daniels, Mei Francis, Evelyn Fredericksen, Michael Gilmartin, Carlos Guerrero, John Hsieh, Chris Metzen, Glenn Rane